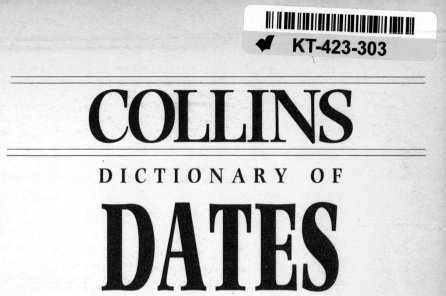

COLLINS

DICTIONARY OF

DATES

COLLINS

DICTIONARY OF

DATES

Audrey Butler

HarperCollins*Publishers*

HarperCollins Publishers
PO Box, Glasgow G4 0NB

First published as *Everyman's Dictionary of Dates* 1911
Second edition 1940
Third edition 1954
Fourth edition 1964
Fifth edition 1967
Sixth edition 1971
Seventh edition 1986

This edition © HarperCollins Publishers 1996

Reprint 10 9 8 7 6 5 4 3 2 1 0

ISBN 0 00 470898 9

A catalogue record for this book is available from the British Library

Printed in Great Britain by
HarperCollins Manufacturing, Glasgow

CONTENTS

PREFACE

The basic purpose of this work is to make useful dates accessible to the general reader, but even this seemingly simple objective involves a number of problems. It was necessary to include most of the 'obvious' events lest the compiler be accused of 'not even putting in the *Battle of Hastings*,' and yet it was clearly desirable to add many matters – such as the *Shoguns* – which are hard to find quickly elsewhere.

To solve the resulting difficulties of selection, the compiler was guided by a number of principles. Considerable prominence was given to countries, institutions and dynasties of universal influence. Then room was found for notices (however short) on other countries, cities, provinces, institutions and families of historical repute. Thirdly, considerable space was devoted to arts, sciences, philosophy, religion, invention and technology. And, lastly, a large number of miscellaneous facts have been included on grounds of general interest.

Broadly speaking there are three types of headings: short entries relating to particular matters, e.g. *coach*; narratives, e.g. *United States of America*; and classified entries, e.g. *sieges*. Logic and exclusiveness have been sacrificed to convenience wherever it was thought desirable, and I have not hesitated to repeat myself if necessary.

Generally the classified entries are the longest, then the narratives, so that if the subject sought by the user is not to be found under its own name he or she should scan likely general headings in that order. It should be borne in mind that this is *not* a biographical dictionary, so that in order to look up 'the dates of George V' one must first know whether the individual in question was the King of England or the last ruler of Hanover of that name, and so on. In the same way, Graham Greene appears under *English Literature*; Leonardo de Vinci in the Italian section of *arts, the*; W.G. Grace under *cricket*, etc.

This *Dictionary of Dates* was first planned over eighty years ago, and has since been extensively revised several times. This eighth edition, while retaining the basic character and objectives of its predecessors, is considerably more comprehensive (containing over 500 completely new entries) and there have been extensive changes in content to meet the demands of the fast-changing world of today. The lists of classical emperors, etc., remain; in addition, there are now many newer entries such as *European Union; Gulf War; Ordination of Women; drug addiction; Commonwealth of Independent States* and *Press Complaints*

Commission. Many articles have been expanded, e.g. *newspapers* now includes lists of major foreign newspapers as well as British ones, and *Stock Exchange* provides a list of important stock exchanges world wide. There is considerably greater sports coverage than in previous editions and the growth in popular travel is reflected in extended articles on numbers of cities to include many of their most notable buildings, etc. and some new articles on famous institutions and landmarks, e.g. *Uffizi* and *Prado* museums, *Trafalgar Square*, and so on.

Traditional English spelling and usage is adopted for place-names; thus main entries appear under *Canton* and *Peking*, but with cross-references from *Guangzhon* and *Beijing* and while there is a main article at *Burma* there is a cross-reference from *Myanmar*. When an asterisk appears within an article, this indicates a cross reference and the word/words so marked will have a separate entry within the dictionary section. Where there have been place-name changes or reversions in East Europe in recent years, the present name is used in the main article, e.g. St Petersburg; Volgograd, with appropriate cross references; but historical events associated with a previous name remain under the former title, e.g. at *Sieges* the names *Leningrad* and *Stalingrad* are retained. In general, *European Economic Community* (*EEC*) is used when referring to events before the Single European Act of 1 July 1987; *European Community* (*EC*) from 1987 until 1 November, 1993; thereafter, *European Union* (*EU*). The Chronological section of 'timebanding', from *c.* 30,000 BC to the present day, is intended to complement the dictionary section, as well as to be used as a 'ready reckoner' of dating in its own right. It is the publishers' belief that this completely revised and enlarged edition of a well-tried, favourite reference book will prove a worthy successor to those of the past half-century.

1996   AUDREY BUTLER

CALENDARS

1. The Old Style and New Style Calendars

The present system of Christian dating originated as follows:

(a) The Roman Era began with the foundation of Rome in 753 BC. By 46 BC, owing to various imperfections the Roman Calendar had fallen into confusion and Julius Caesar then reformed it.

(b) The year 46 BC was therefore made to consist of 445 days, and is called the 'Year of Confusion'. Thereafter each year consisted of 365 days except that *every* fourth year was a leap year. This Julian or Old Style Calendar remained in general use in Europe until 1582.

(c) By 1582 there was a difference of 10 days between the Julian and the tropical year. In that year Pope Gregory XIII ordered that 5 Oct. should be called 15 Oct., and that of the end-century (00) years only the fourth should be a leap year. This Gregorian or New Style Calendar is still in use. It was adopted in:

1582 Italy, France, Spain, Portugal
1583 Prussia, Switzerland, Holland, Flanders, German Catholic States
1586 Poland
1587 Hungary
1700 German Protestant States, Denmark
1872 Japan
1912 China
1915 Bulgaria
1917 Turkey, USSR
1919 Yugoslavia, Romania
1923 Greece

In Sweden the change was made between 1700 and 1740 by the omission of 11 leap-year days.

In Britain (including N America and the then Colonies) the change was made in 1752 (3 Sept. being called 14), and the beginning of the official year was altered from 25 Mar. (which was the date of the vernal equinox when the Julian Calendar was introduced) to 1 Jan. at the same time.

2. Jewish Calendar

A system by which the beginning, length and sub-division of the year is fixed. Nothing is certain concerning the calendar in use during biblical times. Later the beginning of a month was ascertained by observation of the new moon, but about the middle of the fourth century a constant calendar was introduced, based on earlier practice.

The day is the period between two successive sunsets although, for calendar purposes, it is computed to commence at the beginning of the seventh hour after noon, i.e. at 6 p.m. The week consists of seven days, ending with the Sabbath, the other days having no special name, but being designated as the first day, the second day of the week, etc. A month is the period between two revolutions of the moon. Ordinarily, twelve months containing alternately 30 and 29 days, make a year, which should therefore contain 354 days. But since the Bible ordains that Passover must be celebrated in the month of *Abib* (the fresh ears of grain) and since vegetable growth is dependent on the sun, it is necessary to adjust this lunar year to the solar one of 365¼ days. This is done by intercalating a month of 30 days before the last month of the religious year seven times during every 19 years (the Metonic cycle), viz. in the third, sixth, eighth, 11th, 14th, 17th, and 19th years of each cycle. These intercalary or leap years therefore ordinarily contain 384 days. But there are certain factors which make it necessary to lengthen or shorten the regular year of 354 days and the leap year of 384 days by one day.

The Day of Atonement must not fall on the first or sixth day of the week, nor the seventh day of Tabernacles on Sabbath. Consequently the New Year festival must not fall on the first, fourth or sixth day. Again, the New Year festival must be celebrated on the day on which the new moon becomes visible; consequently if the lunar conjunction occurs at noon or later the festival is postponed to the next day, since the new moon will be seen only at 6 p.m. or later, which period belongs to the following day. For these and other reasons, the eighth month, *Cheshvan*, sometimes has 30 instead of 29 days (when the year is described as 'redundant') and the ninth month, *Kislev*, 29 instead of 30 days (a 'defective' year). Thus the ordinary year may contain 353, 354, or 355 days and the leap year 383, 384, or 385.

The character of a Jewish year is therefore definitely known by the determination of its first day, that which is to be celebrated as its New Year Festival, and by its length, dependent on whether it is an ordinary or leap year and regular, redundant, or defective (i.e. whether any variation is required in the lengths of *Cheshvan* and *Kislev*). Each of the possible 14 types of year, seven for ordinary and seven for leap years, is described by a 'characteristic' consisting of three Hebrew letters, the first of which intimates the day of the week on which the New Year festival falls, the second whether the year is regular, redundant, or defective, and the third the day of the week on which the first day of Passover falls. The last is not really necessary and is included in the 'characteristic' only because when the incidence of Passover is known the days of the week on which the principal festivals of the following year fall may easily be ascertained. To these three letters is, of course, added the Hebrew word for 'ordinary' or 'leap' as may be required.

The times when the solstices and equinoxes (*Tekufah*) fall must also be computed, since the petition for rain has to be interpolated in the *Amidah* prayer on and after the 60th day from the autumnal equinox. Each *Tekufah* is 91 days 7½ hours distant from another, being a quarter of the 365¼ days which, according to Samuel Yarchinai, make up the solar year. Each *Tekufah* returns to the same day of the week and to the same hour every 28 years, which period is termed a 'greater cycle' or a 'solar cycle'. The calculation of the civil date with which any particular Jewish date corresponds and vice versa, is of a complicated character. There is, however, a mathematical formula (that of

Gauss), which gives the date of the Passover in any year; from this that of the next New Year festival may easily be calculated, since the number of days between these two festivals is constant.

Jewish months (with the seasonal equivalent in brackets) are as follows:

Nisan	(Mar./Apr.)
Iyar	(Apr./May)
Sivan	(May/June)
Tammuz	(June/July)
Av	(July/Aug.)
Ellul	(Aug./Sept.)
Tishri	(Sept./Oct.)
Cheshvan	(Oct./Nov.)
Kislev	(Nov./Dec.)
Tevet	(Dec./Jan.)
Shevat	(Jan./Feb.)
Adar	(Feb./Mar.)*

* In leap years the extra month is known as Adar 2.

Among major Jewish commemorations, with dates, are:

Purim (Festival of Lots), Feb./Mar.
Pesch (The Passover), Mar./Apr.
Yom Hashoah (Holocaust Day), which commemorates the millions of Jews killed during the Nazi *Holocaust and takes place in Apr. on the 27th day of Nisan: it has been an official Remembrance Day in Israel since 1951.
Rosh Hashanah (New Year), Sept., on the first day of Tishri
Yom Kippur (Day of Atonement), Sept./Oct.
Hanukah (Festival of Lights), Dec.

3. Roman Calendar

The ecclesiastical or liturgical year begins on the first Sunday of Advent, which is the first Sunday next, whether before or after the feast of St Andrew the Apostle (30 Nov.). There follow the four weeks of Advent and the Christmas festivals ending with the Epiphany. The ensuing Sundays are the First, Second, etc. 'of the year'. Following Ash Wednesday, Lent has six Sundays, the last of which is known as Passion or Palm Sunday. The week beginning with Palm Sunday is called Holy Week. Easter Sunday, the feast of the Resurrection, upon the date of which the foregoing festivals depend, falls on the Sunday next following the full moon first occurring after 20 Mar.

The weeks between Easter and Pentecost (seventh Sunday or 50th day after Easter) are Paschal time, and the Sundays are Second, Third, etc. 'of Eastertide.' Forty days after Easter (always on a Thursday) is the feast of the Ascension. Trinity Sunday follows, on the Thursday after which the Church celebrates the feast of Corpus Christi, and after its Octave day the feast of the Sacred Heart of Jesus.

The remaining Sundays of the year, are now known as Tenth, Eleventh etc. 'of the year.'

Concurrently with the above series of celebrations there runs the calendar of festivals fixed to particular days of the month. This varies considerably from country to country, from diocese to diocese, and even between the calendars of certain religious orders. The calendar printed in this volume shows major festivals of universal (excepting certain religious orders) observance. There are rules governing the order of celebration when two feasts of different rank coincide.

Saints and festivals marked with an asterisk occur in the Calendar prefixed to the Anglican *Book of Common Prayer*. Those in square brackets were officially removed from the list of saints by *motu proprio* of Paul VI on 1 Jan. 1970.

Abbreviations

Ab.	Abbot	K.	King
Ap.	Apostle	M.	Martyr
B.	Bishop	P.	Pope
C.	Confessor	V.	Virgin
D.	Doctor of the Church	W.	Widow

JANUARY
1 Octave of Christmas. – Solemnity of Mary, the Mother of God. – *The Circumcision
2 SS Basil the Great and Gregory Nazianen
3
4
5 St Telesphorus, P.M.
6 *The Epiphany
7
8
9 *St Lucian
10 The Baptism of Our Lord
11 St Hyginus, P.M.
12
13 *St Hilary
14 St Hilary, B.C.D. – St Felix, M.
15 St Paul, 1st hermit – St Maurus, Ab.
16 St Marcellus, P.M.
17 St Anthony, Ab.
18 St Peter's Chair at Rome – *St Prisca, V.M.
19 St Marius and Companions, MM. – St Canute, K.M.
20 SS Fabian* and Sebastian, MM.
21 *St Agnes, V.M.
22 SS Vincent* and Anastasius, MM.
23 St Raymund of Peñfort, C. [St Emerentiana, V.M.]
24 St Timothy, B.M.
25 Conversion of St Paul
26 St Polycarp, B.M.
27 St John Chrysostom, B.C.D. – St Angela Merici, V
28 St Thomas Aquinas, D.
29 St Francis de Sales, B.C.D.
30 [St Martina, V.M.]
31 St John Bosco, C. – St Peter Nolasco, C.

FEBRUARY
1 St Ignatius, B.M.
2 *Presentation of Our Lord
3 *St Blaise, B.M.
4 St Andrew Corsini, B.C.
5 *St Agatha, V.M.
6 St Titus, B.C. – St Dorothy, V.M. – SS Paul Miki, M. and others
7 St Romuald, Ab.
8 St John of Matha, C.
9 St Cyril of Alexandria, B.C.D. – St Apollonia, V.M.
10 St Scholastica, V.
11 Our Lady of Lourdes
12 The Seven Founders of the Servite Order
13
14 *St Valentine, M.
15 SS Faustinus and Jovita, MM.
16
17
18 St Simeon, B.M.
19
20
21
22 St Peter's Chair at Antioch
23 St Peter Damian, B.C.D.
24 *St Mathias, Ap. – St Polycarp, B.M.
25
26
27
28
Note. In leap year the feast of St Mathias is kept on 25 Feb.

MARCH
1 *St David
2 *St Chad
3
4 St Casimir, C. – St Lucius, P.M.
5
6 SS Perpetua and Felicity, MM.
7 St Thomas Aquinas, C.D. – *St Perpetua
8 St John of God, C.
9 St Frances of Rome, W.
10 The Forty Martyrs. – St John Ogilvie, M
11
12 *St Gregory the Great, P.C.D.
13
14
15
16
17 St Patrick, B.C. – *St Edward, King of the West Saxons
18 St Cyril of Jerusalem, B.C.D.
19 St Joseph
20
21 *St Benedict, Ab.
22
23

24 St Gabriel the Archangel
25 *The Annunciation
26
27 St John Damascene, C.D.
28 St John Capistran, C.
29
30
31

APRIL
 1
 2 St Francis of Paula, C.
 3 *St Richard
 4 St Isidore, B.C.D. – St Ambrose
 5 St Vincent Ferrer, C.
 6
 7
 8
 9
10
11 St Leo the Great, P.C.D.
12
13 St Hermengild, M.
14 St Justin, M. – SS Tiburtius and Vale-
    rian, MM.
15
16
17 St Anicetus, P.M.
18
19 *St Alphege
20
21 St Anselm, B.C.D.
22 SS Soter and Caius, PP. MM.
23 *St George, M.
24 St Fidelis of Sigmaringen, M.
25 *St Mark the Evangelist
26 SS Cletus and Marcellinus, PP., MM.
27 St Peter Canisius, C.D.
28 St Paul of the Cross, C. – St Vitalis, M.
29 St Peter, M.
30 St Catherine of Siena, V

MAY
 1 *SS Philip and James, App.
 2 St Athanasius, B.C.D.
 3 *Finding of the Holy Cross – SS Alex-
    ander, P., and others
 4 St Monica, W. – Blessed Martyrs of
    England and Wales.
 5 St Pius V, P.C.
 6 *St John before the Latin gate

 7 St Stanislaus, B.M.
 8 Apparition of St Michael the Archangel
 9
10 St Antoninus, B.C. – SS Gordian and
    Epimachus, MM.
11
12 SS Nereus and others, MM.
13 St Robert Bellarmine, B.C.D.
14 St Boniface, M.
15 St John Baptist de la Salle, C.
16 St Ubald, B. C.
17 St Pascal Baylon, C.
18 [St Venantius, M.]
19 *St Peter Celestine, P.C. – [St Pudenti-
    ana.] – *St Dunstan
20 St Bernardine of Siena, C.
21
22
23
24
25 St Gregory VII, P.C. – St Urban,
    P.M.
26 St Philip Neri, C. – St Eleutherius, P.M.
    – *St Augustine of Canterbury
27 *St Bede, C.D. – St John, P.M.
28 St Augustine of Canterbury, B.C.
29 St Mary Magdalen dei Pazzi, V.
30 St Felix, P.M.
31 St Angela, V. – St Petronilla, V.

JUNE
 1 *St Nicomede
 2 SS Peter and Marcellinus, MM.
 3 St Charles Lwanga and others MM.
 4 St Francis Carraciolo, C.
 5 *St Boniface, B.M.
 6 St Norbert, B.C.
 7
 8
 9 SS Primus and Felician
10 St Margaret, Queen, W.
11 *St Barnabas, Ap.
12 St John of St Facundo, C. – SS Basilides
    and others, MM.
13 St Antony of Padua, C.
14 St Basil the Great, B.C.D.
15 St Vitus and others, MM.
16
17 *St Alban
18 St Ephrem, C.D. – SS Mark and
    Marcellianus, MM.

19 St Juliana, V. – SS Gervase and Protase, MM.
20 St Silverius, P.M. – Translation of St Edward
21 St Aloysius, C.
22 St Paulinus, B.C. – SS John Fisher and Thomas More MM.
23 Vigil of St John the Baptist
24 Nativity of *St John the Baptist
25 St William, Ab.
26 SS John and Paul, MM.
27
28 St Irenaeus, B.M.
29 SS Peter and Paul, App. – *St Peter
30 Commemoration of St Paul

JULY
1 The Most Precious Blood – Octave of St John the Baptist
2 *The Visitation of Our Lady – SS Processus and Martinian, MM.
3 St Leo II, P.C.
4 *Translation of St Martin
5 St Antony Zaccaria, C.
6 Octave of SS Peter and Paul – St Maria Goretti, V.M.
7 SS Cyril and Methodius, BB., MM.
8 St Elizabeth, Queen, W.
9 *St Thomas More
10 The Seven Brethren, MM.
11 St Pius, P.M.
12 St John Gualbert, Ab. – SS Nabor and Felix, MM.
13 St Anacletus, P.M.
14 St Bonaventure, B.C.D.
15 St Henry, C.
16 Our Lady of Mount Carmel
17 [St Alexius, C.]
18 St Camillus of Lellis – St Symphorosa and her Sons, MM.
19 St Vincent de Paul, C.
20 St Jerome Emilian, C. – [St Margaret, V.M.]
21 St Praxedes, V
22 *St Mary Magdalene
23 St Apollinaris, B.M. – St Liberius, B.C.
24 Vigil of St James – St Christina, V.M.
25 *St James the Apostle – [St Christopher, M.]
26 *St Anne, and St Joachim, Parents of Our Lady

27 St Pantaleon, M.
28 St Nazarius and others, MM.
29 St Martha, V. – SS Felix and others, MM.
30 SS Abdon and Sennen – St Peter Chrysologus, B.C.D.
31 St Ignatius Loyola, C.

AUGUST
1 St Peter's chains
2 St Alphonsus, B.C.D. – St Eusebuis of Vercelli, B.M.
3 Finding of St Stephen, 1st martyr
4 St Dominic, C. – St John Mary Vianney
5 Dedication of Our Lady of the Snow
6 *The Transfiguration of our Lord – SS Xystus and others, MM.
7 St Cajetan, C. – St Donatus, B.M. – Name of Jesus
8 SS Cyriacus and others, MM.
9 Vigil of St Laurence – St Romanus, M.
10 St Laurence, M.
11 SS Tiburtius and Susanna, MM.
12 St Clare, V.
13 SS Hippolytus and Cassian, MM.
14 Vigil of the Assumption – St Eusebius, C. - St Maximilian Kolbe, M.
15 The Assumption of Our Lady
16
17 St Hyacinth, C. – Octave of St Laurence
18 St Agapitus, M.
19 St John Eudes, C.
20 St Bernard, Ab. D.
21 St Jane Frances de Chantal, W.
22 Octave of the Assumption – St Timothy and others, MM.
23 St Philip Benizi, C. – St Rose of Lima, V.
24 *St Bartholomew, Ap.
25 St Louis, K.C.
26 St Zephyrinus, P.M.
27 St Joseph Calasanctius, C.
28 *St Augustine, B.C.D. – St Hermes, M.
29 *Beheading of St John the Baptist – St Sabina, M.
30 St Rose of Lima, V. – SS Felix and Adauctus, MM.
31 St Raymund Nonnatus, C.

SEPTEMBER
1 St Giles, Ab. – The Twelve Brethren, MM.

2 St Stephen, K.C.
3
4
5 St Lawrence Justinian
6
7 *St Evurtius
8 *Nativity of Our Lady – St Hadrian, M.
9 St Gorgonius
10 St Nicholas of Tolentino
11 SS Protus and Hyacinth, MM.
12 Holy Name of Mary
13
14 Exaltation of the Holy Cross – *Holy Cross Day
15 Seven Dolours of Our Lady – St Nicomedes, M.
16 SS Cornelius and Cyprian, BB., MM. – SS Euphemia and others, MM.
17 Stigmata of St Francis – *St Lambert
18 St Joseph of Cupertino, C.
19 St Januarius and others, MM.
20 [St Eustace and others, MM.] – SS Andrew Kim Taegon and others MM.
21 *St Matthew, Ap.
22 St Thomas of Villanova, B.C. – SS Maurice and others, MM.
23 St Linus, P.M.
24 Our Lady of Ransom
25
26 SS Cyprian* and Justina, MM.
27 SS Cosmas and Damian
28 St Wenceslaus
29 Dedication of St Michael – *St Michael and All Angels
30 *St Jerome, C.D.

OCTOBER
1 *St Remigius, B.C.
2 The Holy Guardian Angels
3 St Thérèse of the Child Jesus
4 St Francis of Assisi, C.
5 St Placid and others, MM.
6 St Bruno, C. – *St Faith
7 The Holy Rosary – St Mark, P.C. – St Sergius and others, MM.
8 St Bridget, W.
9 *St Denys and others, MM.
10 St Francis Borgia, C.
11

12
13 St Edward, K.C. – *Translation of St Edward
14 St Callistus, P.M.
15 St Teresa, V.D.
16 St Hedwige, W.
17 St Margaret Mary Alacoque, V. – *St Etheldreda
18 *St Luke the Evangelist
19 St Peter of Alcantara, C.
20 St John Cantius
21 St Hilarion, Ab. – St Ursula and others, VV., MM.
22
23
24 St Raphael, Archangel
25 Forty English Martyrs. – SS Chrysanthus and Darias, MM – *St Crispin
26 St Evaristus, P.M.
27 Vigil of SS Simon and Jude
28 *SS Simon and Jude, App.
29
30
31 Vigil of All Saints

NOVEMBER
1 *All Saints
2 All Souls
3
4 St Charles Borromeo, B.C. – SS Vitalis and Agricola, MM.
5
6 *St Leonard
7
8 Octave of All Saints – The Holy Crowned Martyrs
9 Dedication of St John Lateran – St Theodore, M.
10 St Andrew Avellino, C. – SS Tryphon and others, MM.
11 *St Martin, B.C.
12 St Martin I, P.M. – St Mennas, M.
13 St Didacus, C. – *St Britius
14 St Josaphat, B.M.
15 St Gertrude, V. – *St Machutus
16
17 St Gregory Thaumaturgus, B.C. – *St Hugh of Lincoln
18 Dedication of the Basilicas of St Peter and St Paul

19 St Elizabeth, Queen, W. – St Pontianus, P.M.
20 St Felix of Valois, C. – *St Edmund, K.M.
21 Presentation of our Lady
22 *St Cecilia, V.M.
23 *St Clement, P.M. – St Felicitas, M. – St Columbanus, A.
24 SS Andrew Dung-Lac and others MM – St Chrysogonus, M.
25 *[St Catherine, V.M.]
26 St Sylvester, Ab. – St Peter, M.
27
28
29 Vigil of St Andrew – St Saturninus, M.
30 *St Andrew the Apostle

DECEMBER
1
2 [St Bibiana, V.M.]
3 St Francis Xavier, C.
4 [St Barbara, V.M.]
5 St Sabbas, Ab.
6 *St Nicholas, B.C.
7 St Ambrose, B.C.D.

8 The Immaculate Conception of Our Lady – *Conception of the B.V.M.
9
10 St Melchiades, P.M.
11 St Damasus, P.C.
12
13 *St Lucy, V.M.
14 St John of the Cross, C.D.
15 Octave of the Immaculate Conception.
16 *O. Sapentia
17
18
19
20 Vigil of St Thomas
21 *St Thomas the Apostle
22
23
24 Christmas Eve
25 *The Nativity of Our Lord
26 *St Stephen, 1st martyr. – The Holy Family
27 *St John the Evangelist, Ap.
28 *Holy Innocents, MM.
29 St Thomas of Canterbury, B.M.
30
31 *St Sylvester, P.C.

4. Orthodox Calendar

The ecclesiastical year of the Orthodox Church begins on 1 Sept. and it is called 'Indiction'. (See 9 below.) On 14 Nov. fasting before Christmas starts. Christmas Festivals end with Epiphany. Then, one to four Sundays follow (it depends on the date of Easter Sunday) and 'Triodion' and the movable feasts begin, which consist of two parts: (a) a period of four Sundays, which is as an introduction to the Lent before Easter, and (b) the whole period of seven weeks of the Lent. The most important Sundays of the second period are: the first, in which the reintroduction of the Holy Ikons is celebrated. The third in which the Holy Cross is worshipped for spiritual strengthening of those who fast. And Palm Sunday, after which the Great and Holy Week begins. Special services, called the 'Akathist Hymn,' are held in honour of Holy Virgin in the afternoons of the first five Fridays of Lent. Easter falls on the first Sunday after the full moon of the Spring Equinox, but if it happens to coincide with the Jewish Passover it is postponed to the next Sunday. This is one reason for the differences in the dating of Easter Sunday between Eastern and Western Churches. The weeks between Easter and Pentecost are Paschal time. The Ascension of Our Lord is 40 days after Easter and always on Thursday. On the 50th day after Easter the feast of Pentecost is celebrated and it is followed by Trinity Monday. The Sunday next is the day of All Saints. The first fortnight in August is dedicated to the Holy Mother of God, when special services are held and it is kept as a fasting period.

With the above runs the Calendar of Festivals – given below in abridged form owing to lack of space – fixed to particular days of the months.

CALENDAR OF FESTIVALS
(Proper names transliterated from modern Greek orthography)

JANUARY
1 Circumcision. St Basil the Great
2
3
4
5
6 The Epiphany
7 St John the Baptist
8
9
10 St Gregory, Bishop of Nyssis
11 St Theodosius
12
13
14
15
16
17 St Antonius the Great
18 St Athanasius and St Cyril, Patriarchs
      of Alexandria

19
20 St Efthymios the Great
21 St Maximus the Confessor
22
23
24
25 St Gregory the Theologian
26
27 Removal of the Holy remains of St John
      Chrysostom
28
29
30 St Basil the Great, St Gregory the Theo-
      logian, and St John Chrysostom
31

FEBRUARY
1
2 Purification of Our Lady
3 SS Symeon and Anna

4
5
6 St Photius the Great, the Confessor
7
8
9
10 St Charalambos
11
12
13
14
15
16
17
18
19
20
21
22
23 St Polycarpos, Bishop of Smyrna
24
25
26
27
28
29 St Cassianos

MARCH
1 St Evdokia and others
2
3
4
5
6
7
8
9 Forty Martyrs
10
11
12
13
14
15
16
17
18 St Cyril, Archbishop of Jerusalem
19 SS Chrysanthos, Daria, Claudius
20
21
22
23

24
25 The Annunciation
26
27
28
29
30
31

APRIL
1
2
3
4
5
6 St Eftychius, Patriarch of Constantinople
7
8
9
10 St Gregory, Patriarch of Constantinople
11
12
13 St Martinos, Bishop of Rome
14
15
16
17
18
19
20 St Theodorus of Trihina
21
22
23 St George's Day
24 St Elisabeth
25 St Mark the Apostle and Evangelist
26
27
28
29
30

MAY
1
2 Removal of the Holy remains of Athanasius the Great
3
4
5 St Irene
6
7
8 St John the Theologian

9
10
11
12 St Epiphanius, Bishop of Cyprus and
St Germanos, Archbishop of Constantinople
13
14
15
16
17
18
19
20
21 St Constantine the Great and St Helena
22
23
24
25
26
27
28
29
30
31

JUNE
1 St Justin the Apologist and Philosopher
2
3
4
5 St Dorotheos, Bishop of Tyros
6
7
8 St Theodoros the Stratilat
9
10
11
12
13
14
15
16
17
18
19
20
21
22
23
24 Nativity of St John the Baptist

25
26
27
28
29 St Peter and Paul
30 The Twelve Apostles Day

JULY
1 St Kosmas and Damianus, the Anargyroi
2
3
4
5
6
7 St Kyriaki
8
9
10
11 St Effimia
12
13
14
15
16
17 St Marina
18
19 St Makrina
20 St Elias the Prophet
21
22
23
24 St Christine
25 Assumption of St Anna
26 St Paraskevi
27 St Panteleimon
28
29
30
31

AUGUST
1
2 Removal of the Holy remains of St
Stephanos the Protomartyr
3
4
5
6 The Transfiguration of Our Lord
7
8 St Emilianus, Bishop of Kyzikos
9 St Mathias the Apostle

10
11
12
13
14
15 The Assumption of Our Lady
16
17
18
19
20
21
22
23
24
25
26
27
28
29 Beheading of St John the Baptist
30
31

SEPTEMBER
1 Indiction. St Symeon the Stylite
2
3
4
5 St Zacharias the Prophet
6
7
8 Nativity of Our Lady
9 St Joachim and Anna
10
11
12
13
14 The Exaltation of the Holy Cross
15
16 St Effimia
17
18
19
20 St Efstathius
21
22
23 St Thecla the Martyr
24
25
26 Assumption of St John the Evangelist
27

28
29
30

OCTOBER
1
2 St Cyprianus
3 St Dionysios the Areopagite
4 St Herotheos, Bishop of Athens
5
6
7
8
9
10
11
12
13
14
15
16
17
18 St Luke the Apostle and Evangelist
19
20 St Artemios
21
22
23 St Jacobus the Brother of Our Lord
24
25
26 St Demetrius
27 St Nestorius
28
29
30
31 St Stachios the Apostle, first Bishop of
      Byzantium

NOVEMBER
1
2
3
4
5
6
7
8 SS Michael and Gabriel the Archangels
9
10
11
12

13 St John Chrysostom, Archbishop of Constantinople
14 St Phillipos the Apostle
15
16 St Matthew the Apostle and Evangelist
17
18
19
20
21 Presentation of Our Lady
22 St Phillimon the Apostle
23 St Amphilochius, Bishop of Ikonium
24
25
26
27
28
29
30 St Andrew the Protoklite

DECEMBER
1
2
3
4 St Barbara, St John of Damascus
5 St Savva

6 St Nicholas, Bishop of Myra
7 St Ambrosius, Bishop of Mediolana
8
9 Conception of St Anna
10
11
12 St Spyridon, Bishop of Trimythoundos
13
14
15 St Elefterios
16
17 St Dionysios, Archbishop of Aegina
18
19
20 St Ignatius
21
22 St Anastasia
23
24
25 The Nativity of Our Lord
26
27 St Stephen, First Martyr
28
29
30
31

5. Muslim Calendar

The Muslim calendar takes as its basis the migration of the Prophet Mohammed from Mecca to Medina in 622 AD (an event known as the hegira, hejirah, hijrah which took place on 16 Apr.). This event inaugurated Year 1. It is a lunar calendar, going from one new moon to the next. Months have either 29 or 30 days, and the extra minutes per month total 11 days over 30 years. There are therefore 11 leap years within each 30-year period. There are 354 days in the calendar, 355 in a leap year.

Months are as follows:

Muharram
Safar
Rabi' Ul-Awwal
Rabi' Ul-Thani
Jamada Al-Awwal (Jamada al Ula)
Jamada Al-Thani (Jamada al Akhira)
Rajab
Sha'ban
Ramadan
Shawwal
Dhul-Qi'Da
Dhul-Hijjah

The holy day of the week (Day of Assembly) is the 6th, Friday. Ramadan is the annual fast of the ninth month of the lunar year.

Muslim festivals include:

1 Muharram (New Year's Day)
1–10 Muharram (New Year Festival Period)
12 Rabi' Ul-Awwal (Birthday of the Prophet)
26 Rajab (Festival of the Prophet's Night Journey and Ascension)
15 Sha'Ban (Night of Forgiveness)
1–29/30 Ramadan (Month of Fasting)
1 Shawal (Breaking of Fast)
Dhul-Hijjah (Day of Arafat)
10 Dhul-Hijjah (Festival of Sacrifice)

The calendar's structure allows for considerable variations in the celebrations as related to the Western secular calendar, e.g. In Hegira 1416, Muharram 1 (New Year's Day) is 30 May 1995 and Ramadan starts on 21 Jan. 1996. In Hegira 1420, Muharram 1 is on 16 Apr. 1999; Ramadan starts on 8 Dec. 1999.

6. *The Buddhist Era*, taken by Theravada Buddhists as beginning 543 BC. Most other Buddhists now take the date of Gautama Buddha's death (marking start of Buddhist era) as *c*. 486 BC.

7. *The Coptic Era* begins AD 29 Aug. 284.

8. *The Parsee Era* begins AD 16 June 632.

9. *The Japanese Era* begins 11 Feb. 660 BC.

10. *The Roman Indiction* was a cycle of 15 years introduced by Constantine for purposes of taxation. The indictions began on AD 1 Sept. 312.

11. *The Olympiad* was a four-year period used for dating by the Greeks. The first year of the first Olympiad was 776 BC.

12. *The French Republican Era* lasted from 22 Sept. 1792 until 31 Dec. 1805. The first days of the months of the French Revolutionary Calendar as they occurred in the year 1 of the Era are shown in the preceding secular Calendar; in calculating Gregorian dates from Republican dates the following must be borne in mind:

(*a*) The Republican Calendar was only in actual use from 26 Nov. 1793 till 31 Dec. 1805.
(*b*) The Republican Year begins with the first Vendémiaire.
(*c*) In leap years a sixth Sansculottide was added in Sept. Therefore between 28 Feb. and 22 Sept. 1796 it is necessary to *subtract* one day from each date according to the Gregorian Calendar.
(*d*) On the other hand the year VIII was a leap year, whereas the Gregorian year 1800 was not. Therefore from 23 Sept. 1800 until 31 Dec. 1805 it is necessary to *add* one day to each Gregorian date except in the period 28 Feb.–23 Sept. 1804 (XII), when the clash between the Gregorian and Republican leap years cancels it out.

13. *Hinduism* relies on two principal lunar calendars: the *Purnimanta* and the *Amanta*, but there are other variants. Principal Hindu festivals include:

Holi (Spring festival), celebrated in Feb./Mar., especially in N India
Divali (Festival of Lights), in Oct./Nov.

AA. *See* AUTOMOBILE ASSOCIATION.

Aachen or **Aix-la-Chapelle,** Germany. Founded by Romans, AD 125. Charlemagne made it his capital, 795. He *d.* and was buried here, 814. For treaties signed here see AIX-LA-CHAPELLE, TREATIES OF.

Aarau, Treaty of 11 Aug. 1712, ended the Second Villmergen War. Helvetic republic proclaimed at, 1798.

Aargau. Swiss canton in the basin of the River Aare, which had been conquered by the Franks under Clovis (*c.* 465–511), is first mentioned, as a county, 763. Ceded some SW territory to Berne in the 14th C. Subject to the Swiss Confederacy, from 1415. Joined, 1798, the Helvetic Confederation, and from then until 1803 was divided into two cantons of Baden and A. Joined the Sonderbund (separate Catholic confederation), 1845.

Abadan, Iran. First oil refinery at, 1909.

Abbasids, Islamic dynasty 750–1258, *see under* CALIPHATE.

Abbaye Prison (Paris), France. Built 1631–5. Massacre at, 2–3 Sept. 1792.

Abbeville, France. Treaties of A. (1) between Henry III of England and Louis IX of France renouncing continental Normandy was made at Paris, 28 May 1258, and confirmed in London, 1259. (2) Between Henry VIII and Francis I, 1527.

---

abdications of sovereigns (including forced abdications and 'desertions'):

Diocletian, Roman emperor AD 305
Stephen II of Hungary 1131
Albert the Bear of Brandenburg 1142
Wladislaw III of Poland 1206
Pope Celestine V 13 Dec. 1294
John Balliol of Scotland 1296
Otho (of Bavaria) of Hungary 1309
Edward II of England 1327
Richard II of England 29 Sept. 1399
Eric VII of Denmark 1439
Pope Felix V 1449
Charles V, as Emperor of Germany 25 October 1555
Charles V, as King of Spain 16 Jan. 1556
Mary, Queen of Scots 24 July 1567
Christina of Sweden 16 June 1654
John Casimir of Poland 1668
James II of England (fled) 11 Dec. 1688
Frederick Augustus II of Poland 1704
Philip V of Spain (resumed) 1724
Victor Amadeus of Sardinia 1730
Charles of Naples 1759
Stanislaw II of Poland 1795
Charles Emmanuel IV of Sardinia 4 June 1802
Francis II of Germany, who became Emperor of Austria 11 Aug. 1804
Charles IV of Spain, in favour of his son 19 Mar. 1808
Charles IV of Spain, in favour of Bonaparte (*see* SPAIN) 1 May 1808
Joseph Bonaparte of Naples (for Spain) 1 June 1808
Gustavus IV of Sweden 29 Mar. 1809
Louis Bonaparte of Holland 1 July 1810
Jerome of Westphalia, Bonaparte 20 Oct. 1813
Napoleon I of France 5 Apr. 1814
Victor Emmanuel of Sardinia 13 Mar. 1821
Pedro IV of Portugal 2 May 1826
Charles X of France 2 Aug. 1830
Pedro I of Brazil 7 Apr. 1831
Dom Miguel of Portugal 26 May 1834
William I of Holland 8 Oct. 1840
Louis Philippe of France 24 Feb. 1848
Louis Charles of Bavaria 21 Mar. 1848
Ferdinand of Austria 2 Dec. 1848
Charles Albert of Sardinia 23 Mar. 1849
Leopold II of Tuscany 21 July 1859
Bernhard of Saxe-Meiningen 20 Sept. 1866
Isabella II of Spain 25 June 1870

Amadeus I of Spain 11 Feb. 1873
Prince Alexander of Bulgaria 7 Sept. 1886
Milan, King of Serbia 3 Mar. 1889
Pedro II of Brazil 15 Nov. 1889
Oscar, of Norway and Sweden, recognized Norwegian independence; Norway as separate state 27 Oct. 1905
Abdul Hamid II, Sultan of Turkey 27 Apr. 1909
Manoel of Portugal 4 Oct. 1910
P'u-yi of China 12 Feb. 1912
Nicholas of Montenegro. Left his country 1916. Dethroned Apr. 1918
Nicholas II of Russia Mar. 1917
Constantine of Greece 12 June 1917. Restored Dec. 1920. Abdicated again 27 Sept. 1922
Ferdinand I of Bulgaria 4 Oct. 1918
Wilhelm II of Germany 9 Oct. 1918
Charles of Austria 11 Nov. 1918
Mohammed VI of Turkey 17 Nov. 1922
George II of Greece 25 Mar. 1924
Hussein, King of the Hedjaz 5 Oct. 1924
Ali, King of the Hedjaz 19 Dec. 1925
Amanullah, Khan of Afghanistan twice in 1929
Alfonso XIII of Spain 11 Apr. 1932
Prajadhipok of Siam 2 Mar. 1935
Haile Selassie of Ethiopia. Fled 1 May 1936 Restored 5 Apr. 1941
Edward VIII of Great Britain 11 Dec. 1936
Zog of Albania 8 Apr. 1939
Carol II of Romania Sept. 1940
Regent Miklós Horthy of Hungary 15 Oct. 1944
Peter II of Yugoslavia Nov. 1945
Victor Emmanuel of Italy 9 May 1946
Umberto of Italy 12 June 1946
Simeon of Bulgaria Sept. 1946
Michael of Romania 30 Dec. 1947
Wilhelmina of Holland Sept. 1948
Leopold III of Belgium July 1951
Farouk of Egypt 26 July 1952
Talal I of Jordan Aug. 1952
Ahmed Fuad II of Egypt June 1953
Grand Duchess Charlotte of Luxembourg 1964
Idris of Libya Sept. 1969
Zahir of Afghanistan, 24 Aug. 1973
Constantine II of Greece 1974
Haile Selassie of Ethiopia 12 Sept. 1974 (again)
Shah of Iran Jan. 1979
Juliana of Holland Apr. 1980

abduction, defined and punishable in the UK under the Criminal Law Consolidation Act, 1861; Illegal Practices Act, 1883; Criminal Law Amendment Act, 1885; Sexual Offences Act, 1956 and subsequently.

Aberdeen, Scotland, built *c.* 893, made a royal burgh by William the Lion, 1179. Chartered by Robert the Bruce, 1319. Burned by English, 1336. St Machars Cathedral, 1357–1527. University of Aberdeen, King's College, founded by Bishop Elphinstone, 1495. Marischal College, 1593. The two colleges united, 1860. Base for N Sea oil industry since 1970s. The Robert Gordon University at A., 1992, formerly The Robert Gordon Institute of Technology.

Aberfan, mining village near Merthyr Tydfil, Wales, where on 21 Oct. 1966 a coal tip subsided on the village, burying the school and killing over 140 people, mainly children.

Aberystwyth, Wales. Castle founded by Gilbert Strongbow, 1109. Town incorporated by Edward I. Castle used by Charles I as a mint during Civil War, and demolished, 1647. College opened, 1872. Welsh National Library, 1911. *See* WALES, UNIVERSITY OF.

Abingdon, England. Monastery founded *c.* 675 by Cissa. Burned by Danes *c.* 871. Grammar school founded, 1563. Held by Essex against Charles I, 1645. Defenders put prisoners to death without trial, hence term 'A. Law.'

Abjuration, Oath of, was required to be sworn by all entering on certain public offices after 1688 (but especially up to 1702), denying the claims of the house of Stuart. Regulated by the Promissory Oaths Act, 1868. *See* NONJURORS

Abjuration of the Realm, a self-imposed sentence of exile following confession of a crime on account of which the criminal had taken sanctuary. Whole procedure of sanctuary and A. was abolished in the reign of James I (1603–25).

Abkhazia, since 1989 self-proclaimed independent republic in state of rebellion from *Georgia. Georgian offensive against A. began, Aug. 1992. Ceasefire, July 1993, but conflict restarted soon after and Black Sea port of Sukhumi fell to Abkhazis, 27 Sept. 1993. Abkhazis by then controlled more than half of A., but subsequently, with Russian support Georgian position strengthened. May 1994: Russian-Georgian-Abkhaz agreement introduced Russian peacekeepers to A. and provided for return of Georgian refugees. UN observer mission established. Continuing instability.

Abo, Treaty of, 18 Aug. 1743. Sweden ceded part of Finland to Russia.

Abolitionists (USA) Party opposed to slavery. First congress, 1774, but party only became active from 1832 onwards. Merged with the Republican Party, 1868.

abominable snowman or **Yeti.** Footprints described by Col. Howard-Bury, leader of Everest Expedition, 1921, found at 21,000 ft/6405 m. A special expedition set out in search of the A. S., 1954, but its findings were inconclusive. Continued alleged sightings of footprints in 1970s, 1980s and 1990s: announced that Chinese government was mounting further search for the A.S. in 1995.

Abortion Act, 27 Oct. 1967. Came into operation 27 April 1968 and considerably liberalized law governing abortion in England, Wales and Scotland. Time limit on abortions lowered from 28 to 24 weeks by Stillbirth (Definition) Act, 1992. Sept. 1983, referendum voted amendment outlawing abortion into the Irish Constitution. Jan. 1992: President Clinton removed some abortion restrictions imposed in USA by previous Republican administrations. Suggestion that eggs from aborted foetuses might be used in future in *in vitro* fertilisation raised in UK, Jan. 1994. Abortion issue caused split between

ideological groups at UN Population Conference, Cairo, Sept. 1994.

Abrantes, Treaty of, 29 Nov. 1807, ratified at Madrid after which it is sometimes named. *See* PORTUGAL.

Abruzzi National Park, nature reserve around the Gran Sasso d'Italia, founded, 1922.

Abu Dhabi, largest sheikdom and capital of the *United Arab Emirates since 1971. Off-shore oil production started, 1962: international airport opened, 1982.

Abuja, official capital of *Nigeria since Sept. 1982.

Abu Simbel, site of two ancient temples built beside Nile during reign of Ramses II. Moved to higher ground, before site flooded by Aswan High Dam, 1966–7.

Abydos, Asia Minor, was the E end of the pontoon bridge thrown across the Dardanelles by the Persian Army of Xerxes, 480 BC.

Abydos, Upper Egypt, contains a ruined temple of Seti I, where, in 1817, was found the Table of A., key to the genealogy of early Pharaohs.

Abyssinia. *See* ETHIOPIA.

academies, from Academia, a grove outside Athens (sacred to the hero Academus). Plato first taught philosophy here, *c.* 387 BC. Ptolemy Soter founded an academy at Alexandria, 314 BC. First philosophical academy in France founded by Père Mersenne at Paris, 1635. The following are the principal A. with the dates when they were founded. The A. of Great Britain are also under their various titles.

Ancona, Caliginosi, 1642.
Berlin, Akademie der Wissenschaften, 1700; Architecture, 1799.
Bologna, Ecclesiastical, 1687; Mathematics, 1690; Sciences and Arts, 1712.
Boston, Arts and Sciences, 1780.

Brescia, Erranti, 1626. Brescia Academy, 1801.

Brest and Toulon, Military, 1682.

Brussels, Académie Royale, 1773.

Bucharest, Romanian Academy, 1866.

Caen, Belles-Lettres, 1705.

Chicago, Sciences, 1865.

Connecticut, Arts and Sciences, 1799.

Copenhagen, Sciences, 1742.

Cortona, Antiquities, 1726.

Dublin, Royal Irish Academy, 1782.

Erfurt, Saxony, Sciences, 1754.

Faenza, Philoponi, 1612.

Florence, Fine Arts, 1270; Platonica, 1474 (dissolved, 1521); Accademia della Crusca, 1582; del Cimento, 1657; Georgofili, 1752 (agricultural); Antiquities, 1807.

Geneva, Medical, 1715.

Genoa, Painting, etc., 1751; Sciences, 1783.

Göttingen, Gesellschaft der Wissenschaften, 1752.

Haarlem, The Sciences, 1760.

Helsinki, Societas Scientiarum.

Istanbul (formerly Constantinople), Academy of, 1851.

Leipzig, Academy of, 1768.

Lisbon, Portuguese Academy, 1779.

London, Royal Society, 1662 (charter granted); Royal Academy of Arts, 1768; Royal Academy of Music, 1822.

Lyons, Sciences, 1700.

Madrid, Royal Spanish, 1713; History, 1730; Painting and the Arts, 1753.

Mannheim, Sculpture, 1775.

Mantua, Vigilanti (Sciences), 1704.

Marseilles, Belles-Lettres, 1726.

Massachusetts, Arts and Sciences, 1780.

Milan, Sciences, 1719; Academy of, 1838; Architecture, 1880.

Munich, Arts and Sciences, 1759.

Naples, Rossana, 1540; Secretorum Naturae, 1560; Sciences, 1695; Herculaneum 1755.

New Haven, USA, Connecticut Academy of Arts and Sciences, 1799.

New York, Literature and Philosophy, 1814; Sciences, 1818; National Academy, 1863.

Nîmes, Royal Academy, 1682.

Oslo, Academy, 1837.

Padua, Poetry, 1610; Academy of, 1779; Sciences, 1792.

Palermo, Fine Arts, 1300; Medical, 1645.

Paris, Académie Française, 1637; Académie Royale de Peinture et de Sculpture, 1648; Académie de Peinture, 1648; Académie des Inscriptions, 1663; Académie Royale des Sciences, 1666; Académie Royale d'Architecture, 1671. All these A. at Paris were suppressed, 1793, and in 1795 one large one, the Institut National, was founded. This in 1816 was split up into four classes by Louis XVIII: (*a*) Académie Française; (*b*) Académie des Inscriptions et Belles Lettres; (*c*) Académie des Sciences; (*d*) Académie des Beaux-Arts, and in 1832 Académie des Sciences Morales et Politiques.

Parma, Innominati, 1550.

Peking, Academia Sinica (refounded 1949).

Pennsylvania, Academy of Fine Arts, 1805.

Perugia, Insensati, 1561.

Philadelphia, Arts and Sciences, 1749; Natural Sciences, 1812.

Rome, Lincei, 1609; Umoristi, 1611; Fantastici, 1625; Infecondi, 1653; Painting, 1656; Arcadi, 1656; English, 1752; Nuovi Lincei, 1847.

St Petersburg, Academy, (formerly the Imperial Academy), 1728.

Stockholm, Sciences, 1741; Belles-Lettres, 1753; Agriculture, 1781.

Toulon, Military, 1682.

Trondhjem, Academy, 1760.

Turin, Sciences, 1757; Fine Arts, 1778.

Uppsala, Royal Society, 1720.

Venice, Medical, 1701; Academy, 1760.

Verona, Music, 1543; Sciences, 1780.

Vienna, Kaiserliche Akademie, 1487; Sculpture and Arts, 1705; Surgery, 1783; Oriental, 1810; Sciences, 1847.

Warsaw, Languages and History, 1753.

Washington, DC, Smithsonian Institute, 1846; National Geographical Society, 1888; International Academy of Sciences, Arts and Letters, 1910.

Academy Award given since 1927 by the American Academy of Motion Picture Arts and Sciences, in several categories. The gold-plated statuette first nicknamed 'Oscar', 1931. In 1927–8 best film actor was

Emil Jannings; best film actress, Janet Gaynor; best film, *Wings*.

Among those receiving AAs subsequently have been:
Best film actors
George Arliss (1929–30)
Frederic March (1931–32 and 1946)
Charles Laughton (1932–33)
Clark Gable (1934)
Spencer Tracy (1937 and 1938)
Robert Donat (1939)
James Cagney (1942)
Bing Crosby (1944)
Ray Milland (1945)
Laurence Olivier (1948)
Humphrey Bogart (1951)
Gary Cooper (1952)
Marlon Brando (1954 and 1972)
Alec Guinness (1957)
Sidney Poitier (1963)
Rex Harrison (1964)
Paul Scofield (1966)
John Wayne (1969)
Jack Nicholson (1975)
Peter Finch (1976)
Dustin Hoffman (1979 and 1988)
Henry Fonda (1981)
Ben Kingsley (1982)
Paul Newman (1986)
Jeremy Irons (1990)
Anthony Hopkins (1991)
Tom Hanks (1994 and 1995)
Best film actress
Mary Pickford (1928–29)
Katharine Hepburn (1932–33, 1967, 1968 and 1981)
Bette Davis (1935 and 1938)
Vivien Leigh (1939 and 1951)
Greer Garson (1942)
Jennifer Jones (1943)
Ingrid Bergman (1944 and 1956)
Olivia De Havilland (1946 and 1949)
Judy Holliday (1950)
Audrey Hepburn (1953)
Elizabeth Taylor (1960 and 1966)
Sophia Loren (1961)
Julie Andrews (1964)
Maggie Smith (1969)
Glenda Jackson (1970 and 1973)
Liza Minnelli (1972)

Shirley Maclaine (1983)
Jodie Foster (1988 and 1991)
Emma Thompson (1993)
Holly Hunter (1994)
Jessica Lange (1995)
AAs for best film have included:
All Quiet on the Western Front (1929–30)
Mutiny on the Bounty (1935)
Gone With the Wind (1939)
Rebecca (1940)
Casablanca (1943)
The Bridge on the River Kwai (1957)
My Fair Lady (1964)
The Sound of Music (1965)
A Man for All Seasons (1966)
The Godfather (1972)
The Sting (1973)
One Flew Over the Cuckoo's Nest (1975)
The Deer Hunter (1978)
Chariots of Fire (1981)
Gandhi (1982)
Amadeus (1984)
Rain Man (1988)
The Silence of the Lambs (1991)
Schindler's List (1994)
Forrest Gump (1995)

Acadia (Acadie), Name changed to *Nova Scotia, 1713.

Acarnania, Greece. People of A. engaged in Peloponnesian War, 429 BC against Ambracians, conquered by Spartans, 390 BC; by Macedonians, 225 BC. Defeated by Romans, 197 BC. Subjugated, 145 BC, and was included in the province of Achaea.

ACAS (Advisory, Conciliation and Arbitration Service), an independent body set up under the Employment Act of 1975.

accountants, Chartered Institute of England and Wales founded, 1880. Chartered Institute of Scotland founded, 1854. Association of Chartered and Certified A., 1904. Plans, 1995, to merge Institute of Chartered Accountants with the Chartered Institute of Management Accountants and create a new body.

Accra, Capital of *Ghana, since 1876. Founded 17thC as trading post by British and Dutch.

Achaeans, Hellenic tribe (or group of tribes) which played a leading part in the wars and migrations of the Heroic Age (second millennium BC) and eventually settled on the north coast of the Peloponnese, where the **Achaean League** of 12 city-states, renewed in 281 BC, undertook the liberation of its members from Macedonian hegemony. In 251 it was joined by Sicyon, then by Corinth, Sparta, and other cities not strictly belonging to Achaea, defeated the Macedonians and dominated the peninsula until its defeat by the Romans in 146 BC, after which the Greek mainland became the Roman province (and later the Byzantine theme) of Achaea.

acid rain term first used, 1859, in *Quarterly Journal* of the Chemical Society. In 1972 Sweden presented a case study to the UN Conference on Human Environment, which detailed effects of A.R. on Scandinavia allegedly caused by industrial emissions from western European industrial areas. Since then, further evidence of A.R. damage. Britain blamed by Norway for much A.R. damage (due to emissions from coal-fired power stations), 1993.

acoustics. Explained by Pythagoras *c.* 500 BC. Galileo's important discoveries, AD 1600. Speed of sound discovered by Newton, 1698. Brook Taylor's practical demonstrations of Galileo's theory, 1714. Mersenne's discovery of 1636 explained by Helmholtz, 1862.

Acre, Saint Jean d' (OT *Acco*; NT *Ptolemais*; Modern **Akka**). Captured by Arabs, 638. By Crusaders, 1104. By Saladin, 1187. By Richard I after two years' siege, 1191. By Egyptians, 1291. After its capture by the Turks in 1517 it fell into decay. Successfully defended against Napoleon by Sir Sydney Smith, 1799. Captured by Ibrahim, son of Mehemet Ali Pasha of Egypt, 1832. Stormed by Sir Robert Stopford, 4 Nov. 1840, and returned to Turkey, 1841. Occupied by British, 23 Sept. 1918. Awarded to Arabs by UN but taken by the Israelis, 17 May 1948, and became part of Israel. *See* CRUSADES.

Acropolis, at Athens, consisted in the second millennium BC of fortifications, which together with most of the other buildings on the site were destroyed in the Persian invasion of 480. An early temple to Athene was replaced by the Erechtheum (completed 409 BC). The *Parthenon built, 447–432, and Propylaea, built 437–433. The theatre of Dionysus on the southern slope was converted to a stone structure between 338 and 326 BC. Pollution damage to, since 1970s.

actinometer. Invented by Sir John Herschel *c.* 1825.

Acton Burnell, Statute of, legislating for the recovery of debt, passed, 1283.

actors and actresses, film *see under* CINEMATOGRAPHY.

actors and actresses, stage *see* THEATRE.

Acts of Parliament or **Statutes** earliest mentioned Provisions of Merton, 1236. Earliest existing statute roll 6 Edward I (Statute of Gloucester).

actuary, Institute of As. founded, 1848. Scottish Faculty of As. established, Edinburgh, 1856. A. Society of America assembled, 24 Apr. 1890.

Addis Ababa. Founded, 1885. Made capital of Ethiopia by Emperor Menelek, 1892. Treaty with Italy signed at, 1896. Occupation by Italians, 1936. Pillage of by Italians, 19–22 Feb. 1937. Liberated by British, 5 Apr. 1941. New opera house completed, 1955. The National University, Ethiopia's first university, founded 1961. Headquarters of *Organization of African Unity since 1963.

Addled Parliament, 5 Apr.–7 June 1614.

Adelaide. Capital of state of S Australia. Founded by Col. Light, who arrived 27 July 1837. University founded, 1874.

Aden. Taken by Portuguese, 1513, but captured by Turks, 1538. Independent after 1730 till occupied by the E India Co, 19 Jan. 1839. Control transferred from Indian to British Government, 1927. Crown colony, 1 Apr. 1937. 1962–7, Nationalist uprising against Britain. On 30 Nov. 1967 A., and the former federation of S Arabia became an independent state subsequently known as the *People's Democratic Republic of Yemen with A. as the capital until the country united with the Yemen Arab Republic to become the *Republic of Yemen, 1990. Centre of rebel power in brief civil war, 1994: fell to government, July 1.

administrations, British (since the beginning of the modern cabinet system by Sir Robert Walpole, 1721). For list of Prime Ministers, see under PRIME MINISTER

admiral. Word derived from the Arabic *amir* or *emir* (*lord* or *commander*: cf. *amir-al-bahr*, commander of the sea) and was first used in England in the 14th C under Edward III, though the office it denotes is much older. In the USA the A. was declared the 'ranking officer' in the navy, 2 Mar. 1867; rank abolished, 24 Jan. 1873, but revived in 1899, when Admiral Dewey was appointed. *See* famous A.s listed under SOLDIERS AND SAILORS; and SOLDIERS, SAILORS, AND AIRMEN OF THIS CENTURY.

Admiralty. A commission for discharging the duties of the Lord High Admiral whose office certainly dates from 1405, and probably earlier; it was first placed in commission, 1628. Administrative work of the A., whether in commission or not, was done by the Navy Board instituted in 1546; it performed the duties originally performed by the Keepers of the King's Ships the first of whom was appointed in 1214; the Navy Board was abolished in 1832. The last Lord High Admiral (1827–8) was the Duke of Clarence, later William IV. In 1964, when the A. was absorbed by the Ministry of Defence, the Queen again assumed the title, but not the functions, of Lord High Admiral.

Admiralty Arch erected, as a memorial to *Queen Victoria, 1910.

Admiralty Court ceased to have jurisdiction in naval disciplinary affairs under the terms of the Naval Discipline Act, 1866, its only connection with naval matters being its capacity as a Prize Court as defined by the Judicature Acts of 1873 and 1875. *See also* PROBATE COURT.

Admiralty Islands. Discovered by Dutch, 1616. Occupied by Germany, 1885. Seized by Australian troops, 1914, and after 1919 administered by Australia as a mandated territory. Taken by Japanese, 1942; retaken by Americans, 1944. Self-governing part of Papua New Guinea since 1975.

'Admonition to the Parliament'. Puritan demand for the abolition of episcopacy presented to the House of Commons, 1572. A second pamphlet drawn up and suppressed, 11 June 1573.

Adowa, Adwa or **Adua,** capital of Tigré, Ethiopia. Ethiopians inflicted crushing defeat on Italians, 1 Mar. 1896. Taken by Italians, 6 Oct. 1935. Recaptured by British and Ethiopian troops, Apr. 1941.

Adrianople (Turkish **Edirne**). Old town enlarged by Emperor Hadrian (*d.* AD 138). Constantine I defeated Licinius near, 3 July 323; Valens defeated and slain by Goths, 378; seized by Turks under Murad I, 1361; their capital until 1453; captured by Russians, 20 Aug. 1829; restored, 14 Sept. 1829; occupied by Russians, 20 Jan. 1878. During Balkan Wars, Oct. 1912–Aug. 1913, surrendered to Bulgarians after five months' siege, 26 Mar. 1913; recaptured by Turks, 18 July 1913.

Adrianople, Peace of. Ended Russo-Turkish War, 14 Sept. 1829.

Adulite Monument, an inscription on a marble seat found at Adulis (now Zula or Thulla on the coast of Eritrea near Massawa) referring in Greek to Ptolemy Euergetes, King of Egypt, 246–221 BC by Cosmas of Alexandria in the first half of the 6thC AD.

Advertisements, Book of. A book of ecclesiastical discipline put in force by Archbishop Parker, 1565. It is generally taken as marking the beginning of the persecution of Puritans by the Church of England.

Advertising Standards Association, established London, 1962.

Advisory, Conciliation and Arbitration Service, *see* ACAS.

Advocate, The Lord, also **King's** or **Queen's** (Scotland). Office created *c.* 1480 by James III. First mentioned as 'Lord' A., 1598.

Advocate General or **King's Advocate** (England) office vacant since 1872.

Advocates' Library (Edinburgh) established 1682 by Sir George MacKenzie of Rosehaugh. Non-legal books presented to Scottish nation, 1925.

aediles. Minor Roman magistrates to superintend finance, sanitation, police, etc. First appointed, 494 BC. A higher rank of A., Curule A., first appointed, 367 BC. *See* ROMAN REPUBLIC.

Aegina. Ancient island republic in the Saronic Gulf. Independent till *c.* 456 BC, when it was subjugated by Athens.

Aemilian Way, giving its name to the region of Emilia, was named after its builder, the consul M. Aemilius Lepidus, at whose orders it was begun in 187 BC.

aerial warfare. *See* AVIATION.

aerodynamics. Chair instituted at Imperial College, London, 1920.

Aeronautical Society of Great Britain. Established, 12 Jan. 1866.

Aeroplanes. *See* AVIATION.

aether or **ether,** a putative fine substance first so named by Leibnitz in 1671; a thesis of Kant, 1755, presupposed A., while Thomas Young in 1801 regarded it as the vehicle of light. Michelson and Morley, in 1881 and 1887, tried and failed to find evidence of an A.-drift at the earth's surface.

affiliation. Process in England governed by the Bastardy Acts, 1845, 1873, and 1923, the Affiliation Order Act, 1914, the Affiliation Proceedings Act, 1957, the Maintenance Orders Act, 1968, and the Affiliation Proceedings (Amendment) Act, 1972.

afforestation. Forestry Act, 1919, provides for acquisition and A. of land in UK. Amplified by Forestry Act, 1927. Crown forests transferred to Forestry Commission, 1924. Forestry Commission reorganized, Apr. 1992.

Afghanistan. Invaded by Alexander the Great, 330 BC. Unsuccessful Roman attempts to subjugate, 305–255 BC. Tatar dynasty, AD 907. Part of Moghul Empire, 1525. Conquered by Persia, 1737. Became independent under Durrani dynasty, 1747. First Afghan War, 1838–42. Massacre of British at, and disastrous retreat from Kabul, 1841–2. Kabul captured by British, Sept. 1842. Britain helps Afghans by naval support against Persia, 1854. Second Afghan War, Sept. 1878–Nov. 1890. Relief of Kandahar, Aug. 1880. Amir Habibullah murdered, Feb. 1919. His son Amanullah invades India, May–Aug. 1919 (Third Afghan War). Treaty, Nov. 1921. Military coup overthrew monarchy, 1973. President killed in left-wing coup, Apr. 1978 which led to establishment of a pro-Soviet government. Opposition to Russia led to further unrest and in Dec. 1979 Soviet troops invaded. A civil war between pro- and anti-Soviet factions in A. 1979–88 when UN mediated a peace agreement which was never fully effective. Soviet troop withdrawal complete, Feb. 1989 and pressure on Communist government under Najibollah (in power from 1986) increased. 16 Apr. 1992, Najibollah forced to resign. Anti-government forces took Kabul, 25 Apr. New government with former exile Rabbani as interim president, 28 June 1992. A. proclaimed an Islamic State. Rabbani elected head of state for two years, 30 Dec. 1992, in ballot where he was sole candidate. Civil war still continuing sporadically between different Islamic groups and famine widespread, 1995, despite 'power-sharing agreement' between government and main rebel groups, Mar. 1993. UN peace plan involving eventual resignation of Rabbani and establishment of a ruling interim council becoming operative, Feb. 1995, but country still unstable.

Africa Company, Royal, or Guinea Company of Merchants, founded under Charles II, 27 Sept. 1672. Abolished 7 May 1821, when the Crown took possession of all its settlements, forts, and trading posts, etc. Other companies for exploiting the African trade had previously been formed under royal protection in 1588, and in the reigns of Charles I and James I.

Africa, German East. *See* TANGANYIKA.

Africa, North. *See* ALGIERS AND ALGERIA; TUNISIA; MOROCCO; LIBYA; CARTHAGE.

Africa, South. *See* SOUTH AFRICA, REPUBLIC OF.

African coast, early settlements, etc.
Portuguese: Ceuta, 1415. Guinea voyages begun, 1426. Senegal River, 1445. Sierra Leone, 1460. Gold Coast, 1469. Fernando Po, 1481. Elmina, 1482. Congo, 1484. Dias discovers Cape of Good Hope, 1486. Vasco da Gama explores southeast coast on way to India, 1497–9. Sofata occupied, 1505. Mozambique, 1507.
French: St. Louis, 1626.
English: Cormantine, 1618. Fort James, 1663. Cape Coast Castle, 1672.
Dutch: St. Thomé, 1637–48. Cape Town, 1652.
Prussia: Fredericksburg, 1682.

African exploration (interior). Bruce, 1768–73, to discover sources of Nile. Mungo Park: (1) 1795; (2) 1805, to discover the course of the Niger. Livingstone, 1840–73, Great African Lakes area. Stanley, 1868–95, in Central Africa, Nigeria, and Congo. Niger Expedition subsidized by Parliament, 1840–41. Richardson explores Sahara, 1845–6 and 1849.

Afrikander Bond. Association of Dutch-speaking S Africans, formed 1880. Took an active part in the abortive rebellion of 1914.

African National Congress, established 1912 in S Africa to end racial discrimination there and extend franchise to all races. Banned by government of S Africa 1960–90. Suspended armed struggle and began dialogue with government, 1990. 'Power-sharing' envisaged, Feb. 1993.

Agreement between ANC and Nationalist government on establishment of transitional executive council, Sept. 1993. ANC's leader, Nelson Mandela, became S Africa's first black president after April 1994 elections, brought ANC to power and white minority rule in S Africa ended.

Agadir. Morocco, Importance as a port declined after revolution of 1773. Destroyed by earthquake, 29 Feb. 1960.

Agadir Crisis. Germans sent the gun-boat *Panther* to A., Aug. 1911, in support of claims in Morocco in order to test the strength of the Anglo-French Entente (*see* ENTENTE CORDIALE). Britain and France united to compel a withdrawal in 1912.

Aga Khan. Hereditary head of the Ismaili Moslems. First A.K. fled from Persia to Bombay in 1836. The third A. K. (1877–1957) given status of a First Class Indian Prince, 1916, for political services in World War I. Succeeded by his grandson Karim (*b.* 1936).

age in law at which a marriage in England is valid was raised to 16 by an Act of 1929. Age of majority lowered from 21 to 18, 1970, under Family Law Reform Act, 1969. *See also* CONSENT, AGE OF.

Agincourt. *See* BATTLES.

Agra, Uttar Pradesh State, India. Captured by Baber, 1526, when Koh-i-Noor was among the booty. Seat of Mogul Government, 1566–1658. Taj Mahal built, 1630–32. Stormed by Lord Lake, 17 Oct. 1803. Withstood a long siege in Indian Mutiny during which many important buildings were destroyed, 1857. *See* INDIAN MUTINY.

Agricultural Holdings Acts (Great Britain), granted greater certainty of tenure and compensation for improvements to agricultural tenants in Scotland; passed, 1883; amended, 1900, 1908, and 1913. Act applicable to England and Wales passed, 1922. Consolidating Act for England and Wales, 1948; for Scotland, 1949. Modified by the Agricultural (Miscellaneous Provisions Act), 1976 and by further legislation in 1986. New Bill aimed at further encouraging farming tenancies proposed, 1995.

Agriculture, Fisheries and Food, Ministries of. Board of Agriculture set up, 1793. Dissolved, 1822. Reconstituted, 1889. Became the Board of Agriculture and Fisheries, 1903. Raised to ministry status, 1919. Amalgamated with Ministry of Food, 1955.

Agrigento, Sicily, lies slightly to the W of the Greek town of Acragas (Lat. *Agrigentum*), *fl.* 560–406 BC, having been founded in 582 as a colony of Gela. Captured and sacked by the Carthaginians, 405, and again in 255; and twice by the Romans, 261 and 210. During the days of its independence as a Greek city it was famous for its architecture. In AD 828 A. was captured from the Greeks by the Saracens, and from them by the Norman, Roger I, 1086.

Ahmedabad, capital of Gujarat, India. Founded, 1411. Subjugated by Akbar, 1572, it became the capital of the Muslim Kingdom of Gujarat. Stormed by British, 1780. Restored to Mahrattas same year. Reverted to British, 1818.

Ahmednagar, Maharashtra State, India. Founded, AD 1494. Emperor Aurungzeb *d.* here, 1707. Seized by the Peishwa, 1759. Ceded to Scindiah, 1797. Taken by Wellington, 12 Aug. 1803. Finally annexed to British possessions, 1817 under Treaty of Poona.

Ahvenanmää or **Åland Islands.** Swedish till 1809, when they were ceded to Russia at the Peace of Frederikshavn. Finnish from July 1919. Demilitarization convention, 1921, signed by Great Britain, France, Italy and all Baltic powers except Russia.

AIDS (Acquired Immune Deficiency Syndrome), sexually transmitted disease, believed to have originated in Africa, became internationally recognized problem in 1980s, spreading to the USA, Far East and Europe and subsequently world-wide. Caused by human immunodeficiency virus (HIV), first identified 1983. Government campaign to alert public on dangers in Britain, from 1986. Jan 1993: Harvard report estimated 13 million A. cases world-wide by end of 1992. Figure could reach 100 million by year 2000, with big increases in Africa and Asia. As yet (1995) no effective vaccine for A. Home Secretary said passing on A. deliberately would not be made a criminal offence in the UK, 1992.

Aigues Mortes, France. First Tour de Constance built 12th C by Raymond V of Toulouse. Port created by St. Louis (IX), who built the present Tour de Constance, and sailed from here for the Crusades of 1248 and 1270. Walls built by Philippe le Hardi, 1272–5. Meeting of Charles V and Francis I, 1538.

air. Discovered not to be an element by Priestley, who isolated oxygen in 1774. First vacuum by Torricelli *c.* 1646. First A. pump by O. von Guericke *c.* 1650. First liquefied by Cailletet, 1877. *See also* OXYGEN.

Air Council. Formed, 1918, on model of Army Council to administer Royal Air Force. Functions later taken over by Defence Council.

aircraft carrier. First ship fitted to carry seaplanes, *Hermes*, took part in British naval manœuvres, 1913. But the *Ark Royal* (sunk 1941) was the first A.C. to be effectively used in action. Phased out of Royal Navy, 1968 onwards but USA has consistently made global use of A.Cs during and since World War II, notably during the *Gulf War and Bosnian conflict.

Air Force Regiment, Royal, raised, Feb. 1942.

Air Force, Royal, formed in 1918 by amalgamation of the Royal Flying Corps and Royal Naval Air Service (*see under* FLEET AIR ARM).

airmen of this century. *See* SOLDIERS, SAILORS AND AIRMEN OF THIS CENTURY.

air laws. Aerial Navigation Act, 1911, regulated civil air transport in Britain.

Extended to naval and military areas. 1913. Present A.L. in Britain based on the Civil Aviation Act, 1949 which established the Civil Aviation Authority. International A.L. administered by International Civil Aviation Authority, a UN agency, established 1947 and based in Canada. The EC moved to liberalize Civil Aviation within the Community, June 1992.

Air Ministry. Instituted, 1922. Absorbed by Ministry of Defence, 1964.

air pollution. Extensive powers to prevent this available under the Clean Air Acts, 1946, 1956, and 1968. Further powers under Control of Pollution Acts, 1974, 1980, etc.

Air-Raid Precautions Act, 22 Dec. 1937.

air raids. First offensive use of aircraft by Italians in Libya, 1911, and by Greeks against Turks at Dardanelles, Feb. 1913. First raid on a town by German Zeppelin on Lunéville, 9 Aug. 1914. First on Britain by German aeroplanes, Dec. 1914. First British air raid on German hangars at Düsseldorf, 22 Sept. 1914. In World War II daily German A.R. on Britain began 18 June 1940. Flying bomb attacks started June 1944. Heavy allied raids on Germany from Jan. 1943 onwards. American planes dropped first atom bomb on *Hiroshima, 6 Aug. 1945. A.R. played major part in Korean War (from 1950) and in Vietnam, 1964–75. Also important in Arab-Israeli conflict, 1967–94, in Afghanistan, 1979–92, during Falkland Islands campaign, 1982, Gulf War, 1991, conflicts in Balkans since 1991, and Chechenya, 1994–5. (*See* AVIATION and WORLD WARS I and II.

Airships. Invented, 1783. Giffard's steam-driven airship first ascended, 24 Sept. 1852. Gas engine introduced, 1872. Santos Dumont's gasoline-driven airship, 1898. First Zeppelin completed, 1900. Britain abandoned development of A. after the *R.101* disaster at Beauvais, 5 Oct. 1930; USA after the *Akron*, 4 Apr. 1933, and *Macon* disasters, 12 Feb. 1935. The German airship *Hindenburg* was burnt out, May 1937, but the *Graf Zeppelin* remained in

service until 1938. Limited revival in Britain in 1980s for observation or advertising purposes.

Aix-en-Provence (Latin *Aquae Sextiae*). Founded by Romans, 120 BC. Destroyed by Moors and rebuilt, AD 796. University founded, 1409. Captured by Charles V, 1535. Church councils at, 1112, 1374, 1409, 1416, 1585, 1612.

Aix-la-Chapelle (city). *See* AACHEN.

Aix-la-Chapelle, Congress of, To regulate European affairs, 29 Sept.–21 Nov. 1818.

Aix-la-Chapelle, Treaties of.
1. Between France and Spain, 2 May 1668.
2. At end of War of Austrian Succession, 1748.

Ajaccio, Corsica. Bishopric since 7thC: French since 1768. Napoleon *b.* at, 15 Aug. 1769.

Akkerman. *See* BELGOROD-DNESTROVSKIY.

Aksum, Semitic kingdom in Africa 1st–6thC AD which included modern Sudan and much of modern Ethiopia.

Alabama, Explored by De Soto, 1540. Settled by French, 1702. Ceded to Great Britain by Treaty of Paris, 1763. Part occupied by Spain but retaken by USA, 1813. Admitted to the Union as a state, 1819.

***Alabama* Dispute,** A Confederate warship equipped, 1862, in England did great damage to US shipping till sunk by USS *Kearsarge*, 19 June 1864. Treaty of Washington decided that Britain must pay compensation for damage to USA, Dec. 1871.

Alais. *See* ALÈS

Alaska. Discovered by Bering, 1741. Under control of Russian-American company, 1799. Called 'Russian America' till purchased by USA, 1867. Boundary dispute with Britain settled by arbitration, 1903. Became an incorporated territory, 1912. Admitted to the Union as the 49th state, 3 Jan. 1959. Earthquake at Anchorage killed 180 people, 27 Mar. 1964.

Commercial oil production began, 1959. Transalaska Pipeline completed, 1978. Considerable environmental damage from tanker *Exxon Valdez* oil-spill in Prince William Sound, 1989.

Albania. Area in dispute between Bulgars and Byzantines till Michael Comnenus founded Despotate of Epirus, in which A. was included, 1204. Passed to the Orsini family, 1318–58. Conquered by Stephen Dushan, 1358. Scanderbeg's defence of A. against Turks, 1444–66. Venetian attempt to prevent conquest, 1466; fails, 1479–81. Finally became a Turkish province, 1748. Rebellion achieves independence, 1912. Overrun by Austrians and Allies in World War I. Mandated to Italy, 1920. Republic proclaimed with Ahmed Zog as president, 22 Jan. 1925. Zog becomes king, 1928. Italian conquest, Apr. 1939. Invaded by Greeks in Italo-Greek War, Dec. 1940. Tirana recaptured from Italians by Albanian partisans, Nov. 1944. Proclaimed a People's Republic, 11 Jan. 1946. British cruisers fired at in Corfu Straits, 15 June 1946. British destroyers mined in Corfu Straits, Nov. 1946. Hague Court of International Justice ordered A. to pay compensation 1951, but A. failed to do so. In 1960, A. began ideological quarrel with USSR. In 1967, government declared A. first atheist state in the world; religious practice not again permitted till 1990. A. left *Warsaw Pact and after quarrel with China, 1978, was completely isolated until 1990 when some foreign contacts resumed. Enver Hoxha ruled as Communist dictator from 1946 till death in 1985: numerous purges in 1970s and early 1980s. Following collapse of Communism in eastern Europe, 1989–90, elections in A. Mar. 1991 won by former Communists. Unrest followed: elections in Mar. 1992 won overwhelmingly by opposition Democratic party whose leader, Sali Berisha, elected first non-Communist president of A., Apr. 1992. Severe economic problems in A. 1992 onwards and revival of tribal feuding. Hoxha's widow gaoled for nine years for 'squandering public funds', Jan. 1993. Referendum rejected proposed new constitution, Nov. 1994.

Albany, New York. First European settlement, Fort Nassau, planted by Dutch, 1614; occupied and renamed by English, 1664. Became state capital, 1797.

Albany, Dukes of. Title first created, 1398, for cadets of the Scottish royal house, and so used until 1536; borne by Darnley (*b.* 1545), consort of Mary Stuart, 1565–7; held by James I, Charles I, and James II (*see* ENGLISH SOVEREIGNS AND THEIR CONSORTS); by Ernst August, Bishop of Osnabrück, youngest brother of George I and other Hanoverian princes, intermittently from 1716 to 1827; lastly by Leopold George Duncan Albert, youngest son of Queen Victoria (*b.* 1853), 1881–4, and by his posthumous son, Arthur Charles Edward, who became the last reigning Duke of Saxe-Coburg (abdicated, 22 Oct. 1920).

Albert Canal (Belgium). Antwerp to Liège, opened June 1939.

Albert Memorials. Albert Hall, London, opened by Queen Victoria, 29 Mar. 1871: plans (1993) to refurbish completely by 2000, to enable scientific conferences as well as musical concerts to be held there. Memorial in Kensington Gardens, London, opened, 3 July 1872 and paid for by public subscriptions begun 1862, designed by Sir Giles Gilbert Scott. In 1990s in danger of collapse and covered; restoration work taken over by English Heritage, July 1994. Estimated restoration will be completed by 2000 at cost of £14 million. Albert Memorial Chapel, Windsor, opened, 1 Dec. 1875. Albert Bridge, Chelsea, opened, 28 Aug. 1873.

Alberta, Canada. Constituted a province, 1905. University opened at Edmonton, 1908. Crude oil pipeline, 1,150 miles / 1840 km long, from Edmonton oilfields to Superior, Wisconsin, USA, completed, 1951. Extended to Sarnia, Ontario, in 1953 (643 miles), making it the longest pipeline then existing in the world.

Albigenses. Neo-Manichean sect, whose

beginnings in France were discernible before 1022, and whose doctrines were denounced by councils of Arras (1025), Charroux (*c*. 1028), and Rheims (1049). Name A. first appeared *c*. 1181, derived from Albi, where they were specially numerous. Peter of Castelnau, papal legate sent to extirpate the heresy in the domains of Count Raymond VI of Toulouse, was murdered therein, 1208. Innocent III proclaimed the 'Albigensian Crusade,' 1209. Slaughtered included 20,000 inhabitants of Béziers. Raymond VII continued the struggle against the crusaders and Louis VIII; but made peace in 1229, and the persecution of A. was resumed. They disappear from history after the capture of their last stronghold, Mont Ségur, 1245.

Alcantara, Spain. Famous Roman bridge built, AD 105; restored, 1860. *See* KNIGHTHOOD, ORDERS OF.

Alcatraz, island in San Francisco Bay, California, USA. From 1934–63 a notorious US federal prison. A. was originally a Spanish fort, became a US one, 1850 and in 1868 a military prison. Lighthouse at, 1854. Indian agitation to reclaim A., 1969–71. Since 1972 part of the Golden Gate National Recreation Area.

Alcoholics Anonymous established in USA, 1935. *Twelve Steps* written, 1938. First A.A. World Service opened, New York, 1940. Established in Britain, 1947. First World Service Meeting, New York, 1969. European Information Centre established London, 1978. 1992: 3000th A.A. group registered. A.A. groups now world-wide. General Service Office (incorporating European Information Centre) at York since 1987.

Aldeburgh, Suffolk, was the first corporation in England to have a woman mayor – Mrs. Garrett-Anderson, 1908.

Aldeburgh Festival. Musical festival founded at Aldeburgh, Suffolk, 1948, by Benjamin Britten, Eric Crozier and Peter Pears and held annually since. In 1969 Snape Maltings adapted to house some concerts: burned down but rebuilt and used since 1970.

Aldersgate (London). Described as 'Ealdredesgate' *c*. 1000. Gate rebuilt, 1616. Pulled down, 1761.

Aldershot Camp (England). Formed, Apr. 1854.

Aldgate (London). Gate rebuilt, 1608. Pulled down, 1761. Pump renovated, 1908.

Aldine Press. Instituted by Aldo Manuzio (Aldus Manutius), at Venice, 1490. Italics first used, 1501. Aldus *d*. 1515. Press continued till 1597, and printed 908 different works.

Aldwych (London). Modern thoroughfare opened by Edward VII, 18 Oct. 1905.

Alençon, France. Castle built, 1026; Seized by William the Conqueror, 1048; by Henry II, 1135; restored to France, 1219. Captured by English, 1424, who were expelled, 1450.

Aleppo, Syria. Founded earlier than 2000 BC. Taken by the Egyptians, 1460 BC. Fell to the Crusaders under Baldwin II, AD 1124, and to the Tatars under Tamberlaine, 1400. Became Turkish, 1517. Destroyed by earthquake, 1822. *See* SYRIA.

Alès, in the Cevennes, was an important centre of the Huguenots, captured by Richelieu in 1629, who signed with them the Treaty of A., or *Edict of Grace*, depriving them of political privilege but guaranteeing their liberty of conscience. *See also* CAMISARDS.

Alessandria, Italy. Founded, 1168, and named after Pope Alexander III. Academy founded, 1562. French, 1800–14. Cathedral built, 1823. Headquarters of Piedmontese during Lombardo-Venetian rebellion, 1848–9.

Aleutian Isles. Explored by Bering, 1768; Cook, 1778. Japanese got a foothold on Attu and Kiska islands, 1942, but were driven off by Americans, 1943.

Alexandra Land. *See* NORTHERN TERRITORY.

Alexandria, Egypt. Founded by Alexander the Great, 332 BC. Capital of Egypt under Ptolemaic dynasty, 323–9 BC. Captured by Caesar, 47 BC. By Augustus, 29 BC. Rebuilt by Hadrian, AD 122. Captured by Persians, 616; by Arabs, 640. Recovered and retaken, 644. Plundered by Crusaders, 1365. Taken by Turks, 1517. Captured by French, 1798. Taken by British under Abercromby and retaken by French, 1801. Taken by British under Frazer, 1807. Bombarded by British fleet, 1882. British naval base in World War II. Finally evacuated by British, 1947.

Alexandrian Library. Said to have been commenced by Ptolemy Soter *c.* 284 BC. Badly damaged by fire, 47 BC, and again in AD 391. Contained *c.* 700,000 scrolls. Remains finally disappeared at or immediately after Omar's conquest of Alexandria in AD 642.

Alexandrinus, Codex, or **Alexandrian Codex.** Probably a 5thC scriptural MS in Greek presented by Patriarch of Alexandria and Constantinople to Charles I of England, 1628. Transferred to British Museum, 1757.

Algarve, Portugal. Under Moorish rule 8th–13thC. Taken by Alfonso III, 1249. Tourist resort area since 1950s.

algebra. First Greek textbook on this subject by Diophantus of Alexandria *c.* AD 350. Name originates in title of an Arabic textbook *c.* AD 820, '*Al-jebr wa'l-muquábala,*' by Al-Khwarizmi, which was translated into Latin by Robert of Chester *c.* 1146. Study of A. reintroduced to Europe by Leonardo of Pisa, 1202. Cubic equation first solved by Tartaglia, 1555. Descartes linked A. with geometry in 1637.

Algeciras, Spain. Taken by Moors, 711; by Spaniards under Alphonso XI, 1344. Naval engagements: 1. English and Spanish fleets defeated by French, 6 July 1801; 2. Result reversed, 12 July 1801. Conference at, concerning Moroccan affairs, Jan.–Apr. 1906.

Algiers and **Algeria,** Africa. City captured from Turks by Ferdinand of Spain, 1509, but lost again, 1530. The seaboard towns of the province remained the headquarters of the Barbary pirates for three centuries thereafter. The city was bombarded by an Anglo-Dutch fleet in 1816, but the pirates were only finally suppressed when the French invaded and conquered the province in 1830. Annexed to France, Feb. 1842. Kabyle rising, 1871. From 1881 departments of Algiers, Oran and Constantine an integral part of metropolitan France. Allies land during World War II at A., 8 Nov. 1942. Immense deposits of oil discovered at Hassi Messaoud, near Ouazgla, 1952 – two large oilfields in production by 1957 and by 1980 a major oil and natural gas producer. 1 Nov. 1954: Nationalist war against France begun in A., 1958: Algerian war resulted in fall of Fourth Republic in France and return to power of de Gaulle. 1962: peace signed between A. and France: Algerian independence proclaimed, 3 July 1962. French property taken over. Ben Bella became president of the Democratic People's Republic of A. in 1963. Government overthrown by military junta under Boumédienne in 1965. Return to civilian government, 1977. New constitution, Feb. 1989. Rising tide of Islamic fundamentalism and general dissatisfaction with government led to local elections, June 1990 being won by opposition Fundamental Islamic Front (FIS). State of emergency, June 1991. First round of multiparty elections, Dec. 1991, showed FIS lead. President Bendjedid resigned; elections cancelled. Veteran FLN leader Boudiaf became head of state. New state of emergency, Feb. 1992; FIS banned, Mar. 1992 and *de facto* civil war began with fundamentalists in which thousands of Algerians and many foreigners killed. Boudiaf assassinated, June 1992, succeeded by Ali Kafi, July. Defence minister Zeroual president of A., Jan. 1994; promised elections in 1995 but by end of 1994 fundamentalist violence increasing. There were hijackings by fundamentalists of Algerian planes culminating in forced surrenders at Alicante, 28 Feb. and Majorca, 13 Nov. On 24 Dec. a French plane hijacked at Algiers airport, three passengers murdered and forced to fly to Marseilles. Stormed by French police, 26 Dec. and all four terrorists killed. Subsequent murders of French priests in A., and violence escalating, 1995. 40 killed in bomb outrage, Feb. Britons killed in A., May. Peace moves, June, but later deterioration. Elections planned for November, won by President Zeroual. Algerian Islamic extremists responsible for bomb outrages in France.

Algoa Bay, S Africa. So named by Bartholomew Diaz, 1486. First British colonists landed at, 1820.

Alhambra (Arabic **alhamrah**, the red [castle]) at *Granada built by the Nasride emirs, beginning AD 1213, and enlarged during a period extending into the 14thC. Part of the building dates from after the Christian reconquest, and was added in the reign of Charles V (1516–55), being started in 1526, but never finished.

Alicante, Spain. Besieged by Moors, 1331; by French, 1709. Bombarded by Cartagenan insurgents, 1 Oct. 1873. Bombed by Franco's aircraft in Spanish Civil War, 25 May 1938. Tourist centre from 1950s.

Alice Springs. Capital of Central Australia territory from 1927 to 1931, when Central Australia once again became part of the *Northern Territory.

Aliens Acts (Great Britain). Jan. 1793. Act to register A., 1795. A. Act, 1905, came into force, 1 Jan. 1906. British Nationality and Status of A. Act, 1918, prohibited naturalization of Germans for ten years after official termination of World War I. New provisions, 1933. All Germans naturalized after 31 Dec. 1932 liable to internment under Regulation 18B in World War II. British Nationality Act, 1948, defined an alien as a person who was not a British subject, a British protected person, or a citizen of the Irish Republic. Modified by the requirements of the Commonwealth Immigrants Acts of 1962 and 1968, by the British Nationality Act of 1981 (amended, 1983) and also by EC legislation since the 1980s.

Alkmaar, Holland. Besieged by Spaniards under Alva, 1573. Town hall built, 1582. Captured by Duke of York's Dutch expedition, 2 Oct. 1799.

Allahabad, Uttar Pradesh State, India. Very anciently a holy place. Great mosque demolished, 1157. Fort built by Akbar, 1583. Occupied by British, 1765. Finally annexed, 1801. Massacre at, during Indian Mutiny, 1857. University founded, 1887. First Indian National Congress held here, 1885.

Allegiance, Oath of. Statutes requiring: Elizabeth, 1559; William and Mary, 1689; Anne, 1701; combined with *Oaths of Supremacy and *Abjuration; Victoria, 23 July 1858. Power to modify the oath to enable Jews to sit in Parliament, 23 July 1858; amended, 6 Aug. 1860. Form of affirmation in lieu of oath, 8 Apr. 1859.

All Souls' College (Oxford), founded, 1438 by Archbishop Henry Chichele in memory of those killed in the French wars of the period.

almanacs. Earliest known published by Soloman Jarchus, 1150. First printed A. by Purbach, 1450. Bore a stamp duty in Britain, 1710–1834. British almanac first published, 1828. Almanach de Gotha first published, 1763.

Almeida, Portugal. Taken and lost by Spaniards, 1762. Captured from British by French under Soult, 17 Aug. 1810. Recovered by Wellington, 11 May 1811.

Almeria, Spain, anciently **Urci,** became a Roman town, 19 BC. Was a petty kingdom from 1288 to 1489. The cathedral dates from 1524.

Almohades. Muslim sect and dynasty founded in 12thC in N Africa (Berber). Founded by Mohammed Ibn Tumart. He and his successor, Abd-el-Mumin, conquered much of N Africa and Morocco between 1128 and 1149, and invaded Spain. Christian reconquest of Spain checked by them at Allarcos, 1185, but their decline was rapid after their defeat at Navas de Tolosa, 1212. By 1254 they were pinned into Granada, and the last of the line was murdered in 1269. *See* ALMORAVIDES and SPAIN.

Almoravides. Muslim sect and dynasty founded 11thC. They conquered *Morocco and founded Marrakesh *c.* 1080. In 1086 their leader Yusuf-ibn-Tashfin invaded Spain, and after uniting the various Muslim emirates there defeated the Christian Alfonso VI at Zalaca, 1086. After this a decline set in until they were superseded by the *Almohades, who captured Marrakesh in 1147.

Alnwick, England. Besieged by Scots, 13 Nov. 1093; taken, 1136; burnt by King John of England, 1215; by Scots, 1448. Castle ceased to be residence of Dukes of Northumberland, 1945.

Alps. Crossed by Hannibal, 217 BC; by Romans, 154 BC; highest mountain (Mount Blanc) climbed by Paccard and Balmat, 1786; crossed by Napoleon, May 1800. Mont Cenis tunnel through A. completed, 25 Dec. 1870. St. Gotthard tunnel completed, 29 Feb. 1880. Simplon tunnel completed, 24 Feb. 1905. First flight by airman over A., Sept. 1910. Susten Pass post-road opened, 1946. Mont Blanc road tunnel opened, 1965. St Gotthard road tunnel, 1980; Karawanken road tunnel, 1983.

Alsace. Came under French occupation by Peace of Westphalia, 1648. Annexed by Germany, 1871. Returned to France, 1919. Re-annexed to Germany, 1940. Retaken by France, 1945.

Alsatia. Nickname of district around Whitefriars, London, which had certain privileges of sanctuary and consequently became the resort of criminals. Privileges abolished, 1697.

Altamira, caves in N Spain where palaeolithic wall-paintings were found, 1879.

Althing. *See* ICELAND.

Altona, in Schleswig-Holstein, became Danish in 1640. Burnt down during the Dano-Swedish War, 1713. Fiscal and other privileges granted by the Swedish crown withdrawn, 1853. Occupied by troops of the German Confederation, 1864, and became Prussian territory, 1866.

Altmark, supply ship of the German pocket battleship *Graf Spee* in World War II. On 15 Feb. 1940, located by the RAF entering a Norwegian fjord. British destroyer *Cossack* entered fjord, boarded the A. and released 299 British merchant seamen held prisoner there (17 Feb.). They had been held since before sinking of the *Graf Spee* on 17 Dec. 1939.

Altranstadt, Peace of.
1. 24 Sept. 1706, between Charles XII of Sweden and Augustus II of Poland.
2. 7 Mar. 1714, between Louis XIV and the Emperor Charles VI.

aluminium. Discovered by Sir H. Davy, 1807. Wöehler produced A. powder, 1827. First bar made by Deville, 1855.

Alzheimer's Disease, degenerative brain disorder, named after Alois Alzheimer (1864–1915) a German neurologist. Ex-President Reagan announced he had A.D., Nov. 1994.

Amadis of Gaul, Romance of uncertain origin, possibly 14thC or written in its present form by Garcia de Montalvo (late 15thC). Enlarged, 1492. First printed, 1508, in Spanish. Translated into French by Herberay des Essarts, 1540. Abridged English version by R. Southey, 1803.

Amalfi, Italy. Important naval power from 7th C. Fleet repulsed a Saracen invasion of Italy, 848. Independence suppressed by King Roger of Sicily, 1131. Town devastated by flood, 1343. Its Code of Sea Laws (*Tavole Amalfitane*) recognized throughout the Mediterranean till 1570.

Amarapura, Burma. Founded, 1783. Capital of Burma till 1823, and from 1837 to 1860.

Amatongaland (Tongaland), part of Natal, S Africa, annexed to Natal, 1897.

Amazon River, S America, first seen by Europeans under Vicente Yañez Pinzon, 1500. First descended (by Orellana), 1541, from which time the present European name appears to date. First ascended from its mouth as a route to Quito in Bolivia by Pedro Texeira, 1638. Considerable deforestation of A. basin since 1980.

Amboina, Amboyna, or **Ambon,** Moluccas, Indonesia. Trading station in native kingdom of Tidor. Occupied by Portuguese, 1562; seized by Dutch, 1605, who massacred the English merchants there in 1623. It was in British hands, 1790–1801 and 1810–16, when it was returned to the Dutch. Became part of Moluccas government, 1927. Captured by Japanese, Feb. 1942. Surrendered by Japanese, 1945. Capital of Moluccas Province since establishment of the Republic of *Indonesia in 1950.

Amboise, Edict of, 19 Mar. 1563. Conceded freedom of worship to Huguenots.

Amboise, Tumult of, Jan. 1560. Huguenot conspiracy against the Guises suppressed by Catherine de' Medici.

Ambrosian Library (Milan). Founded by Cardinal Borromeo, 1602. Opened, 1609.

America, discovery of. Named in honour of Amerigo Vespucci, a Florentine, who visited land, 1499. Norse colonies established in 10th and 11thC in N America. Columbus first discovered Cuba, Oct. 1492. Cabot discovered Labrador, 1497. Portuguese under Cabral discovered Brazil, 1500.

American Academy of Television Arts and Sciences, responsible since 1949, for awarding Emmys, the television equivalent of the cinema Oscar, for notable television productions. Since 1983 individual performers have been entered into a 'Hall of Fame.'

American Federation of Labor, founded 1881 by Samuel Gompers. Since 1955 merged with the Congress of Industrial Organizations.

American Football. *See* FOOTBALL, AMERICAN.

American literature in English. The fol-

lowing is a list of prominent American authors:

Adams, Henry Brooks 1838–1918, historian.
Adeler, Max. *See* CLARK, this entry.
Albee, Edward, 1928–, dramatist.
Alcott, Louisa May, 1832–88, novelist.
Allen, William Hervey, 1889–1949, novelist.
Allston, Washington, 1779–1843, poet and novelist.
Angelou, Maya, 1928–, novelist and dramatist.
Azimov, Isaac, 1920–92, science fiction writer.
Babbitt, Irving, 1865–1933, critic.
Baldwin, James, 1924–87, novelist.
Bellow, Saul, 1915–, novelist.
Bemelmans, Ludwig, 1898–1962, Austrian-born humorist and cartoonist.
Benchley, Robert, 1889–1945, humorist.
Bromfield, Louis, 1896–1956, novelist.
Browne, Charles Farrar ('Artemus Ward'), 1834–67, humorist.
Bryant, William Cullen, 1794–1878, poet.
Cabell, James Branch, 1879–1958, humorist.
Cable, George Washington, 1844–1925, novelist.
Capote, Truman, 1924–84, novelist, journalist and dramatist.
Cather, Willa Sibert, 1876–1947, novelist.
Chandler, Raymond, 1888–1959, crime novelist.
Clark, Charles Heber ('Max Adeler'), 1841–1915, humorist.
Clemens, Samuel Langhorne ('Mark Twain'), 1835–1910, humorist.
Coolidge, Susan (Sarah Chauncy Woolsey), 1835–1905, children's writer.
Cooper, James Fenimore, 1789–1851, novelist.
Crane, Stephen, 1871–1900, novelist and poet.
Crawford, Francis Marion, 1854–1909, novelist.
Dana, Richard Henry, jnr, 1815–82, miscellaneous writer.
De Vries, Peter, 1910–93, comic writer.
Dickinson, Emily, 1830–86, poet.

Dos Passos, John Roderigo, 1896–1970, novelist.

Dreiser, Theodore, 1871–1945, novelist.

Dunbar, P. L., 1872–1916, poet.

Eddy, Mary Baker Glover, 1821–1910, Christian Scientist.

Emerson, Ralph Waldo, 1803–82, poet and essayist.

Faulkner, William Harrison, 1897–1962, novelist.

Fitzgerald, Francis Scott Key, 1896–1940, novelist.

Friedman, Milton, 1912–, economist.

Frost, Robert, 1875–1963, poet.

Franklin, Benjamin, 1706–90, statesman and journalist.

Galbraith, John Kenneth, 1908–, economist.

Gardner, Erle Stanley, 1889–1970, detective-storywriter.

George, Henry, 1839–97, economist.

Ginsberg, Allen, 1926–, poet.

Greeley, Horace, 1811–72, journalist.

Grey, Zane, 1872–1939, 'Western' novelist.

Habberton, John, 1842–1921, author of *Helen's Babies*.

Harris, Joel Chandler, 1848–1908, miscellaneous writer.

Harte, Francis Bret, 1839–1902, poet and storywriter.

Hawthorne, Nathaniel, 1804–63, novelist.

Hearn, Lafcadio, 1850–1904, miscellaneous writer.

Hecht, Ben, 1904–64, dramatist.

Heller, Joseph, 1923–, novelist.

Hellmann, Lillian, 1907–84, dramatic writer.

Hemingway, Ernest Miller, 1899–1961, novelist.

'Henry, O.' *See* PORTER, this entry.

Holmes, Oliver Wendell, 1809–94, poet and miscellaneous writer.

Howe, Julia Ward, 1819–1910, poet.

Irving, Washington, 1783–1859, miscellaneous writer.

James, Henry, 1843–1916, novelist.

Johnson, James Weldon, 1871–1938, poet.

Kerouac, Jack, 1923–69, novelist.

Lardner, Ringgold (Ring) Wilmer, 1885–1933, journalist and short-story writer.

Lewis, Sinclair, 1885–1951, novelist.

Lindsay, Nicholas Vachel, 1879–1931, poet.

London, Jack, 1876–1916, novelist.

Longfellow, Henry Wadsworth, 1807–82, poet.

Lowell, Amy Lawrence, 1874–1925, critic and poet.

Lowell, James Russell, 1819–91, poet and essayist.

Lowell, Robert, 1917–77, poet.

McCarthy, Mary, 1912–89, novelist and critic.

Mailer, Norman, 1923–, novelist.

Marquis, Donald Robert Perry, 1878–1937, humorist.

Melville, Herman, 1819–91, novelist.

Mencken, Henry Louis, 1880–1956, critic.

Miller, Arthur, 1915–, dramatist.

Miller, Henry, 1891–1980, novelist.

Mitchell, Margaret Munnerlyn, 1900–49, novelist.

Moore, Marianne Craig, 1887–1972, poet.

Morrison, Toni, 1931–, novelist.

Morley, Christopher Darlington, 1890–1957, novelist, poet, and essayist.

Motley, John Lothrop, 1814–77, historian.

Nash, Ogden, 1902–71, humorous poet.

Nathan, George Jean, 1882–1958, critic.

Norris, Frank, 1870–1902, novelist.

Odets, Clifford, 1906–63, dramatist.

O'Neill, Eugene Gladstone, 1888–1953, dramatist.

Parker, Dorothy, 1893–1967, humorist.

Parkman, Francis, 1823–93, historian.

Poe, Edgar Allan, 1809–49, poet and story-writer.

Plath, Sylvia, 1932–63, poet.

Porter, William Sydney ('O. Henry'), 1867–1910, story-writer.

Prescott, William Hickling, 1796–1859, historian.

Riding, Laura, 1901–93, poet and critic.

Robinson, Edwin Arlington, 1869–1935, poet.

Roosevelt, Eleanor, 1884–1962, diarist.

Roth, Philip, 1933–, novelist.

Runyon, Alfred Damon, 1884–1944, humorist.

Salinger, J. D., 1919–, novelist.

Santayana, George, 1863–1952, philosopher.

Scott, Turow, 1949–, novelist.

Sinclair, Upton Beall, 1878–1968, novelist.
Singer, Isaac, 1904–91, Polish-born novelist and short-story writer.
Singer, Israel, 1893–1944, Polish-born writer.
Steinbeck, John Ernst, 1902–68, novelist and short-story writer.
Stevens, Wallace, 1879–1955, poet.
Stockton, Frank Richard, 1834–1902, story-writer.
Stowe, Mrs. Harriet Elizabeth Beecher, 1812–96, novelist.
Stratton-Porter, Mrs. Gene, 1868–1924, novelist and naturalist.
Theroux, Paul, 1941–, novelist.
Thompson, Dorothy, 1894–1961, journalist.
Thoreau, Henry David, 1817–62, naturalist and writer.
Thurber, James Grover, 1894–1960, humorist.
Twain, Mark. *See* CLEMENS, this entry.
Updike, John, 1932–, novelist and short-story writer.
Van Doren, Charles Clinton, 1885–1950, critic and biographer.
Van Druten, John William, 1901–57, dramatist and novelist.
Vidal, Gore, 1925–, novelist.
Walker, Alice, 1944–, poet and novelist.
Wallace, Lewis, 1827–1905, religious novelist.
Ward, Artemus. *See* BROWNE, this entry.
Warren, Robert Penn, 1905–89, novelist.
Webster, Noah, 1758–1843, lexicographer.
Wharton, Edith Newbold, 1862–1935, novelist.
Whitman, Walt, 1819–92, poet.
Whittier, John Greenleaf, 1807–92, poet.
Wiggin, Kate Douglas (Mrs. Riggs), 1856–1923, novelist.
Williams, Tennessee, 1914–83, dramatist.
Wilson, Thomas Woodrow, 1856–1923, historian and essayist.
Woolman, John, 1720–72, Quaker essayist.
Woolsey, Sarah Chauncy, *See* COOLIDGE, this entry.
Wouk, Herman, 1915–, novelist and dramatist.

American republics. Haiti declared its independence, 1804; Chile, 1810; Colombia, 1811 (from this Venezuela and Ecuador seceded, 1830); Argentina, 1816; Paraguay, 1821; Peru, 1821; Mexico, 1821; Central American Confederation, 1828 (from which secession took place as follows: Guatemala, 1839; Costa Rica, 1839; Honduras, 1839; Nicaragua, 1839; Salvador, 1848. All had formed part of Mexico between 1821 and 1823); Bolivia, 1825; Uruguay, 1828 (after successive occupation by Brazilian and Argentine forces); Dominican Republic, 1844; Brazil, 1889; Cuba, 1897; Panama, 1903.

America's Cup, The. Cup originally called the Queen's Cup, presented by the Royal Yacht Squadron in 1851 and won in that year by the American schooner *America*. Presented to New York Yacht Club by the owner in 1887; it has been called the A.C. ever since, and won by the USA until 1983, when Australia won it. Won back by the USA in Feb. 1987. USA retained it in 1988 and 1992. Won by New Zealand, 1995.

Amiens, France. Cathedral built, 1220–88. Treaty of A. Between Henry VIII, represented by Cardinal Wolsey, and Francis I, signed here, 18 Aug. 1527. Taken by Spanish, 11 Mar. 1597; retaken by French, 25 Sept. 1597. Peace treaty signed, 25 Mar. 1802, between England, France, Spain and Holland. Germans entered A., 28 Nov. 1870, during Franco-Prussian War. Threatened by Germans, 24 Apr. 1918. Occupied by Germans, 21 May 1940. Liberated by British, Aug. 1944.

Amiens, Mise of. The award pronounced by Louis XI of France, 23 Jan. 1264, in the dispute between Henry III of England and his barons. *See also* OXFORD, PROVISIONS OF.

Amman, Jordan (Biblical *Rabath-Ammon*; Gr. *Philadelphia*). Became capital of Transjordan, 1921. *See* JORDAN.

Amnesty International, founded in Britain, 1961, to campaign for human rights and release of political prisoners all over the world. Awarded Nobel Peace Prize, 1977.

Amoy or **Hsiamen,** China. Trading with A. permitted, 1676. The fort destroyed by British, July 1840. Town captured, 26 Aug. 1841. Port opened by treaty for trade, 26 Aug. 1842. Occupied by Japanese, 1938. Returned to China, 1945. A. linked to mainland by two stone embankments, 1956.

Amritsar became the headquarters of the Sikh religious movement, 1574. Golden Temple destroyed, 1761; rebuilt, 1764, and roofed with copper gilt by Ranjit Singh, 1802. The 'A. Massacre' took place, 13 Apr. 1919. Indian army stormed Golden Temple, June 1984.

Amsterdam, Holland. Founded, 1204. Charter granted, and Old Church built, 1300. New Church, 1408. Dutch E India Co. established at, 1602. University founded, 1632. Surrendered to Prussians, 1787. To French, 1795. N Holland Canal built, 1819–25. N Sea Canal, 1865–95. Occupied by Germans, 14 May 1940. Liberated, 12 May 1945. Canal linking A. with River Waal opened, 1952. Airport first opened at Schiphol, 17 May, 1920: modern Schiphol Centre airport opened, 26 April, 1967. First road-tunnel under river at A., 1960; second, 1966. Underground system, 1977.

Anabaptists. Said to have been founded by Thomas Münzer *c.* 1520. A. state established under John of Leyden at Münster, 1533–5. Laws against, 1525–34. *See* BAPTISTS.

'Anabasis'.
1. *See* TEN THOUSAND.
2. Arrian's account (AD 166–8) of Alexander the Great's campaigns.

ANC. *See* AFRICAN NATIONAL CONGRESS.

anaesthetics. Nitrous oxide (laughing gas) first used as anaesthetic by Sir H. Davy, 1800. Ether by Morton, 1846. Chloroform by Sir J. Y. Simpson, 1847. Local A. first used, 1884.

anarchism. First formulated as a modern political theory by Godwin, 1793. Elaborated by Proudhon, 1840. Four anarchists hanged at Chicago, 1886. Prominent in Spanish Civil War, 1936–9. Anarchism blamed for some international terrorism since 1960s, notably in Germany, France and Italy.

Anatolia or **Asia Minor.** Conquered by Cyrus, 546 BC. By Alexander the Great, 334 BC. Roman province of 'Asia' established, 133 BC. Roman conquest complete, 63 BC. Invaded by Chosroes II of Persia, AD 616–26. By Arabs, 668. Central A. subdued by Seljuk Turks, 1071–80. Destruction of Seljuk power by Mongols, 1243. Ottoman power established at Brusa, 1307. Final Ottoman conquest, 1481. (For later history *see* OTTOMAN EMPIRE and TURKISH REPUBLIC.)

Anchorage, Alaska. Founded 1918, now (1995) largest city in Alaska. Earthquake at killed 200 people, 27 Mar. 1964.

Ancient Buildings, Society for Protection of. Established, 1877.

Ancient Lights. Law passed, 1 Aug. 1832.

Ancient Monuments Society. Founded 1924, for the study and conservation of ancient monuments, historic buildings and fine old craftsmanship.

Ancona, Italy. Founded by refugees from Syracuse *c.* 390 BC. Rebuilt by Trajan, AD 107. Besieged by Frederick Barbarossa, 1167; by Christian, Archbishop of Mainz, 1173. Annexed to Papal States, 1532. Captured by French, 1797; by Austrians, 1799; by French, 1801. Restored to Papal States, 1802. Occupied by French, 1832; evacuated, 1838. Bombarded by Austrians, 18 June 1849. A. rebelled against Papacy, Sept. 1860, and has been since part of Italian state. Severely damaged by bombardment, 1943.

Andaman and **Nicobar Islands,** in the Bay of Bengal. A British settlement was made on North Andamans, 1789. Used as penal settlement, 1858–1942. Nicobar Islands ceded to Britain by Netherlands, 1869. The Japanese occupied the A.I. 1942–5. Part of India since 1947.

Andean Group, formed 26 May 1969 by

Bolivia, Chile, Colombia, Ecuador and Peru with a free-trade area objective. 1973, Venezuela joined A.G. Chile withdrew, 1977. By Act of Caracas, May 1991, a free-trade zone between members established from 1992, with its ideal, the creation of a 'common market' by 1995. Headquarters in Peru.

Anderida. *See* SUSSEX.

Andorra (officially **Las Valls d'Andorra**). Small semi-independent republic in the Pyrenees. Counts of Foix and Spanish Bishop of Urgel became co-princes of A., 1278. French office of Co-Prince descended through the French monarchy to the President of the French Republic in modern times. First Andorran political party formed, 1976. First prime minister appointed, 1981. Executive and legislative powers separated, 1982. Wholly independent from France from May, 1993; joined UN, July 1993.

Angel Falls, Venezuela. Highest waterfalls in the world, named after aviator James Angel who flew over them, 1935, crash-landing nearby.

Angers, France. Taken from Romans, AD 464; fortified *c.* 859–60. Castle completed by Louis IX. Town burnt by King John of England, 1206; taken by Huguenots, 1585; attacked by Vendéan army, 1793. Church of Saint-Serge built, 1050.

Angevins. *See* ENGLISH SOVEREIGNS.

Angkor, Cambodia. Famous Khmer temple at, built *c.* 9th–12thC.

Anglesey, Wales. Conquered by Romans under Agricola, AD 78. Hugh of Chester's attempt to conquer A. frustrated with Viking assistance, 1098. Subdued and organized by Edward I, 1295–8.

Anglia, East, kingdom founded *c.* AD 500. Submitted to Egbert of Wessex, 826. Subsequently invaded by the Danes, who held it until forced to submit to Edward the Elder, 918. One of the four great earldoms under Canute.

Anglia, East, University of, established at Norwich, 1963.

Anglia Polytechnic University, since 1992, name of former Anglia Polytechnic, at Chelmsford.

Anglican Communion, recognition of, dates from first *Lambeth Conference of 1867. Membership implies acceptance of the Lambeth Quadrilateral of 1888. In 1995 there were 33 independent Anglican provinces world-wide, all recognizing the special position of the archbishop of Cantebury. See also ENGLAND, CHURCH OF.

Anglo-Irish Agreement reached between British and Irish governments at *Hillsborough in 1985. It gave the Irish government in Dublin a greater voice in N Irish affairs and was opposed by Unionist parties in N Ireland. It resulted in both governments having subsequent regular talks on N Ireland and contributed to the eventual *Anglo-Irish Declaration of 1993 and the 'Framework Document' of 1995, under which both governments set out a proposed framework for negotiations by all constitutional parties on the future of N Ireland.

Anglo-Irish Declaration, signed in London, 15 Dec. 1993, by John Major, British premier, and Albert Reynolds, *Irish premier. It was intended to open way for peace in N Ireland and offered *Sinn Fein a seat at the negotiating table once *IRA renounced *violence permanently, while declaring status of N Ireland could only be changed by vote of the majority. IRA 'complete cease-fire' from 31 Aug. 1994, followed by Loyalist cease-fire.

Anglo-Saxon Chronicle, or more correctly **Chronicles**. Of the six different texts which survive all appear to have been begun in the reign of Alfred the Great, probably after 880, though they incorporate matter taken from much earlier chronicles which were kept up in Northumbrian religious houses from the middle of the 7th to the end of the 8th C. Between them they record events in Britain from AD 449 to 1154.

Angola, Discovered, 1486, and colonized by Portuguese. Occupied by Dutch, 1641. Restored to Portugal, 1648. Anti-colonial revolution in A. from 1961, led to a People's Republic of A. being proclaimed, Nov. 1975. Civil war followed, 1975–91, with Cuba supporting the Angolan Marxist government and S Africa aiding Unita rebels. Dec. 1988: Cuba and S Africa agreed withdrawal of all Cuban troops from A. by May 1991. New constitution, 1991, allowed for multi-party state, with Marxist Jose Eduardo dos Santos as president, but when elections in autumn 1992 produced government majority Unita leader Savimbi refused to accept result and civil war restarted, Jan. 1993. Famine and economic disruption endemic in A. as result of years of fighting. Peace agreement brokered by UN initialled between government and rebels, 1994, but government subsequently launched new offensive against rebels. Peace treaty eventually signed in Lusaka, 20 Nov. UN peacekeeping force in preparation, Mar. 1995. British troops join peacekeeping force April.

Angoulême, France. Became English possession by marriage of Henry II with Eleanor of Aquitaine, 1152; annexed to France, 1303; restored to England, 1360; reconquered by French, 1373.

Anguilla, W Indies, discovered and colonized by the British, 1650. Anguillan resentment of government from St Kitts led to British troops being landed there to maintain order, 19 March 1969. Reverted to direct British rule, 1971. Anguilla Act, 1981, confirmed independence from St Kitts.

Anhalt, Germany. Separated from Saxony, 13thC. Continual subdivision between various petty princes continued till 1800. The remaining duchies of A.–Bernburg and A.–Dessau united, 1863, under Leopold of A.–Dessau. Assisted Prussia in war of 1866. Joined German Empire, 1871. Now mainly in the district of Halle.

aniline dyes. Discovered by Unverdorben, 1826.

Anjou, France. Conquered by Henry II of England, 1156; by Philip II of France from King John, 1204; retaken by Edward III and afterwards given up, 1360. Finally annexed to French crown, 1480. Battle of A. (or Beaugé), English defeated by French, 22 Mar. 1421.

Ankara or **Angora** (anciently **Ancyra**). Ottoman capital in 14thC. Became capital of Turkey, 1923.

Annam. Under Chinese rule till AD 968 when local monarchy established. Independent, 1428. First French expedition to, 1787. French protectorate, 1884. Part of Vietnam since 1945. See INDO-CHINA and VIETNAM.

Annapolis, Maryland, USA. US Naval Academy founded, 1845: accepted women from 1976.

Annapolis Royal, Nova Scotia. Settled by French (as Fort Royal), 1605. Taken by English, 1614 and 1710. Ceded to Britain, 1713. Capital of Nova Scotia till 1879. See ACADIA and NOVA SCOTIA.

Annapurna. Mountain in Himalayas, N Nepal. Height 26,493 ft/8075 m. Was first peak of over 26,000 ft/8000 m to be climbed (north face) by Herzog and Lachenal of the French Himalayan Expedition, 3 June 1950 and (south face) by a British expedition, 1970.

Annates, or **First Fruits.** First year's profits of a living claimed by the bishop. Suppressed in France by edicts, 1406, 1417, 1418, 1463 and 1464. Prohibited in England by Henry IV. Parliament granted them to the crown in 1534, but in 1704 Queen Anne applied them to the augmentation of poor livings. See also QUEEN ANNE'S BOUNTY.

Annobon Island. See PAGALU.

Annual Register. A yearly record of public events first published in London, 1759 (for the year 1758). For 30 years Edmund Burke (1729–97) wrote the survey of events.

Ansbach, Bavaria. Grew up round the monastery founded by St Humbert in the

8thC. Acquired by Burgraves of Nürnberg, 1331; combined with Bayreuth to form a margravate, 1398. Monastery dissolved, 1560. United with Prussia, 1791; but awarded to Bavaria by Napoleon, 1806.

Anschluss. Political union of Austria and Germany, 12 Mar. 1938.

Antarctica. *See* ARCTIC AND ANTARCTIC REGIONS and QUEEN MAUD LAND.

Antarctic Ocean. *See* ARCTIC AND ANTARCTIC REGIONS.

Antarctic Territory, British. *See* BRITISH ANTARCTIC TERRITORY.

Anti-Aircraft Command. Established, 1939. Disbanded, 1955.

Anti-Comintern Pact. Between Germany and Japan, 25 Nov. 1936. Joined by Italy, 6 Nov. 1937. By Hungary and Spain, 1939. By Slovakia, Romania, and Bulgaria, 1941.

Anti-Corn Law League. Founded Manchester, 18 Sept. 1838. Deputies assembled London, 8 Feb. 1842. Corn Laws repealed, 6 June 1846. League dissolved, 2 July 1846.

Antigua. Discovered by Columbus, 1493. First English settlement, 1632. Formally ceded to Britain by Treaty of Breda, 1667. Part of Leeward Islands Federation, 1871. Crown colony, 1956: independent, Nov. 1981. Hurricane, Sept. 1995.

Antioch, now **Antakya,** Turkey. Founded 300 BC by Seleucus Nicator. Christians first so-called here, AD 42. Destroyed by Persians, AD 540. Rebuilt by Justinian, 542–5. Conquered by Arabs, 637. Captured by Crusaders, 1098, and became a Christian principality till 1268, when it was taken by Bibars, Sultan of Egypt. Made part of Syria, 1920, but restored to Turkey, 1939.

antipopes. *See* PAPACY.

Antiquaries, Society of. Founded, 1572. Dissolved by James I, 1604. Reconstituted, 1707. Charter, 2 Nov. 1751.

Anti-Saloon League of America. Founded 1893, in Ohio. Succeeded in 1948 by the Temperance League of America, which merged with the National Temperance Movement in 1950 to form the National Temperance League. Prominent in pushing through US prohibition, 1919–33.

Anti-Slavery Association. *See* SLAVE TRADE.

Antonine Wall, Scotland. Built *c.* AD 140–200.

Antwerp, Belgium. Probably founded by Frankish tribes *c.* 8thC. Citadel burnt by Spaniards, 4 Nov. 1576 ('The Spanish Fury'). Besieged and captured by Parma, 1584–5; Marlborough captured, 6 June 1706; Marshal Saxe captured, 9 May 1746; captured by French, 29 Nov. 1792. Part of Netherland kingdom, 1815–30; cession to Belgium confirmed, 1839; besieged by Germans, 4–6 Oct., surrendered, 9 Oct. 1914. Albert Canal linking A. to Liège opened, June 1939. Occupied by Germans, May 1940. Captured by British, Sept. 1944. Bombarded by German V-weapons, Nov. 1944–May 1945.

Anur or **Tarracina,** town of the *Volsci under Roman supremacy, 509 BC. Stormed by Volsci, 397. Retaken by Romans, 312. Sacked by Goths, AD 409, and again, 595. Temple of Jupiter A. built 1stC BC.

Anzac. Landing of As. (i.e. Australia and New Zealand Army Corps) in Gallipoli in World War I, 25 Apr. 1915.

Anzio, anciently *Antium*, conquered by Romans, 468 BC. Revolted and subdued, 338. The beach-head (known to the Germans as the Nettuno beach-head) established here by Allied Forces, 22 Jan. 1944, was maintained until 25 May, when contact by land was made with Fifth Army.

Anzus. Defence treaty modelled on treaty setting up *NATO, signed San Francisco 1951, ratified 1952, dealing with security in the Pacific. Members were Australia, New Zealand, USA. Further strengthened 1954 by the South East Asia Collective Defence Treaty (the Manila Treaty). In 1984 the New Zealand government refused to allow US nuclear ships to visit New Zealand waters and in Aug. 1986 the USA announced suspension of its committment to New Zealand's defence. Since then A. has operated between Australia and the USA (and also between Australia and New Zealand) but biennial meetings now between Australia and USA only.

Aosta, Valle d', came into possession of Counts of Savoy, 1032. Gran Paradiso area, set aside as a game reserve by the Crown Prince of Piedmont in 1836, became a National Park in 1920. Minor adjustment of Franco-Italian frontier, 1945; confirmed by treaty, 1947.

apartheid, legally established system of racial segregation and discrimination in S Africa, existed from establishment of the Union but most critically from 1948. A. denied non-white majority rights of the white minority ruling class. Began to break down in late 1980s; in 1991 de Klerk carried through repeal of several elements of A. though non-whites still denied equal voting rights. This remnant of A. abolished under constitutional agreement, 17 Nov. 1993, between ANC and National government in time for the constituent assembly elections of April 1994 which resulted in an ANC majority and election of Mandela as S Africa's first black president. Land Rights Bill, Nov. 1994, designed to enable non-whites to claim land lost since 1913 in discriminatory legislation under the A. system. *See* SOUTH AFRICA, REPUBLIC OF.

Apollo Belvedere. Found at Porto d'Anzio early in the 16thC. Bought by Pope Julius II, 1511. Taken to Paris by French, 1797. Restored to Vatican, 1815.

Apollo of Rhodes. 'The Colossus', wonder of the world, sculpture of Chares of Lindus 292–280 BC. Overthrown by earthquake, 224 BC. Broken up, AD 653.

Apostles' Creed. *See* CREEDS.

apothecaries. First apothecary in England traditionally John Falcourt of Lucca, 1362. Licensed by Bishop of London, 1511. Society chartered, 1606 (with Grocers); separately, 1617. House of Lords pronounced that A. could prescribe for a sick patient without the advice of a physician, 1704. 1774: Society of A. limited its membership to those who were practising A. (i.e., medical practitioners). 1815: Act of Parliament gave Society power to examine all A. in England and Wales and grant them licences to practise.

Appeal of Felony. *See* BATTLE, WAGER OF.

Appellants or **Lords Appellant.** The nobles who protested against certain ministers of Richard II in 1387. They caused the death of two of these ministers. In 1388 the L.A. convened the Merciless Parliament.

Appenzell, Swiss canton, settled by Allemanni before AD 600. Joined the Confederation, 1513.

Appian Way (Via Appia), Italy. A famous roadway from Rome to Capua via Albano, begun by Appius Claudius Caecus, 312 BC and extended to Brindisi via Benevento. Excavations were instituted by the papal court, 1850–3. Now Strada Nazionale 6.

Appomattox, village in Virginia, USA where Confederate army under General Lee surrendered to Union General Grant, 9 Apr. 1865. This marked end of American Civil War.

Apprentices, Statute of, 1562 (England). No person allowed to work at a trade without previously serving seven years' apprenticeship. Repealed, 1814.

approved schools, i.e. approved by the Home Office. Term came into use with the passing of the Children and Young Persons' Act, 1933. Discontinued, 1969. Suggestions from 1993 for revival of some form of A.S. to deal with juvenile crime wave; 'boot-camps' planned, 1995.

Apsley House (London). Built 1771–8 for Baron Apsley, 2nd Earl Bathurst. Bought by the Duke of Wellington, 1820. Presented by the 7th Duke to the nation, 1947. Opened as a museum 1952.

Apulia or **Puglie,** Italy. Conquered by Rome, 317 BC. Devastated in Social War,

90–88 BC. Became part of the Kingdom of the Two Sicilies, 1134; and of Italy, 1861.

aqueduct. Longest in Britain, constructed by Telford in 1805, is Pont Cysylltau, Clwyd, Wales, length 1006 ft/307 m.

Aquileia, Italy. Founded 181 BC. Strategically important at head of Adriatic. Destroyed by Attila, AD 452. Cathedral dates from 11thC. Part of *Holy Roman Empire then of Austria, until acquired by Italy in 1918.

Aquitaine, E France. Conquered by Franks, AD 507; separate state, 700; united to France, 1137; became part of English crown by marriage of Henry II and Eleanor of A., 1152; province finally lost under Henry VI, 1453.

Arab League. Founded Mar. 1945 and in 1994 consisted of 21 members, including the Palestine Liberation Organization. Egypt's membership was suspended Mar. 1979, when Tunis replaced Cairo as the A.L's headquarters; Egypt readmitted, 1989.

Arabia. Minaean Kingdom in Jauf, 1200–650 BC. Sabaean (Sheba) Kingdom from 1500 BC. Rise of the Himyarite Kingdom, 115 BC. Ethiopian rule in Yemen, AD 525–75. (For later history down to 1917, *see* CALIPHATE; OTTOMAN EMPIRE, etc.) Conquered by Ibn Saud, 1924, and renamed *Saudi Arabia.

Aragon, NE Spain. Recovered from the Moors, 1131. Continuous southward expansion at the expense of the Moors checked at battle of Alarcos, 1185. Catalonia united with it, 1137. In alliance with Castile to win great victory at Navas de Tolosa, 1212. Valencia united with it, 1238. Moors practically subdued by Jaime I (1213–76). King Ferdinand II of A. married Isabella, Queen of Castile, 1469.

Aragon, Sovereigns of:
Ramiro I 1035–63
Sancho I 1063–94
Pedro I 1094–1104
Alfonso I, the Battler 1104–34
Ramiro II 1134–37
Petronilla 1137–62

Alfonso II 1162–96
Pedro II 1196–1213
Jaime I, the Conqueror 1213–76
Pedro III 1276–85
Alfonso III, the Magnificent 1285–91
Jaime II 1291–1327
Alfonso IV, the Fair 1327–36
Pedro IV 1336–87
Juan I 1387–95
Martin I 1395–1410
Ferdinand I 1410–16
Alfonso V, the Magnanimous 1416–58
Juan II 1458–79
Ferdinand II, the Catholic 1479–1516 (from 1474 Ferdinand V of Castile)
See further under SPAIN, SOVEREIGNS OF.

Aral Sea. Man-made irrigation projects since 1960s caused it to be a quarter of its 1950 area by 1995.

arbitration, industrial. Purely voluntary in England until 1896, when legislation placed it on a legal footing, based on the Conciliation Act, 1896, and Industrial Courts Act, 1919. Present practice based on legislation passed in 1970s. *See also* ACAS.

Arbitration, International Court of. Established at The Hague, 1900. Italo-Greek dispute settled by A., 1923. Bulgaro-Greek dispute settled by permanent court of *International Justice, 1924. Ditto Sino-Belgian dispute, 1924, and Franco-Turkish *Lotus* case, 1926. Absorbed in International Court of Justice, under UN auspices, 1945.

Arc de Triomphe de l'Étoile, Paris. Begun, 1806. Finished, 1836.

Archaeological Institute, Royal (London). Established, 1843.

Archangel (Arkhangel'sk), Russia. Founded, 1584. Blockaded by British fleet, 1854. Allied landing against Bolsheviks, 1918: evacuation, 1919. A port of destination on the convoy route to Russia in World War II.

Archbishop. Title first used in the Eastern Church, 320; in Rome, 420.

archery, used from earliest times in war and hunting. In 15thC English bowmen best in Europe. In 20thC, A. has become an international sport. The Fédération Internationale de Tir à l'Arc (FITA) was established 1931. World championships held annually till 1959, since then biennially.

Arches, Court of. Sat in St Mary-le-Bow from *c.* 1085 till removed to Doctor's Commons, 1567. In Lambeth Palace since 1876.

architectural societies (London). Institute of British Architects, 1834. Incorporated and made royal by charter, 11 Jan. 1837. Society of Architects founded, 1884: amalgamated with Royal Institute of British Architects, 1925. A. Association founded, 1847. American Institute of Architects, 1857.

Arcot, former capital of the Carnatic. Its successful defence by Clive in 1751 was the decisive event in the Anglo-French struggle for India. Taken by Hyder Ali, 1780. Ceded to E India Co., 1801.

Arctic and Antarctic regions, principal expeditions before 1912:

Arctic Regions:

Date	Explorer
1496	Sebastian Cabot
1498	John Cabot
1553	Sir Hugh Willoughby and Richard Chancellor
1576 1577 1578	Frobisher
1584 1595	William Barents
1853–55	Kane
1857–59	McClintock
1859–60	Hayes
1870–72	Hall
1871–72	Merriman
1872–73	Green
1875–76	Nares and Stephenson
1879	G.W. DeLong
1880	Leigh Smith
1887	Col. Gilder
1893–96	Dr. Nansen
1893	Peary
1895	Jackson
1897	Andrée

1899	Wellman
	Peary
1902	Sverdrup
1909	Peary (discovery of N Pole, 6 Apr.)
1909–12	Mikkelsen Amundsen Stefansson

Capt. Sedoff's Russian expedition started for Franz Josef Land, 1912; returned, 1915, without Sedoff, who, having set out for N Pole, had perished. Vilkitsky's expedition, 1915. Stefansson's *Karluk*, on Alaskan expedition on behalf of Canadian government, sank 40 miles/64 km from Wrangel Islands, Jan. 1914; in 1915 he discovered new land N of Prince Patrick Islands; in 1916 more new land W of Axel Heiberg Islands, and in 1918 he explored Beaufort Sea, disproving existence of Keenan Land. Amundsen's aeroplane voyage toward N Pole from Spitzbergen, 21 May–15 June 1925. Byrd flew over N Pole, 1926. In 1928 Sir Hubert Wilkins flew from Alaska to Dead Man's Land, Spitzbergen; in the same year General Nobile made three flights in his dirigible *Italia*, but was wrecked off NE Land. He was rescued, but Amundsen, who had joined in the relief expeditions perished. Gino Watkins on the Greenland ice-cap, 1931. Ushakov expedition N of Cape Chelyuskin, 1931–2. Soviet exploration of Nordenskjold Island, 1936; French Polar research ship *Pourquoi Pas* sank off Iceland, Sept. 1936; Otto Schmidt's meteorological survey of N Polar regions, 1937. *Nautilus* first ship to cross N Pole beneath the Arctic ice, 3 Aug. 1958. Japanese explorer Uemura first person to reach N Pole alone by dogsledge after 54-day journey, 30 Apr. 1978. Sir Ranulph Fiennes and Charles Burton (British) reached N Pole, Apr. 1982, thus being first to circle earth from pole to pole at end of three-year expedition.

Antarctic Regions:

1585 1586 1587	John Davis

1602	George Waymouth
1607–11	Hudson
1612–13	Bylot and Button
1614	Bylot and Gibbons
1615–16	Baffin
1631	James
1676	Capt. Wood
1728 1729 1741	Bering
1735	Chelyuskin
1773	Phipps and Lutwidge (Horatio Nelson in this expedition)
1778	Cook and Clerke
1806 1822	Scoresby
1818	John Ross
1818	Buchan and Franklin
1819–22	Franklin
1819–20 1821–23 1824–25	Parry
1824	Lyon
1819 1824–25	Parry
1825–27	Franklin
1826–28	Buchan
1829–33	John Ross
1833–35 1836–37	Back
1836–39	Dean and Simpson
1845–46	Franklin
1846–47	Rae
1848–49	John Ross Richardson
1848–52	Moore
1848–50	Hooper Saunders
1849–51	Pullen
1850–51	John Ross Penny De Haven and Kane
1850–54	M'Clure
1850–55	Collinson
1851–52	Kennedy
1851–54	Rae
1852–54	Maguire Belcher Kellett Pullen

Visited by Cook in 1773 and 1774. Land discovered by Bellingshausen (Peter I and Alexander I Lands), 1821; by Capt. Biscoe, Feb. 1831; by Capt. D'Urville, 1838. Ross discovered and explored Victoria Land, 1839–43; Nares in the *Challenger* first crossed the Antarctic Circle, 1874. Principal expeditions to: Christensen first to set foot on Antarctic continent, 1894; C. E. Borchgrevink landed at Cape Adare, 23 Feb. 1895; second expedition, equipped by Sir George Newnes, reached Cape Adare, 17 Feb. 1899; de Gerlache expedition, 16 Aug. 1897–28 Mar. 1899; German expedition, under Capt. H. Ruser, 11 Aug. 1901; British expedition, under Capt. Scott, 24 Dec. 1901–10 Sept. 1904; Dr Bruce's Scottish expedition, Jan. 1903–July 1904; Dr Jean Charcot, French expedition, 1904–5 and 1908–10; Lieut. (later Sir Ernest) Shackleton's expedition, 1907–9; Dr David, with Mr D. Mawson and Dr Mackay found the S magnetic pole to be at 72° 25′ S, 155° 16′ E on 16 Jan. 1909; Capt. Amundsen's expedition, 1910, S Pole reached, 16 Dec. 1911; Capt. Scott, British expedition, 1910–13, reached S Pole, 17 Jan. 1912 (Capt. Scott was found dead by a search party, 12 Nov. 1913); Sir Ernest Shackleton's *Endurance* left on 'Farther South' expedition, 1 Aug. 1914; returned, 1916; Shackleton, with *Quest*, started, 1921; reached S Georgia, where Shackleton *d.*, 5 Jan. 1922; in 1928 Wilkins flew over Graham Land and proved that it was not part of the main mass of the Antarctic continent; the British Colonial Office, through the 'Discovery Committee', sent out *Discovery I* on whaling research expedition; *Discovery II* was sent out in 1930 and 1931, and between 1935 and 1937 circumnavigated Antarctic continent; Norwegian expeditions, 1935 and 1937; Byrd expeditions (US Navy), 1928–9; 1933–8; 1939–40; 1946; 1947–50: Fuchs organized the Falkland Islands Dependencies Survey in the Antarctic; 1957–8: Expeditions from various countries co-operated in Antarctic exploration to mark the International Geophysical Year; 1957–8: Fuchs and Hillary led British Transantarctic Expedition: Fuchs left

Shackleton Base on Weddell Sea, 24 Nov. 1957; reached S Pole, 19 Jan. 1958; Scott Base on McMurdo Sound, 2 Mar. 1958. Fuchs thus became first man to traverse the Antarctic, completing 2200 miles/3520 km in 99 days. Antarctic Treaty, 1 Dec. 1959 signed between major powers regulating status of territorial claims in Antarctica and reserving Antarctica for research. 1962: first nuclear plant operational, McMurdo Sound. 1964: British survey team landed on Cook Island by helicopter. 1964: New Zealanders surveyed one of last remaining uncharted areas of Antarctica. In 1991 39 nations signed treaty agreeing to 50-year ban on commercial mining in Antarctica. Attempt by Sir Ranulph Fiennes and Dr. Michael Stroud to cross Antarctica on foot, 1992–3 reached S Pole (halfway) 16 Jan. 1993; completed crossing of Antarctica, 7 Feb. 1993, a world record. Announced, May 1994 that Antarctica to be a whale sanctuary: This came into force, Dec. *See also* QUEEN MAUD LAND.

Arezzo, anciently *Arretium*, an Etruscan city, made a treaty with Rome, 308 BC. Besieged by Gauls, 283. Defeated in a war with Florence, AD 1289, and became a Florentine possession, 1348. Church of St Francis built, 1322.

Argentaeus, Codex, discovered in the abbey library of Werden, Westphalia, by the topographer Mercator (alias Gerhard Kraemer, 1512–94), and brought to Prague for the collection of the Emperor Rudolf II (reigned 1576–1611); on the storming of the city by the Protestants in 1648, the MS was taken to Stockholm by Count Königsmark. It was presented to Uppsala University, 1669. It was first printed, 1665.

Argentina. Rio de la Plata visited by Spaniards, 1515. *Buenos Aires founded 1536 by Pedro de Mendoza, and made part of the Viceroyalty of Peru. Buenos Aires captured by British expedition from Cape Town, 1806, but British surrendered shortly after. Viceroy deposed, 25 May 1810. Independence proclaimed at Congress of Tucuman, 9 July 1816. Independence recognized by Britain and USA,

1823. By Spain, 1842. Republic extended to Rio Negro, 1878–80. Patagonia divided with *Chile by treaty, 1881. Peron became president, June 1946 and carried through sweeping radical changes involving considerable nationalization. Revolution by dissident factions resulted in Peron's deposition (22 Sept. 1955) and exile. Peronists in power again 1973–6, but unstable economic and political situation led to a series of military coups. Argentine forces invaded the *Falkland Islands 2 Apr. 1982: defeated by the British and surrendered 14 June. Galtieri resigned as president, succeeded by Bignone. Democratic elections, 1983 and radical Alfonsin elected. Trials of junta leaders followed. Economic chaos, with hyperinflation, followed by business revival 1990 onwards: Menem regime encouraged privatization. Diplomatic relations with Britain re-established, 1990. A. and Britain agreed joint policy to preserve Falkland Islands fish stocks, Dec. 1992. Bomb destroys Jewish centre in Buenos Aires, July 1994: 96 killed. Menem offers cash to Falkland Islanders if they will support some form of Argentine rule over islands: rejected, Oct. Prince Andrew visits A., Nov. Menem again returned as president of A., May 1995. Joint oil exploration in S Atlantic agreed with Britain, Sept. 1995.

Heads of the State (Presidents) from the Establishment of the Republic, 1853:

Urquiza 1853–60
Derqui 1860–62
Mitre 1862–68
Sarmiento 1868–74
Avellaneda 1874–80
Roca 1880–86
Celman 1886–90
Pellegrini 1890–92
Pena 1892–98
Roca 1898–1904
Quintana 1904–06
Alcorta 1906–10
Pena 1910–14
De la Plaza 1914–16
Irigoyen 1916–22
Alvear 1922–28

Irigoyen 1928–30
Uriburu 1930–32
Justo 1932–38
Ortiz 1938–42
Castillo 1942–43
Rawson (two days) June 1943
Ramirez June 1943–44
Farrell 1944–46
Peron 1946–55
Lonardi (3 weeks) 1955
Arambru 1955–58
Frondizi 1958–62
Guido 1962–63
Illia 1963–66
Ongania 1966–70
Levingston 1970–71
Lanusse 1971–73
Cámpora 1973
Peron 1973–74
Maria Peron 1974–76
Videla 1976–81
Galtieri 1981–82
Bignone 1982–83
Alfonsin 1983–89
Menem 1989–

Arianism. Propounded by Arius (256–336) c. 321. Synod of Bithynia upheld him against St. Athanasius, who was banished, 323. Condemned by Council of Nicaea, 325. His doctrines have since been condemned by numerous councils, but were the basis of 'State' churches in the *Gothic and *Vandal kingdoms. As an organized creed A. died out before 600.

Arizona. Discovered by Marcos de Niza, 1539; first settled by Spanish missionaries c. 1772. Largely ceded as a result of the Mexican War, 1848; the remaining territory, comprising modern A., was acquired by the Gadsden Purchase of 1853, and its present boundaries were fixed in 1863: admitted to the Union, 14 Feb. 1912.

Arkansas, explored by De Soto, 1541, and settled by French, 1686. Purchased by US Government, 1803; organized as a territory, 1819; admitted to the Union, 1836.

Arles, France. Greek colony refounded by the Romans c. 47 BC. Roman theatre and

amphitheatre built, 2ndC AD. Became capital of Gaul and an archbishopric in 4thC, and capital of the kingdom of Provence or Arelate at end of 9thC. First Synod of A., 314. Cathedral built, 11thC: rebuilt 12thC and 14thC. Amphitheatre converted into a fortress, 12thC. Archbishopric abolished, 1790.

Armagh, city in the district of A., (until 1973 county of) N Ireland. Seat of Celtic kings of Ulster from 400 BC–AD 333. Present city grew from 4thC fort of Ard Mhacha. St Patrick established his principal church at A., 445; present St Patrick's cathedral (Church of Ireland) built 1834, on his site. Brian Boru died at, 1014. Destroyed by Shane O'Neill, 1566; subsequently under Protestant control. Royal School, 1627; observatory, 1765. Roman Catholic cathedral, 1840–73. Made an official city, July 1994.

Armada, The Spanish. Left Lisbon, 29 May 1588; arrived off Lizard Point, Cornwall, 19 July; Howard met A., 21 July, and kept up running fight until 25 July; A. anchored in Calais Roads, 26 July; met there by Howard and pursued until 22 Aug., though organized fighting ended 30 July.

Armagnacs or **Orléanists.** The anti-Burgundian (and therefore patriotic) party formed in 1396, first under the leadership of the Duke of Orleans. They played a decisive part in driving the British from France. Their objects being achieved by the Treaty of Arras, 1435, the faction ceased to exist.

Armed Forces Act. 1981 *see under* COURTS MARTIAL.

'Armed Neutrality'. Confederacy of northern powers against maritime policy of England, commenced by Russia, 1780: its objects defeated, 1781; renewed, 16 Dec. 1800; dissolved after Nelson's victory at Copenhagen, 16 Dec. 1801.

Armenia (Hayastan), Asia. Subject in turn to Assyrians, Medes and Persians. Conquered by Alexander, 325 BC. Under

Roman influence in early part of Christian era. Christianity introduced by St. Gregory the Illuminator in 3rdC. Conquered by Mongols, 1242. Reigning dynasty overthrown by Saracens, 1375. Continually persecuted by Turks. Massacres, 1895–7. In 1918, during the Russian Revolution, an independent 'Republic of Transcaucasia' was formed by union of A. with Azerbaijan and Georgia. Occupied by Red Army, 1920, and transformed into a Soviet republic, which in 1922 was included in the Transcaucasian Federal Republic of the USSR. When this was abolished, 1936, A. became a constituent republic of the USSR. Serious earthquake in A., Dec. 1988 with over 50,000 deaths. Declared independence, 23 Sept. 1991: member of the Commonwealth of Independent States since Dec. 1991. Intermittent fighting between A. and *Azerbaijan over disputed territory, since early 1988; by 1994 Armenians had made considerable gains but at heavy cost, and sporadic fighting continued despite official June 1993 cease-fire. Elections July 1995 increased Presidential power.

Arminianism. A doctrine of free will propounded by Jacobus Arminius, who was professor at Leyden University from 1603 till his death in 1609. A. savagely persecuted by Calvinists after the *Synod of Dort, 1618–19.

Armistice between Germany and Allies signed at Compiègne, 11 Nov. 1918. Between France and Germany at Compiègne, 22 June 1940. Between France and Italy, near Rome, 24 June 1940. Between N Korea and the UN forces, 27 July 1953.

Army, British. Oldest English corps, the *Yeomen of the Guard, founded, 1485. *Gentlemen-at-Arms, 1509. Honourable Artillery Company, chartered 1537. 1st Foot (Royal Scots), 1633. Household troops established, 1661. Standing armies declared illegal in First Mutiny Act, 1689; Second Act, 1803. E India Co.'s army absorbed, 1858. Flogging abolished in peacetime, 1868. A. Act, 1881. Short Service Act, 1870, and abolition of commission by purchase, 1871 – part of the Cardwell

(Secretary of War, 1868–74) reforms. Haldane's new A. scheme, 1906. Territorial and Reserve forces Act, July 1907. Kitchener's A., 1915. Derby Scheme, 1915. Conscription introduced, 1916; ended, 1918. Territorial A. formed, 1920. Southern Irish regiments disbanded and cavalry regiments reduced, 1922. Field Punishment No. 1 abolished, 1923. Mechanization, 1935. *Conscription into militia introduced, 9 May 1939; ended, 1960. Army reorganization, complete by the end of 1962, included reducing the number of line cavalry and infantry regiments by amalgamation. Further reorganization involving more regimental amalgamations took effect, 1993 but four regimental mergers originally proposed, were abandoned Feb. In July 1994 further sweeping cuts proposed. Proposal to restructure army ranks, Apr. 1995. *See also* REGIMENTS OF THE BRITISH ARMY and VOLUNTEERS.

Army Act, 1881. *See* COURTS MARTIAL.

Army Act, 1992, under which the Ulster Defence Regiment merged with the Royal Irish Rangers to form the Royal Irish Regiment.

Army Council. When office of Commander-in-Chief abolished A.C. was set up under the Secretary of State for War, 1904. Now superseded by the Defence Council.

Army Plot, a rumoured attempt by the Royal A. to coerce Parliament to obey Charles I, 1641.

Arnhem, Holland. Sir Philip Sidney *d.* at 1586. Fortified by Cohoorn, 1702. Taken by French, 1795; by Prussians, 1813. Scene of the famous and ultimately unsuccessful landing of the British Airborne Divisions and Polish Parachute Brigade, 17–26 Sept. 1944.

Aroostook Dispute. Boundary dispute, 1839–42 between New Brunswick and Maine, so named on account of the Aroostook River.

Arras, Treaties of. Armagnacs and Burgundians, 1414; France and Burgundy, 20 Sept. 1435; Louis XI and Flemings, 1482.

Catholic union between Hainault, Douai, and Artois signed at A., 5 Jan. 1579.

arrest, freedom from, a privilege enjoyed by members of Parliament from very early times, confirmed by Edward I, 1290. Recognized by Act of Parliament, 1433. *See also* PARLIAMENT.

Arromanches, harbour of. Artificial prefabricated harbour used during Anglo-American invasion of Normandy, 1944. Prototype constructed in Scotland, 1943. Equipment dispatched across Channel, 6 June 1944, and harbour functioning by the end of June. Remnants still remain, 1995.

arrondissements or sub-prefectures, territorial divisions of French departments, under the administrative system introduced in 1799.

arson remained a capital crime in England until the passing of the Malicious Damage Act, 1861. Now covered by Criminal Damage Act, 1971.

Articles, The Six, statute passed, 1539; repealed, 1547.

Articles, The Thirty-nine, as now printed in the Prayer Book, are based on the Forty-Two Articles of 1553 (*see next article*), which were revised by Archbishop Parker and submitted to Convocation in 1562, and finally authorized by Parliament, 1571, the Declaration preceding them being drawn up by Archbishop Laud and added in 1628. Subscription thereto ceased to be obligatory on proceeding to a degree at Oxford or Cambridge, 1871.

Articles of Religion (Anglican), other than those mentioned above, were drawn up as follows:

Ten A., 1536.
Institution of a Christian Man (Bishop's Book), 1537.
Thirteen A., 1538.
Necessary Doctrine, etc. (King's Book), 1543.
Forty-two A., 1553.

Articles of War continued to form the legal basis for the discipline of the British Army until the *Mutiny Act of 1789.

artificial insemination, originally used by animal breeders, developed in 20thC to overcome human infertility, later extended to cover '*in vitro* fertilization', resulting in 'test-tube babies' of which the first was *b.* in Britain, 1978. Surrogacy agencies banned in Britain, 1985. Human Fertilization and Embryology Act, 1990. Suggestions that eggs from aborted foetuses might be used in A.I. in future, 1994.

artificial silk or **rayon.** Idea of imitating silk expressed by Réaumur, 1754; thread obtained from nitro-cellulose and called A.S. by Audemars in 1855. Process developed by de Chardonnet, 1886.

Artois, northern French province, conquered by Franks in the 5thC, but ruled by the Counts of Flanders until they ceded it to the Kings of France, 1180, who made it into a county, 1237, but in the 14thC ceded it to Burgundy, whence it passed to Austria, but returned to France under the Treaty of the Pyrenees, 1659. In 1789 it became the department of Pas-de-Calais. First artesian well in Europe sunk in A., 1126 (hence the name).

arts, the. *See* ENGRAVING and PAINTING for history. Prominent performers in these departments include:

American:
Allston, Washington, 1779–1843, painter.
Audubon, John James, 1785–1851, painter.
Cassatt, Mary, 1855–1925, painter.
Copley, John Singleton, 1738–1815, painter.
Eakins, Thomas, 1844–1916, painter.
French, Daniel Chester, 1850–1931, sculptor.
Homer, Winslow, 1836–1910, painter.
Moses, Mrs. Anna Mary Robertson, 1860–1961, painter.
O'Keeffe, Georgia, 1887–1986, painter.
Pollock, Jackson, 1912–56, painter.
Saint-Gaudens, Augustus, 1848–1907, sculptor.

Sargent, John Singer, 1856–1925, painter.
Warhol, Andy, 1928–87, painter.
West, Benjamin, 1738–1820, painter.
Whistler, James Abbott McNeill, 1834–1903, painter and etcher.
Wright, Frank Lloyd 1869–1959, architect.
Chinese:
Chao Mêng-fu, 1254–1322, painter.
Ch'i Pai-shih, 1863–1957, painter.
Chien Lung, 1722–96, painter and architect.
Fu Pao-shih, 1904–65, painter.
Han Kan, *fl*. 600–50, painter.
Hsieh-Ho, *fl*. 450–500, painter.
Hsu Peihung, 1895–1953, painter.
Hua Yen, 1660–1740, painter.
Huang Ping-hung, 1864–1955, painter.
Jen Po-min, 1840–95, painter.
Kao Ch'i-p'ei, *c*. 1698–1734, painter.
Kao Chien-fu, 1879–1951, painter.
Kao Chi-feng, 1889–1933, painter.
Ki K'ai-chih, *fl*. 350–400, painter.
Kung Hsien, *fl*. 1600, painter.
Kuo Hsi, *fl*. 1100–50, painter.
Liu Danshai, 1931–, painter.
Liu Hai-su, 1896–1994, painter.
Liu Shou-Kwan, *d*. 1977, painter.
Liu Xian, 1915–, woodcut artist.
Mei Ching, 1623–97, painter.
Shih-Tao, 1667–1714, painter and calligrapher.
T'ay Yiu, 1470–1523, painter.
Tung Ch'i Ch'ang, 1555–1636, painter, calligrapher and art theorist.
'The Four Wangs':
Wang Shi-Min, 1592–1680 ⎫
Wang Chien, 1598–1680 ⎬ painters
Wang Hui, 1632–1720 ⎪
Wang Yuan Chi, 1642–1715 ⎭
Wang Meng, 1308–85, painter.
Wang Wei, 698–759, painter.
Wu Ch'ang-shih, 1844–1927, painter.
Wu Tao-Tzu, *fl*. 700–50, painter.
Wu Wei, 1458–1508, painter.
Dutch:
Bosch, Hieronymus (Jerome van Acken), active 1480–1516, painter.
Brouwer, Adrian, 1605–38, painter.
Cuyp, Aalbert, 1620–91, painter.
Gogh, Vincent Willem van, 1853–90, painter.
Hals, Frans, 1580–1666, painter.

Heem, Jan Davidsz van, 1606–1684, painter.
Hobbema, Meindert, 1638–1709, painter.
Hooch, Pieter de, 1630–*c*. 1681, painter.
Israels, Josef, 1824–1911, painter.
Jongkind, Johann Barthold, 1819–91, painter and engraver.
Mauve, Anton, 1838–88, painter.
Metsu, Gabriel, 1630–67, painter.
Mondrian, Piet, 1872–1944, abstract painter.
Ostade, Adriaan van, 1610–85, painter and etcher.
Ostade, Isaack van, 1621–49, painter.
Rembrandt van Rijn, 1606–69, painter.
Ruisdael, Jakob Isaac van, *c*. 1628–82, painter.
Terborch, Gerard, 1617–81, painter.
Vandevelde, Adrian, 1636–72, painter and etcher.
Vandevelde, Jan, 1593–after 1641, engraver.
Vandevelde, Willem (I), 1611–93; and (II), 1633–1707, draughtsman.
Vermeer van Delft, Jan, 1632–75, painter.
English, Scottish, Irish, and Welsh:
Abercrombie, Sir Patrick, 1879–1957, architect.
Adam, Robert, 1728–92, architect.
Allan, David, 1744–96, Scottish painter.
Allingham, Helen, 1848–1926, water-colourist.
Alma-Tadema, Sir Lawrence, 1836–1912, painter.
Arup, Ove, 1895–1988, Danish-born architect.
Bacon, Francis, 1909–92, painter.
Barry, Sir Charles, 1795–1860, architect.
Beardsley, Aubrey, 1872–98, illustrator.
Bewick, Thomas, 1753–1828, engraver.
Blake, William, 1757–1827, engraver.
Bonington, Richard Parkes, 1802–28, painter.
Bratby, John, 1928–92, painter.
Brown, Ford Madox, 1821–93, painter.
Browne, Hablôt Knight ('Phiz'), 1815–82, caricaturist.
Burne-Jones, Sir Edward, 1833–98, painter.
Chase, Marian Emma, 1844–1905, water-colourist.
Chippendale, Thomas, *c*. 1718–79, furniture designer.

Clausen, Sir George, 1852–1944, painter.
Constable, John, 1776–1837, painter.
Cooper, Samuel, 1609–1702, miniaturist.
Cooper, Susie (Susan Vera Barker), 1902–1995, ceramic artist.
Cooper, Thomas Sidney, 1803–1902, painter.
Cotman, John Sell, 1782–1842, painter.
Cox, David, 1793–1859, painter.
Cozens, John Robert, 1752–99, painter.
Crome, John, 1769–1821, painter.
Cruikshank, George, 1792–1878, caricaturist and illustrator.
Dobson, Frank, 1889–1963, sculptor.
Epstein, Sir Jacob, 1880–1959, sculptor.
Etty, William, 1787–1849, painter.
Flaxman, John, 1755–1826, sculptor.
Forbes, Stanhope Alexander, 1857–1947, painter.
Foster, Sir Norman, 1935–, architect.
Frampton, Sir George, 1860–1928, sculptor.
Freud, Lucian, 1922–, painter.
Frink, Dame Elisabeth, 1930–93, sculptor.
Gainsborough, Thomas, 1727–88, painter.
Gibbons, Grinling, 1648–1721, sculptor and woodcarver.
Gibbs, James, 1674–1754, architect.
Gilbert, Sir Alfred, 1854–1934, sculptor and woodcarver.
Gilbert and George (Gilbert Proesch, 1943– and George Passmore, 1942–), painters.
Giles, Carl, 1916–95, cartoonist.
Gill, Eric Rowland, 1882–1940, sculptor, engraver, and typographer.
Gillray, James, 1757–1815, caricaturist.
Girtin, Thomas, 1775–1802, painter.
Guthrie, Sir James, 1859–1930, painter.
Hawksmoor, Nicholas, 1661–1736, architect.
Heath Robinson, William, 1872–1944, cartoonist.
Hepworth, Dame Barbara, 1903–75, sculptor.
Hilton, Roger, 1911–75, painter.
Hockney, David, 1937–, painter.
Hogarth, William, 1697–1764, painter and engraver.
Hone, Evie, 1894–1955, Irish painter.
Hoppner, John, 1758–1810, painter.
Hunt, William Holman, 1827–1910, painter.
John, Augustus Edwin, 1879–1961, painter.

John, Gwen, 1876–1939, painter.
Jones, Inigo, c. 1573–c. 1652, architect.
Keene, Charles Samuel, 1823–91, illustrator.
Kiff, Ken, 1935–, painter.
Kneller, Sir Godfrey, 1646–73, German-born painter.
Knight, Dame Laura, 1877–1970, painter.
Landseer, Sir Edwin, 1802–73, painter.
Lavery, Sir John, 1857–1941, painter.
Lawrence, Sir Thomas, 1769–1830, Dutch-born painter.
Leach, Bernard, 1887–1979, potter.
Lear, Edward, 1812–88, writer of nonsense verse and painter.
Leighton, Frederick Leighton, Baron, 1830–96, painter and sculptor.
Lely, Sir Peter, 1618–80, Dutch-born painter.
Lewis, Percy Wyndham, 1884–1957, painter.
Lorimer, Hew, 1907–93, sculptor.
Low, David, 1891–1963, cartoonist.
Lowry, Laurence Stephen, 1887–1976, painter.
Lutyens, Sir Edwin Landseer, 1869–1944, architect.
Mackintosh, Charles Rennie, 1869–1928, architect and designer.
Makepeace, John, 1939–, furniture designer.
May, Philip William, 1864–1903, illustrator.
Millais, Sir John Everett, 1829–96, painter.
Moore, Henry, 1898–1986, sculptor.
Morland, George, 1763–1804, painter.
Moser, Mary, 1744–1819, painter.
Munnings, Sir Alfred, 1878–1959, painter.
Nash, John, 1752–1835, architect.
Nash, Paul, 1889–1946, painter and theatrical designer.
Nevinson, Christopher Richard Wynne, 1889–1946, painter.
Nicholson, Ben, 1894–1982, painter.
Opie, John, 1761–1807, painter.
Opie, Julian, 1958–, painter.
Orchardson, Sir William Quiller, 1835–1910, painter.
Orpen, Sir William, 1878–1931, painter.
Piper, John, 1910–92, painter.
Potter, Beatrix, 1866–1943, children's illustrator and writer.
Rackham, Arthur, 1867–1939, painter and illustrator.

Raeburn, Sir Henry, 1756–1823, painter.
Rennie, John, 1761–1821, architect.
Reynolds, Sir Joshua, 1723–92, painter.
Richardson, Sir Albert, 1880–1965, architect.
Rie, Lucie, 1902–95, Austrian-born English potter.
Riley, Bridget, 1931–, painter.
Rogers, Sir Richard, 1933–, architect.
Romney, George, 1734–1802, painter.
Rossetti, Dante Gabriel, 1828–82, painter.
Rothenstein, Sir William, 1872–1945, painter and etcher.
Rowlandson, Thomas, 1756–1827, caricaturist.
Scarfe, Gerald, 1936–, cartoonist.
Scott, Sir George Gilbert, 1811–78, architect.
Scott, Sir Giles Gilbert, 1880–1960, architect.
Shepard, Ernest Howard, 1879–1976, illustrator.
Sheraton, Thomas, c. 1751–1806, furniture designer.
Sickert, Walter Richard, 1860–1942, painter.
Sisley, Alfred, 1840–99, painter.
Spear, Ruskin, 1911–90, painter.
Spence, Sir Basil, 1907–76, architect.
Spencer, Sir Stanley, 1892–1959, painter.
Steer, Philip Wilson, 1860–1942, painter.
Stevens, Alfred, 1818–75, sculptor.
Stirling, Sir James, 1936–92, architect.
Stone, Marcus, 1840–1921, painter.
Stone, Nicholas, 1586–1647, sculptor.
Stubbs, George, 1724–1806, painter.
Sutherland, Graham, 1903–80, painter.
Tenniel, Sir John, 1820–1914, cartoonist and illustrator.
Turner, Joseph Mallord William, 1775–1851, painter.
Vanbrugh, Sir John, 1664–1726, architect.
Varley, John, 1778–1842, painter.
Watts, George Frederick, 1817–1904, painter and sculptor.
Weight, Carel, 1908–, painter.
Wilkie, Sir David, 1785–1841, painter.
Wilson, Richard, 1714–82, painter.
Wint, Peter de, 1784–1849, painter.
Wren, Sir Christopher, 1632–1723, architect.
Yeats, Jack Butler, 1871–1957, Irish painter.

Flemish:
Breughel, Jan, 1568–1625, painter.
Breughel, Pieter the Elder, 1520–69, painter.
Breughel, Pieter the Younger, 1564–1637, painter.
Eyck, Hubert van, c. 1379–1426, painter.
Eyck, Jan van, c. 1390–1441, painter.
Hoorenbault, Gerard, 1480–1540, painter.
Mabuse, Jan van, c. 1475–1536, painter.
Matsys, Quintin, 1466–1530, painter.
Memlinc, Hans, c. 1430–94, painter.
Rubens, Peter Paul, 1577–1640, painter and etcher.
Teniers the Younger, David, 1610–94, painter.
Van der Weyden, Rogier, c. 1400–64, painter.
Van Dyck, Sir Anthony, 1599–1641, painter and etcher.
French:
Arp, Hans (Jean), 1887–1966, painter and sculptor.
Blanche, Jacques Émile, 1861–1942, painter.
Boucher, François, 1703–70, painter.
Bourdelle, Émile Antoine, 1861–1929, sculptor.
Braque, Georges, 1881–1963, painter.
César, 1921–, sculptor.
Cézanne, Paul, 1839–1906, painter.
Chagall, Marc, 1887–1985, Russian-born painter.
Chardin, Jean Baptiste Siméon, 1699–1779, painter.
Claude de Lorraine, 1600–82, painter.
Clouet, or Janet, François, c. 1510–72, painter.
Corot, Jean Baptiste Camille, 1796–1875, painter.
Courbet, Gustave, 1819–77, painter.
Dalon, Jules, 1838–1902, sculptor.
Daubigny, Charles François, 1817–78, painter.
Daumier, Honoré, 1808–79, caricaturist and painter.
David, Jacques Louis, 1748–1825, painter.
Degas, Edgar Hilaire Germaine, 1834–1917, painter and engraver.
Delacroix, Eugène, 1798–1863, painter.
Diaz de la Peña, Narcisse Virgile, 1808–76, painter.

Doré, Gustave, 1832–83, illustrator and engraver.

Duchamp, Marcel, 1887–1968, painter.

Dufy, Raoul, 1877–1953, painter and designer.

Duvet, Jean, c. 1485–1561, engraver.

Fantin-Latour, Ignace Henri Jean Théodore, 1836–1894, painter.

Fragonard, Jean Honoré, 1732–1806, painter.

Gauguin, Paul, 1848–1903, painter and sculptor.

Greuze, Jean Baptiste, 1725–1805, painter.

Houdon, Jean Antoine, 1741–1828, sculptor.

Ingres, Jean Auguste Dominique, 1780–1867, painter.

Lalique, René Jules, 1860–1945, glass designer.

Le Brun, Charles, 1619–90, painter.

Lebrun, Elisabeth Vigée, 1755–1842, painter.

Le Nain, Antoine, 1588–1648, painter.

Le Nain, Louis, 1593–1648, painter.

Le Nain, Mathieu, 1607–77, painter.

Maillol, Aristide, 1861–1944, sculptor.

Manessier, Alfred, 1911–93, abstract painter.

Manet, Édouard, 1832–83, painter.

Matisse, Henri, 1869–1954, painter.

Méryon, Charles, 1821–68, engraver.

Millet, Jean François, 1814–75, painter.

Monet, Claude Oscar, 1840–1926, painter.

Pissarro, Camille, 1830–1903, painter.

Poussin, Nicolas, 1594–1665, painter.

Renoir, Pierre August, 1841–1919, painter.

Rodin, François Auguste, 1840–1917, sculptor and etcher.

Rouault, Georges, 1871–1954, painter.

Rousseau, Henri Julien, 1844–1910, painter.

Rousseau, Pierre Étienne Théodore, 1812–67, painter.

Seurat, Georges Pierre, 1859–91, painter.

Signac, Paul, 1863–1935, painter.

Toulouse-Lautrec, Henry de, 1864–91, painter.

Troyon, Constant, 1810–65, painter.

Utrillo, Maurice, 1883–1955, painter.

Viollet-le-Duc, Eugène Emmanuel, 1814–79, architect.

Watteau, Antoine, 1684–1721, painter.

German:

Altdorfer, Albrecht, c. 1480–1538, painter and engraver.

Carstens, Asmus Jakob, 1754–98, Danish-born painter.

Corinth, Lovis, 1858–1925, painter.

Cornelius, Peter von, 1783–1867, painter.

Cranach, Lucas, 1472–1553, painter.

Dürer, Albrecht, 1471–1528, painter, engraver, and etcher.

Elsheimer, Adam, 1578–1610, sculptor.

Friedrich, Caspar David, 1774–1840, painter.

Gropius, Walter, 1883–1969, architect: became US citizen.

Grosz, Georg, 1893–1959, painter became US citizen.

Grünewald, Matthias, c. 1470–1529, painter.

Holbein the Elder, Hans, c. 1460–1524, painter.

Holbein the Younger, Hans, 1497–1543, painter.

Kampf, Arthur von, 1864–1950.

Kaulbach, Wilhelm von, 1805–74, painter.

Kiefer, Anselm, 1945–, painter.

Liebermann, Max, 1847–1935, painter.

Marc, Franz, 1880–1916, painter.

Mengs, Anton Raphael, 1728–79, painter.

Nolde, Emil, 1867–1956, painter.

Schadow, Johann Gottfried, 1764–1850, sculptor.

Schongauer, Martin, c. 1445–c. 1499, painter and engraver.

Schwind, Moritz von, 1805–71, painter.

Strigel, Bernhardin, 1460–1528, painter.

Wilhelm of Cologne, fl. 1358, d.c. 1378, painter.

Greek, Ancient:

Apelles, fl. 350 BC, painter.

Lysippus, c. 336–270 BC, sculptor.

Myron, 5thC BC, sculptor.

Pheidias, c. 500–432 BC, sculptor.

Polyclitus of Argos, c. 452–412 BC, sculptor.

Polygnotus, fl. 500–425 BC, painter.

Praxiteles, fl. 364–330 BC, sculptor.

Scopas, fl. 395–350 BC, sculptor.

Italian:

Alberti, Leon Battista, 1404–1472, architect.

Andrea del Castagno, c. 1423–1457, painter.

Andrea del Sarto, 1488–1530, painter.
Angelico, Fra Giovanni da Fiesole, 1387–1455, painter.
Annigoni, Pietro, 1910–88, painter.
Bartolommeo, Fra, of S. Marco, 1475–1517, painter.
Bellini, Giovanni, 1422–1516, painter.
Bernini, Giovanni Lorenzo, 1598–1680, sculptor, painter, and architect.
Boccioni, Umberto, 1882–1916, painter.
Borromini, Francesco, 1599–1677, architect.
Botticelli, Sandro, 1445–1510, painter.
Bramante da Urbino, 1444–1514, architect.
Brunelleschi, Filippo, 1379–1446, sculptor and architect.
Canaletto, or Antonio Canale, 1697–1768, painter.
Canova, Antonio, 1757–1822, sculptor and painter.
Caravaggio, Michelangelo Amerighi da, 1573–1610, painter.
Cellini, Benvenuto, 1500–71, sculptor and jeweller.
Cimabue, Giovanni, 1240–1302, painter.
Correggio, Antonio da, 1494–1534, painter.
Donatello (Donato di Betto Bardi), 1386–1466, sculptor.
Duccio di Buoninsegna, c. 1260–1319, painter.
Ghiberti, Lorenzo, 1378–1455, sculptor.
Ghirlandaio, Domenico, 1449–94, painter.
Giorgione da Castelfranco, 1477–1511, painter.
Giotto, 1266–1337, painter, sculptor, and architect.
Gozzoli, Benozzo, 1421–97, painter.
Guardi, Francesco, 1712–93, painter.
Lippi, Filippino, c. 1457–1504, painter.
Lippi, Fra Filippo, 1406–69, painter.
Luca della Robbia, 1399–1482, sculptor.
Mantegna, Andrea, 1431–1506, painter.
Masaccio di S. Giovanni, 1401–28, painter.
Michelangelo Buonarotti, 1475–1564, painter, sculptor, and architect.
Modigliani, Amadeo, 1884–1920, painter.
Moroni, Giambattista, 1510–78, painter.
Palladio, Andrea, 1508–80, architect.
Perugino, Pietro, 1446–1523, painter.
Piero della Francesca, 1416–92, painter.
Piranesi, Giovanni Battista, 1720–78, engraver.

Pollaiuolo, Antonio, 1432–98, painter.
Raphael of Urbino, 1483–1520, painter and architect.
Sansovino, Andrea, 1460–1529, sculptor and architect.
Sansovino, Jacopo, 1486–1570, sculptor and architect.
Segantini, Giovanni, 1858–99, painter.
Tiepolo, Giovanni Battista, 1696–1770, painter.
Tintoretto (Jacop Robusti), 1518–94, painter.
Titian, or Tiziano Vecellio, 1477–1576, painter.
Uccello, Paolo, 1397–1475, painter.
Veronese, Paolo, 1528–88, painter.
Verrocchio, Andrea del, 1435–88, sculptor and painter.
Vinci, Leonardo da, 1452–1519, painter and sculptor.
Japanese:
Cho Denshu, 1351–1427, painter.
Doncho, *fl.* 6thC, Korean painter.
Hamada Shoji, 1894–1978, painter.
Hidari Jingaró, *d.* 1634, sculptor.
Hiroshige, 1797–1858, wood block prints.
Hishigawa Moronobu, 1618–94, painter of engravings.
Hokusai, 1760–1849, painter of engravings.
Ikeda Yosou, 1895–1988, painter.
Jositsu, *fl.* 15thC, painter.
Kano Eitko, 1543–90, screen painter.
Kikutako Kiyonori, 1928–, architect.
Kosé-no-Kanaoka, *fl.* 850, painter.
Maeda Seison, 1885–1978, painter.
Munakata Shiko, 1905–77, wood block printer.
Ogata Korin, 1678–1716, painter.
Saito Kiyoshi, 1907–, print artist.
Tange Kenzo, 1913–, architect.
Taniguchi Yoshiro, 1904–78, architect.
Umehara Ryuzaburo, 1888–1986, painter.
Utamaro, 1753–1806, painter of engravings.
Yokoyama Taikan, 1868–1958, painter.
Russian:
Bakst, Leon, 1866–1924, painter and stage designer.
Chagall, *see under French.*
Dionysii, *fl.* 1502, ikon painter.
Dubuzhinsky, Matislav, 1875–1957, painter.

Fabergé, Peter Carl, 1846–1920, goldsmith and lapidary.

Feodotov, Pavel, 1815–52, painter.

Goncharova, Natalya, 1881–1962, painter and stage designer.

Kandinsky, *see under Various*.

Larinov, Mikhail, 1881–1964, painter.

Malevich, Kasimir, 1878–1935, painter.

Repin, Ilya Yefimovich, 1844–1918, painter.

Rodchenko, Alexander, 1891–1956, painter.

Rublev, Andrei Theophanes 'The Greek', *fl*. 1378–1405, ikon painter.

Tatlin, Vladimir, 1885–1953, abstract painter.

Ushakov, Simon, 1626–86, ikon painter.

Scandinavian:

Burgesson, John, d. 1910, Icelandic sculptor.

Jensen, Georg, 1866–1935, Danish silversmith.

Milles, Carl, 1875–1955, Swedish sculptor.

Munch, Edvard, 1863–1944, Norwegian painter.

Thorvaldsen, Bertel, 1770–1844, Danish sculptor.

Vigeland, Gustaf, 1869–1943, Norwegian sculptor.

Zorn, Anders Leonard, 1860–1920, Swedish etcher and engraver.

Spanish:

Cano, Alonso, 1601–67, painter, sculptor, and architect.

Dali, Salvador, 1904–89, painter.

Fortuny y Carbo, Mariano José Bernardo, 1839–74, painter.

Gaudi, Antonio, 1852–1926, architect.

Goya y Lucientes, Francisco José de, 1746–1828, painter and etcher.

Greco, El, or Domenico Theotocopoulos, 1541–1614, Greek-Spanish painter.

Miro, Joan, 1893–1984, surrealist painter.

Murillo, Bartolomé Estéban, 1617–82, painter.

Picasso, Pablo, 1881–1973, painter.

Pradilla, Francisco,1847–1921, painter.

Ribera, Jusepe de, 1588–1656, painter.

Velázquez, Diego de Silva y, 1599–1660, painter.

Zurbaran, Francisco, 1598–1662, painter.

Various:

Brancusi, Constantin, 1876–1957, Romanian sculptor.

Christo (Christo Javacheff), 1955–, Bulgarian-born artist in materials, naturalized US citizen.

De Kooning, Willem, 1904–, Dutch-born naturalized US abstract painter.

Ensor, James, 1860–1947, Belgian painter.

Giacometti, Alberto, 1901–66, Swiss sculptor.

Kandinsky, Wassily, 1866–1941, Russian-born painter.

Kauffmann, Angelica, 1741–1807, Swiss painter.

Klee, Paul, 1879–1940, Swiss painter.

Kokoschka, Oskar, 1886–1980, Austrian-born painter.

Le Corbusier (Charles Édouard Jeanneret), 1887–1965, Swiss-French architect.

Magritte, René, 1898–1967, Belgian painter.

Meunier, Constantin, 1831–1905, Belgian sculptor.

Mylsbec, Joseph Wenceslas, 1848–1922, Czech sculptor.

Nolan, Sir Sidney, 1917–92, Australian painter.

Arts Council of Great Britain, name adopted on 9 Aug. 1946 by former *CEMA.

Arts, Royal Society of, London, established, 1754; incorporated, 1847. Granted title 'Royal', 1908, and members took title of 'Fellow', 1914. Edinburgh, established, 1821; incorporated, 1841.

Arya Samja, Reformist Hindu society founded about 1866 by Dayananda Sarasvati (1825?–82).

Ascalon (modern **Ashkelon**), Israel, Biblical Philistine city. Captured by Saladin, 1187, and by Bibars, Sultan of Egypt, who demolished its fortifications, 1270, *See* CRUSADES.

Ascension Island, discovered on A. Day, 1501, by João da Nova. First occupied by British, 1815, and administered by the Admiralty until 1922, when it was made a dependency of St Helena. Fuelling post for Falklands Campaign, 1982.

Ascot, England, first race meeting held at, 11 Aug. 1711: Gold Cup first awarded, 1807.

ASEAN. *See* ASSOCIATION OF SOUTH EAST ASIAN NATIONS.

Ashanti, Ghana. First British expedition to, 1807. Wars with Great Britain: (1) 1863–4; (2) 1873–4; (3) 1895–1900 (relief of Kumasi), Protectorate, 1896; annexed, 1901.

Ashburton Treaty, 1842, settled the frontiers between USA and Canada.

Ashes, The, non-existent cricket trophy, competed for between England and Australia, first mentioned 29 Aug. 1882. Subsequently bails from England–Australia match played in Australia were burned and presented in an urn to the English captain. Kept at Cobham Hall, Kent, till 1927: since then, in the Memorial Gallery at Lord's. By 1995, England had won the A. 28 times, and Australia 30 (retaining the A. in the 1994–5 Test series).

Ashmolean Museum, Oxford, Founded, 1683, by Elias Ashmole (1617–92). Its contents separated, 1860, 1886, and 1894, and the bulk of them placed in the present building.

Asia Pacific Economic Co-operation (APEC), forum established 1989 for regular discussion between members on trade and economic matters. Members in 1995 included the USA, Canada, Japan, S Korea, Taiwan, Indonesia, etc. 1993 'summit' in Seattle: 1994 one in Jakarta, attended by 18 nations, envisaged Asian free-trade area by 2020.

Asiento, The, Contract originally between France and Spain for supplying Negro slaves to Spanish colonies, 1702. Transferred by Spain to Britain, 1713. Twice lost, it was finally restored for remaining period of two years, 1748.

Asmaia, capital of independent Eritrea since 1993. Rebellion in 1974 marked beginning of independence struggle against Ethiopia.

Assam. State of India since 1947. Conquered by British, 1826. Tea planting inaugurated, 1835. Separate province, 1919. Immigration from Bangladesh after 1972 led to rioting and murders from 1983. Rebel movements fighting independence campaign from 1987. India imposed direct rule, 1990.

assassinations. The most famous victims of assassination include:

Hipparchus of Athens, by Harmodius and Aristogiton, 514 BC.
Artaxerxes III of Persia, by Bagoas, 338 BC.
Philip II, of Macedon, by Pausanias, 336 BC.
Darius III of Persia, by Bessus, 330 BC.
Julius Caesar, by Brutus and others, 15 Mar. 44 BC.
Caius Caligula, by a tribune, AD 41.
Claudius I, poisoned by his wife, Agrippina, AD 54.
Edmund, St, King of E Anglia, 870.
Edmund the Elder of England, 26 May 946.
Edward the Martyr of England, 18 Mar. 978.
Albert I of Germany, by his nephew John, 1 May 1308.
Edward II of England, 27 Sept. 1327.
St Thomas Becket, Archbishop of Canterbury, 29 Dec. 1170.
James I of Scotland, by nobles, 21 Feb. 1437.
Edward V of England, July 1483.
James III of Scotland, by nobles, 11 June 1488.
David Rizzio, Mary Stuart's secretary, by Darnley's followers, 9 Mar. 1566.
Lord Henry Darnley, Mary Stuart's husband, by persons unknown, 10 Feb. 1567.
William the Silent, of Orange, by Balthazar Gérard, 12 July 1584.
Henry III of France, by Jacques Clément, 1 Aug. 1589.
Henry IV of France, by Ravaillac, 14 May 1610.
George Villiers, Duke of Buckingham, by John Felton, 23 Aug. 1628.
Gustavus III of Sweden, by Ankarström, 29 Mar. 1792.
Marat, by Charlotte Corday, 13 July 1793.

Paul, Tsar of Russia, by nobles, 24 Mar. 1801.

Spencer Perceval, British Prime Minister, by John Bellingham, 11 May 1812.

Abraham Lincoln, President of USA by Wilkes Booth, 14 Apr. 1865.

Michael, Prince of Serbia, 10 June 1868.

Abdul Aziz, Sultan of Turkey, alleged suicide, 4 June 1876.

Mehemet Ali Pasha, by Albanians, 7 Sept. 1878.

Alexander II of Russia, 13 Mar. 1881.

General Garfield, President of USA, by Charles Jules Guiteau, d. 19 Sept., 2 July 1881.

Chief Secretary for Ireland, Lord Frederick Cavendish, by Fenians, 6 May 1882.

Sadi Carnot, President of France, by Santo Caserio, 24 June 1894.

Nasr-ed-Deen, Shah of Iran, by Mullah Reza a Sayyid, 1 May 1896.

Elizabeth, Empress of Austria, by Luccheni, 10 Sept. 1898.

Humbert I of Italy, by Gaetano Bresci, 29 July 1900.

William McKinley, President of U.S.A., by Leon Czolgosz, d. 14 Sept., 5 Sept. 1901.

Alexander I of Serbia and wife, Draga, 10 June 1903.

King Carlos and Crown Prince of Portugal, by Buica and Da Costa, 1 Feb. 1908.

Peter Stolypin, Russian premier, 14 Sept. 1911.

Francisco I. Madero, President of Mexico, and Vice-President José Pino Saurez, 23 Feb. 1913.

George I of Greece, 18 Mar. 1913.

Archduke Francis Ferdinand of Austria-Hungary and wife, by Gabriel Princip, 28 June 1914.

Jean L. Jaurès, French Socialist leader, 31 July 1914.

Tsar Nicholas of Russia and family, at Ekaterinburg, by the Bolsheviks, 16 July 1918.

General Venustiano Carranza, President of Mexico, 20 May 1920.

Field-Marshal Sir Henry H. Wilson, in London, 22 June 1922.

Dr. Walter Rathenau, German Foreign Minister, 24 June 1922.

Michael Collins, by rebels, near Bandon, County Cork, 22 Aug. 1922.

Gabriel Narutowicz, first President of Polish Republic, by Capt. Niewadowski, 16 Dec. 1922.

Giacomo Matteoti, Italian Socialist leader, kidnapped by Fascists, body found 15 Aug., 10 June 1924.

Kevin O'Higgins, Vice-President of Irish Free State, 10 July 1927.

Paul Doumer, President of France, by Paul Gargolov, 6 May 1932.

Luis M. Sanchez Cerro, President of Peru, by Abelardo Hurtado de Mendoza, 30 Apr. 1933.

Nadir Shah, King of Afghanistan, by Abdul Khallig, student, 8 Nov. 1933.

Ernst Roehm, General Schleicher, his wife, and others, by Nazi Party, 30 June 1934.

Engelbert Dollfuss, Austrian Chancellor, by Otto Planetta, 25 July 1934.

Alexander, King of Yugoslavia, and French Foreign Minister Louis Barthou, at Marseilles, by Georgief, 9 Oct. 1934.

Senator Huey Long of Louisiana, by Carl Weiss, 8 Sept. 1935.

Ernst von Rath, German diplomat, by Herschel Grynszpan, in Paris, 7 Nov. 1938.

Leon Trotsky, exiled Russian leader, at Coycacán, Mexico, by Jacques Mornard, 21 Aug. 1940.

Darlan, Jean François, French admiral, at Algiers, 24 Dec. 1942.

Benito Mussolini, dictator of Italy, and his mistress, by Italian partisans, 28 Apr. 1945.

Ananda Mahidol, King of Thailand, 9 July 1946.

Mohandas Karamchand Gandhi, by Natheram Jodre, 30 Jan. 1948.

Imam Yahya of the Yemen, 17 Feb. 1948.

Count Folke Bernadotte, United Nations mediator, by Israeli terrorists, at Jerusalem, 17 Sept. 1948.

President Chalbaud of Venezuela, 13 Nov. 1950.

King Abdullah of Jordan, 20 July 1951.

Liaquat Ali Khan, Prime Minister of Pakistan, by Said Akbar, 16 Oct. 1951.

President Somoza of Nicaragua, 29 Sept. 1956.

King Feisal II of Iraq, his family and Prime Minister, by revolutionary nationalists, 14 July 1958.

Mr. Bandaranaike, Prime Minister of Sri Lanka, by Buddhist extremists, 25 Sept. 1959.

General Rafael Trujillo, dictator of the Dominican Republic, 30 May 1961.

President Sylvanus Olympio of Togo, 13 Jan. 1963.

President Ngo Dinh Diem of S. Vietnam, 1 Nov. 1963.

John F. Kennedy, President of USA, at Dallas, Texas, 22 Nov. 1963.

Pierre Ngendandumwe, Premier of Burundi, 15 Jan. 1965.

Mr. Mansur, Premier of Iran, 21 Jan. 1965.

'Malcolm X', leader of the US Black Muslims, 21 Feb. 1965.

Sir Abubakar Balewa, Premier of Nigeria, c. 15 Jan. 1966.

Hendrik Verwoerd, Premier of S Africa, 6 Sept. 1966.

Dr. Martin Luther King, US black leader, at Memphis, Tennessee, 4 Apr. 1968.

Senator Robert Kennedy, brother of President John F. Kennedy, at Los Angeles, 5 June 1968: he d. 6 June.

Tom Mboya, leading Kenyan politician, in Nairobi, 5 July 1969.

Sir Richard Sharples, Governor of Bermuda, 10 Mar. 1973.

President Allende of Chile, 11 Sept. 1973.

King Feisal of Saudi Arabia, 25 Mar. 1975.

Mujibar Rahman, President of Bangladesh, 15 Aug. 1975.

President Daoud of Afghanistan, Apr. 1978.

Airey Neave, MP, by INLA, 30 Mar. 1979.

Lord Mountbatten of Burma, by IRA, 27 Aug. 1979.

President Park of S Korea, 1979.

President Tolbert of Liberia, 12 Apr. 1980.

Archbishop Romero, in San Salvador cathedral, May 1980.

John Lennon, British popular musician, in New York, 9 Dec. 1980.

President Ziaur Rahman of Bangladesh, 30 May 1981.

President Sadat of Egypt, 6 Oct. 1981.

President Bashir Gemayel of Lebanon, 14 Sept. 1982.

Benigno Aquino, Philippine opposition leader, 21 Aug. 1983.

Four S. Korean cabinet ministers, at Rangoon, 10 Oct. 1983.

Maurice Bishop, Premier of Grenada, and three of his ministers, 20 Oct. 1983.

Indira Gandhi, Indian Premier, 31 Oct., 1984.

Olof Palme, Swedish premier, Stockholm, 28 Feb. 1986.

Lebanese premier, Rashid Karami, 1 June 1988.

Ian Gow, MP, by INLA, 30 July, 1990.

Rajiv Gandhi, Indian politician, 21 May 1991.

President Boudiaf of Algeria, 29 June 1992.

Hakija Turajlic, Bosnian vice-president, 8 Jan. 1993.

Chris Hani, black S African Communist leader, 10 Apr. 1993.

Ranasinghe Premadase, President of Sri Lanka, 1 May 1993.

Melchior Ndadaye, President of Burundi, 21 Oct. 1993.

Presidents of Rwanda and Burundi (in suspect plane crash), 6 Apr. 1994.

Gamini Dissanayake, Sri Lankan opposition leader, 25 Oct. 1994.

Fathi Shqaqi, Islamic Jehad leader, 29 Oct. 1995.

Yitzhak Rabin, Israeli premier, 4 Nov. 1995.

assassins, powerful Muslim secret society founded in Syria by Hassan ibn Sabbah (*fl.* 1080), the original 'Old Man of the Mountain' (*Sheikh-el-Jebel*). Massacre of 1255 virtually exterminated the sect.

assay officer. *See* HALLMARKS.

Assent, Royal, last refused to a parliamentary bill, 1707.

assignats and **mandats,** French revolutionary paper currency, first issued, 1790. Withdrawn 1797.

Assiniboia. Name previously applied to two districts in Canada. First formed, 1835, by the Hudson's Bay Co. and ceased to exist, 1870, on the transference of Rupert's Land to Canada. Second created, 1882, as a provisional district within the NW Territories, and became part of Saskatchewan in 1905.

Assisi, Umbria, Italy was town in Roman times. Birthplace of St Francis (1182–1226). Founder of the *Franciscan order (1209) and with St Clare of the Poor Clares (1212). A. has been centre of pilgrimage since Francis's death. Basilica of St Francis (begun 1228; consecrated 1253) contains tomb of St Francis and frescoes by Cimabue, Giotto, etc. Basilica of St Clare (begun 1257) has St Clare's tomb and the 'speaking Crucifix' of St Francis, originally in St Damian's. St Mary of the Angels, begun 1569, houses the saint's original chapel of the Porzunciola (outside A. proper).

Assize Courts. *See* COURTS, ENGLISH.

Assize of Clarendon, 1166, first legislative direction to employ the *jury.

Association of South East Asian Nations (ASEAN), established at Bangkok, 1967. Consists of Brunei, Indonesia, Malaysia, the Philippines, Singapore and Thailand. Took over non-military role of South East Asia Treaty Organization, 1975. Agreed to cooperate with European Community, 1980. Summits held: 1976; 1977; 1987; 1992. Vietnam joined, July 1995.

Assumption of the Virgin Mary established as an article of the Roman Catholic faith by a papal pronouncement *ex cathedra*, 1950.

Assyria became independent of *Babylon 17thC BC; rose into prominence under Tiglath-Pileser I *c*. 1120 BC, who conquered Babylon. Nineveh became capital under Tiglath-Pileser III (745–727 BC), whose empire was maintained by Sargon II, 722–705, and Sennacherib, 705–681 (*see* BIBLE). Essarhaddon, 681–668, conquered Egypt, but on his death the empire was divided and an alliance of Medes and Babylonians stormed and destroyed Nineveh and overthrew the Assyrian Empire, 612 BC.

Assyrians (Modern). About AD 1400 the Chaldaean Christians of N Iraq who had survived the reign of Timur-i-Leng the Mongol, fled to the Hakkiari mountains N of Mosul. Their tradition stated that they were the descendants of the ancient A., converted to Christianity in the first century AD by Thaddaeus. Between 1550 and 1750 various sections submitted to Rome as 'Chaldaean Uniates'. Surviving descendants comprise small Christian communities in present-day Iraq, Iran and Syria.

asteroids, designation given to minor planets, 1802, by Sir William Herschel (1738–1822). First and largest asteroid, Ceres, discovered by Piazzi at Palermo on 1 Jan. 1801. First photographs of dark side of an A. taken by British astronomers, Dec. 1992.

Aston University, Birmingham, established 1966.

Astronomer Royal. Office established 1675. Title was given to the Director of the Greenwich Observatory until 1975; since then, honorary. The following have held the title:

John Flamsteed, 1675
Edmund Halley, 1720
James Bradley, 1762
Nathaniel Bliss, 1762
Nevil Maskelyne, 1765
John Pond, 1811
Sir George Airy, 1835
Sir William Christie, 1881
Sir Frank Dyson, 1910
Sir Harold Jones, 1933
Sir Richard Woolley, 1955
Sir Martin Ryle, 1972
Sir Francis Graham-Smith, 1982
Arnold Wolfendale, 1991
Sir Martin Rees, 1995

Astronomical Association, British. First meeting, 24 Oct. 1890.

Astronomical Society, Royal. Founded, 1820. Incorporated, 1831.

astronomy. Copernicus (founder of present system), *b*. 1473, *d*. 1543; Kepler discovered planetary motions, 1609, 1619; Galileo discovered Jupiter's moons, sunspots, 1610; Newton's discoveries, 1666, etc.;

Greenwich Observatory, 1675; Halley's observations, 1705, etc.; Herschel's observations, 1781, etc.; Lord Rosse completed famous telescope, 1845; Lick telescope erected at Mt. Hamilton, California, 1887; Professor Perrine discovered new satellites of Jupiter, 1904–5, 1908. The work of stellar spectroscopy begun in America in 1872 by Henry Draper (1837–82). Spectra interpreted, 1913; Michelson measured angular diameter of a star, 1920, at the Mt Wilson Observatory. Solar telescopy developed specifically since *c.* 1900; notably since 1930s. Jodrell Bank Radio Telescope, then largest in the world, completed, 1958. Kitt Peak National Observatory Telescope, USA, 1970; Anglo-Australian Telescope installed at Siding Spring, NSW, 1974. Hubble Space Telescope put in orbit round earth, Apr. 1990, by space shuttle *Discovery*; impact of comet Shoemaker Levy on planet Jupiter seen clearly on Hubble, July 1994.

Asunción, capital of Paraguay. Founded, 1537.

Aswan or **Assuan,** Egypt. Dam built, 1902. Raised, 1912. Raised again, 1929–31. High Dam commenced 1955: stored water from 1964: operational, 1970.

asylum, right of. Exercised by embassies in Europe, 1862 (Greece) and 1875 (Spain). In 20thC exercised intermittently in S America, more recently in Europe. Nov. 1956: Nagy the Hungarian Prime Minister, sought asylum in the Yugoslav Embassy, and Cardinal Mindszenty, Hungarian primate, in the US embassy in Budapest. Pentecostal Russians sought A. in US embassy in Moscow, 1978; allowed to emigrate to Israel, 1983. In UK new House of Lords ruling on A., 1988: further curbs envisaged, 1991 onwards. Tightening of US and Western European rights of A, following collapse of Soviet bloc, post-1989. Germany restricted right of asylum, May 1993.

Athanasian Creed. *See* CREEDS.

Athelney, Somerset. King Alfred fled here in 878–9. The Alfred Jewel found, 1693.

Athenaeum, The. Literary weekly founded, 2 Jan. 1828. Absorbed into the *Nation*, Feb. 1921; amalgamated with *New Statesman*, 1931.

Athenaeum Club (London). Founded, 1824.

Athens. *History:* Draco's legal code, 621 BC. Reforms of Solon, 594. Tyranny of the Peisistratids, 560–510. Reforms of Cleisthenes, 508. Persian Wars, 490; 480–479; 468; 450–449. First Delian League, 478–404; second, 377–338. Age of Pericles, 443–429. Peloponnesian War, 431–421; 416–413; 412–404, when A. surrendered to Lysander. Government of the Thirty, 404–403, when the democracy was restored. A. again at war with Sparta, 378–371. Social War, 357–355. Athenian and allied forces defeated by Philip II of Macedon at Chaeronea, 338. Lamian War, 323–322, when A. was occupied by Antipater and compelled to modify her constitution. The democracy restored by Demetrius Poliorcetes, 307. A. included in the Roman province of Achaia, 146. Captured by Sulla, 86 BC. Philosophical schools closed by Justinian, AD 529. A. captured by Latins, 1205, and remained a Latin duchy till 1261. Captured by Turks, 1454; by Venetians, 1466; recaptured by Turks, 1479. Venetians attack and explode the Parthenon, which had been made a powder magazine, 1687; retaken by Turks, 1690. Captured by Greeks, 1822; retaken by Turks, 1827. Became capital of Greece, 1834. Occupied by French and English, 1854–6; by Allies, Dec. 1916. Germans occupied A., 27 Apr. 1941. British liberated A., 14 Oct. 1944. Fighting between Communists and Allied forces, 5–30 Dec. 1944. *Ancient Buildings:* A. sacked and destroyed by Persians, 480 BC. City wall, built by Themistocles soon after 479 BC; reconstructed by Conon in 393 and by Lycurgus *c.* 333; enlarged by Hadrian. Erechtheum: building started between 431 and 421; completed, 409; repaired after fire, early 4thC; W front reconstructed, 1stC AD. Long Walls: N and Phaleric completed *c.* 457 BC, Middle or S *c.* 445; all destroyed, 404. N and Middle restored, 393; both finally destroyed by Sulla, 86 BC. Monument of Lysicrates, 335–334. Odeum of Herodes Alticus, *c*. AD 162. Parthenon: begun, 447 BC; dedicated, 438; sculptures completed, 432. Propylaea, 437–433. Stadium, *c*. 330 BC; rebuilt *c*. AD 143; restored, late 19thC. Stoa of Attalus *c*. 158 BC restored, AD 1955. Temple of Hephaestus, 5thC BC. Temple of Olympian Zeus: Begun by Hippias *c*. 520 BC; continued, 175–164; completed, AD 132. Theatre of Dionysus: site first used for temporary wooden structure, 490 BC; permanent stone structure, between 338 and 326; alterations to stage and orchestra under Nero and Hadrian. Tower of the Winds, 2nd or 3rdC.

athletics. Evidence of organized running events in ancient Egypt, *c*. 3500 BC. Vase found in Cyprus dated *c*. 1250 BC has paintings of A. First *Olympic Games probably held 776 BC. 19thC revival of A. on organized scale in British public schools and universities. 1864: first Oxford–Cambridge A. match held at Oxford. 1880: establishment of Amateur Athletics Association (AAA); first championships held. 1896: Olympic Games revived. Henceforth increasing world interest in A. with growing African dominance in second half of 20thC. International Amateur Athletic Federation (IAFF) formed, 1912. Women's AAA, 1922. 1951: first Pan-American, Mediterranean and Asian games championships. First World A. championship held Helsinki, 1983, then every fourth year. 1975: IAAF introduced automatic suspension for athletes found to have taken anabolic steroids.

Atlanta, capital and largest city of Georgia, USA. Founded, 1837. Partially destroyed by Union Gen. Sherman, 1864. Important car, aeroplane and soft drinks manufacturing centre. To host Olympic Games, 1996.

Atlantic Charter. Declaration of the Four Freedoms issued by Franklin Roosevelt and Winston Churchill from a warship in the Atlantic, 11 Aug. 1941.

Atlantic flights. *See* AVIATION.

Atlantic passage record since the first crossing by a steamer, *Sirius*, in 1838, was held by the *Queen Mary*, 1938, until broken by the *United States*, 7 July 1952, with a time of three days, 10 hours, 40 minutes. Bid by Richard Branson's British *Virgin Challenger* failed when boat sank, Aug. 1985, but he subsequently beat the record in *Virgin Challenger II*, 1986.

Atlantic telegraph cable, begun Aug. 1857. First message, 5 Aug. 1858. Relaid 1866. (First transatlantic radio telegraphic transmission, 1901).

Atlantic telephone cable, First one successfully laid and opened to traffic, 1956.

atom. First split by Lord Rutherford, 1919.

atomic bomb. First detonated experimentally, 16 July 1945; first used operationally at Hiroshima, 6 Aug., and at Nagasaki, 9 Aug. 1945.

Atomic Energy Agency, International, established 29 July 1957 and reports annually to the UN. Aims to promote and speed contribution of atomic energy for peaceful uses, and to encourage research and training in nuclear power. Given task of drawing up safeguards in accordance with Non-Proliferation Treaty of 1968. Formed, with World Health Organization and Food and Agricultural Organization, international consultative group on food irradiation, 1983.

Atomic Energy Authority, United Kingdom (AEA Technology), established under the Atomic Energy Authority Act, 1954. Since April 1986, operates on a commercial footing. Adopted trading name **AEA Technology,** 1990.

Atomic Energy Research Establishment. Established at Harwell, England, 1945.

atomic power. Radioactivity discovered by Becquerel, 1896. Einstein's equation, 1905.

ATS (Auxiliary Territorial Service). *See* WOMEN'S ROYAL ARMY CORPS.

Attainder, Act of. First Bill of A. recorded against Despenser family, 1321. Most famous against Strafford after his impeachment had failed, 1641. Last against Lord E. Fitzgerald for participation in the Irish Rebellion, 1797.

Atterbury's Plot. Abortive Jacobite plot led by Francis Atterbury, Bishop of Rochester (1662–1732) in 1721. Atterbury was banished.

Attorney-General. William de Giselham, first recorded A.-G., 1278. A.-G. has sat in House of Commons since 1673. Ceased to practise at the Bar privately in return for increased salary, 1945.

Auckland. Founded 1840. Was capital of New Zealand till 1865.

Augmentation, Court of, set up, 1536, under Act of Dissolution. Dissolved, 1553.

Augsburg. Founded by Romans *c*. 15 BC (as *Augusta Vindelicorum*). Free city, 1276. Confession of A. drawn up by Luther and Melanchthon and presented to Charles V at Diet of A., 25 June 1530. Interim of A., 15 May 1548. Religious peace of A., 1555. League of A. against France, 9 July 1686. Annexed by Bavaria, 1806.

Augustales, games, sacred to the memory of the Emperor Augustus, held on his birthday, beginning in 11 BC.

Augusteo, Roman concert hall on the site of the Mausoleum of Augustus, opened in 1908.

Augustinian Canons, religious order established consequent on the Lateran synod of 1059.

auk, great. Last known specimen killed, 4 June 1844, on the Stack of Eldey, off SW Iceland.

Aulic Council. Established by Emperor Maximilian I, 1497, to assist in governing the Holy Roman Empire.

Aurora, former Tsarist Russian cruiser anchored in the River Neva at St Petersburg, and now a museum and training ship. It was a blank shot fired from the A. which signalled the assault on the Winter Palace, 1917, which marked the start of the Russian revolution.

Auschwitz, notorious Nazi concentration camp. *See under* its present Polish name of OSWIECIM.

Ausgleich (compromise). A treaty governing the joint affairs of the Dual Monarchy, concluded between its several partners, Austria and Hungary, in 1867, and renewed in 1878, 1887, 1902 and 1907.

Australia. N coast sighted by various Dutch voyagers, 17thC. Explored by Capt. Dampier, 1688; by Capt. Cook, 1769–70; Bass and Flinders, 1798. Colonized by British convicts from 1783. Last convicts landed, 1840. Divided into provinces, 1829, 1834, 1850, 1859. New South Wales Constitution, 1842. Australian Colonies Act passed, 1850; granted power to various provinces to draw up own constitution. Gold rush began, 1851. S Australian Constitution, 27 Oct. 1856. Victoria Parliament opened at Melbourne, 17 Jan. 1867. Commonwealth Bill of A. Constitution, 9 July 1900. First governor-general appointed, 14 July 1900. Australians played major role in World War I campaigns, notably at Gallipoli. Australian Federal Parliament was opened at *Canberra by Duke of York, 9 May 1927. Increased urbanization and growth of unions increased power of Labor movement between World Wars 1919–39. Unsuccessful attempt by WA to secede from Commonwealth, 1933–5. A. played major role in World War II, notably in N Africa and Far E. Troops sent to Vietnam, 1965. Increased non- British immigration after 1945 and constitutional crisis, 1975, led to growth of republican movement, 1975 onwards, emphasized by election of Labor gov. under Hawke, 1983. Australia Act, 1986, abolished last traces of British legal authority in A. but republicanism further increased after resignation of Hawke and premiership of Keating, Dec. 1991. Queen to be dropped from allegiance oath, Dec. 1992. Peacekeeping force sent to Somalia, 1993. Labor under Keating again re-elected, Mar. 1993. In Sept. 1993 Keating told Queen he would like A. to be a republic by 2000. Worst bush-fires for 200 years in New South Wales, Jan. 1994.

Governor-Generals since 1901:
Earl of Hopetoun 1901–02
Lord Tennyson 1902–04
Lord Northcote 1904–08
Earl of Dudley 1908–11
Lord Denman 1911–14
Visc. Novar 1914–20
Lord Forster 1920–25
Lord Stonehaven 1925–30
Lord Somers (acting) 1930–31
Sir Isaac Alfred Isaacs 1931–36
Lord Gowrie 1936–44
Sir Winston Dugan (acting) 1944–45
HRH the Duke of Gloucester 1945–47
Sir Winston Dugan (acting) 1947
Sir William John McKell 1947–52
Sir William Slim 1953–60
Lord Dunrossil 1960–61
Viscount De L'Isle 1961–65
Lord Casey 1965–69
Sir Paul Hasluck 1969–74
Sir John Kerr 1974–77
Sir Zelman Cowen 1977–82
Sir Ninian Stephen 1982–89
Bill Hayden, 1989–
Heads of Administrations (Prime Ministers) from 1901:
Barton 1901–03
Deakin 1903–04
Watson (Apr.–Aug.) 1904
Reid 1904–05
Deakin 1905–08
Fisher 1908–09
Deakin 1909–10
Fisher 1910–13
Cook 1913–14
Fisher 1914–15
Hughes 1915–23
Bruce 1923–29
Scullin 1929–31
Lyons 1931–39
Menzies 1939–41
Fadden (Aug.–Oct. 1941
Curtin 1941–45
Chifley 1945–49
Menzies 1949–66

Holt 1966–68
McEwen (acting) 1968
Gorton 1968–71
McMahon 1971–72
Whitlam 1972–75
Fraser 1975–83
Hawke 1983–1991
Keating 1991–

Austria (German **Oesterreich**). Roman provinces of Rhaetia, Noricum, and Pannonia *c.* 33 BC. Organized as a march (*Ostmark*) of the * Holy Roman Empire by Charlemagne, AD 791–6. Created a duchy, 1156. Given by Emperor Rudolf I of Hapsburg to his son Rudolf, 1282. Carinthia annexed, 1335. Defeated twice by Swiss at Zürich, 1358. Annexation of Tyrol, 1363. Leopold III killed by Swiss at battle of Sempach, 1386. Albert V becomes King of Bohemia and Hungary, 1437–40. Created archduchy, 6 Jan. 1453. Recognizes Swiss independence, 1474. Vienna captured by Matthias of Hungary, 1485. A. given to Ferdinand, brother of Emperor Charles V, 1521. Annexation of Bohemia and Silesia, 1526. First Turkish siege of Vienna, 1529. 'Imperial' Hungary ceded to A., 1541. Truce of Adrianople with Turks, 1545. Zapolya renounces Hungary to A., 1570. *Thirty Years War, 1618–48. *Peace of Westphalia, 1648. Hungary conquered from Turks, 1688; acquisition confirmed by Treaty of Carlowitz, 1699. War of Austrian Succession, 1741–8. *Seven Years War, 1756–63. French Revolutionary Wars begun, 1792. Lombardy and the Netherlands secured by France, 1797. Defeat at battle of Hohenlinden, Dec. 1800. Pact of Lunéville, Feb. 1801. Defeat at battle of Ulm, 1805. At Austerlitz, Dec. 1805. Pact of Pressburg, Dec. 1805. Battle of Wagram, 1809. Battle of Leipzig, 1813. Treaty of Paris, May 1814. Congress of Vienna, 1814–15. The Karlsbad Decrees, 1819. Revolution and resignation of Metternich, Mar. 1848. Czech revolt suppressed, June 1848. Hungarian rebellion under Kossuth, Sept. 1848. Windischgrätz suppressed Vienna insurrection, Oct. 1848. Hungarians capitulate to Russians at Vilagos, Aug. 1849.

Convention of Olmütz (Olomouc), 1850. Occupation of Romania, 1854. Austro-Prussian invasion of Denmark 1864. War with Prussia, 1866. Battle of Sadowa, 3 July 1866. Sardinia annexed Venetia, 1866. The *'Ausgleich'* ('compromise') with Hungary, 1867. Alliance with Russia and Germany (*Dreikaiserbund*), 1873. Renewed 1881, 1884. Annexation of Bosnia-Herzegovina, 1908. Archduke Franz Ferdinand assassinated at Sarajevo, 28 June 1914. *World War I 1914–18. *Bundesrepublik* (Federal Republic) declared secession from Dual Monarchy, 12 Nov. 1918. New boundaries settled by Treaty of St. Germain, 10 Sept. 1919. Federal Constitution, Nov. 1920. Dollfuss suppresses Socialists in Vienna by military force, Feb. 1934; assassinated by Nazis, 25 July 1934. A. annexed by Germany, 12–14 Mar. 1938. Russian armies invaded A., 1945, and captured Vienna, 13 Apr. Karl Renner (1870–1950) elected president, 1945, of revived *Bundesrepublik*. Agreement with Italy on S Tyrol, 6 Sept. 1946. Austrian peace treaty signed, 15 May 1955. Last occupation forces left A., Sept. 1955. Growth of right-wing extremism in 1990s. First applied to join European Community, 1989. Joined European Economic Area, Jan. 1994; agreed terms for joining European Union, Mar. 1994; referendum approved terms, June; A. became EU member, 1 Jan 1995. Coalition government resigned, Oct. 1995.

Austria, Emperors of:
The rulers of the house of Hapsburg (Grand Dukes of Austria) took the title of Emperor of A. on 11 Aug. 1804, and Francis II renounced the crown of the *Holy Roman Empire, 6 Aug. 1806. The following were the Emperors of A.:

Franz II and I 1804–35
Ferdinand I 1835–48
Franz Josef 1848–1916
Karl (abdicated) 1916–18

Effective Heads of Administration:
The government of the Austrian Empire cannot be compared with the system of responsible government existing in England at the same time. Its heads relied in the last resort upon the emperor, and his personal policy could decide which member of the administration was to be the effective head, regardless of their actual titles of office. The following is a list of the most influential figures in Austrian government. It does not purport to be a list of the holders of one particular office.

Stadion 1806–09
Von Metternich 1809–48
Kolowrat 1848
Ficquelmont 1848
Von Pillersdorf 1848
Wessenberg 1848
Schwarzenberg 1848–52
Bach 1852–59
Goluchowski 1859–60
Von Schmerling 1861–65
Belcredi 1865–67
Beust 1867–70
Taaffe 1870–71
Hohenwart 1871
Von Auersperg 1871–78
Stremayr 1878–79
Taaffe 1879–93
Windischgrätz 1893–95
Badeni 1895–97
Gautsch 1897–98
Von Thun 1898–99
Clary-Aldringen 1899
Von Körber 1900–04
Gautsch 1905–06
Von Hohenlohe 1906
Beck 1906–08
Biernerth 1908–11
Gautsch 1911
Stürgkh 1912–16
Von Körber 1916
Clam-Martinic 1917
Von Seidler 1917–18
Hussarek 1918
Lammasch 1918
Presidents, since 1920:
Hainisch 1920–28
Miklas 1928–38 (13 Mar.)
Renner 1945–50
Koerner 1951–57
Schärf 1957–65
Jonas 1965–74

Kirchsläger 1974–86
Waldheim 1986–92
Klestil 1992–
Heads of Administration since 1919 (Chancellors):
Renner Mar. 1919–Oct. 1919
Mayr Oct. 1919–July 1920
'Proporz' Cabinet July 1920–Nov. 1920
Mayr Nov. 1920–May 1921
Schober July 1921–May 1922
Seipel May 1922–Nov. 1924
Ramek Nov. 1924–Oct. 1926
Seipel Oct. 1926–Apr. 1929
Steeruwitz May 1929–Sept. 1929
Schober Sept. 1929–Sept. 1930
Vaugoin Sept. 1930–Nov. 1930
Ender Dec. 1930–June 1931
Sepiel 18 June 1931–20 June 1931
Buresch June 1931–May 1932
Dollfuss May 1932–July 1934
Von Schuschnigg July 1934–12 Mar 1938
Seyss-Inquart was nominally chancellor from 12–14 Mar. 1938. After 'inviting' Hitler to annex Austria, he became first governor of *Ostmark.*
Renner Apr. 1945–Oct. 1945 (provisional)
Figl Nov. 1945–53
Raab 1953–59
Gorbach 1959–64
Klaus 1964–70
Kreisky 1970–83
Sinowatz 1983–86
Vranitzky, 1986–

Austrian Succession, War of the. Broke out, 1741. Ended by Treaty of Aix-la-Chapelle, 1748.

Authorized Version of the Bible, rendered into English by a commission of 47 translators working, 1607–10, and first published, 1611.

Authors, Society of, founded 1884. Its headquarters are at 84 Drayton Gardens, London SW10 9SB.

auto-da-fé, ceremonial burning of heretics by the Inquisition, last carried out in Mexico, 1815.

Automobile Association (AA). Founded, 1905.

Autun, France, ancient *Augustodunum*, founded by Augustus, who removed thither the population of nearby Gallic Bibracte. Destroyed, AD 240; but rebuilt 340; sacked by Vandals, 406; Burgundians, 414; Huns, 451; Franks, 534; Arabs, 739; Normans, 895; English, 1379.

Auxiliary Territorial Service *See* WOMEN'S ROYAL ARMY CORPS.

Avebury, Wiltshire, built *c.* 2600 BC. Largest (though now incomplete) stone circle in Europe.

aviation. Borelli's artificial wings, 1670; Sir George Cayley's machine, 1796; Henson's aerostat, 1843; Wenham's aeroplane, 1866; Dr. Pettigrew's elastic screws demonstrated, 1867; Moy's aerial steamer, 1874; Langley's steam-driven model, 1893; Sir H. Maxim's experiments, 1880–90, 1893–4; Lilienthal killed on gliding machine, 1896; W. and O. Wright's experiments begun, 1900; they first flew, 1903; S. Dumont's aeroplane, 1906; Farman biplane, 1907; Blériot flew across Channel, 25 July 1909; Paulhan's altitude record, Jan. 1910. First air mail service between Hendon and Windsor, 1911. Single-seater planes used solely for fighting first used by British, Dec. 1914. First airship and aeroplane crossing of Atlantic, 1919. First solo transatlantic flight, New York–Paris, by Lindbergh, in just over 33 hours, reaching Paris, 21 May 1927. First jet-propelled plane in service (German), 1944. First pilotless plane to cross Atlantic, Oct. 1947. Maiden flights of both French and British models of the Anglo-French supersonic *Concorde*, 1969. First 'Jumbo-jet' flew Atlantic on commercial flight, 1970. *Solar Challenge* flew across English Channel using only solar power, 1981. Worst single A. accident Aug. 1985 (Boeing 747 in Japan: 520 died). First aircraft flew non-stop round world without re- fuelling (California USA to California), Dec. 1986. First flight of Bell-Boeing V-22 Osprey, combination aeroplane/helicopter, 1989.

Avignon. Popes went into residence at, 1309. Purchase from France, 1348. Papal

Palace built, 1342–60. Popes left for Rome, 1377. French antipopes at A., 1378–1408. Became an archbishopric, 1475. Annexed by France, 1797.

Avlona. *See* VLÖNE.

avoirdupois weight. First Act directing use of, 1532. *See* WEIGHTS AND MEASURES.

Avon, non-metropolitan county established 1974 under the Local Government Act of 1972 and based in *Bristol. Abolition envisaged 1995.

Avranches, Concordat of, whereby Henry II of England withdrew all his demands concerning jurisdiction over 'criminous clerks', and other causes of his disputes with Becket, and in return was absolved of all complicity in the archbishop's murder, 1172.

'Axis', The, Italo-German alliance of 1936.

Aylesbury Election Case, 1704, or **Ashby v. White**. Decided that the courts would protect any one whose right to vote was wrongfully denied.

Aynthia, Thailand. Founded, 1351. Capital of Siam till 1782, when it was sacked by Burmese.

Azerbaijan (Iranian). Russian attempt to subvert frustrated, 1946.

Azerbaijan republic of, Soviet republic, 1920. Included in the Transcaucasian Republic, 1922, 1936, a constituent republic of the USSR. Declared independence, 30 Aug. 1991: independence recognised as member of the CIS, Dec. 1991, but left in 1992, not rejoining till Sept. 1993. Fighting between Muslim A. and Christian *Armenia over disputed area of Nagorno-Karabakh since 1988, with A. in retreat since 1993. Government fell following defeats in 1993; president Aliyev succeeded (elected Oct. 1993). Opposition crushed by Mar. 1995.

Azores. Discovered by Portuguese under Cabral, 1431–2. First settled, 1444. British allowed temporary naval and air bases, 1943.

Azov, Russia. Founded, 12C. Taken by Tamerlane, 1395; by Russians, 1696; restored to Turks, 1711. Fortifications demolished, 1739. Ceded to Russia, 1774. Occupied by Germans, 1941; retaken, 1943.

Aztecs. Settled in *Mexico *c*. AD 1200. Overthrown by Cortes, 1519.

Baader-Meinhof Gang, or **Red Army Faction,** German anarchist terrorist group named after two of its founders, Andreas Baader (1943–77) and Ulrike Meinhof (1934–76). The third founder member was Gudrun Esslin. The gang was active against US and German capitalist targets in Germany from 1968. Arrested in 1968, the leading members escaped 1970, were rearrested 1972 and sentenced to life imprisonment, 1977. Meinhof committed suicide in her cell, May 1976: the remaining captive members of the gang committed suicide in Stammheim gaol, Stuttgart, in Oct. 1977. Other anarchist groups have appeared in Germany since 1977, but none with the notoriety of the original B.-M.G. They have, however committed a number of notorious acts e.g., murder of the head of Deutsche Bank, 30 Nov. 1989.

Baal, major figure in several Syriac-Palestinian cults, co-existent with the Old Testament, in which B. is specifically mentioned.

Baalbeck, or **Heliopolis,** Syria. Captured by Assyrians, 738 BC. Became a Roman colony under Augustus (31 BC–AD 14). Sanctuary built, 150–210. Converted into church c. 330. Captured by Arabs, 635. Dome removed to the 'Dome of the Rock' in Jerusalem c. 710. Walls demolished, 745. Sacked by Mongols, 1400. Earthquake, 1759. Laid waste, 1760–70, by Turks.

Babi. *See* BAHA'I.

Babington's Conspiracy. Anthony B. (1561–86) and others plotted to kill Queen Elizabeth and liberate Mary, Queen of Scots. Leaders of plot executed, Sept. 1586.

Babylon (town). Settled about 4000 BC by the Sumerians; first mentioned in a cuneiform tablet c. 2700 BC. Capital c. 2200 BC. After 1100 B. became subject to or dependent on Assyria until the New Babylonian Empire (620–539) was founded by Nebuchadnezzar. 'New Palace' built, 604. The town was destroyed by Sennacherib the Assyrian, 696 BC, and rebuilt by Essarhaddon, 680–670. Captured by Cyrus, 538. The most important excavations of the city took place, 1899–1917.

Babylonia. First mentioned as an independent state c. 2200 BC. Elamites driven out by Hammurapi (the biblical Amraphel) c. 2037. Kassite conquest of B. c. 1743. Rise of Assyria, 1900–1400. Assyrians became supreme under Shalmanezer I, 1300. First Assyrian Empire reaches its climax under Tiglath-Pileser I c. 1110. Civil war, 824–746, leads to establishment of Second Assyrian Empire by Pul (Tiglath-Pileser III), 745. Pul crowned at Babylon, 729. Merodach-baladan leads rebellion against Assyria, 722–710. Assyrian power destroyed by the Babylonians and Medes c. 610, and end of B.'s independence, 538, by Persian conquest.

Babylonian Captivity. Jewish historical term to describe the period between the capture or destruction of Jerusalem by Nebuchadnezzar, 599 or 586, and the deportation of its inhabitants, to the edict of Cyrus, 538, allowing the tribes of Judah, Benjamin and Levi to return home.

'Babylonish Captivity'. Name applied by critical contemporaries to the Papacy's residence at *Avignon, 1309–77.

Bachelor of Arts. Degree first conferred in various universities in the 13thC.

Bachelor Tax. Imposed in England, 1695 and 1785.

bacteria. Discovered by van Leeuwenhoek, 1680. F. J. Cohn (1828–98) founder of modern bacteriology.

Bactria. Old Persian province now part of *Afghanistan. Conquered by Cyrus *c.* 540 BC, by Alexander, 325. After 323 ruled by Seleucids until the beginning of the independent Graeco-Bactrian kingdom (255–140) founded by Diodotos which was conquered by the Scythians, who ruled until AD 560.

Badajoz (Roman *Pax Augusta*), Spain. Originally a Celtic settlement, then a town in Roman times. Capital of a Moorish kingdom, 1031. Besieged very frequently, the most recent being the sieges by the Portuguese, 1385, 1396, 1542 and 1705; the French, 1808–9, and Feb. 1811; the British, May and June 1811. It was finally stormed by British, 6 Apr. 1812. During Spanish Civil War taken by nationalists, Aug. 1936.

Badakhshan visited by Marco Polo, 1272–3, was part of the Graeco-Bactrian kingdom (*See* BACTRIA). From the 13thC until the time of Nadir Shah of Persia (1688–1747), ruled by a local dynasty claiming descent from Alexander the Great. Conquered by the Uzbeks *c.* 1800; Afghan supremacy was restored, 1859. Part of Tajikistan since 1929.

Baden, Grand Duchy and Republic of, split between several rulers of the Zähringen family till 1771, when it was united under one margrave. Became a Grand Duchy and substantially enlarged, 1806. Constitution granted, 1818. Hecker and Struve established a republic, 1848; grand duke reinstated, 1849. Joined Austria against Prussia, 1866. Joined German Empire, 1871. Republic declared, 1918. Suppressed by Hitler 1934. *Land* of Baden-Württemberg, since 1952.

Baden-Baden, Germany. Founded as *Aurelia Aquensis* by Hadrian, in the 2ndC AD. The ruins on Castle Hill (Schlossberg) are of a castle destroyed by the French in 1689, as was the original 'new castle' built in the 16thC, of which the extant building is a facsimile. Famous 19thC spa and gambling resort.

Badminton. Seat of the Dukes of Beaufort in Gloucestershire, came into the hands of the Somerset family, 1608; the present building was erected by Henry Somerset (1629–99), first Duke of Beaufort in 1682, one of the finest surviving examples of the Palladian style. The game of B. was invented at B. House, 1868: first world championships held, 1977. B. Horse Trials established after World War II.

Baffin Bay. Discovered by William Baffin, 1616.

Baghdad, Iraq. Founded, AD 763, by the Abbasid Caliph Al-Mansur, it reached its highest splendour in the reign of Haroun-al-Rashid (786–809). Besieged and stormed by Persians under Tahir (812–13). Seljuk Sultan Toghrul Beg acclaimed here, 1055. Seljuks ousted, 1181. Kwarismian attack, 1216. Sacked by Hulagu, the Mongol emperor, 1258. Captured by Timur, 1393. Turkish from 1638. Captured by British, 11 Mar. 1917. Became capital of Iraq, 1921. Headquarters of the *B. Pact, 1955–8. Revolution overthrowing the monarchy originated in B., July 1958. Bombed, 1991, during *Gulf War.

Baghdad Pact. Defensive and economic pact, so called because it was first signed at Baghdad between Turkey and Iraq in Feb. 1955. Subsequently Britain (Apr.), Pakistan (Sept.), and Iran (Nov.) signed it. In 1958 Iraq left the organization which was renamed *CENTO (Central Treaty Organization).

Baha'i or **Babi.** Followers of an originally Persian sect founded *c.* 1844 by Mirza Ali Mohammed (1819–*c.* 1850) of Shiraz. After the martyrdom of its founder at Tabriz in 1850 the sect spread through the Ottoman Empire, about two-thirds of its present-day adherents being converts from Islam or the descendants of such, the remainder mostly western Europeans and Americans.

Bahamas (formerly **Lucayos**). Discovered by Columbus, 1492. The first island colonized was Eleuthera, 1646; then New Providence, 1666. English expelled by French and Spaniards, 1703; re-colonized by English, 1717; reduced by Spain, 1781;

restored, 1783, by treaty. Extensive cyclone damage, 1866, 1883, 1945. Duke of Windsor (formerly Edward VIII) appointed governor, 1940–45. Independent within Commonwealth, 1973.

Bahrain. Archipelago in Persian Gulf, B. was occupied by the Portuguese for the whole of the 16thC, who were then dispossessed by Arab subjects of the Shah. Britain undertook B.'s defence and foreign relations under treaties of 1882 and 1892. Oil discovered, 1931. Independent, 1971.

Baia, formerly **Bahia,** Brazil. Visited by Amerigo Vespucci, 1510. Colonized, 1536. Refounded, 1549, and seat of viceroys of Brazil until 1763.

Bailey or **Old Bailey.** The street in London (first extant reference, 1444–5) in which have stood a succession of courts for the trial of criminals. One, built 1773, was destroyed, 1780; re-built, 1785–6; enlarged, 1808. Re-built on site of Newgate Prison, 1902–7.

Bailey bridge, invented by Donald Bailey, 1941, and successfully used during World War II and since.

Baireuth. *See* BAYREUTH.

Bakelite, invented 1909, in USA by Leo Baekeland (1863–1944). First plastic.

Baku, capital of republic of *Azerbaijan since Dec. 1991. Under Persia, 1509–1723. Under Russia, 1723–35. Persia, 1735–1806. Finally annexed by Russia, 1806. Oil refineries severely damaged in civil disturbances, 1904–5, 1914–21 and in World War II. Riots and clashes between Azeri majority and Armenian minority in 1990: Armenians subsequently fled from B. Fire on B. underground railway killed over 300, Oct. 1995.

Balaklava or **Balaclava,** town in the republic of *Ukraine, anciently *Portus Cymbolorum,* became a Genoese 'factory' in the 14thC, and remained so until the Turkish conquest of the *Crimea. Became a garrison town under Catherine the Great (1762–96). Held by British expeditionary

force, 1854–6; scene of the battle in which the ill-fated Charge of the Light Brigade occurred, 25 Oct. 1854. *See* BATTLES.

Balasore was the first English settlement in India, 1642, and the last (as distinct from the Portuguese and French possessions) of the other European stations; the Danish 'factory' here was sold to the E India Co., 1846.

Balearic Islands. Colonized by the Phoenicians *c.* 4thC BC. Conquered by Romans, 123 BC; by Vandals, *c.* AD 426; by Moors, 798. Independent Moorish kingdom, 1009–1232. Independent Christian kingdom of Majorca, 1276–1349, when it became a dependency of Aragon. *See* MAJORCA and MINORCA.

Balfour Declaration, 2 Nov. 1917, suggested British approval for a Jewish state in Palestine. *See* PALESTINE, MODERN.

Bali. During the period of Muslim expansion in the 15thC AD many Buddhists and Brahmins fled to B. and the religion of the island is a synthesis of these two faiths, both in a more archaic form than any extant elsewhere. Trade relations with the Dutch began in 1597, but Dutch rule was not firmly established until 1908. B. was occupied by the Japanese, 1942–5, and in 1946 there was a battle in western B. between western Indonesian nationalists and the Dutch. Part of Indonesia since 1946. Volcanic eruption, Mar. 1963, killed over 1,000 people on B. Major tourist area since 1960s.

Balkan Entente. Between Yugoslavia, Romania, Turkey and Greece, signed in Athens, 9 Feb. 1934. Bulgaria signed non-aggression pact with B.E., 31 July 1938. Renewed for seven years, 3 Feb. 1940, but a dead letter after 1941.

Balkan Mountains. Became frontier line of Turkish dominions by Treaty of Berlin, 13 July 1878.

Balkan Wars, Oct. 1912–Aug. 1913, fall into three divisions: 1. First B. War – the war of the B. League against Turkey in which the League conquered Macedonia, Albania and a large part of Thrace.

Armistice, Dec. 1912. 2. Greece continued the war. The armistice denounced, Feb. 1913, and the other allies continued the war. 3. Second B. War. B. League broke up, June 1913, then followed the war of Serbia, Greece, and Montenegro against Bulgaria, assisted by Romania, which now intervened, and Turkey. The first B. War ended by Treaty of London, 30 May 1913; the second by Treaty of Bucharest, 10 Aug. 1913, and by the treaty between Bulgaria and Turkey, 18 Sept. 1913.

ball-point pen, invented 1888 in USA but not popularized till produced by Biro family in Hungary, 1938.

Ballarat goldfield was opened up, 1851. The rebellion of miners at Eureka Stockade, 3 Dec. 1854, is the only battle ever fought on Australian soil.

ballet. The culmination of a long tradition of European dance technique, difficult to trace historically, but perhaps first reaching a form which would be recognizable today at the courts of England, Scotland and France late in the 15thC. To this was added the influence of Italian pantomime; the kind of entertainment devised *c.* 1555 for Catherine de Medici by her Master of Music Baltazarini (who *d. c.* 1587) is the first to be called B. In the classical comedy of 17thC France, B. forms an integral part of the entertainment and it did not become finally disengaged from 'legitimate' drama and opera until the mid-19thC. The classical European B. of today derives from the Russian school of St Petersburg, the formative period of which was 1840–80, though the Imperial B. had been founded in 1735, largely under French and Italian tuition. The return impact of Russian dancing on the W. had its greatest force in the years 1910–20, just after the influence of Isadora Duncan (1878–1927) had been felt in St Petersburg. Nijinsky became Imperial B. Master, 1913. Massine produced his first B., 1917. British ballet reached new heights, period 1960–90.

Prominent names in the world of modern B. include:

Ashton, Sir Frederick (British dancer and choreographer), 1906–88.
Balanchine, George (Russian-born choreographer), 1904–83.
de Valois, Dame Ninette (British ballerina and choreographer), 1898–
Baryshnikov, Mikhail (Latvian-born dancer), 1948–
Diaghilev, Sergei (Russian impressario and choreographer), 1872–1929.
Dolin, Sir Anton (British dancer and choreographer) 1904–83.
Duncan, Isadora (American dancer), 1878–1927.
Fokhine, Mikhail (Russian dancer and choreographer), 1880–1942.
Fonteyn, Dame Margot (British ballerina), 1919–91.
Helpmann, Sir Robert (Australian dancer and choreographer), 1907–86.
Macmillan, Sir Kenneth (British choreographer), 1930–92.
Markova, Dame Alicia (British ballerina), 1910–
Massine, Leonid (Russian dancer and choreographer), 1896–1979.
Mille, Agnes de (U.S. choreographer), 1905–93
Nijinsky, Vaslav (Russian dancer), 1890–1950.
Nureyev, Rudolf (Russian-born dancer), 1939–93.
Pavlova, Anna (Russian ballerina), 1885–1931.
Rambert, Dame Marie (Polish-born ballerina), 1889–1982.
Ulanova, Galina (Russian ballerina), 1910–

balloons. Principal experiments, etc., with: Joseph Montgolfier made first fire balloon, 1782. Brothers Montgolfier successfully made an ascent in a fire balloon, 1783. First ascent in balloon filled with hydrogen at Paris by Professor Charles, Aug. 1783. First ascent in England by Vincent Lunardi, Sept. 1784. Channel crossed by Blanchard and Jefferies, 7 Jan. 1785. Nassau balloon left London and descended at Nassau, 1836. Nadar's balloon ascended with 14 persons, 4 Oct. 1863 (the first balloon with steering apparatus).

Glaisher and Coxwell rose to a height of seven miles in a balloon, 5 Sept. 1862. Godard's Montgolfier balloon ascended, 28 July and 3 Aug. 1864. Giffard's experiments with dirigible, 1852. Zeppelin, 1900, 1908. Alberto Santos Dumont's experiments with steerable balloon, July–Oct. 1901; Feb. 1902. B. were used for observation purposes by the French, 1794, but Napoleon disbanded the Balloon Corps, 1798. Used as artillery observation posts in Italian War of Liberation, 1860: *American Civil War in Franco-Prussian War, 1870–71; and in Spanish-American War, 1898. German Balloon Corps formed, 1884; British Balloon Corps, 1879. B. first used by the Royal Navy at Gallipoli, 1915, and on the western front during World War I; and in mass as a barrage against aircraft, World War II. First Atlantic balloon crossing, 1978; first Pacific balloon crossing, 1981.

ballot box. First used in England at election of London aldermen, 1526. Bills authorizing parliamentary voting by ballot thrown out by Lords, 1710; passed, 18 July 1872. First parliamentary election in England by secret ballot at Pontefract, 15 Aug. 1872.

Ballymote, Book of. A MS in Middle Irish, a miscellany of prose and verse copied in 1391 by the monks of B. in Sligo.

Balmoral Castle. Purchased by Prince Albert, 1852; present building commenced, 1853; completed, 1855.

Baltic and Black Sea Canal. Projected by Peter the Great (1682–1725), said to have been completed 70 years after his death, afterwards fell into disuse.

Baltic and White Sea Canal (142 miles/227 km). Begun, Dec. 1931; opened, 1933.

Baltic Entente. Alliance between Estonia, Latvia, Lithuania and Poland, Mar. 1922.

Baltic Exchange. The Baltic merchants began in Elizabethan times to meet in the Virginia and Baltic inns. In the 18thC merchants interested in Baltic trade met in the Baltic Coffee House. The Baltic Club founded, 1823. The association thus formed was united in 1899 with the London Shipping Exchange to form the modern B.E. Building bombed by the IRA, 10 Apr. 1992.

Baltic expeditions.
1. Under Admirals Parker and Nelson, 1801.
2. Under Admiral Gambier and Lord Cathcart, 1807.
3. Under Admiral Napier, 11 Mar. 1854.
4. Under Rear-Admiral Dundas, 4 Apr. 1855.

Baltic Sea. Whole surface frozen over, 1658, 1809. Holstein Canal, connecting River Eider with Baltic, opened, 1785; B. and N Sea Canal for large vessels, 1895.

Baltic states. Estonia, Lithuania and Latvia (*see* all these) proclaimed independent republics, 1918. All these states were annexed to the USSR, July 1940. Occupied by Germany, 1941–4, and incorporated in the Reich Commissariat *Ostland*. Reconquered by the USSR, 1944–5. Subsequently reincorporated into the USSR but regained their independence, Aug. 1991, and last Russian troops left B.S., Aug. 1994.

Baltimore, Maryland. Founded, 1729. Named after the first Lord B. Incorporated, 1796; first Roman Catholic diocese in the USA, 1789. John Hopkins University founded, 1876. Art Museum, 1914. Greater part of business area destroyed by fire, 1904. Subsequent rebuilding and considerable expansion. *See* MARYLAND.

Baluchistan, Asia. Occupied by British successively, 1839, 1840, 1841. British B. incorporated in India, 1887. Became part of *Pakistan, 15 Aug. 1947.

Bamberg, Germany. Prince Bishopric founded, AD 1007. University existed between 1648 and 1803. Secular power finally abolished, 1806.

Bamburgh Castle. The stronghold of the *Bernician kings, built by Ida the Anglian chief, 547; besieged by the Mercian pagan King Penda, 641. Destroyed by Olaf of Dublin, 993. Besieged by William II, 1095. Extensively added to in Norman times, especially under Robert de Mowbray, Earl of Northumberland, 1080–93; and often restored, especially in 1721, and by Lord Armstrong in 1894.

Bampton Lectures in divinity at Oxford founded by Rev. John B. (1690–1751). Begun, 1780.

Banat, the. Area between Transylvanian Alps and rivers Tisza, Mures and Danube. Originally ruled by Hungary, but under the Austrian crown, 1849–60. Treaty of Trianon, 1920, divided it between Yugoslavia and Romania.

Banbury, England. Castle erected at by Alexander, Bishop of Lincoln, 1125. Battle of (Wars of Roses), 1469. Surrendered to Charles I, Oct. 1642; besieged, 1643, 1644 and in 1646, when it surrendered to parliamentary forces.

Band of Hope. Temperance association for juveniles, started in Leeds, 1847. Organized into the Band of Hope Union, 1855.

Banda Islands discovered (1512) and settled (1520) by Portuguese; occupied by Dutch, 1814, who had expelled the Portuguese, 1580. Formal cession by Britain to Netherlands, 1816. Joined Indonesia, 1950.

Bandoeng or **Bandung,** Indonesia, on island of Java. The Bandoeng Conference, a meeting of Afro-Asian delegates, held here, 18–27 Apr. 1955.

Banff, Scotland. Granted charter by Malcolm IV, 1163; by Robert Bruce, 1324; and Robert II, 1372. Present castle built, 1750.

Bangkok, Thailand. Became capital of Siam (now Thailand) after Burmese destroyed Aynthia, 1782. The Emerald Buddha chapel built, 1785.

Bangladesh. Independent republic since 1971, formerly E Pakistan. Original constitution provided for parliamentary democracy but this ceased Jan. 1975 with presidency of Mujibur Rahman (assassinated Aug. 1975). Zia elected president, 1978: martial law lifted but Zia assassinated, 1981. Coup by Gen. Ershad, 1982: he became president after elections in 1986 but popular unrest and economic grievances forced his resignation, 1990. Elections, 1991 won by B. Nationalists under Begum Khaleda Zia, and in Aug. 1991 B. reverted to parliamentary rule. Abdur Rahman Biswas president since Oct. 1991. During period since B.'s independence, periodic cyclonic floodings have hampered progress. Government under pressure to hold elections, from Nov. 1994 when opposition parties quit parliament. 1995: elections promised for 1996.

Bangor, Wales. Bishopric and cathedral reputed founded by St Deiniol c. 550. Old cathedral destroyed, 1071. Present cathedral dates from 1496 to 1532. N Wales University College opened, 18 Oct. 1884.

Banjul. Capital of *Gambia. Founded as **Bathurst**, 1816. Name changed to B., 1973.

bank. Chinese said to have had a paper currency c. AD 800. In 808 Lombard Jews established a B. in Italy. Private Bs. existed in Venice in 1270. Bank of St George, Genoa, 1407. The Banco di Rialto was established in Venice, 1584 and 1587 – the first public B. in Europe. Banco del Giro, or B. of Venice, established, 1619; B. of Amsterdam, 1609; first B. established in England by Francis Child, c. 1603; Bank of Hamburg, 1619–1873; Riksbank of Stockholm established, 1656; issued the first bank-note, 1658.

bank amalgamations (UK). Major stage completed, 1918, when 'big five' emerged; Barclays Bank, founded, 1896; Lloyds Bank, founded, 1865; National Provincial Bank, founded, 1833; Midland Bank, founded 1836; Westminster Bank, founded, 1836. Gurney & Co., last of the English private provincial Bs., founded, 1809, bought up by Barclays, Feb. 1953. National Provincial took over the District Bank, 1962. In 1968 National Provincial and Westminster Banks merged to form the National Westminster: and in 1969 Barclays absorbed Martin's Bank. The Midland B. was taken over by the Hong Kong and Shanghai B., 1992, but retains its name. Announced agreed take-over of Trustee Savings B. by Lloyds B., Oct. 1995.

Bank Holidays Act. Introduced by Sir John Lubbock; passed, 25 May 1871.

Bank of Credit and Commerce International, founded 1972: closed down 1991 after discovery of massive fraud running into billions of pounds sterling, and criminal prosecution of executives followed.

Bank of England. Founded by William Paterson, who is said to have originated the project in 1691. Incorporated by charter, 27 July 1694. Special privileges: monopoly conferred, 1709; restricted, 1826, 1833. Cash payment suspended, 1797; resumed, 1821. Under Bank Charter is remodelled, 19 July 1844; Bank Charter suspended 25 Oct. 1847; 12 Nov. 1857; 11 May 1866. Important changes in management, 16 June 1892. Rebuilding begun, 24 Nov. 1924. Nationalized, 1946. Banking Acts of 1979 and 1987 set out B. of E.'s authoritative power over UK banks (not building societies). Thus B. of E. closed down Bank of Credit and Commerce International, 1991, but subsequently criticized for acting too late. Suggestions that B. of E. should be made independent of government being made in 1990s. B. of E. failed to broker rescue of Barings Bank, Feb. 1995, which then went into administration. Barings was subsequently taken over by the Dutch bank ING. B. of E. report on Barings collapse published, July 1995.

Bank of France. Founded by Napoleon, 1800. Nationalized, 2 Dec. 1945.

Bank of Ireland. Established, 1 June 1783. Irish Banking Act passed, 21 June 1845. Central Bank of Eire established, 1 Feb. 1943.

Bank of Scotland. Set up at Edinburgh by Act of Scottish Parliament, 1695.

Bankruptcy (UK). Court of, established by Act of Parliament, 1831. Originally only traders could be subject to bankruptcy. B. Act. 1861 made all debtors subject to B. proceedings. Subsequent legislation includes B. Act. 1914; B. (Amendment Act) 1926; Insolvency Act, 1976. The Insolvency Act of 1986 included a category of 'administration' aimed at keeping companies from B.

Bankruptcy Acts (USA). Bill passed by Congress, 19 Aug. 1841; repealed, 3 Mar. 1843. National B. A., 1898 forms basis of subsequent bankruptcy laws; was amended by legislation enacted in 1938, 1978 and 1989.

banks, American. Congress chartered the Bank of N America, 26 May 1781; opened in Philadelphia, 1782; second bank established at Boston, 1784; Bank of USA established Philadelphia, 20 Dec. 1790; Bank of New York established, 1790; first Bank of the United States chartered, 1791–1811; second, 1816–36. National Bank Acts, 1863 and 1864, authorized privately-owned banks chartered by the federal government. Financial crises led to Federal Reserve Act, 1913, enabling federal government to control bank reserves. Depression/slump 1920s/30s resulted in Glass-Steagall Banking Act, 1933. Subsequent legislation concentrated on securing financial stability of banks. 'Thrift bank' scandals and failures resulted in legislation, 1989, to correct situation permanently, including setting up the Resolution Trust Corporation.

Bannockburn. *See* BATTLES.

Baptists (for earlier history of, *see* ANABAPTISTS). First English Baptist church founded in Amsterdam by John Smyth and Thomas Helwys, 1609–11. Helwys formed first Baptist church in England, London, 1612 (General Baptist, or Arminian). First Particular Baptist (Calvinist) church formed, Southwark, 1633. Confession of Faith published by the seven Particular Baptist churches in London, 1644. Baptist Missionary Society founded, 1792. General and Particular B. united as Baptist Union of Great Britain and Ireland, 1921; name changed to Baptist Union of Great Britain, 1988. Roger Williams formed first regular congregation of

B. in America in Rhode Island, *c.* Mar. 1639. Baptist World Alliance formed, 1905. More than 38 million Bs. worldwide, 1995.

Bar, Confederation of the. An anti-Russian coalition of Polish nobles, formed 1768 and dissolved, 1776.

Bar, Trial at, i.e., a trial in the King's Bench division before a full bench of judges, was the usual procedure up to 1285; the last Trial at B. was that of Sir Roger Casement, for treason, 1916.

Baralong **Case.** German prize crew on board American ship killed by crew of British auxillary 'B', 19 Aug. 1915. German Government threatened Zeppelin warfare in retaliation, Dec. 1915.

Barbados, W Indies. First mention, 1518. Thought to have been visited by Portuguese *c.* 1536; formally acquired by English, 1625. Independent state within the Commonwealth, 30 Nov. 1966. Labour victory in Sept. 1994 elections.

barbed wire invented in America, 1873. Introduced to Britain, 1880, by 5th Earl Spencer. B.W. Act, concerning the fencing of land adjoining highways, passed, 1893.

barbers, as a guild, were incorporated in England, 1461, and separated from surgeons, 1745.

Barbican Arts Centre, London EC2, opened 3 Mar. 1982, comprises theatre, concert hall, cinemas, art gallery, library and restaurants.

Barcelona, Spain. Said to have been built by Hamilcar Barca, 3rdC BC. Became a Roman colony; conquered by Visigoths, AD 415, and Moors, 713. Independent county, 762; incorporated with Aragon, 1164. Cathedral begun, 1289. University founded, 1450; Autonomous University of B., 1968. Treaty of B. between France and Spain, 1493. Captured by the French under Vendôme, 1697; by the English under Peterborough, 1706. Taken by the Duke of Berwick (James Fitzjames), for Philip V, 1714; by Napoleon, 1808. Restored to Spain by Treaty of Paris, 1814. Church of Holy

Family (designed by Gaudi) begun, 1882. Execution of Ferrer for conspiracy at, 13 Oct. 1909. Metro system started, 1924. Last capital of the republic, 1937. Surrendered to Franco, 1939. Olympic Games held at, 1992; opera house burned down, Jan. 1994.

Barebones Parliament, or Little Parliament, of members, selected from nominees of the congregations in each county. Met, 4 July 1653; dissolved, 12 Dec. 1653. Named after Praise-God B. or P. Barbon (1596?–1679), who attended as member for London.

Barfleur, France. William, son of Henry I of England, wrecked and drowned, in the *White Ship*, off B., 28 Nov. 1120. Destroyed by English, 1346. French fleet destroyed off B. by Admiral Russell, 19 May, 1692.

Bargain and Sale. An obsolete form of real estate conveyance, facilitated by the Statute of Uses, 1535; fell into desuetude after the passing of the Real Property Act, 1845.

Bari (ancient *Barium*) Apulia, first mentioned, 180 BC. Captured by Saracens, AD 812; retaken by Greeks, 885; by Robert Guiscard, 1071. Annexed to Kingdom of Naples, 1558. After Sept. 1943 was temporary seat of Badoglio's provisional government.

Barings Bank. British merchant bank established London, 1762. Collapsed, Feb. 1995 when losses in Far East overweighed bank's assets. *See* also BANK OF ENGLAND.

Barking, England. Benedictine abbey founded by St Erconwald, 670, burnt by Vikings, 870. All Hallows, B. by the Tower, belonged to the abbey and was built in the 7thC; burnt down, 1087; rebuilt before 1100; rebuilt again in the 13thC and largely destroyed by bombing 29 Dec. 1941; but rebuilt after 1945.

Barnard Castle (County Durham). Built by Guy Baliol B. (1112–32). Taken from the rebel John Baliol by the English, 1296.

Barnardo's Homes, Dr, originally for orphans, founded 1866 by Thomas John B.

(1845–1905). From the 1960s large institutions gave way to small home units: all homes closed by 1981. Charity continues with family and child welfare projects

Barnburners. Political faction in the USA, active 1844–52.

Baroda, India. *See* MAHRATTAS.

barometer. First made by Torricelli, a Florentine, *c.* 1643. Pascal's experiments, 1646. Aneroid B. said to have been invented by Conté, 1798. The English patent, however, was registered by Vidi for his invention of 1844. Vidi *d.,* 1866.

Baron.
1. Peerage title first used in England after Norman conquest, 1066. First created by patent, 1387. Wensleydale peerage case, 1856, decided that it must be hereditary to carry a seat in the House of Lords (*see* LORDS, HOUSE OF). This principle amended by Appellate Jurisdiction Act, 1876, and Life Peerages Act, 1958. Further modified by Peerages Act, 1963.
2. County Palatine of Chester had its own Bs. till 1679.
3. Ditto of Durham till 1716.
4. The Cinque Ports still have Bs. elected for life.

Baronet. Order of knighthood instituted by James I of England, 22 May 1611, to replenish his exchequer. The first B. was Sir Nicholas Bacon of Redgrave.

Barons' War. Caused by disputes between Henry III of England and the B. First important engagement, the taking of Northampton for the king by Prince Edward, 4 Apr. 1264; king's army defeated at Lewes, 14 May 1264; De Montfort killed and B. defeated at battle at Evesham, 4 Aug. 1265. The name B.W. also given to conflict between King John and his barons, 1215–17.

Barrier Act passed by the General Assembly of the Church of Scotland, 1697.

Barrier Treaties. By the first B. Treaty between Great Britain and the States-General (29 Oct. 1709), 'Great Britain undertook to procure for the Dutch an adequate *barrier* . . .' to secure Holland against French aggression. The second (29 Jan. 1713) modified the first; by it British undertook to obtain right for Dutch to garrison the frontier fortresses 'from the future sovereign of the Spanish Netherlands.' The third, signed 15 Nov. 1715, was supplemental.

Barrow-in-Furness became industrially important with the discovery of haematite ore locally, 1840. Docks opened, 1867. Last surviving shipyard called in receivers, May 1993.

Bartholomew, Massacre of St, (of Huguenots), at Paris started 24 Aug. and lasted until 17 Sept. 1572. Outside Paris it continued until 3 Oct. Estimated death toll: 25,000.

Bartholomew, St. Fair held on festival of St B. in London, 1133–1855. Hospital of St B. (London) founded by Rahere, 1123; re-founded, 1547; rebuilt, 1730–66. Medical college founded, 1843. Hospital first threatened with closure, 1992: after High Court ruling, July 1994, government announced hospital to be closed by year 2000, but patients won right to judicial review on closure, July 1995.

baseball, derived from English game usually known as rounders, played in England *c.* 1600 onwards. Mentioned by Jane Austen, 1798. B. spread across eastern USA in early 1800s; modern game said to have been evolved by Doubleday (1819–83) and by Alexander Cartwright of New York, who started the Knickerbocker B. Club of New York, 1845, and drew up a set of rules (added to, 1848 and 1854). National League founded, 1876. Rules standardized, 1887. American League formed, 1900. World Series began, 1903, played annually (except 1904 and 1994). Famous B. players include Babe Ruth (1895–1948) and Joe di Maggio (1914–), both played for New York Yankees. World Series cancelled, Sept. 1994 due to industrial dispute between players and owners. Strike settled, Mar. 1995.

Basel or **Bâle,** Switzerland. Council of, 1431–49. University founded, 1460. Joined Swiss Confederation, 1501. The bishopric abolished, 1529. Treaty between France and Prussia, 22 July 1795. Canton divided into two half-cantons, 1833 (Basel-Stadt and Basel-Land).

Bashkiria. Autonomous republic of Russia, set up, 1919. Demanding more independence, since 1989.

BASIC, computer-programming language. First developed, 1964.

basic English, first word-list of printed, 1929. First dictionary published, 1932. Committee of ministers reported on, 1943, and Government purchased copyright in, 1947.

basketball invented in the USA, 1891, by James Naismith. First men's European championships, 1935; women's 1938. First men's world championships, 1950; women's 1953. National Championships held in England for both men and women since 1982, annually.

Basques, pre-Indo-European racial group. United in *Navarre 10th–11thC. In modern times divided between communities in France and Spain. Fought for Republicans in Spain, 1936–9. Separatist movement post-1968; its militant wing (*ETA) campaigns for an independent Basque state. Autonomous Basque region established 1979 but ETA violence continuing, 1995.

Basra, Iraq. Founded by Caliph Omar, 637. Severely damaged during Gulf War, 1991, when heavily bombed by US planes. Further damaged by abortive Shiite uprising, Mar. 1991, subsequently crushed by Iraqi government.

Bassein, Burma. Founded *c.* 1250.

Bassein, India. Ceded to the Portuguese, 1534. Taken by the Mahrattas, 1739. Taken over by the British, 1818.

Bass Rock, Firth of Forth, Scotland. St Baldred (*d.* 756) had a hermitage here. It was bought by the English Government, fortified and made into a political prison,

1671, where leading Covenanters were detained. In 1691 four young Jacobites captured the island by a trick and held it against the Williamite forces from June 1691 to Apr. 1694. Fort demolished, 1701.

Bastaards or **Bastards.** *See* GRIQUAS.

Bastard. *See* LEGITIMACY.

Bastille (Paris). Built, 1369–83, destroyed, 14–15 July 1789.

Basutoland. *See* LESOTHO.

Bataan, Philippine Islands. Famous stand against Japanese by MacArthur's troops, 9 Dec. 1941–9 Apr. 1942.

Batavia. *See* JAKARTA.

Batavian Republic. Holland was reorganized under this name under French hegemony, May 1795–June 1806.

Bates's Case. Tried before Court of Exchequer, 1606. John Bates, a Levant merchant, refused to pay excess duty not authorized by Parliament, but four Barons of the Exchequer found against him.

Bath, England (Roman *Aquae Sulis*). Roman baths begun, AD 84. Used until *c.* 400. Cathedral founded, AD 775. King Edgar crowned at B., 973. Bishopric amalgamated with Wells, 1139. Present abbey, founded 1405–99, superseded cathedral. Grammar school founded, 1552. Roman baths uncovered, partly, 1788, but not excavated. Rediscovered, 1879, and excavated, 1888–90, 1923 and during 1980s. Pump room built as a result of resolution by the corporation of 1705. Rebuilt, 1751 and 1795. National Hospital for Rheumatic Diseases founded, 1738, largely at the instance of Beau Nash (1674–1761). University established, 1966.

battery, electric, invented by Alexander Volta (1745–1827), 1800.

Battersea, first mentioned in a document of 693. The park was opened, 1853. In connection with Festival of Britain, 1951, Pleasure Gardens opened at, 28 May, later discontinued.

Battle, Wager of, and **Appeal of Felony.** Last waged in Court of Common Pleas 1571. Court of Chivalry, 1631. Court of Durham, 1638. As a result of an attempted Trial by Combat in 1818 both were formally abolished, 1819.

Battle Abbey. Founded by William the Conqueror on site of battle of Hastings, 1067. Consecrated, 1094. Its abbot sat in the House of Lords until the *Dissolution of the Monasteries, 1539.

Battle Abbey Roll, purporting to be a nominal roll of Norman officers present at the battle of Hastings, is a forgery, probably of the 14thC.

battles. *See also* WORLD WARS I and II and SIEGES. Most famous or important battles are printed in **bold type**. Those described in Creasy's *Fifteen Decisive Battles of the World* are marked¶. See also Bruce, George, *Collins Dictionary of Wars* (Harper Collins, 1995).

On Land
B. connected with Napoleon are marked N, with Wellington W, with Marlborough M, and with Frederick the Great F.
Aboukir,
    (1) 25 July 1799 (N)
    (2) 8 Mar. 1801
Abu Klea, 17 Jan. 1885
Acs, 2 and 10 July 1849
Adowa, 1 Mar. 1896
Adrianople,
    (1) 3 July 323
    (2) 9 Aug. 378
    (3) 20 Aug. 1829
Agincourt, 25 Oct. 1415
Agnadello, 14 May 1509
Aisne
    (1) 13–28 Sept. 1914
    (2) 16–20 Apr. 1917
    (3) 27 May–6 June 1918
Ajnadain, 30 July 634
Akhalzikh, 24 Aug. 1828
Alamein, 23 Oct.–7 Nov. 1942
Alamo, 24 Feb.–6 Mar. 1836
Alarcos, 1185
Albans, St,

    (1) 22 or 23 May 1455
    (2) 17 Feb. 1461
Albuera, 16 May 1811 (W)
Albufera, 4 Jan. 1812 (W)
Alexandria,
    (1) 21 Mar. 1801
    (2) 11–13 July 1882
Alford, 2 July 1645
Aliwal, 28 Jan. 1846
Allia, 16 July 390 BC
Alma, 20 Sept. 1854
Almansa, 25 Apr. 1707
Almenara, 28 July 1710
Angora, 28 July 1402
Anjou, 22 Mar. 1421
Antietam, 16–17 Sept. 1862
Antioch, 28 June 1098
Anzio, 22–25 May 1944
Arbela, 1 Oct. 331 BC
Arcis-sur-Aube, 20–21 Mar. 1814
Arcole, 14–17 Nov. 1796 (N)
Ardennes, 16–22 Dec. 1944
Argaum, 29 Nov. 1803
Argentario, 378
Arklow, 10 June 1798
Arnhem, 17–26 Sept. 1944
Arques, 13–28 Sept. 1589
Aspern, 21–22 May 1809 (N)
Aspromonte, 29 Aug. 1862
Assandun (Ashingdon), 1016
Assaye, 23 Sept. 1803 (W)
Asunden (Lake), Jan. 1520
Atbara, The, 8 Apr. 1898
Atherton Moor, 30 June 1643
Atlanta, 22 July 1864
Auerstädt, 14 Oct. 1806 (N)
Aughrim, 12 July 1691
Auneau, 24 Nov. 1587
Austerlitz, 2 Dec. 1805 (N)
Ayacucho, 9 Dec. 1824
Aylesford, *c.* 455
Badajoz, 6 Apr. 1812 (W)
Balaklava, 25 Oct. 1854
Bannockburn, 24 June 1314
Bapaume, 2–3 Jan. 1871
Barnet, 14 Apr. 1471
Barrosa, 5 Mar. 1811 (W)
Bassano, 8 Sept. 1796
Bastogne, Dec. 1944
Bautzen, 20–21 May 1813 (N)
Baylen, 20 July 1808 (W)

Beaugé. *See* ANJOU
Belfort (siege), 3 Nov. 1870–8 Feb. 1871
Belgrade (siege), 22 July–4 Sept. 1456
Belmont, 23 Nov. 1899
Benevento, 26 Feb. 1266
Bennington, 16 Aug. 1777
Beresina, 26–28 Nov. 1812 (N)
Berlin, 15 Apr.–2 May 1945
Big Bethel, 10 May 1861
Bir Hakim, 26 May–11 June 1942
Bitonto, 27 May 1734
¶**Blenheim, 13 Aug. 1704** (M)
Blore Heath, 23 Sept. 1459
Blumenau, 22 July 1866
Borghetto, 30 May 1796 (N)
Borisov, 27 Nov. 1812
Borodino, 7 Sept. 1812 (N)
Bosworth Field, 22 Aug. 1485
Bothwell Bridge, 22 June 1679
Bouvines, 27 July 1214
Boxtel, 17 Sept. 1794
Boyne, 1 July 1690
Braila, 19 June 1773
Brandywine, 11 Sept. 1777
Brechin, 18 May 1452
Brentford, 12 Nov. 1642
Breslau, 22 Nov. 1757 (F)
Briars Creek, 3 May 1779
Brienne, 29 Jan. 1814 (N)
Brunanburh, *c.* 937
'Bulge, The'. *See* ARDENNES
Bull Run,
    (1) 21 July 1861
    (2) 29–30 Aug. 1862
Bunker Hill, 17 June 1775
Burlington Heights, 6 June 1813
Busaco, 27 Sept. 1810 (W)
Buxar, 1764
Caen, 25 June–8 July 1944
Calatafimi, 15 May 1860
Camden (USA),
    (1) 16 Aug. 1780
    (2) 25 Apr. 1781
Cannae, 2 Aug. 216 BC
Caporetto, 24 Oct.–18 Nov. 1917
Carberry Hill, 15 June 1567
Carrhae, 53 BC
Cassano,
    (1) 16 Aug. 1705
    (2) 27–29 Apr. 1799
Cassino, 5 Feb.–8 May 1944

Castalla, 13 Apr. 1813
Castelnuovo, 21 Nov. 1796
Castiglione, 5 Aug. 1796 (N)
Castillion, 17 July 1453
Castlebar, 7 Aug. 1798
Cawnpore,
    (1) 16 July 1857
    (2) 27–28 Nov. 1857
    (3) 6 Dec. 1857
Cedar Creek, 19 Oct. 1864
Cerignola, 28 Apr. 1503
Cerisoles, 14 Apr. 1454
Ceva, 1796 (N)
Chaeronea,
    (1) 7 Aug. 338 BC
    (2) 86 BC
Chalgrove, 18 June 1643
¶**Châlons,** AD **451**
Champaubert, 10 Feb. 1814 (N)
Chancellorsville, 2–4 May 1863
Chataila, 17–18 Nov. 1912
Châteaudun, 18 Oct. 1870
Château Thierry,
    (1) 13 Feb. 1814 (N)
    (2) 27 June 1918
Chattanooga, 23–25 Nov. 1863
Chebrëiss, 24 July 1798 (N)
Chickahominy, 26 June–1 July 1862
Chickamauga, 19–20 Sept. 1863
Chilianwála, 13 Jan. 1849
Chippewa, 5 July 1814
Citate, 6 Jan. 1854
Clifton Moor, 18 Dec. 1745
Clontarf, 23 Apr. 1014
Cold Harbor, 1 and 3 June 1864
Colenso, 15 Dec. 1899
Corinth, Miss., 3–4 Oct. 1862
Corunna, 16 Jan. 1809 (W)
Courtrai, 1302
Coutras, 20 Oct. 1587
Craonne, 6–7 Mar. 1814 (N)
Crécy or Cressy, 26 Aug. 1346
Crete, 20 May–3 June 1941
Cropredy Bridge, 29 June 1644
Culloden, 16 Apr. 1746
Custozza,
    (1) 23–25 July 1848
    (2) 24 June 1866
Cynoscephalae, 190 BC
Czaslau or Chotusitz, 17 May 1742 (F)
Dannevirke,

(1) 1331
(2) 23 Apr. 1848
Dego, 14 Apr. 1796 (N)
Delhi,
    (1) 8 Sept. 1803
    (2) 7–16 Oct. 1804
    (3) after siege, 14–20 Sept. 1857
Dennewitz, 6 Sept. 1813
Desert Storm, 24–27 Feb. 1991
Dettingen, 27 June (N.S.) 1743
Devizes, 13 July 1643
Dien-Bien-Phu, Apr.–May 1954
Dieppe, 14 Aug. 1942
Donnington, Glos., 21 Mar. 1645
Dorylaeum, 1097
Douro, 12 May 1809 (W)
Dresden, 27 Aug. 1813 (N)
Dreux, 19 Dec. 1562
Drumclog, 1 June 1679
Drummossie. *See* CULLODEN
Dunbar,
    (1) 27 Apr. 1296
    (2) 3 Sept. 1650
Dunes, 4 (14 N.S.) June 1658
Dungan Hill, 8 Aug. 1647
Dunkirk,
    (1) *See* DUNES
    (2) **(Evacuation of) 29 May–3 June 1940**
Eckmühl, 22 Apr. 1809 (N)
Edgehill, 23 Oct. 1642
Edington, summer 878
Elandslaagte, 21 Oct. 1899
Elchingen, 14 Oct. 1805
Enghien, 3 Aug. (N.S.) 1692
Enslin, 25 Nov. 1899
Espierres, 22 May 1794
Essling. *See* ASPERN
Eutaw, 8 Sept. 1781
Evesham, 4 Aug. 1265
Eylau, 7–9 Feb. 1807 (N)
Fair Oaks, 31 May–1 June 1862
Falkirk,
    (1) 22 July 1298
    (2) 17 Jan. 1746
Famars, 23–24 May 1793
Fehrbellin, 1675
Firozshahr, 21–22 Dec. 1845
Fleurus,
    (1) 1622
    (2) 1 July 1690

(3) 26 June 1794
Flodden Field, 9 Sept. 1513
Flushing, 15 Aug. 1809
Fontenoy, 11 May (N.S.) 1745
Formigny, 1450
Fornovo, 6 July 1495
Fredericksburg,
    (1) 13 Dec. 1862
    (2) *See* CHANCELLORSVILLE
Friedland, 14 June 1807 (N)
Fuentes de Onoro, 3–5 May 1811 (W)
Gaugamela. *See* ARBELA
Gembloux, June 1578
Germantown, 4 Oct. 1777
Gettysburg, 1–3 July 1863
Gitschin, 29 June 1866
Glencoe (S Africa), 20 Oct. 1899
Goose Green, Falkland Islands, 28 May 1982
Gorey, Co. Wexford, 4 June 1798
Gravelotte, 18 Aug. 1870
Great Meadows, July 1754
Grochow, 19–20 Feb. 1831
Gross Beeren, 23 Aug. 1813 (N)
Gross Jaegerndorf, 30 Aug. 1757 (F)
Grozny, 31 Dec. 1994–Feb. 1995
Guadalajara, 1937
Guinegatte, 16 Aug. 1513
Gujerát, 21 Feb. 1849
Halidon Hill, 19 July 1333
Hanau, 30 Oct. 1813
Harlaw, 24 July 1411
Hasbain, 23 or 24 Sept. 1408
¶**Hastings, 14 Oct. 1066**
Hatfield, 632
Hennersdorf, 23 Nov. 1745 (F)
Herrera, 24 Aug. 1837
Hexham, 8 May 1464
Himera, 408 BC
Hochkirch, 14 Oct. 1758 (F)
Hochstädt. *See* BLENHEIM
Hohenfriedberg, 3–4 June 1745
Hohenlinden, 3 Dec. 1800
Homildon, 14 Sept. 1402
Idstädt, 25 July 1850
Imjin River, 23–25 Apr. 1951
Ingogo, 8 Feb. 1881
Ingour, 6 Nov. 1855
Inkerman, 5 Nov. 1854
Ipsus, 301 BC
Isandlhwana, 22 Jan. 1879

Ivry, 14 Mar. 1590
Jarnac, 13 Mar. 1569
Jemappes, 6 Nov. 1792
Jena, 14 Oct. 1806 (N)
Kalisz, 1706
Kalka, 1224
Katzbach, 26 Aug. 1813 (N)
Kazan, 1552
Kesselsdorf, 15 Dec. 1745 (F)
Khart, 19 July 1829
Killiecrankie, 27 July 1689
Kilsyth, 15 Aug. 1645
Kirk-Kilisse, 22–24 Oct. 1912
Kissingen, 10 July 1866
Klissow, July 1702
'Knightsbridge' (N. Africa), 28 May–15 June 1942
Kohima, 10 Apr.–18 May 1942
Kolin, 18 Jan. 1757 (F)
Konieh, 21 Dec. 1832
Königgrätz. *See* SADOWA
Kossovo,
    (1) 1389
    (2) 1448
Krasnoi, 15–17 Nov. 1812
Kulikovo, 1380
Kumanovo, 23–25 Oct. 1912
Kunersdorf, 12 Aug. 1759 (F)
Kurdla, 1795
Kursk, 5 July–23 Aug. 1943
La Bicocca, 29 Apr. 1522
Laffeldt, 2 July 1747
Laingsnek, 28 Jan. 1881
Landen, 29 (19 O.S.) July 1693
Landshut, Apr. 1809 (N)
Langensalza, 27 June 1866
Langport, 10 July 1645
Langside (Glasgow), 13 May 1568
Lansdown, 5 July 1643
Laon, 9–10 Mar. 1814 (N)
Largs, 1263
Lauffeld, 2 July 1746
Leipzig, 16–19 Oct. 1813 (N)
Lens, 20 Aug. 1648
Leuctra, 371 BC
Leuthen, 5 Dec. 1757 (F)
Lewes, 14 May 1264
Lexington,
    (1) 19 Apr. 1775
    (2) 20 Sept. 1861
Liaoyang, Sept. 1904

Libenau, 25 June 1866
Liegnitz, 15 Aug. 1760 (F)
Ligny, 16 June 1815 (N)
Lincelles, 18 Aug. 1793
Lincoln,
    (1) 2 Feb. 1141
    (2) 20 May 1217
Linlithgow Bridge, Sept. 1526
Lioppo, 16 May 1860
Lipau, 1434
Lippstadt, 6 Nov. 1632
Lissa. *See* LEUTHEN (F)
Lodi, 10 May 1796 (N)
Lonato, 3 Aug. 1796 (N)
Lüle Burgas, 28–30 Oct. 1912
Lundy's Lane, 25 July 1814
Lützelberg, 10 Oct. 1758
Lützen,
    (1) 6 (16 N.S.) Nov. 1632
    (2) 2 May 1813 (N)
Magenta, 4 June 1859
Magersfontein, 11 Dec. 1899
Magnano, 5 Apr. 1799
Magnesia, 190 BC
Maharajpur, 29 Dec. 1843
Maida, 4 July 1806 (W)
Majuba, 27 Feb. 1881
Malplaquet, 11 Sept. 1709 (M)
Malvalli, 27 Mar. 1799
Mantinea,
    (1) 418 BC
    (2) *c.* 367 BC
    (3) 295 BC
    (4) 242 BC
    (5) 207 BC
Manzikert, 1071
¶**Marathon, 28 or 29 Sept. 490** BC
Marengo, 14 June 1800 (N)
Margus,
    (1) 285
    (2) 505
Marignano,
    (1) **13–14 Sept. 1515**
    (2) *See* PAVIA
    (3) 8 June 1859
Marne, The,
    (1) **6–9 Sept. 1914**
    (2) **15 July–31 Aug. 1918**
Marston Moor, 2 July 1644
Maserfield, 641
Mechanicsville, or White Oaks, 26 June 1862

Medina del Rio Seco. *See* RIO SECO
¶**Metaurus, 207** BC
Metz, 31 Aug. 1870
Milazzo, 20 June 1860
Millesimo, 13–14 Apr. 1796 (N)
Milli Duzov, 1–2 June 1829
Milvian Bridge, 312
Mincio,
    (1) 29 May 1796 (N)
    (2) 8 Feb. 1814
Minden, 1 Aug. 1759
Möckern,
    (1) 5 Apr. 1813
    (2) 16 Oct. 1813
Modder River, 28 Nov. 1899
Moeskirch, 5 May 1800
Mohács,
    (1) **29 Aug. 1526**
    (2) 12 Aug. 1687
Mohilev, 23 July 1812
Mollwitz, 10 Apr. 1741 (F)
Monastir, 15–18 Nov. 1912
Moncontour, 3 Oct. 1569
Mondovi, 22 Apr. 1796 (N)
Mons, Aug. 1914
Mons Badonicus c. 500
Montebello,
    (1) 1796 (N)
    (2) 1805
Montebello Casteggio,
    (1) 9 June 1800
    (2) 20 May 1859
Montenotte, 12 Apr. 1796
Montinirail, 11 Feb. 1814 (N)
Mookerheede, 1574
Morat, 22 June 1476
Morgarten, 15 Nov. 1315
Mortimer's Cross, 2 Feb. 1461
Mount Tabor, 16 Apr. 1799 (N)
Mudki, 18 Dec. 1845
Mukden, 1–9 Mar. 1905
Multan, 7 Nov. 1848
Münchengrätz, 28 June 1866
Munda, 45 BC
Muret, 12 Sept. 1213
Murfreesboro,
    (1) 31 Dec. 1862
    (2) 2 Jan. 1863
Naas, 24 May 1798
Nachod, 27 June 1866
Najara, 3 Apr. 1367

Nantwich, 25–28 Jan. 1644
Narva, 30 Nov. 1700
Narvik, 28 May–10 June 1940
Naseby, 14 June 1645
Navas de Tolosa, 1212
Nedao, 454
Neerwinden, 18 Mar. 1793
Nesbit, 7 May 1402
Neville's Cross, 17 Oct. 1346
Newburn, 28 Aug. 1640
Newbury,
    (1) 20 Sept. 1643
    (2) 27 Oct. 1644
New Ross, 5 June 1798
Newtownbutler, 30 July 1689
Nicholson's Nek, 30 Oct. 1899
Nive, 9–13 Dec. 1813
Nivelles, 10 Nov. 1813
Nördlingen,
    (1) 27 Aug. 1634
    (2) 3 Aug. 1645
Northallerton. *See* STANDARD, THE
Northampton, 10 July 1460
Novara, 23 Mar. 1849
Novi,
    (1) 15 Aug. 1799
    (2) 8 Jan. 1800
Obidos, 17 Aug. 1808
Okinawa, 1 Apr.–21 June 1945
Oltenitza, 4 Nov. 1853
Omdurman, 2 Sept. 1898
Oporto. *See* DOURO
¶**Orleans,**
    (1) **29 Apr. 1429**
    (2) 11 Oct. 1870
Ormuz, 1622
Orthez, 27 Feb. 1814
Ortona, Dec. 1943
Ostrolenka, 26 May 1831
Otterburn, 15 Aug. 1388
Oudenarde, 11 July 1708 (M)
Oulart, 27 May 1798
Ourique, 25 July 1139
Paardeberg, 16, 18–27 Feb. 1900
Palestro, 31 May 1859
Palo Alto, 8 May 1846
Panipat,
    (1) 1526
    (2) 1556
    (3) 1761
Parma, 29 June 1734

Passchendaele, 26 Oct.–10 Nov. 1917
Patay, 18 June 1429
Pavia, 24 Feb. 1525
Pelekanon, 1326
Pelusium, 525 BC
Pfaffendorf, 15 Aug. 1760
Pharsalia or Pharsalus, summer of 48 BC
Philiphaugh, 13 Sept. 1645
Piacenza, 16 June 1746
Pinkie, 10 Sept. 1547
Pirmasens, 14 Sept. 1793
Plassey, 23 June 1757
Plataea, 479 BC
Plevna, July, Sept., and Dec. 1877
Podoll, 26 June 1866
Poitiers, 19 Sept. 1356
Polotzk, 30–31 July 1812
¶Poltava, 8 July 1709
Port Arthur, 21 Nov. 1894
Porto Novo (S India), 1 July 1781
Prague, 6 May 1757 (F)
Preston,
    (1) 17 Aug. 1648
    (2) 12–13 Nov. 1715
Prestonpans, 21 Sept. 1745
Pultusk, 26 Dec. 1806
Pusan Perimeter, 1 Sept.–1 Oct. 1950
Pyramids, The, 13, 21 July 1798
Pyrenees, The, 25 July–2 Aug. 1813
Quatre Bras, 16 June 1815 (W)
Ramillies, 23 May 1706 (M)
Rathmines, 2 Aug. 1649
Raucoux, 11 Oct. 1746
Ravenna, 11 Apr. 1512
Redinha, 12 Mar. 1811
Resaca de la Palma, 9 May 1846
Rheinfelden, 3 Mar. 1638
Rietfontein, 24 Oct. 1899
Rieti, 7 Mar. 1821
Rio Seco, 14 July 1808
Rivoli, 14–15 Jan. 1797 (N)
Rocroi, 19 May 1643
Rolica, 17 Aug. 1808
Rorke's Drift, 22 Jan. 1879
Rosebecque or Roosebeke, 26 or 27 Nov. 1382
Rossbach, 5 Nov. 1757 (F)
Roveredo, 4 Sept. 1796 (N)
Ruremonde, 18 Sept. 1794
Saarbrücken (an undefended assault), 2 Aug. 1870

Sadowa, 3 July 1866
Sagunto, 25 Oct. 1811
Saint-Antoine, 2 July 1652
Saint-Denis, 10 Nov. 1567
Saint-Dizier, 27 Jan. 1814 (N)
Saintes, 22 July 1242
Saint-Quentin,
    (1) 10 Aug. 1557
    (2) 19 Jan. 1871
Sakaria, The, 23 Aug.–13 Sept. 1921
Salamanca, 22 July 1812 (W)
Salerno, 9 Sept.–1 Oct. 1943
Sangro, 2 Nov.–27 Dec. 1943
Santa Lucia, 6 May 1848
Saragossa,
    (1) 20 Aug. 1710
    (2) 20 Feb. 1809
Sarantoporon, Oct. 1912
¶**Saratoga, 17 Oct. 1777**
Schwechat, 30 Oct. 1848
Sedan, 29 Aug.–1 Sept. 1870
Sedgemoor, 6 July 1685
Seidlitz, 10 Apr. 1831
Selby, 11 Apr. 1644
Seminara, 21 Apr. 1503
Sempach, 9 July 1386
Seneffe, 11 Aug. 1674
Seringapatam,
    (1) 15 May 1791
    (2) 6 Feb. 1792
Sesia, The, Jan. 1524
Sheriffmuir, 13 Nov. 1715
Shiloh, 6–7 Apr. 1862
Shrewsbury, 21 July 1403
Simancas, 939
Skalitz, 28 June 1866
Smolensk,
    (1) 16–17 Aug. 1812 (N)
    (2) 1941
Sobraon, 10 Feb. 1846
Soissons, 486
Solferino, 24 June 1859
Solway Moss, 24 Nov. 1542
Soor,
    (1) Sept. 1745 (F)
    (2) 28 June 1866
Somme,
    (1) **1 July–18 Nov. 1916**
    (2) **21 Mar.–5 Apr. 1918**
    (3) **21 Aug.–5 Sept. 1918**
Spion Kop, 24–25 Jan. 1900

Spottsylvania, 7–21 May 1864
Spurs, The. *See* GUINEGATTE
Stalingrad, Sept. 1942–Jan. 1943
Standard, The, 22 Aug. 1138
Steenkirk, 23 July (3 Aug. N.S.) 1692
Stoke, 16 June 1487
Stone River. *See* MURFREESBORO
Stow-on-the-Wold. *See* DONNINGTON
Strasburg, 20 Dec. 1888
¶**Syracuse, 413 BC**
Szegedin, 4 Aug. 1849
Tagliacozzo, 1268
Talavera, 27–28 July 1809 (W)
Tannenberg,
    (1) 1410
    (2) 26–30 Aug. 1914
Tara, 26 May 1798
Tarbes, 20 Mar. 1814 (W)
Tchernaya, 16 Aug. 1855
Teb, El, 29 Feb. 1884
Tel-el-Kebir, 13 Sept. 1882
¶**Teutoburger Wald, AD 9**
Tewkesbury, 4 May 1471
Thabor, 16 Apr. 1799
Thapsus, 46 BC
Thermopylae, 480 BC
Torgau, 3 Nov. 1760 (F)
Toulouse, 10 Apr. 1814 (W)
Tournai, 25 Apr. 1794
¶**Tours, 10 Oct. 732**
Towton, 29 Mar. 1461
Trautenau, 28 June 1866
Trebbia,
    (1) 218 BC
    (2) 17–19 June 1799
Truellas, 22 Sept. 1793
Tudela, 23 Nov. 1808
Ucles, 13 Jan. 1809
Ulm, 20 Oct. 1805 (N)
Vareggio, 25 July 1848
¶**Valmy, 20 Sept. 1792**
Valteline, 19 Aug. 1812
Valtezza, 27 May 1821
Varna, 10 Nov. 1444
Vilagos, 25 Apr. 1521
Vauchamps, 14 Feb. 1814 (N)
Villafranca, 10 Apr. 1812
Villaviciosa, 10 Dec. 1710
Vilna, 18 June 1831
Vimiero, 21 Aug. 1808 (W)
Vimy Ridge, 9–10 Apr. 1917

Vinegar Hill, 21 June 1798
Vitebsk, 14 Nov. 1812 (N)
Vitoria, 21 June 1813 (W)
Volturno, 1 Oct. 1860
Vouillé, 507
Wagram, 6 July 1809 (N)
Waitzen, 14–17 July 1849
Wakefield, 30 Dec. 1460
Wandiwash, 22 Jan. 1760
Warsaw,
    (1) 28–30 July 1656
    (2) 17 Apr. 1794
    (3) 4–8 Nov. 1794
    (4) 7 Sept. 1831
    (5) 14–27 Sept. 1939
    (6) 19–28 Apr. 1943
    (7) 1 Aug.–3 Oct. 1944
¶**Waterloo, 18 June 1815 (N, W)**
Wavre, 18, 19 June 1815
Wawz, 31 Mar. 1831
White Mountain, 1620
White Oak Swamp, 30 June 1862
White Oaks. *See* MECHANICSVILLE
White Plains, 28 Oct. 1776
Wilderness, 5–6 May 1864
Williamsburg, 5 May 1862
Winwaed, 654
Worcester,
    (1) 23 Sept. 1642
    (2) 3 Sept. 1651
Wörth, 6 Aug. 1870
Wurschen, 21 May 1813
Würtzburg, 3 Sept. 1796
Ximena, 10 Sept. 1811
Yenidje Vardar, 2, 3, 5 Nov. 1912
Yarmuk, 20 Aug. 636
Ypres,
    (1) **19 Oct.–31 Oct. 1914**
    (2) **22 Apr.–25 May 1915**
    (3) **31 July–10 Nov. 1917**
    (4) **Sept. 1918**
Zallaca, 1086
Zama, 202 BC
Zela, 47 BC
Zenta, 11 Sept. 1697
Zorndorf, 25–26 Aug. 1758 (F)
Züllichau, 23 July 1759
Zürich, 24–25 Sept. 1799

Naval Battles
B. connected with Nelson are marked N.

Aboukir. *See* NILE, THE
Acre, 3 Nov. 1840
Actium, 2 Sept. 31 BC
Aegadean Isles, 241 BC
Aegospotami, 404 BC
Aix Roads, 11–12 Apr. 1809
Alexandria bombarded, 11–13 July 1882
Algeciras, 6 and 12 July 1801
Algiers bombarded, 27 Aug. 1816
Altmark (boarding), 15 Feb. 1940
¶Armada, 21–30 July 1588
Basque Roads. *See* AIX ROADS
Beachy Head, 30 June 1690
Bismarck (pursuit and sinking), 22–27 May 1941
Bismarck Sea, 1–3 Mar. 1943
Cadiz, 1587
Camperdown, 11 Oct. 1797
Cartagena, 1588
Champlain, 1814
Chesapeake Bay, 5 Sept. 1781
Copenhagen,
    (1) 2 Apr. 1801 (N)
    (2) 25 Sept. 1807
Coral Sea, 4–8 May 1942
Coronel, 1 Nov. 1914
Dannoura, 1185
Dogger Bank,
    (1) 5 Aug. 1781
    (2) 24 Jan. 1915
Dominica. *See* SAINTS, THE
Dover,
    (1) 19 May 1652
    (2) 2–3 June 1653
Downs, The, 3 June 1666
Dungeness, 1652
Dunkirk, 1666
Falkland Islands, 8 Dec. 1914
Finisterre, Cape,
    (1) 3 May 1747
    (2) 14 Oct. 1747
    (3) 1805
Gibraltar Bay, 13 Sept. 1782
Guadeloupe. *See* SAINTS, THE
Hampton Roads, 8–9 Mar. 1862
Hangö, 27 July 1714
Harwich, 1666
Heligoland, 28 Aug. 1914
Itamarca, 1640
Japan Sea, 14 Aug. 1904
Java, 27–8 Feb. 1942

Jutland, 31 May 1916
Lagos, 18 Aug. 1759
La Hogue, 14–16 May 1692
Lake Champlain, 11 Sept. 1814
Lemnos, 18 Jan. 1913
Lepanto, 7 Oct. 1571
Lissa, 20 July 1866
Macassar Strait, 23–25 Jan. 1942
Malaga, 13 Aug. 1704
Malaya, 10 Dec. 1941
Manila, 1 May 1898
Matapan, 28 Mar. 1941
Messina, 1676
Midway, 3–6 June 1942
Minorca, 1756
Narvik, 10 and 13 Apr. 1940
Navarino, 20 Oct. 1827
Negapatam, 6 July 1782
New Orleans, 25 Apr. 1862
Newport News. *See* HAMPTON ROADS
Nile, The, 1 Aug. 1798 (N)
North Foreland,
    (1) 2–3 June 1653
    (2) 1 June 1666
    (3) 25–6 July 1666
Oran, 3 July 1940
Passaro Cape, 11 Aug. 1718
Pearl Harbor, 7 Dec. 1941
Philippine Sea, 23–25 Oct. 1944
Plate River, 14–15 Dec. 1939
Portland, 18–20 Feb. 1653
Quiberon, 20 Nov. 1759
Rosas Bay, 1 Nov. 1809
St. Vincent,
    (1) 16 June 1693
    (2) 16 Jan. 1780
    (3) 14 Feb. 1797 (N)
Saints, The, 12 Apr. 1782
Santa Cruz,
    (1) 20 Apr. 1657
    (2) 1797
Salamis, 480 BC
Samos, 16–17 Aug. 1824
Santiago, 3 July 1898
Sevastopol bombarded, 17 Oct. 1854
Sinope, 30 Nov. 1853
Sirte, 22–4 Mar. 1942
Sluys, 24 June 1340
Sole or Southwold Bay, 28 May 1672
Taranto, 11 Nov. 1940
Tchesiné, 7–9 July 1770

Texel, 9 Aug. 1653
Trafalgar, 21 Oct. 1805 (N)
Tsu Shima, 27–8 May 1905
Ushant,
   (1) 27 July 1778
   (2) 1 June 1794
Yalu, 17 Sept. 1894
Yellow Sea (two battles), 10 Aug. 1904
Zeebrugge, 23 Apr. 1918

Air Battles
Britain, 8 Aug.–29 Oct. 1940

---

battleship. First ship with turrets the *Rolf Krake* designed for Danish Navy by British Capt. C. P. Coles, RN, 1860. First turret ship in action the USS *Monitor*, 9 Mar. 1862. B. design revolutionized by launching of HMS *Dreadnought*, 1906. German 'pocket B.' *Deutschland* launched, May 1931; famous Ger. pocket Bs. were the **Graf Spee* scuttled 17 Dec. 1939, the *Bismarck*, sunk by the British, 27 May 1941, and the *Tirpitz* (destroyed 12 Nov. 1944 by RAF bombers in a Norwegian port.) Bs. obsolescent by 1960.

Bavaria (German **Bayern**). One of the original 'tribal duchies' of Germany. Earliest (probably Celtic) inhabitants subdued by Romans *c*. 10–5 BC. Ravaged by Odoacer, AD 476–86. Settled by Germanic tribes, 488–520. Conquered by Franks, 555, and governed by Frankish dukes till Charlemagne deposed Tassilo III, 788. Wittelsbach family take throne from Henry the Lion, 1180. Duchy divided till accession of the Emperor Louis the Bavarian, 1314. Becomes an electorate, 1623. Annexes the Upper Palatinate, 1648. Alliance with France leads to occupation by British and Austrian troops before battle of Blenheim, 1704. Attempts to dismember Austria with Prussian help, leads to defeat and occupation, 1742. Becomes a kingdom, 1805. Allied to Austria in Austro-Prussian War, 1866. Makes military convention with Prussia, Aug. 1866. Joins in Franco-Prussian War, 1870, against France. Joins German Empire, 1871. Jesuits expelled, 1873. Wittelsbachs deposed and

Communist Republic proclaimed by Kurt Eisner, 1918. Eisner murdered, Feb. 1919. Moderate Government re-established by force, 1 May 1919. Attempted Munich *putsch* of Hitler and Ludendorff, 8 Nov. 1923. Democratic government abolished by Hitler, 1933. Occupied by American forces, 1945. Separate *Land* government set up 1946. Christian Social Union has since dominated Bavarian politics.

Heads of State.
From the foundation of the electorate, 1623, until the declaration of the republic, 1918.

Electors:
Maximilian I 1597–1651
Ferdinand Maria I 1651–79
Maximilian II 1679–1726
Karl Albrecht I 1726–45
Maximilian III 1745–77
Karl Theodor I 1777–99
Maximilian IV (*elector*) and I (*king*) 1799–1825

Kings:
Ludwig I 1825–48
Maximilian II 1848–64
Ludwig II 1864–86
Otto I (incurably insane) 1886–1913
Luitpold (Regent) 1886–1912
Ludwig (Regent) 1912–13
Ludwig III 1913–18

Bay of Pigs, abortive invasion of Cuba by anti-Castro dissidents, with US connivance, 17–20 Apr. 1961.

Bayeux, Normandy, has a cathedral built from the 11th to the 13thC. Bishopric dates from the 4thC. Taken by Rollo, 890. Pillaged by Henry I of England, 1106. It was the first French town to be recaptured by the Allies in June 1944.

Bayeux Tapestry of panoramic scenes embroidered in worsted on a linen ground, and depicting the events of the reign of King Harold II of England, which culminated in the battle of *Hastings, was almost certainly executed shortly after Oct. 1066, probably under the patronage of Odo (d. 1097), Bishop of B. and Earl of Kent and half-brother of William the Conqueror. First recorded mention, 1476. Formerly kept in Old Bishop's Palace: now in a specially-constructed museum in B., 1995.

bayonet. 'Plug B.', supposed to have been invented at Bayonne c. 1647, but in use before; external screw allowing the firelock to be fired without unfixing B., invented by Gen. Hugh Mackay (1640–1692), after battle of Killiecrankie, 1689.

Bayonne, France. Meeting-place of Catherine de Medici and the Spanish Duke of Alva, 1565. Ferdinand VII of Spain was here induced by his father, the ex-king Charles IV, to abdicate in favour of Napoleon, 2 May 1808. Invested by British, 1814. Convention of B., signed, 10 May 1808.

Bayonne Decree, 17 Apr. 1808. Napoleon ordered seizure of all American vessels.

Bayreut(h), Bavaria, founded 1194, became in 1248 a dependency of *Nürnberg and later combined with Ansbach to form a principality ruled by a cadet branch of the Hohenzollerns before becoming Prussian in 1791, finally passing to Bavaria, 1810. The Wagner Theatre was opened in 1876, when the B. Festival was first held; the Opera House proper, 1748.

BBC. See BRITISH BROADCASTING CORPORATION.

BCCI. See BANK OF CREDIT AND COMMERCE INTERNATIONAL.

bear-baiting in Britain banned by Act of Parliament, 1835.

Beaufort scale standard for measuring velocity of wind invented, 1805, by Rear-Admiral Sir Francis B., naval hydrographer (1774–1857).

Beauvais, France. Cathedral choir built, 1227–1347. Unsuccessfully besieged by

Charles of Burgundy, 1472, owing to valour of Jeanne Lainé (La Hachette). Transepts and tower of cathedral completed, 1547. Tower (the highest in Europe) fell, 1573. Monument to La Hachette, 1850. British airship *R.101* crashed at B., Oct. 1930.

Bec, Normandy, a Benedictine abbey, founded, 1034, by Herlwin, became famous for the school founded there, 1045, by Lanfranc (1005–89), later Archbishop of Canterbury. Though decline set in during the 13thC it survived until 1789, and its last pre-Revolutionary prior was Talleyrand (1754–1838). Abbey church then demolished. In 1948, abbey restored by French government and Benedictines returned.

Bechuanaland. See BOTSWANA.

Bedford, England. Burned by Danes, 1010. B. School refounded, 1552. B. Modern School founded, 1566. Bunyan imprisoned, 1660–72.

Bedford Level, England. The large area of the Fens drained, c. 1640, by Cornelius Vermuyden at expense of the third Duke of B.

Bedlam, from Bethlehem Hospital, founded in London by Simon Fitzmary, 1247. Became madhouse, 1407. Moved to Moorfields, 1676; to Lambeth, 1815; to Beckenham, Kent, 1930. Now (1995) known as the Bethlehem Royal Hospital, and linked with the Maudsley Hospital.

Béguines. Order of sisters devoted to education, etc., founded at Liège in the 12thC by Le Bèghe. Most famous house was at Bruges.

Beijing. See PEKING.

Beirut, capital of the Lebanon. Destroyed by earthquake in the 6thC. Seized by Ibrahim Pasha, 1832; Egyptian Army totally defeated at, Oct. 1840; massacre at, May 1860. Bombarded during Italo-Turkish war, 1912. Occupied by Allenby's army, 8 Oct. 1918. Captured from French by British, July 1941. Became capital of the independent republic of the Lebanon, 26 Nov. 1941. From 1968 scene of considerable fighting in Arab/Israeli conflicts. B. airport raided by Israelis, 1968. B. temporarily largely occupied by Israelis, 1982, who were superseded by a UN peacekeeping force, 1983, which withdrew, 1984. Heavy fighting in B. followed between Christian east B. and Moslem west B. Kidnapping of foreign hostages in B., 1980s: all those still alive freed by 1992. Peace in B. following treaty of 22 May 1991, between *Lebanon and *Syria.

Belarus (Belorussia or **Byelorussia),** independent republic since 1991. Medieval B. subject to Lithuania and Poland; from 16thC, divided between Russia and Poland. Independent, 1918–19; part of the USSR from 1922. After World War II, Polish B. acquired by USSR. B. contaminated by radioactive material from *Chernobyl accident, 1986. Declared independence from USSR, Aug. 1991; member of Commonwealth of Independent States from Dec. 1991. In July 1994 anti-corruption candidate Alexander Lukashenko, a pro-Russian, was elected president of B. Protests against the government ended when troops stormed parliament, Apr. 1995.

Belau. *See* PALAU.

Belfast, Ireland. Castle built *c.* 1177; destroyed by Edward Bruce, 1316. B. attacked by Earl of Kildare, 1503, 1512. Town and castle repaired by Hugh O'Neill, who acquired them in 1552. B. granted by James I to Sir Arthur Chichester, 1612, received its charter, 1613. Taken by Gen. Monck, 1648; by Lord Montgomery, 1649. Mayor became Lord Mayor, 1892. University founded as Queen's College, 1845; received royal charter, 1909. Parliament Buildings at Stormont opened, 1932. Queen Elizabeth Bridge opened by the Queen, 1966. Scene of riots, murders and bombings caused by Catholic and Protestant extremists, 1968–94, when extremists on both sides announced a 'cease-fire'. Daytime patrols by British troops in B. ended, Jan. 1995.

Belfort, France. Ceded to France, 1648. Famous for its defence by Col. Denfert-Rochereau, Nov. 1870–Feb. 1871 against the Prussians. The General Delegation for Occupied France was set up here by Fernand de Brinon, 7 Sept. 1940.

Belgae. A mixed Celtic-Germanic group of tribes in NE Gaul, part of whom migrated to S Britain *c.* 75 BC.

Belgium. Its Celtic inhabitants conquered by Julius Caesar, 51 BC. Was southern part of Spanish Netherlands, the northern part of which broke away in 1579. A separate kingdom under Spanish ruler, 1598–1621. Ceded to Austria by Peace of Utrecht, 1713. Overrun by the French, 1744–8. Republic, 1787–90. Passed to France by Treaty of Campo Formio, 1797. Restored to Austria, 1814. United with Holland, 1815. Revolution commenced, 25 Aug. 1830. Treaty between Holland and B. regarding latter's independence signed at London, 19 Apr. 1839, and guaranteed by principal European powers; commercial treaty with Great Britain, 22 Aug. 1862. Neutrality violated by German Army, 4 Aug. 1914. 'Pact of Mutual Guarantee' (for security of Belgian independence) signed at London, 1 Dec. 1925. Equality of Flemish and French languages recognized, 1932. Invaded by Germany, 10 May 1940. Leopold III capitulated, 28 May. B. liberated Sept.–Nov. 1944. Minor modifications in B.'s favour on Belgian-German frontier, Apr. 1949. Monarchy crisis, 1944–51. 1950: Referendum pronounced narrowly in favour of recalling Leopold III; his return followed by rioting, and in Aug. he delegated his powers to his son, finally abdicating in his favour, July 1951. Member of the European Economic Community, 1957. Congo (*see* ZAIRE) became independent of B., 30 June 1960. 'Language frontiers' established, 1962–3. Legislation 1971–80 established considerable regional autonomy, based on 'language frontiers'. New federalist proposals, 1993, further reduced royal powers. End of conscription announced, 1995. Government corruption scandal, 1995, and foreign minister resigns, Mar. Elections in May showed little change.

Kings
Leopold I 1831–65
Leopold II 1865–1909
Albert I 1909–34
Leopold III 1934–51*
Prince Charles, Regent 1944–50
Leopold III (20 July–10 Aug.) 1950
Baudouin, Prince Royal (since 11 Aug.) 1950
Baudouin I 1951–93
Albert II 1993–
*Prisoner of war, May 1940–May 1945. Prince Charles was Regent from Aug. 1944 to July 1950. Leopold exercised his prerogatives during July and Aug. 1950, but Prince Badouin took them over in the latter month. Leopold abdicated, 16 July 1951, and Baudouin was enthroned, 17 July 1951.

Belgorod-Dnestrovskiy, Ukraine, formerly **Akkerman** (Romanian **Cetatea Alba**). Taken by Russians from Turks, 1770; restored, 1774; ceded to Russia, 1806. Russo-Turkish Treaty of, 4 Sept. 1826. Romanian 1918–40 and 1941–4. Re-named B.-D., 1944.

Belgrade (Serbian, **Beograd**), capital of **Serbia** and **Yugoslavia**. Roman town of *Singidunum*, said to have stood on an earlier Celtic settlement. Destroyed by the Avars in the 6thC. Seized by Hungarians from Greeks, 1124, besieged by Turks unsuccessfully, 1444, 1456; captured by Turks, 1522; imperial forces, 1688; Turks, 1690; Prince Eugene, 1717; restored to Turks, 1739; captured by Austrians, 1789; restored to Turks, 1792; surrendered to Serbia, 1867; independence of Serbia declared at B., 22 Aug. 1878; king and queen murdered by army, 10 June 1903; captured by von Mackensen, 7 Oct. 1915; capital of *Yugoslavia 1919–92, since then, in theory, of its rump, and also of Serbia, bombed by Germans, 6 Apr. 1941; occupied, 12 Apr. 1941; liberated by partisans and Russians, 20 Oct. 1944. *See also* Serbia and Yugoslavia.

Belize, Central America, probably discovered by Columbus, 1502. First settled by British woodcutters from Jamaica *c.* 1638 and Spain acknowledged British rights, 1670. Governed as a colony from Jamaica, 1862–84. Independent since Sept. 1981: British garrison stationed at B. since independence, withdrawn, by end of 1994.

Bell Rock Lighthouse (N Sea). Built by Robert Stevenson, 1807–11. The rock is famous through Southey's ballad, *The Inchcape Rock.*

bells. Used in France *c.* 550. In the capitulation of Jerusalem, AD 637, the 12th article stipulated that the Christians 'shall not ring, but only toll their bells'. Prominent among the ritual objects of the Celtic Church, in the 6thC. First mentioned as used in churches in England in 7thC by the Venerable Bede. Largest B. in the world is the 'Tsar Kolokol' of Moscow, cast 1773–5.

Belorussia. *See* Belarus.

Belsen (Germany). Concentration camp set up in 1933, and taken by British troops, Apr. 1945. Its commandant, Josef Kramer, and 11 of his staff were sentenced to death for torture and murder of prisoners, 17 Nov. 1945.

Belvoir Castle (England). Seat of the dukes of Rutland, built 1808 after a fire had destroyed the previous building.

Benares or **Banaras,** India. Holy city of great antiquity. Sacked by the Moslems, 1194. Annexed by E India Co., 1775. College opened, 1791. Hindu university opened, 1916.

Benedictine Order. Founded by St Benedict, 529. Introduced into England, 596. Its oldest foundation is *Montecassino.

Benefit of Clergy, by which after Becket's murder (1170) English clerics, and later all who could read, were exempt from punishment by a civil court. After 1489 B. of C. could be claimed only once. Ben Jonson escaped gallows by, 1598. Finally abolished, 1827.

Benelux. Economic union of Belgium, the Netherlands and Luxemburg, came into force, 1 Jan. 1948. Fully operative from 1 Nov. 1960.

Benevento, Italy. Captured by Romans *c.* 277 BC; conquered by Lombards, 571; ceded by Emperor Henry III to Pope Leo IX, 1052. Charles of Anjou defeated Manfred of Sicily at B., 26 Feb. 1266. Seized by King of Naples, but restored, 1773; taken by French, 1798; restored to pope, 1815; Napoleon made Talleyrand prince of B., 1806; annexed to Italy, 1866.

Benevolences. Forced loans levied by English monarchs; so called from reign of Edward IV onwards. Parliament declared them unlawful, 1484, but they continued to be levied. Finally declared illegal by *Bill of Rights, 1689.

Bengal, independent, 1340. Annexed to Mogul Empire, 1576. Under British influence after battle of Plassey, 1757. Ceded to E India Co., 1765. Made chief presidency of India, 16 June 1773. Warren Hastings governor of, 1772–83. Assam annexed to B., 1826–74. Divided into two parts, 1905. This partition revoked, 1911, and B. reconstituted, 1912, Bihar, Orissa, and Chota Nagpur being made a separate province (*see* BIHAR). Famine killed three million in, 1943. E.B. and part of Assam became part of Pakistan, 15 Aug. 1947: part of *Bangladesh since 1971. Area subject to frequent disastrous flooding, e.g. tidal wave May 1985 causing thousands of deaths.

Benghazi, Libya. Occupied by Italians, 20 Oct. 1911. Captured by Australians, 7 Feb. 1941; lost again, 3 Apr.; recaptured, 24 Dec. 1941; lost, 29 Jan. 1942, and finally recaptured by the British, 20 Nov. 1942. *See* WORLD WAR II.

Benin, formerly **Dahomey,** W Africa. French protectorate, 1863; annexed, 1894. Independent republic, 1960; name changed from Dahomey to People's Republic of B., 1975. In 1989 B. abandoned Marxism; constitution revoked. Mar. 1990 and name amended to Republic of B.

Elections, Feb./Mar. 1991: Nicéphore Soglo president, Apr. 1991.

Ben Nevis observatory built, 1883; abandoned, 1904.

Berar, India. Formerly part of Hyderabad State, leased by British Government, 1853–1947. Now part of Madhya Pradesh State.

Berchtesgaden, Bavaria. Has salt-mines which have been worked since 1140. Priors of B. made princes of the Empire, 1495. Principality secularized, 1803. The Berghof, B., was Hitler's country residence and here he interviewed Neville Chamberlain about the Sudeten crisis, 15 Sept. 1938. Bombed by Allied air forces, Apr. and May 1945; living-quarters destroyed but solid stone mountain pavilion or 'Eagle's Nest' was undamaged until taken by the French First Armoured Division, 5 May 1945. Now (1995) a tourist attraction.

Berg, a county of Westphalia from early in the 12thC, became a duchy, 1380, and passed to the electorate of Bavaria, 1799. Made a Grand Duchy, and handed to Joachim Murat by Napoleon, 1806. Awarded to Prussia by Treaty of Vienna, 1815.

Bergen, Norway. Seaport founded by King Olaf the Peaceful, 1070–5. Cathedral founded, 1248: rebuilt, 1537. Germans landed and occupied port, 9 Apr. 1940. German naval command in Norway surrendered to British and Norwegians, 15 May 1945. Museum founded, 1825. University established, 1946, opened 30 Aug. 1948.

Bergen op Zoom. Fortified, 1576, unsuccessfully besieged by Spaniards, 1588, 1605, 1622. Held by the French from 1795 to 1815.

Berkshire, historic English county, its abolition (except for ceremonial purposes) suggested by Local Government Commission, 1994, widespread protests followed and the High Court granted objectors a stay, Oct. 1995.

Berlin, Germany. First became important

during reign of Frederick William the Great Elector (*d.* 1688). Charlottenburg Schloss built, 1696–1841; rebuilt, 1950. Palace of Sans Souci began, 1745. Brandenburg Gate 1788–91; goddess of Victory surmounting it, 1789–93 removed by Napoleon 1806–7, restored 1814. Gate and statue damaged in World War II, restored, 1956. Seized by Russians and Austrians, Oct. 1760; entered by French after battle of Jena, 1806. Capital of German Empire from 1871 to 1918. Victory Column built 1872–3 to commemorate victorious wars of 1864, 1866 and 1871. Kaiser Wilhelm Church, 1891–5 was destroyed during World War II and totally rebuilt on modernist lines, 1961–3. The Reichstag, 1884–94 was damaged by fire in 1933 and by bombardment, 1945; now (1995) being rebuilt in modified form. Two-week wrapping of Reichstag by controversial architect Christo, June 1995. B. Congress, June–July 1878. Metro begun, 1902. Became capital of Third Reich, 1933. Surrendered to Russians, 2 May 1945, after heavy bombing and fighting had destroyed about 75 per cent of the city proper but extensive rebuilding took place in 1950s and 1960s. Deutsche Opera, 1961, replaced pre-war building. Outstanding modern architecture includes Corbusier Haus, 1954. Subsequently partitioned into Russian, American, French and British sectors; from 1948 effectively only into Russian and Western sectors. Its blockade by the Russians, 28 June 1948–12 May 1949, failed in the face of allied air supply. W Berlin a *Land* of the Federal German Republic, and simultaneously a city, under constitution of 1 Sept. 1950. E Berlin the capital of the German Democratic Republic from 1949. Riots in Soviet sector (E Berlin) suppressed, 17 June 1953. Scene of four-power Conference, 26 Jan.–17 Feb. 1954. 13 Aug. 1961: E. Germany sealed off the Berlin border, and began constructing a permanent concrete wall along it, subsequently reinforced with anti-tank barriers, etc. Would-be escapers shot on sight. On Nov. 9 1989 the Berlin Wall was reopened and subsequently almost completely demolished. Following the reunification of the two Germanies, B. was proclaimed the capital once more in Oct. 1990, and (Oct 1993) announced all government administration to be moved there by 2000. President Clinton visited B., July 1994: in Sept. 1994 the last British, French and US troops left B., the Russians having already gone. E and W Berlin became united 16th *Land* of the Fed. Republic.

Berlin Decrees, 21 Nov. 1806. *See* CONTINENTAL SYSTEM.

Bermudas or **Somers Islands,** Atlantic Ocean. First recorded on map, dated 1511. Visited and named by Juan Bermudez, 1515; settled, 1609, by Sir George Somers. Administration transferred from B. Company to crown, 1684. Colonized in 17thC from Virginia, and during the American Revolution by Loyalists. Air and naval bases leased to USA for 99 years in 1941. Royal naval dockyard closed, 1951. Self-governing colony since 1968. Sir Richard Sharples, governor-general, assassinated, 10 Mar. 1973. Referendum organized by government. Aug. 1995 voted against independence from Britain and Bermudan premier resigned.

Bern or **Berne.** Joined Swiss League, 1353. The town of B. resisted Rudolph of Hapsburg, 1288; surrendered to French, 12 Apr. 1798; capital of Switzerland, 1848. Bears have been kept in B. at public expense ever since 1513.

Bernicia. The more northerly of the two Anglian kingdoms which later merged into Northumbria (see under N. for list of rulers). Its area roughly corresponded to that of the counties of Northumberland and Durham, but it was only a kingdom distinct from *Deira from AD 547 to 605 and from 633 to 655. *See also* BAMBURGH.

Berrow's Worcester Journal, the oldest surviving British newspaper, was founded in 1690, but did not acquire the name B. until 1753.

Berwick-on-Tweed. Given up to England by Scotland, 1176; seized by Robert Bruce, 1318; surrendered to English, 1333. Independent of England and Scotland,

1551. Peace of Berwick, between England and Scotland, 1639. Surrendered to Cromwell, 1648; to Gen. Monck, 1659.

beryllium. Discovered in the form of oxide in the mineral beryl, 1798. Isolated by Wöhler, 1828.

Besançon, France. Became a free city of the empire, 1184. In Spanish hands, 1648–78. Became capital of *Franche-Comté when that province was ceded to France, 1678.

Bessarabia (Ukrainian **Budzhak**). Region on the W coast of the Black Sea between the Danube and the Dniestr, called after the Basarab dynasty or else after the Bessi, a Thracian tribe who lived in the area. Romania controlled part of B. 1918–40 and 1941–4 but this subsequently incorporated with the rest of B. in the USSR, confirmed by the peace treaty of 1947. Since 1991, divided between independent republics of *Moldova and *Ukraine.

Bessel's Functions, in mathematics, indicate certain relationships between two variables. Introduced by F.W. Bessel, 1817.

Bessemer process, for purifying iron and steel, invented by Sir Henry Bessemer, 1856.

Bethlehem (modern **Beit-Lahm**), Israel. The village dates from before 1000 BC. Christian pilgrimage began earlier than 132 (see NATIVITY, CHURCH OF THE), but the village was devastated in 1244 and again in 1489.

Béthune, France. Founded in the 11thC. Ceded to France at the Treaty of Nijmegen, 1678. Severely damaged in World War I and II. Since 1960s, car industry has replaced coal-mining as main industry of B.

betting. B. Acts of 1853 and 1874, and the B. and Lotteries Act of 1934, regulated B. in Britain until the B. and Gaming Act, 1960, provided for the establishment of licensed B. shops. Consolidating Act, 1963. Amendments 1968, 1971 and 1980. On-course Sunday B. allowed in England from Jan. 1995. See also GAMING AND GAMBLING AND NATIONAL LOTTERY.

betting-houses (Great Britain). Suppressed, 1853. Licensed betting shops allowed under the Betting and Gaming Act, 1960. Relaxation of restrictions proposed, 1993. Open on Sundays, 1995.

Beveridge Plan. National insurance scheme signed by Lord Beveridge (1879–1963), chairman of the Inter-departmental Committee on Social Insurance and Allied Services, 1941–2, and published by HM Stationery Office, 20 Nov. 1942. It formed the basis of post-war legislation in the fields of social insurance and social security. Principal of 'welfare' state being questioned increasingly in 1990s.

Beverley, England. Its principal church, of the 12thC, is built on the site of that founded by St John of B. (c. 640–721), who is also the reputed founder of B. grammar school. A charter of the town is mentioned as having been granted in 925, but is not extant; but one granted between 1120 and 1135 is. Weaving was an important industry 14th–17thC.

Bhopal. Former Indian princely state, merged into Madhya Pradesh since 1956. Founded by Dost Mohammed Khan, 1723. Over 2000 killed and possibly over 200,000 affected by emission of poison gas from US-owned factory, 3 Dec. 1984.

Bhutan (Bhotian, **Druk-Yul**) was invaded by Tibetans in 9thC AD and Indian population driven out. Treaty with E India Co., 1774. Dispute with Britain terminated by treaty, 1865 and further treaty, 1910. British representation in B. succeeded by Indian, Aug. 1947. Treaty of friendship with India, 1949.

Biafra, name given 1967–70 to the Eastern States of *Nigeria by secessionists who on 30 May 1967 announced their withdrawal from the federal republic of Nigeria, and renamed the region B. The name B. and the act of secession were never recognized by Nigeria, which mounted a full-scale military campaign to reconquer B. B.

suffered severe famine and finally capitulated Jan. 1970 and the area was reunited with Nigeria.

Bible, translations of. The first translation of the Old .Testament into Greek, called the Septuagint, made in stages between 284 BC and AD 100. Origen's collection of versions, *Hexapla*, commenced, AD 231. Psalms believed to have been translated into Old English before Alfred's time. Cædmon's metrical paraphrase of a portion of the B. *c.* AD 670. Bede's St John, 735, and Aelfric's partial Old Testament, 990. Division into chapters, often ascribed to Lanfranc (11thC), was probably a result of the labours of Hugh de Sancto Caro (*c.* 1200–63). Wycliffe's English versions *c.* 1382 and 1388. The whole Bible divided into verses first in the Geneva version of 1557–60. Tyndale's (New Testament) printed, 1525; Coverdale's (first complete English B.) printed, 1535; Cranmer's B. first authorized, 1539; authorized version published, 1611 (*see* HAMPTON COURT CONFERENCE); revised version, New Testament, 1881; Old Testament, 1884. Dr. James Moffat's translations published: New Testament, 1913; Old Testament, 1924. New version of the New Testament in modern English, 1961; Old Testament new version, 1970, the combined new Old and New Testaments being put together as 'The New English Bible'. Several further modern versions since 1970, including *Good News* and abbreviated versions; *New International Bible*, 1973. For Latin B., and translations therefrom, *see* separate article, VULGATE.

Bible Society, British and Foreign. Begun, 1803; organized, 1804. American B.S. organized at Philadelphia, 1808; various American B.Ss. amalgamated to form the American and Foreign B.S., 1839.

Bibliothèque Nationale. The building in Paris which now houses the collection was bought for the purpose by the crown in 1721, having been built in the mid-17thC. The nucleus of the collection is the books owned by Louis XI (*d.* 1483).

bicycle. *See* CYCLE.

bigamy in England is punishable under the Offences against the Person Act, 1861; in Scotland it is merely another form of perjury punishable by statute of 1551; in the USA the law of B. varies from state to state, but in general it is based on an English statute of 1603.

Big Bang, popular term for radical reform of London Stock Exchange, came into operation, Oct. 1986.

Big Bang, theory of, astronomic hypothesis regarding origin of the universe in which B.B. thought to have occurred *c.* 15 billion years ago.

Big Ben (London). First hung, 1858. Clock in use from 1859. Chimes first broadcast, 1923. Named after Sir Benjamin Hall (1802–67), Commissioner of Works at the time: he became Baron Llanover, 1859.

'Big Bertha'. Nickname given to German long-range gun which fired on Paris during 1918.

Bihar, India. Separated from Bengal, 1911. From Orissa, 1935. Serious riots in 1942, 1946 and 1971. Scene of world's worst rail disaster, 6 June 1981, when over 800 were killed when a train plunged into a river.

Bilbao, Spain. Founded *c.* 1300; taken by French, July 1795, and in 1808; bombarded by Carlists, but relieved, 1874; fell to Nationalist forces, 18 June 1937.

billiards. Known in England in Shakespeare's time. It has been ascribed to Henri Devigne, 1571.

Billingsgate, London. Tolls collected there from 10thC. Opened, 1588, as a landing-place for provisions; free market, 1699; extended, 1848; rebuilt, 1852, 1875: site of fish market moved to Isle of Dogs, Jan. 1982.

Bill of Rights. *See* RIGHTS, BILL OF.

Bills of Exchange Act, 1882, codified existing practice concerning B. of E. in the UK.

Bills of Exchequer first issued, 1696.

Bills of Sale or **Chattel Mortgages** are

regulated by the Acts of 1878 and 1882 in England and Wales only.

Bingen, Rhineland-Palatinate, was important for the water-borne traffic of the Rhine as the nearest harbour to the dangerous rapids of Bingerloch until these were cleared by blasting in 1834. The statue of Germania – *'Die Dame ohne Verhältnisse'* – was erected, 1877–83.

bingo. Game which reached height of popularity in 1950s and 1960s, when many British cinemas converted to B. halls. Remains a popular club game. B. Act, 1992, amended Gaming Act of 1968 with respect to B.

Binomial Theorem. First published by Isaac Newton, 1676.

Birdcage Walk. Perhaps really Bocage W., but James I (1603–25) built an aviary there, and the nearby cock-pit was not done away with until 1816.

Birkbeck College. Founded as the London Mechanics' Institute by Dr. George Birkbeck, 1823. Became a constituent college of London University, 1920.

Birkenhead, England. Dock opened, Aug. 1847. *See* LIVERPOOL.

Birmingham, England. Appears in Domesday Book, 1086. Market charters granted, 1166, 1189, 1249, 1295. Sacked by Royalists, 1643. Canal opened, 1767. 'Church and king' riots in, 1791. Chartist riot, 15 July 1839. John Bright first elected MP for, 1857. Became a city, 1889. Office of lord mayor created, 1896. University chartered, 1900. Became a bishopric, 1904. *University of Aston established in B., 1966. IRA bomb attack in B. kills 21, injures 162, 24 Nov. 1974. B. Polytechnic became University of Central England at B., 1992. Rebuilding of B. 'Bull-Ring', 1960s: proposed demolition and rebuilding, 1993. Opening of Gas Hall art gallery, Oct. 1993.

Birmingham Royal Ballet (1990) was formerly the Sadler's Wells Royal Ballet (1946).

Birmingham Six. *See* TRIALS AND CAUSES CÉLÈBRES.

birth, concealment of, in Scotland, was considered to be proof of infanticide, a capital offence, until 1803, when it was made punishable by a maximum penalty of imprisonment, as in England and Wales. From 1861, a misdemeanour under the Offences Against the Person Act.

birth control. *See* CONTRACEPTION.

Bishoprics (England and Wales). Following are dates of foundation of the Anglican sees (not suffragan sees):

Bangor *c.* 550
Bath and Wells 1139
Birmingham 1904
Blackburn 1927
Bradford 1919
Bristol 1541
Canterbury 597
Carlisle 1133
Chelmsford 1927
Chester 1541
Chichester 1075
Coventry 1919
Derby 1927
Durham 995
Ely 1109
Exeter 1050
Gloucester 1541
Guildford 1927
Hereford 676
Leicester 1919
Lichfield 669
Lincoln 1067
Liverpool 1880
Llandaff *c.* 550
London 605
Manchester 1847
Monmouth 1920
Newcastle 1882
Norwich 1094
Oxford 1542
Peterborough 1541
Portsmouth 1927
Ripon 1877
Rochester 604
St Albans 1877
St Asaph *c.* 550
St Davids *c.* 550
St Edmundsbury and Ipswich 1914

Salisbury 1075
Sheffield 1914
Sodor and Man *c.* 1134
Southwark 1905
Southwell 1884
Swansea and Brecon 1920
Truro 1876
Wakefield 1888
Winchester *c.* 650
Worcester *c.* 680
York 625

Bishops (UK). Earliest British B. *c.* 180. For dates of foundation of sees, *see* BISHOPRICS. In Scotland replaced by superintendents, 1561. Restored, 1573. Abolished, 1638. Abolished in England, 1646. Restored in both countries, 1661. Expelled by Scottish convention, 1689.

Bishops (USA). Samuel Seabury, Bishop of Connecticut, Nov. 1784, first Protestant bishop consecrated for USA. First bishop of New York consecrated in London, 4 Feb. 1787.

Bishops, Seven, committed to the Tower for seditious libel (i.e. opposing the Declaration of Indulgence), but found not guilty at the Bar of the King's Bench, 29 June 1688.

Bisley, England. Scene of National Rifle Association meetings since 1890.

Bismarck Archipelago. Discovered by Dampier, 1699, and named New Britain, but by agreement of 1885 assigned to the German sphere of influence and their name changed to B.A. Occupied by Australian forces, Sept. 1914, and after 1918 attached to the Australian-mandated territories in New Guinea. Parts of the independent state of Papua New Guinea since 1975.

Bismarck. *See under* BATTLESHIP.

Bithynia, Asia Minor. Became part of the kingdom of Lydia, 570 BC, but absorbed with it by the Persian Empire, 546. After recovery of its independence Nicomedia was founded by 264 BC. The last king of B. bequeathed his state to Rome, 74 BC. Conquered by Turks, AD 1298.

Bizerta, Tunisia, N Africa (anciently *Hippo Zarytis*). Occupied by French, 1881. Captured from Germans, 9 May 1943. French maintained base at B. till 1961.

Black and Tans. Force specially recruited by Britain, 1921, and used in Ireland to fight Sinn Fein. So called from colour of the uniform.

Black Death. Identical with bubonic plague. Supposed to have originated in China. Raged there, 1340–48. In Europe, 1346–9, 1361–2, and 1369.

Blackfriars Bridge (London). Old bridge, 1760–1860; new bridge opened, 6 Nov. 1869; enlarged, 1909.

Black Friday.
1. 6 Dec. 1745. Young Pretender's entry into Derby announced in London, causing a run on the bank and closing of shops.
2. 11 May 1866. Overend, Gurney & Co., the bankers, stopped payment, causing commercial panic; partners tried for conspiracy to defraud, but acquitted, Dec. 1869.

Blackheath, England. Wat Tyler's men assembled on, 12 June 1381; Jack Cade, 1 June 1450. Cornish rebels defeated at, 22 June 1497.

Black Hole of Calcutta. Suraj-ud-Dowlah, Nawab of Bengal, imprisoned 146 English people in, on 19 June 1756: only 23 survived the night there.

Black Monday in medieval England, certain Easter Mondays upon which tradition recorded disasters to the English: (1) 29 Mar. 1209. 500 settlers massacred by Irish at Collenswood, Dublin; (2) 9 Apr. 1357. Black Prince's army sustained terrible losses through a storm; (3) 13 Apr. 1360. In Edward III's army near Paris many men died of cold.

Black Monday. 19 Oct. 1987, when on London Stock Exchange share values fell by over £100 billion.

Black Muslims, black separatist religious group founded, USA, 1929. Underwent radicalization and revival 1946–64 under

Malcolm X: further revival under Louis Farrakhan in 1990s.

Blackpool, England, was a small fishing village until growth into major seaside resort began in 18thC with then-new fashion for sea-bathing. Railway links in 19thC brought workers from the N industrial towns to B. and it became extremely popular. Had over 5000 hotels at height of its seaside popularity in 1950s. B. Tower, built 1889–95, as a miniaturist replica of the *Eiffel Tower and 520 ft/152 m high, is centre of vast amusement complex. Since 1950s B. has hosted many business and political conferences.

Black Prince, popular title of Edward, eldest son of Edward III; *b.* 15 June 1330; at battle of Poitiers, 1356; *d.* 8 June 1376 and is buried in Canterbury cathedral.

Black Rod. Office instituted, 1349.

Blackwall Tunnel, London, begun, 1892; opened, 1897. Reopened after £1,000,000 improvements, Apr. 1969.

Black Wednesday, 16 Sept. 1992, when collapse of sterling led to Britain leaving the European Exchange Rate Mechanism. Subsequently called **White Wednesday** by those opposed to British membership of the ERM.

Blair House Agreement, named after Washington, DC building where it was signed in Nov. 1992 by EC and US negotiators after two years of talks on reducing farm subsidies. Subject was for long a major obstacle in concluding Uruguay Round of *GATT.

Blanc, Mont, highest mountain in the Alps. *See* MONT BLANC.

Blandford, England. Whole town almost destroyed by fire, 1731.

Blarney Castle, Co. Cork, Ireland, gave its name to the phrase for flattery which cannot be traced – in writing – further back than 1819. Castle stands on the site of one founded by Cormac McCarthy in 1446, the date also inscribed on the B. Stone.

Blasket Islands, Ireland. Gaelic-speaking stronghold, evacuated July 1953.

blasphemy. Act of 1697 was repealed by the Criminal Law Act, 1967. B. against Christianity remains an offence in Britain (1995), though in 1985 Law Commission had suggested this should be changed. *See* FATWA.

bleaching. Artificial B. invented by Dutch early in 18thC; first bleach-field in Scotland established at Salton *c.* 1730; introduced into England, 1768; Berthollet's discoveries with chlorine *c.* 1785; Tennant's patent, 1798; Mather's improvements, 1885.

Blenheim Palace, England. Built by Sir J. Vanbrugh at national expense for the first Duke of Marlborough between 1705 and 1722. Sir Winston Churchill (1874–1965) *b.* at., 30 Nov. 1874.

Bloemfontein, capital of the Orange Free State, S Africa. Founded, 1846.

Blois, France. Sold to Louis, Duke of Orleans, 1391; States-General held at, 1576 and 1588; Henry of Guise assassinated at, 23 Dec. 1588.

blood, circulation of the. Pulmonary circulation discovered by Servetus, 1540; but principal discoveries regarding, due to William Harvey between 1616 and 1628.

Blood's (Colonel) Conspiracy. Attempt to steal crown jewels from Tower of London, 9 May 1671, by Col. Thomas B., *b. c.* 1628, *d.* 1680.

blood transfusion was practised on animals as early as the 17thC. Janssky in 1907 discovered the principle of the four human blood groups. A method of B. T. not direct from artery to artery was discovered in 1916, as was refrigeration. Plasma, as opposed to whole blood, first transfused on a large scale, 1940. In 1990s evidence that haemophiliacs had contracted *AIDS through receiving transfusions of infected blood: stringent checks introduced in western Europe and USA subsequently.

'Bloody Assize'. The trials by Judge George Jeffreys (1648–89), in Aug. 1685, after *Monmouth's rebellion.

'Bloody Sunday'. 30 Jan. 1972, when 13 Catholic civil rights protesters were shot dead by the British Army in Londonderry.

Blue-Books. Parliamentary and state reports, so called from their blue paper wrappers. These reports first printed in 1681.

blue-stocking. Term originated *c.* 1750, when a literary circle was established in London, consisting of ladies and gentlemen among whom was Benjamin Stillingfleet, who habitually wore blue stockings.

Board of Trade, founded 1661, but modern form dated from 1786. Became **Department of Trade and Industry**, 1970, and has undergone a number of changes since then. In 1992 the incoming Minister, Michael Heseltine, revived the title of President of the B. of T.

boat people. Term applied to Vietnamese attempting to enter Hong Kong illegally by boat, after Communist victory in Vietnam in 1975. Detained in camps by Hong Kong government which began forcible repatriation of B.P., from 1990.

boat race, Oxford and Cambridge. First held in 1829, this did not become an annual event until 1856. A dead-heat was rowed in 1877. Score to date (1995) Cambridge 72, Oxford 68, one dead-heat. Oxford boat sank, 1951; Cambridge, 1977, and in 1984 Cambridge boat sank before race started. Cambridge subsequently lost in a borrowed boat. Record time was rowed by an Oxford crew in 1984.

Bodleian Library. *See* LIBRARIES, MODERN.

Boeotia, Greece. United under Theban leadership, *c.* 1100 BC. Victory over Spartans at Leuctra, 371 BC, gave B. supremacy in Greece till death of Epaminondas at battle of Mantinea, 362 BC.

Boers. Emigrated from Cape Colony, 1835–7; founded Orange Free State, 1836; Transvaal Republic, 1848. *See* SOUTH AFRICAN WAR; CAPE COLONY; TRANSVAAL, etc.

Boer Wars, First B. War, 1880–1. Virtually ended by the British defeat at Majuba Hill, 27 Feb. 1881. Second B. War, 1899–1902. Concluded by the Peace of Vereeniging (*See under* TREATIES), 31 May 1902.

Bogomils, Old Slavonic for 'God's beloved', were a sect of heretics in the Balkans first mentioned in Greek sources, 1115. Their leader Basil was interrogated by the Emperor Alexius Comnenus, and then burnt by his orders, 1118. Slavonic sources mention the sect earlier, in the mid-10thC, as of Manichaean (*See* MANICHAEISM) type. Driven out of Serbia *c.* 1200, they took refuge in Bosnia, where they survived until the 15thC.

Bogotá, formerly **Santa Fé de Bogotá,** capital of Colombia since 1831, was founded in 1538 and became an episcopal see in 1561, capital of the viceroyalty of New Granada in 1598.

Bohemia. Christianity introduced from Moravia during 9thC. Dukedom, AD 891. Rulers known as kings soon after. 'Good King Wenceslas' murdered by Boleslav the Cruel, 929. Recognized as a kingdom by emperor, 1088. Reign of Ottokar begins, 1253. Extinction of Przemyslid dynasty, 1306. John of Luxembourg elected king, 1310. Killed at Crécy, 1346. University of Prague founded, 1348. John Hus *b. c.* 1373. Hussites adopt heretical doctrines, 1390 onwards. Hus burned by Council of Constance, 1415. 'The Twelve Years (Hussite) War', 1419–31. Battle of Taus, 1431. Destruction of the Taborites at battle of Lipau, 1434. Religious Pact of Iglau, 1436. George of Podebrad elected king, 1457. Ferdinand of Hapsburg became king, 1526. Ferdinand had himself declared hereditary ruler of B., so that B. became a permanent Hapsburg appanage, 1547. Toleration of Protestantism promised by Emperor Rudolf's *Letter of Majesty*, July 1609. The *Letter* violated by Ferdinand II. Defenestration of Prague, 1619. Battle of the White

Mountain, 1620. Thirty Years War, 1618–48. After Treaty of Westphalia, 1648, history of B. became generally coincident with that of *Austria, until 1918, thereafter with that of *Czechoslovakia. Sudeten territories incorporated in Germany, Oct. 1938. With Moravia became the 'Protectorate of B.-Moravia', and liberties suppressed under Germany, Mar. 1939. Liberated by Russians and Americans, 1945. Sudeten Germans forcibly driven out, 1945–6.

Rulers of, from the beginning of the historical period, *c.* 922, until 1918.

Princes:
Wenceslas I (Saint), the Good *c.* 922–*c.* 929
Boleslav I, the Cruel *c.* 929–967
Boleslav II 967–999
Boleslav III 999–1002
Vladivoj I 1002–03
Jaromir I 1003–12
Ulrich I 1012–37
Bretislav I 1037–55
Spytihinev II 1055–61
Vratislav II (King) 1061–92
Bretislav II 1092–1110
Borivoj II 1110–20
Vladislav I 1120–25
Sobeslav I 1125–40
Vladislav II (as King, I) 1140–73
Sobeslav II 1173–89
Conrad Otho I 1189–91
Wenceslas II 1191–92
Kings:
Premysl Ottokar I 1198–1230
Wenceslas I 1230–53
Premysl Ottokar II 1253–78
Wenceslas II 1278–1305
Wenceslas III 1305–06
Rudolf I of Hapsburg 1306–07
Henry of Carinthia 1307–10
John 1310–46
Charles I (IV) 1346–78
Wenceslas IV 1378–1419
Sigismund 1419–37
Albert of Hapsburg 1437–39
Ladislas Posthumus 1439–57
George of Podebrad 1458–71
Vladislav II 1471–1516
Louis I 1516–26

Ferdinand I 1526–64
Maximilian I 1564–76
Rudolf II 1576–1612
Matthias 1612–19
Frederick of the Palatinate *1619–20
Ferdinand II *1619–37
Ferdinand III 1637–57
Leopold I 1657–1705
Josef I 1705–11
Karl II (VI) 1711–40
Maria Theresa *1740–80
Karl of Bavaria *1740–43
Josef II 1780–90
Leopold II 1790–92
Franz I 1792–1835
Ferdinand IV (I) 1835–48
Franz Josef 1848–1916
Karl III (I) 1916–18
*Disputed succession

Bohemian Brethren. *See* Moravian Brethren.

Bokhara or **Bukhara,** Asia. Conquered in 7thC by Arabs, under whom it *fl.* until 1220. Seized by Uzbeks *c.* 1500. Emirate abolished and Soviet regime established 1921. Since 1991 part of the republic of *Uzbekhistan.

Bolivia. Conquered by Spain during the 16thC, and formed part of the viceroyalty of Peru. Separated from Peru, 1776, and added to the viceroyalty of Buenos Aires. War of Independence, 1810–24; royalists defeated at battle of Ayacucho, and independence granted, 1825. Boundary dispute with Chile, 1879–83; with Brazil, 1903. War over Gran Chaco with Paraguay 1933–6. Frontier with Paraguay settled by arbitration, 1938. Political instability since 1945 has been caused by economic problems: frequent military coups. A democratic government, 1951–64, was toppled by an army coup. In 1982, democracy restored, but B. has had serious economic problems since, with hyperinflation: and US pressure on B. to reduce coca crops has resulted in populist anti-American feeling. Sanchez de Lozada elected president, Aug. 1993.

Bologna, Italy (Latin *Bolonia*). Roman colony, 189 BC. University grew out of schools of liberal arts, which *fl.* in 11thC; first statutes, 1252. Pope Julius II took and entered, 11 Nov. 1506. Taken by French, 1796; by Austrians, 1799; by French 1800; restored to pope, 1815; taken by Austrians, 16 May 1849, who evacuated, 12 June 1859, and papal legate left. Became part of Italy, 1860. Terrorist bombing of B. station, 2 Aug. 1980, caused 82 deaths.

Bolsheviks. That part of the revolutionary Socialist party which professed Marxist Communism and happened to be in a majority (*bolshestvo*) at the end of the Second Congress of the Russian Social-Democratic Labour Party, in 1903, when several delegates had already left the congress. Independent Bolshevik Party founded (calling itself Social-Democratic Labour Party), 1912. Led by Lenin and Trotsky it seized power in Russia in Nov. 1917. Known by name 'Communist Party' ('Bolsheviks') from 1918; word 'Bolsheviks' dropped, 1952, and term now only used in Russia in an historical sense. *See* OCTOBER REVOLUTION; RUSSIA; MENSHEVIKS; COMMUNISM.

Bolton Abbey (England). Founded 1121, at Embassy, and transferred to the site in Wharfedale, 1151. Really a priory, not abbey, of Augustinians. Dissolved, 1540.

Bombay, India. Acquired by Portuguese, 1509; given to Charles II of England as marriage portion of Catherine of Braganza, 1661; granted to E India Co., 1668. University founded, 1857. Capital of Maharashtra state, 1960. Clashes between Muslims and Hindus 1992–3, over 600 dead. Bomb attacks in B., 12 Mar. 1993: over 200 killed. B. known officially as **Mumbai** from 1 May 1995.

bomber. The first specialized military aircraft for this purpose was the German Gotha, twin-engined push-bi-plane, taken into service, 1917.

Bomber Command, British, established 1936. Saturation bombing of Germany by B.C. under Sir Arthur Harris, 1942–5.

bombs of a type similar to the modern mortar-bomb first mentioned in English, 1588. The word was also used to describe *shells*, an expression not used until the middle of the 17th century.

Bonaparte, House of. Following are the principal members of this family of Corsican origin: 1. *Joseph, b.* 1768. King of Naples 1806–8. King of Spain, 1808–13; *d.* Florence, 1844. 2. *Napoléon I, b.* 1769. First Consul of France, 1800. Consul for life, 1802. Emperor of the French, 18 May 1804. Abdicated, Apr. 1814. At Elba, May 1814–Feb. 1815. Landed at Antibes, Feb. 1815. Abdicated again, June 1815; *d.* St. Helena, 5 May 1821 3. *Lucien, b.* 1775. President of the Council of Five Hundred, 1799. Prince of Canino; *d.* 1840. 4. *Louis, b.* 1778. King of Holland, 1806–10. Father of Napoléon III below; *d.* 1846. 5. *Jerome b.* 1784. King of Westphalia, 1806–13. Marshal and President of the French Senate under Napoléon III; *d.* 1860. 6. *Napoléon III, b.* 1808. President of French Republic, Dec. 1848. Emperor, 1852. Abdicated, 2 Sept. 1870; *d.* 9 Jan. 1873, at Chislehurst, England. 7. *Eugène Napoléon, b.* 1856. Prince Imperial. Killed at battle of Ulundi, 1879.

Bond Street, New. Built, 1721.

Bond Street, Old. Built 1686, by Sir Thomas Bond, who in 1683 bought and demolished Clarendon House for a building site.

Bonin or **Ogasawara Islands.** Discovered by Quast and Tasman, 1639. British, 1827. Japanese, 1878. Administered by the USA, 1945–68, then returned to Japan.

Bonn, Germany. Became residence of the electors and archbishops of Cologne during the Middle Ages. Became Prussian after 1815. Academy founded, 1777; made a university, 1786; abolished, 1802; restored and enlarged, 1818. Albert (Prince Consort) educated at, from 1837. Occupied by Allied troops after World War I until 31 Jan. 1926. Seat of German Federal Government from 5 May 1949; when Berlin became the capital of the united Federal Republic, 1990. B. remained its administrative centre; but this to move to Berlin by 2000.

Book of Common Prayer. *See* PRAYER, BOOK OF COMMON.

Booker Prize. British literary prize, presented annually for a work of fiction since 1969, when the winner was P. H. Newby (*Something to Answer*). Other winners have included Iris Murdoch (*The Sea, The Sea*), 1978; Salman Rushdie (*Midnight's Children*), 1981; Kingsley Amis, (*The Old Devils*), 1986; Ben Okri (*The Famished Road*), 1991. Worth £20,000, the B. is funded by Booker plc. In 1993 Salman Rushdie awarded the Booker of Bookers (ie prize to mark best B.P. in its 25-year history); the 1994 winner was James Kelman (*How Late It Was, How Late*), and the 1995 winner Pat Barker (*The Ghost Road*).

boomerang, probably existed in Australia by about 4800 BC.

Bophuthatswana. Self-governing 'black homeland' of S Africa from 1977–94, when it was absorbed into the S African state (12 Mar.).

Bordeaux, France. Taken by Goths, AD 412; by Clovis, 508; became subject to England in 1154 by reason of the royal marriage in 1151; surrendered to France, 14 Oct. 1453; entered by British troops, 27 Feb. 1814. Temporary seat of French Government, Sept.–Dec. 1914 and 15–30 June 1940.

Border, The, between England and Scotland, dates in its present form as to the eastern sector from 1018 when the Scots under Malcolm II recovered Lothian, and as to the western sector from the reconquest of Cumberland by the English in 1157 (*See* STRATHCLYDE). It ceased to be a political frontier in 1603. Following are some battles important in the annals of B. warfare.

Halidon Hill, 1333
Otterburn, 1388
Nisbet, 1402
Homildon, 1402

Hedgeley Moor, 1464
Flodden, 1513
Solway Moss, 1542
Ancrum Moor, 1544

Borneo, Indian Ocean. First European resident in B., Francisco Serrão (Portuguese), 1511–21. Visited by Magellan's comrades in 1522. Dutch established trading posts, 1604. Dutch B. became part of *Indonesia after World War II. The nucleus of British North B. was territory acquired in 1878 by a syndicate which transferred to the British N B. Co., chartered, 1881. *Sarawak became, 1841, the rajahship of Sir James Brooke, and his descendants; enlarged, 1861, 1882, 1884, 1890, 1904. British N B., Sarawak, and the diminished state of Brunei became British protectorates in 1888. Sarawak and British N B. annexed by British Government, 15 July 1946, to form British B., which also included Brunei and the island of Labuan. N B. (excepting *Brunei) joined the federation of *Malaysia, 1 Aug. 1963, and from then on was known as the state of Sabah.

Bornu, Kingdom of. First discovered by Europeans, 1823. Partitioned about 1900 between Nigeria and French W Africa.

borough. The Municipal Corporations Act, 1835, defined what was and what was not a municipal B., and reformed their constitutions. It was superseded by the Municipal Corporations Act, 1882, and the Local Government Acts of 1933, 1958 and 1972, the last of which abolished the B. in its historic form though it continued to have honorary status.

Borough, The. *See* SOUTHWARK.

borstal. Originally at B., near Chatham, 1902. Made a regular part of prison system, 1908, under heading of B. detention; name changed to B. training, 1948; system revised completely after 1983 (when name B. was dropped) and again in 1988, when B. replaced by Young Offenders' Institutions.

Boscobel, parish in Shropshire. Charles II hid in an oak tree there after his defeat at Worcester in 1651.

Bosnia. Incorporated with Turkey, 1463; rebellion against Turkish rule, 1849–51 and 1875; occupied by Austria, 1878, and formally annexed by her, 1908. Became part of Yugoslavia, 1918, as Bosnia-Herzegovina. *See also* HERZEGOVINA; for history after 1918, *see* BOSNIA-HERZEGOVINA.

Bosnia-Herzegovina. A national committee sat at Sarajevo from Oct. 1918, in close touch with the Yugoslav national council at Zagreb. On formation of the state of *Yugoslavia, *Bosnia and *Herzegovina, became part thereof. B.-H. became one of the federated republics of Yugoslavia, 1945. In 1990 elections nationalists (mainly Muslims) overturned communists; declared sovereignty of B.-H., 15 Oct. 1991. Referendum approved independence, 20 Feb. 1992 but this not recognized by government in Belgrade or by Bosnian Serbs. Fighting began between Serbs, Croats and Muslims in B.-H., with Serbia supporting Bosnian Serbs. B.-H. independence recognized by USA and EC, Apr. 1992. Bosnian Croats first helped Muslims, later turned against them. Serb troops made big gains and Sarajevo, under virtual siege since Apr. 1992, cut off by Dec. Serb atrocities alleged; charges of 'ethnic cleansing' and much civilian hardship. EC and UN made repeated attempts to mediate a ceasefire and lasting settlement during 1992–3. Peace talks in Geneva, New York, etc., conducted by Owen and Vance (later Stoltenberg replaced Vance) envisaged first a B.-H. divided into 10 ethnic areas, but this idea not accepted (Feb. 1993 by Muslims or US government). Airdrops on starving Bosnians cut off in remote areas begun 28 Feb. 1993 by US planes from Frankfurt. In Mar. 1993 peace talks reopened in New York: agreed by June that the original peace plan was dead and Owen asked to convene further talks in Geneva. By Aug. 1993 a plan to divide B.-H. into separate Serb, Croat and Muslim states, with Sarajevo administered by the UN: but this rejected in effect by Muslims, Sept. Fighting continued throughout 1993; Sarajevo remained surrounded but siege partially lifted by summer with UN supervising importing of food and medicine. European Union initiated new peace talks with warring Bosnian factions, Nov. 1993 but these broke off without settlement. Dec.: Serbs rejected plan to cede more territory to Muslims in return for lifting some sanctions. Further negotiations early in 1994 inconclusive, and in July Serbs again threatening Sarajevo. In Aug. 1994 Bosnian Serbs rejected latest peace plan (envisaging a division of former B. between Serbs, Muslims and Croats); during the year Bosnian Serb defiance of UN led to NATO air strikes. Bosnian Serb isolation increased when *Serbia disowned the Bosnian Serbs and enforced embargo against them; Muslim/Croat coalition won back some territory in Oct./Nov. 1994. US threatened to lift arms embargo against Muslims if no peace agreement agreed by all parties within six months, Oct. 1994. Serb attacks increased: NATO, EU and UN divided on future policy towards B.-H. Former US President Carter attempts mediation at Bosnian Serb request, Dec. 1994; reaches agreement for four-month cease-fire with both sides, but situation remained critical, 1995. Ceasefire expired at end of Apr., fighting more widespread. After NATO bombed Serbs they took UN peacekeepers hostage (including British troops): but all released by mid-June. France and Britain agreed on 'rapid reaction' force for B., June: mediator Lord Owen retired and was succeeded by Carl Bildt of Sweden. As result of Serb bombardment of Sarajevo, 22 Aug., prolonged NATO airstrikes resulted and subsequent Serb weaknesses enabled Muslims and Croats to win back substantial territory lost earlier. American- brokered cease-fire Oct., envisaged eventual peace being enforced by NATO. Bosnian peace talks in Dayton, Ohio, USA, Nov. Peace agreement initiated by Presidents of B.-H., Croatia and

Serbia 21 Nov. 1995: B.-H. to remain separate entity comprising a Muslim/Croat federation and Bosnian Serb republic

Boston, England. St Botolph founded a monastery here, 654, which was destroyed by the Danes in 870. In the Guildhall (1450) those subsequently famous as the Pilgrim Fathers were imprisoned, 1607.

Boston, Mass., USA. Founded by John Winthrop, 1630. First American newspaper, *Boston News-Letter*, Apr. 1704 (*See* NEWSPAPERS). Tea chests destroyed in B. Harbour, 16 Dec. 1773, in event known as the B. Tea Party. Many educational establishments founded in B. moved to *Cambridge in the 20thC. Subway began 1897 was first in USA.

Botanic Gardens, Royal (Kew). Established, 1759; enlarged, 1841–65. A board of trustees, set up under the National Heritage Act, 1983 to administer the Gardens, became an independent body, 1984. B.Gs were established in Italy in the 16thC (Padua and Pisa) and at Oxford in the 17thC. In Scotland, the **Royal Botanic Garden**, Edinburgh, originated in the Physic Garden, established 1670.

Botany Bay, Australia. Discovered 28 Apr. 1770, by Capt. Cook. Capt. Arthur Phillip, RN, commissioned to form penal colony here in 1787, but found locality unsuitable (Jan. 1788), and removed to site on which Sydney now stands. Transportation of convicts ceased, 1840.

Botswana, formerly **Bechuanaland,** independent republic within the Commonwealth. Ravaged by Matabele tribe, 1817. London Missionary Society established at Kuruman, 1818. Boer encroachments led to British protectorate being established, 10 Sept. 1884. Whole country under British protection, 30 Sept. 1885. S Bechuanaland added to Cape Colony, 1895, but rest of country remained a British protectorate. Caprivi Appendix, formerly part of German SW Africa, incorporated, 1922. On independence, 30 Sept. 1966, Bechuanaland was renamed Botswana.

Seretse Khama became its first President, d. 1980.

Boulder Dam on the Colorado River between Nevada and Arizona completed, 1935–6.

Boulogne, France. Sacked by the Normans, 882. Unsuccessfully besieged by Edward III, 1347. Seized by Duke of Burgundy (1419), seizure confirmed by Treaty of Arras, 1435; united to France, 1477. Treaty between Henry VIII (of England) and Francis I at B., 28 Oct. 1532. Besieged by English, 1492; taken by English, 14 Sept. 1544; restored, 1550. Napoleon I mustered his forces at B. with the intention of invading England, 1803. British defence of, 22–24 May 1940. Liberated by Canadian First Army, 19 Sept. 1944.

***Bounty* Mutiny.** HMS *Bounty* sailed in Dec. 1787 to the Society Islands on a scientific mission under command of Capt. William Bligh (1754–1817). On 28 Apr. 1789, in the Indian Ocean, the crew mutinied and put Bligh and 18 others in an open boat which he sailed to Timor, reaching that island on 9 June. The mutineers returned to Tahiti, which nine of them left in 1790 for Pitcairn Island, accompanied by Tahitian wives and some Tahitian men. *See also* PITCAIRN ISLAND. Bligh published his narrative of the mutiny and his subsequent voyage, 1792.

Bourbon, House of. First Duke of B., 1327. From this house sprang royal families of France, Naples, Parma and Spain and also the grand dukes of Luxemburg.

Bourbonnais, ancient province united to the French crown on the confiscation of the Constable of Bourbon's domains by Francis I in 1527. From 1661 to 1789 held by the house of Bourbon Condé. Became the *départmente* of Allier, 1794.

Bourges, capital, under the name of *Avaricum*, of the Gallic Biturigan territory. Avaricum was sacked by Julius Caesar, 52 BC. The cathedral was built, 1200–60, but not consecrated until 1324. Pragmatic

Sanction of B., 1437. For a period *c.* 1440 was capital of France.

Bournemouth University, since 1992, name of former Bournemouth Polytechnic.

Bouvetoya (Bouvest Island). Island in the S Atlantic, was discovered by the Frenchman Pierre Bouvet, 1739; in 1825 the British flag was hoisted. Britain waived claim to B., 1928, and it was proclaimed Norwegian territory, 27 Feb. 1930.

Bouvines. *See* BATTLES.

bovine spongiform encephalopathy (BSE), or 'mad cow disease', causing brain sponginess and madness in cattle. Warnings of outbreak in UK first given in 1970s. BSE became an epidemic from 1986. By 1995 it had killed more than 154,000 cattle in Britain, and was running at the rate of more than 800 deaths a week. In June 1994 German government threatened ban on British beef, as result of BSE fears: threat later withdrawn. Possible links between BSE and *Creutzfeld-Jakob disease in humans suggested from 1990s.

Bowling. Played in Germany and the Low Countries, and in England under the name 'skittles', since the 14thC. Taken to America in the 17thC by Dutch settlers, and played out of doors until 1840. B. alleys opened in Britain, 1959 onwards.

bowls, outdoor and indoor, has been played in England since at least 1299 and is now (1995) played in many other English-speaking countries. Word first occurs in Act of 1511. Sir Francis Drake said to have been playing B. at Plymouth when told of the approach of the Spanish Armada, 1588. Men's B. world championships held since 1966; women's, since 1969, in addition to regional and national championships.

Bow Street. Magistrates' court first sat, 1735; present court building erected 1881, replacing that of 1749, which was sacked by the Gordon rioters, 1780. The street was first built up in 1637. Covent Garden Theatre built, 1858. B.S. Runners formed the only criminal detection force in London *c.* 1750–1829, after which date their functions were taken over by the police.

Boxers. Chinese secret society founded 1896, encouraged in 1899 by the agents of the Dowager Empress to provoke antiforeign incidents. For Boxer Rising of 1900, *See* CHINA.

Boxgrove Man. Human shin bone found at Boxgrove, Sussex in May 1994, claimed to be that of oldest European yet discovered, and dated as about 500,000 years old. Human tooth of same period found, 1995.

boxing. First B. booth opened in London, 1719. Queensberry rules formulated, 1867. Became a legal sport in England, 1901. Following serious injuries and deaths of some boxers, validity of B. being questioned, notably in Britain, during 1990s. Famous world heavyweight champions in B. include:

Bruno, Frank, 1961–
Carnera, Primo, 1906–67
Dempsey, Jack, 1895–1983
Louis, Joe, 1914–81
Marciano, Rocky, 1923–69
Mohammed Ali (Cassius Clay) 1942–
Tunney, Gene, 1898–1978
Tyson, Mike, 1966–

Boxing Day. Officially recognized as a Bank Holiday in England and Wales, 1874.

boycott. Term derived from Capt. Charles B. (1832–97), land agent to Lord Erne in Co. Mayo, Ireland, who was the victim of a B. in 1880, organized by the *Land League in retaliation for certain evictions.

Boyles' Law. Formulated, 1662, by Robert Boyle (1627–91).

Boys' Brigade. Founded, 1883, by Sir W. Smith (*d.* 1914). Amalgamated with Boys' Life Brigade, 1926. There is a girls' equivalent organization, founded 1893. Proposal to merge boys' and girls' sections, 1995.

Boys' Clubs, National Association of. Founded, 1925.

Boys' Club of America. Founded, 1906.

Boy Scouts. Organization began in 1908 in the UK. Adopted by Chile, 1909, the USA, France and Scandinavia, 1910, and ultimately over one hundred other countries. First World Jamboree, 1920. First Chief Scout, the founder, Sir Robert Baden-Powell (who became Baron Baden-Powell of Gilwell in 1929), was *b.* 1857 and *d.* 1941. Movement prohibited in Nazi Germany, 1933, and in territories subsequently occupied by Germany. Restarted there after 1945 but not in territories controlled by Communist regimes until the collapse of the Soviet system in the late 1980s. Hungary and Czechoslovakia admitted to Scout World Organization, July 1990; scouting growing in former Soviet Union territories from 1991. Scout promise last revised, 1967. Supplemental Charter, 19 July, 1991, enabled girls to join the Scout movement provided certain requirements were met.

Brabant, Low Countries. Duchy, 1190, passed through the house of Burgundy to Philip II of Spain. At the division of the Spanish Netherlands, 1579, N B. became part of the United Provinces and was recognized as belonging to them at the *Treaty of Westphalia, 1648. This is the modern Dutch province of N B. S B. remained Spanish till 1714, when it was transferred to Austria. When Belgium was annexed by France at Treaty of Campo Formio, 1797, S B. was further divided into what are now the Belgian provinces of B. and Antwerp.

Bradford, England, existed during the reign of Edward the Confessor. Besieged in 1642 and 1643 by royalist forces. First woollen weaving mill opened, 1798 but wool and cloth-making industry in decline from 1970s. Incorporated, 1847; became city, 1897. University established 1966. Considerable Jewish immigration, 19thC; Asian immigration, 20thC. Fire at B. football stadium, May 1985, with over 50 fatalities. Racial riots in B., June 1995.

Braganza. Family descended from Alfonso (*d.* 1461), son of King John I (1357–1433), who was made Duke of B., 1442. The family ruled *Portugal, 1640–1910, and *Brazil, 1822–89. Catherine of B. (1638–1705) married King Charles II in 1662.

Braille, reading system for the blind, invented by Louis B. (1809–52), in 1829.

Brandenburg. Frederick of Hohenzollern became margrave of, 1415. Neumark acquired, 1455. Kottbus, 1462. Züllichen, 1482. Zossen, 1490. Reversion of Prussia secured by agreement, 1569. Ravensberg, Mark and Wesel acquired, 1614. Prussia acquired, 1618. E Pomerania, 1648–79, from Sweden. Elector of B. takes title of King in Prussia, 1701. Henceforth known as *Prussia, except for a district, corresponding to the Altmark, which became in 1949 a province of the German Democratic Republic. On 14 Oct. 1990, upon the reunification of Germany, B. was reconstituted as a *Land* of the German Federal Republic.

Electors of B., 1415–1701:
Frederick I 1415–40
Frederick II the Iron 1440–70
Albert Achilles 1470–86
John Cicero 1486–99
Joachim I 1499–1535
Joachim II 1535–71
John George 1571–98
Joachim Frederick III 1598–1608
John Sigismund 1608–19
George William 1619–40
Frederick William, 'The Great Elector' 1640–88
Frederick III 1688–1713
(From 1701, Frederick I, King of Prussia.)

See further under PRUSSIA, KINGS OF.

branding, was abolished for civilians in England and Wales, 1822; in France, 1832. In 1858 the British Mutiny Act ordered deserters to be branded below the left armpit; this Act was repealed in 1879. Concentration camp prisoners in Nazi Germany were branded 1936–45.

Brasilia, capital of *Brazil. Inaugurated, 21 Apr. 1960.

Bratislava (Hungarian **Pozsony;** German **Pressburg**). Founded *c.* AD 1000. Became capital of 'imperial' Hungary after capture of Buda by Turks, 1541 until 1784. The Hungarian kings were crowned in the cathedral of St. Martin, 1526–1916, and the Hungarian Parliament met in the Landhaus down to 1848. Incorporated in Czechoslavakia, 1918. Capital of 'independent' Slovakia, 1939–44; capital of the Slovak Republic since 1 Jan. 1993.

brawling in church was punishable under statutes of Edward VI, which replaced the pre-Reformation canon laws on the offence. The B. Act of 1860 applies to places of worship of all denominations; hitherto only the Anglican churches had been so protected since the Reformation.

Brazil. Treaty of Tordesilhas, drawing a dividing line between Spanish and Portuguese colonial interest, giving the southern American continent to Portugal, 1494. Pedro Alvares Cabral landed on the coast of B., 22 Apr. 1500, and formally took possession of the country for the crown of Portugal. Treaty of Tordesilhas ratified, 1506. Martin Alfonso de Souza arrived at Pernambuco, 30 Jan. 1530. Appointed first governor-general, 1531. Colonization started effectively. Traffic in African slaves begun, 1532. Foundation of the city of Bahia, which becomes capital of B., 1549. São Paulo founded, 1554. Rio de Janeiro founded 1567 after driving the French back from their foothold. B. partitioned, ruled by two governors from Bahia and Rio de Janeiro, 1572–81. Spanish domination 1581–1640. Dutch try to colonize parts of B., 1630–61. Portuguese rebellion and Dutch naval victory over the Spaniards at Itamarca result in re-establishment of Portuguese rule, 1640. Dutch expelled during Anglo-Dutch wars of the English Commonwealth, 1654. Gold found in Minas Gerais, 1699. Coffee plant brought to B., 1727. Progress of commercial cultivation only about 100 years later. Bandeirantes found diamonds in Minas Gerais, 1730.

The colony became state of viceroyalty. Rio de Janeiro became capital, 1763. Napoleon's invasion of Portugal results in D. João VI moving to B., with the Portuguese royal family, 1808. B. declared kingdom, 1815. D. João VI, returning to Portugal, leaves the regentship to his son, D. Pedro, 1821. D. Pedro declared independence of B. and crowned as first Emperor of B, 7 Sept. 1822. First constitution, 1824. D. Pedro I was forced to abdicate in favour of his five-year-old son, 7 Apr. 1831. Slave trade abolished, 1850. War against Argentina, 1851. War against Paraguay, 1865–70. Complete abolition of slavery, 1888. Proclamation of republic, 15 Nov. 1889. Civil war, 1893–4. Begins great industrial revolution, especially in São Paulo, 1920. Civil war, 1930. New constitution: Vargas was elected president and ruled for 15 years on steadily increasing totalitarian principles, 24 Oct. 1930. Military revolution dismissed Vargas, 30 Oct. 1945, but he returned to power, 1951, and *d.* 1954. Period of economic expansion in 1970s ended, in the early 1980s, with heavy international debts. Return to civilian democracy, 1985. 1989: programme to safeguard environment of the Amazon: but deforestation continued. International banks agreed to restructure B.'s debts, 1992: in June 1992. B. was venue for ecological Earth Summit. In same year President Collor de Mello impeached for corruption and resigned: succeeded by Vice-President Itamar Franco. Referendum approved continuation of presidential government, Apr. 1993. Election in Oct. 1994 was won by Cardoso. Collor de Mello cleared of charges, Dec. 1994.

Presidents of the Republic:
Marshal Manuel Deodoro da Fonseca 1890–91
Marshal Floriano Peixoto 1891–94
Dr Prudente José de Moraes Barros 1894–98
Dr Manuel Ferraz de Campos Salles 1898–1902
Dr Francisco da Paula Rodrigues Alves 1902–06

Dr Alfonso Augusto Moreira Penna 1906–09

Dr Nilo Peçanha 1909–10

Marshal Hermes Rodrigues da Fonseca 1910–14

Dr Wenceslau Braz Pereira Gomes 1914–18

Dr Francisco da Paula Rodrigues Alves 1918

Dr Delfim Moreira da Costa Ribeiro 1918–19

Dr Epitácio da Silva Pessoa 1919–22

Dr Arturo da Silva Bernardes 1922–26

Dr Washington Luiz Pereira de Souza 1926–30

Dr Getúlio Dornelles Vargas 1930–45

Dr José Linhares 1945–46

Gen. Eurico Gaspar Dutra 1946–51

Dr Getúlio Dornelles Vargas 1951–54

Carlos Coimbra de Luz (3 days) 1955

Nereu Ramos, 1955–56

Juscelino Kubitscheck 1956–61

Dr Janio Quadros (6 months) 1961

Dr João Goulart 1961–64

Gen. Castelo Branco 1964–66

Marshal Costa e Silva 1967–69

Garrastazu Medici 1969–74

Ernesto Geisel 1974–79

Baptista de Oliveiro Figueiredo 1979–85

Tancredo Neves 1985.

José Sarney 1985–90

Collor de Mello 1990–92

Itamar Franco 1992–94

Cardoso 1995–

Brazzaville, cap. of Congo. Founded by the French explorer, Count P. P. F. C. S. de Brazza (1852–1905) in 1886.

breathalyzer. Instrument used for measuring alcohol in the human system in UK since 1967.

Breda, Holland. Captured from Spaniards by Prince Maurice of Nassau, 1590; retaken by Spaniards, 1625; by Dutch, Oct. 1637. Compromise of B., 1566. Charles II's Declaration from B., 1660. Peace of B., 1667. Taken by French, 1794; French expelled, 1813.

Brehon Laws. Ancient laws of Ireland, going back to the 3rdC (reign of Cormac MacArt), and prevailing until the middle of the 17thC century. Penalties against submitting to, 1366.

Bremen, Germany.
1. City. Principal member of *Hanseatic League, 14thC. Free city, 1646. Taken by Denmark, 1712. Sold to Hanover, 1715. Independence recognized by George II, 1730. Taken by French, 1757. Restored 1758. Annexed by Napoleon, 1810. Independence restored, 1813. Joined German Empire, 1871. Heavily bombed in World War II and fell to the British Second Army, 23–8 Apr. 1945.
2. Archbishopric. Became an ecclesiastical principality early in the 13thC. Secularized and acquired by Sweden, 1648. Territory taken by Denmark, 1712, and sold to Hanover, 1715.
3. Verden from 1405 to 1550 was a free city of the empire, on the River Aller some 23 miles SE of B. At the Peace of Westphalia (1648) it became Swedish; until 1715 it had the same history as B. Purchase confirmed by Treaty of Stockholm, negotiated by George I of England, 1719.

Brenner Pass first traversed by a carriageway, 1772, and by railway, 1864–7. Motorway completed after World War II.

Breslau, *See* WROCLAW.

Brest, France. Founded, 1240; in English hands, 1342–97. Last attacked from the sea by English, 1694. The *Scharnhorst*, *Gneisenau*, and *Prinz Eugen* in the docks attracted RAF bombing, 1941–2. German garrison surrendered, 19 Sept. 1944, after six-week siege. Largely rebuilt after 1944.

Brest-Litovsk (Russian or Polish **Brzesc Nad Bugiem**). A fortress town since 1017; became Lithuanian, 1319; Polish, 1569; Russian, 1795; Polish 1918. Has been Russian since Sept. 1939, except for German military occupation during World War II. At a synod held here, 1594, the Uniate Church of Ruthenia was brought to the Roman obedience. In 1831 the old town was demolished by the Russians and a fortress built on the site. The Russian and

German armies made contact here after the Polish campaign of 1939, 18 Sept.

Brest-Litovsk, Treaty. Imposed on Russia by Germany, 3 Mar. 1918.

Brethren, Church of the. *See* GERMAN BAPTISTS.

Brethren of the Common Lot or **Life.** The name given to a brotherhood founded in the Low Countries by Gerard Groote of Deventer, *c.* 1380. Erasmus was at one of the their schools in 'S Hertogenbosch *c.* 1483. They began to decline in the 16thC, and died out in the 17th.

Brétigny, Peace of, 8 May 1360. *See* HUNDRED YEARS WAR.

Bretton Woods Agreement. An international monetary and financial conference at B.W., begun 1 July 1944, and signed its Final Act, 22 July. This was ratified first by the US Congress in 1945.

bribery of voters in the UK first punishable under the Corrupt Practices Act, 1854. Later dealt with under the Representation of the People Act, 1949.

Bridewell (London). Saxon palace on site of a Roman fort. Rebuilt by Henry I. King John held council, 1210. Wolsey rebuilt palace, 1522. Edward VI granted manorhouse and palace of B. to the city of London as a house of correction for vagrants, 1552. Destroyed in Fire of London, 1666. Women's prison built after 1666. Pulled down, 1864.

bridge, card game which evolved from *whist. Known in England by 1886. *Pocket Guide to Bridge* published, 1895. Auction B., 1904; Contract B., 1925.

Bridgewater Canal. Begun, 1755. Opened, 17 July 1761.

Brighton, England. Originally Brighthelmstone. Pavilion begun, 1784, by Prince of Wales (later George IV) and finished, 1827. W Pier built, 1866. Palace Pier, 1900. University of Sussex opened at, Oct., 1961. IRA bomb at B. hotel failed to wipe out British Cabinet, 12 Oct. 1984. B.

Polytechnic became B. University, 1992.

Brindisi, Italy. Ancient Greek colony founded 5thC BC. Taken from the Sallentini by the Romans, 267 BC. Cathedral founded, 1089. Base of Italian fleet in 1866 and of the Otranto Barrage in World War I. Seat of Badoglio's pro-Allied government, Sept. 1943.

Brisbane, Australia. First occupied as penal settlement by Thomas B., 1824. Became capital of Queensland, 1859.

Bristol, England. Importance as a town began *c.* 1000. Came by marriage into possession of Earl of Gloucester, 1119. Cathedral founded, 1148. First charter, 1171. Recognized as a staple town, 1353. Church of St Mary Redcliffe built *c.* end of the 14thC. Brothers Cabot sailed for N America from, 1497. Slave trade *fl.* 1580–1640. Taken by Prince Rupert, 1643; by Fairfax, 1645. Attempt to fire shipping in harbour, 1777. Modern harbour constructed, 1809. Half city burnt in rioting, 1831. Clifton suspension bridge begun, 1836. University College founded, 1876. University established, 1909; HQ of *Avon since 1974. Bristol Polytechnic became University of the West of England at Bristol, 1992.

Britain. Invaded by Julius Caesar, 55 and 54 BC, Cunobelin, King of the Catuvellauni *c.* AD 5. Invaded and conquered by Romans under Aulus Plautius, AD 43–7. Caractacus defeated by Ostorius and deported to Rome, 50. Romans massacred by Boudicca, 60. Boudicca defeated, 61. Christianity said to have been taught, 64. Agricola reforms government and defeats the Picts, 78–85. Hadrian's Wall begun *c.* 122. Antonine Wall built by Lollius Urbicus, 142, on site of Agricola's field fortifications. Hadrian's Wall strengthened by Severus, 208. Constantine proclaimed emperor at York, 25 July 306. Saxon raids on coastal areas, from beginning of 3rdC onwards. British bishops attend Council of Arles, 314. War with Picts and Scots, 360; invasion of southern B., 367. Driven out, 368. Romans finally quit

B. some time shortly before 429, and abandon responsibility for the defence, 446. Anglo-Saxon invasions begin on a large scale c. 449. See ENGLAND.

Britain, Battle of. Name for the air attack on B. by day, 8 Aug.–29 Oct. 1940, intended to be the first stage of a series of operations culminating in *Operation Sealion, which would have been the seaborne invasion of southeast England. In the phase 8–18 Aug. the Luftwaffe attacked shipping, ports and later fighter airfields between Harwich and the Isle of Wight. 13 Aug. – 'Eagle Day' in the German planning timetable – was the date by which it was hoped that all RAF fighter stations would be out of action. In the second phase up to 5 Sept. similar objectives farther west and north along the coast and farther inland to the northwest were attacked by formations relatively stronger in fighters and weaker in bombers. A mass daylight attack on London (7 Sept.) by 350 bombers began the third phase: until 5 Oct. there were 37 more day attacks on London, besides diversionary attacks on other southeastern targets. The last phase consisted of night attacks on London by fighters and fighter-bombers and lasted until the end of Oct.

Britannia. Naval training ship for officer cadets, 1859–1903. The Royal Naval College, Dartmouth, became officially HMS B. in 1921. Royal yacht B. (4,000 tons) built to replace the Victoria and Albert, and completed in Jan. 1954. Future in doubt, 1995, and possible privatization envisaged. Due to be decommissioned, 1997.

British Academy. Incorporated 18 Aug. 1902, after foundation in 1901 to promote study of the moral and political sciences.

British Antarctic Territory, established 3 Mar. 1962 as consequence of coming into force of the Antarctic Treaty. B.A.T. consists of area south of latitude 60°S, previously included in Falklands Islands Dependencies.

British Association for the Advancement of Science. Established, 1831. Kew Observatory presented to, by Queen Victoria, 1842.

British Broadcasting Corporation (BBC). Succeeded B.B.Co., which was formed, 1922, and established, on national footing, 1923; Chelmsford long-wave station opened, 1924. B.B.Co's charter expired, 31 Dec. 1926. Daventry stations opened, 1925 and 1927; Chelmsford (short-wave), 1927. Chartered Corporation, 1927. Droitwich took over long-wave from Daventry, 1934. Television from Alexandra Palace, 1936. Foreign broadcasts commenced, 1937. Television service reopened, June 1946. Television monopoly broken with introduction of first commercial channel, 1954; radio monopoly similarly broken in early 1970s. First colour television in Europe started on B.B.C. 2, 1 July 1967. Launch of Radio 5, 1990. Licence fee collection became responsibility of the BBC, and not the Post Office, 1 Apr. 1991. B.B.C.'s contribution and finances governed by royal charter which was due to expire Dec. 1996, but, in 1994, was further extended to 2006.

British Columbia, western Canada. Discovered by Perez, 1774; visited by Cook, 1778. Made a British colony, Aug. 1858. Vancouver Island incorporated with, 1866. Annexed to Canada, 1871.

British Council. Established, Nov. 1934, and inaugural meeting held, 2 July 1935; Charter granted, 1940.

British Guiana. See GUYANA.

British Honduras. See BELIZE.

British Indian Ocean Territory. Purchased from Mauritius, 1965, for joint UK/US base. Some outlying islands returned to Seychelles, 1976.

British Industries Fair first held, 1915. Moved to Olympia, 1930. Closed, 1956.

British Legion. Originally the name of numerous now forgotten military organizations in the service of foreign powers or revolutionary movements (e.g. in the Spanish American wars of Liberation c. 1810–25), but now usually referring to the combined ex-service organization which was formed 1 July 1921. Royal charter, Apr. 1925. Now the Royal B.L.

British Library, established July 1973 under the British Library Act, 1972. Its reference section embraces the former library departments of the *British Museum including the Newspaper Library at Colindale, the India Office Library and Records and the Science Reference Library. The Lending Division is made up of the former National Central Library and the former National Lending Library for Science and Technology. The former Copyright Receipt Office and British National Bibliography Ltd comprise the Bibliographic Service Division. The B.L. is also responsible for the National Sound Archive and HMSO Binderies. In 1995 its collection included over 18 million books, 60,000 hours of tape recordings and one million discs, kept at 18 buildings in London and at one major complex in W Yorkshire. The B.L.'s new premises at St Pancras, London due to open to the public, 1996. HQ of the B.L. is at 2 Sheraton St., W1.

British Medical Association (BMA). Founded 1832; took its present name in 1856.

British Museum. Grant made by Parliament, 5 Apr. 1753. Old Royal Library presented to, 1757. Building opened, 1 Jan. 1759. New buildings erected, 1823–47. Elgin Marbles acquired, 1816; Grenville Library, 1847. Reading-room opened, 18 May 1857; Natural history collection removed to S Kensington, 1881. Foundation-stone of extension laid by Edward VII, 2 June 1907; the extension opened, 1914. £100 million development plan for B.M. announced, 1994, to mark its 250th anniversary in 2003. British Museum Act, 1963, separated the Natural History Museum from the British Museum. *British Library established July 1973 under British Library Act, 1972. *See also* LIBRARIES and COTTONIAN LIBRARY.

British Standard Time, operated 1968–71. Abolished due to public outcry.

British Standards Institution. Founded as the Engineering Standards Committee, 1901; royal charter and present title, 1929.

British Telecom, public corporation established under the Telecommunication Act, 1981, to operate the telecommunications network formerly controlled by the *Post Office. Privatized by Conservative government, 1984.

British Tourist Authority, established 1969, under the Development of Tourism Act, to promote tourism from overseas.

British Union of Fascists. *See* FASCISM (2).

Brittany. Conquered by Julius Caesar, 57–6 BC and called *Armorica* by the Romans. Large influx of Celts from Britain to B. in the 5th and 6thC. Independent duchy *c.* 1000. Under Norman suzerainty, 1066. Bestowed as a duchy by Henry II on his brother Geoffrey, 1159. Succession disputed, 1161, 1171, 1186, 1343. By marriage of Charles VIII of France and Anne of Brittany, 1491, united under crown of France. Finally and irrevocably incorporated into France, 1532.

Brixham, England, scene of William of Orange's landing, 1688.

Broad Bottom Administration. Formed out of a coalition, 24 Nov. 1744. Dissolved by death of the Premier Henry Pelham, 6 Mar. 1754.

Broadcasting Standards Council. Instituted, 1988; given statutory authority under the Broadcasting Act, 1990. The B.S.C. publishes codes of practice, monitors programme standards, etc.

Broadmoor Institution. State institution for the criminally insane, in Berkshire. Opened, 1863.

Broads Authority. Established 1988 under the Norfolk and Suffolk Broads Act, with responsibilities similar to those of the National Parks authorities; HQ, Norwich.

Brooklyn, New York, USA. Settled (as Breuckelen) by Dutch, 1636. Incorporated as a city, 1834. Bridge to New York City opened, 24 May 1883. Borough of New York since 1898.

Bronx, the. One of the five New York original boroughs. The Indians called it **Keskeskeck** and sold it to the Dutch, 1639. In 1641 Jonas Bronck bought 500 acres, hence the name B. Part of Westchester Co. till 1898 when incorporated into New York.

brucellosis. Cattle disease which can be transmitted to humans, discovered by David Bruce (1855–1931).

Bruges (French) or **Brugge** (Flemish), Belgium. Capital of Flanders till 1180. Town hall begun, 1376. Belfry, end of 13thC. Order of the Golden Fleece instituted here, 1430. Ceased to be an important port after final silting up of the River Zwyn, 1490. Market hall built, 1561–6. Docks and canal built, 1885–95. Greatly extended, 1930–9 and since 1945.

Brumaire, Coup d'État of. On 18 B. of the year VIII (9 Nov. 1799) Napoleon abolished the *Directory. See FRANCE.

Brunei, northwest Borneo. Treaty between Britain and Sultan of B., 1847. British protectorate, 1888. Declined to become part of Malaysia, 1962–3. Became fully independent of Britain, 1 Jan. 1984.

Brunel University, Uxbridge, established 1966.

Brunswick (German **Braunschweig**), a fragment of the old tribal duchy of Saxony, which in the 10thC was the fief of one Bruno from whom the name derives. When in 1181 Saxony was dismembered Duke Henry the Lion was allowed to keep that part which he had personally inherited; in 1267 the territory was divided into separate duchies of B.-Lüneburg and B.-Wolfenbüttel under two branches of the house of Guelf. Alternate reunification and repartition took place down to 1735, the most significant partition being that of 1596, which led to the rise of the ducal house of Lüneburg-Celle, from which the electoral house of *Hanover derived. The duchy was merged in the kingdom of Westphalia, 1806–14. The ducal house ab-

dicated, 1918, and the territory constituted a free state under the Weimar Republic (1919–33). The Third Reich (1933–45) reduced B. to an administrative province. Since 1945 part of the Lower Saxon *Land.*

Brussels, Belgium. Mentioned in 8thC as *Bruchsella.* Church of Sainte-Gudule completed, 1273. Town Hall, 1402–54. Capital of Low Countries, 1507. Alva's rule, 1567. Union of B., 1578. Mannekin-Pis Fountain, 1619. Bombarded by Villeroi, Aug. 1656. Taken by French, 1701; by Duke of Marlborough, 1706; by Saxe, 1746; by Dumouriez, 1802. Capital of Belgium, 1830. University founded, 1834. King's House rebuilt, 1873–95. Germans occupied city from Aug. 1914 to Nov. 1918. Again occupied by Germans, 17 May 1940. Liberated, 3 Sept. 1944. Serious rioting in B. during the crisis over the monarchy, 1950. NATO HQ since 1967 and HQ of EEC Commission (later EC then EU) since 1958. Riot in Heysel stadium, 1985, between Liverpool and Juventus football fans: over 50 deaths. New European Parliament building opened, Sept. 1993.

Brussels, Treaty of, signed 17 Mar. 1948, an instrument of the *Western Union policy. Signatories were Great Britain, France, Belgium, Holland, Luxemburg. Federal Germany and Italy acceded to the Treaty, 1954.

BSE. *See* BOVINE SPONGIFORM ENCEPHALOPATHY.

Bubastis (Arabic **Tel Basta**), city of Lower Egypt, famous for its temple of Pasht or Basht, the cat (originally lioness) goddess, the ruins of which were excavated in 1887, the city having been in ruins since shortly after its capture by the Persians, 352 BC.

bubonic plague. According to the World Health Organization, reappearing in Asia and Africa during 1990s. *See* BLACK DEATH.

Buccaneers. 16thC associations of piratical adventurers, chiefly French and English. In 1630 they captured Tortuga and used it as a stronghold. In 1655 they helped the Commonwealth Navy to capture Jamaica. In 1685 they defied the Spanish fleet in the Bay of Panama. Their last great achievement was the capture of Cartagena, 1697.

Buchan's Predictions. Meteorological forecasts of periodic cold snaps by Alexander Buchan (1829–1907), made in 1869.

Bucharest (Bucuresti), Romania. Became capital, 1859. Held by Germans, Dec. 1916–Nov. 1918. Treaty between Romania and Central Powers, 7 May 1918, nullified, 11 Nov. 1918. Metro built, 1979. During anti-Communist revolution of 1989, fierce fighting in B.

Buchenwald, near Weimar. Site of a notorious German concentration camp, opened in 1934. Liberated by the Americans, 11 Apr. 1945.

Buckingham Palace. Built, 1703. Property of Queen Charlotte, 1761. New building occupied by Queen Victoria, 13 July 1837, after extensive alterations, started in 1825, had been completed. New façade, 1913. Art gallery opened to the public, 25 July 1962. Palace itself opened to the public for two summer months annually from 1993, initially for five years. Profits to go towards paying for repairs after fire at *Windsor Castle.

Buckingham University, founded as the University College at Buckingham, 1973, independent of government assistance. Chartered, 1983.

Budapest, Hungary. Buda, capital of Hungary, 1320–1526. Captured by Turks, 1541. Recovered, 1686. Palaces built, 1770. University, 1784. Buda and Pest united as one city, 1872. Occupied by Rumanians, Aug.–Nov. 1919. Prolonged fighting between Russian and German troops in 1944–5; finally captured by the Russians, 13 Feb. 1945. The city was largely rebuilt after World War II, but again suffered heavy damage during the abortive revolt of Oct.–Nov. 1956.

Buddhism. The Buddha, or Gautama Siddhartha, *c.* 563–480 BC.

Budget. The, statement of the Chancellor of the Exchequer's financial proposals and tax changes, usually made annually, occasionally bi-annually. Term first used in a pamphlet, 1733, *The Budget Opened.* Word derives from French *bouge,* meaning small bag. Most Bs. announced in Mar. up to 1993: thereafter in the autumn, starting 30 Nov. 1993.

Buenos Aires. Capital of Argentina. City founded, 1535; refounded, 1580. Taken by British, 27 June 1806; retaken by Spaniards, 12 Aug.; British attack repulsed, 5 July 1807. Independent state, Oct. 1853; reunited to Argentina, Nov. 1859.

Buffalo, New York. Founded, 1803 as New Amsterdam; got its present name, 1810. Burned by British, 1813. President McKinley assassinated at, 5 Sept. 1901.

Buganda, *Uganda. British officials became the Kabaka's accepted advisers, 1890. Kabaka exiled by British Government on grounds of non-cooperation, 1953–5. In 1963 the Kabaka, Mutesa II, became President of Uganda: he was deposed by the Ugandan premier (1966), who took over his office. The Kabaka fled to Britain, where he *d.* in 1969. His son, Ronald Mutebi, crowned Kabaka, 24 July 1993.

building societies. Earliest recorded B.S. founded Birmingham *c.* 1780. Free to take on certain banking functions and even become banks, 1986. So far (1995) this only done by Abbey National, in 1989; but restrictions on B.S. banking activities lifted further, July 1994. Halifax B.S. wins approval to merge with the Leeds B.S. Mar. 1995: merged Society will become a bank, 1996/7.

Bukovina, originally part of historic Moldavia, inhabited principally by Slavs of the Ruthenian (Ukrainian) linguistic division, was under Turkish sovereignty from 1512 until its occupation by the Russians in 1769, but was taken from them by the Austrians, 1774, to whom it was ceded by Turkey, 1775, becoming part of Galicia until 1849, when it was separated and made a crown land of the Hungarian kingdom. Granted autonomy, 1861. Sèvres treaty of 1920 recognized all B. as Romanian territory. Northern B., together with Bessarabia, was ceded to the USSR to comply with an ultimatum of 27 June 1940, but was again Romanian from 1941 to 1944. It was finally ceded to Russia under the peace treaty of 1947 and since 1991 forms part of the republic of the Ukraine.

Bulgaria. For early history *see* BULGARS. Treaty of Berlin set up the principality of B. and the autonomous province of Eastern Rumelia, 13 July 1878. Prince Alexander of Battenburg elected ruler, 1879; after his abdication, Prince Ferdinand of Saxe-Coburg elected, 7 July 1887. Independence proclaimed, 22 Sept. 1908, and the prince took title of Tsar. B. entered World War I on German side, Oct. 1915, and surrendered to the Allies unconditionally, Oct. 1918. Tsar abdicated, 3 Oct. 1918, in favour of his son, Boris III. By Treaty of Neuilly, 1919, B. ceded territory to Greece, Romania, and Yugoslavia. Military *coup d'état*, 1934; from 1935 Boris ruled as virtual dictator. Treaty of Craiova, 8 Sept. 1940, ceded S Dobrudja to B., thus restoring the frontier of 1912. German troops entered B., Mar. 1941. B. invaded Yugoslavia and Greece, Apr. 1941, and occupied Thrace and Macedonia until 26 Aug. 1944. The peace treaty with the Allies was signed at Paris, 10 Feb. 1947, and a separate treaty with Yugoslavia, 27 Nov. Communist republic 1946–89 when Communist leader Zhivkov resigned and was imprisoned. In 1990 elections returned former Communists to power but government brought down by public protest. New constitution, July 1991; elections Oct. 1991, won by non-Communists who formed a government. Improved relations with western Europe since 1991; Socialists (mainly former Communists) won elections, Dec. 1994 as economic problems menaced but pledged to continue democratic and free-market policies.

Rulers of B., 1879–1946:
Alexander (Prince) 1879–86

Ferdinand (King 1908) 1887–1918
Boris III 1918–43
Simeon II 1943–46

Bulgars, originally a Ural-Altaic people from Central Asia, occupied the space between the Urals and the Volga in the 4thC AD. After splitting (433) into two main groups, one of them formed a strong state on the northern shore of the Black Sea which was destroyed about 560 by the Avars. The other branch, after a period of subjection, first to the Avars and then to the Turks, recovered its independence, 582, and founded a state on the Volga known as Great Bulgaria (Volgaria), which persisted into the 13thC. A faction split off from this state, under pressure from the Khazars, migrated westwards, and crossed the Danube, 679, into Moesia, where they conquered the local population compounded of Illyrians and more recent Slavonic immigrants. The Slavonic immigration into Moesia, which became the country now known as Bulgaria, was still in progress, and the Slavonic language was adopted by the B., who soon lost all memory of their original non-Aryan tongue. In 811 the Bulgar Khan Krum defeated and slew the Emperor Nicephorus. The Khan Boris (857–88) adopted Orthodox Christianity in 870. After a period of maximum expansion and power under Simeon (893–927) Tsar Samuel was defeated by the Emperor Basil II Bulgaroktonos – 'the slayer of B.' – in 1014. The whole Bulgar territory was subject to the empire from 1018 until 1186, when the northern part became independent under the Asen dynasty, who in the reign of Ivan II (*c.* 1230) ruled the Balkan peninsula as far west as Albania and Epirus. The dynasty died out, 1280, and the B., weakened by internal dissension and Mongol invasions, were defeated and subjected to Serbian rule, 28 July 1330, at the battle of Kustendil; this lasted until 1356, but only 40 years of Bulgar independence remained before conquest by the Turks and the end of the first Bulgarian kingdom in 1396. The B. remained under Turkish rule until 1878; the 'Bulgarian atrocities' of 1876 led to Russia declaring war on Turkey (1877), and this paved the way for Bulgarian independence. *See further under* BULGARIA.

The following is a list of medieval Bulgar rulers:

Khans:
Krum *c*. 802–14
Omurtag 814–*c*. 30
Malomir (Presiam) *c*. 830–52

Princes:
Boris I (Saint) 852–88
Vladimir 888–93

Tsars:
Simeon I, the Great 893–927
Peter 927–69
Boris II 969–71
Samuel *c*. 971–1014
Gabriel Roman 1014–15
Ivan Vladislav 1015–18

Bulgaria subject to Byzantium 1018–1186
Ivan Asen I 1185–94
Peter Asen 1185–95
Kalojan Asen 1195–1207
Boril 1207–18
Ivan Asen II 1218–41
Kaliman I 1241–46
Michael Asen 1246–54
Kaliman II 1254–57
Constantine Asen 1257–78
Ivail 1278–79
Ivan Asen III 1279–80
George Terteri I 1280–82
Smilec 1282
Choki 1282
Theodore Svetslav 1282–1322
George Terteri II 1322
Michael 1322–30
Ivan Istvan 1330
Ivan Alexander 1330–65
Ivan Sracimir 1365
Ivan Sisman 1365–95

bull-baiting made illegal in Britain, 1835.

bullfighting. Probably originated from fertility rites in ancient Minoan civilization. A form of B. brought to Spain by invading Moors from 9thC, but modern B. dates from 18thC Spain, where first permanent modern bull-ring built. Spread with modifications to Portugal, France and Mexico.

Bull Moose. Name of a third party formed in 1912 by the supporters of Theodore Roosevelt, in the USA. It ceased to exist, 1916, when Roosevelt declined to stand for it again.

Bundesbank, Deutsche (German Federal Bank). In 1948 the *Bank deutscher Länder* established at Frankfurt as the central bank of the German Federal Republic. Aug. 1957 this merged with the Berlin central bank to form the B. (Since German reunification in 1991 the former central bank of the German Democratic Republic has become a commercial bank, while its credit arm has been acquired by Deutsche Bank and Dresdner Bank.) The B. is independent of the government but its Governor is appointed by the government for an eight-year term. Governor in 1994: Hans Tietmeyer. The B's principal task is to defend the stability of the country's currency. From the 1970s the B. emerged as the dominant western European financial force.

Bundesrat, Federal Council:
1. The supreme executive of the Swiss confederation, seven men elected for four years by the *Bundesversammlung. The vice-president of this body is a first magistrate co-equal with the President of the Confederation, according to the constitution of 1874, modifying that of 1848.
2. Body corresponding to the Privy Council or Cabinet of the N German League, 1866–71, and the Hohenzollern 'Second Reich', 1871–1918.
3. In Austria, a second chamber of provincial representatives, under the federal constitution of 1929; readopted, 1945.
4. Upper house, Federal German Republic, 1949, which, since reunification in

1990, includes representatives from the whole of Germany.

Bundestag, German for Federal Diet was the name (1) of an assembly of representatives of the German League (*Deutscher Bund*), 1815–66 (not a legislative body, more like a Council Ambassadors); (2) or lower house of the Federal German Republic Parliament from 1949, which since German unification in 1990, includes representatives from the whole of Germany.

Bundesversammlung. German for Federal Assembly, name given to the two legislative houses of the Swiss Confederation, the *Ständerat* and the *Nationalrat*, when sitting jointly, under the constitution of 1874.

Bunhill Fields (London). Used by Dissenters. Burying ground first used, 1665; John Bunyan buried, 1688; Defoe, 1731; Susannah Wesley, 1742; Issac Watts, 1748; William Blake, 1827. Opened as a public garden, 1869.

Bunsen burner, invented by R. W. von Bunsen (1811–99) at Heidelberg, 1855.

Buonaparte. *See* BONAPARTE, HOUSE OF.

Burgos, Spain. Burial place of the Cid, *d.* 1099. Cathedral begun, 1221. Attacked by the Duke of Wellington, 18–19 Sept. 1812; another attempt failed, 18 Oct.; French blew up castle and retired, 12 June 1813. Franco's headquarters, 1936–9.

Burgundy, France. Burgundians, Germanic tribe arrived in SE Gaul *c.* 411. Region around Worms-Mainz became known as B., but the centre of gravity of Burgundian kingdom shifted to Rhône valley, 475. Conquered by Franks, 534. After death of Charlemagne partitioned between France and Lotharingia by Treaty of Verdun, 843. There then arose (1) a *kingdom* of B. (888–1032), dependent on Lotharingia, later in the empire; (2) a *county* of B. (Franche-Comté), which first merged with the duchy *c.* 1470, but in 1483 passed to the empire, and ultimately, with the southern Netherlands, to the crown of Spain; (3) a *duchy* of B., independent *c.* 888–1363, then a fief of France, under duke of the French royal house. On the death of Duke Charles the Bold, 1479, B. became an ordinary province of France.

burial acts in the UK still wholly or partly in force are those of 1852, 1855, 1879, 1880, 1906, and the Cremation Acts, 1902 and 1952. Present (1995) practices covered by the Local Government Act, 1972, and Cremation Regulations, 1979.

Burke's Peerage. Started 1826 by John Burke (1787–1848).

Burkina Faso, formerly **Upper Volta.** This was made a separate French colony from Upper Senegal and Niger, 1919. Abolished, 1932, but reconstructed, 1947. Independent, 1960. Series of military coups between then and 1987. Name changed to B.F., 1984. New constitution, 1991, and elections confirmed position of Blaise Compaoré, in power since 1987.

Burlingame Treaty, between USA and China. Negotiated Washington, 1868; confirmed Peking, 23 Nov. 1869. Authorized mutual immigration. Anson B. (1820–70) was the American representative in China.

Burlington House (London). Built for 1st Earl of Burlington, 1665–8; reconstructed by 3rd Earl, 1716; bought by Government, July 1854. Royal, Linnean, and Chemical Societies' quarters at, 1857. Exhibition rooms date from 1866, 3rd Earl's colonnade removed same year. Royal Academy acquired lease of building and garden behind it, 1867. Royal Academy first opened at, 3 May 1869. New building erected, 1869–72.

Burma, known officially as the **Union of Myanmar** since 19 June 1989. Divided in earliest times into a number of principalities of fluctuating size, among which the two dynasties established at Tagaung play a leading part. According to legend these were succeeded by establishment of a kingdom at Tharakhetara, 483 BC–AD 84. A new dynasty was established at Pagân, 95. B. Calendar era established by Thenga Raja, 639. Most of B. united under King Anoarahta Soa, who established Buddhism permanently (1044?–1077?). Conquest of Arakan by Alaungsithu, 1103. Pagân, captured by Mongols, 1287. Collapse of the Pagân monarchy, 1298. B. divided between two Shan monarchies at Panya and at Sagaing, 1298–1364. Ava founded, 1364. B. in state of civil war under Shan monarchy at Ava until rise of the Burmese Taungu dynasty, 1530–1752. Arrival of Portuguese at Martaban, 1519. B. united under Bureng Naung, 1551–81. Again divided into Pegu and B., 1581–99. Taungu dynasty unites B., 1599. Portuguese expelled from Martaban, 1613. Capital moved to Ava, 1629. Chinese freebooting invasion, 1658–61. Chinese refugee emperor surrendered to a Manchu Army, 1662. Taungu dynasty extinguished at capture of Ava by Talaings, 1752. Alaungpaya reconquers Ava, 1753. Founds Rangoon, 1755. Subdues the whole country, 1758. Invades Siam, 1759. Siam conquered, 1767. Chinese invasions, 1767–9. Amarapura made capital, 1783. First war with Britain, 1824–6. British annex Lower B., 1826. British resident appointed, 1830. Second Burmese War, 1852. Lower B. annexed to Britain, 1853. Accession of Thibaw, 1878. Deteriorating situation led to whole of B. becoming part of the British Empire, 1885, though pacification of Upper B. took several years. Province of British India, 1923–37. Road to China built, 1936–8. Invaded by Japanese, 8 Feb. 1942. Allies recapture Rangoon, 3 May 1945. Becomes independent republic, 4 Jan. 1948. New constitution, 1973 under which U Ne Win became Head of State of the People's Republic. Military coup, 1988; martial law declared, 1989; armed opposition to government since 1988 and abuse of human rights. Opposition leader Aung San Suu Kyi won Nobel Prize for Peace, 1991, from prison. Military refused to hand over power after defeat in 1990 elections. Junta leadership changed, 1992. Some hints of moderating tendencies, 1994 on. Onslaught against Karens, Jan. 1995. Opposition leader Aung San Suu Kyi freed after six years house arrest, 10 July 1995.

Burma Road. Constructed 1936–8 from Lashio to Chungking.

Burschenschaft, was an association of German undergraduates of all universities, started at Jena in 1817 under the patronage of the Grand Duke of Saxe Weimar. Suppressed by the Carlsbad Decrees of 1833, it was revived in 1848. *See also* WARTBURG.

Burundi, Africa. Independent kingdom created by the granting of independence to *Ruanda-Urundi on 1 July 1962; became a republic, 1966. Several coups including 1976; 1980; 1987. Serious unrest with tribal divisions causing suffering and famine since 1980s. Multiparty elections, July 1993 but elected president overthrown in military coup, Oct. President murdered and situation confused thereafter, with extreme civilian suffering. In April 1994 new president probably murdered in plane crash which also killed president and premier of *Ruanda, but though this caused further unrest in B. it was not on the scale of the civil war which erupted in Rwanda. Situation deteriorating in 1995.

Buryat, formerly (until 1958) **Buryat-Mongolia,** autonomous Soviet republic 1920–91; since then, autonomous republic of the Russian Federation.

Bury St Edmunds, England. Named after St Edmund, King of E Anglia, martyred 870, whose remains were transferred hither from Hoxne, 903. Grammar school refounded by Edward VI, 1550. Plague, 1636. Diocese of St Edmundsbury and Ipswich founded, 1914.

Buxton, England. Hot springs patronized by Rome. Became a fashionable spa town in the 18th and 19thC under patronage of the Dukes of Devonshire; 5th duke built The Crescent (being restored, 1995) 1780–84, on site of a Roman hot bath. Poole's Cavern opened to public, 1854. Devonshire Royal Hospital, 1859.

Bydgoszcz, (German **Bromberg**). Polish till 1772. Prussian, 1772–1919. Polish, 1919–39. German, 1939–45. Polish since 1945.

Byelorussia. *See* BELARUS.

Byzantine Authors: Some earlier B. historians wrote in Latin, e.g. Eunapius (*c.* 400), Olympiodorus and Priscus (*c.* 450), Malchus (*c.* 490), and Zosimus (*c.* 500). Some authors writing in Greek are:

Nonnus, *c.* 400, epic poet.
Procopius of Caesarea, *b. c.* 500, *d.* after 559, historian.
Jordanes, *fl. c.* 500 historian.
George Pisiaes, 7thC, panegyrist.
Agathias, 522–88, historian.
Andreas of Crete, *c.* 650–720, hymnologist.
Theodorus of Studium, 759–812, epigrammatist.
Theophanes Confessor, *fl.* 800–13, chronicler.
George Syncellus, *d. c.* 800, chronicler.
Photius, 820–91, philologist.
Leo of Salonika, *c.* 829–56, encyclopaedist.
Leo the Deacon, *fl.* 995, chronicler.

Constantine VII Porphyrogenitus, 905–959, historian.
Cometas Chartularius, *fl.* 950?, epigrammatist.
Theodosius Diaconus, 10thC, panegyrist.
Michael Psellus, 1018–78, historian.
Christopher of Mytilene, 11thC, lyric poet.
Anna Comnena, 1083–1145, historian.
Nicephorus Bryennius, late 11thC, historian.
Johannes Cimnanus, *c.* 1143–85, historian.
John Scyltizes, *d.* after 1081.
Constantine Manasses, *fl.* 1143–80, rhyming chronicler.
Theodorus Prodrumus, *d.* after 1159, epic poet.
George Cedrenus, early 12thC, chronicler.
Nicetas Acominates, *c.* 1140–1220, historian.
George Acropolita, *c.* 1250, historian.
Critobulos of Imbros, late 15thC.

Byzantium. *See* CONSTANTINOPLE and ROMAN EMPIRE, EASTERN.

Romans *c.* 206 BC. Remained part of Roman Empire under name of *Gades* till conquest of Spain by Visigoths, AD 409–20. Reconquered after Justinian's reconquest of Africa *c.* 535. Taken by Moors, 711. Sacked by Normans, 813, and joined to Castile by Alfonso X, 1262. Spanish fleet destroyed by Drake ('singeing of the King of Spain's beard'), 1587. Sacked by Earl of Essex, 15 Sept. 1596. Bombarded by British, July 1797. Blockaded by Lord St. Vincent, 1797–9. Besieged by French, July 1812. Constitution of 1812 promulgated here.

cab. Abbreviation for cabriolet de place, invented by Nicolas Sauvage, *c.* 1660, became current *c.* 1825. C. first licensed in London, 1823. Hansom C. patented, 1834. Cabmen's shelters established, 1875. London C. Act, 1896, and London C. and Stage Carriage Act, 1907, are still in force, as amended by the London Cab Act, 1968. London Cab Act, 1973, restricts private hire cars from being in unfair competition with London taxis. Overhaul of C. laws announced, 1995. *See also* HACKNEY COACHES.

cabal. In later Stuart times the term used for the group of politicians who held power. Originally the so-called C. Ministry of 1671. The letters of the word stood for Clifford, Arlington, Buckingham, Ashley, Lauderdale, its principle members.

Cabinet. *See* COUNCIL.

Cabinet, Imperial War. First met, 1917.

cable. First successful submarine C. between S Foreland and Sangatte, 1851. Atlantic C. laid successfully, 5 Aug. 1858. New pattern C. laid to Holland, Dec. 1947. First transatlantic telephone cable from Scotland to Newfoundland, 1956. Pacific C. laid, 1962; cable Hawaii–Japan, 1964; cable USA–France, 1965.

cable television. *See* TELEVISION.

Cade's Insurrection. Mob led by Jack C., May 1450. Entered London, 27 June. C. killed, 11 July.

Cadiz, Spain. Traditionally founded by Phoenicians *c.* 1000 BC. Captured by

cadmium. Discovered by Strohmeyer, 1817.

Caen, France. Old capital of Normandy and burial-place of William the Conqueror (*d.* 1087) and his queen. Taken by English, 1346, 1417. University founded by Duke of Bedford, 1432. Taken by French, 1 July 1450. Heavily bombarded and half destroyed by Allies, 5–9 June 1944. Restored university inaugurated, 1957.

Caerleon on Usk. Site of Roman fortress (*Isca Silurum*), planned by Sextus Julius Frontinus, governor of Britain AD 74–8, about AD 75. Excavations, 1926 and 1939, showed occupation at least down to 350, possibly later. Excavations in 1954 discovered a large town on an adjacent site.

Caernarvon or **Carnarvon,** Wales. A Roman military station and residence of a Welsh prince till *c.* 893. Castle built by Edward I, 1284. First English Prince of Wales (afterwards Edward II) *b.* at, 25 Apr. 1284. Edward VIII invested as Prince of Wales at C., 1911; Charles, Prince of Wales, eldest son of Queen Elizabeth II, invested at, 1 July 1969. Since 1974 administrative HQ of county of Gwynedd.

Caesaraea (Kaisarieh), Israel. Built by Herod the Great, 25–13 BC. Jewish rising against Romans, AD 66. After AD 70 capital of Roman Palestine and residence of the procurators, and the ecclesiastical capital until 451. Occupied by Arabs, 638. Taken by Crusaders, 1101; by Saladin, 1187; by Richard Coeur-de-Lion, 1191. Demolished by Bibars, 1265.

Caesaraea Philippi (Banias), Syria. Founded by Philip the Tetrarch, 3 BC. Taken by Crusaders, 1129, but lost, 1132. Burnt out, 1157.

caesarean section, performed at least as early as AD 1500, although one tradition asserts that Julius Caesar was delivered by this method, hence the name.

caesium. Discovered by Bunsen at Kirchoff, 1860.

Cagliari, Italy. Traditionally founded by the Phoenicians. Important in Carthaginian and Roman times. Taken by Vandals, 485; by Byzantines, 533; by Saracens, 12thC. Aragonese from 1326 until 1714. Cathedral begun *c.* 1257. University founded, 1606. *See* SARDINIA.

Cahors, France, became a banking centre in 13thC. Liberties suppressed by French kings, 1316. University founded by Pope John XXII, 1331 United with University of Toulouse, 1751.

Caicos Island, or **The Keys.** Discovered *c.* 1512. Settled (from Bermuda), 1678. Jurisdiction transferred to Bahamas, 1804; to Jamaica, 1854. Became Jamaican dependency, 1874.

'Ça ira!' Famous French revolutionary song, traditionally by Ladié, first heard, 5 Oct. 1789.

Cairo, capital of Egypt. Founded by Amr *c.* AD 641 as *Masr.* Became independent capital under Ibn Tulun, 868–83. El Azhar University founded, 941. Refounded on new site a mile from old by Jauhar el-Kaid, 968, as El-Kahira, eventually corrupted to C. Citadel built by Saladin, 1176. Captured by Turks, 1517. Great earthquake, 1754. Taken by Napoleon, 23 July 1798. Recaptured with British help, 27 June 1801. Capital of Mehemet Ali's independent kingdom, 1811. British occupation, 1882–1946. Earthquake, 12 Oct. 1992, killed over 500 people and caused considerable damage in poor quarter of C.

Cairo Declaration, 1 Dec. 1943, by China, Great Britain, and USA regarding war aims and the future of Korea and Formosa (Taiwan).

Calabar, Nigeria. Came under British influence, 1884; protection, 1889. Ceased to be known as Old C., 1904.

Calabria, Italy. The *Iapygia* of the Greeks conquered by Romans, 266 BC; subdued by Odoacer, AD 476; part of the Ostrogothic kingdom of Theodoric, 493; recovered for empire by Belisarius, 536. After 873 C. constituted part of the SW peninsula. Invaded by Otho I, 968, who defeated Greeks, 969; invaded by Peter of Aragon, 1283; invaded by Sicilians, 1296. Part of kingdom of the Two Sicilies, 1597.

Calais, France. Became important port, 10thC. Taken by Edward III, 4 Aug. 1347; finally taken from the English by the Duke of Guise, 7 Jan. 1558; taken by Spaniards, Apr. 1596; restored, 1598. Captured by Germans 22–7 May 1940. Invested, 20 Sept., and taken, 30 Sept. 1944 by Canadian First Army. French end of Channel Tunnel near, 1994.

calcium. First isolated in 1808 by Sir Humphry Davy in his electrolytic researches.

calculating machines. Constructed by Napier of Merchiston, 1617; Blaise Pascal, 1642; Moreland, 1666; Leibnitz, 1671; Visc. Mahon, 1775; Hahn, 1779; Müller, 1784; C. Babbage, 1822. Colmar's arithmometer *c.* 1850. First cash-adding machine by Burroughs, 1888. First electronic C. M. built 1939–44. In general business use throughout world since 1960s; desk and pocket C.M.s in common use from 1970s.

Calcutta, India. Founded, 1687, by Job Charnock, an East India merchant. Fort built, 1696. Confinement of prisoners in Black Hole, 19 June 1756, after capture of town by Dowlah; retaken, Jan. 1757; centre of British India, 1773–1912. Mother Teresa (*b.* 1910) founded her charitable order here, 1948.

Calder Hall, Cumbria. Britain's first industrial nuclear power-station, located at *Sellafield. Construction began, 1949;

formally opened by Queen Elizabeth II, Oct. 1956.

Caldey, island off the Pembrokeshire coast. A Cistercian priory was established here in 1929.

Caledonian Canal (Scotland). Building begun, 1804; opened, 1822; but work not complete until 1847.

Calgary, Alberta, Canada, founded as Fort C. in 1875. Railway reached C., 1885. Oil discovered here, 1914. Developed into a major business centre since 1920. Winter Olympics held at C., 1988.

California, USA. Discovered by Spaniards, 1542; visited by Drake, 1579; subject to Mexico, 1822; occupied by US Army, 1847; ceded to USA, 1848; admitted to Union as a state, 1850. University of C. opened, 1869. Californian gold-rush, 1849–56. Silicon Valley in southern C., area of high-technological microchip industry since 1960s. Very serious forest fires in southern C., Oct.–Nov. 1993. Anti-immigration legislation approved. Nov. 1994. Serious flooding in C., Jan. 1995.

caliphate. The spiritual and political headship of Islam in succession to Mohammed. The first three 'Orthodox' caliphs were: Abu Bekr, 632–4; Omar I, 634–44; Othman, 644–56. At the murder of Othman a civil war between Ali, elected at Mecca, and Moawiya of the Ommayad House led eventually to the establishment of the Ommayad C., 661, which was in its turn overthrown by the Abbasids, 750, who reached their greatest prosperity under Haroun al Rashid, 786–809, and were destroyed effectively at the capture of Baghdad by Hulagu Khan the Mongol, 1258. A puppet C. under the domination of the Mamelukes continued, however, in *Egypt, 1261, until its conquest by the Turks, 1517. In 1520 the last of these puppets, Al Motawakkil, surrendered his office to the Turkish Sultan Suleiman the Magnificent, and the title was borne by the Turkish sultans till Nov. 1922, when it was made elective in the Turkish imperial family. On 3 Mar. 1924 the C. was abolished by the Turkish parliament.

caliphs. Following is a list of C. from the death of Mohammed until the extinction of the genuine caliphate at Baghdad in 1258. Those marked 'O' were of the Ommayad House. Thereafter the remainder were Abbasids. Those marked 'B' were dominated by Buweiyid princes and ministers. Those marked 'S' were virtually vassals of the Seljuk Turks.

Abu Bekr 632–34
Omar I 634–44
Othman 644–56
Ali 656–61
Hasan 661
Moawiya I (O) 661–80
Yezid I (O) 680–83
Moawiya II (O) 683–84
Merwan I (O) 684–85
Abd-el-Melik (O) 685–705
Welid I (O) 705–15
Suleiman (O) 715–17
Omar II (O) 717–20
Yezid II (O) 720–24
Hisham (O) 724–43
Welid II (O) 743–44
Yezid III (O) 744
Ibrahim (O) 744
Merwan II (O) 744–50
Abul Abbas (as Saffah) 750–54
Al Mansur 754–75
Al Mehdi 775–85
Al Hadi 785
Haroun al Rashid 786–809
Al Amin ⎫
Al Mamun ⎬ 809–13
Al Mamun alone 813–33
Al Motassim 833–42
Al Wathik 842–47
Al Mutawakil 847–61
Al Muntasir 861–62
Al Mustain 862–66
Al Motazz 866–69
Al Muhtadi 869–70
Al Motamid 870–92
Al Motadid 892–902
Al Muktafi 902–07
Al Muktadir 907–32

Al Kahir 932–34
Ar-Radi 934–40
Al Muttaki 941–44
Al Mustakfi 944–46
Al Muti (B) 946–74
Al Tai (B) 974–91
Al Kadir (B) 991–1031
Al Kaim (B) 1031–75
Al Muktadi (S) 1075–94
Al Mustazhir (S) 1094–1118
Al Mustarshid (S) 1118–35
Ar Rashid (S) 1135–36
Al Muktafi (S) 1136–61
Al Mustanjid (S) 1161–70
Al Mustadi (S) 1170–80
An-Nasir (S) 1180–1225
Zahir (S) 1225–35
Al Mustansir (S) 1235–42
Al Mustasim 1242–58

Callao, Peru. Old city destroyed by earthquake, 1746.

calotype. Photographic method invented by Fox Talbot, 1841.

Calvinists. Protestant movement named after John Calvin (1509–64).

Cambodia. The Khmer Kingdom was founded in AD 5thC. Rose to its zenith in 9thC. Angkor-Thom completed by Yasovarman c. 900. Angkor-Vat built, 12thC. Empire reached its greatest extent under Jayavarman VII early in 13thC. Angkor abandoned for Lovek in 15thC. Lovek abandoned end of 16thC. By 17thC the Khmer monarchs were puppets alternately under Thai and Annamese influence. C. became a French protectorate in 1863. Became Associated State of French Union, 1949. Complete independence from France, Jan. 1955. Communist guerrilla movement existed in C. from 1945 and Prince Sihanouk was deposed, Mar. 1970 and C. renamed the Khmer Republic. Civil war continued with US and Vietnamese intervention, 1970–3. Khmer Rouge established brutal regime, 1975, but this was opposed by Vietnam. 1976, C. renamed Democratic Kampuchea. Full-scale war between C. and Vietnam, 1977–8, when Khmer Rouge government overpowered and a Vietnam-backed People's Republic of Kampuchea established, Jan. 1979. In 1982 a coalition government was set up, which included an allegedly reformed Khmer Rouge. Talks in Jakarta, 1988, and Paris, 1989, to try to solve Cambodian problem. Last Vietnamese troops withdrawn, Sept. 1989 and Kampuchea reverted to name of C. In Aug. 1990 the UN set up a Supreme National Council in C. and main government agencies placed under UN supervision until elections could be held. In Oct. 1991 the four main Cambodian factions agreed cease-fire, to be monitored by UN troops. March 1992 UN Transitional Authority for C. (UNTAC) started trying to implement peace agreement, but fighting continued and renewed problems caused by Khmer Rouge revival and kidnapping and harassment of UN representatives. Elections, May, 1993, but Khmer Rouge did not participate: moderates secured victory. UN troops began leaving C., July 1993; in Sept. Sihanouk enthroned as king of C. under new constitution. Khmer Rouge remained powerful threat, controlling large parts of the countryside outside the capital, despite failed coup, July 1994. In Oct. 1994, Khmer Rouge murdered three European hostages. Instability continuing, 1995.

Cambrai, France. Church councils at, 1064, 1303, 1383, 1565. League of C., 10 Dec. 1508; Paix des Dames Treaty, 1529. Captured by the Emperor Charles V, 1544; by French, 1667; cathedral destroyed, 1793; French defeated by British under Duke of York, 24 Apr. 1794; taken by Austrians, 10 Sept. 1798; by British under Sir Charles Colville, 1815. *See* BATTLES.

Cambridge, England. Taken by barons, 1215. University charter, 1231. Residence of Henry II, who repaired castle, 1265. Castle possessed by Cromwell, 1643. Historic buildings include church of Holy Sepulchre (1130–15thC.) one of four remaining round Norman churches in England; and King's College chapel 1446–1515. Observatory, 1820. *Fitzwilliam Museum founded at, 1816.

High-technological industrial development in and near since 1970s. Royal Observatory moved to C., 1990.

Cambridge, Mass., USA. *Harvard College founded here, 1638. One of the earliest printing presses was set up at C., which published the *Bay Psalm Book*, the first book printed in British America, in 1640. Massachussetts Institute of Technology (founded Boston, 1861), moved to C., 1916; Radcliffe College founded, 1917. Smithsonian Astrophysical Observatory, formerly in Washington, DC, moved to C., 1955. John F. Kennedy Memorial Library opened at, 1978. Subway connection with Boston completed, 1912.

Cambridge University. Traditionally founded 1209, by migrant students from *Oxford. First charter, 1231; formally recognized, 1318. Records burnt by Wat Tyler, 1381. Written examinations introduced, 1772. New statutes, 1856. Religious tests abolished, 1871. Oxford and Cambridge Act, 1882. Present statutes date from 1926. Women admitted as full members, 1947. First women undergraduates admitted to traditional men's colleges, 1972: first women's college admitted men, 1979. The only college now (1995) admitting only women is Lucy Cavendish. The following are (1995) the principal colleges and halls, with the dates of their foundation:

Ayerst Hall, opened, 21 Apr. 1884; closed, 1896.

Caius (Gonville and Caius College), founded by Edmund Gonville, 1348. John Caius, MD, in 1557 obtained royal charter.

Clare Hall, 1966.

Cavendish College, founded 1876 by County College Association; closed, Dec. 1891.

Christ's College, founded 1505 by Lady Margaret Beaufort, Countess of Richmond and Derby, mother of King Henry VII.

Churchill College, founded 1960.

Clare College, founded by Richard Badew as University Hall, 1326; refounded, 1338, by Lady Elizabeth, sister of Gilbert, Earl of Clare.

Corpus Christi, founded 1352; owes foundation to two tradesmen's guilds in the town, called the Guilds of Corpus Christi and of the Blessed Virgin Mary.

Darwin College, founded 1964.

Downing College, founded under will of Sir George Downing, Bt., dated 20 Dec. 1717; received charter, 22 Sept. 1800.

Emmanuel College, founded 1584 by Sir Walter Mildmay, Chancellor of the Exchequer.

Fitzwilliam House (non-collegiate), founded 1869; college, 1966.

Girton College, founded at Hitchin, 1869. Removed to Girton, near Cambridge, 1873. Admitted as a college of the university, 1947.

Homerton College, founded 1924.

Hughes Hall, founded 1885.

Jesus College, founded 1496 by John Alcock, Bishop of Ely.

King's College, founded 1441 by Henry VI.

Lucy Cavendish College, founded 1965.

Magdalene College, founded 1542 by Thomas, Baron Audley, of Walden. Replaced Buckingham College, founded by Henry Stafford, Duke of Buckingham (1455–83).

New Hall, founded 1954.

Newnham College, founded 1871. Admitted as college of the University, 1947.

Pembroke College, founded 1347 under name of Valence-Mary, who was in reality Mary de St. Paul, widow of Aymer de Valence, Earl of Pembroke. Henry VI was a liberal benefactor, and is known as second founder.

Queens' College, founded 1448 by Margaret of Anjou, wife of Henry VI; refounded 1465 by Elizabeth Woodville, wife of Edward IV.

Robinson College, founded 1977.

St Catherine's College, founded 1473 by Robert Wodelarke, DD, Chancellor of the University.

College of St John the Evangelist (St John's College), founded 1511 by Lady Margaret Beaufort (founder of Christ's College, *above*).

St Peter's College (Peterhouse), founded 1284 by Hugh de Balsham, Bishop of Ely.

Selwyn College, founded 1882, built by public subscription in memory of George Augustus Selwyn, Bishop of Lichfield.
Sidney Sussex College, founded 1596 under will of Lady Frances Sidney, Dowager Countess of Sussex.
Trinity College, founded 1546 by Henry VIII, who combined three other smaller colleges into one, and added to revenues.
Trinity Hall, founded 1350 by William Bateman, Bishop of Norwich.
Wolfson College, founded 1965.

Cambridge University Press. University given power to appoint a printer, 1534: began printing, 1584.

Cambuskenneth Abbey. Founded by, David I of Scotland, 1147. First Scottish Parliament assembled at, 1326.

camera obscura. Known to Euclid, 300 BC and described by Alhazen of Cairo (d. AD 1038), but popularized by Giovanni Battista della Porta, 1569. First used for photographic purposes by Thomas Wedgwood, 1794.

Cameroons, Africa. Colonized by Germans, 1884. Conquered by French and British, 1914–17. Under British and French mandates, 1922. The French mandate became independent under the name of the Cameroon Republic, 1 Jan. 1960. N part of British mandate joined Nigeria and S joined Cameroon Republic, 1961. Unitary and bilingual one-party state of the United Republic of Cameroon established after referendum, 1972. Renamed Republic of C., 1984. After opposition to one-party state grew, multi-party elections took place, March 1992, followed by a coalition government. A draft bill on constitutional reform followed, May 1993.

Camisards. Huguenots of the Cévennes who rebelled after the revocation of the Edict of Nantes (1685). Camisard war, 1702–6, in which the royal forces were commanded successively by Marshals Montrevel, Villars, and Berwick. Jean Cavalier, the chief Camisard leader, d. in 1740, having been made a British brigadier-general in 1735.

Camorra. Secret society founded in Naples jail c. 1820. Entered political field, 1848. Suppressed 1911 but many former C. members subsequently found in the *Mafia.

Camp David Agreement. In Sept. 1978 President Carter of the USA convened a conference at Camp David at which agreement on a peace formula was reached between *Israel and *Egypt. A resultant peace treaty was signed in Washington, 26 Mar. 1979.

Campaign for Nuclear Disarmament (CND), first prominent in Britain in the 1950s, Canon Collins being its chairman 1958–64. Subsequently declined, but revived in 1980s, gaining official Labour Party support for a time. Committed to unilateral nuclear disarmament and banning (or removal) of US Cruise missiles from Britain, but after formal end of 'Cold War', 1989, and subsequent dissolution of the USSR. 1991, CND's numbers fell and its influence waned. Missile removal from Britain in 1990s further diminished CND.

Campbellites (Disciples of Christ). Sect founded in the USA by Alexander Campbell (1788–1866) in 1812.

Campo Formio, Treaty of, 17 Oct. 1797, between Napoleon and Austria, by which (*inter alia*) the republic of Venice was abolished.

Canada. Probably discovered by Norsemen c. 1000. Discovered by John Cabot, 1497. The St Lawrence discovered by Jacques Cartier, 1535. Quebec founded by Champlain, 1608. C. explored by La Salle, 1669, 1678. Hudson's Bay Co. founded, 1670. C. given up to England by France, 1763, after war of 1759–60 (See QUEBEC). C. divided into two provinces, 1791; reunited, 1840; again separated on establishment of the Confederation, 1867. British N America Act for union of C., Nova Scotia, and New Brunswick, under title of Dominion of C., passed 29 Mar. 1867. Territories of Hudson Bay (Manitoba) added, 1869; of British Columbia, 1871; of Prince Edward Island,

1873; of Alberta and Saskatchewan, 1 Sept. 1905. Canadian Pacific Railway opened, 8 Nov. 1885. *Statute of Westminster approved, 30 June 1931. Privy Council judgment upholding abolition of Appeals to Privy Council, 13 Jan. 1947. Newfoundland entered Dominion, 31 Mar. 1949. C. signed North Atlantic Treaty, 4 Apr. 1949. Opening of the St Lawrence Seaway, 1959. Trans-C. Highway opened, 3 Sept. 1962. Growth of separatism in French-speaking C., 1970s onwards. Amended constitution to replace the British N America Act received Royal Assent, Mar. 1982. 1986 Constitution Act amended Commons distribution. 1989: Meech Lake Accord, attempt to contain Quebec separatism, but lapsed when Manitoba and Newfoundland legislatures refused to approve it, 1990. New proposals turned down in a referendum, Oct. 1992. Kim Campbell becomes C's first woman premier, 1993; in June C. government offered Eskimos limited self-rule. Liberal landslide victory, 25 Oct. 1993: Chrétien becomes premier with Bloc Québécois largest opposition group. Separatists win Quebec provincial elections, Sept. 1994, but narrowly defeated in sovereignty referendum in Quebec, 31 Oct. 1995. Dispute between C. and the European Union regarding fishing rights, Mar.–Apr. 1995. For Canadian writers, *see under* ENGLISH LITERATURE.

The following are the Governors-General since the union:
Lord Monck 1867–68
Lord Lisgar 1868–72
Lord Dufferin 1872–78
Marquess of Lorne 1878–83
Lord Lansdowne 1883–88
Lord Stanley of Preston 1888–93
Earl of Aberdeen 1893–98
Earl of Minto 1898–1904
Earl Grey 1904–11
Duke of Connaught 1911–16
Duke of Devonshire 1916–21
Viscount Byng of Vimy 1921–26
Viscount Willingdon 1926–31
Earl of Bessborough 1931–35
Lord Tweedsmuir 1935–40

Earl of Athlone 1940–46
Viscount Alexander 1946–52
Vincent Massey 1952–59
Georges Philias Vanier 1959–67
Roland Michener 1967–74
Jules Leger 1974–79
Edward Schreyer 1979–84
Mrs Jeanne Sauvé 1984–89
Ramon Hnatyshyn 1989–94
Romeo Le Blanc 1995–

The following are the Prime Ministers of Canada, from 1867:
Macdonald 1867–73
Mackenzie 1873–78
Macdonald 1878–91
Abbott 1891–92
Thompson 1892–94
Bowell 1894–1986
Tupper 1896
Laurier 1896–1911
Borden 1911–20
Meighen 1920–21
Mackenzie King 1921–26
Meighen 1926
Mackenzie King 1926–30
Bennett 1930–35
Mackenzie King 1935–48
St Laurent 1948–57
Diefenbaker 1957–63
Pearson 1963–68
Trudeau 1968–79
Clark 1979–80
Trudeau 1980–84
Turner 1984
Mulroney 1984–93
Campbell 1993
Chrétien, 1993–

canals. For the principal ones in Great Britain and Ireland, *see* under various headings. The following (except for the Panama and Suez Cs.) are among the most noted C. outside Great Britain, with the dates of their openings:

Aichi (Japan), 1961
Albert (Antwerp to Liège) 1939
Alentejo (Portugal), 1959
American Erie 1817

Amsterdam 1876
Amsterdam and N Sea 1876
Amsterdam-Rhine, 1952
Baltic and N Sea (Kiel Ship Canal) 1895
Bordeaux and Narbonne 1884
Bourbon 1790
Burgundy 1775
Corinth 1893
Damodar Valley (India) 1958
Du Midi (Languedoc) 1681
Erie (USA) 1817
Ganges 1854
Gliwice (Poland) 1939
Gothenburg 1832
Grand Canal (China) 500 BC–1292 AD
Holstein 1785
Karakumsky (Russian) 1981
Kattegat and Baltic 1806
Kiel 1914
Michigan-Mississippi 1900
Mittelland (Rhine–Ems to Königsberg) 1938
Moscow-Volga 1932–37
Orleans 1675
Princess Juliana (Netherlands) 1935
St Petersburg and Kroustadt 1884
Seine et Loire 1791
Sorraia Valley (Portugal) 1958
Twenthe (Zutphen to Enschede) 1936
Welland (Erie to Ontario) 1824–9; 1932
White Sea and Baltic (Archangel to St Petersburg) 1933

See also SUEZ; PANAMA.

Canary or **Fortunate Islands,** off northwest Africa. Granted by Pope Clement VI to Juan de la Cerda, 1346; since 1496 under Spanish rule.

Canberra. Officially became capital of Australia, 20 Jan. 1910. Foundation stone laid, 12 Mar. 1923. Parliament opened by Duke of York, 9 May 1927. Centre of Australian federal administration; of increasing international importance since 1945.

cancer, in 1995 second most common cause of death in Britain. Word first used in the 17thC (derives from 'canker'). Radium treatment began to achieve cures from 1920s. Chemotherapy treatment, from 1950s. Increased prevention methods: e.g. cervical smear tests from 1960s, breast scanning from 1980s. Government health campaigns against presumed causes of some Cs. (e.g. anti-smoking campaigns) from 1960s. Marie Curie Memorial Foundation established 1948. Vaccine with potential to prevent certain Cs. developed by Patterson Institute, Manchester, Jan. 1993. Genetic basis for some Cs. suggested, 1993; smoking, sunbathing and alcohol blamed for C. rise in UK, 1995.

Candia. *See* CRETE.

Candia, War of, 1635–94. *See* CRETE and VENICE.

Candlemas. Christian feast of Presentation of Christ in the Temple and Purification of Blessed Virgin Mary, celebrated 2 Feb. Became widespread after Emperor Justinian ordered its observance, 542.

cannabis, illegal drug, the dried leaves (marijuana) and resin (hashish) a derivative of the hemp plant, *cannabis sativa.* C. mentioned as a herbal remedy in China c. 2800 BC. In modern times its main growing area was originally Mexico. There were restrictions against its use in the USA from the 1930s but its popularity as an illegal drug in the Western world began in the 1950s and in the UK attempts to prevent its use and sale include legislation passed in 1964, 1965, 1967, 1973 and 1977. In some countries there has been some relaxation of penalties for using C. since the 1980s (e.g. Spain, Holland and (1994) Germany). *See also* DRUG ADDICTION.

Cannes, France. Popularity as a resort dates from Lord Brougham's visit, 1834. Film festival held annually at since World War II: subsequently annual venue for television festival.

Canon. The office of C. appears to have been introduced into the church in the 8thC, and arose from the desire to impose a type of monastic rule on the cathedral clergy.

canonization was not known before the 10thC, but traditionally the first C. was celebrated by Leo III, AD 804. The canonizing of any deceased Christian without the bishop's consent was prohibited in the 9thC. John XV was the first pope who exercised the right, and in AD 993 made Udalric, Bishop of Augsburg, a saint. *Douleia* of 'canonized saints' enjoined by Council of Trent (1545–63). Among those added to calendar in recent times: Joan of Arc, 16 May 1920; Jean Baptiste Vianney, 1925; Theresa of Lisieux, 1925; John Bosco, 1934; Sir Thomas More and Bishop John Fisher, 19 May 1935: Forty Martyrs of England and Wales, 25 Oct. 1970: Oliver Plunket, 1975; John Ogilvie, 1976; Maximilian Kolbe, 1982.

Canon Law. *See* DECRETALS.

Canossa. Emperor Henry IV submitted to Pope Gregory VII at, Jan. 1077.

Canterbury, England. Walls of the Roman *Durovernum* were built in the 2ndC AD. Jutish settlement at, 5thC. St Augustine arrived from Rome at C., AD 596. See founded, 597. Castle taken by Louis of France, 1216. Kentish rebels under Wat Tyler left C. for London, 1381. Cathedral founded by Augustine, 602; pillaged by Roric, 851; entirely rebuilt by Archbishop Lanfranc, 1070; choir completed, 1130. Thomas Becket murdered in choir, 1170. Choir burnt down, 1174: rebuilt, 1174–84. Shrine to Becket erected, 1175; demolished and robbed of its valuable gifts by Henry VIII, 1538. St Martin's Church, frequented by Queen Bertha before the landing of Augustine, said to be the oldest Saxon church in England. Chequers Inn for pilgrims mentioned by Chaucer, built 1400; mostly burnt down, 1865; bombed and badly damaged, 1 Jan. 1942; rebuilding after 1945 led to discovery of Roman town plan. University of Kent. established at, 1965. Pope John Paul II visited C. cathedral, 1982.

Canterbury, Archbishops of. The following is a list since the foundation of the see:

Augustine 597–605
Laurentius 605–19
Mellitus 619–24
Justus 624–27
Honorius 627–53
Deusdedit 655–64
Theodore 668–90
Berhtwald 693–731
Taetwine 731–34
Nothelm 734–40
Cuthbert 740–58
Breogwine 759–62
Jaenberht 763–90
Æthelheard 790–803
Wulfred 803–29
Fleogild 829–30
Ceolnoth 830–70
Æthelred 870–89
Plegemund 891–923
Æthelm 923–25
Wulfelm 928–41
Odo 941–58
Ælsine 958–59
Dunstan 959–88
Æthelgar 988–89
Sigeric 990–94
Ælfric 995–1005
Ælfeath or Alphege 1006–12
Lyfing 1013–20
Æthelnoth 1020–38
Eadsige 1038–50
Robert of Jumièges 1051–52
Stigand 1052–70
Lanfranc 1070–89
Anselm 1093–1109
Ralph de Turbine 1114–22
William de Corbeuil 1123–36
Theobald 1139–61
Thomas Becket 1162–70
Richard 1174–84
Baldwin 1185–90
Reginald Fitz-Jocelin 1191
Hubert Walter 1193–1205
Stephen Langton 1207–28
Richard Wethershed 1229–31
Edmund Rich (of Abingdon) 1233–40
Boniface of Savoy 1240–70
Robert Kilwardby 1273–78
John Peckham 1279–92
Robert Winchelsea 1293–1313
Walter Reynolds 1313–27

Simon de Meopham 1327–33
John Stratford 1333–48
John de Ufford 1348–49
Thomas Bradwardin 1349
Simon Islip 1349–66
Simon Langham 1366–68
William Wittlesey 1368–74
Simon Sudbury 1375–81
William Courtenay 1381–96
Thomas Fitzalan 1396–98
Roger Walden 1398
Thomas Arundel 1399–1414
Henry Chicheley 1414–43
John Stafford 1443–52
John Kemp 1452–54
Thomas Bourchier 1454–86
John Morton 1486–1500
Henry Deane 1501–03
William Warham 1503–32
Thomas Cranmer 1533–56
Reginald Pole 1556–58
Matthew Parker 1559–75
Edmund Grindal 1575–83
John Whitgift 1583–1604
Richard Bancroft 1604–10
George Abbot 1611–33
William Laud 1633–45
William Juxon 1660–63
Gilbert Sheldon 1663–77
William Sancroft 1678–91
John Tillotson 1691–94
Thomas Tenison 1694–1715
William Wake 1716–37
John Potter 1737–47
Thomas Herring 1747–57
Matthew Hutton 1757–58
Thomas Ecker 1758–68
Frederick Cornwallis 1768–83
John Moore 1783–1805
Charles Manners-Sutton 1805–28
William Howley 1828–48
John Bird Sumner 1848–68
Charles T. Longley 1862–68
Archibald Campbell Tait 1868–82
Edward W. Benson 1882–96
Frederick Temple 1896–1902
Randall Davidson 1903–28
Cosmo Gordon Lang 1928–42
William Temple 1942–44
Geoffrey Francis Fisher 1945–61
Arthur Michael Ramsey 1961–74

Donald Coggan 1974–79
Robert Runcie 1979–91
George Carey 1991–

Canterbury Tales, by Geoffrey Chaucer (1340?–1400); composed *c.* 1380 and first printed by Caxton, 1477.

Canton (**Guangzhou** or **Kwangchow**), China. King of Portugal obtained right to trade with, 1517. First visited by English, 1634; besieged and taken by Sir Hugh Gough, 31 May 1841; Convention of C., July 1841; captured by Japanese, 21 Oct. 1938. Restored to China, 1945.

CAP. *See* COMMON AGRICULTURAL POLICY.

Cape Coast, Ghana. Early settlement of Portuguese, 1610, when castle built; taken from them by Dutch, 1642; ceded to England by Peace of Breda, 1667.

Cape Horn. Sighted by Drake, 1578; so named by Dutch explorer Willem Schouten (1616) after his birthplace of Hoorn.

Cape Province (formerly Cape Colony). Cape of Good Hope discovered by Bartholomew Diaz, 1488. Cape Town founded by Dutch, 1652. Colony of Cape Town captured by English, 16 Sept. 1795; restored, 1802; retaken, 9 Jan. 1806. Wars with Kaffirs, 1811–12, 1817–19, 1834–5, 1846–8, 1850–3. Finally ceded to English by Netherlands, 13 Aug. 1814. Boers in large numbers crossed Orange River and left colony ('The Great Trek'), 1835. Natal annexed to C.C., 22 Aug. 1843. Orange River territory annexed to C.C., Mar. 1851. Orange River territory formed into a free state, Mar. 1854. Discovery of diamonds, 1867–70. Transvaal Republic annexed, 12 Apr. 1877. Transvaal independent as S African Republic, 1880 (*See* TRANSVAAL). Houses of Parliament opened, 1885. Annexation of *Orange Free State, 28 May 1900; of Transvaal, 3 Sept. 1900. Became a province of the Union of S Africa after the passing of the S Africa Act, 1909. *See* SOUTH AFRICA, REPUBLIC OF.

Capet Dynasty. *See* FRANCE.

Cape Town (Kaapstad), S Africa. Factory established by Dutch E India Co., 1652. Occupied by British when Holland became French dependency, 1806; restored by Treaty of Amiens, 1810; but reoccupied by British, 1814, to whom the province was finally awarded same year. Castle built, 1666; observatory, 1820; university built, 1873.

Cape Verde. Discovered 1443, by Nuño Tristao.

Cape Verde Islands. Annexed to Portugal, 1441–56. Independent republic, 5 July, 1975. Constitution amended, 1990, abolishing one-party rule. Multi-party elections, Jan. 1991, won by opposition Movement for Democracy, and an independent president instituted.

capital gains tax, first levied in Britain under Finance Act, 1965. Amended in 1971 and 1976. Capital Gains Tax Act, 1979 amended and consolidated previous legislation. Index-linking allowed to 1982, from 1988. From Apr. 1990 married women no longer assessed jointly with husband for C.G.T.

capital levy. First recorded demand for a C.L. in Britain made by a private member in the House of Commons in 1914. Remained part of Labour Party programme until 1927 and revived several times since. The 'Special Contribution' levied by the Labour Government in 1948 is the closest approach to a C.L. so far.

capital punishment, British law relating to, reformed, 1826 (in the light of Beccaria's *Treatise on Crime and Punishments*, 1764), when varieties of capital crime reduced from over 200 to treason, arson, piracy, murder only. Homicide Act, 21 Mar. 1957, divided murders into capital and noncapital categories. The Murder (Abolition of Death Penalty) Act suspended C.P. in Britain for all murder cases, Nov. 1965 for an experimental five-year period. In Dec. 1969, on a free vote, Parliament approved the permanent abolition of the death penalty in Britain except for treason where it remains on the statute book but has not

been used since 1946. Abolition of C.P. in Republic of Ireland, 1990. Still (1995) retained in many countries, including the USA where some states have reintroduced it in recent years.

capital transfer tax, in Britain, replaced *Estate Duty from Mar. 1975: substantially changed after Mar. 1986 by *Inheritance Tax legislation.

Capitol. *See* ROME; WASHINGTON.

Capri Island. Residence of Emperor Tiberius, AD 27–37. Captured by British, 1806; by French, 1808. Restored to Naples and Sicily, 1814.

Capua, Italy. Alliance with Rome, 338 BC. Went over to Hannibal, 216 BC; captured by Romans, 211 BC; captured by Vandals, AD 456; destroyed by Saracens, 840; rebuilt 9thC. Councils at, 391, 1087, 1118. Captured by Caesar Borgia, 24 July 1501; occupied by French, 23 Jan. 1799; surrendered to British, 28 July 1799; capitulated to Sardinian forces, Nov. 1860.

Capuchins. Offshoot of Franciscans, founded by Matteo di Bassi, 1528. Became an independent order, 1619.

Caracas, capital of Venezuela, founded 1567.

Carberry Hill, Midlothian. Mary Stuart and James Bothwell surrendered to the confederate lords of Scotland, 15 June 1756.

carbolic acid. Discovered by Runge, 1834.

Carbon-14 dating. *See* RADIO-CARBON DATING.

Carbonari. Secret society, originated in Naples between 1806 and 1814. Spread to the whole of Italy by 1820. Adherence made high treason in Piedmont and Naples, 1821. Active, 1830–31.

Carcassonne, France. Oldest fortifications still existing, 7thC. Completed in present form, 13thC. Restored late 19thC by Viollet-le-Duc. C. occupied by Saracens, 725–c.750.

Cardiff, S Wales. Site occupied since first century AD, when Roman fort established. Besieged by Owen Glendower, 1404. Oldest charter extant, dated 14 Oct. 1338. Docks opened, 1839. University College of S Wales and Monmouthshire established at, 1883. C. made capital of Wales, Dec. 1955.

Cardinals (*see also* CONCLAVE). Term first applied to chief priest of a Roman parish. Pope Stephen III, about AD 770, seems to have been the first to select seven bishops out of the Roman See and give them the title of Cardinal. The Council of Rome, under Pope Nicholas II, 1059, granted the College of C. the sole voice in the election of a pope. The number in the College of C. was fixed at 70 in 1586. Number increased by Pope John XXIII (1958–63). Style of 'Eminence' conferred by Urban VIII.

cards, playing, and games of cards. Earliest written allusion quotes a manuscript of 1299 (Italian). Chinese dictionary of 17thC claims for China the invention in 1120. They spread rapidly in 15thC. Before 1643 C. were manufactured in England, where a duty was first imposed in 1615.

Caribbean Community and Common Market (CARICOM), formed as result of Treaty of Chaguaramas, 1973, and had 13 members in 1994. Function primarily furtherance of economic integration between member states, but played part in re-establishment of law in *Grenada, 1983. In 1990 members agreed to aim to establish a 'common market' by 1994, and some common tariffs being applied, 1991 and 1992; in 1992, discussions started with the *Central American Common Market with view to forming a Caribbean and Central American free trade area.

Caribbean Federation. Established by the British Federation Act, 1956, and the W Indies Order in Council, 1957. Dissolved, Apr. 1962.

Carinthia (Kärnten), duchy of the Holy Roman Empire and Austrian province. Last independent duke, Boruch, accepted Bavarian suzerainty and baptism, 738. Conquered by Franks under Charlemagne, 791–7. Became part of Ostmark, 811. Part of kingdom of Bohemia, 1270. Acquired by Rudolph of Hapsburg, 1276. Pawned to the counts of Gorizia, but recovered, 1335. Occupied by French, 1809–13; partly by Serbs and Slovenes, 1919 and 1945; by British, 1945.

Carlisle, England. *Luguvallium* of Roman Britain, the Celtic *Caer-luel*. Mentioned by Bede under the year 687 as an inhabited 'city'. Sacked by Danes under Halfdan Ragnarsson, 875. Fortified by William Rufus, 1092; diocese of, 1133; charter, 1158; grammar school, 1170; surrendered to Young Pretender, 15 Nov. 1745; submitted to Duke ('Butcher') of Cumberland, 15 Dec. 1745. Public-houses and breweries all acquired by state, 1916; Licensing Act of 1921 transferred the wholesale and retail licensed trade of C. to the Home Secretary. This state monopoly abolished by the Licensing (Abolition of State Management) Act, 1971.

Carlists (Spain). Supporters of Don Carlos of Bourbon's claim to the Spanish throne. Principally to be found among the Basques, they fought two civil wars, 1834–9 and 1872–6, and there were abortive short-lived Carlist risings in 1846 and 1848. Finally suppressed, 1875.

Carlsbad or **Karlsbad,** now **Karlovy Vary,** Bohemia. Medicinal hot springs patronized by Emperor Charles IV, 1358; baths founded 1364. Congress of Powers, 1819, to repress Liberal press, etc.

Carmelite Order. Founded by Berthold, Count of Limoges, about 1156 on Mt Carmel; received its first rule from Albert, Patriarch of Jerusalem, 1209; sanctioned by Pope Honorius III, 1226. Driven out of Palestine by the Saracens, 1238. Pope Innocent IV changed the Carmelites from hermits to mendicant friars, 1247. First general chapter held in England, 1247. Nuns affiliated to the order from 1452. Discalced Cs., 16thC. Teresa of Avila reformed the Carmelite nuns, 1562.

Carnarvon. *See* CAERNARVON.

Carnatic, India. Taken under direct British rule, 1801.

Carnegie Trust Funds. Administered by a corporation set up, 1911, and also by the Carnegie Foundation for the Advancement of Teaching (instituted 1906), both in USA. Carnegie Trust for universities of Scotland was instituted, 1901, and Carnegie United Kingdom Trust, 1914. Carnegie Endowment for International Peace instituted, 1910.

Caroline Islands, Pacific Ocean. First sighted by Portuguese under Diego da Rocha, 1537. Ruled successively by Portugal and Spain, 1537–1899; sold to Germany, 1899. Mandate entrusted to Japan, 1919. Administered by USA from 1947 as a UN Trusteeship, became *Federal States of Micronesia, 1979. See further under* MICRONESIA

Carolingian Dynasty. *See* FRANCE.

carpet-bagger. absentee political candidate in USA, especially of the 'Re-construction' period in the S *c.* 1865–7.

Cartagena, Spain. Founded by Carthaginian Hasdrubal as capital of Carthaginian Spain *c.* 227 BC. Captured by Scipio Africanus the Elder, 210 BC. Sacked by Goths, AD 425, and by Drake, 1588. Republican naval base during civil war, 1936–9.

cartel, term first used in Germany, 1879, to describe a combine of railway material manufacturers. *See also* TRUSTS.

Carthage. Phoenician city founded near site of modern Tunis *c.* 700 BC. Attempt to conquer Sicily defeated at Himera, 480. N African empire reached its height, 4thC BC. First war with *Rome (First Punic War), 264–241 BC. Second Punic War begun, 218, as result of Hannibal's capture of Saguntum in previous year. His victory at Cannae, 216. The destruction of Hannibal's brother Hasdrubal's army at the Metaurus, 207, led to the conquest of Carthaginian Spain by the Romans, and their invasion of Africa resulted in Hannibal's defeat at Zama, 202. C. accepted terms of peace, 201. In the Third Punic War (149–146 BC) the Romans destroyed the city after a three-year siege. Rebuilt, 10 BC–AD 10 and named *Colonia Julia Carthago*. Captured by Vandals, AD 439, who made it their capital till its reconquest by Belisarius, 533. Finally destroyed by the Arabs, 697.

Carthusian Order. Founded by St Bruno, AD 1086; recognized by pope, 1176. In England the Carthusians settled in 1180, and had a famous monastery in London, since called the 'Charterhouse', founded 1371. Female branch instituted at Salette, France, 1229.

Casablanca, Morocco. Founded 15thC by Portuguese. Taken by French, 1907. Conference of allied statesmen at which unconditional surrender of Axis powers decided upon 14–24 Jan. 1943. C. possesses the world's largest mosque, the Great Hassan II, completed and opened, 1993, intended to hold 100,000 worshippers.

Cashel, Rock of, Tipperary. Fortress built by Cormack MacCarthy, King of Munster, 1127, and cathedral built, 1169.

Casket Letters. Documents relating to the events of 1567 and the murder of Darnley, produced by the Earl of Morton before Commissions at London and York; the originals were lost after 1584 and never recovered. Authenticity doubted by many historians.

Cassel or **Kassel,** Germany. Fortified, 1526. Refuge for French Protestants after 1685. Taken by French, 1760; besieged by Count Lippe, 1761, and by Prince Ferdinand, who took it, 1 Nov. 1762; fortifications destroyed, 1767; occupied by French, 1806. Capital of kingdom of Westphalia, 1807–13.

Cassino. *See* MONTECASSINO.

Castel Gandolfo. Papal villa near Lake Albano, in the Castelli area outside Rome, built by the architect Carlo Maderno (1556–1629) on estate bought by Clement VIII, 1596. It was used by the popes as a summer residence until 1870, and again since 1929, when C.G. was declared part of the Vatican City.

Castile, Spain. First Count Roderic, AD 791. Subject to Leon till 1028, when it was seized by Sancho, King of Navarre, who gave it as a kingdom to his son Ferdinand, first King of C., 1039. Alfonso VI captured Toledo, 1085, but severely defeated by the *Almoravides at Zallaca, 1086. Alfonso VIII defeated by *Almohades at Alarcos, 1195, but in alliance with Aragon and Navarre won crushing victory at Navas de Tolosa, 1212. Ferdinand and Isabella sovereigns of, 1474. Moors finally driven out, 1492. United with Aragon under Spanish crown, 1504.

Castile and Leon, Heads of State of (from 1033). Though Ferdinand I ranks as the first King of C. proper, this monarchy traced its history back to the Christian remnant which continued to resist at the height of Mohammedan power in Spain. This early history, however, is obscure, and many of the kings mentioned are known merely as names. C. and L., although often ruled by the same sovereign, were not finally united until 1230, under (Saint) Ferdinand III.

Sovereign	Leon	Castile
Ferdinand I, the Great	1037–65	1039–65
Sancho II		1065–72
Alfonso VI	1065–1109	1072–1109
Urraca	1109–26	1109–26
Alfonso VII	1126–57	1126–57
Sancho III		1157–58
Ferdinand II	1157–88	
Alfonso VIII, the Good		1158–1214
Alfonso IX, the Slobberer	1188–1230	
Enrique I		1214–17
Ferdinand III, the Saint	1230–52	1217–52

Kings of Castile and Leon:
Alfonso X, the Wise 1252–84
Sancho IV, the Fierce 1284–96
Ferdinand IV 1296–1312
Alfonso XI, the Avenger 1312–50
Pedro I, the Cruel 1350–68
Enrique II, the Bastard, or the Magnificent 1368–79

Juan I 1379–90
Enrique III, the Sickly 1390–1406
Juan II 1406–54
Enrique IV, the Impotent 1454–74
⎰ Isabella the Catholic 1474–1504
⎱ Ferdinand V, the Catholic 1474–1504
 (from 1479 Ferdinand II of Aragon)
Joanna and Philip 1504–06
Ferdinand V (again) 1506–16

See further under SPAIN.

Catalonia, Spain (Spanish **Cataluña**; Catalan **Catalunya**). Conquered by Moors, 712. By Charlemagne, 788. United with *Aragon, 1137. Philip IV of Spain attempted to suppress liberties, 1640. Occupation by French, 1640–59, 1694–7. Liberties and cortes abolished by Philip V, 1714. Civil war, 1823. Divided in four provinces, 1833. Granted local autonomy, 1932–4: then declared a federal republic. Deprived of autonomy, 1939: re-established, 1978, when regional government inaugurated; C.'s first post-Franco parliament elected, March 1980. Threatened to withdraw support from government, 1995.

Catania, Sicily. Founded by Greeks, 729 BC. Population removed by Hiero I to Leontini, 467 BC; returned, 461 BC. C. plundered by Dionysius I, 403 BC. Became subject to Rome, 263 BC. Cathedral built 11th–18thC; fort, AD 1237; university, 1434. Volcanic disasters, 123 BC, AD 1669, 1693.

Câteau Cambrésis, Peace of. Between Philip II of Spain and Elizabeth of England of the one part and Henry II of France of the other, 2–3 Apr. 1559. Calais was finally ceded to France by this treaty.

catechisms, the earliest written schemes extant are those of Kero of St Gall (8thC) and Otfried of Weissenburg (9thC). For early Protestant C. *see* REFORMATION; these provoked the *Summa Doctrinarum* of Peter Canisius, 1566; that of the *Council of Trent; and other C. of the Counter-Reformation, e.g. those of Bellarmine, 1603; Bossuet, 1687. A modern Roman catechism is the *Schema de Parvo*, 1870. The

Calvinists used the *Geneva Catechism*, 1536, and, in Scotland, Craig's, 1592. The Church of England produced a catechism contemporaneously with the Prayer Book in 1549, expanded in the reign of James I; subsequent C. was compiled by the Assembly of Divines, 1648. New Catholic C., 1992.

Cathars or **Catharists.** Heretical Christian sect, which spread to Bulgaria (Bogomils) and in the 10thC to France (Albigensians), where it was brutally eradicated in the 14thC. *See* ALBIGENSES.

cathedrals, Anglican, in England. The following are the principal Anglican cathedrals with dates of foundation (F.) and of the major part of the present building (P.)

	F.	P.
Birmingham		1711–19
Blackburn		1826
Bradford		14thC
Bristol	11thC	1306–37
Canterbury	600	1174–1400
Carlisle		1092–1419
Chelmsford		19thC
Chester	1053	1200–1315
		and 1485–1537
Chichester	1108	1187–1210
Coventry[1]	15thC	1956–62
Durham	995	1104–33
Ely	673	1100–1327
Exeter	1050	1260–91
Gloucester	681	1089–1100
		and 1450–1500
Guildford	1936	1936–61
Hereford	c. 680	1110–1220
Leicester		14th C
Lichfield	672	1200–1321
Lincoln	628	1140–1280
Liverpool	1904	1904–
London:		
(1) Westminster Abbey	618	13th–16thC
(2) St Paul's	7thC	1674–1710
Manchester	1847	19thC
Newcastle		1400–74
Norwich	1094	1274–1446
Oxford	727	1180–1480
Peterborough	667	1118–1237
Portsmouth	1190	1683–95
Ripon	678	1330–1450
Rochester	601	1080–1137
St Albans	793	c. 1360
St Edmundsbury		15thC
Salisbury		1220–58
Sheffield		15thC
Southwark	c. 7thC	12thC
		and 1470–1500
Southwell		1110–1250
Truro	1880	1887–1903
Wakefield		15thC
Wells	704	1306–33
Winchester	c. 7th C	12thC
		and 1367–1404
Worcester	964	1224–1374
York	627	1227–1361

[1]Original fabric, except for the spire, destroyed by bombing, 14 Nov. 1940.

cathedrals, Roman Catholic, in England and Wales (O = Opened; C = Consecrated):

Birmingham (of St Chad) (O) 1808, (C) 1841; Brentwood (of St Helen) and the Sacred Heart, (O) 1861, (C) 1869 as St Mary and St Helen, opened; rebuilt, and dedicated, 1991; Cardiff (of St David). Destroyed by enemy action, 1941. Since rebuilt. (O) 1836, (C) 1887; Clifton (of the Apostles) (O) 1848, (C) 1848 (rebuilt after World War II); Hexham and Newcastle (of St Mary) (O) 1844, (C) 1860; Lancaster (of St Peter) (O) 1799, (C) 1859; Leeds (of St Anne) (O) 1838, (C) 1904; Liverpool ((old) of St Nicholas) (O) 1807, (C) 1815; ((new) of Christ the King), (O) 1933, (C) 1967; Menevia (Wrexham) (of Our Lady of Dolours) (O) 1857, (C)1907; Middlesbrough (of St Mary) (O) 1868, (C) 1911; Northampton (of St Mary and St Thomas) (O) 1825, (C) 1864; Nottingham (of St Barnabas) (O) 1842, (C) 1844; Plymouth (of St Mary and St Boniface) (O) 1858, (C) 1880; Portsmouth (of St John, Evangelist) (O) 1882, (C) 1887; Salford (of St John (O) 1848, (C) 1890; Shrewsbury (of Our Lady Help of Christians and St Peter of Alcantara) (O) 1856, (C) 1891; Southwark (of St George). Seriously damaged during World War II. Restored since. (O) 1841, (C) 1894; Westminster (of the Most Precious Blood) (O) 1903, (C) 1910. St John the Baptist, Norwich, became cathedral of diocese of E Anglia, 1976: it was started, 1884; completed, 1910.

cathedrals, Church of Wales. Prior to the disestablishment of 1920 there were only four dioceses in Wales – Bangor, Llandaff, St David's, and St Asaph's. On the formation of a disestablished Anglican Church in Wales, 1920, two new dioceses were created, and existing churches in Brecon and Newport became Cs.

The following are the principal Welsh cathedrals with dates of foundation (F.) and of the major part of the present building (P.).

	F.	P.
Bangor	before 545	1496–1532
Brecon	1923	13th–14thC
Llandaff	before 612?	12thC
Newport	1921	c. 1150
St Asaph's	6thC	15thC
St David's	before 601?	1180

Catholic Apostolic Church (Irvingites). Founded by Edward Irving (1792–1834), who seceded from the Presbyterian Church having been deposed from the ministry. The sect assumed the name C.A.C., 1832.

Catholic Association, Irish. Organized, 1824; Act for its suppression, 1825, but continued until 1829, when it was voluntarily dissolved.

Catholic emancipation from sundry disabilities under the Penal Laws (1665, etc.) was begun in Britain by an Act introduced by Sir George Saville, 1778. This provoked the *Gordon Riots in England and disturbances in Scotland, and remained a dead letter. In 1791, a further Act was passed for England, and extended to Scotland, 1792. Some disabilities removed from Irish Catholics by Acts of 1774, 1778, 1782, and 1790. More comprehensive was the C.E. Bill which became law in 1829, and also applied to Ireland. The offices of sovereign, regent, and lord high commissioner (to the Church of Scotland) remain closed to Catholics, the office of lord chancellor being effectively opened to Catholics by the Lord Chancellor (Tenure of Office and Discharge of Ecclesiastical Functions) Act, 1974. *See* CLARENDON CODE.

Catholic League in France. Organized against *Huguenots by the Duke of Guise.

See HOLY LEAGUE (4).

Catholics, Old. *See* OLD CATHOLICS.

Catholic Truth Society. Established, 1872.

Cato Street Conspiracy. Formed by Arthur Thistlewood, 23 Feb. 1820, to murder Lord Castlereagh and other ministers. Thistlewood executed with four accomplices, 1 May 1820.

Cattaro. *See* KOTOR.

Cavell Memorial. London, 1920; inscription added, 1924; commemorates British nurse, Edith Cavell, executed by German military authorities, 12 Oct. 1915. Remains subsequently buried in grounds of Norwich Cathedral.

Caves of a Thousand Buddhas. Rock cut shrines of Kansu, China, date from the mid-4thC AD, but mostly dug out and embellished between 618 and 1276.

Cawnpore. *See* KANPUR.

Caxton, William (c. 1422–91), set up the first printing press in England at Westminster Abbey, 1476; but printed his first book, (the first to be printed in English), 1473.

Cayman Islands. A dependency of *Jamaica, described by Columbus, 1503, then by William Jackson, 1643. Victualling point for the Commonwealth Navy, 1655. Separate dependent territory of UK since 1959. New constitution, 1972.

Celebes was a Portuguese possession, 1545–1660, and finally came into Dutch hands, 1669. Became part of Indonesia, 1950.

celibacy of the clergy. Spanish synod of Elvira first council to enjoin it on clergy, AD 305; condemned by Vigilantius, a presbyter of Barcelona, AD 406; strictly enjoined by council of 649; strictly enforced by Gregory VII, 1073. Reaffirmed by Vatican Council. II, 1962–5: but increasing questioning of C. within the Catholic Church from the mid-1960s. Successive popes have subsequently reaffirmed belief in its continuance despite increasing pressures for change.

celluloid. Patented in Britain by Parkes, 1855; improvements made in America by Hyatt, 1870. Superseded by cellulose acetate in 20thC.

Celsius. *See* CENTIGRADE.

CEMA (Council for the Encouragement of Music and the Arts). Set up 1 Jan. 1940. Became the *Arts Council of Great Britain, 9 Aug. 1946.

Cenotaph (Whitehall, London). Temporary structure, July 1919; permanent, 1920.

censorship of drama (Britain) was formerly exercised by the Lord Chamberlain, whose activities in this sphere began before 1509, at first through a functionary of his department called the Master of the Revels. The powers of the Lord Chamberlain became statutory by an Act of 1737 under the terms of which the Examiner of Plays was appointed. He was allowed complete discretion until 1843, when the Theatres Act laid down principles on which plays were to be licensed or refused licence, and also permitted the licensing of playhouses, hitherto the prerogative of the crown alone, by other authorities. The Theatres Act, 1968, abolished theatre censorship and amended the laws relating to theatres and theatrical performances.

censorship of films (Britain). British Board of Film Censors established, 1912. After passing of the Video Recordings Act, 1984, name changed to the British Board of Film Classification (1985), which now classifies videos as well as films. There are restrictions on under-18s regarding viewing of certain films and hiring or buying of certain videos. Announced that laws relating to violence on videos to be tightened, Apr. 1994.

census. A C. Bill was introduced into Parliament, 1753, but rejected on the plea that a C. was dangerous to the liberties of freeborn Englishmen. The first C. taken in Great Britain, 1801. C. extended to cover British Empire, 1871. First C. in Australia, 1871. In USA the first C., 1790.

Centigrade, temperature scale invented by the Swedish astronomer Anders Celsius (1701–44), 1742. C. then **Celsius** used increasingly in Britain from 1965 onwards.

CENTO (Central Treaty Organization). Formerly the *Baghdad Pact. Name of organization changed to CENTO on 21 Aug. 1959. A dead letter after Iranian revolution, Jan. 1979.

Central African Federation. *See* RHODESIA AND NYASALAND, FEDERATION OF.

Central African Republic. Formerly one of the four territories of French Equatorial Africa (Ubangi Shari), became independent, Aug. 1960. From 1976–9 known as the Central African Empire under Bokassa I (formerly president). Bokassa overthrown, 1979: new constitution, 1981, was subsequently suspended and military rule followed, 1981–5. Some relaxation 1986 onwards. Agitation for multi-party state, 1991 and revision of constitution approved. Elections, 1993, when dictator Kolingba defeated. Bokassa freed from prison. Elections and new president chosen, 27 Sept. 1993.

Central American Common Market (CACM), established by treaty signed in Managua, 15 Dec. 1960, ratified 1963. Members are Costa Rica, Guatemala, El Salvador, Honduras and Nicaragua. Agreement with EC, Nov. 1985. Revitalized in 1990s: in 1992 discussions with the *Caribbean Community and Common Market on possible formation of a Caribbean and Central American free-trade area.

Central Criminal Court. *See* OLD BAILEY.

Central Electricity Generating Board. In 1948 the British Electricity Authority was established and took over the functions, plant and other assets of private and municipal electrical undertakings, as well as those of the Central Electricity Board (established 1927). In 1954 the title of the British Electricity Authority was changed to the Central Electricity Authority, subsequently to the C.E.G.B. It disappeared following privatization of the electricity industry in 1989. *See* ELECTRICITY ACT, 1989.

Central England in Birmingham, University of, name of Birmingham Polytechnic changed to, 1992.

Central European Time. Proposal by EC that UK should adopt it, 1993.

Central Intelligence Agency (CIA), US intelligence organization, established 1947, most widely known of the US intelligence branches. Congressional controls upon, since 1980.

Central Lancashire, University of, name of Lancaster Polytechnic changed to, 1992.

Central Provinces and Berar. See MADHYA PRADESH.

Central Treaty Organization. See CENTO.

Centre for Cooperation with European Economies in Transition. Set up, 1990, by the *OECD to liaise with the newly non-Communist economies of E and Central Europe.

CERN. See EUROPEAN ORGANIZATION FOR NUCLEAR RESEARCH.

Cetatea Alba. See BELGOROD-DNESTROVSKIY.

Cetinje. Ancient capital of *Montenegro, founded, 1485. Captured but not held by the Turks, 1683, 1714, 1785. Captured by Austrians, 13 Jan. 1916, and by Serbs, 4 Nov. 1918.

Ceylon. See SRI LANKA.

Chaco or **Gran Chaco.** For wars in *see* BOLIVIA *and* PARAGUAY.

Chad. French protectorate 1900, part of French Equatorial Africa from 1908. Ceased to be a dependency of Ubangi-Shari Colony, 1920. French penetration of the region had begun in 1885. Under its African governor, Felix Eboué (*d*. 1944), C. was the first French colony to declare for Fighting France, 26 Aug. 1940. Forces based on C. began to raid Axis outposts in the Fezzan, Jan. 1941. In the winter of 1942–3 they completed the conquest of the Fezzan, and effected a junction with the Eighth Army between Tripoli and Sfax. Member state of the French Community,

28 Nov. 1958. Became an independent republic, 11 Aug. 1960. Civil war between government and secessionist groups in N C. lasted 1965–79, and restarted after Libyan intervention, 1980, on rebel side. French troops sent to C., Aug. 1983, as 'advisers', Libyans decisively defeated, 1987. C. and Libya resumed diplomatic relations, 1988, and submitted disputed territorial claim to International Court of Justice, Sept. 1990. In December 1990 government overthrown in a coup led by Idriss Deby, which promised multi-party rule after period of transition and consultation.

Chalcedon (Turkish **Kadikeui**). Founded as a colony by the Megarians, 685 BC, but was absorbed by *Pergamum whose king bequeathed it to Rome, 133 BC. Ravaged by the Goths, notably in AD 256, and the Persians, 616–26. The Council of C., 451, determined the bounds of the sees of Rome and Byzantium, C. being by then virtually a suburb of the latter, though separated from it by the Bosporus. It was destroyed by the Turks after 1075.

Chaldea. See BABYLONIA, where the Chaldeans formed the ruling class from the 8thC BC until the death of Labashi Marduk, 556. See also UR.

***Challenger* Expedition.** British scientific expedition under Capt. George Nares left England in the steamship *Challenger*, 7 Dec. 1872, and returned, 24 May 1876. *Challenger* was also name given to ill-fated US space shuttle which exploded on take-off, 28 Jan. 1986, killing whole crew.

Châlons, Battle of. Name of a battle now believed to have been fought near Troyes, in which Attila, King of the Huns, was defeated by Aetius and Theodoric, AD 451.

Chamberlain, Lord. In Britain, one of the chief officers of state from the 13thC. Parliament declared he must be a member of the Council *ex officio*, 1406. Today an officer of high standing in the royal household.

chambers of commerce. First Chamber of Commerce founded in France, 1599. The oldest in Great Britain is at Glasgow, incorporated 1 Jan. 1783; Manchester Chamber of Commerce instituted, 1794; London, 1881. New York Chamber instituted, 1768; incorporated, 1770.

Chambres Ardentes. French courts originally for trial of nobles. Notably those instituted under Francis I in 1535 for trials of heretics, and revived by Henry II, Oct. 1547. Under Louis XIV a *chambre ardente* tried poisoners, and condemned the Marquise de Brinvilliers in 1676; this court was abolished in 1682; but C.A. for trials of embezzling farmers of the public revenues operated during the minority of Louis XV.

Chambres de Réunion Established by Louis XIV of France for the purpose of asserting claims, through old feudal titles, to territories on German frontier, 1679.

Champagne, France. Annexed to crown of Navarre by Theobald, 1234; passed to French crown by marriage of Philip IV to Joanna of Navarre, 1284; invaded by Emperor Charles V, 1523; entered by Prussians under Duke of Brunswick, 1792. The wine known as C. was invented by a Benedictine monk, Dom Perignon, in 1668 and the grapes are grown and the wine produced only in the C. region.

Champ de Mars, Paris. First Grand Federation of the, 14 July 1790; the second, 14 July 1791, at which a petition was signed praying for the abdication of Louis XVI.

Champlain, Lake, USA. Discovered by Samuel de C., 1609. Scene of British naval defeat by the Americans, 1814.

Chanak, Asia Minor. Occupied by British as a check to Kemalist advance, Sept. 1922; evacuated, Oct. 1923.

Chancellor, Lord High (Latin *Cancellarius* = Usher or Chief Clerk). Originally an official responsible for preparation of writs and who acted as clerk of the council. Name C. said to have been used first in England during reign of Edward the Elder, 920. Was nearly always a cleric in the Middle Ages, and rose into prominence by

administering equity and by presiding for the king over the House of Lords. First recorded as sitting in the chancery as a judge, 1377. Independent jurisdiction existed by 1474. The following are the most notable since Henry VII:

Cardinal Wolsey, 1515.
Sir Thomas More, 1529.
Stephen Gardiner, Bishop of Winchester, 1553.
Sir Francis Bacon, 1617.
Edward Hyde, Earl of Clarendon, 1660.
Anthony Ashley Cooper, Earl of Shaftesbury, 1672.
George, Lord Jeffreys, 1685.
Philip Yorke, Lord Hardwicke, 1737.
Edward, Lord Thurlow, 1778, 1783.
John Scott, Lord Eldon, 1801, 1807.
Thomas, Lord Erskine, 1806.
John Singleton Copley, Lord Lyndhurst, 1827, 1834, 1841.
Henry, Lord Brougham and Vaux, 1830.
Robert Monsey Rolfe, Lord Cranworth, 1852, 1865.
Frederic Thesiger, Lord Chelmsford, 1858, 1866.
John, Lord Campbell, 1859.
Richard Bethell, Lord Westbury, 1861.
Hugh McCalmont Cairns, Lord Cairns, 1868, 1874.
William Page Wood, Lord Hatherley, 1868.
Roundell Palmer, Lord Selborne, 1872, 1880.
Sir Hardinge Stanley Gifford, Lord Halsbury, 1885, 1886, 1895, 1902.
Sir Farrer Herschel, Lord Herschel, 1886, 1892.
Robert Threshie Reid, Lord Loreburn, 1905.
Richard Burdon Haldane, Lord Haldane, 1912, 1924.
Sir Stanley Owen Buckmaster, Lord Buckmaster, 1915.
Sir Robert Bannatyne Finlay, Lord Finlay, 1916.
Frederick Edwin Smith, Lord Birkenhead, 1919.
George, Lord Cave, 1922.
Sir Douglas McGarel Hogg, Lord Hailsham, 1924, 1935.

Sir John Sankey, Lord Sankey, 1929, 1931.
Sir Frederic Herbert Maugham, Lord Maugham, 1938.
Sir Thomas Inskip, Lord Caldecote, 1939.
Sir John Simon, Lord Simon, 1940.
William Allen, Visc. Jowitt, 1945.
Gavin Turnbull Simonds, Lord Simonds, 1951.
David Patrick, Maxwell Fyfe, Visc. Kilmuir, 1954.
Reginald Manningham-Buller, Lord Dilhorne, 1962.
Gerald Gardiner, Lord Gardiner, 1964.
Quinton Hogg, Lord Hailsham, 1970.
Lord Elwyn-Jones, 1974.
Lord Hailsham, 1979.
Lord Mackay, 1987.

Chancellor of the Exchequer. *See* EXCHEQUER.

Chancellor of Ireland, Lord High. Earliest nomination that of Stephen Ridel during Richard I's reign, 1189. Office abolished, 1922.

Chancellor of Scotland, Lord High. Office abolished in 1707.

Chandernagore, India. Former French settlement in Bengal, founded 1673. Transferred to India, 1952.

Chang Jiang. *See* YANGTSE KIANG.

Channel Islands. Formed part of the duchy of Normandy when William I conquered England, 1066, and remained English after all other French territories were lost by the English crown. Part of the diocese of Coutances until 1568; then in the diocese of Winchester. Occupied by Germans, July 1940–May 1945; controversial public papers concerning C.I. during World War II made public, Jan. 1993. Hague Court confirms British, not French, title, to Minquiers and Ecrehous reefs, 17 Nov. 1953. *See* ABBEVILLE Treaties (1).

Channel Tunnel. First suggested (to Napoleon I) by the French engineer Mathieu, and again after 1825 by English and French railway engineers. A horse roadway was planned by W. Low in 1867, and a model exhibited at the Paris Exhibition of that year. An English C.T. Co., formed in 1872, actually began digging, but work was stopped by the representations of the War Office. The company continued in being, first as the Submarine Continental Railway, 1881, until after 1940. A British parliamentary committee also reported favourably, 1930, but on 30 June 1930 the House of Commons rejected the project. Renewed interest in scheme after World War II. Anglo-French committee considered a Channel tunnel or bridge, 1961, and recommended a rail tunnel, Feb. 1964. Project cancelled, 1975. Revived, 1984. Anglo-French agreement signed, 1986 and work started. First link-up (service tunnel), 1990: breakthrough of two rail tunnels, 1991. Officially opened by Queen Elizabeth II and President Mitterand of France, 6 May 1994: regular train service started through, Nov. 1994. Scheduled car service from 1995. Length, 31.03 miles/49.9 km. Anglo-French (Eurotunnel) private consortium has concession till 2042; suspended interest payments on its debts for 18 months, from Sept. 1995.

Chantrey Bequest. A fund left by Sir Francis Chantrey (1781–1841) to the Royal Academy for the encouragement of British painting and sculpture. First purchases made, 1877.

Chapel Royal of England existed, as a body of clergy and musicians, in the reign of Edward IV (1461–83), possibly earlier.

Chapel Royal of Scotland, founded by Alexander I (1107–24) at Stirling Castle, and moved by Mary Stuart (1542–87) to Holyrood Abbey Church.

Chappaquidick, island near Martha's Vineyard, Massachussetts, USA. Scene of accident on 18 July 1969 when Senator Edward Kennedy drove his car off an unmarked bridge and his companion Mary Jo Kopechne drowned. Kennedy later found guilty of leaving the scene of an accident; in consequence he did not seek presidential nomination in 1972, nor later.

Charing Cross, London. The original C.C. was erected by Edward I in memory of his wife Eleanor, 1291, on the site of a former village called C., immediately S of Trafalgar Square. This cross was condemned and removed by order of Parliament, 1647. The present reproduction in the courtyard of C.C. Station was erected, 1865.

charities. In England and Wales the Charitable Trusts Acts, 1853–1939, form the basis of modern charity administration. Charity Commission instituted under the Act of 1853 and reconstituted under the C. Act of 1960. Charity Commissioners' powers of investigation and supervision strengthened, 1992, and new controls over charity fundraising established. Modifications suggested, 1993.

Charlemagne or **Charles I.** King of the Franks, the son of Pepin and Bertha; *b.* probably AD 2 Apr. 742, *d.* 28 Jan. 814. Crowned Emperor of the West by Pope Leo III, 800.

Charleston, S Carolina, USA. Founded by William Sayle *c.* 1670. (*See* FORT SUMTER.) There was a severe earthquake here in 1886.

Charlotte Amalie, capital of the Virgin Islands, was known between 1921 and 1937 as St Thomas.

Charlottenburg. Former town of Brandenburg, Germany, incorporated into Berlin, 1920. Grew up round the palace started there in 1696 by Frederick I of Prussia.

Charter, The Great. *See* MAGNA CARTA.

Charterhouse. Corruption of *Chartreuse.* Carthusian (*see* CARTHUSIAN ORDER) monastery founded in Clerkenwell, London, 1371, but when monasteries were dissolved by Henry VIII it was made a depository for the king's tents and pavilions, until granted to the Duke of Norfolk, 1539. Purchased by Thomas Sutton, who founded a school and hospital, 1611. School transferred to Godalming, Surrey, 1872.

charters of corporate towns, granted by Henry I, gave security to industry and promoted manufacturers, 1132; remodelled by Charles II, 1682; the new charter resisted at Nottingham, accepted by Plymouth and other corporations, 1684. Ancient C. restored, 1698; revised by Royal Commission, 1833; altered by Municipal Reform Act, 1835; whole system transformed by Local Government Act, 1972.

Chartism. A movement in Great Britain for extension of political power to the working classes, caused by economic distress. It began in 1836. In 1838 was drawn up by certain 'representatives of the people' the 'People's Charter', and riots known as Chartist riots were enacted all over the country. By 1848 extremists dominated the movement, which petered out by 1858.

Chartres, France. Besieged by Normans, 845 and 911. Henry I of England interviewed Pope Innocent II at, 1131; English from 1417 to 1431; taken by Count of Dunois, 1432; besieged by Duke of Condé, 1568. A fire is recorded in the cathedral as early as AD 753; extensive rebuilding, 1020–8. Towers built, 1145–65; main part of present structure finished by 1260.

Chartwell, near Sevenoaks, Kent, former county home of Sir Winston Churchill (1874–1965), now administered by a trust and devoted to his memory.

Chatham, England. Dockyard and arsenal built by Queen Elizabeth, 1588; removed to its present position, 1662. Surprised by Dutch under De Ruyter, 1667. New docks opened, 21 June 1871; naval dockyard closed, 1983.

Chatham Chest. Charitable fund established by Sir Francis Drake and Sir John Hawkins in 1588. It was removed to Greenwich, 1802, and the fund incorporated with Greenwich Hospital.

Chatham House, St James's Square, London, has been since 1923 the headquarters of the Royal Institute of International Affairs, which originated in 1919.

Chatham Islands, now under New Zealand administration, were discovered, 1791, by Lieut. W. R. Broughton. Conquered, 1831, by a Maori expedition; the aboriginals virtually exterminated by 1849.

Chatsworth House, Derbyshire, England. Original 16thC building demolished after Civil War. Present one, known as 'Palace of the Peak' built for the 1st Duke of Devonshire, 1687–1707. N Wing addition: 1820–7. Chatsworth Park (1,100 acres) includes the Cascade (completed 1696, rebuilt 1701) and garden designed by Brown (18thC) and Paxton (19thC). House and gardens have been open to the public since their inception.

Cheapside, originally Chepe = The Market, was the commercial centre of medieval London. Laws regulating this market were codified under Edward I (1272–1307). Chaucer about 1380 and Lydgate in the early 15thC often refer to Chepe.

Cheb (German **Eger**). Acquired by the Holy Roman Empire, 1000. Colonized by Germans under leadership of Bavarian Cistercian abbots, from 1100. *Reichstag met at C., 1213, and Imperial Chamber of Princes, 1239. Became part of the kingdom of Bohemia for the first time in 1279, and finally in 1322. Wallenstein murdered in C. castle, 1634. From 1621 to 1918 the district had its own provincial Diet. Became a headquarters of the Sudeten German movement until 1939; after 1945 reverted to Czechoslovakia: in Czech Republic since 1 Jan. 1993. *See* SUDETENLAND.

Chechenya, or **Chechenia,** self-proclaimed republic independent 1991–5 when, under Dzhokhar Dudayev, it broke away from the Russian Federation. Criminal gangs from C. have spread not only to Moscow and other Russian cities but also worldwide. Dudayev sworn in as C. president, March 1993, but not recognized by Russia. Russia first tried to create a Chechen 'opposition' but this defeated militarily, Nov. 1994 and 21 Russian soldiers killed. Thereafter Russia threatened reannexation by force: Russian bombing began, Dec., followed by invasion. Capital of C. *Grozny scene of fierce fighting Dec. 1994–Feb. 1995 when it finally fell to Russians. Limited cease-fire from mid-Feb. 1995; but opposition to Russia continued in rural areas, and Dudayev defiant. War caused international condemnation of Russian bombardment of Chechen civilians and internal divisions in Russia. Resistance confined to isolated areas by June 1995, when a Chechen raid inside Russia led to hostage-taking and many deaths. Peace signed July 1995, but conditions in C. remain confused.

Cheddar, England. C. cheese said to have been made here as early as 13thC. C. Gorge contains more than 400 caves, many containing stalagmites and stalactites. Gough's Cave Museum has collection of Stone Age tools and weapons and skeleton of an inhabitant of the cave *c.* 10,000 BC (discovered in 1903).

Cheka. Name applied to Russian Soviet Secret Police, 1917–22.

Chelmsford, England. Remains of Roman settlement of *Caesaromagus* in vicinity. Judicial centre since 13thC. Diocese of C. created, 1915; 1951, parish church of St Mary's designated Anglican cathedral. Anglia Polytechnic University, 1992. Formerly an agricultural centre, modern C. supports important electronics industries. From the C. Marconi premises, 23 Feb. 1920, was transmitted the first wireless-telegraph broadcasting service in the world.

Chelsea Flower Show, first held, 1913. Now takes place annually in May in grounds of the Royal Hospital, Chelsea, London.

Chelsea Royal Hospital or **College** (London), for old and disabled soldiers of British Army. Foundation stone laid, 1682; building by Christopher Wren opened, 1694.

Cheltenham, England. Priory of Benedictines founded about 790. Edward the

Confessor lord of the manor and granted a charter in 1041. The grammar school and almshouses founded, 1578, by Richard Pate. The C. waters were first discovered, 1716. The C. College was established in 1840, followed by the Ladies' College, 1854. C. racecourse famous for the C. Gold Cup. run there since 1924. Government Communications Centre since World War II.

Chelyabinsk-65, secret Soviet nuclear plant in the Urals. Scene of an explosion, Sept. 1957 when the coding system failed. There was massive contamination and many subsequent fatalities. Also known as the *Kyshtim disaster.*

chemical warfare, banned by Geneva Protocol, 1925 and UN, 1989. Used against Kurds in 1980s by *Iraq, 1990. USA and USSR agreed to reduce stockpiles of C.W. weapons. Alleged Iraqi C.W. weapon plants bombed during *Gulf War, 1991. Convention banning chemical weapons signed by 120 countries, including Britain, in Paris, 13 Jan. 1993, ending 20 years of negotiations. The Arab League refused to sign. C.W. used, against dissident 'marsh people' by Iraq, Oct. 1993.

chemistry. In earlier times known as alchemy, inaugurated in Egypt. Diocletian ordered the destruction of all the works of the alchemists, AD 297. A licence for practising alchemy was granted to Richard Carter in London, 1476. C. not a science until the 17thC. In 1772 Joseph Priestley published his discoveries, which commenced a new era in the science.

Chemnitz, German industrial city. Scene of a Swedish victory during the Thirty Years War (1618–48). Under the German Democratic Republic C. was renamed Karl-Marx-Stadt, 1953, reverting to C. in 1990.

Chequers (Court). Bequeathed to the nation, with a trust fund for its upkeep for the use of successive Prime Ministers, by Lord Lee of Fareham (then Sir Arthur Lee), 1917. First occupied by David Lloyd George, 8 Jan. 1921.

cheques. Lawrence Childs, a banker, first printed C. *c.* 1761. Rules with regard to bills of exchange, defined in the Bill of Exchange Act, 1882, also apply to C. By the Cheques Act of 1947 an unendorsed C. which appears to have been paid by the drawer's banker is evidence of receipt by the payee of the sum payable by cheque. Payment by cheque permissible to any employee from 1 Mar. 1963, subject to the employee's agreement. Passing of worthless C. a specific offence under Theft Act, 1978. Cheques Act, 1992 made C. nontransferable if bearing words 'account payee' or 'a/c payee' and amended related laws.

Cherasco.
1. Armistice of, between Napoleon I and the King of Sardinia, 28 Apr. 1796.
2. Treaty of, between Louis XIII of France and Victor Amadeus of Savoy, 6 Apr. 1631.

Cherbourg, France. Captured by Henry V of England, Aug. 1418; retaken by French, 12 Aug. 1450; harbour-works planned by Vauban, 1686, but not finally completed until 1856; fortifications destroyed by English, Oct. 1758; further harbour-works constructed, 1886; occupied by Germans, 18 June 1940; captured from them by Americans, 25 June 1944.

Cherkassy, Ukraine. Belonged to Kiev in the Middle Ages; Lithuanian in 1362; Polish, 1569, Russian, 1793.

Chernobyl, Ukraine. Scene of world's worst nuclear power accident, 26 Apr. 1986, resulting in many immediate fatalities and world-wide repercussions as far away as Sweden and the UK. Two reactors restarted at C., 1992, but complex said to be still potentially dangerous, and minor accident in 1993. One reactor shut down, Jan. 1994; in Mar. 1994 international observers pronounced whole plant to be basically unsafe; in July 1994 Western powers offered Ukraine £1 billion in return for closure of C. 1995: Ukraine promises European Union it will close C. by year 2000 but requests aid of £4 billion.

Cherokees. Tribe of N American Indians. Have a written alphabet of 85 letters invented by a Cherokee, George Guess, in 1821.

Chesapeake Bay, USA. Explored by Capt. John Smith, 1607, who arrived there with colonists. British incursions in 1779. Comte de Grasse with French fleet arrived at, 30 Aug. 1781, and battle took place between French and English fleets, 5 Sept. 1781. Blockaded by English, 5 Feb. 1812.

chess. Learnt by the Persians from India or China where it was known in the 7thC. Persians' name for it was *shatranj*. In AD 950 an Arabic author, Masudi, spoke of the game as having existed before his time. *The Game and Playe of the Chesse*, second book printed by Caxton, probably appeared, 1475. The first important writer on modern C. was the Spaniard, Ruy López de Segura, 1561. First world champion was Wilhelm Steinitz of Austria, 1866. Official world champions since then:

1894–1921	Lasker, Germany
1921–27	Capablanca, Cuba
1927–35	Alekhine, France.
1935–37	Euwe, Netherlands
1937–46	Alekhine, France
1948–57	Botvinnik, USSR
1957–58	Smyslov, USSR
1958–59	Botvinnik, USSR
1960–61	Tal, USSR
1961–63	Botvinnik, USSR
1963–69	Petrosian, USSR
1969–72	Spassky, USSR
1972–75	Fischer, USA
1975–85	Karpov, USSR
1985–	Kasparov, USSR (then Russia)

In 1992, Fischer (USA) beat Spassky (Russia) in Belgrade, but this was not recognized as a world championship contest. In Jan. 1993 Short (Britain) beat Timman (Netherlands) in Barcelona, becoming the first British world champion finalist for over 100 years: played Kasparov for the world title in London

later in 1993, though both were expelled from the World Chess Federation in March 1993. Kasparov won, Oct. 1993.

Chester, England. Called by the Britons *Caerleon*. The *Deva* of the Romans, whose XXth Legion was stationed there until the end of the 4thC. Taken by Ethelfrid, King of Northumbria, 607. Occupied by a Danish army in 894, which retained it till rebuilt by Ethelfleda, Countess of Mercia, *c.* 908. Britons once more masters *c.* 918, but soon driven out by Edward the Elder (*d.* 924). Taken by parliamentary forces, 1645. Castle attacked by Fenians, 1867. C. cathedral (originally a Benedictine abbey) dated from 1053.

Chevening, 18thC house in Kent, given to the nation by the 7th Earl Stanhope, 1959, and at present used as a residence by the Foreign Secretary.

Chicago, USA. Site visited by Joliet and Marquette, 1673; Fort Dearborn built, 1803; Indians massacred the settlers, 1812; fort rebuilt, 1816; C. received first city charter, 1837; almost entirely destroyed by fire, 7–11 Oct. 1871; rebuilt, 1872–3; world's first skyscraper at, 1887–8; private University of C. founded, 1891; C. Art Institute, 1893. Federal Reserve Bank, 1914. Severe race riots at, 1919. Stockyard fire, 1934; stockyards finally closed after World War II. Sears Centre, then tallest building in world, (110 floors, 1454 ft/443 m) completed, 1973.

Chichester, England. Site of Roman town, *Noviomagus*. Cathedral completed *c.* 1108; rebuilt, 1187. City captured by Parliamentarians, 1643; fortifications destroyed, 1648. New theatre opened, 1962. Serious flooding in, 1994.

Child Benefit. *See* FAMILY ALLOWANCES.

Child Support Act, 1991, in effect from 1993, established the Child Support Agency, whose activities in demanding payments from absent parents in respect of their children caused controversy, 1993/4; amended, 1995.

Children Acts. That of 1908 was introduced into the House of Commons by Visc. (then Sir Herbert) Samuel, and much amended by the Children and Young Persons Act, 1933, and the Children Acts of 1948 and 1952, the Children and Young Persons Act of 1969, and the Children Act of 1975. Act of 1989, aiming to give children more protection and safeguard their rights and parental rights, came into operation, 1991.

Children, National Society for Prevention of Cruelty to, established by Benjamin Waugh (1839–1908) in 1884, and incorporated under royal charter, 1895.

Chile. Peruvians acquired territory from Indians inhabiting C., 1450. Discovered by Magellan, 1520. Peruvian dominion ceased, 1533. Spanish invasion, 1435–6, driven back. Detached from Peru, 1568. Treaty of Spain and C. fixing boundary, 1722. Chileans declared independence of Spain, 18 Sept. 1810. Constitution established, 25 May 1833. War declared against Spain, 29 Sept. 1865. Treaty with Peru against Spain, 14 Jan. 1866. War with Bolivia and Peru, 1 Mar. 1879. Peace treaty with Spain confirmed, Sept. 1881. Peace treaty with Bolivia, 25 Jan. 1882; war resumed, July 1882. Peace with Peru, 20 Oct. 1883, by which Peru ceded southernmost province of Tarapaca. Treaty ending territorial dispute between C. and Bolivia signed, 17 Oct. 1905. Tacna ceded to Peru, 1929. Roman Catholic Church disestablished, 1925. Marxist rule 1970–3 followed by a right-wing coup, 1973 and repressive regime. New constitution, 1981, provided for return to democracy within eight years. A plebiscite in Oct. 1988 refused to endorse Pinochet for another eight years. Elections followed in Dec. 1989 when Aylwin victorious. Subsequent return to democratic rule.

The following are the presidents of C.:
O'Higgins 1818–23
Freire 1823–30
Prieto 1830–41
Bulnes 1841–51
Montt (Manuel) 1851–61
Perez 1861–71
Zanartu 1871–76
Pinto 1876–81
Santa Maria 1881–86
Balmaceda 1886–91
Montt (Jorge) 1891–96
Errazuriz 1896–1901
Riesco 1901–06
Montt (Pedro) 1906–10
Albano 1910
Figueroa Larrain 1910
Luco 1910–15
Sanfuentes 1915–20
Alessandri 1920–24
Altamirano 1924–25
Bello 1925
Alessandri (restored) 1925
Barros 1925
Figueroa Larrain 1925–27
Ibañez 1927–31
Opazo 1931 (1 day only)
Montero 1931
Trucco 1931
Montero (again) 1931–32
Socialist Junta 1932
Davila 1932
Blanche 1932
Oyanedel 1932
Alessandri 1932–38
Aguirre 1938–41
Mendez 1941–42
Rios 1942–46
Duhalde 1946
Merino 1946
Gonzalez 1946–52
Ibañez (again) 1952–58
Alessandri 1958–64
Frei 1964–70
Allende 1970–73
Pinochet 1973–90
Aylwin 1990–94
Frei 1994–

Chiltern Hundreds. An ancient statute was amended in 1707 to provide that a Member of Parliament might resign only provided he held an office of profit under the crown. By the Place Act, 1742, the stewardship of the C.H. and of the manor of Northstead in Yorkshire were accounted offices of profit for this purpose. A steward of the C.H. was first appointed as a pretext for resignation, 1750.

Chimborazo. Volcanic mountain (height 20,660 ft/6267 m)) in Ecuador. First ascent by Edward Whymper, 1880.

chimneys. First introduced into England about 1200. Tax on C. called 'hearth-money' levied, 1662; abolished, 1689.

China. Recent research shows period of cultural flowering in C., 5000–4000 BC. Hsia Dynasty founded, 2205 BC, and overthrown 1766 BC by T'ang, who founded the Shang Dynasty, which lasted until 1122 BC, and had its capitals at Po, Nao, and Yin. In 1122 Wu Wang founded the Chou Dynasty. In 771 BC capital established at Loyang. 479 BC is the beginning of the period of the seven 'Warring States'. China conquered by Ch'in, one of the seven states, and the Chou Dynasty overthrown, 256 BC. The first emperor of the Ch'in Dynasty, Shih Huang Ti, is said to have ordered the building of the Great Wall c. 220–210 BC. Ch'in Dynasty overthrown by revolution led by Lio Pang, who as the Emperor Kao Ti established the Han Dynasty, 206 BC. Beginning of the wars against the Huns, 133 BC. Conquest of Sinkiang, 130–120 BC. Conquest of S C. and Canton, 111 BC. Conquest of Laklang in Korea, 108 BC (Japan). Submission of the Hun c. 54 BC. Usurpation of Wang Mang, AD 9, and civil war ending in re-establishment of the Han Dynasty, AD 25. Diplomatic contacts with the Roman Empire, 166. Civil war, end of the Han Dynasty, 220, and the period of the Three Kingdoms, 220–65, followed by the Tsin Dynasty. Hun invasions begin again c. 304, leading to the establishment of a Hun kingdom at Loyang, 311, and the Tsin emperors established a new capital at Nanking, 316, and repel Hun attempt to conquer the S at the battle of Fei Shui, 387. C. reunited under Wen Ti, founder of the Sui Dynasty, 581. This dynasty was overthrown in 618, and authority was re-established by Kao Tsu, who founded the T'ang Dynasty, and consolidated by his son, the emperor T'ai Tsung. Rebellion of the unpaid army in Annam led by Huang Ch'ao, 875, leads to capture of Chang An, 881, and overthrow of the T'angs, 907. C. reunited once more by Chao K'uang-yin, who as T'ai Tsu founded the Sung Dynasty, 960. N C. conquered by the Kin ('Golden') Horde, 1126, and established the Southern Sung Dynasty at Hang Chou, 1127. Mongols under Ogotai capture Kai Feng and destroy the Kin state in N C., 1233. Under Bayan they capture Hang Chou, 1276, extinguish the Sung Dynasty, 1279, and with the accession of Kublai Khan establish the Yüan Dynasty at Peking, 1260. The weakness of the Mongols after Kublai's death, 1294, leads to a Chinese revolt, 1348, which results in the Mongols being driven out of Nanking, 1356, and from Peking, 1368. Chu Yüan-chang (Tai Tsu) establishes Ming Dynasty 1368, at Nanking. Yen seizes the throne, 1402, and reigns as Ch'eng Tsu. Capital moved to Peking, 1404, which was completed in its present form, 1422. Great Wall rebuilt, 1406–25. Christianity introduced by Jesuit missionaries, 16th and 17thC, and made considerable progress in court circles. Portuguese ship under Perestrello reaches Canton, 1516. Portuguese allowed to settle at Macao, 1557. Rebellion led by Li Tzu-cheng overthrows Ming Dynasty, 1644. Manchus found the Manchu Dynasty, 1644. Accession of Kang Tsi (1662–1722) marked period of intellectual progress and great Christian influence at court. His successor, Yung Cheng, began the policy of 'exclusion'. The 'Opium War' between Britain and C., 1840–2, ends with Treaty of Nanking, 29 Aug. 1842, under which Hong Kong was ceded to Britain. Tai-ping (Christian) rebellion in Kwangsi begins under leadership of Hung Hsiu-chuan, 1850. Kung-Elgin Peace convention, 1860, by which in return for the management of the Chinese Customs the English and French were to assist in the suppression of the Tai-ping revolt. Korea becomes independent, 1876. Japan attacks C., 25 July 1894, and declares war, 2 Aug. Naval defeat at battle of the Yalu, 17 Sept. Massacre of Chinese at Port Arthur by Japanese, 21 Nov. 1894. Peace Treaty ratified with Japan, 8 May 1895. Boxer riots, 1900. War between Russia and Japan in Manchuria, Korea and the Chinese seas, 1904; by the Treaty of Portsmouth, USA, Aug. 1905, Port Arthur and Dalny were leased to Japan; Korea annexed to Japan, 23 Aug. 1910; revolution, 1911–12, abdication of the last Manchu emperor P'u-yi, 12 Feb. 1912, and the establishment of a republic with Yuan Shih-k'ai as provisional president, 15 Feb. 1912. Civil war breaks out, Dec. 1925 and by 1930 Chiang Kai-Shek was effective ruler of C. Japanese attack Manchuria, Sept. 1931 and set up puppet republic. Goes on to attack C. proper. Armistice with Japan, 1933: by this time Communists a strong force in C. and independent of the official government. 1937: The Peking 'Incident', 7 July. War breaks out again between Japan and C. Japanese take Peking, 8 Aug: Shanghai, 9 Nov.: Nanking, 12–13 Dec. Chungking made capital of Nationalist China: Burma Road completed, Dec. 1938. C. breaks off relations with Axis, July 1941; Japanese surrender in C., 12 Sept. 1945. War between Communists and Nationalists, 1946–9, ends in establishment of People's Republic, 1949. Nationalists flee to Taiwan. Communist Chinese intervened in Korean War, 1950; invaded Tibet, 1950 which was forced to accept Chinese suzerainty, 23 May 1951 and has since been subject to Chinese repression. By 1961, serious disagreements with Soviet Russia; in 1962, border fighting with India. C. exploded first atomic test bomb, Oct. 1964. In 1966 'Cultural Revolution' launched: purge of intellectuals. Increased Chinese aid to N Vietnam. In Oct. 1968 Liu Shao-ch'i, Chairman of the Republic since 1959, was expelled from the Communist party and deprived of office. C. admitted to the UN in 1971 in place of Nationalist Taiwan government. 'Cultural Revolution' over by 1972: President Nixon visited China. Chiang Kai-Shek *d.*, 1975. Mao Tse-Tung *d.*, 10 Sept. 1976. Hua Kuo-feng headed government and party radicals, the 'gang of four' (including Mao's widow) arrested and found guilty of treason, 1981. US recognized Peking government, 1979. Growing contacts with W after 1976 and some liberalization of government. Agreement with British over future of Hong Kong, 19 Dec. 1984; to return to C. in 1999. 'Open-door' policies reaffirmed at 13th party congress, 1987. Student-led pro-democracy demonstrations Apr.–May 1989 crushed by People's Liberation Army in Tiananmen Square, Peking, 3–4 June, 1989. Purge followed, thousands were killed or imprisoned. Hard-line policies adopted by Deng Xiaoping, though economic liberalization continued. Deng retired from all official posts, 1989, but (1995) retains influence in government. Martial law lasted from Mar. 1989 to Apr. 1990. After 1989 events C. isolated by most of world; gradual return to more normal international relations from 1991. Russian-Chinese agreement, 1991. Friction with Britain over Hong Kong constitutional reforms, 1992–5. Last Tiananmen Square agitators released from prison, Feb. 1993. Continuing suppression of freedom in Tibet in 1993: in Oct. 1993 C. carried out underground nuclear test in defiance of Western appeals for a moratorium. Chinese president meets US president in Seattle, Nov. 1993. Unification of Chinese exchange rates, 1 Jan. 1994. USA retains 'most favoured nation' trade status for C. despite Chinese poor human rights' record, May 1994. Britain and C. finally agree on development of new airport at *Hong Kong, 4 Nov. 1994. US-China trade war averted, Feb. 1995. May and August, 1995, C. again tests underground nuclear device and intercontinental ballistic missile system. June 1995, law passed requiring compulsory sterilization of mentally handicapped. C. said to have enabled *Iran to make nuclear warheads, 1995: UN Women's Conference held in Peking, Sept.

Dynasties, 2697 BC–AD 1126. Dynasties and Emperors, 1127–1911:

The Five Sovereigns (Legendary Epoch) 2697–2205 BC

The Hsia Dynasty 2205–1766 BC

The Shang or Yin Dynasty 1766–1122 BC

The Chou Dynasty 1122–255 BC

The Ch'in Dynasty 255–206 BC
The Han Dynasty 206 BC–AD 220
San Kuo (The Epoch of the Three Kingdoms) 220–65
The Tsin Dynasty 265–420
The Southern Dynasties 420–589
The Northern Dynasties 386–581
The Sui Dynasty 581–618
The T'ang Dynasty 618–907
Wu Tai (The Epoch of the Five Dynasties) 907–960
The Sung Dynasty 960–1279
(From 1127 the Sung Dynasty controlled diminishing area of S C. only.)

The Sung Dynasty (Southern Line), 1127–1279:
Kao Tsung (S. Sung) 1127–62
Hsiao Tsung 1162–89
Kuang Tsung 1189–94
Ning Tsung 1194–1224
Li Tsung 1224–64
Tu Tsung 1264–74
Kung Ti 1274–76
Tuan Tsung 1276–78
Ti Ping 1278–79

The Mongol (Yüan) Dynasty, 1206–1368 (Imperial title from 1279):
T'ai Tsu (Jenghiz Khan) 1206–29
T'ai Tsung (Ogotai Khan) 1229–46
Ting Tsung (Kuyak Khan) 1246–51
Hsien Tsung (Mangu Khan) 1251–60
Shih Tsu (Kublai Khan) 1260–94
Ch'eng Tsung 1294–1307
Wu Tsung 1307–11
Jen Tsung 1311–20
Ying Tsung 1320–23
T'ai Ting Ti 1323–28
Yu Chu 1328
Ming Tsung 1328–29
Wen Tsung 1329–32
Ning Tsung 1332–33
Shun Ti 1333–68

The Ming Dynasty, 1368–1644:
T'ai Tsu (Chu Yuan-chang) 1368–98
Hui Ti 1398–1402
Ch'eng Tsu 1402–24

Jen Tsung 1424–25
Hsuan Tsung 1425–35
Ying Tsung 1435–49
Tai Tsung 1449–57
Ying Tsung (restored) 1457–64
Hsien Tsung 1464–87
Hsiao Tsung 1487–1505
Wu Tsung 1505–21
Shih Tsung 1521–66
Mu Tsung 1566–72
Shen Tsung 1572–1620
Kuang Tsung 1620
Hsi Tsung 1620–27
Ssu Tsung 1627–44

The Manchu (Ch'ing) Dynasty, 1644–1911:
Shih Tsu 1644–61
Kang Tsi 1662–1722
Yung Cheng 1723–35
Kao Tsung 1735–95
Jen Tsung 1795–1820
Hsuan Tsung 1820–50
Wen Tsung 1850–61
Mu Tsung 1861–75
Teh Tsung 1875–1908
P'u-yi 1908–11

Effective Heads of Administration from 1911 to the Present Day:
Yuan Shih-k'ai: President of the Republic of C., 1911–16.
Sun Yat-sen: President of the Republic of C., 1921–5.
Chiang Kai-shek: Commander-in-Chief, Northern Armies, 1926; Generalissimo of the National Republic of C., 1928; Director-General of the Kuomintang, 1938; President of the National Republic of C., 1943; effective ruler of the National Republic of C. 1925–49, then rule confined to Taiwan, 1949–75.
Mao Tse-tung: Chairman of the Council of People's Commissars in Communist S C., 1931; Chairman of the Central People's Council of the People's Republic of C., Sept. 1949; Chairman of the Central Committee of the Chinese Communist Party only since Dec. 1958; but effective ruler of all C., excluding Taiwan, 1949–76.
Hua Kuo-feng: Prime Minister of the

People's Republic of C. and Chairman of the Central Committee of the Chinese Communist Party, 1976–81. Subsequently Hu Yaobang was effective ruler, followed by Deng Xiaoping. In June 1983 Li Hsien-nien was appointed first president since disgrace of Liu in 1969. Succeeded, 1988, by Yang Shangkun in turn, succeeded by Jiang Zeuin, April 1993. Li Peng prime minister, 1992. *See also* TAIWAN; KOREA.

Chinese Eastern Railway, a Russian-built extension of the Trans-Siberian Railway, was sold to the Government of Manchukuo in 1935. 1945–75, part of the Chinese system, jointly owned and operated by China and the USSR; reverted to China in 1975.

Chinese Literature. (*All poets unless otherwise indicated.*) Prominent figures include:

Chang Chao, 16thC AD
Chang, Eileen (Zhang Ailing). 1921–95, novelist and translator.
Chang Fang-sheng, 4thC AD
Chang Tsai, 3rdC AD
Ch'en Tzu-lung, AD 1607–47
Ch'en Tzu-ang, AD 656–98
Cheng Hsiao, *c.* AD 250
Cheng Hsuan, 127–200, commentator
Cheng-kung Sui, 3rdC AD
Chien Wen-ti, 6thC AD
Chi Kang, AD 223–62
Chi Yun, 1724–1805, story-teller
Chin Chia, 1stC AD
Chu Hsi, *fl.* 1150, commentator
Chü Yuan, 332–295 BC
Fu Hsüan, 3rdC AD
Han Yu, 768–824, essayist and philosopher
Hsi Chün, 2ndC BC
Hsiao T'ung, 501–31, anthologist
Hsü Ling, AD 507–83
Kung Fu-tze (Confucius the philosopher), 551–478 BC
Lao-tzu 570–490 BC, traditional founder of Taoism
Li Po, AD 701–62
Liu-Shahe, 1931–
Liu-Shaotang, 1936–, novelist

Lu Hsu, 1881–1936 essayist and critic
Lu Yu, AD 1125–1209
Lu Yün, 4thC AD
Ma Chih-Yuan, 1260–1321, dramatist
Miu Hsi, 3rdC AD
Pao Chao, 5thC AD
Po Chü-i, AD 772–846
P'u Sung-ling, 1640–1715, novelist
Qu Yuan, *fl.* 3000 BC
Ssu-ma Ch'ien, *c.* 145–90 BC, historian
Ssu-ma Kuang, 1019–86, historian
Su Tung-po, AD 1036–1101
Su Wu, *c.* 100 BC
Sung Tsu-Lou, 2ndC AD
Sung Yü, 4thC BC
T'ao Ch'ien, AD 365–427
T'ao Yün, *c* AD 400
Tsang Chih, 6thC AD
Tsao Chic (Prince), AD 192–233
Tsao Hsueh-ch'in 1715–64, novelist
Tsao Sung *c.* AD 900
Tso Ssu, 3rdC AD
Tu Fu, AD 712–70
Wang Chi, *c.* AD 700
Wei Wen-ti (Emperor), AD 188–227
Wu Cheng-en, 1500–82, novelist
Wu-ti (Emperor), 157–87 BC
Wu-ti (Emperor), AD 464–549
Yang-ti (Emperor), 7thC AD
Yüan Chi, AD 210–63
Yuan Chieh, 8thC AD
Yuan Mei, 1716–98, critic
Yuan-ti, AD 508–54

Chinon, France. Geoffrey of Anjou imprisoned in castle of C., 1068–96. Henry II of England *d.* at, 6 July 1189. Arrival of Joan of Arc at, to meet Charles VII, 24 Feb. 1429.

Chios. Anciently one of the more powerful Ionian maritime states, submitted to the Persians, 546 BC, but liberated by the battle of Mykale, 479, when C. joined the Delian League. Revolted against Athenian domination, 413 BC; renewed alliance with Athens, *c.* 403, but finally left the League, 357 BC. Became part of the Roman Empire, 133. Under Genoese influence from AD 1346; conquered by Turks, but given considerable local autonomy, 1566; massacre by the

Turks, 1822. C. became Greek territory after the First Balkan War in 1812. Devastated by earthquake, 1881. Used by British and French forces as a base for the Dardanelles operation, 1915. Revolt which led to fall of Constantine I began in C., 1922.

Chitral, NW Frontier Province, Pakistan, virtually independent until 1895, when the British political agent and an Indian Army garrison were besieged in the fort of C., 4 Mar.–20 Apr., after which C. became a dependency of Kashmir.

Chivalry, Court of. Species of court-martial for officers, established in Edward III's reign (1327–77), was regulated by Richard II, 1390. Between 1737 and 1955 tried no cases. In 1955 upheld Manchester Corporation's claim that a certain theatre should not display the civic coat of arms.

Chivalry, Orders of. *See* KNIGHTHOOD, ORDERS OF.

chlorine. Discovered by Scheele, 1774; experiments of Gay-Lussac and Thénard, 1809; Davy proved it to be an element, and gave it its present name, 1810; apparatus for making C. invented by Smith, 1847; used in warfare by the Germans, Apr. 1915, the British, Sept. 1915, and the Iraqis, 1983–4.

chloroform. Discovered by Liebig, 1831. First used in 1847 by Bell and Simpson.

cholera, bacillus isolated by Koch, 1883; last epidemic in Britain, 1866. The World Health Organization announced (1993) that since 1961 there had been three million cases of C. worldwide, with tens of thousands of deaths; C. outbreak among Rwandan refugees kills thousands, 1994.

Chongqing. *See* CHUNGKING.

Chouans were Breton smugglers, at first under the leadership of Jean Cottereau (1767–94), who rose in revolt against the republican government, 1793. Their activities were mainly confined to the departments of Morbihan and Eure. The Vendéans proper, together with peasants of Anjou, Poitou, Maine, and Mayenne, rose in protest against the Convention's conscription decree of Feb. 1793, their Christian Army (later called Royal and Catholic Army) had possession of most of Brittany and Poitou by Sept. 1793, though they could not capture Nantes. Defeated at Châtillon in Oct., and at Savenay in Dec., guerrilla warfare continued, until the failure of the Quiberon expedition, 20 July 1795. State of siege declared at an end, 30 July 1796. In 1815 there was a Vendéan rising, and another in 1832 against the Orléans monarchy, led by Mme de Berry.

Christ, Disciples of. *See* CAMPBELLITES.

Christadelphians. Sect founded in the USA, 1848, by an Englishman, John Thomas (1805–71).

Christchurch, New Zealand. Founded, 1851, by the Canterbury Association.

Christian Aid, charity backed by several Christian denominations, but aiming to provide international relief on an interfaith basis. Founded 1945. A Catholic counterpart, CAFOD (Catholic Fund for Overseas Development) was founded in 1962.

Christiania. *See* OSLO.

Christianity. Jesus Christ *b.* Bethlehem *c.* 4 BC. Term C. not used until second half of first century AD. Official religion of Roman Empire from 313 AD. Great Schism (separation of Orthodox Christians). 1054: Reformation, which established Protestantism, 16thC. One billion adherents, worldwide, 1995.

Christian Knowledge, Society for Promoting. Founded, 1698.

Christian Science. Theory of C.S. discovered by Mrs Mary Baker Eddy, 1866. Her book, *Science and Health with Key to the Scriptures,* 1875. By 1995 one-third of its over 2,500 groups outside the USA, including over 200 in UK. *Christian Science Monitor* established, 1908. Church of Christ, Scientist established in Boston, Massachusetts, 1879.

Christmas, Christian festival on 25 Dec. celebrating the birth of Christ, though the actual birth-date is not known. 25 Dec. coincides with Roman pagan festivals of Saturnalia and Celtic celebration of winter solstice and was traditionally chosen by Emperor Constantine (280–337) though Church had previously favoured 6 Jan., Epiphany (Coming of the Magi). Church attempted to sanctify festival with special religious services and sacred singing (carols) but pagan rites of feasting and present-giving continued alongside. St Francis (1182–1226) introduced representation of the Nativity scene. C. plays traditional in several English towns in Middle Ages, but these abolished after Reformation. Puritans attacked C. celebrations, 17thC: Parliament banned celebrations in England, 1647 and in 1859 in Massachusetts, USA, fines imposed on those observing the feast.

Modern 'commercial' celebration of C. dates from 19thC. C. Day made a public holiday in England and Wales, 1834. Dickens' *Christmas Carol* 1843, popularized C. as time of giving and celebration. First Christmas card invented by Henry Cole, 1843. C. tree custom said to have been introduced to Britain from Germany by Prince Albert in 1840s. (In Germany custom said to go back to sanctification of pagan spruce by St Boniface in 7thC.) Dutch St Nicholas transformed into Santa Claus in USA and associated with C. present-giving on 24/25 Dec. he was depicted in rich robes by illustrator Thomas Nash in 1870s but now-traditional red dress not established till 1931 and abode not Greenland till 20thC. C. reindeer mentioned in Thomas Moore's poem 'Twas the Night Before Christmas', 1822 and 'Rudolph the Red-Nosed Reindeer' invented by US marketing man, 1939. Festival increasingly commercialized and secularized as 20thC progressed: US global influence after World War II led to it being recognized as a holiday and present-giving occasion in several non-Christian countries, e.g. Japan.

Christmas Island, or **Kiritimati.** In the W Pacific, discovered by Cook, 1777. Annexed by Britain, 1898. Part of the Gilbert and Ellice Islands colony 1919–79: since then part of Republic of *Kiribati. Chosen as the site for British H-bomb tests, 1957, and subsequently used also for American tests.

Christ's Hospital (The Bluecoat School). Founded, 1552, on site of the monastery of the Grey Friars, Newgate Street, London. Charter dated 26 June 1553. School moved to W Horsham, 29 May 1902. New buildings for the girls' school at Hertford (since 1798) opened 1906.

chromium. First isolated by Vauquelin, 1797.

chromosomes. Study begun *c.* 1883 by German biologists Weismann (1834–1914) and Boveri (1862–1915). *See also* DNA

Chronicles, Anglo-Saxon. *See* ANGLO-SAXON CHRONICLES.

chronometers. Invented by John Harrison, 1726.

Chrysler Building, New York, USA, designed by William Van Alen, built 1926–30, briefly tallest building (1048 ft/ 319.4 m) until Empire State Building opened, 1931. Plans to restore, 1994.

Chungking, or **Chongqing,** China, capital of China, 1941–5. *See* BURMA ROAD.

Church Army. Mission of the Church of England, established, 1882.

Church Assembly. Set up in 1920 under the Church of England Assembly Powers Act, 1919. Abolished under the Synodical Government Measure, 1969, which substituted the *General Synod.

Church Commissioners. Set up, 1947, to unite Queen Anne's Bounty and the Ecclesiastical Commissioners. Role change suggested, 1995.

Church of England. *See* ENGLAND, CHURCH OF.

Church Missionary Society, founded 1799.

Church Union. Formed, 1859.

Cid Campeador (real name Rodrigo Diaz de Vivar), *c.* 1035–99. As the almost legendary champion of Spanish Christendom against the Moors he was the subject of a ballad-cycle, *Poema de mio Cid*, composed about 1140; of a drama, *Los Mocedades del Cid*, by Guillen de Castro, 1618, which was the basis of Corneille's tragedy, 1636; and of Southey's *Chronicles of the Cid*, 1808.

cigarettes. Popularized in England by soldiers returning from the Crimean War. First factory established at Walworth, 1856. Royal College of Physicians report, 'Smoking and Health', alleged a casual relationship between cigarette-smoking and lung cancer, Mar. 1962. Ban on television advertising of cigarettes, 1965. Subsequent voluntary agreements on limits of cigarette advertising. Tougher health warnings on C. advertisements from 1992. 'Passive smoking' an issue from the 1990s, and specifically targeted in British government anti-smoking campaign, 1993; further restrictions suggested 1994. In USA increased restrictions since 1970s most notably in California and New York.

cigars. Introduced into Britain *c.* 1812, by soldiers returning from the Peninsular War.

Cimbri. Germanic tribes from the SW Baltic area, and the Jutland Peninsula. They advanced into Illyricum and defeated the consul Papirius Carbo, 113 BC; repulsed by Drusus in Thrace 112 BC, defeated the consul Junius Silanus, in Gaul, 109; ravaged the country till checked in Thrace by Minucius Rufus, 109; victorious over the consul Aurelius Scaurus, 108; forced their way into Roman Gaul, where they defeated the consul Cnaeus Mallius and the proconsul Caepio, 105; invaded Spain, 104; driven out by the natives, 103; defeated the proconsul Lutatius Catulus, 102; forced a passage into Italy, were totally crushed by Marius at Vercellae, their league dissolved, 101.

Cincinnati, Ohio, USA. Maj. Doughty, in 1789, built Fort Washington, around which grew the present town.

Cincinnati, Order of. A republican society formed by Americans, 1783; first general meeting, May 1784.

cinematography. Principle on which C. is based – the persistence of vision – described as early as the 2ndC AD and demonstrated by Dr Peter Mark Roget, 1824. Thaumatrope, 1826. J.A. Plateau's Phenakistiscope, 1833. The principle crudely embodied in the Zoetrope patented by W.G. Horner, 1833. Marey of Paris and Heyl of Philadelphia, by 1870, had both devised cameras for recording consecutive photographs of glass discs. Goodwin (US) invented the celluloid film, 1887. Augustin le Prince granted a British patent for employment of perforated gelatine film, to reproduce a sequence of images taken through a single objective, 1888. William Friese-Greene (1855–1921) of Bristol filed English patent for camera and projector with intermittent movement and a single lens, using ribbon of sensitized celluloid, 21 June 1889. Edison's kinetoscope, on a different principle (no projection), was in use same year. A French patent for a 'cinématographe' taken out by brothers Auguste (1862–1954) and Louis (1864–1948) Lumière, 1895. A film passion-play produced in New York, 1897. First colour films ('Kinemacolor' of Smith and Urban), 1906; followed by 'Technicolor' *c.* 1929; by 'Kodachrome', 1935. 'Talking' film developed in America, 1928. 'Cinerama', 1952. 'Cinemascope', 1953. *Academy Award system instituted, 1927. Among prominent film and film actresses (some also notable stage performers) are:

Allen, Woody (American), 1935–
Andrews, Julie (British), 1935–
Arbuckle, Roscoe 'Fatty' (American), 1887–1933
Arletty, (French), 1898–1992
Astaire, Fred (American), 1899–1987
Astor, Mary (American), 1906–87
(Lord) Attenborough, Richard (British), 1923–

Bankhead, Tallulah (American), 1902–68
Bardot, Brigitte (French), 1934–
Barrault, Jean-Louis (French), 1910–94
Barrymore, John (American), 1882–1942
Bergman, Ingrid (Swedish-American), 1915–82
Bogart, Humphrey (American), c. 1900–57.
Bow, Clara (American), 1905–65
Boyer, Charles (French), 1899–1978
Brando, Marlon (American), 1924–
Burton, Richard (British), 1925–84
Cagney, James (American), 1899–1986
Caine, Michael (British), 1933–
Cantor, Eddie (American), 1893–1964
Chaplin, Charles (British-born), 1889–1977
Chevalier, Maurice (French), 1888–1972
Connery, Sean (British), 1930–
Cooper, Gary (American), 1901–61
Crosby, Bing (American), 1901–77
Cruise, Tom (American), 1962–
Davies, Marion (American), c. 1897–1961
Davis, Bette (American), 1908–
Dean, James (American), 1931–55
de Havilland, Olivia (American), 1916–
del Rio, Dolores (Mexican-born), 1905–83
Dietrich, Marlene (German-American), 1904–92
Dors, Diana (British), 1931–84
Evans, Dame Edith (British), 1888–1976
Fairbanks, Douglas (American), 1883–1939
Fernandel, (French), 1903–71
Fields, Dame Gracie (British), 1898–1979
Fields, W. C. (British-born), 1879–1946
Fonda, Henry (American), 1905–82
Gabin, Jean (French), 1904–76
Gable, Clark (American), 1901–1960
Garbo, Greta (Swedish-American), 1905–90
Garland, Judy (American), 1922–69
Gielgud, Sir John (British), 1904–
Gilbert, John (American), 1897–1936
Granger, Stewart (British), 1913–1993
Gish, Lilian (American), 1896–1993
Grant, Cary (British-born), 1904–86
Guinness, Sir Alec (British), 1914–
Hanks, Tom (American), 1956–
Hardy, Oliver (American), 1892–1957
Harlowe, Jean (American), 1911–37
Harrison, Rex (British), 1908–73
Hayes, Helen (American), 1900–93
Hepburn, Audrey (Dutch-British), 1929–93
Hepburn, Katharine (American), 1909–

Heston, Charlton (American), 1923–
Hope, Bob (British-born), 1903–
Hopkins, Sir Anthony (British), 1937–
Howard, Trevor (British), 1916–88
Jannings, Emil (German), 1884–1950
Johnson, Dame Celia (British), 1908–82
Jolson, Al (American), 1888–1950
Kaye, Danny (American), 1913–87
Keaton, 'Buster' 1895–1966
Kelly, Grace (American), 1929–82
Lamarr, Hedy, (Austro-American), 1914–
Lamour, Dorothy (American) 1914–
Lancaster, Burt (American), 1913–1994
Laughton, Charles (British), 1899–1962
Laurel, Stan (British), 1890–1965
Leigh, Vivien (British), 1913–67
Lloyd, Harold (American), 1893–1971
Lollobrigida, Gina (Italian), 1928–
Loren, Sophia (Italian), 1934–
Loy, Myrna (American), 1905–93
Maclaine, Shirley (American), 1934–
Magnani, Anna (Italian), 1909–73
Marx, Groucho (American), 1895–1977
Mason, James (British), 1909–84
Mastrianni, Marcello (Italian), 1924–
McQueen, Steve (American), 1930–80
Millan, Ray (Welsh-born), 1905–86
Mills, Sir John (British), 1906–
Monroe, Marilyn (American), 1926–62
Montand, Yves (French), 1921–
More, Kenneth (British), 1914–82
Neagle, Dame Anna (British), 1904–86.
Negri, Pola (Polish-born), 1894–1987
Newman, Paul (American), 1925–
Nicholson, Jack (American), 1937–
Niven, David (British), 1909–82
Oberon, Merle (British), 1911–79
Olivier, Laurence Lord (British), 1907–89
O'Toole, Peter (British), 1933–
Peck, Gregory (American) 1916–
Pickford, Mary (American), 1893–1979
Poitier, Sidney (American), 1924–
Powell, William (American), 1892–1983
Presley, Elvis (American), 1935–77
Price, Vincent (American), 1911–93
Rains, Claud (British), 1889–1967
Rathbone, Basil (British), 1892–1967
Redford, Robert (American), 1937–
Redgrave, Sir Michael (British), 1908–85
Richardson, Sir Ralph (British), 1902–83
Robeson, Paul (American), 1898–1976

Robinson, Edward G. (American), 1893–73
Robson, Dame Flora (British), 1902–84
Rogers, Ginger (American), 1911–95
Rogers, Will (American), 1879–1935
Rooney, Mickey (American), 1920–
Rutherford, Dame Margaret (British), 1892–1972
Scofield, Paul (British), 1922–
Sellers, Peter (British), 1925–80
Shearer, Norma (British-born) 1904–1983
Sim, Alastair (British), 1900–76
Sinatra, Frank (American), 1915–
Stewart, James (American), 1908–
Swanson, Gloria (American), 1898–1983
Temple, Shirley (American), 1928–
Thompson, Emma (British), 1959–
Tracy, Spencer (American), 1900–1967
Valentino, Rudolph (Italian-born), 1895–1926
Wayne, John (American), 1915–85
Welles, Orson (American), 1915–85
West, Mae (American), 1893–1980

Notable filmmakers/directors include:
Bergman, Ingmar (Swedish), 1918–
Cocteau, Jean (French), 1889–1963
Disney, Walt (American), 1901–66
Durand, Jean (French), 1882–1946
Duvivier, Julien (French), 1896–1967
Eisenstein, Sergei (Russian), 1898–1948
Fellini, Federico (Italian), 1920–93
Ford, John (American), 1895–1973
Godard, Jean Luc (French), 1930–
Griffiths, David Wark (American), 1875–1948
Hitchcock, Alfred (British), 1899–1980
Ho Dasuke (Japanese), 1898–1981
Jarman, Derek (British) 1942–94
Korda, Alexander (Hungarian), 1893–1956
Kubrick, Stanley (US-born), 1928–
Kurosawa, Akira (Japanese), 1910–
Lang, Fritz (German), 1890–1976
Lean, David (British), 1908–91
Loach, Ken (British), 1936–
Losey, Joseph (American), 1909–84–
Lubitsch, Ernst (German), 1892–1947
Mankiewiecz, Joseph (American), 1909–
Ozu, Yasujiro (Japanese), 1903–63
Pasolini, Pier Paolo (Italian), 1922–75
Polanski, Roman (Polish), 1933–
Powell, Michael (British), 1905–90

Preminger, Otto, (Austrian), 1906–86
Pressburger, Emeric (Hungarian), 1902–88
Puttnam, David (British), 1941–
Ray, Satyajit (Indian), 1922–92
Reed, Carol (British), 1906–76
Renoir, Jean (French), 1894–1979
Roach, Hal (American), 1892–1992
Rossellini, Roberto (Italian), 1906–77
Schlesinger, John (British), 1926–
Schlondorff, Volker (German), 1939–
Scorsese, Martin (US), 1942–
Spielberg, Steven (American), 1947–
Truffaut, François (France), 1932–84
Vadim, Roger (French), 1928–
Vidor, Charles (Hungarian), 1900–59
Wilcox, Herbert (British), 1892–1977
Winner, Michael (British), 1935–
Zeffirelli, Franco (Italian), 1923–

Several famous stage and screen actors have also directed films: among them Richard (Lord) Attenborough, Charlie Chaplin, Orson Welles, Laurence (Lord) Olivier and Woody Allen. (*See separate lists.*)

Cinque Ports, England. Originally five in number: Dover, Hastings, Hythe, Romney and Sandwich; Rye and Winchelsea were added by Richard I. Fortified by William I, 1067; Henry III granted privileges to, 1216. Charter surrendered to the crown, 1688.

Cintra, Portugal. Convention of, concluded between Sir Hew Dalrymple and Marshal Junot, 30 Aug. 1808.

Circassia, ceded to Russia by Turkey, 1829, but did not finally submit to Russian rule until 1859.

circulation of the blood. *See* BLOOD, CIRCULATION OF THE.

Cirta. *See* CONSTANTINE.

CIS. *see* COMMONWEALTH OF INDEPENDENT STATES.

Cisalpine Gaul. *See* GAUL.

Cisalpine Republic. N Italian republic set up by Napoleon, 1797. Later known as the

Italian republic, and converted into the Napoleonic kingdom of Italy, 1805.

Ciskei, from 1981. 'Bantu homeland' in S Africa, though only S Africa recognized its independence. Absorbed into S Africa, Mar. 1994.

Cistercian Order, founded at Cîteaux by St Robert, Abbot of Molêsme, 1098.

Citizen's Charter, published in July 1991 as a White Paper and covering all privatized public utilities and public services.

City Companies. See LIVERY COMPANIES.

City of London University, name and status of former City of London Polytechnic since 1992.

City University, London EC, established 1966.

Ciudad Trujillo. See SANTO DOMINGO.

Civic Forum, dissident pro-democracy Czech movement, formed under leadership of Vaclav Havel, 1989, instrumental in restoring democracy to *Czechoslovakia.

Civic Trust, founded 1957.

Civil Defence Bill. Passed, June 1939.

Civil List. The revenue awarded to the sovereigns of England in return for the crown lands. From 1697 C.L. fixed by Parliament. Scope reduced, 1993.

Civil Rights Bill. Introduced into US Senate, 29 Jan. 1866; passed 13 Mar. 1866; amended, 1875. New C.R.B. became law, 1964.

Civil Wars in Great Britain:
King Stephen and Matilda, 1139–53.
King John and Barons, 1215–16.
Henry III and Barons, 1263–65.
Edward II and Barons, 1321–27.
Henry IV and Owen Glendower, 1403–05.
*Wars of the Roses, 1455–71, also 1485.
Covenanters and Scottish Episcopalians, 1638–43, 1666, 1679 and intermittently until 1688.
Charles I and Parliament, 1642–46.

Charles II and Parliament, 1650–51.
James II and Duke of Monmouth, 1685.
See also JACOBITES.

Civil Wars. Major modern C. Ws., other than in Great Britain include:

Civil War, American, 1861–65.
Civil War, Russian, 1917–22.
Civil War, Spanish, 1936–39.
Civil War, Vietnamese, 1959–75.
Civil War, Yemeni, 1962–68; 1994
Civil War, Nigerian, 1967–70.
Civil War, Jordanian, 1970.
Civil War, Zimbabwe-Rhodesia, 1970–79.
Civil War, Uganda, 1979.
Civil War, Lebanon, 1975–91.
Civil War, Angola, 1975–91; 1993–4.
Civil War, Afghanistan, 1979–88; sporadic fighting since.
Civil War, Cambodia, 1977–92 (officially; but some fighting continuing).
Civil War, Ethiopia, 1978–91.
Civil War, El Salvador, 1980–92
Civil War, Nicaragua, 1982–90
Civil War, Sri Lanka, 1983–
Civil War, Sudan, 1988 (but origins in 1960s).
Civil War, Rwanda, 1989–94.
Civil War, Liberia, 1989–
Civil War, Georgia, 1991–
Civil War, Somalia, 1991–94.
Civil War, *Croatia, 1991–92.
Civil War, *Bosnia, 1992–95
Civil War, Algeria, 1992–
Civil War, Burundi, 1993–94.

---

*These C.W. part of a larger C.W. which involves parts of the former Yugoslavia, with the Serbs generally opposed to the other ethnic groups.

Clarendon Code. A series of English statutes designed to establish the political supremacy of the Anglican Church and to destroy the power of the Presbyterians. The principal Acts were: Corporation Act, Dec. 1661. Act of Uniformity, May 1662. Conventicle Act, July 1664; Five-Mile Act, Oct. 1665.
The C.C. was called after Edward Hyde,

Earl of Clarendon, who was Lord Chancellor, 1661, until banished, 1667.

Clarendon, Constitution of. Drawn up chiefly by Richard de Lucy at Council of C., near Salisbury, to limit the power of the clergy, 25 Jan. 1164. Abandoned by Henry II at Avranches, Sept. 1172.

Clarendon Press. The original name of the press of the University of Oxford, founded, 15thC; printing house erected by Sir John Vanburgh, 1711–13 (with profits of Clarendon's *History of the Rebellion*, Oct. 1713).

Clayton-Bulwer Treaty. Negotiated in Apr. 1850 by John Middleton Clayton of the USA and Sir Henry Bulwer of Great Britain, superseded by new treaty, Feb. 1902.

Clearing-House. Bankers' C.-H. for exchange of drafts and bills set up in Lombard Street, 1770; joined by Bank of England, May 1804.

Cleopatra's Needles. Two granite obelisks erected by Thothmes III at Heliopolis (*c.* 1475 BC) and re-erected by Augustus at Alexandria. (1) Transferred to London and placed on the Victoria Embankment, 1878. (2) Presented by the khedive to the USA and erected in Central Park, New York, 1881.

Clerkenwell (London). Grew up round St John's Church, founded, 1140. C. Bridewell (house of correction) built, 1615; burnt down, 1669, but rebuilt. Succeeded by a House of Detention, 1775. Scene of a Fenian outrage, 1867; closed, 1877.

Cleveland, English administrative county established 1974 under the Local Government Act of 1972. Abolition suggested by boundary commission review, 1993; to be effective, 1996.

Cleves (Kleve). County, afterwards duchy, Germany. War of succession, 1609; concluded, 1614. C. given to Elector of Brandenburg; settlement confirmed, 1666. Seized by French, 1757; restored to Germany, 1763. In 1795 Prussia ceded the

part on left bank of Rhine to France. Exchanges took place, 1803–15; outcome: France gave up all to Prussia and Holland.

clocks. Chinese claim invention *c.* 2000 BC. Water-C. (Clepsydrae) used in ancient Greece, 4thC BC. Introduced into Rome *c.* 160 BC. Earliest C. of mechanical type in Europe, 12thC AD. First reliable C. set up in palace of Charles V of France by de Vick, 1379. Law of pendulum first applied to C. by Huygens *c.* 1657. First successful electric clocks invented by Hope-Jones and Bowell, 1894: quartz-crystal C., 1929: atomic C., 1952.

closure. First authorized in the House of Commons by the Urgency Rules of 1881. Power first vested in Speaker, but transferred to House, 19 Mar. 1887.

Cloth of Gold, Field of the. Abortive conference between Henry VIII of England and Francis I of France, held near Guisnes, 6 June 1520.

clubs. First heard of in England during Elizabeth I's reign. Shakespeare and his friends met at the Mermaid Tavern. Ben Jonson set up a club at the Devil Tavern. The Rota instituted, 1659; White's, 1693; the Kit-Kat, 1700; Beef-steak, 1735; Boodles', 1762; Johnson's, 1764; Brooks's 1764; Almack's 1765; Travellers', 1819; Athenaeum, 1823; Garrick, 1831; Carlton, 1832; Reform, 1836; Savage, 1857; Savile, 1868; Turf, 1868; National Liberal, 1882; Canning, 1910; Lansdowne, 1934; Groucho, 1985.

Cluny, France. Benedictine abbey, founded 910. By 1150, 314 European monasteries had embraced Cluniac regime and were completely subject to C. Abbey suppressed during French Revolution and closed, 1790. Most of it demolished, early 19thC and material used for building work; but S transept remains and is now preserved by the state. Town of C. granted charter by St Hugh, abbot of C., 1190. C. Museum is housed in abbot's former town house (built *c.* 1480). Collection of medieval arts and crafts, assembled by du Sommand, its owner, from 1833, acquired by state in 1842; reorganized in 1950s.

Clwyd. Welsh administrative county established 1974 under the Local Government Act of 1972; plans to abolish, 1995

Cnossos. *See* KNOSSOS.

coach. First used in England in mid-16thC. Bill to prevent men from riding in coaches as too effeminate, 1601. Stage-coaches used for public conveyance in England from the mid-17th–19thC.

coal seems to have been used for fuel in pre-Roman times in Britain: written evidence that it was being mined in Newcastle, 1233; forbidden to be burnt in England, 1273. Nobility and gentry of London petition against use of, 1306. Not in general use in England until 1625. C. Commission established by C. Act, 1938, in which the ownership of all C. vested as from 1 July 1942. Mines nationalized as from 1 Jan. 1947; decline of industry in Britain from 1960s. Coal strike, 1984–5. Proposed closure of 31 pits by government caused public outcry, Oct. 1992, but pits nevertheless continued to be closed prior to coal privatization. British C. ceased to exist, 31 Oct. 1994, becoming the C. Authority, with power to licence, etc., Privatization complete, Dec.

coalition of European states against France, generally brought about by British influence:
1. Great Britain, Austria and Prussia, 1793.
2. Great Britain, Germany, Russia, Naples, Portugal and Turkey, 1799.
3. Great Britain, Austria, Naples and Russia, 1805.
4. Great Britain, Prussia, Russia and Saxony, 1806.
5. Great Britain and Austria, 1809.
6. Prussia and Russia, 1813.

coalition governments in Britain, 1757, 1782, 1783, 1852, 1915, 1931, 1940.

cobalt. Isolated in 1735 by Brandt.

Cobden Club. Founded London, 1866, to spread principles of Richard Cobden.

Coburg, in *Franconia, is first mentioned in documents, 1056, and became a city in 1331. It became the capital of the duchy of Saxe-Saalfeld-C., 1735, and of Saxe-C.-Gotha, 1926. During the 19thC members of its royal house succeeded to the thrones of Belgium, Bulgaria and Great Britain. *See* all of these.

cocaine. First used as an anaesthetic by Koller, 1884. Recognized as an addictive drug after First World War: major illegal world traffic in, from 1980s emanating in the first instance notably from Bolivia and Colombia.

Cochin, Kerala state, India, was once part of the kingdom of Kerala, where Jews and Christians of St Thomas settled in the 1stC AD; these communities still exist. Vasco da Gama sighted the coast, 1498, and Portuguese settled in C. city, 1502, with the permission of the local kings, independent since the 9thC, to build a fort. The Dutch expelled the Portuguese, 1663. C. became subject to Hyder Ali of Mysore, 1776, but was ceded to the British by Tippu Sahib, 1791.

Cochin China. *See* INDO-CHINA.

cock-fighting. Prohibited by Edward III, 1365; by Cromwell, 1653, and finally in 1849. Still occasionally illegally held in UK, 20thC.

Cock Lane Ghost. Sensation caused by fraudulent representations of William Parsons, his wife, and daughter in 1760–1 at Cock Lane, London. Parsons and wife convicted and imprisoned, 10 July 1762.

cocoa and chocolate. Cocoa beans first brought to Europe by Columbus, 1494. Cortez found Aztecs using chocolate as a beverage, 1519, and introduced it to Spain. First 'chocolate house' opened in London, 1657. Eating chocolate first produced in Britain, 1847.

Cocos (or **Keeling**) **Islands,** discovered by Capt. William Keeling, 1609. British protectorate, 1856. Territory under the Commonwealth of Australia, 22 Nov. 1955. A referendum in 1984 voted for integration with Australia.

Code Napoléon. Codification of French civil law was promised by the constitutions of 1791 and 1793, but commissions did not begin work until 1800. The task lasted until 1802, and the necessary measures passed by the Assemblies, 1803–4. The name C.N. was suppressed between 1814 and 1852, but the third and final revision appeared in 1816. The C.N. in French criminal law was replaced by a new Criminal Law, 1994.

Codex Alexandrinus. *See* ALEXANDRINUS, CODEX.

Codex Sinaiticus. *See* SINAITICUS, CODEX.

coelacanths. Group of specialized crossopterygian fishes. Originally thought to have become extinct 50 million years ago. But one caught off E London, Cape Province, 1938; second specimen caught near Madagascar, 1952.

coffee. Introduced to Europe in the 17thC. First English coffee-house opened in Oxford, 1650.

Cognac, Treaty of, between the parties to the *Holy League of 1526.

Coimbra. Capital of Portugal, 1139–1260. Portugal's oldest university, founded at Lisbon, 1290, settled at C., 1537. Its library 1716–23, contains over one million books. Inez de Castro murdered at C., 1355.

Colchester, England (Latin *Camulodunum*). Oldest recorded town in Britain. Cunobelinus reigned in C., 5 BC–AD 43. Became Roman headquarters in Britain, 43. Burnt by Boudicca, 61. End of Roman occupation *c.* 367. First charter, 1189. Castle surrendered to Fairfax in civil war, 1648; University of Essex opened at, 1964.

Cold War, popular term for the ideological, economic and political conflicts existing between the Western democracies and the Soviet-dominated regimes in Europe and elsewhere from 1945 until the collapse of the Soviet system in 1990.

Colditz, castle near Leipzig, Germany, used as a high-security camp for Allied prisoners during the Second World War. Famous escape from there, 1942.

Coleraine, Ulster. New University of Ulster established at, 1965.

Cologne (German **Köln**; Latin *Colonia Agrippina*). Founded *c.* 37 BC by the Ubii. Colony of Roman veterans established there by Agrippina the Younger, AD 51. Diet held at by Charlemagne, 782, and made an archbishopric, 785. Joined Hanseatic League, 1201. Cathedral founded by Archbishop Conrad von Hochstaden, 1248. Town established its independence of the archbishop at the battle of Worringen, 1299. C. incorporated with France at the peace of Campo Formio, 1797, but annexed by Prussia, 1815. Cathedral completed, 1880. Garrisoned by British Rhine Army, 1918–25. City heavily bombed, 1942–5. Captured by American troops, 7 Mar. 1945, centre rebuilt since. Extensive flooding Dec. 1993 and Jan.–Feb., 1995.

Colombia. South American republic. Coast traditionally said to have been visited by Columbus, 1502. Area revolted against Spain, 1811, and achieved independence, 1819. Part of Greater Colombia, 1819–30; when Venezuela and Ecuador seceded, C. called itself the Republic of New Granada, 1831–50. Confederation Granadina, 1858; United States of Colombia, 1863; Republic of Colombia, 1886. *Panama seceded from C., 1903. Civil unrest from 1950s and from 1957–74. C. governed under agreement whereby the two main parties held the Presidency in turn. In elections for constitutional assembly, 1990 former guerrilla movement got 30% of votes. New constitution, 1991. Colombian government waging war against drug barons since 1980s. C. main source of illegal cocaine trade; bombings, murders caused by drug barons increased in 1990s. Escobar, major Colombian 'drug baron', shot dead by police in Medellin, 2 Dec. 1993. Earthquake in SW C., Feb. 1995, killed over 30. Orejuela, whose Cali drug cartel said to control 80% of the world's cocaine trade, arrested in Medellin, 10 June 1995; he escaped, but was recaptured, Aug.

Colombo, capital of *Sri Lanka. First mentioned by European sources, 1346, was taken by the Portuguese, 1517; from them by the Dutch, 1656; surrendered to the British, 1796.

Colombo Plan for Co-operative Economic Development in S and SE Asia, published 28 Nov. 1950, in force 1 July 1951, originally with seven Commonwealth members. Subsequently joined by USA and Japan and several countries in the Pacific area.

Colonial Office. Founded as the Council 'for the Plantations', 1660. Secretary of state for the colonies first appointed, 1854. Merged with the *Commonwealth Relations Office, 1966.

Colonies (British), most of which have since had a change of name and status, were declared as such on the dates given below:

Aden, 1839.
African Forts, 1618.
Anguilla, 1666.
Antigua, 1632.
Ascension, 1815.
Australia, S, 1834.
Australia, W, 1829.
Bahama Islands, 1629. Restored, 1783.
Barbados, 1605.
Bengal, 1652.
Berbice, 1803.
Bermudas, 1609.
Bombay, 1662.
British Burma, 1862.
British Columbia, 1858.
British Guiana, 1814.
British Honduras, 1862.
British Indian Ocean Territory, 1965.
British N Borneo, 1946.
British Somaliland, 1884.
Canada, 1760.
Cape Breton, 1763.
Cape Coast Castle, 1667.
Cape of Good Hope, 1806.
Ceylon, 1815.
Cyprus, 1878.
Demerara and Essequibo, 1803.
Dominica, 1763.
Elmina and Dutch Guinea, 1871.
Falkland Islands, 1833.
Fiji, 1874.
Gambia, 1843.
Gibraltar, 1704.
Gilbert and Ellice Islands, 1915.
Gold Coast, 1874.
Grenada, 1763.
Hong Kong, 1841.
Jamaica, 1655.
Keeling (Cocos) Islands, 1857.
Kenya, 1920.
Kermadec Islands, 1886.
Labuan, 1846.
Lagos, 1861.
Leeward Isles, 1763.
Madras, 1640.
Malacca, 1795(–1818), 1824, 1946.
Malta and Gozo, 1800.
Mashonaland, 1890.
Matabeleland, 1890.
Mauritius, 1814.
Montserrat, 1632.
Natal, 1843.
Nevis, 1628.
New Brunswick, 1713.
Newfoundland, 1583.
New Guinea, 1884.
New Hebrides (Condominium), 1906.
New S Wales, 1787.
New Zealand, 1840.
Niger districts, 1886.
Norfolk Island, 1787.
Nova Scotia, 1622.
Orange Free State, 1902.
Pegu, 1852.
Penang, 1786, 1946.
Pitcairn Island, 1898.
Port Phillip, 1840.
Prince Edward Island, 1745.
Prince of Wales Island, 1786.
Queensland, 1860.
Rhodesia, Northern, 1924.
Rhodesia, Southern, 1923.
St Helena, 1673.
St Kitts, 1623.

St Lucia, 1803.
St Vincent, 1763.
Sarawak, 1946.
Seychelles, 1810.
Sierra Leone, 1787.
Singapore, 1819.
Socotra, 1886.
Straits Settlements, 1826.
Tasmania, 1803.
Tobago, 1763.
Tortola, 1666.
Transvaal, 1901.
Trinidad, 1797.
Tristan da Cunha, 1816.
Vancouver Island, 1781.
Victoria. *See* Port Phillip.
Virgin Isles, 1666.
Windward Isles, 1803.

See also PROTECTORATES, BRITISH.

Colorado was partly acquired by the USA from France under the Louisiana Purchase, 1803, and partly from Mexico, 1848. Gold was found in 1858, and until 1910 C. was the leading US state for the production of this metal. Indian wars, 1860–5. Admitted to the union, 1876.

Colorado beetle. Potato pest which reached Europe from the USA, 1922. There have been sporadic outbreaks of the pest in Britain since 1933.

Colosseum, Rome. Begun, AD 72, by Vespasian. Finished, 80, by Titus.

Colossus of Rhodes. *See* APOLLO OF RHODES.

Colour Bar. *See* APARTHEID; RACIAL DISCRIMINATION.

Columbia, District of, originally an area of 100 square miles, was ceded by Virginia and Maryland, 1790–1, divided by the Potomac; but in 1846 Virginia recovered her portion. Congress first met in the district, 1800. By its Act of 1895 the city of *Washington became co-extensive with the district. Citizens of C. were given the right to vote in national elections by the 23rd Amendment to the US Constitution, 30 Mar. 1962. *See* WHITE HOUSE.

Columbia University (New York, USA). Founded, 1754, as King's College; re-incorporated as C. College, 1784; the title of university adopted, 1896.

Columbus, Christopher (Cristobal Colón), *b. c.* 1446, *d.* 20 May 1506. Voyages:
1. 3 Aug. 1492–15 Mar. 1493 to San Salvador, Cuba, Haiti.
2. 24 Sept. 1493–11 June 1496 to W Indies.
3. 30 May 1498–Summer 1499. Possibly American mainland.
4. 9 May 1502–7 Nov. 1504. Gulf of Mexico.

combat, trial by, or **wager of battle** does not appear to have been customary in England before 1066, except perhaps in the Danelaw. The custom was brought to Normandy from Scandinavia and thence to England, where it was condemned by the Church, 1215, and thus fell into desuetude though still legal. An accused murderer challenged his accuser – who shirked the challenge – and was acquitted, 1817; this led to the immediate abolition of T. by C.

Combination Laws. Various measures, repealed 1824, which had the effect of rendering trade unions or manufacturers' associations illegal.

Comecon. *See* COUNCIL FOR MUTUAL ECONOMIC AID.

Comédie Française. In 1658 the touring company of Molière (*see* FRENCH LITERATURE) settled in the Rue Guénégaud, Paris, under the name of the Illustrious Theatre, where it had only one serious rival, the Hôtel de Bourgogne players. The two troupes were ordered by Louis XIV to amalgamate in 1680, and moved to the Rue de l'Ancienne-Comédie, 1687, and to the Tuileries, 1771. The company split in 1790 into two rival political groups – Théâtre de la Nation and Théâtre de la République, both of which perished before the C. was revived in 1802 by Napoleon, who in 1812 laid down regulations which are still largely binding on the company.

Cominform ('Communist Information Bureau'). A body formed at Russian dictation to direct the activities of the Communist parties of Europe, 1947. Yugoslav Communist Party expelled from, 28 June 1943. Dissolved, 17 Apr., 1956.

Comintern ('Communist International'). Founded, 1919. Formally dissolved, 10 June 1943.

commando, an Afrikaans word for a military unit, mobile column of varying size under a *Commandant* (roughly, lieutenant-colonel); became familiar to the British when the Second S African War entered its guerrilla phase (1900 onwards), but had been in use since the early 19thC. British Cs. were formed from special service battalions, which themselves were made up of companies, once independent, of volunteers from the Army and Royal Marines, first raised in June 1940, and controlled and trained by Combined Operations Command under Sir Roger Keyes, who was succeeded, 27 Oct. 1941, by Lord Louis Mountbatten. Dates of some C. operations are: 6 Mar. 1941, Lofoten; Nov., Beda Littoria and Cyrene; 27 Dec., Vaagsö; 27 Feb. 1942, Breuneval; 28 Mar., St Nazaire; May, Diego Suarez, Madagascar; 19 Aug., Dieppe; June 1944; Normandy; Oct., Walcheren. Cs. reverted to Marine command in Oct. 1945.

Committee of Imperial Defence, organized, 1890. Abolished on creation of Ministry of Defence, 1946.

Committee of Public Safety.
1. USA. In Massachusetts, 1774.
2. France. In Paris, 6 Apr. 1793.

Committee of Safety. Formed by officers of the army after retirement of Richard Cromwell from the protectorship, 29 Oct. 1659.

Common Agricultural Policy (CAP) established by the Treaty of Rome, 1957. One of the most controversial aspects of the European (Economic) Community, the CAP was radically reformed, May 1992, after prolonged and bitter negotiations.

Common Carrier, liabilities of, governed by Carriers' Act, 1830; Railway and Canal Traffic Act, 1854; Road and Rail Traffic Act, 1933; Transport Act, 1947. Carriage of Goods by Road Act, 1965; Civil Aviation Acts, 1949–71; Carriage of Passengers by Road Act, 1974; Merchant Shipping Act, 1974.

Common Council of London has existed since the 14thC; the constitution of its court is virtually unchanged from that period (except that members formerly elected by trades are now elected by ratepayers of wards). Elections take place annually, 21 Dec.

Common Market. *See* EUROPEAN ECONOMIC COMMUNITY; EUROPEAN COMMUNITY; EUROPEAN UNION.

Common Penny, The (German **das gemeine Pfennig**). Tax first levied in the Holy Roman Empire to raise money for the Turkish Wars, 1471; renewed, 1496; renewed again for the Venetian War, 1512.

Common Pleas, Court of. One of the old common law courts existing as a superior court of record. Merged in the C.P. division of the high court, 1873, and finally transferred to the Queen's Bench Division by an Order in Council, 1881.

Common Prayer, Book of. *See* PRAYER, BOOK OF COMMON.

Commons, House of. Originated in 13thC practice of calling up knights and burgesses to give information to the government at Westminster. In embryonic form at Simon de Montfort's Parliament, 1265. 'Model' Parliament, 1295. Claimed right to take part in legislation, 1322. Claimed right to originate direct taxation, 1407. Committee of the whole House instituted *c.* 1600. Privileges confirmed by Petition of Right, 1628, and Bill of Rights, 1689. Franchise and basis of representation altered by Reform Act, 1832. Franchise further extended, 1867, 1884. Power to overrule the *House of Lords given by Parliament Act, 1911, and extended by further legislation under the Labour Government, 1949. Franchise extended to women, 1918 and 1928. Further alterations in system of representation, 1945, 1969. Chamber bombed, 1941; restored and re-opened, 1950. House of Commons proceedings first televised live, 1989. *See* PARLIAMENT.

Commonwealth, association of independent states (*see* separate articles), the majority being former colonies of Britain. The C. Secretariat has been established at *Marlborough House, London since 1965. Since the 1950s, meetings of C. heads of state (C. Conferences) have superseded the *Prime Ministers Meetings. They are held biannually, in different member countries. (1991, Zimbabwe; 1993, Cyprus; 1995, New Zealand). In 1993 the C. had 50 members. States which have left the C. are: Republic of Ireland (1949); S Africa (1961: but rejoined 1994); Pakistan (1971: rejoined 1989); Fiji (1987).

Commonwealth Day, inaugurated, 1902, as **Empire Day**, on 24 May. Queen Victoria's birthday. Name changed to C.D., 1958. and date changed from 1966–76 to the sovereign's official birthday. Since then, held on second Monday in March, with multifaith service in Westminster Abbey.

Commonwealth, English. Lasted from 1649 until 1653.

Commonwealth Games, first held, 1930, in Hamilton, Canada, as the British Empire Games. Became British Empire and Commonwealth Games, 1954; British Commonwealth Games from 1970, though word 'British' now (1995) dropped in practice. Held every four years in a Commonwealth city. Were in Auckland, New Zealand, 1990; in Victoria, Canada, 1994.

Commonwealth Immigrants Act, 1962. Provided for restrictions on the number of Commonwealth citizens entering the UK, and enabled alleged undesirables to be deported to their place of origin. Provisions became law during 1962 (May–July). Further Acts, 1968 and 1971 the latter of which assimilated control of Commonwealth immigrants with that of aliens.

Commonwealth Institute (London). Built to commemorate Queen Victoria's Jubilee, 1887, and named the Imperial Institute; opened 1893. Changed its name to the C.I. under the Commonwealth Institute Act, 1958. Queen Elizabeth II opened the Institute's new buildings in Kensington, Nov. 1962.

Commonwealth of Independent States (CIS) was instituted, 8 Dec. 1991, on break-up of the *USSR. It comprises (1995) the 12 former constituent republics of the USSR – Russia, Ukraine, Azerbaijan, Uzbekhistan, Kazakhstan, Belarus, Moldova, Tajikstan, Kirghizia Bishek, Armenia, Turkmenistan and Georgia. Azerbaijan left the CIS in 1992 but rejoined in Sept. 1993. Georgia originally refused to join but acceded, Mar. 1994 in return for Russian military aid in its civil war. On 21 Dec. 1991 the then members endorsed the idea of a 'single economic space' and also the principle of unitary control of strategic nuclear arms, but both concepts have so far (1995) been found difficult to put into practice. Russia and six other members signed a 'charter of integration', Jan. 1993. HQ of CIS is at Minsk. Agreement among 12 members on closer economic ties, Oct. 1994 marked Russian ascendancy.

Commonwealth Relations Office was separated from the Colonial Office, 1925 (under name of Dominions Office), and called C.R.O. from July 1947. The *Colonial Office merged with the C.R.O., 1966; it was itself merged with the Foreign Office, 1968.

Commune of Paris.

1. The name of the City Council of Paris, set up 21 May 1791, and suppressed, 17 July 1794.
2. The revolutionary socialist government set up in Paris, 18 Mar., and suppressed, 28 May 1871. *See* FRENCH REVOLUTION, THE.

Communism. Karl Marx (1818–83) issued Communist manifesto, 1848. First volume *Das Kapital* issued, 1867. Communist Party of Great Britain founded, 1920. Break-up of Soviet communism began 1985 onwards and complete, 1991. By 1994 even Chinese C. much modified, and C. survived in relatively pure form only in a limited number of minor states, e.g. Cuba and N Korea. *See* INTERNATIONAL; RUSSIA; BOLSHEVIKS.

Community Charge, local tax which replaced the rating system, 1 April 1990. Based on individual rather than property liability, it was highly unpopular, being popularly known as the 'Poll Tax' and non-payment was widespread. Its unpopularity helped to overthrow Thatcher premiership, 1990. Government decided to abolish C.C., 1991, replacing it with the *Council Tax from 1 Apr. 1993.

Community Relations Commission, established 1968 under the Race Relations Act and replaced 1977 by the Commission for Racial Equality (*see* RACIAL EQUALITY, COMMISSION FOR.)

Comoros Islands. French protectorate from 1886 to 1912 (Mayotte from 1841); then a French colony. Attached to Madagascar 1914–47: French Overseas Territory 1947–75: independent republic since 1975: Federal Islamic Republic since 1978; new constitution, 1992. Attempted coup quashed by France, 1995.

compact discs, first introduced, 1983: by 1990s had largely superseded long-playing records. Essential part of computer software.

Companion of Honour, order instituted 1917. Membership limited to 65 (excluding honorary members.)

compass. Chinese claim to have invented it, 2634 BC. Once thought that Marco Polo introduced it to Europe, but now considered that Europeans invented it independently during the 12thC.

Compromise League of certain Dutch and Flemish nobles petitioned Philip II of Spain to cease religious persecution in Netherlands, 1566. Petition rejected.

comptometer. Invented by Felt, 1884.

computer. Forerunner of analogue C.

developed 1620 by English mathematician Edmund Gunter. First mechanical digital calculating machines built 1642 by Pascal. Babbage (1792–1871) investigated the first mechanical C., but first complete electronic one built in America, 1939–44. Direct forerunners of both digital and analogue systems being produced *c.* 1940. Eckert and Mauchly completed first all-purpose all-electronic digital computer, 1946; Ragazzui and others completed first all-purpose analogue C., 1948. Modern hybrid Cs. introduced during 1950s. C. science established as a discipline in 1960s. Development of 'home' and 'desk-top' Cs. in 1980s: of C. 'games' in 1990s; and of the information 'superhighway' by the C. internet system.

Computer Act, 1990, made 'computer hacking' illegal in Great Britain.

Comrades of the Great War (UK). Founded, Aug. 1917, and absorbed in the *British Legion, 1921.

concentration camps. Existed in Nazi Germany, 1933–45. Term derives from camps established by British in S Africa to intern Boers, 1899. Since 1945 also loosely applied to camps set up for dissidents under Soviet regimes; and to prisoner-of-war camps run by Serbs in Bosnia. *See* separate articles on BUCHENWALD, DACHAU, OSWIECIM.

Concepción, Chile. Founded by Pedro de Valdivia, 1550, on a site seven miles NNE of the present city. Destroyed by earthquakes in 1730 and 1751 but rebuilt.

conclave, papal. Papal election by two-thirds majority of *cardinals, instituted 1179 by Alexander III. Council of Lyons, 1274 (Gregory X), decreed that cardinals should be locked up until the election was completed.

Concord, Book of, a synthesis, together with the Nicene and Athanasian and Apostles' Creeds, of the following Lutheran theoretical works: Luther's Smaller Catechism, 1529; Luther's Larger Catechism, 1529; Augsburg Confession,

1530; Apology for Melanchthon's Confession, 1530; Luther's Articles of Schmalkald, 1537; Formula of Concord, 1577, made 25 June 1580 by order of Elector Augustus of Saxony.

concordats. Treaties regarding ecclesiastical affairs between the pope and a temporal power. The following is a selection: Worms between Emperor Henry V and Calixtus II, 1122. Nürnberg between German Electors and Eugenius IV, 1447. Vienna between Emperor Frederick IV and Nicolas V, 1448. Against the Pragmatic Sanction of Bourges between Emperor Charles V and Clement VII, 1526, and again between Ferdinand VI of Spain and Benedict XIV, 1753. 'The Concordat' between Napoleon I and Pius VII, July 1801. Annulled, 1905. Between Frederick William III of Prussia and Pius VII, 16 July 1821. Between Mussolini and Pius XI, 11 Feb. 1929; revised C. between Italy and Papacy, Feb. 1984, whereby Vatican City lost territorial rights. Between General Franco and Pius XII, 27 Aug. 1953 (to replace that abrogated in 1931); abrogated Dec. 1978, since when there has been no established religion in Spain. *See also* VATICAN.

Concorde. *See* AVIATION.

Confederate States of America. The following states seceded from the USA: S Carolina, 20 Dec. 1860; Mississippi, 8 Jan. 1861; Florida and Alabama, 11 Jan.; Georgia, 19 Jan.; Louisiana, 26 Jan.; Texas, 1 Feb.; Virginia, Apr.; N Carolina and Arkansas, May. Jefferson Davis elected president of the Confederation at Montgomery, Alabama, 18 Feb. 1861. Constitution adopted, 11 Mar. 1861. *See* USA.

Confederation, Articles of (USA). Signed, 9 July 1778.

Confederation of British Industry, formed Aug. 1965 from an amalgamation of the *FBI, the British Employers' Federation, and the National Association of British Manufacturers.

Confederation of the Rhine. Formed by Napoleon I, 1806, after abolition of the Holy Roman Empire. Dissolved, 1813.

Conference on Security and Co-operation in Europe (CSCE) set up on initiatives from *NATO and *Warsaw Pact 1975, at Paris Summit. Conferences at Belgrade (1977–8); Madrid (1980–83); Stockholm (1984–6); Vienna (1986–9). At Paris Summit, 1990, members signed treaty for reduction of conventional forces in Europe and agreed to exchange of military information. End of Cold War brought CSCE membership up to 48 by Jan. 1992.

Confucianism. Ethical and philosophical system evolved during the Han era in China (206 BC–AD 220), but based on the teachings of Confucius (Chinese *Kung Futze*), 551–479 BC. System in its original form abandoned after 1912.

Congo (Brazzaville), formerly **Middle Congo**, one of the four territories of French Equatorial Africa. It became an independent republic on 15 Aug. 1960; Marxist 1970–90. New constitution allowing for multiparty elections, 1992. These eventually held May/June 1993; results disputed and situation continues unstable.

Congo. *See* ZAÏRE.

Congo Free State was set up under the auspices of the Association Internationale Africaine after the expeditions of Cameron, 1875, and Stanley, 1877, and internationally recognized by the Treaty of Berlin, 1885. Formally annexed to Belgium, 1908. *See* further under ZAÏRE.

Congo, River. Discovered by Diego Cão, the Portuguese explorer, in 1482. Known as **Zaïre River** since 1971.

Congregationalists (Independents, Brownists), under their first leader, Robert Browne (1550–1630), emigrated to Holland, 1581, and to Scotland, 1584. Their greatest period of power and expansion was 1645–60. Congregationalist Union of Scotland formed, 1811; of England and Wales, 1831. Combined with Evangelical Union, 1896. C. established in America, 1620; revival, 1730–40. United with the

American Christian Church, 1931. Merger agreed with the Evangelical and Reformed Church, 1956. Congregational Church in England and Wales formed, 1966; united with Presbyterian Church in England to join the *United Reformed Church, 1972.

Congress of Industrial Organizations formed (USA), as Committee for Industrial Organization, 9 Nov. 1935.

Congress of the United States. The first C. met in 1789, in succession to the *Continental C.

Congresses, Diplomatic. Principal occasions when sovereigns or their representatives have met to settle diplomatic affairs:

Aix-la Chapelle, 29 Sept.–22 Nov. 1818.
Berlin, 13 June–13 July 1878.
Cambrai, 1722–5.
*Carlsbad, Aug. 1819.
Châtillon, 4 Feb.–18 Mar. 1814.
Constantinople, 23 Dec. 1876–20 Jan. 1877.
Ferentino, 1223.
Frankfort, 16–31 Aug. 1863.
Laibach, 1821.
Paris, Jan.–Apr. 1856.
Prague, 5 July–9 Aug. 1813.
Rastadt, 9 Dec. 1797–8 Apr. 1799.
Reichenbach, 27 June 1790.
Soissons, 1 June 1728; moved to Fontainebleau, 18 Dec. 1729; ended by Treaty of Seville, 28 Sept, 1729.
Troppau, Oct. 1820.
Verona, Aug. 1822.
Vienna, 1 Nov. 1814–9 June 1815.

Connecticut. State of the USA, one of the original 13. First settled, 1635; written constitution, 1639, confirmed by Charles II, 1662. Replaced by a state constitution, 1818.

conscientious objectors. Term came into prominence during World War I. Special measures taken to deal with C.O. in the Military Service Act, 1916; provision also made for them in the Military Training Act, 1939. C.O. after World War II released

from further obligations by the National Service (Release of Conscientious Objectors) Act, 1946.

conscription. Introduced by Jourdan into France, 5 Sept. 1798. Modern system of call-up by age groups introduced in Prussia, 1806. C. introduced in Austria, 1868; Russia, 1870; Germany, 1871; Italy, 1873. Militia service compulsory in Canada, 1868. Introduced in UK, Jan. 1916–Dec. 1920, and from 3 June 1939 (*but see* MILITIA). C. of women, 1941–6. C. in UK ended in 1962. Germany, Austria and Bulgaria forbidden C. by peace treaties after World War I, but Germany resumed it in 1935. C. re-established in E Germany, 1956, and W Germany, 1957. USA adopted selective C., 19 Oct. 1940, and revived it temporarily during the Vietnam War in the 1970s. Value of C. increasingly questioned in Europe from 1990s; notably in the Netherlands, 1994. Belgium announced abolition of, 1995.

consent, age of, in UK, established at 12 in 1828; moved to 16 in 1885 by the Criminal Law Amendment Act. Sexual Offences Act, 1967, made an effect in A. of C. of 21 for homosexuals, by legalizing sexual relations between men of 21 and over. Commons voted to reduce this to 18, Feb. 1994.

conservation, World interest in since 1950s. In UK ten National Parks established in England and Wales, 1950s. Wildlife and Countryside Act, 1981 gave legal protection to many plants and species. Royal Commission, set up in 1970, advises on many aspects of C., and legislation to counter pollution passed in several areas, since then. World 'Summit' on ecology held in Rio de Janeiro, 1992.

Conservative. Word said to have been invented by J. W. Croker, in the *Quarterly Review*, Jan. 1833, as a more appropriate word than *Tory.

Conservative Party. History goes back to Restoration, but only towards end of 18thC. begins to assume form like that of present. Disraeli founder of modern

Conservatism. Created Conservative Central Office in 1870. 1895, Liberal Unionists (dissenters from Gladstone's Home Rule Bill) coalesced with Cs. in Lord Salisbury's third government. Between 2 World Wars, except 1924 and 1929–31, C.P. either in power or dominating group in 'National' governments. 1940, Coalition government took office with Churchill, a C., as Prime Minister. 1945 general election: defeated by Labour. Returned to power 1951 and remained until 1964 under Churchill, Eden, Macmillan and Douglas-Home. After losing general election of 1964, C.P. leader to be elected by parliamentary party, instead of 'emerging' as formerly. Douglas-Home resigned July 1964; Edward Heath succeeded him. Defeated by Labour, 1966. Returned, 1970. Defeated by Labour, 1974. Returned, under Margaret Thatcher, 1979: returned again, 1983, 1987 and 1992. John Major succeeded Margaret Thatcher as leader (and prime minister) 1990. July 1995, John Major defeated John Redwood in leadership election.

Consolidated Fund, first so-called, 1786.

Consols (Consolidated Annuities). An Act of 1731 consolidated certain perpetual and lottery annuities bearing interest at 3 per cent, and these consolidated annuities form the basis of Cs. Interest rate subsequently altered.

Constance. *See* KONSTANZ.

Constantine, Algeria, the Roman *Cirta.* Town destroyed, 311, but rebuilt by Constantine the Great, 312; taken by the Arabs, 710, and the French, 1837.

Constantinople (Turkish **Istanbul**, its official name since 1930). The ancient Byzantium (founded from Megara, 667 BC) rebuilt as capital of the Roman Empire by Constantine the Great, AD 330. First St Sophia built, 347; present building begun in 537 by Justinian I. It became a mosque after 1453 and has been a museum since 1935. Seized by Venetians and Crusaders, Apr. 1204, when it became capital of the Latin Empire of the East. Recaptured by Byzantine emperor, Michael Palaeologus, 1261. Captured by Turks, who made it their capital, 29 May 1453. The Topkapi Palace, begun 1462, is now a museum complex. The Blue Mosque was begun, 17thC. Gates include the Golden Gate, commemorating victory of Theodosius I over Maximus in 388; the Selviria Gate, marking C.'s recapture from the Crusaders, 1261; and the Gate of St Romanus, where the triumphant Sultan entered, 1453. Ceased to be capital of Turkey, 1923. Industrial expansion and a major tourist centre since 1945. *See* OTTOMAN EMPIRE; TURKISH REPUBLIC; COUNCILS OF THE CHURCH; ROMAN EMPIRE, EASTERN.

Consulate, The. French regime, lasted from 1799 to 1804.

consuls (mercantile) were first appointed by Italian republics about 1100. Except for a revival in the 16thC the custom died out, only to become universal in the 19thC. In 1943 the British Consular Service amalgamated with the Diplomatic Service to form the Consular Service.

Consuls (highest ordinary magistrates in republican Rome). Two elected annually and took office on 15 Mar. until 153 BC; thereafter on 1 Jan. Office open to patricians alone until *Lex Licinia* (367 BC) required one Consul to be a plebeian. C. still appointed in the W until AD 534, and in the E until 541.

consumer law in England and Wales, regulated by the Trades Description Act, 1968; the Hire Purchase Act, 1965; the Consumer Credit Act, 1974; the Unfair Contract Terms Act, 1977; the Fair Trading Act, 1973; the Sale of Goods Act, 1979 and the Food Safety Act, 1990. There are parallel Acts applying to Scotland.

Consumer Credit Act, 1974, forms the basis of modern credit law in the UK.

Contempt of Court Act, 1981, restricts court reporting in certain cases.

Continental Congress first met at Philadelphia, 1774, where all states, except Georgia, sent unofficial delegates to discuss ways and means of resisting the Stamp Act of 1765, and thereafter annually down to 1783.

continental drift. Concept put forward in detail by Wegener (1880–1930) in 1910 to explain movements within the earth.

Continental System. The name given to Napoleon I's embargo on trade between Britain and Europe. Begun by the Berlin Decrees, 21 Nov. 1806. Britain retorted by establishing a counter-blockade by the Orders in Council of 7 Jan. 1807. The Russian tsar's refusal to co-operate with the C.S. led directly to Napoleon's invasion of Russia, 1812, whilst the English system was partly the cause of the American war of 1812.

contraception. First clinic opened in Amsterdam, 1881; first in Britain (in London), 1921. Under National Health (Reorganization) Act, 1973, C. administered under the National Health Service. Oral contraceptive first used, 1955.

contributory pensions (UK). Introduced, 1909. Scope enlarged, 1925 and 1937. National Insurance Act, 1946 forms basis of state pension system in UK, but being questioned from 1993.

Conventicle Acts. First passed, 1593. Revised, 17 May 1664. Repeal by Act of Toleration, 1689.

Convention. *See* FRENCH REVOLUTION, THE.

Convention Parliaments. The two English Parliaments convened without royal authority: (1) 25 Apr. 1660, to restore Charles II. (2) 22 Jan. 1689, to offer the crown to William III and Mary II.
Also the Scottish Parliament convened by William III, 1689, for the same purpose as (2).

Convocation.
1. Of Canterbury, first summoned by Archbishop Peckham, 1283. Practically suspended, 1717–1852.
2. Of York, first summoned *c.* 1300. Met only formally between 1717 and 1852. *See* ENGLAND, CHURCH OF.

Conway Castle. Built by Edward I, 1284.

Cook Islands or **Hervey Islands.** Discovered by James Cook, 1773; annexed by Great Britain, 1888; by New Zealand, 1901.

Co-operative Movement. Producers' C. started by Robert Owen at New Lanark, 1799, but declined from about 1828. Consumers' C. opened in Toad Lane, Rochdale, Lancashire, 1844–5. Federation of English Cs., founded 1863 as English Wholesale Society. Central C. Union founded, 1869. First C. bank opened, 1872, in England, though such banks had existed in Germany since 1849. C. Party in Britain established 1917; first MP elected, 1919.

Copenhagen, Denmark. Grew up round Axelhuus, a fortress built by Bishop Absalon, 12thC. Became capital of Denmark, 1443. University founded, 1479. Surrendered to Christian I, 1479; to Christian III, 1536. Captured by Charles X of Sweden, 1658. Danish fleet attacked at, by Nelson and Parker, 2 Apr. 1801. Besieged and taken by British, 5 Sept. 1807. Seized by Germans, 9 Apr. 1940; liberated, May 1945.

Coptic Church. Monophysite Christian Church to which the Ethiopians also belong. It separated from the Orthodox, AD 451.

copyhold tenure. Abolished in England, 1922.

copyright (Great Britain). First known grant to Richard Pynson, King's Printer, 1518. In 1642 it was ordered that no book be printed without the author's permission. First C. Act came into operation, 10 Apr. 1710, and gave protection to booksellers for 21 years. Authors protected for a life or 28 years, 1814. For a life plus 7 years, or 42 years at least, 1842. Act of 1911 (life plus 50 years) came into force, 1 July 1912. Modern law (Copyright Act, 1956) came into force, 1 June 1957. Jurisdiction extended by the Copyright Designs and Patents Act, 1988, and the Broadcasting Act, 1990.

copyright, international. International C. laws passed in Britain, 1838 and 1852. In USA, 1891. International C. Convention at Berne, Sept. 1886. Revised at Paris, 1896; Berlin, 1908; Rome, 1928; Brussels, 1948; Geneva, 1952; Stockholm, 1967; Paris, 1971. USA joined Berne Copyright Union, 1989.

copyright (USA). Petition of Dr D. Ramsay for C., 5 Apr. 1789. Bill passed, 1790. C. Act, 1831. Further legislation, 1870, 1874, 1909, 1928, 1956. Last major revision, 1978. Act extending C. protection to certain computer material, 1984.

Cordeliers.
1. *See* FRANCISCANS, MONASTIC ORDER OF.
2. Since early 15thC applied to the Récollets or Observant Franciscans.
3. One of the earliest political clubs during the French Revolution, named after the convent in which they met. Many members executed, 24 Mar. 1794. Ordered to be discontinued, 1795.

Cordoba, Spain. Occupied by Romans under the Consul Marcellus, 152 BC. Taken by Visigoths, AD 572. Capital of Moorish Spain, 756. Mosque, built 8th to 10thC is now the cathedral. Reconquered by Spanish, 1236. Captured by French, 1808. Plundered by Carlists, 1836.

Corfe Castle, Dorset, England. Dates from the 11thC. King Edward the Martyr murdered on its site, 978. Captured and sacked by Parliamentarians, 1645.

Corfu (ancient *Corcyra*), Greece. First colonized from Corinth, *c.* 700 BC. Allied with Athens, 443 BC, and so caused the Peloponnesian War. Taken by Romans, 229 BC. Held by Robert Guiscard, AD 1081–5. By Roger, King of *Sicily, 1147–54. Semi-independent till annexed by *Venice, 1386. Attacked by Turks, 1536, 1716–18. Ceded to France, 1797. British protectorate, 1815, till united with Greece, 1863. Bombarded by Mussolini, 31 Aug. 1923 ('The C. Incident'). British destroyers mined by Albanians in C. Channel, 1946.

Corinth, Greece. Legendary foundation by Sisyphus *c.* 1350 BC. Reached highest prosperity under tyranny of Cypselus and Periander, 655–582 BC. Oligarchy restored 581 BC. War with Athens, 459 BC. Starts Peloponnesian War, 431 BC. Destroyed by Romans, 146 BC. Rebuilt by Julius Caesar, 46 BC. One of earliest Christian churches established at, *c.* AD 40. Attacked by Alaric, 395. Captured by Franks, 1205; by Turks, 1458. Held by Venetians, 1687–1715; by Turks, 1715–1822. Destroyed by earthquake, Feb. 1858. C. Canal opened, 1893. Town again destroyed by earthquake, 1928.

Cork, Ireland. Occupies site of a 7thC monastery. Burned by Vikings 821, 846 and 1012. Charter, 1172. Rose in favour of Oliver Cromwell, 1649. Taken from Jacobites, 21 Sept. 1690 by Duke of Marlborough. Centre of resistance to British, 1919–20. Protestant cathedral, 1880, on 18thC site; Catholic cathedral, 1808. Queen's College, 1849, became part of the National University of Ireland, 1908; renamed University College.

Corn Laws (English). Passed to raise price of C. Robinson's Act, 1815, only allowed importation when price reached 80s. a quarter. Principle regulated by sliding scale under Act of 1828. Agitation against begun, 1836. New sliding scale introduced, 1842. Repealed by C. Importation Act, which came into force, 1 Jan. 1847, but was suspended 1847–8 temporarily.

Cornish language, a Celtic tongue, was virtually identical with Breton until the 16thC. The last C. speaker died in the early 19thC, but the last recorded use of the language took place about 1780, though it has been revived in language societies since the 1970s.

Cornwall, England. The Celtic inhabitants of Dyvnaint (*Dumnonia*) who had once occupied Devon, C., Somerset, and Dorset, were driven W of the Parret, and thus cut off from S Wales, by King Coenwalh of Wessex, 658. Egbert, King of Wessex, began campaign against Cornishmen, 815, until they acknowledged his supremacy,

823. The last war of the Cornish against the W Saxons was undertaken in alliance with the Danes, 836–7. The allies defeated and slew Æthelhelm, Alderman of Dorset, at Portland, but were finally beaten at Hingston Down by Egbert. Made a duchy vested in the heir to the throne by charter, 1337.

Coronation Oath settled in new form for William and Mary, 1689. Modified, 1706, 1821, 1910, 1937, 1953.

Coronation Stone. *See* SCONE, STONE OF.

Corporation Acts (UK). *See* CLARENDON CODE and BOROUGH.

Corporation Tax, levied in UK in present form since 1970, being a replacement for the *Profits Tax.

Corsica. Successively a Phocaean, Etruscan, Carthaginian and Roman settlement. Seized by Saracens, 10thC. Given to Pisa by papal bull, 1090. Ceded to Genoa, 1367. Rebellion, 1735, reduced by France for Genoa, 1739. Sold by Genoa to France, 1768. Occupied by British, 8 June 1794. Insurrection, 8 June 1796, led by P. Paoli (1725–1807). Abandoned by British, 22 Aug. 1796. Reoccupied by French, 22 Oct. 1796. Last bandit sentenced to death, 1935. Italian occupation, Nov. 1942–4 Oct. 1943. Anti-French nationalist movement in, since 1970s.

cortes, parliaments or 'estates' (of gentry, clergy, and burghers), once the legislative body in each Christian kingdom of the Iberian peninsula. They began to assume some importance at the beginning of the 11thC, that of Leon being quite powerful in 1020. Their decline set in in the 15thC. The modern Portuguese and Spanish C. (revived firstly in the early 19thC and more recently in the 20th with ending of dictatorships in both countries) are constitutional assemblies modelled on other western European parliamentary institutions, and have no real historical continuity with the original C. *See* SPAIN and PORTUGAL.

Corunna, Spain. Armada anchored here on the way to England, 1588. Part of town burnt by Drake and Norris, 1589. Sir John Moore killed at C., 1809.

corvée. Forced labour. Unsuccessful attempt by Holy Roman Emperor, Joseph II, to abolish, 1775. Abolished in France, 1792. In Egypt, 1888–91.

cosmic rays. Experiments indicating existence of C.R. carried out by Rutherford and McLennan from 1903 onwards. Actual discovery attributed to Millikan, 1925.

Cossacks. Took Azov from Turks, 1637. Rising against Poles, led by Hetman Chmielnicki, 1648. Defeated at Khotin by John Sobieski, King of Poland, 1673. Treaty with Charles XII of Sweden, 1707. Mostly hostile to Soviet Government during civil war, 1917–22.

Costa Rica, Central America. First settled by Spanish, 1502. Revolted from Spain and joined Mexican Empire, 1821. Independent, 1823. Part of Central American Confederation, 1824–39. Boundary dispute with Nicaragua settled, 1888; with Colombia, 1921; with Panama, 1921. Army abolished, 1948. Constitution last modified, 1949.

Côte d'Ivoire, official name, since 1986, of the **Ivory Coast,** W Africa. Territory of French W Africa from 1904. Independent republic, 7 Aug. 1960. Houphet-Boigny, president since independence, *d.* Dec. 1993.

Cotopaxi. Volcano in the Andes, in Ecuador, S America. Height 19,613 ft/5897 m. Most violent eruption, 1768. First ascent made by Reid and Escobar, 1872.

cotton. Introduced by Muslims into Europe. Manufactured in Spain, 13thC. Italy, 14thC. England, 17thC. Bombay, 19thC. First machines, 18thC: cotton 'gin', 1794. Cotton industry in England declined rapidly from 1950s: virtually extinct by 1990.

Cottonian Library (England). Founded by Sir R. Bruce Cotton (1571–1631). Placed in Ashburnham House, Westminster, 1731, and partly burned. Formed part of original nucleus of the British Museum, 1753.

Council or **Curia Regis.** *See also* WITAN. From Norman feudal King's C. sprang (1) *c.* 1100–*c.* 1250 The Common Law Courts (*see under* COURTS). (2) *c.* 1250–1300 *The House of Lords. (3) *c.* 1350 The High Courts of Chancery and Admiralty. (4) *c.* 1460 The Star Chamber. (5) Early Tudor period other conciliar courts. (6) *c.* 1700–30 The Cabinet. (7) 1833 The Judicial Committee of the Privy Council. *See* COURTS and PRIVY COUNCIL.

Council for Mutual Economic Aid. E European counterpart to the *European Economic Community popularly known as 'Comecon'. Formed 1949. Its members at the height of its influence in the 1980s were the Soviet Union, the German Democratic Republic, Poland, Czechoslovakia, Hungary, Romania, Bulgaria, Mongolia, Cuba and Vietnam. Albania ceased to be a member in 1962. Dissolved, 26 Sept. 1991.

Council of Europe. Established 1949 by agreement of the consultative council of the Brussels Treaty Organization. Since 1989 a number of E European and central European states permitted to be nonvoting members. Convention on Human Rights, 1950; Social Development Fund, 1956. 1970: European Youth Centre established in Strasbourg, HQ of the C. of E.

Council of Industrial Design. *See* DESIGN COUNCIL.

Council of the Marches. Instituted by Henry VII at Ludlow. Abolished, 1641.

Council of Ministers. Established under the Treaty of Rome, 1957. Headquarters, Brussels. Ministers representing all member states of the *European Union normally meet about once a month, to further the implementation of various policies and for decision making. Amendments to the Treaty of Rome in 1986 (the *Single European Act) restricted the right of individual members to veto decisions arrived at by the

majority. Heads of state or heads of government of the member states normally meet twice a year in the capital of that member state which then holds the presidency of the C. of M. (a six-month term, taken in rotation), or in Brussels. These meetings were less frequent up to 1975.

Council of the North. Instituted, 1537, by Henry VIII after the *Pilgrimage of Grace at York. Abolished, 1641.

Council of the West. Instituted, 1540. Abolished, 1550.

Councils of the Church. All churches recognize the general councils of Nicaea, 325; Constantinople, 381; Ephesus, 431; Chalcedon, 451. The Greek Church recognizes three others in addition: Constantinople II, 553; Constantinople III, 680–1; Nicaea II, 787. The Roman Church another 13: Constantinople IV, 869–70, Lateran I, 1123; II, 1139; III, 1179; IV, 1215. Lyons I, 1245; II, 1274. Vienne, 1311–12. Florence, 1438. Lateran V, 1512–17. Trent, 1545–63. Vatican I, 1869–70. Vatican II, 1962–5. Some French authorities substitute for Lyons, Florence, and Lateran V those of Pisa, 1409; Constance, 1414–18; and Basel, 1431–43.

Council Tax, replaced the *Community Charge, 1 Apr. 1993.

Counter-Reformation. The Roman Catholic reaction to the *Reformation. First definite move organization of the Oratory of Divine Love, 1517. *Franciscans reformed, 1526. *Jesuits formally founded, 27 Sept. 1540. Roman Inquisition set up, 21 July 1542. Doctrinal codification carried out by Council of Trent, 1545–63. Establishment of the Congregation *de propaganda fide*, 1622.

Countess of Huntingdon's Connexion, sect of Calvinistic Methodists founded, 1748, by Selina, Countess of Huntingdon (1707–91), widow of the ninth earl. Most of the chapels still existing are now (1995) served by ministers of the *United Reformed Church.

Countryside Act, 1968, by which the

National Parks Commission became the Countryside Commission with extended powers. Funded by an annual government grant since Apr. 1982; since Apr. 1991 the Countryside Commission's responsibilities in Wales have been undertaken by the **Countryside Council for Wales**.

Countryside Commission for Scotland, *see under* SCOTTISH NATIONAL HERITAGE.

county councils created by Local Government Act, 1888 and amended by Act of 1972. Discussions concerning possible modification or abolition of C.C. started, 1991, but subsequently the majority were retained.

county courts established by Act of Parliament, 1846; amended 1924, 1934, 1955; further amendments since, including C.C. Act, 1971; Litigants in Person Act, 1975; Administration of Justice Act, 1977; Supreme Court Act, 1981, and C.C. Act, 1984.

County Hall, Lambeth, London headquarters first of the London County Council; and 1964–86 of the Greater London Council; built 1908 onwards; formally opened, 1922. Closed after abolition of G.L.C., 1986; sold to Japanese property company, 1993.

'Coupon Election'. British General Election of Dec. 1918, which returned Lloyd George's Coalition Government.

Court of Session, supreme civil tribunal of Scotland established, 1532. Sits Oct. 15–Mar. 20 and May 12–July 20.

courts (English). The following are the dates of the institution and abolition of the principal English C.:
N.B. – C. still in existence in *italics*.
1. Palatine C.: Chester, 11thC–1830. Lancaster, 1351–1972. Durham, 13thC–1972.
2. Common Law C.: Common Pleas, 12thC–1875. King's Bench, 13thC–1875. Exchequer, Henry I–1875. Exchequer Chamber, 1357–1875.
3. Travelling Commissions: Trailbaston, 1290–1380. Of Assize *c.* 12thC–1972. Of Oyer and Terminer, 12thC–1972. Of Gaol Delivery, 12thC–1972. General Eyre, *c.* 1150–*c.* 1360.
4. Statutory Civil C.: Wards and Liveries, 1541–1660. Requests, 18thC–1846. *County Courts*, 1846. High Commission, 1558–1641. Probate, 1857–1875. Divorce, 1857–75.
5. Statutory Criminal C.: *Central Criminal Court*, 1834. *Justices of the Peace*, 1590. Quarter Sessions, 1362–1972. Crown Cases Reserved, 1848–1907. Criminal Appeal, 1908–66. *Crown Courts*, 1972 (replacing the Assize and Quarter Sessions).
6. Conciliar C.: *House of Lords c.* 1250. Chancery, *c.* 14thC–1875. Requests, 1493–1642. Appeal in Chancery, 1851–75. Admiralty, *c.* 1340–1875. Star Chamber, 15thC–1641. *Judicial Committee*, 1833.

In 1875 the Common Law C., and the Cs. of Chancery, Probate, Divorce and Admiralty were amalgamated into a single High Court of Judicature, from which there was to be appeal to a new Court of Appeal, which took the place of the Exchequer Chamber. In 1880 the Exchequer and Common Pleas Divisions were amalgamated with the King's Bench Division. Court of Criminal Appeal transferred to the Criminal Division of the Court of Appeal, 1966. *See also* COUNCIL or CURIA REGIS. In Dec. 1993 Lord Chancellor announced that solicitors in private practice would be allowed to work in higher courts. In June 1995 proposals announced to make civil justice swifter and cheaper.

courts martial, instituted in England, 1625–49; up to 1640, officers were tried under royal ordinance by *Courts of Chivalry. Military law, largely influenced by continental custom, did not receive parliamentary sanction up to 1689 (*see* MUTINY ACTS), but from that date until the Army Discipline Act, 1879, C.M. administered discipline according to articles of war. The Army Act of 1881 (under which 3060 British soldiers were condemned to death between 1914 and 1920) was in force until amended in 1951 and 1955 by legislation prompted by the Lewis Committee, which reported as a result of the trial for mutiny of some 200 British parachutists in Malaya, Oct. 1946. Naval C.M., also affected by the Lewis report, were hitherto regulated by the Naval Discipline Acts, 1866, 1884; these replaced by the Naval Discipline Act, 1957. Similarly Air Force C.M. were from 1955 governed by the Air Force Act, 1955. The C.M. Acts of all three services amended and continued by the Armed Forces Act, 1981. European Commission for Human Rights asked to review 12 British C.M. cases, 1995.

Covenant, Day of the. *See* DINGAAN'S DAY.

Covenanters. Supporters of the *Solemn League and Covenant, financed by Richelieu, raised an army, 1639. Negotiated with Charles I, 1640. Beaten at Rullion Green, 1666, and subsequently persecuted, but rose in revolt and defeated Graham of Claverhouse at Drumclog, 1 June 1679. Defeated by Monmouth at Bothwell Brig, 22 June 1679.

Covent Garden Market. The 'Covent' was, in fact, the Abbey of Westminster, and its garden included Long Acre. The whole parcel was granted to John Russell, 1st Earl of Bedford (1486?–1555) in 1552. The square, with St Paul's Church (by Inigo Jones), was laid out by the 4th earl, 1631. Piazzas built on N and E sides, 1633–4. Market opened, 1634, but present buildings date from 1831. The Market was moved to Nine Elms, Battersea, in 1974, and C.G.M. then developed as a shopping and leisure area. E piazza burnt down, 1769. St Paul's Church burnt down, 1795, and restored according to the original plans; rebuilt, 1872. Theatre dates from 1732; present building opened, 1858. Known as Royal Opera House since Oct. 1968. Theatre museum at, since 1987.

Coventry, England, is first mentioned in a document dated 1043, referring to the foundation of a monastery by King Knut Sveinsson, 1016. The first charter to the town was issued by Earl Ranulf of Chester, 1155, and a corporation established, 1345,

under Edward III. The legend of Lady Godiva was a tradition, first written down in Roger of Wendover's *Flores Historiarum c.* 1235, and has been fixed on to the historical Godgifu (*c.* 1040–80), a pious lady who was the consort of Earl Leofric of Mercia (*d.* 1057), the mother of Hereward the Wake and grandmother of the earls Edwin and Morcar. The expression 'send to Coventry' is said by Clarendon, in his *History of the Revolution*, 1701, to have originated in the concentration of Royalist prisoners here by the Parliamentarian garrison of Birmingham, 1647. A German airraid, 14 Nov. 1940, destroyed the 15thC cathedral church. Cathedral rebuilding began, 1956. Consecrated in the presence of Queen Elizabeth II, 25 May 1962. University of Warwick established at, 1965. C. polytechnic became C. University, 1992.

Cracow, Poland. Founded *c.* 700. University established, 1364. Capital of Poland, *c.* 1320–1595. Taken by Charles XII of Sweden, 1702. By Russians, 1768. Annexed by Austria, 1795. Independent republic, 1815. Again annexed by Austria, 1846. Restored to Poland, 1919. Taken by Germans, 6 Sept. 1939, and became centre of German administration in Poland until stormed by Russians, Jan. 1945.

'Cradle of American Liberty'. Faneuil Hall, Boston, erected, 1742. Burned and rebuilt, 1761. Meeting-place of American patriots during revolution.

Creeds, formulations of Christian faith.
Apostles': Earliest mention by Rufinus, 410.
Athanasian: Ascribed to Hilary, Bishop of Arles, 429–49. No direct connection with Athanasius (*c.* 326–73).
Nicene: Based on C. of Eusebius, 325. Reaffirmed at Council of Constantinople, 381, rest of the present creed except word *filioque* being then added.

cremation was customary practice for disposal of the dead in Britain until the reintroduction of Christianity, or until *c.* AD 600. C. was not practised thereafter until 1884, by the Society for Promotion of C., founded 1874. First crematorium in UK at Woking, 1885. The C. Acts, 1902 and 1952 control C., which is now extremely common in the UK, over 70% of deaths there by 1995 being treated by C.

Cremona, Italy. Founded by Romans, 218 BC. Destroyed by Vespasian, AD 70; by Goths, 540, and by the Lombards, 605. Passed to the Viscontis in the 15thC. Under Spanish control from 1535; Austrian from 1814, and Italian, 1859. The cathedral was begun in the 12thC.

Crespy or **Crespi**, France, **Treaty of.** Between Francis I of France and Emperor Charles V, 17 Sept. 1544.

Crete or **Candia,** Mediterranean island. Seat of Minoan civilization c. 3500–1000 BC (see KNOSSOS). Roman province from 66 BC. Greeks expelled from Carthage by Hassan retire to C., AD 698; Saracens seize and make pirate centre, 823; recovered by Greeks 960; sold to Venetians, 1205; besieged and finally taken by Turks, 1645–69; Turkey accepted the major powers' ultimatum in 1898 and withdrew its army; palace of Minos and 'Labyrinth' discovered at Knossos, 1899. At the outbreak of the Balkan War, Cretan deputies were admitted to the Greek chamber, and the island annexed by Greece, 14 Oct. 1912; formally handed over to Greece by the Treaty of Peace between Greece and Turkey, 1 Nov. 1913; the annexation of C. by Greece acknowledged by the powers, Dec. 1913; attacked by German airborne troops, 20 May 1941; flight of Greek Government and evacuation of allied forces, 2 June 1941. Germans withdrew, autumn 1944. Tourism main industry since 1970s.

Creutzfeld-Jakob disease, affects the human central nervous system and is similar to *bovine spongiform encephalopathy (BSE) in cattle. So far (1995) incurable, it is named after the German neurologists Hans S. Creutzfeld (1885–1964) and Alfons Jakob (1884–1931).

cricket. Said to be a development of medieval 'club ball'. Word first used, 1598. In 1654 Eltham men fined for playing C. on a Sunday. First C. club formed (Hambledon Club), 1750. Marylebone Cricket Club (M.C.C.) founded, 1787. Round-arm bowling legalized, 1835. First Eton v. Harrow C. match, 1805; first Oxford University v. Cambridge University, 1827; first Gentlemen v. Players match, 1866. County C. established 1864, *Wisden's* first published same year. First county C. champions were Surrey, 1864. Since 1980, county C. champions have been:

Middlesex, 1980
Nottinghamshire, 1981
Middlesex, 1982
Essex, 1983
Essex, 1984
Middlesex, 1985
Essex, 1986
Nottinghamshire, 1987
Worcestershire, 1988
Worcestershire, 1989
Middlesex, 1990
Essex, 1991
Essex, 1992
Middlesex, 1993
Warwickshire, 1994
Warwickshire, 1995

First Test match, England v. Australia, 1877. Test matches now (1995) played regularly between various countries of the former British Commonwealth. International panel of umpires for Tests from 1994. S African Test Series resumed, 1994. Increasing role of professional cricketers after 1918, and more so after 1945. 'Bodyline' C. controversy, 1932–3. One-day C. started, 1960s; Sunday League introduced, 1969. World Cup C. first held, 1975, since then, every four years. World Cup winners:

1975, West Indies
1979, West Indies
1983, India
1987, Australia
1992, Pakistan.

Most outstanding figure in C. History, William Gilbert Grace of Britain, 1848–1915. Other outstanding cricketers include:

Ames, Leslie (British), 1905–90
Atherton, Mike (British) 1968–
Border, Allan (Australian), 1955–
Botham, Ian (British), 1955–
Boycott, Geoffrey (British), 1940–
Bradman, Donald (Australian), 1908–
Compton, Denis (British), 1918–
Fry, Charles (British), 1872–1956
Gooch, Graham (British), 1952–
Gower, David (British), 1957–
Hadlee, Richard (New Zealand), 1951–
Hobbs, Jack (British), 1882–1963
Hutton, Len (British), 1916–90
Imran Khan (Pakistan), 1952–
Kapil Dev (India), 1952–
Lara, Brian (West Indies), 1969–
Larwood, Harold (British), 1904–95
Richards, Viv (West Indies), 1952–
Sobers, Garfield (West Indies), 1936–
Sutcliffe, Herbert (British), 1894–1978
Trueman, Fred (British), 1931–
Tyldesley, John (British), 1873–1930
Verity, Hedley (British), 1905–43
Warner, Pelham (British), 1873–1963

Among outstanding modern C. commentators are the Britons, John Arlott (*d.* 1991), Brian Johnston (1912–94) and Ernest William Swanton (1907–).
Women's Cricket. Women said to have played cricket from 1740s. First women's C. club, at Nun Appleton, Yorkshire, 1887; closed, 1950. Women's C. Association formed, 1926. First overseas' tour and first Test v. Australia, 1934. First women's World Cup C., 1973. Won by England for first time for 20 years, 1993. Outstanding woman cricketer, Rachel Heyhoe-Flint of Britain, 1939–.

Crimea, Black Sea. S C. colonized by Greeks in the 7thC BC. Later belonged to Rome and Byzantium, and from the 13thC to Venice and Genoa. Conquered by the Turks, 1475. Annexed by Russia from Turks, 1783; war declared against Russia by England and France, 28 Mar. 1854;

allied armies landed, 1854; war concluded, Apr. 1856. Crimean Autonomous Republic formed, 1921. Occupied by Germans, 1941–3. Crimean Autonomous Republic abolished, 1945, after deportation of the Tatar population for alleged collaboration with the Germans. Reduced to region status, 1945; population allowed to return from 1987. Since 1991 part of the *Ukraine which does not recognize Crimean independence claims. In 1994 voting in C. showed overwhelming majority in favour of either independence or union with Russia: Crimean parliament voted for independence in May though situation subsequently calmed and status quo continued. Ukraine squashes ideas of Crimean independence, Mar. 1995. *See* ALMA, BALAKLAVA, INKERMAN, SEBASTOPOL, *under* BATTLES, SIEGES, and WORLD WAR II.

Criminal Investigation Department, (CID), the detective branch of the Metropolitan Police, was set up, 1878. Its Special Branch, for the protection of state personages and the suppression of terrorism, was established in 1883 to combat Fenian outrages.

criminal laws of England. Committee formed to inquire into their severity, 2 Mar. 1819; two Acts restricting capital punishment, 1820; eight further mitigating Acts passed soon afterwards, chiefly at the instance of Sir Robert Peel, notably five in 1823; Habitual Criminals Act, 1869; Criminal Law Amendment Act (relating to females), 1885; Aliens Act, 1905; Criminal Appeal, 1907; the Prevention of Crime Act, 1908; the Children Act, 1908; the Criminal Law Amendment Act, 1912. Criminal Justice Act, 1948, transferred responsibility for persons 'detained during His Majesty's pleasure' from Home Office to Ministry of Health. Further modifications as a result of Criminal Justice Acts, 1961 and 1967, by the Criminal Appeals Act, 1968 by the Criminal Justice Act, 1983 and the Criminal Justice Act, 1991. Royal Commission on Criminal Justice set up, Mar. 1991, to undertake a major review of the criminal justice system in England and Wales. Flaws acknowledged and changes promised to Criminal Justice Acts of 1991 in 1993, when a new Criminal Justice Bill was introduced (Nov.), which included provision to end defendants' 'right to silence'. Riots in London against the Bill, Oct. 1994, but Bill became law later the same month.

Cripplegate (London). Rebuilt, 1244 and 1491. Demolished, 1760–1. Institute opened, 1896.

Croatia (Hrvatska). Independent Croat kingdom, 10th–12thC, now an independent republic. Linked with Hungary until the middle of the 15thC, then under Turkish domination until the beginning of the 18thC. Part of Illyria, 1809–13; subsequently part of Austria-Hungary. At the dissolution of the Austro-Hungarian monarchy, the National Assembly of C. and Slovenia proclaimed their independence of Hungary, 30 Oct. 1918. A composite ministry for the Serb, Croat and Slovene kingdom (*Yugoslavia) was formed, 29 Dec. 1918. After conquest of Yugoslavia by Germans C. was declared an independent (puppet) kingdom, 18 May 1941. In 1948 the province became a federal republic. Historic resentment of Serbia continued, and began resurfacing in 1970s. First free elections, 1990, returned non-Communist majority. Croat law declared superior to federal and in a referendum, 19 May 1991, nearly 83% voted for an independent C. Serb enclaves (e.g. in the Krajina area) wished to join *Serbia and war between the rump Yugoslavia (now, effectively consisting only of Serbia) and C. started. Serbs made considerable inroads into Croat territory and during 1991 *Dubrovnik badly damaged by bombardment. C.'s independence first recognized by Germany, 23 Dec. *1991; by rest of EC, 15 Jan. 1992. UN-organized cease-fire in 1992 left much Croat territory in Serb hands, under auspices of a UN peace-keeping force. In Jan. 1993 C. launched an offensive in the Krajina area but fighting ceased within days. In *Bosnia-Herzogovina C. at first assisted Muslims, but later joined with Serbs there. During 1994 C. again joined with Muslims in Bosnia in attacking Bosnian Serbs. The Croatian Serbs, however, co-operated with Bosnian Serbs in renewed attacks in Bosnia, from autumn 1994. During first half of 1995 C. regained much territory previously lost to the Serbs, notably in the Slavonia region and joined Bosnian Muslims in offensive against Bosnian Serbs in Bosnia itself. Elections confirmed President Tudjman's dominance in C. Oct. 1995. C. initialled agreement to end Bosnian war, 21 Nov. 1995. *See* SERBO-CROAT LITERATURE.

crofters. Small landholders in Scotland. Royal Commission appointed to inquire into condition of, 22 Mar. 1883–28 Apr. 1884; Act for their benefit passed, 25 June 1886; amended, 1888. Further safeguards for C. in the Crofters (Scotland) Act, 1955.

Croix de Guerre. French military decoration, instituted 8 Apr. 1915.

croquet, properly **lawn-croquet**, outdoor game, derives from *paille-maille* (pall-mall), played in France from the 13thC and in England at least from the 16th. It became very popular in Victorian England and in parts of the USA, where it became known as *roque*, with slightly different rules. First English C. championships were at Evesham, 1867. The original national association was the 'All-England Croquet and Lawn Tennis Association, 1870' but this soon was devoted only to tennis and in 1896 the Croquet Association was formed. Game declined at the beginning of the 20thC but popularity revived since 1945. C. Association headquarters is the Hurlingham Club. C. is also played in Australia, S Africa and New Zealand.

crossword puzzles first invented in the USA, 21 Dec. 1923. *The Times* crossword first appeared, 1930.

Crown Courts, established 1972 as part of Supreme Court under the Court Act of 1971. *See* COURTS.

Crown Jewels. *See* LONDON, TOWER OF.

crown pieces. Gold crown first struck by Henry VIII (1509–47). The first silver crown struck by Edward VI (1547–53). The half-crown originated with Edward VI: and was demonetized, 31 Dec. 1969. Since that reign whole crowns have usually been minted only for commemorative purposes, e.g. Queen Victoria's two jubilees, 1887 and 1897, the Festival of Britain, 1951, the coronation of 1953, in commemoration of Sir Winston Churchill, 1965, for the silver jubilee, 1977 and for the marriage of the Prince and Princess of Wales, 1981. Since then five-pound coins have replaced the C.P.; and these have been struck to celebrate the 80th and 90th birthdays of the Queen Mother, in 1980 and 1990 respectively; and to mark the 40th anniversary of Elizabeth II's coronation, 1993.

Crown, Suit against the, made possible by Act of Parliament in 1947. The crown of Great Britain, in the person of the responsible minister, not of the sovereign, can now be sued, as a result of appeals which went to the House of Lords, 1945.

Croydon, military airfield in World War I, opened as Britain's main commercial airport, 1920. Replaced by *Heathrow after 1946.

Crufts, annual British dog show, named after Charles Cruft (1852–1938), British dog-breeder who held his first dog show at Islington in 1886. These became annual events. Moved to Olympia, 1948; to Earls Court, 1979.

Cruise, nuclear-capable missile. US-controlled ground-launched C. sited in Britain from 1983, removed 1991–2. First use in combat in non-nuclear capacity by USA in *Gulf War, 1991. Used by NATO against Bosnian Serbs, 1995.

Crusades. Jerusalem was captured by the Seljuk Turks, 1071. In 1095 Pope Urban II was roused by the preachings of Peter the Hermit and appeals from Constantinople to consider a crusade. In Nov. 1095 the Council of Clermont invoked western Europe to defend the Holy Land. The following are the eight great C.:
First: 1096. Led by (a) Walter the Penniless, a Burgundian, (b) Peter the Hermit, (c)

Gottschalk, a German monk. These were disorganized bands and met with failure. The military crusade of 1096 divides itself into four sections: (a) Godfrey de Bouillon from the Rhine and N Germany; (b) Hugh, Comte de Vermandois, and others from Central France, Normandy and Britain; (c) Bohemond of Taranto from Italy; (d) Raymond, Comte de Toulouse, from Provence, Spain and Lombardy. Nicaea captured, June 1097, and on 1 July of the same year the Sultan Solyman was defeated at Dorylaeum. Antioch taken, 3 June 1098. Jerusalem, 15 July 1099; and Godfrey de Bouillon elected king, 22 July 1099. Battle of Ascalon, 12 Aug. 1099. *St Jean d'Acre reduced, 1104.
Second: Louis VII of France and Emperor Conrad III, 1146. Damascus attacked, July 1148.
Third: Commenced by siege of *St Jean d'Acre, 1189. Emperor Frederick Barbarossa led an army to Cilicia, 1190. Arrival of Richard I of England and Philip Augustus, 1191. Richard won battle of Azotus, captured Jaffa and Caesarea, 1191. Jerusalem reached, 1192.
Fourth: Set in motion by Pope Innocent III in 1200. Started from Venice, 1202. Led by Boniface of Montserrat and the Counts of Flanders and Blois. Diverted by Venetians to attack Constantinople, which was stormed, Apr. 1204, and a Latin empire established there.
Fifth: To assist John of Brienne, titular King of Jerusalem, against the Sultan Saphadin, the successor of Saladin, 1217. Led by Andrew of Hungary, the Duke of Austria, the Earl of Salisbury, etc. Damietta captured by the English, 1219. The Emperor Frederick II obtained a ten years' treaty, including free access to the Holy City, 1228.
Sixth: Christians driven out of Jerusalem, 1238, caused two distinct C. together known as the Sixth. (a) French knights led by Thibaud of Champagne and the Comte de Bretagne; (b) arranged at Council of Northampton, led by Richard, Earl of Cornwall, which in 1240 arranged a treaty similar to that of Frederick II.
Seventh: Proclaimed by the Council of Lyons, 1245. Led by Louis IX (St Louis) of

France who, with William Longsword of Salisbury and others, set out from Cyprus in spring, 1249. Louis taken prisoner at the battle of Mansurah, 1250.

Eighth: Led by Louis IX of France and Charles of Anjou. Louis IX *d.* at Carthage, 2 Aug. 1270.

Children's C., 1212 was not a C. in the usual military sense of term.

Crystal Palace. Originally the building of the International Exhibition of 1851. Its re-erection begun at Sydenham, 5 Aug. 1852; opened by Queen Victoria, 10 June 1854; purchased by the Earl of Plymouth to hold in trust for the nation, 1911; destroyed by fire, 30 Nov. 1936; remaining tower removed, May 1941. Sports stadium opened, 1965.

CSCE. *See* CONFERENCE ON SECURITY AND CO-OPERATION IN EUROPE.

Ctesiphon, Iraq. Capital of Parthian Empire *c.* 150 BC. Captured by Romans, AD 116 and 196. Became capital of Persia under Sassanids, 4thC. Persians defeated at, by Julian the Apostate, 363. Destroyed by Arabs, 637. Scene of a battle between British and Turks, 22 Nov. 1915.

Cuba. Discovered by Columbus, 27 Oct. 1492; colonized by Spaniards, 1511; Havana fortified, 1584; insurrections of slaves, 1844 and 1848; López's expedition against, 1851; revolt for expulsion of Spaniards, 1868–71; frequent other revolts, notably that starting 1895; occupied by USA after Spanish-American War, 1898–1901, when it became a republic; Gómez insurrection, 1906; Taft of USA proclaimed provisional governor, Sept. 1906; evacuation of US troops, 1908; further revolutions, interspersed by relatively settled government, 1917, 1924, 1931 and 1933. Batista became president for the second time, 1952, and instituted a dictatorship. Revolutionary movement against him initiated July 1953 by Fidel Castro, who overthrew the government, 1958, and instituted a left-wing regime, with drastic land reform, expropriation and nationalization of foreign assets, and close ties with the Soviet bloc. USA broke off diplomatic relations with C., 3 Jan. 1961. C. invaded from Florida by anti-Castro forces, 17–20 Apr. 1961 ('Bay of Pigs' incident); the invasion was crushed. Soviet arms build-up in C. apparent in 1962. On Oct. 22 President Kennedy alleged that Soviet offensive-missile sites were being erected in C. and announced a US naval blockade of the island, to start on 24 Oct. Russia retaliated by putting her army on the alert. On 28 Oct. Khruschev announced that Russia would dismantle the rocket bases in C. and ship them home. On 8 Nov. Russia stated she would allow US Navy to inspect the ships removing the missiles from C. and on 20 Nov. the US blockade was lifted. From mid-1960s C. actively encouraged left-wing agitation in S and Central America. Che Guevara killed in Bolivia, leading left-wing guerrillas there, 1967. Cubans involved in left-wing regimes and revolutionary movements in Africa from 1970s, notably in *Angola where Cuban troops were involved 1975–91. Cuban troops killed during US invasion of *Grenada, 1983. Some improvement in US-Cuban relations, 1985 onwards. Russian withdrawal of aid to C. from 1990 increased economic problems; but more tourism from non-Communist countries some counterbalance. Law of Dec. 1991 provided for 'parliamentary' elections. These, held Feb. 1993 required all candidates to be approved by the Communist party. Mass exodus of Cubans to the USA during summer 1994 led to USA depriving Cubans of 30-year-old automatic asylum right. In September 1994 US-Cuban agreement which allowed 20,000 Cubans per annum to obtain US visas in return for C. promising to halt illegal emigration by force if necessary.

Heads of Administration since the end of Spanish Rule (1898).

United States Military Governors:
Brooke 1899
Wood 1899–1902
President of the Republic:
Estrada Palma 1902–06

United States Provisional Governors:
Taft 1906
Magoon 1906–09
Presidents of the Republic:
Gomez 1909–13
Menocal 1913–21
Zayas y Alfonso 1921–25
Machado y Morales 1925–33
Provisional Junta 1933
San Martin 1933–34
Mendieta 1934–35
Barnet 1935–36
Gómez y Arias 1936
Bru 1936–40
Batista 1940–44
San Martin 1944–48
Socarras 1948–52
Batista (again) 1952–59
Urrutia (Jan.–July) 1959
Torrado 1959–76
Castro 1976–

(Castro has been the effective ruler of C. since 1 Jan. 1959; in 1985 was President of Council of State: President of the Council of Ministers and First Secretary of the Cuban Communist Party.)

Cubism. Term first used by artist Henri Matisse, 1908. Exhibitions at Paris and Brussels, 1911.

Culdees (Irish = Companions of God). Religious community, drawing their inspiration from the rule of St Chrodigang, Archbishop of Metz from 742 to 766, which they introduced into Ireland and into Scotland before 800; converted into canons regular in the reign of David I, King of Scotland (1107–53) on the recommendation of his mother, St Margaret (*d.* 1902). As a separate body, had disappeared by 1300.

Cullinan diamond, found, Jan. 1905, at Premier Mine, Transvaal. Presented to Edward VII, 1907.

'Cultural Revolution', in China. Launched 1966, allegedly an attempt to 'purify' Chinese Communism by eradicating vestiges of 'middle-class' structures and ideas. Caused considerable suffering and ad-

versely affected many aspects of Chinese life. Diminishing by 1969; over by 1972. *See* CHINA.

Cumbria, administrative county of England established 1974 under the Local Government Act of 1972, and based on *Carlisle.

Curaçao. Principal island of the Netherlands Antilles. Discovered by Spanish explorers, 1527, and acquired by the Dutch, 1634.

curfew. Said to have been introduced in England by William I, 1068, but probably existed earlier. Still resorted to in various areas during periods of civil unrest, e.g. in Cyprus, 1956, and in the principal cities in Algeria, 1954–62. Criminal Justice Act, 1991, empowers courts in England and Wales to issue C. orders against certain offenders. 1994 Act strengthened these powers.

Curzon Line. Proposed E frontier of Poland recognized by the Allies in Dec. 1919 on suggestions by Lord C. but not adopted because of Poland's victory over Russia in 1920. The E frontier awarded Poland in 1945 (agreed by the Allies at Teheran in 1943) is based on the C.L., with some minor modifications in Poland's favour.

Customs. Granted to the crown in 1275. Commissioners appointed, 1671; consolidation of C., 26 Feb. 1787. C. Consolidation Act, 1876, may be regarded as the principal statute relating to C. Excise Department, formerly under the Inland Revenue, amalgamated with C., 1909. C. and Excise dealt with collection of VAT from 1973: C. duties amended as result of coming into effect of Single European Market, 1 Jan. 1993. Custom House, London, founded, 1559; rebuilt, 1718; new (the present) building, 12 May 1817.

Cuzco. Peru, capital of the Inca empire. Built *c.* 11thC it was captured by Pizarro in 1533.

cyclamates. Use as a food additive banned in Britain, Oct. 1969, with effect from 1 Jan. 1970.

cycle. Four-wheeled velocipede invented in France by Blanchard and Magurier in 1779; pedals applied to a tricycle by a Dumfriesshire blacksmith, McMillan, 1834; rubber tyres, 1868; bicycles made in England by Coventry Sewing Machine Co., 1869; improved by J.K. Starley, 1874; Starley's 'Rover', with nearly equal wheels, 1885. First C. club, Pickwick Bicycle Club, founded, London, 1870; National Cyclists' Union and Cyclists' Touring Club, 1878. First manufactured in America by A.A. Pope, 1878. First cycling race said to have been in France, 1868. Tour de France race started, 1903; British Milk Race began, 1951. British cyclist Chris Boardman won 4 km. Individual Pursuit Cycle race in 1992 Olympics on revolutionary new cycle. Tour de France ran part of 1994 race in Britain, to celebrate opening of *Channel Tunnel.

Cyprus. Greeks began to colonize C. before 1200 BC; Phoenicians followed, 1000–800 BC. Subject in turn to Egypt, Assyria, Persia, Greece, and Rome. Arab raids in 7thC. Seized by Richard I of England, 1192, and sold by him to Guy de Lusignan, whose successors ruled C. as independent kings. Made tributary to the Mamelukes, 1426. Catherine Cornaro, widow of James II, ceded C. to Venice, 1489. C. was conquered by Turks, 1570–1; ceded to Britain by Anglo-Turkish Convention, 4 June 1878; annexed by Britain, 5 Nov. 1914. Crown colony, 1925. Church plebiscite showed overwhelming support for *enosis* (i.e. union with Greece), 1950. EOKA terrorist campaign to promote *enosis* began, Apr. 1955. Archbishop Makarios exiled to the Seychelles, 1956–7. Agreement signed in London by British, Greek and Turkish premiers, and ratified by Greek and Turkish Cypriots, which provided for C. to become an independent republic within the Commonwealth, 19 Feb. 1959. Makarios became President of C., 14 Dec. 1959. Independence day, 16 Aug. 1960. Attempted right-wing coup against Makarios, and Turkish resentment of Greek majority rule led to Turkish invasion, 1974; since then C. divided. Makarios

d., 1977. Turkish C. declared itself independent, Nov. 1983, but independence only recognized by Turkey. Several UN efforts to reunite C. since 1989. Nationalist Clerides elected president of C., Feb. 1993.

Cyrenaica. *See* LIBYA.

Cyrene. A colony founded from Mediterranean island of Thera, *c.* 630 BC, became a republic about 431. *See* LIBYA.

Czech Republic, came into existence, 1 Jan. 1993 as the result of the Czechs and Slovaks opting for separate states in July 1992. Vaclav Havel became first president of the C.R., Jan. 1993. Announced, 1994 that the C.R. would apply to join the EU, 1995.

Czechoslovakia. Czechoslovakian Republic proclaimed, with Thomas Masaryk as first president, 15 Nov. 1918. Masaryk re-elected president, 1927; resigned, 1935; succeeded by Beneš. Masaryk *d.*, 14 Sept. 1937. Germans incorporated Sudeten territories, 1 Oct. 1938. Poland took possession of zone beyond the Olza, 2 Oct.; Beneš resigned presidency, 5 Oct.; Father Tiso appointed minister for Slovakia (autonomous), 10 Oct.; Brody first premier of autonomous Ruthenia, 12 Oct.; Germany and Italy fixed new frontiers, 2 Nov.; Poles invaded Ruthenia, 24 Nov.; Emil Hacha elected president.
Slovakia seceded from the Czechoslovak State and proclaimed itself an independent republic, 14 Mar. 1939. Germany invaded and annexed the whole country and proclaimed protectorates of Bohemia, Moravia and Slovakia, 15 and 16 Mar.; Hungary occupied Ruthenia, and granted it autonomy, 16 Mar.; Czechoslovak National Committee under Beneš formed in Paris, 17 Nov. Provisional Government recognized by Britain, 21 July 1940.
Ruthenia annexed by Russia, but rest of country recovered independence at surrender of Germany, May 1945, and President Beneš returned to Prague. Communist *coup d'état*, Feb. 1948. Jan Masaryk, Minister for Foreign Affairs, committed suicide. Beneš resigned, June, and *d.*, Aug. Archbishop Beran imprisoned, 1951. Some

liberalization, 1963 onwards, and Beran allowed to leave C. and reside in the Vatican, Feb. 1965. In Jan. 1968 Dubcek succeeded. Novotny as Party Secretary and a rapid programme of liberalization followed. On 20 Aug. Russian troops invaded C., claiming that action was necessary to prevent a counter-revolution. The end of the new freedoms soon followed. In April 1969 Dubcek forced to resign: replaced by 'hard-liner' Husak. Repressive regime followed. Break-up of Soviet bloc from 1989 led to rapid reforms in C. In Nov. 1989 Communist monopoly of government abolished and Havel succeeded Husak as president of C. In Dec. 1989 the Czechoslovak Communist Party denounced the 1968 invasion as 'unjustified and incorrect'. In April 1990 country renamed the Czech and Slovak Federative Republic but separatist tendencies increased. In July 1992 Czechs and Slovaks opted for separate states and Havel resigned the presidency. Czechoslovakia ceased to exist on 1 Jan. 1993, when the *Czech Republic and the Republic of *Slovakia came into being.

Presidents of C. since 1918:
Masaryk 1918–35
Beneš 1935–38
Hacha 1938–39
(*and President of Bohemia-Moravia, under German 'protection', 1939–45*)
Beneš 1940–48
(*administration in London, 1940–45*)
Gottwald 1948–53
Zápotocky 1953–57
Novotny 1957–68
Svoboda 1968–75
Husak 1975–89
Havel 1989–92.

Czechoslovak language and literature.
The 6thC Byzantine mission of Cyril and Methodius to the Bohemians and other Slavs N of the Middle Danube gave rise to a certain amount of vernacular church literature. The Caroline University founded by the patronage of the Emperor Charles

IV, whose reign (1346–78) coincided with the first flowering of Czech culture, gave Bohemia predominance in arts and letters over the whole W Slav area. The first printed book in C. was produced at Pilsen in 1468 – a *Troan Chronicle* – just six years before Caxton's first English book, *Recuyell of the Historyes of Troye*, came out. *Lexicon Symphonicum*, the first scientific dictionary of the C.L., 1537, the *Elucidation of Grammar*, by Jan Blahoslav, 1571, the Kralice Bible, 1579–93, and V.B. Nudozersky's complete Czech grammar, 1603, served to stabilize the language which had finally evolved from its medieval to its modern form before the battle of the White Mountain (1620) began a period of cultural as well as political stagnation, during which German instead of Latin became the official language of the Czech lands (1774) and similarly Magyar replaced Latin in Slovakia. The Prague National Theatre was founded in 1883. Czech early became the literary language of Slovakia, though there exist Slovak glosses to medieval Latin texts. By the middle of the 19thC written Slovak was stabilized largely through the efforts of Ludovit Stúr (1815–56), Mihal Miloslav Hadz (1811–70), and Jozef Miloslav Hurban (1817–88), round the dialects of central Slovakia; Stúr published in 1846 a *Treatise on Slovak Speech*, which was reinforced by M. Hattala's Slovak grammar of 1852–65. Slovak an official language of the Czechoslovak republic from 1918 until its demise on 31 Dec. 1992. The following is a short list of authors writing in Czech, including some of Slovak birth mentioned above.

Březina, Otoka (Václav Jevabý), 1868–1929, poet.
Čapek, Josef, 1887–1945, dramatist.
Čapek, Karel, 1890–1938, dramatist and journalist.
Čapek-Chod, 1860–1927, novelist.
Čech, Svatopluk, 1846–1908, poet.
Comenius (Komensky), Jan Amos, 1592–1670, educationist.
Dobrovský, Josef, 1753–1829, philologian and historian.

Hálek, Vitězslav, 1835–74, poet and novelist.

Hašek, Jaroslav, 1884–1923, satirist.

Havel, Václav, 1936–, dramatist.

Jirasek, Alois, 1851–1930, poet, novelist, and dramatist.

Jungmann, Josef, 1773–1847, lexicographer and historian.

Kollar, Jan, 1793–1852, poet.

Lützow, Count Francis, 1849–1916, historian.

Mácha, Karel Hynek, 1810–36, poet.

Masaryk, Tómaš Garrigue, 1850–1937, logician and sociologist.

Neruda, Jan, 1834–91, poet and critic.

Palacký, František, 1798–1876, historian.

Šafarik, Pavel J., 1795–1861, critic.

Sládek, Josef Václav, 1845–1912, poet and translator.

Vrchlicky, Jaroslav, 1853–1912, poet.

Zeyer, Julius, 1841–1901, poet.

Czestochowa, Poland. Prominent Polish Marian shrine. Monastery plundered by Hussites, 1430. Defended against Swedes, 1655. Bombed, 1939, but since restored.

Dacca, or **Dhaka,** capital of Bangladesh since 1971. Lal Bagh fort built, 1678. Capital of province of E Bengal and Assam, 1905–12.

Dachau, near Munich, Upper Bavaria, was the site of a notorious concentration camp, 1933–45.

Dacia. Roman province, partly corresponding to modern Romania. Conquered by Trajan, AD 101–6; Aurelian withdrew Roman forces and left D. to the Goths, forming a new province of same name S of Danube c. 275; added to Eastern Empire by Gratian, AD 379. See VLACHS.

Dadaism, art style, current 1915–22.

Dagestan or **Daghistan,** Asia. Conquered by Peter the Great, 1723; restored to Persia under Tsarina Anne, 1735; re-annexed to Russia, 1813. D. autonomous republic formed, 1921; since 1991 it has had full republic status.

daguerreotype. Invented by Louis Daguerre (1789–1851), a French painter, with the help of J.N. Niepce (d. 1833), between 1825 and 1839.

Dahomey. See BENIN.

Dail Eireann.
1. Name of a Sinn Fein Assembly, which sat in the Mansion House at Dublin, 1919.
2. Since 1922 the name of the Lower House of the Parliament of the Irish Republic.

Daily Express, etc. See under NEWSPAPERS.

Dairen, Dalny, or **Talienwan,** Manchuria. Leased by China to Russia as terminus for the Chinese Eastern Railway, 1898. Ceded to Japan, 1905. Restored to China, 1945. See also PORT ARTHUR.

Dakar, capital of Senegal. Formal possession taken by French, 1857: became capital of independent Senegal, 1960.

Dalai Lama. See TIBET.

Dalmatia. Balkan area subdued by Statilius Taurus, 23 BC, and by Tiberius, AD 9. Diocletian b. at Salona (Solin) 245, d. at Split, 313. Occupied by Marcellinus, 461. Conquered by Coloman, King of Hungary, 1102–5. Under Venice, 997–1358. Venetian power destroyed by Wars of Chioggia and Negropont (see under EUBOEA), 1358–1573. Ceded to Austria by Treaty of *Campo Formio, 1797. Made part of kingdom of Illyria by Napoleon, 1805. Ceded to Austria, 1814. N D. and D. Islands promised to Italy by Pact of London, 1915, but given to Yugoslavia, 1920. Italy seized Fiume and Zara, 1920. Annexed whole of D., 21 May 1941. Whole of D. returned to Yugoslavia at German surrender, May 1945. After breakup of Yugoslavia, 1990–2. Most of D. in *Croatia though some areas subsequently occupied by Serb forces. See DUBROVNIK; SPLIT; ZADAR.

Dalriada, ancient name of the northern half of County Antrim, home of a Scottish tribe whose eponymous ancestor was called Riada; they migrated across the N Channel to Kintyre, and founded a new kingdom of D. c. AD 500, of which the nucleus was Argyllshire. The D. Scots were defeated in Ireland at Magh Rath, County Down, 637. By their union with the Picts under Kenneth MacAlpin, 843, the kingdom of Alban was founded. See SCOTLAND.

Damascus, Syria. Taken by Assyrians after battle of Karkar, 853 BC. Finally conquered by Assyrians under Tiglath-Pileser III, 733. Captured by Alexander the Great, 333. Taken by Romans, 63 BC. Captured by Arabs, AD 635. Capital of the Caliphate, 661–750. Attacked by Crusaders, 1126 and

1148. Sacked by Mongols, 1260 and 1399. Conquered by Turks under Selim, 1516. Captured by T.E. Lawrence and the Arabs, 1918. Occupied by French, 1920. Taken by combined Free French and British troops, 21 June 1941. Syrian independence proclaimed at D., 27 Sept. 1941, and D. became the Syrian capital. D.'s Great Mosque was built 5thC as a Christian church.

Dambuster Raid. RAF Lancaster raid to destroy the Möhne and Eder dams in the Ruhr, using bomb developed by Barnes Wallis, 16/17 May 1943. Raid successful in that dams were pierced and widespread flooding resulted: but they were rapidly repaired and 42% of bombers were lost. On the ground, approx. 1500 people died, a high proportion being foreign 'slave' labourers.

Danegeld. Tax to buy off attacks by foreign pirates first levied, 991, by Ethelred II. From 991 to 1012, 158,000 silver pounds was so spent. After the murder of Archbishop Aelfheah in 1012 a special tax, called *heregeld*, was levied to pay a standing army. This tax was still collected by the Danish kings Knut, Harald, Hardaknut (1016–42), and by Edward the Confessor, who abolished it in 1051. No recorded use of the actual *term* D. before 1066. William I reimposed the *heregeld* tax, under the name D., and his successors continued to collect it until 1163.

Danelaw. Territory covering most of E England ceded to Guthrum by Alfred the Great in 878, after the battle of Edington. It was largely reconquered by Edward the Elder, but in 940 Edmund I was forced to cede part of the D. to Olaf Guthfrithson, the Viking king of Dublin. Edred had reasserted English authority throughout the D. by 955.

Danes, a Scandinavian tribe unknown to Roman authors, even by name. Their kings play a large part in the English epic *Beowulf,* which is now thought to have an historical basis in events of the late 5thC AD. They were then settled in what is now southern Sweden (Scania). The D. probably did not move into Jutland and the islands E of it until these had been vacated by the Angles and allied tribes when they migrated to Britain in the 5th and 6thC. The Skjoldung ('Children of Scyld') Dynasty began to dominate the whole Danish group in the 8thC under Ivar Widefathom, whose uncle Gudröd's (Godred's) reign in Scania can be tentatively dated 720–40. *See* DENMARK, KINGDOM OF, for later history.

Dangerous Dogs Act, 1991 made compulsory licensing and neutering of certain breeds of dogs considered dangerous, e.g. pit bull terriers. Efficacy subsequently questioned.

Danish literature. The following is a list of prominent writers in D., both inhabitants of Denmark and authors of Norwegian, Faroese, or Icelandic origin. Some medieval D. writers not mentioned here will be found under LATIN LITERATURE, POST-CLASSICAL, because they produced no vernacular work which has survived. The order is that of date of birth.

Christian Pedersen, *d.* 1554, Bible translator.

Hans Tausen, 1494–1561, Protestant apologist.

Anders Sørensen Vedel, 1542–1616, translator of Saxo Grammaticus.

Arild Huitfeldt, 1546–1609, historian.

Anders Arreboe, 1587–1637, religious epic poet.

Anders Bording, 1619–77, poet and editor of the first D. newspaper, *Dansk Merkur,* which appeared in 1666.

Ludvig Holberg, 1684–1754, historian, poet, dramatist.

Hans Adolf Brorson, 1694–1764, lyric poet.

Johan Herman Wessel, 1742–85, poet, dramatist.

Johannes Ewald, 1743–81, poet, dramatist.

Peder Andreas Heiberg, 1758–1841, poet.

Adam Oehlenschläger, 1779–1850, poet and dramatist.

Steen Steensen Blicher, 1782–1848, novelist, poet.

Nikolai Fredrik Severin Grundtvig, 1783–1872, poet, especially song-writer.

Bernhard Severin Ingemann, 1789–1862, novelist, poet.

Johan Ludvig Heiberg, 1791–1860, critic, dramatist.

Poul Møller, 1794–1838, novelist, essayist.

Emil Aarestrup, 1800–56, poet.

Hans Christian Andersen, 1805–75, storyteller.

Frederik Paludan-Müller, 1809–76, novelist, poet.

Søren Kierkegaard, 1813–55, philosopher.

Holger Drachmann, 1846–1908, poet, novelist.

Herman Bang, 1857–1912, novelist.

Henrik Pontopiddan, 1857–1943, novelist.

Karl Gjellerup, 1857–1919, novelist.

Jakob Knudsen, 1858–1917, novelist.

Gustav Wied, 1858–1914, novelist, dramatist.

Ludvig Holstein, 1864–1943, poet.

Jeppe Aakjer, 1866–1930, poet.

Gyrithe Lemche, 1866–1945, novelist.

Martin Andersen Nexo, 1869–1954, novelist.

Helge Rode, 1870–1937, poet, dramatist.

Karin Michaelis, 1872–1949, novelist.

Johannes Vilhelm Jensen, 1873–1950, novelist.

Harry Søiberg, 1880–1954, novelist.

Isak Dinesen (Karen Blixen), 1885–1962, miscellaneous writer.

Nils Petersen, 1897–1943, novelist.

Kaj Munk, 1898–1944, dramatist.

Jorgen Franz Jacobsen, 1900–38, novelist.

Mogens, Klitgaard, 1906–45, novelist.

Dannebrog, Danish royal standard, first flown at the siege of Reval, 1219 (*see under* TALLIN).

Dannevirke, fortified boundary dike laid out by King Godred of Denmark (*d.* 810) along his frontier with the empire, 808; extended by Thyra, consort of King Gorm the Old (reigned 900–40). Demolished by the Prussians after their victory over Denmark in 1864.

Danube, River. Navigation set free by Treaty of Paris, 1856; regulated by Berlin Treaty, 1878; treaty restoring rights to Russia, 1883; Iron Gates Canal opened, 1898;

International Commission for regulating navigation, 1904. Danubian Convention Aug. 1948, at Belgrade, resulted in the Danube Commission, 1949, with headquarters at Budapest since 1954, which monitors all rulings of the Convention. Federal Germany a consultative member since 1957. Economic blockade of Serbia along D., 1992, not wholly effective; lifted 1994.

Danubian Principalities, The. Moldavia and Wallachia formed into independent states by Convention of Paris, 19 Aug. 1858; united under title of *Romania, 23 Dec. 1861.

Danzig. *See* GDANSK.

Dardanelles, Turkey, or **Strait of Gallipoli** (the ancient *Hellespont*). Here Xerxes crossed into Europe, 480 BC and Alexander the Great crossed into Asia, 334 BC. Swum by Lord Byron, 1810; Treaty of, signed in London after conclusion of Syrian War, 1841; British and French fleets entered at the Sultan's invitation, 8 Oct. 1853. British and French naval expedition at, 19 Feb.–18 Mar. 1915, was a failure. Land attack, 25 Apr. 1915–8 Jan. 1916; internationalized by the Treaty of Lausanne, 1923; League of Nations agreed to its refortification by Turkey, 1936. *See under* TURKISH REPUBLIC and WORLD WAR I.

Darien Scheme, The. A Scottish attempt to colonize the isthmus of D. (Central America), organized by Paterson, the founder of the Bank of England, 1695. Parliament voted supplies, and the expedition sailed on 26 July 1698; arrived after many difficulties, 30 Oct. 1698; left, 18 June 1699. In 1715 the sufferers from the scheme received compensation.

Dartford, England. Wat Tyler's insurrection began here, 1381. First paper mill in England erected here, 1590. Road tunnel under Thames completed, Nov. 1963; bridge over Thames at completed, 1991.

Dartmoor Prison (S Devon). Founded, Mar. 1806, for the reception of French prisoners of war. It fell into disuse after 1815; reorganized as a civil prison, 1855.

Dartmouth, England, was the rendezvous of the fleet destined for the Holy Land, 1190 (*see* CRUSADES). French pirates repulsed at D. after burning Plymouth, 1404; taken after four weeks' siege by Prince Maurice, 1643; retaken by Gen. Fairfax, 1646. Naval college founded at, 1905.

Dartmouth College (New Hampshire, USA). Chartered, 1769.

darts. A form of D. was played in medieval times and is said to have been a favourite sport of Henry VIII. The Pilgrim Fathers took D. to America, 1620. D. became popular in British public houses and inns from the 19thC onwards, more so during the 20thC. The National Darts Association was founded in Britain in 1953; the US Darting Association dates from 1969.

Darwin, capital of Northern Territories, Australia, devastated by cyclone, 1974, but since rebuilt.

Darwinism. Charles Darwin's (1809–1882) works, *On the Origin of Species by Means of Natural Selection*, published in 1859, and *The Descent of Man*, 1871, new edition, 1874.

Data Protection. The Data Protection Tribunal was established under the D.P. Act, 1984, to determine appeals against rulings of the D.P. Registrar.

Daugavpils (Russian, **Dvinsk**), founded by Livonian Knights, 1278. Polish till 1773. Russian 1773–1919. In Latvian Republic until its annexation by USSR, 1940. Again Latvian, from 1991. Known as Dünaburg until 1893.

Dauphin. A southern French title, which from 1364 was always borne by the eldest son of the French king. The first royal D. was Charles (afterwards Charles VI of France), on his birth, 1368. The last D. was Louis Antoine, Duke of Angoulême, son of Charles X, who assumed the title on 16 Sept. 1824. It was abolished after the revolution of 1830.

Dauphiné, having belonged successively to the Burgundian and Frankish domin-ions, passed to the empire in 1032, and was immediately ruled by the counts of Vienne, one of whom, called Dolphin, gave his name to the province *c.* 1130. The Emperor Charles IV granted it as a fief to the King of France, 1356, and from 1364 to 1830 it was the customary apanage of the heir to the French throne. In 1794 the province was split up into the departments of Isère, Hautes-Alpes, and Drôme.

David Cohen Prize, British literary prize of £30,000, making it the richest single UK literary prize, established 1992 by the Arts Council in association with Coutts & Co. Awarded every two years, starting 1993, to a living writer in recognition of a lifetime's achievement.

Davis Cup. International tennis trophy presented by Dwight F. Davis of St. Louis, USA., in 1900 and competed for annually by teams from different countries. Not won by Britain since 1936. Open to professional players from 1970. USA (1995) holds most wins in D.C.

Davis Strait. Separating N America from Greenland, discovered by John Davis, 1585.

Davy safety lamp (for miners). Invented by Sir Humphry Davy (1778–1829) in 1816.

Dawes Plan to provide payments by Germany and to stabilize German currency; settled by a committee of which the US General Charles G. Dawes (1865–1951) was leading member; submitted to Reparations Commission, 9 Apr., and accepted, 17 Apr. 1924. Superseded by *Young Plan in 1930.

Day of Dupes. 11 Nov. 1630, when Marie de' Medici and Anne of Austria were outwitted by Cardinal Richelieu.

daylight saving. *See* SUMMER TIME.

D-Day, 6 June 1944, when allied troops landed in Normandy to begin the invasion of Nazi-occupied Europe. Major commemoration at 50th anniversary of, 1994.

DDT, or Dichlorodiphenyltrichloro-ethane. First prepared by Zeidler, 1874, but not used as an insecticide until 1939. Use severely restricted in most Western countries from 1970s.

Dead Sea Scrolls, ancient scrolls or parts of scrolls found in caves at Khirbet Qumran, 7 miles S of Jericho, between 1947 and 1956. The first discoveries were made by goatherds when the caves were in Jordanian territory. The scrolls were purchased by the Hebrew University in Jerusalem and dated between c. 167 BC and c. 200 AD. After the Arab–Israeli War, 1948, territory of the caves in Israel, and area was systematically excavated 1949, and 1951–5; with many archaeological finds. Scrolls religious in character and linked to Essence or other sects. Revival of Qumran monastery after 68 AD coincided with rise of Christianity. Search for more scrolls continuing, 1995.

Deal, England. Attempted landing by Perkin Warbeck, 3 July 1495. Outpost of Sandwich until 1699, when it was incorporated.

Dean, Forest of (Gloucestershire). Royal demesne before the Norman Conquest. The Charter of the Swainmote, or Verderers Court, was granted by Knut in 1016. The deer, limited to 800 head by an Act of 1668, had dwindled to ten by 1810, and the last were killed by order of the crown in 1850. Free miners born in the Hundred of St Briavels, under a charter of Edward I or Edward II, were entitled to mine in the forest on payment to the crown of 1d. per ton royalty. Iron, first worked in prehistoric times, was last worked, 1941.

'Death on the Rock', popular term (from TV programme of that name) for the killing, in Gibraltar by the SAS, on 6 Mar. 1988, of three IRA terrorists. European Court of Human Rights subsequently found against Britain (27 Sept. 1995).

Debt, National. *See* NATIONAL DEBT.

Decameron. Written by Giovanni Boccaccio (1313–75) between 1348 and 1358.

Deccan, India. *See* INDIA.

deceased wife's sister, marriage with. Bill to legalize first introduced, 1841. Became law in 1908.

Decembrists (Dekabrists). Conspirators involved in the Russian mutiny of officers at St Petersburg, 26 Dec. 1825 (14 Dec., Orthodox style). The survivors of those who were neither hanged nor shot were pardoned by Alexander II in 1856, after banishment to Siberia.

Decemviri. Magistrates appointed at Rome in 451 BC to draw up a code of laws that would secure the plebeians against magisterial caprice (*see* TWELVE TABLES). In 367 BC a permanent board of D. was created to look after the Sibylline Books and to celebrate the Apolline and Secular Games.

decimal coinage. First used in modern times in USA, 1792: in France, 1799. Under Decimal Currency Act, 1967, Britain changed to D.C., 15 Feb. 1971. Half penny withdrawn, 31 Dec. 1984: £1 coin in circulation from 1983. Old florin (10p) coin ceased to be legal tender, 1993. S Africa adopted D.C. in 1960; Australia 1966, New Zealand in 1967.

Declaration of Arbroath. Letter to Pope John XXII from nobles and clergy, supporters of Robert Bruce, declaring Scottish independence, 6 Apr. 1320.

Declaration or **Bill of Rights** (English). The foundation of the Bill of Rights declared amongst other things William and Mary King and Queen of England, passed, 1689.

Declaration of Human Rights. Drafting begun, 1946, and subscribed, 10 Dec. 1948, by all member states of the UN except six members of the then Soviet bloc, S Africa and Saudi Arabia. First conference on human rights since dissolution of USSR, held at Vienna, 1993: made some progress on fuller implementation of 1948 declaration.

Declaration of Independence, 4 July 1776. *See* UNITED STATES OF AMERICA.

Declaration of London. Concerning

contraband and blockade, provisionally ratified by European powers and by USA, 1909. Promulgated by Order in Council, 29 Oct. 1914. Withdrawn by Order in Council, 7 July 1916.

Declaration of Paris, signed by powers attending the Congress of Paris, 1856, renouncing privateering and defining contraband of war.

Declaration of Rights (American). Passed by first American Congress at Carpenter's Hall, Philadelphia, Sept. 1774.

Declaration of Rights (Irish). Drawn up by Grattan, demanding legislative independence for Ireland; accepted by Irish Parliament, Apr. 1782, and practically confirmed by the English Parliament in the same year. *See* IRELAND.

Declarations of Indulgence.
1. By Charles II in 1672, by which all Acts against the Nonconformists and Roman Catholics were suspended; this was withdrawn and the *Test Act passed, 1673.
2. By James II in 1687, similar to the above.
3. By James II in 1688, which was commanded to be read in the churches (*see* SEVEN BISHOPS, TRIAL OF THE). *See* also NONCONFORMISTS.

decretals. Collection of papal decrees or decretal letters; part of canon law. First collection made by Dionysius Exiguus about AD 550; word generally applied to the compilation of Gratian in 12thC; first official collection, 1210. What are known as the False D. were supposed to have been written between 425 and 450, but had no existence as a whole until about 850.

Defence, Ministry of. Created 5 Oct. 1946; formally instituted, 1 Jan. 1947. Reconstructed and expanded, 1964.

Defence of the Realm Act. *See* DORA.

Defender of the Faith (*Fidei Defensor*). Title conferred on Henry VIII of England by Pope Leo X, Oct. 1521, in recognition of his tract against Luther entitled, 'On the Seven Sacraments, against Martin Luther,

the Heresiarch, by the Illustrious Prince Henry VIII'. Continued by Parliament, 1544, and since then borne by all British sovereigns.

Defense, Department of, US government department, with headquarters in the Pentagon, Washington DC, established by the National Security Act, 1947.

De Haeretico Comburendo. *See* HERESY, LAWS CONCERNING.

Deira, a kingdom of the Angles, founded by Aelle (reigned 560–88). Ethelfrid had united D. with *Bernicia by 605, and from then onwards, apart from the period 633–55, the two kingdoms were merged into one as *Northumbria.

Delaware, USA. First explored by Hendrik Hudson, 1609. Takes its name from Thomas West, third Baron de la Warr (1577–1618), who entered D. Bay, 1610. Settled by Swedes and Finns, 1638. Dutch from 1655 to 1664, when it was surrendered to the English. In 1682 the territory was leased to William Penn, and was part of Pennsylvania until 1776. D. – Maryland border stabilized and delineated, 1767. Declared itself independent, 1776. Was the first state to ratify the US Constitution in 1787.

Delegates, Court of. Established, 1534. Abolished, 1832, and its powers transferred to the Privy Council.

Delft, Holland. Founded by Godfrey le Bossu, 1075. The famous earthenware first manufactured here late in the 16thC. Diet of D. agreed to throw off allegiance to King of Spain, 1575. Estates of Holland and Zeeland assembled in congress at D. and signed a new Act of Union, 25 Apr. 1576. Assembly of the United Provinces arranged constitution, 13 Jan. 1581. William the Silent assassinated at, 10 July 1584.

Delhi, India. Old D. dates from the mid-17thC AD. (The Red Fort was built in 1652.) Previously taken by Tamerlane, 1398; by Nadir Shah, 1739; by Mahratta, 1759; possessed by Great Britain, 1804. During Indian Mutiny seized by Sepoys, who massacred the British there, 1857; recaptured, 20 Sept. 1857. D. became the official capital of India (see CALCUTTA) at the Coronation Durbar of 12 Dec. 1911, when the foundation stone of New D., S of the old city, was laid. New D. was inaugurated as capital of India, 1931 and remained so after independence, 1947, name of whole city reverting to D. D. Conference, 1940.

Delian League. Organization of Greek states formed 477 BC. under Athens to prosecute war against Persia.

Delos. Smallest of the Cyclades Islands, Aegean Sea. Now known as **Mikra Dili.** Became a great trading centre after the fall of Corinth in 146 BC. Devastated, 87 BC, during the Mithridatic War.

Delphi (modern **Kastri**). The oracle of Apollo at D. in Phocis was a holy spot before the Hellenic invasion. The fame of the oracle declined after the 5thC BC, and the treasure-houses in the walled precincts were sacked by the Phocians between 356 and 346 BC. The *Pythian Games were held under the protection of the shrine. The last oracle was uttered at the request of the Emperor Julian (reigned AD 361–3).

Delphin Classics. Collection of Latin authors prepared by 39 scholars in the reigns of Louis XIV and Louis XV, *Ad usum Delfini* (for the use of the *Dauphin). Published, 1674–1730.

Demarcation, Bull of, 1493. Issued by Pope Alexander VI, dividing New World discoveries between the Spanish and Portuguese.

Demerara, Guyana. Surrendered to British, 1781; again taken by Gen. White, 1796; restored to Dutch, Mar. 1802; recaptured by British, 25 Sept. 1803; ceded to Great Britain, 1814.

Democratic Party, in the USA. 'Democrats' became the only familiar title for the party of Jefferson (anti-Federalist), in 1828. Since the 1930s the D.P. has tended to be the party more favoured by working-class and black Americans. It has controlled the presidency for the following periods: 1801–41; 1845–9; 1853–61; 1885–9; 1893–7; 1913–21; 1932–52; 1960–8; 1976–80; 1993–. Lost control of Congress, 1994.

De Montfort University, name adopted by former Leicester Polytechnic, 1992.

Dendermonde or **Termonde,** Belgium. Famous interview between William the Silent and Counts Horn, Egmont and Hoogstraaten, regarding Flanders's relationship with Spain held, 1566. Sluices opened against Louis XIV, 1667. Captured by Marlborough, 1706.

Denmark, Kingdom of. Danes began to achieve European prominence as searovers during the 9thC. Kingdom consolidated by Gorm the Old, 900–35. Jutland ecclesiastical see established, 948. Harald Bluetooth (936–86) baptized, 965. Defeated by Emperor Otto II, 974. Independence established, 983. Svein (986–1014) besieges London, 994. Conquers Norway and kills King Olaf at battle of Svold, 1000. Knut the Great (1018–35) loses Norway, 1015. Becomes King of England, 1016. Defeats Swedes and Norwegians at battle of Helge-aa, 1025. Re-conquers Norway, 1028. Breakup of Danish Empire, 1035–42. Valdemar I (the Great, 1157–82) conquers Rügen, 1168. Valdemar II (1202–41) conquers Estonia, 1219. Is defeated by Germans at Bornhöved, 1227. Christopher II concedes royal prerogative to the estates, 1320. Valdemar III cedes Schleswig to Duke of Holstein, 1326. Defeated by Holsteiners at battle of the Dannevirke (see under BATTLES), 1331. Margaret (1387–1412) becomes Regent of Norway and Denmark, and 'Sovereign Lady' of Sweden, 1388. Defeat and conquest of Sweden at battle of Falköping, 1389. Union of *Kalmar, 1397. Kings of D. become Dukes of Schleswig-Holstein, 1460. Defeated by Swedes under Sten Sture the Elder at battle of Brunkeberg, 1471. Revival of union, 1497. Swedish rebellion, 1521; ends union, 1523. Decisive defeat of Hanseatic League, 1535. Reformation, 1537. Wars with Sweden, 1563–70, 1611–13 (Peace of Knaeroed). Christian IV defeated by Tilly at battle of Lutter, 1626. Jutland overrun, 1627. Peace of Lübeck, 1629. War with Sweden, 1644–5. Loss of Scania, Blekinge, and Halland by Treaty of Brömsebro, 1645. Treaty of Roskilde, 1658. Peace of Copenhagen, 1660. War with Sweden, 1676–9 (Peace of Fontainebleau). Cession of Oldenburg to Prussia, 1773. Joins the Northern Confederacy against Britain, 1800. Nelson attacks Copenhagen, 1801. British seize Danish fleet, 2–5 Sept. 1807. D. allied with Napoleon, Oct. 1807. Norway ceded to Sweden at Treaty of Kiel, 1814. Cession of Schleswig-Holstein to Prussia by Peace of Vienna, 30 Oct. 1864. Self-government given to *Iceland, 1874. Prince Charles elected King of Norway as Haakon VII, 1905. Plebiscite in N Schleswig, which is returned to D., 1920. German invasion, 9 Apr. 1940. German forces surrender, 5 May 1945. D. signed the North Atlantic Pact, 1949. New Succession Law, 1953, admitted sovereign's daughter to the line of succession: Princess Margarethe succeeded father, 1972. Joined EC, 1973; voted in referendum against ratifying Maastricht Treaty, June 1992; voted in favour in second referendum, May 1993.

Denmark, Sovereigns of:
Gorm the Old *d. c.* 940
Harald Bluetooth 936–86
Svein Forkbeard *c.* 986–1014
Harald II 1014–18
Knut the Great 1018–35
Hardicanute 1035–42
Magnus the Good (of Norway) 1042–47
Svein II Astridsson 1047–74
Harald III (Hein) 1074–80
Knut IV the Good (Saint) 1080–86
Olaf Hunger 1086–95
Eric the Evergood 1095–1103
Nils 1103–34
Eric Emune 1134–37
Eric Lam 1137–47
Svein III 1147–57
Knut V (for three days) 1157
Valdemar I the Great 1157–82
Knut VI 1182–1202
Valdemar II the Victorious 1202–41
Eric Plough-penny 1241–50

Abel 1250–52
Christopher I 1252–59
Eric Klipping 1259–86
Eric VI Maendved 1286–1319
Christopher II 1319–26
Valdemar III 1326–30
Christopher II (again) 1330–32
Period of civil war 1332–40
Valdemar IV Atterdag 1340–75
Olaf 1375–87
Margaret, Queen 1387–97
Regent 1397–1412
Eric of Pomerania (of Sweden, D., and Norway) 1397–1439
Christopher III of Bavaria 1440–48
Christian I (Oldenburg) 1448–81
John 1481–1513
Christian II 1513–23
Frederick I (not of Sweden) 1523–33
Period of civil war 1533–34
Christian III 1535–59
Frederick II 1559–88
Christian IV 1588–1648
Frederick III 1648–70
Christian V 1670–99
Frederick IV 1699–1730
Christian VI 1730–46
Frederick V 1746–66
Christian VII 1766–1808
Frederick (Crown Prince Regent) 1784–1808
Frederick VI (not of Norway after 1814) 1808–39
Christian VIII 1839–48
Frederick VII 1848–63
Christian IX 1863–1906
Frederick VIII 1906–12
Christian X 1912–47
Frederick IX 1947–72
Margarethe 1972–

Deodand. Objects which had caused human death were forfeited to the crown as Ds. till 1846.

deoxyribonucleic acid. *See* DNA

Department of Economic Affairs (DEA), established 1964; abolished 1970.

Départements. France divided into 83, 1790. Napoleon divided France into 130 D., but the number of metropolitan D. is now (1995) 96.

Deposition, Bull of.
1. 1535, issued by Pope Paul III, excommunicating Henry VIII.
2. 1570, issued by Pius V excommunicating Elizabeth I.

Deptford. Henry VIII's dock (established 1512) here used until 1869; Peter the Great (*see* RUSSIA) came here to study shipbuilding, 1689. Royal victualling yard of the Navy established at, 1745.

Deputies, Chamber of.
1. Lower house of French legislature so named under Louis XVIII, 1814. Dissolved by Charles X, 1827, and 16 May 1830. Superseded by National Assembly, 4 May 1848. Restored by Louis Napoleon, 2 Dec. 1851. During the Second Empire (1852–70), replaced by a *Corps législatif*. Restored under Third Republic (1871–1940). Replaced by National Assembly, 1946.
2. Lower house of Belgian Parliament so named, 1831. Known as the Chamber of Representatives since 1921.

Derby, England. The original Anglian settlement was called Northworthige; captured *c.* 870 by the Danes, who renamed it D. It was retaken by the English, 917. First sent burgesses to Parliament, 1295. Grammar school built, 1554. Silk mills set up, 1717: porcelain manufactured from 1770. Canal opened, 1836. Bishopric created, 1907. Major rail centre from 19thC; luxury car-maker and aero-engine works in 20thC (Rolls-Royce) at, from 1906.

Derby Day, originally second day of the summer meeting at Epsom, in late May or early June, when the D. Stakes, instituted 4 May 1780, are run for. Until 1891 Parliament adjourned specially on this day. Race now run on Saturdays, starting 1995. The Kentucky D. (started, 1876) is a celebrated annual horse race in the USA.

Derry, name adopted, 1984, as official title of *Londonderry.

Desert Shield, name given to US contri-

bution to the UN military coalition against Iraq, 1990–1. Eventually US force totalled over 400,000 persons.

Desert Storm, 1) air and land campaign waged by US-led UN coalition against Iraq Jan. 16–Feb 28, 1991; 2) term confined to the land battle against Iraq, 24–7 Feb. 1991. *See* BATTLES; GULF WAR.

Design Council, first established as the Council of Industrial Design, Dec. 1944. Design Centre, Haymarket, 1956–94: Glasgow 1956–94. D.C. at Oxendon St, London from 1994; Scottish Design based in Glasgow. Design Museum opened at Docklands, London, 1990.

Despard's Plot, to assassinate George III, 1802. Col. D. and plotters executed, 21 Feb. 1803.

Detroit, Michigan, USA. First settled by Antoine Cadillac, 24 July 1701. Originally called *La Ville d'Étroit*. Centre of US car industry since the beginning of the 20thC.

Deventer, Holland. Taken by Maurice of Saxony from Spaniards, 10 June 1591.

Devil's Island. In the Îles du Salut group, NW of Cayenne, French Guiana. Was notorious for its penal settlement, 1854–1938.

Devil's Parliament. Met at Coventry, 1459.

Devonport. *See* PLYMOUTH.

Dhaka. *See* DACCA.

diamond. Manilius spoke of it, AD 16; Pliny said it was known only to kings, AD 100, and described six varieties. Mined in India from earliest times till the close of the 19thC; S America from the middle of 18thC; S Africa (discovered accidentally), 1870. Phosphorescence produced by friction discovered by Robert Boyle, 1663; combustibility established by Florentine academicians, 1694. Smithson Tennant demonstrated carbon composition of Ds., 1796. *See also* KOH-I-NOOR and CULLINAN DIAMOND.

Diamond Necklace Affair (France). Queen Marie Antoinette, the Comtesse de Lamotte, the impostor Cagliostro, and the

Cardinal de Rohan were implicated, 1785; Rohan's trial, 14 Apr. 1786. The countess was condemned, but escaped; Rohan was acquitted.

Diamond Sculls. Race for amateur single rowers instituted at Henley, 1844.

dictionary. A Chinese D. by Hü Shin, containing 10,000 characters, published, 150 BC; Italian D. of the Academia della Crusca published, 1612; Samuel Johnson's D., 1755; Noah Webster's, 1828 (expanded into *Webster's New International Dictionary*, 1936); Sir William Smith's *Dictionary of Greek and Roman Antiquities*, 1842, *Biography*, 1849, *Geography*, 1857; Liddell and Scott's, 1843; Littré's French D., 1863–72; *Dictionary of National Biography*, first edited by Leslie Stephen and Sidney Lee, 1885–1900: Funk's, 1893–5; Murray's *New English Dictionary* initiated, 1857; preparation for publishing began, 1879; first fascicule published, 1884; completed 1928; re-issued with supplement, as *Oxford English Dictionary*, 1933; *Dictionary of Dates*, first published by Dent, 1911.

Dien-Bien-Phu, Vietnam. Scene of the final battle between French and Viet Minh forces in the 1945–54 Indo-China War. The Viet Minh captured the French positions, May 1954, with heavy losses to both sides.

Dieppe, Normandy. Occupied by the English, 1420–35. Bombarded by British, July 1694; 1794; 14 Sept. 1803. Occupied by Germans, Dec. 1870–July 1871, and again 10 June 1940. Anglo-Canadian landing at, 18–19 Aug. 1942 suffered heavy casualties. Liberated, 1 Sept. 1944, by same Canadian unit as had landed in 1942.

diesel engine. First model built, 1893–7, by Rudolf Diesel (1858–1913).

Diet. The following are the principal Ds. of the Holy Roman Empire, with their dates:
Augsburg, (*a*) 1530; (*b*) 1555.
Maglione, 1502.
Roncaglia, 12 Nov. 1158.
Speyer, (*a*) 1526; (*b*) 1529.

Worms, (*a*) 1495; (*b*) 1521 (associated with Martin Luther); (*c*) 1547; (*d*) 1578.
See also REICHSTAG.

'Dieu et mon Droit' ('God and my Right'). The parole of the day at the battle of Gisors, 20 Sept. 1198, at which Richard I was present. It first appeared on the Great Seal of Henry VI; discontinued by Queen Anne, but restored by George I.

Diggers, associated with the *LEVELLERS.

Diggers' Conference, in Victoria, Australia, was a 'shadow' parliament, which demanded representation on the Legislative Council, 1854.

Dijon, France. Roman *Divonense Castrum.* Capital of Burgundy, 1180. Joined to French crown, 1477. Capitulated to Germans, Oct. 1870.

Dingaan's Day, anniversary of the victory of Pretorius's commando over D. at Blood River, 16 Dec. 1838. Later known as the **Day of the Covenant.** *See* VOORTREKKERS; ZULUS; TRANSVAAL.

Directors' Liability Act (Great Britain). Passed, 18 Aug. 1890, now contained in amended form in the Companies Act, 1948 further amended by the Acts of 1967, 1976 and 1980.

Directory, French. The Government established in France after the Convention, 27 Oct. 1795; abolished, 9 Nov. 1799.

Directory of Public Worship drawn up by Westminster Assembly of Divines, 1644; accepted by Scottish General Assembly, Feb. 1945.

disestablishment. For D. of Anglican Church in Ireland, *see* IRELAND; in Wales, *see* WALES, CHURCH OF. The Church of Scotland virtually disestablished itself at the time of its union with the United Free Church in 1929. In France the Roman Catholic Church was disestablished in 1793–1801, and again in 1906. Renewed interest in possible D. of the Church of England in 1990s.

Dissenters. *See* NONCONFORMISTS and PURITANS.

dissolution of monasteries. *See* MONAS-TERIES.

district councils (England and Wales) first established by Local Government Act, 1894: a new form of D.C. resulted from the Local Government Act of 1972.

Divine Comedy. Begun probably in 1300 by Dante Alighieri (1265–1321). First printed, 1472.

divine right of kings. The doctrine emphasized in opposition to the temporal claims of the Papacy and used as theoretical justification of secular interference in ecclesiastical affairs during and after the *Reformation, and of royal supremacy in secular affairs especially in England by James I (1603–25) and Charles I (1625–49).

diving bell. First used in Europe *c.* 1538.

divorce (Britain). D. Court established, 1857; D. Amendment Act passed, 21 July 1868. Lord Buckmaster's Bill received royal assent, 1923. A.P. Herbert's Matrimonial Causes Act gave new grounds for decrees both of nullity and of D. – notably, incurable insanity, 1937; operating, Jan. 1938. Matrimonial Causes Act, 1973, radically liberalized divorce laws in Britain, making sole ground for D. irretrievable breakdown of marriage. Further amendments, 1984 and, under the Children Act of 1989. Modifications suggested by Lord Chancellor and others, 1993: including proposals for 'no-fault' D. New reform proposals, Apr. 1995.

Djibouti, republic in Gulf of Aden, formerly French Somaliland. Acquired by France 1856–83. Independent 1977, with capital at D.

DNA (Deoxyribonucleic acid), organic chemical of complex two-stranded molecular structure, found in all living cells, organized into chromosomes and which codes genetic information. DNA was first discovered by Friedrich Mieschen, 1869, but its part in genetic inheritance not established till 1943. Structure determined by Crick, Franklin, Watson and Wilkins at Cambridge University, 1953 and Crick,

Watson and Williams jointly awarded Nobel Prize for Medicine, 1962, for work in elucidating structures of DNA. Use developed in *genetic engineering since 1980s. DNA 'finger-printing' invented by Alec Jeffreys, 1985, first used in murder trial in UK, 1987, but some doubts on total reliability expressed, 1993. DNA testing established that bones found in grave at Ekaterinburg were those of murdered Tsar Nicholas of Russia, wife and three daughters, July 1993 (by British scientists at Harwell, Berks.) Confirmed by US DNA tests, 1995. Ten-year-old rape case (committed in UK, 1983) solved by DNA fingerprinting, Dec. 1993. National DNA database established in Birmingham, UK, Mar. 1995.

Dobruja, Bulgaria and Romania. Ceded to Romania, 1878 and 1913. To Bulgaria by Treaty of Bucharest, 1918. To Romania again, 1919. Southern part to Bulgaria, 1940; confirmed by peace treaty of 1947.

Docking and Nicking of Horses Act, 1947. Makes docking of horses illegal (except on veterinary advice).

Docklands Light Railway, London, opened 1987. *See under* LONDON TRANSPORT EXECUTIVE.

Doctors' Commons. College for doctors of civil and canon law established by Dr Harvey, 1567. Charter, 1768. Dissolved, 1857.

Doctors of the Church. These were, traditionally, SS Gregory the Great, Ambrose, Augustine of Hippo, Jerome, John Chrysostom, Basil, Gregory Nazianzen and Athanasius.
The foregoing were acknowledged as D. of the C. by the early Middle Ages. The following were so declared, in the years shown, by papal decree:
SS Thomas Aquinas, 1568; Bonaventure, 1588; Anselm, 1720; Isidore, 1722; Peter Chrysologus, 1729; Leo I, 1754; Peter Damian, 1828; Bernard of Clairvaux, 1830; Cyril of Alexandria, 1833; Cyril of Jerusalem, 1833; John of Damascus, 1833; Hilary of Poitiers, 1851; Alphonsus Liguori, 1871;

Francis de Sales, 1877; The Venerable Bede, 1899; Ephrem, 1920; Peter Canisius, 1925; John of the Cross, 1926; Albert the Great, 1931; Robert Bellarmine, 1931; Anthony of Padua, 1946. In 1970 the first two women to be declared Doctors of the Church were SS Catherine of Siena and Teresa of Avila. From 1993, campaign to make Thérèse of Lisieux a D. of the C.

Dodecanese Islands. Seized by Italy from Turkey, 1912. Greece gave up claim in favour of Italy, 1920. Formally incorporated in Greece, 1948.

dodo. Last living specimen seen 1681.

Dodoma, capital of *Tanzania, since 1974.

dog licence, fixed at 7s. 6d. per annum (later 35p.) 1878, by Act of Parliament; subsequently abolished.

Doge. See VENICE.

Doggett's Coat and Badge. Thomas Doggett the actor (d. 1721) awarded prize of coat and badge to winner of annual race on Thames by six water-men, instituted 1 Aug. 1715, in honour of George I's accession.

dole. Popular name for unemployment benefit, first became current, 1919–20. It originated at least as early as the 15thC, in the D. given in the form of goods to poor people at the church porch. A D. porch still exists at Eye, Suffolk.

dollar, thaler, taler, originally **Joachimsthaler.** Coins, the currency of the Hapsburg dominions, were so called from the place in Bohemia (Cz. Jachymov), where they were first coined in 1519. Brought into common use in the USA c. 1794, having been officially introduced in 1787. Australia adopted a D. in its decimal coinage system, 1966.

dollar diplomacy. Associated with the Taft administration in the USA, 1908–13, and repudiated by its Democratic successor.

Dolly's Brae, near Newcastle, County Down, was scene of a fatal riot, 12 July 1849, between Orange and Catholic factions.

Domesday or **Doomsday Book.** Compiled as a survey for taxing and administrative purposes and also to obtain general information about his new territories by order of William the Conqueror, 1085–6.

Dominica, Commonwealth of, largest of the Windward Islands. Discovered by Columbus, 1493; settled by French, 1632; ceded to Great Britain by Treaty of Paris, 1763; French possession, 1778–83; to Great Britain by Treaty of Versailles, 1783; attacked by French, 2 Feb. 1805; finally restored to Great Britain, 1814. Independent republic, 3 Nov. 1978. Severe hurricane, 1979; aided US invasion of Grenada, 1983. United Workers Party won elections, June 1995, ending 15-year rule of the Freedom Party.

Dominican Order. Founded by St Dominic (1170–1221) in 1216, who obtained a bull from Pope Honorius III. First chapter held at Bologna, 1220. In England they were known as Black Friars, and in 1221 set up a house in Oxford.

Dominican Republic or **Santo Domingo.** E portion of *Hispaniola. Discovered by Columbus, 1492; colony founded by his brother, Bartholomew, 1496. Ceded by Spain to France, 1795. Part of independent state of *Haiti, 1798–1801, French, 1801–3. Part of Haiti again, 1804–8. British helped Spaniards to drive out French, 1809. Assured to Spain by Treaty of Paris, 1814. Declared its independence, as 'Columbia', 1821. Part of Haiti again, 1822–43. Became the independent D.R., 1844. Once more Spanish, 1861–3. Republic reconstituted, 1865. Occupied by US forces, 1916–23. Rafael Trujillo carried out *coup d'état* and became dictator of the D.R., 1930–61. In 1965 the USA sent a force of Marines to D., fearing a Communist take-over. Constitutional government restored, 1966. 87-year-old Balaguer won election as president, May 1994, though opposition alleged fraud.

Dominions of the Commonwealth. *Canada became the first D. within the

Commonwealth in 1867. Subsequently many former British colonies became Ds. (*see under separate entries*) but following decision after World War II of many former colonies to adopt republican status while remaining in the *Commonwealth, the term dominion has now fallen into disuse (1995).

Dominions Office. *See* COMMONWEALTH RELATIONS OFFICE.

Doncaster, England. First charter granted by Richard I, 1194. Conference held here at which Henry VIII granted pardons (later dishonoured) to partakers in the *Pilgrimage of Grace, 6 Dec. 1536. Famous horse race instituted by Col. St. Leger, 1786.

Dongan Charter, granted to *New York City by Thomas Dongan, governor of the city, 1686.

Donnybrook Fair, outside Dublin, was licensed 1204; abolished, due to public disorder, 1855.

DORA (Defence of the Realm Acts). First of the series was passed 27 Nov. 1914; extended to supply and sale of liquor, May 1915. Ceased to operate, 31 Aug. 1921; but the DOR (Acquisition of Land) Acts, 1916 and 1920, operated for five years after end of World War I.

Dorchester (Dorset). Roman foundation. Besieged and burnt by the Danes, 1003; fortified by Parliamentarians, 1642–3. The famous *Bloody Assizes held here, 1685.

Dorchester (Oxon). Roman foundation. Cynegils, King of the W Saxons, baptized here by St Birinus, AD 634.

Dordrecht or **Dort,** Netherlands. The meeting-place of the States of Holland after their revolt from Spain, 1572. The Synod of D., the first general synod of the Protestants, assembled 13 Nov. 1618, and finished 25 May 1619.

Dorset, historic English county, celebrated in the novels of Thomas Hardy. Abolition (except for ceremonial purposes) recommended by Local Government Commission, 1994 but later dropped.

Dortmund-Weser-Ems Canal. Stretch of the Ems canalized, 1892–9. The banks breached by the RAF, causing virtual draining of the canal, 4 and 21 Nov. 1944; 1 Jan. and 3 Mar. 1945; since repaired.

Douai, France. Taken from Flemings by Philip the Fair, 1297; restored, 1368. Acquired by Spain, 1529. Attempted seizure by Admiral Coligny failed, 6 Jan. 1557; taken by Louis XIV, 1667; surrendered to Marlborough, 26 June 1710; retaken 8 Sept. 1712; Roman Catholic English College founded at, 1568; refounded in England at Ushaw and Ware after the French Revolution. Catholic school for English boys at D. from 1818 to 1903, when it moved to Woolhampton, Berks. The D. version of the Old Testament, published here, 1609–10.

Douglas Rebellion. Headed by William, Earl of Douglas, 1451, as a result of the appointment of Sir William Crichton by James II of Scotland. Douglas murdered by James II in Feb. 1452. Rebellion carried on by relatives, but finally suppressed in 1484.

Dover, England. Originally *Dwyr*, latinized as *Dubris*. One of the *Cinque Ports. King John resigned his kingdom to the papal legate at, 13 May 1213. The Emperor Charles V met by Henry VII at, 1520. Charles II landed here after his exile, 26 May 1660. Treaty of D. between Charles II and Louis XIV, 1670. New naval harbour opened, 1909. Repeatedly bombarded, 1941–4. English terminal for *Channel Tunnel, near, 1994.

Dover Patrol. Established during World War I to maintain cross-Channel communications (1914–8). Monitors added, 1915. Frequent small raids by enemy, 1915–7. *Broke* and *Swift* defeated six destroyers, Apr. 1917. War memorial to D.P. erected on French coast after World War I destroyed by the Germans during World War II. Rebuilt memorial unveiled, 7 July 1962.

Downing Street (London). Named after Sir George Downing (*c.* 1623–84). Number 10 has been the official residence of the

Prime Minister since the time of Sir Robert Walpole. Renovated 1960–3. Attacked by the IRA, with mortar-bomb, while Cabinet in session, 7 Feb. 1991.

D'Oyly Carte Opera Company. Richard D'Oyly Carte (1844–1901) in 1875 produced *Trial by Jury*, the first of the works of W.S. Gilbert (1836–1911) and Arthur Sullivan (1842–1900) to be publicly performed; he built the Savoy Theatre, 1881, and the English Opera House (now Palace Theatre, Cambridge Circus), 1891. The company controlled the copyright in words and music of Gilbert and Sullivan until 1961. Disbanded, 1982.

draft riots (New York), to resist drafting of citizens into the Union Army, 1863.

drama. Comedy said to have been introduced from Megara into Attica *c.* 580 BC. Theatrical exhibitions first seen in Rome, 364 BC. Mystery plays, the origin of D. in England, were performed as early as 1136 at Dunstable. The first original secular play extant is Udall's *Ralph Roister Doister*, written about 1531. The servants of the Earl of Leicester obtained in 1574 a patent for performing plays in any part of England, and in 1576 they built a theatre at Shoreditch, which was the first public building of its kind in England. Shakespeare, with others, received a similar patent, 19 May 1603. The theatres were all closed by a Parliamentary Act on 2 Sept. 1642. In 1737 plays were ordered to be revised and licensed by the Lord Chamberlain; this abolished, 1968. Women did not take part in Greek D. and in Rome were an under-class. First professional actresses in Europe were in Italy in 16thC but in England women not on stage till after 1660. Acting became a profession in western Europe in 16thC. *See also* CENSORSHIP OF THE THEATRE; for **Actors and Actresses**, *see under* THEATRES.

drama (American). In 1733 there appears a mention of a theatrical performance in New York. A performance of Otway's *Orphans* was enacted in 1750. *The Beaux' Stratagem* was performed by a company of London actors at Annapolis, 1752.

Drapier's Letters. In 1722 the English Government gave contract for making Irish copper coinage to a Mr William Wood, of Wolverhampton. This aroused the resentment of the Irish, resulting in the publication of *Drapier's Letters*, by Dean Swift, 1724 and the withdrawal of the coinage.

Dreadnought, name of a battleship launched in 1906, the prototype of a class of Royal Naval battleships known as Ds., which continued to be built up to 1914. First British nuclear-powered submarine named D. (1960).

Dred Scott Case (US), a test case in the slavery question, arose in 1848, and was finally decided on appeal to the Supreme Court, 1857.

Dresden, Germany. Capital of the Margravate of Meissen, 1270; seat of the Albertine line from 1485. Destroyed by fire and rebuilt in 1685; celebrated congress held by Napoleon, 1812; besieged by the allied armies on 26 Aug. 1813; capitulated after Napoleon had left on 11 Nov. 1813; occupied by Prussians, 1866. Bombed and severely damaged by British and American air forces, 13–14 Feb. 1945 when up to 30,000 civilians may have died. Entered by the Russians, 8 May 1945. 'D. china' has been made at *Meissen since 1710. Plan to restore the Frauenkirche, damaged in Feb. 1945 bombing, with international help, 1994.

Dresden, Treaty of, between Frederick the Great and Maria Theresa of Austria, 25 Dec. 1745.

Dreyfus Case (France). Capt. Alfred Dreyfus (1859–1935) sentenced for high treason, Dec. 1894. New trial ordered through Émile Zola's exertions. Dreyfus again found guilty, 1899, but pardoned. Case reopened and Dreyfus declared innocent, July 1906. Dreyfus awarded the Legion of Honour, 1919.

driving licences. First issued, 1903. Procedure governed by the Road Traffic Acts of 1930, 1934, 1956, 1960, 1972 and 1974, the

Vehicle and Driving Licences Act, 1969 and the Road Traffic Acts of 1976 and 1983, together with the Motor Vehicle (Driving Licence) Regulations, 1977.

driving tests (Britain), first conducted on a voluntary basis, from 16 March 1935. Made compulsory to obtain driving licence, 1 June 1935. From 1 July 1993 those convicted of dangerous driving must retake the D.T.

Drogheda, Republic of Ireland. Here the chiefs of Ulster did homage to Richard II, 1395, and *Poyning's Law was enacted, 1494. Stormed by Oliver Cromwell and garrison massacred, 11 Sept. 1649. Surrendered to William III, 1690.

drug addiction first became a social problem in Britain in the 1960s, notably among a section of the young. The Misuse of Drugs Act, 1971, was intended to consolidate existing anti-drug legislation, i.e. the Pharmacy and Poisons Act, 1933, the Drugs (Prevention of Misuse) Act, 1964, and the Dangerous Drugs Acts, 1965 and 1967 and to distinguish between unlawful possession and trafficking, substantially increasing the penalties for the latter. Amended by Misuse of Drugs Act, 1973. Sports Council established independent drug-testing regime, 1988. British government running major anti-drug campaigns since 1985.

Drunken Parliament (Scotland), 1661.

Drury Lane was known as Aldwych Way until the reign of Elizabeth I, when it was an aristocratic quarter taking its present name from Drury Place, a 15thC house owned by the Drury family. The street became increasingly disreputable, until the clearance of the whole neighbourhood when Aldwych and Kingsway were built, 1899–1905. D.L. Theatre Royal is the fourth to be built on this site; the first opened, 1663, and was burnt down, 1672. The second, designed by Wren, opened, 1674. Sheridan and his partners acquired it from David Garrick, 1776; they pulled it down in 1791, and opened the third theatre, 1794, but this was destroyed by fire, 1809. The

fourth theatre, opened 1812, is now (1995) the oldest theatre open in London for regular performances.

Druses. Reformed Muslim sect in Syria and the Lebanon, whose separate existence dates from the early 11thC. They led an unsuccessful rebellion against the French, 1925–6, and were on the Muslim side in the civil war in Lebanon, 1975–91.

Dual Alliance between France and Russia. Began with contacts established, 1887; agreement to co-operate in the Far E, 1891; understanding maintained at accession of Nicholas II, 1894; alliance proclaimed, 26 Aug. 1897; pact of mutual assistance between France and USSR signed, 2 May 1935.

Dual Monarchy. Name given to the Austrian Empire, formed by the union of Austria and Hungary from 1867 until 1917.

Dublin (Baile-atha-Cliath), Ireland. St Patrick is said to have visited D. in 448, but the Norsemen are regarded as the real founders of the city (8thC). D. was sacked by the Danish leader Ragnar, 831, and captured by Olaf the White, 852. Battle of Clontarf fought near, 1014. Christ Church founded by Sihtric, 1038. Possessed by Crovan, King of Man, 1066. The Earl of Pembroke (Strongbow) captured it, 1170. Many citizens murdered by Irish of surrounding hills, Easter Monday, 1209 – the day known as 'Black Monday'. Castle completed, 1220. Besieged by Edward Bruce, 1315. Visited by Richard II, 1394. Bull for the foundation of a university published, 1475. Trinity College founded, 1591. Oliver Cromwell arrived at, Aug. 1649. Visit of James II, who held a Parliament, 1688. Catholic pro-cathedral completed, 1825. National University of Ireland founded, 1909. Sinn Fein rebels, in rising that began 24 Apr. 1916, held General Post Office, City Hall, Four Courts, and Stephen's Green. G.P.O. burned in last days of Apr. Since the treaty of 1921 the capital of the Irish Free State, now the Republic of Ireland. Insurgents opposed to treaty took possession of Four Courts, 14 Apr. 1922, and maintained their hold until 30 June, when, after three days' siege (by Free State troops), they wrecked the building by explosion, destroying the records. Extensive rebuilding since 1970s.

Dubrovnik, formerly **Ragusa**, Croatia, founded in the 7thC by fugitives from the neighbouring town of Epidaurum. In the Middle Ages was a rival of Venice, but its importance declined after 1497. The republic preserved its independence, though under Turkish suzerainty until 1808, when it was incorporated in *Dalmatia. A popular tourist centre from 1950s. D. was badly damaged in fighting between Serbs and Croats, 1991. Again shelled, Aug. 1995. *See* CROATIA.

duelling. Forbidden in England by an Act of Oliver Cromwell, 1654. Charles II also issued a proclamation against D., 1679. Anti-D. Association formed in England, May 1843; and three articles of war were issued in 1844 to prevent the practice in the Army. Last recorded duel in England was fought at Egham Hill, Surrey, in 1852.

Famous Duels:
Duke of Hamilton and Lord Mohun, both died. 15 Nov. 1712.
S. Martin wounded John Wilkes, MP. 16 Nov. 1763.
Lord Byron killed Mr Chaworth. 26 Jan. 1765.
Charles James Fox wounded by Mr Adam. 30 Nov. 1779.
William Pitt and George Tierney. 27 May 1796.
Henry Grattan wounded Isaac Corry. 15 Jan. 1800.
Lord Castlereagh wounded George Canning. 21 Sept. 1809.
Duke of Wellington and Earl of Winchelsea. 21 Mar. 1829.
Duc de Grammont-Caderousse killed Mr Dillon, Paris. Oct. 1862.
Don Enrique de Bourbon killed by Duc de Montpensier, near Madrid. 12 Mar. 1870.
Léon Gambetta and De Fortou, neither hit. 21 Nov. 1878.

Gen. Boulanger, seriously, and M. Floquet, slightly wounded, 13 July 1888.

Duke of Edinburgh Award, British youth scheme, founded, 1956. Absorbed *Outward Bound, 1995.

Dukhobors. Russian heretic sect, sprang up during the 18thC. From 1755 to 1864 their leaders claimed to be reincarnations of Christ. Migrated to Canada, 1898–9.

Dulwich College. Founded and endowed by Edward Alleyn, 1619. In 1857 the college was reconstituted by special Act of Parliament and formed into D.C. and Alleyn's School (also in Dulwich).

Duma (Russian). Council of State created, 6 Aug. 1905. Abolished at Oct. Revolution, Nov. 1917; but title revived after elections of Dec. 1993, and applied to lower house of Russian parliament.

Dumbarton Oaks, Washington DC, USA, was the scene of a conference between the USSR, Great Britain and the USA, 21 Aug.– 27 Sept., and between Great Britain, the USA and China, 29 Sept.–7 Oct, 1944, the outcome of which was the *United Nations Organization.

Dumfries, Scotland, derived its early importance from a bridge over the Nith, built 1280. John Comyn the Red was here assassinated by Bruce's followers for compounding with the English, 1306. Robert Burns (*d.* 1796) lived in D. for the last five years of his life, and is buried here.

Dunces, Parliament of. Met at Coventry, 1404; also known as Unlearned Parliament, so called because no lawyer had a place in the assembly.

Dundee, Scotland. Taken by English under John of Gaunt, 1385. Sacked by Montrose, 1645. Besieged by Gen. Monk after battle of Worcester, 1651. Tay Bridge disaster, 28 Dec. 1879. University established, 1967.

Dunedin, New Zealand. Founded, 1848. University opened, 1871.

Dungannon Convention. Meeting of Irish Volunteers under Grattan, passed resolution for parliamentary reform for Ireland, 8 Sept. 1785.

Dunkirk or **Dunkerque,** France. Traditionally sprang up round a church built by St Eloi in the 7thC. Sacked by the English, 1388. Taken by French, 1646; recovered by Archduke Leopold, 1652; given up to the English, 1658; sold to Louis XIV by Charles II, 17 Oct. 1662; bombarded by English, 26 July 1694. Works ordered to be demolished by Treaty of Utrecht, 1713. Duke of York forced to raise siege of, Sept. 1793. Allied troops evacuated from, May–June 1940. Fifty-year Anglo-French Treaty of Alliance signed at D., 4 Mar. 1947. War memorial at D. unveiled by Queen Elizabeth the Queen Mother, July 1957.

Dunkirk, Treaty of, between Britain and France, signed 4 Mar. 1947 (*see* preceding article).

Dunmow Flitch, first competed for, 1244; names of successful competitors first recorded, 1445. The D.F. (side of bacon) instituted by Robert Fitzwalter as a prize to any married couple who had not quarrelled within a year and a day of their marriage. They had originally to swear the truth of this before the prior of Little Dunmow, in Essex. Prize still claimed in modern times.

Dunwich. The residence of the kings of *E Anglia and the seat of their bishops, then of the more northerly of the two E Anglian sees, 673–870. The first E Anglian church was built here in 627 by order of King Sigeberht (*d.* 637?) for St Felix (*d.* 648). It began to be swallowed up by the sea in the 14thC. As a rotten borough its parliamentary representation was abolished, 1832; it had sent two burgesses to Parliament since 1296. Corporation abolished, 1886.

Duquesne, Fort (Pennsylvania, USA). Erected by French, 1754. Captured by Gen. Forbes and renamed Fort Pitt after the English statesman, 1758.

Durazzo. *See* Durresi.

Durban, Natal, S Africa. Founded, 1824, received its present name, 1835. Salisbury Island naval base built, 1939–45.

Durham, England. Called by the Normans **Duresme**. Episcopal see, originally at Lindisfarne, then (from 883) at Chester-le-Street, transferred, AD 995. Besieged by Duncan of Scotland, 1040; entered by William the Conqueror, 1067. The present cathedral begun, 1092. Headquarters of Edward III and his army, 1327. Battle of Neville's Cross near, 1346. Henry VI visits shrine of St Cuthbert, 1448. University founded, 1832.

Durham Report by the Earl of Durham on the state of *Canada after Papineau's rebellion, 1838. Published, 1839.

Durresi ancient *Epidamnus* and *Dyrrachium*, formerly **Durazzo.** Founded 7thC BC by settlers from Corinth and Corcyra. Captured by the Romans, 4thC BC. Destroyed by earthquake, AD 345. Besieged, 481, 1082 and 1115. Venetian, 1392–1501, and subsequently Turkish (until 1913). Now Albanian.

Dusseldorf, N Rhine Westphalia, Germany. Made a city, 1288; capital of the duchy of Berg. 1385, passed to the Palatinate, 1609. Taken by Ferdinand of Brunswick, 1758; by French, 6 Sept. 1795; incorporated in Prussia, 1815.

Dutch Guiana. *See* Surinam.

Dutch and Flemish literature. The following is a list of prominent writers in the Dutch and Flemish languages, now identical (in their literary form). Except where 'Belgian' is specified the nationality of the writers is Dutch (Netherlands).

Bijns, Anna (poet), *c.* 1494–1575.
Bilderdijk, Willem (poet), 1756–1831.
Bredero, Gerbrand (poet, playwright), 1585–1618.
Cats, Sir Jakob (poet), 1577–1660.
Cauwelaert, August van (Belgian poet and novelist), 1885–1945.
Claus, Hugo (poet), 1929–
Coornhert, Dirk Volckertszoon (humanist), 1522–90.

Gerrit of Komrij (poet and essayist), 1944–.

Gezelle, Guido Pierre Théodore Joseph (Belgian poet), 1830–99.

Haasse, Hella (Belgian historical novelist), 1918–.

Heijermans, Herman (novelist and playwright), 1864–1924.

Hermans, Willem Frederik (novelist), 1921–.

Holst, Henriette Roland (poet), 1869–1953.

Hooft, Pieter (poet, playwright, historian), 1581–1647.

Huygens, Sir Constantine (poet), 1596–1687.

Mulisch, Harry (novelist), 1927–.

Potgieter, Everhard Johannes (publicist), 1808–75.

Querido, Israel (novelist, critic), 1873–1932.

Van den Vondel, Joost (poet, playwright), 1587–1679.

Van Eeden, Frederik Willem (poet, novelist), 1860–1932.

Van Lennep, Jakob (poet, novelist), 1802–68.

Vermeylen, August (Belgian novelist and essayist), 1872–1945.

Dutch Republic. *See* HOLLAND.

Dvinsk. *See* DAUGAVPILS.

Dyarchy. A system of semi-popular government introduced into British India, 1919, as a result of the Montagu-Chelmsford report. Superseded, 1937.

Dyfed, administrative county of Wales, created 1974 under Local Government Act of 1972; but plans to abolish, 1996.

dynamite. Patented by Nobel (*see* NOBEL PRIZE), 1867.

Earl Marshal of England. This office has been hereditary in the family of Howard, Dukes of Norfolk, since 1672.

Earl Marshall (Mariscal) of Scotland. This office in the 14thC became hereditary in the family of Keith, who retained it until its suppression in 1716.

Early Bird, world's first commercial communications satellite, launched from the Kennedy Center, Cape Canaveral, USA, 6 Apr. 1965. First television programme using it was shown to 24 countries on 2 May 1965.

early closing. Movement to reduce shop assistants' working hours inaugurated, 1842. Act for E.C. of shops passed 1919. Amended by Shops Acts, 1928, 1937 and 1950. Moves to counter, 1980 onwards, combined in UK with growth in part-time shop working and resulted in legislation of 1994, which meant that from 1 Dec. most legal restrictions on shop opening hours were abolished.

Early English Text Society. Founded by F. J. Furnivall (1825–1910). First publications, 1864.

earthquakes. Many recorded in Greek and Japanese history. An earthquake accompanied the famous eruption of Vesuvius in AD 79. An earthquake affecting all the known world occurred 6 Sept. 543. The following is a list of the most notable subsequent E. Figures in brackets denote the approximate number of fatal casualties.

Constantinople, 553 or 555
Thrace and Asia Minor, 26 Oct. 740
Syria and Palestine, 746
Glastonbury destroyed, 11 Sept. 1275
Lisbon, 26 Jan. 1531 (30,000)
Shensi, China, 24 Jan. 1556 (830,000)
London (damaged St Paul's), 6 Apr. 1580
Japan, Aug. and Sept. 1596
Naples, July–Dec. 1631
Jamaica, 7 July 1692
Japan, 30 Dec. 1703 (200,000)
China, Oct.–Nov. 1731
Calcutta, 11 Oct. 1737 (300,000)
Peru, 28 Oct. 1746
Cairo, 2 Sept. 1754
Lisbon, 1 Nov. 1755 (60,000)
Messina, 5 Feb. 1783 (60,000)
Aleppo, 1822 (20,000)
Salerno, 16 Dec. 1857 (12,000)
Quito, 22 Mar. 1859
Peru, 13–15 Aug. 1868
Ischia, July–Aug. 1883
Charleston (S Carolina), 1886
Japan, 28 Oct. 1891
Assam, 12 June 1897
Mont Pelée, W Indies, 1902 (20,000)
Kangra (India), 1905 (20,000)
San Francisco (USA), 18 Apr. 1906
Valparaiso, 17 Aug. 1906
Kingston (Jamaica), 14–15 Jan. 1907
Messina, 28 Dec. 1908 (120,000)
Luristan, (Iran), 1909
S Mexico, 1911
Avezzano, Italy, 1915 (30,000)
Kansu, 1920 (180,000)
Tokyo and Yokohama destroyed, 1 Sept. 1923 (180,000); same area, 15 Jan. 1924
Horta (Azores), destroyed, 1926
Herzegovina and Dalmatia, 1927
N Japan and Kamchatka, 16 Feb. 1927
Tajima (Japan), 7 Mar. 1927
Palestine, 11 July 1927
Chile (Talca), Dec. 1928
S Italy, 23 July 1930
New Zealand, 3 Feb. 1931
Nicaragua, 31 Mar. 1931
Mexico, 3 June 1932
China, 1932 (70,000)
Quetta destroyed, 31 May 1935 (60,000)
Rabaul (New Britain), 2 June 1937
Alaska, 22 July 1937

Anatolia (Turkey), 19–20 Apr. 1938
S Chile, 26 Jan. 1939, (over 20,000)
Anatolia, 26–9 Dec. 1939, (over 23,000) (also July 1940 and Dec. 1942)
Karachi, Nov. 1945
Dominican Republic, Aug. 1946
N Peru, Nov. 1946
S Japan, Dec. 1946
Fukui, Japan, June 1948
Central Ecuador, 5 Aug. 1949
N Assam, Aug. 1950
El Salvador, 6 May 1951
Turkey, 18 Mar. 1953
Ionian Islands, 12 Aug. 1953
Cyprus, 10 Sept. 1953
Orléansville, Algeria, 9 Sept. 1954
Afghanistan, 10–17 June 1956
Iran, 4 Nov. 1956
Jangchal, Iran, 2–11 July 1957
Iran, 13 Dec. 1957
Agadir, Morocco, 29 Feb. 1960 (14,000)
Iran, 25 Apr. 1960
Chile, 21–5 May 1960 (5,000)
S Italy, 21–2 Aug. 1962
S Italy and Greece, 28 Aug. 1962
W Iran, 1 Sept. 1962 (14,000)
Barce, Libya, 21 Feb. 1963 (over 250).
Skopje, Macedonia, 26 July 1963 (over 1,000)
Alaska, 27 Mar. 1964 (130)
Chile, 28 Mar. 1965 (400)
E Turkey, 20 Aug. 1966 (3,000)
Gediz, W Turkey, 28 Mar. 1970 (over 1,000)
Huaraz and N Peru, followed by resultant avalanche and flood, 31 May 1970 (over 66,000)
San Fernando, USA, 9 Feb. 1971 (65)
Managua, Nicaragua, 23 Dec. 1972 (5,000)
Pakistan, 26 Dec. 1974 (5,200)
Guatemala, 4 Feb. 1976 (22,800)
Tangshan, China, 28 July 1976 (650,000)
Romania, 4 Mar. 1977 (1,540)
Severe earthquakes, Iran, 1977 and 1979
NW Algeria, 10 Oct. 1980 (4,500)
S Italy, 23 Nov. 1980 (4,800)
Popayán, Colombia, 31 Mar. 1983 (over 500)
Erzurum, Turkey, 30 Oct. 1983 (over 1,500)
Mexico City, 19–21 Sept. 1985 (over 4,000)
NE Ecuador, 5–6 Mar. 1987 (over 4,000)

Nepalese-Indian border, 20 Aug. 1988 (over 1,000)
Burma-China border, 6 Nov 1988 (over 1,000)
NW Armenia, 7 Dec. 1988 (over 55,000)
San Francisco (USA), 17 Oct. 1989 (63)
NW Iran, 21 June 1990 (over 40,000)
Luzon, Philippines, 16 July 1990 (over 1,800)
E Turkey, 13–15 Mar. 1992 (over 4,000)
Flores, Indonesia, 12 Dec. 1992 (over 2,000)
Japan, off Hokkaido, July 1993 (over 250)
San Fernando (USA), 17 Jan. 1994 (61)
Algeria, 18 Aug. 1994 (over 150)
Kobe, Japan, 16 Jan. 1995 (over 5,000)
Sakhalin island (E Russia), 28 May 1995 (over 2,000)
SW Greece, 15 June 1995 (over 20)
Mexico, 9 Oct. 1995 (over 100)

'Earth Summit', name popularly given to the international meeting held in Rio de Janeiro, June 1992, to discuss and formulate measures of global environmental protection. Its official title was the United Nations Conference on Environment and Development.

East Anglia. Founded by Uffa on basis of existing Anglian settlements, 575. Submitted to Wessex, 826. The last three E Anglian kings, Ethelweard, Oswald, and the martyred Edmund, were sub-kings or viceroys under W Saxon protection, but belonged to the old royal house of Uffa. On the re-conquest of the Danelaw about 920 it was administered directly by the W Saxon crown. Knut made it one of the four principal earldoms of England (c. 1017), and so it remained until 1066.

Kings of E Anglia: Uffing Dynasty:
Redwald 593–617
Eorpwald 617–28
State of anarchy 628–31
Sigeberht 631–34
Egric 634–35
Anna 635–54
Ethelhere 654–55
Ethelwald 655–64
Ealdwulf 664–713

Elfwald 713–49
Beorna 749–?
Ethelberht ?–794
Kings of *Mercia 794–823
Athelstan of Wessex ? 829–? 839
Ethelweard ? 839–? 854
Oswald ? 854–? 856
Edmund (St)? 856–870

Danish Kings:
Guthrum I (Guttorm) 878–90
Eohric (Eric) 890–902
Guthrum II 902–17

East Anglia, University of. Opened at Norwich, 1963.

East Asia Economic Caucus. A suggested SE Asian 'economic fortress' to counter the protected single markets in Europe and the Americas, to be led by Japan. Idea first suggested by Malaysia, 1991. By 1993 idea being supported by Singapore, Thailand, Indonesia, the Philippines and Brunei. It arose from the *Asia Pacific Economic Co-operation (APEC) Forum.

East, Empire of the. *See* ROMAN EMPIRE, EASTERN.

Eastern Question, Near. *See* TURKISH RE-PUBLIC; SYRIA; PALESTINE; EGYPT; CYPRUS; GREECE, MODERN; IRAQ; ARABIA.

East India Company, The Honourable. Incorporated by Queen Elizabeth I, 31 Dec. 1600. Charter renewed, 1609. Settlement established at Surat, 1613. Conflict with Dutch E.I.C., 1621–3. Factories established at Canton, 1637, Madras, 1639. St Helena occupied, 1651. Fort William (Calcutta) founded and Bombay given to H.E.I.C., 1668. Factory at Calcutta established, 1690. A rival New E.I.C. chartered, 1691. New E.I.C. charter extended, 1698. Bengal reorganized by Sir Charles Eyre, 1700. New E.I.C. merged with H.E.I.C., 1708 (*see* SEVEN YEARS WAR). Defeat of Oudh at battle of Buxar, 1764. Clive reforms Indian administration, 1765–7. Annexation of N Circars, 1766. International complications arising out of the vast economic and

political activities of the company led to the Regulating Act, 1773. H.E.I.C.'s trading monopoly abolished, 1822. As a result of the *Indian Mutiny its political and administrative powers were abolished, 1858. Company finally wound up, 1873, its army having been absorbed into the forces of the crown by 1861.

East India Companies, Foreign.
1. Dutch. Founded, 1602.
2. French. Founded, 1604. Refounded, 1664. Dissolved, 1770.
3. Danish. Founded, 1614.
4. Austrian. Founded, 1720. Dissolved, 1727.

In 1621, having together eliminated the Portuguese, the English and Dutch quarrelled, and the Dutch massacred the English at Amboina in 1623. After the virtual blockade of Holland in the Anglo-Dutch wars of 1652–4, 1665–7, the French company was able to take its place and the struggle between it and the English company reached its climax in the *Seven Years War, 1756–63, and the total defeat of the French company. The Danish company never became a political organization, and the Austrians were persuaded by Walpole to dissolve their company.

East London, Cape Province, S Africa. Site discovered, 1836, by John Baillie; city founded, 1847, and originally known as Fort Glamorgan.

East London University, name and status acquired, 1992 by the former East London Polytechnic.

East Prussia. *See* PRUSSIA.

East Timor. *See* TIMOR.

Easter. Christian celebration of the Resurrection of Christ. Method of calculating date of E. settled by Council of Nicaea, 325.

Easter Island (Spanish **Isla de Pascua**; Polynesian **Rapa-nui**), Chile (since 1888). Discovered by Dutch in 1722. All traditions concerning the colossal E.I. statues, their origin and purpose, perished *c.* 1850–90 when missionaries burned images and engraved tablets and 'blackbirders' carried off most of the male population to work in the guano islands of Peru. After 1888 survivors were repatriated, but the population was decimated by disease, the ruling class of Polynesians became extinct, and there was a cultural breakdown. Considerable archaeological research since 1950s.

Eboracum. *See* YORK.

EC. *See* EUROPEAN COMMUNITY.

Ecbatana, Asia Minor. Founded on site of the modern Hamadan, 700 BC. Captured, 550 BC by Cyrus, who made it the capital and summer residence of the Persian kings, and by Alexander, 330 BC.

Ecclesiastical Commission. Appointed 1835. Amalgamated with *Queen Anne's Bounty, 1947, after which the two bodies together were known as the Church Commission. *See* CHURCH COMMISSIONERS.

Ecclesiastical Courts. *See* HIGH COMMISSION and ARCHES, COURT OF.

ecology, term invented, 1866, by the German biologist Ernst Häckel, but not in common use until the second half of the 20thC. *See* CONSERVATION; EARTH SUMMIT.

Economics and Political Science, London School of. Founded, 1895.

Economist, The. See under NEWSPAPERS.

ecu. EC currency unit, established 1979, on the formation of the European Monetary System, and based on a 'basket' of currencies: suggested, 1995, that name E. be changed to *euro.*

Ecuador. After battle of Cajamarca, 1532, Spanish presidency of Quito established. Then became part of the new Gran Colombia republic by declaration of 17 Dec. 1819. Effective Spanish rule ended at battle of Pichincha, 24 May 1822. Constituted separate republic on breakup of the original state of *Gran Colombia, 1830. A new constitution, 1945, was followed by a series of coups and dictatorial regimes. New democratic constitution, 1979. Economic difficulties following decline in oil revenues since 1980s, compounded by serious earthquake, 1987. Attempt at market economy, with privatization of state concerns, etc., following 1992 election, has led to opposition and unrest. Border dispute with Peru, 1995.

Ecumenical or Oecumenical Councils. *See* COUNCILS OF THE CHURCH.

Eddas. Compilations of Scandinavian mythology and legend made in Iceland. The 'Elder' or 'Poetic Edda' compiled *c.* 1200 by an unknown editor. The 'Younger' or 'Prose Edda' *c.* 1230 by Snorri Sturluson.

Eddystone Lighthouse, England. Built, 1696. Destroyed, 1703. Rebuilt, 1706. Burnt, 1755. Rebuilt, 1759. Burnt, 1770. Rebuilt, 1774. Present edifice opened, 18 May 1882.

Edessa (now **Urfa**), Turkey. Ancient city, originally Urhai. Rebuilt by Antiochus IV *c.* 170 BC. Became capital of an independent kingdom of E. *c.* 132 BC. Hadrian (AD 117–38) made it a Roman dependency. In 216 it became a Roman military colony and the chief frontier fortress of the Near E. Besieged by Persian King Kavad, 503. Withstood a determined siege by Persian King Chosroes, 544–5. Seized by Baldwin of Flanders and became Crusader principality, 1097. Captured by Zenghi Emir of Damascus, 1151. Lapsed into obscurity thereafter.

Edict, Perpetual. Arose out of the custom by which Roman judicial officials announced, by an edict at the beginning of their year of office, the manner in which they intended to administer justice. The form of this E. began to be standardized, *c.* 200 BC, and was finally fixed into an unalterable code by Salvius Julianus at the order of the Emperor Hadrian, AD 132.

Edict of Châteaubriant. By Henry II of France against Calvinists, 27 June 1551.

Edict of Nantes. By Henry IV of France, giving toleration and a number of cities of refuge to the *Huguenots, 15 Apr. 1598. Revoked by Louis XIV, 24 Oct. 1685.

Edict of Restitution. By the Emperor Ferdinand II of Germany, ordaining surrender of certain Church lands, 1629.

Edinburgh, Scotland. Founded by and named after Edwin, of Northumbria, c. AD 617. Part of Northumbria till 936. Robert Bruce held Parliament at E., 1327 and 1328. Replaced *Perth as Scottish capital, 1437. Pillaged by Henry VIII, 1544 and 1547. John Knox *d.* at, 1572. University established, 1583. Assembly of Convention of States, 10 Dec. 1599. Charles I crowned King of Scotland at, 16 May 1633. Castle surrendered to Cromwell, Dec. 1650. *Porteous Riots, 1736. Young Pretender occupies, 15–17 Sept. 1745. Building of New Town begun, 1767. Anti-Catholic riots, 1779. Royal visit of George IV, 17–28 Aug. 1822. Scottish National Gallery opened, 21 Mar. 1859. Forth Bridge opened, 4 Mar. 1890. Scottish National War Memorial opened, 1927. Annual international music and dramatic festival inaugurated, 1947. Heriot-Watt University established, 1966. Napier Polytechnic became Napier University, 1992. Opera house in course of construction, 1995.

Edinburgh Review. Founded, Oct. 1802. Last issue, Oct. 1929.

Edinburgh Summit, conference of EC leaders, under chairmanship of Britain, held at Edinburgh, 11–12 Dec. 1992. Notable for agreeing modifications to enable *Denmark to accept *Maastricht Treaty at a future referendum.

Edinburgh University. Founded, 1583, by charter of James VI.

Edirne. *See* ADRIANOPLE.

Edmunds Law against polygamy passed by US Congress, 1882.

Education (UK).
1. England and Wales. First grant of public money for E., 1833. Privy Council committee on E. formed, 1839. E. department established in two divisions: (*a*) Popular E. (*b*) Development of science and art, 25 Feb. 1856. Royal Commission appointed, 1858. Regulations published, 1860. Royal Commission reported, 1861. New regulations, 1862. Elementary E. Act passed, 9 Aug. 1870.

Made compulsory, 1876. Free, 1891. Board of E. established, 1899. E. Act passed, 18 Dec. 1902. Royal Commission on university E. in London, 1909. New E. Act, 1918. R. A. Butler's Act, 1944, revolutionized E. in England and Wales. Modified by subsequent E. Acts. School-leaving age raised by Acts of 1962 and 1976. E. Reform Act, 1988 made major changes, including providing for central funding for 'opt-out' schools and the establishment of a National Curriculum (subsequently modified). Parents' right of choice and access to information increased by E. Act of 1992. Board of E. replaced by a Ministry of E. Known as Ministry of E. and Science since 1964; merged with the Department of Employment, 1995.
2. Scotland. Act to compel all barons and freeholders to send their sons to school, 1494. Act taxing agricultural land for maintenance of schools, 1633. Act for providing schools, 1696. Elementary E. compulsory, 1872. E. (Scotland) Act, 1945 and subsequent Acts brought Scottish E. broadly in line with that in England and Wales.
3. N Ireland. N Ireland became a self-governing unit, 1920. First E. Act, 1923. Second Act, 1947, follows the pattern of the English Act of 1944 and subsequent legislation broadly follows pattern of rest of UK.

Government plans nursery vouchers for parents of four year olds, July 1995, to apply in England, Wales, Scotland and N Ireland.

Education (Ireland). Kildare Place Society for Promoting E. of the poor founded Dublin, 1811. Gladstone's University Bill thrown out by Commons, 1873. Intermediate E. Act passed, 1878. Compulsory E. Act, 1892. National University of Ireland founded, 1909. Compulsory instruction in Irish language introduced, 1922.

Education (USA). E. Act, 1884. Blair E. Bill, Mar. 1886. Compulsory E. Act, 4 Apr. 1892. *See also* UNIVERSITIES, and various colleges and academies.

Edward, Lake, Africa. Discovered by Stanley, 1889.

Edward VI Prayer Book. *See* PRAYER, BOOK OF COMMON.

EEC. *See* EUROPEAN ECONOMIC COMMUNITY.

EFTA. *See* EUROPEAN FREE TRADE ASSOCIATION.

Eger. *See* CHEB.

Egypt, Ancient. The following dates are approximate down to 945; all are BC. *Earliest Dynasties:* I, 3200–3000; II, 3000–2780. *Old Kingdom:* III, 2780–20; IV, 2720–2560; V, 2560–2420; VI, 2420–2270. *First Intermediate Period:* VII and VIII, 2270–40; IX and X, 2240–2100. *Middle Kingdom:* XI, 2100–2000; XII, 2000–1788. *Second Intermediate Period:* XIII–XVI, 1788–1600; XVII, 1600–1555. *The Empire:* XVIII, 1555–1350; XIX, 1350–1200; XX, 1200–1090; XXI, 1090–945; XXII, 945–*c.* 745; XXIII, *c.* 745–18, XXIV, 718–12. *Late Period:* XXV 712–663; XXVI, 663–525 (from 663 to 610 Egypt was subject to the suzerainty of Assyria); XXVII (Persian), 525–332: meanwhile Egyptian rebellion, which gradually ousted the Persians, establised XXVIII, 405–399; XXIX, 399–79; XXX, 379–41. In 332 Egypt was conquered by Alexander the Great, at whose death (323) Ptolemy established the Greek dynasty. This lasted, with varying fortune, until 30, when Egypt was made a Roman province.

Egypt, Modern. Christianity existed in E., 2ndC AD. Roman E. conquered by Arabs, 640 and Islam introduced. Conquered for Moawlya the Ommayad, 658. Conquered by Abbasids *c.* 750. Coptic revolt crushed, 832. Ruled by Tulunid dynasty, 808–903. Returned to allegiance of Baghdad, 906. Conquered, 969, by the Fatimids, who ruled till 1171, when the country was conquered by Saladin. From 1261 country ruled by *Mamelukes under nominal *caliphs, until conquered by the *Ottoman Empire under the Sultan Selim, 1517. Invaded by French, under Napoleon, 1798. Expelled by British and Turks. Virtually independent after revolts of Mehemet Ali Pasha, 1831 and 1839. Mehemet Ali made

hereditary khedive, 15 July 1841. De Lesseps obtained concession for the construction of the Suez Canal, 1856. Suez Canal opened for navigation, 1869. Britain purchased Suez Canal shares. Government defaulted on loans, 1876, and instigated anti-foreign rioting which led to British bombardment of Alexandria, July 1882, and Arabi's religious war, 24 July 1882. Arabi defeated at Tel-el-Kebir, 13 Sept. 1882. British interests in E. recognized by France (*see* ENTENTE CORDIALE), 1904. Khedive Abbas II deposed as pro-Turkish by British, 1914. British protectorate established, with Hussein Kamil as sultan, 20 Dec. 1914. Hussein *d.,* 9 Oct. 1917. Succeeded by Fuad. E. declared kingdom, 16 Mar. 1922. King Fuad *d.,* Apr. 1936; succeeded by Farouk 1 (*b.* 11 Feb. 1920). E.'s sovereignty and independence recognized by treaty with Britain, 26 Aug. 1936. British troops evacuated from Cairo and Alexandria, 1947. Israel invaded, 15 May, 1948. Israeli troops entered Egyptian territory, Dec. 1948. A truce, 7 Jan. 1949, followed by a general armistice, 24 Feb. 1949. *Coup d'état* by Neguib, 22 July 1952. King abdicated and Prince Ahmed Fuad (*b.* 16 Jan. 1952) proclaimed, 28 July. Republic proclaimed with Neguib as first president, 18 June. Neguib resigned, April 1954. Government carried on by a council of ministers until 1956, when Nasser became premier, and subsequently president and virtual dictator of E. E. took over defence of the Suez Canal from Britain, Nov. 1955. Last British troops left E., 31 Mar. 1956, and Nasser nationalized the Suez Canal Co. Hostilities broke out between E. and Israel again, Oct.; Israel invaded E. and an Anglo-French force occupied Port Said. E. blocked the Suez Canal with sunken ships. E. accepted a cease-fire on UN conditions, 7 Nov. Withdrawal of Anglo-French forces complete by 22 Dec. Suez Canal re-opened to traffic, 30 Apr. 1957. Union of Egypt and Syria proclaimed by Presidents of both countries, 1 Feb. 1958; two countries to be known henceforth as the *United Arab Republic though name subsequently applied to E. only. Syria left the UAR in 1961,

Yemen shortly after, and E. reverted to old name, 2 Sept. 1971. In June 1967 war broke out between E. and Israel, E. being utterly defeated, losing the Sinai peninsula, the Gaza strip and the Gulf of Aqaba. Suez Canal blocked by E.; Nasser *d.* 1970; succeeded by Sadat. Unsuccessful war against Israel, 1973; Suez Canal re-opened 1975; peace treaty with Israel, 1979. Sadat assassinated, 6 Oct. 1981; succeeded by Mubarak who improved relations with other Arab states. E. part of UN force in *Gulf War, 1991. Resurgence of Islamic fundamentalism in E., 1980s onwards, leading to murders of Copts, 1992 and attacks on Western tourists. Government crackdown on religious extremists from 1993. Flooding and associated fuel explosions killed over 500 in S E., Nov. 1994. President Mubarak survives assassination attempt in Addis Ababa, 26 June 1995. *See also* SUDAN; SUEZ CANAL; ISRAEL; ARAB LEAGUE; SYRIA.

Eidsvold, Norway. Norwegian constitution drawn up at and signed, 17 Mar. 1814.

Eiffel Tower, Paris. Built, 1887–9 designed by Gustave Eiffel (1832–1923) for the Paris Exhibition of 1889. 7500 tons of iron used in construction. Height 984 feet (300 metres) made it tallest building in world at time. Tower at *Blackpool, UK is miniaturized copy of E.T.

Eight Articles. Drawn up by Cranmer, Ridley and Latimer, 1555.

Eikon Basilike. Published, 1649, immediately after execution of Charles I and ascribed to Charles himself, though Gauden, later bishop of Worcester, also claimed authorship.

Einsiedeln, Switzerland. St Meinrad, the hermit, was murdered here, 861, and an abbey founded on the site of his cell *c.* 934. Paracelsus *b.* in E., 1493, and Zwingli a parish priest here, 1516–18.

Eire. For previous history *See* IRISH FREE STATE. New constitution passed, 14 June 1937. British sold all naval bases in E. to E. Government for £50,000,000, and a trade agreement, 25 Apr. 1938. Douglas Hyde first president, 4 May 1938. Neutrality in World War II announced, 28 Sept. 1939. General Election of 4–10 Feb. 1948 won by Fine Gael and Clann na Poblachta combination, and Costello became prime minister. Thereafter *see under* IRELAND: *Republic of Ireland.*

Eisteddfod. Welsh festival of the arts, with origins at least as early as the 6thC BC said to have been formally instituted by Prince Rhys ap Griffith, 1176, but not called Es. before 1450. Modern conception of the E. dates back to the Corwen E. of 1789. National E. of Wales established 1880, and now held annually.

Ekaterinburg (Sverdlovsk from 1924–91). Tsar Nicholas II and his immediate family murdered at, July 1918; use of *DNA to identify remains of, 1993 and 1995.

El Alamein. Eighth Army offensive in the W Desert, N Africa, marking decisive turning-point of World War II, begun there, 23 Oct. 1942.

ELAS (Ellenikos Laiko Apelevtherotikos Stratos), Greek Communist armed movement, active against the Germans after June 1941; engaged in civil war, Dec. 1944, 12 Feb. 1945, and 1947–9, when finally defeated.

Elba, Isle of, Italy. Taken by Nelson, 9 Aug. 1796. Given, 1814, to Napoleon, who escaped from it, 26 Feb. 1815.

Elders of Zion. Their alleged 'Protocols' published in Russia, 1903, 1905, 1907, were said to have been drawn up, 1897. Exposed as a forgery in *The Times*, 16, 17, 18 Aug. 1921.

Elections (UK). *See* FRANCHISE.

Electors of the Holy Roman Empire. The highest ranking princes of the H.R.E., to whom was accorded exclusively the right to elect the Holy Roman Emperor. Their position and rights were settled by the *Golden Bull of Charles IV, 1356, and their number restricted to seven, viz.: the Archbishops of Cologne, Mainz, and Trier, the King of Bohemia, the Count Palatine of the Rhine, the Margrave of Brandenburg, and the Duke of Saxony. To this number were added Bavaria 1623, Hanover, 1692. Electoral rights ceased at abolition of H.R.E., 1806, though the title 'Elector' was used by the Duke of Hesse till 1859.

electricity. Thales of Miletus said to have noticed the magnetic qualities of rubbed amber, 600 BC. William Gilbert of Colchester (1540–1603) experimented with magnetic needle. Robert Boyle (1627–91) conducted experiments. Experiments of Royal Society, 1676, following observations of Sir Isaac Newton (1642–1727). Francis Hawksbee experimented with mercury, 1705, and published results, 1709. Dufay (1699–1739) distinguished experimentally two kinds of E. Leyden jar invented by Cunaeus, 1745, improved by Sir W. Watson (1715–1787). Royal Society experiments on velocity of E., 1747. Benjamin Franklin (1706–90) presented theory of positive and negative E. and identified lightning with electric spark. John Canton (1715–72) demonstrated induction. Experiments in atmospheric E. by Beccaria (1716–81), with silk by Robert Symmers, 1759. With metals and salts by Sir D. Brewster (1781–1868). With gases by Henry Cavendish (1731–1810). By Galvani, 1790, and Volta, 1800, which led to invention of galvanic battery and voltaic pile. Magnetic action of E. discovered by Oersted of Copenhagen, 1819. Ampère's theory, 1820. Faraday discovered electro-magnetic rotation, 1821. Seebeck discovered thermoelectricity, 1822. Ohm's law, 1827. Weber invented electro-dynamometer, 1832. Induction and transformer elaborated by Faraday, 1831. Lenz's Law, 1835. Daniell battery, 1836. Grove's battery, 1836. Bunsen battery, 1842. Sir William Thomson (Lord Kelvin)'s inventions, 1851 *et seq*. Siemens dynamo, 1867. Fauré accumulator, 1881. First electric power station in England opened at Godalming, 1881. DC and AC converter by Salomons and Pyke, 1892. Electric theory of matter by Niels Bohr, 1913. First power station producing E. from nuclear power opened at *Calder Hall, 1956.

Electricity Act, 1989, provided for the privatization of electricity in the UK by establishing 12 private electricity supply companies which were publicly floated in Nov. 1990. Other companies, formed from the former state-run Central Electricity Board, were publicly floated in Feb. 1991. Electricity generation and supply had been nationalized since 1948. These privatized from 1994.

electric light. Carbon arc first produced by Sir H. Davy, 1810. Staite's patented lamp, 1847. Serrins ditto, 1857. S Foreland lighthouse lighted by E.L., 1857. Edison and Swan's incandescent lamp, 1878–80. Tungsten filament, 1904. Neon tubes for street advertisements, 1931. Mercury and sodium vapour lamps for street and floodlighting, 1937. Halogen bulbs, from 1950s.

electric railway. First experiments by Robert Davidson, 1837. Siemens exhibited dynamo traction at Berlin, 1879. Permanent E. R. opened near Berlin, 1882. E. trams at Leytonstone, 4 Mar. 1882. The same Portrush to Bushmills, early 1882. Liverpool overhead E.R., 1893. City and S London, 1890. Chicago, 1895 (first in USA). Underground Waterloo to Mansion House electrified, 11 July 1898. Central London line, 27 June 1900. Mersey railway, 1903. Subsequently considerable electrification of English railways; all underground railways electrified, suburban services, and, since 1950s, all main line routes.

electric telegraph. *See* TELEGRAPHY.

electronics. Derives from a number of experiments with electricity, notably by Thomas Edison (USA), in the 1880s. In 1897 the British physicist J. J. Thomson found the 'Edison effect' due to emission and passage of particles, and called these *electrons. Fleming's thermionic valve, *c.* 1900, improved by Lee de Forest, 1907. Electronic breakthrough started with transistor produced by Bell Laboratories of the USA, 1947. This resulted in a progressive miniaturization of electronic components. Within 30 years a sod state instrument could be produced containing three million transistors on one single silicon chip.

E. now (1995) the basis of an enormous range of industrial, military and consumer products.

electrons. Discovered by Sir Joseph John Thomson (1856–1940), 1897.

Elgin Marbles brought to England *c.* 1812 by Thomas Bruce, Lord E. (1766–1841) and bought for the *British Museum, 1816. Greek government sought return to Greece, 1983 onwards.

Ellis Island. New York Harbor, USA, reception centre for immigrants 1892–1943. A museum of immigration, was opened at E.I. in 1990, following restoration of the original buildings in the 1980s. *See* STATUE OF LIBERTY.

El Salvador. *See* SALVADOR, EL.

Ely, England. Abbey founded by St Etheldreda, 673. Burnt by Danes, 870. Refounded by Ethelwold, Bishop of Winchester, 970. Present building begun, 1083. Resistance of Hereward the Wake, 1068–71. Barons' stronghold taken by Prince Edward, 1267. Cathedral octagon finished, 1328. King's school founded, 1543.

Elysée (Paris). Built, 1718. Became the presidential residence, 1870.

Élzevir or **Elsevier Press.** Founded at Leyden, 1580, by Louis E. (1540–1617): ceased to exist, 1712.

Emergency Powers Acts, include those of 1920, 1939 and 1964.

Emmet's Insurrection. Headed by Robert E. (1778–1803) in Ireland, 23 July 1803. E. arrested 25 Aug. and executed 20 Sept. 1803. *See* UNITED IRISHMEN.

Emmy. *See* AMERICAN ACADEMY OF TELEVISION ARTS AND SCIENCES.

Emperor of India. Title proclaimed for British sovereigns, 1 Jan. 1877. Abolished 15 Aug. 1947.

Empire Day. *See* COMMONWEALTH DAY.

Empire Settlement Act passed, 1922.

Empire State Building, New York. Built 1929–31, at that time and until 1954, the tallest building in city (1,250 ft. or 381 metres high).

Employment Act, 1980, made secondary picketing unlawful.

Employment, Department of, superseded the former *Ministry of Labour, April 1968. Ministry of E. merged with Ministry of Education, July 1995.

Employers' Liability Acts, the first passed in 1880. In 1946 the E.L.A. was repealed by the Law Reform (Personal Injuries Act) which, together with the National Insurance (Industrial Injuries) Act (1946), effected far-reaching reforms in the field of workmen's compensation. Further considerably amended by the E.L.A. of 1969 and subsequent industrial legislation.

Employment Exchanges. Instituted 1905 in UK under management of local authorities. Transferred to central government control from 1909 (when they were known as Labour Exchanges, now Job Centres).

EMS. *See* EUROPEAN MONETARY SYSTEM.

Ems Telegram from King William of Prussia to Bismarck, July 1870, which, when published by Bismarck, with parts deliberately suppressed, helped to provoke the 1870 war against France.

encyclopaedia. Speusippus (*d.* 339 BC) is alleged to have compiled an E. which has not survived; neither has the work of Varro (*d. c.* 27 BC) entitled *Nine Books of Instruction.* The *Natural History* of Pliny the Elder (AD 23–79) is virtually an E. The most important medieval Es. in Latin were those of Martianus Capella the African (5thC), Isidore of Seville (570–636), and the *Speculum Triplex* of Vincent de Beauvais (*d. c.* 1264). At the same time the Arabs both translated Greek Es. and compiled their own, of which the geographical E. by Yaqut ibn 'Abdullah er-Rumi (1179–1229), a bookseller of Greek extraction, is the best known; it quotes the only surviving passages of Ibn Fadhlan's description of Scandinavians (*Rus*) in S Russia, written in

921. The greatest Chinese E. was compiled in the reign of Yung Lao (*d.* 1425). Pierre Bayles's *Dictionnaire Historique et Critique* (1697) was the first E. of modern European type, of which the first English example was the *Cyclopaedia* of Ephraim Chambers (*d.* 1740). Diderot and D'Alembert's *Encyclopédie* (1751–72) was based on a translation of it. The *Encyclopaedia Britannica* was first printed, 1768–71; all editions from the 11th (1910–11) onwards produced under American proprietorship. *Chambers's Encyclopaedia* was first edited 1850–68 by Dr Andrew Findlater. *Everyman's Encyclopaedia*, was first published by Dent in 1911; it was the forerunner of a succession of concise, low-cost Es.

Endeavour, vessel in which Capt. Cook (1728–79) set out on his voyage to New Zealand, 1768. It was also the name given to the US space shuttle which in Dec. 1993 carried out repairs to the Hubble telescope in space, and from which the longest space walks then undertaken were made.

Enderby Land, Antarctica. Visited by John Biscoe, 1831, and named after his employers. Now part of Australian Antarctic Territory.

Enforcing Act (USA). Passed by Congress, 9 Jan. 1809, for preserving strict neutrality in Napoleonic War. *See* BAYONNE DECREE.

Engagement, The. Agreement between Charles I and the Scots Commissioners in the Isle of Wight, 1647.

England, Church of. Christianity was brought to England by Roman soldiers in 1stC AD, but Romano-Celtic Church overwhelmed by Anglo-Saxon invasions, although it survived in the W and in Wales. St Augustine sent from Rome, 596, and first church founded at Canterbury, 597 (traditionally on the site of a former Romano-Christian basilica). Metropolitan province of Canterbury set up, and that of York planned, by Pope Gregory, 601. Irish Celtic monks had settled at Iona, 563, and begun the evangelization of the N. Church of Northumbria founded by Paulinus, 627;

of E Anglia by Felix, 631; of Wessex by Birinus, 634. Real evangelization of Northumbria work of St Aidan, an Iona monk, from 635 onwards. Dispute with Celtic Church settled at Synod of Whitby, 664. *Ecclesiastical History* written by Venerable Bede, who *d.* 735. Third province, with arch-episcopal seat at Lichfield, set up by King Offa in Mercia, but it lasted only from 787 to 802. Separation of church and lay courts, 1086. Murder of Becket, 1170. Legatine Council at London, 1237. Convocations organized *c.* 1283. Wycliffe condemned, 1382. Lollard Act, 1414. Papal authority repudiated and Henry VIII declared head of the church, 1534. Suppression of monasteries, 1536 and 1539. Ten Articles, 1536. Great Bible authorized, 1538. Act of Six Articles, 1539. English Litany, 1544. First Book of Common Prayer, 1549. Clerical marriage permitted, 1549. Second Book of Common Prayer, 1552. Forty-two Articles, 1553. Reconciliation with Papacy by Mary I, 1554. Independence re-established, 1559, by Queen Elizabeth I. Act of Uniformity restored the 1552 Prayer Book but with certain Catholic amendments. Thirty-nine Articles, 1563. *Hampton Court Conference, 1604. Authorized Version of Bible, 1611. Solemn League and *Covenant, 1643. Establishment (temporary) of Presbyterianism, 1646. Savoy Conference, 1667. Trial of Seven Bishops, 1688. Establishment of *Queen Anne's Bounty, 1704. *Ecclesiastical Commission incorporated, 1836. Church Discipline Act, 1840. Oxford Movement begun, 1833; its first phase ended with Newman's conversion to Rome, 1845. Welsh Church disestablishment, 1920. Lambeth Conferences (held periodically since 1867) increasingly concerned with Christian reunion. Church Assembly proposed a new Prayer Book, 1927, but this was rejected by Parliament, 1928. Archbishop of Canterbury visited Pope John XXIII, Dec. 1960. Many Prayer Book revisions put into practice, 1964 onwards. Pope John Paul II visited Canterbury Cathedral, 1982. General Synod first voted for ordination of women, 15 Nov 1984; but measure only achieved necessary two-thirds majority, 11 Nov. 1992. First 32 women priests ordained in Bristol Cathedral, 12 Mar. 1994. Changes in governing structure suggested, 1995.

See BISHOPRICS; GREAT BRITAIN; BIBLE, TRANSLATIONS OF; PRAYER, BOOK OF COMMON; ODINATION OF WOMEN, etc.

English Heritage. Government body established 1984 under the National Heritage Act, to further the preservation of ancient buildings and monuments, e.g. *Stonehenge, etc.

English history. *See* BRITAIN. English mercenaries hired by King Vortigern of Kent mutiny, and make their leader Hengest king, *c.* 450. His descendant, Ethelbert of Kent, marries Christian Frankish wife, 550. Arrival of St Augustine (*see* ENGLAND, CHURCH OF), 597. From 617 the leading English power was Northumbria, but in 730 supremacy of Mercia was established till battle of Ellendun, 821. Egbert, King of Wessex, becomes first king of the English, 829. He defeats first Danish invasion at battle of Hingston Down, *c.* 835. Arrival of the Danish *Here in England, 864. It storms York, 865. Defeats Alfred the Great at Battle of Ashdown, 870. Alfred driven into Athelney, 877. His great victory at Edington and Truce of Chippenham, 878. English Danes conquered by Edward the Elder, 901–25. Athelstan's great victory over Irish, Danes, Norwegians, Welsh and Scots at Brunanburh, 937. *Danegeld instituted, 991. At death of Ethelred the Unready and Edmund Ironside, 1016, Knut of *Denmark becomes king of the English. He visits Rome, 1027; conquers Norway, 1028, and Scotland, 1031. Wessex dynasty restored by Edward the Confessor, 1042. Death of Earl Godwin, 1053. Battle of Fulford, 21 Sept. 1066. Battle of Stamford Bridge, 25 Sept. Harold II killed at battle of Hastings, 14 Oct. 1066.

*Domesday Book, 1085–6. Henry II reconquers Normandy, 1106. *Investiture compromise, 1105. Civil war and French attacks in Normandy, 1111–25. Civil war throughout reign of Stephen, 1135–54. Constitutions of *Clarendon, 1164. Murder of Becket, 1170. Invasion of Ireland by Strongbow, 1171.

Richard I leaves England for Palestine, 1190. Arrives Acre, 8 June 1191. Returns to England, 13 Mar. 1194. French War, 1194–9.

John loses Normandy, 1204–5. Excommunicated, 1209. Reconciled with Papacy, 1213. Battle of Bouvines, 1214. Grants *Magna Carta, 1215.

Simon de Montfort killed at battle of Evesham, 1265. Model Parliament, 1295. Edward of Caernarvon proclaimed Prince of Wales, 1301. Robert Bruce's rebellion, 1305–7. Battle of Bannockburn, 1314. Hundred Years War begins, 1338. Naval victory at Sluys, 1340. Edward III claims French throne, 1340. Battle of Crécy, 1346. Capture of Calais, 1347. Battle of Neville's Cross, 1346. Black Death, 1346–7. Battle of Poitiers, 1356. Death of Black Prince, 1376. Peasants' revolt under Wat Tyler, 1381. Death of Wiclif, 1384. Death of John of Gaunt, 1399. Lancaster's revolt and deposition of Richard II, 1399. Glendower's rebellion, 1400. Persecution of *Lollards, 1401. Rebellion of Percys, 1403. Hundred Years War resumed, 1415. Battle of Agincourt, 25 Oct. 1415. Rouen captured, 1419. Treaty of Troyes, 1420. Orléans relieved by Joan of Arc, 29 Apr. 1429. Cade's rebellion, 1450. All France, except Calais, lost, 1454. *Wars of Roses begin at battle of St Albans, 22 May 1455. Henry VI deposed after battle of Towton, 1461.

Death of Warwick the Kingmaker at battle of Barnet, 1471. Caxton sets up printing press at Westminster, 1476. Edward V murdered ('The Princes in the Tower'), 1483. Wars of Roses end in death of Richard III (killed at battle of Bosworth, 1485): succession of Henry VII (Tudor).

Wolsey becomes Chancellor, 1515. Field of the Cloth of Gold, 1520. Fall of Wolsey, 1529. Henry VIII's church reforms, 1531–40 (*see* ENGLAND, CHURCH OF). Somerset Lord Protector, 1547. First Prayer Book of Edward VI used, 1549. Northumberland Protector, 1550. Second Prayer Book, 1552. Northumberland's attempt to put Jane Grey on throne foiled by Mary I, 1553. She marries Philip II of Spain, 1554. Lady Jane Grey executed, 1554. Reconciliation with Rome, 1554. Persecution of Protestants and burning of Cranmer, Latimer, and Ridley, 1555–6. War with France, 1557. Calais lost, 1558. Acts of Uniformity and Supremacy, 1559. Papal Bull of Deposition issued against Elizabeth, 1570. Drake sails round the world, 1576–9. Throgmorton's plot, 1584. Babington's plot, 1587. Execution of Mary Queen of Scots, 1587. Drake attacks Cadiz, 1587. Defeat of the *Armada, July–Aug. 1588. Essex storms Cadiz, 1596. Foundation of *E Indian Co., 1600. Spanish expedition to Ireland, 1601. *D.* of Elizabeth I and succession to throne as James I of James VI of Scotland, 1603. (*For later history see* GREAT BRITAIN, HISTORY OF.)

English literature. The following is a list of prominent writers in the English language (excepting American, for whom *see* AMERICAN LITERATURE IN ENGLISH):

Abercrombie, Lascelles, 1881–1938, poet.

Abse, Danny, 1923–, Welsh poet

Achebe, Chinua, 1930–, Nigerian novelist

Acton, John E. E. Dalberg-Acton, Lord, 1834–1902, historian.

Addison, Joseph, 1672–1719, poet and essayist.

Aelfric, 955 – *c.* 1022, theologian and educationist.

Agate, James Evershed, 1877–1947, dramatic critic.

Ainsworth, William Harrison, 1805–82, novelist.

Aldington, Richard, 1892–1962, poet, novelist, and biographer.

Alfred the Great, King, *c.* 849–99, translator.

Allingham, Margery, 1904–66, detective writer.

Amis, Sir Kingsley, 1922–95, novelist.

Amis, Martin, 1949–, novelist.

Arbuthnot, John, 1667–1735, Scottish satirist (originator of the term 'John Bull').

Arnold, Matthew, 1822–88, poet and critic.

Arnold, Thomas, 1795–1842, historian.

Ascham, Roger, 1515–68, didactic writer.

Ashmole, Elias, 1617–92, antiquarian.

Atwood, Margaret, 1939–, Canadian poet and novelist.

Aubrey, John, 1626–97, antiquarian.

Auden, Wystan Hugh, 1907–73, poet.

Austen, Jane, 1775–1817, novelist.

Austin, Alfred, 1835–1913, poet laureate.

Ayckbourn, Alan, 1939–, dramatist.

Bacon, Francis, 1561–1628, philosopher.

Bacon, Roger, *c.* 1214–92, scientist and philosopher.

Bagehot, Walter, 1826–77, writer on economics, politics, and L.

Baillie, Joanna, 1762–1851, Scottish poet.

Bainbridge, Beryl, 1934–, novelist.

Balfour, Arthur J., Earl of, 1848–1930, statesman and essayist.

Baring, Maurice, 1874–1945, poet and novelist.

Baring-Gould, Sabine, 1834–1924, novelist and hymn-writer.

Barker, Harley Granville-, 1877–1947, dramatist and critic.

Barrie, Sir James Matthew, 1860–1937, novelist and dramatist.

Bates, Herbert Ernest, 1905–74, novelist.

Baxter, Richard, 1615–91, theologian and hymn writer.

Beaconsfield, Earl of (Benjamin Disraeli, 1804–81, novelist.

Beaumont, Francis, 1584–1616, dramatist.

Beckett, Samuel, 1906–89, Irish author and dramatist.

Bede, the Venerable, *c.* 673–735, historian.

Beerbohm, Sir Max, 1872–1956, critic and miscellaneous writer.

Beeton, Mrs Isabella, 1836–65, cookery writer.

Behan, Brendan, 1924–64, Irish dramatist.

Behn, Aphra, 1640–89, dramatist.

Beith, Maj.-Gen. J. H. *See* HAY.

Bell, Gertrude Margaret, 1868–1926, oriental traveller.

Belloc, Hilaire, 1870–1953, poet, essayist and historian.

Bennett, Alan, 1934–, essayist and dramatist.

Bennett, Enoch Arnold, 1867–1931, novelist.

Benson, Edward Frederick, 1867–1940, novelist and essayist.

Benson, Stella, 1892–1933, novelist.

Bentham, Jeremy, 1748–1832, political writer.

Bentley, Edmund Clerihew, 1875–1956, journalist and novelist.

Bentley, Phyllis, 1898–1971, novelist.

Berkeley, George, 1685–1753, philosopher.

Berlin, Sir Isaiah, 1909–, philosopher.

Betjeman, Sir John, 1906–84, poet.

Binyon, Laurence, 1869–1943, poet and dramatist.

Birkenhead, Lord, 1872–1930, jurist.

Birmingham, George (Canon J. O. Hannay), 1865–1952, novelist.

Birrell, Augustine, 1850–1933, essayist.

Blackie, John Stuart, 1809–95, scholar and man of letters.

Blackmore, Richard Doddridge, 1825–1900, novelist.

Blackstone, Sir William, 1723–80, jurist.

Blackwood, Algernon, 1869–1951, novelist.

Blake, William, 1757–1827, poet and painter.

Bland, Edith ('E. Nesbit'), 1858–1924, children's writer.

Blunden, Edmund, 1896–1974, poet.

Blunt, Wilfrid Scawen, 1840–1922, poet.

Blyton, Enid (Mrs. Kenneth Waters), 1897–1968, children's writer.

Boece or Boethius, Hector, 1465?–1536, Scottish historian.

Bond, Edward, 1935–, dramatist.

Booth, Rt. Hon. Charles, 1840–1916, sociologist.

Borrow, George, 1803–81, miscellaneous writer.

Boswell, James, 1740–95, biographer.

Bowdler, Thomas, 1754–1825, editor of Shakespeare.

Bowen, Elizabeth (Dorothea Cole), 1899–1973, novelist.

Bradbury, Malcolm, 1932–, novelist and critic.

Brenan, Gerald, 1894–1987, miscellaneous and travel writer.

Bridges, Robert Seymour, 1844–1930, poet.

Bridie, James (pseudonym of A. H. Mavor), 1888–1951, Scottish dramatist.

Brink, André, 1935–, S African novelist.

Brontë, Anne, 1820–49, novelist.

Brontë, Charlotte, 1816–55, novelist.

Brontë, Emily, 1818–48, poet and novelist.

Brooke, Rupert, 1887–1915, poet.

Brookner, Anita, 1938–, novelist.

Brophy, John, 1899–1965, novelist.

Brougham and Vaux, Henry Lord, 1778–1868, essayist, founder of *Edinburgh Review*.

Brown, George Mackay, 1921–, Scottish poet, novelist, short-story writer and dramatist.

Browne, Sir Thomas, 1605–82, physician and miscellaneous writer.

Browning, Elizabeth Barrett, 1806–61, poet.

Browning, Robert, 1812–89, poet.

'Bryher' (Annie Winifred Ellerman), novelist, 1894–1983.

Buchan, John (Lord Tweedsmuir), 1875–1940, novelist and historian.

Buchanan, George, 1506–82, Scottish historian.

Bunyan, John, 1628–88, allegorist.

Burgess, Anthony, 1917–93, novelist.

Burke, Edmund, 1729–97, statesman and political philosopher.

Burnet, Gilbert, 1643–1715, historian.

Burnett, Frances Hodgson (Mrs Stephen Townsend), 1849–1924, novelist.

Burney, Fanny. *See* D'ARBLAY.

Burns, Robert, 1759–96, Scottish poet.

Burton, Sir Richard Francis, 1821–90, anthropologist.

Burton, Robert, 1577–1640, humorist.

Butler, Samuel, 1612–80, satirist.

Butler, Samuel, 1835–1902, philosophical writer and novelist.

Byatt, Antonia Susan, 1936–, novelist.

Byron, George Gordon, Lord, 1788–1824, poet.

Cædmon, *d. c.* 680, Northumbrian poet.

Caine, Sir Thomas Henry Hall, 1853–1931, novelist.

Camden, William, 1551–1623, antiquary.

Campbell, Thomas, 1777–1844, Scottish poet.

Canetti, Elias, Bulgarian-born novelist, 1905–94.

Carew, Thomas, 1595–1640, poet.

Carey, Henry, *c.* 1687–1743, dramatist and song writer.

Carlyle, Thomas, 1795–1881, historian and essayist.

Carman, William Bliss, 1861–1929, Canadian poet.

'Carroll, Lewis.' *See* DODGSON.

Cartland, Dame Barbara, 1901–, romantic novelist.

Cary, Joyce, 1888–1957, Irish novelist.

Chambers, Ephraim, *c.* 1680–1740, published first English encyclopaedia.

Chapman, George, 1559–1634, dramatist and translator.

Charteris, Leslie, 1907–1993, crime writer.

Chatterton, Thomas, 1752–70, poet.

Chatwin, Bruce, 1940–89, novelist and travel-writer.

Chaucer, Geoffrey, 1340?–1400, poet.

Chesterfield, Philip Dormer Stanhope, Earl of, 1694–1773, letter-writer.

Chesterton, Gilbert Keith, 1874–1936, poet and critic.

Christie, Dame Agatha, 1890–1976, detective novelist.

Churchill, Sir Winston S., 1874–1965, statesman and historian.

Cibber, Colley, 1671–1757, poet, actor, and dramatist.

Clare, John, 1793–1864, poet.

Clarendon, Edward Hyde, Earl of, 1609–74, historian. *See* CLARENDON PRESS.

Clark, Lord Kenneth, 1903–83, art historian.

Clarke, Arthur Charles, 1917–, science fiction writer.

Clemens, Jack, 1916–94, poet.

Clough, Arthur Hugh, 1819–61, poet.

Cobbett, William, 1763–1835, publicist.

Coetzee, J. M., 1945–, S African novelist.

Coke, Sir Edward, 1552–1634, jurist.

Cole, George Douglas Howard, 1889–1959, political writer.

Coleridge, Hartley, 1796–1849, poet.

Coleridge, Samuel Taylor, 1772–1834, poet, philosopher, and critic.

'Collins, Tom.' *See* FURPHY.

Collins, William Wilkie, 1824–89, novelist.

Colman, George, 1732–94, dramatist.

Compton-Burnett, Dame Ivy, 1892–1969, novelist.

Congreve, William, 1670–1729, dramatist.

Connolly, Cyril, 1903–74, novelist and critic.

Conrad (Korzeniowski), Joseph, 1857–1924, novelist.

Cookson, Catherine, 1906–, romantic novelist.

Cooper, Lettice, 1897–1994, novelist

Coppard, Alfred Edward, 1878–1957, short-story writer and poet.

Corelli, Marie, 1855–1924, novelist.

Coverdale, Miles, 1488–1568, translator. *See* BIBLE.

Coward, Sir Noël, 1899–1973, playwright and composer.

Cowley, Abraham, 1618–67, poet.

Cowper, William, 1731–1800, poet.

Crabbe, George, 1754–1832, poet.

Craik, Dinah Maria, 1826–87, novelist.

Cranmer, Thomas, 1489–1556, liturgist.

Crashaw, Richard, 1612?–49, poet.

Crompton, Richmal, 1890–1969, children's writer.

Cynewulf, *fl.* 750, Northumbrian poet.

Dahl, Roald, 1916–90, novelist and children's writer.

D'Arblay, Frances (Burney), 1752–1840, novelist.

Darwin, Charles Robert, 1809–82, naturalist. *See* DARWINISM.

Darwin, Erasmus, 1731–1802, botanist and poet.

D'Avenant, Sir William, 1606–68, poet and dramatist.

Davidson, John, 1857–1909, poet.

Davies, William Henry, 1871–1940, poet.

Day Lewis, Cecil, 1904–72, poet.

Defoe, Daniel, 1660–1731, journalist and novelist.

Dekker, Thomas, *c.* 1570–*c.* 1632, dramatist and pamphleteer.

Delafield, E. M. (Edmée de la Pasture), 1890–1943, novelist.

De la Mare, Walter John, 1873–1956, poet and novelist.

De la Ramée, Marie Louise ('Ouida'), 1839–1908, novelist.

De la Roche, Mazo, 1885–1961, Canadian novelist.

De Quincey, Thomas, 1785–1859, essayist and miscellaneous writer.

Dicey, Albert Venn, 1835–1922, jurist.

Dickens, Charles, 1812–70, novelist.

Dilke, Charles Wentworth, 1789–1864, journalist.

Dinesen, Isak (Karen Blixen), 1885–1962, Danish-born novelist and prose writer.

Disraeli, Benjamin. *See* BEACONSFIELD.

Dobson, Austin, 1840–1921, poet and essayist.

Dodgson, Charles Lutwidge ('Lewis Carroll'), 1832–98, writer of nonsense and mathematician.

Donne, John, 1573–1631, poet and divine.

Douglas, Gavin, 1474–1522, Scottish poet.

Douglas, Keith, 1920–44, poet.

Douglas, Norman, 1868–1952, Scottish novelist and miscellaneous writer.

Doyle, Sir Arthur Conan, 1859–1930, novelist.

Drayton, Michael, 1563–1631, poet.

Drinkwater, John, 1882–1937, poet and dramatist.

Drummond, William (of Hawthornden), 1585–1649, poet.

Dryden, John, 1631–1700, poet, dramatist, and satirist.

Dugdale, Sir William, 1605–86, antiquarian.

Du Maurier, Dame Daphne (Lady Browning), 1907–1989, novelist.

Dunbar, William, 1460?–1520?, Scots poet.

Durrell, Lawrence, 1912–90, novelist.

Edgeworth, Maria, 1767–1849, Irish novelist.

Eliot, George. *See* EVANS.

Eliot, Thomas Stearns, 1888–1965, American-born poet and dramatist.

Ellis, Henry Havelock, 1859–1939, psychologist.

Elyot, Sir Thomas, 1490?–1546, miscellaneous writer.

Evans, Mary Ann ('George Eliot'), 1819–1880, novelist.

Evelyn, John, 1620–1706, diarist.

Farjeon, Eleanor, 1881–1965, poet and children's writer.

Farjeon, Herbert, 1887–1945, critic and playwright.

Fielding, Henry, 1707–54, novelist.

Firth, Sir Charles Harding, 1857–1936, historian and critic.

Fisher, Herbert A. L., 1865–1940, politician and historian.

Fisher, St John, 1459–1535, theologian.

FitzGerald, Edward, 1809–83, translator.

Flecker, James Elroy, 1884–1915, poet and dramatist.

Fleming, Ian, 1908–65, thriller writer.

Fletcher, John, 1579–1625, poet and dramatist.

Ford, Ford Madox (Hueffer), 1873–1939, poet and novelist.

Forester, Cecil Scott, 1899–1966, novelist.

Forster, Edward Morgan, 1879–1970, novelist.

Fortescue, Sir John, 1394–1476, jurist.

Fox, George, 1624–91, Quaker diarist.

Foxe, John, 1516–87, martyrologist.

Frame, Janet, 1924–, New Zealand novelist.

Francis, Sir Philip, 1740–1818, reputed author of *The *Letters of Junius.*

Frankau, Gilbert, 1884–1952, novelist.

Franklin, Miles, 1879–1954, Australian novelist.

Frazer, Sir James George, 1854–1941, anthropology and comparative religion.

Froude, James Anthony, 1818–94, historian.

Fry, Christopher, 1906–, dramatist.

Fry, Roger E., 1866–1934, art critic.

Fugard, Athol, 1932–, S African dramatist.

Fuller, Thomas, 1608–61, antiquary and biographer.

Furnivall, Frederick James, 1825–1910, lexicographer, editor *Oxford English Dictionary.*

Furphy, Joseph ('Tom Collins'), 1843–1912, Australian novelist.

Galsworthy, John, 1867–1933, novelist and dramatist.

Gardiner, Samuel Rawson, 1829–1902, historian.

Garnett, Edward, 1868–1937, critic.

Garvin, James Louis, 1868–1947, journalist.

Gaskell, Mrs Elizabeth Cleghorn (Stevenson), 1810–65, novelist.

Gay, John, 1685–1732, poet and dramatist.

Gibbon, Edward, 1737–94, historian.

Gibbons, Stella, 1902–89, novelist.

Gibbs, Sir Philip Hamilton, 1877–1962, journalist and novelist.

Gilbert, Sir William Schwenck, 1836–1911, humorist and dramatist.

Gissing, George, 1857–1903, novelist.

Gladstone, William Ewart, 1809–98, statesman and man of letters.

Glyn, Mrs. Elinor, 1864–1943, Canadian novelist.

Godwin, Mrs Mary Wollstonecraft, 1759–97, miscellaneous writer.

Godwin, William, 1756–1836, philosopher and novelist.

Golding, Louis, 1895–1958, novelist.

Golding, Sir William Gerald, 1911–1993, novelist.

Goldsmith, Oliver, 1728–74, poet, dramatist, and essayist.

Gordimer Nadine, 1923–, S African novelist.

Gordon, Adam Lindsay, 1833–70, Australian poet.

Gosse, Sir Edmund William, 1849–1928, poet, critic, and essayist.

Gower, John, 1325?–1408, poet.

Grahame, Kenneth, 1859–1932, writer on child life.

Graves, Robert von Ranke, 1895–1985, poet.

Gray, Alisdair, 1934–, Scottish novelist.

Gray, Thomas, 1716–71, poet.

Green, John Richard, 1837–83, historian.

Greene, Graham, 1904–1991, novelist and dramatist.

Greene, Robert, 1558–92, poet and dramatist.

Greer, Germaine, 1939–, Australian feminist writer.

Gregory, Augusta, Lady, 1852–1932, Irish dramatist.

Grenfell, Julian Henry Francis, 1888–1915, poet.

Greville, Charles Cavendish Fulke, 1794–1865, diarist.

Greville, Sir Fulke, Lord Brooke, 1554–1628, poet.

Grossmith, George, 1847–1912, miscellaneous writer (*Diary of a Nobody*).

Gunn, Neil, 1891–1973, Scottish novelist.

Guthrie, Thomas Anstey ('F. Anstey'), 1856–1934, humorist.

Haggard, Sir Henry Rider, 1856–1925, novelist.

Hakluyt, Richard, 1552?–1616, collector of voyages.

Haldane, Richard Burdon, 1856–1928, critical philosopher.

Haliburton, Thomas Chandler ('Sam Slick'), 1765–1865, Nova Scotian humorist.

Hall, Edward, *c.* 1499–1547, chronicler.

Hall, Margaret Radclyffe, 1886–1943, novelist.

Hammerton, Sir John Alexander, 1871–1949, editor and critic.

Hammond, Barbara, *d.* 1961, economist.

Hannay, J. O. *See* BIRMINGHAM.

Hardy, Thomas, 1840–1928, poet and novelist.

Harington, Sir John, 1561–1612, miscellaneous writer.

Harrison, Mary St Leger ('Lucas Malet'), 1852–1931, novelist.

Harrison, William, 1534–93, chronologist and topographer.

Hartley, Leslie Poles, 1895–1972, novelist.

Hawkins, Sir Anthony Hope, 1863–1933, novelist.

Hazlitt, William, 1778–1830, essayist and critic.

'Hay, Ian' (John Hay Beith), 1876–1952, novelist.

Heaney, Seamus, 1939–, Irish poet.

Heber, Reginald, 1783–1826, hymn-writer.

Hemans, Felicia Dorothea, 1793–1835, poetess.

Henley, William Ernest, 1849–1903, poet and critic.

Henryson, Robert, 1425?–1506, Scots poet.

Henty, George Alfred, 1832–1902, writer for boys.

Herbert of Cherbury, Edward, Lord, 1583–1648, philosopher and historian.

Herbert, George, 1593–1633, poet.

Herrick, Robert, 1591–1674, poet.

Hervey, John, Lord, 1696–1743, memorialist.

Hilton, James, 1900–54, novelist.

Hobbes, Thomas, 1588–1679, philosopher.

Hoccleve or Occleve, Thomas, 1368?–1450?, poet.

Hodgson, Ralph, 1871–1962, poet.

Hogg, James ('the Ettrick Shepherd'), 1770–1835, poet.

Holdsworth, Sir William, 1871–1943, jurist.

Holinshed or Hollingshead, Raphael, ?–1580?, historian.

Holtby, Winifred, 1898–1935, novelist.

Hood, Thomas, 1799–1845, poet and comic writer.

Hooker, Richard, 1554?–1600, theologian.
Hope, Anthony. *See* HAWKINS.
Hopkins, Gerard Manley, 1844–89, poet.
Housman, Alfred Edward, 1859–1936, poet.
Housman, Laurence, 1865–1959, dramatist and poet.
Howard, Henry. *See* SURREY.
Hudson, William Henry, 1841–1922, essayist and novelist.
Hughes, Ted, 1930–, poet.
Hughes, Thomas, 1822–96, novelist.
Hume, David, 1711–76, philosopher and historian.
Hunt, James Henry Leigh, 1784–1859, essayist and poet.
Huxley, Aldous Leonard, 1894–1963, novelist and poet.
Hyde, Douglas, 1860–1949, poet in Irish and English and authority on Irish folklore.
Isherwood, Christopher, 1904–86, novelist and dramatist.
Ishiguro, Kazuo, 1954–, Japanese-born novelist.
Jacobs, William Wymark, 1863–1943, short-story writer.
James, (Baroness) Phyllis Dorothy, (Mrs. C. B. White) 1920–, crime writer.
James, C(yril) L(ionel) R(obert), 1901–89, Trinidadian novelist, historian and critic.
Jefferies, Richard, 1848–87, naturalist and novelist.
Jennings, Elizabeth, 1926–, poet.
Jerome, Jerome Klapka, 1859–1927, novelist and dramatist.
Jerrold, Douglas William, 1803–57, dramatist.
Johnson, Samuel, 1709–84, essayist and lexicographer.
Jonson, Benjamin, *c.* 1573–1637, poet and dramatist.
Jowett, Benjamin, 1817–93, scholar.
Joyce, James, 1882–1941, Irish novelist.
Julian of Norwich, 1342–1416, mystical writer.
Kavanagh, Patrick, 1904–67, Irish poet, novelist and critic.
Kaye-Smith, Sheila, 1887–1956, novelist.
Keats, John, 1795–1821, poet.
Keble, John, 1792–1866, poet and divine.

Ken, Thomas, 1637–1711, hymn-writer.
Kendall, Henry Clarence, 1841–82, Australian poet.
Keneally, Thomas, 1935–, Australian novelist.
Keynes, John Maynard, Lord, 1883–1946, economist.
Kilvert, Robert Francis, 1840–72, diarist.
Kingsley, Charles, 1819–75, novelist.
Kipling, Rudyard, 1865–1936, poet, novelist, and short-story writer.
Knox, John, *c.* 1513–72, Scottish reformer and historian.
Knox, Ronald (Monsignor), 1888–1957, theologian, translator, and miscellaneous writer.
Koestler, Arthur, 1905–83, Hungarian-born novelist.
Kyd, Thomas, 1558–94, dramatist.
Lamb, Charles, 1775–1834, essayist and poet.
Lamb, Mary, 1764–1847, miscellaneous writer.
Landor, Walter Savage, 1775–1864, poet, etc.
Lanfranc, Archbishop, *c.* 1005–89, theologian.
Lang, Andrew, 1844–1912, Scottish poet and mythologist.
Langland, William, 1330?–1400?, poet.
Larkin, Philip, 1922–86, poet and essayist.
Lawrence, David Herbert, 1885–1930, novelist.
Lawrence, Thomas Edward, 1888–1935, historian and translator.
Layamon, *fl.* 1200, poet.
Leacock, Stephen, 1869–1944, Canadian essayist, etc.
Lear, Edward, 1812–88, writer of nonsense verse.
Leavis, Frank Raymond, 1895–1978, academic and critic.
Lecky, William Edward Hartpole, 1838–1903, historian.
Lee, Laurie, 1914–, miscellaneous writer and poet.
Le Fanu, Joseph Sheridan, 1814–73, novelist.
Lehmann, Rosamund, 1901–90, novelist.
Leland, John, *c.* 1506–52, antiquary.
Lessing, Doris, 1919–, novelist.
Lewis, Alun, 1915–44, Welsh poet.

Lewis, Clive Staples, 1898–1963, novelist.

Lewis, Dominic Bevan Wyndham, 1894–1969, biographer and journalist.

Linacre, Thomas, *c.* 1460–1524, physician and scholar.

Lindsay or Lyndsay, Sir David, 1490–1555, Scots poet.

Lingard, John, 1771–1851, historian.

Locke, John, 1632–1704, philosopher.

Lodge, Thomas, 1558?–1625, poet and dramatist.

Lovelace, Richard, 1618–58, poet.

Lucas, Edward Verrall, 1868–1938, story-writer and essayist.

Lydgate, John, 1370?–1450?, poet.

Lynd, Robert, 1879–1949, Irish essayist and critic.

Lytton, Edward Bulwer-Lytton, Lord, 1803–73, novelist and statesman.

Lytton, Edward Robert Bulwer-Lytton, Earl of ('Owen Meredith'), 1831–91, statesman and poet.

Macaulay, Rose, 1887–1958, novelist and poet.

Macaulay, Thomas Babington, Lord, 1800–59, historian and essayist.

MacBeth, George, 1932–92, Scottish poet.

MacCarthy, Sir Desmond, 1878–1952, critic.

MacDonald, George ('Phantastes'), 1824–1905, poet and novelist.

McGonagall, William, *c.* 1825–1902, Scottish versifier.

MacNeice, Louis, 1907–63, poet.

Maitland, Sir Frederic William, 1850–1906, historian.

Maitland, Sir Richard, Lord Lethington, 1496–1586, Scottish poet.

'Malet, Lucas.' *See* HARRISON, MARY ST LEGER.

Malory, Sir Thomas, *fl.* 1470, romancer.

Malthus, Thomas Robert, 1766–1834, economist.

Mansfield, Katherine, 1890–1923, New Zealand novelist.

Marlowe, Christopher, 1564–93, dramatist.

Marryat, Frederick, 1792–1848, novelist.

Marsh, Ngaio, 1895–1982, New Zealand crime writer.

Martin, (Basil) Kingsley, 1897–1969, journalist.

Martineau, Harriet, 1802–76, novelist and economist.

Martineau, James, 1805–1900, Unitarian theologian.

Marvell, Andrew, 1621–78, poet and satirist.

Masefield, John Edward, 1878–1967, poet, playwright and novelist.

Massinger, Philip, 1583–1640, dramatist.

Massingham, Henry William, 1860–1924, journalist and editor.

Maugham, William Somerset, 1874–1965, novelist and dramatist.

May, Sir Thomas Erskine, Lord Farnborough, 1815–86, constitutional jurist and historian.

Mehta, Ved, 1934–, Indian prose writer.

Meredith, George, 1828–1909, novelist and poet.

Meynell, Alice Christiana, 1847–1922, poet and essayist.

Meynell, Wilfrid, 1852–1948, journalist, poet, and essayist.

Middleton, Thomas, 1580–1627, dramatist.

Mill, James, 1773–1836, philosopher and historian.

Mill, John Stuart, 1806–73, philosopher.

Milne, Alan Alexander, 1882–1956, journalist, novelist, children's writer, and dramatist.

Milton, John, 1608–74, poet.

Mitford, Mary Russell, 1787–1855, novelist and dramatist.

Mitford, Nancy, 1904–73, novelist and biographer.

Moffat, Dr James, 1870–1944, theologian and translator of Bible.

Monro, Harold, 1879–1932, poet.

Montagu, Lady Mary Wortley, 1689–1762, letter-writer.

Montague, Charles Edward, 1867–1928, journalist and novelist.

Montgomery, James, 1771–1854, poet.

Montgomery, Lucy Maude, 1874–1942, Canadian novelist.

Moore, George Augustus, 1852–1933, dramatist and novelist.

Moore, Thomas, 1779–1852, poet.

More, Hannah, 1745–1833, miscellaneous and religious writer.

More, Sir (St) Thomas, 1475–1535, historical and political writer.

Morgan, Charles, 1894–1958, novelist and playwright.

Morley of Blackburn, John, Visc., 1838–1923, statesman and man of letters.

Morris, William, 1834–96, poet and artist.

Mulock, Dinah Maria, *see* Mrs CRAIK.

Murdoch, Dame (Jean) Iris, (Mrs J. O. Bayley), 1919–, novelist.

Murray, George Gilbert, 1866–1957, classicist.

Murry, John Middleton, 1889–1957, critic.

Naipaul, Sir, V.S., 1932–, W Indian-born novelist.

Nairne, Carolina Oliphant, Baroness, 1766–1845, Scots poet.

Nashe, Thomas, 1567–1601, dramatist and novelist.

Neale, John Maşon, 1818–66, hymn-writer.

Nesbit, *see* BLAND.

Newbolt, Sir Henry, 1862–1938, poet.

Newman, John Henry (Cardinal), 1801–90, theologian and poet.

Newton, Sir Isaac, philosopher and scientist.

Newton, John, 1725–1807, hymn-writer.

Nicolson, Sir Harold George, 1886–1968, biographer and novelist.

Nichols, Robert Malise Bowyer, 1893–1944, poet.

Northcliffe, Alfred Harmsworth, 1st Viscount, 1865–1922, journalist and newspaper proprietor.

Nolan, *see* O'BRIEN, FLANN.

Noyes, Alfred, 1880–1958, poet.

O'Brien, Edna, 1936–, Irish novelist.

O'Brien, Flann (Brian Nolan), 1911–66. Irish essayist, novelist and dramatist.

O'Casey, Sean, 1884–1964, Irish dramatist.

O'Connor, Frank, 1903–66, Irish short-story writer.

O'Faolain, Sean, 1900–91, Irish short-story writer, novelist and biographer.

Oman, Sir Charles William Chadwick, 1860–1946, historian.

Ondaatje, Michael, 1943–, Canadian poet and novelist.

Onions, Charles Talbut, 1873–1965, philologist.

Oppenheim, Edward Phillips, 1866–1946, novelist.

Orczy, Emmuska, Baroness, 1865–1947, novelist.

Orwell, George (Eric Blair), 1903–50, novelist and essayist.

Osborne, Dorothy (*Lady Temple*), 1627–95, letter-writer.

Osborne, John, 1929–94, dramatist and essayist.

O'Shaughnessy, Arthur William Edgar, 1844–81, poet.

Otway, Thomas, 1652–85, dramatist.

Ouida. *See* DE LA RAMÉE.

Owen, Wilfrid, 1893–1918, poet.

Page, Dr. William, 1861–1934, editor of *The Victoria County Histories*.

Paine, Thomas, 1737–1809, pamphleteer.

Palgrave, Francis Turner, 1824–97, poet and anthologist.

Pares, Sir Bernard, 1867–1949, historian and Slavonic philologist.

Paris, Matthew, *c.* 1195–1259, chronicler.

Park, Mungo, 1771–1806, traveller.

Parker, Sir Gilbert, 1862–1932, Canadian novelist.

Parnell, Thomas, 1679–1718, poet.

Passfield, Sidney James Webb, Baron, 1859–1947, historian and economist.

Pater, Walter Horatio, 1839–94, essayist and critic.

Paterson, A.B. ('Banjo'), 1864–1941, Australian poet.

Patmore, Coventry Kersey Dighton, 1823–96, poet.

Paton, Alan, 1903–88, S African novelist.

Pattison, Mark, 1813–84, scholar and biographer.

Peacock, Thomas Love, 1785–1866, novelist, critic, and poet.

Peake, Mervyn Laurence, 1911–68, novelist.

Pearse, Padraic, 1879–1916, Irish poet.

Pepys, Samuel, 1633–1703, diarist.

Peters, Ellis (Edith Pargeter), 1913–95, historical novelist.

Phillpotts, Eden, 1862–1960, novelist and dramatist.

Pickthall, Marjorie, 1883–1922, Canadian poet.

Pinero, Sir Arthur Wing, 1855–1934, dramatist.

Pinter, Harold, 1930–, dramatist.

Piozzi, Hester Lynch (Salusbury) (Mrs Thrale), 1741–1821, miscellaneous writer.

Pope, Alexander, 1688–1744, poet.

Porson, Richard, 1759–1808, scholar and critic.

Porter, Jane, 1776–1850, novelist.

Potter, Beatrix, 1866–1943, children's writer and illustrator.

Potter, Dennis, 1935–94, television dramatist.

Powell, Anthony Dymoke, 1905–, novelist.

Powys, John Cowper, 1872–1963, novelist.

Powys, Llewellyn, 1884–1939, novelist.

Powys, Theodore Francis, 1875–1953, novelist.

Prichard, Katharine Susannah, 1883–1969, Australian novelist and journalist.

Priestley, John Boynton, 1894–1984, novelist and dramatist.

Priestley, Joseph, 1733–1804, chemist and theologian.

Pringle, Thomas, 1789–1834, S African poet.

Prior, Matthew, 1664–1721, poet.

Pritchett, Sir Victor S. 1900–, novelist.

Prynne, William, 1600–69, antiquarian and pamphleteer.

Pusey, Edward Bouverie, 1800–82, theologian.

Quennell, Sir Peter, 1905–93, miscellaneous writer.

Quiller-Couch, Sir Arthur Thomas, 1863–1944, novelist and critic.

Radcliffe, Mrs Ann, 1764–1823, novelist.

Raine, Katherine, 1908–94, poet and critic.

Raleigh, Sir Walter, 1552?–1618, explorer, historian, etc.

Ramsay, Allan, 1686–1758, poet.

Randolph, Thomas, 1605–35, poet and dramatist.

Ransome, Arthur, 1884–1967, children's novelist and miscellaneous writer.

Rao, Raja, 1908–, Indian novelist and short-story teller.

Rattigan, Sir Terence, 1911–83, dramatist.

Rawlinson, Sir Henry, 1810–95, orientalist.

Ray, John, 1627–1705, naturalist.

Read, Sir Herbert Edward, 1893–1968, poet and critic.

Reade, Charles, 1814–84, novelist.

Rendell, Ruth, 1930–, crime writer.

Rhys, Ernest, 1859–1946, poet, critic, and editor of *Everyman's Library*.

Rhys, Jean, 1890–1979, novelist.

Ricardo, David, 1772–1823, economist.

Richard of Cirencester, *d. c.* 1401, historian.

Richardson, Henry Handel (Ethyl Florence), 1870–1946, Australian novelist.

Richardson, Samuel, 1689–1761, novelist.

Rigg, James McMullen, 1855–1926, biographer and translator of the *Decameron*.

Robert of Gloucester, *c.* 1260–1300, metrical chronicler.

Roberts, Sir Charles George Douglas, 1860–1943, Canadian poet.

Robertson, John Mackinnon, 1856–1933, Shakespearian scholar.

Robinson, Henry Crabb, 1775–1867, journalist and diarist.

Rochester, John Wilmot, Earl of, 1647–80, poet.

Roger of Wendover, *d. c.* 1236, historian.

Rolle, Richard, *c.* 1300–49, mystic.

Rose, John Holland, 1855–1942, historian.

'Ross, Martin' (Violet Florence), 1862–1915, novelist.

Rossetti, Christina Georgina, 1830–94, poet.

Rossetti, Dante Gabriel, 1828–82, poet.

Rowe, Nicholas, 1674–1718, dramatist and poet.

Rowley, William, *c.* 1585–*c.* 1642, dramatist.

Rowse, Alfred Leslie, 1903–, historian.

Rushdie, Salman, 1947–, Indian-born novelist.

Ruskin, John, 1819–1900, writer on art, economics, etc.

Russell, Bertrand Arthur William, 3rd earl, 1872–1970, philosopher.

Russell, George William ('A.E.'), 1867–1935, Irish poet.

Russell, Sir William Howard, 1820–1911, journalist.

Rutherford, Mark, *See* White, W. H.

Rymer, Thomas, 1641–1713, poet and critic.

Sackville, Thomas, 1536–1608, poet.

Sackville-West, Hon. Victoria, 1892–1962, poet, novelist, and biographer.

Sadleir, Michael T. H., 1888–1957, biographer and novelist.

Saintsbury, George, 1845–1933, critic.

'Saki' (Hector Hugh Munro), 1870–1916, short-story writer.

Sala, George Augustus, 1828–95, novelist and journalist.

Sandys, George, 1578–1644, traveller and translator.

Sassoon, Siegfried Lorraine, 1886–1967, poet and novelist.

Savage, Richard, *c.* 1697–1742, poet.

Sayers, Dorothy Leigh, 1893–1957, novelist, essayist, and playwright.

Schreiber. *See* GUEST.

Schreiner, Olive, 1855–1920, S African novelist and social reformer.

Scott, Charles Prestwich, 1846–1932, 57 years editor *Manchester Guardian*.

Scott, Paul Mark, 1920–78, novelist.

Scott, Sir Walter, 1771–1832, novelist and poet.

Seaman, Sir Owen, 1861–1936, poet, sometime editor of *Punch*.

Sedley, Sir Charles, 1639?–1701, poet and dramatist.

Seeley, Sir John Robert, 1834–95, historian and essayist.

Selden, John, 1584–1654, jurist and scholar.

Sewell, Anna, 1820–78, novelist.

Shadwell, Thomas, 1642?–92, dramatist and poet.

Shaffer, Peter, 1926–, dramatist.

Shaftesbury, Anthony Ashley Cooper, Earl of, 1671–1713, philosopher.

*Shakespeare, William, 1564–1616, dramatist and poet.

Sharp, William (Fiona Macleod), 1856–1905, novelist and poet.

Shaw, George Bernard, 1856–1950, Irish dramatist.

Shelley, Mary Wollstonecraft, 1797–1851, novelist.

Shelley, Percy Bysshe, 1792–1822, poet.

Sheridan, Richard Brinsley, 1751–1816, dramatist.

Shirley, James, 1596–1666, dramatist.

Shirley, John, 1366–1456, translator.

Shute, Nevil, 1899–1960, novelist.

Sidney or Sydney, Algernon, 1622–83, political writer.

Sidney, Sir Philip, 1554–86, poet.

Sigerson, Dr George, *d.* 1925, Gaelic scholar.

Simpson, Helen de Guerry, 1897–1940, Australian novelist.

Sinclair, May, 1870–1946, novelist.

Sitwell, Dame Edith Louise, 1887–1964, poet.

Sitwell, Sir Osbert, 1892–1969, poet and novelist.

Skeat, Walter William, 1835–1912, Anglo-Saxon scholar.

Skelton, John, 1460?–1529, poet.

Smart, Christopher, 1722–71, poet.

Smiles, Samuel, 1812–1904, biographer and miscellaneous writer.

Smith, Adam, 1723–90, philosopher and economist.

Smith, Stevie (Florence Margaret), 1902–71, poet and novelist.

Smith, Sydney, 1771–1845, miscellaneous writer.

Smollett, Tobias George, 1721–71, Scottish novelist.

Snow, Baron Charles Percy, 1905–80, novelist.

Somerville, Edith Oenone, 1858–1949, Irish novelist.

Somerville, Mary, 1780–1872, mathematician.

Southerne, Thomas, 1660–1746, dramatist.

Southey, Robert, 1774–1843, poet and biographer.

Southwell, Robert, 1561?–95, poet.

Soyinka, Wole, 1934–, Nigerian dramatist, novelist and critic.

Spark, Dame Muriel, 1918–, novelist.

Speke, John, 1827–64, explorer.

Spelman, Sir Henry, 1564?–1641, historian.

Spencer, Herbert, 1820–1903, philosopher.

Spender, Sir Stephen, 1909–95, poet.

Spenser, Edmund, 1552?–99, poet.

Stanley, Arthur Penrhyn (Dean of Westminster), 1815–81, historian, biographer, and theologian.

Stanley, Sir Henry, 1841–1904, traveller.

Stark, Dame Freya, 1893–1993, travel writer.

Stead, Christina, 1902–83, Australian novelist.

Stead, William Thomas, 1849–1912, journalist.

Steed, Henry Wickham, 1871–1956, journalist.

Steele, Sir Richard, 1672–1729, essayist and dramatist.

Stephen, Sir Leslie, 1832–1904, biographer and critic.

Stephens, James, 1882–1950, Irish story-writer and poet.

Stephens, James Brunton, 1835–1902, Australian poet.

Sterne, Laurence, 1713–68, novelist.

Stevenson, Robert Louis, 1850–94, Scottish novelist and essayist.

Stoker, Bram, 1847–1912, Irish novelist.

Stoppard, Tom, 1937–, dramatist.

Stow, John, 1525?–1605, historian and antiquary.

Strachey, Giles Lytton, 1880–1932, biographer.

Strachey, John St Loe, 1860–1927, critic and biographer.

Strickland, Agnes, 1796–1874, historical writer.

Strong, Leonard Alfred George, 1896–1958, poet and novelist.

Stubbs, William (Bishop), 1825–1901, historian.

Suckling, Sir John, 1609–42, poet.

Surrey, Henry Howard, Earl of, 1517?–47, poet.

Swift, Jonathan (Dean), 1667–1745, satirist.

Swinburne, Algernon Charles, 1837–1909, poet.

Symonds, John Addington, 1840–93, historian, etc.

Symons, Arthur, 1865–1945, poet and symbolist writer.

Synge, John Millington, 1871–1909, Irish dramatist.

Tagore, Sir Rabindranath, 1861–1941, Indian poet.

Tate, Nahum, 1652–1715, poet.

Taylor, Alan John Percival, 1906–1990, historian.

Taylor, Jeremy, 1613–67, essayist.

Taylor, John, 1580–1653, the 'water-poet'.

Temple, Sir William, 1628–99, essayist.

Temple, William (Archbishop), 1881–1944, theologian and philosopher.

Tennyson, Alfred, Lord, 1809–92, poet.

Thackeray, William Makepeace, 1811–63, novelist.

Thomas, Dylan Marlais, 1914–53, Welsh poet.

Thomas, (Philip) Edward, 1878–1917, essayist and poet.

Thomas, Ronald Stuart, 1913–, Welsh poet.

Thompson, Flora Jane, 1876–1947, autobiographical writer.

Thompson, Francis Joseph, 1860–1907, poet.

Thomson, James, 1700–48, Scottish poet.

Thomson, James, ('B.V.'), 1834–82, Scottish poet.

Thrale, See PIOZZI.

Tolkien, John Ronald, 1892–1973, novelist.

Tomlinson, Henry Major, 1873–1958, novelist.

Toynbee, Arnold, 1852–83, economist.

Traherne, Thomas, 1638–74, poet and theological writer.

Tresell, Robert, 1870–1911, Irish-born novelist.

Trevelyan, George Macaulay, 1876–1962, historian.

Trevelyan, Sir George Otto, 1838–1928, historian.

Trevor, William, Anglo-Irish novelist, 1928–.

Trevor-Roper, Hugh (Lord Dacre), 1914–, historian.

Trollope, Anthony, 1815–82, novelist.

Tupper, Martin Farquhar, 1810–89, versifier.

Tutuola, Amos, 1920–, Nigerian short-story writer.

Tynan, Katherine (Mrs Hinkson), 1861–1931, Irish novelist and poet.

Tynan, Kenneth, 1927–80, critic.

Tyndale, William, c. 1490–1536, translator of the Bible.

Udall, Nicholas, 1505–56, dramatist and scholar.

Urquhart, Sir Thomas, 1611–60, Scottish translator of Rabelais.

Usk, Thomas, d. 1388, poet.

Ussher, James, 1581–1656, divine and scholar.

Vachell, Horace Annesley, 1861–1955, novelist.

Vanbrugh, Sir John, 1664–1726, dramatist.

Vaughan, Henry, 1622–95, poet.

Vaux, Thomas, Lord, 1510–56, poet.

Waddell, Helen Jane, 1899–1965, scholar.

Wain, John, 1922–94, novelist.

Walcott, Derek Alton, 1930–, West Indian poet and dramatist.

Waley, Arthur, 1889–1966, orientalist and translator.

Wallace, Edgar, 1875–1932, dramatist and novelist.

Waller, Edmund, 1606–87, poet.

Walpole, Horace, 1717–97, miscellaneous writer.

Walpole, Sir Hugh Seymour, 1884–1941, novelist.

Walsingham, Thomas, d. c. 1422, historian.

Walton, Izaak, 1593–1683, essayist.

Ward, Mrs. Humphry (Mary Arnold), 1851–1920, novelist.

Warton, Joseph, 1722–1800, critic.

Warton, Thomas, 1728–90, historian of English poetry.

Watts, Isaac, 1674–1748, poet and theologian.

Waugh, Evelyn Arthur St John, 1903–66, novelist.

Webb, Beatrice, 1858–1943, economist and political philosopher.

Webb, Mary, 1881–1927, novelist.

Webster, John, 1580?–1625?, dramatist.

Wells, Herbert George, 1866–1946, novelist and writer on sociology.

Wesker, Arnold, 1932–, dramatist.

Wesley, Charles, 1707–88, hymn writer.

Wesley, John, 1703–91, theological writer.

West, Dame Rebecca, 1892–1983, novelist and dramatist.

Whiting, John, d. 1963, dramatist.

White, Antonia, 1899–1979, novelist.

White, Gilbert, 1720–93, naturalist.

White, Patrick Victor Martindale, 1912–1990, Australian novelist.

White, William Hale (Mark Rutherford), 1831–1913, novelist.

Wiclif, or Wycliffe, John, c. 1324–84, translator.

Wilde, Oscar O'Flahertie, 1854–1900, poet and dramatist.

Wilkes, John, 1727–97, journalist, MP.

Wilson, Sir Angus Frank, 1913–91, novelist.

William of Malmesbury, c. 1092–c. 1143, historian.

Williamson, Charles Norris, 1857–1920, novelist.

Williamson, Henry, 1895–1979, novelist.

Winchilsea, Anne Finch, Countess of, 1661–1720, poet.

Wither, George, 1588–1667, poet.

Wodehouse, Sir Pelham (Grenville), 1881–1975, humorist.

Wolfe, Humbert, 1885–1940, poet, critic, and biographer.

Wollstonecraft, Mary, *see* GODWIN.

Wood, Anthony à, 1632–95, antiquarian.

Wood, Ellen (Mrs Henry), 1814–87, novelist.

Woodforde, James, 1740–1803, diarist.

Woolf, Leonard Sidney, 1880–1969, publisher.

Woolf, Virginia, 1882–1941, novelist.

Wordsworth, Dorothy, 1771–1855, diarist.

Wordsworth, William, 1770–1850, poet.

Wotton, Sir Henry, 1568–1639, poet.

Wyatt, Sir Thomas, 1503–42, poet.

Wycherley, William, 1640?–1716, dramatist.

Wyndham, George, 1863–1914, critic.

Wyndham, John, 1903–69, science-fiction writer.

Yates, Edmund, 1831–94, novelist and dramatist.

Yeats, William Butler, 1865–1939, Irish dramatist, poet, and critic.

Yonge, Charlotte Mary, 1823–1901, novelist.

Young, Arthur, 1741–1820, writer on agriculture and travel.

Young, Edward, 1683–1765, poet.

Young, Emily Hilda, 1880–1949, novelist.

Young, Francis Brett, 1884–1954, novelist.

Zangwill, Israel, 1864–1926, novelist and dramatist.

English National Opera Company, began playing in Sadler's Wells theatre, Islington, London, 1931, but on tour 1940–5 while the theatre closed. Reopened after World War II but moved to the Coliseum, 1968. Name changed to E.N.O.C., 1970.

English sovereigns and their consorts. The names of some kings of the English tribes (notably Offa I) are known when they were still in S Jutland, 4thC. Cerdic led the tribe which formed the nucleus of the W Saxon kingdom to England, c. 500, and the 16th King of *Wessex was Egbert, first king of all the English, from whom all subsequent English sovereigns are descended except those in *italics* in the following list:

House of Cerdic

Egbert	802–39	Edmund I	939–46 assassinated
Ethelwulf	839–58	Edred	946–55
Ethelbald	858–60	Edwy	955–59
Ethelbert	860–65	Edgar	959–75
Ethelred I	865–70	Edward the Younger	975–78 assassinated
Alfred the Great	871–99	Ethelred II (the	
Edward the Elder	899–924	Unready)	979–1016
Athelstan	924–39	Edmund II (Ironside)	1016

House of the Skjöldungs or of Denmark

Canute the Great	1016–35	*Harold I* (alone)	1035–40
Harthacanute	1035	*Harthacanute* (again)	1040–42
Harold I			

House of Cerdic (again)

Edward the Confessor 1042–1066

House of Godwin

Harold II 1066 (killed at Hastings)

House of Normandy

Sovereign		Consort
William I (the Conqueror)	1066–78	Matilda of Flanders, *m.* 1053, *d.* 1084
William II (Rufus)	1087–1100	
Henry I	1100–35	1. Matilda of Scotland (grand-daughter of Edmund Ironside), *m.* 1100, *d.* 1119
		2. Adela of Louvain, *m.* 1121, *d.* 1151
Stephen	1135–54	Matilda of Boulogne, *m.* 1124, *d.* 1151

House of Anjou or Plantagenet

Henry II	1154–89	Eleanor of Aquitaine, *m.* 1152, *d.* 1204
Richard I	1189–99	Berengaria of Navarre, *m.* 1191, *d. c.* 1230
John	1199–1216	1. Hadwisa or Avis of Gloucester, *m.* 1189, divorced 1200
		2. Isabel of Angoulême, *m.* 1200, *d.* 1246
Henry III	1216–72	Eleanor of Provence, *m.* 1236, *d.* 1291
Edward I	1272–1307	1. Eleanor of Castile, *m.* 1254, *d.* 1296
		2. Margaret of France, *m.* 1299, *d.* 1308
Edward II (deposed and murdered)	1307–27	Isabella of France, *m.* 1308, *d.* 1358
Edward III	1327–77	Philippa of Hainault *m.* 1328, *d.* 1369
Richard II (deposed and murdered)	1377–99	1. Anne of Bohemia, *m.* 1382, *d.* 1394
		2. Isabella of France, *m.* 1396, *d.* 1409

House of Lancaster

Henry IV	1399–1413	1. Mary de Bohun, *m.* 1380, *d.* 1394
		2. Joan of Navarre, *m.* 1402, *d.* 1437
Henry V	1413–22	Catherine of France, *m.* 1420, *d.* 1437
Henry VI (deposed)	1422–61	Margaret of Anjou, *m.* 1445, *d.* 1482

House of York

Edward IV	1461–70	Elizabeth Woodville, *m.* 1464, *d.* 1492
Henry VI (again)	1470–71	
Edward IV	1471–83	
Edward V (murdered in the Tower)	Apr.–June 1483	
Richard III (killed at battle of Bosworth)	1483–85	Anne Neville, *m.* 1474, *d.* 1485

House of Tudor

Henry VII	1485–1509	Elizabeth of York, *m.* 1486, *d.* 1503
Henry VIII	1509–47	1. Catherine of Aragon, *m.* 1509, divorced 1533, *d.* 1536
		2. Anne Boleyn, *m.* 1533, executed 1536
		3. Jane Seymour, *m.* 1536, *d.* 1537
		4. Anne of Cleves, *m.* Jan. 1540, divorced June 1540, *d.* 1557
		5. Catherine Howard, *m.* 1540, executed 1542
		6. Catherine Parr, *m.* 1543, *d.* 1548
Edward VI	1547–53*	
Mary I and Philip (1554)	1553–58	Philip II of Spain, *m.* 1554, *d.* 1598
Elizabeth I	1558–1603	

* Lady Jane Grey was proclaimed queen and 'ruled' for 10 days in 1553, but was never crowned, and was subsequently beheaded.

House of Stuart

James I	1603–25	Anne of Denmark, *m.* 1589, *d.* 1619
Charles I (beheaded)	1625–49	Henrietta Maria of France, *m.* 1625, *d.* 1669

Commonwealth and Protectorate 1649–60

Charles II	1660–85	Catherine of Braganza, *m.* 1662, *d.* 1705
James II (fled)	1685–88	1. Anne Hyde, *m.* 1660, *d.* 1671
		2. Mary of Modena, *m.* 1673, *d.* 1718
William III* and Mary II	1689–94	*m.* 1677
William III alone	1694–1702	
Anne	1702–44	George of Denmark, *m.* 1683, *d.* 1708

† William III, whose mother was a Stuart, was himself a member of the House of Orange.

House of Hanover

George I	1714–27	Sophia of Brunswick, *m.* 1682, *d.* 1726
George II	1727–60	Caroline of Ansbach, *m.* 1705, *d.* 1737

George III	1760–1820	Charlotte of Mecklenburg-Strelitz, *m.* 1761, *d.* 1818
George IV	1820–30	Caroline of Brunswick, *m.* 1795, *d.* 1821
William IV	1830–37	Adelaide of Saxe-Meiningen, *m.* 1818, *d.* 1849
Victoria	1837–1901	Albert of Saxe-Coburg, *m.* 1840, *d.* 1861

House of Saxe-Coburg, Gotha

Edward VII	1901–10	Alexandra of Denmark, *m.* 1863, *d.* 1925

*House of Windsor**

George V	1910–36	Mary of Teck, *m.* 1893, *d.* 1953
Edward VIII (abdicated)	36	Mrs Ernest Simpson (Duchess of Windsor) *m.* 1936.
George VI	1936–52	Lady Elizabeth Bowes-Lyon, *m.* 1923.
Elizabeth II†	1952–	Philip Mountbatten, Duke of Edinburgh, *m.* 1947

* George V renounced the surname of Saxe-Coburg-Gotha and adopted that of Windsor for himself and his descendants in 1917.

† Heir to the throne (1995) is the Prince of Wales, Charles Philip Arthur George, *b.* 1948, *m.* Lady Diana Frances Spencer, 1981 (separated, 1992) and has issue William Arthur Philip Louis, *b.* 21 June, 1982 and Henry (Harry) Charles Albert David, *b.* 15 Sept. 1984.

See also the separate kingdoms for the period before 802, viz. BERNICIA, DEIRA, EAST ANGLIA, ESSEX, KENT, MERCIA, SUSSEX, WESSEX.

---

engraving on metal and stone. First metal plate from which impressions on paper were taken apparently executed, 1452. Early books with metal engravings, the *Kalender*, 1465, and the *Monte Santo di Dio*, 1477. First specialist in engraving, Marcantonio Raimondi (1475–1530). In England the earliest line engravings are in *The Birth of Mankind*, 1540. Earliest English engraver known by name, William Rogers (*fl.* 1580–1610). Mezzotint process invented by Ludwig von Siegen *c.* 1642. Introduced into England, 1660, by Prince Rupert, who had seen Siegen at work. Aquatints said to have been invented by Saint-Non (1730–1804) and first used in England, 1780. Lithography invented by Aloys Senefelder, 1796. *See* ARTS.

engraving on wood. Practised by Chinese some centuries BC. Modern process, however, dates from 15thC, earliest dated example (1423) being at Memminingen (Germany). Caxton's second edition of *The Game and Playe of the Chesse*, 1476, contains earliest English woodcuts. The art was revolutionized by Albrecht Dürer (1471–1528) of Nürnberg. In England George, Edward, John and Thomas Dalziel were very active from 1839 till process blocks began to supersede engraving *c.* 1879.

Enosis. Campaign for the union of Cyprus with Greece, originated, 1912, and continued until the establishment of the Republic of *Cyprus in 1960.

ensign, military rank in British infantry units, was superseded by the term second lieutenant, 1871.

ensign, national flag flown by shipping, is worn according to a convention adopted in 1864.

Entente Cordiale between England and France (partly brought about by the exertions of King Edward VII) and Anglo-French Agreement signed, 8 Apr. 1904.

environment. Protection of the E. of increasing concern in second half of 20thC, notably in Western countries. Government department of the E. established in Britain, 1970, but legislation to safeguard the E. pre-dates this. UN involvement typified by Conference on Human Settlements, 1976, and by Conference on Environment and Development (*'Earth Summit') held in Brazil in 1992. EC also concerned with E. and 1987 was European Year of the E. Recent British legislation concerned with E. includes the Control of Pollution Act, 1974; Wildlife and Countryside Act, 1981; the Environmental Protection Act, 1990 and the E. Act, 1994. New E. Protection Agencies proposed, 1994. *See also* CONSERVATION; ECOLOGY etc.

Environment, Department of, established 1970, then combining former ministries dealing with housing, planning and ancient monuments. The last-named one now (1995) the responsibility of *English Heritage and the Department of *National Heritage.

EOKA. Cypriot guerrilla force organized 1954, to fight for *Enosis. Disbanded, 1960.

Ephesus, Asia Minor. Founded *c.* 1000 BC. Fell under Lydian domination, 6thC. The Artemisium or Temple of Artemis, founded *c.* 750 BC; sacked by Cimmerii *c.* 650; rebuilt *c.* 545–425 in the form which was one of the *Seven Wonders of the World. Destroyed by Herostratus, 356 BC, but restored shortly after. E. became the administrative capital of the Roman province of Asia *c.* 140 BC, was visited by St Paul (*see* Acts) *c.* AD 56. Temple destroyed by the Goths in AD 263. Church councils held at E., 197, 245, 431, 446, 447, 449.

Epirus, Greece. Rose to prominence for a short period during the wars of its King Pyrrhus against the Romans, which ended 275 BC.

Episcopal Church of the USA. *See* PROTESTANT EPISCOPAL CHURCH.

Episcopal Ordination Act (Scotland). Passed, 1662.

Epping Forest. Ancient royal forest bought and opened to the public by the City of London, 1882.

Epsom (Surrey). Sulphate of magnesia springs discovered, 1618. Races run at E. from about 1620. *Derby Day takes place there.

Equal Opportunities Commission, established 1975, as a result of the passing of the Sex Discrimination Act, 1974. Baroness Lockwood being its first chairman. There is an equivalent body for N Ireland. The E.O.C. has campaigned to enforce the Equal Pay Act, 1970, whose scope was extended, 1984, to meet the more stringent requirements of the European Commission.

Equatorial Guinea, as **Spanish Guinea** acquired by Spain at end of 18thC. Became independent, 1968. Marxist 1968–79 but subsequent military coup re-established economic links with Spain. New constitution, 1982; elections, 1989. Elections, 1993, largely boycotted.

Erastians. A religious sect following the teachings of Erastus (1524–83). Their ideas advocated at Westminster Assembly, 1643–9.

Erfurt, Germany. Bishopric, 741; ceded to the Elector of Mainz, 1648. Luther lived in the monastery of St Augustine, 1508–11. Incorporated into Prussia, 1802. Brandt, Chancellor of the Federal Democratic Republic and Stoph, premier of the German Democratic Republic, met at E., March 1970.

Erie Canal (USA), opened 1817.

ERM. *See* EXCHANGE RATE MECHANISM.

Eros, statue erected in Piccadilly Circus, London, 1893, to commemorate the philanthropist, the 7th Earl of Shaftesbury (1801–85). Restored; 1985; repaired, 1992/3.

Eritrea. Italians purchased Assab, 1870. Occupied Massawa, 1885. Province of E. organized, 1890. Amalgamated with Ethiopia in Italian E Africa, 9 May 1936. British invasion begins, Dec. 1940. Under British Military administration, 1941–8. E. pronounced integral part of Ethiopia, 1962, but Eritrean agitation against this, 1966 onwards. E.'s right to seek independence recognized by new Ethiopian government 1991. After referendum, independence proclaimed, 24 May 1993. *See* ETHIOPIA.

Erzurum, Turkey. Citadel founded *c.* 415 by Theodosius the Younger. Taken by Turks, 1517. By Russians, 1829 and 1878. Armenians massacred at, 1895 and 1915. Captured by Russians, Mar. 1916. Abandoned on Communist orders, Jan. 1918. Reoccupied by Turks, Mar. 1918.

Escheat. Abolished in England, 1925.

Escorial or **Escurial, royal establishment** outside Madrid consisting of palace, church, monastery and college within a single precinct, founded by Philip II of Spain, 23 Apr. 1563. Charles V's remains conveyed there, 1574. Building completed, 1584. Philip II *d.* there, 1598.

Esperanto. International language, invented, 1887, by Dr L. Zamenhof, a Warsaw oculist (1859–1917).

Essex, Kingdom of. Established by the E Saxons *c.* 6thC. There was not always one ruler, power and territory being sometimes divided, though the kings were of a common dynasty. Between *c.* 600 and 824 the names of 15 kings are known. As an independent kingdom it came to an end *c.* 830, and was ceded by Wessex to the Danish kings of E Anglia under the Treaty of *Wedmore, 878.

Essex University, established at Colchester, 1964.

estate duty (UK). First levied, 1894, on real property. Abolished, 1975, and replaced by *Capital Transfer Tax.

Estates, Committee of the. Appointed by Scots Parliament, 1640–8.

Este, Italy. Dukes of became dukes of *Reggio and *Modena, 1452 and of Ferrara, 1471. Family of the Estensi died out in Italy, 1803.

Estonia, Republic of. Two branches of the Finnish group of tribes originating on the Upper Volga – the Ests and the Livs – were settled respectively N and W of the Gulf of Riga by the beginning of the Christian era. The Russians from Novgorod built a fort at Tartu, in E., 1036. Danes under Bishop Albert of Riga, who founded Reval, conquered E., 1219. They sold their gains to the *Teutonic Knights, 1346, who amalgamated E. with Livonia. After dissolution of the Teutonic Order, 1560, northern E. passed to Sweden while southern E. went first to Poland until 1629, thence to Sweden, which ceded the whole country to Russia, 1720. Independent republic proclaimed, 24 Feb. 1918. Russian forces marched into E., 18 June 1940, and E. joined the USSR, as a constituent republic, 6 Aug. The Germans invaded E., Aug. 1941, and remained in occupation of the country, which became part of 'Ostland', 17 Nov. 1941, until ejected by Soviet troops, Feb. 1945. Nationalist movement gained force throughout 1980s; in 1988 E. was declared 'autonomous'. After collapse of Soviet regime, 1989 onwards, E. became fully independent, 20 Aug. 1991. Unrest among and discrimination against Russian minority in E. since 1991. Last Russian troops leave, 1994.

Estonia, roll-on, roll-off car ferry and passenger ship, lost in heavy seas in Baltic, 28 Sept. 1994, on voyage from Estonia to Sweden with loss of over 900 lives. Worst civilian shipping disaster in Europe since loss of *Titanic in 1912. Resulted in car-ferry door checks and decision of Scandinavian shipping companies to seal bow doors of such ferries.

ETA, name of Basque extremist separatist organization, aiming to achieve a separate Basque state, if necessary by terrorist violence. It has bases in both the Spanish and French areas of the Basque country, but since 1968 its main battleground has been on the Spanish side of the frontier, where it has been responsible for bombings and assassinations in several parts of Spain. Spanish legislation in 1979 which established considerable autonomy in Spain's Basque region, did not satisfy ETA. ETA plot to assassinate King Juan Carlos failed, Aug. 1995. *See also* BASQUES.

Etaples, Treaty of, between Henry VII of England and Charles VIII of France, 3 Nov. 1492.

etching. First E., on iron by Albrecht Dürer *c*. 1500. *See* ENGRAVING.

ether (physics). *See* AETHER.

ether (chemistry). Faraday (1791–1867) discovered its soporific qualities, 1818. First used as an anaesthetic, 1846.

Ethiopia or **Abyssinia.** Former royal house claimed descent from Solomon and the Queen of Sheba. Kingdom of Axum *fl.* 1st–7thC. Christianity introduced by St Frumentius *c*. AD 330. El-Esbaha conquered Yemen, 525–75. Revolution and country divided between Axum and Shoa, 1000. Reunited under the Solomonean dynasty by Tekuno Amtak, 1268. Arrival of the Portuguese Pedro de Covilha, 1490. Jesuit attempt at conversion of Copts to Roman Catholicism ends in expulsion of Portuguese by King Fasilidas, 1633. Victory of Kassai of Amhara at Gorgora, 1853. He proclaims himself Emperor as Theodore III, 1853. Defeat by British and suicide of Theodore at Magdala, 1868. Kassai of Tigré proclaimed Emperor as John I, 1872–89. Emperor Menelek (1889–1913) defeats Italians at Adowa, 1896. Regency of Empress Zauditu and Ras Tafari, 1916–30. Tafari becomes Emperor as Haile Selassie, 1930. Italian conquest of E., Oct. 1935–May 1936. Reconquest by British and Haile Selassie begun, Jan. 1941. Completed, Nov. 1941. Federation with Eritrea became effective, Sept. 1952; Eritrea fully integrated, 1962. Haile Selassie granted a more liberal Constitution on his Silver Jubilee, 1955. Haile Selassie deposed, 1974, and a left-wing republic established. Haile Selassie died in captivity, 1975. In 1977

Mengistu led a Marxist coup. Years of terror and civil war followed and a prolonged drought exacerbated the consequent famine in which millions *d.*, despite international aid. Mengistu overthrown, 1991 and a more moderate regime followed. Eritrean independence achieved from and recognized by E., May 1993. Former Ethiopian leaders, including Mengistu, put on trial in E. accused of genocide, etc., Dec. 1994.

Etna, Sicily. 10,952 ft/3323 m. Several serious eruptions since 476 BC. These include eruptions in 125 and 43 BC, and in AD 1169 (when Catania was overwhelmed), 1444, 1537, 1553, 1669 (when a 12-ft/3.5-m abyss was opened up in the mountainside), 1830, 1852, 1879, 1892, 1899, 1910, 1923, 1928, 1971, 1981, 1983, 1985 and 1992.

ethnic cleansing, term became prominent from 1991, when Serb forces in *Bosnia-Herzegovina alleged to have driven Muslim communities from areas occupied by Muslims for centuries, and engaged in murder and atrocities. Term later used to describe racial violence between Hutus and Tutsis in *Rwanda, notably in 1994, when thousands died: also E.C. by Croats against Serbs in Krajina alleged, Aug. 1995.

Eton College (England). Founded, 1440, for poor scholars, by Henry VI and William of Waynflete. Supplementary charter, 1441, when buildings were commenced. Mutinies took place, 1743, 1768, 1783, 1810 and 1832. Prince William at, from 1995.

Etruria, Italy. Inhabited by a people speaking a non-Indo-European language, who may have come from Asia some time before 800 BC and who probably supplied the Tarquin kings to Rome in 7thC BC. Finally conquered by Cornelius Dolabella, 283 BC. Received Roman franchise, 91 BC.

Euboea or **Negropont,** Greece. Struggle between Chalcis and Eretria for leadership of, 8thC. Euboean colonies founded in Chalcidice 8th and 7thC BC. In Sicily and Italy, 760–648. Eretria assists Ionian revolt against Persia, 499. Eretria sacked by Persians, 490. Athenian colony at Histiaea,

445. Athenian influence shaken off, 404. Joins Athenian confederation again, 357. Submits to Macedon, 336; to Rome, 146. Seized by Venetians, AD 1204. Conquered by Turks, 1470. Becomes Greek, 1832.

Euratom. *See* EUROPEAN ATOMIC ENERGY COMMUNITY.

Eureka Stockade. *See* BALLARAT.

European Association. Founded in London by Mazzini and others to promote republicanism in Europe, 1855.

European Atomic Energy Community (Euratom). Constituted, 1 Jan. 1958, to promote a powerful nuclear industry for peaceful purposes among members of the European (Economic) Community.

European Bank for Reconstruction and Development. This was proposed by President Mitterand of France, 1989, to help in the financial and economic reconstruction of the former Communist states of central and Eastern Europe. Inaugurated in London, 15 April 1991, with Attali of France as its first president (resigned July 1993).

EC. *See* EUROPEAN COMMUNITY.

European Central Bank, due to be established by 1 January 1999 under the terms of the *Maastricht Treaty. (1992).

European Coal and Steel Community (ECSC). Established, 10 Aug. 1952, to pool the European (Economic) Community countries' resources of coal, iron, and steel in a single market.

European Commission. Important arm of the *European Community or *Union. Originally the ECSC, Euratom and the EEC each had its own commission, but these merged into one, the E.C., 1 July 1967. Commissioners are nominated by the various member states of the European Union and have extensive powers. Jacques Delors (France) president of the E.C. 1975–94; succeeded by Jacques Santer (Luxemburg), 1995. It is based in Brussels. Commission enlarged, Oct. 1994.

European Community (EC) Term used increasingly from mid-1980s to embrace *ECSC, *Euratom and the *EEC, though strictly not replacing the term European Economic Community until all 12 signatory governments had ratified the Maastricht Treaty of 1992, which (*see* MAASTRICHT), marked high point of European Community centralism. For history before 1986 *see* European Economic Community. *Single European Act signed 1986, became effective, 1987. Single European Market in being, 1 Jan. 1993. Maastricht Treaty finally ratified by all signatories, Oct. 1993. EC *Common Agricultural Policy radically reformed, 1992. *Blair House Agreement, 1992, between EC negotiators and USA, to promote completion of GATT Uruguay Round (Dec. 1993). Increased EC links with Eastern Europe from 1989 onwards. Several countries, e.g. Austria, Cyprus, Malta, Norway, applied to join EC, 1993. Reunification of Germany and recession in Europe and USA put increasing strains on EC, typified by financial crisis of July 1993 which resulted in EC's future economic and political timetable being called into question. From Nov. 1993 term EC being replaced by *European Union.

European Court of Auditors, established Oct. 1977. It is responsible for ensuring the sound financial management of the *European Community and its allied and dependent bodies, and is based in Luxemburg. Heavily criticised EU for tolerance of large-scale fraud, Nov. 1994.

European Court of Human Rights, established, 1959, as a consequence of the European Convention on Human Rights, 1950, by the *Council of Europe. The European Commission of Human Rights, in Strasbourg, investigates complaints brought by individuals, bodies or governments. The court's findings are binding on both parties. Britain condemned by court, Sept. 1995, for SAS 1988 killing of three IRA suspect terrorists in Gibraltar.

European Court of Justice, with headquarters in Luxemburg, dates from the Treaty of Rome, 1957, and exists to interpret the European Community's laws and rule on breaches of those laws. A Court of First Instance established, 1988. In 1991 the C. of J. had over 300 new cases brought before it and delivered 204 judgments.

European Defence Community (EDC). Proposed defensive federation of France, Belgium, Italy, Luxemburg, the Netherlands and the German Federal Republic. Treaty establishing EDC signed, May 1952, but the French National Assembly rejected it, 30 Aug. 1954, and it was subsequently superseded by the defence arrangements made under the *London and *Paris agreements.

Eurodisney, theme park in Maine-la-Vallée, France, opened Apr. 1992 and covering nearly 140 acres.

European Economic Area, comprising states of the European Union and of the *European Free Trade Area (apart from Switzerland) came into being, 1 Jan. 1994.

European Economic Community (EEC), formerly popularly known as the **Common Market**. Came into being 1 Jan. 1958, following ratification of the Treaty of Rome (signed 25 Mar. 1957). Original members ('The Six') were: Belgium, France, Federal Germany, Italy, Luxemburg and the Netherlands. Aim: to eliminate the traditional economic frontiers between member states by gradual abolition of customs barriers and adoption of common policies on agriculture, transport and commerce. Some kind of eventual political unity vaguely envisaged. The Six were also members of the European Coal and Steel Community (ECSC) established 1952 and the European Atomic Energy Community (Euratom) established 1958. Britain formally applied for membership, 10 Aug. 1961 but on 29 Jan. 1963 talks on Britain's entry broke down, due to French pressure. The Commissions of the EEC, Euratom and the ECSC merged, 1 July 1967. Negotiations for Britain's entry restarted, 1970. In 1973

Britain, Ireland and Denmark joined the EEC, public referenda declaring in favour; but Norway remained outside, after a referendum against entry. Removal of trade barriers with European Free Trade Area begun, 1973. Greece joined EEC, 1981. Britain reached agreement on Budget deficit, 1984. Spain and Portugal joined EEC, 1 Jan. 1986. Since 1984, when the *European Parliament approved the treaty establishing the European Union, and the Single European Act (signed 1986; in force from 1 July 1987) the term *European Community was increasingly used to embrace EEC, Euratom, and the ECSC, although strictly it did not replace EEC as the collective term until all 12 signatories had (Oct. 1993) ratified the Maastricht Treaty. (*see* MAASTRICHT) *See further under* EUROPEAN COMMUNITY; EUROPEAN UNION.

European Football Championships. *See* UEFA.

European Free Trade Association (EFTA). Founded 1960, when membership consisted of Austria, Denmark, Norway, Portugal, Sweden, Switzerland and the UK. Finland associated with EFTA, 27 Mar. 1961: Iceland from 1970. UK and Denmark left EFTA, 1973, on joining the *European Economic Community, and after Portugal joined the EEC in 1986 membership in 1993 consisted of Austria, Iceland, Norway, Sweden, Switzerland and Finland, with Liechtenstein an associate member since 1991. All members except Switzerland joined European Economic Area, 1 Jan. 1994. Membership subsequently modified, 1995, after Austria, Finland and Sweden voted to join the EU.

European Investment Bank (EIB), established 1958 under the Treaty of Rome, with headquarters in Luxemburg. Its purpose is to finance capital investment projects within the EC, ensuring the Community's steady development along planned lines.

European Monetary System (EMS) was formed in 1977 and consists of an *Exchange Rate Mechanism (ERM), a

European Currency (see ECU) and expanded short and medium-term credit facilities. Britain participated in it from its foundation but did not join the ERM until Oct. 1990. Britain left the ERM, Sept. 1992, when the pound was devalued. The Maastricht Treaty (see MAASTRICHT) provided for the introduction of a single European currency by 1 Jan. 1999 but after the financial crisis of July 1993 this timing increasingly called in question.

European Monetary Institute. It was announced, Oct. 1993 that this would be based in Frankfurt.

European Monetary Union. In June 1995 European Union ministers agree that EMU could not take place before 1999.

European Organization for European Research (CERN), with headquarters in Geneva, was established in 1954.

European Parliament, originated from the Assembly of the *European Coal and Steel Community. It became the European Parliamentary Assembly, based in Strasbourg, 1958. Name change to E.P., 1962. Members were originally nominated but the first direct elections to the E.P. took place in 1979; subsequent elections, 1984, 1989, 1994. Influence of the E.P. has increased since the *Single European Act extended its powers. It had a Socialist majority in 1995.

European Space Agency, established 31 May 1975 as the result of a merger between the European Space Research Organization and the European Launcher Organization. It is based in Paris and aims at the implementation of a united European space policy.

European Union (EU), term increasingly applied after 1 Nov. 1993 to the body also known as the *Common Market, the *European Economic Community and the *European Community. Gave cool reception to Delors plan for massive borrowing to promote jobs within the EU, Dec. 1993; in same month signed joint declaration of cooperation and partnership with Yeltsin of Russia (9 Dec.) and on 14 Dec. agreed deal with USA which opened door to *GATT agreement the following day. *European Economic Area created 1 Jan. 1994. Britain finally accepts dilution of voting rights, Mar. 1994 but vetoes Dehaen (Belgium) as Delors' successor, June: Santer (Luxemburg) eventually chosen, July. Germany raises 'two-speed Europe' issue, Sept.; Commission enlarged Oct. On 1 Jan. 1995 Austria, Finland, Sweden join EU, after referenda in favour; Norway, however, again voted (Dec. 1994) against membership. EU's efforts towards peace settlement in *Bosnia-Herzegovina 1991–5. Political crisis in Britain regarding increased British payments to EU, Nov. 1994; EU lifted eight-year trade embargo with Syria, Nov. 1994. Trade agreement signed with Russia, July 1995. Heads of EU governments' meeting, in Majorca, Sept. 1995, showed wide differences.

Europol. It was announced, Oct. 1993, that this organization, which will coordinate cross-border police cooperation within the EU is to be based at The Hague.

Eurotunnel, see CHANNEL TUNNEL

Eurovision. Direct television link-up between various European countries. Developed after 1953, when the BBC coverage of Elizabeth II's coronation was relayed successfully to Western Europe. See TELEVISION.

Euston Station, London. Doric arch, a landmark, at entrance, demolished, 1962: in 1994 an attempt made to find ruins.

euthanasia, or 'mercy killing', given some legal standing in the Netherlands since 1983. This considerably increased by parliamentary vote, Feb. 1993. Not so far permitted elsewhere in W, and House of Lords ruled against legalization of E., Feb. 1994.

Evacuation (UK) of mothers and children from danger areas before World War II began, 1 Sept. 1939.

Evacuation Day (New York, USA). Anniversary of the British evacuation of New York, 25 Nov. 1783.

Evangelical Alliance of German protestant states, 1608, opposed by Holy Alliance (founded 1609).

Evangelical Alliance, World's. Founded in London, 1846.

Evangelic League. Founded by certain Lutherans and Calvinists against the Emperor Mathias, 1613.

Evans Case. Timothy Evans was hanged for the murder of his baby daughter at 10 Rillington Place, London, in 1950. Subsequently John Christie, of the same address, was executed (1953) after confessing to the murder of several women, including Mrs. Evans. First inquiry into Evans's case, 1953, found that Evans killed both his wife and child. Second inquiry, 1965–6, reported that Evans probably did not kill his child, but possibly killed his wife. Evans's body reinterred in consecrated ground, 1965, and Evans granted a posthumous free pardon, Oct. 1966. Case and its aftermath influenced the campaign for the abolition of capital punishment in Britain (1965, and, permanently, 1969). *See also* TRIALS AND CAUSES CÉLÈBRES.

Evening News. See NEWSPAPERS.

Evening Standard. See NEWSPAPERS.

Everest, Mount, world's highest mountain (29,108 ft/8872 m as measured by satellite) in the Himalayas. First climbed by Hillary and Tensing, 29 May 1953. First woman to reach summit, Junko Tabei, 16 May 1975. First man on summit without oxygen, Reinhold Messner, 8 May 1978; first woman, Alison Hargreaves, 13 May 1995 (killed in K2 avalanche later same year).

Everyman's Library. Early popular selection of the classics, first published by J. M. Dent & Sons Ltd in 1906.

Evian Conference on refugees, 6–15 July 1938.

Evian Agreement, between France and the Algerian nationalists to end the civil war in Algeria and acknowledge Algeria's independence, signed 18 Mar. 1962.

Evil May Day. 1 May 1517. A riot of London apprentices which arose out of complaints against foreigners and the consequent conspiracy of 30 Apr. 1517.

Evora, Convention of, ended Portuguese civil war, 1834.

Exarch.
1. (of Ravenna). Title of the Byzantine governor of Italy, 584–782.
2. Title of the Patriarch of the Bulgarian orthodox church instituted, 1876.

Excess Profits Duty. Imposed Sept. 1915 to Mar. 1921.

Excess Profits Tax. Imposed 3 Sept. 1939. Abolished 1 Jan. 1954.

Exchange Rate Mechanism (ERM), intended to control exchange rates within the *European Monetary System in which EU currencies are held within prescribed bands. Instituted, 1977. Britain joined, 1990: left, 1992. ERM considerably weakened by financial turmoil from 1991 on and future form in doubt after crisis in July 1993 forced bands to be widened to 15%.

Exchange, Royal (London). Founded by Sir Thomas Gresham, 7 June 1566. Queen Elizabeth I visited it, Jan. 1571, since when it has been called 'Royal'. Burnt, 1666. Rebuilt by Edward German, 1668. Burnt again, 1838. Present building, 1840–4.

Exchequer. Originally part of the *Council, it was already a separate department by reign of Henry II (1154–89), and also distinct from the court of the same name (*see* COURTS). Chancellor of E. office founded, 1221. E. Office founded, 1399. Chancellor of the E.'s judicial functions ceased to exist after 1735. E. and Audit Department instituted, 1866.

Chancellors of the Exchequer since 1924:
Philip Snowden 1924
Winston S. Churchill 1924–29
Philip Snowden 1929–31
Neville Chamberlain 1931–37
Sir John Simon 1937–40

Sir Kingsley Wood 1940–43
Sir John Anderson 1943–45
Hugh Dalton 1945–47
Sir Stafford Cripps 1947–50
Hugh Gaitskell 1950–51
R. A. Butler 1951–55
Harold Macmillan 1955–57
Peter Thorneycroft 1957–58
Derek Heathcoat-Amory 1958–60
Selwyn Lloyd 1960–62
Reginald Maudling 1962–64
James Callaghan 1964–67
Roy Jenkins 1967–70
Iain Macleod 1970
Anthony Barber 1970–74
Denis Healey 1974–79
Sir Geoffrey Howe 1979–83
Nigel Lawson 1983–89
John Major 1989–90
Norman Lamont 1990–93
Kenneth Clarke 1993–

Exchequer, Court of the. *See* COURTS.

excise (UK). Introduced by Long Parliament, 1643. Sir R. Walpole fails to pass a new E. scheme owing to strong opposition, 1733. Board of Inland Revenue founded, 1849. Transferred to control of the Board of Customs and E., 1909.

excise (USA). E. bill on liquor introduced into Congress, 1791. Caused rioting, 1794.

Exclusion Bill to disable the Duke of York (later James II) as a Roman Catholic from succeeding to the throne, introduced, 1679. It was passed three times by the House of Commons, but on each occasion Charles II dissolved Parliament.

Exeter, England. Originally *Isca Dumnoniorum* and a Roman military station. Known to the W Welsh as **Caer Wisc**. Sacked by Sweyn, King of Denmark, 1003. Made a bishopric, 1050. Retaken by William the Conqueror after a rising in the W, 1068. Cathedral begun, 1112. E. school established, 1629. Captured by Prince Maurice, 1643. Retaken by Fairfax, 1646. The University College of the SW

(incorporated 1922) was created University of E., 1955.

Exeter Book. Leofric, Bishop of E. from 1050 to 1071, gave this book to the cathedral library. Written before 1050, first transcribed, 1831, first printed, 1842.

Exhibition of 1851, The Great (London). Royal Commission appointed and building begun in Hyde Park, 3 Jan. 1850. Opened by Queen Victoria, 1 May 1851. *See* CRYSTAL PALACE.

Exile, known in British law as *Transportation.

existentialism, as a philosophy, was expressed in *Sein und Zeit* by Martin Heidegger, 1926; *Gegenwart: eine Kritische Ethik* by E. Grisebach, 1928; *Philosophie*, by Karl Jaspers, 1932; and from *c*. 1940, but especially since 1944, by the plays of Jean-Paul Sartre (1905–80). E. was condemned by the Pope, 1948.

extradition laws. Court of Exchequer declared a form of E.L., 1749. Ashburton Treaty with USA, 1842; extended, 1890. With France, 1843. Present procedure in Great Britain based on the E. Acts of 1870–3 and the amendments of 1906 and 1932. Modified in practice by other legislation e.g., Misuse of Drugs Act, 1971; Hijacking Act, 1971; British Nationality Act, 1982; Taking of Hostages Act, 1982 and The Child Abduction Act, 1984.

Eyre, Lake, Australia. Discovered by Edward E. (1815–1901) in 1840.

Eyre, Commissions of General. (Latin *Iter*.) Bodies of commissioners were sent round the kingdom at intervals to investigate the working of the Government and redress grievances, etc. Instituted by Henry II (1154–89). Henry III (1216–72) compelled to promise that they would not be held more often than once in seven years. Famous E. of Cornwall, 1221. E. of Kent, 1313, lasted a year. Declined in reign of Edward III (1327–77), disappeared under Richard II (1377–99).

Fabian Society. An intellectual society of non-revolutionary Socialists, founded in London, 1884, profoundly influenced by G.B. Shaw and the Webbs.

facsimile transmission, *see* FAX.

Factory Acts. First F. Act introduced by Sir Robert Peel the Elder passed, 1802, providing for F. inspectors. Second F. Act, 1819, relating to cotton mills. Sir Robert Peel's F. Act, 1844, provided a 10-hour limit for women and children. Mining Act, 1842, forbade female and child labour in mines. F. Act extension and Workshop Regulation Acts, 1867, included all Fs. in the previous Acts. Later important F. A. included those of 1901, 1911 and 1937. Present law based on F. A. of 1961, and subsequent amendments and on the Health and Safety at Work Act, 1974, which established the Health and Safety Executive.

Faenza, Italy. 'Faïence' pottery manufactured at since the end of 13thC.

Faeroe. *See* FAROE.

Fahrenheit scale. Temperature divisions invented *c.* 1712 by G.D. Fahrenheit (1686–1736). Popularly used in Britain until the 1960s, but then largely superseded by Centigrade and Celsius.

Fair Isle, the most probable identification of the island known to the ancients as *Thule*; mentioned by Pytheas (300 BC), whose description would fit the F.I., and by Ptolemy, AD 150. For the rest of its history, *see* SHETLAND ISLANDS.

Fair Trading Act, 1973, established an Office of a Director General for Fair Trading and a Consumer Protection Advisory Committee. The Act covered monopolies and mergers, pyramid selling and trade descriptions. *See also* OFFICE OF FAIR TRADING.

Falaise, France. Treaty of, between Henry II of England, his son Henry, and Louis VII of France, 1174. Besieged by Henry V of England, 1417. Captured from English, 1450. Scene of the celebrated 'gap' in the Normandy battle through which the German troops escaped, 7–22 Aug. 1944.

Falangists, member of the Falange Español, founded by José Antonio Primo de Rivera (1903–1930), 29 Oct. 1933, were Fascists of the radical type. On the outbreak of the civil war the F. leader was in Government hands, having been arrested, 15 Mar. 1936. He was executed at Alicante, 20 Nov. 1936. Franco took over the leadership officially, 1938. At the end of the civil war (1939) they were the only political party tolerated in Spain; dissolved, 1966.

Falashas. *See* TIGRE.

Falciu, Romania. Peace between Russia and Turkey, 1711.

Falkland Islands (Spanish, **Islas Malvinas**), British Crown colony. Discovered by John Davis, 1592. French settlement existed, 1764. Partly taken by British, 1765. Ceded by France to Spain, 1767. Spain yielded by convention, 1771. Argentine settlement, 1829. New British settlement, 1833, and Argentinians expelled. Naval battle between British and Germans, 8 Dec. 1914. Argentine claims to became increasingly vocal 1946 onwards. In 1964 the UN recommended Britain and Argentina to seek a peaceful solution to the problem. Inconclusive Anglo-Argentine talks followed in 1970s, foundering on islanders' desire to remain British.

Falkland Islands War, 1982:
19 Mar. – Over 50 Argentine troops landed on S Georgia.

2 Apr. – Argentine invasion of F.I. British marines outnumbered and surrendered.

5 Apr. – British task force sails from UK; British Foreign Secretary, Lord Carrington, resigns.

25 Apr. – British recapture S Georgia.

30 Apr. – US orders sanctions against Argentina following peace talks breakdown.

2 May – Argentine cruiser *Belgrano* sunk by Navy; 4 May, HMS *Sheffield* sunk by Argentine Exocets.

21 May – British invade main F.I. and establish beachhead at San Carlos.

28 May – Darwin and Goose Green recaptured.

14 June – Ceasefire; Argentine general Menendez surrenders nearly 10,000 troops.

Governor returned to F.I., 25 June 1982. Subsequently measures taken to increase financial aid to F.I.; to grant all islanders British citizenship; and to build international airport (opened 1985). New constitution, 1985: Britain reiterated then and subsequently that F.I. sovereignty not negotiable. 1987: conservation zone round F.I., and licensing of vessels to fish within this zone, Feb. 1987. Improved relations with Argentina from 1983 onwards: in Dec. 1992 British and Argentine governments signed agreement to preserve F.I. fish stocks. Geological surveys, 1993, indicated massive oil reserves in sea around F.I. Oct. 1994: President Menem of Argentina offered individual payments to islanders who would agree some form of Argentine sovereignty; this rejected. Anglo-Argentine agreement on oil exploration in S Atlantic, Sept. 1995.
See also ARGENTINA.

family allowances, first provided in Manitoba, Canada, 1915. In France, 1932. F.A. Act in Great Britain became law, 15 June 1945; name later changed to **Child Benefit**.

Family Compact. Name given to three agreements between the French and Spanish branches of the House of *Bourbon. (1) 1733, between Louis XV and Philip V

against English commerce. (2) Treaty of perpetual alliance signed at Fontainebleau, 25 Oct. 1743; (3) 15 Aug. 1761.

Family Law Reform Act, 1969. *See* AGE.

famines. Have occurred since Biblical times and before. There were severe but localized F. in Europe during the 14th, 15th, 16th and 17thC caused by crop failures, droughts, wars and pestilences. In India, a serious famine occurred under the Moguls in the 17thC. Some attempt to measure F. since the 18thC and those of spectacular dimensions include the following (figure given indicates approximate deaths):

Bihar and Bengal areas of India, 1769–70: possibly 10 million

Ireland, potato famine 1854–8: 500,000 died, over one million emigrated

India, 1876–8: about five million

N China, 1876–9: nine–13 million

India, 1896–1900: six million

USSR 1921–2: probably about four million

China 1928–34: three million

USSR 1932–4 (Stalinist collectivization programme): five million

Leningrad, Russia 1941–3 (siege): about one million

India 1943–4: three million

Biafra, Nigeria 1967–70: one million

Sahel (Sahara), 1969–74: one million

Cambodia, 1975–9: one million

Sudan, 1980s onwards: at least two million

Ethiopia 1985: over 500,000

Somalia 1990–93: over 500,000

Since the 1980s there have also been serious famines in Angola, Mozambique, Burundi and Rwanda. In Europe, Balkan conflict resulted in some deaths from starvation in *Bosnia in 1992–5.

Faneuil Hall. *See* 'CRADLE OF AMERICAN LIBERTY.'

Fanning Island, or **Tabuaeran**. Annexed by Great Britain, 1888; part of Gilbert and Ellice colony 1915–75: of *Kiribati since 1976.

fan vaulting. Earliest example of F.V. is in timber F.V. in the chapel of Winchester College *c.* 1390. Earliest stone F.V. at Gloucester *c.* 1420.

Far Eastern or **China Republic.** Declared its independence of Moscow, 1921. Annexed to Soviet Russia, 1922 and is now the Chita region of the Russian Federation.

'Farmer's Letters, The'. A series of letters by the American John Dickinson against English official measures. First appeared in *Pennsylvania Chronicle*, 2 Dec. 1767.

Farne Islands. Inner F. was the hermitage of St Cuthbert between 664 and 687. On its site a Benedictine priory was founded, 1082,of which St Cuthbert's tower still stands. The famous rescue by Grace Darling took place here, 1838. F.I. acquired by the *National Trust, 1925, as a bird sanctuary.

Farnese family. Following are the most distinguished members: 1. Alessandro Farnese, who became Pope Paul III (1534–49). 2. Pierluigi, his natural son. 1st Duke of Parma, 1503–47. 3. Alessandro (1520–89), who completed the famous F. palace at Rome. 4. Alessandro, 3rd Duke, 1545–92, famous Spanish general. 5. Elizabeth, 1692–1766, who married, 1714, Philip V of Spain.

Farnley Wood Plot against Charles II, 1663. Leaders executed, 19 Jan. 1664.

Faroe or **Faeroe Islands,** N Atlantic. Irish hermits driven out by Norse pirates *c.* 795. More heavily settled by Norse immigrants up to *c.* 900. Annexed to Norway, 1035. Became Danish, 1380. Occupied by British troops, Apr. 1940–May 1945. Self-governing, 1948. Fishing limits around the F.I. extended, 1959 and 1963. In EFTA 1968–72. The F.I. is not a member of the *EU.

Farringdon Market (London). Act for establishing of, 1824. Opened, 20 Nov. 1826. Discontinued, June 1892.

farthing. First coined by Edward I (1272–1307) instead of quartering pennies. Ceased to be legal tender, 31 Dec. 1960.

Fascism.
1. Founded as a politically organized creed by Benito Mussolini, at Bologna, 1919. In Oct. 1922 the Fascists took over the Italian Government by force in the 'March on Rome'. (*See* ITALY.)
2. In Britain Mosley's British Union of Fascists (founded 1932) got notoriety by the use of violence at meetings in London and Oxford, 1936, which led to passing of the Public Order Act, 1936. Revived after World War II under name of British Union Movement, later, National Front; main British Fascist group, 1995, was British National Party, but numbers minute. Name changed to National Democrats, July 1995.

Fashoda Question. French Major Marchand occupied F. on the Upper Nile, 10 July 1898. This resented by Britain. After the Dervish defeat at Omdurman (2 Sept. 1898), and further exchanges nearly leading to war, Marchand was withdrawn, 11 Dec. 1898.

Fathers of the Church (*Patres Ecclesiastici*).

The Apostolic F. (believed to have been disciples of the Apostles):
Clement of Rome *fl.* 93–101
Ignatius *fl. c.* 101
Polycarp *d. c.* 155
Barnabas *fl. c.* 120
Hermas *fl. c.* 150

The principal ante-Nicene F. are:
Justin Martyr *c.* 100–65
Irenaeus *c.* 130–202
Clement of Alexandria *c.* 150–*c.* 216
Tertullian *c.* 155–*c.* 222
Origen 185–254
Cyprian *c.* 200–58
Gregory Thaumaturgus *c.* 213–*c.* 270

The principal post-Nicene F. are:
Eusebius of Caesarea *c.* 260–340
Hilary of Poitiers *c.* 403–49
Athanasius *c.* 296–373
Basil *c.* 329–79
Cyril of Jerusalem *c.* 315–86
Gregory Nazianzus *c.* 328–90
Gregory of Nyssa *c.* 301–*c.* 394
Ambrose *c.* 340–*c.* 397
Epiphanius *c.* 330–403
John Chrysostom *c.* 334–407
Jerome 331–420

Augustine of Hippo 354–430
Cyril of Alexandria 376–444
Leo the Great *c*. 540–604
Bede *c*. 673–735
John of Damascus *d. c.* 752

Fatima, in Portugal, was the scene of a vision in which the Virgin is said to have appeared to three country children, and the sun stood still, 13 Oct. 1917.

Fatimites. Family claiming descent from Fatima, daughter of Mohammed, who ousted the Aghlabid dynasty from Tunis, and founded an anti-Caliphate at Al-Mehidiya, near Tunis, 909. After repeated attempts Egypt and Syria conquered from Abbasids, 969, and capital moved to Cairo, where the dynasty remained until extinguished at Saladin's conquest of *Egypt, 1171.

fatwa, Islamic doctrinal ruling. In 1989 the Ayatollah Khomeini of Iran issued a F. ordering death of British novelist Salman Rushdie on charge of blaspheming the Prophet in his novel *The Satanic Verses*.

Faversham, England. Abbey founded, 1147–9.

Fawkes, Guy. *See* GUNPOWDER PLOT.

fax, popular abbreviation for **facsimile transmission**, transmission of information in image form by means of a telecommunications link. Increasingly used since the 1970s, a F. was first patented by Caithness crofter Alexander Bain, 1843, using heather for springs and cattlebones for hinges, but he lost interest and *d*. penniless.

FBI (Federal Bureau of Investigation), set up, 1908, as a branch of the US Department of Justice, independent of State police forces. J. Edgar Hoover (1895–1972) became Director of FBI, 1924. Between 1945 and 1989 the FBI was most prominent in anti-Communist activities, though its prestige later diminished in counter-espionage activities by the growing influence of the Central Intelligence Agency (*CIA) since the 1960s.

FBI (Federation of British Industries). Established, 1916; granted royal charter of incorporation, 1924. Absorbed in *Confederation of British Industry, Aug. 1965.

Federal Convention (USA). Representatives of 12 states assembled at Philadelphia, 1787, to prepare a constitution for USA.

Federal German Republic. *See* GERMANY, FEDERAL REPUBLIC OF.

Federal Reserve System, reform of American finance and banking methods, introduced by Congress, 1913, and modified by the Banking Act, 1935, which led to the creation of the F.R. Board, 1936.

Federal Trade Commission. Set up by the US Government in 1914 to check trusts and monopolies.

Federalist Party (USA). Advocates of national constitution, 1788. Defeated, 1800, by the election of Jefferson as president. Disbanded, 1820.

Federation of Rhodesia and Nyasaland. *See* RHODESIA AND NYASALAND, FEDERATION OF.

Fehmic Courts (Femgerichte), ancient native courts of Westphalia, corresponding to the English *Folkmoot* or Scandinavian *Thing*, first came into prominence, 1180; by the Emperor Charles IV's Westphalian statute of Nov. 1371 they could try crimes of violence. The Fs. attained summit of power, 1430–40, spreading southwards to Switzerland. Reforms took place, 1437 and 1442. Jerome Bonaparte's edict of 1811 abolished F.C. Assassination by right-wing terrorists, 1922–4 (e.g. of Walter Rathenau, 24 June 1922), vulgarly called Fehmic murders, had nothing in common with the original F. court.

Fenian Association. Name (derived from Irish legend) adopted by John F. O'Mahony (1816–77) for the American section founded by him of the Irish Republican Brotherhood, 1858. The main section in Ireland was led by James Stephens

(1825–1901) and the name Fs. came to be applied to the whole membership. Attempted raid into Canada, 1866. Abortive attempt at rebellion in Ireland, and outrages in England, 1867. Attempt to blow up Clerkenwell jail, 13 Dec. 1867. Further raids into Canada, 1870. Plot of the 'Irish Invincibles', 1882.

Fens (UK). *See also* BEDFORD LEVEL. Romans made attempts to drain the F. Unsuccessful attempt to drain Deeping Fen during reign of William I (1066–87). Vermuyden's efforts *c*. 1640. As a whole the major drainage operations in the F. were completed in 1807. Measures to strengthen flood defences announced, Nov. 1947. Extensive flooding, 1 Feb. 1953. Flood-protection scheme begun, 1954; complete by 1964 but said (1995) to be threatened increasingly by rising sea-levels.

Fernando Po, W coast of Africa. Discovered by Portuguese Fernão do Po, 1472. Spanish from 1778, repossessed 1844 and then part of Spanish Guinea, now *Equatorial Guinea.

Ferrara, Italy. Ancient city in the Exarchate of Ravenna *c*. AD 753–4. *Este family became rulers, 1208. University founded, 1391. A council which unsuccessfully tried to reconcile Roman and Greek churches held, 1438. Taken by French, 1796. Given to Papacy, 1814. Held by Austrian garrison, 1849–59. Annexed by Sardinia, Mar. 1860.

Ferrers arrest. George F., MP for Plymouth, was arrested by the sheriffs of the City of London for debt, Mar. 1542. The Commons had them imprisoned for contempt, 28 Mar. 1542, but released on 30th.

Festival of Britain, 3 May–30 Sept. 1951.

Fettmilch Insurrection led by Vincenz F. and others at Frankfurt-am-Main against municipal tyranny 1612–6. Leaders executed, 1616.

feudalism. Theoretically, a medieval system of society based on land in which a division of labour is achieved by committing governmental functions to those prepared to render military protection in return for agricultural and other services. Said to have arisen out of the anarchy of Western Europe in the 8th and 9thC, and then introduced into England and Wales in modified form after 1066. Its externals began to decline almost immediately, the principal dates being: Introduction of Judicial Circuits (*temp.* Henry II, 1154–89). Statute *Quïa Emptores*, 1290. Introduction of the Use, 14thC. Statute of Uses, 1535. Statute of Wills, 1540. Act for the Abolition of Military Tenure, 1660. The last traces of F. were swept away by the Law of Property Acts, 1922–5. In the present century the rigid applications of F. have been increasingly questioned with the theory being claimed as a 12thC legal invention.

Feuillants. Religious order in France, founded 1577, as a reformed branch of the Cistercians by Jean de la Barrière.

Feuillants Club. Founded 1791 by the moderate section of the 'Amis de la Constitution' (organized at Versailles, 1789). Their meeting-place was a disused Feuillant monastery. Disbanded, 10 Aug. 1792.

Fez, Morocco. Founded by Idris II, 808. Mosque of Mulai Idris built, 810. Occupied by French, Mar. 1911. Treaty of F. established French protectorate over Morocco, 1912, which terminated 2 Mar. 1956.

FFI (Forces Françaises de l'Intérieur). Designation adopted by all French resistance forces when placed under unified command once the Allied invasion of June 1944 had started.

Fianna Fail (Irish, meaning Soldiers of Destiny), followers of Eamon de Valera (1882–1975) organized as a party in 1926; formed government, 1932–48; again, 1951–4, 1957–81, 1982 and 1987–1994.

Fidei Defensor. *See* DEFENDER OF THE FAITH.

FIDO (Fog, Intensive Dispersal Operation). Device for clearing airfield fog, invented by A. C. Hartley, 1942.

Field-Marshal (UK). Rank first conferred by George II on the Duke of Argyll, 1736.

Field of the Cloth of Gold. *See* CLOTH OF GOLD, FIELD OF THE.

Fiery Chamber. *See* CHAMBRES ARDENTES.

Fieschi's Plot to kill Louis Philippe of France, 28 July 1835. F. and accomplices executed, 19 Feb. 1836.

FIFA (Fédération Internationale de Football Association), founded 1904. Headquarters, Zurich, Switzerland. Most important international football body, popularized sport world-wide through World Cup, first held 1930.

Winners of World Cup
1930: Uruguay
1934: Italy
1938: Italy
1950: Uruguay
1954: West Germany
1958: Brazil
1962: Brazil
1966: England
1970: Brazil
1974: West Germany
1978: Argentina
1982: Italy
1986: Argentina
1990: West Germany
1994: Brazil

The 1994 World Cup was held in USA for first time, and Brazil beat Italy in the final match in a penalty shoot-out, 3–2.

fifth column. Expression originating in 1936 at the outset of the Spanish Civil War, attributed to the Nationalist Gen. Mola. Used by the Germans in their invasions of Scandinavia and France and the Low Countries, 1940.

Fifth Monarchy Men. Religious anarchical sect founded in England, 1645. Admonished by Cromwell's council, Dec. 1653, and leaders imprisoned, Jan. 1654. Revolted against Charles II, 1661, and leaders executed.

Fifth Republic, France. Constitution came into force, 4 Oct. 1958.

Fighter Command, British, set up July 1936. Played crucial role under Dowding during Battle of Britain, 1940.

Figueras, Spain. Fortress built by Ferdinand VI, 1746–57. Taken by French, 24 Nov. 1794, 2 Mar. 1808, and 19 Aug. 1811. Restored to Spain by Treaty of Paris, 1814.

Fiji Islands, Polynesia. Discovered by Tasman, 1643. Visited by Capt. Cook, 1773. British protectorate, 1874. Independent, 10 Oct. 1970. Leftist, mainly Indian coalition won elections, 12 Apr. 1987 but overthrown in a military (Melanesian) coup, 14 May led by Col. Rabuka. On 25 Sept. 1987 Rabuka declared F.I. a republic and F.I. left Commonwealth. New constitution, 1990 established Melanesian dominance. Elections, 1992, led to a coalition government with Rabuka's party sharing power.

Film Commission, British. established Jan. 1992 to promote use of British locations, technicians, etc. in international film-making.

Film Institute, British. Founded 1933 and reconstituted, 1948.

Film Stars. *See* CINEMATOGRAPHY.

Financial Times. *See* NEWSPAPERS.

Fine Gael, Irish political party, considered to the right of *Fianna Fail, founded by W.J. Cosgrave, 1933. Its leader 1977–87 was Garret Fitzgerald who was Taisoeach 1981–2 and 1982–6. F.G. regained power as head of a coalition government under John Bruton, Dec. 1994.

fingerprints. First used in England and Wales, 1901. Recording of F. of certain accused persons authorized by Criminal Justice Act, 1948. Under the Criminal Justice Act, 1967, palm prints are accepted as F.

Finland (in Finnish **Suomi**). Finns said to have settled in F. during 8thC. Swedish colonies in from 8thC onwards. Swedes under Jarl Birger Magnusson conquer S F. and Tavestehus, 1230–49, and the Finns adopted Christianity. Swedish influence extending to White Sea, 1293. Treaty of Göteborg (Russo-Swedish), 1323. Karl Knutsson sets out from F. to claim Swedish crown, 1448. Overrun by Russian troops, 1710–11. Province of Viborg (Viipuri) ceded to Russia by Treaty of Nystad, 1721. Swedish troops driven out by Russians, 1808. Emperor Alexander recognized as Grand Duke of F. by Finnish estates, 1809. Finnish estates suppressed and national leaders exiled, 1898. Exiles recalled and Diet reopened, 1904. Independence proclaimed, 6 Dec. 1917. Republican constitution adopted, 17 July 1919. Russian invasion, 30 Nov. 1939. Peace with Russia (Viipuri ceded), 12 Mar. 1940. F. joins Axis, June 1941. Britain declares war on F., 7 Dec. 1941. Allied armistice with F., 4 Sept. 1944. Treaties of peace with Allies, by which Petsamo was ceded and Porkkala leased to Russia (returned to F., 1956) as well as territory ceded and leased under the 1940 treaty, came into force, 15 Sept. 1947. Treaty of friendship with Russia, Apr. 1948, subsequently extended. Member of Nordic Council, 1955; EFTA, 1961; Council of Europe, 1989. Applied to join EC Mar. 1992, and member of the *European Economic Area, 1994. Voted in favour of EU membership, Oct. 1994: joined, Jan. 1995.

Presidents of Finland:
J. K. Ståhlberg 1919–25
L. Relander 1925–31
P. E. Svinhufvud 1931–37
K. Kallio 1937–40
R. Ryiti 1940–44
G. C. Mannerheim 1944–46
J. K. Paasikivi 1946–56
U. Kekkonen 1956–82
M. Koivisto 1982–94
M. Ahtisaari 1994–

Finnish Literature. The following is a list of some prominent F. authors:

Aho, Juhani, 1861–1921, novelist.
Brofeldt (real name of Aho above).
Cajander, P. E., 1846–1913, poet.

Canth, Minna, 1844–97, playwright.
Haarla, Lauri, 1890–1944, novelist.
Ivalo, S., 1866–1937, historical novelist.
Järneveldt, Arvid, 1861–1932, novelist.
Jötuni, Marja, 1880–1943, playwright.
Kallas, A., 1878–1947, novelist.
Kivi, Alexis, 1834–72, playwright.
Leino, Einol, 1879–1926, poet.
Lehtonen, J., 1881–1946, novelist.
Linnankosi, Johannes, 1876–1913, poet.
Lönnbohm, A.E.M. (real name of Leino above).
Lönnrot, Elias, 1802–84, folklorist.
Oksanen, A., 1826–99, poet.
Paivärinta, P., 1827–1913, novelist.
Pakkala, T., 1862–1925, novelist.
Peltonen (real name of Linnankosi above).
Sarkia, Kaarlo, 1902–45, novelist.
Stenval, Alexis (real name of Kivi above).
Von Numers, G., 1848–1913, playwright (also in Swedish).

Finns and **Finnish language.** The designation F. was not a native one, but bestowed on them by their western neighbours, perhaps by the Balts. Tacitus in the 1stC AD mentions Fenni and Ptolemy mentions Phennoi about a hundred years later: this could be a rendering of a W Germanic name, cognate with *fen* and meaning 'people from the marshes', which adequately translates the western F.'s own name for themselves – Suomalaiset. Credit for reducing Finnish to writing is usually given to Bishop Michael Agricola (*d.* 1557). *See also* ESTONIA; KARELO-, etc.; LIVONIA.

fire brigades and appliances. First reference to a fire brigade relates to China *c.* 4000 BC. Egyptian F.B., 2000 BC. Romans formed F.B. under a *praefectum vigilum c.* 150 BC. Machine built by Hautsch of Nürnberg, 1657. Flexible hose introduced by Jan Vanderheide, 1672. First fire insurance office founded in London, 1680, and first English fire brigade then organized. Newsham's engine patented, 1700. In 18thC all insurance companies had their own fire brigade, and first fire engine acquired by a London insurance company, 1722. London parishes obliged to keep a fire engine by Act of Parliament, 1774. First steam fire engine invented by Braithwaite, 1829. All London private brigades united, 1833. Metropolitan fire brigade set up, 1865, by which time steam engines general. Motor fire engines introduced, 1905. National Fire Service started, 1940. Repartitioned into local F. services, 1948.

Fire of London, The Great, broke out, 2 Sept. 1666, and burned until 6 Sept. Previous to this the term 'Great F, of L.' had meant the catastrophe of 1136.

firearms. Crude cannon in use in Europe by 1300. Edward III used them against the Scots, 1327. First handguns made at Perugia, 1364, and at Augsburg by 1380. Wheel lock in use by 1575; flint-locks c. 1640. Percussion detonator patented by Forsyth, 1810. Automatic pistols c. 1900.

First Empire, in France, the reign of Napoleon I, 1804–14.

First Offenders Act, 1887, repealed by Probation of Offenders Act, 1907, which was amended by the Criminal Justice Acts, 1925, 1948, 1961, 1967, 1983, 1991 and 1994.

First Republic, in France, 27 Sept. 1792 until 1804.

fishing limits. British F.L. were extended to 12 miles by Fisheries Limits Act, 1964. From 1983 the EU Common Fisheries Policy has increasingly opened British waters to the fishing fleets of all EU members. In Dec. 1994 Britain obliged to accept opening of 'Irish Box' to Spanish and Portuguese fishermen. Canadian fishing dispute with EU, 1995.

Fitzwilliam Museum, Cambridge. A collection of paintings, MSS and books was bequeathed to the university by Richard, Visc. F. of Meryon (1745–1816). The building was begun, 1837; entrance hall (E.M. Barry), 1875. Marlay Galleries added, 1924; McClean MSS Room, 1925; Courtauld Galleries, 1931; Henderson Galleries and Charrington Print Room, 1936; Graham Robertson Room, 1955.

Fiume. *See* RIJEKA.

Five Boroughs. Lincoln, Nottingham, Derby, Stamford, and Leicester established as Danish colonies c. 850. They retained certain Danish customs ('by-laws') till well into the 13thC. *See* VIKING AGE.

Five Hundred, Council of. The lower house of the French legislature under the constitution of the year III (1795), the upper house being called the Council of Ancients. Lucien Bonaparte elected president of, 22 Oct. 1799. Dissolved by Napoleon, 10 Nov. 1799. *See* BRUMAIRE.

Five Members of the Long Parliament, Pym, Hampden, Hazelrigg, Strode, and Holles, whom Charles I attempted unsuccessfully to arrest, 4 Jan. 1642.

Five Mile Act. *See* CLARENDON CODE.

Five Power Naval Treaty signed at London, 22 Apr. 1930, between Britain, USA, Japan, France and Italy restricting the size of their respective navies.

Five-Year Plan (USSR). To industrialize Russia. First F.-Y.P., 1928–33. Second, 1933–8 (completed by 1937). Third, 1938–42, but interrupted by war. Fourth, 1946–50. Fifth, 1951–5. Sixth, 1956–60. Succeeded by a 7-year plan, 1959–65, which in turn was superseded by a 20-year plan, 1961–81. Theory of comprehensive planning subsequently discredited and collapsed after dissolution of the USSR, 1991.

Flagellants. Most famous outbreaks of this ascetic sect, 1348–9 and 1417. Condemned by bull of Clement VI, 20 Oct. 1349.

Flamboyant architecture. *See* GOTHIC ARCHITECTURE.

Flaminian Way (Latin *Via Flaminia*) from Rome to Rimini was built during the consulship of Flaminius, 220 BC.

Flanders, Belgium and N France. Colonized by Franks, 800–2. Annexed to France, 843. Famous for woollen manufactures, 962. Counts of F. refuse to recognize Hugues Capet as King of France, 987.

Flemings take part in William I's conquest of England and in Earl Tostig's unsuccessful invasion, 1066. St Omer first Flemish city to receive a charter, 1127. Zeeland Islands transferred from F. to Holland, 1256. French influence in F. becomes considerable after 1210. Flemings defeat French at Courtrai, 1302. Rebellion of Jacob van Artevelde of Ghent, 1337. He calls for English assistance which being given signals the start of the Hundred Years War, 1338. Anglo-Flemish victory over French at Sluys, 1340. Flemin crushed at Ghent, 1349. Victory over the French at Roosebeke, 1382. Acquired by dukes of Burgundy, 1384. Collapse of Burgundians after death of Charles the Bold at Nancy, 1477. *Great Privilege, 1477. Artois annexed by France, 1483. Margaret of Burgundy, Regent of F., supports Lambert Simnel, 1487, and Perkin Warbeck, 1492–6. Abandons Warbeck in return for trading privileges called *'The Great Intercourse', 1497. The 'Bad Intercourse', 1506. French feudal rights in F. surrendered to Emperor Charles V at Treaty of Cambrai, 1529, and remained loyal to Spain when N half of Spanish Netherlands broke away, 1579. For history after this date, *see* BELGIUM.

Fleet Air Arm. The Royal Naval Air Service fused with Royal Flying Corps, 1918, to form the Royal Air Force, which controlled *all* aviation, even that attached to the fleet. In 1922, an element of the naval air component, thenceforth called the F.A.A., was placed under complete operational and partial administrative and disciplinary command of the Admiralty. In 1937 complete command passed to the Admiralty, but F.A.A. as a distinct unit dissolved in reorganization after World War II.

Fleet Ditch (London). Covered in, 1733.

Fleet Market (London). Instituted, 30 Sept. 1737. Superseded by *Farringdon Market. Swept away, 1829.

Fleet marriages (London) occurred in the Liberties of the Fleet and in the Liberty of the Savoy (notably in the Fleet Chapel)

from 1614 until abolished by Lord Hardwick's Act, 1753.

Fleet Prison (London), for debtors, existed as early as 1197, possibly earlier. Burnt by Wat Tyler, 1381. Star Chamber prisoners incarcerated in till 1641. Burnt in *Great Fire of London, 1666. Burnt by *Gordon rioters, 1780. Abolished, 1842. Demolished, 1844.

Fleet Street (London) was part of the quarter burnt down in 982. In 1228 it was called F. Bridge Street, and F.S. first in 1311. Its connection with printing begins with Wynkyn de Worde (*d.* 1534), who set up his press at No. 32 in 1500. It became the centre of the British newspaper industry, and synonymous with it, from the second half of the 19thC until the 1980s, when with the introduction of new printing processes the major newspapers removed to sites in E London.

Flemings in Britain. *See* WEAVING.

fleur-de-lis. Emblem of the French monarchy. Origin traditionally ascribed to Clovis, AD 496. Definitely connected with the monarchy under Louis VII *c.* 1147. Number in the French royal arms reduced to three, 1376.

flogging and whipping. Powers of the British courts to pass a sentence of corporal punishment were abolished by the Criminal Justice Act, 1948, both for adults and juvenile offenders.

Florence (Latin *Florentia*), Italy. The ancient Roman colony was rebuilt by Julius Caesar, 59 BC. Baptistery built *c.* AD 1100. Independent republic, 1198. Defeated by Siena, 1260. Cathedral built, 1294–8. City partly burnt in rioting, 1304. University founded, 1321. Ponte Vecchio built, 1345. Papal attack repelled, 1375. Revolution of the Ciompi, 1378. Rule of the Albizzi, 1382–1434. Medici come to power, 1434. Library founded, 1444. Rule of Lorenzo de' Medici (the Magnificent), 1470–92. Founds Platonic Academy, 1476. The Pazzi Conspiracy against the Medici, Giuliano killed, Lorenzo escapes, Apr. 1478. Medici expelled, 1494. Death of Savonarola, 1498. Medici restored, 1512; again expelled, 1527. Again restored, 1530. Giovanni de' Medici becomes pope as Leo X, 1513–21. Uffizi Gallery, 1560, built by Vasari; Medici become Grand Dukes of Tuscany, 1569. Accademia della Crusca founded, 1582. End of Medici family, 1737. F. presented by Napoleon to his sister Elise, 1808. Provisional capital of Italy, 1864–71. Heavily damaged during allied capture, 4–11 Aug. 1944. Further severe damage during unprecedented floods, Nov. 1966. Uffizi Gallery and some paintings and sculpture damaged in bomb outrage, May 1993.

Florida, USA. Discovered by Ponce de Leon on Easter Day, 1512. Conquered for Spain by Narvaez, 1528, and de Soto, 1539. Santo Augustino sacked by Sir Francis Drake, 1586. Ceded by Spain to Britain in exchange for Cuba at Treaty of Paris, 1763. Again ceded to Spain, 1783. Taken by USA, 1811. Returned to Spain, 1812. Purchased from Spain, 1819. Admitted to union as a state, 8 Mar. 1845. Tourist and retirement centre since beginning of 20thC but most notably since 1950s.

florin. First struck in gold at Florence, 11thC. Silver F. first struck, 1181. Gold F., value 6s., first struck in England, 1343, by Edward III. Silver F., value 2s., struck, 1849, and called 'Godless and Graceless', because *Dei Gratia* omitted from the superscription. Omission rectified, 1852. Name 'Florin' disappeared from superscription at accession of George VI. Decimal equivalent since 1971, 10 pence; old F. coin withdrawn, 1993.

flower shows in England were started by the Royal Horticultural Society of London, 1804. *See also* CHELSEA FLOWER SHOW.

fluoride, properly **sodium floride**. Theory that F. in drinking water could prevent tooth decay demonstrated in the USA by McKay (1874–1959). In Britain, 1976, Royal College of Physicians recommended F. be added to drinking water with low F. levels and this practise now (1995) affects water used by millions of people in the UK.

fluorine. Isolated by Moisson, 1876.

Flushing, Holland (Dutch **Vlissingen**). Jakobskerk founded, 1328. Fort dismantled, 1867. Harbour opened, 1873.

flying bombs (Vergeltungswaffe I, pilotless aircraft, jet propelled) were used against London, June–Aug. 1944, and against Antwerp and Liège, 13 Oct. 1944–31 Mar. 1945.

Flying Squadron. Scots political party led by Lord Tweeddale founded *c.* 1705, and secured settlement of the union question, 1706.

fog signals first regularized by the International Maritime Code, 1862.

Foix, France. County in the Pyrenees independent from *c.* 100 until Count Francis Phoebus became King of Navarre, 1479. His sister married Jean d'Albert and F. passed with *Navarre eventually to the Bourbons, and then to the French crown on the accession of Henry IV, 1589. Its counts were co-princes of *Andorra. At the revolution it became the department of Ariège.

Fokker. Invention by Anton Fokker (1890–1940) of a wireless-directed bombing plane announced, Sept. 1919: responsible for design of planes in World War I and after.

Fommonah, Treaty of. Between Britain and the King of Ashanti, 1874.

Fontainebleau, France. Treaty of F. between Napoleon and Godoy, the minister of Charles IV and the *de facto* King of Spain, 1807. Decree against British commerce, 1810. Napoleon signed abdication at, 6 Apr. 1814. The palace of F. was traditionally founded in the 12thC, but, as it exists today, was begun by Francis I in the 16thC. *SHAPE functioned from F., 1950–66.

Foochow, Fuchow or **Fuzhou**, China. Bridge of Ten Thousand Ages built *c.* 1000. Visited by Marco Polo *c.* 1290. Opened to British trade, 1842.

Food and Agriculture Organization. Agency of the UN, established, 16 Oct. 1945, with headquarters in Rome.

food control (UK). Food Ministry under Lord Devonport formed, 1917. Maximum prices and rationing introduced, Sept. 1917. F. Ministry abolished, 1921. In World War II W.S. Morrison appointed F. Minister, 6 Apr. 1939. Price-fixing orders, 3 and 11 Sept. 1939. F. rationing in Britain began, 1939, and ended, 1954, and in 1955 the Ministry of F. was amalgamated with the Ministry of Agriculture and Fisheries.

football. Evidence that Chinese played a game like modern F. (Tsu Chu) and Japanese had similar (Kemari) *c.* 1000 BC. In 1175 William Fitzstephen described 'the famous game of ball' played on Shrove Tuesday in London. Modern F. (popularly known as soccer) originates from founding of the *Football Association in London, 26 October 1863. Growing professionalism recognized by foundation of English *Football League in 1888. Popularity of F. rapidly spread worldwide. Federation International de Football Association (*FIFA), set up, 1904. Olympic F. began, 1908 but world F. dominated by FIFA's World Cup from 1930. UEFA (*Union of European Football Associations) established 1954 and responsible for European Football Championship, first held 1960. Women's F. established by late 1980s. Transfer fee system in doubt after European court ruling, 1995. Famous football players include: (British, unless otherwise stated)

George Best, 1946–
Sir Matt Busby (player-manager), 1909–94
Eric Cantona (France), 1966–
Jack Charlton, 1935–
Bobby Charlton, 1937–
Paul Gascoigne, 1967–
Alex James, 1901–53
Kevin Keegan, 1951–
Gary Lineker, 1960–
Diego Maradona (Argentina), 1960–
Sir Stanley Matthews, 1915–
Bobby Moore, 1941–93 (captain of England when England won World Cup, 1966)

Edson Pele (Brazil), 1940–
Bob Wright, 1924–94

football, American, game played in N America, evolved second half of 19thC from British soccer and rugby football. Different versions at start, but game codified after first match played between Harvard and McGill universities, Montreal, under 'Harvard Rules', May 1874. Intercollegiate Football Association, 1876. First professional game (Latrobe v. Jeanette) played in Pennsylvania, 1895. A.F. was the US national game by 1900. First Rose Bowl game between college teams, 1902. American Professional Football Association, 1920, became the National Football Association, 1922 (NFL). American Football League (AFL) formed 1960 was rival to NFL. NFL and AFL merged 1970 and divided into two conferences (AFC and NFC). The Superbowl championship, started in 1966, is between the AFC and NFC champions at the end of the A.F. season and is currently the US's greatest domestic sporting event. On 1 Feb. 1993, the Superbowl was won by the Dallas Cowboys who beat the Buffalo Bills: this win repeated, 1994. Won by San Francisco 49ers, 1995.

Football Association, English, established in London, 26 October 1863, marked the beginning of modern *football. It launched the Challenge Cup (which became the F.A. Cup) in 1871 and organized its first international match, against Scotland, in 1872. Professionalism in the game legalized from 1885. Establishment of *Football League, 1888. The first Cup Final winners (1872) were Wanderers, who beat Royal Engineers, 1–0. From 1885 professional players dominated. Cup Final winners since 1980:

1980: West Ham United
1981: Tottenham Hotspur
1982: Tottenham Hotspur
1983: Manchester United
1984: Everton
1985: Manchester United
1986: Liverpool
1987: Coventry City

1988: Wimbledon
1989: Liverpool
1990: Manchester United
1991: Tottenham Hotspur
1992: Liverpool
1993: Arsenal
1994: Manchester United
1995: Everton

Football Association, Irish. Established 1880: covered all Ireland until 1921 when the **Football Association of Ireland** was formed to cover the Irish Republic.

Football Association, Scottish, established 1873. Scottish Cup Finals have been held since 1874, when the winners were Queen's Park. For much of its history Scottish football has been dominated by the two Glasgow clubs of Rangers and Celtic. Winners of the Scottish Cup from 1980:

1980: Celtic
1981: Rangers
1982: Aberdeen
1983: Aberdeen
1984: Aberdeen
1985: Celtic
1986: Aberdeen
1987: St Mirren
1988: Celtic
1989: Celtic
1990: Aberdeen
1991: Motherwell
1992: Rangers
1993: Rangers
1994: Dundee United
1995: Celtic

Football Association of Wales. Established 1876. Welsh F.A. Cup instituted, 1878.

Football League, English, established, 1888. League Championship first awarded, 1889, when winners were Preston North End, who beat Aston Villa, with Wolverhampton Wanderers in third place. League Championship winners since 1980:

1980: Liverpool
1981: Aston Villa
1982: Liverpool
1983: Liverpool
1984: Liverpool
1985: Everton
1986: Liverpool
1987: Everton
1988: Liverpool
1989: Arsenal
1990: Liverpool
1991: Arsenal
1992: Leeds United
1993: Manchester United
1994: Manchester United
1995: Blackburn Rovers

Premier League established for 1992–3 season.

Football League, Scottish, established, 1891, when the first winners were Dumbarton and Rangers (tied). Winners since 1980:

1980: Aberdeen
1981: Celtic
1982: Celtic
1983: Dundee United
1984: Aberdeen
1985: Aberdeen
1986: Celtic
1987: Rangers
1988: Celtic
1989: Rangers
1990: Rangers
1991: Rangers
1992: Rangers
1993: Rangers
1994: Rangers
1995: Rangers

Scottish Premier League established for 1992–3 season.

Force Act. Passed by US Congress, 1870, authorizing Federal agencies to interfere in individual states for the maintenance of order in certain cases.

Foreign Enlistment Act (UK). 1) 1919. Forbade British subjects to enlist in a foreign service at war with any state friendly to Great Britain. 2) 1870.

Forefathers Day, USA, commemorates 21 Dec. 1620 when an exploring party of the *Pilgrim Fathers arrived at what is now Plymouth, Massachusetts.

foreign legions. The French 'Foreign Legion' is a group of *Régiments Étrangers*, of which the first was raised by Louis Philippe, 9 Mar. 1831; its nucleus was the recently discharged soldiers of the two Guard and four Line regiments of Swiss, disbanded after the revolution of July 1830: between 1871 and 1914 it consisted largely of Alsatians and Lorrainers. In 1854 Napoleon III raised an *ad hoc* legion, mainly Swiss, for the Crimea, and in 1855 Great Britain raised two, one German-Swiss and one Italian, for the same purpose. F.L., including English, Scots and Irish in some numbers, fought in Spanish interests in the war of French intervention, 1823; the First, 1834–8, and Second, 1872–6, Carlist Wars; and the Civil War of 1936–9 (International Brigade on Republican side and the professional *Tercio*, together with O'Duffy's volunteers, for Franco); also in the Graeco-Turkish wars of 1821–33 and 1897, on the Greek side. The French *Régiments Étrangers* were disbanded, 1940, but reconstituted, 1945. They fought with distinction in Indo-China, 1946–54, and Algeria, 1954–62. On 28 Apr. 1961, the First Foreign Legion Parachute Regiment was disbanded for its part in the abortive army mutiny in Algeria earlier that month. Sent to *Chad, 1983; to Tahiti, 1995.

Foreign Office. Dates as such from 1872, when the redistribution of functions among Secretaries of State resulted in all foreign affairs being concentrated in the hands of one. The combined Foreign Service resulted from the merger of the F.O. and Diplomatic Service, the Commercial Diplomatic Service, and the Consular Service in 1943. Merged with the Commonwealth Relations Office, 1968.

British Secretaries of State for Foreign Affairs since 1924:

J. Ramsay MacDonald 1924
Sir Austen Chamberlain 1924–29
Arthur Henderson 1929–31
Lord Reading 1931
Sir John Simon 1931–35
Sir Samuel Hoare 1935
Anthony Eden 1935–38
Lord Halifax 1938–40
Anthony Eden 1940–45
Ernest Bevin 1945–51
Herbert Morrison 1951
Sir Anthony Eden 1951–55
Harold Macmillan 1955
Selwyn Lloyd 1955–60
Lord Home 1960–63
R.A. Butler 1963–64
Patrick Gordon Walker 1964–65
Michael Stewart 1965–66
George Brown 1966–68
Michael Stewart 1968–70
Sir Alec Douglas-Home 1970–74
Anthony Crosland 1974–77
David Owen 1977–79
Lord Carrington 1979–82
Francis Pym 1982–83
Sir Geoffrey Howe 1983–89
John Major 1989
Douglas Hurd 1989–95
Malcolm Rifkind 1995–

Forest Laws. Introduced into England by William I, who destroyed several villages to make the New Forest, 1079–1085. Their severity was much mitigated by the F. Charter of Henry III, 1217, and the F. courts fell into disuse by the middle of 16thC. In 1631–2 they were revived by Charles I as a means of raising revenue, but the outcry which resulted prevented their penal jurisdiction ever being exercised again.

Formigny, Battle of, 1450. English defeated by French, who for the first time had artillery which could outrange the English long-bow.

Formosa. *See* TAIWAN.

Fort Augustus, built at Kilchumin,

Inverness-shire, after the 1715 rebellion (*see* JACOBITES), and taken by the Highland Army, 1745. Reoccupied by Hanoverian troops, 1746, and named after the Duke of Cumberland.

Forth and Clyde Canal (Scotland). Begun 1768. Opened, 1790.

Forth Bridge (rail) (Scotland). Act passed, 1882. Begun, Jan. 1882. Finished, 1889. Opened, 4 Mar. 1890.

Forth Road Bridge (Scotland). Begun, 1958. Opened, 4 Sept. 1964.

Forties oilfield, first major British oilfield, discovered 1970: first oil brought ashore Nov. 1975.

Fort Sumter (USA), on an island in Charleston harbour, bombarded by Confederates, 12 Apr. 1861. This action is regarded as the beginning of the American Civil War. Captured by the Federal fleet, 1865. Became a national monument, 1948.

fortune-telling. First specifically mentioned in English law as a form of witchcraft, and therefore a capital offence, in a statute of 1563. Now punishable under the Vagrancy Act, 1924 and Criminal Justice Act, 1948.

Fotheringhay Castle (Northants, England). Founded, 1066. Richard III *b.,* Oct. 1452. Mary Queen of Scots executed, 8 Feb. 1587. Demolished by James I, 1604

foundling hospitals.
1. London (St Pancras), projected by Thomas Coram. Royal charter, Oct. 1739. Closed, 1926, and hospital transferred to Berkhamsted, Herts.
2. Dublin, instituted, 1704.

Fountains Abbey. Founded, 1132, by a body of Benedictine monks who seceded from the Abbey of St Mary's, York, on land granted them by Archbishop Thurstan, and joined the Cistercians. Abbey dissolved, 1539, and much of the stone used to build F. Hall. Now (1995) National Trust property.

Four Cantons (Switzerland). Schwyz, Uri, Unterwalden, original members of the Swiss confederation, 1315, were joined by Lucerne, 1332. *See* SWITZERLAND.

Four Freedoms, peace aims for the Allies, enunciated while the USA was still neutral, by Franklin D. Roosevelt, 6 Jan. 1941.

Four Power Pact for peace of Europe between Britain, France, Germany and Italy initialled at Rome, 1933.

Fourteen Points propounded by President Wilson in an address to US Congress, 8 Jan. 1918, as a basis for a peace settlement with Germany. Considered at Allied Supreme War Council, 3 Nov. 1918, when Britain, Belgium and Italy raised detailed objections. Reply sent to Wilson same day.

Fourth Party. Short-lived independent group of Conservative politicians formed 1880 and led by Lord Randolph Churchill and A.J. Balfour.

Fourth Republic of France. Existed from 24 Dec. 1946 until 4 Oct. 1958.

France (Latin *Gallia, Gaul*). Conquered by Romans, 121–51 BC. Frankish incursions began *c.* AD 250. Settlement of Visigoths in F., 415–23. Defence of F. by Aëtius against Salian Franks, 425–30. With Frankish and Gothic help he repulses Attila at battle of *Châlons, 451. Collapse of Roman direct authority, 470–6. Clovis, king of Salian Franks, 481, defeats Syagrius at Soissons, 486; the Alemanni, 496; and embraces Christianity, 496. Defeats Alaric, king of the Visigoths, at Vouillé, 507; *d.* 511. Merovingian era, 481–716. Collapse of Merovingian power at death of Dagobert, 638.

Charles Martel, Mayor of the Kingdoms, 716. He defeats the Moors at Tours, 732. Pepin becomes king of the Franks, 751. Charlemagne sole king of the Franks, 771. Count Roland killed at Roncesvalles, 778. Charlemagne crowned Roman Emperor at Rome, 25 Dec. 800: *d.* 814. At Treaty of Verdun Carolingian Empire divided into three, 843. Viking invasions begin *c.* 850. They besiege Paris, 885–6. End of the Carolingian House, 987.

Hugh Capet elected king of France, 987. French defeat by William (Conqueror) at Varaville, 1058. Norman invasion of England, 1066. First *Crusade, 1095. Statutes of the *Templars drawn up by St Bernard, 1128. With accession of Henry II of England Aquitaine and Anjou pass to the English kings, 1154. Conquest of Normandy by Philip Augustus, 1200–04. Philip's great victory over the emperor and the Flemings at Bouvines, 1214. Albigensian Crusades, 1208–29. Death of Philip Augustus, 1223. Under Louis IX (St Louis) F. reached the height of its medieval greatness, 1226–70. Alliance with Scotland and quarrel between Philip IV and Pope Boniface VIII, 1295. Boniface seized at Anagni, 1302. Clement V crowned pope at Lyons, 1305, and fixed his residence at Avignon, 1309 ('Babylonish captivity'). Templars suppressed, 1312.

*Hundred Years War begins, 1338; interrupted by Treaty of Brétigny, 1360. Resumed, 1369. Truce of Bruges, 1375. Duke of Orléans murdered in Paris, 1407. English resume the war, 1415. Duke of Burgundy murdered, 1419. Treaty of Troyes, 1420. Joan of Arc drives the English from Orléans, 1429, and crowns Charles VII at Rheims, 1430. Treaty of Arras, 21 Sept. 1435. Paris goes over to the French king, 1436. The *Ordonnance sur la Gendarmerie*, 1439. The *Praguerie*, 1440. Battle of *Formigny, 1450. English driven out of all F. except Calais, 1453.

Charles VIII invades Italy, 1494–6. He marries Anne of Brittany, 1491. Captures Naples, 1504. League of Cambrai, 1508. *Holy League, Oct. 1511. Louis XII assumes title of *Pater Patriae*, 1513. Peace and alliance with England, 1514. Concordat of Bologna, 1516, between Francis I and Leo X.

Franco-Hapsburg Wars, 1521–59:
1. 1521–26 ending with Treaty of Madrid (battle of Pavia, 1525)
2. 1527–29 ending with Treaty of Cambrai
3. 1535–38 ending with Treaty of Nice
4. 1542–44 ending with Treaty of Crespy
5. 1552–59 ending with Treaty of Câteau Cambrésis

The Wars of Religion (between Huguenots and Catholics):
The First. 1562–63: ending with the Peace of Ambroise
The Second. 1567–68: ending with the Peace of Longjumeau
The Third. 1569–70: ending with the Peace of Saint-Germain
Massacre of St Bartholomew, 1572, leading to:
The Fourth. 1572–73: ending with the Peace of La Rochelle
The Fifth. 1574–76: ending with the Peace of 'Monsieur'
The Sixth. 1577: ending with the Peace of Bergerac
The Seventh. 1579–80: ending with the Peace of Fleix
The Eighth. 1585–98: ending with the Treaty of Vervins, 1598.

Henry of Guise murdered, 1588. Henry of Navarre acceded as Henry IV, 1589, becoming a Catholic in 1593. Treaty of Vervins, 1598. Edict of Nantes, 15 Apr. 1598. Henry IV assassinated by Ravaillac, 1610. Rebellion of Condé, 1614. Richelieu, first minister, 1624. Huguenot power broken by capture of La Rochelle, 1628. War with Spain, 1635. Death of Richelieu, 1642. Mazarin, first minister, 1643. Treaty of *Westphalia, 1648, whereby F. obtained Metz, Toul and Verdun, and Lorraine.
The first or Parliamentary Fronde, 1648–9. Second or Aristocratic Fronde, 1650–3. English Alliance (Treaty of Westminster), 1654. Peace with Spain at the Treaty of the Pyrenees, 1659. Death of Mazarin, 1661. Louis XIV takes over the government and appoints Colbert finance minister, 1661. French E India Co. founded, 1664. War of Devolution against Spanish Netherlands, 1667–8. Dutch War, 1672. Revocation of the Edict of Nantes and the Dragonade, 1685. War of the League of Augsburg, 1688–97. Peace of Ryswick, 1697. War of the *Spanish Succession, 1701–13, ends by Treaty of * Utrecht, 1713. Death of Louis XIV, Sept. 1715.
Triple Alliance (England, F., and Holland), Jan. 1717. Quadruple Alliance (England,

F., Austria, Holland), 2 Aug. 1718. F. joins in War of the *Austrian Succession against Austria, 1740. Britain joins in an alliance with Austria ('The War of Jenkins's Ear'), 1742. Battle of Fontenoy, 1745. Peace of Aix-la-Chapelle, 1748. The *Seven Years War, 1756–63. Loss of major part of French colonial possessions in America and India, 1759–60. Intervention in the War of American Independence, 1778. Treaty of Versailles, 1783. Meeting of the States-General, 5 May 1789.

The *French Revolution, 1789–92. Monarchy overthrown, 10 Aug. 1792. The First Republic proclaimed, 22 Sept. 1792. Louis XVI executed, Jan. 1793. The *Directory comes into force, 1795. Napoleon conquers Italy and makes peace with Austria at Campo-Formio, 17 Oct. 1797. Napoleon in the Middle E, July 1798–Aug. 1799, when he returned to France. He overthrows the Directory (*Brumaire), 10 Nov. 1799. The Consulate. Napoleon First Consul of F., 15 Dec. 1799. Battle of Marengo, 14 June 1800. Treaty of Lunéville, 9 Feb. 1801. The Concordat, 1802. Treaty of Amiens, 1802. *Code Civile* published, 1804.

The First Empire: Napoleon crowns himself emperor, 2 Dec. 1804. Battle of Ulm, 20 Oct. 1805. Battle of Trafalgar, 21 Oct. 1805. Battle of Austerlitz, 2 Dec. 1805. Holy Roman Empire abolished and Confederation of the Rhine formed, 1806. Battle of Jena, 1806. Treaty of Tilsit, 1807. Battle of Baylen, 1808. Pope Pius VII deported to F., 1809. Russia deserts the *Continental System, 1810. Retreat from Moscow, 1812. Battle of Leipzig, Oct. 1813. Napoleon abdicated, 11 Apr. 1814. First Treaty of Paris, 1814. Napoleon returns to Paris, 20 Mar. 1815. Battle of Waterloo, 18 June 1815. Second Treaty of Paris, 15 Nov. 1815.

The Restoration: War with Spain, 1822–1827. Capture of Algiers, 1830. Polignac issues the July Ordinances, 1830. Revolution in Paris. Charles X abdicates, 2 Aug. 1830. The July Monarchy: Louis Philippe of Orléans proclaimed king of the French, 7 Aug. 1830. Conquest of Algeria, 1830–2. Revolution breaks out in Paris, 23 Feb. 1848. Louis Philippe abdicates, 24 Feb. 1848.

The Second Republic proclaimed, 26 Feb. 1848. Louis Napoleon *Bonaparte elected president by universal suffrage, 11 Dec. 1848. Republic overthrown by Bonaparte, 2 Dec. 1851.

The Second Empire: Napoleon III proclaimed emperor, 2 Dec. 1852. Joins with Britain against Russia in Crimean War, 1854–6. Treaty of Paris, Mar. 1856. War with Austria, 1859. Battle of Solferino, July 1859. Truce of Villafranca, 11 July 1859.

Franco-Prussian War, 1870–1. Battle of Sédan, 2 Sept. 1870. Revolution in Paris, 3 Sept. 1870.

The Third Republic proclaimed, 4 Sept. 1870. Paris surrenders, 28 Jan. 1871. Proclamation of the Commune at Paris, Feb. 1871. Peace of Frankfort, 10 May. Commune suppressed, 21–8 May 1871. Republican constitution promulgated, 1875. The Panama scandal, 1888–92. Franco-Russian alliances, 1891, 1896, 1900. Gen. Boulanger flees the country, 1891. The Dreyfus case, 1894–1906.

Anglo-French Alliance (*Entente Cordiale*), 8 Apr. 1904. Rupture with Vatican, 1904. Separation Law (Church and State), 1906; Devolution of Church Property Bill passed, 1908. 1914–18: *see* WORLD WAR I. French troops occupied Ruhr, 1922. Bayonne municipal bank failed, involving Stavisky scandal, 30 Dec. 1933. 1934: Stavisky shot himself, 8 Jan.; King of Yugoslavia and French Foreign Minister (Barthou) murdered at Marseilles, 9 Oct.

1936: Triumph of Popular Front, May. Subsequent frequent changes of government.

1938: Daladier and Bonnet visited London to confer about Czechoslovakia, 17 Sept.; Ribbentrop, in Paris, signed declaration that no territorial question existed between Germany and F., 6 Dec.

1939: F. declared war on Germany, 3 Sept. 1940: Reynaud became Premier, 21 Mar.; German troops entered Paris, 14 June; F. capitulated and accepted armistice terms of Germany and Italy, 22 June. De Gaulle carried on the fight from London. Government set up at Vichy, 1 July; diplomatic relations with Britain broken off, 5 July;

Pétain becomes head of state, with Laval as successor, 12 July; German-occupied zone announced, 28 July.

1942: Germans occupy Vichy F., 11–12 Nov. French fleet scuttled at Toulon, 27 Nov. Assassination of Darlan, 24 Dec.

1944: Invasion of France by Allies, 6 June. Most of France liberated by Sept. De Gaulle's Committee recognized as Provisional Government, 23 Oct.

1946: De Gaulle resigned, Jan. Fourth Republic came into being, 24 Dec. Beginning of Indo-China war.

1949: France signed *North Atlantic Treaty, 4 Apr.

1954: Fall of *Dien Bien Phu, May. Geneva conference of foreign ministers, May–July; as a result an armistice ending the Indo-China war signed there on 21 July. Civil war broke out in Algiers, Nov.

1956: Moroccan independence announced in Mar. Egypt nationalized the Suez Canal. Outbreak of the Israeli-Egyptian war; an Anglo-French force landed at Port Said, 5 Nov., withdrawal was completed by 22 Dec.

1957: F. a signatory to the Treaty of Rome, establishing the *European Economic Community, 25 Mar. Critical Algerian situation.

1958: Growing impatience in the French Army coupled with serious rioting in Algeria led to the collapse of the Fourth Republic, 13 May. De Gaulle formed a 'Government of National Safety', 29 May. De Gaulle elected President of the Fifth Republic, 21 Dec.

1961: Referendum in F. and Algeria approved de Gaulle's Algerian policy, 8 Jan. Army revolt in Algeria, 19–26 Apr. This was suppressed, and European resistance there to de Gaulle went underground (*see* OAS).

1962: Franco-Algerian peace talks held in secret near Franco-Swiss border, 11–8 Feb., ended with agreement made at *Evian ending the Algerian war and providing for an independent Algeria. In July Adenauer paid an official visit to F. A public show of Franco-German reconciliation reached its climax with a Mass in Rheims Cathedral attended by de Gaulle and Adenauer. De Gaulle threatened to resign if a referendum on the proposed new way of electing a president went against him. In the referendum, on 28 Oct. de Gaulle got 61.75 per cent of the votes cast, and his supporters won the General Election in Nov.

1963: De Gaulle made it clear that he did not want Britain in the EEC, 14 Jan. On 24 Jan. de Gaulle and Adenauer signed the Franco-German 'reconciliation treaty' in Paris. After initialling of the nuclear Test Ban Treaty in Moscow, de Gaulle announced (29 July) that France would not sign it.

1966: French withdrawal from NATO.

1967: In Nov. de Gaulle vetoed Britain's new application for entry to the EEC.

1968: While de Gaulle was in Romania students joined workers in marches in Paris and other French cities; but in June de Gaulle had an overwhelming electoral victory. France again vetoed British entry to EEC, Sept.

1969: Worsening economic situation brought disenchantment with de Gaulle's regime. De Gaulle resigned (30 April).

1970–80: F. agreed to Britain's entry into EEC, 1973.

1981: Socialist election victory, and Mitterand elected president.

1986: Right-wing government under Chirac; this fell in 1988, and Socialist government under first Rocard, then Bérégovoy in power 1988–93. Domestic problems caused by modernization programmes and the recession of the 1990s led to growth of anti-socialist feeling. Elections, Mar. 1993: landslide right-wing victory and Balladur became prime minister. Franc under increasing pressure: on 2 Aug. *ERM drastically altered, allowing virtual flotation of franc and other currencies, but franc remained tied to German mark despite adverse domestic economic consequences. Privatization programme started, May 1993. Government scandals affected popularity of Balladur regime throughout 1994 and threatened right-wing chances in 1995 Presidential election. In Apr. 1994 Nazi collaborator Touvier sentenced to life imprisonment for ordering killing of Jews in World War II: 6 May;

Mitterand joined Queen Elizabeth II in official opening of *Channel Tunnel. In Dec. Delors announced he would not contest presidential elections in 1995. Air France plane hijacked at Algiers by Muslim fundamentalists, 24 Dec.: stormed by French police at Marseilles, 26 Dec. Presidential election, 1995, won by Jacques Chirac. French commandos storm Greenpeace ship *Rainbow Warrior* in S Pacific, July 1995. Bomb explosion in Paris Metro, July 1995, thought to be work of Islamic extremists. Underground nuclear testing at *Muraroa, from Sept. 1995, caused world-wide protests and rioting in *Tahiti.

France, Heads of State.

1. *Monarchy:*
   Merovingian Dynasty 481–716
   Carolingian Dynasty 771–987
   Capetian Kings
   Hugh Capet 987–96
   Robert 996–1031
   Henry I 1031–60
   Philip I 1060–1108
   Louis VI 1108–37
   Louis VII 1137–80
   Philip II, Augustus 1180–1223
   Louis VIII 1223–26
   Louis IX, the Saint 1226–70
   Philip III 1270–85
   Philip IV 1285–1314
   Louis X 1314–16
   John I 1316
   Philip V 1316–22
   Charles IV 1322–28
   House of Valois
   Philip VI 1328–1350
   John 1350–64
   Charles V 1364–80
   Charles VI 1380–1422
   Charles VII 1422–61
   Louis XI 1461–83
   Charles VIII 1483–98
   Louis XII 1498–1515
   Francis I 1515–47
   Henry II 1547–59
   Francis II 1559–60
   Charles IX 1560–74
   Henry III 1574–89

   House of Bourbon
   Henry IV 1589–1610
   Louis XIII 1610–43
   Louis XIV 1643–1715
   Louis XV 1715–74
   Louis XVI 1774–93
2. *First Republic*
   Robespierre 1792–94
3. *The Directory*
   Barras 1795–99
   Rewbell 1795–99
   La Révellière-Lépeaux 1795–99
   Carnot 1795–97
   Letourneur 1795–97
   Barthélemy 1797
   Merlin 1797–99
   François 1797
   Siéyès 1799
   Gohier 1799
   Roger Ducos 1799
   Moulin 1799
4. *The Consulate*
   First Consul. Napoleon 1799–1804
   Second Consul. Siéyès 1799–1800
   Cambacérès 1800–04
   Third Consul. Ducos 1799–1800
   Le Brun 1800–04
5. *Empire*
   House of Bonaparte
   Napoleon I (abdicated) 1804–14
6. *Monarchy*
   House of Bourbon (restored)
   Louis XVIII 1814–24
   Charles X (abdicated) 1824–30
   House of Bourbon-Orléans
   Louis Philippe (abdicated) 1830–48
7. *Second Republic*
   President: Louis Napoleon Bonaparte 1848–52
8. *Empire*
   House of Bonaparte (restored)
   Napoleon III (abdicated) 1852–70
9. *Presidents of the Third Republic*
   Adolphe Thiers 1871
   Marshal MacMahon 1873
   Jules Grévy 1879
   Sadi Carnot 1887 (assassinated, 1894)
   Jean Casimir-Périer 1894
   François Félix Faure 1895
   Émile Loubet 1899
   Armand Fallières 1906
   Raymond Poincaré 1913

Paul Deschanel 1920
Alexandre Millerand 1920
Gaston Doumergue 1924
Paul Doumer 1913 (assassinated, 1932)
Albert Lebrun 1932
Re-elected, 1939. Deposed, 1940
10. *Chief of the French State*
Marshal Pétain 1940–44
11. *Head of the French Resistance*
Charles de Gaulle 23 June 1940
(Recognized as head of the Provisional Government of France, 23 Oct. 1944)
12. *Presidents of the Fourth Republic*
Vincent Auriol 1947
René Coty 1953
13. *Presidents of the Fifth Republic*
Charles de Gaulle 1958–1969
Georges Pompidou 1969–1974
Giscard d'Estaing 1974–1981
François Mitterand 1981–95
Jacques Chirac 1995–

Franche-Comté (the *County* of *Burgundy). Acquired by the *dukes* of Burgundy, 1384. Occupied by French, 1482–3. Seized by Louis XIV, 1678, and ceded to France by Treaty of Nijmegen, 1679.

franchise, elective (Britain).
1. *Counties:* Under Edward I county MPs were elected by freeholders. Conduct of county elections first regulated by statute, 1406. F. restricted to 40-shilling freeholders, 1430 till 1832.
2. *Boroughs:* There was no general statute on borough F. till 1832, voting qualifications depending exclusively on the terms of the borough charter.
3. *From 1832:* The local government F. in respect of both counties and boroughs was, until the passing of the Representation of the People Act, 1945, based on the occupation of rateable property, but that Act assimilated the local government F. with the parliamentary F. by making the normal basis that of residence. Successive classes of the population admitted to the F. by Acts of 1832, 1867, 1884; all males over 21 and females over 30 admitted, 1918; females

between 21 and 30, 1929. Business F. of spouses abolished, 1945. University and business F. abolished, 1948. Universal suffrage for all over 18 years of age, effective, 1970.

Franciscans, Monastic Order of. Called also Minorites. Founded by St Francis of Assisi (1182–1226) in 1209 (the female order, the Poor Clares founded, 1212). First came to England, 1220, where they first founded monasteries at Canterbury (1224) and Northampton. *See also* ASSISI.

Franco-Prussian War. Lasted from 15 July 1870 until signing of peace on 10 May 1871, although the Paris Commune continued fighting for a few days longer.

Franconia (Franken). Since the Treaty of Verdun, 843, it has meant a duchy comprising the land of the E Franks, on both sides of the valley of the Main, from which the Franks first set out to conquer Gaul (*see* FRANCE) and the Low Countries in the 4thC. Since *c.* 1500 it has been restricted to three counties (Upper, Middle, and Lower F.), centring upon Bamberg, Nürnberg and Würzburg respectively, in NW Bavaria. These were organized in 1837 by the Bavarian crown, which acquired all F., 1803.

francs were first struck for John of France, 1360, then again in 1576. In 1793 the franc became the monetary unit of France and maintained the same value until 1914, since when it has been devalued several times. Introduced by the Helvetic Republic, 1799. By the kingdom of the Belgians, 1831. De Gaulle 'New' or 'Heavy' F., 1960.

Frankfurt-am-Main, Hesse, was first mentioned by Einhard, AD 793. Diets held at, 822, 823, 951, 1015, 1069, 1109, etc. Became place for election of German emperors, 1152. Placed under an interdict during dispute between Louis the Bavarian and Papacy, 1329–49. By the *Golden Bull declared the principal seat of imperial elections, 1356. Free city, 1372. Joined League of Schmalkalden, 1536. Garrisoned by Gustavus Adolphus, 1631; bombarded by French, 1796; made capital of Grand

Duchy of Frankfurt, 1810; entered by Prussians, 16 July 1866. Frankfurt Peace signed, 1871. Heavily bombed, 1943–5, rebuilt, and since 1950s effective financial capital of Germany. HQ of the Bundesbank: chosen as HQ for *European Monetary Institute, 1993. *See also* FETTMILCH INSURRECTION.

Frankfurt-an-der-Oder, Brandenburg. Incorporated, 1253. Joined Hanseatic League, 1368; taken by Sweden, 1631; Russians, 1759; French, 1806; Russians, 1945.

franking of letters (Great Britain). Members of Parliament had the right from 1660; abolished on institution of penny postage, 10 Jan. 1840. *See* POST OFFICE.

Fredrickshald. *See* HALDEN.

Free Church Federal Council. Formed in 1940 by the union of the Free Church Council (established 1892) and the Federal Council (established 1919).

Free Church of Scotland. Formed by opponents of private patronage, 1843. Amalgamated with the Cameronians, 1876. Amalgamated, 31 Oct. 1900, with the United Presbyterian Church, the union assuming the name United F.C. The United F.C. united with the Church of Scotland on 2 Oct. 1929. The present F.C. is strongest in the Highlands, and stems from a dissentient fraction of the larger body, being popularly known as the Wee Frees (1995). It is a relatively small body (about 18,000 members).

Free Presbyterian Church of Scotland, established 1893 by two dissident members from the *Free Church of Scotland. Strictly Sabbatarian and adheres to 1648 Confession of Faith. About 5000 members in 1995.

freemasonry (Britain and general). The first grand lodge in England was established, 1717; in Ireland, 1725; in Scotland, 1736. Freemasons' Hall, London, built, 1775. Pope Clement XII issued a bull of excommunication against freemasons in 1738. Banned in Germany, 1934–45.

freemasonry (USA). F. was introduced into America in 1730. In 1733 a lodge was established at Boston by Henry Price. First masonic hall built at Philadelphia, 1754.

Free Soil Party (USA). Founded on 9 Aug. 1848, against extension of slavery in various territories; disbanded, 1854.

Freiburg (French **Fribourg**). Swiss canton, first belonged to the dukes of Zaehringen, one of whom, Bernard IV, founded the city in 1157. On the extinction of this dynasty, 1218, F. passed to the dukes of Kyburg; to the Hapsburgs, 1277–1452; to Savoy until 1477; joined the Swiss Confederation, 1481.

Freiburg-im-Breisgau. Founded, 1120, by dukes of Zaehringen; became separate county, 1218, until it passed to the Hapsburgs, 1369, who retained it until the dissolution of the empire in 1806; ceded to the Grand Duchy of Baden.

French Equatorial Africa. First settled 1839. Its four territories became independent republics in Aug. 1960 under the names of *Central African Republic, *Congo, *Chad, and *Gabon.

French Fury, The. Francis, Duke of Anjou, in Jan. 1583, occupied Antwerp. The citizens resisted and massacred over 2,000 of his troops, officers and nobles.

French Guiana (Cayenne). F. settlement began in 1604, and involved a long struggle with the Dutch, finally decided by the transplantation of dispossessed *habitants* from *Acadia *c.* 1760. Occupied by the Portuguese during the Napoleonic Wars. Convicts were first sent out in 1854 (*see* DEVIL'S ISLAND). Transportation abolished, 1938 but last convicts did not leave until 1953. Became Overseas Department of France, 19 Mar. 1946 and an administrative region, 1974.

French Guinea. *See* GUINEA, REPUBLIC OF.

French literature. The following is a list of prominent authors in the F. language, whether of F., Belgian, Swiss, Canadian, etc., nationality. Among medieval authors writers in the N F. dialect, the *langue d'œil,* including Anglo-Normans are in this list.

But writers in the S F. dialect (*langue d'oc*) of this period will be found in the list of PROVENÇAL AND CATALAN authors.

Abbo of Fleury, 945–1004, theologian.

Abélard, Pierre, 1079–1142, philosopher, famous for letters to Héloïse.

Adam de la Halle ('the Hunchback of Arras'), ?–1286, dramatist.

Adam, Paul Auguste Marie, 1862–1920, novelist.

Aicard, Jean François Victor, 1848–1921, poet and dramatist.

Amiel, Henri Frederic, 1821–81, Swiss philosopher.

Amyot, Jacques, 1513–93, translator.

Aragon, Louis, 1897–1983, poet.

Arnauld, Antoine, 1612–94, Jansenist theologian.

Arnault, Antoine Vincent, 1767–1834, dramatist, etc.

Arouet, François Marie. *See* VOLTAIRE.

Assoucy, Charles Cuypeau d', 1604–c. 1679, poet.

Aubigné, Jean Henri Merle d', 1794–1872, Swiss historian.

Aubigné, Théodore Agrippa d', 1552–1630, historian, poet, etc.

Augier, Guillaume Victor Émile, 1820–1889, dramatist.

Aymeric of Peyrac, ?–1400, chronicler.

Bachelard, Gaston, 1884–1962, philosopher and critic.

Baillon, André, 1875–1932, Belgian novelist.

Balzac, Honoré de, 1799–1850, novelist.

Balzac, Jean Guez, Baron de, 1594–1654, miscellaneous.

Barbusse, Henri, 1873–1935, novelist.

Baron, Michel Boyron, 1653–1729, dramatist.

Barrès, Auguste Maurice, 1862–1923, novelist and political writer.

Bartas, du. *See* DU BARTAS.

Barthélemy, Abbé Jean Jacques, 1716–95, miscellaneous writer.

Barthes, Roland, 1915–80, writer and critic.

Baudelaire, Charles Pierre, 1821–67, poet and critic.

Bazin, René François, 1853–1932, novelist.

Beaumarchais, Pierre Augustin Caron de, 1732–99, dramatist.

Beauvoir, Simone de, 1908–86, novelist.

Bellay, Joachim du. *See* DU BELLAY.

Belleau, Remi, *c.* 1528–77, poet.

Belloy, Pierre Laurent Beyrette de, 1727–75, dramatist.

Benoît de Sainte-Maure, 12thC, poet.

Benserade, Isaac de, 1613–91, poet.

Béranger, Pierre Jean de, 1780–1857, ballad-writer.

Bergson, Henri Louis, 1859–1941, philosopher.

Bernanos, Georges, 1888–1948, novelist.

Bernard, Charles de, 1805–50, novelist.

Bernard, Paul (Tristan), 1866–1947, novelist and dramatist.

Bernard, St, of Clairvaux, 1090–1153, theologian.

Bertaut, Jean, 1552–1611, satirical and religious poet.

Beyle, Marie Henri (Stendhal), 1783–1842, novelist.

Bèze, Théodore de, 1519–1605, historian and theologian.

Blanc, Louis, 1811–82, historian.

Blondel de Nesle, living in 1193, ballad-writer.

Bloy, Léon, 1846–1917, essayist.

Bodin, Jean, 1530–96, sociologist.

Boëtie, Étienne de la, 1530–63, poet and political writer.

Boileau-Despréaux, Nicolas, 1636–1711, historian and satirist.

Bossuet, Jacques Bénigne (Bishop), 1627–1704, historian and theologian.

Boulle, Pierre, 1912–94, novelist.

Bourget, Paul Charles Joseph, 1852–1935, poet, novelist and essayist.

Boursault, Edmé, 1638–1701, dramatist.

Brantôme, Pierre de Bourdeille, Seigneur de, 1540–1614, memoir-writer.

Brébeuf, Guillaume de, 1618–61, poet.

Brémond, Henri, 1865–1939, essayist.

Brieux, Eugène, 1858–1932, dramatist.

Brillat Savarin, Anthelme, 1755–1826, writer on gastronomy.

Broglie, Achille Victor, Duc de, 1785–1870, political writer.

Broglie, Albert, Duc de, 1821–1901, political and historical writer.

Brueys, David Augustin de, 1640–1723, dramatist.

Calvin (Cauvin), Jean, 1509–64, theologian and philosopher.

Cammaerts, Émile, 1878–1955, Belgian poet, theologian and essayist.

Camus, Albert, 1913–61, novelist, essayist and dramatist.

Carton de Wiart, Henry, 1869–1951, Belgian sociologist and novelist.

Casaubon, Isaac, 1559–1614, theologian.

Celine, Louise-Ferdinand, 1894–1961, novelist.

Chamfort, Nicolas Sébastien Roch, 1741–94, dramatist and miscellaneous writer.

Chapelain, Jean, 1595–1674, poet.

Chardin, Pierre Teilhard de, 1881–1955, philosopher and palaeontologist.

Charles, Duke of Orléans, 1391–1445, poet.

Charron, Pierre, 1541–1603, philosopher.

Chartier, Alain, c. 1385–1433, poet, historian, etc.

Chastellain, Georges, c. 1404–75, poet and chronicler.

Chateaubriand, François René, Vicomte de, 1768–1848, miscellaneous writer.

Chénier, André Marie de, 1762–94, poet.

Chrétien de Troyes, ?–1195, poet.

Christine de Pisan, 1363–1430, poet, historian, etc.

Cixous, Hélène, 1937–, feminist essayist.

Cocteau, Jean, 1891–1963, poet and dramatist.

Colette (Madame Henri de Jouvenel), 1873–1954, novelist.

Collé, Charles, 1709–83, poet and dramatist.

Collin d'Harleville, Jean François, 1755–1806, dramatist.

Commines or Commynes, Philippe de, 1455–1509, diplomatist and historian.

Comte, Auguste, 1798–1857, philosopher.

Constant de Rebecque, Henri Benjamin, 1767–1830, novelist and philosopher.

Coppée, François Édouard Joachim, 1842–1908, poet.

Coquillart, Guillaume, 1450–1510, satirist.

Corneille, Pierre, 1606–84, dramatist.

Corneille, Thomas, 1625–1709, dramatist.

Coster, Charles de, 1827–79, Belgian storywriter.

Courteline, Georges, 1860–1929, novelist.

Crébillon, Claude-Prosper Jolyot de, 1707–77, novelist.

Crébillon, Prosper Jolyot de, 1674–1762, dramatist.

Crétin, Guillaume, ?–1525, poet.

Crousez, Jean Pierre de, 1663–1750, philosopher.

Cyrano de Bergerac, Savinien, 1619–55, novelist and dramatist.

D'Alembert or Dalembert, Jean le Rond, 1717–83, encyclopaedist.

Dancourt, Florent Carton, 1661–1725, dramatist.

Daudet, Alphonse, 1840–97, poet and novelist.

Daudet, Léon, 1867–1942, critic, novelist, and journalist.

Deffand, Mme du, 1697–1780, letter-writer.

Delavigne, Casimir, 1793–1843, dramatist.

Déroulède, Paul, 1846–1914, poet and dramatist.

Derrida, Jacques, 1930–, philosopher and critic.

Descartes, René, 1596–1650, scientific and philosophical writer.

Deschamps, Eustache (called Morel), 1338–1415, poet.

Destouches, Philippe (Néricault), 1680–1754, dramatist.

Diderot, Denis, 1713–84, miscellaneous writer.

Dierx, Léon, 1838–1912, poet.

Du Bellay, Joachim, c. 1524–60, poet and antiquarian.

Dudevant, Amandine Lucile Aurore (Dupin), Baronne ('George Sand'), 1804–76, novelist.

Dufresny, Charles Rivière, 1648–1724, dramatist.

Duhamel, Georges, 1884–1966, novelist.

Dumas, Alexandre Davy de la Pelleterie (père), 1803–70, novelist and dramatist.

Dumas, Alexandre (fils), 1824–95, novelist and dramatist.

Du Perron, Jacques Davy (Bishop), 1556–1618, essayist and poet.

Duras, Marguerite, 1914–, dramatist and writer.

Du Ryer, Pierre, 1606–68, dramatic poet and translator.

Eekhoud, Georges, 1854–1927, Belgian novelist and critic.

Elskamp, Max, 1862–1931, Belgian poet.

Eluard, Paul, 1895–1952, poet.

Erckmann Chatrian. The compound name of Émile Erckmann (1822–99) and Alexandre Chatrian (1826–90), who collaborated in fiction and drama.

Estienne. The name of a family of printers and scholars who lived in the 16thC.

Fénelon, François de Salignac de la Mothe (Archbishop), 1651–1715, miscellaneous writer.

Feuillet, Octave, 1821–90, novelist.

Feydeau, Georges, 1862–1921, farcical dramatist.

Flaubert, Gustave, 1821–80, novelist.

Fléchier, Espirit, 1632–1710, preacher.

Florian, Jean Pierre Claris de, 1755–94, novelist and poet.

Fontenelle, Bernard le Bovier de, 1657–1757, philosopher, etc.

Foucault, Michel, 1926–84, philosopher and historian of ideas.

Fournier, Alain, 1886–1914, novelist.

France, Anatole, *See* THIBAULT.

François de Sales (St), 1567–1622, theologian.

Froissart, Jean, *c*. 1338–1406, chronicler.

Fustel de Coulanges, Numa Denis, 1830–89, historian.

Gaguin, Robert, 1433–1501, poet and historian.

Garnier, Robert, *c*. 1545–90, dramatist.

Gautier, Théophile, 1811–72, poet, novelist and dramatist.

Genlis, Stephanie Félicité Ducrest, Comtesse de, 1746–1830, romantic writer.

Gerlache, Étienne Constantin de, Baron, 1785–1871, Belgian historian.

Gerson, Jean Charlier de, 1363–1428, theologian and philosopher.

Gide, André Paul Guillaume, 1869–1951, novelist and dramatist.

Gilbert, Nicolas Joseph Laurent, 1751–80, poet.

Gilkin, Iwan, 1858–1924, Belgian poet, critic and historian.

Giraud, Albert (A. Kayenbergh), 1860–1929, Belgian poet.

Giraudoux, Jean, 1882–1944, dramatist and essayist.

Gobineau, Arthur de, 1816–82, novelist, historian, etc.

Goncourt, Edmond de, 1822–96, } joint novelists.
Goncourt, Jules de, 1830–70, }

Gourmont, Rémy de, 1858–1915, journalist and critic.

Gras, Félix, 1844–1901, Provençal poet and novelist.

Green, Julian, 1900– , US/French novelist.

Gregory of Tours (St), 538?–93, historian.

Grévin, Jacques, 1538–70, poet.

Guérin, Charles, 1873–1902, poet.

Guérin, Georges Maurice de, 1810–39, poet.

Guillaume de Nangis, ?–*c*. 1300, historian.

Guimond de la Touche, Claude, 1729–60, dramatist.

Guizot, François Pierre Guillaume, 1787–1874, historian.

Gyp. *See* MARTEL DE JANVILLE.

Halévy, Élie, 1870–1937, historian.

Halévy, Ludovic, 1834–1908, dramatist.

Héloïse, 1101–71. *See* ABÉLARD.

Helvétius, Claude Adrien, 1715–71, philosopher.

Heredia, José Maria de, 1842–1905, poet.

Herzog, Émile. *See* MAUROIS.

Hugo, Victor-Marie, Vicomte, 1802–85, novelist and poet.

Hugues de la Bachelerie, 12thC, poet.

Huysmans, Joris Karl, 1848–1907, novelist.

Jacques de Guise, ?–1399, chronicler.

Jacques de Vitry (Bishop), ?–1240, chronicler.

Jaurès, Jean, 1859–1914, publicist.

Jean de Meung (Jean Clopinel), *c*. 1280–?, translator.

Jean de Troyes, living in 1480, chronicler.

Jean le Bel, ?–1370, chronicler.

Jodelle, Étienne, 1532–73, dramatist.

Joinville, Jean, Sire de, *c*. 1224–1317, historian.

Jouy, Victor Joseph Étienne, *c*. 1764–1846, novelist and dramatist.

Juvénal des Ursins (Archbishop), 1380–1422, historian.

Kervyn de Lettenhove, Joseph, Baron, 1817–91, Belgian historian.

Labaud, Valéry, 1881–1957, poet and essayist.

Labé, Louise ('La Belle Cordière'), 1526–1566, biographer and poet.

La Bruyère, Jean de, 1645–96, philosopher and moralist.

La Calprenède, Gautier de Costes de, 1614–63, novelist and dramatist.

La Chaussée, Pierre Claude Nivelle de, 1692–1754, dramatist.

Lacroix, Paul, 1806–54, novelist and historian.

La Fayette, Marie, Madeleine Pioche de la Vergne, Comtesse de, 1634–93, novelist.

La Fontaine, Jean de, 1621–95, fable-writer and poet.

Laforgue, Jules, 1860–87, poet and story-writer.

La Harpe, Jean François de, 1739–1803, dramatist.

Lamartine, Alphonse Prat de, 1790–1869, historian and poet.

Lamennais, Hugues Félicité Robert de, 1782–1854, theologian and journalist.

La Motte, Antoine Houdart, 1672–1731, dramatist and critic.

La Rochefoucauld, François, Duc de, 1613–80, writer on morals.

Larousse, Pierre, 1817–75, lexicographer.

La Salle, Antoine de, 1398–1462, romantic writer.

Leconte de Lisle, Charles Marie René, 1818–94, poet.

Lefreuc, Abel, 1862–1952, critic.

Legouis, Émile, 1861–1937, writer on English literature.

Le Maire de Belges, Jean, 1473–1524?, historian and poet, etc.

Lemonnier, Antoine Camille, 1845–1913, Belgian novelist and critic.

Lerberghe, Charles van, 1861–1907, Belgian poet and dramatist.

Lesage, Alain René, 1668–1747, novelist, author of *Gil Blas*.

Lorens or Laurent (Frère), 13thC, writer on morals.

Loti, Pierre. *See* Viaud.

Maeterlinck, Maurice, Count, 1862–1949, Belgian poet, dramatist and philosopher.

Maintenon, Françoise d'Aubigné, Marquise de, 1635–1719, letter-writer.

Maistre, Joseph, Comte de, 1754–1821, publicist and philosopher.

Maistre, Xavier de, 1763–1852, novelist.

Malebranche, Nicolas, 1638–1715, philosopher.

Malherbe, François de, 1555–1628, poet and critic.

Mallarmé, Stéphane, 1842–98, poet.

Malraux, André, 1901–76, miscellaneous writer.

Marguerite de Valois-Angoulême (Queen of Navarre), 1492–1549, poet and tale-teller.

Marie de France, 12thC, poet.

Maritain, Jacques, 1882–1973, philosophical writer.

Marmontel, Jean François, 1723–99, dramatist, poet, and novelist.

Marot, Clément, 1497–1544, poet.

Martel de Janville, Sibylle Gabrielle Marie Antoinette, Comtesse de ('Gyp'), 1849–1932, novelist.

Martin, Thérèse (St Thérèse of Lisieux), 1873–97, mystical writer.

Masson, Pierre Maurice Alexandre, 1879–1916, critic.

Maupassant, Guy de, 1850–93, novelist and short-story writer.

Mauriac, François, 1885–1970, novelist.

Maurois, André (pseudonym of Émile Herzog), 1885–1967, writer and biographer.

Maurras, Charles Marie, 1868–1952, poet, critic and miscellaneous writer.

Ménage, Gilles de, 1613–92, scholar.

Mendès, Catulle, 1841–1909, poet, novelist and dramatist.

Mérimée, Prosper, 1803–70, novelist.

Merrill, Stuart, 1863–1915, poet of American birth.

Meschinot, Jean, *c.* 1415–91, poet.

Michelet, Jules, 1798–1874, historian.

Mirabeau, Victor Riqueti, Marquis de, 1715–89, economist.

Mistral, Frédéric Joseph Étienne, 1830–1914, Provençal poet.

Mockel, Albert, 1866–1945, Belgian poet and critic.

Moliére, Jean Baptiste Poquelin de, 1622–1673, dramatist.

Montaigne, Michel Eyquem, Seigneur de, 1533–92, essayist.

Montalembert, Charles Forbes René de, 1810–70, historian and political writer.

Montesquieu, Charles Louis de Secondat, Baron de, 1689–1755, sociologist.

Musset, Alfred de, 1810–57, poet and dramatist.

Necker, Jacques, 1732–1804, statesman and miscellaneous writer.

Nerval, Gérard de, 1805–55, poet and novelist.

Noailles, Anna, Comtesse de, 1876–1933, poet.

Pascal, Blaise, 1623–62, philosopher and poet.

Pasquier, Étienne, 1529–1615, historian.

Péguy, Charles, 1873–1914, poet.

Perrault, Charles, 1628–1703, writer of fairy-tales.

Picard, Edmond, 1836–1924, Belgian essayist, dramatist and poet.

Pigault-Lebrun, Charles Antoine Guillaume Pigault de l'Épinoy, 1753–1835, novelist.

Pirenne, Henri, 1862–1935, Belgian historian.

Poincaré, Jules Henri, 1854–1912, mathematician and philosopher.

Prévost d'Exiles, Antoine François, Abbé, 1697–1763, novelist.

Prévost Eugène Marcel, 1862–1941, novelist and dramatist.

Prévost, Jean, 1901–44, miscellaneous writer.

Proudhon, Pierre Joseph, 1809–65, socialist writer.

Proust, Marcel, 1871–1922, novelist.

Prudhomme, Sully. *See* SULLY-PRUDHOMME.

Quinault, Philippe, 1635–88, dramatist.

Rabelais, François, *c.* 1490–1553, satirist.

Racan, Honorat de Bueil, Marquis de, 1589–1670, poet, dramatist and biographer.

Racine, Jean, 1639–99, poet and dramatist.

Regnard, Jean François, 1655–1709, poet and dramatist.

Régnier, Henri François Joseph de, 1864–1936, poet and novelist.

Régnier, Mathurin, 1573–1613, poet.

Renan, Ernest, 1823–92, historian and philosopher, etc.

Restif de la Bretonne, Nicolas Edmé, 1734–1806, novelist.

Retz, Jean François Paul de Gondi, Cardinal de, 1614–78, writer of memoirs and *pensées*.

Richepin, Jean, 1849–1926, poet and dramatist.

Ricoeur, Paul, 1913–, philosopher and essayist.

Rimbaud, Jean Nicolas Arthur, 1854–91, poet.

Rivarol, Antoine de, 1753–1801, scholar.

Robbe-Grillet, Alain, 1922–, novelist.

Robert de Sorbon, 1201–74, philosopher, founded the Sorbonne.

Roland, Marie Jeanne Phlipon, Mme, 1754–93, writer of memoirs and letters.

Rolland, Romain, 1866–1944, novelist, dramatist and essayist.

Rollin, Charles, 1661–1741, historian.

Ronsard, Pierre de, 1524–85, poet.

Rostand, Edmond Eugène Alexis, 1868–1918, dramatist and poet.

Roumanille, Joseph, 1818–91, Provençal poet and story-writer.

Rousseau, Jean-Jacques, 1712–78, novelist, philosopher, etc.

Rutebeuf, *c.* 1230–80, poet.

Sagan, Françoise, 1935–, novelist.

Saint-Amant, Marc Antoine, Seigneur de, 1594–1661, poet.

Sainte-Beuve, Charles Augustin, 1804–69, critic, poet, moralist, historian, etc.

Saint-Évremond, Charles de Marguetel de Saint-Denis, Seigneur de, 1613–1703, miscellaneous writer.

Saint-Exupéry, Antoine de, 1900–44, novelist.

Saint-Gelais, Mellin de, 1491–1558, translator and epigrammist.

Saint-Gelais, Octavien de (Bishop), 1466–1502, poet.

Saint-Pierre, Charles Castel, Abbé de, 1658–1743, sociologist.

Saint-Pierre, Jacques Henri Bernardin de, 1737–1814, novelist and traveller.

Saint-Simon, Claude Henri de Rouvroy, Comte de, 1760–1825, philosopher.

Saint-Simon, Louis de Rouvroy, Duc de, 1675–1755, historian.

Sales. *See* FRANÇOIS DE SALES.

Samain, Albert, 1858–1900, poet.

Sand, George. *See* DUDEVANT.

Sartre, Jean-Paul, 1905–80, dramatist and existentialist philosopher.

Scarron, Paul, 1610–60, novelist and satirist.

Scève, Maurice, *c*. 1510–60, poet.

Scribe, Augustin Eugène, 1791–1861, dramatist.

Scudéry, Georges de, 1601–67, dramatist.

Scudéry, Madeleine de (sister of the above), 1607–81, novelist.

Segrais, Jean Regnauld de, 1624–1701, poet, memoir- and story-writer.

Séverin, Fernand, 1867–1934, Belgian poet.

Sévigné, Marie de Rabutin-Chantal, Marquise de, 1626–96, letter-writer, etc.

Simenon, Georges, 1903–1989, Belgian detective novelist.

Sorel, Albert, 1842–1906, historian.

Sorel, Charles, 1602–74, novelist.

Sorel, Georges, 1847–1922, philosopher.

Staël-Holstein, Anne Louise Germaine (Necker), Baronne de, 1766–1817, novelist.

Stendhal. *See* BEYLE.

Sue, Eugène (Joseph Marie Sue), 1804–57, novelist.

Sully, Maximilien de Béthune, Duc de, 1560–1641, memoir-writer.

Sully-Prudhomme, René François Armand, 1839–1907, poet.

Taine, Hippolyte Adolphe, 1828–93, critic and historian.

Thérèse of Lisieux *See* MARTIN.

Thibault, Jacques Antoine Anatole ('Anatole France'), 1844–1924, novelist and satirist.

Thierry, Amédée S.D., 1787–1873, historian.

Thierry, Jacques Nicolas Augustin, 1795–1856, historian.

Thiers, Louis Adolphe, 1797–1877, historian, critic, and statesman.

Thou, Jacques Auguste de, 1553–1617, historian.

Tocqueville, Alexis Clerel de, 1805–59, historian.

Tristan L'Hermite, François, 1601–55, poet.

Turgot, Anne Robert Jacques, Baron de l'Aulne, 1727–81, philosopher and political economist.

Tyard, Pontus de (Bishop), 1521–1605, poet.

Urfé, Honoré d', 1568–1625, novelist.

Valéry, Paul, 1871–1945, poet and dramatist.

Vauquelin de la Fresnaye, Jean, 1536–1608, poet.

Verhaeren, Émile, 1855–1916, Belgian poet.

Verlaine, Paul, 1844–96, poet.

Verne, Jules, 1828–1905, novelist.

Viau, Theophile, de (called Théophile), 1590–1626, poet.

Viaud, Julien ('Pierre Loti'), 1850–1923, novelist.

Vigny, Alfred, Comte de, 1797–1863, poet and novelist.

Villehardouin, Geoffroi de, 1155?–1213?, historian.

Villiers de l'Isle Adam, Philippe Auguste Mathias, Comte de, 1840–89, poet, story-writer, and dramatist.

Villon, François de Montcorbier (called), 1431–85?, poet.

Voltaire (François Marie Arouet de), 1694–1778, poet, dramatist, philosopher, novelist, etc.

Wace, Robert, of Jersey, *fl.* 1170, chronicler.

Weil, Simone, 1909–43, mystical writer.

Yourcenar, Marguerite, 1903–87, novelist.

Zola, Émile, 1840–1902, novelist.

French Revolution, The. Jean-Jacques Rousseau (1712–78) did much to prepare France for the revolution by his *Social Contract*. Meeting of the States-General, 5 May 1789, when the Third Estate demanded that the assembly should be composed of one order instead of three. The Third Estate met and took title of National Assembly, 17 June 1789. Louis XVI ordered Three Estates to separate. Led by Mirabeau, they refused, 23 June 1789. Royal troops sent to Paris, July 1789. Necker dismissed by Louis XVI, 11 July 1789. The *Bastille captured by the mob, 14 July 1789. Mob marched to Versailles and forced royal family to go to Paris, 5 Oct. 1789. Death of Mirabeau, 2 Apr. 1791. Massacre of the Champ de Mars, 17 July 1791. New constitution formed called the Legislative Assembly, 30 Sept. 1791, and the National Assembly dissolved. Mob invaded the Tuileries, 20 June 1792. The monarchy overthrown, 10 Aug. 1792. Dumouriez defeated the Prussians, who issued a manifesto against the French people, at the battle of Valmy, 20 Sept. 1792. National Convention took place of Legislative Assembly, and declared France a republic, 22 Sept. 1792. Louis XVI executed, 21 Jan. 1793. Committee of Public Safety formed, Jan. 1793. England, Holland, Spain, Portugal, Tuscany, Naples and the Holy Roman Empire joined against France, 1 Feb. 1793. Girondists overthrown, 2 June 1793. Robespierre triumphant, Mar. 1794, but executed, 28 July 1794. Paris mob demands bread, Apr. 1795. Napoleon fires on mob, 5 Oct. 1795. *See* FRANCE.

French Somaliland. *See* DJIBOUTI.

Friedewald, Treaty of, 1552, between Henry II of France and the German Protestant princes, led by Maurice of Saxony.

Friendly Isles. Explored by Capt. Cook, 1773. *See* TONGA.

Friendly Societies (UK). First legalized by Act of Parliament, 1793. Registration made compulsory, 1923. Part of F.S. in National Insurance and social security came to an end under the terms of the National Insurance Act, 1946.

Friends, Society of. *See* QUAKERS.

Friends of the Earth, environmental pressure group, formed in Britain, 1971, but now (1995) has branches in more than 30 countries.

Friends of the People. Society formed 1792, to obtain parliamentary reform by constitutional means.

Friesland. From 1579 to 1795 one of the constituent parts of the republic of the United Provinces. William IV became hereditary stadtholder of F. (and all the other provinces) in 1747. Since 1815 a province of the Kingdom of the Netherlands.

Friesland, East. Region in NW Germany. A county in the 15thC, and later an independent duchy. Passed to Prussia, 1744, and annexed by Napoleon to Holland, 1806. Passed to Hanover, 1815.

frigate.
1. Single-decked three-masted warship. First was the *Constant Warwick*, launched, 1646, and purchased for the Navy, 1649. Term abolished in the Royal Navy, 1883.
2. A type of all-purpose small warship introduced by Royal Navy in World War II, 1941. Since 1975, small escort warship.

Friuli, Province of, Italy and Slovenia. A county founded by the Carolingian emperors *c.* 780. Divided, 1500, between Venice and Austria. Rest of it went to Austria at the fall of the Venetian Republic, 1797, and was ceded to Italy in 1866. Small portion ceded to Yugoslavia, 1947; Slovene from 1991. *See* VENETIA.

Frobisher Bay, Arctic Ocean. Discovered by Sir Martin F., 1576.

Froebel system. Educational system founded by F.W.A. Froebel (1782–1852) as expounded in his book, *Die Menschenerziehung*, 1826. Froebel's first kindergarten opened in Switzerland, 1837.

Fronde, The. The First or Parliamentary F. originated in the Paris *Parlement*, June, 1648, against abuses in the Government. Closed with the Treaty of Rueil, 1 Apr. 1649. The Second or Aristocratic F. led by certain nobles under Condé, principally against Cardinal Mazarin, 1650; suppressed, 1653.

Fucino, Lake (ancient *Lacus Fucinus*). Overflow tunnel from, to Liri River, built at orders of Emperor Claudius, AD 37. Attempts to reopen it from 1240 onwards failed. Completely drained, 1876.

Fugitive Offenders Act, 1881, was replaced by the **Fugitive Offenders Act,** 1967.

Fugitive Slave Laws, passed by US Congress, 1850; repealed, 1864.

Fujiyama (Mount Fiji). Volcano on Honshu Island, Japan. Height 12,400 ft (3,788 metres). Has a prominent Shinto shrine; volcano extinct since 1707.

Fulda, Germany. Abbey founded, 744, by Winfrith (Boniface) of Crediton, Apostle of Germany (680–755), who is buried there.

Fulham (London). Manor given to bishopric of London *c*. 691. First rector appointed, 1242. Bishops of London have resided at F. Palace since 1141, but present building not started until *c*. 1510–20.

futurism. Movement founded by Marinetti, 1909. First Italian futurist exhibition held in Paris, 1911. Transferred to London, 1912. Movement collapsed *c*. 1915.

Fuzhou. *See* FOOCHOW.

G7, term applied since 1975 to the Group of Seven, i.e. Germany, Japan, Italy, France, USA, Canada and Britain, when their representatives meet in concert to discuss global economics and finance.

Gabelle. Certain taxes levied in France, especially on salt; first levied, 1286, finally abolished, 1790.

Gabon. Discovered by Portuguese, 1485. First French settlement, 1839. Libreville, founded 1848, made capital, 1849. Territory of French Equatorial Africa, 1946; member of the French Community, 1958; independent republic, 17 Aug. 1960. One-party state, 1968. Opposition parties legalized, 1990 and elections held, though claims of manipulation followed.

Gadsden Purchase. In 1853 the US Government bought certain lands from Mexico. The negotiations were managed by Gen. James G. (1788–1858), hence the name.

Gads Hill, Kent. Dickens bought a house here, 1856, and lived in it, 1860–70.

Gaeta, Italy. Besieged by Alfonso V of Aragon, 1435; by Austrians, 1707; by Charles of Naples, 1734; by French, 1806; by Austrians, 1815; by Italian National Party, 1860–1. Pope Pius IX took refuge here, 1848–9.

Gainsborough, England. Marriage of Alfred the Great at, AD 868. Destroyed by the Danes, 1013. Church founded by Templars, 1209. Captured from Parliamentarians, 1643.

Galapagos Islands. Discovered 1535, by Fra Tomas de Balanga, 3rd Bishop of Panama. Annexed by Ecuador, 1832. Darwin's visit during his expedition, 1831–36, inspired the formulation of his theory of evolution. 20thC development threatens G.I.'s unique natural character. Serious fire in, Apr. 1994.

Galatia. Ancient district of Asia Minor. The Gaulish or Galatian immigrants who settled there about the 3rdC BC were defeated by Attalos I of Pergamum, 230 BC. Came under Roman rule, 133 BC.

Galicia, Spain. Settled at some time BC by the *Gauls, after whom it is named. G. became a Roman province, AD 137. The Suevi founded a kingdom of G., 411, which was overthrown by the Visigoths, 528. In the 8thC after a short spell of Saracen rule G. was absorbed into the kingdom of the Asturias, and in 1072 was incorporated with Leon and Castile.

Galicia (former Austrian crown-land), named after the principality of Halicz, was settled towards the E by *Ruthenians and towards the W by Lechs (Poles) in the 6thC AD. W G., finally passed to Poland in the 10thC. E G. was converted to Orthodox Christianity and Russian hegemony in the reign of Vladimir the Great of Kiev (*d.* 1015). G. formed, together with Volhynia, a short-lived independent principality (1199) which was absorbed by Lithuania, 1321, but fell to Poland under Casimir the Great, 1349. In 1371 a Galician Patriarchate, independent of Kiev, was set up, which at the Union of Brest-Litovsk, 1596, transferred its obedience to Rome (*see* RUTHENIAN CHURCH). The entire Galician territory passed to Austria in the Partitions of 1772 and 1795, and the Polish (less so the Ukrainian) element managed to retain considerable autonomy down to 1918. Polish, 1919–39. Occupied by the Russians from Sept. 1939 to July 1941. By treaty of 17 Aug. 1945 all G. E of the San River passed to the Soviet Republic of Ukraine (now, 1995. the Republic of the Ukraine).

Galilee became part of the Assyrian Empire, 734 BC, but was given up to the Israelites after their return from the Captivity. Under the rule of the Idumean princes Herod the Great (37–4 BC) and his son Herod Antipas (4 BC–AD 39), the former being also King of Judea, but the latter only Tetrarch of G. Under Roman procurators from AD 44, G. became the chief refuge of the Jews after their expulsion from Jerusalem, 135. *See* SAFAD. After the war of 1948 much of the Arab population fled to Jordan

Gallia Cisalpina or **G. Citerior,** practically identical with the modern regions of Piedmont, Lombardy and Venetia, was divided into G. Cispadana on the right bank and G. Transpadana on the right bank and G. Transpadana on the left bank of the Po respectively. The Gauls penetrated into the Po valley from the N in the 5thC BC. A Roman colony was established at Sena Gallica (Senegaglia), 282 BC, and the whole country reduced, 203–191, the last Gallic tribe to resist being the Boii.

Gallia Transalpina or **G. Ulterior,** consisting of G. Narbonensis (Provence), Aquitania (basin of the Garonne), G. Lugdunensis (central plateau) and G. Belgica, which extended up the Rhine, is dealt with under FRANCE.

Gallican Church. Owing to its independent attitude towards the Roman See, the Church in France was often called the G.C. The Pragmatic Sanction of 1269 provided that the laws of the Church should conform with the common law. Philip IV in 1302 opposed Pope Boniface VIII and imprisoned him; and again in 1438, the Pragmatic Sanction of Bourges aimed at the encroachments of Rome. This last was superseded by the Concordat of Bologna, between Pope Leo X and Francis I. The declaration of the French clergy in 1682 (the Four Propositions) declared the Pope incompetent to interfere in civil affairs. Condemned by Pope Alexander VIII, 1690; by Clement XI, 1706 and by Pius VI, 1794. Declaration of 1682 was again put into force by Napoleon, 1810. In 1826 the French bishops confirmed this. However, at the Vatican Council, 1869–70, they declared the Pope competent to intervene.

Gallican Confession. Profession of faith of the French Reformed Church adopted at the Synod of La Rochelle, 1571.

Gallipoli, Turkey. Captured by Turks, 1357. British and French armies landed at, Apr. 1854, and proceeded against the Russians. For G. campaign, 1915–16, *see* Dardanelles, *under* WORLD WAR I.

gallon, standardized for the UK, 1824, as the volume of 10 lb. of distilled water at 62°F. and 30 in. barometric pressure superseded by the litre by 1995. The present standard G. in USA is the archaic wine G. of Queen Anne, standardized in 1707 at 231 c. in.

Gallup Poll, invention, of George Horace G. (1901–85), who founded the G. Institute, 1935, which correctly forecast the results of several US presidential elections. His methods form the basis of modern public opinion polling.

Galveston, Texas. Settled 1837. Captured by the Federals, 1862, and retaken by the Confederates, 1863. Seriously damaged by fire, 1885, and by the sea, 1900. Centre of oil industry since 1920s.

Galway, Ireland. Fortified *c.* 1244; surrendered to parliamentary forces, 10 July 1641. Gavazzi riots at, Mar. 1859.

Galway Election. In May 1872 a successful petition was presented to unseat Capt. Nolan, MP for G., owing to alleged intimidation of certain Irish Roman Catholics.

Gambia, W Africa. Settlement founded by English on initiative of Portuguese in London, 1588. English factory established at, 1620. English right to G. confirmed by Treaty of Paris, 1815; separated from Sierra Leone, 1843; included in W African Settlements, 1866; again made a separate crown colony, 1888. On 18 Feb. 1965 became an independent state within the Commonwealth. G. became a republic in April 1970: joined with Senegal to form Confederation of Senegambia, 1982; this dissolved, 1989. Government overthrown in military coup, July 1994.

gaming and gambling, laws regulating (Great Britain). Act of Charles II, 1665, by which persons losing more than £100 at one time were not compelled to pay. An Act of 1710 provided that bonds and other securities won at play were not recoverable, and any person losing more than £10 might sue and recover this amount from the winner. Acts to amend, previous laws, 1845, 1854, 1860, 1892 and 1922. Betting and Gaming Act, 1960, radically modified British gambling laws. Amended, 1968. Gaming Board established, Oct. 1968. Betting and Gaming Duties Act, 1972; Betting, Gaming and Lotteries (Amendment) Act, 1980, etc. *See* BETTING.

gamma rays. Discovered by Villard, 1900.

Gandamak, Treaty of, between Britain and Afghanistan, 1879.

Garde Nationale. First raised, 1789, under Lafayette, in Paris; they helped to crush the Parisian mob in 1795 (13th Vendémiaire), but in 1830 and 1848 declared for the revolutionaries. Disbanded after the suppression of the Commune at Paris, May 1871.

garden city. Idea first mooted by Ebenezer Howard (1850–1928) in his book *Tomorrow* (1898). First (Letchworth), G.C. founded, 1903, and second (Welwyn), 1920. *See* NEW TOWNS.

Garhwal, ravaged by Gurkhas, 1803 (*see* NEPAL, *also* SIKKIM), came under British protection, 1814, and was included in United Provinces. Now part of Uttar Pradesh.

gas. Illuminating power demonstrated experimentally by Dr John Clayton, Dean of Kildare, *c.* 1691. Illumination by, first attempted in Cornwall to replace candles and lamps at a factory, 1792. In London it was introduced, 1807, and generally used, 1816. G. flame used for cooking in J. Sharp's ovens, 1835. First practical internal combustion G. engine made by Lenoir, 1860. Used in conjunction with refrigerating plants, 1908. First used for illumination in USA at Boston, 1823. Natural gas discovered under N Sea in Dutch waters, after World War II. Substantial British N Sea gas finds, 1965 onwards. Conversion of British gas supplies to N Sea gas begun, 1968.

Gas, British. Gas in Britain nationalized, 1949, under Gas Act of 1948. Gas Corporation replaced Gas Council, 1972. Privatized, 1986, as British Gas plc. In 1993 this company had a virtual monopoly of British gas supplies: it had 3,400 miles of pipeline and six reception terminals. Proposals to break British Gas's monopoly put forward, 1993; British Gas's monopoly of domestic gas to be ended, 1996. Public outcry regarding executive pay rises, 1995.

gas, poison, first used by Germans against Russians, Apr. 1915, and against British, Sept. 1915. Geneva Protocol of 1925 banned its use in warfare. Used by Iraq against Iran, 1983–4 and also against Kurds.

Gascony, France. *See* AQUITAINE.

Gastein, Convention of, between Austria and Prussia at close of the Schleswig-Holstein War, 14 Aug. 1865.

GATT (General Agreement on Tariffs and Trade), signed at Geneva, 1947. In force from 1 Jan. 1948. There were 104 contracting members at the beginning of 1992. 'Rounds' of G.A.T.T. talks on various global economic matters have been:

1. Geneva, 1947
2. Annecy, 1949
3. Torquay, 1951
4. Geneva, 1956
5. Geneva (the Dillon Round), 1960–1
6. Geneva (the Kennedy Round), 1964–7
7. Geneva (the Tokyo Round), 1973–9.
8. Geneva (the Uruguay Round) intended to break down trade barriers began, Sept. 1986. Tentative agreement (*see* BLAIR HOUSE AGREEMENT) was reached between the US and EC on agriculture, 1992, but this subsequently challenged by France, and when cleared, other sub-

jects, e.g. films, insurance and financial services, threatened to jeopardize completion. But agreement eventually signed, Geneva, 15 Dec. 1993. though various subjects omitted from it. Round officially ended by final signatures at Marrakesh, 15 Apr. 1994. Ratification of Uruguay Round by USA, Nov. 1994. GATT organization, superseded by World Trade Organization (*WTO), Jan. 1995.

Gatwick, Sussex, was flying-club airfield from Aug. 1930 and handling commercial flights by 1936. In 1953 it was designated as diversionary airport for *Heathrow; named as London's official 'second' airport, 1954 and rapidly developed. Officially opened as such by the Queen, 1958; major runway extension work, 1964. Further phase completed, 1978. Satellite building, 1983. By 1987 was world's second busiest airport (overtaking JFK, New York). North Terminal opened by the Queen, 1988. Handled over 20 million passengers, 1991–2; estimated will handle 30 million by year 2000.

Gaul. *See* FRANCE.

Gauls. A branch of the Celts, whose language does not survive. Their main body spread outwards from the Alps and settled widely in *Gallia, *Cisalpina and *Transalpina in the 5thC BC. The La Tène culture of the early Iron Age (500–1 BC) represents the peak of Gallic art. In the 4thC they invaded central Italy, taking Rome, 390, unopposed. At the same time elements migrating SW from France reached *Galicia; another section pressed E and settled in the interior of Asia Minor, 275 (*see* GALATIA). In the 2ndC German tribes drove the Gallic Helvetii and allied tribes out of what is now Baden and Württemberg W over the Rhine and S into the Jura. For the history of the W and S branches, *see* FRANCE and GALLIA CISALPINA. For that of the eastern, *see* GALATIA.

gavelkind. An ancient English form of land tenure, under which the inheritance was divided equally among all the sons. It existed only in Kent and was abolished by the Law of Property Act, 1925.

Gaza, Israel, Town mentioned in Genesis (x. 19) and other biblical books. Captured by Alexander the Great, 332 BC; ravaged by Saladin, 1170; citadel captured by him, 1187. Captured by Khwarizmians, 1244, and held by Muslims until taken by the French under Kléber, 1799. Taken by the Egyptians, 1831; by the British, Nov. 1917. Israeli from 1967; scheduled to become Arab self-governed under PLO-Israeli agreement, Sept. 1993. Israelis finally withdrew from G., May 1994 and Arafat installed there from 1 July 1994. (*See* GAZA STRIP.)

Gaza Strip came into existence as a result of the armistice agreement between Israel and Egypt, 1949. It represented the area of Palestine left in Egyptian hands after the 1948 fighting. Israel expelled Egyptian forces from the G.S., Nov. 1956, but in Mar. 1957 Israel troops withdrew and a UN force took their place. Egypt resumed the civil administration of the G.S. At Egypt's request, the UN force withdrew, 19 May 1967. 8 June 1967, Israel won control of the G.S. in the 'June war'; and despite Arab and international opposition from 1970 proceeded to try to turn the G.S. into a permanent Jewish settlement. Increased Arab militant resistance, from the mid-1980s. Sealed off by Israelis after Arab violence, April 1993. G.S. became self-governing Arab territory when PLO-Israeli agreement of Sept. 1993 operative; this occurred when Israelis withdrew from G.S., 17 May 1994 and Yassir Arafat returned to take up residence there, 1 July 1994. Police clash with Islamic fundamentalists, Nov. and subsequent threats from Islamic militants continued sporadically.

Gdansk, German **Danzig,** by which name it was known until 1945. Capital of Dukes of Pomerania, 1230. Occupied by Teutonic Knights, 1308; reconquered by Poland, 1455; place of refuge of Charles VIII when driven from Sweden, 1457; an autonomous free city, 1466–1793; seized by Russians and Saxons, 29 June 1734; ceded to Prussia, 1793; surrendered to Napoleon, who declared it a free city again, 26 May 1807; restored to Prussia, 1814. Declared a free city by the Treaty of Versailles, 1919. Germany annexed G., 1 Sept. 1939. Heavily bombed by Anglo-US and Russian air forces in World War II. Ceded to Poland by Yalta agreement. German population largely driven out, 1945–6. Scene of *Solidarity anti-Communist action from 1980 which eventually led to collapse of Communism in *Poland.

Gdynia (Polish), **Gdingen** or **Gotenhafen** (German). Built by Poles as a Baltic port, 1921–30. Occupied by Germans, 14 Sept. 1939. Returned to Poland, 1945.

Geiger counter. Invented by Rutherford and Geiger, 1908, and developed by Geiger and Müller, 1928.

Gelderland, Holland. Formed part of the Burgundian possessions, 1472–92. Formed part of the Burgundian Circle of the Holy Roman Empire, 1512. Passed to the Emperor Charles V, 1543. Province of the United Netherlands, 1578. Part of the kingdom of the Netherlands, 1815.

Gelnhausn, Compact or **Agreement of,** by the Electors of the Empire to resist the reforms of the Emperor Maximilian, June 1502.

General Agreement on Tariffs and Trade. *See* GATT.

General Assembly. *See* CHURCH OF SCOTLAND.

General Strike (Britain), 3–13 May 1926.

General Synod (of the Church of England), established 1970, under the Synodical Government Measure of 1969, to replace the *Church Assembly. The G.S. meets three times annually and consists of a House of Bishops, House of Clergy and House of Laity. It carried a proposal for the *ordination of women by the required two-thirds majority, 11 Nov. 1992.

genetic engineering has developed since

1960s, alongside growing knowledge of DNAs which play a crucial role in G.E. Gene therapy in Britain approved by the Committee on the Ethics of Gene Therapy, 1992, which led to the establishment of the Gene Therapy Advisory Committee, 1993, to monitor developments in G.E. A European genetic information centre (European Bioinformation Institute) planned, 1993, with possible HQ at Cambridge. Isolation of certain genes possibly related to various serious diseases, e.g. cystofibrosis and certain cancers, 1993, gave hope of future successful treatment by G.E. Genetically-engineered vaccines becoming increasingly important, 1994. *See also* DNA

genetics, science founded by the Austrian biologist, Gregor Johann Mendel (1822–84) whose theories on particular inheritance, known as Mendelism, were published 1865–9, but importance not fully recognized until several years after his death.

Geneva (German **Genf**), Switzerland. Republic founded, 1512; allied with Freiburg, 1519, and Berne, 1526; adopted Protestant doctrines, 1535. Calvin (*see* CALVINISTS) went there, 1536, and exiled from, 1538; recalled, Sept. 1541; d. at, 1564. G. annexed to France, 1798. Joined Swiss Confederation, 1815. *See* LEAGUE OF NATIONS.

Geneva Conferences. Among the most notable conferences held at Geneva are:
1. Held by foreign ministers of 19 countries at Geneva, Apr.–July 1954, to discuss (*a*) unification of Korea, (*b*) a settlement in Indo-China. No settlement was reached over Korea; but an armistice ending the Indo-China war was signed, 21 July.
2. Heads of governments of Britain, France, Russia and the USA met at Geneva, 18–23 July 1955, first such meeting since Potsdam (1945).
3. Talks held under UN auspices between US and Iraqi representatives to try to avert *Gulf War, 1990. These failed.
4. Negotiations between EC mediators, Lord Owen and Cyrus Vance (later, Torval Stoltenberg) and representatives of Bosnia, Serbia, Croatia and the Bosnian

Serbs to try to settle conflict in Bosnia-Herzogovina, began 1992. Transferred to New York, 1993. Returned to G., July 1993, but further negotiations foundered, Nov. In 1994 more negotiations took place in G: a peace plan with UN backing formulated April, but Bosnian Serbs rejected this, August. Bosnian peace-talks restarted at G., Sept. 1995 when agreement in principle reached.

Geneva Conferences (Disarmament).

1. 1927: Sequel of the Washington Conference of 1922, on naval disarmament. Its sequel was the London Conference of 1930.
2. 1932: Came to an abrupt end in Oct. 1933 when Hitler announced Germany's withdrawal from the conference and from the League of Nations.
3. 1962: Between UN members, began 14 Mar.; little progress made subsequently, though these discussions indirectly influenced the events leading to the Test Ban Treaty initialled in Moscow between the USSR, USA and Britain in July 1963. and eventually to the SALT Agreements 1972–9.
4. 1981: Talks begun on limiting nuclear forces in and around Europe. In 1982: START talks began, leading eventually to the signing in Moscow in 1991 between USA and Russia of START I and US/Russian agreement, in Geneva on draft treaty for START II, Dec. 1992. *see* also SALT; START.

Geneva Convention.
Signed by the representatives of 12 countries, 22 Aug. 1864, and dealt with the treatment of wounded during war. Revised 1906, to which 57 nations became parties in 1929, when paragraphs relating to the civil population were raised. A new convention was signed in 1949. Additional Protocols, 1977.

Genoa,
Italy (Latin *Genua*, Italian **Genova**). Submitted to Romans *c.* 200 BC; a free republic, AD 1000. Joins the First Crusade, 1095–9; and Third Crusade, 1191–6. Alliance with Venice, 1238; with the Pope, 1239; with Florence and Lucca, 1251. Quarrel with Venice at Acre, 1256. Defeat at naval battle of Acre, 1258. Assists the Greek Emperor Michael Palaeologus to retake Constantinople from the Latins, 1261. Treaty of Cremona, 1270. Naval battle of Curzola, 1298. War of *Chioggia, 1350–81. Annexes Corsica from Pisa, 1367. Commercial treaty with the Turks, 1452. Refuses help to the Knights of St John, 1520. Sacked by Spanish and Italians under Colonna, 1522. Battle of Prevesa, 1540. Sends nominal contingent to fight at Lepanto, 1571. Walls built, 1626–32. Bombarded by French, 1684; by British, 1745. Sells Corsica to France, 1768. Converted into the Ligurian republic under French domination by Napoleon, July 1797. Annexed by France, 1806. Incorporated with Piedmont-Sardinia, 1815. Bombarded by the British fleet, Feb. 1942.

Gentlemen-at-Arms, Honourable Corps of.
English royal bodyguard, founded 1509. First went into action as Henry VIII's bodyguard at Guingatte, 1513, then at the siege of Boulogne, 1544. It also took up action stations at St James's Palace, 1848, in face of an alleged Chartist march on Westminster. Since the 19thC the Government Chief Whip in the House of Lords is also Captain of the Corps.

Geographical Society, American.
Established, 1852.

Geographical Society, Royal,
was founded, 1830. Responsible for the establishment of a school of geography, the first in an English university, at Oxford, 1899.

Geological Society,
Great Britain. Founded, 1807, and incorporated, 1826.

Geophysical Year, International.
July 1957–Dec. 1958, during which observations of the action of natural physical forces on the earth were made by scientists from approximately 40 countries at locations throughout the world.

George Cross.
Honour instituted, 1940, to reward the performance of deeds of valour by civilians. It ranks immediately after the *Victoria Cross. The G.C. was awarded to

the island of *Malta on 17 Apr. 1942, in recognition of its gallantry under enemy bombardment.

George Washington Bridge over the Hudson River opened, Nov. 1931.

Georgia, Caucasus (Russian **Gruzia**; Georgian **Karthveli**). The 'Iberia' of the ancients. Converted to Christianity, 318. Invaded by Tartars, 1236; laid waste, 1386 and 1393–4, by Timur, who was driven out in 1403; invaded by Persians, 1618. The last king was George XIII, who resigned the crown in favour of Paul, Emperor of Russia, 1800; formally annexed to Russia, 1801. Soviet Socialist Republic proclaimed, 25 Feb. 1921. Became constituent republic of the USSR, 1936. Nationalist uprisings, 1989, led to repression by Russian troops. Following breakup of USSR, G. declared independence 8 Apr. 1991 with Gamsakhurdia as president, but (Dec.) did not join CIS. Opposition to Gamsakhurdia led to civil war, 1991–2; Gamsakhurdia fled G. and military council chose former Soviet foreign minister Shervardnadze (a Georgian) to head government (1992). G. joined Conference on Security and Economic Co-operation in Europe, 1992. S Ossetia declared independence from G., 1992 but this not recognized by G. and fighting has continued sporadically between S Ossetia and G. since 1990. Fighting between Abkhazi (*see* ABKHAZIA) rebels and G. since 1989 intensified from 1992. Short-lived Russian-brokered cease-fire, July 1993 but in Sept. 1993 Abkhazis captured Sukhumi on Black Sea, thus controlling more than half Abkhazia. G. applied to join CIS in effort thereby to obtain Russian military and economic aid. Gamsakhurdia returned to G., autumn 1993 and established military base; G. in state of anarchy, but Russian aid started having effect, Oct. Gamsakhurdia in flight, committed suicide, Jan. 1994, by which time Shervardnadze had regained control of most of G. G. joined CIS, Mar. 1994. Unsuccessful assassination attempt on Shevardnadze, Aug. 1995; presidential election, Nov.

Georgia, USA. Founded by royal charter,

granted 9 June 1732; named after George II; State constitution adopted, 5 Feb. 1777. State university at Athens chartered, 1785. One of original 13 states of the Union. Seceded, 1861; readmitted to union, 1870. New constitution adopted, 1976.

Georgetown, capital of *Guyana. Founded 1781, named after George III. Controlled and largely rebuilt by Dutch (who named it Starbroek), 1784–1812. Renamed G. 1812. University founded, 1963.

Georgetown, now part of Washington, DC, area settled late 17thC. Planned as a town, 1751, called George. Incorporated as G., 1789. In 1871 merged with District of Columbia and in 1878 annexed to Washington city. G. University founded, 1789. Congress legislation to preserve old streets and buildings of G., 1950.

German Baptists. A sect founded, 1708; settled in America early in the 18thC. The first congregation there was organized at Germantown, Pennsylvania, 25 Dec. 1723; their press in 1743 printed the first Bible to appear in a European language in America. J.C. Beissel (1690–1768) seceded with his followers, who are now known as the Seventh Day Baptists. Another faction, the Old Order Brethren, seceded, 1880–90, and a Radical or progressive group, 1882. G.B. known as Church of the Brethren from 1908; in 1939 split into the Brethren Church and the Grace Brethren.

German Catholics. A sect in Saxony and Silesia, which seceded from the Church of Rome, 1844. Can be regarded as forerunners of the *Old Catholics.

German Federal Bank. *See* BUNDESBANK, DEUTSCHE.

German literature. The following is a list of principal authors in the G. language, whether Germans, Austrians, or Swiss:

Arnim, Bettina von, 1785–1859, poetess.
Arnim, Ludwig Achim von, 1781–1831, miscellaneous writer.
Auerbach, Berthold, 1812–82, novelist.

Auersperg, Graf Anton Alexander von, 1806–76, poet.

Bernhard, Thomas (Austrian), 1931–, novelist.

Bodenstedt, Friedrich Martin von, 1819–92, poet.

Böhme, Jakob, 1575–1624, philosopher.

Böll, Heinrich, 1917–85, novelist.

Bonhoeffer, Dietrich, 1906–45, theologian.

Brant, Sebastian, 1458–1521, satirist.

Brecht, Bertolt, 1898–1956, dramatist.

Breitinger, Johann Jakob, 1701–76, miscellaneous writer.

Brentano, Clemens, 1788–1842, romantic writer.

Brockes, Barthold Heinrich, 1680–1747, poet.

Büchner, Georg, 1813–37, dramatist.

Bunsen, Christian Karl Josias, Baron von, 1791–1860, antiquarian.

Burckhardt, Jakob, 1818–97, Swiss art historian.

Canitz, Friedrich Rudolf Ludwig, Freiherr von, 1654–99, poet.

Carossa, Hans, 1878–1956, story-writer.

Dach, Simon, 1605–59, poet.

Döblin, Alfred, 1878–1957, novelist.

Droste-Hülshoff, Annette von, 1797–1848, poet.

Ebeling, Christoph Daniel, 1741–1817, historian.

Ebers, Georg, 1837–98, romance writer.

Eck, Johann Maier von, 1486–1543, theologian.

Eckhart, Johannes (Meister), 1260–1327, mystic.

Egestorff, Georg, pseudonym. *See* OMPTEDA.

Ekkehard of St Gall, *fl. c.* 930, poet.

Fallada, Hans, 1893–1947, novelist.

Feuchtwanger, Leon, 1884–1958, novelist, dramatist and critic.

Fichte, Immanuel Hermann von, 1797–1879, philosopher.

Fichte, Johann Gottlieb, 1762–1814, philosopher.

Fischart, Johann, *c.* 1546–90, satirist.

Fischer, Ernst Kuno Berthold, 1824–1907, philosopher.

Fischer, Johann Georg von, 1816–97, poet and dramatist.

Fleming, Paul, 1609–40, poet.

Fontane, Theodor, 1819–98, novelist and poet.

Fouqué, Friedrich Heinrich Karl de la Motte, 1777–1843, novelist.

Freiligrath, Hermann Ferdinand, 1810–97, poet.

Freud, Sigmund, 1856–1939, psychologist.

Freytag, Gustav, 1816–95, novelist.

Frisch, Max, 1911–91, Swiss novelist and dramatist.

Geiler von Kaysersberg, Johannes, 1445–1510, mystic.

George, Stefan, 1868–1933, poet.

Gessner, Salomon, 1730–88, poet.

Goethe, Johann Wolfgang von, 1749–1832, poet.

Gottfried von Strassburg, *c.* 1210, poet.

Gottschalk, Rudolf von, 1823–1909, dramatist, novelist, poet and critic.

Gottsched, Johann Christoph, 1700–66, poet and dramatist.

Grass, Günter, 1927–, novelist and poet.

Grillparzer, Franz, 1791–1872, Austrian poet and dramatist.

Grimm, Jakob, 1785–1863, } philologists and folklorists; Grimm, Wilhelm, 1786–1859, } brothers who collaborated

Grimmelshausen, Hans Jakob Christoffel von, *c.* 1624–76, picaresque novelist.

Gryphius, Andreas, 1616–49, poet and dramatist.

Gunther, Johann Christian, 1695–1723, poet.

Hagedorn, Friedrich von, 1708–54, poet.

Hagelstange, Rudolf, 1912–84, poet and novelist.

Haller, Albrecht von (Swiss), 1708–77, poet.

Hardenberg, Friedrich von, 1772–1801, poet.

Hartmann von Aue, *c.* 1170–*c.* 1210, poet.

Hauptmann, Gerhard, 1862–1946, dramatist.

Hebbel, Christian Friedrich, 1813–63, poet.

Hegel, Georg Friedrich, 1770–1831, philosopher.

Heidegger, Martin, 1889–1976, philosopher.

Heine, Heinrich, 1797–1856, poet and dramatist.

Heinrich von Meissen ('Frauenlob'), *c.* 1250–1318, poet.

Heinrich von Morungen, end of 12thC, poet.

Heinrich von Veldeke, *c.* 1170, poet.

Herder, Johann Gottfried von, 1744–1803, poet and philosopher.

Hesse, Hermann, 1877–1962, Swiss-domiciled novelist and poet.

Heyse, Paul Johann, 1830–1914, poet and storywriter.

Hochhuth, Rolf, 1931–, dramatist.

Hoffmann, Ernst Theodor Wilhelm, 1776–1822, romanticist.

Hoffmann, Heinrich, 1809–94, children's writer.

Hofmannsthal, Hugo von, 1874–1929, poet and dramatist.

Hölderlin, Johann Christian Friedrich, 1770–1843, poet.

Hölty, Ludwig, 1748–76, poet.

Humboldt, Friedrich Heinrich Alexander von, 1769–1859, traveller and scientist.

Humboldt, Karl Wilhelm von, 1767–1835, critic and philologist.

Husseil, Edmund Gustar Albrecht, 1859–1938, philosopher.

Hutten, Ulrich von, 1488–1523, poet and controversialist.

Johnson, Uwe, 1934–, writer.

Kafka, Franz, 1883–1924, novelist.

Kant, Immanuel, 1724–1804, philosopher.

Kästner, Erich, 1899–1974, children's writer.

Kautsky, Karl, 1854–1938, historian of Socialism.

Keller, Gottfried, 1819–90, novelist and poet.

Keyserling, Count (Hermann Alexander), 1880–1946, philosopher and essayist.

Kirsch, Sarah, 1935–, poet.

Kleist, Ewald Christian von, 1715–59, poet.

Kleist, Heinrich von, 1777–1811, dramatist.

Klopstock, Friedrich Gottlieb, 1724–1803, poet.

Knapp, Georg Friedrich, 1842–1926, economic historian.

Konrad von Würzburg, 1230?–87, poet.

Körner, Karl Theodor, 1791–1813, dramatist and poet.

Kotzebue, August Friedrich Ferdinand von, 1761–1819, dramatist.

Lassalle, Ferdinand Johann Gottlieb, 1825–64, economic writer.

Lavater, Johann Kasper, 1741–1801, Swiss poet.

Leibnitz, Gottfried Wilhelm, Freiherr von, 1646–1716, philosopher.

Lessing, Gotthold Ephraim, 1729–81, dramatist and critic.

Logau, Friedrich, Freiherr von, 1604–55, epigrammist.

Ludwig, Emil, 1881–1948, biographer.

Ludwig, Otto, 1813–65, poet and dramatist.

Luther, Martin, 1483–1546, hymn-writer and theologian.

Mann, Heinrich, 1871–1950, novelist.

Mann, Thomas, 1875–1955, novelist and critic.

Marx, Heinrich Karl, 1818–83, economist and philosopher.

Melanchthon, Philipp, 1497–1560, theologian.

Meyer, Konrad Ferdinand, 1825–98, Swiss novelist.

Mommsen, Theodor, 1817–1903, historian.

Mörike, Eduard Friedrich, 1804–75, poet.

Müller, Wilhelm, 1794–1827, poet.

Musil, Robert, 1880–1942, novelist and playwright.

Neidhart von Reuenthal, *c.* 1180–1250, poet.

Nestroy, Johann, 1801–62, dramatist.

Nietzsche, Friedrich Wilhelm, 1844–1900, philosopher.

Ompteda, Baron Georg von, 1863–1931, novelist.

Opitz von Boberfeld, Martin, 1597–1639, poet.

Oswald von Wolkenstein, 1367–1445, poet.

Ranke, Leopold von, 1795–1886, historian.

Remarque, Erich Maria, 1898–1970, novelist.

Reuter, Heinrich Ludwig Christian Friedrich ('Fritz'), 1810–74, story-writer.

Richter, Johann Paul Friedrich, 1763–1825, novelist, etc.

Rilke, Rainer Maria, 1875–1926, lyric poet.

Rosegger, Petri Kettenfeier, 1843–1918, novelist and poet.

Sachs, Hans, 1494–1576, poet and dramatist.

Schiller, Johann Christoph Friedrich von, 1759–1805, poet and dramatist.

Schlegel, August Wilhelm von, 1767–1845, poet, essayist and translator.

Schlegel, Friedrich von, 1772–1829, novelist, dramatist, and critic.

Schleiermacher, Friedrich Ernst Daniel, 1768–1834, theologian and philosopher.

Schnitzler, Arthur, 1862–1931, dramatist and novelist.

Schopenhauer, Arthur, 1788–1860, philosopher.

Schubart, Christian Friedrich Daniel, 1739–91, poet and musician.

Schumacher, Fritz, 1911–1977, economist.

Schweitzer, Albert, 1878–1965, Alsatian-born ethical writer.

Spengler, Oswald, 1880–1936, philosopher.

Sperr, Martin, 1944–, dramatist.

Spitteler, Carl Friedrich, 1845–1924, poet.

Spyri, Johanna, 1829–1901, Swiss children's novelist.

Stein, Edith (Sister Teresa Benedicta), 1891–1942, philosopher and religious writer.

Stefan, Andres, 1906–70, novelist.

Storm, Theodor Woldsen, 1817–88, poet and novelist.

Strauss, David Friedrich, 1808–74, theologian and biographer.

Sudermann, Hermann, 1857–1928, dramatist and novelist.

Sylva, Carmen (Elisabeth, Queen of Romania), 1843–1916, miscellaneous writer.

Tauler, Johannes, c. 1300–61, mystic.

Tieck, Johann Ludwig, 1773–1853, dramatist.

Toller, Ernst, 1893–1939, dramatist and poet.

Treitschke, Heinrich von, 1834–96, historian.

Uhland, Johann Ludwig, 1787–1862, poet.

Wagner, Wilhelm Richard, 1813–83, dramatist and musician.

Walther von der Vogelweide, c. 1168–c. 1228, poet.

Wedekind, Frank, 1864–1918, dramatist.

Werfel, Franz, 1890–1945, Austrian novelist.

Wieland, Christoph Martin, 1733–1813, novelist, poet, and translator.

Wildenbruch, Ernst von, 1845–1909, dramatist.

Winckelmann, Johann Joachim, 1717–68, art historian.

Wolf, Christa, 1929–, novelist and essayist.

Wolfram von Eschenbach, c. 1170–1220, poet.

Wyss, Johann Rudolf, 1781–1830, children's novelist.

Zweig, Stefan, 1881–1942, novelist and poet.

German Volga Republic. The region on both sides of the Lower Volga was settled by Germans at the invitation of Catherine the Great, 1760. In 1918 they set up a commune, which in 1924 was transformed into an autonomous republic. In 1941, the republic forfeited its autonomy, and its German inhabitants were deported. It became part of the Saratov region, 1947. Since the collapse of the USSR many people of German descent have left Russia and settled in Germany, 1989 onwards.

germanium. Chemical element discovered by Winkler in 1886.

Germany. For history previous to 12 July 1806, *see* HOLY ROMAN EMPIRE, also PRUSSIA. Confederation of the Rhine formed under Napoleon's mediation, 12 July 1806. German Confederation formed under Austrian presidency, 1815. N German *Zollverein founded, 1819. S German Zollverein, 1828–31. Central German Zollverein, 1828. Revolutions, 1848–50. Resumption of the German Diet, 1851. German-Danish War, 1864. Austro-Prussian War leads to the exclusion of Austria from Confederation and the formation of the N German Confederation under Prussia, 1866. Franco-Prussian War, 1870–1. German Empire proclaimed at Versailles, 1871. Peace of Frankfurt-on-Main, 10 May 1871. First German Imperial Parliament, Mar. 1871. Triple Alliance constituted between Austria, Italy and G., 1883. Togo,

Cameroons and SW Africa acquired, 1884; E Africa, 1885; William II came to the throne, 1888. Bismarck resigned, 1890. Kiaochow seized, 1897. Steady rise of Socialism with strong Marxist tendencies, from 1900 onwards. Expansion of navy by Navy Bill, 1900; G. refused at Hague Conference of 1907 to abate naval building. Morocco crisis between G. and France, 1905, and *Agadir incident, 1911. War declared on Russia, 1 Aug.; on France, 3 Aug.; on Belgium, 4 Aug. 1914.

*World War I: Revolution breaks out, Nov. 1918. Kaiser William II flees, 9 Nov. The Weimar Republic established, 31 July 1919. G. declared herself unable to meet reparations, July 1922, and French troops occupied Ruhr, 10 Jan. 1923. Partial evacuation of Ruhr, Nov. 1924. Death of Ebert, 28 Feb.; election of President Hindenburg, 26 Apr. 1925. Locarno Treaty signed, Oct. 1925. Treaty with Soviet, Apr. 1926. Admission to League of Nations, 8 Sept. 1926. Hindenburg re-elected, 10 Apr. 1932.

1933: Adolf Hitler became Chancellor, 30 Jan.; legal Government of Prussia deposed, 6 Feb.; Reichstag fire, 27 Feb.; freedom of speech and press abolished, 28 Feb.; Hitler triumphant at polls, 5 Mar.; persecution of Jews began, 8 Mar.; Social-Democratic Party suppressed, 23 June; Centre Party wound up, 29 June; notice of withdrawal from League of Nations given, 14 Oct.; Hitler's policy approved by plebiscite, 12 Nov.

1934: 90 dissentient Nazis shot, including Schleicher, former Chancellor, and Röhm, chief of the S.A., 30 June; Hindenburg *d.*, and office of president was abolished, Hitler becoming supreme as Führer, 2 Aug.

1935: Saar plebiscite, 13 Jan., returned to G., 1 Mar.; Hitler denounced Treaty of Versailles, 16 Mar.

1936: Troops reoccupied Rhineland, 8 Mar.; Edgar André, Communist leader beheaded at Hamburg, 5 Nov.; Anti-Comintern Pact with Japan, 25 Nov.

1938: German troops entered Austria, 11 Mar.; union of Austria with the Reich ('Anschluss') proclaimed, 13 Mar.; Chamberlain flew, 29 Sept., to Munich, where four-power agreement regarding Czechoslovakia (between Britain, France, Italy and Germany) signed, 30 Sept.; German occupation of the claimed portions of Czechoslovakia completed, 10 Oct.

1939: *Czechoslovak republic destroyed by G., 15 Mar.; Slovakia a German protectorate; Memel transferred from Lithuania to the Reich by forced agreement, 22 Mar.; Poland rejected G.'s demands as to Danzig, etc., 5 May; 'Axis' announced to have become a military pact, 6–7 May; military alliance with Italy embodied in treaty, 22 May; Russo-German non-aggression pact signed at Moscow, 23 Aug.; Poland invaded, and Danzig's return to Reich proclaimed, 1 Sept. (*See* WORLD WAR II.) Britain and France declared war on G., 3 Sept.; Gdynia surrendered to G., 14 Sept. Warsaw surrendered to G., 28 Sept.; Western Poland annexed, Germans in Latvia invited to return to Reich, 8 Oct.; first shipload of Baltic Germans left Riga for Gdynia, 14 Oct.; repatriation of Germans from Estonia announced, 16 Oct.; Hitler nearly killed in Bürgerbräukeller at Munich by a time-bomb, 8 Nov.

1940: Invasion of Denmark and Norway, 9 Apr.; and of Belgium and Holland, 10 May; France accepted armistice terms of G. and Italy, 22 June; *Tripartite Pact with Italy and Japan signed in Berlin, 27 Sept.; German troops began occupation of Romania, 13 Oct.; Hungary signs pact in Vienna, 20 Nov.; Romania and Slovakia sign pact, 23 Nov.

1941: German troops occupy Bulgaria, which joins Axis (Tripartite) Pact, 1 Mar.; invasion of Yugoslavia and Greece, 6 Apr.; both countries occupied by end of Apr.; flight to Britain of Rudolf Hess, deputy Führer, 10 May; attack on Russia began, 22 June. Heavy bombing of G. by Britain begins, 1942. (For further German history till 1945 *see* WORLD WAR II).

Hitler presumed dead in Berlin, 30 Apr. 1945. Final surrender, 8 May 1945. Four allied commanders-in-chief assumed supreme power and established zones of occupation, 5 June 1945. Potsdam Conference, July 1945. Formation of State governments begun in US zone, Jan. 1946.

Fusion of British and American zones begun, Dec. 1946. Four-power negotiations in the Council of Foreign Ministers in London broke down on the future of a politically and economically united G., Dec. 1947. Britain, France and the USA therefore (1948) integrated their zones politically and economically. Currency reform in Western zones, June 1948, followed by Russian blockade of *Berlin, 28 June 1948–12 May 1949. Parliamentary Council met in Bonn to begin the task of drafting a constitution for W G., Sept. 1948. For subsequent history of G. *see* the next two articles.

Germany, Democratic Republic of (E Germany).

German Democratic People's Republic set up in Russian zone, 7 Oct. 1949. Pieck (1876–1960) became first President, but real power in Ulbricht's hands. After Stalin's death a more 'liberal' policy begun, June 1953, but after rioting in Berlin and several other cities had had to be crushed by Russian tanks, 16–17 June, a harsher policy was readopted. 'National people's army' created, 18 Jan. 1956. Due to defections to the W, the population of the republic fell by nearly 2,000,000 between 1948 and 1959. After Pieck's death (7 Sept. 1960) the presidency was abolished. Instead a council of state was established whose first chairman (Ulbricht, *d.* 1973) had dictatorial powers. Friction between the republic and the W increased during 1960–1, due to steady flow of refugees to the W through Berlin, and on 13 Aug. 1961 (by which time three million people had left for the W) the republic closed the Berlin border and subsequently built a heavily fortified wall along it (20 Aug.). Many killed by E German guards trying to get over the Berlin Wall. Some liberalization from 1970s; meetings between GDR and FRG leaders and Honecker, E German leader 1976–89, paid controversial official visit to Federal Republic. Breakup of Soviet regime from 1989 led to thousands of GDR families leaving the country and seeking refuge in other E European cities. In Oct. 1989 Honecker forced to resign (sub-sequently charged with crimes against E German citizens killed crossing the Wall, but trial abandoned on medical grounds). Nov. 1989, border between two Germanies opened, and subsequently, 9 Nov., Berlin Wall pulled down (*see* BERLIN). In Aug. 1990 the GDR agreed to reunify with the FRG. Formal reunification date, 3 Oct. 1990. For subsequent history, *see under* GERMANY, FEDERAL REPUBLIC OF (Next article).

Germany, Federal Republic of.

A constitution for a Federal Republic in W G. was approved by the Western Occupying Powers, 12 May 1949, and the republic came into being, with its capital at Bonn, 23 May. First elections to Federal Diet (Bundestag), 15 Aug. First chancellor, Konrad Adenauer, elected, 16 Sept. State of war between Western Powers and G. ended, 1951. Member of the Council of Europe, 1951. Reparations agreement concluded with Israel, 1952. Member of the European Coal and Steel Community, 1952. Diplomatic relations were established between Russia and the federal republic, and several thousand German prisoners repatriated from Russia. The republic joined Western Union and NATO, May 1955. Saar reunited to Germany at midnight on 31 Dec. 1956. Member of the European Economic Community, 1958. A foreign ministers' conference at Geneva, attended by representatives of both German republics, failed to reach agreement on reunification of Germany, 1959. Franco-German friendship demonstrated by Adenauer's official visit to France, July 1962, when there was a ceremony of reconciliation between the two countries. 1963: Franco-German 'reconciliation treaty' signed in Paris, 24 Jan. In the elections Sept. 1969 the Social Democrats made big gains: on 21 Oct., Brandt was elected chancellor of a coalition of Socialists and Free Democrats. Schmidt succeeded as Chancellor, 1974. Christian Democrats regained power under Helmut Kohl, 1983. Improved relations with GDR from 1970s; increased numbers of E Germans settling in FRG from 1980s, notably after softening of Soviet regime after 1986. Border between two Germanies opened, Nov. 1989; subsequently, Berlin Wall (*see* BERLIN) pulled down, 9 Nov. During 1990 four former occupying powers and representatives of both Germanies reached agreement on German reunification. Monetary union of both Germanies began, July and formal political reunification occurred, 3 Oct. 1990. Berlin declared capital of the reunited state. First free all-German elections since 1932 held, Dec. 1990 with Christian-Democrat victory. Reunified state retained name of Federal Republic of Germany. Since reunification severe economic problems in FRG. Rising unemployment and growing hostility to immigrant workers led to increased far-right support in local elections, 1992–3. Recession affecting FRG from 1992. FRG dominant force in EC from 1980s but after reunification strong German mark caused serious financial difficulties in EC and world-wide, resulting in ERM crisis, 1993. From 1993 Germans again allowed to serve in armed forces abroad (peace-keeping only). Strike for parity of pay with W German workers by E German steelworkers, May 1993. Legislation passed to limit right of asylum, May 1993. Maastricht Treaty ratified by FRG, Oct. 1993. Recession easing, 1994, but problems remaining in former E Germany and in elections, Oct. 1994 former Communists gained parliamentary representation, but Kohl returned as Chancellor though with reduced majority. June 1995: German combat troops to support UN in Bosnia. Oct.: neo-Nazis given long sentences for racial killings.

Chancellors of the Federal Republic of Germany since 1949:

Adenauer	1949–63
Erhard	1963–69
Brandt	1969–74
Schmidt	1974–83
Kohl	1983–

Gertruydenberg. Conference to end War of *Spanish Succession frustrated, 1710.

Gestapo (GEheimeSTAatsPOlizei) was first set up in Prussia by Goering, 1933. Other federal states of Germany followed and the separate forces amalgamated into one for the whole Reich under Himmler, 1934. Pronounced a criminal organization, at the Nuremberg trials, 1946.

Getty Museum, art collection founded at Malibu, California, USA by J. Paul Getty (1892–1976), an oil billionaire. The J. Paul Getty Trust (1982) grew from this. It is planned to move most of the collection to a new complex in Los Angeles by 1996.

Gettysburg, Pennsylvania, USA. The Federal Army of the Potomac defeated the confederates under Lee and thereby saved the union from defeat in the civil war, 1–3 July 1863. Lincoln's celebrated speech was made in Nov. 1863, at dedication of the cemetery.

Ghana. Came into being, 6 Mar. 1957, on attainment of Dominion status by the former colony of the *Gold Coast and the trusteeship territory of *Togoland. Name is that also held by a powerful medieval W African monarchy. Became a republic, 1 July 1960, with Nkrumah as President. While Nkrumah was visiting China a 'National Liberation Council' under Gen. Ankrah took over the government, 18 Feb. 1966, and declared Nkrumah deposed. Mar. 1969, Ankrah resigned; replaced by Afrifa. Free elections, August 1969, and Busia became prime minister. Army coups, 1972, 1978 and 1979. Civilian government, 1979–81, then further military coup under Flt. Lt. Rawlings, 31 Dec. which established a Provisional National Defence Council. Rawlings won landslide election victory as president-elect, Dec. 1992.

Ghent, Belgium. Said to have been founded in the 5thC. Given to Count Baldwin IV, 1007; capital of *Flanders, 12thC; John of Gaunt *b.* at, 1340. Insurrection of Jakob van Artevelde at, 1379; rebelled against the Emperor Charles V,

1539; surrendered to Spaniards, 1584; taken by Louis XIV of France, 1698; by Duke of Marlborough, 1706; seized by French, 1793; incorporated with Netherlands, 1814; became part of Belgium, 1830 (*see* FLANDERS).

Ghent, Convention of, granted the *Great Privilege, 1477.

Ghent, Pacification of, agreed to expulsion of the Spaniards and the establishment of Protestantism, 8 Nov. 1576.

Ghent, Treaty of, between USA and Great Britain ratified, 17 Feb. 1815.

ghetto. Jewish quarter of any city, named after the G. of Rome, instituted, 1556, and demolished, 1885, though Gs. had existed at Valencia, 1239; Frankfurt-on-Main, 1462; Venice, 1516. Its counterpart in London was the Old Jewry, a Jewish quarter from 1066 to 1291, where pogroms took place in 1261 and 1264. After the conquest of Poland in 1939 a quarter of Warsaw was walled off by the Germans and designated G. (*Judengasse*); its inmates rose against the Germans, 18 Apr. 1943, the quarter was burnt out and razed to the ground, as was the G. of Bialystok after a similar rising in Sept. 1943, which lasted a fortnight, and involved 40,000 Jewish casualties. Since the 1950s the term G. has been loosely applied to city areas housing a particular ethnic group which for economic or other reasons is not able to move out of it, e.g. Harlem, New York, has become known as a Black-Puerto Rican G.

Ghibellines. *See* GUELPHS.

Gibraltar. Taken by Moors, 711; captured by Spaniards, 1462; formally annexed to Spain, 1502; surrendered to combined English and Dutch fleet under Sir George Rooke, 1704; finally ceded to Great Britain by Treaty of Utrecht, 1713; frequently besieged by Spaniards, most famous attempt, 1779–83. Spain renewed her claim to G. after World War II. In Sept. 1967 the Gibraltarians voted to remain British but Spain refused to accept this vote. Spain closed land frontier with G., May 1968; and

the ferry service from Algeçiras suspended by Spain, 26 June. New constitution, 1969. Further Anglo-Spanish talks, resulting in reopening of frontier, Jan. 1985 but some friction remains (1995) over G. between Britain and Spain. British Army handed defence of G. over to Gibraltar Regiment, Mar. 1991. Socialists in power after election victory, Jan. 1992. Scene of killing of three IRA suspects by SAS, 6 Mar. 1988. European Court of Human Rights ruled against Britain on this, 27 Sept. 1995. In 1994 Spanish allegations that G. being used as base for smuggling; Spain imposed new border controls, but withdrew these, Dec. Renewed tension between G. and Spain, June 1995.

Gilbert and Ellice Islands, Pacific. British protectorates (1892) annexed to the Crown as colonies, Nov. 1915. Ellice Island severed connection on 1 Oct. 1975 and became *Tuvalu and Gilbert Island became independent, 1976, and a republic, 1979, as *Kiribati.

Gilbertine Order, founded in England by St Gilbert of Sempringham, 1135. Suppressed at the Reformation.

Gin Act, 1736. Imposed duty on G. sold by retail. Repealed, 1743.

gypsies. Local authorities in England and Wales expected to erect permanent sites for G. under 1968 Act, but by 1995 few had complied fully.

gypsies, Acts against (UK). Banished from England, 1531. From Scotland, 1541. Act forbidding intercourse with G., 1562. Acts repealed, 1783. Criminal Justice Act, 1994, altered trespass laws and expected to affect gypsies adversely.

Girl Guides. *See* GUIDE ASSOCIATION.

Girls' Public Day School Trust. Founded, 1872; one of the pioneers of girls' public day schools in England and Wales.

Girondists or **Girondins.** A party of moderate republicans led by Danton during the French Revolution, 1791. The earliest members were returned by the Gironde district of France. Louis XVI formed a Girondist ministry, 1792. On 1 Oct. 1793 many of them were tried before the National Convention, and several executed. The party had disappeared by 1794.

gladiators (Latin for swordsmen) were originally either performers in funeral games or the victims of funeral sacrifices. Professional G. were said to have been first employed by Marcus and Decimus Brutus at their father's obsequies, 264 BC. The revolt of G. under Spartacus took place, 73–71. Gladiatorial displays were finally abolished by Theodoric, 500.

Glamorgan University, formerly the Polytechnic of Wales, achieved present name and status, 1992. It is at Pontypridd.

Glasgow, Scotland. St Mungo (Kentigern) founded a bishopric here *c.* 560. See restored by David, prince of Cumbria, 1115. Present cathedral structure begun, 1175. G. made a burgh of barony *c.* 1176; made a burgh of regality by James II, 1450. University founded by Bishop Turnbull, 1450–1; endowed by James, Lord Hamilton, 1460, and a new deed of erection granted by James VI, 1577. University of Strathclyde established at, 1964. In a disaster at Ibrox football ground, G., 2 Jan. 1971, 66 people died. Burrell Collection opened, Oct. 1983. European 'City of Culture', 1990. McLellan Galleries reopened, 1990; Glasgow Royal Concert Hall, 1990; St Mungo's Gallery, 1993. 1992, Glasgow Polytechnic and Queen's College merged to become Glasgow Caledonian University. G. chosen as site of new Scottish Art Gallery, Nov. 1993. HQ of *Strathclyde Region since 1974.

Glasnost, term internationally used from 1986 to denote Gorbachev's policy of 'openness' in Soviet politics.

Glastonbury (Somerset). Abbey traditionally said to have been founded by Joseph of Arimathea about AD 63. It is historically certain that a British monastery was founded here *c.* 610, and was replaced *c.* 708 by a Saxon abbey built by Ina. The Chapel of St Joseph built, 1101–20;

destroyed by fire, 1184. The last abbot, Richard Whiting, was hanged on G. Tor for his adherence to the Roman Catholic faith, 15 Nov. 1539. A Celtic lake-village was discovered at G. in 1892.

Glencoe, The Massacre of. The Government issued a proclamation in Scotland promising pardon to all who before 31 Dec. 1691 would lay down their arms. One of the heads of clans, Alexander MacIan Macdonald of G., was late in doing so, and he and others of his clan were ruthlessly killed by a company of Argyll's Regiment quartered upon them, 13 Feb. 1692.

Gleneagles Agreement, 1977, whereby the British Government bound itself to sever sporting links with S Africa. Dead letter since 1990s, following dismantling of *apartheid in S Africa.

global warming. *See* GREENHOUSE EFFECT.

Globe Theatre (London). Erected by Richard and Cuthbert Burbage, 1599; associated with William Shakespeare; burnt, 1621; rebuilt shortly afterwards; destroyed by Puritans, 1649. In 1989 partial remains of G.T. excavated, now protected as an ancient monument. Modern reconstruction of G.T. now (1995) underway. This was inspiration of US actor director Sam Wanamaker (1919–93) who founded the Shakespeare Globe Trust, 1971. Work began, 1989; first two bays unveiled by Prince Edward, 1993. G.T. to open 1996.

Glorious First of June. Usual name of a naval victory over the French, won by Howe in the open sea off Ushant, 1794. Known in France as the battle of Prairial of the year II.

Gloucester, England. The Roman *Glevum* (later *Claudia Castra*). Founded by Nerva, AD 96–8; Abbey of St Peter founded, 681; fabric of present cathedral erected by Abbot Serlo (1072–1104); first charter granted by Henry II, 1155; incorporated by Richard III, 1483; made a bishopric, 1541.

Glyndebourne Festival. An operatic season held annually at Glynde, Sussex, in a private opera house erected by John Christie (1882–1962). First year, 1934. New theatre at G. completed, Jan. 1994: opened for first performance, May.

Gnostics, religious-philosophic sect of 2nd and 3rdC centuries AD. Opposed by orthodox Christians.

Goa, India. Discovered, 1498, by Vasco da Gama. Seized, 1510, by Portuguese under Alfonso de Albuquerque, and made capital of their Indian Ocean trading empire, 1511. St Francis Xavier visited G., 1542–52. By 1570 it had become one of the wealthiest cities in India, but after 1580 it declined commercially. In 1946 it was given the status of a metropolitan province. On 18 Dec. 1961 Indian troops invaded G., which was subsequently incorporated in India proper; became a state, 1987.

Gobelin tapestry. Called after a family of dyers, who set up dye works in Paris in the 15thC, and added tapestry-making in the 16thC. The business was acquired by Colbert in 1662 for Louis XIV as royal upholstery works. Tapestry-making only, from 1697.

Godesberg was the scene of a conference between Hitler and Neville Chamberlain, 22–24 Sept. 1938.

Godiva legend. *See* COVENTRY.

God Save the King (or **Queen**), British national anthem, said to have been the first authentic national anthem. Authorship disputed, but it was first performed in London in 1745 to celebrate the victory over the Jacobites at Prestonpans, and since used on ceremonial and royal occasions.

God's Truce. An instrument for suspending hostilities on holy days and seasons used during the Middle Ages. Originated in S France at the synod of Tuluges, in Rousillon, 1027; confirmed by Council of Clermont, 1095, and other councils. Fell into disuse in the 13thC.

Goeben and **Breslau**. German warships which in 1914 escaped from Messina, 6 Aug., into Dardanelles, 10 Aug. Nominally sold to Turkey, 13 Aug. Sank monitor *Raglan*, 20 Jan. 1918. *Breslau* sunk, 20 Jan. 1918. *Goeben* surrendered, Oct. 1918.

Gog and Magog, figures in the Guildhall of London, were perhaps first placed there in the reign of Henry V, but were destroyed in the fire of 1666. Replaced by new figures, 1708, which were seriously damaged in the fire of 29 Dec. 1940. New figures were erected in 1951.

Golan Heights, on Israeli-Syrian border, annexed by Israel, 14 Dec. 1981. Suggestion, Jan. 1994, that Israel might eventually be prepared to return G. H. to Syria as part of Middle East peace process but position unchanged, 1995.

Golconda, India. City and kingdom which *fl.* independently from 1512 until conquered by the Mogul emperor Aurungzebe, 1687, and placed under the viceroyalty of *Hyderabad.

Gold Coast, W Africa. Possessed by Portuguese, 1481–2; by Dutch, 1642; war between English and Dutch over settlements, 1664–5; Dutch forts and territory purchased by Great Britain, 1871; created a separate crown colony, 1874. Northern Territory added, 1897. Became the dominion of Ghana, 6 Mar. 1957. For subsequent history *see* GHANA.

Golden Bull, The, of Charles IV. Issued in its first form at the Diet of Nürnberg, 10 Jan. 1356, and in its final form at Diet of Metz, 25 Dec. 1356. It laid down the major principles of the constitution of the *Holy Roman Empire, confirmed the powers of the Diets, and of the *Electors. It remained in force till 1806.

Golden Horde, name given to Mongol-Tatar invaders of Europe from 1237. Defeated by Tamerlane, 1394: Ivan III of Russia ceased paying tribute to, 1480.

Gold rushes. California, 1848; Australia, 1851; S Africa, 1886; Klondike 1897; Brazil, 20th century.

Gold standard. First introduced into Britain, 1821. Internationally established when adopted by India, 1893. Abandoned during World War I, 1914–19. Slowly re-established, 1919–28. Finally abandoned by Britain, 1931.

golf, game which in its modern form is of Scottish origin, though games with golfing characteristics were played in ancient Rome, 1stC Japan, 12thC France and Flanders (*chole*) and 13thC Netherlands (*kolven*), etc. First recorded reference to G. is Act of Scottish Parliament, 1457, in which James II of Scotland tried to ban the game and concentrate the population on archery instead. James VI of Scotland (I of England) brought game to England, but after 1688 English interest generally declined until 19thC. In Scotland, in 1744, Honourable Company of Edinburgh Golfers held first competition at Leith, and established first set of G. rules. Club moved to Musselburgh, 1836; Muirfield, 1892. Royal and Ancient Golf Club founded at St Andrews, 1754 (now governing joint body of G., with US Golf Association, established, 1891). By 1800, only ten G. courses in Britain; but by 1880s G. established throughout British Empire (Calcutta Club, 1829; Bombay Club, 1842). In USA and Canada G. played from 17thC but not organized until 1888, when St Andrews Golf Club, Yonkers, New York, established by two Scots. 1000 G. clubs opened in the USA in 1890s. Increased professionalism from 20thC, coupled with increased US domination of G., combined with its spread to continental Europe and Far East. Rules revision, 1984.
Major G. championships (with dates of foundation) under:
British Open, 1860; US Open, 1895; US Masters, 1934; US PGA, 1958; World Matchplay, 1964; British PGA, 1975.
Major Cups: Walker Cup, 1922; *Ryder Cup, 1927; Curtis Cup (women), 1932.
Major golfers include: (nationality mentioned where not British)

Ballesteros, Severano (Spain), 1957–
Braid, James, 1870–1950
Cotton, Sir Henry, 1907–88
Davies, Laura, 1963–
Faldo, Nick, 1957–
Hagen, Walter (US), 1892–1969
Hogan, Ben (US), 1912–
Jacklin, Tony, 1944–
Jones, Bobby (US), 1902–71
Langer, Bernhard (Germany), 1957–
Morris Sr, Tom, 1821–1908
Morris Jr, Tom, 1851–75
Nicklaus, Jack (US), 1940–
Norman, Greg (Australia), 1955–
Palmer, Arnold (US), 1929–
Player, Gary (S Africa), 1935–
Sarazen, Gene (US), 1902–
Taylor, J.H., 1871–1963
Thomson, Peter (Australia), 1929–
Trevino, Lee (US), 1939–
Vardon, Harry, 1870–1937
Watson, Tom (US), 1949–
Woosnam, Ian, 1958–

Goncourt. Academy and Prize were founded under the will of Edmond de G., who *d.* 1896 (*see* FRENCH LITERATURE). Academy constituted, 1903. Recent prize-winners include: Jean Rouault (*Les champs d'honneur*, 1990); Patrick Chamoisease (*Texaco*, 1992): and Amin Malalouf (*Le Roche de Tanios*, 1993).

Good Parliament, 1376. The only medieval parliament in which the Commons made sufficient show of independence to secure reforms in their favour.

Gordon Riots. After an Act, passed in 1778, had repealed certain laws against Roman Catholics. On 2 June 1780 Lord George G. headed a mob, which almost succeeded in forcing its way into the House of Commons. During the next few days much property was attacked, including Newgate Prison. The army dispersed the mob, and many of the ringleaders were executed. Lord George G. was acquitted of high treason; but was imprisoned, 28 Jan. 1788, on another account, and *d.* insane in Newgate, 1 Nov. 1793.

Gorizia (Slovene **Gorica**; German **Goerz**). Seat of an important county under the Carolingian Empire, which was divided,

1001, between the county of *Friuli and the bishopric of Aquileia. Inherited by the Hapsburgs, 1500. The city was founded, 1307. Demanded by Italy as part of the price of her defection from the Triple Alliance, 1915, and entered by King Victor Emmanuel at the head of Italian troops, 9 Aug. 1916. Recaptured by Austrians, 28 Oct. 1917, but awarded in 1919 to Italy, which retained it against Yugoslav claims after 1945.

Gorky. See NIJNI NOVGOROD.

Goshen, Land of. Boer republic, set up in southern Bechuanaland, 1882, and dissolved, 1884.

Gothenburg or **Göteborg,** Sweden. Founded, 1609–11, by Charles IX of Sweden. Destroyed by the Danes, 1611. Under the Treaty of Knäred Danes occupied Alvsborg, 1613, until indemnified. Dutch financiers raised indemnity and after the departure of the Danes G. was refounded, 1615–20. Successful defence against Danes, 1789. G. Canal built, 1832.

Gothic architecture. Term used to cover western European architectural styles c. 1140–c. 1550. It embraces the English terms of Early English, Decorated and Perpendicular, and the European Early Gothic, Rayonnant and Flamboyant. The Gothic revival in architecture began in the 18thC but achieved its height in the 19th, lasting into the first decades of the 20th.

Gothic language, said by Procopius (d. c. 560) in his book, *The Vandal War,* dealing with events of 530–40, to be identical with the Vandal and Gepidic languages, is preserved in the Ostrogothic dialect of Moesia, the Arian bishop Ulfilas (d. 383) having translated considerable passages of the scriptures into Moeso-Gothic.

Goths. First known to history as settlers on the middle Vistula in 1stC AD. According to their own tradition they had arrived there from Sweden (probably the island of Gotland), via Pomerania. About AD 150 they migrated again SE to the N shore of the Black Sea and the Crimea. In the 3rdC

they invaded the Roman province of Moesia on the lower Danube; they conquered Dacia and raided Thrace, 321, but were beaten off by the Emperor Constantine. Their king, Hermanaric, d. c. 370, after conquering numerous other German tribes as well as Slav and Estonia neighbours. Thereafter, see OSTROGOTHS and VISIGOTHS.

Gotland (island in Baltic). Not improbably, as the name implies, the former home of the *Goths, but they must have left the island about or just before the birth of Christ. St Olaf introduced Christianity there, 1030. Island acknowledged Swedish suzerainty after battle of Roma, 1288. King Birger Magnusson repulsed, 1313. Island conquered by Danish king Waldemar, 1361. Reconquered by King Karl Knutsson of Sweden, except Visborg, 1449. Ravaged by constant wars between Sweden and Denmark till 1526. Finally passed to Sweden, 1644–5.

Göttingen, Germany. Joined *Hanseatic League c. 1360. Captured by Tilly, 1626. By Saxons, 1632. University founded, 1734, by George II of England. Opened, 1737.

Gowrie Conspiracy, 5 Aug. 1600. The Earl of G. and his brother, Alexander Ruthven, attempted to murder James VI of Scotland at G. House. An alarm was raised, however, and the two brothers were killed.

GPU, OGPU (Russian state political department), new designation for the *Cheka, adopted 1922–34, after which the name was changed to *NKVD.

Graeco-Turkish Wars.
1. 1897: broke out 18 Apr., the result of anti-Christian excesses and anti-Turkish risings in *Crete, then part of the Ottoman Empire, but claimed by Greece. Turks entered Larissa, 23 Apr. Greeks defeated in Epirus, but won battle in Thessaly, 29 Apr. Turkish mountain position of Imaret-Grimbovo stormed, 12–15 May. Greek volunteers who had been landed in Crete before the outbreak of war (Feb.) were withdrawn, 9 May, under pressure from the

Concert of Europe, and the terms finally settled at Constantinople, 6 Dec., included only slight frontier adjustments and the payment by Greece of £4,000,000 indemnity. Turks evacuated Thessaly, June 1898.

2. 1921–2: Greek offensive in Asia Minor, 23 Mar. 1921. Greeks defeated near Eskishehr, Apr. 1921; resumed offensive from Ushak and Brusa, July 1921; entered Eskishehr, 20 July. Turks fell back on Sakaria River; Greeks heavily defeated, Sept. 1921; retired on Eskishehr and repulsed Turkish attacks at Afion Karahissar, Oct. 1921. Main Turkish offensive opened, 26 July 1922; Greeks in headlong flight, Aug.–Sept. 1922; Mudania Armistice, Oct. 1922; terminated the war.

Graf Spee, Admiral. German 'pocket' battleship engaged and crippled by three British cruisers off River Plate, took refuge in Montevideo, 14 Dec. 1939; scuttled by order of Hitler, 17 Dec.; captain committed suicide, 20 Dec.

Grampian, Scottish administrative region since 1972, with headquarters at Aberdeen.

gramophone (American 'phonograph') was invented by Edison, 1877, perfected by E. Berliner, 1888. Electrical recording first practised, 1920. Superseded by the *record-player after World War II.

Granada, Spain. Invaded by the Moors, AD 745. Wall of the Alhambra built *c.* 1019. Part of the Arab kingdom of Murcia, 1229–38. Fell into hands of Abu Abdullah Mohammed Ibn al Ahmar, who formed the kingdom of G., 1238. Alhambra Palace begun, 1213. Captured by Christians, 1492.

Grand Alliance.

1. Against France, began with the Treaty of Vienna, May 1689, between the emperor and the Dutch. It came to include Spain, Holland, Sweden, Savoy and Great Britain. Renewed, 1696; ended, 1697.
2. Concluded at The Hague, 7 Sept. 1701, between England, Holland, and the empire; joined by Prussia, 20 Jan. 1702; by Portugal, 16 May 1703; by Savoy, 25 Oct. 1703. It dealt mainly with the conquest of Spain. *See* SPANISH SUCCESSION, WAR OF.

grand juries (England). Abolished except for a few minor exceptions, 1933: finally abolished, 1948. Still part of US judicial system, 1995.

Grand National, horse race at Liverpool instituted at, Aintree, 1839. Race declared void after false starts, 1993.

Grand Remonstrance. *See* REMONSTRANCE, THE GRAND.

Grantham, England. Mentioned in Domesday Book, 1085. Incorporated by Edward IV, 1463. Captured by royalists, 1642–3.

Grattan's Parliament. The Irish parliament, whose legislative independence was granted, May 1782, through the exertions of Henry G. (1746–1820). It came to an end, 2 July 1800.

Gravelines, France. Founded by Henry Count of Flanders, 1160. Defeat of French by Spanish Army, 1558. Defeat of Spanish *Armada by the English at, 1588. Taken by French, 1658, and ceded to them, 7 Nov. 1659.

Gravesend, England. Mentioned in Domesday Book, 1085. Burned by the French, 1380. Incorporated, 22 July 1562. Princess Pocahontas *d.* at G., 1617.

Great Britain, history of (for previous history *see* ENGLISH HISTORY; SCOTLAND; ENGLISH SOVEREIGNS). G.B. formed by union of the crowns of England and Scotland, 10 Apr. 1603. Hampton Court Conference and peace with Spain, 1604. Gunpowder Plot discovered, 5 Nov. 1605. Plantation of Ulster, 1607. War with France, 1624–9. Petition of Right, 1628. Dissolution of Parliament and beginning of the personal rule of Charles I, 1629. Charles attempts to introduce C. of E. Prayer Book into Scotland, 1637. The Ship Money trial (R. *v.* Hampden), 1637. Scots sign the National Covenant, 1638. First Bishops' War begins, May 1639. The Long Parliament meets, 3 Nov. 1640. Root-and-Branch Petition, Dec. 1640. Strafford beheaded, Star Chamber and High Commission abolished, May 1641. Irish Rebellion, Oct. 1641. Grand Remonstrance, Nov. 1641. Charles I attempts to arrest the Five Members, Jan. 1642. Civil war begins, Aug. 1642. Charles I surrenders to Scots, May 1646. Scots begin Second Civil War, Apr. 1648. Pride's Purge, Dec. 1648. Charles I beheaded, 30 Jan. 1649. England declared a Commonwealth, 29 May 1649. Scots defeated at Dunbar, Sept. 1650. Charles II defeated at Worcester, Sept. 1651. War with Holland, 1652–4. Cromwell becomes Protector, 1653. War with Spain, 1656–9. Oliver Cromwell d., 3 Sept. 1658. Long Parliament restored, 7 May 1659. Richard Cromwell resigns the Protectorship, 25 May 1659. Convention Parliament called by Monck, 15 Apr. 1660. The Restoration, 25 May 1660. Charles II sells Dunkirk to France. Act of Settlement, 1662. Second Naval War with Holland, 1665–7. Great Plague, 1665. Fire of London, 1666. Secret Treaty with Louis XIV, 1667. Secret Treaty of Dover, 1670. The 'Popish Plot', 1678. Habeas Corpus Act, 1679. Monmouth's rebellion defeated at Sedgemoor, July 1685. James II's Declaration of Indulgence, 2 Apr. 1687. Trial of the Seven Bishops, 29–30 June 1688. William III lands at Torbay, 15 Nov. 1688. Bill of Rights, Oct. 1689. James II defeated at battle of the Boyne, July 1690. War with France, 1690–7. Massacre of Glencoe, 1692. French naval defeat at La Hogue, 1692. National Debt established, 1693. Bank of England, 1694. Treaty of Ryswick, 1697. *Partition Treaties, 1698–1700. War of the Spanish Succession, 1701–13. Parliamentary Union of England and Scotland, 1 May 1707. Treaty of Utrecht, 1713. Jacobite rising, 1715; Septennial Act, 1716. S Sea Bubble, 1720. War of Jenkins's Ear, 1739–48. Jacobite Rebellion in Scotland, 1745. Defeated at Culloden, 16 Apr. 1746. Treaty of Aix-la-Chapelle, 1748. *Seven Years War, 1756–63. American Stamp Act, 1765, Royal Marriage Act, 1772. Boston Assembly threatens seces-

sion, 1772. The Boston Tea-party, 1773. First congress of American colonies, 1774. Quebec Act, 1774. War of American Independence begins with battle of Lexington, 19 Apr. 1775. American Declaration of Independence, 1776. British defeat at battle of Saratoga, Oct. 1777. France declares war on Britain, 1778. Spain, 1779. British capitulation at York-town, 1781. Independence of USA recognized at Peace of Versailles, 1783. War with *France, 1793–1802. Treaty of Amiens, 1802. War with *France, 1803–14, 1815. 'Battle of Peterloo', 1819 Six Acts, 1819. First Burma War, 1824. Trade unions legalized, 1825. First steam locomotive railway opened, 1825. Catholic emancipation and Metropolitan police established, 1829. Reform Act passed, 1832. Municipal Corporations Act, 1835. Chartist agitation, 1838–9. Penny postage introduced by Rowland Hill, 1840. Chartist riots, 1842. Factory Act, 1844. Repeal of Corn Laws 1846. Oregon Treaty with USA, 1846. Great Exhibition, 1851. Crimean War, 1854–6. Peace of Paris, 1856. Divorce legalized, 1857. First Atlantic cable laid, 1857. Ionian Islands ceded to Greece, 1863. Second Reform Act, 1867. Queen Victoria proclaimed Empress of India, 1877. Gladstone defeated on Home Rule Bill, 1886. S African War, 1899–1902. *Entente Cordiale* between Britain and France, 8 Apr. 1904. Anglo-Japanese alliance, 1905. Lords reject Lloyd George's finance bill, Nov. 1909. Parliament Act, 1911. National Insurance Act, 1912. *World War I, 1914–18. Welsh Church disestablished, 1920. General Strike, 3–13 May 1926. Two million unemployed by Dec. 1929. 'Landslide' election for a 'National' government, Oct. 1931. George V d., 20 Jan. 1936. Edward VIII abdicated, 10 Dec. 1936. Coronation of King George VI, 12 May 1937. Eden resigned Foreign Secretaryship, 20 Feb. 1938. Chamberlain sees Hitler at Munich, 17 Sept. Godesberg, 22 Sept. Munich agreement, 29 Sept. 1938. British guarantee to Poland, 31 Mar. 1939; to Greece and Romania, 13 Apr.; Military Training Act, 27 May. British ultimatum to Germany, 1 Sept. followed by *World War II, 3 Sept. 1939–12 Sept. 1945. Churchill forms coalition government, 10 May 1940. Roosevelt and Churchill issue Atlantic Charter, 11 Aug. 1941. Education Act, 1944. General Election, 5 July 1945; Labour government returned and sweeping programme of *nationalization and social reform follows.

'Austerity' government. India and Pakistan independent, 1947. Princess Elizabeth marries Lt. Philip Mountbatten, 20 Nov. 1947. Britain signs N Atlantic treaty, 4 Apr. 1949: Korean War breaks out, June 1950 and British troops in action there by Sept. 1951: Festival of Britain opened 3 May: General Election in October returns Conservative government under Churchill. King George VI *d.* 6 Feb. 1952, succeeded by Elizabeth II, who is crowned, 2 June 1953. Food rationing ended, 1954. Agreements with Egypt over Suez and Iran over oil. Eden succeeds Churchill as premier, 1955: Suez crisis Oct.–Nov. 1956 and Eden is succeeded by Macmillan, 1957. Britain joins EFTA, 1959. S Africa leaves Commonwealth, 1961 and President Kennedy visits London, June: Britain applies unsuccessfully for membership of the EEC. Macmillan signs Nassau Agreement with Kennedy, 1962, under which Britain agrees to accept Polaris nuclear missiles. Profumo affair, June, 1963, undermines confidence in Government. Philby granted asylum in Moscow, July; Ward trial, July–Aug.; Great Train Robbery, Aug.; Macmillan resigns and succeeded by Douglas-Home, Oct. 1964: Labour wins General Election in Oct.; Wilson Prime Minister. Churchill *d.* 1965 and given state funeral. Rhodesia declared unilateral independence, Nov. Labour increases its majority in 1966 General Election. Economic crisis and sterling devalued, 1967. Growing unrest in N Ireland from 1968; Prince of Wales invested at Caernarvon, 1 July. Conservatives returned to power under Heath, 1970: Decimalization of coinage, Feb. 1971. Britain joins EEC (*see* EUROPEAN ECONOMIC COMMUNITY), 1973. Serious economic difficulties and Labour returned to power, 1974. Margaret Thatcher Conservative leader, 1975; Callaghan succeeds Wilson as premier, 1976. Conservatives

returned under Margaret Thatcher, 1979; UDI in Rhodesia ends, Dec. 1979, resulting in independent republic of *Zimbabwe, April 1980. Prince Charles marries Lady Diana Spencer, July 1981. Falklands War, 1982 (*see under* FALKLAND ISLANDS). Social Democrats' rise, 1982. Conservatives returned with increased majority, June 1983, and Kinnock Labour leader, Oct. Coal strike, Mar. 1984–5. IRA attempt to assassinate Cabinet at Brighton fails, Sept. 1984. Anglo-Irish agreement, 1985; Westland crisis and GLC abolished, 1986. 1987: Terry Waite kidnapped in Beirut, Jan: Tory landslide in June General Election. 'Big Bang' revolutionized City financial practices, Oct. but hurricane hit SE England 15 Oct. and Stock Exchange crash (*'Black Monday') 19 Oct. 1988: Merger of Liberals and Social Democrats: economic boom but number of financial scandals; growing Thatcher distrust of Europe; growth in terrorist activity. Disasters include Piper Alpha rig explosion, 6 July; Clapham rail crash, 12 Dec. and *Lockerbie air disaster, 21 Dec. 1989: Rising opposition to Mrs Thatcher within Conservative party, and Chancellor of the Exchequer Lawson resigns, 2 Nov.; Thatcher survives leadership challenge, 23 Nov. 1990:*Community Charge starts, April; protests follow. Iraq invades Kuwait, Aug. and Britain begins sending troops and aircraft to the Gulf. Britain enters *Exchange Rate Mechanism but in Nov. Mrs Thatcher forced to resign after party revolt and replaced by John Major. 1991: *Gulf War in which Britain took part; IRA attacks 10 Downing Street, 7 Feb. Growing recession with unemployment over 2 million. Terry Waite released, Nov. In Dec. Britain agreed to sign Maastricht Treaty (*see* MAASTRICHT) with 'opt-outs', (actual treaty signed, 7 Feb. 1992). 1992: Major wins April General Election with reduced majority. Kinnock replaced as Labour leader by John Smith. Sterling crisis; Britain leaves ERM, Sept: announcement of massive pit closures causes national outcry, Oct., but eventually goes ahead. In Nov. Queen agrees to pay income tax from 1993; separation of Prince and Princess of Wales, Dec.; British 'peace-keeping' troops sent to Bosnia. 1993: *Council Tax replaces Community Charge, April; government defeated in Commons on debate on Maastricht ratification but Britain finally ratifies, 2 Aug. Inflation lowest for 25 years; unemployment starts falling. Defence cuts announced, Oct. Britain signs *GATT agreement, 15 Dec.; on same day British and Irish governments sign declaration designed to bring peace to N Ireland, promising talks with *Sinn Fein if IRA announces end to violence permanently. 1994: Recession easing but government remains unpopular. Heavy Conservative losses in European and local elections, May. Queen and President Mitterand of France officially open *Channel Tunnel. Labour leader John Smith dies suddenly, 12 May; Tony Blair succeeds him, 21 July. Government reshuffle, July; terrorists bomb London Israeli embassy, 26 July. IRA announce cease-fire, 31 Aug.; this gives impetus to Anglo-Irish talks and some restrictions on Sinn Fein lifted, Sept. Queen pays state visit to Russia, Oct. Government announces establishment of commission to examine standards in public life (see NOLAN COMMMITTEE); abandonment of plans to privatize the *Post Office; Government drops projected VAT increase on fuel after backbench revolt in Budget. Dudley by-election loss in Dec. marks biggest Conservative by-election defeat since 1935. Forced to accept EU fisheries policy, Dec. Year ends with first balance-of-payment surplus since 1987 but government remains unpopular despite continuing fall in unemployment and low inflation. 1995: N Ireland 'Framework Document' published in Belfast by British and Irish governments, Feb. Conservatives do badly in local elections, Apr./May. In June the Prince of Wales makes first official visit to the Irish Republic since its independence. Prime Minister John Major announces Conservative leadership contest: result, on 4 July, was a victory by Major over his opponent John Redwood. Cabinet reshuffle followed. First person charged under War Crimes Act (1991) in July 1995. N. Ireland secretary Sir Patrick

Mayhew has secret talks with *Sinn Fein leaders, July; Liberal by-election victory reduces Conservative majority to nine. European Court rules against Britain in *Death on Rock case, 27 Sept. Director of Prisons dismissed Oct.; Commons Committee reports on Nolan Committee Nov.; subsequent Government climb-down on detail.

Great Council of Peers. *See* MAGNUM CONCILIUM.

Great Plague. In London and Derbyshire, 1665.

Great Privilege (*Groote Privilegie*). On 3 Feb. 1477 a congress of the Netherlands met at Ghent. The Duchess Mary, then regent, granted to this assembly a charter known as the G.P. on 11 Feb. 1477. It has been called the 'Magna Carta of Holland'.

Great Schism. After the return of the Papal Court from Avignon, 1378. Urban VI was elected pope, but the French Party elected Clement VII as a rival. The two parties continued to elect rival popes until 1409, when Gregory XII at Rome was deposed and Alexander V and John XXIII successively elected in his place. As Gregory XII refused to recognize his successors there were therefore three rival popes until 1415, when at the Council of Constance John XXIII was deposed and Gregory XII resigned. Martin V was then elected pope at Rome in their stead in 1417. This is generally called the end of the G.S., though a French anti-papacy continued (as successors to Clement VII) till 1429. *See* PAPACY.

'Great Train Robbery'. The Scotland to London Post Office express was ambushed near Cheddington, Buckinghamshire on 8 Aug. 1963 and over £2½ million stolen. A number of men were subsequently sentenced to heavy terms of imprisonment but some subsequently escaped from prison. Only a small proportion of the money was ever recovered.

Great Wall of China, built 3rdC BC as a defence against invading Mongols:

restored since 19thC. Present length: 1,450 miles (2,250 km.).

Greater London Council, established under the London Government Act of 1963. It superseded the *London County Council, and embraced a much larger area and population. G.L.C. abolished, 1986.

Greece, Ancient. Earliest settlements known at Tiryns and Mycenae, c. 3000 BC. Minoan supremacy in the Aegean, c. 2300–1400. Achaeans' invasion of G., c. 1270–1250. They attack Egypt, 1223, and sack Troy (*The Iliad*), c. 1180. Dorians overrun G., c. 1100–1000. Ionian settlements of Asia Minor, c. 1040. Athenian monarchy made elective, 683. Sparta threatened by the First, 736–716, and the Second, 650–630, Messenian wars; introduces the Reforms of Lycurgus c. 610. Ionia falls under the power of Croesus of Lydia, 560–546, when Lydia was conquered by the Persians under Cyrus. Persian Darius invades Thrace, 516. Ionian revolt, 499. Helped by Athens, 498; defeated at naval battle of Lade, 494. Persian invasion of G., 491; battle of Marathon, 490. Second Persian invasion, 480. Battle of Thermopylae and Salamis, 480. Battles of Plataea and Mycale, 479.
Delian confederacy formed under Athens, 478. Battle of the Eurymedon, 466. Athenians attack Egypt, 459. Delian Treasury moved to Athens, 454. Thirty years' peace between Athens and Sparta signed, 445. Peloponnesian War begins, 431. Battle of Pylos (Sphacteria), 425. Battle of Amphipolis, 422. Peace of Nicias, 421. Athenian expedition to Syracuse, 415, and final defeat at, 18 Sept. 413. Decelean War, 413. Resumption of Peloponnesian War, 412. Battle of Aegospotami, 405. Surrender of Athens, 404. Sparta supreme in G., 404; till overthrown by Thebes at battle of Leuctra, 371. Thebes collapses after death of Epaminondas at battle of Mantinea, 362. Philip becomes king of Macedonia, 359. Checked by Athenians at Thermopylae, 352. Demosthenes delivers First Philippic, 351. Battle of Chaeronea, 338. Philip forms Pan-Hellenic League at Corinth, 338. Murdered, 336. Alexander the Great puts down Theban revolt, 335. Alexander conquers Persian Empire and dies, 323. Aetolian League founded, 323. Achaean League revived, 281. Romans defeat Macedon at Cynoscephalae, 197. Macedon conquered and made a Roman province, 146. Rest of G. conquered the same year. Remained a Roman province until the Turkish Conquest, AD 1440–60. *See* ROMAN EMPIRE; OTTOMAN EMPIRE; GREECE, MODERN.

Greece, Modern. For previous history *see* GREECE, ANCIENT; ROMAN EMPIRE; OTTOMAN EMPIRE; ROMAN EMPIRE, EASTERN. War of independence began, 25 Mar. 1821, and practically ended in the battle of Navarino, 20 Oct. 1827, when the Egyptian fleet was destroyed by Britain, France, and Russia. On 7 May 1832, G. declared independent kingdom under British, French and Russian protection. War with Turkey (*see* GRAECO-TURKISH WARS (1)). Otto I expelled, 1862 *Ionian Islands incorporated, 1863. The powers compelled Turkey to withdraw her forces from Crete, 1898, and Crete was granted autonomy under a Greek prince; *Balkan Wars, Oct. 1912–Aug. 1913; Salonika captured by the Greeks, 9 Nov. 1912; King George of G. murdered, 18 Mar. 1913; Crete ceded to G., Nov. 1913; Venizelos (pro-Ally), Premier, 1914–15, invited allied troops to Salonika, Oct. 1915. Constantine repudiated invitation and Venizelos resigned, Oct. 1915. Bulgarian invasion, Aug. 1916. Cretan revolution under Venizelos, Sept. 1916. Allies bombarded Athens, 1 Dec. 1916. Constantine abdicated, June 1917, and succeeded by Alexander, who *d.* 1920. Constantine king again, 1920–2. *Graeco-Turkish War (2), 1921–2. Republic proclaimed, 25 Mar. 1924. Royalist revolt in Athens, 9 Sept. 1935; end of the republic, 10 Oct. 1935; plebiscite, and restoration of King George II, 3 Nov. 1935. Parliamentary government suspended after *coup d'état* by Gen. Metaxas, 4 Aug. 1936. Italian invasion of G., 28 Oct. 1940; Greek forces thrust back Italians into Albania, 1940. British troops landed in G., Mar. 1941; German invasion, 6 Apr. 1941; removal of Government to Crete, 23 Apr. 1941; occupation of Greek mainland by

Germans completed, 2 May 1941. Withdrawal of German troops, Sept. 1944. Communists start civil war, 12 Oct. 1944. Truce negotiated, Dec., and peace agreement signed, 12 Feb. 1945. Monarchy restored by plebiscite, 1946; and Communist rising. King George II *d.*, Apr. 1947; succeeded by Paul I. Annexation of Dodecanese, 7 Mar. 1948; total defeat of Communists, Aug. 1948. G. joined NATO, 1951. From 1953 Greek politics increasingly influenced by *Cyprus question. King Paul *d.*, Mar. 1964 and was succeeded by his son as Constantine II. In Apr. 1967 a group of army officers took over government. In Dec. 1967 Constantine went into exile. Military regime ousted, 1974. Monarchy abolished, 1973: formally voted out, 1974. New constitution, 1975. G. joined EEC, 1981. Socialist government returned, 1981, with anti-American bias. Campaign to restore *Elgin Marbles to G. revived 1981. Domestic scandals helped cause socialist defeat in 1989; but socialists returned again, Oct. 1993. Trade blockade of Macedonian Republic, 1994. Ex-King Constantine and family stripped of citizenship and property, Apr. 1994. Agreement with Macedonian Republic, and blockade lifted, Sept. 1995.

Kings of Modern Greece:
Otto (Prince Otto of Bavaria) 1833–62
George I (Prince William of Denmark) 1863–1913
Constantine I 1913–17
Alexander 1917–20
Constantine I (again) 1920–22
George II 1922–23
Republic 1924–35
George II (again) 1935–44
Regency 1944–46
George II (again) 1946–47
Paul I 1947–64
Constantine II 1964–74

Greek authors, Classical, of whom complete works or fragments survive:

Aeschines, 389–14 BC, orator.
Aeschylus, 525–456 BC, tragedian.

Agathon, *c.* 448–400 BC tragedian.
Alcaeus, *fl.* 606 BC, lyric poet.
Anacreon, 570–*c.* 485 BC, lyric poet.
Apollonius Rhodius, *c.* 222–180 BC, poet and grammarian.
Appian (Roman of Alexandria who wrote in Greek), 2ndC AD, historian.
Archilochus, *fl. c.* 700 BC, lyric poet.
Archimedes, 287–12 BC, mathematician.
Aristarchus of Samos, *c.* 280 BC, mathematician and astronomer.
Aristophanes, *c.* 445–*c.* 385 BC, comic poet and playwright.
Aristotle, 384–322 BC, philosopher.
Arrian, *c.* AD 95–*c.* 170, historian and philosopher.
Asclepiades of Samas, 3rdC BC, lyric poet.
Aurelius, Marcus, AD 121–80, philosopher.
Bacchylides, *fl. c.* 460 BC, lyric poet.
Bion, *c.* 280 BC, bucolic poet.
Callimachus, *c.* 305–*c.* 250 BC, poet and grammarian.
Corinna, *fl. c.* 500 BC, lyric poet.
Critias of Athens, *d.* 403 BC, orator.
Democritus, *c.* 460–361 BC, natural philosopher.
Demosthenes, *c.* 384–22 BC, orator.
Dio Cassius, *c.* AD 150–235, historian.
Diodorus Siculus, late 1stC BC, historian.
Diogenes Laertius, 2nd or 3rdC AD, biographer.
Dionysius of Halicarnassus, *fl. c.* 30 BC, historian and rhetorician.
Epictetus, *fl. c.* AD 55–138, philosopher.
Epicurus, 341–270 BC, philosopher.
Epimenides, 6thC BC, poet.
Euclid, *c.* 330–283 BC, geometrician.
Euripides, *c.* 484–407 BC, tragedian.
Galen, AD 130–200, physician.
Heliodorus of Emesa, 3rdC AD, romantic writer.
Heraclitus of Ephesus, *c.* 540–*c.* 475 BC, philosopher.
Herodas, 3rdC BC, dramatist.
Herodotus, *c.* 484–24 BC, historian.
Hesoid, ? *c.* 700 BC, didactic poet.
Hippocrates, *c.* 460–377 BC, physician.
Homer, *fl.*? between 810 and 730 BC, epic poet.
Isaeus, *c.* 420–*c.* 350 BC, orator.
Isocrates, 436–338 BC, rhetorician.

Lucian, *c.* AD 125–90, satirist.
Lycophron, *fl.* 285–47 BC, grammarian and poet.
Lysias, 458–380 BC, orator.
Menander, 342–292 BC, comedian.
Mimnermus, *fl. c.* 634–600 BC, elegiac poet.
Moschus, *fl. c.* 150 BC, bucolic poet.
Pausanias, 2ndC AD, geographer.
Pindar, 518–442 BC, poet.
Plato, *c.* 428–357 BC, philosopher.
Plutarch, *c.* AD 46-after 120, biographer and philosopher.
Polybius, *c.* 204–122 BC, historian.
Sappho, *b. c.* 612 BC, poet.
Simonides of Amorgos, *fl. c.* 664 BC, iambic poet.
Simonides of Ceos, *c.* 556–467 BC, lyric poet.
Sophocles, 496–406 BC, tragedian.
Stesichorus, *c.* 640–*c.* 555 BC, lyric poet.
Strabo, *c.* 63 BC–*c.* AD 24, geographer.
Theocritus, *c.* 310–*c.* 267 BC, bucolic poet.
Theognis, *b. c.* 540 BC; elegiac poet.
Theophrastus, *c.* 370–286 BC, philosopher.
Thucydides, *c.* 464–*c.* 402 BC, historian.
Tyrtaeus, *fl. c.* 685–68 BC, poet.
Xenophon, *c.* 430–*c.* 356 BC, historian.

See also BYZANTINE AUTHORS.

Greek fire, pre-eminently a naval weapon, but also used in sieges, was invented by Callinicus of Heliopolis, a Syrian in the employ of the Emperor Constantine Pogonatus (648–85); this so-called 'wet fire' (because the liquid when it came in contact with water was self-igniting) is the true G.F. as used during the Crusades.

Greek Orthodox Church. First signs of disunion between the Greek and Roman Churches in AD 385, when celibacy of priests was enforced, and a demand that the Pope should be recognized as supreme, and doctrinal differences were raised. In AD 484 the two Churches separated for a period of 40 years. In 734 the Greeks condemned image worship (Iconoclastic Controversy). The final separation was the Great Schism of 1054, when Pope Leo IX excommunicated the patriarchs of Constantinople. The 'Orthodox Confession' was drawn up in 1643. On 7 Dec. 1965 Orthodox Church annulled its 1054 excommunication of the Church of Rome.

Greenback Party, advocating that treasury notes, as opposed to bank-notes, should be the sole legal tender of USA, *fl.* 1874–84.

green belt, means of preventing 'urban sprawl' in Britain after World War II, first G.Bs. established, 1947.

Greenham Common, England. Following siting there of US Cruise missiles, women's anti-nuclear 'peace-camp' established from 1981. After removal of US *Cruise missiles from G.C. 1991–2, and announcement of sale of G.C. by government 1993, camp subsequently disbanded.

greenhouse effect, term first used by Trewartha in *Introduction to Weather and Climate,* 1937. With increased concern about global warming and the depletion of the ozone layer from the 1960s, G.E. frequently used to describe in easily-understood terms what the consequences of these could be in the future. G.E. said to be increasing, 1995; international conference held in Berlin agrees to cuts in 'greenhouse gases' i.e. carbon dioxide.

Greenland. Original Scandinavian settlement, begun in 982, died out *c.* 1480. Visited by Frobisher, 1577. Danish settlements refounded, 1721. On 5 June 1953 G. became an integral part of the Danish kingdom (had been a colony since 1261), with same rights and measure of self-government as the rest of Denmark. Full internal self-government, 1981. Left EC, February 1985.

Greenpeace, international organization founded in British Columbia, Canada, 1971, initially to oppose US Alaskan nuclear testing. Greenpeace UK, 1971. Now (1995) has international branches worldwide. Has campaigned aggressively against commercial whaling and in Britain against nuclear waste dumping, etc., On 10 July 1985, Greenpeace ship *Rainbow*

Warrior blown up in harbour at Auckland, New Zealand, and two French intelligence agents subsequently gaoled for causing this, though later released. In June 1995 a campaign by G. forced the oil company Shell not to sink an obsolete oil platform, the Brent Spar, in the N Atlantic. In Sept., G. ships banned by France from nuclear exclusion zone round Muraroa atoll.

Greens, the, originally groups or individuals aiming at environmental protection. Came to prominence from 1970s and began to enter politics. German G. Party founded 1979 by Petra Kelly (*d.* 1992) and others; won seats in federal parliament, 1983, but influence declined from 1990s and German reunification. 'Brussels G.' founded, Jan. 1974. A British G. party has fought last three European elections and several parliamentary elections but with no success, but G. has (1995) a number of seats in the European Parliament and is represented in several European parliaments.

Greenville, Treaty of. Between USA and the NW Indian tribes, 3 Aug. 1795.

Greenwich, London, celebrated for its hospital and observatory (*see* succeeding articles). A palace was built here by Humphrey, Duke of Gloucester, in 1428, and later came into Henry VI's possession. It was a favourite residence of the Tudors; Mary I and Elizabeth I were *b.* there, and Edward VI *d.* there. The Queen's House was designed 1616, by Inigo Jones, for the wife of James I: completed *c.* 1635 for Henrietta Maria, wife of Charles I. Charles II started to rebuild the whole palace but in 1694 William and Mary decided on its conversion to a sailors' hospital. In 1934 this became the National Maritime Museum and the Queen's House, previously used as a naval orphanage was added, 1937. Queen's House restored in style of Henrietta Maria, 1980s.

Greenwich Hospital (England). Founded, 1694, on the site of G. Palace. Opened, 1705. Ceased to be a pensioners' hospital, 1869. Became Royal Naval College, 1873;

future closure announced, Dec. 1994 and sale planned, 1995.

Greenwich Observatory (London). Built, 1675, by Wren. Opened, 1675–6. Removed to Herstmonceux, 1947–58; to Cambridge, 1990. Restoration of building (now part of National Maritime Museum) completed, 1993. Greenwich Mean Time, based on the Greenwich meridian, replaced by co-ordinated universal time, 1986.

Greenwich, University of, name and status of the former Thames Polytechnic, from Sept. 1992.

Greenwich Village, area of Lower Manhattan, New York City, started as a rural village in 17thC. In early 20thC. became a centre of intellectual and artistic activity, based on and around Washington Square-Washington Arch, 1895. Since 1980s G.V. has become principally an expensive residential area and artistic activity has moved on to East Village, Soho, etc.

Gregorian chants. Named after Pope Gregory I (540–604), who is traditionally said to have added extra tones to the Ambrosian chants then in use.

Grenada, W Indies. Discovered by Columbus, 1498; colonized by French, 1651; ceded to England by Treaty of Paris, 1763; recaptured by French, 1779; restored to England by Treaty of Versailles, 1783. 'Brigands' War', 1795. Massacre of governor and loyal subjects, 1796. Crown colony, 1876; member of W Indies Federation, 1958–62; associated state, 1967; independent within the Commonwealth, 1974. Left-wing coup, 13 Mar. 1979, and constitution suspended. Extremist left-wing coup, Oct. 1983, in which premier and three ministers murdered. USA and several Caribbean states invaded G., 23 Oct. and 1974 constitution restored. US troops left, 1985.

Grenadiers. A few G. were first attached to the French *Régiment du Roi* in 1667. Formed into companies in 1668–70. The British Grenadier Guards (First Foot Guards) were organized in 1660. They received their present name in 1815 after Waterloo, as a result of the conspicuous part taken by them in defeating the G. of the French Imperial Guard. G. in the German Army derived prestige from the traditions of the Prussian G., the élite infantry units of the Seven Years War and other mid-18thC campaigns, most of which had been raised by King Frederick William I (reigned 1713–40).

Gresham's Law, or the proposition 'Bad money drives out good', was formulated in 1560 by Sir Thomas G. (1519–79), founder of the *Stock Exchange, and of the school at Holt, Norfolk, which bears his name.

Gretna Green, Scotland. After the abolition of *Fleet marriages in 1754, those in England wishing to marry clandestinely, crossed the border to G.G. to take advantage of the Scottish marriage laws. By a law passed in 1856, these marriages were invalid unless one of the parties had resided in Scotland for three weeks: completely illegal after 1940.

Grey Friars. Franciscan monastery established in London, 1224. Afterwards *Christ's Hospital.

greyhound racing. US invention, derived from hare-coursing, but using an electric-driven bait; first demonstrated at Emeryville, California, 1920s; first racetrack at St Petersburg, Florida, 1925. It was introduced to Britain, 1926, and became more popular there than in the USA. The National Greyhound Racing Club was set up in Britain in 1928.

Grisons (German **Graubünden**; Italian **Grigioni**; Romansch **Grischun**). Largest of the Swiss cantons. The Raetians living about the sources of the Rhine and Inn were conquered by Rome, 15 BC, and the district formed the nucleus of Rhaetia Prima. Christianity was introduced, AD 400. Conquered by the Franks, 536, who entrusted civil government to the Bishop of Chur. In 806 Charlemagne separated the civil power and placed it under a count. The 'Grey League' from which the canton

takes its name was founded, 1395; this *Graubund* joined in federation with the League of God's House (founded, 1367), and the League of Ten Laws (founded, 1436) to form the Free State of Ten Leagues, which became associated with the original Swiss Confederation from 1497 to 1524. In 1794 Veltlin (Valtellina) seceded, and was attached by Napoleon to the Cisalpine Republic, 1797, since when it has been Italian with a short interval of Austrian hegemony. The rest of G. joined the Helvetic Republic, 1797, but regained its independence in 1803. Finally adhered to the Swiss Confederation, 1854.

groats. First coined, 1351. Discontinued, 1662. Revived, 1838. In Scotland first issued, 1358. In Ireland, 1460. Last coined in Great Britain, 1856, except for a special issue coined for Maundy money. *See* MAUNDY THURSDAY.

Groningen, Holland. Joined *Hanseatic League *c.* 1282. Part of United Netherlands, 1594.

Ground-nuts Scheme, Tanganyika, launched early in 1947; wound up. 1955. Caused contemporary government scandal.

Grozny, or **Grozni,** capital of *Chechenya. Fortress founded, 1818. Oil production centre since 1890s; new oil finds in 1950s. Petroleum Institute, 1920. Battle of G., Dec. 1994–Feb. 1995 left G. in ruins.

Grotte Chauvet, cave 40 miles NW of Avignon, France, where prehistoric paintings discovered, 18 Dec. 1994. Age of paintings estimated 18,000–20,000 years old.

Guadalajara, second city in Mexico, founded by the Spanish, 1530. Cathedral built, 1561–1618. Rapid industrialization since 1950s. Devastated by leaking gas explosion, 22 Apr. 1992, when over 250 people died.

Guadalcanal. One of the largest and most important of the *Solomon Islands. Scene of a protracted campaign against the Japanese, who landed powerful forces there in summer, 1942. American and Australian forces landed shortly afterwards and drove the Japanese out by 9 Feb. 1943.

Guadalupe-Hidalgo, Treaty of. Between USA and Mexico, signed, 2 Feb. 1848.

Guadeloupe, W Indies. Discovered by Columbus, 1493, colonized by France, 1635; captured by Britain, 1759; restored to France, 1763; ceded to Sweden, 1813; restored to France, 1814. Overseas Department of France, 19 Mar. 1946; administrative region, 1973. Its dependency, St Martin, was simultaneously occupied by the French and Dutch, but partitioned, 1648.

Guam, Pacific island, discovered by Magellan, *c.* 1521; ceded to USA by Spain, 1898; occupied by Japanese, 10 Dec. 1941, and scene of heavy fighting, July–Aug. 1944, when Americans recaptured it. From 1950 administered by the USA Interior Department. Voted for commonwealth status in referendum, 1982.

Guangzhou. *See* CANTON.

Guardians of the Poor. Abolished, 1929, by Local Government Act. *See* POOR LAWS.

Guatemala, Central America. Declared independent of Spain, 1821. Boundary treaty with Britain, 1859. Common boundary with Salvador and Honduras agreed, Mar. 1936. From Feb. 1948 to May 1951 the frontier with British Honduras (now *Belize) was closed as part of the recurrent claim, dating from Spanish colonial days, that this is Guatemalan territory. This claim still maintained. Arbenz's regime, 1951, instituted a left-wing policy and became increasingly pro-Communist till overthrown, 1954. Series of unstable regimes resulting in a bloodless coup, 1982, by military junta: this overthrown by a rival right-wing coup, 1983. Democracy re-established under new constitution, 1985; Government of national unity, 1990. President Serrano deposed, June 1993, and Carpio succeeded m, to serve till 1996.

Guatemala City, capital of the preceding

and before that of a Spanish colonial province, was founded, 1776, on the destruction of the previous capital, Antigua, in the earthquake of 1773. Another severe earthquake, 1976.

Guelph, Welf. Surname of the dukes of Saxony since the 11thC, and thence surname of the Hanoverian royal family of Great Britain. Proclamation changing name to Windsor, July 1917.

Guelphs and Ghibellines. Two factions caused by the rivalry between emperor and pope, after the death of Henry V in 1125. The Ghibellines, or emperor's party, took their name from Waiblingen, a castle in Württemberg, Italianized into Ghibellino. The G. or papal party had their name from Welf, the name of many princes of the House of Bavaria. The first outbreak of hostilities between the two parties occurred in 1154, when the Emperor Frederick Barbarossa made an expedition into Italy. After the Hohenstaufen defeat at Tagliacozzo, 1268, the struggle began to lose its real force. The names were temporarily revived during the French campaigns in Italy at the beginning of the 16thC.

Guernica, Spain. Famous because on 27 Apr. 1937, during the Spanish Civil War, it was heavily bombed by German planes supporting the Falangists.

Guernsey, Channel Islands. Probably granted to abbot of Dol by Childebert the Merovingian, AD 550. Became part of Normandy on its formation in 10thC. Its fortress, Castle Cornet, held out against the parliamentary forces, 1643–51. French made ineffectual attempts to land, 1779 and 1780. Occupied by Germans, 1 July 1940–9 May 1945. Constitution modified from 1 Jan. 1949.

Gueux ('Beggars'). During the revolt of the Netherlands against Spain a confederacy of nobles drew up, in 1565, a 'Compromise' (*see* COMPROMISE LEAGUE) which in Apr. 1566 they presented to the regent, Margaret of Parma. The demonstration caused some alarm, but she was reassured by a councillor: 'Madam, is your Highness afraid of these beggars?' The 'Beggars of the Sea', under de la Marck, did much damage to the Spanish fleet, and captured Brill in 1572.

Guiana, S America. *See* FRENCH GUIANA; GUYANA; SURINAM.

Guide Association, name, since 1994, of the movement until then known as the **Girl Guides**, founded 1910 by Lord Baden-Powell as a parallel organization to the *Boy Scouts. Pledge revised, 1993.

Guildford, England. Abbots Hospital founded, 1619. Diocese, 1927. Cathedral founded, 1936; consecrated, 1961. University of Surrey established at, 1966.

Guildford Four. *See* TRIALS AND CAUSES CÉLÈBRES.

Guildhall, London. An important hall has stood on this site since the 11thC. A new building was erected, 1411–26, but much of this was destroyed in an air raid on 29 Dec. 1940. A new Great Hall was completed in 1954 to the designs of Sir Giles Gilbert Scott.

guillotine. Supposed to have been invented by Joseph Ignace Guillotin (1738–1814), but in fact he merely recommended the use of the instrument, long known to the Scots and in certain parts of the N of England. It was first used to execute a highwayman in Paris, 25 Apr. 1792. Discarded when capital punishment abolished in France, 1981.

guinea. Gold coin first used in England, 1664. Last issued, 1813.

Guinea, Republic of, formerly French Guinea. Britain recognized France's rights in the area, 1882. Made a separate colony from Senegal, 1891. Boundaries finally settled, 1899. Became an independent republic on 2 Oct. 1958. Agreement of unity with Ghana (Nov. 1958) and Ghana-Mali (Dec. 1960) never had practical effect. Military coup, 1984; new constitution, 1991. Multiparty system introduced, 1992.

Guinea Bissau, formerly **Portuguese Guinea**, discovered by Nuno Tristao, 1446, and made a separate colony of Portugal, 1879. Independent, 1974. Ruled by a Revolutionary Council from 1980–4, when a new constitution established. Elections, July 1994, won by Party for the Independance of Guinea and Cape Verde (PAIGC).

Guinea, Spanish. *See* EQUATORIAL GUINEA.

Guines, Treaty of. *See* CLOTH OF GOLD, FIELD OF THE.

Gulf Co-operation Council, set up in Mar. 1991 following the liberation of *Kuwait. Bahrain, Kuwait, Oman, Qatar, Saudi Arabia and the United Arab Emirates, together with Egypt and Syria, by the Declaration of Damascus, proposed the establishment of an armed regional peacekeeping force, and political and economic co-operation between members. An aid fund was established, April 1991, to help economic progress in Arab states which had assisted in Kuwait's liberation.

Gulf War, 1) 16 Jan.–28 Feb. 1991, between *Iraq and the USA together with a coalition of 28 other countries whose chief members were Britain, France, Saudi Arabia, Kuwait, Syria, Egypt and Italy. The USA and its allies were operating under the auspices of the United Nations and in fulfilment of UN resolutions which Iraq had ignored.

The war originated in Iraq's invasion of *Kuwait, 2 Aug. 1990. Iraq had previously made territorial claims on Kuwait in 1961 and 1973. These were raised again during a dispute centering on oil in July 1990. Iraqi forces overran Kuwait in 48 hours and proclaimed it part of Iraq. The Emir fled to Saudi Arabia. The USA immediately began raising a coalition against Iraq. On 7 Aug. 82nd US Airborne Division sent to Saudi Arabia to forestall Iraqi invasion there ('Desert Shield'). British planes were in the Gulf by 12 August. By November *c.* 250,000 US forces in Gulf. Negotiations to achieve a peaceful withdrawal from Kuwait proved futile and on 29 Nov. 1990 UN Resolution 678 sanctioned use of 'all necessary means' to liberate Kuwait if Iraqi troops had not withdrawn by 15 Jan. 1991. Foreign hostages held in Iraq (including foreigners trapped in Kuwait by the Iraqi invasion) from Aug. 1990; last allowed to return home, 7 Dec.

When Iraq failed to comply with Resolution 678 by midnight 15 Jan. 1991, air war began against Iraq, 16 Jan., waged by US and allies. British Tornado aircraft played important role. Baghdad and Iraqi missile sites heavily bombed: but some Scuds not destroyed and these used by Iraq on attacks on both Israel and Saudi Arabia. Air campaign lasted 33 days and virtually destroyed Iraqi air force. On 22 Feb. President Bush issued 'final' ultimatum to Iraq to withdraw from Kuwait. When there was no response coalition forces attacked from Saudi Arabia on 24 Feb., under US Gen. Norman Schwarzkopf in an action popularly known as *'Desert Storm'. Iraqis abandoned a devastated Kuwait almost without a struggle. By 27 Feb. Iraqi forces in retreat, road to Baghdad open, Kurdish uprisings in N, Shiite rebellion in S Iraq. Bush announced all military objectives met. 28 Feb., Iraqi ambassador to UN said Iraq accepted all UN resolutions and hostilities ended. Battle had lasted approximately 100 hours. For subsequent history *see* IRAQ; KUWAIT; KURDS; etc.

2) Gulf War also used to describe Iraq–Iran war, 1980–8.

gun-cotton. Invented by Braconnot, 1832. Put to practical use by Schönhein (German), 1845. First manufactured in England, 1847.

Gundulph Bible, a Vulgate MS copied in Amsterdam, was brought to England by G., a monk of Bec. In 1077 he became Bishop of Rochester, and his Bible was kept in the cathedral until 1540, when it disappeared. In Mar. 1952 it was rediscovered in a library at San Marino, California.

gunpowder. The precise era of the invention and application of G. in Europe is doubtful but it was clearly known before the middle of the 14thC, and, before the end of the same, the use of artillery was familiar to the states of Germany, Italy, Spain, France and England. G. is said to have been made by Berthold Schwartz of Brunswick *c.* AD 1320, although Roger Bacon mentions its composition in a work published, 1216.

Gunpowder Plot. Originated by Robert Catesby early in 1604, to blow up the Houses of Parliament. In July 1605, Guy Fawkes was commissioned to commit the deed, and 5 Nov. 1605, the day on which Parliament was to meet, was the day chosen. Catesby was killed during his flight from the Government officers. Fawkes and other leaders executed, Jan and Feb. 1606. Since 1605, firework and bonfire celebrations on 5 Nov. in England and Wales.

Gupta. A famous dynasty under which India reached great prosperity, AD 320–480.

Gurkhas. Predominant ethnic group of *Nepal, from which were recruited 10 regiments of Gurkha Rifles of the army of British India. By an agreement of Aug. 1947, eight of the 19 Gurkha battalions then in being took service under the British crown, the rest entering the Indian service. British Gurkha contingent steadily reduced from 1980s: but recruiting to recommence, 1995.

Guyana, formerly **British Guiana**, independent state within the Commonwealth. First partially settled by Dutch W India Co. *c.* 1630. Captured by British, 1796, and ceded to Britain, 1814. G. independent under the name of Guyana, 26 May 1966. Republic, 22 Feb. 1970. Mass-suicide of 911 mostly American followers of religious leader Jim Jones in G., Nov. 1979. New constitution, 1980. Presidential and legislative elections, 1992, won by People's Progressive Party under Cheddi Jagan.

Guy's Hospital (London). Founded by Thomas Guy, 1721. 1993 proposals envisaged eventual amalgamation of G.H. and St Thomas's hospital; plans to downgrade G.H., Feb. 1994.

Gwalior, India. City and state founded by Mahadji Sindhia, 1769. Under British influence, 1782. British intervention, 1843.

Nucleus of the Union of Minor States, known as Madhya Bharat, formed 15 June 1948, with G. city as its capital; part of Madyha Pradesh from 1 Nov. 1956.

Gwent, Welsh county authority established, 1974 under terms of Local Government Act of 1972. Headquarters are at Cwmbran. Abolition envisaged, 1996.

Gwynedd, Welsh county authority established, 1974 under terms of 1972 Act: abolition envisaged, 1996.

gymslip. Invented at Hampstead College of Physical Education by a student, Mary Tait, 1893. Rapidly became standard girl's school uniform in Britain, but declined after 1940s.

Haarlem, Holland. Charter, 1245. Captured by peasants during rebellion, 1492. Medieval cloth centre. Attracted artists 16th–17thC: Frans Hals (*d.* 1666) buried in St Bavo's Cathedral (1397–1496). Besieged by Duke of Alva and the Spaniards, Dec. 1572–July 1573.

Habeas Corpus Act (Great Britain). Passed, 1679, to prevent illegal imprisonment; extended to cases other than criminal, 1816. In Scotland the Wrongous Imprisonment Act, passed 1701, is equivalent to the English Act; Irish Act passed, 1781–2.

Habsburg. *See* HAPSBURG.

hackney coaches. First used in London, 1625. Laws regarding hire of, 1831, 1853, 1869, 1896 and 1907. The London Cab Order, 1934, and the London Cab Acts of 1968 and 1973, regulate the London taxi service, the modern equivalent of H.C. Law overhaul announced, 1995.

Hadfield's (James) attempt to assassinate George III at Drury Lane Theatre, 15 May 1800. Tried and acquitted, 26 June 1800.

Hadrian's Wall (England). Designed by the Emperor Hadrian during his visit to Britain in AD 122, but the work was executed largely by the legate Aulus Platorius Nepos, 122–6. Extended from the Tyne to the Solway Firth; repaired by Severus about 208. Wall abandoned, AD 383. Used as quarry in building of military road 18th/19thC. Major excavations in 20thC: a growing tourist attraction since World War II. Serious erosion during 1990s as a result of tourism.

Hague, The, or **'s Gravenhage**, Holland. Founded, 1248. Spanish supremacy abjured at, 1580; the de Witts killed, 1672; captured by French, 19 Jan. 1795; evacuated by the French, Nov. 1813; the Permanent Court of Arbitration at The H. established in 1899; the Palace of Peace at The H., instituted by the Carnegie Foundation inaugurated Aug. 1913. Academy of International Law founded, Jan. 1914. Permanent Court of International Justice founded, 1920; name changed to International Court of Justice, 1946.

Hague, The, Peace Conferences at.
1. Met, 18 May 1899.
2. Met, 15 June–18 Oct. 1907.

Hague, The, Treaties of.
1. between England, France and Holland to enforce Peace of *Roskilde, 21 May 1659;
2. between England and Holland, July 1659;
3. between England, France and Holland, Aug. 1659;
4. between Great Britain and Holland, 23 Jan. 1668; receives name of Triple Alliance after Sweden joins, 25 Apr. 1668;
5. between Portugal and Holland, 7 May 1669;
6. between the Emperor, Holland, and Spain against France, 25 July 1672;
7. *Grand Alliance renewed, 1696;
8. second *Triple Alliance, 4 Jan. 1717;
9. between Spain, Savoy, and Austria, 17 Feb. 1717;
10. convention between Great Britain, Austria, Holland; and Sardinia against France and Spain, 26 Jan. 1748;
11. between France and Holland, 16 May 1795.

Haifa, Israel. Developed commercially since *c.* 1890. Harbour completed, 1933. Oil refineries begun, 1939. University founded, 1964. Arab population left, from 1950s.

Haileybury and Imperial Service College (England). Founded 1806 by the E India Co., at Hertford Castle, but removed to its present site, 1809. In 1862 it was reopened as a public school, and incorporated, 1864. The Imperial Service College was amalgamated with it in 1942.

Hainan, Chinese province (since 1988) when it was separated from Canton.

Hainaut (Hainault, Henegouwen) acquired as part of a dowry by Baldwin, Count of Flanders, 1051; passed to Bavaria, 1345; Burgundy, 1433; Austria, 1477; Spanish Netherlands, 1555; France, 1659; Austrian Netherlands, 1714. Became French province, 1794; was ceded to the United Netherlands, 1814; became Belgian province, 1830.

Hair-powder Tax. In Great Britain, 1795. Repealed, 1869.

Haiti. Once signified the W Indian island of *Hispaniola. Now the name of the W portion of the island. Jean Jacques Dessalines, an ex-slave, proclaimed himself Emperor of H., 1804; assassinated, 1806. Henri Christophe, in the N, proclaimed life-president, 1807. Rival Government, headed by Alexandre Pétion, formed at Port-au-Prince, 1807–18. Christophe proclaimed king, 1811; crowned, 1812; committed suicide, 1820. Pétion's successor, Jean Pierre Boyer, seized Christophe's dominion, drove Spaniards from E portion, and ruled the whole island, 1822–43. For subsequent history of E. portion, *see* DOMINICAN REPUBLIC. H. proper proclaimed an empire by Faustin Soulouque, 1849; republic restored, 1859. Many revolutions since. USA intervened, 1915. Treaty with USA, 1916, brought H. under US protection. US marines left, 15 Aug. 1934. *Coup d'état,* 10 May 1950, led by Col. Paul Eugène Magloire, the first president (Oct. 1950) to be elected by universal direct suffrage. François Duvalier was elected President, Sept. 1957 and soon established a notorious dictatorship: became president for life, 1964: succeeded by son, Jean-Claude Duvalier, 1971: he was deposed in a coup, 1986. Period of unrest followed by free elections won by populist Jean-Bertrand Aristide, Dec. 1990. Ousted

in military coup, Sept. 1991 and fled to USA. Trade embargo imposed on H. by USA. Ferry disaster off H., Feb. 1993; thousands drowned. Agreement by military rulers to restore Aristide by July, later disowned, Oct., and US ships denied entry to H. on 18 Oct. US imposed oil and arms blockade; increased sanctions against H., in May 1994. By July, many Haitians fleeing to USA and on 31 July UN approved US request for permission to invade H. to restore Aristide. In Sept. US forces assembled off H., and ex-President Carter brokered agreement for military junta to relinquish power within a month. US forces landed in H., 19 Sept. and situation generally calm. Junta leader Cedras agreed to go into exile in Panama, and Aristide returned to H., 15 Oct. 1994 to mass welcome. UN-supervised elections, June 1995, confirmed Aristide's position.

Halden, formerly **Fredrickshald,** Norway. Charles XII of Sweden killed at siege of, 11 Dec. 1718.

Halicarnassus. City of Asia Minor on SW coast of Caria, founded by Dorians from Troezane and Argos. Became subject to Persia, 6thC BC. The satrap Lygdamis obtained power as tyrant; his daughter and successor, Artemisia I, present with Xerxes at Salamis, 480 BC. H. was a member of the Delian League until the Peace of Antalcidas restored it to Persian suzerainty, 387 BC. The satrap Mausolus (377–353 BC) made himself independent. His wife and successor, Artemisia II, built the Mausoleum *c.* 352 BC. H. was destroyed by Alexander, 334 BC.

Halifax, W Yorkshire, became a major textile centre from the 18thC. Church, 15thC; town hall (by Barry), 1863. Britain's largest (1995) building society originated here, 1853.

Halifax, Nova Scotia. Founded, 1749: garrisoned by British troops until 1906; explosion in harbour caused 5,800 casualties, 16 Dec. 1917.

Halifax Fisheries Award. At Halifax, Nova Scotia, 5 June 1877. Great Britain awarded $5,500,000 for allowing fishing privileges to the USA for 12 years.

Halifax Law (summary trial and execution by guillotine for certain types of larceny) arose in Halifax, Yorkshire, in the 15thC and was last enforced in 1650.

hallmarks (Britain).
1. The London assay office established by statute, 1300. The earliest marks of this office now known date from 1390. The date letter series begins, 1478. Its marks were:
   1478–1697: A crowned leopard's head. 1697–1719: Britannia. 1719–1820: A crowned leopard's head. 1820 to now: Leopard's head uncrowned.
2. The Birmingham office opened, 1773. Its mark is an anchor.
3. The Sheffield office opened, 1773. Its mark is a crown.
4. The Edinburgh office was in existence, 1485, from which its earliest marks date. The date letter series begins, 1681. Its mark is a three-towered castle on a rock.
5. The following offices have also existed:
   (a) The Chester office probably existed before 1300. Date letter series begins, 1701. Its marks were:
       1300–1701: A shield with three sheaves and a dagger. 1701–19: As before, halved with three English leopards. 1719: The London leopard's head was added. In 1779 the old shield was readopted. In 1839 the London mark was dropped. Office closed, 1962.
   (b) Exeter date, letter series begins, 1544. Mark, a three-towered castle. Office closed, 1883.
   (c) The Glasgow office instituted, 1819. Its mark is the fish, tree, bell, and bird of the Glasgow arms. Closed, 1964.
   (d) Newcastle founded, 1423. Date letter series begins, 1658. Mark is three towers on a shield. Office closed, 1864.
   (e) Norwich founded, 1423. Date letter series begins, 1565. Marks are a crowned rose, and a shield with a gate tower over a leopard. Office closed, 1697.
   (f) York founded, 1423. Date letter series begins, 1562. Marks are a fleur-de-lys and a crowned leopard's head halved with each other, and a cross charged with five leopards. Office closed, 1857.

The Excise Duty Mark (the sovereign's head in profile) was used between 1784 and 1890. The heads of both sovereigns were used in the year 1935 only. Since Jan. 1975 all assay offices in the UK have used same style of date shield and letter for all articles.

In Ireland, the Dublin office existed by 1500. Date letter series begins, 1638. Its mark is a crowned harp.

Halle, Saxony. Part of Archbishopric of Magdeburg from 968. Member of Hanseatic League, 1281–1478; passed to Brandenburg, 1648. Cathedral built, 1520–36. Martin Luther University founded, 1694; incorporated with University of Wittenberg, 1817.

Hallé Orchestra. Established in 1857 in Manchester by Sir Charles Hallé (1819–95).

Halley's Comet observed, 1682, by Edmund Halley (1635–1742), who correctly predicted its reappearance in 1758. Again appeared 1835, 1910 and 1986. Next expected appearance, 2061. The comet which appeared in 1066, 1456, 1531 and 1607 was almost certainly H.C.

Hambledon, Hampshire, England. Traditional birth-place of modern *cricket, 1750.

Hamburg, Germany. Founded by Charlemagne, AD 808; bishopric, 831; archbishopric, 834; made a free imperial city, 1189; allied with Lübeck, 1241; Bank of, founded, 1619; opera house, 1678; peace of, 1762; occupied by French, 1806; evacuated by French on approach of Russians, 1813; freed from French, 1814; joined German Confederation, 1815; one-third of the town destroyed by fire, 1842; art gallery founded, 1850; new constitution granted by the senate, July 1860; joined the *N German Confederation, Aug. 1866; joined the Zollverein in Oct. 1888; university founded, 1919. Dock area mostly destroyed by allied bombing, 1942–3; later rebuilt and modernized. Captured by British, 3 May 1945. Severe flooding, 16–17 Feb. 1962. *See* HANSEATIC LEAGUE.

Hamas or **Hammas,** Islamic fundamentalist terrorist movement, opposed to any settlement between the *PLO and *Israel, established, Dec. 1987. Since the 1994 peace between the PLO and Israel H. has operated against both Israeli and Palestinian authorities in Gaza, Jericho and Israel proper, killing over 100 Israelis between May–Dec. 1994 H. is committed to building an independent Palestinian Islamic state.

Hampshire, **The.** British cruiser on the way to Russia mined and sunk off Marwick Head in the Orkneys, Lord Kitchener and staff perishing, 6 June 1916.

Hampton Court Conference. Held at H.C., 12–18 Jan. 1604, between the Church party and the Puritans.

Hampton Court Palace (England). Built by Cardinal Wolsey, and presented by him to King Henry VIII, 1526; Edward VI *b.* there, 12 Oct. 1537; enlarged by Christopher Wren for William III, 1694, when the famous chestnut avenue was planted; vine planted, 1768; state apartments opened to public, 1837; excavation of moat completed and restoration, 1910. Partially destroyed by fire, 1 March 1986; restoration completed, 1992.

Hampton Roads Conference (USA) between Lincoln and Seward for the Federal Government and Confederate vice-president Stephens, 3 Feb. 1865.

Hanaper Office of the Court of Chancery founded *c.* 1670. Abolished, 1842.

Hangchowfu, China. Described (as Kinsai) by Marco Polo, who visited it *c.* 1280. Capital of Sung dynasty, 1127–1278. Held by Taiping rebels, 1851–4. Nationalist stronghold in civil war, 1926.

Hankow, China. Founded during Ming

dynasty (1300–1644). Sacked and largely destroyed in the Taiping rebellion, 1851–1854. Opened to European trade, 1862.

Hanoi, capital of N Vietnam, 1954–76, since 1976 capital of Vietnam. Some 11th and 12thC buildings survived massive US bombing in 1965, 1968 and 1972.

Hanover, Germany. Made an electorate, 1692. Elector George acquired Celle by marriage, 1705. Became King of Britain, 1714. Acquired Bremen and Verden from Sweden, 1715. Made a kingdom, 1814. Acquired E Friesland, 1815. At accession of Victoria crown of H. went to Ernest Augustus, hitherto deputy-elector of H. and Duke of Cumberland, 1837, because Salic Law obtained in H. Joined Austria in the Austro-Prussian War of 1866, and annexed by Prussia, 26 Sept. 1866. Monarchy abolished after World War I.

Hanover, House of. *See* ENGLISH SOVEREIGNS AND THEIR CONSORTS.

Hanover, Treaties of.
1. Between England, France and Prussia, signed, 3 Sept. 1725, to oppose the secret Treaty of Vienna (20 Apr. 1725) between Spain and Austria, who pledged themselves to assist in the restoration of the Stuarts, joined by Holland, 9 Aug. 1726; by Sweden, 26 Mar. 1727; by Denmark, 18 Apr. 1727.
2. Between George II and Maria Theresa, 24 June 1741.
3. Between H. and England, 1834.

Hanoverian Succession. Established by law, 12 June 1701; arranged that the Princess Sophia of Hanover and her heirs should succeed to the British throne after the death of Queen Anne, provided the latter *d.* without issue.

Hansard. Record of parliamentary debates, begun 1774 by Luke Hansard (1752–1828), a printer. The name 'Hansard' was dropped from the *Parliamentary Debates* between 1889 and 1943, but then restored and officially adopted.

Hanseatic League, or **Hansa**. Hamburg and Lübeck in alliance, 1241. First meeting of Hanse towns (The Wendish Group), 1256. Gothland association existed in 1229, but subsequently absorbed by the H.L. Was given privileges in England, 1237. The Free Counter at Bruges established, 1309. At Bergen, 1343. Wars with Denmark, 1361–70. Lübeck recognized as head of the H.L., 1418. Baltic trading monopoly broken by Peace of Copenhagen, 1441. Novgorod counter closed, 1494. Bruges counter closed, 1540. Last general assembly held, 1669. Counters at Bergen closed, 1775; London, 1852; Antwerp, 1863.

Hapsburg or **Habsburg, House of.** Family called after H., in Switzerland, to which they came in 1028. Rudolf of H. elected Holy Roman Emperor, 1273. Austria and Styria acquired soon after. Carinthia and Carniola, 1335. Tirol, 1363–4. Franche-Comté, 1493 (lost, 1555). Württemberg and Breisgau, 1520 (lost, 1534). Bohemia, Moravia, Croatia, Silesia, and Christian Hungary, 1526. Rest of Hungary reconquered from the Turks, 1650–99. Netherlands, 1712 (lost, 1797). Milan, 1714 (lost, 1797). Banat of Temesvar, 1718. Craiova and Serbia, 1718 (lost, 1739). Parma, 1735 (lost, 1748). Tuscany, 1737 (lost, 1801). Silesia lost, 1742. Galicia, 1772. Lublin, 1795 (lost, 1809). Venetia, 1797 (lost, 1805). At Vienna Congress (1814–15) Hs. obtained Tuscany, Modena, Parma, Milan, Venetia, which were all lost, 1859–66, and permanently acquired Trento and Salzburg. Through marriages with the houses of Burgundy and Spain the Emperor Charles V was also King of Spain, but at his death the Spanish and the Germanic lands descended in different branches of the family until the extinction of the Spanish Hs., 1700 (*see* SPANISH SUCCESSION). The death of the Emperor Charles VI, 1740, extinguished the true Austrian branch, but through the marriage of his daughter Maria-Theresa with Prince Charles of Lorraine the family was known as H.-Lorraine. At abolition of the *Holy Roman Empire, 1806, the Hs. took the title of Emperor of Austria. They ceased to reign in Austria and Hungary, 1918.

hara-kiri. Japanese form of honourable suicide required on certain occasions, customary during the Middle Ages. Abolished officially, 1868, but practised by several Japanese officers during World War II.

Harar or **Harrar,** Ethiopia. Became seat of Arab government of Zelia, 1521. Occupied by Egyptians, 1875–85. Conquered by Ethiopian Emperor Menelek II, 1887. Capture by British forces, Mar. 1941, heralded the collapse of Mussolini's colonial empire.

Harare, capital of *Zimbabwe. Founded, as Fort Salisbury, 1890. Capital of S Rhodesia, 1923. Capital of Zimbabwe, under name of H., since 1980.

Harfleur, Normandy. Captured by Henry V of England, 1415. English expelled, 1433. Recaptured by English, 1440. Driven out by Dunois, 1450. Sacked by Huguenots, 1562.

Harleian Collection. Valuable MSS, books, and pamphlets, whose collection was started by Robert Harley (1661–1724), 1st Earl of Oxford, and continued by his son. Much of it was acquired in 1753 by the British Museum.

Harlem, district of New York City, established 1658 as Niewe Haarlem by Peter Stuyvesant, governor of New Netherlands. Battle of H. Heights, 16 Sept. 1776. Remained rural till mid-19thC, then built up and became predominantly black. Was base for 'Harlem Renaissance' of 1920s but after World War II prosperity declined. Growing Puerto Rican population from 1950s.

Harper's Ferry, W Virginia, USA. The scene of John Brown's celebrated raid before the American Civil War, 16 Oct. 1859.

Harrier, vertical take-off and landing fixed-wing aeroplane. The Hawker-Siddeley AV-8A first flew, 1960. In service from 1966. Sold to US Marine Corps, 1971. *Sea-H.* developed from H., first flown 20 Aug. 1978, first one handed over to Royal Navy, 18 June 1979. Used in Falklands campaign, 1982: in Gulf War, 1991, etc.

Harrow School. Founded by John Lyon, a Harrow butcher, 1571. Originally intended for education of poor boys of the parish. Original red-brick school house built, 1608–15. Mutinies at, 1771 and 1815.

Hartford, Connecticut, USA. Settled by the Dutch, 1633, by the English, 1635.

Hartford Conventions.
1. 20 Oct. 1779, to inquire into the depreciation of continental paper money.
2. 15 Dec. 1814, to deliberate upon security and defence.

Harvard University (USA). Founded by the general court of Massachusetts Bay Colony, 10 Oct. 1638, and subsequently named H. College after Revd John Harvard (*b.* 1607), who went to America in 1637, and bequeathed in 1638 his library and a sum of money towards the foundation of the college at *Cambridge, Mass. Charter granted, 1650. Transformed into a university, 1780. Under control of state until 1865, since when it has been self-governing. *Radcliffe College founded for women, 1879, now merged with H.U.

Harwich, England. Danes defeated off, AD 885; incorporated, 1318, and charter further extended, 1604; Isabel, queen of Edward II, landed at, 1326; Dutch fleet defeated by Duke of York near, 3 June 1665.

Hastings, England. Chief of the Cinque Ports, founded *c.* 893. King Athelstan established a mint here. H. was a borough before 1086. The battle of H. was fought six miles inland; William's army halted at H. on the night of 13–14 Oct. 1066, preceding the battle. Importance as a port declined after English loss of Normandy in 1204. Burned by French, 1377 and 1380.

Hastings, Warren, Trial of. Commenced before the House of Lords, 12 Feb. 1788; lasted until 23 Apr. 1795.

Hatfield, Council of (England). Held to declare the orthodoxy of the English Church regarding Monothelite heresy; also accepted the decrees of the five first general councils, 17 Sept. 680.

Hatfield House (England). Old Palace built *c.* 1496 by Archbishop Morton, Henry VII's minister. Later it passed to the crown. Elizabeth I succeeded to crown here. James I gave it to Robert Cecil, Earl of Salisbury, in exchange for Theobalds. Substantial rebuilding between 1607 and 1611.

Hatteras Expedition. The Confederate forts at H. Inlet (USA), attacked by Federal army, under Gen. Butler, and a small fleet, 28 Aug. 1861; Confederates surrendered on following day.

Havana, capital of *Cuba, founded, 1509, capital of the island from 1529. University of, 1728 (reorganised, 1976), when city boundaries extended. Palace of Captains General, 1793.

Havana, Declaration of, published by Pan-American Conference, 30 July 1940.

Havre, Le France. Originally *Havre de Notre-Dame de Grâce*. Founded by Louis XII, 1509; given to Queen Elizabeth by Huguenots, 1562; besieged and captured by Montmorency, 1563; bombarded unsuccessfully by English, 1678, 1694, 1759, 1794, 1795.

Hawaiian or **Sandwich Islands.** Shipwrecked Spaniards settled here, 1527. Juan Gaetano made landfall, 1555. Rediscovered by Capt. Cook, 1778. Cook murdered by the natives here, 1779. Constitution granted by reigning king, 1840; independence guaranteed by Great Britain and France, 1844; revolution at, 1893, when Queen Liliuokalani (*d.* 11 Nov. 1917) was deposed. Republic proclaimed, 1894; annexed to USA, 1898. Became a state of the Union, 1959.

hawkers or **pedlars,** Acts respecting, in Great Britain. Pedlars Act, 1871, by which they were placed under surveillance of the police; extended, 1881. H. Act, 1888, repealed by Local Government Act, 1966.

Hawthornden Prize, founded by Miss Alice Warrender in 1919, awarded annually to author of best work of imaginative literature during the previous year.

Haymarket Square Riot by anarchists in Chicago, 1886.

Hay-Pauncefote Treaty. Between Britain and USA, 1901, to amend Clayton-Bulwer Treaty regarding canal scheme between Atlantic and Pacific.

Head Act (Ireland), 1465, permitting wholesale slaughter of the Irish.

health centre. The first H.C. to be set up under the National Health Service Act, 1946, was opened at Stoke Newington, 14 Oct. 1952.

Health, Ministry of. Established by Act of 1919. First minister appointed, 1920. Part of the **Department of *Health and Social Security** from 1968 to 1988.

Health and Safety Commission established under the Health and Safety at Work Act, 1974. Works through the Health and Safety Executive. *See* FACTORY ACTS.

Health and Social Security, Department of, department of state, formed from the former ministries of Health and Social Security, 1968. The departments split again, 1988.

heart transplants. *See* TRANSPLANT SURGERY.

Hearth or Chimney Money. A tax on every hearth introduced in England, 1663. Abolished, 1689.

Heathrow, Britain's leading airport, and the world's busiest (over 42 million passengers 1991–2), named after the ancient Middlesex village on site of present Terminal 3. In 1929 Richard Fairey opened Great West Aerodrome, mainly for experimental flying. Development of H. as a military airfield begun, 1944, but subsequently changed to civilian airport and H. officially opened as London Airport, 31 May 1946. Europa Building (now Terminal 2) opened, 1955. Oceanic Terminal, 1962: renamed Terminal 3, 1968, and much developed subsequently. Terminal 1 formally opened, 1969; Terminal 4, 1986. Plans for fifth Terminal revealed, 1991. Underground line from central London to H. opened, 1975–7; 'loop' complete, 1984. Approval for construction of express rail-link Paddington-Heathrow, 1991; tunnelling accident put completion back a year, Oct. 1994. Plans for further runway dropped, May 1994. Three mortar bomb attacks by the IRA on H. perimeter, Mar. 1994: no mortars exploded and there were no casualties. Application to build a fifth terminal at H. announced, Dec. 1994.

heavy hydrogen (deuterium). Discovered by Urey in 1931.

heavy water. Discovered by Urey in 1931; first prepared by Lewis, 1933.

Hebdomadal Board (Oxford). Instituted, 1631.

Hebdomadal Council, supplanted preceding, 1854.

Hebrides. Settled and Christianized by the Scots of Dalriada, 6thC. Immigration from Norway begun *c.* 800. H. subjugated by Harald Fairhair, King of Norway, *c.* 875, and granted to the Jarls of Sudreyar (*Lords of the Isles), who remained Norwegian vassals until 1266. Thereafter *see under* SCOTLAND.

Heidelberg, W Germany. University founded by Elector Rupert I, 1385; reconstituted by Charles Frederick, Grand-Duke of Baden, 1803. H. plundered by Tilly, 1622, by the Swedes, 1633, and by the Imperialists, 1635; sacked by the French, 1688 and 1693.

Hejaz, Arabia. Sherif Hussein of Mecca proclaimed independent of Turkey, June 1916. Recognized as King of the H., 29 Oct., and enthroned, 4 Nov. After unsuccessful war with Ibn Sa'ud, Hussein abdicated, 1924. Hejazi independence extinguished, 1932.

Hejira. The name given to Mohammed's flight from Mecca to Medina, AD 622.

helicopter. First constructed, 1872; first successful model (built by Crocker and Hewitt) flown, 1918. Used extensively for air-sea rescue during and since World War II. First heliport opened in London, 1959.

Used extensively in Vietnam War, 1959–75; in Falklands' campaign, 1982; in Gulf War, 1991, and after; in Balkans since 1992, and since 1950s in N Sea oil industry. Chinook H. crashed in N Sea, Oct. 1986, killing 45; 2 June 1994, an RAF Chinook H. flew into mountainside, Mull of Kintyre, killing 29.

Heligoland (Frisian island off mouth of Elbe) was pagan place of pilgrimage for the Angeles and Frisians, containing sacred groves. The former building was destroyed by St Ludger, first Bishop of Münster (*d*. 809). Ceded to Britain, 1814. Exchanged for certain German E African possessions, 1890. Fortress blown up by British, 1945–7. Formally returned to Federal German Republic, 1 Mar. 1952.

helium. Discovered in the sun by Sir Joseph Lockyer (1836–1920), 1868. Onnes (1853–1926) of Leyden succeeded in liquefying it, 1908.

Helsinki or **Helsingfors,** Finland. Founded by Gustavus I of Sweden in 1550; plague, 1710, destroyed by fires, 1713 and 1708; made capital of Finland instead of Abo, 1812; bombarded by allied fleets, Aug. 1855; largely rebuilt during 19thC when Great Church (1852) constructed; bombed by Russians during Russo-Finnish wars, 1939–40 and 1941–4. *See* FINLAND.

Helsinki Accords or **Agreement,** 1 Aug. 1975, signed by the USA, Great Britain and USSR to safeguard human rights, was final act of the *Conference on Security and Cooperation in Europe. First review conference (Belgrade 1977–8) got no further on human rights; second (Madrid 1980) shifted to disarmament.

Helvetic Confession. First H.C. drawn up, 1536, by the Swiss theologians assembled at Basel. H.C. at Zürich, 1566, formed basis of union between Calvin's party and the Zürich reformers.

Henley-on-Thames regatta, first held, 1839. Women competed over full course for first time, June 1993.

Herald of Free Enterprise*. See* ZEEBRUGGE.

Heralds' College of Arms. Founded by Richard III of England, 1483.

Herculaneum (Italian **Ercolano**). Damaged by a severe earthquake, AD 63. H. was destroyed by the eruption of Vesuvius, 79, as described by Pliny the Younger (62–*c*. 120). Excavations on a small scale began, 1719, and were continued more ambitiously, 1927–30 and since 1960.

Hereford (England) was a Mercian outpost in AD 600, but was retaken by the Welsh, who in 1055 destroyed a castle built by Ralph, the Norman earl installed by Edward the Confessor. Chartered as a city by Richard I, 1189. The cathedral, founded 680, was also destroyed, 1055, but a new Norman building was finished in 1140. Other portions built between 1220 and 1500. The cathedral's Mappa Mundi is the oldest extant example of its kind, executed *c*. 1300; its proposed sale caused outcry in the 1980s, and was subsequently abandoned. The county of H. was merged with Worcester as result of 1972 Local Government Act; in 1994 Local Government Commission recommended its restoration as a separate county. *See also* THREE CHOIRS' FESTIVAL.

Heregeld ('Army Tax'), levied after the murder of Archbishop Alfheah in 1012, to pay Danish mercenaries who had deserted from Knut's army. Abolished, 1051.

heresy, laws concerning (England). In 1382 provided that sheriffs should arrest 'persons certified by the bishops to be heretics'. By the *De Haeretico comburendo* Act, 1401, the bishops themselves were empowered to punish H. This Act was enlarged, 1414. In 1533 an Act declared that offences against the See of Rome were not H. The Bill of the Six Articles, 1559, defined various heretical acts. Punishment of death for H. abolished, 1677.

heretics. The following are some of the better-known sects regarded as heretical by the Roman Catholic Church.
Gnostics. Appeared in 1stC AD, but had pre-Christian origins. Among the principal exponents were Simon Magus (1stC);

Marcion, Basilides, and Valentinus (2ndC), Mani (3rdC).

Montanists. Montanus *c.* 156 proclaimed himself prophet of the Spirit. Tertullian joined the sect *c.* 202, and it lingered on in Africa and the E until *c.* 400.

Monarchians. (*a*) Dynamists (or Adoptionists) founded by Theodotus of Byzantium *c.* 190–200; died out in the middle of the 3rdC; (*b*) Sabellians (or Patripassians or Medalists) arose *c.* 215 with the arrival of Sabellius in Rome. Condemned at Council of Nicaea, 325.

Donatists. Followers of Donatus, Bishop of Carthage, in opposition to Majorinus, 311; opposed by Pope Melchiades, 313, the Council of Arles, 314, and finally condemned by the Council of Carthage, 411. The sect disappeared after the Saracenic invasion of Africa.

Arians. Commenced at Alexandria in 313, when Arius (*c.* 250–336) quarrelled with the Bishop Peter. Condemned at Nicaea, 325, and lost its hold after the Second Council of Constantinople, 381. Its continuation among the barbarian kingdoms was of political rather than doctrinal significance.

Pelagians. Pelagius began to preach, *c.* 405, at Rome. Doctrine condemned at councils of Carthage, 418, and Orange, 529. The Semi-Pelagians, founded by Cassian (*c.* 360–*c.* 435), Abbot of St Victor; condemned at Orange, 529.

Nestorians. Nestorius (*d. c.* 451), a disciple of Theodore of Mopsuestia (*c.* 350–428) was condemned at the councils of Ephesus, 431, and Chalcedon, 451. His doctrines already preached by Diodorus of Tarsus (*d. c.* 392). The sect survives in the E.

Monophysites. Principal teachers were: Eutyches (*c.* 378–*c.* 454). Dioscurus (*d.* 454) who was condemned at Chalcedon, 451, and Timothy Aelurus (*d.* 477). The teaching survives among the Copts and Syrian Jacobites.

Monothelites. The doctrine first appears *c.* 622 in an address delivered before the Emperor Heraclius by Paul, head of the Acephali; but the principal exponent was Sergius (*d.* 638), patriarch of Constantinople. Monothelitism was finally condemned at Constantinople, 680–1.

Cathars. Originated in Bulgaria, 10thC, spread to S France and centred round city of Albi (hence alternative name for C., = Albigenses or Albigensians). Eradicated by force in 14thC.

Modernism. Condemned by papal decree *Lamentabili*, 3–4 July 1907, and by the encyclical *Pascendi*, 8 Sept. 1907. Chief exponents: A. Loisy (1857–1940) in France and G. Tyrrell (1861–1909) in England.

Heriot Watt University, Edinburgh, Established, 1966.

Heritable Jurisdictions Act abolished hereditary jurisdictions in Scotland, 1746, as a result of the 'Forty-Five'.

Heritage. *See* NATIONAL HERITAGE, DEPARTMENT OF.

Hermandad (Spanish for brotherhood), a defensive alliance of Castilian and Aragonese cities, formed *c.* 1250, and reinforced, 1295. Ceased to exist *c.* 1550.

Hermitage, art museum in St Petersburg, formerly part of the Winter Palace. Its art collection originated, 1764, as the private collection of the Empress Catherine II and includes paintings bought from the Walpole estate at Houghton Hall, Norfolk, England, in the 18thC.

Hertfordshire, University of, name and status of the former Hatfield Polytechnic since Sept. 1992.

Hertogenbosch (French **Bois-le-Duc**), Netherlands. Became a fortified town, 1184. Taken by the Duchy of Brabant, 1629. In French hands, 1794–1814.

Herzegovina. United with *Bosnia, 1326; formally ceded to Turkey, 1699, by Peace of Carlowitz; rebelled against Turkish rule, 1875; occupied by Austrians, Aug. 1878; formally annexed to Austria-Hungary, 7 Oct. 1908; became part of Yugoslavia, 1918. Formed, with Bosnia, one of the federal republics of Yugoslavia, 1945–91. *See* BOSNIA-HERZEGOVINA.

Hesse, Germany. Became a principality, 1292. Divided into four, 1567. By 1622 there were three Hs., viz. H.-Darmstadt, H.-Homburg, H.-Cassel. The two latter annexed by Prussia, 1866. H.-Darmstadt became a republic, 1919. The province, reunited, became a *Land* of the Federal German Republic after 1945.

Hexham (Northumberland). The early English abbey church is on the site of the church of St Andrew, which St Wilfrid founded 673. It was the seat of a Northumbrian bishopric associated with the sub-kingdom of *Bernicia. The see finally merged into that of Lindisfarne, 821, and was absorbed by that of Durham. A district called Hexhamshire surrounding H. was under the jurisdiction of the Archbishop of York, until 1545.

Hezbollah or **Hizbullah,** 'Party of God'. Muslim extremists, originating in Iran, active in Lebanon from early 1980s and responsible for much of the Western hostage-taking which took place during that decade. Possible involvement in Lockerbie bombing alleged, 1994.

High Church Party. Term first used in England *c.* 1703, and referred to the faction who opposed the Dissenters (*see* NONCON- FORMISTS), and enforced the laws made against them.

Highland Clearances, forcible eviction of tenants from several Scottish estates at the end of the 18th and first half of 19thC. Many went to Glasgow area or England: thousands emigrated to N America.

High Commission, The Court of. Established by Queen Elizabeth I, 1559, to investigate ecclesiastical cases; abolished by the Long Parliament, July 1641. James II in 1686 revived it, but it was finally abolished by the Bill of Rights in Dec. 1689. A similar court existed in Scotland, 1608–38.

Highland Garb Act forbade the wearing of H. dress, 1746. Repealed, 1782.

high school, term denoting, in USA, school maintained by the state from *c.* 1850; high school roughly equivalent to modern British comprehensive school. Term commonly used in Scotland and also used in England and Wales historically of some state grammar schools: still (1995) used by many schools run by the Girls' Public Day School Trust.

Highway Code (Britain), first published April 1931. Since revised in 1935, 1946, 1959, 1969, 1978, 1987 and 1993.

Hijacking, term first used in USA, 1923, as a slang expression to describe thefts of and from lorries. Since 1960s an accepted term generally denoting seizure of aircraft together with crew and passengers, usually during flight, and usually culminating in a ransom demand, often involving political aims. First H. of this sort in America occurred, 1 May 1961. From mid-1960s Hs. became more frequent in Europe and Middle E. International treaties against H. include those of 1963, 1970 and 1971. In Sept. 1971 four aircraft were hijacked and subsequently destroyed within 11-day period, involving over 300 passengers. 1978: seven-nation meeting in Bonn agreed sanctions against future hijackers and the European Community acted equally firmly. Aircraft H. has declined since 1980s, but not eradicated and in 1994 H. used three times by Algerian Islamic fundamentalists to advance cause. In third instance, 24–6 Dec., a French plane hijacked at Algiers airport and three passengers murdered. Plane eventually stormed by French police after flying to Marseilles and all hijackers killed. H. of ships has also occurred, notably that of the *Achille Lauro*, hijacked in the Mediterranean, 7 Oct. 1985, when a US passenger was murdered. Brit legislation against H. includes the Hijacking Act, 1971; Protection of Aircraft Act, 1973; Taking of Hostages Act, 1982. Jumbo jet hijacked on internal flight, Japan, 21 Mar. 1995, but passengers and crew released unharmed. Air H. used increasingly as method of financial blackmail in Russia since 1990.

Hillsborough Agreement. *See* ANGLO- IRISH AGREEMENT.

Hillsborough Disaster, Britain's worst

sporting disaster occurred at the Hillsborough Football Stadium in Sheffield, 15 April 1989, in a stampede resulting from overcrowded terraces. 95 people died then and soon after: in 1993 the 96th victim, in a coma since 1989, was 'allowed' to die after House of Lords decision.

Hindenburg Line. *See* WORLD WAR I.

Hire Purchase Act (Britain) came into force, 1 Jan. 1939, since superseded by the Consumer Credit Act of 1974.

Hiroshima, Japan. Castle founded at 1594; military centre from 1868. First atomic bomb dropped at H., 6 Aug. 1945; estimated 70,000–80,000 *d.* as result. Atomic Bomb Casualty Committee established at, 1947. Up to 90,000 buildings destroyed by 1945 bomb; rebuilding began *c.* 1950, with new Inari bridge. Castle restored, 1957, and houses museum of the city. Major industrialization and population over 1 million, 1994. Peace Festival at H. annually on 6 Aug.

Hispaniola. Name given to the island that now contains Haiti and the Dominican Republic, by Columbus, on his discovery thereof, 1492. Santo Domingo, first European town in W hemisphere, founded by Bartholomew Columbus, 1496. Negroes, introduced 1505, soon displaced native population. W portion, invaded by French buccaneers, ceded to France by Treaty of Ryswick, 1697; negroes of W portion rose against whites, 1791. E portion ceded by Spain to France, 1795. Toussaint l'Ouverture quelled British invaders, 1798; crushed mulatto revolt, 1799; completed conquest of whole island, but was deported by the French, 1801. French had to leave, 1803. E portion reoccupied by Spain, 1816–21; for later history, *see* HAITI and DOMINICAN REPUBLIC.

Hitler Youth (*Hitlerjugend***),** official National Socialist (*see* NATIONAL SOCIALISM) youth movement initiated in 1926 and made virtually compulsory for all 'Aryan' children in Germany, 1936.

Hittites. Settled in Asia Minor by 2000 BC.

Rose to greatest power under Shuppiluliuma (*c.* 1375–1340 BC). Fell *c.* 1200 BC.

HIV. *See* AIDS.

Hoare-Laval Pact, proposing for Ethiopia unacceptable terms as the price of peace with Italy, signed Dec. 1935. *See* ETHIOPIA.

Hobart, capital of Tasmania, founded as a penal settlement, 1804.

Ho Chi Minh City, founded as a trading post, 1623, when it was called **Saigon**. Capital of French Cochin China, 1869. Capital of S Vietnam, 1954–76, when it was captured by N Vietnamese and renamed H.

hockey, or **field hockey**, game of which a form was played in ancient Egypt. Often associated with Gaelic hurling, played in Ireland, 1272 BC. A type of H. played in S America in the 16thC, but the modern game derives from that played in English public schools from the early 19thC. The H. Association formed, 1886. Game spread to India (H. club formed in Calcutta, 1885) and in 20thC India and Pakistan have produced several champion teams. H. first played in the Olympic Games, 1908, but omitted from 1924 Games, after which International H. Federation formed. European Cup matches first played, 1970. H. played in girls' schools from late 19thC and in 1895, Ladies H. Association (later All-England Women's H. Association) established.

Hohenstaufen, a German family who, as *Holy Roman Emperors, 1138–1254, conducted a controversy with the Papacy until the male line was extinguished by the murder of Conradin in 1268.

Hohenzollern. Name of the Swabian family which became successively Electors of *Brandenburg, kings of *Prussia, and German emperors. The regime of the senior branch ended in Germany, Nov. 1918, and the last H. to have ruled Prussia *d.* 4 June 1941, but the Sigmaringen branch continued on the throne of *Romania till abdication of King Michael, 30 Dec. 1947.

Holland. *See* NETHERLANDS, KINGDOM OF THE.

Holland House, Kensington, built 1608–10, by Sir Walter Cope. Henry Richard Vassall Fox, 3rd Baron H. (1773–1840), nephew of Charles James Fox, made H.H. a headquarters of the Whig Party from 1800 until his death. Demolished after World War II and grounds now a public park.

Holloway. Prison for women built, 1849–51.

Holocaust, 1933–45, when the Hitler regime carried out the extermination of over 15 million people, about 6 million of whom were Jews. Began within a month of Hitler becoming German chancellor in Jan. 1933. Nüremberg Laws, 1935, deprived Jews of German citizenship. *Kristallnacht*, anti-Jewish pogrom, 9–10 Nov. 1938. 20 Jan. 1942: discussion of the 'Final Solution' after which extermination accelerated. In Israel Holocaust Day observed in April (anniversary of Warsaw Ghetto uprising, 1943).

Holy Alliance. Signed at Paris, 26 Sept. 1815, between the rulers of Russia, Prussia and Austria. It was offered for signature to the other powers, and all except Great Britain signed.

Holy Island (Lindisfarne). St Aidan (*d.* 651) founded a priory, 635, which was destroyed, 793 (*see* VIKING AGE). The Lindisfarne Gospels traditionally produced here. After about 90 years of actual harassing, or the threat of it, by Scandinavian pirates (*see* VIKING AGE), the first monastery was abandoned in 883 (*see* DURHAM). Benedictines from Durham reestablished a cell on H.I., 1082.

Holy Leagues, The.
1. Formed in 1511 between Pope Julius II, the Emperor Maximilian I, Henry VIII of England and Ferdinand, King of Aragon, to crush France; dissolved, 1513.
2. Formed by Pope Clement VII in 1526 against the Emperor Charles V; France, Venice and Milan were also in the league.
3. Formed by Pope Pius V, Spain and Venice against the Turks, 1570.
4. Formed by the Catholic party against the Huguenots in 1576, also known as the Catholic League.
5. Formed by Catholic princes of Germany under Maximilian of Bavaria in 1609 as a counterblast to Protestant Union of 1608.
6. Formed by Pope Innocent XI, the Emperor, Poland, Venice and Russia, against the Turks in 1684.

'Holy Maid of Kent'. Elizabeth Barton, during Henry VIII's reign. She prophesied the violent death of the king if he married Anne Boleyn. She and her confederates executed, 1534.

Holy Places. *See* CRUSADES. Dispute over their custody ultimately caused war in *Crimea, 1854.

Holy Roman Emperors. (Rivals and Anti-Caesars in *italics*)

Charles I (Charlemagne) 800–14
Louis I (the Pious) 814–40
Lothar I 840–55
Louis II (in Italy) 855–75
Charles II (the Bald) 875–81
Charles III (the Fat) 882–87
Guido (in Italy) 887–94
Lambert (in Italy) 894–96
Arnulf 896–99
Louis the Child 899–901
Louis III of Provence (in Italy) 901–11
Conrad I 911–15
Berengar (in Italy) 915–18
Saxons
Henry I (the Fowler) 918–36
Otto I. King of the E Franks 936–62
    H.R. Emperor 963–73
Otto II 973–83
Otto III 983–1002
Henry II (the Saint) 1002–24
Salians
Conrad II (the Salic) 1024–37
Henry III (the Black) 1037–56
Henry IV 1056–1106
Rudolf of Swabia 1077–1081
Hermann of Luxemburg 1081–93

Conrad of Franconia 1093–1106
Henry V 1106–25
Lothar II 1125–38
Hohenstaufen
Conrad III 1138–52
Frederick I (Barbarossa) 1152–90
Henry VI 1190–97
Philip⎫
Otto IV⎭ as rivals 1197–1208
Otto IV, alone 1208–12
Frederick II 1212–50
Henry Raspe 1246–47
William of Holland 1247–56
Conrad IV 1250–54
Interregnum 1254–57
Richard of Cornwall⎫
Alfonso of Castile⎭ 1257–72
Rudolf I of Hapsburg 1273–91
Adolf of Nassau 1292–98
Albert I of Hapsburg 1298–1308
Henry VII of Luxemburg 1308–13
Louis IV of Bavaria 1314–47
Frederick of Austria 1314
Charles IV of Luxemburg 1347–78
Günther of Schwartzburg 1347
Wenzel of Luxemburg 1378–1400
Rupert of the Palatinate 1400–10
Sigismund of Luxemburg 1410–37
Jobst of Moravia 1410
Hapsburgs
Albert II 1438–40
Frederick III 1440–93
Maximilian I 1439–1519
Charles V 1519–58
  (Abdicated 25 Oct.)
Ferdinand I 1558–64
Maximilian II 1564–76
Rudolf II 1576–1612
Matthias 1612–19
Ferdinand II 1619–37
Ferdinand III 1637–57
Leopold I 1658–1705
Joseph I 1705–11
Charles VI 1711–40
Charles VII of Bavaria 1742–45
Francis I of Lorraine 1745–65
Joseph II 1765–90
Leopold II 1790–92
Francis II 1792–1806
  (Abdicated)

NB: Francis I was elected as husband of
Maria Theresa of Austria because no
woman had ever held the throne. Charles
VII is therefore the only true exception to
the permanent Hapsburg tenure beginning in 1438. Ferdinand I and his successors were never crowned by the Pope.

Holy Roman Empire. Leo III crowns
Charlemagne Roman Emperor at Rome, 25
Dec. 800. Civil war, 840, leads to Partition
of Verdun, 843. Deposition of Charles the
Fat, 887. Henry the Fowler defeats the
Magyars at battle of the Unstrut, 933. Mag-
yars finally defeated by Otto I on the Lech,
955. Otto I crowned emperor of the H.R.E.
of the German nation by John XII, 963.
Henry III reforms Papacy at Synod of
Sutri, 1046. Choice of popes transferred
from H.R. Emperor to the cardinals 1059.
Hildebrand (Gregory VII) denounces *Lay
Investiture 1075. Henry IV submits to
Gregory VII at Canossa, 1077. War of Investiture, 1077–1122. Concordat of Worms
(Investiture Compromise), 1122. Elective
principle asserted at election of Lothar,
1125. Frederick Barbarossa begins war
with Lombard cities, 1158. Defeated at battle of Legnano, 1176. Peace of Constance,
1183. Frederick II leaves Sicily for his
Peaceful Crusade, 1228. Papal deposition
of Frederick II at Council of Lyons, 1245.
Hohenstaufen defeat and destruction at
battle of Tagliacozzo, 1268. Election of Rudolf of Hapsburg, 1273. He conquers Austria from Bohemia, battle of the Marchfeld,
1278. First Union of Swiss Cantons, 1307.
Battle of Morgarten, 1315. Charles IV establishes Electoral Constitution of the
H.R.E. by the Golden Bull, 1356. John Hus
burned by Council of Constance, 1415.
Bohemian (Hussite) War, 1419–36, ends
with Compact of Iglau, 1436. Turkish raids
begin after battle of Kossovo, 1448. Maximilian fails to introduce effective reforms
at Diets of Worms, 1495. Augsburg, 1500.
After battle of Mohacs (1526) Turks besiege Vienna, 1529. Charles V rejects confession of Augsburg, 1530. Formation of
League of Schmalkalden (Protestant),
1530. Truce of Frankfort, 1539. Protestant
defeat at battle of Mühlberg, 1547. Interim

of Augsburg, 1548. Peace of Augsburg, 1555. War of Dutch Liberation begins, 1572. Union of Utrecht, 1579. Counter Reformation, 1551–1620. Defenestration of Prague, 1618. Thirty Years War, 1618–48. Wallenstein becomes Imperial C.-in-C., 1625. Dismissed, 1630. Tilly sacks Magdeburg, 1631. Defeated by Swedes at battle of the Breitenfeld, 1631. Wallenstein defeated and Gustavus Adolphus of Sweden killed at battle of Lützen, 1632. Wallenstein murdered, 1634. Peace of *Westphalia, 1648. Repulse of the Turks from Vienna, 1683. War of *Spanish Succession, 1701–14. Treaty of Utrecht, 1713. Treaty of Rastatt, 1714. Pragmatic Sanction guaranteed by Prussia, 1728. War of Austrian Succession, 1740–2. Second Silesian War, 1744–5. Peace of *Aix-la-Chapelle, 1748. *Seven Years War, 1756–63. Napoleon forms Rhenish Confederation, 12 July 1806. Francis II renounces crown of H.R.E., 6 Aug. 1806. *See* AUSTRIA.

Holyrood Abbey and Palace (Edinburgh). Abbey founded, 1128, by David I of Scotland. The palace was built in 1501 by James IV of Scotland; destroyed by English, 1544, but immediately rebuilt; Rizzio murdered at, 1566; burned by Cromwell's troops, 1650; rebuilt by Charles II, 1670–79. The monastery was dissolved at the Reformation, and the chapel became the parish church until James II made it a chapel royal (1687).

Holy Shroud (of Turin), *see* TURIN SHROUD.

Home Guard came into being as a voluntary defence force, May 1940. Members reached their peak – about two million men – about June 1943. The force stood down, 1 Nov. 1944, and was disbanded, 31 Dec. 1945. Re-formed, Jan. 1952. Placed on a reserve basis, 1956. All activities suspended, 1957. *See also* VOLKSSTURM.

Home Office. Department of state, dates in present form from 1792, but powers much increased after 1914 and again since 1939. Prison service an executive agency of the H.O. from 1 Apr., 1993. Home Secretaries since 1914:

Sir John Simon 1915
Herbert Samuel 1916
Sir George Cave 1916
Edward Shortt 1919
William Bridgeman 1922
Arthur Henderson 1924
Sir William Joynson-Hicks 1924
John Clynes 1929
Sir Herbert Samuel 1931
Sir John Gilmour 1932
Sir John Simon 1935
Sir Samuel Hoare 1937
Sir John Anderson 1939
Herbert Morrison 1940
Sir Donald Somervell 1945
James Chuter Ede 1945
Sir David Maxwell-Fyfe 1951
Gwilym Lloyd-George 1954
R.A. Butler 1957
Henry Brooke 1962
Sir Frank Soskice 1964
Roy Jenkins 1965
James Callaghan 1967
Reginald Maudling 1970
Robert Carr 1972
Roy Jenkins 1974
Merlyn Rees 1976
William Whitelaw 1979
Leon Brittan 1983
Douglas Hurd 1986
David Waddington 1989
Kenneth Baker 1990
Kenneth Clarke 1992
Michael Howard 1993

Home Rule. *See* IRELAND.

Homestead Act.
1. New Zealand, passed 1885, providing free land for emigrants.
2. W Australia, similar Act, 1893.

Homestead Act (USA). Passed by Congress, 1862, by which every US citizen of the age of 21 years was entitled to claim a certain portion of unappropriated land.

Homicide Act. *See* CAPITAL PUNISHMENT.

Homilies, Book of. The Convocation of 1542 decided to publish it for the guidance of preachers. First published, 1547; reprinted, 1560. Second book published, 1563.

Homs (Hims), Syria, the Roman city of Emesa, was taken by the Saracens, AD 636, and by the Crusaders, 1098. Ibrahim Pasha defeated the Turks at, 1832. *See* FIRST CRUSADE.

Honduras, republic of Central America. Discovered by Columbus, 1502. First settlements, 1524 (Spanish). Independent of Spain, 1821. Independent of the Federation of Central America, 1838. Frequent wars with other states till 1876, and several civil wars, notably in 1883 and 1903. Pan-American Highway completed, 1943. Dispute with El Salvador led to the 'football war', July 1969; settled, 1980. New constitution, 1982. Liberal presidential victory, 1993.

Honduras, British. *See* BELIZE.

Hong Kong, China. Occupied by British, 1841. Ceded to Britain at Treaty of Nanking, 1842. Kowloon added, 1860. Chinese government grant 99-year lease of other mainland areas, 1898. University opened, 1912. Bombed by Japanese, 21 Feb. 1939. Captured by Japanese, 7–25 Dec. 1941. Liberated, 30 Aug. 1945. Considerable influx of refugees from China, from 1950s until 1990s; also arrival of *Vietnamese 'boat people'. Leading commercial and financial centre in Far E since beginning of 20thC, but notably since 1950s. Agreement signed in Peking, 19 Dec. 1984, that H. should return to China on 1 July 1997. First direct elections in H., May 1991. Christopher Patten made governor of H., 1992: publishes reform plans in defiance of China, Mar. 1993. Subsequent negotiations with China; when these failed, Patten announced he would continue plans despite Chinese objections. H. legislature narrowly endorsed Patten reforms, June 1994, but China said it would disregard after 1997. Anglo-Chinese agreement to develop new airport at H., 4 Nov. 1994. Last elections under British rule, Sept. 1995, produced overwhelming pro-democracy vote but on a low turn-out.

Honourable Artillery Company (HAC). Founded 1537 in London as a guild for Trained Band instructors. In 1638 some members of it migrated to America and founded the Ancient and H.A.C. of Boston (Massachusetts).

hops. First introduced from Netherlands into England *c.* 1525. Prohibited temporarily, 1528, because certain physicians thought them harmful.

hormone replacement therapy (HRT), increasingly used since 1970s, but remains controversial (1995).

Horse Guards, Royal. Present regiment raised by Earl of Oxford in 1661, out of the remains of Cromwell's New Model. Their headquarters, in Whitehall, London, erected, 1758.

horse-racing, sport going back to classical times and beyond. Type of H. featured in the original Olympic Games. H. popular with medieval Arabs, and thought Crusaders introduced it to western Europe from the 11thC. By 17thC it was a recognized sport, and Charles II established Newmarket as the sport's English HQ. H. also becoming popular in New England and France. Jockey Club founded at Newmarket *c.* 1750. This controlled H. in UK until British Horseracing Board assumed responsibility, June 1993. On-course Sunday betting allowed in England from Jan. 1995. British race-horse *Red Rum* (three times *Grand National winner, 1973, 1974, 1977) d. Oct. Famous races (with dates of establishment) include:

1779: Oaks, at Epsom
1780: Derby, at Epsom
1786: St Leger, at Doncaster
1807: Ascot Gold Cup, at Ascot
1809: Two Thousand Guineas, at Newmarket
1812: Goodwood Cup, at Goodwood
1814: One Thousand Guineas, at Newmarket
1839: Grand National, at Aintree
1924: Cheltenham Gold Cup, at Cheltenham

Famous races outside Britain include (with foundation dates):

Prix du Jockey Club, Chantilly, France, 1836
Prix de l'Arc de Triomphe, France, 1920
Kentucky Derby, Louisville, Kentucky, USA, 1876
Irish Sweep Stake, The Curragh, Ireland, 1866

Hospitallers, Knights. *See* MALTA, KNIGHTS OF.

Housing and Local Government, Ministry of. Established, 1951. Subsequently absorbed in Department of the *Environment.

hovercraft. First public service began between Rhyl and Wallasey, 20 July 1962. Cross-Channel service, 1966. SRN4, then world's biggest H., launched at Cowes, 4 Feb. 1968.

Hoxne Treasure. Roman treasure (coins, jewellery and tableware) dug up in field at Hoxne, Suffolk, Nov. 1992. Largest collection of Roman coins yet discovered in Britain, buried in 5thC. Declared treasure trove. Sept. 1993. Bought by British Museum, April 1994.

Hubble space telescope, placed in orbit round the earth by the US space shuttle *Discovery,* Apr. 1990. Fault impaired performance from start. US space shuttle team sent to repair, Dec. 1993. 11-day journey included a record five space walks lasting over 35 hours, and cost $629 million. Repairs confirmed successful, Jan. 1994. *See* SPACE FLIGHTS.

Hubertusburg, Treaty of, 1763, between Prussia and Austria at end of Seven Years War. By it the Empress Maria Theresa finally ceded Silesia to Frederick the Great.

Huddersfield, University of, name and status of the former Huddersfield Polytechnic from 1992.

Hudson Bay Territory or **Prince Rupert's Land,** NW America. Discovered by Cabot, 1498; revisited and explored by Hudson, 1610; Hudson's Bay Co. formed, 1670; English factories at captured by French, 1685; restored by Peace of Utrecht, 1713; part of territory became *British Columbia, remainder was purchased by Canada, 1858; formal transfer to the Dominion, 19 Nov. 1869. Most of the H.B.T. has formed part of the *N-W Territories since 1918.

Huguenots. The name originated between 1510 and 1535 at Geneva, when those in favour of an alliance with Freiburg were called *Eidgenossen* ('partakers of an oath'), a popular French adaptation having introduced association with the personal name Hugues. They joined with the Bernese, who had declared for the reformed religion. The name gradually came to be attached to the French Protestants. *See* BARTHOLOMEW, MASSACRE OF ST, and FRANCE.

Hull (Kingston-upon-), England. Chartered by Edward I, 1299. Defences built, 1541. Manor granted, 1552. University college founded, 1927; reconstituted as the University of Hull, 1954. *Humber road bridge completed, 1981.

Human Fertilization and Embryology Authority, established London under the Human Fertilization and Embryology Act, 1990. It advises the minister of health, and licences persons engaged in activities involving the creation or use of embryos outside the body for treatment of infertility. *See* ARTIFICIAL INSEMINATION

human rights. *See* DECLARATION OF HUMAN RIGHTS.

Humane Society, Royal, founded, 1774.

Humber Bridge, 1981, has (1995) largest single central span (4626 ft/1410 m) of any suspension bridge in the world.

Humberside, England, administrative county established 1974 under Local Government Act of 1972. Headquarters are at Beverley. H. embraces areas formerly in Lincolnshire and Yorkshire. Its continued existence questioned from 1990, and abolition envisaged, 1996.

Humberside, University of, name and status, from 1992, of former Humberside Polytechnic.

Humble Petition and Advice. The second paper constitution of the English Protectorate, 1657. The petition collapsed on the dissolution of Parliament by Cromwell in 1658.

Hundred Associates, The. Cardinal Richelieu, in 1627, annulled a charter of the Trading Co. of New France in America belonging to a family of Huguenots, and organized a company known as the H.A., to drive out the Huguenots and colonize the district.

Hundred Years War, 1338–1453. France assists Scotland against England, 1334. All Englishmen in Flanders arrested, 1336. Rebellion of Jacob van Artevelde of Ghent, 1338. Edward III renews claim to the French crown, 1340. Naval battle of Sluys, 1340. English sack Poitiers, win battle of Crécy and Neville's Cross, 1346; capture Calais, 1347. Black Death, 1347–50. Battle of Poitiers, 1356. The *Jacquerie*, 1358. Peace of Brétigny, 8 May 1360. War resumed, 1369. English driven out of most of France by Bertrand de Guesclin, 1369–75. Peasants revolt in England, 1381. Duke of Orléans murdered by Burgundy, 1407. England resumes war again, 1415. Harfleur captured and battle of Agincourt, 1415. Burgundy murdered, 1419. Treaty of Troyes, 1420. Joan of Arc relieves Orléans, May 1429. Dauphin crowned at Rheims, 1430. Joan of Arc burnt, 28 May 1431. Burgundy changes sides at Treaty of Arras, 1435. *Ordonnance sur la Gendarmerie*, 1439. *La Praguerie*, 1439–43. Battle of Formigny, 1450. English driven out except at Calais by 1453.

Hungarian literature. The following is a list of some prominent Hungarian authors:

Ady, Endve, 1871–1915, poet.
Arany, Janos, 1817–82, poet.
Babits, Mihaly, 1883–1941, poet.
Balassi, Balint, 1554–94, poet.

Bessenyei, György, 1747–1811, dramatist.
Csiky, Gregor, 1842–91, dramatist.
Döbrentei, Gabor, 1786–1851, philologist.
Eötvös, Baron József, 1813–71, poet.
Fejer, György, 1766–1852, historian.
Jókai, Maurus, 1825–1904, novelist.
Jozsef, Attila, 1906–37, poet.
Kazinczy, Ferenc, 1759–1831, literary reformer and critic.
Kemény, Baron Zsigmund, 1816–75, novelist.
Kisfaludy, Károly, 1788–1830, poet and dramatist.
Kosztolanyi, Dezsö, 1885–1939, poet.
Miksáth, Kálmán, 1847–1910, novelist.
Molnar, Ferenc, 1878–1952, dramatist.
Petöfi, Sandor, 1823–49, poet.
Szigligeti, Ede (József Szatmáry), 1814–78, dramatist.
Vörösmarty, Mihály, 1800–55, poet and dramatist.

Hungary. The Hungarians or Magyars crossed the Carpathians, AD 889. Were driven out of Germany after battle of Unstrut, 933, by Henry the Fowler. Last invasion of Germany defeated by Otto I at the Lech, 955. Converted by King Stephen to Christianity, 1000. Stephen II abdicates, 1131. Invaded by Mongols, 1226. Turkish slave raids begin after their capture of Adrianople, 1361. Defeat of Christian confederacy by Turks at the first battle of Kossovo, 1389, and of crusades at Nicopolis, 1396. Rise of John Hunyadi, 1437. His victory at the Haemus, 1444. Defeated at Varna, 1444. Decisive defeat by Turks at second battle of Kossovo, 1448. Election of Matthias Corvinus to the throne, 1458. Invades Bohemia, 1468. Seizes Vienna, 1485. Conquest of H. at battle of Mohacz, 1526. Treaty of Torok, 1606. Turks repulsed at second siege of Vienna, 1683. Prince Eugene reconquers H., 1683–99. Peace of Carlowitz, 1699. Maria Theresa appeals to the Hungarians against Prussia, 1741. Rebellion against Hapsburg rule, 1848. Defeated by Jellaçic at battle of Schwechat, 30 Oct. 1848. Capitulation of Villagos, 14 Aug. 1849. The *Ausgleich*, Feb. 1867. (For events during the war of 1914–18 *see* WORLD WAR I.) Declared a republic, 1918; succeeded by Bela Kun's Communist dictatorship, Mar. 1919. Right-wing Regency under Horthy, 1920–45. Claimed part of Czechoslovakia and occupied it, Oct. 1938. Joined Anti-Comintern Pact, 2 Feb. 1939. Gained half of Transylvania from Romania by Vienna Award, 30 Aug. 1940; signed Axis Pact, Nov. 1941: invaded Yugoslavia, Apr.: declared war on Russia, 27 June (*see* WORLD WAR II). Occupied by Russia, 1945: republic, Feb. 1946; People's Republic, 18 Aug. 1949. Cardinal Mindzenty sentenced to life imprisonment for treason: persecution of Catholic Church. In Oct. 1956 an anti-Soviet rising in Budapest; Nagy became premier, 24 Oct. and Mindszenty released. Russian troops crushed uprising. Nov.: Mindszenty took refuge in US embassy and died in Rome, 1975; Nagy took refuge in Yugoslav embassy but subsequently abducted and shot. Thousands of refugees fled to western Europe and policy of repression followed. From early 1960s there was liberalization and economic progress. Crown of St Stephen, in US custody since 1945, returned to H., 1978. Communist leader Kadar forced to resign, May 1989; constitution amended, Oct. Multiparty election. Mar/April 1990 won by the Democratic Forum. Rapid economic expansion followed. Queen Elizabeth II paid state visit to H., 1993. After elections of May 1994 former Communists won largest vote and formed coalition with centre left, June. Economic reform programme continued.

Huns. A Turanian group of tribes which invaded Europe in 4th and 5thC, and were defeated at battle of Châlons, 451.

Hussars, light cavalry of Hungarian origin, first raised by Matthias I (Corvinus), 1458. For the dates of conversion of British Light Dragoon regiments to H., *see under* REGIMENTS OF THE BRITISH ARMY.

Hussites. The followers of John Hus (*b.c.* 1373) who was burned as a heretic by the Council of Constance, July 1415. Led by Ziska they carried out the 'Defenestration of Neustadt', 1419, and took up arms to prevent Catholic reconquest. Establishment of Tabor, 1420, and the split between the Taborites and the Calixtines. Death of Ziska, 1424. Rise of Procopius the Great, 1425. Victory over Cesarini at battle of Tauss, Aug. 1431. Annihilation of Taborites by Calixtines at battle of Lipari, 1434. Maintained a position of semi-independence until battle of the White Mountain, 1620.

Hyde Park (London). Originally belonging to Westminster Abbey it became crown property, 1536. Opened to public, 1670. Serpentine formed, 1730–3. Underground car park opened, 15 Oct. 1962. 'Speakers' Corner' at H.P. famous since the 19thC. Queen Elizabeth Gate at, opened 6 July 1993.

Hyderabad, India. At the conquest of the Deccan by Aurungzebe, 1687, H. became the residence of the governor of the Deccan. By 1748 this official under the title of the Nizam of H. had made himself virtually independent of the Moguls. He ceded the Circars to the French, 1755. Defeated by Marathas at battle of Kurdla, 1795. Accepted permanent British alliance, 1799. Acquired Berar from the Marathas, 1804. Loyal to Britain, 1857; new treaty, 1860. At division of India, 15 Aug. 1947, delayed accession. Indian troops entered the State and set up military government, Sept. On 1 Dec. 1949 the State acceded to the Indian Union. Redrawing of state boundaries in 1956 meant that H. was partitioned between various units, and the Nizam became a private Indian citizen.

hydro-electric power. First hydro-electric station in the British Isles begun in 1883, in N Ireland.

hydrofoil, first fitted to a boat, 1906. First commercial H., 1956.

hydrogen. Discovered by Paracelsus *c.* 1500; experiments by Boyle, 1672; proved to be an element by Cavendish, 1766; presence in water was discovered by Watt and Cavendish, 1781.

hydrogen bomb. US Atomic Energy Commission announced on 16 Nov 1952 that tests involving 'thermo-nuclear weapons' had taken place on Eniwetok Atoll, Marshall Islands. This was generally taken to mean that explosions felt in the Pacific area 1–4 Nov. had been caused by the detonation of a H.B. Voroshilov claimed Russia had H.B., Nov. 1952. H.B. first officially detonated by USA in the Marshall Islands on 1 Mar. 1954. Russia detonated their first H.B. in Sept. 1954; Britain in 1957. First Chinese H.B. exploded, Oct. 1964. French exploded a H.B., 24 Aug. 1968. Now (1995) believed capacity for producing H.Bs. widespread and there may be more than 20,000 thermo-nuclear devices scattered throughout the world.

hypnotism, first investigated in modern times by Paracelsus (1493–1541). Used therapeutically by Mesmer, 1774 (whence *mesmerize*). Brought into disrepute by Cagliostro (1743–95). The word H. was coined by Dr. Braid of Manchester, 1841.

Hythe, one of the original *Cinque Ports under Edward the Confessor (1042–66), lost its maritime importance with the silting up of the River Leman. Its ancient liberties were conferred by King John, 1205. The Royal Military Canal from H. to Rye was cut *c.* 1809.

ice hockey. Canada's national sport. Has developed rapidly since the formulation of rules in 1879, at a game between two teams from McGill University, Montreal. National Hockey League, 1917. Game spread to Europe after World War I. Played in Winter Olympics from 1920. World Hockey Association, amalgamated with National League, 1979. 1994 World Champions: Canada.

Iceland. Discovered by Irishmen at the beginning of 9thC. Colonized by Norwegians *c.* 870–90. (*See* Viking Age.) First Parliament (*Althing*), 930. Christianity officially adopted, 1000. Inhabitants acknowledged sovereignty of Norway, 1262–4. United to Denmark with Norway, 1380; at separation of Norway and Denmark in 1814 became part of Denmark. Danish-Icelandic Federal Constitution, making both I. and Denmark independent states under the same sovereign, 1 Dec. 1918. Occupied by British troops, 10 May 1940. As a result of separation from Denmark crown prerogatives assumed by the *Althing*, 16 May 1941. American troops landed, July 1941. Declared a republic, 17 June 1944. Signed *North Atlantic Treaty 1949, and agreed to US forces being stationed in I., 30 June 1958. Fishing dispute with Britain, 1953–61. I. joined EFTA, Mar. 1970. First woman president, Vigdis Finnbogadottin, elected 1980; re-elected 1984, 1988 and 1992. I. declared itself nuclear-free zone, 1985.

Icelandic language and literature. Great period of Old Icelandic literature *c.* 1000–1200. Old I. authors include:

Arnor Jarlaskald, *d.* 1067?, poet.
Egil Skallagrimsson, 900–83, poet.
Einar Jinglescale (Skalaglamm), *fl.* 1130–60, poet.
Eysteinn Asgrimsson, *fl.* 1350.
Halldor Skvaldri, *fl.* 1110.
Hallfred Vandradaskald, *fl.* 995–1000, poet.
Jon Arason, 1484–1551, poet and historian.
Sighvat Thordarson, *fl.* 1015–30, poet.
Snorri Sturluson, 1179–1242, historian.
Sturla Thordarson, 1214–84, poet.
Thorarin Stuttfeldr, *fl.* 1110.
Thord Sigvaldi's Skald, *fl.* 1000–30, poet.

Modern I. letters begin with the Reformation and the introduction of the printing-press, as in the rest of Northern Europe. The last of the Catholic bishops of Holar, Jon Arason (*see above*), may be regarded as also the last of the older poets in the skaldic tradition, and it was he who in 1525 brought the first printing-press to Iceland. It was not used to produce the first vernacular version of the New Testament (which was printed at Copenhagen 1540), but in 1584 this press at Holar printed the first I. edition of the entire Bible.

Iceni British tribe, inhabiting and around present-day Colchester. Revolted under Boudicca against the Romans, AD 61.

'Ich Dien'. Motto of John of Luxemburg, King of Bohemia, found on his helmet after the battle of Crécy, 26 Aug. 1346. Thereupon adopted as the motto of the Prince of Wales by the Black Prince.

Iconoclasts (Greek for 'image breakers'). Name given in the 8thC to those who opposed the use of images in the Church. The Emperor Leo the Isaurian issued edicts against images in AD 726 and 730. Images allowed in churches, 787. Images restored in the E, 843.

Idaho, USA. Territory formed, 1863; present limits defined, 1868; state admitted to Union, 1890.

identity cards (Britain). Issued 30 Sept. 1939 and following days. Abolished, Apr. 1952. Proposal to revive a form of I.C. for social security beneficiaries (to combat fraud), 1993 onwards; in Oct. 1994 Home Secretary announced investigation into establishment of a voluntary I.C. Government produced a consultative document on I.C., May 1995.

Ido, adapted from Esperanto, 1907.

Iglau, Treaty of, 1436, ended the war of the Emperor Sigismund against *Hussites.

Ijsselmeer. Remnant of Zuider Zee formed by irruption of N Sea through W Frisian coastline in 13thC. Bill for reclamation became law, 1918. Work begun, 1923. Wieringer Polder completed, 1930; wrecked, 1945; restored, 1946. NE Polder completed, 1942; E Flevoland, 1957; Zuidelijk Flevoland, 1967. Whole 'Delta project' completed by 1980.

Illinois, USA. Explored by Jacques Marquette, Jesuit missionary, and Louis Joliet, representing the Government of New France, 1673. By treaty passed to English, 1763, ceded to USA, 1783; admitted into the Union as a state, 3 Dec. 1818.

Illyria (more properly **Illyricum**). Greek colonies on coast, 6thC BC. Country except Dalmatia annexed by Romans, 168 BC. Dalmatia also annexed, AD 9. At partition of empire fell to Byzantium, 379. The Napoleonic 'Kingdom of I.' formed 1809 and attached to 'Kingdom of Italy'; ceded to Austria, 1814. Now (1995) divided between Italy, Croatia and Slovenia.

Imitatio Christi (The Imitation of Christ). Generally held to be the work of Thomas à Kempis (c. 1379–1471). First printed at Augsburg c. 1471. Translated into English at least as early as 1438 (MS now in Magdalen College, Oxford).

Immaculate Conception. Established as an article of the Roman Catholic faith by the bull *Ineffabilis Deus*, 8 Dec. 1854.

impeachment. The first recorded exercise of the power was in 1376, when an attack was made on Richard Lyons and Lord Latimer by the 'Good Parliament'. Fell into disuse owing to the more general employment of Acts of Attainder until the I. of Sir Giles Mompesson, 1620. By Act of Settlement, 1701, a royal pardon cannot be pleaded in bar of I. Last British I., 1806. In USA President Andrew Johnson impeached, 1868; Nixon resigned presidency, 1974, to avoid I.

Imperial College of Science, Technology and Medicine, S Kensington, part of University of London formed by the fusion in 1907 of the City and Guilds Technical College, Royal College of Science (founded 1881), the Royal School of Mines (founded 1851). The St Mary's Hospital Medical School was united to I.C.S.T.M., as a constituent college, on 1 Aug. 1988.

Imperial Conference of Premiers of Great Britain and Self-Governing Dominions. Resolution of Colonial Conference of 1907 to hold such conferences every four years. First held, 1911. After 1937 superseded by *Prime Ministers' Meetings.

Imperial Defence College. Formed in London, 1927.

Imperial Institute. *See* COMMONWEALTH INSTITUTE.

Imperial War Museum, London. Founded, 1917.

Inauguration Day, USA, 20 Jan., the day on which (at four-year intervals) the newly elected President takes the oath of office.

Incas (Peru). The Inca dynasty was probably established in Peru in AD 13thC. Tupac Inca Yupanqui conquered Chile c. 1450. Huayna Capac conquered Quito c. 1490. Accession of Atahualpa, 1525. He massacred many I., 1532. Was seized and murdered by Pizarro, 1533.

Incitement to Disaffection Act, 1934, enables the police, on leave given by a High Court judge, to search the premises of persons suspected of endeavouring to seduce members of H.M. forces from their allegiance.

income tax first imposed in Great Britain, 1799, at rate of 2s. per £ on incomes over £200. Discontinued during Peace of Amiens, and again in 1815. Reintroduced by Peel in 1842 at 7d. in the £. 'Pay-as-you-earn' (PAYE) system instituted, 1944. Queen paid I.T. on personal income from April 1993.

income tax (USA). First enacted by Congress, 1 July 1862.

Indemnity Acts (Britain). Usually passed to relieve servants of the Crown of the consequences of any illegal act done by them in an emergency. Originated, 1715.

Independence Day, 4 July, public holiday in USA since 1776.

Independent Labour Party. Formed at Bradford, 1893. Dominated *Labour Party until 1914. Seceded, 1932, under James Maxton (1885–1946). Last I.L.P. MP joined Labour Party, 1948.

Independent Television Authority. Set up under the Television Act of 1954 to provide television services additional to those provided by the British Broadcasting Corporation. Succeeded by the **Independent Television Commission**, 1991 under the terms of the Broadcasting Act, 1990.

Independents. *See* CONGREGATIONALISTS; *also* NONCONFORMISTS.

Index Expurgatorius. Part of the Prohibitory Roman Index (*see* following entry); a list of books to be expurgated before being sanctioned to be read. First printed, 1601.

Index Librorum Prohibitorum (List of Prohibited Books). Drawn up by the Council of Trent, submitted for papal approval, and published, 1564; it was revised by the Congregation of the Index, and underwent modifications under Leo XIII. The first Roman Index was issued in 1557 and 1559 under Paul IV. Abolished, 1966.

India. Punjab invaded by Alexander the Great, 327–325 BC. Rise of Asoka and an-nexation of Baluchistan from Seleucus Nicator c. 250 BC. Kushan invasions, AD 150. Kushan decline c. 330. Rise of Guptas under Samudragupta, 340. Conquest of Gujarat from Sassanids by Chandragupta, 400. First Mohammedan raid, 664. I. split into numbers of small states till the conquest of the Punjab by Mahmud of Ghazni, 1000–1. Afghans conquered most of the country, 1206–10, and founded the 'Slave Dynasty', which *fl.* till 1250, and declined on Tamerlane's invasion, 1398. Marco Polo visits I. c. 1290–3. Formation in S I. of Vijayanagar, 14thC. Vasco da Gama reaches I., 1498. Defeat of Egyptians at Diu by Francisco d'Almeida, 1509. Albuquerque's viceroyalty and establishment of Portuguese trading empire, 1509–15. Babar's invasion, 1525, and establishment of Mogul Empire (1525–50), which reached its peak under Akbar, 1556–1605. Destruction of Vijayanagar at battle of Talikota, 1565. Accession of Jehangir, 1605. Dutch blockade of Goa, 1606. Death of Jehangir and accession of Shah Jehan, 1629. Reign of Aurungzebe, 1659–1707. Invasion of Nadir Shah from Persia, 1739. Rise of Marathas, 1720 onwards. Clive's defence of Arcot, 1751. Cession of Northern Circars to French, 1753. Suraj-ud-Dowlah's capture of *Calcutta, 1756. Seven Years War, 1756–63. Battle of Plassey, 1757. French defeat at battle of Wandewash and Marathas capture Delhi, 1760. First Mysore War, 1767–9. Warren Hastings governor of *Bengal, 1772. Second Mysore War, 1780. Arrival of French fleet under Suffren, 1782. Third Mysore War, 1790. Capture of Pondicherry, 1793. Fourth Mysore War, 1799. Storming of Seringapatam and death of Tipu Sahib, 1799. Treaty of *Bassein, 1802. Maratha Wars, 1802–5. E I. Co.'s trading monopoly abolished, 1813. Nepal War, 1814. Pindari War, 1817–18. First Burma War, Dec. 1825–Feb. 1826. Measures against *Thugs and *Suttee, 1829. Mysore rebellion, 1830. First Afghan War, 1837–42. Sind War, 1843. First Sikh War, 1845–6. Annexation of Sattara, 1848. Second Sikh War, 1848–9. Annexation of Punjab, 1849. Second Burma War, 1852. Treaty with Afghanistan,

1855. Persian War, 1856. *Indian Mutiny, 1857. Assumption of Government of I. by the crown, 1858. Queen Victoria proclaimed Empress of I., 1 Jan. 1877.

Frontier War, 1897–8. Mohmand incursions, joined by the Afghans, 1908. Government of I. Bill passed, June 1912. Seat of government transferred from Calcutta to Delhi, and changes were made in the constitution of Bengal and Assam. World War I: Indian Expeditionary Force sent to France, Aug.–Sept. 1914; in action, 28 Oct. 1914. Indian National Congress demanded self-government for I., 1917. Delhi and Punjab disturbances and martial law in Punjab, Apr. 1919. Amritsar riots, in which Brig.-Gen. Dyer ordered troops to fire on the mob, 13 Apr. 1919; Indian Legislature established, 1919. Council of State and Legislative Assembly inaugurated, 8 Apr. 1921. Round Table Conference met in London, Oct. 1930; second conference 1931. Gandhi's third civil disobedience campaign began, 1932. He transferred charge of Congress to Nehru, 1935. In 1936 Government of I. Bill became law, but was rejected by Congress. Burma and Aden separated from I., 1937. World War II, Sept. 1939: Congress continued opposition to British rule but first Indian troops reached France, Dec. Some Indian troops joined dissident Indian National Liberation Army, 1942–4. Cripps's proposals rejected by Congress, 1942. By 1945 Muslim and Hindu Nationalists irreconcilably divided. 1947: I. given Dominion status and *Pakistan separated from it; religious massacres and migrations followed. Gandhi assassinated, 30 Jan. 1948; Nehru prime minister, Oct. Revolt in Kashmir, 1948. In 1949 Hindi declared the official language but in practice has not superseded English. I. proclaimed a republic, 26 Jan. 1950. Between 1952 and 1954 all former French settlements in I. transferred to I. At Afro-Asian Conference held at Bandoeng, 1955, I. established itself as spokesman for the 'uncommitted nations'. 1956: Acts dividing I. into 14 states and six centrally administered territories came into force. 1959: Dalai Lama of *Tibet given political asylum in I., 1961: Indian forces occupied Goa, Dec. In 1962 there was border fighting with China. Nehru d., May 1964, succeeded by Shastri, who d. 1966. He was succeeded by Mrs Indira Gandhi, daughter of Nehru, who continued policy of non-alignment. From 1967 economic crises and government corruption led to discontent culminating in Mrs Gandhi's defeat by Janata coalition, 1977, but this later fell apart. Mrs Gandhi re-elected, 1980, but assassinated by Sikh extremists, 31 Oct. 1984. Succeeded by son, Rajiv Gandhi, who won landslide election victory, Dec. 1984 but defeated after corruption allegations, 1989: assassinated, 1991. Many clashes with Sikh militants from 1980s, and continued dispute with Pakistan over Kashmir. Rising Hindu fundamentalism caused destruction of Ayodha Mosque, Dec. 1992 and rioting in Delhi, Bombay, etc. with several hundred fatalities, mostly Muslim. Kashmiri problem increased 1993–5; in Oct. 1994, Europeans taken hostage in Delhi by Kashmiri separatists but later freed by government action; further European hostages seized in Kashmir, July 1995 and one murdered, Aug.

India, Governors-General (or Viceroys) of:

Warren Hastings, 1774.
Sir John Macpherson, 1785.
Marquess of Cornwallis, 1786.
Sir John Shore, 1793.
Marquess of Cornwallis, 1796.
Sir Alured Clarke, 1798.
Marquess of Wellesley, 1798.
Marquess of Cornwallis, 1805.
Sir George Barlow, 1805.
Earl of Minto, 1807.
Marquess of Hastings, 1813.
Hon. John Adam, 1 Jan.–1 Aug. 1823.
Lord Amherst, 1823.
Hon. W. Butterworth Bayley, 1828.
Lord William Bentinck, 1828.
Sir Charles Metcalfe, 1835.
Earl of Auckland, 1836.
Earl of Ellenborough, 1842.
Viscount Hardinge, 1844.
Marquess of Dalhousie, 1848.

Earl Canning, 1856.
Earl of Elgin, 1862.
Sir John Lawrence, 1864.
Earl of Mayo, 1869.
Lord Northbrook, 1872.
Earl Lytton, 1876.
Marquess of Ripon, 1880.
Earl of Dufferin, 1884.
Marquess of Lansdowne, 1888.
Earl of Elgin, 1894.
Lord Curzon, 1899.
Earl of Minto, 1905.
Lord Hardinge, 1910.
Lord Chelmsford, 1916.
Earl of Reading, 1921.
Lord Irwin, 1926.
Earl of Willingdon, 1931.
Marquess of Linlithgow, 1936.
Viscount Wavell, 1943.
Earl Mountbatten, 1947.

India, Dominion of, Governors-General of: Earl Mountbatten, 15 Aug. 1947–21 June 1948.
Mr. Rajagopalachari, 21 June 1948–24 Jan. 1950.

Indian Mutiny. Began at Meerut, 10 May 1857; at *Lucknow, 30 May; Delhi taken, 20 Sept.; rebels defeated at Agra, 10 Oct.; Lucknow relieved, 17 Nov.; Gwalior captured, 19 June 1858.

Indian National Congress. First met, 1885. Combined with the Muslim League in a declaration for Indian Home Rule, 1917.

Indian Ocean Territory, British. *See* BRITISH INDIAN OCEAN TERRITORY.

Indian Territory, former name of *Oklahoma.

Indian Union, Presidents of (Presidents of the Republic of India).

Rajendra Prasad 1950–62
Sarvepalli Radhakrishnan 1962–67
Zazir Husain 1967–69
Varaha Giri 1969–77
Sanjiva Reddy, 1977–82
Zail Singh 1982–87
Sharma 1987–92
Venkataraman 1992
Sharma 1992–

Indiana, USA. First settled by French, who had trading posts *c.* 1672. Made part of Canada by Quebec Act, 1774. Passed into American control, 1779. Indian Wars, 1785–95. Territory partitioned from NW Territory, 1800. Further partitioning, 1809. Admitted to the Union as state, 1816.

Indo-China. French influence in Tongking and *Annam dates from the 17thC. Cochin-China was invaded by French and British forces, 1861. Annam and Tongking proclaimed a French protectorate, 1884, and finally united to Cambodia, 1887. The local Vichy Government surrendered to the Japanese, 1941, who ejected them in favour of Viet Nam republican authority, Mar. 1945. Peace between re-established French authorities and Viet Minh lasted, 6 Mar.–19 Dec. 1946. French military operation began in Tongking, Oct. 1947. A treaty between the Emperor Bao Dai and the French republic, signed 8 Mar. 1949, theoretically marked the end of the French colonies in I.-C. and the beginning of Viet Nam 'independent within the French Union'. In Jan. 1950 China and the USSR recognized the rival government of Ho Chi Minh. Viet Minh invaded kingdom of Laos, 14 Apr. 1953. French defeats culminated in the final defeat at *Dien Bien Phu in May 1954. As a result of the Geneva Conference, an armistice ending the I.-C. war was signed there on 21 July 1954, and this marked the end of French authority in the area. *See also* CAMBODIA and VIET NAM.

Indonesia, formerly **Netherlands E Indies**. Republic of I. proclaimed by Sukarno and Hatta on 17 Aug. 1945, but not recognized by the Dutch, who, except for a brief period during the Napoleonic wars, had controlled the territories concerned since *c.* 1620. Sporadic fighting, interspersed by negotiations, between Dutch and Indonesian nationalists, 1945–50. The United States of I. were officially inaugurated in Aug. 1950. Netherlands-

Indonesian Union dissolved, 1954. Bandoeng Conference, Apr. 1955; this established I. as one of the principal 'uncommitted nations'. Under agreement signed between Holland and I., 15 Aug. 1962, W New Guinea was transferred to Indonesian control on 1 May 1963. I. encouraged the nationalist revolt in Brunei, Dec. 1962, and in 1963 asserted ultimate claim to Australian New Guinea. I. protested against creation of Malaysia, 1963, and began a 'confrontation' which lasted until 1966. A coup in 1966 resulted in Sukarno's being deprived of all real power. In Aug. 1966 I. signed a treaty with Malaysia, ending confrontation. Sukarno dismissed, 1967 and Suharto took over government. Forced annexation of E Timor, 1976; massacres of Christians in E Timor, 1991, and violations of human rights there thereafter. President Clinton visits I., Nov. 1994. *See* New Guinea; Netherlands.

Indulgence, Declaration of, allowing liberty of conscience, 1687. A second declaration was issued in 1688. *See* Seven Bishops.

indulgences. Commenced in the Roman Catholic Church *c.* AD 800 by Pope Leo III. In the 12thC they were given principally as rewards to the Crusaders. Clement V in 1313 instituted the public sale of I. Leo X's abuse of the issue of I. led amongst other things to the publication of Luther's theses at Wittenberg, 1517.

Industrial Design, Council of. *See* Design Centre.

Industrial Revolution, British, took place *c.* 1740–1840. Arnold Toynbee first used the term, 1884.

infallibility, Papal, defined by Vatican Council, 1870.

infantile paralysis. *See* Poliomyelitis.

Information, Ministry of, formed, Sept. 1909, from publicity department of Foreign Office, and succeeded by:

Information, Central Office of, in Apr. 1946.

Inheritance Tax, 1986, substantially changed conditions of *Capital Transfer Tax. Queen to remain exempt from I.T., 1993.

Ingolstadt, Germany. Danube diverted to pass it, 1363. University was founded, 1472. City fortified, 1539.

Inkatha, Zulu political organization in S Africa, established 1973 by Chief Buthelezi and in frequent conflict with the *African National Congress until agreement reached with government, Apr. 1994. I. took part in the S African elections and the position of Zululand (Kwa-Zulu) as an independent state was recognized. Buthulezi awarded a post in Mandela's government, but friction between I. and government continuing, 1995

INLA. *See* Irish National Liberation Army.

Inland Revenue, Board of, originated in the Commissioners of Stamps, appointed, 1694. Commissioners of Taxes appointed, 1719. Consolidated Board of Stamps and Taxes established, 1834. Commissioners of Excise absorbed, 1849. Excise matters transferred to Customs Board, 1908.

Innsbruck, *Tirol. Became a city, 1232. Taken by Maurice of Saxony, 1552. By Bavarians, 1703. By French and Bavarians, 1805. University founded, 1669. Site of Winter Olympics, 1964; 1976.

Inns of Court and Chancery.
Lincoln's Inn moved to present site, 1415, but existed 150 years earlier. To it were attached the following Inns of Chancery: Thavies', 1550–1769; Furnival's, 1406–1890.
Gray's Inn. Established *c.* 1295. Freehold of present site acquired, 1733. Inns of Chancery: Staple, end of 14thC; Barnards, *c.* 1440–1894.
Inner Temple. Established by 1326. Freehold of present site acquired, 1609. Inns of Chancery: Cliffords, 1345; Clements, *c.* 1460.
Middle Temple. See Inner Temple. Separate by 1404. Inn of Chancery: New Inn, 1485.

Serjeants' Inn. Fleet Street, 1443–1758. Chancery Lane, 1416–1876.

Only Lincoln's Inn, Gray's, and the Inner and Middle Temple now exist as organizations.

Inquisition or **Holy Office of the Church of Rome.** Was constituted when the imperial rescripts of 1220 and 1224 were adopted into the ecclesiastical criminal law in 1231. The direction of the court was entrusted chiefly to the Dominican Order, 1233, when the bishops of S France also were instructed by Pope Gregory IX. It operated principally in the Latin countries, and in the Spanish and Portuguese possessions. In Spain it became a political instrument wielded by the Spanish kings.

insemination, artificial. *See* ARTIFICIAL INSEMINATION.

Institute of International Affairs, Royal. *See* CHATHAM HOUSE.

Instrument of Government. Passed by English Parliament, 16 Dec. 1653, constituting Oliver Cromwell Lord Protector of England.

insulin for diabetes introduced 1921 by Frederick Banting (1891–1941) of Canada.

insurance (Great Britain). The earliest record of any life policy being issued was on 15 June 1523, at the 'Office of Insurance within the Royal Exchange'. First fire insurance office opened in London, 1680. The first general I. company was established in 1696 under the name of the 'Amicable Contributionship for the I. of Houses'; it was using 'Hand-in-Hand' as subtitle in 1706. Absorbed by the Commercial Union Assurance Co. Ltd, 1905. The oldest *life* I. office was the 'Society of Assurance for Widows and Orphans', started in 1699.

insurance (USA). The first I. company was established in Boston, Mass., by the Sun I. Co. (English), 1728. The first fire I. policy was issued in Hartford, Conn., 1794. First accident I. company established at Hartford, Conn., 1863.

interdict. The most famous are those issued (1) against Poland by Gregory VII after the murder of Bishop Stanislaus, 1080; (2) against Scotland by Alexander III, 1181; (3) against France by Innocent III, 1200; (4) against England under King John by Innocent III, 1208; (5) against England under Henry VIII by Paul III, 1535.

Interim of Augsburg. A system of doctrine issued by the Emperor Charles V, May 1548, attempting to reconcile religious differences.

Intermediate Nuclear Forces Treaty, signed by USA and USSR, 8 Dec. 1987. Important stage in international nuclear arms reduction.

International.
First: Developed from I. Working Men's Association formed by Marx and Engels, 1864.
Second: Held its First World Congress at Paris, July 1889.
Third: Identical with *Comintern.

International Bank for Reconstruction and Development, popularly known as the 'World Bank', established by the *Bretton Woods Agreement in 1944.

International Federation of Free Trade Unions, formed, 1949, with HQ in Brussels, and representatives from over 100 countries in 1993. Was breakaway from Communist-dominated World Federation of Trade Unions, formed 1945, and after 1949 of little practical significance.

International Justice, Permanent Court of. Established at The Hague, 1920. Superseded after 1945 by the **International Court of Justice**, the judicial arm of the United Nations.

International Labour Office. Established at Geneva in 1919. In 1946 the I.L.O. became a specialized agency associated with the UN. Won Nobel Peace Prize, 1969.

International Monetary Fund. One of the institutions established by the *Bretton Woods Agreement of 1944 and operating since 1947.

Internet. International computer 'high-way', established throughout the world during the 1990s.

Interpol (International Criminal Police Commission). Established, 1923, in Vienna; reorganized after 1945 and since then based in Paris.

Intifada. Palestinian uprising, began 1987, in 'occupied' territories of Israel, involving violence as well as civil disobedience. Officially ended after PLO-Israeli agreement, 1993, but some extremist action continued intermittently.

Intolerable Acts, or **Coercive Acts**, name of four punitive measures enacted by the British government in retaliation at the recalcitrance of the New England colonists, 1773. They were the Boston Post Bill, the Massachussetts Government Act, the Administrative Justice Act and an Act to reintroduce compulsory billeting. The resentment created led to the first Continental Congress of 1774.

Invalides, Hôtel des (Paris). Established by Louis XIV for wounded soldiers, 1670. Dome built, 1693. Endowed by Napoleon I, 1811. His remains deposited at, 1861.

invasions of British Isles. From the Norman Conquest, the following are the principal invasions of the British Isles:

William the Conqueror, 1066.
The Scots, 1091.
Robert of Normandy, 1103.
The Scots, 1136.
Empress Maud, 1139.
Ireland, by Fitz-Stephen, 1169.
Ireland, by Edward Bruce, 1315.
Queen Isabel, 1326.
Duke of Lancaster, 1399.
Queen Margaret, 1462.
Earl of Warwick, 1470.
Edward IV, 1471.
Queen Margaret, 1471.
Earl of Richmond, 1485.
Lambert Simnel, 1487.
Perkin Warbeck, 1497.
Ireland, by Spaniards and Italians, 1580.

Ireland, by Spaniards, 1602.
Duke of Monmouth, 1685.
William of Orange, 1688.
Ireland, by James II, 1689.
James Stuart, the Old Pretender, 1708.
Second invasion of Pretender, 1715.
Glenshiel, by Spaniards and Jacobites, 1719.
Charles Edward Stuart, the Young Pretender, 1745.
Wales, by the French, 1797.
Ireland, by the French, 1798.
Channel Islands, by the Germans, 1940.

---

in-vitro **fertilization.** *See* ARTIFICIAL INSEMINATION.

investiture, lay. The power of a lay sovereign to control the appointment of ecclesiastical dignitaries. Condemned by Gregory VII (Hildebrand), 1075. Urban II forbade ecclesiastics to do homage to any layman, 1095. Holy Roman Emperor surrendered his rights of I. at the Concordat of Worms, 1122. *See also* REFORMATION.

iodine. Discovered by Courtois at Paris, 1811.

Iona, Hii, Y, Icolumcille. Monastery founded by St Columba (Columcille, 521–97), a native of Donegal, AD 563. I. was an episcopal see from the 9thC until 1507, when the title and boundaries were changed to that of 'The Isles' (and later to 'Sodor and Man' the present designation: *see* LORD OF THE ISLES): the see depended on *Trondhjem *c.* 1000–1263. Since 1938 the I. Community has restored the ancient monastery buildings. John Smith, Labour leader, buried on I., 1994.

Ionia, narrow strip of land with adjacent island on the W coast of Asia Minor. Colonized by Greeks in prehistoric times. Historically, there were 12 Ionian cities, forming a league with its sanctuary on Mt Mycale.

Ionian Islands, Mediterranean. In 1081 Corfu and Cephalonia were seized by Robert Guiscard. Corfu became Venetian property, 1386. Ceded to France, 1797.

Seized by Russia and Turkey, 1799, when they were formed into the republic of the Seven United Islands. Restored to France by Treaty of Tilsit, 1807. After Napoleonic Wars, 5 Nov. 1815, formed into the United States of the I.I. under British protectorate. Incorporated with Greece by treaty, 14 Nov. 1863. *See* CORFU.

Iowa, USA. Territory formed 1838 by partition of Wisconsin Territory and its boundaries reduced to present limits on formation of state, 1846.

Ipswich, England. First charter, 1200; incorporated, 1446. Medieval wool centre. Cardinal Wolsey *b.* here, *c.* 1475. Christchurch Mansion (16thC) is now a museum and art gallery.

IRA. *See* IRISH REPUBLICAN ARMY.

Iran, formerly **Persia.** Establishment of Achaemenid dynasty when Cyrus defeated Medes at battle of Pasargadae, 550 BC. Reached their zenith under Darius I, 522–485. Xerxes I was defeated by Greeks at Salamis, 480. The dynasty fell with the conquest of P. by Alexander the Great, 331, and the assassination of Darius III. At Alexander's death, 323, P. was ruled by the Seleucids until conquered by the Arsacid (Parthian) dynasty, 129. Scythian invasions repelled by Mithridates the Great, 123–90. Defeat of Crassus at Carrhae, 53. Phraates IV enters into a treaty of dependency with Rome, 4 BC. Arsacids overthrown by the Sassanids under Ardashir I, AD 226. Unsuccessful wars under Sapor I (240–73) with Rome. Sassanids reach their greatest power under Kavad I, 488–531. Chosroes I, 531–79. Defeat and destruction of Sassanids by Arabs at battles of Kadisiya, 637, and Nehavend, 641. Population converted to Islam, 8thC. P. divided and in confusion until conquered by the Mongols under Hulagu, 1256. Mongol rule continued till death of Tamerlane, 1404. After civil wars Safavid dynasty seized power, 1499. Defeat of the Uzbegs, 1510. War with Turkey, 1514–55. Zenith of Safavids under Shah Abbas I, 1587–1628. Russian and Turkish invasions, 1722–7. Nadir Shah overthrows Safavids, 1736. Invades India, 1738. Bokhara and Khiva, 1740. Nadir assassinated, 1747. Zand dynasty, 1750–94. Kajar dynasty takes the throne, 1794. Treaty of Tehran with Britain, 1814. Defeated by Russia in war for Georgia, 1812–28. Invasion of Afghanistan, 1837–8. Anglo-Russian agreement fixes spheres of influence in P., 1907. Constitutional revolution, 1909. Last Kajar Shah deposed and succeeded by Reza Shah Pahlavi, 1925. Anglo-Russian action forces Reza to abdicate, 1941, in favour of his son, Mohammed Reza Pahlavi (1919–80). Government troops drive Soviet puppet government from Azerbaijan, 11–3 Dec. 1946; and from Kurdistan, 15 Dec. 1946. Anglo-Iranian Oil Co. nationalized under Mussadeq, 1952; oil dispute with Britain settled, 1954. Overthrow of Shah, Jan. 1979, and establishment of hard-line Islamic republic under Ayatollah Khomeini (*d.* 1989). US hostages held in I., 1979–80. *Iraq invaded I., Sept. 1980: war ended, 1988. Khomeini pronounced *fatwah against British author Salman Rushdie, 1989. Kurds fled to I. following *Gulf War, 1991. Earthquake in I. killed 40,000, 1990. During 1994–5 claimed that I. was supporting militant Muslims in Bosnia to bolster support for weak domestic regime and Iranian extremists said to be linked to anti-Semitic outrages in Argentina, July 1994. From 1990s supplied with nuclear material by Russia and China; capability to make nuclear warheads by end of 1995. Worsening of relations with the W, notably with the USA, which imposed a trade ban against I., May 1995. Iranian hijacks plane to Israel, Sept. 1995, and asks for political asylum in USA.

Irangate, name given to scandal in USA, 1986–7, when it transpired that some members of the Reagan administration had sanctioned arms sales to Iran, 1985, in exchange for release of hostages in *Labanon. Moneys obtained had been spent on arms for Contras in *Nicaragua. Weinberger, former Defence Secretary, pardoned for any part in I., Dec. 1992.

Iraq. Conquered from Turkey by British forces, 1914–18. Entrusted to Great Britain as a mandate, 1919, and name officially adopted, 1921, when Feisal became first king of I. British mandate ended, 1932. I.–Mediterranean pipeline inaugurated, Jan. 1935; Baghdad railway completed, July 1940. Pro-German coup crushed by British, Apr. 1941; most British troops withdrawn from I. by 1947. Mass exodus of Iraqi Jews to Israel, 1950–1. In 1958 a left-wing coup, led by Kassem, overthrew the monarchy and the royal family was murdered and a republic established. In 1959 I. withdrew from the Baghdad Pact (signed in 1955). Coup, and Kassem shot, 1963. Rise of Saddam Hussein; in complete control from 1968. War with *Iran, 1980–8. Attacks on Kurds, 1984–9, including use of chemical weapons. Annexation of *Kuwait 1990, resulted in *Gulf War, 1991. I. heavily defeated but Saddam Hussein kept power and there were limited air strikes by US planes against I., Jan 1993 until I. complied with disputed UN resolutions. Kurdish 'safe haven' established in I. after Gulf War, but many Kurds fled to Iran, 1991 onwards. UN reaches agreement with I. on inspection of missile sites, July 1993. Several incidents on Iraqi-Kuwait border, 1993. I. agrees to UN long-term weapons monitoring, Nov. In Oct. 1994 I. started moving troops towards Kuwaiti border: US and Britain sent reinforcements to Kuwait. I. withdrew troops and in Nov. 1994, following Russian mediation, formally recognized Kuwait. Internal situation deteriorating, 1995: UN sanctions against I. (imposed after *Gulf War) continuing. Members of Saddam's family fled to Jordan, Aug. In Sept. I. claims draining of marshes complete between Tigris and Euphrates, marking end of 'Marsh Arab' culture and threatening ecological disaster.

Ireland. Until the arrival of St Patrick from Rome in AD 432 the history of I. is poorly documented. The five chief kingdoms of I. in the 5thC were: Ulster, Leinster, Meath, Connaught and Munster. According to Celtic tradition, Tara was the chief residence of the Irish kings in ancient times, a central monarchy being established here, and 150 monarchs reigned till it was destroyed in 563. In the 10thC Brian Boru conquered the country; he was killed at Clontarf, where the Scandinavian power in I. was finally destroyed, 1014 (*see* VIKING AGE). After his death various dynasties disputed the overlordship of I. Church reforms put in hand at Synod of Kells, 1152. When Strongbow invaded I. Roderick O'Connor, High King of I., did homage to Henry II, and at Synod of Cashel Henry enforced papal claims on Irish Church, 1172. I. divided into a series of virtually independent palatinates by the Anglo-Normans. Division of English pale into counties by King John, 1212. Statute of Kilkenny, forbidding intermarriage of Anglo-Normans and Irish, 1367. Richard II landed with armed force, 1394. Poynings' Law, 1494. Insurrection of Tyrone, 1601. Maguire's rebellion (Ulster Civil War) to expel English, massacres, 23 Oct. 1641. Oliver Cromwell subdued the whole land with great cruelty, 1649–50. Landing of the deposed James II, 1689. Landing of William III, 14 June 1690. Battle of Boyne, 1690. Treaty of *Limerick, 3 Oct. 1691. Irish Parliament declared independent (*see* GRATTAN'S PARLIAMENT), 1782. Act of Union, which joined English and Irish Parliaments, 1 Jan. 1801; followed by Robert Emmet's insurrection, 23 July 1803. Act of Catholic Emancipation, 1829. Daniel O'Connell's agitation for repeal of Act of Union commenced, 1842; trial of O'Connell, 15 Jan. 1844. Irish famine; subsequent decades saw large-scale Irish emigration to the USA, 1846. Disestablishment of Anglican Church in I., 1869. Murder of Lord Frederick Cavendish, chief secretary for I., and T.H. Burke, permanent under-secretary, in Phoenix Park, 6 May 1882. Gladstone's first Home Rule Bill brought and defeated, Mar. 1886; Gladstone's second Home Rule Bill passed by Commons, but thrown out by Lords, 1893. Irish Land Act, Aug. 1907; Irish Universities Act, 1908; Irish Land Act, Dec. 1909. Home Rule Bill introduced by Asquith, 11 Apr. 1912; second reading moved by Churchill, 30 Apr., carried by 372 votes to 271 on 9 May; committee stage begun, 11 June; in Ulster there was an anti-Home Rule movement led by Sir Edward Carson, and on 28 Sept. a covenant was signed by Ulster men at Belfast against the Bill; the Bill was twice passed by the Commons and twice rejected by the Lords between 1 Jan. and 14 Aug. 1913. A Home Rule Bill was placed on statute book in 1914, with suspensory clause for duration of World War I. A hopeless rebellion, 'organized' by Sinn Fein ('Ourselves Alone'), broke out, 24 Apr. 1916. Irish Convention met, 25 July 1917; report, Apr. 1918. After the war, Home Rule Act was superseded by Government of Ireland Act, 1920, most of Ulster electing to remain united with Great Britain. The Republicans or Sinn Fein Party rejected the Act, and a state of war between I. and England existed until a peace treaty was signed, 6 Dec. 1921, by which the *Irish Free State was set up in southern I. British evacuated 1921. *See* IRELAND, NORTHERN; FENIAN ASSOCIATION; IRELAND, LORDS LIEUTENANT OF. For events 1921–1948 *see* IRISH FREE STATE *and* EIRE.

Republic of Ireland, brought into existence by R.o.I. Act, 1948, which came into operation, 18 Apr. 1949. President Kennedy visited I., summer 1963. In Jan. 1965 the premiers of the republic of I. and of N I. met in Belfast, the first such meeting for 40 years. Joined EEC, 1973: approved Maastricht Treaty, 1992.

Papal visit to I., 1980. Anti-abortion amendment to constitution approved by referendum, 1983. Unsuccessful joint efforts by I. and Britain to solve N I. problem, 1970–85. Anglo-Irish Agreement, 1985. Increasing economic problems in late 1980s; General election, Nov. 1992 led to coalition of Fianna Fail and Labour. Punt devalued, Jan. 1993. Government expressed interest in Ulster SDLP – Sinn Fein negotiations, Oct. 1993 and in Dec. the Irish premier met British premier Major in London and they signed joint declaration which it was hoped would open way to peace in N I. IRA announced 'complete cease-fire' from midnight on 31 Aug. 1994 and Loyalist paramilitaries soon followed suit. Following this Irish premier Reynolds put pressure on British government to speed up N Irish 'peace process', and held 'Peace Forum' in Dublin, Oct., not attended by British government or Unionist representatives. As result of domestic crisis in Nov., Reynolds' government fell and Bruton, leader of Fine Gael, became premier of I., Dec. With Britain drew up 'Framework Document' in effort to achieve solution in N I., Feb. 1995; release of several IRA prisoners from Irish gaols. Subsequently 'peace process' stalling on 'decommissioning of weapons' issue. Referendum, Oct. 1995. Divorce referendum, 24 Nov. (small majority in favour of divorce). President Clinton to visit I., Dec. 1995.

Presidents of Ireland:
Douglas Hyde 1938–45
Sean O'Kelly 1945–59
Eamonn de Valera 1959–73
Erskine Childers 1973–74
Cathal O'Daly 1974–76
Patrick Hillery 1976–90
Mary Robinson 1990–

Ireland, Church of, arose from the Irish Supremacy Act, 1537. Established by legislation of 1560 but never accepted by majority of population. Irish Articles, 1615, accepted by clergy of C of I., 1634. Act to disestablish passed, 1859; came into operation, 1871. Divided into provinces of Armagh and Dublin; *c.* 375,000 members in 1995.

Ireland, Lords Lieutenant and Lords Deputy of:

Hugh de Lacy, 1172.
Richard, Earl of Pembroke, 1173.
Raymond le Gros, 1176.
Prince John, 1177.
Lord Justices, no Lord Deputy, 1184.
Hugh de Lacy, 1189.
Meyler FitzHenry, 1199.
Hugh de Lacy, 1203.
Meyler FitzHenry, 1204.
Hugh de Lacy, 1205.
Geoffrey de Marisco, 1215.

Piers Gaveston, 1308.
Edmund le Botiller, 1312.
Roger de Mortimer, 1316.
Thomas Fitzgerald, 1320.
John de Bermingham, 1321.
Earl of Kildare, 1327.
Prior Roger Outlow, 1328.
Sir John d'Arcy, 1332.
Sir John de Cherlton, 1337.
Prior Roger Outlow, 1340.
Sir Raoul de Ufford, 1344.
Sir Roger d'Arcy
Sir John Moriz } 1346.
Walter de Bermingham, 1348.
Maurice, Earl of Desmond, 1355.
Thomas de Rokeby, 1356.
Almaric de St Amand, 1357.
James, Earl of Ormonde, 1359.
Lionel, Duke of Clarence, 1361.
Gerald, Earl of Desmond, 1367.
William de Windsor, 1369.
Maurice, Earl of Desmond
James, Earl of Ormonde } 1376.
Edmund, Earl of March, 1380.
Robert, Earl of Oxford, 1385.
Sir John Stanley, 1389.
James, Earl of Ormonde, 1391.
Thomas, Duke of Gloucester, 1393.
Roger de Mortimer, 1395.
Reginald Grey, Lord
Thomas de Holland, Justice } 1398.
Sir John Stanley, 1398.
Thomas, Earl of Lancaster, 1401.
Sir John Stanley
Sir John Talbot } 1413.
James, Earl of Ormonde, 1420.
Edmund, Earl of March, 1423.
Sir John Talbot, 1425.
Sir John Grey, 1427.
Sir John Sutton, 1428.
Sir Thomas Stanley, 1431.
Lionel, Lord de Wells, 1438.
John, Earl of Shrewsbury, 1446.
Richard, Duke of York, 1449.
George, Duke of Clarence, 1461.
Tiptoft, Earl of Worcester, 1470.
George, Duke of Clarence (again), 1472.
John de la Pole, Earl of Suffolk, 1478.
Gerald, Earl of Kildare, 1483.
John de la Pole, Earl of Lincoln, 1484.
Jasper, Duke of Bedford, 1488.

Henry, Duke of York (afterwards Henry VIII), 1494.
Gerald, Earl of Kildare, 1496.
Thomas, Earl of Surrey, 1521.
Henry, Duke of Richmond, 1529.
Thomas, Earl of Sussex, 1560.
Robert, Earl of Essex, 1599.
Charles, Lord Mountjoy, 1603.
Henry, Visc. Falkland, 1622.
Thomas, Earl of Strafford, 1629.
James, Marquess of Ormonde, 1643.
Philip, Lord Lisle, 1647.
Oliver Cromwell, 1649.
Henry Cromwell, 1657.
James, Duke of Ormonde, 1662.
John, Lord Robartes, 1669.
Lord Berkeley of Stratton, 1670.
Arthur, Earl of Essex, 1672.
James, Duke of Ormonde, 1677.
Henry, Earl of Clarendon, 1685.
Richard, Earl of Tyrconnel, 1687.
Visc. Sydney of Shepey, 1692.
Lord Capell of Tewkesbury, 1695.
Laurence, Earl of Rochester, 1700.
James, Duke of Ormonde, 1703.
Thomas, Duke of Pembroke, 1707.
Thomas, Earl of Wharton, 1709.
Thomas, Duke of Ormonde, 1710.
Charles, Duke of Shrewsbury, 1713.
Charles, Duke of Bolton, 1771.
Charles, Duke of Grafton, 1721.
Lord Carteret, 1724.
Lionel, Duke of Dorset, 1731.
William, Duke of Devonshire, 1737.
Earl of Chesterfield, 1745.
William, Earl of Harrington, 1746.
Lionel, Duke of Dorset 1751.
William, 4th Duke of Devonshire, 1755.
John, Duke of Bedford, 1756.
George, Earl of Halifax, 1761.
Earl of Northumberland, 1763.
Earl of Hertford, 1765.
George, Visc. Townshend, 1767.
Simon, Earl Harcourt, 1772.
Earl of Buckinghamshire, 1777.
Earl of Carlisle, 1780.
Duke of Portland
Earl Temple } 1782.
Earl of Northington, 1783.
Duke of Rutland, 1784.
Marquess of Buckingham (the

Earl Temple, appointed 1782), 1787.
Earl of Westmorland, 1790.
Earl Fitzwilliam, ⎫ 1795.
Earl Camden, ⎭
Marquess Cornwallis, 1798.
Earl of Hardwicke, 1801.
Duke of Bedford, 1806.
Duke of Richmond, 1807.
Visc., afterwards Earl, Whitworth, 1813.
Earl Talbot, 1817.
Marquess of Wellesley, 1821.
Marquess of Anglesey, 1828.
Duke of Northumberland, 1829.
Marquess of Anglesey (again), 1830.
Marquess of Wellesley, 1883.
Earl of Haddington, 1834.
Visc., afterwards Marquess of, Normanby, 1835.
Lord, afterwards Earl, Fortescue, 1839.
Earl de Grey, 1841.
Lord Heytesbury, 1844.
Earl of Bessborough, 1846.
Earl of Clarendon, 1847.
Earl of Eglinton, 1852.
Earl of St Germans, 1853.
Earl of Carlisle, 1855.
Earl of Eglinton (again), 1858.
Earl of Carlisle (again), 1859.
Lord Wodehouse (Earl of Kimberley), 1864.
Marquess of Abercorn, 1866.
John, Earl Spencer, 1868.
James, Duke (formerly Marquess) of Abercorn, 1874.
Duke of Marlborough, 1876.
Earl Cowper, 1880.
John, Earl Spencer, 1882
Henry Herbert, Earl of Carnarvon, 1885.
Earl of Aberdeen, 1886.
Marquess of Londonderry, 1886.
Earl of Zetland, 1889.
Lord Houghton (afterwards Earl of Crewe), 1892.
Earl Cadogan, 1895.
Earl of Dudley, 1902.
Earl of Aberdeen (again), 1905.
Lord, afterwards Visc, Wimborne, 1915.
Visc. French of Ypres, 1918.
Visc. FitzAlan, 1921.

Ireland, Northern (*see also* ULSTER). King George V opened Parliament, 1921. Sir James Craig, later Visc. *Craigavon, first Prime Minister of N.I. IRA outrages 1937–9. 1949: Ireland Act (UK Parliament) further defined N.I.'s constitutional position: limited IRA activity, 1954–62.

By 1965 relations between N.I. and the Irish republic much improved at government level.

1967–8: Growth of the 'civil rights' movements in N.I. and hardening by extremists on both Catholic and Protestant sides. There were disturbances in Londonderry, Oct. 1968.

1969–70: Civil rights agitation grew. Following serious rioting in Aug., 1969, British troops took over responsibility for law and order in N.I. *'Bloody Sunday', 30 Jan. 1972. Under legislation of 1973 and 1974 N.I. directly governed from Westminster. Subsequent attempts, 1980 and 1982, to produce a representative N.I. Assembly failed. 1969–94 the IRA and Protestant extremists have pursued a campaign of violence in N.I. and, sporadically by the IRA and INLA, in mainland Britain. Anglo-Irish Agreement, 1985, opposed by Unionist parties in N.I. Negotiations between SDLP leader and Sinn Fein, 1993, and Irish foreign minister proposed joint British–Irish sovereignty in N.I., but this rejected by Unionists. British government admitted communications with the IRA had taken place during year, Nov. 1993. Anglo-Irish Declaration of 15 Dec. was hoped to open way to peace in N.I. but met with hostile response from Unionists. IRA 'complete cease-fire' from 31 Aug. 1994 was followed by cease-fire from Loyalist paramilitaries and N.I. mainly peaceful after 25 years of violence. Major visited Belfast, Oct. and EU promised aid to rebuild N.I. economy. Government talks with Protestant terrorist groups, Dec. 'Framework document', published by British and Irish governments in Belfast, Feb. 1995. Mar. 1995: Queen visits Belfast and President Clinton invites Sinn Fein leader Gerry Adams to a St Patrick's Day reception. British troops withdrawn from regular patrols in Belfast and elsewhere. A British minister meets Sinn Fein leaders (first time for 23 years), 10 May. Riots in

Belfast following release of Private Lee Clegg, June. Sept. 'summit' between British and Irish premiers postponed; London and Dublin disagreement on 'decommissioning of weapons issue.' President Clinton to visit I., Dec. 1995.

Irish Free State. (For early history *see* IRELAND.) Civil war, 1921–3. Michael Collins murdered, 1922. I.F.S. Agreement Act, 1922, enforced Treaty of, 6 Dec. 1921, conferring Dominion status on Ireland. I.F.S. Constitution Act, 1922. British soldiers attacked at Queenstown, 21 Mar. 1924. Protection adopted, 1924. Fianna Fail Party formed, 1926. Kevin O'Higgins (Minister of Justice) murdered, 10 July 1927. Republicans renounced abstention from Dail and took their seats, 12 Aug. 1927. Oaths of allegiance to king, and appeals to Privy Council abolished, 1933, by de Valera's administration. Name changed to *Eire, a 'sovereign independent and democratic state' with directly elected president, 30 Apr. 1937.

Irish National Liberation Army (INLA), formed as an extreme splinter group from the Irish Republican Army in the late 1970s. Marxist, and responsible for many murders in Northern Ireland and the UK including those of Airey Neave, MP, 1979, and Ian Gow, MP, 1990. Did not join in 1994 terrorist 'cease-fire'.

Irish Republic. Sinn Feiners declared themselves 'the Provisional Government of the I.R.' in 1916. *See* IRELAND.

Irish Republican Army (IRA). Formed in 1920 to fight for complete independence of the whole of Ireland. Active until the end of 1921; and in Northern Ireland and England in 1938 and 1939 in terrorist bombing. Declared illegal by the Government of Eire, 23 June 1939. After World War II the IRA became active again in both N Ireland and England. There was a minor campaign of violence, 1957–62: but a concentrated campaign of violence and murder was waged 1969–94 in N Ireland, the British mainland, and even in mainland Europe. IRA (1995) constitutes a break-away (Pro-

visionals) from the original movement, which took place in the 1960s and there was a further splintering in the 1970s. Outrages in recent years include major bombings in the City of London (Apr. 1992 and Apr. 1993) and a bomb attack on a shopping centre in Warrington, Lancashire, March 1993, which killed two children. Attempt by SDLP leader John Hume to get IRA to renounce violence through negotiations with *Sinn Fein, Sept./Oct. 1993: but on 23 Oct., IRA bombs in Belfast shop killed 10, including two children. British and Irish premiers agreed on fresh attempt to settle N Ireland problem, Oct. 1993; in Nov. Britain admitted secret communications with IRA/Sinn Fein during 1993. In Dec. the joint British/Irish declaration on Ulster said Sinn Fein could be admitted to talks 'if IRA gave up armed struggle permanently' and IRA announced 'complete cease-fire' from 31 Aug. 1994. Talks with British government representatives at Stormont, Dec., and with British ministers, 1995, but progress stalling on issue of 'decommissioning' of terrorist weapons.

Irish Volunteers. Formed by Sinn Feiners, Sept. 1913, following a speech by John Redmond. In Nov. 1915 they joined forces with the Citizen Army, and thereafter planned rebellion against British government.

Iron Cross. Prussian Order instituted by Frederick William III in 1813 for service in the War of Liberation; revived (by William I), 19 July 1870; again in the war of 1914, and by Hitler in 1939.

Iron Crown of Lombardy, containing a circlet said to have been made from one of the nails of the Cross, c. 591. Used by all emperors who were kings of Lombardy, including Napoleon I, crowned at Milan, 26 May 1805.

Iron Curtain. Description, used in Mar. 1946 by Winston Churchill to denote the barrier then separating Communist and non-Communist states in Europe, which has passed into popular usage. Its derivation much earlier; possibly phrase first used (to denote barrier separating Russia from western Europe) by Vasili Rozanar (1856–1919): repeated by Ethel Snowden (of the Soviet Union), 1920.

Iron Mask, The Man in the. An unknown prisoner of the Bastille, supposed to have been imprisoned, 18 Sept. 1698, and who almost certainly *d.* 19 Nov. 1703.

Iroquois. Name given by the French to one of the great confederations of N American Indians. The I. reached the height of their power *c.* 1720; they always sided with the English against the French and fought on the English side in the War of Independence.

Isfahan, Ispahan, capital of Iran (Persia), AD 1587–1800. Masjid-i-Shah (Royal Mosque) built *c.* 1600; Masjid-i-Juma (Friday Mosque) begun, 760; completed 11thC: rebuilt, 17thC; Palace of Forty Pillars remodelled, 1700; Madrasseh-i-Shah Husain, 1710; Maidan-i-Shah (Royal Square) and Chahar Bagh (Four Gardens Avenue) laid out, 1600–23. Sacked by Afghans, 1722, and ceased to be royal residence, 1749.

Islam or **Mohammedanism,** religion founded by Mohammed (571–632). He started preaching between 600 and 610 and fled to Medina, 622. I.'s holiest shrine is at Mecca; between the 7th and 16thC I. spread across Asia Minor and N Africa and into western Europe, and penetrated SE Asia. Revival of militant I. since 1970s, notably in Iran, Algeria, Libya, Sudan and Egypt.

Islamabad, capital of Pakistan since 1967, a 'new' city, designed and laid out in the 1960s.

Islamic Conference, established May 1971. It had 44 members in 1993. Egyptian membership was suspended 1979–84 and Afghan, 1980–9. The 'Turkish Republic of Cyprus' and Mozambique have observer status.

Ismailis. Muslim sect, founded in the mid-8thC.

Israel. (For history prior to 1948 *see* PALESTINE, ANCIENT *and* PALESTINE, MODERN.) State proclaimed, 14 May 1948. Trans-

jordan Arab Legion reached Old Jerusalem, and Egyptian Army entered Beersheba, 20 May 1948. Armistice, June–Oct. 1948. United Nations mediator Count Folke Bernadotte murdered, 17 Sept. Jews overrun Negeb and destroy Palestinian Arab Army in Galilee, Nov. 1948. King Abdullah makes peace with Israelite Government, Dec. 1948. Truce with Egyptian forces, 7 Jan. 1949. General armistice with Arab League signed at Rhodes, 24 Feb. 1949. Large-scale exodus of Arabs from I., 1949 onwards; equally large influx of Jews from all over the world. Knesset (legislative assembly) first met, 8 Mar. 1949. Chaim Weizmann, first president (*b.* 1874), *d.,* 9 Nov. 1952. Treaty with W German Federal Republic concluded, 1952. I. invaded *Egypt and occupied Sinai Peninsula and Gaza Strip, Oct. 1956. Anglo-French intervention and arrival of UN forces in area followed. Premier Ben Gurion announced capture of Adolf Eichmann, a leading Nazi war criminal, May 1960; he was tried in I., 1961, and executed there, 1962. War broke out between I. and Egypt (with Jordan, Lebanon, Iraq and Syria), 5 June 1967, ending in an overwhelming Israeli victory. Egypt accepted a cease-fire, 8 June, by which time I. had won control of the Sinai Peninsula, Gulf of Aqaba, Gaza Strip and Old Jerusalem. Arab guerrilla resistance to I. increased 1968 onwards. I. retaliated severely when Arabs attacked her: in Dec. 1968 an attack by Arabs on Israeli airliners at Athens was followed by an Israeli attack on Beirut airport. Japanese *'Red Army' attack passengers at Lod airport, May 1972. Egyptian attack repulsed, 1973: cease-fire, 1975: *Camp David conference, 1978: Peace Treaty signed with Egypt, 26 Mar. 1979: I. withdrew from Sinai, 1982. Intervened in Lebanon, 1978–83. Arab uprising in occupied territories (*Intifada) began, 1987. Attacked by Iraqi missiles during Gulf War, 1990. Direct negotiations with Palestinian Arabs begun 1991: ceased 1992 and future talks in doubt after I. deported 400 Arabs to a 'no man's land' between I. and Lebanon, 1993. Restarted, May 1993, and agreement signed in Washington, DC, USA, 13

Sept. between Israel and *PLO under which the PLO recognized existence of I. and I. proposed internal self-government to Arabs in *Jericho and the *Gaza Strip. Israeli attacked *Hezbollah bases in Lebanon, Nov. Accord between I. and Vatican signed, Dec. Israelis leave Gaza, May 1994: peace agreement with Jordan signed, Oct. 1994, but US fails to broker peace with Syria. Intermittent Arab terrorist attacks continued in I., condemned by Arafat but in July 1994 Arab extremists bombed the Israeli embassy in London. Peace talks resume between I. and Syria, Mar. 1995 but failed to progress. I. and the PLO agree Palestinian autonomy deal for West Bank (signed in Washington, 28 Sept. 1995). Israeli premier Rabin assassinated by Jewish extremist in Tel Aviv, Nov. 1995.

Presidents of Israel:
Weizmann 1949–52
Ben-Zvi 1952–63
Shazar 1963–68
Katzir 1968–78
Navron 1978–83
Herzog 1983–93
Weizmann, 1993–

Istanbul, official name since 1930, of *Constantinople.

Istria. Conquered from the Illyrians by Rome, 177 BC; from the Ostrogoths by Byzantium, AD 539. Incorporated in the kingdom of Lombardy by Charlemagne, 788. Under Dukes of *Carinthia, 1173, and Patriarchs of Aquileia, 1209. In the 14thC partitioned between Venice and the Hapsburgs. By Treaty of Campo Formio, 1797, the whole peninsula came to Austria, which retained it until 1918 except during Napoleon's 'Illyrian Kingdom' (1805–9), who developed Pola as a naval base. After 1918 the greater part of it was incorporated in Italy. After 1947 most of it went to Yugoslavia; now (1995) mostly in Croatia.

Italy. (For early history of I. *see* ROME.) Odoacer deposed the last Western emperor, 476. Invasion of I. by Theodoric,

King of the Ostrogoths, AD 489. Reign of Theodoric, 493–526. Power of Goths overthrown, 553. Lombard invasion under Alboin, 568. Charlemagne's invasion, 774; he was crowned emperor at Rome, 800. Hildebrand (Gregory VII) becomes pope, and the great struggle between Guelph and *Ghibelline begins, 1073. During the 14th and 15thC I. was split up between five principal powers (*see under* titles of various duchies, Ferrara, Venice, etc.). Invasion of Charles VIII of France, 1494. Louis XII assumed titles of King of Naples and Duke of Milan, 1499. Treaty between him and Ferdinand of Spain, Ferdinand to have Calabria and Apulia, and Louis the remainder of Neapolitan kingdom, 1501. France and Spain at war in I., 1502. French driven out of I. by Holy League, 1513. Francis I conquered Milan, 1515; lost it, 1521; captured at battle of Pavia, 1525. Emperor Charles V sacked Rome and made pope prisoner, 1527. After another campaign, Francis renounced Italian claims at the Peace of Cambrai, 1529. Charles took possession of Milan for Spain, 1535, and Naples came to be governed by Spanish viceroys for 200 years. Savoy again independent, 1574. Francis, with allies, warred against Spain in N I., 1635–59; Neapolitan revolt under Masaniello, 1647. Austrian predominance assured by end of reign of Louis XIV. Sicily, wrested from Spain, exchanged by Savoy for Sardinia; Duke of Savoy took title King of Sardinia, 1720. Bourbons established in the Two Sicilies (kingdom of Naples), 1734–5; obtained Parma and Piacenza, 1748. 45 years of peace ended, 1793. Napoleon Bonaparte entered I., 1796 (*see* BONAPARTE); crowned himself King of I., 1805. By Congress of Vienna, 1815, I. was reorganized, and French rule ended. States of central I. annexed to kingdom of Victor Emmanuel, Mar. 1860. First Italian Parliament met at Turin, Feb. 1861, and Victor Emmanuel proclaimed King of I. Emancipation of I. completed by Victor Emmanuel's triumphal entry into Rome, 2 July 1871. I. joined Germany and Austria in Triple Alliance, 1882; seized Massawah on Red Sea, 1885, and established colony of Eritrea. Set up a protectorate over Somaliland, 1889–92. War with Ethiopia, 1896, and (29 Feb.–1 Mar.) the disaster of Adowa. Assassination of King Umberto, 29 July 1900, by an anarchist. War with Turkey on the question of Tripoli, 29 Sept. 1911, ended by the Treaty of Lausanne, 18 Oct. 1912; Electoral Reform Bill passed, May 1912. Socialist rising in the N suppressed, June 1914 (see WORLD WAR I). Protectorate over *Albania proclaimed, 20 June 1917. D'Annunzio seized *Fiume, Sept. 1919 (see RAPALLO). Fascisti's first success, in suppressing Bologna riots, Nov. 1920. Venice Conference with Austria, 8 Oct. 1922. Fascisti 'march on Rome', 28 Oct. 1922; came into office, 31 Oct. Corfu occupied, 31 Aug. 1923 (see JANINA). Vatican established as a sovereign state, 7 June 1929. Fighting with *Ethiopia began at end of 1934. Sanctions against I. by 50 countries began, 18 Nov. 1935. Chamber of Deputies replaced by National Assembly of Corporations, 23 Mar. 1936. 1937: Adherence to German-Japanese Anti-Comintern Pact (formed 1936), 6 Nov.

1939: I. invaded Albania, 7 Apr.; the King of I. accepted the Albanian crown, 13 Apr.; military alliance with Germany signed in Berlin, 22 May.

1940: I. declared war on Allies, 10 June (see WORLD WAR II); France accepted armistice terms of Germany and I., 22 June; mutual assistance pact with Germany and Japan (Tripartite Pact), 27 Sept.; ultimatum to and invasion of Greece, 28 Oct.

1941: War declared on Yugoslavia, 6 Apr.; crown of 'independent' *Croatia offered to House of Savoy, 18 May; Dalmatia annexed, 21 May; war declared on Russia, 22 June.

1943: Mussolini overthrown and succeeded by Badoglio, 25 July; surrender to Allies, 9 Sept.; I. declared war on Germany, 13 Oct.

1945: Mussolini executed by partisans, 28 Apr.

1946: King Victor Emmanuel III abdicates in favour of Prince Umberto, 9 May; referendum, 2 June, led to proclamation of I. as a republic, 11 June, and departure of King Umberto, 13 June;

1947: Peace treaty signed with Allies at Paris, 10 Feb.; Lateran treaties adopted as part of constitution, July; peace treaty finally ratified, 6 Sept.; Istria ceded to Yugoslavia. I. joined NATO in 1949. In 1954 I. and Yugoslavia settled their 9-year dispute over *Trieste; death of de Gasperi, architect of post-war I. I. joined the EEC in 1958. Kidnappings and murders by 'Red Brigade' terrorists during 1970s and 1980s, including murder of politician Aldo Moro, May 1978. Financial scandals involved the Vatican, 1982–3. A new concordat, 1984, resulted in the Catholic Church being no longer the state religion in I., and Vatican lost its territorial rights. Corruption in public life reached scandalous proportions in the 1990s and destabilized Italian politics. Growth of regional parties. Former premier charged with corruption, 1993. Referendum, April 1993, voted for sweeping electoral reform. Local elections, June, gave Northern League power in N I. New non-political premier Ciampi (appointed April) led drive on corruption in government and industry. Protest bombings in Milan and Rome. In Nov. 1993 local elections, further gains by Northern League and extreme right and left parties decimated Christian Democrats and Socialists. General election, Mar. 1994 won by right-wing parties and right-wing coalition formed in April under premiership of Silvio Berlusconi. Subsequent unrest due to economic reforms attempted by Berlusconi to cure government deficit. Severe flooding in N I., Nov. 1994 causes over 60 deaths. Berlusconi ordered to face magistrates over alleged corruption charges, Nov. Resigned, Dec., 1995 when Dini became premier. Former premier Andreotti on trial for alleged Mafia crimes, Sept. Economic weakness and political instability continuing.

Presidents of Italy:
Einaudi 1948–55
Gronchi 1955–62
Segni 1962–4
Saragat 1964–71
Leone 1971–78

Pertini 1978–85
Cossiga 1985–92
Scalfaro 1992–

Italian literature. The following is a list of prominent I. writers:

Alberti, Leone Battista, 1404–72, humanist.
Alfieri, Vittorio, Count, 1749–1803, poet and dramatist.
Amicis. *See* De Amicis.
Ammirato, Scipione, 1531–1601, historian.
Angiolieri, Cecco, *c.* 1260–*c.* 1312, poet.
Aretino, Pietro, 1492–1556, dramatist.
Ariosto, Lodovico, 1474–1533, poet and dramatist.
Bandello, Matteo, *c.* 1485–1561, writer of tales.
Baretti, Giuseppe, 1719–89, miscellaneous writer.
Basile, Giovanni Battista (Count of Morone), 17thC writer of tales.
Bassani, Giorgio, 1916–, novelist.
Belli, Giuseppe Giocchino, 1791–1863, poet.
Bello, Francesco, *c.* 1450–1505, poet.
Bembo, Pietro (Cardinal), 1470–1547, poet and historian.
Bentivoglio, Ercole, 1506–73, poet.
Berni, Francesco, *c.* 1497–1535, poet.
Betti, Ugo, 1892–1953, dramatist.
Boccaccio, Giovanni, 1313–75, writer of tales and poet.
Bruni, Leonardo, 1369–1444, biographer.
Bruno, Giordano, 1548–1600, poet.
Calvino, Italo, 1923–85, novelist.
Campanella, Tommaso, 1568–1639, poet.
Carducci, Giosuè, 1836–1907, poet.
Caro, Annibale, 1507–66, poet and translator.
Casa, Giovanni della, 1503–56, poet.
Casanova de Seingault, Giovanni Jacopo, 1725–98, diarist and adventurer.
Castiglione, Baldassare, 1478–1529, author of *The Book of the Courtier*.
Cavalcanti, Guido, *c.* 1250–1300, poet and philosopher.
Cellini, Benvenuto, 1500–71, artist and autobiographer.
Cena, Giovanni, 1870–1917, novelist and poet.

Cinzio. *See* Giraldi.
Colonna, Vittoria, 1490–1547, poet.
Compagni, Dino, ?–1324, chronicler.
Coppetta, Francesco, 1510–54, poet.
Costanzo, Angelo di, 1507–*c.* 1591, poet and historian.
Croce, Benedetto, 1866–1952, philosopher and critic.
D'Annunzio, Gabriele, 1863–1938, poet and novelist.
Dante Alighieri, 1265–1321, poet.
De Amicis, Edmondo, 1846–1908, novelist, writer of travel books, etc.
Deledda, Grazia, 1875–1936, novelist.
Eco, Umberto, 1932–, novelist.
Ficino, Marsilio, 1433–99, humanist.
Filelfo, Francesco, 1398–1481, humanist.
Filicaja, Vincenzo da, 1642–1707, poet.
Fo, Dario, 1926–, dramatist.
Folengo, Teofilo ('Merlino Coccaio'), 1491–1544, macaronic poet.
Foscolo, Ugo, 1778–1827, poet.
Ginzburg, Natalia, 1916–91, novelist and dramatist.
Giraldi, Giovanni Battista (Cinzio), 1504–73, writer of tales.
Goldoni, Carlo, 1707–93, dramatist.
Gregory I, Pope, 540–604, theologian.
Guarini, Giovanni Battista, 1537–1612, poet and dramatist.
Guicciardini, Francesco, 1483–1540, historian.
Guidiccioni, Giovanni, 1500–41, poet.
Guinizelli, Guido, *c.* 1230–1306, poet.
Jacopone da Todi, *c.* 1230–76, poet.
Lampedusa, Guiseppe di, 1896–1957, novelist.
Lanzi, Luigi, 1732–1810, art historian.
Latini, Brunetto, 1230–94, poet.
Leopardi, Giacomo, 1798–1837, poet and philosopher.
Levi, Carlo, 1902–75, novelist.
Levi, Primo, 1919–87, novelist, critic and poet.
Lorenzo de' Medici, 1449–92, poet and patron of letters.
Machiavelli, Niccolò, 1469–1527, historian and political writer.
Manzoni, Alessandro, 1785–1873, poet and novelist.
Maraini, Dacia, 1938–, novelist and dramatist.

Marino, Giovanni Battista, 1569–1625, poet.

Mazzini, Giuseppe, 1808–72, patriotic writer.

Meli, Giovanni, 1740–1815, poet.

Metastasio (Trapassi), Pietro, 1698–1782, poet and dramatist.

Michelangelo, Buonarotti, 1475–1564, poet.

Molza, Francesco Maria, 1489–1544, poet.

Monti, Vincenzo, 1754–1828, poet.

Morante, Elsa, 1918–85, poet and novelist.

Moravia, Alberto, 1907–90, novelist.

Niccolini, Giovanni Battista, 1782–1861, dramatist.

Oriani, Alfredo, 1852–1909, novelist.

Parini, Giuseppe, 1729–99, poet.

Pascoli, Giovanni, 1855–1912, poet.

Pellico, Silvio, 1789–1854, poet and dramatist.

Petrarca, Francesco (Petrarch), 1304–74, poet.

Pirandello, Luigi, 1867–1936, dramatist.

Pius II, Pope (Aeneas Sylvius Piccolomini), 1405–64, humanist.

Poliziano (Angelo Ambrogini), 1454–94, poet and dramatist.

Polo, Marco, 1254–1324, traveller.

Prati, Giovanni, 1815–84, poet.

Pratolini, Vasco, 1913–, novelist.

Pulci, Luigi, 1432–84, poet.

Rossetti, Gabriele, 1783–1854, translator.

Rucellai, Giovanni, 1475–1525, poet.

Sacchetti, Franco, c. 1330–99, writer of tales.

Sannazaro, Jacopo, 1458–1530, poet.

Sarpi, Pietro (Fra Paolo), 1552–1623, natural philosopher.

Sciascia, Leonardo, d. 1989, novelist.

Serao, Matilde, 1856–1927, novelist.

Sforza, Count Carlo, 1873–1952, political writer and philosopher.

Silone, Ignazio, 1900–78, novelist.

Stampa, Gaspara, 1523–54, poet.

Straparola, Giovanni Francesco, d. c. 1556, story-writer.

Tansillo, Luigi, 1510–68, poet.

Tasso, Bernardo, 1493–1569, poet.

Tasso, Torquato, 1544–95, poet.

Tassoni, Alessandro, 1565–1635, poet.

Testi, Count Fulvio, 1593–1646, poet.

Todi, Jacopone da. *See* JACOPONE DA TODI.

Tozzi, Federigo, 1883–1920, novelist.

Troya, Carlo, 1784–1858, historian.

Uberti, Fazio degli, c. 1310–c. 1370, poet.

Vanini, Lucillo (Giulio Cesare), c. 1585–1619, poet.

Vasari, Giorgio, 1511–74, biographer.

Verga, Giovanni, 1840–1922, novelist.

Villani, Giovanni, c. 1275–1348, historian.

Villari, Pasquale, 1827–1917, historian.

Vinci, Leonardo da, 1452–1519, artist, and writer on painting and natural philosophy.

Ivory Coast. *See* CÔTE D'IVOIRE.

Iwo Jima, in the W Pacific, was annexed by Japan, 1891. US forces captured it, 1945; returned to Japan, 1968.

Jack the Ripper. Between 1887 and 1889 eight women were murdered and mutilated in the E End of London by a criminal popularly nicknamed 'J. the R.', who was never caught. A series of murders in the N of England prior to 1982, eventually leading to the conviction of Peter Sutcliffe, led to the murderer being popularly named 'The Yorkshire Ripper'.

Jacobins. Members of an extremist political club, formed during French Revolution, originally known as *Club Breton*, founded at Versailles, 1789, by members of States-General. Later called J. because of their meetings in a building in the Rue St Honoré, Paris, which belonged to the Dominican Order. Practically dissolved at the death of Robespierre, 1794; formally closed, 9 Nov. 1794.

Jacobites. Followers of the exiled Stuarts. Name first adopted after revolution of 1688, especially in the Irish war of 1689–90 between Williamites and J.
Insurrection of 1715: An attempt to set James Edward Stuart, son of James II, on the throne after Queen Anne's death, 1714. Earl of Mar (John Erskine, 1675–1732) set up James's standard at Braemar, 6 Sept. 1715. Indecisive battle against the Duke of Argyll at Sheriffmuir, 13 Nov. James landed at Peterhead, 22 Dec., but re-embarked with Mar in Feb. 1716 (OS 1715) and left for Avignon, France.
1719: Highland rising began Apr. under George Keith (the last Earl Marshal of Scotland, 1603–1778), but only Mackenzies and Macraes 'came out'. Ended June in drawn battle at Glensheil. Some 300 Spanish troops sent to support the Highlanders laid down their arms.
Rebellion of 1745: Led by Charles Edward Stuart, son of James Edward, who gained victory at Prestonpans, 21 Sept. Reached Derby, 6 Dec. (*see* BLACK FRIDAY). Defeated at Culloden by ('Butcher') Cumberland, 16 Apr. 1746. It led to the abolition of heritable jurisdictions in Scotland, 1746.
Last Jacobite executed (Dr. Archibald Cameron), 7 June 1753.
The last Stuarts: James Francis Edward: 'James III' – *The Old Pretender*, 1688–1766. Charles Edward: 'Charles III' – *The Young Pretender*, 1720–80. Henry Benedict Maria: 'Henry IX' – *Cardinal York* 1725–1807. James Fitzjames, Duke of Berwick: *Marshal of France and political adviser to the Old Pretender*, 1670–1734.

Jacquerie. A rebellion of French peasants in 1358. Word taken from 'Jacques Bonhomme', the name given by the nobles to the peasants; finally suppressed at battle of Meaux, 9 June 1358.

Jaffa, Israel (Arabic, **Yafa**; Greek, **Joppa**). Within the Roman province of Syria from 64 BC. Captured by Crusaders, 1099. Incorporated as a fief in the kingdom of Jerusalem, 1100. Captured by Saladin, 1187. Recaptured by Crusaders under Richard I, 1190. Sacked by Bibars, 1267. Captured by Napoleon, 1799; and by British, 1917. Centre of Arab nationalism until 1948. Administration united with that of Tel-Aviv in Oct. 1949.

Jaffna, town and district of N Sri Lanka. Leading centre of Tamil separatist agitation from 1980s.

Jaipur, India. The capital was transferred to J. city, newly founded in 1728. J. joined Rajasthan 30 Mar. 1949.

Jakarta, Indonesia. City of NW Java founded by the Dutch as **Batavia** in 1619. Headquarters of Dutch E India Co. Name reverted to J. after 1945.

Jamaica. Discovered by Columbus, 1494; possessed by Spaniards, 1509; British expedition sent out by Cromwell conquered J., 1655; ceded to England by Treaty of Madrid, 1670; earthquake at Kingston, destroying practically whole town, 14 Jan. 1907. Various defence sites leased to USA, Nov. 1940. Member of *Caribbean Federation, 1956; independent within the Commonwealth, 6 Aug. 1962. Increased links with USA from 1980s. Severe hurricane damage, Sept. 1988.

Jameson Raid. An invasion of the Transvaal by the forces of the British S Africa Co., 31 Dec. 1895–2 Jan. 1896. The leader was Dr Jameson, who was tried in July 1896 under the *Foreign Enlistment Act and sentenced to imprisonment. He was later premier of Cape Colony, 1904–8.

Jamestown, Virginia. Named after James I by English settlers who landed, 13 May 1607. Earliest permanent European settlement in New England.

Jammu and Kashmir, India. *See* KASHMIR.

Janina (Albanian), **Ioannina** (Greek), or **Yannina** (Turkish), Epirus. Murder of Gen. Tellini and other Italian members of boundary commission in Albania, Aug. 1923. Result was the 'Corfu Incident', Sept. 1923. Siege of, by Greeks in Second Balkan War, 25 Nov. 1912–6 Mar. 1913.

Janissaries. Troops originally recruited exclusively from Christian children for the Ottoman Army. First raised by Sultan Orkhan *c*. 1330. Reorganized by Murad I *c*. 1360. Insurrection of, 14 June 1826, resulted in their destruction.

Jan Mayen Island, Arctic Ocean. Sighted by Hudson, 1607. Said to have been rediscovered by Jan Mayen, 1614. Annexed to Norway, 1929.

Jansenism. Religious movement based on ideas of Cornelius Jansen (1585–1638) in France. His work *Augustinus* (published, 1640) led to the foundation of the *Port Royal community. It was condemned in 1642, and the controversy led to Pascal's *Provincial Letters,* 1656–7; continual persecution and the practical dissolution of the

movement in 1713, though the ideas of the Jansenists continued to influence French Catholicism throughout the 19thC.

Japan. (Traditional date of the foundation of the Japanese Empire by the Emperor Jimmu, 11 Feb. 660BC. This date is, however, discredited.) Japanese missions visit Korea, AD 57, 107. War with Korea under the Empress Jingu early 3rdC. Japanese naval defeat by Koreans, 516. Buddhism introduced, 552. Religious and political rivalry of the Soga and Nakatomi clans, 554–93. Issue of the Code of Shōtoku Taishi, 604. First embassy to China, 607. Death of Shōtoku Taishi, 621. Soga overthrown by Nakatomi-no-Kamatori, 645. The Taikwa or Great Reform Edict introduced a new system of Land Tenure, 646. The Taiho edict sets up administration on Chinese model, 702. Nobility reorganized on Chinese model, 707.

Nara founded, 710. Fujiwara family in power, 710–59, and from 782 to 1068. Capital moved to Nagaoka, 784; to Heian (Kyoto), 794. Wars against the Ainu in N J., 782. Ainu subdued, 812. Decline of the Fujiwara with the rise of the Cloistered Emperors, 1087–1156. Taira supremacy, 1156–85. Taira clan overthrown by Minamoto Yoritomo at naval battle of Dannoura, 1185.

Kamakura made capital of the *Shogun Yoritomo, 1185. Hojo family became regents on behalf of the Minamoto Shoguns, 1205. Defeat of the Mongol invasions, and Mongol fleet destroyed in a storm ('Divine Wind'), 1281. End of the Hojo regency and the destruction of Kamakura, 1333.

Establishment of a Northern Court at Kyoto and a Southern Court at Yoshino and civil war between them, 1336–92. With the settlement of the dynastic dispute power passes to the Shoguns of the Ashikaga family, who move the capital to Muromachi, a suburb of Kyoto, 1392. The Onin Civil War, 1467–77. Total collapse of government and civil war, 1480. Portuguese reach J., *c*. 1542. Order restored by Hobunaga, 1568. Hideyoshi destroys power of western feudatories, 1577. First Christian persecution, 1587.

Yedo founded, 1590. Hideyoshi's unsuccessful invasion of Korea, 1592. Jyeyasu establishes himself by defeat of the Toyotomi clans at Sekigahara, 1600, and by storming Osaka, 1615. 'Law of the Military Houses', 1615. Spaniards expelled, 1624. Shimabara rebellion, 1637. Japanese forbidden to go abroad, 1638. Portuguese expelled, 1638. Christians virtually wiped out. All other Europeans expelled, 1640, except Dutch, who were confined to Deshima, 1641. Beginning of the Nito School of Historians, 1660. The 'Genroku' period, 1688–1703. Relaxation of edicts against western learning, 1716. American Commodore Perry compels the Shogun to conclude commercial treaty, 1854. End of Shogunate, 1867, and rise in real power of the emperor. Feudal system abolished 1871, and westernization begun. By First Treaty of Shimonoseki China cedes Formosa (see TAIWAN) and Liaotung, 17 Apr. 1895. By Second Treaty Russia, France, and Germany take Japanese gains except Formosa, 8 May 1895. Anglo-Japanese alliance, 1902. Russo-Japanese War, 8 Feb. 1904. Russian defeat on land at battle of Mukden, 1–9 Mar. 1905. At sea in battle of Tsushima, 27–8 May 1905. Treaty of Portsmouth, 5 Sept. 1905. Annexation of Korea, 1910. On Allied side in World War I. Leaves League of Nations, 1933: Anti-Comintern Pact with Germany, 1936. The Peking Incident, 7 July 1937 (for war with China, see CHINA). J. joins the Axis, 27 Sept. 1940. 1941–5 see WORLD WAR II. 1945: Atomic bombs dropped on Hiroshima and Nagasaki, Aug. 6 and 9; J. surrenders unconditionally, 14 Aug. New constitution in force, 1947: Liberal Democrats continuously in power, 1959–93. Peace treaty signed between J. and representatives of 48 countries, 8 Sept. 1951; Security Treaty with USA ratified, 26 Oct. J. joins UN, 1956. 1960: J.-US Mutual Security Treaty; from 1960 increasing Japanese prosperity and massive penetration of traditional Western markets. 1971: Okinawa Reversion Treaty, 1972. Corruption scandals increased from 1980s. Akihito emperor, 1989. From 1992 Japanese armed forces permitted to send up to 2000 troops abroad for UN

peacekeeping. Ruling Liberal Democrats lost power after 30 years, July 1993; Hosokawa became 'reformist' premier. In Sept. he apologized to Britain for Japanese ill treatment of British prisoners of war during World War II. Hosokawa himself resigned after corruption allegations, April 1994. In June Muryama became premier. Strong yen and imbalance of exports/imports continued to cause international problems, notably with the USA. Serious earthquake in *Kobe, 16 Jan 1995, killed over 5,000 people. Poison nerve gas released on Tokyo underground, 20 Mar. 1995, caused 12 deaths, hundreds suffered ill-effects. Attack blamed on Aum Shinriko cult and its leader Shoko Asahar subsequently arrested. Hijacking of an internal flight, June, ended peacefully with no casualties.

Japanese literature.
Japanese writers include:
Abé Kobo, 1924–93, novelist and dramatist.
Akutagawa Ryunosuke, novelist, 1892–1927.
Dazai Osamu, novelist, 1909–48
Endo Shusako, novelist, 1923–
Higuchi Ichigo, storyteller, 1872–96
Ihara Saikaku, novelist, 1642–93
Ishikawa Takoboku, poet, 1885–1912
Jippensha Ikku, humorist, 1765–1831
Kawabata Yasunari, novelist, 1899–1972
Mishima Yukio, novelist, 1925–70
Murusaki Shikibu, epic writer, *fl.* 998
Natsume Soseki, novelist, 1867–1916
Ooka Shohei, novelist, 1909–88
Osaragi Jiro, 1897–1973, novelist
Tanizaki Junichiro, 1886–1965, novelist

Jarrow, County Durham. The Venerable Bede was associated with the Benedictine abbey founded here, 682, by Benedict Biscop (628–90). Sacked by Vikings, 794. March of unemployed from J. to London, 1936.

Jassy (Romanian **Iasi**) was a centre of Greek as well as Vlach culture, and capital of Moldavia, in the 16thC. Here Alexander

Ypsilanti (1792–1828) proclaimed the independence of Greece, 1821, but his forces were defeated by the Turks, and he fled into exile.

Java, Indonesia. Dutch founded a factory in, 1610; Dutch rule began, 1619. Occupied by British, 1811. Regained by Dutch, 1816. Conquered by Japan, Feb.–Mar. 1942. Became part of the republic of Indonesia, 1950. *See* INDONESIA.

jazz, rhythmic, syncopated music, with origins in black American and other 'folk' music, which developed from a base in New Orleans, USA in the early 20thC. Its emphasis on personal interpretation and improvisation has led it to diversify in several directions. With the marketing of the first J. record, 1917, the style spread rapidly world-wide, but by the 1920s its US centre had moved to Chicago. Early J. included Dixieland and swing, the latter giving rise to the 'Big Band Era', from the mid-1920s to 1940s. Later J. forms were less populist, and there was further fragmentation and specialization from rise of rock music in the 1950s (*see* ROCK AND ROLL). Among famous names in the J. world are:

Armstrong, Louis, 1901–71
Baker, Josephine, 1906–75
Basie, 'Count', 1904–84
Beiderbecke, 'Bix', 1903–31
Brubeck, Dave, 1920–
Coltrane, John, 1926–67
Davis, Miles, 1926–93
Eckstine, Billy, 1913–93
Ellington, Duke, 1899–74
Fitzgerald, Ella, 1918–
Gillespie, 'Dizzy', 1917–93
Goodman, Benny, 1909–86
Hall, Adelaide, 1901–93
Herman, Woody, 1913–87
Holiday, Billie, 1915–59
Horn, Lena, 1917–
Mingus, Charles, 1922–79
Monk, Thelonius, 1917–82
Miller, Glenn, 1904–44
Morton, 'Jelly Roll', 1885–41
Parker, Charlie, 1920–55
Smith, Bessie, 1894–1937

Smith, Tommy, 1967–
Tatum, Art, 1909–56
Waller, 'Fats', 1904–43

The ragtime pianist and composer Scott Joplin (1868–1917) had considerable influence on J. development, and the music form was used by the Gershwins and other mainstream composers.

Jedburgh, Scotland. Abbey founded by David, I, 1118–47. Burned by English, 1544–5.

Jehovah's Witnesses, international fundamentalist religious sect founded *c.* 1872 by C. T. Russell as the Watch Tower Bible and Tract Society and the International Bible Students' Association. Took title J.W. under Russell's successor, J. F. Rutherford in 1931. World-wide membership, but strongest in English-speaking countries, and in Mexico, Japan, Nigeria and Italy. Estimated over 4,700,000 members (1995).

Jena, Germany. First documentary mention of, AD 863. Granted municipal rights in 13thC. Came into hands of the Saxon Wettin dynasty, 1331, and was an independent dynasty known as Saxe-Jena, 1672–90. Came by inheritance to the principality of Saxe-Weimar, 1741, whose ruler, Karl August (reigned 1775–1828), was a great patron of the arts and of J. University (founded 1558). Battle of J., between Napoleon I and the Prussians, 14 Oct. 1806.

Jenkins's Ear (War of). Robert Jenkins, master of the brig *Rebecca*, had his ship boarded off Havana, 9 Apr. 1731, by Spanish coastguards, who, Jenkins alleged, cut off the ear in question. He complained to his own Government with no result, but in 1738 was called to the bar of the House of Commons, where he repeated his story, which was used as a *casus belli* for the war of 1739–42. Jenkins *d.* 1745.

Jericho. The walls traditionally destroyed by Joshua were excavated earlier this century, and would appear to have been continuously occupied from 2000 to 1600 BC, the outer works dating from *c.* 1800 BC. Further investigations, 1952–8, have shown that J. probably existed as early as 9000 BC. The first J. was abandoned after the Babylonian Exile, 586 BC. The second J. was excavated, 1950–1, and Herodian remains found. Modern J. dates from the Crusader period. It expanded after its incorporation into Jordan, 1949: in Israeli hands from 1967, but under PLO-Israeli agreement, Sept. 1993 to have internal Arab self-government; this implemented, May 1994, and Israeli troops left J.

Jersey. United to the English crown, 1066. Occupied by Germans, June 1940–9 May 1945. British military government lasted, 12 May–25 June 1945. Legislative reforms, 1948. *See* CHANNEL ISLANDS.

Jerusalem (Arabic **al Qds**, colloquially **'Udes**). Letters signed by the ruler of 'Urusalim', and written *c.* 1375 BC, are extant. Taken by David *c.* 1050 BC. Hezekiah repels Assyrian siege, 701. Destroyed by Nebuchadnezzar, 586. Rebuilt by Nehemiah, 445. Taken by Alexander the Great, 332. Temple destroyed by Antiochus Epiphanes, 168. Rebuilt by Maccabees *c.* 150. J. taken by Pompey, 65. Temple plundered by Crassus, 54. Rebuilt by Herod, 35–34. Sacked by Titus, AD 70. Captured by Arabs, 637. Dome of the Rock begun, 643. Occupied by Crusaders, 1099–1244 (*see* CRUSADES). Captured from Turks by Allenby, 1917. British evacuate, 1948. During the Israeli-Arab War of 1948–9, Jordan forces occupied the Old City and Israeli forces the New, which the Knesset proclaimed as the capital of Israel, 23 Jan. 1950. In the 'June War' of 1967, Israel conquered and occupied the Old City declaring, 1980, the united J. to be the Israeli capital. This is not recognized by the UN, etc. Right-wing mayor elected, 1993.

Jervaulx Abbey (Yorkshire). Founded 1156. Last Abbot hanged, 1537 for alleged role in the Pilgrimage of Grace.

Jesuits (Society of Jesus). Founded, 1534, by Ignatius Loyola (1491–1556). Constitutions approved by papal bull, 1540. First colleges in Portugal, 1542; France (at Billom), 1545; Paris, 1550. Expelled from France, 1594. Restored, 1603. Again expelled, 1764; again restored, 1814. Again expelled, 1880. Expelled from England, 1579, 1581, 1586, 1602, 1829. Prominent in mission work in Japan, China, N and S America in 16th, 17th and 18thC. Suppressed by Pope Clement XIV, 1773. Restored by Pius VII, first in Russia, 1801, then in the Two Sicilies, 1804; completely, 1814. Today permitted in most countries.

jet propulsion. Basic principles first stated by the French engineer, René Lorin, 1913. In 1930 Sir Frank Whittle, then a RAF cadet, began work on gas turbines, which received official support from the Air Ministry, 1937. His first J.P. aircraft flew, 14 May 1941. Independent experiments started by the German, Heinkel, 1939, and the J.P. Heinkel 53B was flown on 27 Aug. that year. Jet engine principal form of aircraft engine since 1970s.

Jew, the Wandering. First mentioned in the Chronicle of St Alban's Abbey, 1228.

Jews in England. Mentioned in ecclesiastical documents as early as AD 740. Came to England in large numbers after the Norman Conquest (1066). Riots against them in 1189 at coronation of Richard I. Driven from England by Edward I, 1290; but from 1580 to 1640 Portugal was conquered by and annexed to Spain, and a great many Jewish refugees from Portugal, settled in Bristol and London between 1590 and 1600. This *fait accompli* was acknowledged, and J. officially readmitted by Cromwell, 1656. Bill passed to naturalize J., 1753, repealed, 1754. Allowed to obtain freedom of City of London, 1832. Act to relieve J. elected to municipal offices from taking oaths, 1845; extended when they were admitted to Parliament, 1858. Universities Tests Act, 1871, enabled J. to graduate at the universities. First admitted to House of Lords, 1885. Considerable influx of J. to Britain from E Europe, 1880–1910; from Nazi Germany, 1933–8.

Jibuti. *See* DJIBOUTI.

Jodrell Bank, Cheshire site of the Lovell Telescope (completed 1957: modified, 1970), the largest instrument in the Nuffield Radio Astronomy Laboratory there.

Johannesburg, Transvaal. Founded, 1886, and probably named after Johannes Meyer, the Mining Commissioner of that time. *Jameson Raid organized at, 1895. Made into a city, 1928 and now (1995) largest in S Africa.

John Bull. Personification of the English nation. Name and character first popularized in 1712 by John Arbuthnot, an anti-Whig pamphleteer.

Johns Hopkins University, USA. Founded by a gift from Johns Hopkins, of Baltimore, made 1867. Opened, 1876. The present buildings are on a site outside Baltimore, Maryland, presented by the city in 1902.

Johore, former Unfederated Malay State, entered into treaty relations with Britain, 1885. Became a member state of the Malay Federation, 1948; of Malaysia, 1963.

Joinville, Treaty of, 1584, between Philip II of Spain and Henry of Guise.

Jordan (formally **Transjordan**). Conquered by Moslem armies, 637. Hashemite Kingdom established when, after the expulsion of the Emir Feisal from Syria (1920), his brother, Sharif Abdullah, was dissuaded from invading Syria again (which he threatened to do, Apr. 1921) by being recognized as emir of the territory E of J., between Es Salt and Ma'an. An independent, though mandated, state, proclaimed by the British, 1923. Boundary with Nejd province of Saudi Arabia fixed by Treaty of Hadda, 1925.
Britain recognized total independence by treaty of 22 Mar. 1946. Name changed to J. officially, 17 June 1946. In the war with Israel, 1948, J. conquered *c.* 2,000 square miles of Arab Palestine, and subsequently annexed this, Apr. 1950. King Abdullah murdered, 20 July 1951; grandson Hussein

enthroned, 1953. All British military and air bases handed back to J. by May 1957. The kings of J. and *Iraq united their kingdoms in the 'Arab Federation', 14 Feb. 1958; this lapsed after 14 July 1958, and was officially dissolved, 1 Aug. 1958. J. joined the 'June War', 1967, on side of Egypt but her forces were pushed back from the Old City of Jerusalem and the left bank of the Jordan. Arab guerrillas made J. their base, 1968 onwards and constituted a 'state within a state'. Hussein's army launched an attack against them, 1970, and Arab guerrilla activity subsequently moved to *Lebanon. About 1 million Arab Palestinians living in J. by 1990. Economy suffered during *Gulf War, 1991. First parliamentary elections since 1967 took place, 1989. Better relations with Israel sought after PLO-Israeli agreement, Sept. 1993. Nov 1993: first multiparty elections since 1956 results in success for moderates. Peace treaty with Israel signed, Oct. 1994.

Juan Fernandez Island, Pacific. Discovered in 16thC by Juan Fernandez. Alexander Selkirk lived here, 1704–9. Occupied by Spain, 1750, and passed to Chile in 1810.

Judaism. Origins appear to date *c.* 2000 BC. Formalized *c.* 1200 BC. *c.* 20 million Jews world-wide, 1994, about 50% in USA. *See also* JERUSALEM; ISRAEL; PALESTINE, ANCIENT and MODERN.

Judicature Acts passed 1873, 1875, 1925 and 1981. The Act of 1925 consolidated Acts, 1873–1910; radical changes made by 1981 Act. *See* COURTS, ENGLISH.

Judiciary of the USA. Supreme Court organized, 1789; Court of Claims established, 1855; Circuit Court of Appeals established, 1891. Women admitted to practise in the Supreme Court, 15 Feb. 1879.

judo, sport which is a modified form of jujitsu, said to have been developed as a means of self defence by Chinese monks in the 12thC. It spread to Japan where the Samurais adopted it. In 1882 Prof. Jigoro Kano established a school of 'judo' ('gentle way') in Tokyo. J. was introduced to the

USA *c*. 1900 and has since spread world-wide. There have been World J. championships since 1956: introduced into Olympic Games, 1964.

Jülich. Occupied in Roman times, the medieval city was chartered in the 13thC, ruled from 1336 by margraves, and from 1386 by dukes; captured by Maurice of Orange, 1610, during the J.-Cleves succession dispute (1609–14). Became part of Prussia, 1814, having been included in the French Empire since 1801. *See* CLEVES.

jumbo jet, popular name for the Boeing 747. Developed as a passenger plane in the 1960s, first flew 9 Feb. 1969. Early version carried 350–490 persons: subsequent ones could carry up to 650.

'June War' (1967). Fought between Israel, on the one hand, and Egypt, Lebanon, Jordan, Syria and Iraq on the other. Began, 5 June: Israel made immediate and sweeping military gains and Egypt and her allies agreed to a cease-fire, 8 June. Israel had gained control of Old Jerusalem, the Gulf of Aqaba, the Gaza Strip (awarded Palestinian self-rule, 1994), and the Sinai peninsula (returned to Egypt, 1982).

'Junius, Letters of.' A series of seventy political letters signed 'Junius', which appeared in the *Public Advertiser* between 21 Jan. 1769 and 21 Jan. 1772. The printer and publisher, H. S. Woodfall, was prosecuted in Dec. 1769 for a certain letter which appeared against King George III, but acquitted. Sir Philip Francis (1740–1818) reputed to have been the author. Claims have also been made for the authorship of Burke, Wilkes, Horace Walpole, etc.

Juia, new canton established in Switzerland, 1 Jan. 1979.

jury, trial by. Use of juries first appears in compilation of *Domesday Book, 1085–6. Established as a method of trial by Henry II, 1154–89, in civil cases. In criminal cases, *c*. 1215, as a result of abolition of trial by ordeal. Introduced by Act of Parliament for civil cases in Scotland, 1815. Grand Juries abolished for most purposes, 1933;

totally, 1948. Majority verdicts permissible under Criminal Justice Act, 1967. Juries Act, 1974, made voters over 18 eligible for jury service. Juries (Disqualification) Act, 1984 made certain persons ineligible. Runciman Report, July 1993 suggested end of automatic right to T. by J. in some cases.

Justice of the Peace. Knights to keep the peace appointed by royal proclamation in England, 1195. *Custodes Pacis* appointed by Simon de Montfort, 1262–4. Regular provision for their appointment made by an Act of 1327. Known as J.P.s since 1362. Commissions of the Peace finally settled, 1590. Women have been eligible to become J.P.s since 1919. Justices of the Peace Act, 1949, imposed an age limit on J.P.s. Justices of the Peace Act, 1968, and Administration of Justice Act, 1973, imposed further conditions on J.P.s.

Justice, Royal Courts of. From the Norman Conquest to 1873, situated at Westminster Hall. Then reorganized and transferred to the present building in the Strand.

'Justification', The, of William of Orange. In 1567 the Council in Spain declared William (the Silent) of Orange an outlaw if he did not surrender himself for trial. William's reply was his 'J.', published in 1568, and sent to all the courts of Europe.

Justinian's Legislation. The following are the principal legal works issued at J.'s orders:
Codex Vetus, 529.
The Fifty Decisions, 529–31.
The Digest or Pandects, 533.
The Institutes, 533.
Codex Repetitae Praelectionis supersedes the *Codex Vetus*, 534.
The Novels, 534–65.

Jutland. N Slesvig ceded to Prussia, 1864, but returned to Denmark after a plebiscite, 1920.

Juvenile Offenders Acts. Act for instituting a prison for the correction of J.O., 1838.

Act for committal to reformatories, 1854. J.O. Act, 1901. By the Act of 1908, separate courts set apart for trial of children. Children and Young Persons Act of 1933 provided for less formal court procedure. Criminal Justice Acts of 1948, 1961, 1972, 1983 and 1991 made various changes in the procedures for dealing with delinquent juveniles, as did the Children Acts of 1948, 1952, 1975 and 1989. Serious crimes by some juveniles in 1990s led to proposals for further modification in treatment, 1993, embodied in new Criminal Justice Act, 1994.

K-2, Himalayas, otherwise known as Mount Godwin-Austen (28,250 ft/8611 m). First climbed, 31 July 1954, by an Italian expedition. Six climbers, including two Britons, *d.* after ascent, 1986. Alison Hargreaves and four companions killed in avalanche on, Aug. 1995.

Ka'aba (Mecca). Present building erected, 1626, but so as to preserve the essential features of the original building and some part of the fabric of the mosque which the Caliph Mahdi left unfinished at his death (AD 785). The holy black stone 'cube' built into the wall of the pre-Islamic shrine was carried off by raiders, AD 930, but restored, AD 952.

Kabul, *Afghanistan. Captured by Tamerlane, 1394; by Nadir Shah, 1702. Made capital of Afghanistan, 1774. Fell to anti-Communists, 25 April 1992.

Kaffir Wars with British: 1779–81, 1789–93, 1799–1802, 1811–12, 1817–19, 1834–5, 1846–8, 1850–3.

Kaffraria, S Africa. British colony from 1847 till 1865, then joined to Cape Colony.

Kalashnikov. *See* RIFLE

kaleidoscope. Invented, 1817, by Sir David Brewster.

Kaliningrad, USSR. Founded as Koenigsberg by Teutonic Knights *c.* 1255. Acquired by Brandenburg-Prussia, 1618 (*see* PRUSSIA). Annexed by USSR, and name changed to K., 1945. Now (1995) in Russia.

Kalmar, Union of, June 1397. Norway, Sweden and Denmark united dynastically by Queen Margaret of Denmark under a Danish dynasty. *Sweden seceded from the Union when Gustavus Vasa was elected king of Sweden at the Diet of Strängnäs, 6 June 1523. *See* KIEL, TREATY OF.

Kamchatka. Discovered by Cossacks, AD 1690; Russian, 1697; visited by Bering, 1728; unsuccessful attempt made on fort of Petropavlovsk by British and French fleets, 1854.

Kampala, Uganda. British flag hoisted at K. fort, 1 Apr. 1893. Capital of *Uganda since 1962.

Kampuchea, name of *Cambodia, 1976–89.

Kandahar, Afghanistan. Capital of Afghanistan, 1747–74. Held by British from 1839 until 1842; finally evacuated by British, Apr. 1881. *See* AFGHANISTAN.

Kandy, Sri Lanka. Capital of the kingdom of K., 1480–1815; site of an important Buddhist shrine.

Kangchengjunga, Himalayas, (28,208 ft/8598 m), first climbed, 1955, by a British expedition.

Kanpur, formerly **Cawnpore**, India, formally possessed by Britain, 1801. Besieged by Nana Sahib, 1857: massacre of women and children by mutineers, 6 June 1857.

Kansas, USA. The greater part of the territory was acquired by the Louisiana Purchase, 1803; more territory taken over from Mexico, 1850. The K.-Nebraska Act, 1854, regulated the boundaries of these two states, allowed local option in the slavery question. Admitted to the Union, 1861.

Kappel, Switzerland. First Peace of, between the Forest Cantons and the Zwinglian Party, June 1529; second Peace of, 11 Oct. 1531, after Zwingli had been killed in battle there.

Karachi, Pakistan. Founded, 1843. Became capital of *Pakistan, 1947–1959; remains capital of Sind province. University at, 1951.

karate (Japanese for 'empty hand'), evolved over centuries in E Asia: became organized in Okinawa in 17thC. Reached mainland Japan *c.* 1920. Popular sport in the W and USA since Second World War.

Karelia, autonomous NW Russian republic, occupies the area of the White Sea, and is populated chiefly by people of Finnish origin. Known under the tsars as Olonets Province it became the Karelian Autonomous Soviet Socialist Republic, July 1923. From 31 Mar. 1940, all territory ceded by *Finland to the USSR was included in the territory and name changed to Karelo-Finnish Soviet Socialist republic. But in 1946 the areas containing Vyborg (*see under* VYBORG) and Käkisalmi were transferred to the Russian RSFSR, reverting to autonomous states in 1956. In Nov. 1991 the republic declared its present title.

Karen Rebellion, 1947. *See* BURMA.

Kariba Hydro-electric Scheme. Building of the dam begun, 6 Nov. 1956; opened by Queen Elizabeth the Queen Mother, 17 May 1960.

Karl-Marx-Stadt, 1953–90, *see* CHEMNITZ.

Karlovy Vary. *See* CARLSBAD.

Karlsbad or **Carlsbad Decrees, 1819.** Issued against liberalism in Germany at Congress of K. at the instance of Metternich.

Karnataka. *See* MYSORE.

Kashmir, India. Part of Mogul Empire, 1587: became part of Sikh monarchy, 1819 and Jammu dynasty of Gulab Singh established by British influence, 1846. Hindu maharajah acceded to India, 1947, and Muslim uprising followed. In 1949 K. was partitioned between India and Pakistan, the Indian section forming state of Jammu and K. Dispute concerning final disposition of K. between India and Pakistan caused armed conflicts between, 1965–6 and 1971. These temporarily settled by Tashkent Declaration, 1966 and Simla Agreement, 1972 but dispute still basically unresolved, 1994. During 1990s repeated complains of Indian repression in Jammu and K. and renewed Pakistani and Indian claims to all K., Aug. 1994 plus growth of separatist extremists. Renewed violence from 1994 and extremists kidnapped Europeans in Delhi, released after armed intervention, Oct. Foreigners, including British, taken hostage by guerrillas, July 1995: one (a Norwegian) later murdered.

Kassel, Germany. *See* CASSEL.

Katanga, richest state in *Zaïre. It declared itself independent of the central government, 11 July 1960. K. eventually reintegrated into Zaïre, Jan. 1963 and was subsequently renamed **Shaba**. Tribal warfare in from 1990s.

Katmandu, capital of Nepal, founded 8thC. British residency at 1817.

Katrine, Loch, Scotland, has supplied Glasgow with water since 1859.

Kazakhstan Republic, created 1920. Became a constituent republic of the USSR, 1936. Its territory formerly was included in Siberia and Russian *Turkestan. Kazakhs not reconciled to this regime emigrated to *Sinkiang, Kansu and Chinguin in western China. In 1950 they fled again into Tibet, ultimately reaching Kashmir. In 1952 those who did not wish to settle in Kashmir settled permanently in Turkey. K. is now (1995) an independent republic, and member of the *Commonwealth of Independent States: it was the last of the former USSR republics to declare its independence, 16 Dec. 1991. A referendum in April 1995 approved an extension of the president's rule until Dec. 2000.

Kazan, Russia. Captured by Russians, 1552, from Tatars who founded it, mid-13thC, and made it their capital, 1445. Destroyed during the Cossack mutiny of Pugachev, 1774, and rebuilt by Catherine II. Capital of Tatar Soviet Republic, 1920: since 1990, capital of the Tatar Republic.

Kedah, former Unfederated Malay State. The ruling house converted to Islam *c.* 1500. Known since 1516 to the Portuguese, who attacked it, 1611. English traders dealt with K. merchants in the 17thC but the Dutch obtained a concession, 1641, and drove out the English company, 1683. By Treaty of 1791 the government of K. was subsidized by the E India Co. Conquered by Siam, 1821. By treaty between Siam and Britain, 1909, the whole territory, except Setul, was transferred to British suzerainty. K. adhered to the Malay Union, 1946, the Malay Federation, 1948, and has been part of *Malaysia since Sept. 1963.

Keele, University of. Formerly the University College of N Staffordshire. Granted charter, 1962.

Keeling Islands. *See* COCOS ISLANDS.

Kelantan, former Unfederated Malay State. Conquered by Mahmud, last Sultan of Malacca, who reigned, 1488–1511. Became temporarily independent under a prince from Johore at end of 16thC. Adhered to Malay Union, 1946, Malay Federation, 1948, and part of Malaysia since 1963.

Kellogg Pact. For 'outlawry of war'. Signed by representatives of 15 nations, 27 Aug. 1928; called after its negotiator, Frank B. Kellogg (1856–1937), US ambassador in London, 1923–5. Eventually 59 nations signed it; but it had little practical effect.

Kenilworth (England). Castle founded by Geoffrey de Clinton *c.* 1120. Given by Queen Elizabeth to the Earl of Leicester, 1563.

Kenilworth, Dictum or **Ban of,** 31 Oct. 1266, enacted that all who took up arms against the king should pay the value of their lands for five years.

Kennedy Space Center. Cape Canaveral, Florida, USA. Used for space flight launches since 1960s. The first manned flight to land on the moon launched from here, 1969.

Kensington. Holland House, built 1608–10. Serpentine formed, 1733. K. Gardens generally opened to the public, early 19thC. Victoria and Albert Museum established, 1857. Natural History Museum,

1881. Science Museum organized, 1909. Commonwealth Institute's new buildings opened at, Nov. 1962.

Kensington Palace. Originally Nottingham House. Bought by William III from the 2nd Earl of Nottingham, 1689. Queen Victoria *b.* at, 1819. London Museum at, 1951–76. Again used as a royal residence since 1960s.

Kent, Kingdom of. The arrival of Hengest and Horsa in K. as *foederati* in the service of the British king Vortigern is said by the early chroniclers to have taken place during the reigns of Martian and Valentinian III, Roman emperors of the E and W, and is thus dated between 449 and 455. The laws of Ethelberht, written down late in the 6thC, show a social organization and system of land tenure different from that of other Old English kingdoms. The kingdom of K. was co-terminous with the modern county. Christianity established, 597. Between 673 and 685 a second code of law, which survives, was issued by King Hlothere, in whose reign there were two destructive invasions, one by the Mercians *c.* 675, and one by the W Saxons under Caedwalla and his brother Mull, beginning in 685. After *c.* 780 K. ceased to have any real independence, and if native kings ruled they did so only as the clients first of Mercia, then (after 825) of Wessex.

Rulers of, c. 449–860:
Hengest *fl.* 449–*d.* 488
Oisc ?
Octa ?
Eormenric ?
Ethelberht I *c.* 560–616
Eadbald 616–40
Eorcenberht 640–64
Egbert I 664–73
Hlothere 673–85
Eadric 684–86
State of anarchy 686–94
Wihtred 694–725
Eadberht 725–48
Ethelberht II 748–62
Kent divided among several kings, subject to Mercia 762–98

Cuthred of Mercia 798–805
Baldred (*probably subject to Mercia*) 805–23
Ethelwulf of Wessex 825–39
Athelstan of Wessex 839–c. 40
Ethelwulf of Wessex (*again*) 856–58
Ethelberht of Wessex 858–60

Kent, University of. Established at Canterbury, 1965.

Kentucky, USA, was originally part of Virginia, and its early history is closely connected with that of W Virginia and *Tennessee. Settlement made by Daniel Boone, 1775. Admitted to the Union, 1792.

Kenya. Prospected in 1880 by the Imperial E Africa Co., which was chartered, 1885. Protectorate over coastal area leased from Sultan of *Zanzibar set up under name of British E Africa, 1895. Came under Colonial Office administration, 1905. United with Zanzibar Protectorate, renamed K., and made a colony, 1920. N boundary agreement with Ethiopia, 1947. *Mau-Mau disturbances among Kikuyu tribe lasted 1952–7. Internal self-government, June 1963; full independence, Dec. K. became a republic, Dec. 1964, with Kenyatta, former Mau-Mau leader, as first president; on his death, 1978, Daniel arap Moi succeeded him. One-party state, 1982. Despite growing prosperity, government corruption led to movement for multiparty democracy in 1990s. Elections in Dec. 1992 won by arap Moi but opposition refused to accept result. Attempts to enforce repatriation of Somali refugees from K., 1993. Human rights infringements alleged, 1994. Britain freezes most aid to K., July 1995.

Kerala, state of SW India since 1956, from territories formerly states of Cochin and Travancore.

Kerch (ancient *Panticapaeum*), town in the E Crimea. Founded by Greeks, 6thC BC. Capital of the Bospor Kingdom, from the 5thC BC to the 4thC AD; then Byzantine, Tatar and Turkish. Russian 1774–1991; since then in Ukraine. Destroyed during Crimean War and 1941–3.

Kerguelen Islands, Indian Ocean. Discovered by Kerguélen-Trémarée (1745–97), 1772; annexed by France, 1893, but occupation only effective since 1949.

Kett's Rebellion. Instigated by Robert Kett, a Norfolk tanner and small landowner, in July 1549. The rioters met at Norwich, but were soon disbanded. Kett, defeated at Dussindale, 26 Aug., was hanged at Norwich Castle, 7 Dec. 1549.

Kew, England. Royal Botanic Gardens founded, 1759; open to the public since 1840.

Keys, House of. *See* TYNWALD.

KGB (Russian abbreviation for **Committee of State Security**). Name of Soviet security service, 1953–1991, when it was replaced by the Russian Federal Security Agency.

Khalifa. Title taken by Abd'allah at Taashi, the successor of the Mahdi. He was defeated by Kitchener at Omdurman, 1898, and killed at Om Debrikah, 1899.

Kharkov, city of the Ukraine, founded 1656. Provincial government seat, 1732. Industrialization in 20thC: capital of Ukraine, 1917–34. Changed hands frequently during World War II: severely damaged, since rebuilt. Has a 17thC and 19thC cathedral. University, 1805. Underground railway, 1975.

Khartoum, capital of Sudan. Founded *c.* 1822 by Mehemet Ali; defended against the Mahdi, 1884–5, by Gen. Gordon, who was killed there, 26 Jan. 1885; after the battle of Omdurman. 2 Sept. 1898, K. was recovered from the *Khalifa.

Khedive, Persian word meaning prince, conferred as an hereditary title by the Turkish sultan on the rulers of *Egypt 1867, and borne by them till 1914.

Khmer Rouge, extreme left-wing movement in *Cambodia, initially backed by N Vietnam, which rose to influence and power during the late 1960s. From 1975, when it gained total power, until 1979, it exercised a regime of terror under Pol Pot and tens of thousands died. Thereafter a guerilla movement until 1991 when it declared itself 'reformed' and joined government coalition, but boycotted 1993 elections and subsequently renewed guerrilla warfare against government. In control of many rural areas, 1994, though failed to overthrow government in coup, July. In Oct. K.R. murdered three European hostages.

Khyber Pass, Afghanistan. Twice crossed by British Army during first Afghan War, 1841, 1842, and again in the second Afghan War, Nov. 1878. The Treaty of Gandamak, 1879, stipulated that the pass should be fully controlled by the British authorities, and these rights were acquired by Pakistan, 1947.

Kiakhta, Treaty of. Between China, Russia and Outer Mongolia, for settlement of boundaries, 1915.

Kiaochow, now usually known as **Tsingtao.** Seized by Germans, 1897; ceded to Japan, 1919; restored to China, 1922, and again in 1945.

Kiel, founded, 1240; chartered, 1242; joined Hansa, 1248. Naval base developed *c.* 1890–1914 and 1934–9. Heavily bombed by the British, 1941–4.

Kiel Canal. Completed in July 1914.

Kiel, Treaty of, ceding Norway to Sweden, between Great Britain, Sweden and Denmark, 14 Jan. 1814.

Kiev, capital of Ukraine. According to the *Chronicle of Nestor* was founded by the Slav brothers, Kiy, Shchek and Khoriv, 864, but seized by the Rus (Swedes), Askold and Dir, same year (*see* VIKING AGE.) Capital of Russian Varangian principality by AD 880. Became centre of Russian Christianity after baptism of Vladimir, 988. Said to have had 400 churches and eight markets by Thietmar, Bishop of Merseburg (975–1018). Captured by Andrei Bogolyubski, 1169. Destroyed by Tatars under Batu, 1240. Passed to Lithuania, 1320. Sacked by Crimean Tatars, 1483. Obtained the 'Magdeburg Right' (Civil Liberties), 1499. Ceded to Poland, 1569. Poles driven out,

1654. Elective magistracy instituted, 1667. Annexed by Russia, 1686. Dubno Contract Fair moved to K., 1797. Rebellion at, 1905. Ukrainian Rada at, Feb. 1917. Stormed by Communists, Dec. 1919. Occupied by Poles, May–June 1920. Bitter fighting at, and serious damage, 1941–3. *See* WORLD WAR II.

Kilimanjaro, Tanzania, highest mountain (19,340 ft/5895 m) in Africa. First climbed, 1889.

Kilkenny, Statute of. Forbade amongst other things (1) marriage between English and Irish; (2) Englishmen to use Irish names or wear Irish apparel; passed, 1367.

Kilmainham Treaty, Apr. 1882, between Gladstone and Parnell, by which the latter promised to assist in the restoration of order in Ireland. It was abortive because of the *Phoenix Park murders, which immediately followed.

Kimberley, S Africa. Relieved, 15 Feb. 1900, after a three-month siege in S African War.

King's Bench Prison (London). Burnt during Gordon Riots, 7 June 1780; rebuilt, 1781; demolished, 1880.

King's Champion, an office dating from the reign of William I, and has been discharged by the family of Dymoke since 1377. The earliest written claim to perform the service is dated 1327. The last Champion actually to challenge all comers at the coronation banquet to deny the sovereign's title was the Champion of George IV in 1820.

King's (or Queen's) Counsel. Title first granted in England by James I in 1604 to Sir Francis Bacon.

King's Cross disaster, occurred, 18 November 1987, when a fire under an escalator at King's Cross Underground Station killed 31, and led to safety changes, including a total smoking ban on the London Underground.

King's Cup. Aeroplane race instituted,

1922 and continued annually until the Second World War.

King's Evil or **scrofula.** Supposed to have been cured by the touch of the sovereign. The custom was maintained from the time of Edward III, but fell into disuse with the accession of George I in 1714.

Kings and Queens of England and Great Britain. *See* ENGLISH SOVEREIGNS AND THEIR CONSORTS.

King's Prize for rifle shooting instituted, as Queen's Prize, 1860. Name subsequently reverted.

Kingston, *Jamaica. Founded 1693 after earthquake (1692) had destroyed Port Royal; became commercial capital on destruction of Port Royal by fire, 1703; capital, 1872. Almost totally destroyed by earthquake, 1907.

Kingston-upon-Thames, England. Incorporated in the time of Henry II; but first extant charter dated 1200. Saxon kings crowned here. Castle captured by Henry III during Barons' War, 1264. Fairfax made it his headquarters during civil war, 1647. University at, 1992.

Kingston University, name and status, since 1992 of the former Kingston Polytechnic.

Kinshasa, Zaïre, formerly **Leopoldville.** Founded by H. M. Stanley, 1882. Name changed to K., 1966.

Kirghizstan became an autonomous republic, 1926, and a constituent member of the USSR, 1936. Its inhabitants, the Kara-Kirghiz and Kirghiz Kazaks, recognized Russian suzerainty in 1864 and 1810 respectively. Declared itself independent, 31 Aug. 1991: member of the *Commonwealth of Independent States. Fighting between Kirghiz and Uzbeks, 1991 caused over 500 deaths. Referendum, Jan. 1994, gave overwhelming endorsement to President Akayev's plan of faster moves towards capitalist economy. First democratic assembly elected, Feb. 1995.

Kiribati, Pacific, formerly the Gilbert Islands (*see* GILBERT AND ELLICE ISLANDS) took the name K. when it became a republic, 12 July 1979.

Kiritimati. *See* CHRISTMAS ISLAND.

Kit-Cat Club, founded *c.* 1703 in London as a literary society, grew into a club patronized by influential supporters of the Hanoverian succession. Dissolved, 1720.

Klaipeda, German **Memel,** founded 1253, by Livonian knights. Given to Lithuania under Treaty of Versailles, 1919. German agitation for return to Germany from 1933. Ceded to Germany, 22 March 1939: annexed by USSR. 1940. German-occupied 1941–4; thereafter part of Lithuanian SSR, since 1991 independent republic of Lithuania.

Kleve. *See* CLEVES.

Klondike gold rush began, 1896.

Klosterzeven, Convention of, concluded by the Duc de Richelieu (1696–1788) and the Duke of Cumberland (*d.* 1760), respectively for the French and Anglo-Hanoverians, 1757.

Knighthood, Orders of. The following are the principal historical orders (many not now extant), with the dates of their foundations:

Great Britain
Bannerets, said to have been in existence, 1282.
Bath, 1399; renewed, 1725.
British Empire, 1917.
Garter, *c.* 1346–48.
Indian Empire, 1877.
Royal Victorian Order, 1896.
St Michael and St George, 1818.
St Patrick, Ireland, 1783.
Star of India, 1861.
Thistle, 1687.

Foreign
Albert (Saxony), 1850. Albert the Bear (Anhalt), 1382 traditionally; revived, 1807 and 1836. Alcantara (Spain), 1156. Alexander Nevsky (Russia), 1725. Amaranta (Sweden),

1645. Andrew, St (Russia), 1698. Anna, St (Bavaria), 1784. Anne, St (Russia), 1735. Annunciation (Italy), 1362 traditionally. Anthony, St (Bavaria), 1382. Apostolic Order of St Stephen (Hungary), 1764. Aviz, St Benedict of (Portugal), 1147; became a spiritual order, 1162.

Bavarian Crown (Bavaria), 1808. Bear (Austria), 1213. Black Eagle (Prussia), 1701. Blood of Our Saviour (Austria), 1608.

Calatrava (Spain), 1158. Catherine, St (Russia), 1714. Charles III (Spain), 1771. Charles XIII (Sweden and Norway), 1811. Charles Frederick (Baden), 1807. Christ (Portugal), 1317. Crescent (Turkey), 1801. Crown (Rumania), 1881.

Dannebrog (Denmark), 1219 traditionally; revived, 1671. De la Scaura (Spain), 1320. Ducal House (Oldenburg), 1838.

Elephant (Denmark), 1693. Ernest (Saxe-Coburg), 1690.

Falcon (Iceland), 1921. Faustin, St (Haiti), 1849. Ferdinand, St (Spain), 1811. Fidelity (Denmark), 1732. Francis Joseph (Austria), 1849. Frederick (Württemberg), 1830.

George, St (Austria), 1470. George, St (Bavaria), 1729. George, St (Russia), 1769. George of Alfaura, St (Spain), 1201. Golden Fleece (Spain and Austria), 1429.

Henry the Lion (Brunswick), 1834. Hermingilde, St (Spain), 1814. Hubert, St (Bavaria), 1444.

Iron Cross (Prussia), 1813. Iron Crown (Austria), 1805. Iron Helmet (Hesse), 1814. Isabella, St (Portugal), 1801. Isabella the Catholic (Spain), 1815.

James, St (Portugal), 1310. James of Compostella, St (Spain), 1175. John, St (Prussia), 1812. John of Malta, St (Austria), 1043.

Legion of Honour (France), 1802. Leopold (Austria), 1808. Leopold (Belgium), 1832. Lily of Aragon (Spain), 1410. Louis (Bavaria), 1827. Louisa, St. (Prussia), 1814.

Maria Louisa (Spain), 1792. Maria Theresa (Austria), 1757. Maurice, St (Italy), 1434. Maximilian (Bavaria), 1853. Medjidie (Turkey), 1852. Mercy (Spain), 1261. Merit (Prussia), 1740. Michael, St (Bavaria), 1693. Military Merit (Russia), 1792.

Netherlands Lion, 1815. Nicani-Iftihar (Turkey), 1831.

Olaf, St (Norway), 1847. Our Lady of the Conception (Portugal), 1818. Our Lady of Mercy (Spain), 1218. Our Lady of Montesa (Spain), 1317.

Palatine Lion (Bavaria), 1768. Polar Star (Sweden), 1748.

Red Eagle (Prussia), 1734. Redeemer (Greece), 1833. Rosary of Toledo (Spain), 1212.

Saviour (Spain), 1118. Saviour of the World (Sweden), 1561. Savoy (Italy), 1815. Seraphim (Sweden and Norway), 1280. Sincerity (Prussia), 1705. Slaves to Virtue (Austria), 1662. Stanislaus (Russia), 1765. Star (Romania), 1877. Starry Cross (Austria), 1668. Swan (Prussia), 1449. Sword (Sweden and Norway), 1525.

Teutonic Order (Austria), 1191. Theresa (Bavaria), 1827. Tower and Sword (Portugal), 1459.

Ulrica (Sweden), 1734.

Vasa (Sweden and Norway), 1772. Vladimir (Russia), 1782.

White Eagle (Russia), 1713. White Falcon (Saxe-Weimar), 1732. William (Netherlands), 1815. Wing of St Michael (Portugal), 1172.

Knights of Labor. A labour association founded at Philadelphia, USA, 1869.

Knights Hospitallers. *See* MALTA, KNIGHTS OF.

Knights Templars. *See* TEMPLARS.

Knights' War, The, 1522–3, waged by the knights of Germany under Franz von Sickingen and Ulrich von Hutten, who espoused the Lutheran cause against the empire.

Knock, Ireland. Marian shrine dates from alleged apparition there of the Virgin Mary, 21 Aug. 1879.

Knossos. Ancient city of Crete, originating before 4000 BC; neolithic beds contain pottery, stone implements, and idols; copper utensils from *c.* 3000 BC. Its great palace (*c.* 2000 BC), whose complicated structure may have given rise to the legend of the Labyrinth was destroyed by fire *c.* 1800 BC, but immediately rebuilt. This second

Minoan civilization was somehow destroyed in 14thC BC. In 12th and 11thC BC Achaean culture superseded Minoan and K. ceased to be the principal city. Excavations by Sir Arthur Evans, 1900–8, and his account of them published, 1921–36. His account questioned by experts, 1961, and subsequently.

Kobe. Japan, capital of Hyogo prefecture. With Kyoto and Osaka, K. is part of the Keihanshin Industrial Zone, Japan's second largest urban/industrial conurbation. Kobe Steel founded, 1905. Grew from a fishing village after opening of Japan to foreigners in 1860s. Railway, 1874; city charter, 1892. After 1923 Tokyo and Yokohama earthquake, K. acquired much of their former trade. Severe earthquake devastated K., 16 Jan. 1995, killing over 5,000.

Koenigsberg. *See* KALININGRAD.

Koh-i-Noor Diamond. Owned by Nadir Shah, 1739. Given to Queen Victoria by E India Co., 1850.

Konstanz (French **Constance**). Germany, on the Rhine on its exit from Lake K. Bishopric since the 6thC. Free Imperial city, 1192. Council of K. (Constance) 1414–8. John Hus burnt here, 1415. Occupied by Austrians, 1548: besieged by Swedes, 1633. Became part of Baden, 1805. Bishopric suppressed, 1821.

Koran. Mohammed wrote none of the *suras* (chapters) himself. Some portion of his teaching would appear to have been written down as early as 615, and revised by him later; the remainder was collected after his death in 632 by Zaid ibn Thabit, his last secretary. (*See* ISLAM.) Translated into Latin, 1143.

Korea (Tai-Han: in Japanese, **Chosen).** A Chinese possession from *c.* 200 BC. Anti-Japanese riots, 1882. Treaties with Britain, 1883; Russia, 1888. Invaded by Japan, 1894. Independence proclaimed, 1895. Annexed by Japan, 1910. Abortive revolt suppressed with great cruelty, Mar.–July 1919. NW coast swept by tidal wave, 1923. Divided into Russian and American occupation zones, divided by the 38th parallel of latitude, Sept. 1945. Russian-American talks about the unification of the country broke down, May 1946. Elections were held in May 1948 in the American zone, and in July Syngman Rhee was elected first President of the Republic of K. which was proclaimed on 15 Aug. N of the 38th parallel a Korean People's Republic (KPR), claiming authority over the whole country, was proclaimed in Pyongyang, 12 Sept. 1948.

Korean War, 1950–3. Northern troops crossed the 38th parallel and invaded the southern republic of K., 25 June 1950. The Security Council of the UN demanded a N Korean withdrawal and asked member countries to enforce its demands, 27 June. First US troops landed in K., 30 June; MacArthur made Supreme Commander of the UN forces in K., 7 July. 1st Battalions of the Middlesex and Argyll and Sutherland regiments from Hong Kong were the first non-American UN forces to reach the theatre of war (29 Aug. 1950), where existing forces had been driven into a small perimeter round Pusan, out of which they broke, 15 Sept., when the US X Corps from Japanese bases landed at Inchon and captured Seoul, 28 Sept. 3rd Battalion Royal Australian Regiment joined British units in 27th Commonwealth Brigade, Oct. S Korean units crossed the 38th parallel, 1 Oct., and US troops, 9 Oct. By the end of Oct. UN troops had almost reached the Manchurian border, but on 26 Nov. Chinese troops, which had been in K. since about 25 Oct., counter-attacked at several points. UN retreat terminated at Imjin River, end Mar. 1951. Ridgway replaced MacArthur, 11 Apr. 1951. Truce talks started 10 July 1951; armistice eventually signed, 27 July 1953. Since then there have been intermittent negotiations between N and S Korea aiming at eventual unification, so far (1995) unsuccessful.

N Korea since 1953. N Korea was dominated from 1953–94 by Kim Il-Sung, premier, 1948–72, and then president (re-elected for fifth time, 1990). His son Kim Chong Il succeeded him, 1994. Slight easing in repression in 1990s; admitted to UN,

1991. Signed non-aggression accord with S Korea, Dec. 1991 and an agreement on de-nuclearization of Korean peninsula, Feb. 1992, but from 1993 threatened to abandon this. UN pressed N Korea to open nuclear programme to UN inspection, 1993 and by June 1994 situation critical as USA, Japan and S Korea sought sanctions against N Korea which was threatening to leave the International Atomic Agency. Situation eased when in Oct. 1994, following intervention by former US President Carter, accommodation was reached on major outstanding nuclear issues. In June 1995 N K. agreed to end its nuclear weapons programme. N K. subsequently threatened to terminate the 1953 armistice agreement.

S Korea since 1953. Regime operated a free market but remained basically politically authoritarian for many years. Coups and student unrest in 1961 and 1980, and further anti-government demonstrations in 1991 led to political reforms, and the first 'democratic' elections for 30 years, held Dec. 1992, resulted in election of Kim Young-Sam, a civilian, who called immediately for Korean unification. Economically S Korea became an important world trading power from the 1960s, often competing successfully with the Japanese. The country underwent rapid modernization on Western lines following the end of the Korean War. Severance from N Korea remained total, 1995. For relations with N Korea, *see* preceding section.

Kosovo or **Kossovo,** region of S Serbia with predominantly Albanian population. Autonomous region 1974–90: formally annexed to Serbia, Sept. 1990. Kosovo assembly referendum, 1991 (not recognized by Serbia) voted overwhelmingly for independence but (1995) K. remains part of Serbia, and human rights abuses by Serbia against Albanian population, there alleged, 1993 onwards.

Kotor (Italian **Cattaro**), a small Adriatic republic in the Middle Ages, absorbed by Venice, 1420. Ceded to Austria, 1814. Occupied by Italians, Nov. 1918, but ceded to Yugoslavia, 1919. Became part of Montenegro, 1945. Had severe earthquakes, 1563 and 1667.

Kowloon. China. The peninsula ceded to Britain, 1861, by the terms of the Convention of Peking, 1860. Further adjacent area leased to Britain for 99 years by China, 1898. K. forms part of the Crown Colony of *Hong Kong.

Krajina, area on Croatian-Bosnian border, with majority Serb population. It declared itself an autonomous Serbian province, 1991, and fierce fighting took place there between Croats and Serbs, 1991–2. Taken by the Serbs, 1992, it was recaptured and largely integrated into *Croatia, Aug. 1995, when Serb population expelled.

Krakatoa. Volcano in E Indies, which had a celebrated eruption in 1883.

Krakow. *See* CRACOW.

Kremlin (Russian **Kreml'**). A citadel, especially that of Moscow, which once (in the early 15thC) comprised the whole area of the city. It contains within fortified walls the cathedral of Uspensky (1474) and other contemporary churches and palaces. Has been the seat of government for all Russia, except for the period 1703–1917. Closed to the public during Stalin's regime, but gradually reopened from 1955.

Kriegspiel (From German for war-game). Marshal Keith (1693–1788), a Scottish officer in the Prussian employ, invented a form of K., but its present form was evolved by von Reisswitz, 1824.

Kristallnacht ('night of crystal'), 9–10 Nov. 1938 marked a night of anti-Jewish attacks throughout Germany and Austria. It was allegedly caused by the shooting in Paris of a German diplomat by a Polish Jew on 7 Nov. Nearly 100 Jews died: businesses were destroyed and thousands arrested. Escalation of anti-Jewish measures followed.

Kronstadt, Russia. Founded by Peter the Great, 1703; K. Canal, 1884.

Kuibishev. *See* SAMARA.

Ku Klux Klan. A secret society said to have been founded in Tennessee in 1865. It gradually came to have far-reaching powers, but was disbanded, Mar. 1869, and had ceased to exist by 1871. The second organization of this name was started by W. J. Simmons in 1915, at a meeting near Atlanta, Georgia. Like its predecessor, it opposed negroes and stood for white Protestant domination in politics. It reached the height of its power in 1928, and was revived again after World War II by Dr Samuel Green (1945). It had a temporary revival, 1960–5, and was the subject of a Senate investigation, 1965–6. Since then there have been localized and limited revivals of minor significance.

'Kulturkampf'. Name given to the conflict between Bismarck and the Roman Catholic Church in Germany, 1871–87.

Kuomintang. Chinese radical republican party formed, Aug. 1912, to carry out political programme of Sun Yat-sen, who was its chairman till his death in 1925. By 1928 it was dominated by Chiang Kai-shek, who by defeating Chang Tso-lin at Peking made it the only party in *China, apart from the Communists, who originally formed part of the K., but were expelled in 1927. 1995: still controlled the government in *Taiwan but with reduced support.

Kurds. Since 1920 divided between Turkey, Iraq and Iran. Turkish K. rebelled following abolition of the caliphate, 1925. Iraqi K. have attempted to assert their independence, 1922–3, 1944–5, 1960–2, 1934–89 and, notably, 1991, when they rose against Saddam Hussein at the end of the *Gulf War. Between 1984–9 thousands of K. said to have been killed by Iraqi chemical weapons: further thousands *d.* as result of 1991 uprising, though limited 'safe havens' for K. established in N Iraq under UN auspices. K. in Iran have also come into conflict with the government, and in Turkey K. are subject to discrimination and their political parties outlawed. Kurdish 'free state' in N Iraq, in economic chaos, 1995. Turkey attacks Kurds in N Iraq, July 1995.

Kurile Islands, formerly Japanese territory, awarded to Russia in 1945 as the price of her participation in the war against Japan, under the terms of the *Yalta agreement.

Kursk, town and region in Russia. Scene of biggest tank battle of World War II, 5 July–23 Aug. 1943. Germans were defeated. Town devastated but later rebuilt. Nuclear power station, 1979. Area of opencast iron ore mining since 1950s.

Kutchuk-Kainardji, Treaty of, between Catherine II of Russia and the Sultan Abdul Hamid I, signed, 1774. By this treaty Turkey gave up the Crimea, Azov and Taganrog.

Kuwait, Persian Gulf. Turkish attempt to occupy prevented by British, 1897. Under British protection, 1899. Britain recognized the emir of K. as an independent ruler, under British protection, 1914. Oil developed from 1934. Britain recognized complete independence of K., 19 June 1961. *Iraq claimed K., 25 June 1961. British troops landed to protect her, 2 July, but had all been withdrawn by 10 Oct. A constitutional monarchy was instituted, Dec. 1961, but political power remains in the hands of the ruling family and the large non-Kuwaiti section of the population cannot vote. 1988: Kuwaiti airliner hijacked by Iranian extremists. Iraq invaded K., 2 Aug. 1990 and declared K. a part of Iraq. The *Gulf War resulted, and the Emir of K. fled to Saudi Arabia. K. was liberated 27 Feb. 1991 and the Emir subsequently returned. Since then there has been limited political reform, but criticism of ill treatment of alleged collaborators. The Iraqi invasion seriously damaged the Kuwaiti economy and caused ecological disasters, but by 1993 the bulk of the damage repaired. Following new Iraqi action, a limited number of US troops were sent to guard the K.–Iraq border, Jan. 1993. In Oct. 1994 Iraq moved large numbers of troops towards K. USA and Britain sent reinforcements to K., and Iraq subsequently withdrew troops and in Nov., under Russian pressure, Iraq recognized Kuwaiti sovereignty and frontiers.

Kwangchow. *See* CANTON.

Kyoto, founded AD 793, was the capital of the Japanese Empire until 1868.

Kyshim Disaster. *See* CHELYABINSK-65

Labor Party of Australia, founded, 1891; first came to power, 1909; but lost power during World War I. Inter-war years period of strong governments under Lyons. Split by Communist issue during 1950s, ensuring long period out of office. Whitlam's L. government fell as a result of constitutional crisis, 1975. L.P. regained power under Hawke, 1983 and retained it under Keating, leader from 1991; party now pro-republican and anti-nuclear.

Labour Day, in Europe, usually 1 May, perhaps because on that date in 1889 the Second International first proposed a workers' festival for all countries. In Great Britain the first Monday in May has been a Bank Holiday dedicated to labour since 1978; this arrangement confirmed, 1993, except that in 1995 the holiday was on second Monday, May 8, to commemorate 50th anniversary of end of World War II. L.D. in the USA is the first Monday in Sept., and was federally adopted in 1894. Canada also celebrates L.D. on the first Monday in Sept.; in New Zealand it is observed on the third Monday in Oct.

Labour Exchanges. Established by Robert Owen in England, 1832–4. Previously established at Cincinnati by Josiah Warren. New Act for L.E., 1909. Name subsequently changed to *Employment Exchanges, now Job Centres.

Labour Party of Great Britain. Arose out of the L. Representation Committee, appointed by representatives of the *ILP, the Fabian Society and the Trades Union Congress, 27 Feb. 1900. It took the name L.P.,

Jan. 1906. In office, 22 Jan.–4 Nov. 1924, and 8 June 1929–24 Aug. 1931. ILP disaffiliated itself from, 30 July 1932. First obtained control of London County Council, 8 Mar. 1934. Leaders entered National Government, 10 May 1940. Victorious at General Election, 5 July 1945. Held office, 27 July 1945–Oct. 1951. Won narrow victory at General Election, Oct. 1964; overwhelming victory at General Election, Mar. 1966; but defeated at General Election, June 1970. Returned to power, 1974, but defeated by the Conservatives in 1979, 1983, 1987 and 1992. Leader John Smith got approval to abolish union block-vote for selection of Labour parliamentary candidates, Sept. 1993. Smith *d.* suddenly, May, 1994; Tony Blair succeeded, July. Succeeds in getting Clause 4 (pro-nationalization) removed from Labour constitution, Apr. 1995 and followed this up by promoting 'New Labour' and 'social democratic' policies.

Labour Party of New Zealand, first returned members to Parliament, 1890: first held office, 1935, retaining it until after World War II. Lost office, 1949: in power, 1954–60, 1972–5 and 1984–90.

Labourers, Statutes of, were all passed in the reign of Edward III, the result of disturbed social conditions which followed the Black Death of 1348. The most important were those of 1349 and 1351; all attempted to fix the agricultural wage at the level of 1347.

Labrador. Visited by Norsemen (who called it Helluland) in the 10th or 11thC; explored by Frobisher, 1576; rediscovered by Hudson, 1610; the peninsula ceded to Britain by France in 1763. The part that drains into Hudson Bay belonged to the Hudson's Bay Co. Remainder given to the province of Quebec by Act of 1774. Newfoundland recovered its strip by Act of 1809. Part of this strip, from Ance Sablon to 52° N, restored to Quebec (Lower Canada), 1825. The Hudson's Bay Co.'s part surrendered to Canada, 1869. Newfoundland, under letters patent of 28 Mar. 1874, exercised jurisdiction along Atlantic coast. The remainder, under order in council of

18 Dec. 1897, was constituted Ungava, an unorganized territory of Canada, annexed to Quebec, 1912. In 1927 the Privy Council decided that Newfoundland was entitled to all that part that drained into the Atlantic. When Newfoundland acceded to the Dominion of Canada, 1949, all L. was brought into the confederation.

Labuan. Ceded to Britain by Sultan of Brunei, 1846: part of N Borneo, 1946; part of *Sabah since 1963.

Laccadive Islands. *See* LAKSHADWEEP.

lacrosse, game of N American Indian origin. 17thC French settlers to Canada saw the Indians playing a form of L. called *baggataway*. First white L. match in Montreal, 1844. Spread to US in 1860s, thence to the UK. Women played L. from early 20thC. Box L. (indoor L.) introduced by Canada, 1930. Men's world championships since 1967; women's since 1969.

Lado Enclave, surrounding the town of L. on the White Nile, was Egyptian from 1878, when Gen. Gordon founded it, to 1885, when it passed to the then Belgian Congo. In 1909 it became part of the Anglo-Egyptian Sudan (now the Sudanese Republic); part transferred to N Uganda in 1914.

Ladrones. *See* MARIANA ISLANDS.

Ladysmith, S Africa. Founded, 1851. Relieved by Sir R. Buller after siege of 121 days during S African War, 28 Feb. 1900.

Lagos, *Nigeria. District ceded from native king, 1861. Created a separate government, 1863; part of British W African Settlements from 1866; made a colony, 1886; part of S Nigeria, 1906. Capital of both colony and protectorate of all Nigeria, 1 Jan. 1914, and of the independent dominion 1960–82.

Lahore, Pakistan. Mogul capital in 16th and 17thC. British Council of Regency established at, 1846. Became capital of Punjab, 1849. Earthquake, 1905.

Laibach. *See* LJUBLJANA.

laissez-faire, laissez-aller, or, more correctly, *laisser-passer*, a phrase denoting a government policy of non-interference in economic matters. Its origin is usually attributed to Legendre, who, *c.* 1680, in an interview with Colbert regarding government interference with commerce, stated: '*Laissez-faire, laissez-aller.*'

Lakshadweep, group of coral islands, formerly known as the **Laccadive Islands**. Discovered by Vasco de Gama, 1499; acquired by Britain, 1877. Indian since 1947: a Union Territory of India, 1956. Name changed to L., 1973.

Lambeth Articles. Drawn up by Archbishop Whitgift, 1595. They embraced Calvinism and were rejected at Hampton Court Conference, 1604.

Lambeth Bridge, built, 1862; demolished, 1929; new bridge opened, 1932.

Lambeth Conferences, of bishops of the Anglican communion from all over the world, originated in a letter from Bishop Hopkins of Vermont in 1851, followed by a request from the Church in Canada, 1865. The following conferences have been held, with their presidents: numbers of bishops attending have increased at each conference, from 76 in 1867 to some 500 in 1968.

1. 1867 – Archbishop Longley
2. 1878 – Archbishop Tait
3. 1888 – Archbishop Benson
4. 1897 – Archbishop Temple
5. 1908 – Archbishop Davidson
6. 1920 – Archbishop Davidson
7. 1930 – Archbishop Lang
8. 1948 – Archbishop Fisher
9. 1958 – Archbishop Fisher
10. 1968 – Archbishop Ramsey
11. 1978 – Archbishop Coggan
12. 1988 – Archbishop Runcie.

Lambeth Palace (London), residence of the Archbishops of Canterbury since 1197, consists now largely of buildings erected, 1430–90, though the chapel, was built *c.* 1230. Sacked in Wat Tyler's rising, 1381.

Lambeth Walk, street in L. of no great antiquity celebrated in street songs current in the 19thC. It inspired a song-and-dance number in the musical comedy 'Me and My Girl', 1937 (revived, 1992), and the dance became popular, 1938.

Lambeth ware. Pottery was first made in L. *c.* 1630, and figures of artificial stone were modelled at Goade's works from 1760. Doulton pottery was first produced in the Vauxhall Walk, L., by the firm of that name, in 1815.

Lampeter, Wales. St David's College for training priests of the Church in Wales was founded, 1822, there, but in 1971 it became part of the University of Wales and its name was changed to St David's University College.

Lancashire Polytechnic. *See* CENTRAL LANCASHIRE UNIVERSITY.

Lancaster, England. Castle said to have been built by Agricola, AD 124; present structure begun by Roger de Poictou *c.* 1094; restored by John of Gaunt in the 14thC; burnt by Scots, 1322 and 1389. L. received its first charter, 1193. 'Lancashire witches' tried here, 1612. Given the title and dignity of a city, 1937. University established, 1964.

Lancaster, Duchy of. Settled on John of Gaunt and his heirs by royal charter, 1362. Annexed to the crown by Edward IV, 1461. The court of the county was abolished by the Judicature Act of 1873.

lancers did not exist in Europe until the 4thC AD, when the Roman Army adopted the stirrup without the use of which no horseman can handle a lance. The lance continued to be the decisive cavalry weapon until about 1600, when the dragoon's pistol began to replace it. Thereafter only the Cossacks and Poles among European cavalry retained the lance, but such was the success of the latter in the French employ under Napoleon (1807–15) that first French (1811) and later other cavalry units readopted the lance (British in 1816). The last British lancer unit to use the weapon in action was probably the 21st L. against the Mohmand rebels in World War I; in Sept. 1918 the 2nd Indian L. used it on the Turks at Lejjun, Palestine. Its use was abolished in the British Army in 1927.

lancers, square dance of five figures, a form of *quadrille invented in Paris, 1836; brought to London, 1850.

Land League. Founded in Ireland by Michael Davitt, 1879, for the purchase of land. Act of Parliament against, 1881.

Land Registry established by Act of 1862; re-formed by L. Transfer Act, 1875, L. Transfer Act, 1897, and L. Registration Act, 1925. Records open to public inspection from Dec. 1990.

Landsknechte, term used for German dismounted mercenaries employed in France (Lansquenets), Italy, and occasionally England in the 16thC. Word first applied to units raised by Emperor Maximilian in (S) Germany, 1492.

land taxes, payable in the UK under an Act of 1798: four new taxes, introduced in 1910, were abolished in 1920.

Lands Tribunal, set up under the Lands Tribunal Act, 1949: now regulated by the Lands Tribunal Rules, 1975 and amendments, 1977.

Languedoc, France. E L. annexed to French crown, 1229. W L. (county of Toulouse), 1271. Estates first convoked, 1302. Civil war in L., 1561–98. Protestant rebellion, 1620–2. Replaced by the eight *départements* of Haute-Loire, Lozère, Ardèche, Aude, Tarn, Hérault, Gard and Haute-Garonne, 1791.

Laocoön, The. Famous ancient sculpture discovered at Rome, 1506, and placed in the Vatican by Julius II. Napoleon brought it to Paris, 1796. Restored, 1814. Fragments of a similar group found in a cave at Sperlonga, 1957.

Laos, independent state in SE Asia. French protectorate, 1893; independent sovereign state within the French Union,

1949. Invaded by Vietminh forces, 1953, aided by Pathet-Lao (pro-Communist Laotian group). Agreement for cessation of hostilities reached at Geneva, 1954; but war between royalists and Pathet-Lao continued till 1973. A coalition government of both sides formed, 1974, but in 1975 king abdicated and People's Democratic Republic of L. proclaimed.

La Paz, Bolivia. Founded, 1548. Bishopric established, 1605. Rose against Spaniards, 1809. Became de facto capital of Bolivia, 1898.

La Plata, Argentine. Founded, 1882.

Lascaux Caves, in France, underground gallery of palaeolithic art (c. 25,000 BC), first entered in modern times, 1940. Deterioration caused by public opening of caves caused closure, 1963. Facsimile opened, 1983.

laser, light-amplifying device, used in modern medicine, industry, defence, etc. Two US physicists, Schawlow and Townes, proposed L. idea in 1958. Similar ideas developing at same time in Russia. First L. (a ruby L.) built by Maiman of the USA, 1960. Trials started in UK for L. treatment of coronary disease, 1993.

Las Vegas, Nevada. USA, founded 1855, known world-wide as a gambling centre.

La Tène, Celtic settlement at the N end of the lake of Neuchâtel, in Switzerland. It was inhabited from c. 500 to 100 BC, first discovered in 1858, and excavated after 1881. The period of prehistory named after it by archaeologists is that following the Hallstadt culture, and is alternatively called the Later Iron Age; it extends from c. 550 to 15 BC.

Lateran, St John (Rome). Palace and church rebuilt in 12thC. Church entirely rebuilt by Sixtus V, 1586. Damaged in terrorist bombing, 1993.

Lateran Treaty, 11 Feb. 1929. *See* PAPACY.

Latin American Integration Association, took over functions of the Latin American Free Trade Association (1960) on 1 Jan 1981. In 1994 it had 11 members and HQ in Montevideo, Uruguay. It aims to promote free trade and integration between member states.

Latin literature, Classical. Principal authors of whom works or fragments survive:

Andronicus, Livius, *fl.* 240 BC, epic and dramatic poet.

Bassus, Caesius, *fl.* AD 60, lyric poet.

Caecilius Statius, *d.c.* 168 BC, comic poet.

Caesar, C. Julius, 102–44 BC, historian.

Calpurnius Sienlus, T., 1stC AD, pastoral poet.

Cato, M. Porcius, 232–147 BC, historian and writer on agriculture.

Cato, P. Valerius, BC, 1stC poet and grammarian.

Catullus, C. Valerius, 84–c. 54 BC, poet.

Catulus, Q. Lutatius, *d.* 87 BC, orator and poet.

Cicero, M. Tullius, 106–43 BC, orator, philosopher, etc.

Cinna, C. Helvius, *d.* 44 BC, poet.

Commodianus, *fl. c.* AD 250, poet.

Cornificius, *fl. c.* 85 BC, rhetorician.

Curtius Rufus, Q., *fl.* AD 41–54, rhetorician.

Ennius, Q., 239–170 BC, epic poet.

Eumenius, *c.* AD 260–c. 312, panegyrist.

Fabius Pictor, Q., *b. c.* 254 BC, historian.

Festus, S. Pompeius, 2ndC AD, grammarian.

Flaccus, L. Valerius, *fl.* AD 70, epic poet.

Florus, 2ndC AD historian.

Fronto, M. Cornelius, *c.* AD 100–70, grammarian and rhetorician.

Gellius, Aulus, *c.* AD 123–65, miscellaneous writer and grammarian.

Graltius, 1stC AD, didactic poet.

Horace (Q. Horatius Flaccus), 65–8 BC, poet.

Justinus, 2ndC AD, historian.

Juvenal (D. Junius Juvenalis), *c.* AD 50–c. 130, satirist.

Livy (T. Livius), 59 BC–AD 17, historian.

Lucan (M. Annaeus Lucanus), AD 39–65, epic poet.

Lucilius, Gaius, *c.* 180–c. 102 BC, satirist.

Lucretius Carus, *c.* 99–55 BC, philosopher and poet.

Manilius, 1stC AD, astronomer and poet.

Martial (M. Valerius Martialis), c. AD 40–c. 104, poet.

Mela, Pomponius, 1stC BC, geographer.

Nepos, Cornelius, 1stC BC, historian.

Ovid (P. Ovidius Naso), 43 BC–AD 17, poet.

Paterculus, C. Velleius, 19 BC–c. AD 40, historian.

Persius Flaccus, A., AD 34–62, satirist.

Petronius, d. AD 66, romance writer and satirist.

Phaedrus, b. c. 30 BC, fabulist.

Plautus, T. Maccius, c. 254–184 BC, comic poet.

Pliny the Elder (C. Plinius Secundus), AD 23–79, polymath.

Pliny the Younger (C. Plinius Caecilius Secundus), AD 61–c. 113, panegyrist and letter-writer.

Propertius, S. Aurelius, c. 50–c. 16 BC, elegiac poet.

Publilius Syrus, 1stC BC, mimeographer.

Quadrigarius, fl. 100–78 BC, historian.

Quintilian (M. Fabius Quintilianus), b. c. AD 40, rhetorician and critic.

Sallust (C. Sallustius Crispus), 86–34 BC historian.

Seneca, L. Annaeus, c. 4 BC–AD 65, Stoic philosopher.

Seneca, M. Annaeus, c. 55 BC–c. AD 41, rhetorician.

Silius Italicus, Tib. Catius Asconius, c. AD 25–c. 101, epic poet.

Statius, P. Papinius, c. AD 61–96, poet.

Suetonius Tranquillus, C., fl. AD 100, historian.

Tacitus, P. Cornelius, c. AD 55–c. 120, historian.

Terence (P. Terentius Afer), c. 195–159 BC, comic poet.

Tibullus, Albius, c. 54–19 BC, elegiac poet.

Valerius Maximus, 1stC AD, historian.

Varro, M. Terentius, 116–27 BC, antiquary and writer on agriculture.

Virgil (P. Vergilius Maro), 70–19 BC, poet.

Latin literature: Chief post-classical authors:

Abélard, Pierre (French), 1079–1142, philosopher, theologian and poet.

Adam of Bremen (German), d. c. 1076, historian.

Adam of St Victor (French), 1130–80, hymn-writer.

Adamnan, St (Irish), 642–704, biographer and topographical writer.

Aeneas Sylvius. See PICCOLOMINI.

Albertus Magnus, Albert of Cologne, or Albrecht von Böllstadt (German), 1193–1280, scientific writer, philosopher and theologian.

Alcuin (Northumbrian), 735–804, educational writer and theologian.

Aldhelm, St (Wessex), c. 640–709, poet and ecclesiastical writer.

Anselm, St (Italian), 1033–1109, philosopher and theologian.

Ascham, Roger (English), 1515–68, educational writer.

Asser (Welsh), d. c. 910, biographer.

Bacon, Roger (English), 1214–92, philosopher.

Bede, the Venerable (Northumbrian), c. 673–735, historian.

Bernard of Clairvaux, St (French), 1090–1158, poet, theologian and mystical writer.

Boccaccio, Giovanni (Italian), 1313–75, poet.

Bourne, Vincent (English), 1695–1747, poet.

Buchanan, George (Scottish), 1506–82, historian.

Calvin, John (French), 1509–64, religious reformer.

Cheke, Sir John (English), 1514–57, classical scholar.

Coffin, Charles (English), 1676–1749, poet.

Columba, St (Irish), d. 597, poet.

Corippus, Flavius Cresconius (African), fl. 550–80, poet.

Dante Alighieri (Italian), 1265–1321, poet and political writer.

Duns Scotus, Johannes, or John the Scot (probably English), d. 1308, philosopher and theologian.

Einhard (German), c. 770–840, historian.

Ekkehard of St Gall (German), d. 973, poet.

Erasmus Desiderius (Dutch), 1466–1536, humanist and critic.

Estienne, Charles, or Stephanus Carolus (French), 1504–64, anatomist.

Florence of Worcester (English), d. 1118, chronicler.

Fortunatis, Verantius (Italian), *fl.* 569, poet.

Fulbert of Chartres (French), *d.* 1029, hymn and didactic writer.

Geoffrey (Norman Welsh) of Monmouth, or Geoffrey Arthur, *c.* 1100–54, chronicler.

Geoffrey of Vinsauf (Norman), *fl.* 1200, poet.

Gerard, John (English), 1564–1637, autobiographer.

Gerbert (Pope Sylvester II French), 999–1003, philosopher, theologian and mathematician.

Gildas, St (British), *c.* 516–70, moralist.

Giraldus Cambrensis, or Gerald de Barri (Norman-Welsh), *c.* 1147–1220, historian and topographical writer.

Godescalc of Orbais (Frankish), *fl.* 730, hagiographer.

Gregory I, Pope St (Roman), *d.* 604, theologian and spiritual writer.

Gregory of Tours, St (Frankish), *d.* 594, historian.

Grève, Philippe (French), *d.* 1236, hymnwriter.

Grossetête, Robert (English), *c.* 1175–1253, theologian and scholar.

Guido delle Colonne (Sicilian), 13thC, novelist.

Heiric of Auxerre (French), *c.* 834–*c.* 881, poet.

Henry of Huntingdon (English), 1080–*c.* 1150, historian.

Hildebert (French), *d.* 1134, poet.

Hrabanus Maurus (German), 784–856, theologian and pedagogic writer.

Hroswitha (German), *d. c.* 1000, poetess and playwright.

Isidore of Seville, St (Spanish), *c.* 560–636, encyclopaedist.

John of Salisbury (English), *c.* 1115–80, philosopher and historian.

Johnson, later Cory, William (English), 1823–92, poet.

Jónsson, Arngrimr (Icelander), 1568–1648, historian.

Jónsson, Finnur (Icelander), 1704–89, ecclesiastical historian.

Jordanes (Romano-Gothic), *fl. c.* 550, historian.

Langton, Stephen (English), *d.* 1228, scriptural writer.

Liutprand (Lombard), *c.* 922–73, historian.

Luther, Martin (German), 1483–1546, religious reformer.

Magnusson, Arne (Icelander), 1633–1730, historian.

Map, Walter (English), *c.* 1140–*c.* 1210, poet and anecdotal writer.

Martin of Braga, St (Spanish), *d.* 580, moralist.

Matthew of Vendôme (French), 11th–12thC, poet.

Melanchthon (Philipp Schwarzerd) (German), 1497–1560, theologian and philologist.

Nennius (Welsh), *fl.* 840, chronicler.

Newton, Sir Isaac (English), philosopher and scientist, 1642–1727.

Notker Balbulus (German), 840–912, poet and historian.

Olaus Magnus or Olaf Stora (Swedish), 1490–1558, historian.

Owen, John (English), *d.* 1622, poet.

Paulus Diaconus (Lombard), *d. c.* 799, historian.

Pecham, John (English), *c.* 1240–92, poet, biographer and letter-writer.

Peter Damian, St (Italian), 1007–72, moralist.

Petrarca (Petrarch), Francesco (Italian), 1304–74, poet and moralist.

Piccolomini, Aeneas Sylvius (Italian), *d.* 1464, humanist and critic. He became Pope Pius II.

Poggio Bracciolini, Giovanni Francesco (Italian), 1380–1459, historian.

Poliziano, Angelo (Politian) (Italian), 1454–94, poet.

Pontano, Giovanni (Italian), 1426–1503, poet.

Prudentius, Aurelius Clemens (Spanish), 348–*c.* 405, poet.

Reuchlin, Johann (German), 1455–1522, critic and grammarian.

Richard of Bury (English), 1286–1345, bibliophile.

Sannazaro, Jacopo (Italian), 1458–1530, poet.

Santeul, Claude de (French), 1628–84, poet.

Santeul, Jean de (French), 1630–97, poet.

Saxo Grammaticus (Danish), *fl.* 1140–1206, historian.

Scaliger, Jules-César (French), 1484–1558, philologist, critic and classical scholar.

Scaliger, Joseph Justus (French), 1540–1609, classical scholar.

Simeon of Durham (English), *fl.* 1130, historian.

Spagnoli, Giovanni Battista (Italian), 1448–1516, poet.

Theodulf (Spanish), *d.* 821, poet and theologian.

Thomas Aquinas, St (Italian), 1226–74, philosopher, theologian and poet.

Thomas of Celano (Italian), *d. c.* 1251, poet.

Torfaeus (Thormodur Torfason), (Icelander), 1636–1719, historiographer.

Verecundus (African), *d.* 552, ecclesiastical writer.

Vergil, Polydore (Italian), *c.* 1470–*c.* 1555, miscellaneous writer.

Vincent of Beauvais (French), *d.* 1264, encyclopaedist.

Walafrid 'Strabo' (German), 807–49, poet and theologian.

William of Malmesbury (English), *d.* 1143?, historian.

Wipo (French), 11th–12thC, historian.

Wycliffe, John (English), 1324–84, religious writer.

Latitudinarians. A school of theologians in England which grew up after 1688. They were the forerunners of the 19thC Broad Church Party.

Latvia. Consisted in the Middle Ages of three provinces: Courland or Kurland, Livonia or Livland, and Zemgale or Semigallia; came under the domination of the Teutonic Order and of (German) prince-bishops, 1158. Under Polish rule from 1562 to 1795, except for Livonia, which was ruled by the Swedes from 1629 to 1721. From 1795 to 1918 L. was one of the Baltic provinces of Russia. Independent republic proclaimed, 18 Nov. 1918. Russian troops entered L., 17 June 1939. Latvian SSR admitted to Soviet Union, Aug. 1940. German occupation of L. complete, July 1941. Reconquered by the Soviet Union, 1944–5. Nationalist agitation increased from 1988; declared unilateral independence from the

USSR, 4 May 1990. Clashes with Soviet troops, 1990–1. Independence formally declared, 21 Aug. 1991, agreed by Russia, 10 Sept. 1991. Subsequent transfer to free-market economy. Elections, 1993, won by right-wing: virtual disenfranchisement of Russian minority in L. Last Russian troops left, 1994.

laureate, poet. The first poet laureate proper was appointed by Queen Elizabeth in 1591. The following is a list of the poets laureate:

Edmund Spenser 1591–99
Samuel Daniel 1599–1619
Ben Jonson 1619–37
Vacant from 1637–60
Sir William Davenant 1660–68
John Dryden 1670–89
Thomas Shadwell 1689–92
Nahum Tate 1692–1715
Nicholas Rowe 1715–18
Laurence Eusden 1718–30
Colley Cibber 1730–57
William Whitehead 1757–85
Thomas Warton 1785–90
Henry James Pye 1790–1813
Robert Southey 1813–43
William Wordsworth 1843–50
Alfred Tennyson 1850–92
Alfred Austin 1896–1913
Robert Bridges 1913–30
John Masefield 1930–67
Cecil Day Lewis 1968–72
Sir John Betjeman 1972–84
Ted Hughes 1984-

Lausanne Conference, of Britain, France, Italy, Belgium and Germany, 1932, ended war debts (with one exception as to Germany) as between those parties, but USA would not assent.

Law Commission. Name of two statutory bodies set up in 1965 to consider ongoing proposals for legal reforms. One sits for England and Wales, and one for Scotland.

League of Nations. Covenant of the L. accepted by Allies, 28 Apr. 1919; subscribed by the signatories of the Treaty of

Versailles, 28 June 1919; came into force, 1 Jan. 1920. President Wilson's action in committing USA to participation repudiated in the presidential election of 1920. League's ineffectiveness shown by events of Italo-Ethiopian war, 1935–6, and Spanish civil war, 1936–9. Final meeting, 8 Apr. 1946. Existence formally terminated, 31 Aug. 1947.

League, The, in full the Holy Catholic L., was organized by the Duc de Guise (1550–88) in 1576 to prevent the accession of Henry of Navarre (Henri IV), the Protestant claimant to the throne of France.

Leasehold Act. Popular name for the Housing and Urban Development Act, 1993, which proposed granting leaseholders of flats the freedom to buy the freehold, and became law, 1 Nov.

Lease-Lend. Bill introduced into both Houses of US Congress, 10 Jan. 1941. Passed by Senate, 9 Mar.; by Representatives, and signed by President, 11 Mar. 1941. L.-L. officially terminated, 20 Aug. 1945.

Lebanon. Under predominantly Maronite influence from *c.* 650 AD; French influence, 1860–1914. Made a state separate from Syria, under French mandate, 1920. Occupied by British and Free French forces, 1941. Independent republic proclaimed at Beirut, 26 Nov. 1941, and French transferred administrative power to L. Government, with effect 1 Jan. 1944. Muslim revolt, May 1958, and L. asked for US aid. US troops in L., July–Oct. 1958: internal peace restored. L. aloof from Arab-Israeli dispute until early 1970s when L. became the main PLO base (*see* PALESTINE LIBERATION ORGANIZATION). L. sank rapidly into civil war. Israeli troops invaded L., 1978, with Lebanese Christian support. Further Israeli invasion, 1982, devastation of Beirut and massacre of Palestinians. Assassination of Christian President Gemayel, Sept. 1982. Partial Israeli withdrawal, 1983, led to increased Syrian domination of Palestinian forces in L. despite presence of UN peacekeeping force, 1983–4. PLO pro-Arafat forces defeated by extremists, Nov. 1983 and left L. UN force withdrawn, 1984. Renewed conflict from 1985 and L. in state of increasing anarchy with Western hostages seized by armed factions. Relatively stable government re-established with Syrian backing, Dec. 1990; treaty of brotherhood with Syria, May 1991. Remaining Western hostages released during 1991. Exodus of many Christians since 1991–2. Economy of L. ruined by civil war: remains weak (1995) with militant groups such as *Hezbollah based in L. and Israel retaining a 'buffer zone' in the S of the country.

Leeds, England. Kirkstall Abbey built at, 1147. Captured by parliamentary forces under Gen. Fairfax, 1643; incorporated, 1626, and again in 1673. Centre of wool-trade from 17thC to *c.* 1800; thereafter tailoring centre. River Aire joined to Calder-Liverpool Canal, 1816. College founded 1874; granted university status, 1904. Leeds Metropolitan University (1992) was formerly Leeds Polytechnic. Planned to move Royal Armoury from Tower of London to L., 1996. Henry Moore Gallery opened, 1993.

Leeward Islands Federation lasted 1871–1956, when its component members separated.

legal aid, series of Acts governing free or assisted L. A. in the UK passed from 1949 onwards. From 1980 Lord Chancellor had responsibility for all types of financial assistance in legal proceedings. Proposals to limit extent of L.A. put forward in the 1990s, and by 1994 some restrictions in place. Proposals to curb L.A. further, Dec. 1994.

Leghorn (Italian **Livorno**), first mentioned, 891, was under Pisa in the 14thC, but *c.* 1400 passed to France, and was sold to the Genoese, 1407. They sold it to the Florentines, 1421, whose Medici princes extended and fortified the port, 1550, and opened it to ships of all nations, 1606. It was a free port from 1691 to 1867. Severe earthquake in 1741. L. was heavily bombed and shelled by the invading US forces, July 1944.

Legion of Honour created by Napoleon I, 1802.

Legionnaire's disease. so-called as first identified after outbreak at an American Legion convention in Philadelphia in 1976, since when outbreaks have been identified at various UK locations.

legitimacy. The Legitimacy Act of 1926 provided for legitimation of children by subsequent marriage of parents. The Act of 1959 carried this process further by enacting that marriage legitimized a person even if the father or mother was married to a third party when the illegitimate person was born. Further amendments resultant on the Matrimonial Causes Act, 1973, and the Legitimacy Act, 1976.

legitimists, word now applied to any partisans of monarchy, or of a particular branch of a royal house as against another branch (cadet) or republican regime, but only current since 1830, when it was coined to describe those royalists who supported the senior Bourbon as opposed to the cadet Orléans branch of the French royal house.

Leicester, England. In Old English *Legerceastre.* Site of Roman *Ratae* on the Fosse Way, AD 120. Seized by the Danes, AD 874. Incorporated by King John, 1199. Cardinal Wolsey *d.* at the abbey, 1530. Captured by royalist forces, May 1645, when the castle was dismantled; retaken by parliamentary forces under Fairfax, June 1645. Hosiery made at from 1674. University College became the University of L., 1957. L. Polytechnic became De Montfort University, 1992.

Leipzig, Germany. First mentioned in 1015. L.'s fair first mentioned, 1268. University founded, 1409. L. Conference between Luther, Eck and Carlstadt, 1519. L. Book Fair instituted, 1545. During the Thirty Years War (1618–48) it was five times besieged and taken; captured by Prussian Army, 1756; allied armies entered

the city after defeat of Napoleon, 16–19 Oct. 1813. Industrial centre from 1880s. Centre of town largely destroyed by allied air attack, 4 Dec. 1943, when famous library also wiped out. Centre of anti-Communist movement that eventually led to German reunification, 1989/90.

Lemnos (Modern Greek **Limni**) was captured from the Venetians by the Turks, 1478. Mudros Bay on the S coast of L. was used as an allied base from 1915, and here the Turks signed an armistice, 30 Oct. 1918.

Lend-Lease. *See* LEASE-LEND.

Leningrad, name of *St Petersburg from 1924–91.

Leon, Spain. Kingdom founded 10thC AD. First united with Castile, 1037. Finally, 1230.
Kings of Leon. See under CASTILE.

Leopoldville. *See* KINSHASA.

Lesotho, formerly **Basutoland**, Africa, kingdom within the Commonwealth. Annexed by Britain, 1868. Annexed to Cape Colony, 1871. Rebellion, 1879–80, resulted in its being made a protectorate under Britain, 1883. 3 Oct. 1966, became an independent kingdom within the Commonwealth, changing its name from Basutoland to L. Unrest from 1970s: in 1986 the government was overthrown and executive and legislative powers vested in King. These revoked, Mar. 1990 and in Nov. 1990, the king was deposed and replaced by his son as Letsie III. Army coup, 1991.

Letters of Marque. Licences first granted, 1295, permitting seizure of an enemy's ships or property. Abolished by Treaty of Paris, 1856.

Lettres de Cachet. Warrants of imprisonment granted by the kings of France from about the 14thC. Abolished by National Assembly, 1 Nov. 1789.

leukaemia, cancer of blood-forming tissues, word first used, 1855. Disease identified by end of 19thC. Much progress on treatment during 20thC. By 1994, 50% cure rate in UK among children.

Levant Company, The. Founded 1581. Chartered by Queen Elizabeth I for trade with Middle E, 1592. British Government took over consular representation from L.C. in Turkey, 1803. Company dissolved, 1825.

level crossings. After a number of accidents on L.C., fresh safety provisions contained in Level Crossings Act, 1983.

Levellers. Ultra-republican party in the parliamentary army during the civil war, 1647. In 1649 it brought about a mutiny, but was suppressed. The leader was Lieut.-Col. John Lilburne (1618–57).

Leyden or **Leiden,** Holland. Settled by the Romans. University founded 1575 by William of Orange in commemoration of the citizens' defence of the town against the Spaniards from Oct. 1573 to Oct. 1574.

Lhasa, *Tibet. Became capital of Tibet in 7thC. Became seat of the Dalai Lama, 1641. The Potala built, 1641–1701. Occupied by the Chinese, Mar. 1959. The Dalai Lama fled to India. Destruction of historic areas of L. and increasing Chinese population in, since 1980s. Sporadic Tibetan resistance ruthlessly crushed.

Liampo. *See* NINGPO.

Liberal Democrats, political party formed in Mar. 1988 as the result of a merger between the *Liberals and the Social Democrats, first known as Liberal and Social Democrats, but since Oct. 1989 as L.D. Parliamentary Leader (1995), Paddy Ashdown.

Liberals. Covenanters termed 'Whigamores', 1679; name Whig came to be fastened on all Scottish Presbyterian zealots, then on English politicians who opposed the court and treated Nonconformists leniently. Terms Whig and Tory came into use, 1679–80, and more advanced Whigs and reformers first named L. in a derogatory sense (meaning French revolutionary) *c.* 1820. Last held office, 1918; last represented in government, 1940–5. In alliance with Social Democratic Party, 1982. In Mar 1988. L. and Social Democrats

merged; known as *Liberal Democrats since Oct. 1989.

Liberia, W Africa. A negro republic originally of liberated slaves. Founded by the American Colonizing Society, 1821; republic constituted, 1847. Boundaries determined by Anglo–Liberian (1885) and Franco-Liberian (1892, 1907, 1910) agreements. In 1911 a small exchange of territory with Sierra Leone took place. Government in hands of few select families till 1980, when President Tolbert assassinated and his government overthrown. Samuel Doe, a former master-sergeant, became head of state. New constitution, 1984. Doe's victory in 1985 elections claimed fraudulent. Full-scale civil war from 1989 after invasion by Charles Taylor. Doe murdered, Sept 1990. Officially, cease-fire from Feb. 1991 policed by pan-African peacekeeping force and peace agreement signed, 25 July 1993, but situation remains confused (1995). Thousands have died, thousands have starved and up to 1 million people have fled from L. Taylor promised future free elections, 1994.

Liberty, name (1994) of the former **National Council for Civil Liberties**, founded 1934, which campaigns for the rights of the individual citizen.

Liberty, Statue of. *See* STATUE OF LIBERTY.

Liberum Veto was written into the Polish constitution in the first half of the 17thC. First exercised, 1652; and abolished, 1791.

libraries, ancient. Chaldean L. said to have existed as early as 1700 BC. First public library founded at Athens by Pisistratus, 540. Founding of the great Alexandrian library by the first of the Ptolemies, 284; partially destroyed when Julius Caesar set fire to the city in 47. First library in Rome brought from Macedonia by Aemilius Paulus, 167. Library at Constantinople founded by Constantine *c.* AD 355.

libraries, modern. The following are among the most famous L., with the dates of their foundation:

Australia: Canberra: National Library, 1960.
Austria: Vienna: Imperial Library, founded by Frederick III, c. 1440.
France: Paris: Royal Library, now the Bibliothèque Nationale, founded by Francis I, c. 1520.
Canada: Parliamentary Library, Ottawa, founded, 1849: since 1950 the National Library.
Denmark: Royal Library, Copenhagen, founded, 1661.
Germany: Berlin: Royal Library, founded, 1659. Dresden: Royal Library, founded, 16thC. Munich: Royal Library, founded by Duke Albert V of Bavaria, 16thC. Stuttgart: Royal Library, founded, 1765.
Great Britain and Ireland: Library Association of the UK, founded, 1877. Aberystwyth: Welsh National Library, founded, 1911. Cambridge: University Library, founded, 15thC, enlarged by George I, 1715. Dublin: King's Inns' Library, founded, 1787; Trinity College Library, founded, 1601. Edinburgh: Advocates' Library founded, 1682; Scottish National Library, 1925. University Library, founded, 1580. St Andrews: University Library, founded, 1456; London: *British Museum, 1757 (since 1973 the *British Library); Royal Society Library, founded, 1660; Royal College of Physicians' Library, founded, 1518; London Library, founded, 1840; University of London Library, founded c. 1838. Oxford: Bodleian Library, founded, 1598 (a restoration and expansion of a collection begun in the 15thC); Radcliffe Library, founded under the will of Dr. Radcliffe, 1714, opened, 1749. Manchester: Chetham Library, founded, 1653, claims to be first free library in England.
Holland: Royal Library, The Hague, founded, 1798.
India: National Library, Calcutta, founded, 1903 (as the Imperial Library).
Italy: Florence: library, founded by Niccolo Nicoli, 1436; Mediceo-Laurenziana, 1571; Marucelliana, 1703; Nazionale (amalgamation of Magliabechiana and Palatina), 1861. Rome: Biblioteca Casanatense, founded, 1701; Vatican Library, founded by Pope Nicholas V, 1446, enlarged by Sixtus V, 1588; Vittore Emanuele Library, 1875.
Portugal: Lisbon: Bibliotheca Naçional, founded, 1796. Oporto: Municipal Library, founded 1833.
Romania: Academic Library, 1867.
Russia: St Petersburg: Public Library, 1795. Moscow: State Library, 1862.
S Africa: Cape Town Library, 1818.
Spain: The Escorial's library, founded soon after the building, which began, 1562. Salamanca: University Library, founded, 1254.
USA: Baltimore: Enoch Pratt Free Library, 1857; Johns Hopkins University, 1876; Peabody Institute Library, 1857. Boston: Public Library, 1871–1905. California: Leland Stanford University Library, 1891; Henry Huntington Library, 1919. Chicago: Newberry Library, 1887; University Library, 1892; John Crerar Library, 1894. Illinois: University Library Urbana, 1867. Massachusetts: Amherst College Library, 1821; Harvard University Library, 1638. Michigan: University Library, 1837. New Haven: Yale College Library, 1701. New Jersey: Princeton University, 1746. New York: Columbia University, 1763; Astor Library, opened, 1854; Lenox Library, 1870; New York Public Library 1894; Pierpoint Morgan Library, 1924. Pennsylvania: Lehigh University Library, 1877; State Library, 1777; University of Pennsylvania, 1749. Washington: Library of Congress, 1800; Bureau of Education, 1868; Geological Survey, 1882; House of Representatives Patent Office, 1836; Folger Shakespeare Library, 1930.

Libreville, capital of Gabon, founded, 1849, for freed slaves.

Libya. Originally a Greek name signifying the N African littoral, not including Egypt. After the Jugurthine War of 106 BC L. proper, known as the *Regio Tripolitana*, was annexed to the province of Africa, but under Diocletian (emperor, AD 284–305), the name L. was reintroduced and the western part named Marmarica. In 476 the

*Vandals conquered the whole of the diocese of Africa, including L. It was recovered by Count Belisarius in 534, and remained part of the *Praefectura Africae* until its conquest by the Arabs, 647. In the 15thC it was conquered by the Turks, who proclaimed the country a vilayet, 1835. Seized from Turks by Italians, 1911. Italian conquest recognized at Treaty of Ouchy, 18 Oct. 1912. 'Pacification' by Italian forces under Marshal Balbo in 1925 necessitated a treaty with Egypt, signed 6 Dec. 1925, whereby the Bay of Sollum was ceded to Egypt in return for the Oasis of Jarabub, a Senussi stronghold, occupied by Italian forces, 7 Feb. 1927. Scene of much fighting in World War II, it was finally conquered by British, Feb. 1943. In June 1949 the British Government recognized Mohammed Idris es Senussi as King of L., and a Federal State came into being with alternating capitals at Benghazi and Tripoli. Massive oil discoveries revolutionized L.'s economy, 1960 onwards. Sept. 1969, a military coup deposed King Idris and a republic was proclaimed, under leadership of Muammar Gadaffi. L. subsequently adopted extreme leftist but Muslim line, interfering in politics of several neighbouring countries. 1972–81, abortive plans to merge with Chad. Egypt and Syria: reconciliation with Egypt, 1989. Policewoman shot, from London Libyan Embassy, 1984 and Britain broke off diplomatic relations with L. In Apr. 1986 USA accused L. of terrorism and bombed L. Following the *Lockerbie air disaster, USA and Britain accused Libyan nationals of organizing the attack, 21 Dec. 1988. Two Libyan suspects named, 1991. L. refused to extradite them and the UN imposed limited sanctions on L. in consequence, 15 Apr. 1992., reviewed in Apr. 1993, and later extended.

licensing laws (Britain). The present law founded on Consolidation Act of 1826. Wine and Beer House Act of 1869 regulated 'off-licence' houses. Act of 1902 increased penalties for drunkenness, convicted habitual drunkards, and compelled clubs to be registered. Children Act, 1908, prohibited presence in bars of children under 14; and it and L. (Consolidation) Act, 1910, restricted sale of liquor to such. 'Permitted Hours' system established, 1921. Sale to persons under 18 restricted by Act of 1923. Licensing Act, 1961, increased permitted hours of drinking in public houses, and selling hours in off-licences, and introduced principle of local option to Wales in respect of Sunday opening. Flexible licensing hours in Scotland since 1976: and in England and Wales since passing of the Licensing Act of 1988. Suggestions for further changes to allow children in public houses in certain circumstances proposed, 1993. Relaxation of Sunday L.L. in England and Wales, 1995. *See also* LOCAL OPTION.

Lichfield, England. The Mercian See founded here in the 7thC by St Chad, first Bishop of L. Cathedral dates from 13thC. Besieged by parliamentary army, and cathedral damaged by, 1643.

Lidice, Czech Republic. After assassination of Heydrich, the German Protector of Bohemia and Moravia, the Germans destroyed the village, 10 June 1942, killed all the adult males, shot the women or sent them to concentration camps and sent the children to German foster homes or concentration camps. Village rebuilt after 1945.

Liechtenstein, Principality of. Named after the L. family, who acquired the county of Vaduz, 1699, and the lordship of Schellenberg, 1713. Became a principality, 1719. Preserved its independence at extinction of the Holy Roman Empire, 1806. Sovereign since 1866. Joined UN, 1990; EFTA, 1991. Women voted for first time, 1986. Prince Hans Adam II succeeded, 13 Nov. 1989. L. votes to join European Economic Area, April 1995.

Liège (Flemish **Luik**), Belgium. Cathedral founded, 712. Captured by Charles the Bold, 1467; by the French, 1691; by the English under Marlborough, 1702; by French, 1794; university founded, 1817.

lifeboat. The first L. patented, 1785, by Lionel Lukin, an Essex coachbuilder. Two

South Shields men produced first purpose-built L., *The Original*, 1790. It survived for 40 years. 31 similar Ls. built by 1804. First steam-propelled L. designed, 1890; first with motor power, 1904. In 20thC improvements with self-righting Ls. and smaller, inflatable Ls. for in-shore rescues. Modernization programme from 1986; last double-ended L. (at Aldeburgh) phased out, 1993.

Lifeboat Institution, Royal National. Founded in 1824 through the exertions of Sir William Hillary and Thomas Wilson, MP for the City of London.

Life Guards. *See under* REGIMENTS.

light, velocity of, determined by Römer, 1675; more accurately by Michelson, 1926.

lighthouses. One at Sigeum on the Hellespont preceded the Pharos at Alexandria which was erected *c*. 280 BC. A Phoenician one at Corunna was re-established *c*. 1634, and modernized in 1847. The oldest extant is at Cordonan at the mouth of the Gironde, built, 1584–1611. The first Eddystone one, mainly of wood, erected, 1696, by Henry Winstanley, was destroyed, 1703, by a storm in which the architect lost his life. Rudyerd's, 1706, was destroyed by fire, 1755. Smeaton's, 1759, though burnt, 1770, was rebuilt and lasted till 1877; demolished then because of wear in rock foundation. Douglass's, farther out, completed, 1882. Northern Lighthouse Board instituted by Act of Parliament, 1786. In America an Act of Congress dated 1789 provided for the building of L. Since 1950s members of manned L. has drastically decreased; all Britain's offshore L. to be completely automated by 1998. Needles' keepers left, Nov. 1994, leaving Hanois L., Guernsey as last manned offshore L. in British waters. *See also* TRINITY HOUSE.

Ligurian Republic. Set up at Genoa by Napoleon on 6 June 1797. Annexed to France, 1805.

Lille, France. Founded in the 11thC by counts of Flanders. Mortgaged to France,

1305; became part of Burgundy, 1369; captured by Louis XIV, 1667; by the Duke of Marlborough, 1708; restored, 1713; bombarded by Austrians, 1792. Wholly automatic underground system opened, 1982.

Lillibullero or **Lilliburlero,** words published in 1687, attributed to Lord Wharton (1648–1715), and set to Purcell's (1658–95) arrangement of an old Irish tune. British Commando units adopted the tune as a march during World War II.

Lilongwe, capital of Malawi since 1975.

Lima, *Peru. Founded, 1535, by Pizarro, who was murdered here in 1541. University founded, 1551. Severe earthquake, 1746. Scene of world's worst football disaster, 24 May 1964, when over 300 spectators killed in a stadium riot.

Limburg. Dutch province, part of a county founded in Carolingian times, which became a duchy in the 12thC, and passed to Brabant in 1228, then to *Burgundy, and thus to the Austrian Netherlands, 1713. Its capital is *Maastricht. Included in the kingdom of the United Netherlands, 1815, it was partitioned in 1839, when the W portion became **Limbourg** or **Limburg,** Belgian province, whose coal-mines were first exploited in 1920.

Limerick, Ireland. Incorporated, 1195. Taken by Ireton, 1651; invested by English and Dutch, Aug. 1690; again invested and surrendered, Oct. 1691. The cathedral founded, 1142; rebuilt, 1490.

limericks. Earliest known, appeared in print *c*. 1820. Popularized through publication of Edward Lear's *Book of Nonsense*, 1846.

Limousin, ancient province of France centring on Limoges, came into English hands, 1152, as the dowry of Eleanor of Aquitaine, bride of Henry II. Restored to France, 1369. Partitioned into the *départements* of Corrèze, Haute-Vienne, Creuze, and (parts of) Charente, Dordogne, 1791.

Limousins, name given to a clerical party,

a group of cardinals native to the above region, dominant at the papal court of Avignon, 1342–78.

Lincoln, England. Bishop of L. present at Council of Arles, 314. Castle commenced by William I, 1068. Cathedral built between 1068 and 1501. Fight known as 'Fair of Lincoln', 1217. Five Parliaments held here between 1301 and 1386. Besieged by parliamentary army under the Earl of Manchester, 1644.

Lincolnshire Insurrection, The. Was largely the outcome of the dissolution of the monasteries and of fiscal oppression. It originated in Oct. 1536 and had been largely suppressed by the end of that month.

Lindisfarne. *See* HOLY ISLAND.

Linnean Society (London). Founded, 1788, by Sir J. E. Smith; incorporated, 1802; named after Carl Linnaeus, the Swedish botanist (1707–78).

Lion League. Formed by the knights against the tax instead of personal service levied by Albert IV of Bavaria, 1488.

Lisieux, France, contains tomb of St Thérèse (1873–97), canonized, 1925. Cathedral begun, 1170: basilica consecrated, 1954. Severe damage during Allied bombardment, June 1944.

Lisbon. Conquered by Moors, AD 716. Retaken by the Portuguese with English assistance and cathedral built, 1147. Portuguese capital since 1260. Vasco da Gama embarked from Belem, 1497, and monastery of Belem commenced, 1500. Seized by Spaniards under Alva, 1580. Retaken by Braganza, 1640. Almost totally destroyed by earthquake, 1 Nov. 1755. Cathedral rebuilt, 1756–7. Held by French, 1807–8. University founded, 1911 (that founded in 1290 was transferred to Coimbra, 1537). Gulbenkian Arts Centre at, 1962.

lithography. Invented by Alois Senefelder (1771–1834) *c.* 1796. *See* ENGRAVING.

Lithuania (Lithuanian **Lietuva**). Lithua-nians first politically united under Mindaugas, Grand Prince from 1236 to 1263. His most prominent successors were Gediminas (1316–41), Algirdas (1345–77), and Vestutis, the last heathen ruler, who was murdered by the Teutonic Knights, 1382. The latter's son, Vytautas the Great, allied with Poland to smash the Teutonic Knights at the first battle of Tannenberg (1410); the alliance became a union with the marriage (1386) of the Grand Prince Jogaila to the Polish princess Jadwiga (1369–99) by which he became King Jagiello (Wladislaw II) of *Poland, and converted the Lithuanians to Christianity. The joint power of L. and Poland extended to the Black Sea and their legislatures were merged at the Union of Lublin, 1569, from which time L. shared the history of Poland, its partitions and suppression. Except for Memel (Klaipeda) most of L. fell to Russia, and became known as the Government of Kovno, 1795. A Soviet republic, established 1918, was overthrown and an independent republic established, 1919. L. was occupied by the Red Army, 15 June 1940. Occupied by Germany, 1941–4; then reconquered by Russia. Anti-Russian independence movement emerged in 1960s, increased from 1980. In 1989 Communists forced to hold multiparty elections, won by Nationalists, Feb. 1990, who declared unilateral independence, Mar. 1990. Clashes followed with Russian troops, who killed several Lithuanians at Vilnius TV Centre, Jan. 1991. Russia and the W reorganized L. as an independent republic, Sept. 1991. Free-market economy changes caused hardship and former Communist leader Brazanskas defeated Landsbergis in Oct. 1992 elections.

Little Entente (Czechoslovakia, Yugoslavia and Romania). Formed, Aug. 1920. Scope enlarged, 1922 and 1923.

Liverpool, England. Founded by King John, 1199. Attacked by Prince Rupert, 26 June 1644. Principal dock-building began, *c.* 1780. University College founded, 1880. Made a city and diocese, 1880. Mersey railway tunnel open, 1886. Chief magistrate made Lord Mayor, 1893. Independent university set up, 1903. Anglican cathedral founded, 1904. Roman Catholic cathedral founded, 1933: opened, 1967. First Mersey road tunnel opened, 1934; second, 1971. Severe bombing by the Germans, 1941. Famous for its football prowess and 'pop' music culture from the 1960s. Labour council abolished office of Lord Mayor, 1983. Tate Gallery, opened 1988. L. Polytechnic became Liverpool John Moores University, 1992.

Livery Companies of London. So called: not all have L. With earliest date at which each is known to have existed (E.), and date of incorporation (I.). Names in square brackets are of extinct companies. Names marked 'NL' are of companies that have no L.:

		E.	I.
1.	Mercers	1172	1393
2.	Grocers	1345	1428
3.	Drapers	1180	1365
4.	Fishmongers	1321	1364
5.	Goldsmiths	1180	1327
6.	Merchant Taylors	1267	1327
7.	Skinners	1272	1327
8.	Haberdashers	1371	1448
9.	Salters	–	Reign of Edward III
10.	Ironmongers	1364	1463
11.	Vintners	1321	1437
12.	Clothworkers	1480	1528

The above are the 'Great Companies'.

	E.	I.
Dyers	1188	1471
Brewers	1345	1438
Leather-sellers	1372	1444
Pewterers	1348	1473
Barbers	1308	1462
Cutlers	1285	1416
Bakers	1155	1486
Waxchandlers	1358	1483
Tallowchandlers	1363	1462
Armourers and Braziers	Reign of Edward II	1453
Girdlers	1180	1448
Butchers	1180	1605
Sadlers	1216	1395
Carpenters	1333	1477
Cordwainers	1272	1439
Painter-Stainers	1466	1581
Curriers	1272	1606
Masons	1356	1677
Plumbers	1365	1611
Innholders	1327 as Hostelers	1515
Founders	1365	1614
Poulters	1345	1504

	E.	I.
Cooks	1311	1482
Coopers	{ Reign of Edward II }	1501
Tylers and Bricklayers	?1502	1568
Bowyers	1488	1621
Fletchers	1371	None
Blacksmiths	1325	1571
Joiners and Ceilers	1309	1571
Weavers	{ Not later than reign of Edward I }	{ Reign of Henry I }
Woolmen	? 14thC	Unknown
Scriveners	1357	1617
Fruiterers	1416	1606
Plaisterers	–	1502
Stationers and Newspaper Makers	?1403	1556
Broderers	–	1561
Upholders	14thC	1626
Musicians	{ 1350 as Minstrels }	1604
Turners	1310	1604
Basket-makers	1422	? None
Glaziers and Painters of Glass	1328	1638
Horners	1376	1638
Farriers	1272	1685
Paviors	{ Before 1479 }	{ 1673 (with-drawn) }
Loriners	1260	1711
Apothecaries	1511	1617
Shipwrights	1456	1605
Spectacle-makers	?1628	1629
Clockmakers	1627	1631
Glovers	14thC	1638
[Combmakers]	–	?1650
Feltmakers	1180	1667
Framework Knitters	–	1657
[Silk-throwers]	–	?1629
[Silkmen]	–	–
[Pinmakers]	–	?1636
Needle-makers	{ Reign of Henry VIII }	{ ?1636 Common-wealth }
Gardeners	1345	1605
[Soap-makers]	–	?1638
Tinplate Workers	{ 1469 as Wire-drawers }	1670
Wheelwrights	–	1670
Distillers	–	1638
[Hatband-makers]	–	?1638

Patten-makers	14thC	1670
Glass-sellers	–	1664
[Tobacco-pipe Makers]	–	(1) 1619
		(2) 1663
Coach and Coach-harness Makers	–	1677
Gunmakers	–	1638
Gold and Silver Wyre Drawers	1423	1623
[Longbow-string Makers]	–	–
Playing-card Makers	–	1628
Fan-makers	c. 1600	1709
[Woodmongers]	–	–
[Starchmakers]	–	?1632
[Fishermen]	–	?1687
Parish Clerks NL	1233	1442
Carmen	1516	1524
[Porters]	–	–
Watermen and Lightermen NL	Unknown	None
[Surgeons]	–	?1308
Solicitors	1909	1944
Master Mariners	1926	1930

Since the 1950s there have been several new L.C. which include:

Furniture Makers	1952	1963
Lightmongers	1953	1984
Tobacco Pipe Makers and Tobacco Blenders	1954	1961
Scientific Instrument Makers	1955	1964
Builders Merchants	1961	1977
Company Directors and Administrators	1956	1976
Environmental Cleaners	1972	1986
Marketors	1975	1977
Chartered Accountants	1976	1977
Chartered Surveyors	1977	–
Insurers	1979	1979
Actuaries	1979	1979
Arbitrators	1981	1981
Engineers	1983	1983

Livingston. Scotland, a 'new town', established 1962.

Livingstonia Mission. Suggested by David Livingstone, the explorer (1813–73), for the abolition of slavery on the E coast of Africa; expedition first fitted out in 1875, and settled at Cape Clear. Moved to Bandawé, 1883.

Livonia (Latvian **Vidzeme**; Estonian **Libmaa**), territory since at least the beginning of the Christian era inhabited by and named after the Livs, a Finnish tribe related to the Estonians; subject to and converted to Christianity by the *Teutonic Order, after whose decline L. submitted to Polish suzerainty, 1561, until 1629, when it passed to Sweden; Russian territory from 1721. In 1918 partitioned between Estonia and Latvia. See LATVIA and ESTONIA.

Ljubljana (German **Laibach**), capital of Slovenia. A Roman settlement (*Emona*), L. was capital of Ilyria, 1749–1849, and of Carniola, 1849–1919. University, 1920. Linked to S Austria by Karawanken Alpine road tunnel, 1979–83.

Llandaff, Wales. Cathedral begun, 1120; restored, 1844–69; bombed, 1941; restored, 1957.

Lloyd's of London, originally **Lloyd's Marine Intelligence Department**. Started in a coffee-house kept by Edward L. (*c.* 1648–1713) in 17thC; moved from Tower Street to Lombard Street, 1691; to Royal Exchange, 1774; parliamentary inquiry into management of, 1810; incorporated, 1871. Ceased to be restricted to marine insurance after Act of 1911. Moved to Leadenhall Street, 1928; further new building, 1958 and 1986. Lloyd's Act, 1982. Financial crises in 1980s–90s led to far-reaching reforms, 1993, which removed the established practice of unlimited liability, and admitted corporate members. Heavy damages awarded against L. to 'names' in a former L. syndicate, Oct. 1994. New settlement offered to names, May 1995; ruling against accountants, Nov.

Lloyd's Register of Shipping had its origins in Lloyd's coffee-house (*see* previous article) *c.* 1760; became an independent organization, 1834.

load line. *See* PLIMSOLL.

Local Defence Volunteers (LDV). *See* HOME GUARD.

local government (UK). Municipal corporations made elective by ratepayers in Scotland, 1832. In England, 1835. County Councils set up, 1888. Urban and Rural District Councils set up, 1894. Franchise extended to all parliamentary electors, 1945. Pattern of L.G. in UK transformed by Local Government Act of 1972: further major changes considered, 1994–5, but plan to produce a largely unitary system of L.G. abandoned, 1995, in England and Wales. L.G. in Scotland to be restructured in 1996, with existing two-tier authorities to be replaced by one tier authority.

Local Government Board (UK). Superseded the Poor Law Board, 1871. Replaced by Ministry of Health, 1919.

Locarno Treaties, 16 Oct. 1925. Three treaties:
1. Mutual guarantee by Germany, Belgium, France, Great Britain and Italy. Denounced by Germany, 1936.
2. France and Poland, against Germany should she break the peace.
3. France and Czechoslovakia, similar to 2.

Lochaber hydro-electric power scheme begun, 1926.

Loch Ness. *See* NESS, LOCH.

Lockerbie air disaster, occurred, 21 Dec. 1988, when Pan Am flight PA 103 (a Boeing 727) travelling Frankfurt–Heathrow, London–New York, blew up, 54 minutes out of Heathrow, over Lockerbie, Scotland. All passengers killed, plus 11 people on the ground in Lockerbie (total of over 260). Investigation proved a bomb responsible. In 1991 two Libyan suspects were named, but so far (1995) no action taken against them. UN imposed limited sanctions against Libya for its failure to extradite the suspects, 15 Apr. 1992. Litigation resulting from the disaster bankrupted the carrier, Pan Am, one of the oldest airline companies. Further UN sanctions against Libya, 1993 onwards but suspects remained in Libya. Possible Syrian connection suggested, Dec. 1993; allegation of *Hezbollah involvement, Nov. 1994, and suggestions of Iranian complicity, Jan. 1995.

Lofoten Islands, Norway, raided by British forces, 6 Mar. and 29 Dec. 1941.

logarithms invented, 1614, by John Napier (1550–1617).

LOGO, computer programming language developed in the 1970s at the Massachussetts Institute of Technology.

Lollards. Name applied, after his death, to the followers of Wyclif (1324–84). In 1395 they presented a petition to Parliament protesting against abuses in the Church. In 1401 the statute *De Haeretico Comburendo* was passed against them, and on 12 Feb. 1401 William Sawtrey, the first victim, was burnt at the stake for his views. Persecution continued spasmodically, Sir John Oldcastle being one of the most famous victims in 1417. An 'underground' Lollard movement continued in unorganized form until the Reformation in the 16thC when many of its ideas incorporated in English Protestantism.

Lombardy, Italy. Occupied by the Lombards or Langobards, AD 568. Joined by Charlemagne to his empire, 774. From 843 ruled by its own kings until 1337, when it passed to the dukes of Milan. Became part of Spain under Charles V, 1529. Fell to Austria, 1714. After Napoleon's campaign and his downfall it was restored to Austria, 1815. Annexed by Savoy, 1859.

London and Paris Agreements (1954) evolved a formula to supersede the defensive arrangements which the European Defence Community (EDC), rejected by France, had been intended to cover.

London Airport, see entries for HEATHROW, GATWICK and STANSTED.

London Bridge. Originally built of wood, the first bridge of which there is documentary evidence (963) was wrecked by Olaf the Saint, when a mercenary in the service of Ethelred II, 1014. Another was built, destroyed by a hurricane in 1091, not rebuilt till 1120, and burnt down, 1136. A temporary structure followed. A new (stone) one commenced, 1176, and completed, 1209. It suffered frequently from fire, and was restored. Toll discontinued, 27 Mar. 1782. New bridge commenced, 15 Mar. 1824, and opened by William IV, 1 Aug. 1831, when the old structure was demolished. This bridge in turn put up for sale, Oct. 1967, and bought by a US company and re-erected in the USA. Present L.B. begun, 1967; completed, 1973.

London, City of. Said to have been founded before AD 43. Burned by Boudicca, 61. Fortified, 350–69. Destroyed by Danes, 839. Tower of L. commenced, 1078. First charter granted to city, 1079. First mayor appointed, 1089. Privileges granted by the regent, Prince John Lackland, 1191. Divided into wards, and aldermen appointed, 1242. Chief magistrate known as 'Lord Mayor' since 1354. First theatre built for, 1576. Royal proclamations against further building, 1580 and 1611. Great Plague, 1665. Great Fire, 1666. Charter forfeited, 1682; restored, 1689. Commercial and financial centre of international importance since 17thC. Great fires caused by German raids, Dec. 1940 and May 1941. Right to send two MPs to Parliament abolished, 1948. Much rebuilding, 1950–90. Major IRA bomb outrages in, Apr. 1992 and Apr. 1993, led to sealing off of major City roads to motor traffic, July 1993; this became permanent, 1994.

London Conference on naval armaments opened, 22 Jan. 1930. Treaty concluded between five powers – Great Britain, USA, France, Italy and Japan – 22 Apr. 1930.

London County Council. County of L. formed by Local Government Act, 1888, and L.C.C. set up to administer the same area as was served from 1855 onwards, by the Metropolitan Board of Works, whose powers the L.C.C. inherited. Labour Party gained control of L.C.C., 1934, retaining it until the L.C.C. was superseded by the *Greater London Council under the London Government Act, 1963. County Hall, Lambeth, (built 1908 onwards) sold to a Japanese property company, 1993.

London, County of. Defined by Local Government Act of 1888, and a county council formed. Formed into 28 municipal boroughs by L. Government Act, 1899. Disappeared under the L. Government Act, 1963 which created Greater London, itself abolished as an administrative entity, 1986.

Londonderry (Irish *Doire*), officially, since 1984, **Derry**, and so called generally until its colonization in the 17thC by the Irish Society of London. Grew up round a monastery founded in AD 546 by St Columba. The 12thC cathedral church was demolished, 1600. Besieged, 19 Apr.–30 July 1689, by Jacobites. Civil rights disturbances in, 1968, serious rioting, Aug. 1969 and 30 Jan. 1972, scene of *'Bloody Sunday' tragedy (*see* IRELAND, NORTHERN). Subsequently scene of sporadic but sometimes considerable IRA violence up to 1994 ceasefire.

Londonderry Air, traditional Irish tune, first printed, 1855.

London, Diocese of. Following is a list of bishops since 1044:

William, 1051
Hugh d'Orivalle, 1075
Maurice, 1086
Richard de Belmeis I, 1108
Gilbert Universalis, 1128
Robert de Sigillo, 1141
Richard de Belmeis II, 1152
Gilbert Foliot, 1163
Richard Fitzneal, 1189
William de Santa Maria, 1199
Eustace de Fauconberg, 1221
Roger Niger, 1229
Fulk Basset, 1242
Henry de Wengham, 1260
Henry de Sandwich, 1263
John de Chishull, 1274
Richard Gravesend, 1280
Ralph de Baldock, 1306
Gilbert Segrave, 1313
Richard de Newport, 1317
Stephen de Gravesend, 1319
Richard de Bintworth, 1338
Ralph de Stratford, 1340
Michael de Northburgh, 1355
Simon de Sudbury, 1362
William Courtenay, 1375
Robert de Braybroke, 1382
Roger Walden, 1405
Nicholas Bubwith, 1406
Richard Clifford, 1407
John Kemp, 1421
William Gray, 1426
Robert FitzHugh, 1431
Robert Gilbert, 1436
Thomas Kemp, 1450

Richard Hill, 1489
Thomas Savage, 1496
William Wareham, 1502
William Barons, 1504
Richard FitzJames, 1506
Cuthbert Tunstall, 1522
John Stokesley, 1530
Edmund Bonner, 1540
Nicholas Ridley, 1550
Edmund Bonner, 1553
Edmund Grindal, 1559
Edwin Sandys, 1570
John Aylmer, 1577
Richard Fletcher, 1595
Richard Bancroft, 1597
Richard Vaughan, 1604
Thomas Ravis, 1607
George Abbot, 1610
John King, 1611
George Mountain, 1621
William Laud, 1628
William Juxon, 1633
Gilbert Sheldon, 1660
Humfrey Henchman, 1663
Henry Compton, 1675
John Robinson, 1714
Edmund Gibson, 1723
Thomas Sherlock, 1748
Thomas Hayter, 1761
Richard Osbaldeston, 1762
Richard Terrick, 1764
Robert Lowth, 1777
Beilby Porteous, 1787
John Randolph, 1809
William Howley, 1813
Charles James Blomfield, 1828
Archibald Campbell Tait, 1856
John Jackson, 1869
Frederick Temple, 1885
Mandell Creighton, 1896
Arthur Foley Winnington-Ingram, 1901
Geoffrey Francis Fisher, 1939
John William Charles Wand, 1945
Henry Montgomery Campbell, 1956
Robert Wright Stopford, 1961
Gerald Alexander Ellison, 1973
Graham Douglas Leonard, 1981
David Michael Hope, 1991.
Richard Chartres, 1995.

London Gazette. *See* NEWSPAPERS.

London Library. Founded 1840, and opened, 3 May 1841. Reading-room opened, 15 May 1843. Removed from 40 Pall Mall to Beauchamp House, St James's Square, 1845. Rebuilt, 1896.

London Museum. Founded, 1910, and opened at Kensington Palace, 1912. Transferred to Lancaster House, St James's, 1913–14, but closed in 1939. Reopened at Kensington Palace, 1951. In 1976 Kensington Palace and Guildhall Museums amalgamated to form the Museum of London in a new building near London Wall in the City.

London, Pact of. Between Britain, France and Russia, who mutually engaged not to conclude peace separately, Sept. 1914. A secret agreement, signed 26 Apr. 1915, by the Allies and Italy, comprising the terms on which Italy would enter the war on the side of the Allies. *See* FIUME.

London Transport Executive, superseded, 1948, the **London Passenger Transport Board**, which had been established in 1933. The Greater London Council was responsible for the L.T.E.'s overall policy 1969–84, when the government took over, renaming the L.T.E. **London Regional Transport**. It was responsible for the construction of the Docklands Light Railway in the 1980s (opened, 1987). Ownership was transferred from the L.R.T. to the Docklands Development Corporation in 1992.

London, Tower of. The present White Tower, the earliest part of the structure, was begun by William the Conqueror *c.* 1078; completed by William Rufus, 1098. In 1140 Stephen used the tower as a residence. In Henry III's reign (1216–72) the regalia were removed to the tower. Additions made, 1680–85. Famous attempt to steal the crown jewels by Col. Blood from the tower, 9 May 1671. Damaged by fire, 1841 and by bombing in World War II. New jewel house opened, 1994. Royal Armoury to move from tower to Leeds, 1996.

London, Treaties of.
1. Between England and Holland; signed, 1674, ending war of 1672.
2. Between England, France and Russia, during Greek War of Independence; contracting parties bound themselves to take action for the purpose of securing the independence of Greece under Turkish suzerainty; signed, 1827.
3. Between Great Britain, France and Holland, providing for the erection of the Flemish and Walloon provinces into an independent kingdom; signed 1833.
4. Between Austria, France, Great Britain, Prussia and Russia, confirming the treaty of 1833.
5. Between England, France, Russia, Austria and Turkey, after conclusion of Syrian War; it provided that the Bosphorus and Dardanelles should be closed to ships of war (also known as the Treaty of Dardanelles); signed, 1841.
6. Between Austria, France, Great Britain, Prussia, Russia and Sweden, settling the succession to the Danish throne; signed, 1852.
7. Treaty of L., 30 May 1913, ending the First Balkan War.
8. Treaty of L. (Naval), defined relative strengths of fleets of the powers, 1936. *See also* LONDON AND PARIS AGREEMENTS.

London University. Institution in Gower Street (now University College) founded, 1828. King's College founded as a rival institution, 1829. University chartered by William IV, 28 Nov. 1836; students from both existing colleges to sit for examinations conducted by the university. Amended charter, 1858. Degrees granted to women, 1878. University of London Acts, 1898 and 1926. New buildings in Bloomsbury begun, 1933; completed, 1936. In 1995 L. U. comprised 14 schools, six medical schools, 11 postgraduate medical centres, 13 Senate institutions and five institutions having recognized teachers.

Long Island, New York, USA, first settled, 1636. L.I. City created, 1870, and officially absorbed by New York City (borough of Queens), 1898.

Long March, 1934–5, 6,000 mile journey by Mao Tse-Tung and his army from SE to NW China, to regroup against Nationalist forces.

Long Parliament. The fifth Parliament summoned by Charles I; met, 3 Nov. 1640 (*see* PRIDE'S PURGE); dissolved forcibly by Oliver Cromwell, 20 Apr. 1653; recalled twice, and finally declared itself dissolved, 16 Mar. 1660.

Lonsdale Belt for boxing first awarded, 1911, by Hugh Cecil Lowther (1857–1944), 5th Earl of L.

Lord of the Isles. Title of the rulers of the Western Isles of Scotland. First conferred by David I of Scotland on Somerled of Argyll, 1135. Somerled's line supplanted by Iain MacDonald of Islay, 1346. The Ls. of the I. were intermittently vassals of Norway until the Treaty of Perth, 2 July 1266, when Haakon of Norway surrendered his claims. Title forfeited to Scottish crown, 1493, and became an apanage belonging to the heir male of the Scottish crown in 1540, which it has since remained.

Lord Privy Seal. Office first held by laymen in reign of *Henry VIII. Specific duties abolished, 1884, and position now generally held by a senior member of the Cabinet.

Lord's Day Observance Society. Founded, 1831.

Lords, House of. Earliest extant writ is dated 1265. Mitred abbots excluded, 1536. Abolished by Commons, 6 Feb. 1649. Cromwell recalled a selection of peers to be called House of Lords, 20 Jan. 1658. House of Lords constituted as before 1649 reassembled, 25 Apr. 1660. Sixteen Scottish peers elected by their order added under Act of Union, 1707. Crown's power to create peers used to secure a Tory majority, 31 Dec. 1711. Twenty-eight Irish peers, elected for life, added, 1801; no election of Irish peers has taken place, however, since the Irish Free State Act of 1922. Proxy voting waived since 1868. L. of Appeal added by Appellate Jurisdiction Act, 1876. Parliament Act restricting Lords' veto to a delaying power of two years became law, 18 Aug. 1911. New bill to restrict delaying power to one year became law in 1948. Life Peerages Act, 1958, empowered the sovereign to create men and women life peers and peeresses. Peerages Act, 1963, allows hereditary peers the option of remaining commoners (in which case they can stand for election to the Commons), though their heirs are free to revive the title. Wilson government proposed radical reforming legislation for H. of L. in a Bill introduced, 19 Dec. 1968, but the Bill was abandoned, 17 April 1969. H. of L. sessions first televised, 1985.

Loreto or **Loretto,** Italy. Virgin Mary's house reputed to have been miraculously translated from Nazareth to L., 1295. The Holy Image was taken to France, 1796; but restored, 1803.

Loro Sae. *See* TIMOR.

Lorraine, founded as kingdom of Lotharingia, AD 843. Duchy of L. given to King of Poland, 1736. Incorporated in France, 1766. Thereafter changed hands in same manner as *Alsace.

Lorraine, Cross of. Carried by Joan of Arc in the 15thC, and adopted as an emblem of French resistance to the Germans by de Gaulle in 1940.

Los Angeles, California, settled in 1781, became the Mexican capital of California, and was seized by a US naval force in 1846. Prospered in California gold rush, 1849. US city charter granted, 1850. Centre of film industry since 1911, and financial centre since 1940s. Aqueduct 233 miles long, Sierra Nevada mountains to L.A., 1913. Grew greatly after World War II and (1995) third largest city in USA. Rioting, Apr. 1992 after acquittal of four white policemen accused of beating a black motorist caused major damage and 53 deaths. Important buildings include the Missions of San Gabriel Arcangel (1771) and San Fernando Rey de Espana (1791); University of S California (1880); University of California (1919) and the County Museum of Art (1913). Earthquakes at, 1971 and 1994.

Lost Ten Tribes of Israel, not accounted for after the deportation of the original 12 Israelite tribes to Media by the Assyrians, 722 BC. Frequently 'rediscovered', e.g. by Antonio de Montezinos, 1644, in America, but first in England by John Sadler, 1649. The doctrine of the British Israelites was first developed by Richard Brothers (1757–1824).

Lottery, National. See NATIONAL LOTTERY.

Loughborough, University of, established, 1966.

Louisbourg, Nova Scotia. Fortified by French, 1713. Taken by British, 1745. Restored to France, 1748. Again captured by British, 1758. Finally ceded to Britain, 1763.

louis d'or. Gold coin in use in France, 1641–1795.

Louisiana, USA. Originally claimed for France by the explorer La Salle (1643–87), who named the territory after Louis XIV. Handed over to the Mississippi Co. (*see* MISSISSIPPI SCHEME), 1719. Ceded to Spain by England, 1762; to France, 1800. Sold to USA by Napoleon, 1803 (part of the **'Louisiana Purchase'*), admitted as a state, 1812. Huey Pierce Long's governorship, 1931–5. Petrochemical manufactures brought prosperity from 1940s.

Louisiana Purchase, sale in 1803 by Napoleon I of France, to the US, of the French territory, then still held in N America – namely over 2 million square miles, covering not only the modern state of Louisiana, but those of Arkansas, N and S Dakota, Iowa, Nebraska, Oklahoma and Missouri.

Lourdes, France. Virgin Mary said to have appeared to a peasant girl, Bernadette Soubirous, 11 Feb. 1858. Church declared the facts to be authentic, 1862. The basilica erected, 1876. St Bernadette canonized, 1933. Underground basilica consecrated, 1958.

Lourenço Marques. See MAPUTO.

Louvain (Flemish **Leuven**), Belgium. University founded, 1426; suppressed, 1797; refounded, 1817, and designated the Catholic University, 1835. Seriously damaged by Germans in 1914 and 1940.

Louvre, The (Paris). Present building started in 1541 by Francis I. Formerly a royal palace, a museum and art gallery since the French Revolution, enlarged during reign of Louis XIV (1643–1715). Controversial glass pyramid by I.M. Pei installed outside entrance, 1984. Richelieu wing opened, 1993.

Loyalists, United Empire, migrated to Canada, 1783, from United States. See ONTARIO.

Lübeck, Germany. Founded by Saxons, AD 1143; held by French, 1806–14; joined N German Confederation, 1866. Relinquished status as free city, 1937. See HANSEATIC LEAGUE.

LSD (Lysergic Acid Diethylamide). Synthetic hallucinogenic drug. In 1960 it was suggested as a cure for neuroses but this claim discredited. Banned in most countries, it attracted drug-users from the 1960s and habit spread from the USA, with a number of fatalities.

Lucca, Italy. Originally *Luca*. Since at least the 11thC the cathedral of St Martin has contained the *Volto Santo* (Holy Face), a wood carving of Christ attributed to His contemporary, St Nicodemus. Made a Roman colony. 177 BC; independent republic from 1369 to 1797; made a principality by Napoleon, 1805; passed to Spain, 1815; ceded to Tuscany, 1847.

Lucerne (Luzern), Switzerland. Benedictine monastery, *c.* 750. Joined Swiss Confederation, 1332.

Lucknow, India. Ancient city. Capital of Oudh, 1775; besieged during the Indian Mutiny, 1 July 1857; reinforced by Gen. Havelock, 25 Sept. 1857; relieved by Sir

Colin Campbell, 17 Nov. 1857; final capture by him, 19–22 Mar. 1858. Now the capital of Uttar Pradesh.

Luddite riots. Broke out first in Nottinghamshire, in reaction to increasing use of industrial and agricultural machinery, in Nov. 1811. The name L. originated with Ned Ludd, said to have been a worker who had broken some machinery some years before, but his actual existence doubtful. Renewed, July 1816, when much further damage was done in the N of England.

Luftwaffe, German Air Force which had existed in fact since at least 1933, first officially mentioned in a proclamation by Goering, Mar. 1935. Post-war L. estab., 1956.

Lundy Island, England, presented to the National Trust, 1969.

Lunéville, Peace of. Signed between Germany and France, 9 Feb. 1801, confirming the Treaty of Campo Formio.

Lupercalia, ancient Roman festival, celebrated on 15 Feb., until its abolition, AD 494, when Pope Gelasius I decreed its replacement by the Christian Lady Day (2 Feb.).

Lusaka. Capital of Zambia (formerly N Rhodesia) since 1935.

Lusatia (Wendish **Lužica;** German **Lausitz**), principally inhabited by the *Wends, was one of the Bohemian crown lands for the period 1160–1360. It was acquired by the Electors of Saxony, 1620. All but a part of Upper L. was ceded to Prussia, 1815. Since 1946 a portion of L. which lies E of the River Neisse, has belonged to Poland.

Lusitania. Unarmed Cunard liner sunk by German submarine off Old Head of Kinsale, 7 May 1915. 1198 passengers and crew, including 124 Americans, were drowned, and the sinking influenced the USA's subsequent decision to enter the war on the Allied side.

Lutheranism, form of Protestantism named after and based on the teachings of Martin Luther (1483–1546) and generally considered as dating from the Augsburg Confession, 1530.

Lutine, **H.M.S.** A 32-gun ship wrecked in a storm off Vlieland, Netherlands, 9–10 Oct. 1799, with specie on board to the then value of £1,175,000. Not until 1823 did the Dutch Government acknowledge that Lloyd's were entitled to half the wreck value, but the underwriters only recovered £22,000. Lloyd's retrieved the ship's bell, known as the **Lutine Bell** and this has since hung in all Lloyd's various buildings. Traditionally rung whenever an important announcement made. Limited salvaging of wreck, 1938, but detailed salvaging in progress since 1990.

Lutterworth, England. Wyclif (*d.* 1384) was rector at the church here, 1374–84. The church, contains many mementoes of the reformer.

Luttrell or **Louterell Psalter.** Illuminated MS of *c.* 1340. Acquired for the nation, 1929.

Lützen, Germany. Wallenstein defeated by Gustavus Adolphus (who was killed), 1632; allies by Napoleon, 1813.

Luxemburg or **Luxembourg,** (in the local Franconian dialect **Letzeburg**). Settled by Franks, AD 459. Independent county, 963. Became Burgundian territory, 1443. Then Hapsburg, 1482; Spanish, 1555; French, 1684–97; Spanish until 1714; Austrian until 1795; then French again until allotted to the United Netherlands at Congress of Vienna, 1815, and garrisoned by Prussia. Seceded from Belgium, 1839, losing thereby Belgian L. Constitution granted, 1848. In 1867, by Treaty of London, it was declared an independent grand duchy, and the Prussians withdrew. The fortifications were at the same time demolished. Occupied by the Germans, 1914–18. Invaded by Germany, 10 May 1940; liberated, 1944. Constitutional revision of 1948, abolished L.'s 'perpetually neutral' status. Joined NATO, 1949. Member of the EEC since 1 Jan. 1958 and site of many of its offices. Grand-Duchess Charlotte abdicated, 1964, succeeded by her son Jean. Jacques Santer of L. became secretary of the EU Commission, 1994.

Lvov. Founded *c.* 1250. Became Polish, 1340. From 1848 centre of the Ukrainian national movement. Part of Austria, 1772–1918, and then Polish until 1939, when it was annexed by the USSR and is now (1995) part of the Ukraine.

Lydia, Asia Minor. Before 700BC known as Maeonia. Conquered by Persians, 546. Independent, 334, but after a period of Syrian and Pergamite domination became part of the Roman province of Asia, 133.

Lynne River flood disaster. On the night of 15–16 Aug. 1952 the E and W L.Rs. burst their banks, and wrecked the town and harbour of Lynmouth, Devon, causing many deaths.

Lyons, France. Roman colony of *Lugdunum* founded, 43 BC. Burnt AD 59; by Romans, 197. Made capital of *Burgundy, 478. United to French crown, 1312. The silk-weaving industry was introduced by Italian refugees about the second decade of the 14thC; it was fostered by Charles VII, Francis I, Henry II, and Henry IV. In 1793 refused to acknowledge National Convention, and was besieged for 70 days and destroyed. Its name was temporarily changed to Ville-Affranchie. Capitulated to Austrians, Mar. 1814 and July 1815. Important centre of French resistance movement, 1940–4; liberated from the Germans by French and American troops, 3 Sept. 1944.

M1. First British motorway intended originally to link London and Birmingham. First section officially opened, Nov. 1959. Marked start of nationwide motorway development which continued into 1990s. M1–A1 link completed, 1993. Proposals to charge for motorway use floated, 1993; testing of electronic tolling planned but subsequently abandoned, Mar. 1995. Proposals to make sections of the M25 14-lane abandoned, April 1995. Speed limits lowered on M25, Aug. 1995.

Maastricht, town in Limburg, Netherlands, place of meeting known as the **Maastricht Summit,** 9–10 Dec. 1991 between 12 heads of government of the *European Community to set out agreed terms for future integration within the community. **Maastricht Treaty** signed, 7 Feb. 1992. Terms endorsed by European Parliament, April 1992. Treaty rejected by Danes in referendum, June 1992 and provoked widespread opposition in UK which had *'Social Chapter' opt-out. In 1993 Danes approved treaty in second referendum. Britain ratified the treaty, 2 Aug. 1993 (the day a year earlier on which the ERM and EMS, basic to the treaty, ceased to fulfil their original function). Germany ratification, Oct. 1993 meant the terms of the treaty could come into force, from Nov. after which the EC was increasingly known as the *European Union (EU).

Mabinogion, The. Title of a collection of eleven medieval Welsh folk-tales found in *The White Book of Rhyd-derch* (c. 1300–25) and *The Red Book of Hergest* (c. 1375–1425) and other MSS.

macadamization of roads. Named after J. L. McAdam (1756–1836). First used in England between 1810 and 1816. Word 'tarmac' registered, 1903.

Macao or **Macau,** China. Portuguese settled at, 1557. Declared a free port, 1845. Treaty with China, 1 Dec. 1887, confirmed Portuguese rights to the territory; under 1974 agreement M., a Chinese territory under Portuguese administration, will revert wholly to China, 1999.

Macassar, Indonesia. First Dutch settlement, 1607. Massacre, 1618.

Macedonia, peopled by Grecian tribes, became united under one government c. 700 BC. Capital: first, Aegae; then, Pella. Persians subdued it c. 490 BC; its king, Alexander I, compelled to help invasion of Greece by Xerxes. Recovered independence after battle of Plataea, 479 BC. Prospered under Archelaus (d. 399 BC). Civil wars till accession, 359 BC, of Philip II, who became leader of Greece. His son, Alexander the Great, ruled 336–323 and was succeeded by Antipater (d. 319 BC). Civil wars ensued; security regained under Antigonus Gonatos, 277–239 BC. Conquered by Rome, 168 BC; became a Roman province, 143 BC; later, part of *Eastern Roman Empire. Overrun by Slavs at end of 6thC AD. Dominated by Bulgarians, 9th–11thC. Mission of Cyril and Methodius, c. 860, led to Macedonian, first among Slavonic languages, being reduced to writing in the Cyrillic and Glagolithic scripts invented by the missionaries. 11thC MSS (Codex Zagrophenic, etc.) still extant. Byzantine rule re-established, early 11thC. Included in Serbia in 14thC, fell to Turks in 15thC. Claimed by Greece, Serbia, and Bulgaria in 19thC; and was in a continuous state of civil war till 1903, when the Bulgarians rose and the Turks were massacred. The Balkan League's victory over Turkey, 1912–3, and the defeat of Bulgaria, resulted in division of M. between Greece, Bulgaria, and Serbia, 1913. Civil war started by

Communists in Greek M., with Yugoslav and Bulgarian assistance; ended, 1948. Macedonian recognized as a separate nationality and language at AVNOJ session of 29 Sept. 1943, and Macedonian Republic set up, as a constituent part of Yugoslavia, 2 Aug. 1944.

Macedonia – former federal republic of Yugoslavia. Independence movement grew during 1980s; in 1990 elections removed ruling Communists. Declared independence, 1992 but this rejected initially by Serbia and name M. refused by Greece which claimed it for Greek M. exclusively. Albanian minority also agitating for independence from 1990. UN sent peacekeeping mission to M. and recognized it in April 1993 as the Former Yugoslav Republic of M. but tensions with Greece continued and economic hardships in M. as result of Greek trade blockade. Elections, Nov. 1994, confirmed position of ruling Alliance Party. Agreement, Sept. 1995 between M. and Greece brokered by the USA. Macedonian flag modified and Greek blockade lifted.

McGill University of Canada, founded as a private college by James McG. of Glasgow (*d.* 1813). Incorporated, 1821 and 1852.

machine gun, invented 1884 by H. S. Maxim (1840–1916).

Machu Picchu, ancient Peruvian city of the Andes, built *c.* AD 800, rebuilt in the 16thC after having been abandoned once. Site rediscovered, 1911, by Hiram Bingham who, in 1948, formally opened a new highway to the city, named after him.

M'Naughten Rules, the answers to a set of questions put to the judges as a body by the House of Lords following the acquittal on grounds of insanity of Daniel M'N., who in 1843 shot dead Sir R. Peel's private secretary. Now superseded.

Madagascar (known as **Malagasy,** 1958–75). Appears on Arab charts of 12thC. Visited by Diego Diaz (Portugal), 1500. Granted, 1642, by Louis XIV to the Compagnie de l'Orient. French massacred by natives, 1672. British took possession, 1814;

French returned after 1815. British ascendancy, 1810–28. Under Queen Rànavàlona I, missionaries were persecuted and trade hampered, 1829. Europeans returned to Antananarivo after 1853. French protectorate established 1895, monarchy abolished. M. made a French colony, 1896. Occupied by British, May–Sept. 1942. French resumed administration, 1944. M. an independent republic, 26 June 1960; military rule, 1972–5. New constitution, 1975; overturned, 1991, when the ruling revolutionary supreme council and national people's assembly dissolved. New constitution, Aug. 1992. Elections, 1992–3 made Zafy first president of a new republic of M. Severe ecological damage in M. since 1960s.

'Mad cow disease'. *See* BOVINE SPONGIFORM ENCEPHALOPATHY.

Madeira, Atlantic. Porto Santo discovered, 1418; M. itself, 1420, by João Gonçalves Zarco. Colonized by Portuguese, 1431. Occupied by British, 1801 and 1807–14, in trust for Portuguese crown. Unsuccessful rebellion against Portuguese rule, Apr.–May 1931: granted partial autonomy 1980.

Madhya Pradesh, India. Present state came into existence, 1 Nov. 1956, with the merger of the states of Madhya Bharat and Vindhya with most of the former Central Provinces (renamed M.P. from 1947 onwards), excluding the Mahratta-speaking districts of the latter.

Mad Parliament, 1258. It appointed the committee which drew up the *Provisions of Oxford.

Madras, *India. City and former state (see TAMIL NADU). English established themselves in, 1639; city captured by French, 1746; restored to English, 1748; besieged by French, 12 Dec. 1758 and shelled by Germans, 1914.

Madras Mutiny, among European officers of the E India Co.'s army, broke out, 1809.

Madrid, Spain. Founded by Moors in 10thC as *Medina Majerit.* Taken by Ramiro II,

King of Leon, 939, but not permanently conquered until 1083. First charter, 1202. Cortes first held there, 1309. Rebuilt, 14thC, by Henry III. Treaty between Charles V and Francis I, 1526. Declared capital of Spain by Philip II, 1561. Palacio Real built on site of old alcazar, 1738–64: Prado Museum built, 1785–1819. Captured from French by allied forces under Wellington, 1812. University of M. was established by the removal of that of Alcalá to the capital, 1836–7. Much expansion and industrialization, 1850–to present day.

Mafeking Night, 18 May 1900, when news reached London that M. had been relieved after a seven-month siege by the Boers.

Mafia, originally, Sicilian secret movement possibly with 16thC origins, but in its modern form founded between 1800 and 1825. It rose to great power, 1860–70, and in the 1890s its influence spread to the USA, where a large number of immigrants to New York were of Sicilian origin. The Fascists claimed to have crushed the organization in 1928, but, partially due to US wartime support of M. influence as a counter to Fascism, there was a recrudescence of violence and extortion in Sicily after World War II which gradually affected several areas of Italian business and government. By the 1980s the M. was prominent in kidnapping, murder, vice and drug dealings in both Italy and the USA. In the 1990s there were a number of successful prosecutions of M. leaders in the USA. In Italy, 1993, several former government leaders and businessmen accused of being involved with the M. Government crisis resulted, and radical constitutional changes followed. Ex-premier Andreotti on trial for alleged M. crimes, Sept. 1995. Term M. also loosely used since 1950s to describe criminal organizations in several parts of the world other than Italy and the USA. *See also* CA-MORRA; ITALY.

Magdeburg, Germany, capital of Saxony-Auhalt since 1990. Founded by Charlemagne, AD 805; destroyed by the Wends, 924, and refounded shortly afterwards by

Editha; made seat of a bishopric, 968; joined Luther, 17 July 1524; joined League of *Schmalkalden, 1531; surrendered to Maurice of Saxony, Nov. 1551; besieged by Wallenstein, 1629; sacked by Tilly, 1631; annexed to kingdom of Westphalia, 1803; restored to Prussia, 1814. Canal link with Rhine, 1938.

Magellan, Straits of, discovered, 1520, by the Portuguese navigator, Ferdinand M. (1480–1521).

Maginot Line. Pre-1939 E fortifications of France, constructed 1928–34. Named after André Maginot (1877–1932), minister of war. 'Turned' during German offensive, 1940.

Magna Carta or **The Great Charter** of England. The barons compelled King John to grant it at Runnymede, 15 June 1215.

Magnum Concilium or Great Council of Peers last met at York, 1640.

Mahabad, Iran. Kurdish town centre of Kurdish resistance to Iran since 1940s. Proclaimed a republic 1945–6, but suppressed.

Mahdi. *See* SUDAN.

Maharashtra, state of W central India, established 1960. Capital is *Bombay.

Mahrattas. First appear in Indian history in the middle of 17thC. Defeated by Afghans, Jan. 1761. From 1780 onwards at war with the British and their allies. Of their leaders the Peishwa of Poona was compelled to accept a British alliance in 1802, the Gaekwar of Baroda in 1803, the Scindiah and the Bhonsla of Nagpur in 1804, the latter being then forced to cede Berar to the Nizam of *Hyderabad. War nevertheless continued and culminated in the submission of the Holkar of Indore in 1817, the British annexation of Poona in 1818, and the abolition of the Peishwaship. The claimant to this office, Nana Sahib, later played a leading part in the *Indian Mutiny. Satara was annexed in 1848, Nagpur in 1853.

maiden, beheading machine used in Scotland and in some northern English boroughs (*see* HALIFAX LAW) in the Middle Ages. That of Edinburgh was first used, 1561; last used, 1710.

Maiden Castle, earthwork in Dorset, one of the largest in Europe, surrounding a site inhabited from *c.* 2000 BC and fortified from *c.* 300 BC until the inhabitants were forcibly evacuated by the Romans after being defeated by Vespasian, AD 43. It was excavated by Sir Mortimer Wheeler, 1934–7. Further excavations and repairs since 1985.

Maine, French province *c.* 1600 up to 1789, with capital at Le Mans. From *c.* AD 800 was ruled by counts who were themselves vassals of the counts of *Anjou. United with Anjou under the Angevins, 1110. English territory, 1154–1204. It belonged to the Count of Provence, 1246–1328, then passed again to the French crown. It returned permanently to the French crown in 1481.

Maine, USA. First permanent settlement, at Pemaquid, 1623. Western territory, known as province of M., 1635, from 1651 to 1820 a detached part of Massachusetts. The present state of M. founded, 1820; boundary dispute with Great Britain settled, 1842.

Mainz or **Mayence,** Germany. Of Celtic origin; Roman military station called *Moguntiacum* dates from 13 BC; cathedral built, AD 975–1009; head of the confederacy of Rhenish cities, 13thC; in French possession, 1797–1814; by Congress of Vienna, 1814–5, ceded to Hesse-Darmstadt; declared a federal fortress, 1870. Heavily damaged during fighting in 1945.

Majorca (Spanish **Mallorca**), Mediterranean, conquered by the Romans, 123 BC; by the Vandals, AD 423; by the Moors, 790; became a Moorish kingdom, 1009; independent Christian kingdom, 1276–1349, when finally annexed by Aragon. Held by the nationalists during the civil war 1936–9; prominent tourist centre since 1950s.

Major-General. Rank was instituted in Britain with special sense by Oliver Crom-

well in 1655, after he had quarrelled with his first Parliament. Each M.-G. was to govern a district. This scheme was dropped in 1657.

Malacca, *Malaysia. Settled by Portuguese, 1511, who held it until 1641, when the Dutch seized it and, in turn, held it until 1795, when the English took possession; restored to the Dutch by the Peace of Amiens, 1801; exchanged with Britain for Sumatra, 1825; made part of Straits Settlements, 1867. Incorporated in the Malayan Union, 1947, in the Malayan Federation, 1948, and in Malaysia, 1963.

Malaga, Spain. Founded by Phoenicians; Moorish from 711. Captured from Moors by Ferdinand and Isabella, 1487. Sacked by French, 1810.

Malagasy. *See* MADAGASCAR.

Malawi, formerly **Nyasaland**, E Africa. Visited by Bocarro, 1616. By Livingstone, 1859. African Lakes Co. established, 1878. Rhodes obtained charter to develop Nyasaland, 1884. Protectorate established, 1891. Suppression of slave trade, 1893–7. John Chelembwe's revolt, 1915. United with the Rhodesias in Central African Federation, 1953. In 1963 became a self-governing colony, nationalist leader Hastings Banda being premier. Federation dissolved, Dec. 1963. On 6 July 1964 Nyasaland, under the new name of **Malawi**, became an independent state within the Commonwealth, subsequently a republic, with Banda as president, July 1966 (life president from 1971). Some liberalization from 1980s but increased calls in 1990s for further reforms. Influx of refugees from Mozambique in 1980s caused social and economic problems. In June 1993, referendum voted for end of one-party rule. In elections, May 1994, Banda's party overwhelmingly defeated. He retired, succeeded by Muluzi. In Jan. 1995, Banda put under house arrest for alleged connivance in political murders carried out during 1980s. *See also* RHODESIA AND NYASALAND, FEDERATION OF.

Malaya. Main treaties establishing British

predominance made with Perak, 1874; Selangor, 1874; Negri Sembilan, 1896; Pahang, 1888. These states were federated in 1896. By treaty with Siam, Siamese suzerainty over Kelantan, Trengganu, Kedah and Perlis ceded to Britain, 1909. Johore came under British influence after 1815, and ceded Singapore to Britain, 1819. Penang was purchased from Kedah, 1786. Malacca ceded by the Dutch, 1825. Japanese invasion began, 8 Dec. 1941. *See* MALAYAN FEDERATION, MALAYAN UNION, MALAYSIA, and all the separate states and territories mentioned above.

Malayan Federation, including all former British colonies and protectorates in the Malay Peninsula and Islands, excluding the colony of Singapore, inaugurated its Legislative Council, 24 Feb. 1948. Communist rebellion broke out, May 1948; crushed by 1955. The M.F. became a self-governing Dominion within the Commonwealth, 31 Aug. 1957. Became part of *Malaysia, 16 Sept. 1963.

Malayan Union. Proposal for reorganization of M. states and colonies published, 22 Jan. 1946. Union inaugurated, 1 Apr. 16. Came to an end, 1 Feb. 1948.

Malaysia, union of the Malayan Federation, Singapore, N Borneo (renamed *Sabah) and Sarawak. M. came into being on 16 Sept. 1963. Indonesia began a policy of aggressive 'confrontation' which ended, Aug. 1966. *Singapore seceded from M. by mutual agreement, 9 Aug. 1965. New Development Policy launched, 1991. Sultans agreed to give up legal privileges, Feb. 1993. M. temporarily stopped trade with Britain, Feb. 1994, owing to *Pergau dam dispute; resumed, Sept.

Maldive Islands, former British protectorate having treaty relations with *Sri Lanka. A new constitution established a sultanate, 1932, which was abolished in 1952 when the M.I. became a republic. Sultanate restored, 1954. Became independent, 26 July 1965; republic since 1968. Full member of the Commonwealth, 1985. Attempted coup failed, 1988.

Mali, independent African republic since 22 Sept. 1960. Military regime, 1968; civil constitution, 1979 but further military coup, 1991. Multiparty elections, 1992. For previous history *see* SUDAN: *French Sudan.*

Malines or **Mechelen,** Belgium. Made a separate fief, 754. Passed to Philip the Bold of Burgundy, 1384. Became archbishopric, 1559. Sacked by Spaniards, 1572.

Mall, The (London), began to have houses built along the N side, 1650–60. Redesigned, 1903. Opened to traffic, 1911.

Malta, G.C. Phoenicians colonized the island, 16thC BC; Greeks dispossessed them, 736 BC; driven out by Carthaginians *c.* 500 BC. Became finally Roman, 201 BC. St Paul shipwrecked at, 1stC AD. Fell to Vandals, then Goths, in the 5thC; liberated by Belisarius, 533, and nominally united with E Empire. Arabs drove out the Greeks, 870, and made M. a centre of piracy. Count Roger of Sicily drove Arabs from, 1090; conquered by Spain, 1282; given by the Emperor Charles V to the Knights of the Order of St John of Jerusalem, 1530, who owned the island until 1798, when the French took possession; the Maltese rebelled, and the island was recognized as British by the Congress of Vienna, 1814–15. Maltese superseded Italian as language of courts, 1934. Severely damaged by Italian and German bombing, 1940–3. Island awarded the George Cross (G.C.) by King George VI, 17 Apr. 1942. Agitation, first for 'integration,' with Britain, and then for independence, from 1945. M. independent state within Commonwealth since 21 Sept. 1964. Labour party under Mintoff gained power 1972. M. became a republic within the Commonwealth, 1974. Non-aligned policy pursued from 1972 and British base closed, 1979. Old and new universities amalgamated as university of M., 1980. After Nationalist regained power in 1980s, privatization programme pursued and closer links with W. Constitutional amendment 1987; applied to join EC, 1991.

Malta, Knights of. Known also as the Order of the Knights of St John of Jerusalem, the Knights of Rhodes, and the Hospitallers; founded by one Gerald or Gerard in a hospital at Jerusalem *c.* 1070; sanctioned by Pope Paschal II, 1113; Frederick Barbarossa took the Order under his protection, 1185; captured Rhodes, 1310, which they held until 1523; Charles V presented them with the island of *M 1530, which they surrendered in 1798, when the Order became a charitable religious institution, establishing its headquarters at Rome in 1878. The modern English Order of St John is a purely secular and philanthropic institution, incorporated by charter in 1888.

Malvern Festival. Founded, 1929, and partially revived in 1970s.

Maluku, formerly known as the **Moluccas.** Indonesian islands which attempted to secede in 1949 but were unsuccessful.

Malvinas, Argentine name for the *Falkland Islands.

Mamelukes. The Turkish M. under Kutuz seized the government of Egypt, 1250. They were superseded by the Circassian M., 1390, and the latter ruled till the Ottoman conquest of 1517.

Man, Isle of. Ruled by Welsh kings, 6th–9thC, when the Norwegians conquered the island; ceded to the kings of Scotland, 1266; inhabitants placed themselves under protection of Edward I of England, 1290; kingdom granted to Sir John Stanley, 1406; surrendered to parliamentary army, 1651; fell by inheritance to the Duke of Atholl, from whom it was purchased by the British Government after prolonged negotiations (1765–1829) and is now a dependency of the crown, retaining its own ancient legislature.

Managua, capital of Nicaragua since 1857. Virtually destroyed by earthquakes, 1931 and 1972. University of M. became part of University of Nicaragua, 1952. Scene of strikes and fighting against Somoza regime, 1978–9.

Manchester, England. There was a Roman fort, called *Mancunium* or *Mamucium*, in the Castleford district of M., founded *c.* AD 79 during Agricola's conquest. It was later called *Mamecestre.* Captured by Edwin, King of Northumbria, 620; King Edward the Elder sent forces to repair and man it, 923; first charter granted, 14 May 1301; grammar school founded, 1515; during civil war Fairfax captured it, 1643; walls and fortifications removed, 1652; Peterloo Massacre at, 1819; University founded (as Owens College), 1851: reorganized 1880 and 1903. Hallé orchestra founded at, 1857. M. Ship Canal built, 1887–94. Centre of cotton industry in Britain from 18th–mid-20thC. University of Salford established at, 1967; M. polytechnic became M. Metropolitan University, 1992.

Manchuria (Japanese **Manchukuo**). Conquered *China, 1644, and founded the Chinese dynasty that reigned there till 1911; the occupation of M. by *Russia caused the Russo-Japanese War, 1904–5. Made into a state separate from China, 18 Feb. 1932, by *Japan who installed the former emperor of China, P'yu yi, as emperor (under the name of Kang Teh) of Manchukuo, 1 Mar. 1934. Absorbed into China, 1945.

Mandalay, built as the capital city of Burma by King Thebaw *c.* 1860. Captured by British, 1885. Largely destroyed by fire, 1892. Held by Japanese, 8 May 1942–13 Mar. 1945.

mandates, trusteeship system of government devised, after World War I, under League of Nations auspices, for former German and Turkish overseas territories. Several M. held by Britain and France: system defunct after 1945.

Manhattan Island, USA. Purchased from Red Indians for Dutch W India Co. by Peter Minuit, 1624. Basis of modern *New York and centre of financial and theatre area.

Manichaeism. A dualistic religion ascribed to Mani (*c.* 215–77). Numerous Persians converted, 241 onwards. Spread to Roman Empire, 280–440. From it are descended the Bogomil, Paulician, Catharist, and *Albigensian doctrines.

Manifest Destiny, term used by John L. O'Sullivan, 1845, in the *U.S. Magazine and Democratic Review*. It implied the inevitability of US expansion W. and even beyond and was used to justify the annexation of Texas and Oregon, and the Mexican War. Revived as a Republican tenet in 1890s with reference to the Philippines, etc.

Manila, capital of the Philippine Islands. Founded by Legaspi, 1571. Attacked by British, 1762. Spanish squadron destroyed by US Navy, May 1898. Occupied by the Japanese, 2 Jan. 1942. Retaken by the Americans, 5–24 Feb. 1945. Scene of fighting during downfall of Marcos regime, 1986, and subsequently during (failed) coups to oust Aquino regime.

Manila Conference.
1. Held 6–8 Sept. 1954, on SE Asia defence, and ended with the signing of the South East Asian Collective Defence Treaty.
2. Held Oct. 1966, attended by Australia, New Zealand, the Philippines, the USA, Thailand, S Korea and S Vietnam in an (abortive) attempt to secure a settlement in Vietnam.

Manipur, NE India, governed from Assam until 1947. Then a Union Territorial State since 1972. Modern *polo said to have originated here.

Manitoba. Fur-trading posts established, 18thC. Known as Red River Colony from 1812 and administered by Hudson's Bay Co. (*see under* HUDSON BAY TERRITORY) till 1869. Became a province of Canada, 1870. Extended boundaries, 1881 and 1912.

Mansion House (London). The official residence of the Lord Mayor, building begun, 1739 by George Dance, Sr, completed 1753.

Mantua, Italy. Ruled by the Gonzagas, 1328–1708. Taken by French, 1797; by Austrians, 1814; surrendered to Italy, 1866.

Maori Wars.
1. Between the settlers of New Zealand and the Maoris, 1843–7; it resulted in the definition of boundaries.
2. Boundary disputes caused war, 1863–Aug. 1864.
3. In consequence of a massacre of Europeans by Maoris, July 1869–Jan. 1870.

Maputo. Mozambique, founded by the Portuguese, 1544, as **Lourenço Marques**; changed name to M., 1975.

Maquis (Corsican dialect for Italian **Macchia**). Mediterranean heath, hence hilly country covered by it; since the Napoleonic Wars, synonym for outlawry, phrase popularized by romances of Prosper Mérimée (1803–70); applied to Frenchmen who took to the hills to avoid forced labour after the occupation by the Germans of 'Vichy' France, Nov. 1942, and became a loose synonym for *FFI.

Marathon, in Attica, scene of the defeat of the Persians by Athenians and Plataeans, 490 BC. Of the several monuments, which were described by Pausanias, AD 110, only the burial mound of the 192 Athenians killed in the action is now known. In 20thC name of long-distance running race; in Olympics since 1896. Several cities now have their annual M. (including London, since 1981, each spring): earliest of these was the Boston M., (USA), begun 1897.

Marble Arch (London). Originally erected in front of Buckingham Palace by Nash, 1828. Moved to present site, 1851. Traffic island since 1908. *Tyburn gallows here till 1783.

Marchioness Tragedy, occurred 20 Aug. 1989 when the pleasure boat *Marchioness* sank in the Thames after colliding with the *Bowbelle*. 51 people died.

Mariana Islands, formerly **Ladrones Islands**, Pacific Ocean. Discovered by Magellan *c*. 1521. *Guam the largest, ceded to USA by Spain, 1898; remainder sold to Germany, 1899; mandated to Japan, 1919. Scene of heavy fighting in World War II. USA took over administration as a trusteeship for the UN, 18 July 1947. In 1976 Congress established a Commonwealth of the M.I., effective from 1986.

Marine Corps (USA). Established by Congress in Nov. 1775; became a permanent arm of the service by the Act of 11 July 1798. Now regulated by National Security Act, 1947, and its amendments of 1952.

marketing boards for agricultural products. Established under Act of 1933; all wound up since 1980s, the last being the Milk Marketing Board in 1994.

Marlborough House (London), built by Wren, 1709, for John Churchill, first Duke of M., who died there, 1722. Occupied by Queen Mary, 1936–53, and given to the nation by Queen Elizabeth II, 17 Feb. 1959, for use as a Commonwealth Centre. Since 1965 HQ of the Commonwealth Secretariat.

Marlborough, Parliament of, 1267, after the *Barons' War.

Maronites, Syrians who adopted Christianity in the 5thC, abandoned Monothelite heresy, 1182, when they adhered to the Church of *Rome, though they left it again temporarily, 1382–1445.

Maroon (from Spanish **Cimarron**, a runaway slave especially in the Caribbean). The Ms. of Jamaica, who lived in the interior mountains, were in a state of rebellion against the English from 1655 till the Maroon War of 1796, most of the survivors of which were transported to Nova Scotia and Sierra Leone.

Marprelate Controversy. Caused by certain writings against episcopacy by Elizabethan Puritans, 1587–9; supposed to have been written by John Penry, who was executed in 1593.

Marquesas Islands, the first European to sight the M.I. was the Spaniard Mendaña de Nera, 1594. Were not all known to navigators until 1701. Became a French protectorate, 1842. Overseas territories of the French Community since 1958; form a part of French Polynesia.

marriage laws (Britain). Lord Hardwicke's Act of 1753 provided that Ms. must be performed in the parish church,

with the exception of those of Jews or Quakers. This Act superseded by the Marriage Act of 1823. Dissenters' M. Act, 1836, permitted Dissenters to marry in their own chapels or churches or enter into a civil contract by giving notice to the registrar. This was followed by several M. Acts, the most important of which are: Deceased Wife's Sister's M. Acts, 1907; Deceased Brother's Widow's M. Act, 1921; Age of M. Act (making void Ms. of persons under 16), 1929. Present statute M.L. contained in the M. Acts, 1949–83. Foreign Marriages Acts, 1892–47, provide for British subjects marrying abroad: the Royal Marriages Act, 1772, legislated regarding royal marriages. M.L. affected by modern divorce laws (*see* DIVORCE) and by 1983 Nationality Act. 1994 Marriage Act legalized marriages in England and Wales that took place in approved locations other than register offices or places of worship (as was already the case in Scotland).

Married Women's Property Act, 18 Aug. 1882, abolished the rule whereby upon marriage a woman's property passed at law to her husband. Amended subsequently, notably in 1893, 1907, 1925, 1935, 1949, 1970 and 1981.

Marseillaise, The, national anthem of the French Republic, was partly written and composed in 1792 by Rouget de Lisle, an officer stationed at Strasbourg. Originally called *Chant de guerre pour l'Armée du Rhin*. It was forbidden under the Restoration and Second Empire, and again became the national song during the Franco-Prussian War of 1870. Official national anthem since 1879.

Marseilles, France. One of the oldest cities in France, being a Greek settlement in the 7thC BC, and known to Romans as *Massalia* or *Massilia*. Captured by Julius Caesar, 49 BC; became a republic, AD 1112; revival as a Crusader port, 11th–14thC; treacherously surrendered to Henry IV; shortly after it finally lost its independence. Basilica dating from 8thC largely rebuilt, 1853, 12thC cathedral. Charité hospital, 1660–1750; 18thC, Fort Saint John. Old port district and port destroyed by Germans 1943–4: since rebuilt.

Marshall Islands, Pacific Ocean, came under German protection, 1885. Mandated to Japan, 1920. Overrun by US forces, 1944. Put under UN trusteeship, 1946, the USA administering. Moves to independence from 1981 blocked by Soviet Union; but after USSR dissolved. Russia withdrew objections and M.I. recognized by UN as an independent republic, 1990.

Marshall Plan or **European Recovery Programme (ERP).** Original proposal made by George M. (1880–1959), US Secretary of State, in speech at Harvard University, 5 June 1947. Interim Aid Bill signed by President Truman, 17 Dec. 1947. Convention for European Economic Co-operation (16 nations) signed at Paris, 16 Apr. 1948. This was the foundation of *OEEC, although the M.P. itself came to an end in 1952.

Marshalsea Prison, in what is now the Borough High Street, Southwark, was built at some time between 1327 and 1377, and first used to confine those who 'broke the King's peace' within a certain radius of Westminster Palace; later housing maritime criminals. It became specifically a debtors' prison *c.* 1560, but at some time the site was changed because the M. prison where the father of Charles Dickens was imprisoned, 1824–5, was farther down the Borough High Street; was united with the King's Bench and Fleet prisons in 1842, and was demolished, 1887.

Martello towers. Built as English coast defences at the end of the 18thC, after the model of a fort on Cape Mortella, Corsica, bombarded by British in 1794.

Martinique. Discovered by the Spaniards, 1493. Settled by French, 1635. Slavery abolished, 1860. An overseas *département* of France since 1946. Overseas region status, 1974. Greater self-government since 1982.

Maryland, USA. Explored by John Smith, 1608. First settled by Capt. William Claiborne, 1634. Named after Henrietta Maria, queen of Charles I. One of the original 13 states of the USA, 1776: official statehood, 1788.

Marylebone Cricket Club, better known as M.C.C., first so called in 1787, when an already existing club began to play in Dorset Square, M.

Mary Rose, warship and flagship of Henry VIII, sank off Southsea 1545 while leaving harbour, with loss of 700 lives; salvaged, 1982 and it and various artefacts since displayed at Southsea. Conservation of ship still continuing, 1995.

Mashonaland, Zimbabwe. Placed under British protection, 1888; powers of administration granted to British S Africa Co., 1889.

Mason-Dixon Line (USA), drawn by two English surveyors, M. and D., who in settlement of a dispute between the proprietors of the various colonies demarcated the boundary between Maryland and Pennsylvania, 1763–7. This line and its westward continuation became from 1820 onwards the boundary between 'slave' and 'free' states and the phrase and its abbreviation 'Dixie' achieved greatest currency in the Civil War (1863) period.

Massachusetts, USA. Explored by Gosnold, 1602; Champlain, 1604; John Smith, 1614. Settled by English Puritans, Nov. 1620, who sailed over in the *Mayflower*. First constitution framed, 1780; amended, 1820. Constitution of USA adopted, 1788.

Master of the King's (or **Queen's**) **Musick,** an office instituted, 1660, was conferred on Sir Malcolm Williamson in 1975.

Masulipatam, India. English settlement founded, 1611. Held by Dutch, 1686–90. Given to French by Nizam of Hyderabad, 1750. Captured by British under Forde, Apr. 1758.

Matabeleland, Zimbabwe. Ceded to the British S Africa Co., 1889. Matabele rebellion, 1896; ended by Rhodes' mediation, Aug. 1896.

Matrix-Churchill Affair. Acquittal of three executives of Coventry-based Matrix-Churchill company who had been charged with illegal exporting to Iraq from 1989, revealed conflicting advice given by different government departments, 1992, and law officers. Scott inquiry into M.-C.A. began, May 1993. Lady Thatcher gave evidence to, Dec; John Major, Jan. 1994. June 1995, rumours of some government ministers withholding information from Scott inquiry.

Matterhorn (Switzerland)(14,688 ft/4478 m). Summit first reached, 14 July 1865. First winter ascent of the N face made by two Swiss climbers, 4 Feb. 1962.

Mau-Mau, revolutionary movement among the Kikuyu tribe from the 1950s aiming to dominate first it and then all other Africans in *Kenya with a view to seizing power in Kenya. Between 1952 and 1957, cattle maimed and several Europeans and others killed. Trial of Jomo Kenyatta, Dec. 1952–Mar. 1953. Kenyatta found guilty of managing M.-M. and sentenced to life imprisonment. By 1957 M.-M. crushed. Kenyatta freed in Aug. 1961 and subsequently became leader of an independent Kenya.

Maumbury Rings, England, late Neolithic or early Bronze Age (*c.* 1800 BC) fortification converted during the Roman occupation (after AD 200) to an amphitheatre (capable of seating 10,000) which was excavated 1908 and 1913. Site used for public executions up to 1767.

Maundy Thursday. The Thursday before Good Friday, also known as Holy Thursday, on which day alms are still given to the aged poor in the form of 'M. money' by the British sovereign. In the form of 'dole' till 1833, since when replaced by a money payment (M. Money). Provisions for this money revised by Acts of 1971 and 1973. The money was traditionally given out at Westminster Abbey; but Elizabeth II varied the venue considerably to cover Anglican cathedrals all over the country.

Mauritania, independent Islamic republic in W Africa, made a French protectorate, 1903, and a colony, 4 Dec. 1920. From Nov. 1958 M. was a member of the French Community, and became an independent republic on 28 Nov. 1960. Under military rule 1978–92, when multiparty elections held but conflict between Arab majority and African minority continues. Got W Sahara from Spain, 1975: conflict with Morocco, 1981–5.

Mauritius, Indian Ocean. Discovered by the Portuguese between 1505 and 1512; occupied by the Dutch, and named M. after Prince Maurice of Orange, 1598; abandoned by Dutch, 1710; occupied by French, 1715; captured by English, 1810; formally ceded to England by Treaty of Paris, 1814. Became an independent dominion, 1968; republic from 12 March 1992. 1968 constitution amended, 1969 and 1991.

mausoleum. Named after the tomb erected for King Mausolus of Halicarnassus, in Caria (377–353 BC), by his widow, Queen Artemisia II, *c.* 352 BC.

Mayas, a race based on the Yucatan in Central America. Its civilisation arose *c.* 2500 BC. The first M. empire lasted 2nd–8thC AD. The second empire was founded, AD 1000, and was still flourishing at the time of the Spanish conquest in the 16thC.

May Day, in pagan times was an almost universal feast in Europe, taking place at or soon after the vernal equinox, as the Roman *Floralia* did. Tolerated in England from the time of Augustine's mission until 1644, when it was banned, but revived in 1661. Public holiday associated with socialist movement in many European countries since 19thC. A M.D. bank holiday on the first Monday in the month, has been observed in the UK since 1978; exceptionally on the second Monday, in 1995 to coincide with 50th anniversary of V-E Day. *See also* LABOUR DAY.

***Mayflower*, The.** Sailed from Plymouth, England, 16 Sept. 1620. The M. compact was signed off Cape Cod, 2 Nov., and the

*Pilgrim Fathers landed in Massachusetts, 21 Dec. 1620. Society of M. Descendants founded, 1894. On 20 Apr. 1957 *Mayflower II*, a replica of the first ship, sailed from Plymouth to Cape Cod, in connection with the 350th anniversary of the first permanent English settlement in N America (at Jamestown, Virginia).

Maynooth College (Ireland). College first established, 1521. Refounded, 1795, by Irish Parliament for education of candidates for Irish Roman Catholic priesthood.

Mayor as a title for the chief dignitary of a city first appears in England *c*. AD 1100.

M.C.C. *See* MARYLEBONE CRICKET CLUB.

Meal Tub Plot, 1679. Pretended conspiracy against the Duke of York originated by Dangerfield.

Mecca (Arabic **Om al Kora**). Holiest of Muslim shrines, containing the Great Mosque and Kaaba. The pilgrimage now (1995) attracts over 600,000 Muslims from all over the world, each year. Known to Ptolemy in the 2ndC AD. Expelled Mohammed, 622, who returned and captured it, 630. Captured by Wahabis, 1803, but ceded to Mehemet Ali, pasha of Egypt, 1833. Captured again by Wahabis under Abdul Aziz ibn Sa'ud, 13 Oct. 1924, who was proclaimed king of the Hejaz here, 1926 (later, Saudi Arabia). Over 400 Iranian pilgrims killed in clash with Saudi police at M., 1987; stampede caused *c*. 1,500 pilgrim deaths there, July 1990.

Mecklenburg, Germany. Became duchy, 1348. Lutheranism became state religion, 1549. Partitioned, 1611. Repartitioned into M.-Schwerin and M.-Strelitz, but with joint diet, 1701. Serfdom abolished, 1819. Joined N German Confederation, 1866. With W part of former Pomerania, region of E Germany, 1946, split into districts, 1952. After German reunification, 1990. M.-W Pomerania revised as one of Federal Germany's five states.

Medallin, Colombia, notorious since 1980s as one of the 'drug-capitals' of the world. Deaths by violence there in 1990s at rate of several thousand per year.

Media, in NW Iran, became independent of Assyria *c*. 708 BC, and overthrew the Assyrian Empire, 612. Amalgamated with Persia, 560. Became part of the Macedonian Empire, 331. After 624 the NW portion became independent and remained so, under the name of Atropatene, until the 1stC AD. The remainder thereafter was alternately in the possession of Persia, Syria and Parthia.

Medici family. Chiefs of the Florentine Republic from 1434. Contributed to the renaissance of literature and the arts in Italy. Cosimo de' M. (1389–1464) was the first chief. Lorenzo de' M. ruled, 1469–92; he was the father of Pope Leo X. Caterina de' M. became Queen of France, 1547; Maria de' M., 1600. The family became extinct, 1737.

Medina (Arabic for 'the city'), in full **Medinat Rasul Allah**, was the residence of Mohammed in AD 622. He *d*. and was buried here, 632.

Medina del Campo, Treaty of, 1489. By it Henry VII of England betrothed his infant son Arthur to Catherine of Aragon.

Medjugorje, Croatia, scene of reported visions of the Virgin Mary by six local children, June 1981, and since a place of pilgrimage.

Meissen, Saxony, a castle founded here by Henry I, 929, as the nucleus of a margravate (border county) established, 966, which became part of the electorate of Saxony, 1423. The manufacture of porcelain began, 1710. Some leading designers were Hörold (1720–35), Kändler (1735–56), Count Marcolini (1774–1813). Most so-called 'Dresden' ware, 1710–1863, was made at M.

Melbourne, Australia. Site first occupied, 1835. Named M., 1837. Made an Anglican diocese, 1849. Became capital of Victoria, 1851. Seat of commonwealth government, 1901–27. University founded, 1854.

Melfi, Apulia, founded, AD 304, became capital of the Norman duchy of Apulia, 1044. Its cathedral, built in 1155, was almost totally destroyed in the earthquake of 1851.

Mellifont (Ireland), first Cistercian abbey in Ireland, founded, 1142, by St Malachy (1094–1148). Ruins first excavated, 1884–5.

Melos (Italian **Milo**), island in the Cyclades, taken by Athenians, 416 BC; by Turks, 1566. The statue of Venus called 'de Milo' found here, 1820.

Melrose Abbey (Scotland). Founded by David I in 1136; partly destroyed by English in 1322 and 1385; reduced to ruin by Lord Hertford, 1545.

Memel, German for *Klaipeda.

Memphis.
1. Capital of Egypt *c*. 3200 BC until replaced by Thebes *c*. 1600; now ruined.
2. Industrial city of Tennessee, USA. Founded 1819.

Menai Straits (Wales). Telford's suspension bridge open, 1826 (reconstructed 1940). Stephenson's tubular railway bridge, 1850, damaged by fire, 1970.

Mendelism. Theory of heredity propounded between 1865 and 1869 by G. J. Mendel (1822–84) while abbot of the Augustinian monastery at Brno. *See* GENETICS.

Menin Gate (Ypres, Belgium). Unveiled by Lord Plumer, 24 July 1927.

Mennonites, pacifist Protestant sect, successors to the Anabaptists, formed *c*. 1537, taking their name from the preacher Menno Simons (1492–1559). Several colonies of M. formed in S Russia, 1786, and the first Mennonite congregation established at Germantown, Pennsylvania, 1683. In 1871, considerable numbers settled in Kansas and Minnesota.

Mensheviks (Russian **menshinstvo**, minority), a wing of the Russian Social Democratic Party, founded, 1903 when they separated from the *Bolsheviks. Suppressed, 1922.

Mental Health Act Commission, established under terms of the Mental Health Act, 1983. This Act established principle of community care for mental patients and led to many institutional closures. Amendments proposed to safeguard public and patients from 1993.

Mercator. Gerhard Kremer, *alias* Gerardus M., born at Rupelmonde, 5 Mar. 1512. His 'Projection' for maps was published, 1568. He *d*. 2 Dec. 1594.

Merchant Adventurers, The. A guild of traders established in Brabant, 1296. The branch in England received the title by patent of Henry VII, 1505; incorporated, 1553. Became known as the Hamburg Company, 1578; dissolved, 1808.

Merchants, Charter of. Granted in 1303 by Edward I to foreign merchants.

Merchants, Statute of. *See* ACTON BURNELL, STATUTE OF.

Merchant Shipping Acts. Consolidating Act, 1854; this superseded by the Act of 1894 which remains the principal Act on the subject, various amendments and additions having been made to it, notably in 1971, 1979, 1981 and 1984.

Merchant Taylors' School (London). Founded, 1561; destroyed during Great Fire of 1666; rebuilt, 1671–4; rebuilt on new site, 1873–4; rebuilt, Northwood, Middlesex, 1931–3.

Mercia. Anglian kingdom, founded 500–50 in central England. Rose to supremacy *c*. 730, which lasted through the reigns of Ethelbald and Offa, and ended by the defeat of Coenwulf at Ellendun, 821, after a period in which it was tributary to Wessex. Completely absorbed in Wessex, 825–9. It was finally conquered by the Danes, 874, and split into English (SW) and Danish (NE) Mercian earldoms; reunited in 1016 under Knut, the territory ceased to be an administrative unit in 1066.

Mercia, rulers of, c. 593–874:
Creoda *d.c.* 593
Pybba *c*. 593–*c*. 606
Cearl *c*. 606–*c*. 626
Penda 626–55

Peada 655–56
Oswy (of Bernicia) 656–59
Wulfhere 659–75
Ethelred 675–704
Cenred 704–09
Ceolred 709–16
Ethelbald 716–57
Beornred 757
Offa 757–96
Ecgfrith 796
Coenwulf 796–821
Ceolwulf I 821–23
Beornwulf 823–25
Ludeca 825–27
Wiglaf 827–29
Egbert (of Wessex) 829–30
Wiglaf (restored) 830–39
Beorhtwulf 839–52
Burgred 852–74
Ceolwulf II 874

Merciless (or **Wonderful**) **Parliament.**
Summoned in 1388 by the Lords Appellant after the defeat of Richard II. It condemned eight of Richard's supporters to
death.

Merit, Order of, instituted, 1902.

Mermaid Tavern (Cheapside, London),
first mentioned, 1464. M. Club founded,
reputedly by Sir Walter Raleigh, 1603.
Burnt down, 1666.

Merovingians, Frankish dynasty, reigning 448–751. *See* FRANCE.

Mersey Tunnel (England), railway tunnel
opened, 1886; first road tunnel opened,
1934; second, 1971.

Mesopotamia. *See* IRAQ.

Messina, Italy. Founded by Greeks c. 8thC
BC. Taken by the Saracens in the 9thC AD
and in 1072 by the Normans. Ruled by
Spain, 1282–1713. Devastated by plague,
1743; by earthquake, 1783 and 1908.

Meteorological Office set up, 1855.
Transferred from Board of Trade control
to that of the Royal Society, 1867. From
1919 administered by the Air Ministry;
subsequently by the Ministry of Defence,

becoming an executive support agency
within the Ministry, April 1992. Headquarters at Bracknell, Berks.

Methodists. Name first given to followers
of John and Charles Wesley at Oxford,
1729; Wesleyan Methodist Society
founded by John Wesley, 1739; first conference, 1744; conference constituted supreme authority, 1784; Dr Coke
constituted 'bishop' of the American M.,
1784; death of Wesley, 1791, after which
the sect split up; union of many divisions
into the 'United Methodist Church', 1907;
Enabling Bill for union of Wesleyan, Primitive, and United M. passed, 1929; final
denominational vote, 1931. Reunion became effective, 1932. Proposals for a two-
stage reunion with the Church of England
published, 25 Feb. 1963. In 1969 the M.
Conference first voted in favour of unity
plan with Church of England: but plan
made defunct by subsequent Anglican re-
jections of it.

Methuen Treaty. Negotiated by Sir Paul
M., English ambassador in Portugal, 1703.
It reduced the duty on Portuguese wines,
thus helping to form the English taste for
port drinking. Annulled, 1836.

metric system. Became the legal system
in France, 1795. Though not in commercial
use the system was made legal in the UK
by an Act of 1864. Britain began adopting
the M.S. over a nominal 10-year period
from 1965: relics of the imperial system
(e.g. the pint for milk and beer) still
remaining, 1995 but metrication of packaged goods in Britain compulsory from 1
Oct. 1995, in compliance with EU directive.
The mile has also been retained.

Metropolitan Museum of Art (New
York), incorporated, 1870, opened, 1872.
Present building complex opened, 1880
and main section completed, 1902.
American art section added, 1924
(incorporates 1823 marble bank façade
from Wall Street). American Wing, 1980.
Lehman Wing, 1975. Rockefeller and
Sackler Wings, 1978. Thomas J. Watson
Library, 1964. The museum's medieval

section in Fort Tryon Park, known as The Cloisters, opened 1938.

metronome, invented *c.* 1814.

Mexico. Had a considerable Indian culture before 1519. In 1519 Hernando Cortes (1485–1547), the Spanish adventurer, landed at Vera Cruz, and conquered the land, 1521. In 1540 M. was united with other American territories and called New Spain. Declared itself independent of Spain, 1821, and Gen. Iturbide made emperor, May 1822. Proclaimed a republic, 1824. War with the USA regarding boundary dispute, May 1846–19 May 1848, when a peace treaty was signed. War with France, 1862–7. Emperor Maximilian shot, 1867. Period of revolution and social change, 1910–21. New constitution, 1917. Campaign against Catholic Church, 1924–31. Trotsky murdered at Coycacán, 21 Aug. 1940. Rapid industrialization following exploitation of Mexican oil industry since 1950: but financial crises caused international repercussions from 1980s: IMF loan, 1986 and debt reduction agreement with USA, 1988. Signatory to NAFTA, 1993. Indian revolt in Chiapas province, Jan. 1994; still continuing, 1995. Collapse of peso, Dec. 1994: subsequent plan to rescue Mexican economy agreed by the USA and the International Monetary Fund.

Heads of State, from 1821. (All presidents, except where otherwise indicated):
Iturbide (Regent) 1821–22
  (Emperor) 1822–23
Victoria 1824–29
Pedraza 1829
Guerrero 1829
Bustamante 1829–32
Pedraza 1832
Santa Anna 1833–36
Bustamante 1836–41
Santa Anna 1841–42
Bravo 1842–43
Santa Anna 1844
Herrera 1844–46
Paredes 1846
Santa Anna 1846–47

Herrera 1848–51
Arista 1851–53
Santa Anna (Dictator) 1853–55
Alvarez 1855–56
Comonfort 1856–57
  (Dictator) 1857–58
Juarez 1858–63
Zuloaga 1858
Miramon 1859–61
Maximilian (Emperor) 1864–67
Juarez 1867–72
Lerdo 1872–76
Diaz 1877–80
Gonzalez 1880–84
Diaz 1884–1911
Madero 1911–13
Huerta 1913–14
Carranza 1914–20
Obregon 1920–24
Calles 1924–28
Portes Gil 1928–30
Ortiz Rubio 1930–32
Rodriguez 1932–34
Cardenas 1934–40
Camacho 1940–46
Alemán Valdes 1946–52
Cortines 1952–58
Lopez Marteos 1958–64
Ordaz 1964–70
Echevarria 1970–76
Lopez 1976–82
Hurtado 1982–88
Salinas 1988–94
Zedillo 1994–

Mexico City. Founded as *Tenochtitlan* by *Aztecs c.* AD 1325. Captured by Spaniards, 1521. Cathedral begun, 1573. Olympic Games at, 1968; World Football Cup finals at, 1970. Earthquake, Sept. 1985, caused great damage and over 4,000 deaths.

MI5. British intelligence service, principally home-orientated, organized by Capt. (later Maj.-Gen. Sir) Vernon Kell (1873–1942) when, in 1909, the Admiralty established the Secret Service Bureau to counter threat posed by the expanding German fleet. Kell was made responsible for counter-espionage within the British Isles. In 1916 his service was incorporated into the Directorate of Military Intelligence and became MI5. Renamed Security Service in 1931. Major role in World Wars I and II and in countering subsequent communist threat. In mid-1980s resources switched from countering communism to combating terrorism. Officially recognized under Security Service Act, 1989. Director-General (Mrs Stella Rimington) first named, 1992. Responsibility for mainland intelligence about Irish terrorism switched from police to MI5, 1992. Public details of service and photographs of its director-general first released, July 1993.

MI6, British secret service (also known as SIS = Secret Intelligence Service). In its modern form, dates from 1909 when Capt. (later Sir) Mansfield Cumming (1859–1923) was put in charge of overseas intelligence operations. A state-run intelligence service had been in operation in some form at least from the reign of Henry VII (1485–1509). One of the earliest English spymasters was Sir Francis Walsingham (c. 1530–90). Reorganization under the elder Pitt (1708–88), then by William Eden, 1st Baron Auckland (1744–1814). Successfully used by Duke of Wellington (1769–1852) during Napoleonic Wars. Its (secret) budgetary arrangements through Foreign Office formalized, 1887. Under Cumming and successors active and effective during World Wars I and II but after 1945 scandals involving agents who defected (e.g. Blake, convicted and sentenced, 1961; escaped prison and fled to Russia, 1966; and Kim Philby, defected to Russia, 1963) tarnished service's image despite its numerous successes. Existence of MI6 officially admitted for first time, 1992. Put on same statutory footing as MI5, Nov. 1993. Documents dating back to 1791 and dealing with creation of modern service placed in Public Record Office, 1993.

Michelson-Morley experiment. Albert Abraham Michelson (1852–1931) and Edward Williams Morley (1822–94) performed an experiment in 1887 to determine the velocity with which the earth moved through the ether. Its negative results led to the hypothesis on which the theory of * relativity is based.

Michigan, USA. Discovered by French, 1618, and settled by French missionaries, 1671. Detroit founded, 1701; possessed by British, 1763; by Americans, 1796; erected into an independent territory, 1805; fell into the hands of the British, Aug. 1812; reconquered by Gen. Harrison, 1813; admitted to the Union as a state, Jan. 1837.

Micronesia, Federated States of, came into being 10 May 1979, comprising the former *Caroline Islands. The US administration of M. ended 3 Nov. 1986 when the USA recognized M, as fully independent and made a 15-year 'free association' agreement. Owing to Russian objections, however, M.'s independence was not recognized by the UN until Dec. 1990. M. became a full member of the UN, 17 September 1991.

microphone, invented by E. Berliner (1851–1929), 1877.

microscope. The first compound M. said to have been made by Janssen, a Dutchman, 1590. It was not, however, of much practical use until the achromatic lens was invented c. 1758.

Middelburg, Holland. St Nicholas Abbey founded, 1106. Bell-tower rebuilt, 1718.

Middlesex, historic English county, absorbed by Greater London, 1965. Name first appears in charter of 704. Still (1995) used to denote postal districts, etc.

Middlesex University, name and status since 1992 of the former Middlesex Polytechnic.

Midway Islands, discovered and annexed to the USA, 1859. Made an American reservation, 1903. Japanese fleet defeated by US Navy off M., June 1942.

Midwives Act, 1951, which previously regulated the profession was repealed by the Nurses, Midwives and Health Visitors Act of 1979. Men are now permitted to become midwives. Further modifications under Nurses, Midwives and Health Visitors Act, 1992.

Mikado, title of the emperors of *Japan, the first of whom traditionally began in his reign, 660 BC.

Milan, Italy (Latin *Mediolanum*). Taken from Gauls by Romans, 222 BC; Constantine's edict in favour of Christians, AD 313; sacked by Huns, 452; by Goths, 539; head of Lombard League from 1167; ruled by Visconti family, 1227–1447, by Sforza family, 1450–1535; from 1535 to 1713 under the rule of Spain, then of Austria; after Napoleonic wars restored to Austria, 1815; capital of Austro-Italian kingdom until 1859, when it became part of Italy; present cathedral founded, 1386; and completed, 1805–13. La Scala opera house, 1778.

Mildenhall Treasure, a hoard of Roman silver-ware found near M. in Suffolk, 1942–3, presumed to have been buried for safety by the occupants of a villa during pirate raids in the 4thC AD. Now in the British Museum.

mile. English statute M. legalized, 1593.

Militant Tendency, extreme left movement, originally within the British Labour Party, prominent in the 1970s especially in local government in Liverpool. Subsequently banned by the Labour Party who expelled several leading members in the 1980s after which its national influence declined, but (1995) retains a power-base in NW England and parts of Glasgow.

Military Training Act, 1939, compelling every male subject between 20 and 21 to undergo six months' training and then to be 3½ years in auxiliary force. Superseded by National Service (Armed Forces) Act, 3 Sept. 1939, and National Service Act, 1947: but ended when conscription abolished in Britain, 1962.

militia (Great Britain). M. statutes, 1661–3; general M. Act passed, 1802; M. Reserve Act, 1867; M. Enlistment Act, 1875; title of M. abolished on introduction of Territorial and Reserve Force Act, 1907; superseded by Special Reserve (1908); Special Reserve

renamed M., 1921, but it remained a merely nominal force. The conscripts under the Military Training Act, 1939, were termed M. *See* FYRD.

militia (USA). Bill for the organization of the M. passed House of Representatives, 27 Mar. 1792.

Millbank Prison (London). Erected, 1813–16; closed, 1890; demolished, 1903; on the site now stands the *Tate Gallery.

Milo, Venus of. *See* MELOS.

Milton Keynes, England. Designated a 'new town', 1967 and expanded rapidly. Covers an area of 119 square miles. *Open University established there, 1969.

Minnesota, USA. Explored by two Huguenots, Groseilliers and Radisson, 1658–9; formally possessed by French, 1671; divided between Spain and Great Britain, 1762–3; visited by Jonathan Carver, 1766; part of territory of Indiana, 1800; purchased by USA, 1803; territory of M. created, 1849; admitted to the Union, 11 May 1858.

Minorca, Mediterranean. Captured by English, 1708, during War of Spanish Succession, ceded to England by Treaty of Utrecht, 1713; recaptured by French, 1756 (as a result of which the English executed Adm. Byng); restored to England by Treaty of Paris, 1763; recaptured by French and Spaniards, 1781; ceded to Spain, 1782; retaken, 1798, but restored to Spain by Treaty of Amiens, 1802.

Minsk, capital of Belarus. Founded in 11thC, became Lithuanian, 1326. Russian, 1793. Heavily damaged in World War II, before which it had a large Jewish population. HQ of the *Commonwealth of Independent States since Dec. 1991.

Mint (Great Britain). Regulations for the government of the M. made by King Athelstan *c.* AD 928; by Act of Parliament the present M. was founded on Tower Hill, 1811; new constitution, 1815; complete change in administration, and a master, deputy master and comptroller appointed,

1850; office of Chancellor of the Exchequer amalgamated with that of master, and the office of deputy master and controller combined, 1870. Mint moved from London to Llantrisant, S Wales, in 1972–4.

Mint (USA). The earliest M. was established at Boston, 27 May 1652. The power of coinage was exercised by several states from 1778 until the adoption of the National Constitution. Establishment of a M. by Act of Congress, 1795, at Philadelphia.

Minton porcelain, first made by Thomas and Herbert M. at Stoke-on-Trent, 1796.

Missal. Tridentine M. ordered to be used in all Roman Catholic churches by *Council of Trent, 1570; largely phased out after 1965, when vernacular M. substituted, but limited use still (1995) permitted.

Mississippi, USA. The lower course of the river discovered by de Soto, 1541; visited by La Salle, 1682; territory of M. created, 7 Apr. 1798; admitted to the Union as a state, 1817.

Mississippi Scheme. A proposal to develop *Louisiana, the country on the borders of the M. The scheme was the idea of John Law (1671–1729), who floated a company in 1717. The scheme was not a success, and in July 1720 the bubble broke.

Missouri, USA. Originally called Upper Louisiana. Ste Genevieve said to have been founded, 1735; by Treaty of Paris, 1763, territory passed to the English; ceded to USA, 1803; admitted into the Union as a state, 10 Aug. 1821.

Missouri Compromise, The. In 1818 the inhabitants of the M. territory petitioned for admission into the Union as a state; a bill was introduced into Congress, 13 Feb. 1819. A question of the abolition of slavery in the territory caused the bill to be delayed and it was not until 27 Feb. 1821 that a final compromise was adopted, and M. admitted to the Union as a state.

Mithraism, a branch of *Zoroastrianism. Introduced into Rome from Asia Minor, 68 BC. It *fl.* in Britain, mainly as a cult in garrison stations, throughout the Roman occupation, and a temple to Mithras was excavated in London in 1953. M. ceased to exist in the W with the victory of Theodosius in 394, when it was superseded by Christianity.

Moabite Stone, The. Probable date of inscription, *c.* 850 BC. Now in the Louvre, Paris. Discovered by Revd F. Klein at Dibon in 1868.

Model Parliament, 1295, summoned by Edward I. From this time knights and burgesses regularly included.

Modena, Italy. Ruled by the Estes, 1288–1860. Made a duchy, 1452; duke expelled by French, 1796; restored, 1814; finally expelled and duchy incorporated in Italy, 1860.

Mogadishu, capital of Somalia. Devastated by civil war from 1970s: captured by rebels, 1991, but fighting between warlords continued till temporarily halted by UN intervention, 1992. Conflict between UN forces and warlord Aidid brought fresh conflict, casualties and destruction in M., 1993 onwards.

Mohammedanism. *See* ISLAM.

Mohawks or **Mohocks, The.** A club of wealthy young London men about town who committed such outrages that on 18 Mar. 1712 they were the subject of a royal proclamation.

Moldova, or **Moldavia,** independent republic and member of the *Commonwealth of Independent States since Dec. 1991. Soviet Moldavian Autonomous republic established, 1921: it absorbed *Romanian Bessarabia, Aug. 1940 and became the Moldavian SSR. Occupied by German and Romanian forces, 1940–4. Achieved independent status, 1991; but subsequent conflict between Slav minority and Romanian majority, 1992, and proclamation of an independent Slav republic of Transdniestr in the E of M., not recognized by M. and protected by Russian troops. Former Communists returned to power in 1994 elections.

Molotov cocktail, crude but effective hand-thrown explosive device said to have been invented by Finns when fighting the USSR in 1940: but earlier versions also used in Spanish Civil War, 1936–9.

Molly Maguires, in Ireland, an anti-landlord society which *fl.* 1835–55. In America, an Irish-led terrorist society which attempted to dominate the Pennsylvanian coal-mining area, 1862–77.

Moluccas. *See* MALUKU.

Mombasa, Kenya. Originally an Arab slave-trading town in E Africa, was first visited by the Portuguese, 1498. Sacked (1500) and occupied by them, 1505. Retaken by Arabs, 1698. Included in British E African protectorate, 1896.

Monaco. An independent principality on the Mediterranean, ruled by the Grimaldi family since 1297; made a French protectorate, 1644; Menton and Roquebrune annexed by Sardinia, 1846; became part of Italy, 1859; sold to Napoleon III, 1861. Until the constitution of 1911 the Prince of Monaco was an absolute ruler. By a treaty of 1918, succession to the throne of M. must be approved by the French government. Rainier III became Prince of M. in 1949; he married Grace Kelly (*d.* 1982), an American film actress, in 1956. A 'good neighbour' treaty was signed between France and M., 23 Dec. 1951. Dispute with France, 1959, settled, 1963. Member of UN, 1993.

monasteries (British Isles). M. on the Celtic pattern existed in SW and NW Britain in the 5thC. The first monastery in England with Benedictine influence appears to have been erected about AD 597 at Canterbury by St Augustine. A large number, belonging to many different orders, grew up in England. In 1535, during Henry VIII's reign, a commission was issued for the visitation of the M. In 1536 an Act was passed for the suppression of the religious houses with an income of less than £200. The large houses were suppressed in 1539. English foundations subsequently set up in France and Low Countries: after French

Revolution a number of these returned to Britain and established themselves there. Some Anglican M. since 19thC. Tractarian revival movement. Scottish M. were suppressed in 1560.

Mongolia, Republic of, since 1991. Chinese province, 1686–1911. Chinese officials expelled by the chiefs, 1911. Again a Chinese province, 1919–21. Communist revolution and proclamation of a People's Government of Outer M., Mar. 1921. Treaty with USSR, Nov. 1921. People's Republic of Outer M. proclaimed, 1924, on death of Khan Bogdo Gezen. Independent M. recognized by China, 5 Jan. 1946; friendship treaty with USSR, 1966. Democratic reforms from 1990; new constitution, 1992 and last Russian troops left M.

Mongolia, Inner, since 1947, autonomous region of China.

Monmouth's Rebellion. Originated by James, Duke of Monmouth (1649–85), who landed on 11 June 1685 at Lyme Regis. He was defeated at Sedgemoor, 6 July 1685, and executed, 15 July.

monopolies. In 1597 Parliament protested to Elizabeth against grants of M. The Parliaments of Charles I protested still more strongly, and by an Act of 1624 most of these M. were abolished, and in 1639, the whole system was done away with. In more modern times, M. have been regulated by the Monopolies and Restrictive Practices Act, 1948, superseded subsequently by the Fair Trading Act, 1973, which established the *Monopolies and Mergers Commission to deal with M.

Monopolies and Mergers Commission, was first the Monopolies and Restrictive Prices Commission, 1948. It became the M. and M.C., 1973, with the duty of investigating and reporting on the existence of possible monopolies referred to it, working in conjunction with the Fair Trading Act, 1973, the Restrictive Trade Practices Act, 1976, the Competition Act, 1980 and the Broadcasting Act, 1990. Former state corporations, now privatized, can be referred to the M. and M.C. by their regulatory authorities.

Monroe Doctrine. Proclaimed by President James M. (1758–1831) of the USA in his message to Congress on 2 Dec. 1823. In the words of M. himself, the doctrine was that the USA 'should consider any attempt on their [the foreign Powers] part to extend their system to any portion of this [the American] hemisphere as dangerous to our peace and safety'.

Monrovia, capital of Liberia, founded 1821 as refuge for freed slaves from USA. Devastated during civil conflicts since 1989.

Montagnards or **Montagne,** extremist republican wing in the French National Convention c. 1792–5.

Montana, USA, first settled, 1809. Organized as a territory, 1864. Indian wars, 1866–7. Admitted to the Union as a state, 1889.

Mont Blanc (France and Italy: 15,771 ft/4807 m). In 1760 Saussure offered a reward for a practicable route to the summit. Two guides in June 1786 gained it. Saussure reached the top himself in 1787. Construction of the M.B. tunnel begun, 1959; opened, 16 July 1965.

Monte Carlo, Monaco. Famous since the 19thC as a luxury gambling resort. Casino opened, 1861; later extended. Opera house, 1878; Sporting Club, 1932. Casino operations taken over by government, 1967. M.C. rally started, 1911.

Mont de Piété or **Monte de Pietà.** Institutions founded for lending money to the poor at low interest, first established at Orvieto, 1463, and Perugia, 1467.

Montecassino, oldest monastic house in Europe, founded by St Benedict, AD 529. Sacked by Lombards, 585; destroyed by Saracens, 884, and by Allied air forces and shell-fire, Feb.–May 1944; occupied by Polish forces, 18 May 1944. Restored after each event: during the restoration of 1950–6, an urn believed to contain remains of St Benedict and his sister Scholastica (missing since c. 1550) rediscovered. Abbey formally reopened, 1956.

Montenegro (Serbo-Croatian **Crnagora**). The history of M. as an independent state begins with the battle of Kossovo, 1389; Cetinje made capital, 1484; captured by the Turks, 1623, 1687 and 1714; fresh war with Turkey, 1853; peace finally restored, Nov. 1858; Turkish supremacy recognized, Sept. 1862; declared independent of Turkey by Treaty of San Stefano, 3 Mar. 1878; first Montenegrin Parliament assembled at Cetinje, Oct. 1906; Prince Nicholas assumed title of king, 28 Aug. 1910. During the first Balkan War, Oct. 1912–May 1913, M. allied with Bulgaria, Serbia and Greece against Turkey; during the second Balkan War, June–Aug. 1913, M. allied with Serbia and Greece against Bulgaria, Romania and Turkey. Invaded by Austria, 1916; in 1918 king deposed and M. voted to join Serbia. Yugoslav republic, 1946. Nationalist movement from 1980s; last king's body reinterred in M., 1989. Multiparty elections in Dec. 1990 returned former Communists to power and since then M. has sided with Serbs in conflicts in *Croatia and *Bosnia-Herzegovina. 'Federated' with Serbia, 1992 (union not recognized by UN); former Communists again returned, 1992.

Montessori method. Education system founded, 1906–9, by Maria Montessori (1870–1952).

Montevideo, Uruguay. First settlement made, 1726; taken by the English, 1807; in 1828 it was made the capital of Uruguay or Banda Oriental. German warship *Graf Spee* driven into M., Dec. 1939 and later scuttled outside it.

Montreal, Canada. Originally *Ville Marie*. Founded by French settlers, 1642; captured by British, 8 Sept. 1760; by Americans, 12 Nov. 1775; recaptured by British, 15 June 1776. McGill College founded, 1813; made a university by royal charter, 1821; new charter granted, 1852. Anglican bishopric founded, 1850. Great fire destroyed the greater part of the town, 8–9

July 1852. Christ Church, the Anglican cathedral, destroyed by fire, 10 Dec. 1856. M. University founded, 1876. Underground railway opened, 1966. M. Expo., 1967; University of Quebec at M., 1968; Concordia University, 1974. Considerable modernization since 1960s; centre of French Canadian separatism since 1970s.

Montserrat, W Indies, discovered by Columbus, 1492: colonized by Irish and British, 1632. Severe hurricane damage, 1989: further hurricane damage and volcanic activity, 1995.

Moonies. Popular name for World Unification Church, founded 1954 by Korean Sun Myung Moon. About 800 adherents in Britain, 1995.

Moorgate disaster, Britain's worst underground train accident, 28 Feb. 1975, caused when a Northern Line train overran the buffers at speed at Moorgate Underground Station in London. The cause was never decided, the driver being among the 42 dead.

Moravia. Occupied in early period successively by Boii (Celts), Quadi (Teutons), Rugii and Heruli, 5thC; soon displaced by Slavs; they sided with Charlemagne in suppressing the Avars on the E, end of 8thC; received part of Avars' territory. Converted to Christianity by Cyril and Methodius, 863. King Svatopluk extended dominions to the Oder and the Gran. Magyars entered at his death, 894. From 1029 usually incorporated with Bohemia. On death of Louis II at battle of Mohácz came under rule of Austria, 1526; made a separate crown land, 1849. Became part of Czechoslovakia, 1918. Part of the German protectorate of Bohemia–Moravia, 15 Mar. 1939 until 1945. Province of Czechoslovakia till 1949; then district. In Czech Republic since Jan. 1993.

Moravian Brethren or **Moravian Church.** A religious sect founded in the E of Bohemia c. 1457; first synod held, 1467. It grew out of the Hussites. In 1749 the British Parliament passed Acts to encourage their settlement in the then English-American colonies.

Moriscos. Moors who remained in Spain after their final conquest in 1492, and who were finally expelled by Philip III, 1609–14.

Morley-Minto Reforms introduced in India by Lord Morley (1838–1923). Secretary of State, and the 4th Earl of Minto (1847–1914), Viceroy, 1909.

Mormons, The, or **Church of Jesus Christ of Latter-Day Saints.** A sect founded by Joseph Smith (1805–44). *The Book of Mormon* was first published in New York in 1830. The first church was founded on 6 Apr. 1830 at Fayette; moved to Kirtland, Ohio, Jan. 1831. Their headquarters at Salt Lake City, Utah, founded, 1847, by Brigham Young (1801–77) who also advocated polygamy, 1852, later rejected by the M., 1890. Over two million M. in USA in 1995 and churches in other English-speaking countries, notably UK.

Morocco (Arabic **Maghreb,** 'Far W'). Occupied by Berbers since at least 1200 BC. Conquered by Arabs, AD 682. Successful Berber revolt, 739. Idrissi dynasty (Arab), 788–988, founded Fez, 808. *Almoravide (Berber) rule, 1061–1149. Marrakesh founded, 1062, by Yusuf Ben Tashfin. *Almohade (Moorish) rule, 1149–1269. Marinid (Tribal Berber) dynasty established, 1269. Yakub II subdued Spain, 1269–86. Ali V took Tlemcen, 1337. Fall of Marinids, 1360–1471. Wattassi dynasty (1471–1548) lost coastal towns to Spanish and Portuguese. Portuguese driven out by Saddi dynasty (Arab), 1550–1668. Conquest of Timbuktu, end 16thC. Present Filali (Berber) dynasty seized Marrakesh, 1668. Unification under Moulay Ismail, 1672–1727. French conquest of Algeria, 1830, resulted in wars, 1844 and 1859. Spaniards took Tetuan, and Ifni ceded to them, 1860. Britain relinquished her interests to France, 8 Apr. 1904. Tangier crisis, 1905. Algeciras Conference, 1906, drafted Act of Algeciras, 7 Apr. French occupied Casablanca, 1907. Agadir crisis, 1911.

Spanish and French protectorates established by treaty of Fez, 30 Mar. 1912. Anglo-Franco-Spanish Convention, 18 Dec. 1923, defined the status of *Tangier. Abd-el-Krim's rebellion against Spanish, 1923–6. Ifric occupied and effectively annexed by Spaniards, 1934. France and the Sultan terminated the treaty of Fez, 2 Mar. 1956; Spanish protectorate ended, 7 Apr.; and the international status of Tangier was abolished, 29 Oct., thus making M. an independent monarchy. Sultan took title of king as from Aug. 1957. Hassan II succeeded to the throne, 26 Feb. 1961. New constitution, 1972. Acquired W Sahara, 1976: subsequent war with Polisario guerrillas. Cease-fire, 1990, but situation remains fluid. Growing fundamentalist Islamic movement in M. since 1980s. Talks with Israel, 1993–4. Constitutional reforms, 1992, left main power with king.

Morse code, invented by Samuel Morse (1791–1872) and Alexander Bain (1810–77).

Mortmain, Statute of, 15 Nov. 1279. It forbade any person to buy or sell or, under cover of any gift, term, or other title, to receive any lands or tenements in such a way that such lands and tenements should come under the ownership of a corporation without royal licence. A second Statute of M. was passed in 1391.

Moscow, capital of Russia. Founded *c.* 1147; captured by the Tatars (i.e. by Toktamish, Khan of the Golden Horde), 1382; *Kremlin built, end of 15thC. Cathedrals of the Assumption, 1475–9; Ciscencion, 1484–9 – rebuilt after fire, 1562–4; Archangel, 1505–8. Burnt by the Khan of the Crimea, 1571. Bell-tower of Ivan the Great, 16thC, damaged 1812 but restored. Tsai Bell cast, 1733–5 but never rung. The city was burnt by the inhabitants in 1812, when Napoleon entered, and he was forced to leave it. Ceased to be Russian capital on founding of St Petersburg, 1712. Again made capital, 1917. Capital of the USSR, 1922–91. Moscow Canal built by forced labour, 1932–7. Metro system begun, 1935.

Mosul. Finally included in Iraq by Treaty of Angora, 5 June 1926.

Mothering Sunday, fourth Sunday in Lent, has origins in England going back to pre-Conquest times; revival in Victorian period. Now often known as **Mother's Day,** which originated in the USA, in Philadelphia, in 1908, and is celebrated there and in Canada, on the second Sunday in May.

motorcycle racing, developed early in the 20thC. The T.T. race (Isle of Man) started, 1907. Belgian Grand Prix began, 1921; German, 1923; Dutch, 1925; Daytona, USA race started, 1937. *Motocross,* a type of M.R., developed since 1950s.

motor racing. First real M. R. was Paris-Bordeaux, 1895. First closed-circuit race in France in 1898. International M.R. since 1901. Le Mans Grand Prix, 1906. First speedway built at Brooklands, UK, 1906. Rally driving started, 1911. World championship for drivers instituted, 1950.

mountains, first ascents of: these include:

Etna (Sicily), Emperor Trajan, approximately AD 100.

Titlis (Switzerland), four peasants, 1744.

Mont Blanc (France-Italy), M.G. Paccard and J. Balmat, 1786.

Gross Glockner (Austria), five local men, 1800.

Jungfrau (Switzerland), J. R. and H. Meyer, 1811.

Ararat (Russia), Parrot, 1829.

Finsteraarhorn (Switzerland), J. Leuthold, 1829.

Piz Bernina (Switzerland-Italy), J. Coaz, 1850.

Monte Rosa, Dufourspitze (Switzerland), five British, 1855.

Dom (Switzerland), J. Ll.-Davies, 1858.

Aletschhorn (Switzerland), F. F. Tuckett, 1859.

Gran Paradiso (Italy), J. J. Cowell, 1860.

Monte Viso (Italy), W. Matthews, 1861.

Weisshorn (Switzerland), J. Tyndall, 1861.

Les Ecrins (France), E. Whymper, 1864.

Grandes Jorasses (France-Italy), E. Whymper, 1865.

Aig Verte (France), E. Whymper, 1865.

Matterhorn (Switzerland), E. Whymper, 1865.

Elbruz (Caucasus), D. W. Freshfield, A. W. Moore, C. C. Tucker, 1868.

Cimone della Pala (Italy), E. R. Whitwell, 1870.

Meije (France), E. B. de Castelnau, 1877.

Grand Teton (USA), N. P. Langford, J. Stevenson, 1872.

Grand Dru (France), C. T. Dent, 1878.

Chimborazo (Ecuador), E. Whymper, 1880.

Mt Cook (New Zealand), W. S. Green, 1882.

Aig du Géant (France-Italy), four Signori Sella, 1882.

Kabru (Himalayas), W. W. Graham, 1883.

Kilimanjaro (Tanzania), Hans Meyer, 1887.

Ushba (Caucasus), J. G. Cockin, 1888.

Aconcagua (Chile-Argentine), M. Zurbriggen, 1897.

Mt St Elias (Alaska), Duke of Abruzzi, 1897.

Mt Kenya (Kenya), H. J. Mackinder, 1899.

Ruwenzori (Central Africa), Duke of Abruzzi, 1906.

Trisul (Himalaya), T. G. Longstaff, 1907.

Mt McKinley (Alaska), Parker-Browne expedition, 1912.

Mt Robson (Canada), W. Foster, A. H. McCarthy, C. Kain, 1913.

Mt Logan (Alaska), A.H. McCarthy, 1925.

Illampu (Bolivia), German-Austrian expedition, 1929.

Kamet (Himalaya), Kamet expedition, 1931.

Nanda Devi (Himalayas), British-American expedition, 1936.

Annapurna (Himalayas), French expedition, 1950.

Everest (Himalayas), E. P. Hillary (New Zealand) and Tensing (Nepal), 29 May 1953.

Nanga Parbat (Himalayas), H. Buhl, 3 July 1953.

K-2 (Himalayas), Italian expedition, 31 July 1954.

Kangchenjunga (Himalayas), British expedition, 25 May 1955.

Manaslu (Nepal), Japanese expedition, 1956.

Lhotse (Himalayas), Swiss expedition, 1956.

Broad Peak, Austrian expedition, 1957.

Rakaposhi, British-Pakistani expedition, led by M. Banks, 1958.

Shisha Pangma, (Tibet), Chinese expedition, 2 May 1964.

Since 1960s concentration on climbing different faces of mountains already climbed.

Mozambique. Discovered by Vasco da Gama, 1498. Colonized by Portuguese from 1505. Large areas chartered to the M. Co., and the Nyasaland Co., 1891, and the Zambesi Co., 1892. Vatua rebellion and siege of Lourenço Marques, Aug. 1894. Vatuas broken by battles of Marracuene, Coolela and Chaimite, 1895. Gazaland reconquered, 1897. Overseas province of Portugal, 1951. Guerrilla activity from 1950s resulted in independence, 1975. M. became a one-party Marxist state in 1977. Peace agreement with S Africa, 1984. Multiparty system under new constitution, 1990. Negotiations with rebel Renamo movement, 1991–2, led to ceasefire, Oct. 1992, with UN presence, March 1993. But over 300,000 refugees still in Malawi and economy destroyed by years of civil war. Elections held under UN auspices, Oct 1994, won by government.

Mufti, Grand, office abolished in Turkey, 1924. The office of M. of Jerusalem was instituted, 1922.

Muggletonians. An ephemeral religious sect which was founded in England *c.* 1651 by John Reeve and Lodowick Muggleton.

Mugwumps, faction of the Republican Party in the USA, first so called, 1889. Obsolete.

Mujahadeen, Islamic guerilla fighters, prominent in Afghanistan from 1970s and primarily responsible there for overthrow of the Marxist regime, 1992. Also groupings in the Middle East (Iran, Lebanon) from 1980s. Divided into several (often conflicting) factions.

Mukden (Chinese **Shenyang**), Manchuria, largely burnt out in the Boxer rising of 1900. Russians defeated by Japanese, Mar. 1905.

Munich or **München,** Germany. Capital of *Bavaria. Traditionally founded, AD 962, by Henry of Saxony; Wittelsbach seat, 1255–1918. Taken by Gustavus Adolphus of Sweden, 1643; plague killed many, 1644; taken by Austrians, 1704, 1741, 1746; by French, 2 July 1800; university founded, 1826. King Ludwig I created modern M., 1825–48. Scene of first National Socialist *putsch*, 8 Nov. 1923 and subsequently a Nazi centre. Agreement on Czechoslovakia, 29 Sept. 1938. Financial and cultural centre since World War II. Murder of Israelis at Olympic Games held at M., 1972, by Arab fanatics.

Münster, Westphalia, by 1186 had grown into a town; declared for the Protestant faith, 1532; famous during 1535 for the Anabaptist disturbances, when the Roman Catholic bishop was temporarily expelled.

Münster, Treaty of. Also known as the *Treaty of Westphalia (see TREATIES), 1648.

Muraroa, Pacific atoll, owned by France. Since 1975 used as test site for over 130 nuclear experiments. Nuclear underground testing at M. in 1995 caused international outcry.

Murder (Abolition of Death Penalty) Act. *See* CAPITAL PUNISHMENT.

Murmansk, founded, 1915, as Romanovna-Murmane, allied base in the abortive Archangel expedition of 1918–19. Besieged by Finns and Germans, 1941–4.

Muscat, Persian Gulf. Occupied by Portuguese, 1508. Driven out by the Sultan of Oman, 1650, who made it his capital, 1741.

musical composers. The following are among the most celebrated of the world's M.C. with their dates:

American:
Berlin, Irving, 1888–1989
Bernstein, Leonard, 1918–90
Buck, Dudley, 1839–1909
Cage, John, 1912–92
Chadwick, George Whitefield, 1854–1931
Copland, Aaron, 1900–90
De Koven, Henry Louis Reginald, 1859–1920
Foster, Stephen, 1826–64
Gershwin, George, 1898–1937
Grainger, Percy (Australian-born), 1882–1961
Griffes, Charles Tomlinson, 1884–1920
Herbert, Victor (Irish-born), 1859–1924
Loeffler, Charles Martin Tornov (French-born), 1861–1935
Loewe, Frederick, 1901–88
MacDowell, Edward Alexander, 1861–1908
Nevin, Ethelbert Woodbridge, 1862–1901
Paine, John Knowles, 1839–1906
Parker, Horatio William, 1863–1919
Rodgers, Richard, 1902–79
Schelling, Ernest, 1876–1939
Sousa, John Philip, 1854–1932
Austrian:
Berg, Alban, 1885–1935
Bruckner, Anton, 1824–96
Czerny, Karl, 1791–1857
Dittersdorf, Karl Ditters von, 1739–99
Fall, Leo, 1878–1925
Goldmark, Karl, 1830–1915
Haydn, Franz Josef, 1732–1809
Kreisler, Fritz, 1875–1962
Lanner, Josef Franz Karl, 1801–43
Mahler, Gustav, 1860–1911
Mozart, Wolfgang Amdeus, 1756–91
Pleyel, Ignaz Josef, 1757–1831
Schubert, Franz Peter, 1797–1828
Schönberg, Arnold, 1874–1951
Strauss I, Johann, 1804–49
Strauss II, Johann, 1825–99
Suppé, Franz von, 1819–95
Wolf, Hugo, 1860–1903
Belgian:
Benoît, Pierre Léopold Léonard, 1834–1901
Des Prés, Joaquin, *c.* 1450–1521
Dufay, Guillaume, *c.* 1400–74
Franck, César August, 1822–90

Gossec, François Joseph, 1734–1829
Grétry, André Ernest Modest, 1741–1813
Jannequin, Clément, c. 1475–1560
Lassus, Roland de (Orlando di Lasso), c. 1552–94
Lekeu, Guillaume, 1870–94
Ockeghem, Jean de, c. 1430–c. 1495
Tinel, Edgar, 1854–1912
Verdelot, Philippe, c. 1530–c. 1567
Vieuxtemps, Henri, 1820–81
Willaert, Adrian, c. 1480–1562
Brazilian:
Villa-Lobos, Heitor, 1887–1959
British:
Arne, Thomas Augustine, 1710–78
Arnold, Malcolm, 1921–
Attwood, Thomas, 1765–1838
Balfe, Michael William, 1808–70
Bateson, Thomas, c. 1575–1630
Bax, Sir Arnold Edward, 1883–1953
Benedict, Sir Julius, 1804–85
Bennett, Sir William Sterndale, 1816–75
Bishop, Sir Henry Rowley, 1786–1855
Blow, John, 1649–1708
Boyce, William, 1710–79
Bridge, Frank, 1879–1941
Bridge, Sir John Frederick, 1844–1924
Britten, Benjamin, Baron, 1913–76
Bull, John, c. 1562–1628
Burney, Charles, 1726–1814
Butterworth, George Sainton Kaye, 1885–1916
Byrd, or Byrde, William, 1543–1623
Campion, Thomas, 1567–1619
Carey, Henry, c. 1687–1743
Cellier, Alfred, 1844–91
Clarke, Jeremiah, 1673–1707
Coleridge-Taylor, Samuel, 1875–1912
D'Albert, Eugene Francis Charles, 1864–1932
Davies, Sir Henry Walford, 1869–1941
Davies, Sir Peter Maxwell, 1934–
Delius, Frederick, 1862–1934
Dibdin, Charles, 1745–1814
Dowland, John, 1563–1626
Dunstable, John, d. 1453
Elgar, Sir Edward, 1857–1934
Farnaby, Giles, c. 1565–c. 1640
Field, John (Irish), 1782–1837
German, Sir Edward, 1862–1936
Gibbons, Orlando, 1583–1625

Greene, Maurice, 1695–1755
Gurney, Ivor, 1890–1937
Handel, George Frederick, 1685–1759 (German-born)
Harty, Sir Herbert Hamilton (Irish), 1879–1941
Henschel, Isidor Georg (Sir George) (German-born), 1850–1934
Heseltine, Philip ('Peter Warlock'), 1894–1930
Holst, Gustav Theodore, 1874–1934
Hullah, John Pyke, 1812–84
Humfrey, Pelham, 1647–74
Ireland, John, 1879–1962
Lehmann, Liza (Mrs Herbert Bedford), 1862–1918
Lloyd, George Walter Selwyn, 1913–
Lloyd Webber, Sir Andrew, 1948–
Locke, Matthew, c. 1630–77
MacCunn, Hamish (Scottish), 1868–1916
Macfarren, Sir George Alexander, 1813–87
Mackenzie, Sir Alexander Campbell (Scottish), 1847–1935
Miles, Philip Napier, 1865–1935
Monckton, Lionel, 1862–1924
Morley, Thomas, 1557–1602
Nares, James, 1715–83
Novello, Ivor (Davies), 1893–1951 (Welsh)
O'Neill, Norman Houston, 1875–1934
Ouseley, Sir Frederick Arthur Gore, 1825–89
Parratt, Sir Walter, 1841–1924
Parry, Joseph, 1841–1903
Parry, Sir Charles Hubert Hastings, 1848–1918
Purcell, Henry, 1659–95
Quilter, Roger, 1877–1953
Ronald, Sir Landon, 1873–1938
Rubbra, Edmund, 1901–86
Sharp, Cecil James, 1859–1924
Somervell, Sir Arthur, 1863–1937
Stainer, Sir John, 1840–1901
Stanford, Sir Charles Villiers, 1852–1924
Seymour, Sir Arthur, 1842–1900
Tallis, Thomas, c. 1505–85
Taverner, John, c. 1495–1545
Tippett, Sir Michael, 1905–
Tomkins, Thomas, 1573–1656
Tosti, Sir Francesco Paolo (Italian-born), 1846–1916
Tovey, Sir Donald Francis, 1875–1940
Tye, Christopher, c. 1500–72 or '73

Vaughan Williams, Ralph, 1872–1958
Wallace, William Vincent, 1812–65
Walton, Sir William, 1902–83
Warlock, Peter. *See* HESELTINE, PHILIP
Weelkes, Thomas, *c.* 1575–1623
Wesley, Samuel, 1766–1837
Wesley, Samuel Sebastian, 1810–76
White, Robert, *c.* 1535–74
Willbye, John, 1574–1638
Williamson, Sir Malcolm, 1931–
Wood, Charles, 1866–1926
Czech:
Dvořák, Anton, 1841–1904
Fibich, Zdenek, 1850–1900
Hammerschmidt, Andreas, 1611–75
Janácek, Leoš, 1854–1928
Kozeluch, Leopold Anton, 1754–1818
Nedbal, Oscar, 1874–1930
Smetana, Bedrich, 1824–84
Suk, Josef, 1874–1935
Danish:
Buxtehude, Diderik, 1637–1707
Gade, Niels Vilhelm, 1817–90
Hartmann, Johan Peter Emil, 1805–1900
Horneman, Christian Frederik Emil, 1841–1906
Lassen, Eduard, 1830–1904
Nielsen, Carl August, 1865–1931
Dutch:
Isaak, Hendrick, 1450–1517
Lassus, Roland de, 1532–94
Obrecht, Jakob, 1430–1505
Röntgen, Julius, 1855–1934
Sweelinck, Jan Pieterszoon, 1562–1621
Finnish:
Kajanus, Robert, 1856–1935
Melartin, Errki Gustav, 1875–1937
Sibelius, Jean, 1865–1957
French:
Alkan (Morhange), Charles Henri Valentin, 1813–88
Auber, Daniel François Esprit, 1782–1871
Audran, Edmond, 1840–1901
Benoist, François, 1794–1878
Berlioz, Hector, 1803–69
Bizet, Georges, 1838–75
Boëllmann, Léon, 1862–97
Boïeldieu, François Adrien, 1775–1834
Bourgault-Ducoudray, Louis Albert, 1840–1910
Bruneau, Louis Charles Bonaventure

Alfred, 1857–1934
Campra, André, 1660–1744
Caplet, André, 1879–1925
Chabrier, Alexis Emmanuel, 1841–94
Chausson, Ernest, 1855–99
Couperin, François, 1668–1733
Daquin, Louise, 1694–1772
David, Félicien César, 1810–76
Debussy, Claude, 1862–1918
Delibes, Léo, 1836–91
Dukas, Paul, 1865–1935
Duparc, Henri, 1848–1933
Erlanger, Camille, 1863–1919
Fauré, Gabriel Urbain, 1845–1924
Godard, Benjamin Louis Paul, 1849–95
Goudimel, Claude, 1510–72
Gounod, Charles François, 1813–93
Guilmant, Félix Alexandre, 1837–1911
Halévy, Jacques Fromental Élie, 1799–1862
Hérold, Louis Joseph Ferdinand, 1791–1833
Indy, Paul Marie Théodore Vincent d', 1851–1931
Lalo, Victor Antoine Édouard, 1823–92
Lecocq, Alexandre Charles, 1832–1918
Lesueur, Jean François, 1760–1837
Lully, Jean Baptiste, 1632–87
Magnard, Albéric, 1866–1914
Massenet, Jules Émile Frédéric, 1842–1912
Méhul, Étienne Nicolas, 1763–1817
Messager, André Charles Prosper, 1853–1929
Messiaen, Olivier Eugene Prosper Charles, 1908–1992
Monsigny, Pierre Alexandre, 1729–1817
Offenbach, Jacques, 1819–80
Onslow, George (Anglo-French), 1784–1853
Philidor, François André, 1726–95
Pierné, Henri Constant Gabriel, 1863–1937
Poulenc, François, 1899–1963
Planquette, Robert, 1848–1903
Rameau, Jean Philippe, 1683–1764
Ravel, Maurice Joseph, 1875–1937
Reyer (Rey), Ernest, 1823–1909
Roussel, Albert, 1867–1937
Saint-Saëns, Charles Camille, 1841–1921
Satie, Erik (Alfred Eric Leslie), 1866–1925
Séverac, Joseph Marie Déodat de, 1873–1921
Thomas, Charles Louis Ambroise, 1811–96
Widor, Charles Marie Jean Albert, 1844–1937

German:
Bach, Carl Philipp Emanuel, 1714–88
Bach, Johann Christian, 1735–82
Bach, Johann Sebastian, 1685–1750
Beethoven, Ludwig van, 1770–1827
Brahms, Johannes, 1833–97
Bruch, Max, 1838–1920
Cornelius, Peter, 1824–74
Draeseke, Felix, 1835–1913
Flotow, Friedrich, Freiherr von, 1812–83
Franz, Robert, 1815–92
Gluck, Christoph Willibald, 1714–87
Goetz, Hermann, 1840–76
Graupner, Christoph, 1683–1760
Handl, Jakob, 1550–91
Hasse, Johann Adolf, 1699–1783
Hassler or Hasler, Hans Leo, 1564–1612
Henselt, Adolf von, 1814–99
Hiller, Johann Adam, 1728–1804
Hindemith, Paul, 1895–1963
Hoffman, Ernst Theodor Amadeus, 1776–1822
Hummel, Johann Nepomuk, 1778–1837
Humperdinck, Engelbert, 1854–1921
Jensen, Adolf, 1837–79
Karg-Elert, Sigfrid, 1877–1933
Keiser, Reinhard, 1674–1739
Kirchner, Theodor, 1824–1903
Kücken, Friedrich Wilhelm, 1810–82
Kuhnau, Johann, 1660–1722
Lachner, Franz, 1804–90
Lortzing, Gustav Albert, 1801–51
Löwe, Johann Karl Gottfried, 1796–1869
Marschner, Heinrich August, 1795–1861
Mendelssohn-Bartholdy, Jakob Ludwig Felix, 1809–47
Meyerbeer, Giacomo, 1791–1864
Moscheles, Ignaz, 1794–1870
Moszkowski, Moritz, 1854–1925
Mottl, Felix, 1856–1911
Naumann, Johann Gottlieb, 1741–1801
Neukomm, Sigismund von, 1778–1858
Nicodé, Jean Louis (Polish-born), 1853–1919
Nicolai, Karl Otto Ehrenfried, 1810–49
Pachelbel, Johann, 1653–1706
Raff, Joseph Joachim, 1822–82
Reger, Max, 1873–1916
Rheinberger, Josef Gabriel, 1839–1901
Scharwenka, Ludwig Philipp, 1847–1917
Scharwenka, Xaver, 1850–1924

Schreker, Franz, 1878–1934
Schumann, Robert, 1810–56
Schütz, Heinrich, 1585–1672
Spohr, Ludwig, 1784–1859
Steibelt, Daniel, 1765–1823
Strauss, Richard, 1864–1949
Telemann, Georg Philipp, 1681–1767
Vogler, Georg Josef, 1749–1814
Volkmann, Friedrich Robert, 1815–83
Wagner, Wilhelm Richard, 1813–83
Weber, Karl Maria Friedrich Ernst von, 1786–1826
Weill, Kurt, 1900–50,
Hungarian:
Bartók, Béla, 1881–1945
Dohnanyi, Ernö, 1887–1960
Erkel, Ferenc, 1810–92
Heller, Stephen, 1814–88
Joachim, Joseph, 1831–1907
Kodaly, Zoltan, 1882–1967
Lehár, Ferencz (Franz), 1870–1948
Liszt, Franz, 1811–86
Mosonyi, Michael Brandt, 1814–70
Italian:
Abbatini, Antonio Maria, c. 1595–1677
Albinoni, Tomaso, 1671–1750
Allegri, Gregorio, 1582–1652
Arditi, Luigi, 1822–1903
Bellini, Vincenzo, 1801–35
Boccherini, Luigi, 1743–1805
Boito, Arrigo, 1842–1918
Bononcini or Buononcini, Giovanni Maria, 1642–78
Bossi, Marco Enrico, 1861–1925
Busoni, Ferruccio Benvenuto, 1866–1924
Caccini, Giulio, 1545–1618
Carissimi, Giacomo, 1605–74
Catalani, Alfredo, 1854–93
Cavalieri, Emilio di, c. 1550–1602
Cavalli, Pietro Francesco, 1602–76
Cherubini, Maria Luigi Zenobio Carlo Salvatore, 1760–1842
Cimarosa, Domenico, 1749–1801
Clementi, Muzio, 1752–1832
Corelli, Arcangelo, 1653–1713
Donizetti, Gaetano, 1797–1848
Durante, Francesco, 1684–1755
Frescobaldi, Girolamo, 1583–1643
Gabrieli, Andrea, 1520–86
Gabrieli, Giovanni, 1557–1612
Gagliano, Marco da, c. 1575–1642

Geminiani, Francesco, 1687–1762
Gesualdo, Carlo, Prince of Venosa, 1560–1613
Jommelli, Niccolò, 1714–74
Legrenzi, Giovanni, 1625–90
Leo, Leonardo, 1694–1744
Leoncavallo, Ruggiero, 1858–1919
Locatelli, Pietro Antonio, 1693–1764
Lotti, Antonio, 1667–1740
Marcello, Benedetto, 1686–1739
Marenzio, Luca, 1553–99
Martucci, Giuseppe, 1856–1909
Mercadante, Giuseppe Saverio Raffaele, 1795–1870
Merulo, Claudio, 1533–1604
Monteverdi, Claudio, 1567–1643
Paer, Ferdinando, 1771–1839
Paesiello or Paisiello, Giovanni, 1741–1816
Paganini, Niccolò, 1782–1840
Palestrina, Giovanni Pierluigi da, 1525–1594
Pergolese, or Pergolesi, Giovanni Battista, 1710–36
Piccinni, or Piccini, Niccolò, 1728–1800
Pinsuti, Ciro, 1829–88
Puccini, Giacomo, 1858–1924
Respighi, Ottorino, 1879–1936
Rossini, Gioacchino Antonio, 1792–1868
Sacchini, Antonio Maria Gaspare, 1734–86
Salieri, Antonio, 1750–1825
Sarti, Giuseppe, 1729–1802
Scarlatti, Alessandro, 1660–1725
Scarlatti, Domenico, 1685–1757
Sgambati, Giovanni, 1841–1914
Spontini, Gasparo Luigi Pacifico, 1774–1851
Steffani, Agostino, 1654–1728
Stradella, Alessandro, 1642–82
Tartini, Giuseppe, 1692–1770
Traetta, Tommaso, 1727–79
Vecchi, Orazio, c. 1550–1605
Verdi, Giuseppe, 1813–1901
Viadana (Grossi), Ludovico, 1564–1645
Vicentino, Nicolà, 1511–c. 1576
Vivaldi, Antonio, c. 1675–1741
Zingarelli, Nicolà Antonio, 1752–1837
Mexican:
Ponce, Manuel, 1882–1948
Norwegian:
Grieg, Edvard Hagerup, 1843–1907
Selmer, Johan Peter, 1844–1910

Svendsen, Johan Severin, 1840–1911
Polish:
Chopin, Frédéric François, 1810–49
Godowsky, Leopold, 1870–1938
Moniuszko, Stanislaus, 1819–92
Noskowski, Zygmunt, 1846–1909
Paderewski, Ignacy Jan, 1860–1941
Szymanowski, Karol, 1882–1937
Russian:
Arensky, Antonin Stepanovich, 1861–1906
Balakirev, Mily Alexeievich, 1837–1910
Borodin, Alexander Porfirievich, 1833–87
Cui, César Antonovich, 1835–1918
Dragomijsky, Alexander, 1813–69
Glazunov, Alexander Constantinovich, 1865–1936
Glinka, Mikhail Ivanovich, 1804–57
Kastalsky, Alexander Dmitrievich, 1856–1926
Khachaturian, Aram Ilyich (Armenian), 1903–78
Liadov, Anatol Constantinovich, 1855–1914
Liapunov, Serge Mikhailovich, 1859–1924
Mussorgsky, Modest Petrovich, 1839–81
Napravnik, Eduard (Czech-born), 1839–1916
Prokofiev, Sergei, 1891–1953
Rachmaninov, Serge, 1873–1943
Rebikov, Vladimir Ivanovich, 1866–1920
Rimsky-Korsakov, Nicolas Andreievich, 1844–1908
Rubinstein, Anton, 1830–94
Scriabin, Alexander Nicolaievitch, 1871–1915
Taneiev, Alexander Sergeievitch, 1850–1915
Taneiev, Serge Ivanovich, 1856–1915
Tchaikovsky, Peter Ilyich, 1840–93
Spanish:
Albeniz, Isaac, 1860–1909
Bretón, Tomás, 1850–1923
Chapi, Ruperto, 1851–1909
Falla, Manuel de, 1876–1946
Granados Campina, Enrique, 1867–1916
Pedrell, Felipe, 1841–1922
Sarasate, Pablo de, 1844–1910
Victoria, Tomás Luis de, c. 1535–1611
Swedish:
Hallén, Johan Andréas, 1846–1925

Hallström, Ivar, 1826–1901
Sjögren, J. G. Emil, 1853–1918
Swiss:
Honegger, Arthur, 1892–1955
Huber, Hans, 1852–1921

musical festivals. Festival of the Sons of the Clergy in St Paul's Cathedral, annual since 1698. Three Choirs Festival held annually in cathedrals of Gloucester, Hereford and Worcester, in succession, from 1715. Norwich Festival held at irregular intervals since 1770. Crystal Palace Handel Festival began, 1857; irregular, and later triennial. Leeds Festival instituted, 1858; held again, 1874; since then, triennial. Bayreuth Festival, 1876. Since 20thC, M. F. in the UK include Glyndebourne, 1934; Cheltenham, 1945; Edinburgh International, 1947; Aldeburgh, Suffolk, 1948; Llandaff, 1958; English Bach (Oxford), 1963. In USA festivals began at Boston and Worcester, 1858; Cincinnati, 1873. Bach Festival at Bethlehem, Pennsylvania, 1900. Berkshire Festivals, established at Pittsfield, Massachusetts, 1918, were in 1931 transferred to Library of Congress, Washington. The Boston Symphony Orchestra acquired Tanglewood, Berkshire, Massachussets, as permanent festival home in 1937. In Europe M.F. include the Lower Rhine, 1817; Salzburg, 1870; Munich, 1901; Zurich, 1909; Florence, 1933; Vienna, 1951.

musical performers. The following are among the world's most famous M.P. (for singers, *see under* OPERA.)

Ashkenazy, Vladimir, pianist and conductor, 1937–
Barenboim, Daniel, pianist and conductor, 1942–
Barbirolli, Sir John, conductor, 1899–1970
Beecham, Sir Thomas, conductor, 1879–1961
Boulez, Pierre, conductor, 1927–
Boult, Sir Adrian, conductor, 1889–1983
Bream, Julian, guitarist and lutist, 1933–
Byng, Sir Rudolf, impresario, 1902–
Casals, Pablo, cellist, 1876–1973
Davis, Sir Colin, conductor, 1927–
Dupré, Jacqueline, cellist, 1945–87

Furtwangler, Wilhelm, conductor, 1886–1954
Goossens, Eugene, conductor, 1845–1906
Halle, Sir Charles, conductor, 1819–95
Hess, Dame Myra, pianist, 1890–1965
Horowitz, Vladimir, pianist, 1904–89
Joyce, Dame Eileen, pianist, 1912–
Karajan, Herbert von, conductor, 1908–89
Kempe, Rudolf, conductor, 1910–76
Klemperer, Otto, conductor, 1885–1973
Krips, Josef, conductor, 1902–74
Menuhin, (Lord) Yehudi, violinist, 1916–
Moisiewitch, Benno, pianist, 1890–1963
Ogdon, John, pianist, 1937–89
Paderewski, Ignacy Jan, pianist, 1860–1941
Previn, André, conductor, 1929–
Rattle, Simon, conductor, 1955–
Rostropovich, Mstislav, cellist, 1927–
Rubinstein, Arthur, pianist, 1887–1982
Solti, Sir George, conductor, 1912–
Sargent, Sir Malcolm, conductor, 1895–1967
Toscanini, Arturo, conductor, 1867–1957
Walter, Bruno, conductor, 1876–1962
Wood, Sir Henry, conductor, 1869–1944

See also under BALLET; JAZZ; MUSICAL COMPOSERS.

Muslim Brotherhood, fundamentalist Islamic organization founded by Hassan al Banna at Ismailia, Egypt, 1928. It spread from Egypt to Sudan, Lebanon and the then Palestine. Began to be politicized after 1938. Sent underground by Egyptian revolution of 1952. After attempted assassination of Nasser, 1954, it was suppressed and leaders executed. Revival in 1980s: implicated in assassination of Sadat, 6 Oct. 1981. Uprising of M.B. in Syria, Feb. 1982, crushed by Assad. Murder of Egyptian Copts and foreign tourists by M.B. extremists, 1992–3, led to government campaign against, 1993 onwards.

Mutiny Acts, the legal basis of military law and hence of the existence of a standing army in the UK, were passed annually from 1689 to 1881, when they were merged in the Army Acts.

MVD, executive forces of the Ministry of the Interior of the USSR, and including frontier and security troops of all arms, and warders and administrative personnel of forced-labour camps, as well as the secret police force, known until 1945 as the *NKVD, and after 1953 as the *KGB. Since dissolution of Soviet Union, 1991, superseded by different bodies in the different states of the CIS, in Russia by the Federal Security Agency.

Myanmar, Union of, official name, since 1989 of *BURMA.

Mysore, India. Continually at war with the British, 1760–99. In 1799 Tipu Sahib finally defeated; M. made to accept a subsidiary alliance and to cede Coimbatore to British, and Kurnool to Hyderabad, 1801. State annexed by British, 1834, but retroceded to a native rajah, 1881. Joined the Indian Union, Dec. 1947; state boundaries enlarged under States Reorganization Act, 1956, and state known as **Karnataka** since 1973.

NAFTA. *See* NORTH AMERICAN FREE TRADE AGREEMENT.

Nagaland, inaugurated as 16th state of India, 1 Dec. 1963. Unrest, 1960–75, theoretically terminated by the Shillong Agreement of 1975, but sporadic fighting has continued since.

Nagasaki, Japan. As a port, it became centre of Catholic mission activity from Spain and Portugal in 16thC, and many Japanese converted. Christianity forbidden, end 16thC and martyrdoms of European and Japanese Catholics at N., 1597 and 1614–44. Catholic church built, 1864, commemorates these. Estimated 20,000 Christians remaining in N. when Japan reopened, 1859. Chinese temple at N. dates from 1629. Coaling station in 19thC, then shipbuilding centre. From 1640 the (Protestant) Dutch were the only European nation permitted to trade with Japan, and they were allowed only one trading post on Deshima, near N. This continued till Japan was opened to trade, 1859. City mostly destroyed by atomic bomb, 9 Aug. 1945; since rebuilt, with Peace Park under site of bomb detonation. About 40,000 *d.* in explosion. N. now (1995) again major shipbuilding centre.

Nagorno-Karabakh, mountainous area within *Azerbaijan since 1923, but with mainly Armenian population. War between the Armenians and Azeris since 1988, with considerable Armenian gains, by 1995.

Nairobi, capital of Kenya. Founded, 1898.

Namibia, formerly S-W Africa. This territory (excluding certain islands and Walvis Bay) proclaimed a German protectorate, 1884. Mandated to S Africa by League of Nations, 17 Dec. 1920. In July 1949 N. virtually incorporated in S Africa; UN mandate terminated, 1966, but this not accepted by S Africa. Guerrilla resistance to S African rule led by SWAPO and based in Mozambique continued from 1960s until 1989, when UN force in N. supervised multiparty elections. Won by SWAPO. Independence, 1990 and agreement with S Africa for joint administration of Walvis Bay, 1991. Free multiparty elections, 1992; National Assembly inaugurated, Jan. 1993. SWAPO won Dec. 1994 elections with increased majority.

Namur, Belgium. Captured by Louis XIV in 1692; recaptured in 1695 by William III; French, 1702–12; bombarded by allies, 1704; subsequently in possession of different powers, and assigned to Belgium, 1830.

Nancy, France. Captured by Charles the Bold, 29 Nov. 1475; lost by him, 5 Oct. 1476; captured by French, 1633 and 1670; restored to Duke Leopold, 1697; became French possession, 1766; put to ransom by the Prussians, 1870.

Nanking or **Nanjing,** China. Capital of China, 1368, till abandoned by Yung-lo, 1405. Captured by British, 1842. By Taipings, 1853. Railways to Tientsin and Shanghai opened, 1909. Became capital again, 1928. Stormed and sacked by Japanese, Nov. 1937. Became capital of Wang Ching Wei's Japanese-sponsored government, 1940–5. Officially ceased to be Chinese capital after Communist victory in 1949.

Nantes, France. Of Roman origin. In possession of Clotaire I, AD 560; held by Normans, 843–936; communal constitution granted by Francis II, 1560; scene of Carrier's *noyades*, 1793.

Nantes, Edict of, by which the Huguenots were permitted to exercise their religion, published on 15 Apr. 1598 by Henry IV of France. Its revocation on 24 Oct. 1685, by

Louis XIV, drove many of the Protestants into permanent exile and settlement abroad notably in Britain, the Netherlands and Prussia.

napalm, mixture of napthemic and palmitic acids, notorious for its use in bombing by the Americans during the Vietnam War, 1961–75, and allegedly used in Bosnian conflict, 1994.

Napier University, name and status since 1992 of the former Napier polytechnic, Edinburgh.

Naples, Italy. The Romans subdued the territory in 326 BC; it fell into the hands of the Goths, but they were driven out by Belisarius in AD 536; Charles of Anjou in possession, 1266; great massacre of the French at Palermo known as the *Sicilian Vespers, 1282; separated from *Sicily, 1303; reunited with Sicily, 1442; annexed to Spain, 1504; insurrection headed by Masaniello, 1647; possessed by Austria, 1713; recovered by Spain, 1734; invaded by French Republican Army, 1789; by Napoleon, 1806; restoration of the Bourbons, 1815; incorporated in the kingdom of Italy, 1860.

Narbonne, France. In 118 BC the first Roman colony in Gaul was founded under the name of *Narbo Martius*; seized by the Visigoths, AD 413; by Saracens after a two years' siege, 719; retaken by Pepin le Bref, 759; united to French crown, 1507; Cinq-Mars arrested at for conspiracy, 1642.

Narvik, formerly **Viktoriahavn,** was connected with the ironstone mines in N Sweden (Kiruna, etc.), 1903. Four German destroyers sunk in N fiord, 13 Apr. 1940; town captured by Allies, 28 May, but abandoned, 10 June.

NASA (National Aeronautics and Space Administration), established 1959 by US government to research and conduct its space programme, from the Kennedy Space Center, Florida, with HQ in Washington. Has expanded its activities to include environmental research (e.g. report on ozone layer depletion, 1992). Mars probe lost from, 1993, but successful mission to repair Hubble telescope revived NASA's flagging reputation, Dec.

Nassau 1) Germany. Early occupied by the Alamanni, who were defeated by Clovis towards the close of the 5thC; became part of German kingdom, 843; annexed to Prussia, 1866.
2) capital of the Bahamas, founded 17thC.

Natal, S Africa. Discovered by Vasco da Gama on Christmas Day, 1497, hence the name; declared part of British dominions, 1843; formally annexed to Cape Colony, 31 May 1844; declared a separate colony, 15 July 1856; Zululand annexed to, 1897; Boers finally driven from, 1900. An original member of the Union of S Africa, 1910.

national anthem. First N.A. said to have been the English *God Save the King* (or *Queen*) first performed in London in 1745 to celebrate the victory over the Jacobites at Prestonpans, and since used on royal and other ceremonial occasions.

National Art Collections Fund. Founded, 1903.

National Assembly, 1789–91. *See* FRENCH REVOLUTION.

National Assistance Act, 1948, replaced by a new principle a system which hitherto had been based on successive modifications of the Elizabethan *Poor Laws.

National Book League. Founded, 1944, as the successor to the National Book Council (founded, 1924).

National Council for Civil Liberties. *See* LIBERTY.

National Curriculum, established 1988 in the UK and intended to ensure study of certain subjects in all state schools. Modifications, 1993 onwards.

National Debt (Great Britain). Originated in the reign of William III, and was introduced by Charles Montagu, Earl of Halifax (1661–1715) on 15 Dec. 1692. Became a permanent institution, 1694.

Deadweight debt on 31 Mar. in years named: 1914, £649,770,091; 1939, £7,130,800,000; 1969, £33,963 million; 1980, over £96 billion; 1992, over £198 billion; 1994, over £300 billion.

National Dental Service provided for under N. Health Service Act, 1946, which came into operation, 5 July 1948.

National Front. *See* Fascism (2).

National Gallery (London). Founded, 1824. Present building completed, 1838; enlarged, 1860, 1869, 1876, 1886, 1930 and 1975. New Sainsbury Wing opened, 1991. *N. Portrait Gallery founded, 1856, transferred to new buildings adjoining N.G., 1896.

National Gallery of British Art. *See* Tate Gallery.

National Governments, coalitions in the UK which came to power in Aug. 1931 and Nov. 1935, and which continued in office during World War II, being, however, largely reconstituted in the spring of 1940. A N. G. continued in office until 1945.

National Guard (France). Introduced into Paris during French Revolution, July 1789; superseded by present military system, 1870.

National Guard (USA). Founded, 1903.

National Health Service Act was evolved from proposals made in the White Paper of Feb. 1944. It became law in 1946, but did not come into operation until 5 July 1948.

National Heritage, Department of, established 1992, responsible for areas previously dealt with by six other departments and all the functions of the former office of Arts and Libraries. It also has responsibility for the *National Lottery.

National Insurance. An insurance against ill health and unemployment, introduced in 1911, and came into force, 15 July 1912. Entire structure of N.I. in Britain changed by the Act of 1946 (*see* next article).

National Insurance Act, 1946, based on recommendations made in the report of the Beveridge Committee, 1942, and developed in a White Paper of Sept. 1944, repealed all previous legislation on the subject of unemployment, etc., insurance and pensions, and became law, 1946, though it has since been considerably amended.

National Lottery. Modern N.L. first proposed for UK, 1992 and began operating, 14 Nov. 1994, first draw 19 Nov. Run by private consortium, profits to be divided between charities, the arts, sport, heritage and the Millenium Fund. Earlier N.Ls. in England include 1569 (for repair of Cinque Ports); 1612 (for support of plantations in Virginia); 1640 (for ransom of English slaves held in Tunis). N.Ls. authorized by parliamentary Act, 1698. N.L. of 1753 used to finance original British Museum building; discontinued due to fraud complaints early in 19thC. N.Ls. exist in many other countries, including Spain, Italy, Ireland, Japan, etc. Many US states have state lotteries. Single win in N.L. of nearly £18 million on 10 Dec. 1994 was then the UK's biggest recorded individual gambling win. Scratch cards (maximum payout £50,000) introduced, Mar. 1995.

National Parks and Access to the Countryside Act, 1949, set up the National Parks Commission with powers to designate national parks and areas of outstanding beauty in England and Wales. Ten national parks had been established by 1969, when the N.P. Commission was succeeded by the Countryside Commission.

National Portrait Gallery, London, founded 1856; present buildings opened, 1896; extended, 1933.

Nationality Act, British, 1981, replaced a previous Act, 30 July 1948, which itself replaced the Act of 1914. It amended the Immigration Act of 1971 regarding rights of abode in the UK and established three categories of citizenship.

nationalization. The following is a list of

principal measures of N. taken in the UK between 1944 and 1977:

Bank of England, 1946; cable and wireless, 1946; coal, 1946; civil aviation, 1946; electricity, 1948; gas, 1948; rail and road transport, 1948; steel, 1949–51; shipbuilding, 1977; aircraft industry, 1977. Since 1979 all these have been denationalized, except for the Bank of England: also some parts of the former British Rail still remained under government control, 1995. Since 1980s considerable denationalization even in countries still Communist (e.g. China).

National Playing Fields Association. Founded, 1925; chartered, 1933.

National Register.
1. Taken, 15 Aug. 1915.
2. Register taken and *identity cards issued, 29 Sept. 1939. Closed, 1952.

National Research Development Corporation. Set up by the Development of Inventions Act, 30 July 1948.

National Rivers Authority, (NRA), established under the Water Act of 1989, an independent body with board appointed by Ministries of Environment and Agriculture and Secretary of State for Wales. Has responsibilities for control of pollution, management of water resources, monitoring of water quality, etc.

National Savings Bank, name given, 1971, to the **Post Office Savings Bank**, established 1861. National Savings Department established 1969.

National Savings Certificates, first issued, Feb. 1916.

National Security Agency (NSA) (USA) established by presidential directive, 1952, largest US national security organization. It grew from US military intelligence services created in World War II and Congress has little control of it.

National Security Council (NSC) established by the US Congress, 1947. The *Central Intelligence Agency (CIA) is subordinate to it.

National Service, Ministry of. Set up as a temporary recruiting expedient, 1917, and dissolved after the war. Revived as part of Ministry of Labour and N.S., 19 Dec. 1938 until conscription ended, 1962.

National Society for the Prevention of Cruelty to Children (NSPCC), established 1884.

National Socialism (Germany). A pan-German party with the title N. Socialist Labour Party was founded in Bohemia in 1912, but had no direct traceable connection with that which Anton Drexler founded at Munich in 1919, and called simply German Labour Party (*Deutsche Arbeiter Partei*). This was used by Hitler as the nucleus of his N. Socialist German Labour Party (NSDAP for short in German). It adopted a detailed pan-German nationalist programme, with some vague socialist tenets, 1920, and from 1933 to 1945 was the only permitted party in the country.

National Temperance League. *See* ANTI-SALOON LEAGUE.

National Theatre, Great Britain. Laurence Olivier its first director, Aug. 1962. First season at Old Vic, 1963: new building completed, 1976.

National Trust, founded by Octavia Hill and others, 1895. Incorporated, 1907. N.T. for Scotland founded in 1931.

Nativity, formally appointed to be observed on 25 Dec. by the Synod of Salzburg, 800, but this was only confirmation of practice general since *c.* 690.

Nativity, Church of the, at Bethlehem. St Helena (*c.* 250–330), mother of the Emperor Constantine, built a church here in 325, over a cave first mentioned as the scene of the N. by Justin Martyr in 155, and which was shown to Origen in 215. St Helena's building was burnt, probably in the Samaritan rising of 529; but by order of the Emperor Justinian (reigned 527–65), a church was built on the same site. On the Muslim conquest of Palestine the church was given special protection by command of the

Caliph Omar (c. 640). From then until 1947, except for the period 1099–1187, the site was in Muslim hands; since 1947, in Israel.

NATO (North Atlantic Treaty Organization). *N Atlantic Treaty signatories set up permanent council of ministers' deputies, May 1950. Defence Committee decided on a permanent integrated force on a war footing on the European mainland, Sept. 1950. Gen. Eisenhower appointed first Supreme Commander, and Field Marshal Montgomery appointed Deputy Commander Land Forces, Dec. Their headquarters, SHAPE, became operational, Apr. 1951. Turkey and Greece joined NATO, 1952. Lord Ismay first Secretary-Gen. Oct. 1952. German Federal Republic joined NATO, Oct. 1954 (effective 9 May 1955), and German units thereafter included in NATO forces. France withdrew her naval Atlantic force from NATO, June 1963, and by 1966 had virtually withdrawn from it altogether. HQ moved from Paris to Brussels, 1967. Spain joined NATO, 1982. Reunited Germany joined NATO, 1990. At London Summit, 1990, strategy and goals redefined after end of 'Cold War'. Agreed to establish 'rapid reaction corps' under British command, May 1991. At Nov. 1991 Rome Summit, strategic concepts and forces reorganized; 30% reduction in strength planned. *North Atlantic Co-operation Council formed. From 1990, USSR (later, Russia) had diplomatic representative at NATO, and Hungary became an associate member in 1991. In 1993, NATO involved in possible future peace-keeping role in *Bosnia. Suggestions that all former Eastern bloc countries in Europe should join NATO put forward by Germany, 1993; but rejected by USA, 1994, and at NATO summit held in Jan. in Brussels idea of E European countries being involved in 'partnership for peace' with NATO, not full membership, accepted. First military action in NATO's history, Feb. 1994, when NATO used air power against Bosnian Serbs. 'Partnership for peace' signed by Russia, June. Further NATO air strikes in Bosnia during 1994.

But division among members on Bosnian policies led to weakening of NATO's authority, 1994–5; this division largely healed, 1995, when far greater NATO air power and 'rapid reaction force' used against Serbs. This played major role in forcing preliminary agreement on Bosnia, Sept. NATO to undertake policing of Bosnian peace agreement, Nov. 1995.

Secretaries-Gen. of NATO:
Lord Ismay 1952–57
Paul-Henri Spaak 1957–61
Dirk Stikker 1961–64
Manlio Brosio 1964–71
Joseph Luns 1971–84
Lord Carrington 1984–88
Manfred Wörner 1988–94
Willy Claes, 1994–5

Supreme Commanders of NATO:
Gen. Eisenhower 1950–52
Gen. Ridgway 1952–53
Gen. Gruenther 1953–56
Gen. Norstad 1956–62
Gen. Lemnitzer 1962–69
Gen. Alexander Haig 1970–79
Gen. Bernard Rogers 1979–87
Gen. John Galvin, 1987–1992
Gen. John Shalikashvili 1992–93
Gen. George Joulwan, 1993–

Naturalization Act (Great Britain). Passed, 1870; a treaty with USA was made the same year, by which both countries pledged themselves to recognize claims of N. British naturalization processes modified by the British Nationality Act, 1981.

Nauru, republic in the Pacific, discovered by Capt. Fearn, 1798; annexed by Germany, 1888, mandated to Britain, 1920. Occupied by Japanese, 1942–5. Administered jointly by Britain, Australia and New Zealand, 1947–68, when N. became independent with 'special member' Commonwealth status.

Naval Discipline Acts began in England with the N. Laws of Olèron, 1194. Henry VIII codified Sea Laws, 1530. Modern naval discipline regulated by the Naval

Discipline Act, 1957 (as amended and continued by the Armed Forces Act, 1981).

Naval Limitation Conference (at Geneva) – Great Britain, USA and Japan – failed to come to any agreement, 4 Aug. 1927. *See* LONDON CONFERENCE.

Navarre. United all Basques, 10th–11thC. United with Aragon, 1076–1134. Vizcaya and Guipúzcoa annexed by Castile *c.* 1200. French dynasty took throne, 1285. Spanish N. annexed by Castile, 1512. French N. united when Henry of N. ascended French throne as Henry IV, 1589. Spanish N. was a viceroyalty till 1833. *See* SPAIN.

navigation laws (Great Britain). Oliver Cromwell in 1650 excluded all foreign ships without a licence from trading with the plantations of America. The N. Act of Cromwell passed, 1651. Act providing that all colonial produce should be exported in English vessels, 1660. Colonies prohibited from receiving goods in foreign vessels, 1663. N. Acts of Charles II, 1672, extended Cromwell's Act and ruined the Dutch Navy. N. Act repealed, 1826, but a new code of regulations still prevented free trade. These laws abolished, 1842, 1846 and 1849.

Navy, Royal (British). Alfred the Great built a fleet to resist the Danes, 897; Richard I equipped a large fleet for the crusades, 1189; Edward III defeated the French at Sluys, 1340; Henry V increased the number and size of the ships, 1413–22; Henry VII built the *Great Harry*, 1488; the English N. defeated the Armada, 1588; the *Sovereign of the Seas* launched, 1637; the first British frigate built, 1649; first steamer built for the Royal N., 1814; screw propeller introduced, 1845; reserve volunteer force established, 1859; first ironclad ship of the N. built, 1860; first armour-clad turret ship built, 1868; breech-loading guns manufactured for the N., 1881; torpedo cruiser built, 1887; first British submarine launched, 1901; first British aircraft-carrier, 1913. *See* WORLD WARS I and II, and BATTLES. Number of Royal N. ships in commission first declared to be exceeded by total USSR strength, Mar. 1953. Work completed on first nuclear-powered submarine, 1963. N. played vital role in Falklands War, 1982; active in *Gulf War, 1990–91. Cuts in ships and manpower since 1980s.

Navy, US. On 13 Oct. 1775, Congress authorized the fitting-out of a gun-carrying vessel. This was the beginning of the US. N. Board of Admiralty established, 1779. Other vessels fitted out, 1775. In 1794, the N. having fallen into neglect, Congress voted a sum of money 'for creating a small N'. *See* WORLD WARS I and II, and BATTLES. Played crucial role in *Gulf War, 1990–91 and also in Bosnian 'peace-keeping' from 1994. In 1995 the US Navy was the most powerful sea force in the world.

Nazi Party. *See* NATIONAL SOCIALISM.

Neanderthal, valley near Düsseldorf, Germany, giving its name to a primitive human race, a skull of one of its members having been found there, 1856.

Nebraska, USA, territory ceded by France to Spain, 1762, returned to France, 1801, and forming part of the *Louisiana Purchase, 1803. Territory organized, 1854; state admitted to Union, 1867.

Negri Sembilan, former Federated Malay State, is largely populated by the descendants of Sumatrans who immigrated in the 16thC. Dominated by *Johore, 1641–1773. A confederation of smaller states gave N.S. its present extent, 1895. Since 1963 part of *Malaysia.

Negropont. *See* EUBOEA.

Nejd. *See* SAUDI ARABIA.

Nelson's Column, in Trafalgar Square, London, commemorates the Battle of Trafalgar and was designed by William Railton and erected 1839–42. The statue of Nelson by E. H. Baily was placed on the top, 1843. Bronze reliefs at base (representing Nelson's achievements and death) made from metal melted from captured French guns. Landseer's bronze lions added, 1867.

NEP (New Economic Policy). Following economic breakdown in Russia, Lenin introduced the NEP as a temporary capitalist dilution of Soviet socialism, 1921–8.

Nepal. Conquered by Harisinha-Deva, 1324. Jayastithi-Malla (1386–1429) introduced caste system. Divided into four states, 1429–1768. Conquered by Gurkhas, 1768–70. War with China, 1790–2. Treaties with British, 1792–1801. First Gurkha War, 1814–16, ended in cession of Kumaon province to British India. British residency established at Katmandu, 1817. Jung Bahadur Rana seizes power ('The Kot Massacre'), 18 May 1845. Rana family consolidated their power and established new system of government, 1845–56. Gurkhas assist British in Indian Mutiny, 1857. Treaty with Britain recognized independence of N., 1923. Constitutional monarchy, 1951, but in 1960 King abolished party government and took absolute powers. After agitation for reform in 1980s, ban on political parties lifted, April 1990. New constitution, Nov. 1990, and multiparty elections, May 1991. King dissolved parliament, July 1994, marking end of '3-year democratic experiment', but elections in Dec. produced a Communist majority.

Ness, Loch (Scotland). Famous for the alleged 'monster' in its waters. According to legend, the monster was pacified by St Columba in the 6thC. First 'photographed' in the 1930s (but this incident now (Mar. 1994) suggested to have been based on a hoax). Since then, countless unsuccessful attempts to prove or disprove the monster's existence. A major tourist attraction since 1950s.

Net Book Agreement, UK, effectively ended, by withdrawal from it of major publishing houses, after c. 100 years, Sept. 1995.

Netherlands, Kingdom of the, popularly known as **Holland,** became a separate entity after the Spanish victory at Gembloux, 1578, had driven the Catholic Netherlanders to make terms and instituted the Union of Arras, 1579 (see BELGIUM). The northern Protestant provinces repudiated Spanish sovereignty in the Act of Abjuration, 26 July 1581, being led by Holland. William I of Orange assassinated, 1584. Jan van Oldenbarneveldt in power, 1586–1618. Spanish naval defeat at Gibraltar, 1607. Truce of Antwerp, 1609. Wars with Britain, 1653–4, 1666–7. Joins Triple Alliance against France, 1668. Wars against France and Britain, 1672–8. William of Orange becomes King of Britain, 1689. Treaty of Ryswick, 1697. Joins in War of Spanish Succession against France, 1701–13. Office of Stadhouder declared hereditary in family of Orange, 1747. French Republican army invades N., 1794; William V expelled, 15 Jan. 1795; Louis Bonaparte declared king, 5 June 1806, abdicated, 1 July 1810. House of Orange restored under William Frederick, 1 Dec. 1813; N. and Belgium united by Treaty of London, 14 June 1814, and William made King of the united N., 15 Mar. 1815. Separated from *Belgium, 12 July 1831; peace between N. and Belgium, 19 Apr. 1839 and William Frederick abdicated; William II succeeded, 1840; William III, 1849; Wilhelmina crowned (after queen-mother's regency), 1898. Ex-Kaiser sought refuge in N., Nov. 1918. German invasion, 10 May 1940. Dutch military surrender, 14 May, but Dutch royal family fled to Britain. Ex-Kaiser *d.* at Doorn, 4 June 1941. British airborne forces land at *Arnhem, 17 Sept. 1944. British land at Walcheren, 1 Nov. 1944. Member of *Benelux, 1949. Wilhelmina abdicated, 4 Sept. 1948 (*d.* Nov. 1962); succeeded by daughter Juliana. N. member of NATO, 1949. Dutch E Indies became republic of *Indonesia, 1950; Indonesia obtained W Dutch New Guinea, 1963. Member of *European Economic Community, 1958. Juliana abdicated, 1980, and succeeded by daughter Beatrix (*b.* 1938). Serious flooding in N., Jan. 1995.

Sovereigns of the Netherlands:
William I* (*d.* 1843) 1815–40
William II 1840–49
William III 1849–90
Wilhelmina 1890–1948

Juliana (*b.* 1909) 1948–80
Beatrix (*b.* 1938) 1980–
* 'I' means first *king*. He would have been sixth Stadhouder of that name.

Neuchâtel, Switzerland. Originally *Novum Castellum*, whose original possessors took the name of count mid-12thC; under Prussian rule from 1707 to 1857, excepting the years 1806–14, when Napoleon granted it to Marshal Berthier; became a full republican member of the Swiss Confederation, 1857.

Neuilly, Treaty of, by which Bulgaria, after World War I, gave up all claims to Macedonia and Thrace, signed 27 Nov. 1919.

Nevada, USA, first settled, 1849. At first, part of the territory of Utah which was set up, 1850 (*see* UTAH), but after expansion due to gold and silver discoveries made a territory on its own, 1861, and became a state, 1864. Since 1930s known as a gambling (Las Vegas) and divorce (Reno) venue.

Nevis, Nievis, or **Mevis,** formed with St Kitts and Anguilla into a presidency, 1882. Discovered by Columbus, 1493. Granted to the Earl of Carlisle, 1627, and colonized from St Kitts, 1628. Devastated by the French, 1706, and again captured by them, 1782, but restored by the Treaty of Versailles in the following year. *Anguilla seceded, 1967. N., with *St Kitts, became independent within the Commonwealth, 1983.

New Brunswick, Canada. Discovered by Cabot, 1497; colonized by French, 1630 and 1672; ceded to Britain, 1713, and in 1784 separated from Nova Scotia and made a separate colony; was incorporated into Dominion of Canada, 1867.

New Caledonia, Pacific, was discovered by Capt. Cook, 1774; closely explored by d'Entrecasteaux, 1793; claimed by France, 1843; British claim withdrawn, 1853. Became an Overseas Territory of France, 1958.

Newcastle upon Tyne, England. Roman *Pons Aelli*. Named after castle erected 1080 by Robert Curthose; besieged by William Rufus, 1095; present castle built, 1172–7; besieged by Scots under Gen. Leslie, 1644; Anglican bishopric founded, 1882 and parish church of St Nicholas (began 14thC) became cathedral. High-level bridge, 1846–9; swing bridge, 1865–76. Tyne Bridge opened, 1928. University founded, 1852; reorganized, 1963. N. polytechnic received name and status of University of Northumbria at N., 1992. N. was a staple town in 1353 and from end of 18thC an industrial centre. Since World War II a major service industries' centre.

New Deal. Name given to policy of Franklin D. Roosevelt, President, USA, adumbrated during his first presidential campaign at Atlanta, 22 May 1932.

New Delhi. *See* DELHI.

New England, USA. Visited by Sir Humphrey Gilbert, 1583, and by Bartholomew Gosnold, 1602; Puritans sailed in the *Mayflower*, and founded settlement, 1620. *See* also MASSACHUSETTS and MAINE etc.

New Forest, England. Already a forest when Canute issued his Laws at Winchester, 1016. William I extended its area, 1079, and enforced the Forest Laws more harshly.

Newfoundland. Discovered by John Cabot, 24 June 1497. Visited by five Anglo-Portuguese expeditions, 1500–5. Formally annexed to England by Sir Humphrey Gilbert, Aug. 1583. Island divided between English and French at Treaty of Ryswick, 1697. Wholly given to Britain by Treaty of Utrecht, 1713. Responsible government, 1855. N. was one of the dominions given independent status under the Statute of Westminster, 1931, but owing to bankruptcy the government was surrendered to a commission nominated by the British Treasury, 18 Dec. 1933. Became a province of Canada, 31 Mar. 1949.

Newgate Prison (London). In existence at least as early as 1190. Being rebuilt when burnt down in the *Gordon Riots, 1780, and building completed, 1783. Executions took place here in public, 1783–1868. Demolished, 1902–3.

New Guinea. Probably sighted by Antonio d'Abreu (Portuguese), 1512. First visit by Europeans: either Jorge de Menesis (Portuguese), 1526, or Alvaro de Saavedra (Spanish), 1528. E India Co. made a settlement in Geelvink Bay, 1793; but in 1814 British government admitted claims of the Netherlands. Dutch proclaimed sovereignty over W half of island, 1848. Remainder divided between Britain (S) and Germany (N), 1884. The British part, called Papua, was placed under the Commonwealth of Australia in 1906. In 1914 the German territory was occupied by Australian forces. Petroleum discovered, 1919. Civil administration of former German territory appointed by Commonwealth, 1921, under League of Nations mandate of 1920. Scene of much fighting in *World War II. Dutch N. G. was handed over to Indonesia on 1 May 1963; independence struggle since by guerilla warfare. The Australian trust territory became the independent state of *Papua N G on 16 Sept. 1975.

New Hampshire, USA, first settled, 1623, founder member of the Union, signatory of the first Declaration of Independence. Has a pre-revolutionary university in Dartmouth College, Hanover (founded, 1769). State, 1788.

New Haven, Connecticut, USA: Originally *Quinnipiac.* First settled by English Puritans, 1637. Collegiate school of Connecticut removed to N.H., 1716. This later became Yale University.

New Hebrides. *See* VANUATU.

New Jersey, USA, discovered by John Cabot, 1497; settlements made in early 17thC by Dutch taken by British, 1664. Founder member of Union. State, 1787.

New Jerusalem Church. *See* SWEDENBORGIANS.

New Mexico, USA, organized as a territory, 1850, admitted to the Union, 1912, as state which, however, consisted only of the rump of the territory, which had ceded large areas to Texas, Utah and Colorado (1861), and out of which the whole of Arizona was carved (1863). First Spanish settlement, 1598. For the Mexican War, ending Feb. 1848, after which Mexico ceded N. M., *see* TEXAS.

New Model Army. The name given to the new parliamentary force raised by Cromwell and Fairfax, 15 Feb. 1645.

New Orleans, Louisiana, USA. Founded, 1718; possessed by Spain, 1763; fell to France, 1800, and purchased from F. as part of the Louisiana Purchase, 1803; attacked by British, Dec. 1814, who were repulsed, 8 Jan. 1815; surrendered to the Federals, Apr. 1862. Serious race riot, July 1866. *Jazz started here, early 20thC. 30-year plan, 1970–2000, to move port from river front to area along Gulf of Mexico.

New South Wales, Australia. Named, 1770, by Capt. Cook. Colony established by transported prisoners, 1788. Transportation ceased, 1840. Gold discovered at Bathurst, 1851. Responsible government, 1855, part of Australian Commonwealth since 1901. *See* AUSTRALIA.

newspapers. In the 15thC in some German towns news-sheets were issued in the form of letters. The first official paper said to be that issued in Venice in 1566, known as the *Notizie Scritte,* published by order of the Venetian Government. First English newspaper, printed by Nathaniel Batter, was the *Courant,* or *Weekly Newes from Foreign Parts* produced, Oct. 1621; but his first entry of *A Currant of Newes* in the [Stationers'] registers is dated 7 June 1622. Civil war pamphlets, produced regularly from the 1640s (e.g. *The Moderate Intelligence*) generally taken to mark beginning of English N. on a significant scale. The *Publick Intelligencer* was first issued by Nedham as a bi-weekly, 1659; after his flight abroad, Oliver Williams issued another with the same title. The *London Gazette* was started by Henry Muddiman, 7 Nov. 1665. In 1662 a press censorship was started and continued until 1695. *Berrow's Worcester Journal* started, 1690; (adopted present name, 1753). First English daily newspaper, the *Daily Courant*, existed from 1702 until 1735. A tax of one halfpenny on N. introduced, 1712, increased by stages to fourpence in 1815; in 1836 reduced to one penny, and abolished altogether, 1855. Steam printing introduced, 1814; rotary press (in UK), 1857; computer technology revolution in printing from 1980s. London papers began move from traditional Fleet Street base, 1980s. Concern over alleged press abuses in 1980s/90s: government legislation being considered, from 1993 onwards.

The following daily papers have ceased to exist:

Morning Chronicle, 28 June 1769–2 Mar. 1865.

Morning Post, Nov. 1772–30 Sept. 1937 (absorbed by *Daily Telegraph*).

Globe, 1803–5 Feb. 1921.

Standard, 21 May 1827–16 Mar. 1916.

Daily News (founded by Charles Dickens), 21 Jan. 1846–31 May 1930.

Pall Mall Gazette, 7 Feb. 1865–27 Oct. 1923.

Echo, 8 Dec. 1868–31 July 1905.

Daily Chronicle, 6 Mar. 1871–31 May 1930.

Westminster Gazette, 31 Jan. 1893–31 Jan. 1928 (absorbed by *Daily News*).

Daily Graphic, Jan. 1890–16 Oct. 1926.

News Chronicle, May 1930–17 Oct. 1960 (incorporated into the *Daily Mail*).

Star, 17 Jan. 1888–17 Oct. 1960 (absorbed by the *Evening News*).

Daily Herald, 15 Apr. 1912–14 Sept. 1964 (replaced by the *Sun*).

Daily Sketch (1909) merged with *Daily Mail*, 1971.

Evening News (1881) merged with *Evening Standard*, 1980.

Today, 1986–17 Nov. 1995

London daily papers still existing, with dates of first issues:

The Times, 1 Jan. 1788 (had been running three years as the *Daily Universal Register*).

Morning Advertiser, 8 Feb. 1794.

Guardian, 1821, formerly the *Manchester Guardian*; began printing a London edition in 1959: now (1995) only printed in London.

Daily Telegraph, 29 June 1855.

Evening Standard, 11 June 1860.

Financial Times, 1888.

Daily Mail, 4 May 1896.

Daily Express, 24 Apr. 1900.

The Mirror, 2 Nov. 1903 (until April 1985, *Daily Mirror*).

Daily Star, 1978 (*The Star*, July 1985)

Morning Star, formerly the *Daily Worker* (name changed, 1966), 1930 (suppressed under Defence Regulations, Jan. 1941–Sept. 1942).

Sun, 15 Sept. 1964.

Independent, 1986

Principal British weekly papers still existing with dates of first issues:

Observer, 4 Jan. 1801.

Sunday Times, 20 Oct. 1822.

Spectator, 5 July 1828 (original *Spectator*, 1 Mar. 1711–20 Dec. 1714).

Economist, 1843.

News of the World, 1 Oct. 1843.

Investor's Chronicle, 1861.

People, 16 Oct. 1881.

Sunday Pictorial, 1915 (renamed *Sunday Mirror*, Apr. 1963).

Sunday Express, 29 Dec. 1918.

New Statesman and Society, 1913

Tribune, 1937

New Scientist, 1956

Sunday Telegraph, 5 Feb. 1961.

Mail on Sunday, 1981.

The European, 1990.

Independent on Sunday, 1991.

Among prominent British weekly N. no longer existing are:

Picture Post (1938–57)

Punch (1841–1992)

British daily N. still existing, but not printed in London, include:

Belfast Telegraph, 1870, printed Belfast

Birmingham Post, 1857 (incorporating

Birmingham Gazette, 1740), printed Birmingham
Daily Record, 1895, printed Glasgow
East Anglian Daily Times, 1874, printed Ipswich
Eastern Daily Press, 1870, printed Norwich
The Herald, 1785, printed Glasgow
Northern Echo, 1870, printed Darlington
The Press & Journal, 1747, printed Aberdeen
The Scotsman, 1817, printed Edinburgh
Western Daily Press, 1858, printed Bristol
Western Mail, 1869, printed Cardiff
Yorkshire Post, 1866, printed Leeds

Proprietors of British N. include:
Conrad Black, 1944–
Lord Beaverbrook (William Maxwell Aitken), 1879–1964
Lord Camrose (William Ewart Berry), 1879–1954
Sir Edward Hulton, 1906–88
Lord Kemsley (James Gomer Berry), 1883–1968
Robert Maxwell, 1923–91
Rupert Murdoch, 1931–
Lord Northcliffe (Alfred Charles William Harmsworth), 1865–1968
Lord Rothermere (Vere Harold Esmond Harmsworth), 1925–
Lord Stevens (David Robert Stevens), 1936–
Lord Thomson (Roy Herbert Thomson), 1894–1976

Foreign daily N. (excepting USA) with dates of foundation, still existing include:
Argentina:
La Nacion, 1870
Austria:
Die Presse, 1848
Australia:
Sydney Morning Herald, 1831 (weekly: daily from 1840)
The Age, 1854
Belgium:
La Libre Belgique (originally, *Gazette de Liège*), 1840.
Het Volk, 1891
Brazil:
Correio Braziliense, 1808

Canada:
Globe and Mail, 1844
Toronto Star (as *Evening Star*, 1892, renamed 1897)
Denmark:
Berlingske Tidende, 1749
France:
Le Figaro, 1826
Le Monde, 1944
Le Parisien, 1944
Le Soir, 1944
Germany:
Berliner Zeitung, 1945
Frankfurter Algemeine Zeitung, 1945
Suddeutsche Zeitung, 1945
Der Tagespiegel, 1945
Die Welt, 1946
Die Zeit, 1946
(Among prominent German weekly N. is *Der Spiegel*, 1947. A major German N. proprietor was Axel Springer, 1912–85.)
Greece:
Eleftherotipia, 1980
Hong Kong:
Wen Wei Pu, 1948
Hong Kong Standard, 1949
India:
The Times of India, 1838
Republic of Ireland:
Irish Independent, 1905
Irish Times, 1859
Italy:
Corriere della Sera, 1875
Il Giorno, 1956
La Stampa, 1868
La Repubblica, 1976
Japan:
Tokyo Shimbun, 1854
Japan Times, 1897
Tokyo Times, 1946
Mainichi Shimbun, 1982
Luxemburg:
Luxemburger Wort, 1848
Mexico:
El Informador, 1917.
La Jornada, 1984.
Netherlands:
De Volkskrant, 1919
Portugal:
Corriero da Manha, 1979

Russia:
Izvestia, 1917: *Izvestia* (Financial), 1992
Nezavisimaya Gazeta, 1990
Pravda, 1912 (as underground magazine);
official Communist N. from 1918: closed
for four weeks, Oct. 1993 then reopened
under new management.
Singapore:
Straits Times, 1845
South Africa:
Argus, 1857
Spain:
El Mundo, 1989
El Pais, 1976
Sweden:
Aftonbladet, 1830
Switzerland:
Baslerszeitung, 1842
Le Matin, 1865
Neue Zurcher Zeitung, 1780

---

newspapers (USA). The first newspaper
issued in America was in 1690 at Boston.
Its title was *Public Occurrences*. It lasted
only a day owing to its outspoken nature.
The first permanent paper was the *Boston
News-Letter*, issued in Apr. 1704. The first
daily paper was the *Pennsylvania Packet* or
General Advertiser (afterwards as *Daily
Advertiser*), first issued in 1784.

Prominent US N., with date of foundation,
include:
Boston Globe, 1872
Chicago Tribune, 1947
Christian Science Monitor, 1908
Los Angeles Times, 1881
New York Times, 1851
Wall Street Journal, 1889
Washington Post, 1877

Daily US N. no longer existing include the
Chicago Daily News (1875–1978) and the
New York Herald Tribune (founded as *The
Tribune*, 1872; merged to form the *New
York Herald Tribune*, 1924; ceased publica-
tion, 1966).

Weekly US journals include:

Forbes Magazine, 1919
Time, 1923
The New Yorker, 1925

Prominent US newspaper proprietors in-
clude:
William Randolph Hearst, 1863–1951
Robert McCormick, 1880–1955
Joseph Pulitzer, 1847–1911

---

new towns. First to be built was Welwyn
Garden City (1920). Seven N.T. round
London initially projected under N.T. Act,
1946. Work begun on the first of these
(Stevenage), 1947. Subsequently 32 N.T.
built in UK – 21 in England, five in Scotland, four in N Ireland and two in Wales.
They include, besides Stevenage, Aycliffe,
Basildon, Corby, Crawley, Cwmbran, Hatfield, Harlow, Livingston, Milton Keynes,
Peterlee and Skelmersdale. N. T. Commission established under N.T. Act 1959 and
in 1993 still retained responsibility in a
number of N.T. *See* also GARDEN CITY.

New York City, New York, USA. Settled
by the Dutch and named N. Amsterdam,
1624; captured by English and the name
changed to N.Y., 27 Aug. 1664; surrendered to the English during War of Independence, 15 Sept. 1776; British evacuated,
25 Nov. 1783, temporary national capital,
1785–89. Five boroughs of N.Y. – the
Bronx, Brooklyn, Manhattan, Queens and
Staten Island – united 1898 to form modern
N.Y.C. Columbia University, 1754. N.Y.
Stock Exchange, 1792; formalized, 1817,
present name, 1863. Central Park acquired
by N.Y., 1856. Brooklyn Bridge (oldest in
N.Y.), 1883. Metropolitan Museum of Art,
1870. Metropolitan Opera, 1883. St
Patrick's R.C. Cathedral, 1858–1906.
Chrysler Building, 1926–30. Empire State
Building, 1929–31; World Trade Center,
1972.

New York State, USA, coast explored by
Verrazano, 1524, and hinterland by Samuel de Champlain (from Canada), 1609.
Dutch from 1614. The British Col. Nicolls
took possession in name of the Duke of

York, 1664. Founder state of the Union, 1777.

New Zealand. Discovered by Tasman, 1642; surveyed by Capt. Cook, 1769; ceded to Great Britain by Treaty of Waitangi, 1840, and colonized the same year; self-government granted, 1852; Wellington made capital, 1865; called Dominion of N.Z., 1907. Women's suffrage, 1893. Earthquake, Feb. 1931. Labour Party won majority for first time in General Election, 27 Nov. 1935. War on Germany declared, 3 Sept. 1939; and on Italy, 11 June 1940. Statute of Westminster adoption Bill passed, 28 Nov. 1947, and New Zealand Constitution (Amendment) Act, 1949, was then enacted. Anti-nuclear Labour government under Lange elected, 1984; *Rainbow Warrior* incident, 1985. Economic difficulties and Labour party differences from 1987. Nationalist elected, 1990. Suggestions that N.Z. might eventually become a republic, 1993. Nationalist losses in Nov. 1993 general election, but retained power with one-seat majority. N.Z. protested strongly at restart of French nuclear testing at Muraroa, in the Pacific, 1995.

Prime Ministers since the granting of dominion status, 1907:
Ward 1906–11
Mackenzie 1911–12
Massey 1912–25
Coates 1925–28
Ward (again) 1928–30
Forbes 1930–35
Savage 1935–40
Fraser 1940–49
Holland 1949–57
Holyoake (2 months) 1957
Nash 1957–60
Holyoake (again) 1960–72
Marshall 1972
Kirk 1972–74
Muldoon 1975–84
Lange 1984–89
Palmer 1989–90
Moore 1990
Bolger 1990–

Governor-Generals since 1917 (date of establishment of the office):
Earl of Liverpool 1917–20
Viscount Jellicoe 1920–24
Sir Charles Fergusson 1924–30
Lord Bledisloe 1930–35
Viscount Galway 1935–41
Lord Newall 1941–46
Lord Freyberg 1946–52
Lord Norrie 1952–57
Viscount Cobham 1957–62
Sir Bernard Fergusson 1962–67
Lord Porritt 1967–72
Sir Denis Blundell 1972–77
Sir Keith Holyoake 1977–80
Sir David Beattie 1980–85
Sir Paul Reeves 1985–90
Dame Catherine Tizard 1990–

Niagara Falls (USA-Canada). Discovered, 1678, by a French priest. Blondin was the first to cross them on a tight-rope, 1859. Rainbow bridge opened, 1941.

Nicaea (Turkish **Isnik**) in *Bithynia, built 316 BC under the name of *Antigonea*, name changed by order of the Macedonian Gen. Lysimachus (*d.* 281). Chosen as capital by the Sultan Soliman 1078; taken by the Franks in the First Crusade, 1096. After the capture of Constantinople by the Latins, 1204, was the temporary capital of the Eastern Empire. Scene of First Ecumenical Council, 325, when Nicene Creed formulated, and the Seventh, held in 787, which dealt with the Iconoclast controversy.

Nicaragua, Central America. Discovered by Columbus in 1502; explored by Gil Gonzalez De Avila, 1522; declared itself independent, 1821; joined Federal Union of the five Central States, 1823; separate republic, 1838; independence acknowledged by Spain, 1865; war with Honduras, Feb.–Apr. 1907. In 1916 US government purchased canal route and naval bases in Fonseca Bay and Corn Island by Bryan Chamarro Treaty, Feb.–June. President Somoza assassinated, Sept. 1956, succeeded by his sons Luis and Anastasio who continued repressive right-wing governments. Bryan Chamarro Treaty abrogated, 1970. Somoza regime overthrown by Sandinista (left-wing) revolt, 1979, and constitution abrogated. USA aided 'Contra' resistance to Sandinistas, but latter won elections, 1984–5. New constitution, 1987. Almost immediately suspended with increased Contra infiltration. Atrocities on both sides. Hostilities ended, 1989; in 1990 an anti-Sandinista government under Violetta Chamarro elected but economic hardship caused intermittent unrest subsequently, notably in Aug. 1993.

Nice, France. Founded by the Phocaeans of Marseilles *c.* 600 BC; Saracens repulsed, AD 729; burnt by Saracens, 880; attached to Savoy from 1388; attacked by Francis I and Barbarossa, 1543; captured by Duke of Guise, 1600; by Catinat, 1691; restored to Savoy, 1696; besieged by French, 1705, and captured; by Treaty of Utrecht was again restored to Savoy, 1713; again captured by French, 1795, who owned it until 1814, when it reverted to Savoy. Finally ceded to France after a plebiscite, 1860.

Nice, Truce of. Between Charles V and Francis I for 10 months from June 1538.

Nicobar Islands. *See* ANDAMAN AND NICOBAR ISLANDS.

Nicosia, Cyprus. Cathedral of St Sophia built, 1209–1325 (converted to mosque, 1571). Pillaged by the Mamelukes, 1426. Fortified by the Venetians, 1567. Taken by the Turks, 1570, and 20,000 Christians massacred in street fighting. Earthquake, 1741. British flag raised over N., 1878. Capital of the Republic of Cyprus since 1960 but divided between Greek-Cypriot and Turkish 'Republic of Cyprus' by 'Green Line', policed by UN since 1974.

Nidaros. *See* TRONDHJEM.

Niger, W Africa. French from 1891; republic with French Community, 1958; independent, 1960. Army coup, 1974. 1991. Tuareg rebellion began in N N. Nov. 1991; state of emergency, Apr. 1992. Elections, 1993, when Third Republic proclaimed. Rebels split, 1993, but conflict continuing, 1995.

Nigeria. Includes what was formerly the Niger Coast (or Oil Rivers) Protectorate, formed, 1844. Remainder of N. acquired by British United African Co., 1879–86. Constituted, 1 Jan. 1900; *Lagos added, 1906. Governments of S and N N. amalgamated, 1 Jan. 1914. Legal status of slavery abolished by Slavery Ordinance, 1917. N. became a Dominion within the Commonwealth, 1 Oct. 1960. N. became a republic within the Commonwealth, Oct. 1963. A series of army coups followed. On 30 May 1967, Ojukwu, military governor of the eastern states, announced his state's secession from N. and proclaimed it the independent republic of *Biafra. A full-scale war followed, but Biafra did not finally capitulate till Jan. 1970. New constitution ratified, 1977–8, confirmed re-establishment of civilian government. *Abuja replaced Lagos as capital, Sept. 1982. In 1983 two million non-Nigerians expelled; military coup, Dec. Babangida took power, 1985–93. New constitution, 1989, allowed multiparty elections, 12 June 1993, but result (an opposition victory) annulled by military government, 27 Aug. Babangida stepped down: succeeded by interim head of state, with full civilian rule promised by 1995. Military rule again, Nov. 1993. Oil strike against military rule, July–Sept. 1994, followed by government measures against opposition groups. World concern at human rights abuses in N.; environmental protesters sentenced to death, Oct. 1995. EU imposes arms embargo on N., Nov. 1995.

Nijmegen, Netherlands, was a residence of the Frankish emperors in the 9thC AD. Devastated in the Allied attack by air and ground forces, Sept. 1944. Severe floods in and around, Jan. 1995.

Nijni Novgorod, Russia, under protection of Suzdal, 1221. Ceased to elect its prince, 1390. Annexed to Moscow, 1392. Fair established at Makaryev, 1641. Repels attack by Stenka Razin, 1667. Fair moves to N., 1817. Revived after Bolshevik Revolution but finally abolished, 1930. Birthplace of writer Maxim Gorky (1863–1936) and name N. changed to **Gorky** in his honour, 1932–90.

Nimes, France. Taken by Romans, 121 BC. Made a military colony under Augustus. Amphitheatre built, 1st–2ndC AD. Belonged to Toulouse, AD 1185–1207. Catholics massacred by Protestants, 1567. Trestaillons and his followers massacred Bonapartists, 1815.

Nineveh, adjoining the modern Mosul, in Iraq, became the capital of Assyria under Sennacherib (704–681 BC). Destroyed, 612, by combined forces of Babylonians, Medes and Scythians. The deserted site was first investigated by western archaeologists early in the 19thC.

Ningpo, formerly **Liampo,** was a Portuguese 'factory', 1522–45. Occupied by British, 1841–2.

nitroglycerine first produced by Sobrero, 1846.

Niue, discovered by Capt. Cook, 1774 and called Savage Island. British protectorate, 1900, annexed to New Zealand, 1901. Internal self-government, 1974. Member of S Pacific Forum. Largest inhabited coral island in the world.

NKGB, the Soviet security service, 1943–6. Succeeded by the MGB (1946–53).

NKVD (Narodnij Kommissariat Vnutrennich Djel = People's Commissariat for Internal Affairs), designation of the Russian Interior Office and its internal security forces, from 1934 to 1943.

Nobel Prize. Founded by Alfred N. (1833–96), the inventor of dynamite, to be awarded annually for excellence in learning (chemistry, physics, medicine, literature) and the furtherance of universal peace. First awarded in 1901. A N. memorial prize for economics first instituted, 1969. Prize winners have included:

Peace:

1901	Jean Dunant (Swiss)
	Frédéric Passy (French)
1906	Theodore Roosevelt (USA)
1917	International Red Cross
1919	Woodrow Wilson (USA)
1926	Aristide Briand (French)
	Gustav Stresemann (German)
1927	Viscount Cecil (British)
1944	International Red Cross
1952	Albert Schweitzer (French)
1961	Dag Hammarskjöld (Swedish)
1964	Martin Luther King (USA)
1971	Willy Brandt (German)
1978	Anwar Sadat (Egypt)
	Menachem Begin (Israeli)
1979	Mother Teresa (Albanian-born)
1981	Office of UN Commissioner for Refugees
1974	Bishop Desmond Tutu (South African)
1990	Mikhail Gorbachev (USSR)
1991	Daw Aung San Sun Kyi (Burmese)
1992	Rigoberta Menchu (Guatemalan)
1993	Nelson Mandela and F.W. de Klerk (South African)
1994	Yassir Arafat (PLO), Shimon Peres and Yitzhak Rabin (Israeli)
1995	Joseph Rotblat (British)

Literature:

1901	René Sully-Prudhomme (French)
1907	Rudyard Kipling (British)
1913	Rabindranath Tagore (Indian)
1925	George Bernard Shaw (Irish)
1936	Eugene O'Neill (USA)
1952	François Mauriac (French)
1953	Sir Winston Churchill (British)
1954	Ernest Hemingway (USA)
1958	Boris Pasternak (USSR): prize declined
1970	Alexander Solzhenitsyn (USSR)
1972	Heinrich Böll (German)
1976	Saul Bellow (USA)
1982	Gabriel Garcia Marquez (Colombian-Mexican)
1990	Octavio Paz (Mexican)
1991	Nadine Gordimer (South African)
1992	Derek Walcott (West Indian)
1993	Toni Morrison (USA)
1994	Kenzaburo Oe (Japanese)
1995	Seamus Heaney (Irish)

Physics:

1901 Wilhelm Röntgen (German)
1909 Guglielmo Marconi (Italian)
1921 Albert Einstein (German-USA)
1935 Sir James Chadwick (British)
1948 Patrick Blackett (British)
1951 Sir John Cockroft (British)
1962 Lev Landau (USSR)
1982 Kenneth Wilson (USA)
1992 Georges Charpak (French)
1993 Russell Hulse and Josephine Taylor (USA)

Chemistry:

1901 Jacobus van't Hoff (Dutch)
1908 Ernest Rutherford (British)
1911 Marie Curie (Polish-French)
1944 Otto Hahn (German)
1954 Linus Pauling (USA)
1961 Melvin Calvin (USA)
1964 Dorothy Hodgkin (British)
1974 Paul Flory (USA)
1982 Aaron Klug (South African)
1991 Richard Ernst (Swiss)
1993 Michael Smith (Canada) and Kary Mullis (USA)
1995 Paul Crutzen (Dutch), Mario Molina (Mexican-born USA) and Sherwood Rowland (USA)

Medicine:

1901 Emil von Baring (German)
1945 Ernest Chain
      Sir Alexander Fleming
      Sir Howard Florey (British)
1960 Peter Medawar (British)
1987 Susumu Tonegawa (Japanese)
1992 Edwin Krebs
      Edmond Fischer (USA)
1993 Richard Roberts (British)
      Phillip Sharp (USA)
1994 Alfred Gilman (USA)
      Martin Rodbell

Winners of the Memorial Prize in Economics include the US economist Milton Friedman (1976). The 1993 prize was shared jointly by Robert Fogel and Douglass North (both USA); the 1994 one jointly by John Harsanyi (*b.* Hungary), John Nash (USA) and Reinhard Selten (German); 1995 winner was Robert Lucas (USA).

Nolan Committee, appointed by government under chairmanship of Lord Justice Nolan, 1994, to examine alleged fall in standards in public life. Sittings held, 1995. First report, May 1995; Commons committee rejected some Nolan proposals, Nov. Subsequent commons vote reinstated these.

Nomanhan, on the borders of Mongolia, was the scene of a six weeks' undeclared war between Mongolian, Japanese and Russian troops in 1939. The Japanese and Mongolian forces had to retire, and the incident led to the Russo-Japanese non-aggression pact of 1941.

Non-Compounders. Extremist section of the Jacobite Party formed *c.* 1692. Were prepared to restore James II unconditionally.

Nonconformists and **Nonconformity,** the religious attitude of Protestant Dissenters against the Established Church, especially the Church of England. Word first used in this sense *c.* 1563, but gaining wider currency at the Restoration, especially with the passing of the Act of Uniformity, 1662. Some disabilities were suspended by Charles II's Declaration of Indulgence, 1672, and by James II's Declaration of Indulgence of 1687. They were accorded freedom of worship by Toleration Act, 1689, but excluded from municipal office by the Occasional Conformity Act, 1711, which was itself repealed, 1718. The Schism Act, 1711, excluded N. from schools and was also repealed, 1718. Political disabilities of N. removed, 1828. Admitted to universities, 1871. During the 16th and 17thC the essence of Nonconformity was the particularism of numerous sects, but in 1730 a phase of amalgamation and consolidation set in which may be said to have culminated in the reunion of the Methodist Church in 1932, previously split into three factions. Formation of *United Reformed Church, 1972, signalled union of English Presbyterian and Congregationalist churches. *See also* FREE CHURCH FEDERATION.

Nonjurors. Clergy in Britain who refused the oath of allegiance to William and Mary. An Act of 1 Aug. 1689 required them to take the oath within six months or suffer deprivation. In Scotland all the bishops refused and episcopacy was abolished.

Nordic Council. Assembly of elected representatives from the Scandinavian parliaments (Denmark, Norway, Sweden and Iceland), established, 1952, to foster closer co-operation between their countries. Finland acceded, 1955; Faeroes and Aland Islands, 1969/70, and Greenland, 1984. Passport regulations between the Scandinavian countries abolished, 1952. Treaty of Helsinki, 1962, amended, 1971 and N.C. of Ministers established.

Norham, Conference of. Between Edward I and the competitors for the crown of Scotland, June 1291. The question of the disposal of the Scottish crown was settled, Nov. 1292.

Normandy, France. Rollo appointed first duke, AD 912; united with the crown of England under William the Conqueror (Duke of N.), 1066; united to crown of France, 1204; English claim formally renounced, 1259; conquered by Edward III, 1346; by Henry V, 1418; English finally driven out, 1449. Invaded by Allies, 6 June 1944. *See* WORLD WAR II.

North American Free Trade Agreement (NAFTA), signed Dec. 1992 between Canada, Mexico and the USA, creating the world's largest free-trade zone, became operational, 1 Jan. 1994. Ratified by USA, Sept. 1993, but Canadian government pressed for amendments, 1994. Mexican peasant revolt, Jan. 1994, partially caused by fears of NAFTA's effects on peasant economy.

North Atlantic Cooperation Council, established by NATO, Nov. 1991, to pursue common security policies with members of the former *Warsaw Pact.

North Atlantic Treaty signed at Washington, 4 Apr. 1949, between Britain, Canada, the USA, France, Belgium, Holland, Luxemburg, Norway, Denmark, Iceland, Italy and Portugal. Greece and Turkey were admitted to the treaty, 1951 (effective, 1952), the German Federal Republic, 1954 (united Germany, 1990) and Spain, 1982. *See* NATO.

***North Briton* newspaper.** Instituted by John Wilkes. 'Number 45', the issue dated 23 Apr. 1763, was publicly burnt by the hangman, 3 Dec. 1763, as containing a libel against the king. *See* WILKES'S CASE.

North Carolina, USA. Coasts said to have been discovered by Cabot, 1498; first settled, unsuccessfully, 1585–6; named after Charles II of England, who, in 1663, granted the region to certain of his courtiers; made a royal province, 1728; declared itself independent of Great Britain, May 1775; state constitution adopted, 1 Dec. 1776. Seceded, 20 May 1861; readmitted to the Union, 25 May 1868.

North Dakota, USA, part of the old territory of Dakota, organized as such, 1861. Admitted to the Union, 1889. First settlements took place c. 1766. *See also* SOUTH DAKOTA.

Northern Ireland. *See* IRELAND, NORTHERN.

Northern Rhodesia. *See* ZAMBIA.

Northern Territory, Australia, formerly **Alexandra Land,** originally part of *New S Wales, but annexed to S Australia, 1863. Placed under direct Commonwealth Government rule, 1911. Divided into N Australia and Central Australia, 1926, but united under a single administration by an Act of 1931. Self-government granted, 1 July 1978. Coast explored by P. P. King, 1818, by J. C. Wickham, 1838, and J. L. Stokes, 1839. Interior explored by A. C. Gregory, 1855.

North German Confederation, league of German states established, 1867, under Prussian leadership. Dissolved in the German Empire, 1871.

North Korea. *See* KOREA.

North London, University of. Name and

status, since 1992 of the former North London polytechnic.

North Ossetia. Area bordering Georgia, a former autonomous republic of the USSR. Population deported by Stalin in 1940s, returned under Khruschev in 1960s. Claimed independence in 1992: sporadic factional fighting and with Russian troops since.

North Pole. First reached, 6 Apr. 1909, by the American Robert E. Peary. *See* ARCTIC AND ANTARCTIC REGIONS.

North Staffordshire, University College of. *See* KEELE, UNIVERSITY OF.

North, The Council of the. Instituted in 1536 by Henry VIII originally to try persons connected with the *Pilgrimage of Grace; abolished by Long Parliament, 1641.

Northstead, Manor of, in Yorkshire, has a stewardship in the gift of the crown, the holding of which by the Place Act, 1742, is not compatible with membership of the House of Commons, and is thus used as a formal excuse for resignation of an MP. *See* CHILTERN HUNDREDS.

Northumbria, Kingdom of. *See* BERNICIA and DEIRA.

Kings of *c.* 457–*c.* 913:
Bernicia:
Ida 547–59
His elder sons 559–86
Ethelric 586–93
Ethelfrith 593–617
Edwin (of Deira) 617–32
Eanfrith 632–33
Oswald 633–42
Oswy 642–70
Deira:
Aelle 560–88
Ethelric (of Bernicia) 588–? 593
Ethelfrith (of Bernicia) ? 593–617
Edwin 617–32
Osric 632–33
Oswald (of Bernicia) 633–42
Oswine 642–51
Ethelwald 651–55
Oswy (of Bernicia) 655–70

Kings of all N.:
Ecgfrith 670–85
Alfrith 685–704
Eardwulf I 704–05
Osred I 705–16
Cenred 716–18
Osric 718–29
Ceolwulf 729–37
Eadberht 737–58
Oswulf 758
Ethelwald Moll 759–65
Alhred 765–74
Ethelred I 774–79
Elfwald I 779–88
Osred II 788–90
Ethelred I (restored) 790–96
Osbald 796
Eardwulf II 796–808
Elfwald II 808
Eardwulf II (restored) 808–10
Eanred 810–40
Ethelred II 840–44
Raedwulf 844
Ethelred II (restored) 844–48
Osberht 848–66
Elle 866–67
Egbert I 867–72
Ricsige 873–76
Egbert II *fl.* 876
Eadwulf ?–913

Northumbria, University of at Newcastle, name and status, since 1992, of former Newcastle polytechnic.

North-West Frontier Province. Created by the British administration in India, 25 Oct. 1901. Now a province of Pakistan.

North-West Mounted Police, raised, 1873; title changed to Royal Canadian Mounted Police, 1920. Mechanized, 1953.

North-West Passage. Sought since 15thC. First completed, 1850–4, by Robert McClure: first sailed by Amundsen, 1906.

North-West Territories of Canada, formed from the former Northern Territory and Rupert's Land, and divided into the districts of Keewatin, MacKenzie and Franklin by Order in Council of 16 Mar. 1918. Under N.-W.T. Act, 1952, government placed under a commissioner with territorial control of part of N.-W.T., handed to Inuits, 1990, and further concessions proposed, 1993. Yellowknife made capital of N.-W.T., 1967.

Norway. Battle of Hafursfjord, 872, and N. united for the first time under Harald Fairhair. First Norwegian settlement in Iceland, 874. Rolf the Ganger's expedition against Normandy, 876. Erik Bloodaxe king, 930. Haakon the Good comes from England and is made king at Trondhjem, 935. Erik Bloodaxe goes to England, 939, and is killed there, 950. Battle of Rastarskalf, 955. Death of Haakon the Good after battle of Stord, 961. N. ruled by Jarl Haakon of Lade, 970–95. Christianity introduced, 998. Death of King Olaf Tryggvason at battle of Svold, 1000. N. under Swedish and Danish rule till battle of Nesjar and election of St Olaf as king, 1015. He makes alliance with Sweden, 1019. Defeated by Knut (Canute) of Denmark at Helge-Aa, 1027. N. conquered by Denmark, 1027–8. Death of St Olaf at battle of Stiklestad, 29 July 1030. Danes driven out by King Magnus the Good, 1035–6. Harald Hardrada king, 1047. Killed at Stamford Bridge, 1066. After Haakon IV, 1217–63, N. declined into chronic civil war (for history down to this point *see* VIKING AGE). It was finally united with Sweden under the Danish crown by the Union of *Kalmar, 1397. N. remained under Danish rule till virtually cut off from Denmark by the British blockade, 1794–1814. As a reward for Swedish participation in the war against Napoleon I, it was proposed that Denmark should cede N. to Sweden (Treaty of Kiel, 14 Jan. 1814). The Norwegians called a national convention which signed a parliamentary constitution at Eidsvold, 17 May 1814, and then accepted the suzerainty of the Swedish crown. Separated from Sweden, Oct. 1905. Haakon VII elected to the throne, 18 Nov. 1905. Prohibition, 1919–26. Christiania renamed Oslo, 1 Jan. 1925. Spitzbergen (Svalbard) annexed, 14 Aug. 1925. Greenland awarded to Denmark by International Court of Justice, 5 Apr. 1933. Part of Antarctica annexed, 14 Jan. 1939. Declarations of neutrality, 2 Sept. and 26 Dec. 1939. *Altmark* incident, 17 Feb. 1940. Attacked by Germany, 9 Apr. Battles of Narvik, 10 and 13 Apr. Liberated, 8 May 1945. Signed *North Atlantic Treaty, 1949. Fishing dispute with Great Britain settled in favour of N. by The Hague International Court, 1951. Member of Nordic Council, 1952. Death of Haakon VII and accession of Olaf VI, 1957. Member of *European Free Trade Association, 1959. Voted against joining *European Economic Community, 1973. Death of Olav VI and accession of Harald V, 1991. N. restarted commercial whaling, 1993, despite international protests. Again voted in referendum to reject membership of the EU, Dec. 1994.

Rulers of c. *839–1349; 1905–51:*
Halfdan the Black *c.* 839–*c.* 860
Harald I Fairhair *c.* 860–933
Erik Bloodaxe 930–35
Haakon I the Good 935–61
Harald II Greyskin 961–70
(Jarl) Haakon of Lade 970–95
Olaf I Tryggvason 995–1000
(Jarls) Erik and Svein 1000–15
Olaf II, Saint 1015–30
Svein Knutsson 1030–35
Magnus I, the Good 1035–47
Harald III, the Stern 1048–66
Olaf III, the Quiet 1067–93
Magnus II 1067–69
Magnus III, Barelegs 1093–1103
Haakon 1093–95
Olaf IV 1103–16
Eystein I 1103–22
Sigurd I, the Pilgrim 1103–30
Magnus IV, the Blind 1130–35
Harald Gille 1130–36
Sigurd II, Mund 1136–55
Inge 1136–61
Eystein II 1142–57
Haakon, II, the Broad-shouldered 1161–62
Magnus V 1162–84
Sverre 1184–1202
Haakon III 1202–04
Anarchy 1204–17
Haakon IV, the Old 1217–63
Magnus VI, 1263–80

Erik 1280–99
Haakon V 1299–1319
Magnus VII 1319–43
Haakon VI 1343–80
Olaf V 1381–87
Margaret (Lady of N.) 1387–89
Eric of Pomerania 1387–1439
(*See further under* DENMARK, KINGS OF,
1439–1814; SWEDEN, KINGS OF, 1814–1905).
Modern Norway:
Haakon VII 1905–57
Olaf VI 1957–91 ·
Harald V 1991–

Norwegian language and literature.
From the Union of Kalmar down to the
end of the 19thC the written language of
Norway, both for official and artistic
purposes, was Danish; therefore some N.
authors have been listed under Danish
literature *supra*. There are two modern
idioms: the urban, or *riksmål*, developed
from the Danish, which is the official
idiom, and the rustic, or *landsmal*, now
generally called *nynorsk*. The progress of
the language was assisted by *Dølen*, the
first newspaper to be printed in it (1858),
under the editorship of Aasmund Olafsen
Vinje (1818–70).
The following are mainly *riksmål* authors not
now living (those marked * wrote *nynorsk*):

Johan Sebastian Welhaven, 1807–73, poet.
Henrik Wergeland, 1808–45, poet.
Peter Christen Asbjørnsen, 1812–85, folk-
lorist.
Jørgen Moe, 1813–82, folklorist.
Henrik Ibsen, 1828–1906, playwright.
Bjørnstjerne Bjørnson, 1832–1910, play-
wright.
Jonas Lie, 1833–1908, novelist.
Amalie Skram, 1846–1905, novelist.
Camilla Collett, 1849–1906, novelist.
A. L. Kielland, 1849–1906, novelist.
*Arne Garborg, 1851–1924, novelist.
Gunnar Heiberg, 1857–1929, playwright.
*Jens Tvedt, 1857–1935, novelist.
Knut Hamsun, 1859–1952, novelist.
Nils Collett Vogt, 1864–1937, poet.
Hans E. Kinck, 1865–1926, novelist and poet.

Tryggve Andersen, 1866–1920, novelist.
Sigbjørn Obstfelder, 1866–1900, poet.
Niels Kjaer, 1870–1924, essayist.
Vilhelm Krag, 1871–1933, poet.
*Olav Duun, 1876–1939, novelist.
Sigrid Undset, 1882–1949, novelist.
*Olaf Aukrust, 1883–1929, poet.
Olaf Bull, 1883–1933, poet.
Olav Nygard, 1884–1924, poet.
Sigurd Christiansen, 1891–1947, novelist.
Ronald Fangen, 1895–1946, novelist.
Rudolf Nilsen, 1901–29, poet.
Nordahl Grieg, 1902–43, poet.

Norwich, England. First mentioned in
Anglo-Saxon Chronicle, 1004, when sacked
by Svein. Cathedral founded, 1096. Charter, 1158; extended, 1194. Julian of N. lived
at, 1349–c. 1429. Cathedral completed *c.*
1500. N. school of painters flourished at,
early 19thC. New city hall, 1938. University of E Anglia opened at N., 1963. R.C.
diocese of E Anglia based at N., 1976.
Sainsbury Centre for Visual Arts at, 1978:
extended 1991. Fire gutted N. library, US
Memorial Library and County Record
Office, Aug. 1994.

Nottingham, England. One of the five
Danish boroughs, 868. Fortified by
Edward the Elder, 922–4. Parliaments held
at N., 1334, 1337, 1357. Charles I set up
standard at, 1642. Castle dismantled, 1644.
Goose Fair instituted under Queen Anne,
1702–14. University College opened, 1881;
made a university, 1948. Nottingham
Trent University, 1992, was formerly N.
polytechnic.

Nova Scotia. Discovered by John Cabot,
1497; partly colonized by the French, as
'Acadia', 1598; French settlements
destroyed by English from Virginia, 1614;
granted by James I to William Alexander,
Earl of Stirling, 1621; ceded to France by
Treaty of Breda, 1667; captured by English,
1689; restored to France by Treaty of
Ryswick, 1697; Port Royal captured by
English under Gen. Nicholson, 1710; ceded
to England by Treaty of Utrecht, 1713
(Cape Breton, French till 1763); became
part of the Dominion of Canada, 1867.

Novaya Zemlya, archipelago off the N coast of Russia, explored by Stephen Borough, 1556, and Baron Nordenskjold, 1895–7. Also by H. J. Pearson, 1895–7, and O. Ekstam, 1900–3. Used as a nuclear testing site by USSR.

Novgorod, formerly **Veliki Novgorod** ('N. the Great'), founded by Scandinavians, traditionally, 862, but probably on the site of an earlier Slav settlement. Though it acknowledged princes of the house of Rurik it was virtually an independent republic of merchants, and obtained a charter from Yaroslav the Wise, 997, which was regarded as the basis of its liberties, of which it was deprived by Ivan III, 1478. It was burnt to the ground by Ivan IV (the Terrible), 1570.

Noyon, Treaty of. Between Charles of Spain and Francis I, signed 1516; by it Francis gave up all claims to Naples, and France's right to Milan was acknowledged.

NRA (USA). National Recovery Administration appointed under National Industrial Recovery Act, 1933, empowered to promulgate codes for industry. The US Supreme Court held codes unconstitutional, 18 Feb. 1935.

Nubia. *See* SUDAN.

nuclear accidents have included that at Windscale (renamed *Sellafield), UK, 1957; *Chelyabinsk-65, 1957; Three Mile Island, U.S.A., 1979; and (most serious to date) *Chernobyl, Ukraine, 1986. In 1993 Russian ex-servicemen claim damage for exposure to nuclear radiation in 1954. Similar claims made by British and US ex-servicemen since 1980s. April 1993, N. A. at Tomsk, Siberia.

Nuclear Non-Proliferation Treaty, 1968, formed basis of subsequent global policies on nuclear arms control. Principal signatories in 1968 were the USA, USSR and Britain: several countries, later suspected of manufacturing nuclear weapons or their potential never signed. N Korea threatened to withdraw from the Treaty, 1993, withdrew threat, 1994. Russia ends pledge not to use nuclear arms first, Nov. 1993. Kazakhstan signed Treaty, 1993. Yeltsin urged new anti-nuclear treaties to take note of changed world conditions, Sept. 1994. Ukraine accedes to Treaty, Nov. 1994. 25-year review of the N.N.P.T., April 1995. Nuclear states win an indefinite extension of the treaty.

nuclear reactor. Harwell, built 1947, was the first British N.R.; the first American N.R. was built at the University of Chicago in 1942.

Nuclear Test Ban Treaty signed, Moscow, between the USA, USSR, and Britain, 5 Aug. 1963. In Dec. 1993 USA admitted to 252 secret nuclear tests 1960–90. China still carrying out underground nuclear testing, in 1995. France announces resumption of nuclear testing, June 1995; explodes underground nuclear devices at *Muraroa, from Sept. but says will sign N.T.B.T. when tests complete.

Nürnberg (German: anglicized as **Nuremberg,** which form is also current in other non-German countries), Germany. Made an Imperial Free City, 1219. Embraced Protestantism *c.* 1525. Annexed by Bavaria, 1806. First Nazi Party congress, 1933. Heavily bombed in World War II when many historic buildings damaged, since restored. Major industrial development since 1945. Historical buildings include Protestant Church of St Sebaldus (13th–15thC): R. C. Frauenkuche (14thC: built on synagogue site) and house of the painter Dürer, which he acquired 1509, and which is now a Dürer museum.

Nürnberg Laws, anti-Semitic code decreed by the Nazi Government, Sept. 1935.

Nürnberg Trials, international trials of war criminals, lasted from Nov. 1945 to Oct. 1946.

Nyasaland. *See* MALAWI.

nylon. Discovered by W.H. Carothers of the Du Pont corporation, USA after experiments conducted during 1920s and 1930s. Went into production, 1938: first products sold commercially, 1940.

Oak-apple Day, anniversary of the restoration of Charles II to the English throne, 29 May 1660. The oak leaves formerly worn on this occasion commemorate his hiding in an oak-tree when a fugitive after the battle of Worcester, 6 Sept. 1651.

OAS (Organisation de l'Armée Secrète). Clandestine, ultra-right-wing organization founded by General Raoul Salan, in Madrid, in May 1961, after the failure of the anti-Gaullist rising in Algiers. Its object initially was to keep Algeria French. After Algerian independence, in 1962, the O.A.S. transferred its activities to France, and attempted to assassinate de Gaulle. Salan was captured, Apr. 1962, and sentenced to life imprisonment for treason, May 1962. After this O.A.S. power declined, and after de Gaulle's resignation, 1969, its *raison d'être* ceased.

OAS (Organization of American States). Charter adopted, 30 Apr. 1948. Meeting at Uruguay in 1967 established the basis of a Latin-American Common Market. Protocol of Buenos Aires, modifying the 1948 charter, effective, 27 Feb. 1970; further modification to O.A.S. by Protocol of Cartagena de Indias, 1985. Had 35 members in 1994.

OAU (Organization of African Unity), established in Addis Ababa, 25 May 1963, to further African political development, unity and solidarity. Had 51 members in 1994, including S Africa, which joined, 1994, at same time as O.A.U.'s Liberation Committee (established 1963) disbanded.

oaths, parliamentary. Oath of supremacy, imposed on MPs, 1534; oath of allegiance, 1610. In 1678 no member could take his seat until the O. of allegiance, supremacy and abjuration were taken. By Act of 1829 Roman Catholics could use special form of oath; provision made for Jews, 1858. In 1866 the three O. were combined in one, and in 1868 the form included all religious denominations. O. Act of 1888 allows an affirmation in lieu of the oath.

Oberammergau (Germany). Passion play commemorates a plague of 1633. The decision to produce a play every 10 years was taken in 1634 in thanksgiving for the town's deliverance. Most recent production, 1994; next planned for 2004.

Observer Corps, Royal. An O.C. was raised in 1925 under War Office auspices; but operational command in 1927, and administration in 1939, passed to the Air Ministry. Later operationally controlled by Fighter Command, the O.C. was given the title Royal in Apr. 1941. It stood down, 12 May 1945, officially terminated, 31 Mar. 1992.

October Revolution, in Russia. So called because it occurred in Oct., according to the Julian Calendar. Kerensky's government overthrown and the Communists established in power, 6–7 Nov. 1917 (24–25 Oct., Old Style calendar).

Oder-Neisse Line. Has formed the official boundary between Germany and Poland since 1946, and most Germans formerly living E of it have been deported W of it. Line reaffirmed by united Germany, 1990/1991.

Odessa, Ukraine. Disputed between Lithuania and Tatars, 14th–16thC. Captured by Turks, 1764. By Russians, 1789. Finally occupied by Russians, 1791. Inhabitants supported the *Potemkin* rising, 1905. Occupied by the Romanians, 1941–4, becoming the capital of Transnistria during that time.

OECD (Organization for European

Economic Co-operation and Development) grew out of the **OEEC (Organization for European Co-operation)** which became effective in the passing by the US Congress of the Economic Co-operative Act, Apr. 1948, with the object of restoring the European economy by the end of 1951. Convention signed in Paris, setting up a permanent constitution, 16 Apr. 1948. After Marshall Aid ended, 1952, OEEC continued as a permanent instrument of European economic co-operation. Spain joined it, 1959. In Dec. 1960 the OEEC organization was reconstituted as the OECD Ceased to be mainly European when US and Canada joined it, 1961. In 1990 the OECD established the *Centre for Co-operation with European Economies in Transition.

Offa's Dyke, built *c.* 785 as a boundary between his dominion and the Welsh (whom he defeated, 779) by O., King of Mercia, who reigned *c.* 755–94, abdicated, and *d.* at Rome, 796.

Office for Fair Trading, non-ministerial government department established under the Fair Trading Act, 1973. The Director-General is charged with protecting consumers from unfair trading practices and also has responsibilities under the Consumer Credit Act, 1974, the Estate Agents Act, 1979 and the Control of Misleading Advertisement Regulations, 1988. Additionally, the Office investigates monopolies and mergers and threats to free competition. It cooperates with the European Commission on consumer matters.

Official Secrets Act, 1989, is the UK Act on which current policy and practice dealing with what is considered confidential government material is based. It permits no defence of public interest.

OFGAS (Office of Gas Supply), regulatory body established under the Gas Act, 1986, to monitor British Gas, where necessary enforcing changes in practice, etc.

OFTEL (Office of Telecommunications), established under the Telecommunications Act, 1984, being the body responsible for monitoring the telecommunications industry.

OFWAT (Office of Water Services), established under the Water Act of 1989, and deals with customer concerns regarding water supplies, quality, etc.

Ohio, USA. First explored by La Salle *c.* 1680; N of the O. River was held by French until 1763, when it was surrendered to the English; unofficially admitted to the Union as a state, 1803; entrance made official retroactive to 1803, 8 Aug. 1953.

Ohm's Law, in electricity, 1827, by the German physicist G.S. Ohm (1787–1854).

Okinawa, largest of the Ryuku Islands in Pacific, captured from the Japanese by US forces, 21 June 1945, after a battle lasting nearly three months. Casualties were heavy and *c.* 145,000 civilians *d.* Returned to Japan, 1972. Protests against US bases on O., 1995.

Oklahoma, USA, then known as the Indian country, was extensively settled from 1866 onwards by government purchase of land from the Choctaw, Cherokee, Creek, Chickasaw and Seminole Indians. Organized as a territory, 1890, and admitted as a state to the Union, 1907. O. City state capital since 1910. Bombing of public building complex in O. City, 19 April 1995. Final death toll estimated 168. Rightwing extremists alleged responsible.

oil pollution. Oil spillages from ships at sea causing major O.P.:

1967: *Torrey Canyon,* off Cornwall, 124,000 tonnes lost
1972: *Sea Star,* Gulf of Oman, 123,000 tonnes lost.
1976: *Urqiola,* off Spain, 91,000 tonnes lost
1977: *Hawaiian Patriot,* mid-Pacific, 101,000 tonnes lost
1978: *Amoco Cadiz,* off Brittany, 221,000 tonnes lost
1979: *Atlantic Express,* West Indies, 257,000 tonnes lost
1979: *Independenta,* in the Bosporus, 75,000 tonnes lost

1983: *Castill de Bellver*, off S Africa, 239,000 tonnes lost

1988: *Odyssey*, mid-Atlantic, 132,000 tonnes lost

1989: *Khark 5*, off Morocco, 76,000 tonnes lost

1989: *Exxon Valdez*, Alaska, 36,000 tonnes lost

1992: *Aegean Sea*, off Spain, 80,000 tonnes lost

1993: *Braer*, off the Shetlands, 85,000 tonnes lost

There was further extensive O.P. in the Persian Gulf in 1991 as the result of Iraqi action at the end of the Gulf War, and also in Kuwait itself. Serious oil spillage was reported from ruptured pipe-lines near Usinsk, in the Komi region of Russia (just below the Arctic Circle), Oct. 1994.

old age pensions (Britain). First proposed in 1772 by Francis Maseres, and again in 1787 by Mark Rolle, MP; other schemes proposed, notably by W.E. Gladstone's royal commission in 1893, but nothing was done until passing of O.A.P. Act, 1908, which came into force on 1 Jan. 1909 and was subsequently amended. Since 1946, covered by the provisions of the *National Insurance Act, and now known as retirement pensions. Plans to standardize retirement age of men and women put forward, 1992 onwards; decision, 1993, to work towards equal pension age of 65 by 2020.

Old Bailey. A court held in a house on 'Balehill' is mentioned in Stow's *Survey of London*, 1603. 60 persons attending the court, including two judges and the Lord Mayor, *d.* of jail fever from the adjacent *Newgate Prison, 1780. The present Central Criminal Court occupies the site of the old sessions and part of the former Newgate Prison, demolished to make way for it, 1902.

Old Catholics. Those Catholics who refused to accept the doctrine of papal infallibility proclaimed at the Vatican Council of 1870. Dogmatic base of all groups of O.C. contained in the Declaration of Utrecht (1889).

Old Contemptibles, name applied to the (predominantly Regular) British Expeditionary Force of Aug. 1914. In Sept. a BEF Routine Order quoted the Kaiser Wilhelm II on 'Gen. French's contemptible little army'; it has never been established when (or whether) this (or a similar) phrase was used, and in 1925 the ex-Kaiser denied that he had ever done so.

Oldenburg, Germany. Independent county, 1180. United with Denmark, 9 June 1667. Ceded to Russia, 16 Oct. 1776. Made an independent duchy under Frederick of Holstein-Gottorp, 22 Mar. 1777. Joined German Empire, 1871. Became a republic, 1918. Since World War II part of the *Land* of Lower Saxony.

Old Vic. A theatre called the Coburg was built on this site in the Waterloo Road, 1818. In the mid–19thC it became a music hall, but classical concerts were given there from 1880 onwards, and in 1914 regular performances of Shakespeare's plays were produced under Lilian Baylis (1874–1937). Rendered unusable in the 1939–45 war; performances recommenced, 1950. Dramatic School closed, 1952. From 1963–76, the theatre was temporary home of the new *National Theatre. In 1983 it was refurbished and reopened as a commercial theatre.

Olive Branch Petition, by moderate Americans to avert war with Britain. Presented, July 1775, to George III, who ignored it.

Olmütz, Convention of. Austro-Prussian agreement of 1850, reviving Austrian influence in Germany at the expense of Prussia, and regarded by the latter as 'the humiliation of Olmütz'.

Olympia, Greece. The site of the original Olympic games. The earliest building is the temple of Hera, *c.* 1000 BC. The method of calculating time by Olympiads or quadrennial periods between celebrations of the games, reckoned from 776 BC, was first adopted *c.* 264 BC. After the year AD 394 the games were discontinued, and in 426 the temple was destroyed. Site of games rediscovered by Richard Chandler, 1776.

Olympic games, first took place at Olympia, in Greece in 776 BC, being discontinued in AD 394. The games were revived at a meeting of delegates from various nations, 16 June 1894. Games were held at Athens, 1896 (when 10 nations took part); Paris, 1900; St Louis, 1904; London, 1908; Stockholm, 1912; Antwerp, 1920; Paris, 1924; Amsterdam, 1928; Los Angeles, 1932; Berlin, 1936; London, 1948; Helsinki, 1952; Melbourne, 1956; Rome, 1960; Tokyo, 1964; Mexico City, 1968; Munich, 1972; Montreal, 1976; Moscow, 1980; Los Angeles, 1984; Seoul, 1988; Barcelona, 1992. Planned for Atlanta, USA, 1996 and for Sydney, 2000. There have been winter Olympics since 1924. From 1994 summer and winter games to be held two years apart. In 1992 a record 172 nations participated.

Olympiad. *See* OLYMPIA.

Omaha Beach (France). Code-name for the stretch of beach from the Vire River to Port-en-Bessin, where the US 5th Corps landed on D-Day, 6 June 1944, and from which they only narrowly averted being dislodged by the defending Germans.

Oman, known till 1970 as **Muscat and Oman** (*see* MUSCAT), independent Arabian state since 1951, with close ties with Britain since early 19thC, confirmed by Treaty, 1951, and Memorandum of Understanding, June 1982. Reigning Sultan replaced in a coup by his son, 1970. More open and liberal policies instituted and name changed to O.

ombudsman. For the parliamentary O., *see* PARLIAMENTARY COMMISSIONER FOR ADMINISTRATION. Subsequently Os. have been established to deal with maladministration in local government, the Health Service, insurance, pensions, banking, etc. First O. was in Sweden, 1809.

omnibus. The first O. to ply in London was run by Shillibeer, 1829. The London General O. Co. was founded, 1856. First

double-decker appeared, 1904; last horse-bus, 1911. Electric trolley-buses from 1911 onwards; diesels took over after 1955.

Ontario, Canada. First settled by the French in the late 17thC; British territory from 1763; its prosperity founded by loyalist emigrants from the USA after the latter had declared its independence; made into a separate province in 1791, and known as Upper Canada, but in 1867 it again received its original name. Increasing industrialization since 1940s.

OPEC. *See* ORGANIZATION OF PETROLEUM EXPORTING COUNTRIES.

Open University, established 1969 with HQ at Milton Keynes, awarding degrees based on tuition by correspondence, in co-ordination with television programmes, summer schools and a locally-based tutorial system. Over 200,000 students at, 1994. O.U. funded by Ministry of Education until April 1993; subsequently by the Higher Education Funding Council.

opera. First O. proper was *Dafne*, 1597, by Peri and Rinuccini; first O. whose music survives complete was *Euridice*, 1600, by the same collaborators.
Famous singers of O. include:

Anderson, Marian (USA), 1899–1993
Baker, Dame Janet (British), 1933–
Billington, Elizabeth (British), *c.* 1765–1818
Brannigan, Owen, (Welsh), 1908–73
Butt, Dame Clara (British), 1873–1936
Caballé, Montserrat (Spanish), 1933–
Callas, Maria (Greek), 1923–77
Carreras, Jose Maria (Spanish), 1946–
Caruso, Enrico (Italian), 1873–1921
Chaliapin, Feodor (Russian), 1873–1938
Christoff, Boris (Bulgarian), 1914–93.
De Rezske, Edward (Polish), 1853–1917
Domingo, Placido (Spanish), 1941–
Evans, Sir Geraint (Welsh), 1922–
Ferrier, Kathleen (British), 1912–1953
Fischer-Dieskau, Dietrich (German), 1925–
Flagstad, Kirsten (Norwegian), 1875–1962
Gigli, Benjamino (Italian), 1890–1957
Gobbi, Tito (Italian), 1915–84

Hammond, Dame Joan (New Zealand), 1912–
Horne, Marilyn (USA), 1934–
Lanza, Mario (USA), 1921–59
Lehmann, Lilli (German), 1848–1929
Lehmann, Lotte (German-USA), 1888–1976
Los Angeles, Victoria de (Spanish), 1923–
Lind, Jenny (Swedish), 1820–87
McCormack, Count John (Irish), 1884–1945
Marchesi, Luigi (Italian), 1754–1829
Melba, Dame Nellie (Australian), 1861–1931
Melchior, Lauritz (Danish-USA), 1890–1973
Moore, Grace (USA), 1901–47
Norman, Jessye (USA), 1945–
Patti, Adelina (French), 1843–1919
Pavarotti, Luciano (Italian), 1935–
Pears, Sir Peter (British), 1910–1986
Robeson, Paul (USA), 1898–1976
Schwarzkopf, Elisabeth (German), 1915–
Söderström, Elisabeth (Swedish), 1927–
Sutherland, Dame Joan (Australian), 1926–
Te Kanawa, Dame Kiri (New Zealand), 1944–
Vishnevskaya, Galina (Russian), 1926–

Opium War. Between China and Britain, 1840–2.

Oporto, Portugal. Originally *Portus Cale*, the origin of the name *Portugal*, to which in the 5thC a new northern quarter, the *Castrum Novum* of the Alani, was added. Captured by Visigoths, AD 540; by the Moors, 716; recaptured by Christians, 997; captured by the Duke of Wellington, 12 May 1809; besieged by Dom Miguel, 1832–3. The 13thC cathedral occupies the site of a church built by Theodomir, king of the Visigoths, 589, to house the relics of St Martin of Tours (316–97).

Oradour-sur-Glane, France, scene of a Nazi atrocity, 10 June 1944, when the men of the town were all shot or hanged and the women and children driven into the church, which was then set on fire.

Oran, Arabic **Ouahran**, Algeria, a Spanish settlement established in 1509, was abandoned, 1792, and occupied by the French, 1831. French fleet attacked after ultimatum by Adm. Somerville, 3 July 1940, in the harbour of Mers-el-Kebir at O. Scene of violent *OAS disturbances, Mar.–June 1962.

Orange Free State, S Africa. Inhabited by the Dutch Boers, 1836; annexed to British crown, 1848; given up to the Boers, 1854; became part of British Empire after Boer War as the Orange River Colony, 1902; joined Union of 1910 as the O.F.S.

Orange, House of. Came to principality of O. (S France), 1393. Philibert of O. given lands in Netherlands by Emperor Charles V, 1522. These lands passed to William of O.-Nassau (William the Silent), 1544. The family held the offices of Stadhouder and Capt.- and Adm.-General of the Netherlands, 1577–1650 and 1672–1702. William III was King of England, 1688–1702. William VI became King William I of the Netherlands, 1815. *See* NETHERLANDS, KINGDOM OF.

Orangemen, The. A term applied to Protestants in Ireland in 1689; the first Orange lodge instituted, 21 Sept. 1796; all Orange societies suspended, 1813–28; of significance in N Ireland since 1921, and notably since civil violence erupted there from 1960s.

Oratory of St Philip Neri, Congregation of the (or Oratorians). A Roman Catholic order founded, 1556, by Philip Neri (1515–95); confirmed by papal bull, 1575, and again in 1612; first congregation in England established, 1847.

ordeal, trial by. O., together with compurgation, was the commoner form of assessing the value of evidence in pre-Conquest English law-courts; for instance, the weight of red-hot iron to be carried by an accused person pleading not guilty is laid down by the Laws of Athelstan (between 925 and 940) as 3 lb. Queen Emma Aelfgifu, widow of Ethelred, was so tried for adultery, and acquitted, 1043. Trial by O. was abolished in England, 1215–19 (except for trial by battle, which was not formally abolished till 1819). It survived longer on the Continent, and unofficially, in the form of witch-ducking, much longer in England. A case of T. by O. was reported from Charleston, N Carolina, 26 Feb. 1951.

Orders in Council (Britain). First issued in 18thC. 'The O. in C.' were issued in 1807 in reply to Napoleon's Berlin Decrees (*see under* CONTINENTAL SYSTEM).

Orders of Knighthood. *See* KNIGHTHOOD, ORDERS OF.

ordination of women. By the end of the 19thC women increasingly officiating as ministers in Nonconformist churches, and by 1975 World Council of Churches reported that over one-third of its member churches ordained women. Congregationalists ordained women from 1919. First Anglican deaconess, Elizabeth Ferrard, ordained London, 1862; order of deaconesses recognized at Lambeth Conference, 1897. First Anglican woman priest was Florence Li Tim Oi (1907–92) ordained by Bishop Hall in China, 1944. Women ordained Anglican priests in Hong Kong from 1971. Episcopal Church in USA voted for O. of W., 1976; in that year Canada and New Zealand also began ordaining women. Practice followed in Australia, Brazil, Cuba, China, Ireland, Kenya, the Philippines, Puerto Rico, etc. There were three Anglican women bishops by 1994: Barbara Harris, USA (1989), Penny Jamieson, New Zealand (1990) and Mary Adelia McLeod, USA (diocesan: 1993). By 1993 over 1500 Anglican women priests world-wide. In Church of England itself progress towards O. of W. slower and met both clerical and lay opposition. General Synod stated no fundamental objection to the O. of W., 1986 and women deacons ordained from 1987. Movement for O. of W., founded, 1979. In Nov. 1992, General Synod passed by required two-thirds majority vote in favour of O. of W. Approved by Parliament, 1993. First women priests in Church of England ordained in Bristol, 12 Mar. 1994, but decision threatens split

in Church, with a number of defections to Rome. *Church in Wales voted against O. of W., April 1994. Lutheran Church already ordains women. Maria Jepsen was Bishop of Hamburg, 1993. Katherine Richardson president of the Methodist Conference, 1993 and Ruth Clarke Moderator of the United Reformed Church. About 1500 Anglican women ordained in the UK by Easter 1995: Church in Wales voting again on O. of W. during 1995 (*see* WALES, CHURCH IN). The Roman Catholic Church, with the Orthodox Churches, remains officially opposed to the O. of W. But a Catholic Women's Ordination Movement was established in London, Mar. 1993.

Ordnance Board existed before 1660, and was recognized as a civil department of state, 1683. The duties of the O.B. were transferred to the War Department, 1855.

Ordnance Survey was formed in 1791, to make a map on the scale of 1 inch to 1 mile of the whole of Great Britain. This task was completed for England, except the six northern counties, 1840. Its establishment was doubled, 1880, after being transferred from the War Department, 1870. Cultivated area of England completely mapped on scale of 1:2500 by 1890. The O.S. became an executive agency, May 1990, being responsible to the Secretary of State for the Environment.

Oregon, USA. Name first applied to whole area of modern O. and Washington. Columbia River discovered by Capt. Gray, 1792. Fur-trading post established on river, 1811. Dispute between Britain and USA about boundary between Canada and USA from the Lake of the Woods to Pacific arose, 1816. Fixed along 49° N by provisional treaty of Nov. 1818 between Lake of the Woods and the Rocky Mountains. Area comprising the modern states of Idaho, O., Washington and the S half of British Columbia in joint Anglo-American occupation till 49° N boundary extended to Queen Charlotte Sound by treaty of 1846. Admitted as state of the Union, 1859. Vancouver Island given to Canada by arbitration, 1872.

Organization of African Unity. *See* OAU.

Organization of American States. *See* OAS.

Organization of Petroleum Exporting Countries (OPEC), established 1960 to represent oil exporting countries and constitutes a price control. OPEC ability to influence cartel declined after 1980.

Organization for European Economic Cooperation and Development. *See* OECD.

Oriental and African Studies, School of, part of London University, opened by King George V, 23 Feb. 1917. Charter issued, 5 June 1916. African branch added, 1938.

Orkney Islands, Scotland. Possessed by Norsemen in 9thC; formally subject to the Norwegian crown, 1098; pledged by Christian I of Denmark for the payment of the dowry of his daughter Margaret, betrothed to James III of Scotland in 1468; the money was never paid, so the islands passed to the Scottish crown. Denmark renounced all claims to the O.I., 1590.

Orissa, NE India, was a subdivision of Bengal, 1803–1912, then joined to Bihar. Separate province, 1936. Area greatly increased before being made a state of India, 1950.

Orleanists. A French political party who supported the royal claims of the house of Orléans, founded shortly after the French Revolution; after the revolution of 1848 it lost importance.

Orléans, France. Originally *Civitas Aureliani*. Vainly besieged by Attila, AD 451; captured by Clovis, 498; entered by Joan of Arc, 29 Apr. 1429; besieged by the Duke of Guise, 1563; held by Huguenots, 1567–8; surrendered to Henry IV of France, 1594.

Orsini Affair. Felix O. and accomplices attempted the life of Napoleon III, 14 Jan. 1858, and were subsequently executed. The plot had been arranged in London, and the French protested so strongly that

the British Government introduced a propitiatory bill into Parliament, and so was forced to resign.

Orthodox Eastern Church. *See* GREEK ORTHODOX CHURCH and CALENDAR.

Orvieto, Italy. Captured by Belisarius, AD 539; Pope Hadrian IV resided at, 1157; cathedral commenced, 13 Nov. 1290, when Pope Nicholas IV laid foundation stone; Miracle Chapel built, 1350–6. O. became part of kingdom of Italy, 1866.

Osaka, oldest city in Japan, capital 4th–8thC AD. Industrial centre since beginning of 20thC.

Osborne House (Isle of Wight). Purchased by Queen Victoria, 1845; Queen Victoria *d.* there, 1901; presented to the nation by Edward VII as a convalescent home for officers, 1902; Royal Naval College at Osborne opened, 1903. State and private apartments open to the public.

Osborne Judgment. Disallowing a forced political levy on trade union members, handed down by the House of Lords, 1909. Largely nullified by the Trades Union Act of 1913.

Oscar. *See* ACADEMY AWARD.

Oslo, Norway. Founded by Harald Hardrada, 1047. King Sigurd the Crusader buried here, 1130. Burnt down, 1624. Rebuilt by Christian IV of Denmark, who renamed it Christiania. Reverted to older name, 1925.

Oslo, Convention of, a free-trade convention between the 'O. Powers' – Belgium, Luxemburg, the Netherlands, Sweden, Norway and Denmark, signed, Dec. 1930. Finland adhered, Feb. 1933.

osteopathy formulated by Andrew Taylor Still (1828–1917), an American doctor, 1874. British School of O. founded, 1917. London College of O. founded, 1946. Creation of General Osteopathic Council envisaged in private bill, 1993, making O. the first 'alternative' treatment to gain official recognition in the UK.

Ostrogoths. Soon after AD 370 the eastern portion of the hitherto united Gothic tribes came under the supremacy of the *Huns. A raid of O. under King Radagais penetrated into Italy as far as Florence, 406. Ostrogothic bands fought in the army of Attila at Châlons-sur-Marne, 451, but after the death of the Hunnish king regained their liberty of action. They sued the Empire for permission to settle in *Pannonia, which was granted in the second half of the 5thC. Their king, Theodoric (Dietrich, 454–526), became a figure of Germanic legend, and founded an Ostrogoth kingdom in Italy c. 500, having first, in the service of the Emperor Zeno, reconquered Dalmatia and the Danube lands from Odoacer, himself probably a Goth. He married his daughter to Alaric II, king of the *Visigoths, effecting a reunion of the E and W Goths, who again separated at his death. Under his grandson and successor Athalaric the Ostrogoth kingdom ended, 555.

Oswiecim, Poland (German **Auschwitz**). The Germans began the construction of a camp here in 1941. By Mar. 1945 a million and a half persons, mostly Jews, had been killed in O. 'destruction camp' by various branches of the *SS. The commandant and other SS officers were tried and executed at Warsaw for crimes against humanity in 1947. 50th anniversary of liberation of O. by Russian troops commemorated, 27 Jan. 1995.

Otranto, anciently *Hydruntum,* taken from the Byzantines by the Norman, Robert Guiscard, 1068. The Romanesque cathedral was consecrated, 1088. Taken by the Turks, 1480. The castle of O., subject of Walpole's novel published in 1764, was built in 1450.

Ottawa, Canada. Discovered by Champlain, 1613; first permanent settlement, 1826, when the Rideau Canal built; originally known as Bytown; name changed to O. (name of an Indian tribe), 1854, when it was incorporated as a city, made capital of Canada, 1858, first Parliament opened at, 1865. University of O., 1848. Parliament buildings erected (on Westminster model), 1860–1920. Rideau Hall, 1938. Extensive redevelopment since 1950. National Arts Center, 1969. *See* CANADA.

Ottawa Conference between Britain and the Dominions (except Irish Free State) agreed upon trade preferences, Britain to raise tariffs against other countries, 1932.

Ottoman Empire. *See* OTTOMAN RULERS and TURKISH REPUBLIC. Ertogrul (*d.* 1288) obtains lands near Ankara from *Seljuks, and later moves to Sugut. Osman conquers Karaja Hissar, 1295. Orkhan takes Brusa, 1326; Karasi, 1338; Gallipoli, 1355. Foundation of the Janissaries by Orkhan, 1326–59. Murad I takes Ankara and Adrianople, 1361. Adrianople becomes capital, 1367. Acquires Kutahiah, 1381. Overthrows the allied Balkan forces at battle of Kossovo, 27 Aug. 1389. Bayazid I besieges Constantinople; takes Salonika, 1395. Recognized as Sultan of Rum by caliph, 1396. Defeated and captured by Tamerlane at battle of Ankara, 1402. Revival of Os. under Mohammed I, 1413–21. Murad II defeats John Hunyadi at Kosovo, 1448. Mohammed II takes Constantinople, 29 May 1453. Naval victory over Venice, 1499. Selim I (the Grim) drives Bayazid II from throne, 1512. Persians defeated, 1515. Syria and Egypt annexed, 1516–17. Assumes caliphate, 1517. O.E. reaches its greatest extent under Soliman I (the Magnificent or the Lawgiver), 1520–66. He annexes Belgrade, 1521. Destroys Hungarian Army at battle of Mohacz; conquers most of Hungary, 1526–47. Baghdad captured from Persians, 1534. Kheir-ed-Din Barbarossa's naval victory over allied Christians at Prevesa, 1538. Peace with Persia, 1555. Unsuccessful attack on Malta, 1563–5. Naval defeat at battle of Lepanto, 1571. First capitulations granted to Britain, 1580. First serious Janissary revolt, 1591. They murder Osman II, 1622; Ibrahim, 1648. Siege of Vienna marks beginning of O. decline, 1683. Defeat of Russia, 1710. Phanariot Greeks given governorships of Moldavia and Wallachia, 1710–1821. Austrian re-conquest of Hungary, 1680–1718. Belgrade passes to Austria by Treaty of Passarowitz, 1718. Popular rising of Patrona Khalil, 1730. Treaty of Belgrade, 1739. Persian war, 1743–6. Women's faces ordered to be veiled, 1755. Russians conquer the Crimea, 1771. Treaty of Kuchuk-Chainardji, 1774. War with Napoleon, 1798–1802. Treaty of Bucharest, 1812. Beginning of Serbian independence, 1817. Greek rising begins, 1821. Mahmud II destroys Janissaries, 1826. Turko-Egyptian fleet destroyed at Navarino, 1827. French occupy Algiers, 1830. Greece independent by Treaty of London, 1832. Governorship of *Egypt made hereditary, 1840. First Straits Protocol, 1841. Crimean War, 1854–6. The 'Bulgarian Atrocities', 1876. War with Russia, 24 Apr. 1877. Treaty of San Stefano, 3 Mar. 1878. Cession of Cyprus to Britain, 4 June 1878. Berlin Treaty, 13 July 1878. Decree of Muharram gives the Turkish debt administration to European delegates, 1881. Bulgaria autonomous, 1885. Armenian revolts and 'massacres', 1894–6. War with Greece, 1897. Germans begin the 'Baghdad–Berlin' railway, 1899. Macedonian insurrections, 1901–3. Austria annexes Bosnia, 1908. Bulgaria declares independence, 1908. Young Turk Revolution and dethronement of Abdul Hamid II, 1909. Italian aggression, 1911; and annexation of Tripoli and Dodecanese, 1912. *See* BALKAN WARS and WORLD WAR I. Sultanate abolished, 1 Oct. 1922. Caliphate abolished, 3 Mar. 1924. For later history *see* TURKISH REPUBLIC.

Ottoman rulers. Those marked 'A' abdicated. Those marked 'M' were murdered. Those whose reigns were ended by the Janissaries were marked 'J'.

Osman I ('Ottoman') 1288–1326
Orkhan 1326–59
Murad I 1360–89
Bayazid I 1389–1403
  Sultan 1396
  Interregnum 1402–13
Mohammed I 1413–21
Murad II 1421–51
Mohammed II (the Conqueror) 1451–81
Bayazid II (A) 1481–1512

Selim I (the Grim) 1512–20
  Caliph 1517
Soliman I (the Magnificent or the Lawgiver) 1520–66
Selim II (the Sot) 1566–74
Murad III 1574–95
Mohammed III 1595–1603
Ahmed I 1603–17
Mustafa I (imbecile) 1617
Osman II (JM) 1618–22
Mustafa I (again) (JA) 1622–23
Murad IV 1623–40
Ibrahim (JM) 1640–48
Mohammed IV (JA) 1648–87
Soliman II 1687–91
Ahmed II 1691–95
Mustafa II (JA) 1695–1703
Ahmed III (JA) 1703–30
Mahmud I 1730–54
Osman III 1754–57
Mustafa III 1757–73
Abdul Hamid I 1773–89
Selim III (JA) 1789–1807
Mustafa IV 1807–08
Mahmud II 1808–39
Abdul Mejid I 1839–61
Abdul Aziz (A) 1861–76
Murad V (insane) 1876
Abdul Hamid II (A) 1876–1909
Mohammed V 1909–20
Mohammed VI (A) 1920–22
Abdul Mejid II (as caliph only) (A) 1922–24

Oudh, India. Became independent of Moguls *c.* 1732. War with the British, 1759–64, ended in defeat at battle of Buxar, 1763, and acceptance of subsidy at treaty of alliance, 1764. Half territory ceded to Britain, 1801. Completely annexed, 1856. Formed, with Agra, the *United Provinces, 1902. Part of Uttar Pradesh since 1949.

Outward Bound, British youth organization founded, 1941. Trust formed, 1946. Mountain school opened, 1950. Training courses for girls from 1951. Merged with the *Duke of Edinburgh Award, 1995.

Owens College (Manchester). Founded from a bequest by John Owens (*d.* 1846). Opened, 1851 and was the nucleus of the present-day Manchester University.

OXFAM (Oxford Committee for Famine Relief), major British charity founded in Oxford in 1942. Its original purpose was to aid the starving in Greece: after 1945 it played a leading part in alleviating suffering in western Europe, after which its activities gradually shifted to the Third World. Its founder, Canon T. R. Milford, of Oxford, *d.* in 1987.

Oxford Brookes University, name and status since 1992 of the former Oxford Polytechnic.

Oxford City, England. Mentioned in the *Anglo-Saxon Chronicle*, 912. Empress Maud besieged in, 1142. Charter, 1199. Mad Parliament held at, 1258. Made a bishopric, 1542. Occupied by Charles I, 1644–6. Charles II holds Parliament at, 19–28 Mar. 1681. Growth of the motor industry transformed Oxford into an industrial city, 1925–38.

'Oxford Group'. A movement started by Frank Buchman (an American) (1878–1961). Having become a Lutheran pastor, 1902, he formed a First Century Christian Fellowship at Oxford, 1921, with which he toured S Africa, 1929, where the S Africans dubbed the party 'the O.G.'. Popularly known as 'Moral Rearmament' rather than the O.G. since World War II.

Oxford Movement. Founded, 1833, by Keble, Newman and others for reforming the Church of England along Catholic lines. When Newman was converted to Rome, 1845, the O.M. lost its initial impetus; nevertheless, its views on matters of liturgy and theology have had a penetrating and lasting effect upon Anglicanism world-wide and its supporters in 1990s prominent in opposing *ordination of women in the Church of England.

Oxford, Provisions of. Drawn up by Simon de Montfort, 1258, and annulled, 1261, by Henry III.

Oxford University. Schools founded early 12thC. Vacarius lectured on Roman law at O., 1149. University as a corporate body dates from late 12thC or early 13thC. A migration from O. to Cambridge traditionally started the latter university, 1209. Earliest known charter, 1214. Recognized as a *Studium Generale* by the Pope, 1296. Famous Town and Gown Riot, 1354. University reorganized, 1571. Given right to representation in the House of Commons, 1604. New statutes, 1636, 1854, 1877, 1926. Women admitted to degrees, 1920. Parliamentary representation abolished, 1948.

The following are the colleges, halls, and societies (most of which are now open to both sexes: after Oct. 1994, when Somerville first admitted men. St Hilda's the only all-women college remaining), with dates of foundation and the names of their founders:

All Souls, 1438. Henry VI and Archbishop Chichele.

Balliol, *c.* 1263. John and Devorguilla Balliol.

Brasenose, 1509. William Smyth, Bishop of Lincoln and Sir R. Sutton.

Campion Hall, 1896. Richard Clarke.

Christ Church, 1546. Henry VIII.

Corpus Christi, 1517. Richard Foxe, Bishop of Winchester.

Exeter, 1314. Walter Stapeldon, Bishop of Exeter.

Green, 1979.

Greyfriars, 1910.

Hertford, 1740. Richard Newton. Dissolved, 1805. 1874: T. C. Baring, MP.

Jesus, 1571. Queen Elizabeth I.

Keble, 1868. Erected by subscription as a memorial to John Keble.

Lady Margaret Hall, 1878.

Linacre, 1962.

Lincoln, 1427. Richard Fleming, Bishop of Lincoln.

Magdalen, 1458. William Waynflete, Bishop of Winchester.

Manchester, 1990; (name changed to Manchester Academy and Harris College, 1994).

Mansfield, 1886.

Merton, 1264. At Merton. 1274: At Oxford, Walter Merton, Bishop of Rochester.

New, 1379. William of Wykeham, Bishop of Winchester.

Nuffield, 1937. Lord Nuffield.

Oriel, 1326. Adam de Brome and Edward II.

Pembroke, 1624. Thomas Tesdale and Richard Wightwick.

Queen's, 1340. Robert Eglesfield.

Regent's Park, 1886.

Rewley House, 1990. (name changed to Kellogg College, 1994).

Ruskin, 1899.

St Anne's, 1952. (Originally Society of Oxford Home Students, 1879.)

St Antony's, 1950. M. Antonin Besse.

St Benet's, 1897.

St Catherine's (as a society), 1868. Refounded as a college, 1962.

St Cross, 1965.

St Edmund Hall, 1270.

St Hilda's, 1893.

St Hugh's, 1886.

St John's, 1555. Sir Thomas White.

St Peter's, 1929.

Somerville, 1879.

Trinity, 1554. Sir Thomas Pope.

University, 1249. William of Durham.

Wadham, 1612. Dorothy and Nicholas Wadham.

Wolfson. Sir Isaac Wolfson, 1966.

Worcester, 1714. Sir Thomas Cooke.

Oxford University Press. Founded, 1478.

oxygen. First obtained, 1727, by Stephen Hales. First described by J. Priestley, 1774. Word 'O.', first used by Lavoisier *c.* 1775.

ozone layer, acts as a shield against ultra-violet radiation from the sun. Concern regarding its depletion since 1970s when it was noticed that certain chemicals (CFCs, or chlorofluorocarbons) were breaking it down. In 1984 the British Antarctic Survey reported thinning of O.L. over S Pole. Under the Montreal Protocol of 1987 the world use of CFCs to be halved by 1998. Subsequently it was decided this target was too low. In 1990 an agreement was reached to attempt to achieve 50% reduction in CFCs by 1995, 85% by 1997 and a total ban by 2000: halons also to be banned by 2000. Problem of enforceability remains. O.L. over Antarctic reached record low, 1993. 1994: hole in O.L. detected over N Pole, though smaller than S Pole's.

Pacific Islands. See MARIANA ISLANDS; MARSHALL ISLANDS; MICRONESIA; PALAU.

Pacific Ocean. First sighted from Panama by Balboa in Sept. 1513. Magellan sailed, 1520, through the strait named after him, and gave the ocean its name.

Pacific War, 1879–83, between Chile and a combination of Peru and Bolivia, in which Chile made territorial gains.

Padua, Italy (Latin *Patavium*), came under Roman supremacy, 215 BC; sacked by Attila, AD 452; under rule of the Franks, 774; university (where Galileo lectured) founded by the Emperor Frederick II in 1222, and the present buildings date from 1493 to 1552; the town was conquered by the Venetians in 1405, who ruled it until 1797, when it was taken by the French; ceded to Austria, 1814; incorporated with kingdom of Italy, 1866.

Paestum (now **Pesto**). Greek colony of *Poseidonia*, founded by Sybarites, *c.* 600 BC. Became subject to Rome, 273 BC. Sacked by Saracens, 871, and partially dismantled by Normans *c.* 1055. Eventually abandoned during 16thC. Temple of Peace, built 2ndC BC, excavated, 1830. Temple 'of Ceres' built *c.* 530 BC. Temple of Poseidon built, 6thC BC. Other remains accidentally uncovered, 1943; since excavated.

Pagalu, formerly **Annobon Island**, in the Gulf of Guinea, discovered by Portuguese, 1 Jan. 1471. Ceded to Spain, 1778. Part of Republic of *Equatorial Guinea since 1968.

Pagan, ancient ruined city of Upper Burma. Capital of the country from 849 to 1287, when it was sacked by Kublai Khan.

Pahang, former Federated Malay State. Became British protectorate, 1888. Invaded by Japanese, 1942. Part of Malaysia since 1963.

painting. P. on canvas known at Rome AD 66, and to Bede, AD 735. The brothers Van Eyck founded Flemish school of P. in oil, 1415. Royal Academy founded, 1768. Modern movements include: Impressionism, 1831, Neo-Impressionism, 1886; Post-Impressionism, 1890; Fauvism, 1906; cubism, *c.* 1908; futurism, 1911; expressionism, 1908; Dadaism, *c.* 1920; surrealism, 1925; op art, 1960s; minimalism, 1980s. For list of eminent painters, *see* ARTS.

Paisley University, name and status since 1992 of the former Paisley College of Technology.

Pakistan. Name first coined, 1933. Agitation in favour of a separate Moslem state in India begun by All India Moslem League, 1938. P. became independent dominion with the Quaid-i-Azam Mohammed Ali Jinnah as first Governor-General, 14 Aug. 1947. Country made a federation of two units – E and W P. – Nov. 1954. Joined Baghdad Pact (later *CENTO), Sept. 1955. Proclaimed an Islamic Republic within the Commonwealth, 23 Mar. 1956. Internal situation unstable, increasingly so from 1956 onwards, and martial law regimes, 1956–70. In Sept. 1965 there was serious fighting between P. and India on the Kashmir border and tension there has flared up intermittently ever since. Elections, 1970, highlighted secessionist feelings in E P. (*see* BANGLADESH). E P., as Bangladesh, seceded from P., 1971, and P. then withdrew from the Commonwealth (but readmitted, 1989). Bhutto came to power, 1971, but was overthrown by a military coup under General Zia, 1977, and executed in 1979. Zia a civilian president following referendum, 1984. In May 1988, he dissolved the national assembly, but was killed in plane crash, Aug. In subsequent elections the People's Party under

Benazir Bhutto gained power but dismissed, Aug. 1990, for alleged corruption, by the president (Ishaq Khan). Elections, Oct. 1990 won by Islamic Democratic Party led by Nawaz Sharif but he was dismissed for alleged corruption, Apr. 1993. Conflict between 'modernists' and 'traditionalists' continued, despite introduction of Islamic law, 1991. In elections, Oct. 1993, Benazir Bhutto again returned to power, with help of coalition partners. Continuing dispute with India over *Kashmir. Inter-Muslim clashes in P. and some foreigners murdered, Mar. 1995.

Pakistan, East. *See* BANGLADESH.

Palace Court instituted, 1631; abolished, 1849.

Palatinate (German **Pfalz**). First Count Palatine, 945–96. P. given to Otto of Bavaria, 1215. Became independent at division of Wittelsbach possessions, 1255. Received electoral vote under Golden Bull, 1356. Divided into four, 1410. Reunited, 1559. Reunited with Bavaria, 1777. Again divided up after the Napoleonic Wars, 1815.

Palau, or **Belau,** republic of. Pacific island group, Spanish in 1886, sold to Germany, 1899. Occupied by Japanese, 1914; mandated to Japan by League of Nations, 1921. Captured by USA, 1944, became part of UN Trust Territory of the Pacific Islands, 18 July 1947, which was administered by the USA in July 1978. P. decided in referendum not to join *Micronesia. Self-governing since 1981 but argument with USA concerning US desire to deploy nuclear weapons on P. delayed proposed free association agreement with USA until Oct. 1994 after which UN Trust status ended and P. linked formally with USA. First president assassinated, 1985; second committed suicide in 1988; Kamura elected president, Nov. 1992.

Palermo, Sicily (Latin *Panormus*). Phoenician foundation, 8thC BC. Conquered by Pyrrhus, 276 BC; by Romans, 254 BC; by Vandals, AD; by Belisarius, 535; by Saracens, 832; by Normans, 1071; cathedral built by Archbishop Walter, an Englishman, 1169–85; university founded, 1777; revolts against the Bourbon kings, 1820 and 1848; incorporated with Italy, 1860. Mafia outrages in, since 1960s.

Palestine, ancient (Arabic **Falastin**). Hebrew monarchy established *c.* 1000 BC. Rise of Jehu, 841. Assyrians take Samaria, 721. Under Persia from *c.* 539. Conquered by Alexander the Great, 333–2. Maccabaean War of Independence, 168. Roman conquest, 65–3. Jewish rebellion and suppression of Jewish state by Titus, AD 70. Another rebellion, 132–5. Conquered by Persia, 616. By Arabs under Omar, 636. Invaded by Seljuk Turks, 1072 (*see* CRUSADES). Taken by Ottoman Turks, 1517.

Palestine, modern. Conquered by Napoleon, 1799; by the Egyptians, 1831. Europeans and many Jews immigrated during 19thC; Jewish agricultural movement began, 1870. Country freed from Turks by British, 1917–18. The Balfour Declaration, 2 Nov. 1917. Britain became mandatory power, 1920. Jerusalem University opened, 1 Apr. 1925. Wailing Wall outrages, 1929. Jews and Arabs began conflict at Jaffa, 19 Apr. 1936. Royal commission proposed partition, 7 July 1937, but World Zionist Congress of Zürich declared partition unacceptable, 11 Aug. P. Conference opened in London, 7 Feb. 1939; P. Conference ended in rejection of British plan by Arabs and Jews, 17 Mar. and outbreaks of Arab and Jewish terrorism in P. Jewish terrorism in P. began again, June 1945. Partition between Jews and Arabs voted by the United Nations, 29 Nov. 1947. British mandate ended, 14 May 1948. *See further under* ISRAEL *and* JORDAN.

Palestine Liberation Organization (PLO), Palestinian resistance movement, formed, 1964, from Al Fatah, which had existed since 1956. Its president from 1969 was Yassir Arafat, one of the founders of Al Fatah. He addressed the UN, 1974. The PLO made its base in *Lebanon from the early 1970s but after the official expulsion of the PLO forces from Lebanon in 1982 its

HQ was Tunisia. PLO support of Iraq in *Gulf War, 1991, antagonized many, though in 1989 it had implicitly recognized Israel's right to exist. Agreement between Israel and PLO signed, Washington, 13 Sept. 1993, with Arab self-government in Jericho and Gaza planned. Mutual recognition of Israel/PLO by each other. From 1994, PLO under Arafat in charge of self-governing *Jericho and *Gaza Strip, but challenged by Arab extremists. PLO signed agreement with Israel, gaining W Bank autonomy, 28 Sept., 1995.

Palma (de Mallorca), capital of Majorca and of the Balearic Islands. Roman colony, 276 BC. Cathedral started, 1230. 20thC tourist centre.

Panama Canal. International Congress for building of canal convened through influence of F. de Lesseps, builder of Suez Canal, 1879. Company formed and surveying begun, Feb. 1881. Company liquidated, 1 Jan. 1889. New company formed, 1894. Work resumed, 1899. Britain conceded her claims to USA by Hay-Pauncefote Treaty, 1891. Company agreed to sell its rights to US government, 16 Feb. 1903. Treaty between USA and Panama, defining use of canal and government of Panama Zone, Nov. 1903. Canal formally opened, 15 Aug. 1914. P.C. Treaty, 1977; Canal Zone handed over to Panama by the USA, 1979 and control of canal itself. Jan. 1990, the US retaining military bases there. Panamanian control to be total by 2000.

Panama City, capital of Panama. Present city founded 1673 after previous one (1519–1671) destroyed by Henry Morgan.

Panama, Republic of. Treaty between USA and Colombia concerning canal concession ratified by US Senate, 18 Mar. 1903. Colombian Senate refused ratification, and P., hitherto a department of Colombia, revolted against *Colombia, 4 Nov. 1903. USA prevented Colombian government from suppressing the revolt and Panamanian independence recognized by Colombia, 13 Nov. 1903. P. then ceded canal zone to USA, 18 Nov. 1903. Independence

recognized by Colombia, 1914, in Treaty of Bogotá with USA, ratified, 1921. Canal Zone handed over to P., 1979. Vice-President Delvalle took power, 1985; in 1988 failed to curb power of army chief Noriega who ousted him. Elections, May 1989 annulled by Noriega who made himself head of state. The USA invaded P., 20 Dec. 1989; Noriega taken to USA and subsequently convicted there of drug trafficking, Apr. 1992. Endara established as president after fall of Noriega; crushed attempted coup, 1991. Legislative assembly abolished armed forces, 1991. Perez succeeded as president, 1994.

Pan-American Conferences. Arranged for by Act passed by US Congress, 1888. First conference: Washington, Oct. 1889–Apr. 1890; 10 nations signed arbitration treaty. The *Organization of American States grew out of the P.-A.C.

Pannonia. Natives conquered by Augustus, 35 BC. Insurrections suppressed, 12 BC and AD 6–9, after which P. was included in the province of Illyricum; separate province, AD 10. Divided into Upper and Lower P. c. AD 105. Conquered by Ostrogoths, 453; then by Lombards, 527; finally by Magyars c. 900. See HUNGARY.

pantomime, in Britain, theatrical spectacle with origins in 18thC harlequinade and 19thC burlesque. First British P. performance took place at Lincoln's Inn Theatre, 22 Dec. 1716.

Papacy. Christianity lawful in Roman Empire by the Edict of Milan, 313. Primacy of the Roman See established by Innocent I, 402–17. P. had acquired considerable temporal power in the district around *Rome by the time of Leo the Great, 440–61. First decree on papal elections issued by Synod of Rome, Mar. 499. Gregory I sends Augustine to England, 596. Gregory II sends Boniface to Germany, 715. Pepin cedes papal states to Stephen II, 753. Leo III crowns Charlemagne emperor at Rome, 25 Dec. 800. Leo IV fortifies Rome, 847. The False Decretals forged in France c. 850. John VIII murdered by Roman nobles, 882.

Martin I the first bishop to become pope, 882. The pornocracy of the two Theodoras and Marozia, 904–63. End of the rule of the nobles, 980. Cluniac reform movement reaches its climax with election of Gerbert of Reims to the P. as Silvester II, 999. The counts of Tusculum hold the P., 1012–45. Synod of Rome pronounces against simony and regulates the P., 1047–8. Papal election by cardinals only established 1059. *Dictatus Papae* outlines papal temporal claims, 1075. The Investiture Dispute, 11th–12thC. Emperor Henry IV humiliated at Canossa, 1077, by Gregory VII (Hildebrand). Only Englishman to become pope, Nicholas Breakspear, reigned as Adrian IV, 1154–9. P. reached the summit of its temporal power under Innocent III (1198–1216) and began to decline after the death of Innocent IV, 1254. Political struggle against the Hohenstaufen emperors ended in the defeat of Conradin at Tagliacozzo, 1268, after which the P. passed under French influence and moved to Avignon, 1309. The return of Gregory XI to Rome, 1377, was followed by the French-provoked 'Great Schism', 1378–1417, when the antipopes resided at Avignon and elsewhere. The schism was ended at the election of Martin V, 1417, by the Council of Constance, 1414–18. Temporary union with the Greek and Armenian Churches, 1439. Owing to inability of the Renaissance popes to reform the abuses of the Church the Reformation began with the issue of Luther's 95 Theses, 31 Oct. 1517. Luther burns the papal bull of excommunication, 1520. Paul III starts internal reforms, 1537, and confirms the Jesuit Order, 1540. Council of Trent redefines Roman Catholic doctrine, 1545–63. Counter-reformation in Germany, 1550–1600. In France, 1623–44. Pius VI taken to France as a prisoner, 1799. During the Roman revolution of 1848, Pius IX fled to Gaeta, but was restored with French help. All the states of the Church, except Rome and the Patrimony of St Peter, annexed to Italy, 1860. Remainder annexed, 1870. Papal infallibility proclaimed by the Vatican Council on 18 July 1870. Rupture of diplomatic relations with France, 1904. Encyclical on modernism, 1907. Temporal sovereignty within Vatican City restored by Lateran Treaty, 11 Feb. 1929, amended by Concordat of 1984. Pope John XXIII convened 4th Ecumenical Council of the Church, Oct. 1962. ('Vatican II'). Council closed, 8 Dec. 1965. Opposition to 'artificial' forms of contraception affirmed in encyclical *Humanae Vitae*, 25 July 1968. New Catechism, 1992. Encyclical *Veritatis Splendor*, Oct. 1993, restated traditional papal position with stand on moral absolutes. Accord with Israel, Dec. 1993. The following is a list of popes, with antipopes in *italics*.

1. St Peter (*d.* between AD 64 and 67)
2. St Linus, 67–76, or 67–79
3. St Anacletus I, 76–88, or 79–91
4. St Clement I, 88–97, or 92–101
5. St Evaristus, 97–105, or 101–5
6. St Alexander I, 105–15
7. St Sixtus I (Xystus), 115–25
8. St Telesphorus, 125–36
9. St Hyginus, 136–40
10. St Pius I, 140–55
11. St Anicetus, 155–66
12. St Soter, 166–75
13. St Eleutherius, 175–89
14. St Victor I, 189–99
15. St Zephyrinus, *c.* 199–217
16. St Calixtus I, 217/18–222
    St Hippolytus, antipope, 217/18–235
17. St Urban I, 222–30
18. St Pontianus, 230–35
19. St Anteros, 235–36
20. St Fabian, 236–50
21. St Cornelius, 251–53
    Novatian, antipope, 251
22. St Lucius I, 253–54
23. St Stephen I, 254–57
24. St Sixtus II, 257–58
25. St Dionysius, 259–68
26. St Felix I, 269–74
27. St Eutychianus, 275–?283
28. St Gaius, 283–?296
29. St Marcellinus, 296–304
30. St Marcellus I, *c.* 308–*c.* 309
31. St Eusebius, 309 (?310)
32. St Miltiades, 311–14

33. St Sylvester I, 314–35
34. St Marcus, 336 (Jan.–Oct.)
35. St Julius I, 337–52
36. St Liberius, 352–66
    Felix II, antipope, 355–65
37. St Damasus I, 366–84
    Ursinus, antipope, 366–67
38. St Siricius, 384–99
39. St Anastasius I, 399–401
40. St Innocent I, 401–17
41. St Zosimus, 417–18
42. St Boniface I, 418–22
    Eulalius, antipope, 418–19
43. St Celestine I, 422–32
44. St Sixtus III, 432–40
45. St Leo I, 440–61
46. St Hilarius, 461–68
47. St Simplicius, 468–83
48. St Felix III, 483–92
49. St Gelasius I, 492–96
50. Anastasius II, 496–98
51. St Symmachus, 498–514
    Laurentius, antipope, 498–c. 505
52. St Hormisdas, 514–23
53. St John I, 523–26
54. St Felix IV, 526–30
55. Boniface II, 530–32
    Dioscorus, antipope, autumn 530
56. John II, 533–35
57. St Agapetus I, 535–36
58. St Silverius, 536–37
59. Vigilius, 537–55
60. Pelagius I, 555–61
61. John III, 561–74
62. Benedict I, 574–79
63. Pelagius II, 579–90
64. St Gregory I, 590–604
65. St Sabinian, 604–606
66. Boniface III, 607 (Feb.–Nov.)
67. St Boniface IV, 608–15
68. St Deusdedit (or Adeodatus), 615–18
69. Boniface V, 619–25
70. Honorius I, 625–38
71. Severinus, 638–40
72. John IV, 640–42
73. Theodore I, 642–49
74. St Martin I, 649–55 (*d.* in exile)
75. St Eugenius I, 654–57
76. St Vitalian, 657–72
77. Adeodatus II, 672–76
78. Donus, 676–78
79. St Agatho, 678–81
80. St Leo II, 681–83
81. St Benedict II, 683–85
82. John V, 685–86
83. Conon, 686–87
    Theodore and *Paschal, rival antipopes,* 687 (Sept.)
84. St Sergius I, 687–701
85. John VI, 701–05
86. John VII, 705–07
87. Sisinnius, 708 (Jan.–Feb.)
88. Constantine, 708–15
89. St Gregory II, 715–31
90. St Gregory III, 731–41
91. St Zacharias, 741–52
92. Stephen II, 752–57
93. St Paul I, 737–67
    Constantine, antipope, 767–68
    Philip, antipope, 768 (July)
94. Stephen III, 768–72
95. Adrian I, 772–95
96. St Leo III, 795–816
97. Stephen IV, 816–17
98. St Paschal I, 817–24
99. Eugenius II, 824–27
100. Valentinus, 827 (Aug.–Sept.)
101. Gregory IV, 827–44
    John, antipope, 844 (Jan.)
102. Sergius II, 844–47
103. St Leo IV, 847–55
104. Benedict III, 855–58
    Anastasius, antipope, 855
105. St Nicholas I, 858–67
106. Adrian II, 867–72
107. John VIII, 872–82
    (wrongly called Martin II)
108. Marinus I, 882–84
109. St Adrian III, 884–85
110. Stephen V, 885–91
111. Formosus, 891–96
112. Boniface VI, 896 (Apr.)
113. Stephen VI, 896–97
114. Romanus, 897 (Aug.–Nov.)
115. Theodore II, 897 (Nov.–Dec.)
116. John IX, 898–900
117. Benedict IV, 900–03
118. Leo V, 903 (July–Sept.)
    Christopher, antipope, 903–04
119. Sergius III, 904–11
120. Anastasius III, 911–13
121. Lando, 913–14

122. John X, 914–28
123. Leo VI, 928 (May–Dec.)
124. Stephen VII, 928–31
125. John XI, 931–35
126. Leo VII, 936–39
127. Stephen VIII, 939–42
128. Marinus II (wrongly called Martin III), 942–46
129. Agapetus II, 946–55
130. John XII, 955–964 (deposed Dec. 963)
131. Leo VIII, 963–965
131. Benedict V, 964–65 or 966

Rivals, one or other of whom may be regarded as an antipope.

132. John XIII, 965–72
133. Benedict VI, 973–74
     Boniface VII, antipope, 974 (June–July), expelled
134. Benedict VII, 974–83
135. John XIV, 983–84 (expelled)
     Boniface VII, antipope, returned, 984–85
136. John XV, 985–96
137. Gregory V, 996–99
     John XVI, antipope, 997–98
138. Sylvester II, 999–1003
139. John XVII, 1003 (June–Dec.)
140. John XVIII, 1004–09
141. Sergius IV, 1009–12
142. Benedict VIII, 1012–24
     Gregory, antipope, 1012 (May–Dec.)
143. John XIX, 1024–32
144. Benedict IX, 1032–44
145. Sylvester III, 1045 (Jan.–Mar.)
146. Benedict IX, 1045 (Apr.–May) resigned
147. Gregory VI, 1045–46
148. Clement II, 1046–47
149. Benedict IX (restored), 1047–48
150. Damasus II, 1048 (July–Aug.)
151. St Leo IX, 1049–54
152. Victor II, 1055–57
153. Stephen IX, 1057–58
     Benedict X, antipope, 1058–59
154. Nicholas II, 1059–61
155. Alexander II, 1061–73
     Honorius II, antipope, 1061–72
156. St Gregory VII, 1073–85
     Clement III, antipope, 1080, 1084–1100
157. Bl. Victor III, 1086–87
158. Bl. Urban II, 1088–99

159. Paschal II, 1099–1188
     Theodoric, antipope, 1100
     Albert, antipope, 1102 (Feb.–Mar.)
     Sylvester IV, antipope, 1105–11
160. Gelasius II, 1118–19
     Gregory VIII, antipope, 1118–21
161. Calixtus II, 1119–24
162. Honorius II, 1124–30
     Celestine II, antipope, 1124 (Dec.)
163. Innocent II, 1130–43
     Anacletus II, antipope, 1130–38
     Victor IV, antipope, 1138 (Mar.–May)
164. Celestine II, 1143–44
165. Lucius II, 1144–45
166. Bl. Eugenius III, 1145–53
167. Anastasius IV, 1153–54
168. Adrian IV, 1154–59
169. Alexander III, 1159–81
     Victor IV, antipope, 1159–64
     Paschal III, antipope, 1164–68
     Calixtus III, antipope, 1168–78
     Innocent III, antipope, 1179–80
170. Lucius III, 1181–85
171. Urban III, 1185–87
172. Gregory VIII, 1187 (Oct.–Dec.)
173. Clement III, 1187–91
174. Celestine III, 1191–98
175. Innocent III, 1198–1216
176. Honorius III, 1216–27
177. Gregory IX, 1227–41
178. Celestine IV, 1241 (Oct.–Nov.)
179. Innocent IV, 1243–54
180. Alexander IV, 1254–61
181. Urban IV, 1261–64
182. Clement IV, 1265–68
183. St Gregory X, 1271–66
184. St Innocent V, 1276 (Jan.–June)
185. Adrian V, 1276 (July–Aug.)
186. John XXI, 1276–77
187. Nicholas III, 1277–80
188. Martin IV, 1281–85
189. Honorius IV, 1285–87
190. Nicholas IV, 1288–92
191. St Celestine V, 1294 (July–Dec.)
192. St Boniface VIII, 1294–1303
193. St Benedict XI, 1303–04
194. Clement V, 1305–14 (to Avignon in 1309)
195. John XXII, in Avignon, 1316–34
     Nicholas V, antipope in Italy, 1328–30
196. Benedict XII, 1334–42 in Avignon

197. Clement VI, 1342–52 in Avignon
198. Innocent VI, 1352–62 in Avignon
199. Bl. Urban V, 1362–70 (in Rome from 1367)
200. Gregory XI, 1370–78 (to Rome 1377)
201. Urban VI, 1378–89
    Clement VII, antipope, 1378–94
202. Boniface IX, 1389–1404
    Benedict XIII, antipope, 1394–1423
203. Innocent VII, 1404–06
204. Gregory XII, 1406–15
    Alexander V, antipope, 1409–10
    John XXIII, antipope, 1410–15
205. Martin V, 1417–31
    Clement VIII, antipope, 1423–9
    Benedict XIV, antipope, 1425–30
206. Eugenius IV, 1431–47
    Felix V, antipope, 1439–49
207. Nicholas V, 1447–55
208. Calixtus III, 1455–58
209. Pius II, 1458–64
210. Paul II, 1464–71
211. Sixtus IV, 1471–84
212. Innocent VIII, 1484–92
213. Alexander VI, 1492–1503
214. Pius III, 1503 (Sept.–Oct.)
215. Julius II, 1503–13
216. Leo X, 1513–21
217. Adrian VI, 1522–23
218. Clement VII, 1523–34
219. Paul III, 1534–49
220. Julius III, 1550–55
221. Marcellus II, 1555 (Apr.)
222. Paul IV, 1555–59
223. Pius IV, 1559–65
224. St Pius V, 1566–72
225. Gregory XIII, 1572–85
226. Sixtus V, 1585–90
227. Urban VII, 1590 (Sept.)
228. Gregory XIV, 1590–01
229. Innocent IX, 1591 (Oct.–Dec.)
230. Clement VIII, 1592–1605
231. Leo XI, 1605 (Apr.)
232. Paul V, 1605–21
233. Gregory XV, 1621–23
234. Urban VIII, 1623–44
235. Innocent X, 1644–55
236. Alexander VII, 1655–67
237. Clement IX, 1667–69
238. Clement X, 1670–76
239. Bl. Innocent XI, 1676–89

240. Alexander VIII, 1689–91
241. Innocent XII, 1691–1700
242. Clement XI, 1700–21
243. Innocent XIII, 1721–24
244. Benedict XIII, 1724–30
245. Clement XII, 1730–40
246. Benedict XIV, 1740–58
247. Clement XIII, 1758–69
248. Clement XIV, 1769–74
249. Pius VI, 1775–99
250. Pius VII, 1800–23
251. Leo XII, 1823–29
252. Pius VIII, 1829–30
253. Gregory XVI, 1831–46
254. Pius IX, 1846–78
255. Leo XIII, 1878–1903
256. St Pius X, 1903–14
257. Benedict XV, 1914–22
258. Pius XI, 1922–39
259. Pius XII, 1939–58
260. John XXIII, 1958–63
261. Paul VI, 1963–1978
262. John Paul I, 1978
263. John Paul II, 1978–

Papal states. Temporal rule of the Papacy began with the bestowal of the Exarchate of Ravenna, hitherto administered from Byzantium, on Pope Stephen II (752–7). Greatly reduced in extent, 1859, and suppressed, 1870. In 1929 a successor to this state, known as the *Vatican City was recognized as a sovereign power by concordat with Italy; amended, 1984.

paper. Said to have been invented in China, AD 105, by Tsai-Lun.

Papua New Guinea. The P.N.G. Act 1949–72 provided for the administrative union by Australia (as a UN nominee) of *New Guinea and Papua. Self-government was granted on 1 Dec. 1973 and P.N.G. became fully independent on 16 Sept. 1975. Separatist agitation in Bougainville from 1988, amounting to virtual civil war. Economic advances since 1990s based on gold industry.

parachute, first used by a human being from an aircraft (balloon), Paris, 22 Oct. 1797.

Paraguay. Explored by Juan Diaz de Sotis, 1515. By Irala, Ayotas, and Garay, 1519–32. First settlement founded by Pedor de Mendoza, 1537. Further exploration by Cabeza de Vaca, 1541–2. First Jesuits arrive, 1557. Foundation by Father Diego de Torres of the Jesuit Missionary State in P. ('The Reductions'), 1608–11. Civil War between the Spanish planters and the Jesuits, 1723–5. Rebellion of the *Comuñeros* led by Mompox, 1726–35. Jesuit rule abolished, 1767. Declaration of P.'s independence from Spain, 1811, and Francia's dictatorship, 1814–40. War with Brazil, Argentina and Uruguay, 1865–70. Brazilian occupation, 1870–6. War with Bolivia, 31 July 1932–12 July 1935. Frontier with Bolivia fixed by arbitration, 10 Oct. 1938. Civil war, Mar.–Aug. 1947, resulted in victory of Colorados. Stroessner became president, 1954, and established a right-wing dictatorship. Stroessner overthrown in military coup, Feb. 1989 by Rodriguez, who became president, May. In multiparty election, May 1993, Wasmosy elected president; moves to civilian rule followed.

paratroops, first demonstrated by Russians, 1936. First used by Germans in Holland, May 1940. Development of British P. from 1942 onwards.

Paris, France. First mentioned by Caesar under title of *Lutetia Parisiorum*. In 52 BC it became a Roman town of some importance; Clovis made it his capital, AD 508; between 1180 and 1223 the cathedral of Notre-Dame was commenced and the University of P. founded; revolution of P. headed by Etienne Marcel, 1358; Louvre begun, 1541; Arc de Triomphe, 1806; reconstruction of the city under Napoleon III, 1851–70. *Eiffel Tower completed, 1889. P. fell to German Army, 1871 and 14 June 1940; liberated by French forces under Leclerc, Aug. 1944. Considerable growth of population and rebuilding since 1945. Market of Les Halles moved to Rungis, 1969; Centre National d'Art et de Culture Georges Pompidou, 1977; Musée d'Orsay (former station), 1990. *See* FRANCE and BASTILLE.

Paris Commune *see* COMMUNE OF PARIS.

Paris, Declaration of. Drawn up at the Congress of P. in 1856. It settled four important points of international law.

Paris, Treaties of. Name of several treaties, the most notable of which are:
1. Between France, Spain and England, by which the Seven Years War was ended and Canada ceded to England, signed Feb. 1763.
2. Between Britain and the American Commissioners, recognizing American independence, 3 Sept. 1783.
3. Between the allies, after the abdication of Napoleon in May 1814.
4. After the close of Napoleon's final campaign in Flanders, 20 Nov. 1815.
5. Between Russia, Turkey, England, France and Sardinia at the close of the Crimean War, signed 30 Mar. 1856.
6. Between England and Persia: amongst other things it abolished the slave trade in the Persian Gulf, signed 3 Mar. 1857;
7. Terminating the Spanish-American War, 10 Dec. 1898.

Parliament (*see also* LORDS, HOUSE OF; COMMONS, HOUSE OF; FRANCHISE). In Jan. 1265 there was a meeting (summoned by Simon de Montfort) of citizens and burgesses, together with knights of the shire; but until 1295 there appears to have been for the most part only one legislative chamber. Acts of P. were first printed in 1501. First P. of Great Britain met, 23 Oct. 1707. Septennial Act became law, 7 May 1716; first P. of the UK of Great Britain and Ireland, 1801; Roman Catholic Relief Act, 1829; Reform Act, 1832; Houses of P. destroyed by fire, 16 Oct. 1834; new buildings commenced, 1840; new House of Lords completed, 15 Apr. 1845; new House of Commons completed, 4 Nov. 1852; Act for enabling Jews to sit, 1858; final rebuilding of P. completed, 1867. Parliamentary Elections Act (as to corrupt practices), 1868; Ballot Act, 1872; closure adopted, 1882; P. Act, 1911, made five years instead of seven maximum length of a P., and curtailed powers of House of Lords, as did that of 1949. MPs first paid, 1911. Franchise extended to women, 1918 and 1928. House of Commons bombed, 1941; restored chambers reopened, 1950. Act of 1948 abolished plural voting, by abolishing university and business franchises. Peerage Bill establishing Life Peerages became law, 31 July 1963. House of Lords reform Bill dropped by government, 1969. Voting age reduced to 18 from 1970. Since 1960s, a campaign for proportional representation waged by Liberals (now Liberal Democrats); joined by some Socialists since 1990. *See* LORDS, HOUSE OF.

Parliament, European. *See* EUROPEAN PARLIAMENT.

Parliamentary Commissioner for Administration (popularly, the 'Ombudsman'), appointed under the Parliamentary Commissioner Act, 1967, to investigate administrative action taken on behalf of the Crown, i.e. alleged maladministration.

Parkinson's disease, progressive disorder of the nervous system, named after Dr James Parkinson, who first diagnosed it, 1817.

Parma, duchy of, created 1545, for Pierluigi Farnese, natural son of Pope Paul III. Conquered by the French, 1796. Assigned to Marie Louise, wife of Napoleon, after 1815. Became part of the kingdom of Italy, 1859.

Parnell Commission. Caused through facsimile reproduction, in *The Times* of 18 Apr. 1887, of a letter purporting to have been written by Charles S. Parnell (1846–1891): it excused the *Phoenix Park murders. The Government (Aug. 1888) appointed a commission, which reported, 13 Feb. 1890. It acquitted Parnell on all charges.

Parthenon at Athens, building begun, 447 BC; dedicated, 438; sculptures completed, 432. Converted into a Christian church, 5thC, and into a mosque, AD 1456. Blown up, 1687. Sculptures removed by Lord Elgin, 1801 to British Museum; demanded back by Greek government from 1983. Restoration work begun, mid-1980s to repair damage to P. caused by air pollution.

Parthia, ancient W Asian kingdom. Controlled a considerable empire between 250 BC and AD 224 when the country was annexed to Persia.

Partition Treaties between William III, representing England and Holland, and Louis XIV, attempted to settle the devolution of the Spanish dominions at the death of the reigning King Charles II.
1. 2 Oct. 1698. By this treaty Spain, its colonies, and the Netherlands were to go to the Electoral Prince of Bavaria, Milan to the Archduke Charles of Austria, Naples, Sicily and other Italian possessions to the Dauphin. This arrangement was frustrated when Charles II left all the Spanish dominions to the Electoral Prince by a will, published 14 Nov. 1698, and the Electoral Prince *d.*, 6 Feb. 1699.
2. 11 June 1699. The Archduke Charles to have the Electoral Prince's share. The Dauphin to have the same as before, plus Milan. This treaty was ratified, 13 Mar. 1700. It was frustrated because the Austrian emperor refused ratification, and Charles II, by a will signed 7 Oct. 1700, gave all the territories to the Duke of Anjou (grandson of Louis XIV). Charles II *d.* 1 Nov. 1700. Louis XIV accepted the Spanish offer, 12 Nov. Acceptance publicly announced, 16 Nov. 1700. *See* SPANISH SUCCESSION, WAR OF.

Passchendaele, Belgium, scene of heavy fighting, July–Nov. 1917, when the British fought an unsuccessful offensive battle, resulting in over 350,000 casualties.

Pass Laws, in S Africa, part of the *apartheid system, repealed 1986.

Paston Letters, The. A series of letters written to or by the Ps., a Norfolk family, between 1422 and 1509; they give an invaluable insight into English life of the 15thC.

Patagonia. Since 1881 part of *Argentina.

patent laws (Britain). First granted for stained glass-making, 1449; for exclusive privilege of printing books, 1591; properties and rights of inventors first protected in 1623; this law was repealed and a new Act passed known as the P. Act in 1883, frequently amended in succeeding years. Important changes contained in Act, 1949 which came into operation, 1 Jan. 1950. Further amendments to P.L. under Patents Act, 1957, Patents Act, 1977, and Copyright Designs and Patents Act, 1988. System of European patents introduced into English law under the 1977 Act (Part II). The Patent Office, an executive agency of the Department of Trade and Industry, is responsible for administering the Patent Acts. Tradesmark Act of 1994 reinforced and radically strengthened existing patents legislation.

Pavia, Italy (ancient *Ticinum*; later **Papia**). Founded by the Ligurii. Taken from the Lombards by Charlemagne, 774. Taken by the Viscontis, 1359. Sacked by the French, 1500. Charles V captured Francis I of France here, 1525. Annexed by Austria, 1744. Became part of a united Italy, 1859. Church Councils held at P., 1081, 1160, 1423.

Pawnbrokers' Acts, 1872–60, repealed by the *Consumer Credit Act of 1974, sections 114–22 of the latter act regulating matters traditionally covered by pawnbroking.

Pay As You Earn (PAYE), part of modern British income tax system, was introduced in 1944.

Peace Ballot, conducted by the League of Nations Union, secured 11,640,066 British votes for adherence to the League, and 10,500,000 for all-round reduction of armaments, 27 June 1935.

Peace Conferences (International). *See also* HAGUE.
1. Met at The Hague, 1899; arbitration court formed at the conference, and founded, 29 July 1899.
2. Met at The Hague, 15 June–18 Oct. 1907.
3. Inter-Allied and Associated Powers held first plenary session, in Paris, on 18 June 1919. Draft treaty handed to German delegates, 7 May 1919. After the treaty was ratified further conferences were held at San Remo, Apr. 1920, and at Hythe, May, and Spa, June 1920, to discuss reparations, disarmament, mandates and the Adriatic question. For P.C. with Turkey *see* TURKISH REPUBLIC.
4. A Peace Conference held in Paris in 1946 resulted in peace treaties between the Allies and Italy, Hungary, Rumania, Bulgaria and Finland being signed and ratified in 1947. The treaty with Austria, however, was not signed until 1955. For other P.C. since World War II *see* GENEVA CONFERENCES.

Peace Corps, a voluntary US government agency. Idea of President John F. Kennedy, created by P.C. Act, 1961. Volunteers serve for two years on projects such as health, education, etc., mainly in the Third World. Within five years of conception had attracted over 10,000 volunteers, but in 1980s became unpopular in certain countries where P.C. accused of political bias.

Pearl Harbor, American naval base in the Hawaiian Islands. Dredging of P.H. completed, 1912; dry dock opened, 1919. Japanese attack on P.H., 7 Dec. 1941, when much of US Pacific Fleet destroyed or damaged, with 2000 fatal casualties. Brought the USA into World War II on the Allied side.

Peasants' Revolt. Accelerated by enforcement of poll tax (1377–81). Rebels suppressed after breaking into Tower of London and murdering the Archbishop of Canterbury, 15 June 1381.

Peasants' War.
1. France. *See* JACQUERIE.
2. Germany: Decay of feudal protection, together with continuance of feudal tyranny, led to a P. League which rose in the Rhine countries in 1502, and to another rising in Württemberg in 1514. Great insurrection began in Swabia,

1524, and spread through S Germany. Demands of P. set out in 12 Articles issued by insurgents of Swabia, Easter, 1525; Under the Anabaptist Münzer, they were overwhelmed by Philip of Hesse at Frankenhausen, 15 May 1525.

Pechenga (Finnish, **Petsamo**, by which name it was known, 1919–44), port at head of P. Bay on the Barents Sea. Formally ceded to Finland by the USSR under Treaty of Dorpat, 1920. USSR gained access to P., 1940, and reacquired it, 1944.

Peenemunde, village in NE Germany, on NW of Usedone Island, in Baltic. Recorded in 13thC. During World War II, site of German rocket research and testing station. Bombed by RAF, Aug. 1943. Captured by Russians, April 1945.

Peine Forte et Dure, form of torture to extort plea or evidence, authorized in England, 1406. Last recorded instance, 1741. Abolished, 1772.

Peking, Peiping or **Beijing**, capital of China. Captured by Khitan Tatars, AD 986; recaptured by Chinese in 12thC; again captured by Tatars, 1151; first settlement of foreigners in 1860; Boxer riots and the siege of the legations, 1900. Capital of China from 1421 until 1928, when Chiang Kai-Shek removed the government to Nanking and renamed Peking Peiping. Occupied by Japanese, 1937–45. Surrendered to the Communists, 1 Feb. 1949, and re-established under its original name of Peking or Beijing as the capital of China, 1 Oct. 1949. In Tianamen Square, in P. over 1000 civilians killed by government forces 3–4 June 1989, when a popular movement to establish democracy was suppressed.

Pelagians. The followers of Pelagius (*c.* 360–420), a British theologian, who was summoned before a synod of bishops at Jerusalem, 415, where he successfully defended his views. Pope Innocent, however, in 416 upheld the opponents of Pelagius, amongst whom was St Augustine of Hippo. The doctrine of Pelagianism finally condemned, 418, by the Western Church, and in 431 by the Eastern Church.

penal servitude, as punishment for felony, substituted for transportation in English law, 1853–7. Abolished, 1948.

Penang. Ceded to E India Co. by Rajah of Kedah, 1785. Incorporated with Singapore and Malacca, 1826. Capital of Straits Settlements, 1837–1936. Part of Malaysia since 1963.

PEN (Poets, Playwrights, Editors, Essayists and Novelists) Club founded, 1921.

penicillin. Discovered, 1928, by Alexander Fleming (1881–1955).

Peninsular War, The (1808–14). Between France and England, begun in consequence of the alliance between Spain and England, July 1808, when the Duke of Wellington, then Sir Arthur Wellesley, was dispatched to the peninsula with troops; there were two campaigns, and the British Army was forced to evacuate the country in Jan. 1809. A fresh force was landed in Apr. 1809; the war had commenced with the battle of Vimiero, 21 Aug. 1808, when Wellington defeated Junot, and ended with the battle of Toulouse, 10 Apr. 1814, when Wellington defeated Soult (*see* PORTUGAL and SPAIN).

Pennsylvania, USA. Founded by William Penn, who in 1681 obtained a grant of land in America from Charles II. In Sept. 1682 Penn embarked on the *Welcome* for America, and landed on 28 Oct. of the same year; as one of the 13 original colonies it became a state of the Union, 1787.

penny. First mentioned in Laws of King Ine (*fl.* 689–726), King of Wessex. Halfpennies not coined before the late 9thC. Copper pence first struck, 1797; bronze substituted for copper, 1860. New P., one-hundredth part of Britain's decimal currency system from Feb. 1971, is worth 2.4 old Ps.

Pensions, Ministry of, created, 1916. Merged with the Ministry of National Insurance, to form the M. of P. and National Insurance, 1953; since 1988 part of the Department of Social Security.

Pentagon Building (Washington, DC, USA), built 1941–3 and declared a national monument.

Pentecostalists. The Pentecostal movement originated in Los Angeles, USA, 1906, and reached Britain, 1907. In Britain, there are four principal groupings of Ps.: the Elim Pentecostal Church, 1915; the Apostolic Church, 1916; the Assemblies of God, 1924; the New Testament Church of God, 1953. In 1995 there were over 22 million Ps. world-wide and about 115,000 in Great Britain. The P.'s charismatic practices have been adopted by some other Christian churches since the 1960s.

Perak, former Federated Malay State, made treaty (1765) with Dutch, who first established factories there, 1650. Ceded Dinding and Pangkor Island to Britain by treaty of 1826, but these were returned, 1934–5. Part of Malaysia since 1963.

Perceval Administration. Spencer P. (1762–1812) at the head. Formed, Oct. 1809; dissolved on assassination of P. in the lobby of the House of Commons, 11 May 1812.

perestroika, term given to the reforms, 1986–91, carried out by Mikhail Gorbachev which led ultimately to the dismantling of Soviet Communism.

Pergamum. Said to have been founded by Aeolian Greeks; a place of some importance by 420 BC. Ruled by Philetaerus, 283–63; Eumenes I, 263–41; Attalus I, 241–197; Eumenes II, 197–59; Attalus II, 159–38; Attalus III, 138–33. Bequeathed to Rome, 133 BC.

Pergau Dam (Malaysia). Britain offered aid to build, 1988, on understanding of arms deal in return; but aid funded from Overseas Aid account. Press allegations of corruption caused *Malaysia to ban British trade for six months, 1994; Foreign Office criticized for conduct in High Court ruling, Nov. and foreign secretary accepted criticism, Dec.

Perlis, former Unfederated Malay State, became subject to Siam, 1821, and inde-pendent, 1841. By treaties of 1909 and 1930 the ruler of P. accepted British protection. Part of Malaysia since 1963.

Persia. *See* IRAN.

Persian authors, classical.

Avicenna (Abu Ibn Sina), 980–1036, philosopher and physician.
Firdausi, Abulkasim Mansur, *c.* 950–1020, poet.
Hafiz, Shamseddin Muhammed, *d. c.* 1390, poet.
Jalaluddin Rumi, 1207–73, poet.
Khayyám, Omar, *d.* 1123, poet.
Saadi, *d.* 1291, poet.
Zoroaster, *c.* 7thC BC, poet and prophet.

Perspex, clear plastic first produced, 1930. Also known as lucite.

Perth, Australia. Capital of W Australia, founded 1829. Grew rapidly after gold rush of 1893.

Perth, Scotland. Traditionally founded by Agricola, AD 70. Made a royal burgh by William the Lion, 1210; besieged and captured by Robert Bruce, 1311; captured by Edward III, 1335; retaken by Scots, 1339; after 1437, the year of the murder of James I, P. was no longer capital of Scotland; captured by Montrose, 1644; by Cromwell, 1651; Old Pretender proclaimed at, 16 Sept. 1715.

Peru, Republic of. Independence proclaimed, 28 July 1821. Declared independent of Colombia, 26 Jan. 1827. Constitution proclaimed, 21 Mar. 1828. United with Bolivia, 1835–9. Joined with Bolivia against Chile in the 'Nitrate War', 1879. Defeated and forced to cede the province of Tarapaca to Chile, 1883. Attempt to end series of alternating military juntas and elected presidents by new constitution, 1980. Dispute with Ecuador revived, 1981. P. increasingly burdened by hyperinflation and violence and terrorism, with serious drug problems. 'Shining Path' guerilla movement active from 1980s. President Fujimori suspended the constitution, 1992. In Jan. 1993 constitutional congress reaffirmed Fujimori as head of state. Referendum, Nov. 1993 approved new constitution proposed by Fujimori. Renewed border dispute with Ecuador, 1995.

Peru, Spanish Viceroyalty of. Conquered by Pizarro, 1531–4. Lima founded, 1534. Manco Inca's unsuccessful revolt, 1535. Pizarro killed, 1541. 'New Laws' according liberty to Indians, 1542. Execution of Inca Tupac Amaru, 1571. Viceroyalty of New Granada separated from P., 1739. Viceroyalty of the River Plate separated from P., 1776. Condorcanqui's rebellion, 1780.

Perugia, Italy. Originally *Perusia*. Captured by Pope Leo X from the Baglioni, 1520; occupied by French, 1797; by Austrians, 1849; united to kingdom of Italy, 1860.

Peter I Island, in the Antarctic Ocean sighted by the Russian Admiral von Bellingshausen, and named by him in 1821; Norwegians landed on, 1929. Under Norwegian sovereignty from 1931; incorporated into Norway as a dependency, 1933.

Peterborough, England. Originally called *Medehamstede*. In 655 Saxulf, a monk, founded a monastery there, and the name was altered subsequently to *Burgus sancti Petri*: cathedral founded, 656; destroyed by Danes, 870; the present building founded, 1117. Catherine of Aragon buried at, 1536. See founded by Henry VIII, 1541. Cathedral despoiled by Cromwell, 1643.

Peterloo Massacre at St Peter's Field, Manchester, 16 Aug. 1819.

Peter's Pence. A tax levied on the English by the popes, and probably dating from a mention in a letter of Canute's dated 1031, from Rome to the English clergy; in 1534 the tax was abolished by Henry VIII; still exists (1995) as a voluntary levy in the Roman Catholic Church in England and Wales.

Petition of Right. Presented to Charles I by Parliament, 28 May 1628; it asked for a reform of various constitutional abuses. Until the Crown Proceedings Act, 1947, a P. of R. was the only way in which the subject could obtain legal relief against the crown.

Petticoat Lane, name given to a famous London market which radiates from Middlesex St., London E1. Held on Sunday mornings, its origins in 18thC probably connected with beginnings of Jewish immigration to and settlement in E London.

Petrograd. *St Petersburg renamed, Aug. 1914 to remove any suggestion of German influence. Name changed to Leningrad, 1924; back to St Petersburg, 1991.

Petsamo. *See* PECHENGA.

Pharmaceutical Society. Founded, 1841; incorporated, 1843. Membership became automatic and compulsory for all qualified chemists and druggists, 1933. Constitution revised, 1953, and the coming into operation of the Pharmacy Act, 1953.

Phi Beta Kappa. Oldest American college fraternity, formed at William and Mary College, Williamsburg, Virginia, 1776. Women eligible since 1876.

Philadelphia, Pennsylvania, USA. Founded by William Penn, 1682. Was capital of Pennsylvania and of United (at first Federal) States, 1790–1800.

Philippine Islands. Discovered by Magellan, who was killed there, 1521. Occupied by Spaniards, who built Manila, 1564–71. Admiral Montojo's fleet destroyed at battle of Manila, 1 May 1898. Ceded to USA by Treaty of Paris, 10 Dec. 1898. Granted local autonomy, 1916. US Congress declares P.I. independent as from 1945 (but this in fact delayed by World War II), 24 Mar. 1934. Japanese attack and occupy Manila, 2 Jan. 1942. Siege of Bataan, 5 Jan.–1 May 1942. Surrender of Corregidor, 6 May 1942. Americans land in P.I., 20 Oct. 1944. Final liberation, 6 Aug. 1945. Republic of the Philippines came into being, 4 July 1946. Marcos's corrupt regime (in power since 1965) overturned, 1986: Mrs Cory Aquino (widow of opposition leader Benigno

Aquino, assassinated 1983) made president. New constitution, 1987. Aquino survived seven attempted coups, 1987–90. Fidel Ramos succeeded her as president, 1992. Increasing industrialization in 1990s; but severe social problems. Fundamentalist Islamic and Communist unrest in outlying islands. Typhoon kills over 500, Nov. 1995.

Phoenicia conquered by Egyptians c. 1600 BC. Became independent again c. 928 BC. Hegemony of Tyre lasted until 876 BC, when Phoenician cities became tributary to Assyria and thereafter to other great powers; but the colony of *Carthage was founded c. 700 BC.

Phoenix Park murders. Lord Frederick Cavendish, Chief Secretary for Ireland, and T. H. Burke murdered by terrorists in Dublin, 6 May 1882.

phosphorus. Discovered, 1669, by Dr Brandt, of Hamburg.

photography. In the 16thC the action of light on chloride of silver was known, but it was not until c. 1802 that Thomas Wedgwood (1771–1805) published his *Account of a Method of copying Painting upon Glass, and of making Profiles by the Agency of Light upon Nitrate of Silver*; in 1819 Sir John Herschel improved Wedgwood's method, and in 1824 Louis J. M. Daguerre produced photographic plates, afterwards known as daguerreotypes; the first *negative* was produced by Talbot in 1839; celluloid roll films introduced by George Eastman, 1889; telephotography invented by T. R. Dallmeyer (1859–1906) in 1891; direct colour P. by the Lumière Autochrome Plate, patented, 1904.

photogravure. Invented by Klietsch (1841–1926), 1895.

Physicians, Royal College of (London). Charter granted through exertions of Dr Linacre, Henry VIII's physician, in 1518.

piano(forte) or **hammerklavier** developed by modification of the harpsichord by Bartolomeo Cristofori (1655–1731).

Picture Post. *See* NEWSPAPERS.

Pietists began to hold meetings, 1670, of German Lutherans under Jakob Spener (1625–1705). Community at Herrnhut founded by Nikolaus Ludwig, Graf von Zinzendorf (1770–60).

Pilgrimage of Grace. The name given to the insurrection caused by the dissolution of the monasteries and the agrarian injustices resulting from enclosures; it originated in Yorkshire and Lincolnshire in 1536; the leaders were executed in Mar. 1537.

Pilgrim Fathers, *émigré* Puritans from Lincolnshire, left England, 1608, for Leyden, sailed from Delftshaven, July 1620; from Southampton, 5 Aug.; from Plymouth, Devon, 16 Sept.; landed at Plymouth, Massachusetts, 21 Dec. 1620.

Pilgrim Trust founded, 1930.

pillory, offences punishable by defined, 1266, in 'Statute of the P'. Limited to cases of perjury and subornation, 1816; last used, 1830; and finally abolished in England, 1837. Abolished in France, 1832; in state of Delaware, 1905; in rest of USA, 1839.

Piltdown man's skull partially dug up, 1912, and further skull fragments found, 1915. It was decided that P.M. must have lived some 50,000 years ago. Detailed modern technical examination 1953–4, resulted in the 'discovery' being exposed as a fraud, 1955.

ping-pong. *See* TABLE TENNIS.

'Pinkville', Massacre of, of Vietnamese civilians, by US troops on 16 Mar. 1968.

Pinyin. Chinese phonetic alphabet, used for places and people, increasingly since 1979, approved by the Chinese government, 1956.

Piper Alpha disaster, 6 Mar. 1987, when fire destroyed an oil-rig platform in the N Sea, and 173 men died. The tragedy led to a revision of safety regulations concerning oil rigs, culminating in the Offshore Safety Act, 1992.

piracy. Notorious pirates included the Vikings, 8th–11thC AD. During 16th and 17thC, English pirates attacked Spanish bullion ships, often with government connivance. In the period 1600–1800, P. was common in the Mediterranean due to decline in Turkish authority. In 1816, when the European powers forced the Barbary States to renounce P., over 3,000 Christian slaves captured by pirates were liberated in Algiers. In the 20thC P. has been rampant in the S China Sea, in the first eight months of 1992, more than 80 acts of P. occurred, chiefly in the Pacific.

Pisa, Italy (ancient *Julia Pisana* or *Julia Obiensequeus*). Independent republic by the 11thC; leaning tower built, 1173–1350; power crushed by Genoa in a naval battle off Melovia, 1284; university founded, 1343; subject to Florence, 1405; independent under French protection, 1494; retaken by Florence, 1509. Increased lean of tower of P. in 1980s led to tower being closed to public, 1990, and remedial work carried out from 1993 but (1995) with little success.

Pitcairn Island, S Pacific. Discovered by Carteret, 1767; occupied by mutineers from the *Bounty*, 1790, and not visited by anyone else from the outside world until 1808. Population removed to Tahiti, 1831, but returned to P.I., 1832. Removed to Norfolk Island, 1856, but most soon returned. Original P.I. Bible returned to P.I., 1949. Under Fijian jurisdiction from 1952–70, since when British Commissioner in New Zealand has been Governor of P.I. *See* BOUNTY MUTINY.

Pittsburgh, Pennsylvania, USA, began to grow *c.* 1785 on the site of Fort Pitt (formerly Fort Duquesne, which was built, 1754).

Plaid Cymru, Welsh nationalist party, founded 1925. Its object is an independent Wales. First MP elected, 1966. Three MPs in Parliament, elected April 1992.

plastics. First plastic (celluloid) discovered by Alexander Parkes, 1865. Bakelite produced from 1908; Perspex from 1930.

Considerable developments since 1950s.

platinum. Discovered, 1538, in Spain; first found in 1741 in England by Brownrigg.

player piano invented, 1842.

plebiscite, originally a law enacted by the Plebs (*see* ROME) in their own assembly, the *comitia tributa*, established 449 BC, as opposed to the Senate. Such laws came to be valid for the whole nation by the *Lex Hortensia*, 286 BC. For modern Ps. *see* CARINTHIA; GREECE, MODERN; ITALY; SAARLAND; SILESIA.

Plebs under King Servius Tullius (578–34 BC) acquired some constitutional rights and the obligation of military service. Office of Tribune of Plebs instituted, 493.

plimsoll line, compulsory load-line, obtained, 1876, by the efforts of Samuel P. (1824–98).

PLO. *See* PALESTINE LIBERATION ORGANIZATION

Plombières. The Pact of P. was signed by Napoleon III and Cavour, 1858. *See* FRANCE and ITALY.

pluralism, forbidden in England by Act of 1529 in certain cases. Also by the Acts of 1838, 1850 and 1885: but terms virtually abrogated by Pastoral Reorganization Measure, 1949 and Pastoral Measure, 1968.

plural voting in Great Britain completely abolished by Representation of the People Act, 1948.

Plymouth, England, was frequently attacked by the French during the 14th and 15thC. First English town to be incorporated by Act of Parliament, 12 Nov. 1439. Witnessed the departure of Drake on his expedition round the world, 1577; of the Elizabethan fleet in the encounter with the Spanish Armada, 1588; and of the *Mayflower*, 1620. Royal Dockyard, P., and adjoining township of P. Dock founded, 1690. P. Dock renamed Devonport, 1824, and dockyard retained name when administrative areas of P., Devonport and Stonehouse amalgamated, 1914. Severely damaged by German bombing, 1941. The South West Polytechnic in P. received name and status of Plymouth University, 1992.

Plymouth, Massachussetts, USA. This town was site of one of the earliest permanent settlements by Europeans in New England. An advance party arrived from shores of Cape Cod, 21 Dec. 1620 (now celebrated annually as Forefathers Day). First fortress commenced, 26 Dec. 1620. Pilgrim Hall Museum, 1824; Pilgrim Monument, 1889. Many early colonial buildings restored during 20thC. *Mayflower II (see under MAYFLOWER, THE)* is berthed in P.

Plymouth Brethren. Religious sect founded *c.* 1830 at P.; John Nelson Darby (1800–82) is generally regarded as the founder.

Poet Laureate. *See* LAUREATE, POET.

Pola. *See* ISTRIA.

Poland, Kingdom of. First appears as independent state, 10thC. Mieszko I (962–92) converted to Christianity. Boleslaw III divides P. between his sons, 1138, but country reunited by Casimir II (1177–94). Teutonic Knights settle in Kulm, 1208. Mongol invasion, 1241; P. again divided. P. reunited under Wladislaw Lokietek, 1306. Kingdom revived, 1320. First Diet, 1331. Casimir the Great, 1333–70. Personal union with Lithuania, 1386. Witowt and Jagiello (Wladislaw II) defeat Teutonic Knights at Tannenberg, 1410. Union of Horodlo, 1413. Prussia acquired from the Knights by Treaty of Thorn, 1466. War with Turkey, 1485 onwards. Escheat of Masovia and Warsaw, 1526. Religious dissensions, 1550–64. Decrees against heretics, 1564. Political union with Lithuania (Union of Lublin), 1 July 1569. Interregnum, 1572–3, following which monarchy becomes elective. Election of Henry of Valois, 1573. Reign of Stephen Báthory, 1575–86. University of Vilna founded, 1579. Sigismund III tried for treason by a Court of Inquisition, 1592. Creation of the Uniate Church, 1596. War with Russia,

1608–18. Defeat of Turks at battle of Czoczim, 1621. Cossack rebellions, 1640–9. Bogdan Khmelnitzki recognized as Hetman of the Cossacks at Zborow, 1649. Khmelnitzki defeated at battle of Beresteczko, 1651. War with Russia, 1651–64. Loss of Ukraine and Smolensk to Russia at Truce of Andrussov, 1667. John Sobieski rescues Vienna from the Turks, 1683. Peace of Karlowitz, 1699. Confederation of Radom, 1767. Russian influence attacked by Confederation of Bar, 1768. First Partition of P., 1772. Second Partition, 1793. Kosciuszko proclaims national insurrection, Mar. 1794. Russians suppress Kosciuszko, 1794. Third Partition, 1795–6. King Stanislaw abdicates, 1795, and *d.* in Russia, 1798. Napoleon creates Grand Duchy of Warsaw, 1806–15. Congress of Vienna creates a kingdom of P. under the Russian crown, usually called 'Congress P.', 1815. Suppressed, 1831, following the rising of 1830. Rising in Russian provinces of P., 1863.

Kings of Poland, 962–1795:
Mieszko I 962–92
Boleslaw I the Brave 992–1025
Mieszko II 1025–34
Casimir I the Restorer 1040–58
Boleslaw II the Bold 1058–79
Wladislaw Herman 1079–1102
Boleslaw III the Wry-Mouthed 1102–38

Partitional Period of Rival Duchies, 1138–1305:
Wladislaw 1138–59
Boleslaw the Curly 1146–73
Mieszko the Old 1173–77
Casimir II the Just 1177–94
Mieszko the Old (again) 1194–1202
Wladislaw Longshanks 1202–06
Leszek the White 1206–27
Henry the Bearded 1231–38
Henry the Pious 1238–41
Boleslaw the Modest 1243–79
Leszek the Black 1279–88
Henry Probus 1289–90
Przemyslaw 1295–96
Waclaw 1300–05

Wladislaw I the Dwarf (King of all Poland, 1319) 1306–33
Casimir III the Great 1333–70
Louis of Hungary 1370–82
Wladislaw II Jagiello 1386–1434
Wladislaw III of Varna 1434–44
Casimir IV 1447–92
John Albert 1492–1501
Alexander 1501–06
Sigismund I 1506–48
Sigismund II 1548–72
Henry of Valois Feb–June 1574
Stephen Báthory 1576–86
Sigismund III 1587–1632
Wladislaw IV 1632–48
John Casimir 1648–68
Michael Korybut 1669–73
John Sobieski 1674–96
Augustus II 1697–1704
Stanislaw Leszczynski 1704–09
Augustus II (again) 1709–33
Stanislaw Leszczynski (again) 1733–34
Augustus III 1734–63
Stanislaw Poniatowski (*d.* 1798) 1764–95

Poland, Republic of. The risings of 1830 and 1863 (*see* preceding article) had really been in support of a republic, which was at last proclaimed, Nov. 1918. Independence guaranteed under Versailles Treaty, 1919. Wars of aggrandizement with Lithuania, W Ukraine and Soviet Russia, Apr. 1919–Mar. 1921 (*see* RUSSIA). *Coup d'état*, with bloodshed, by Marshal Pilsudski, 12 May 1926. Took possession of zone in Czechoslovakia beyond the Olza, 2 Oct. 1938. In 1939 P. rejected German claims to Danzig (Gdansk) and the 'Polish Corridor'; Germans invaded P. at 5.30 a.m., 1 Sept.; Soviet Russian troops crossed into P. at 4 a.m., Brest-Litovsk fell, 17 Sept. and Polish government fled to Romania; Fourth Partition of P. between Germany and Russia announced from Moscow, 22 Sept.; all P. subjugated by Oct. 1, and new Polish government in exile established in France.
1940: Russians massacre 12,000 Polish officers at Katyn *c.* May. Polish government established in London, 21 June 1943: Warsaw ghetto rising, 18 Apr.–1 June. 1944:

Poles rise against Germans in Warsaw, 1 Aug. Russians refuse help, 20 Aug. Rising crushed, 2 Oct. Poles forced to concede Curzon Line to Russia at Moscow Conference, 9–19 Oct. 1945; Russians enter Warsaw, 11 Jan. Communist-dominated Government of National Unity established, 28 June, based on Soviet regime established at Lublin in 1944. Russo-Polish frontier treaty, 17 Aug. Large-scale deportations of Germans from new Polish territories in the W. By 1948 Communist control in P. complete. Persecution of the Catholic Church; Wyszinski, primate of P., imprisoned, 1953–6. Workers and students rioted in Poznan, June 1956; 'liberal' elements gained control of the Communist regime in P.; Gomulka became the real ruler of Poland, Oct. 1956. Gomulka replaced by more liberal Gierek, 1970, but following political and economic unrest Gierek resigned, 1980, and expelled from Communist party, 1981. Brief period of liberality followed by martial law, 1981, and banning of trade unions (*see* SOLIDARITY). Martial law lifted, 1983. Solidarity remained unrecognized until 1988, when massive industrial and political unrest led to a dismantling of the Communist regime. Solidarity was recognized and multiparty elections were held, 1989. Communist party disbanded, Jan. 1990. Nov. 1990: Germany and P. signed treaty confirming P.'s borders. Lech Walesa (Solidarity leader) elected president, Dec. 1990. Treaty agreeing withdrawal of all Russian forces from P., 1991. In elections, Sept. 1993, coalition led by former Communists gained power; subsequent disputes between government and President Walesa. Walesa loses presidential election Nov. 1995; former communist Kwasniewski succeeded.

Polish literature. The following are among the most celebrated P. authors:

Fredro, Count Aleksander, 1793–1876, dramatist.
Krasicki, Ignatius, 1735–1801, poet and critic.

Kraszewski, Jósef Ignacy, 1812–87, novelist, historian and critic.

Kraszinski, Zygmunt, 1812–49, dramatist.

Mickiewicz, Adam, 1798–1855, poet.

Niémcewicz, Julian Ursin, 1757–1841, poet, dramatist and novelist.

Orzeszkowa, Eliza, 1842–1910, novelist.

Przybyszewski, Stanislas, 1868–1927, novelist.

Reymont, Ladislas Stanislas, 1867–1925, novelist.

Sienkiewicz, Henryk, 1846–1916, novelist.

Slowacki, Juljusz, 1809–49, poet and dramatist.

Tetmajer, K., 1865–1939, poet.

Wyspianski, S., 1869–1907, poet and playwright.

Zapolska, Gabriela, 1860–1921, dramatist.

---

police. In Britain the modern police force derives from Sir Robert Peel's reorganization of the Metropolitan Police Force, 1829: extended throughout UK, 1856. Fundamental changes in P. structure suggested in Sheehy Report, 1993, but many of its ideas not accepted by government. More P. to be routinely armed in London from May 1994.

political uniforms. Prohibited in Britain by Public Order Act, 1936.

polio(myelitis), formerly known as infantile paralysis, acute viral disease. Serious epidemics in N America and western Europe in 1940s and 1950s. Since 1960s controlled by vaccines; WHO declared the Americas P.-free, 1994, but P. still a threat in many Third World countries.

polo. Possibly of Persian origin, used as a cavalry training game c. 600 BC. Introduced to India by Muslim invaders, 13thC. Modern P. said to have originated at *Manipur. First European P. club in India, 1859. First P. match in England at Hounslow in 1871. By 1914 popular in England, India and the USA; subsequently in Argentina and S Africa. Not played in Olympic Games since 1936. The Cowdray Park Gold Cup, replaced the Championship Cup (main UK trophy, 1876–1939) in 1958. In the USA the

Westchester Cup, 1886, was surpassed by the Cup of the Americas from 1928. World P. Championships also played.

poll tax. Levied in England, 1377, 1379 and 1380. The latter was a cause of Wat Tyler's rebellion in 1381; revived, 1513; finally abolished, 1689. Name P.T. was adopted for the highly unpopular *Community Charge by its opponents and by the general public, in 1990.

pollution. *See under* CONSERVATION; ECOLOGY, OIL POLLUTION; OZONE LAYER, etc.

Polotsk, independent principality from the 10thC, absorbed by Lithuania, 1307. Retaken by Ivan the Terrible, 1563. Became Polish, 1582; and finally Russian, 1772.

polygamy. *See* MORMONS and UTAH, where it was forbidden by the Edmunds-Tucker Act of 1887.

Pompeii, Italy. Entirely destroyed by eruption of Vesuvius, 24 Aug. AD 79; in 1763 systematic excavations were commenced. Further considerable excavations from 1861, especially since 1920s. Maiuri in charge of excavations at P., 1924–61. By 1980s, three-quarters of P. excavated.

Pondicherry, first settled by French, 1674. Transferred to India *de facto*, 1 Nov. 1954; cession formally recognized by treaty, 28 May 1956.

Pontefract Castle (England). Built c. 1069; Richard II murdered at, 10 Feb. 1400. Castle dismantled, 1649.

Poor Laws (Britain). Overseers were appointed for parishes, 1601; the word 'guardian' first used in this connection in a bill introduced into the Commons, 11 May 1735, by William Hay (1695–1755); first systematization of unions of parishes accomplished by Gilbert's Act, 1782, by which the relief of the poor was entrusted to visitors and guardians appointed by the justices. Poor Law Commission, 1832–3; Poor Law Board appointed, 1834; dissolved, 1846; Poor Law Amendment Act passed, 1834; amended, 1836, 1838, 1846, 1868; New Poor Law Act passed, 1889;

amended, 1890. Overseers abolished by Rating and Valuation Act, 1925, as from 1 Apr. 1927; boards of guardians by Local Government Act, 1929, as from 1 Apr., 1930: these Acts transferred care of poor to the local authorities. Whole system abolished, 1948, by the National Assistance Act.

Poor Persons' Legal Aid, provided by the Poor Prisoners' Defence Act, 1930, superseded by the Legal Aid and Advice Acts, 1949–72, consolidated by the Legal Aid Act, 1974 and amended by subsequent legislation.

Popish Plot. Imaginary Roman Catholic plot against Charles II, invented by Titus Oates. He gave evidence before Sir E. Berry Godfrey, 28 Sept. 1678. Godfrey was murdered, 14 Oct. 1678. Oates convicted of perjury, May 1685. Pardoned and pensioned, 1688. The P.P. resulted in a popular hysterical anti-Catholic reaction, and occasioned the last executions of Catholics to take place in England, 1679–80.

Popular Front, suggested by Comintern, 1935. (*See* FRANCE and SPAIN.) Cripps suggested a similar combination in England, which led to his temporary expulsion from the Labour Party, Apr. 1939.

Port Arthur. Massacre of Chinese by Japanese, 21 Nov. 1894; surrendered by Russian garrison to Japan, 1 Jan, 1905. P.A. was handed over to China in 1955.

Porteous riots. Caused by the hanging of a smuggler in Edinburgh, 1736; Capt. P. ordered the military to fire on the rioters and killed many; he was sentenced to death, but respited; the mob, however, seized and hanged him.

Portland, Maine, USA, first settled, 1632. Capital of Maine, 1820–31.

Portland Vase recovered from a tomb in Italy in the 17thC; bought by Sir William Hamilton from the Barbarini family, 1770, and sold by him to the Duchess of P., who lent it to the British Museum, 1810. Broken by a maniac, 1845, but repaired. Sold to the British Museum, 1946.

Port of London Authority was originally set up under the P. of L. Act, 1908 and is now constituted under the terms of the P. of L. Act, 1968 and the Harbour Revision Order, 1975.

Porto Bello, Panama, built on site of earlier settlement called Nombre de Dios (1502), which was sacked by Drake, 1572. P.B. was built, 1584, and sacked by Henry Morgan, 1668, and John Spring, 1680. Captured by the English for the last time, 1739.

Portobello Road, W London, site of market, on land of 18thC P. Farm (named after 1739 victory, see previous article). Began as solely fruit and vegetable market, 1822. First antique shop there, 1939. By 1961, 200 stalls, of which 35 dealt in antiques. By 1995, 2000 antique dealers there. Antique dealing takes place on Saturdays.

Port Royal des Champs (France). Convent founded, 1204, by Mahaut de Montmorency. It became a Bernardine house. The nuns moved to Paris, leaving P.R. to the lay community, 1626. Schools founded, 1643. The house supported the *Jansenists. Some nuns returned, 1648. Schools suppressed by royal order, 1660. Society reconstituted under the 'Peace of Clement IX', 1669. Angélique Arnauld (1624–84) abbess, 1678. On Louis XIV's suppression of Jansenism the nuns were dispersed and the buildings demolished, 1709.

Port Said, founded on a sand spit at the N end of the *Suez Canal, 1859 and named after Muhammed Sa'id (khedive 1854–63). Breakwater completed, 1868. By 1900, world's largest coal-bunkering station. Severely damaged by air attacks and Anglo-French landings (Oct. 31 and Nov. 5, 1956) during Suez crisis. Restored and extended since 1975.

Portsmouth, England. Granted its first charter, 1194. Importance as a naval dockyard dates from c. 1545. Became seat of a diocese, 1924, and a city, 1926. Scene of the assassination of the Duke of Buckingham, 1628, and the marriage of Charles II to Catherine of Braganza, 1662. P. polytechnic received name and status of P. University, 1992.

Portugal. Conquered by Carthaginians under Hamilcar Barca, 241–230 BC. By Romans, 193–178 BC. Lusitanian revolt, 154–150 BC. Rebellion of Viriatus, 146–139 BC; of Sertorius, 80–72 BC. First mention of Christianity, AD 250. Invasion of Goths, Alans and Vandals, 409–10. Swabian kingdom established in N P., 410–29. Oporto sacked by Visigoths, 456. Swabian kingdom incorporated in Visigothic kingdom by Leovigild, 585. Visigoths converted to Christianity, 586–610. Collapse of Visigothic kingdom in the Moorish invasion, 710–12. Moors conquer P., 712–16. Ommayad rule established, 755. Christian reconquest begun *c.* 747. Rise of the Cordoban monarchy, 796–812. Battle of Simancas, 939. P. overrun by Almanzor, 987–8. Christian conquest of Coimbra, 1064. Portuguese independence from Leon established at, by Alfonso Henrique at battle of São Mamede, 1128. He wins great victory over Moors at Ovrique, and takes title of king, 1139. Anglo-Portuguese conquest of Lisbon, 1147. *Almohade invasion, 1191. Quarrel with the Church and deposition of Sancho II, 1248. Moors finally driven out, 1249. Treaty of Badajoz with Castile, 1267. Treaty of Alcañices, 1297. Victory with Castilians over the Moors at the battle of the Salado, 1340. Ines de Castro, mistress of Pedro, the heir to the throne, murdered by Coelho, 7 Jan. 1355. Civil war ensues, 1355–7. Castilian War, 1369. Burgundian dynasty ends, 1383. John of Avis made regent, Nov. 1383. Proclaimed king, 6 Apr. 1385. Castilians decisively defeated at battle of Aljubarrota, 14 Aug. 1385. Anglo-Portuguese Alliance at Treaty of Windsor, 9 May 1386. Peace with Castile, Oct. 1411. Capture of Ceuta, 1415. Final peace with Castile at Treaty of Medina del Campo, 1431. Trading stations established on African coast, 1448–9. Tangier captured, 1471. Bartholomew Dias rounds the Cape of Good Hope, 1488. Treaty of Tordesilhas fixes Spanish and Portuguese spheres of discovery, 7 June, 1494. Legal reforms of Manoel I, 1498–21.

Vasco da Gama reaches India, 1498. Cabral discovers Brazil, 22 Apr. 1500. Trading empire established in Indian Ocean, 1501–08. Goa made capital of Portuguese India by Albuquerque, 1510. Inquisition introduced, 1536. Loss of most of the N African possessions at battle of Alcazar-Kebir, 1578. End of the house of Avis, 28 Jan. 1580. P. seized by Philip II of Spain, June 1580. Dutch and British reduce most of the Far Eastern possessions, 1595–1620. Independence re-established by John IV, 1 Dec. 1640. Anglo-Portuguese Treaty, 1654. Catherine of Braganza marries Charles II of England, and Bombay becomes British, 25 Apr. 1662. Castelo Melhors palace revolution, 1662. The *Methuen Treaty, 1703. P. enters the War of *Spanish Succession, 1703. Absolute government established, 1706. Lisbon earthquake, 1 Nov. 1755. War with Spain, Feb.–June 1801. French invasion, 1807; royal family fled to Brazil. Sir Arthur Wellesley arrived at Oporto, July 1808 (*see* PENINSULAR WAR). Masséna defeated by British and Portuguese, at Busaco, 27 Sept. 1810. Wellington at Torres Vedras, Oct. 1810. Retreat of Masséna, defeated at Fuentes de Oñoro, 5 May 1811. Popular rising began at Oporto, 29 Aug. 1820. Inquisition abolished. Brazil independent, 1822. Dom Miguel, absolutist regent, proclaimed king, 4 July 1828. Capitulation of Miguel at Evora, 26 May 1834. Constitution of 1822 revived after Sept. *coup d'état*, 1836. Further revolutions, 1846 and 1851. Assassination of Carlos I, 1 Feb. 1908; revolution, 1910; de Arriaga first president of republic, 1911. P. joins World War I on Allied side, 1916. Salazar becomes prime minister with dictatorial powers, 1932. P. neutral during World War II but in 1943 signed agreement with Allies for use of Azores against Germans. Joined NATO, 1949. Discontent with Salazar regime and colonial unrest increased from 1960s. In 1961 India absorbed *Goa. Gaetano replaced Salazar, 1968. Military coup, 1974, resulted in brief neo-Communist regime in P. and independence for P.'s former colonies. Left-wing policies largely reversed by 1979. Constitutional reforms, 1982 and 1989, and election of first democratic president, Soares, 1986; re-elected 1991. P. joined the EEC on 1 Jan. 1986. Considerable privatization and economic growth since mid-80s; but devaluation of escudo in 1990s and increased unemployment. 20,000-year-old Stone Age painting discovered in NE P., Nov. 1994; threatened to be submerged by new dam, 1995 but dam work suspended Nov. 1995. Socialist victory in Oct. 1995 elections. (See also ANGOLA; MOZAMBIQUE; GOA.

Kings of Portugal, 1139–1910:
Burgundian Dynasty:
Alfonso I 1139–85
Sancho I 1185–1211
Alfonso II the Fat 1211–23
Sancho II 1223–48
Alfonso III 1248–79
Diniz 1279–1325
Alfonso IV 1325–57
Pedro I the Cruel 1357–67
Ferdinand 1367–83
Civil War
Aviz Dynasty:
John I 1385–1433
Edward 1433–38
Alfonso V the African 1438–81
John II 1481–95
Manoel I 1495–1521
John III 1521–57
Sebastian 1557–78
Henry 1578–80
Under Spanish Suzerainty *1581–1640
Braganza Dynasty:
John IV 1640–56
Alfonso VI 1656–83
Pedro II 1683–1706
John V 1706–50
Joseph 1750–77
Pedro III 1777–86
Maria I the Mad 1777–1816
John VI 1816–26
Pedro IV 1826
Maria II 1826–28
Miguel 1828–34
Maria II (again) 1834–53
Pedro V 1853–61
Luiz I 1861–89

Carlos I 1889–1908
Manoel II (*d.* in exile in England, 1932) 1908–10
*See Spanish kings, Philip II, III, and IV.

Presidents of the Republic:
Manoel de Arriaga 1911–15
Teofilo Braga May–Oct. 1915
Bernardino Machado 1915–17
Sidonio Paez 1917–18
Admiral de Canto e Castro 1918–19
Antonio de Almeida 1919–23
Manuel Gomes 1923–25
Bernardino Machado 1925–26
Marshal Antonio Carmona 1926–51
Marshal Francisco Higino Craveiro Lopez 1951–58
Rear-Admiral Americo de Deus Rodrigues Tomas 1958–74
General Antonio de Spinola 1974
General Antonio Ramalho Eanes 1974–86
Mario Soares 1986–

Portuguese literature. Prominent Portuguese authors include:

Alcoforado, Marianna, 1640–1723, author of *Letters of a Portuguese Nun.*
Barros, João de, 1496 ?–1570, historian.
Bocage, Manuel Maria Barbosa de, 1765–1805, poet.
Braga, Joaquim Theophilo, 1843–1924, historian and poet.
Camoëns, Luis de, 1524–80, poet.
Castello Branco, Camillo de, Viscount, 1825–90, novelist and dramatist.
Castilho, Antonio Feliciano de, Viscount, 1800–75, poet.
Castro, Lugenio de, 1869–1944, poet.
Deus, João de, 1830–96, poet.
Ferreira, Antonio, 1528–69, poet and dramatist.
Garrett, João Baptista da Silva Leitão de Almeida, Viscount, 1799–1854, poet, dramatist, and novelist.
Goes, Damião de, 1502–74, historian.
Herculano de Carvalho e Araujo, Alexandre, 1810–79, historian and poet.
Lopez, Fernão, 1380 ?–1460 ?, chronicler.

Macedo, José Agostinho de, 1761–1831, poet.

Nascimento, Francisco Manoel de, 1734–1819, poet.

Oliveira Martins, Joaquim Pedro de, 1845–94, historian.

Pascoais, Teixeira de, 1877–1952, poet.

Pinto, Fernão Mendes, 1509–83, adventurer.

Queiroz, José Maria Eça de, 1843–1900, novelist.

Resende, Garcia de, 1470–1536, poet.

Sá de Miranda, Francisco de, 1485 ?–1558, poet and dramatist.

Vicente, Gil, 1465 ?–1536 ?, dramatist.

---

positive rays discovered, 1886, by Goldstein.

Post Office (Britain). Crown service to carry government papers existed from *c.* 1515. The first English postmaster of whom there is any account is Sir Brian Tuke, mentioned *c.* 1533; in 1619 Matthew de Quester was appointed 'Postmaster-General of England for foreign parts'; new postal system organized by the Common Council of London, 1649; rates of postage and rights and duties of postmasters settled by Parliament, 1657. Act for erecting and establishing a P.O. passed, 1660. *Penny Post* instituted in London and suburbs by William Dockwra, 1680; annexed to the crown revenues department, 1690; new Penny Postage Law introduced through exertions of Rowland Hill, 1839; first issue of adhesive stamps, 6 May, 1840. Pillar boxes first erected (at St Helier, Jersey), 1852. London's first six pillar-boxes (green), 1855. The red cylindrical pattern generally adopted, 1876. Sunday letter deliveries ended, 1921. Telegraph system under P.O. control, 1870; telephones, 1880, Girobank, 1968. Biggest robbery suffered by the P.O. took place in a hold-up of the Glasgow–London mail train in Buckinghamshire, Aug. 1963, when over £2,500,000 was stolen. Two-tier letter system introduced, 1968. P.O. reorganized as a public corporation, under the P.O. Act, 1969 (when office of Postmaster-General

abolished). Telecommunications Act, 1981, separated telecommunications from the P.O. and established *British Telecom. Girobank was removed from P.O. control and privatized, 1990. Sunday letter collections (abandoned in 1970s) restarted, 1990. Government abandoned plans to privatize P.O., Nov. 1994.

Post Office Savings Bank. *See* NATIONAL SAVINGS BANK.

potassium. First isolated by Davy in 1807.

potato introduced into Britain from America by Sir Walter Raleigh in 16thC. Crop failure caused famine in Ireland, 1846–9.

Potsdam Agreement, result of conference between Churchill, Attlee, Truman and Stalin at P., 16 July–1 Aug. 1945.

Poynings' Law. Called after Sir Edward P. (1459–1521), lord-deputy of Ireland; passed, 13 Sept. 1494; this law made the Irish legislature subordinate to and completely dependent on the English Privy Council. Repealed, Apr. 1782.

Powys, Welsh administrative county established under the Local Government Act of 1972. Plans to abolish, 1995.

Poznan (Polish) or **Posen** (German). Seat of an episcopal see from 968, which became fused with that of Gniezno in the 12thC. Ceded to Prussia in first and second partitions of 1772 and 1793 (*see* POLAND). Assigned to Poland by Treaty of Versailles, 1919. Annexed by Germany, Sept. 1939. Reassigned to Poland, 1945.

Prado, Museo del (Madrid), art gallery, begun, 1785, under Charles III, completed 1819 under Ferdinand VII. Contains over 3,000 works of art (1994).

Praemunire, Statutes of, passed, 1353 and 1392, for the purpose of restricting papal authority in England.

Praetorian Guard, regular but extralegionary cohorts, nine of which were raised by Augustus, 2 BC. Their barracks NE of the Palatine at Rome were laid out in the reign of Tiberius (AD 14–37). The corps was disbanded by Constantine, 312.

Pragmatic Sanctions.
1. 1385. Against papal interference in the French Church.
2. Of Bourges, 1438, imposed limits on papal authority in France; temporarily annulled, 1461.
3. 1713. Securing the succession of Maria Theresa to the Austrian lands. Ratified by Prussia, 1728. By majority of other German states, 1735. Prussia's disregard of the P.S. caused the War of the *Austrian Succession.
4. Of Naples, 1759, when Charles II of Spain made Naples over to his third son.

Prague, Czechoslovakia. Founded c. 600. Became a bishopric, 973. Rebuilt by Charles IV, 1348 (when Charles University founded). St Vitus Cathedral built from 1344: completed, 1929. Charles Bridge, 1357, reconstructed, 1970. Captured by Swedes, 1648. By French, 1741. By Prussians, 1744. Treaty of P. ended Austro-Prussian War, 23 Aug. 1866. Germans seized P., 15 Mar. 1939. Liberated by the Russians, 10 May 1945. The 'Prague Spring' of 1968 crushed by Russian troops, Aug. 1968. Centre of the democratic movements which led to bloodless revolution of 1989.

Prayer, Book of Common. First P.B. of Edward VI, 1549; second P.B. of Edward VI, 1552. Revised, 1559; suppressed, 1645; restored, 1660; and revised, 1662. A further revision, completed 1927, was placed before Parliament, passed by the Lords, but rejected by the Commons. Several revisions (known as 'Series 2, 3,' etc.) since 1960s.

Preference, Imperial. I.P. on articles produced in and consigned from the British Empire instituted by Finance Act, 1919; extended by Finance Acts, 1925 and 1926. Dismantled after 1945. *See also* TARIFFS

premium bonds. Form of government savings lottery introduced in the Budget of 1956. Prize values greatly increased from 1994.

Premonstratensians. Order founded by St Norbert c. 1120, and following the Augustinian Rule.

Pre-Raphaelite school of painting. Founded c. 1850 by John Everett Millais (1829–96), William Hunt (1827–1910), Dante Gabriel Rossetti (1828–82).

President of the Council, Lord. Became a political office, 1680.

Press Association, The. Founded, 1868. *See also* REUTERS NEWS.

Press Complaints Commission, replaced the *Press Council, Jan. 1991, and intended to have more authority than the latter. In May 1993, it was proposed the P.C.C. should have a lay majority, with an independent chairman.

Press Council, established 1953 on the recommendation of the Royal Commission on the Press, 1947–9. Its constitution was radically amended, 1963 and in 1991 it was replaced by the *Press Complaints Commission.

Pretoria, S Africa. Founded, 1855, by Marthinus Wessels Pretorius (1819–1901). Became capital of *Transvaal, 1860. Surrendered to Lord Roberts, 1900. Became administrative capital of S Africa, 1909. University founded, 1930.

Prevention of Terrorism Act, 1974, was intended to be a temporary measure, but since then it has been renewed annually.

Prices and Incomes, National Board of, established, 1965, and merged with the Monopolies Commission, 1969.

Pride's Purge. The name given to the expulsion and arrest of certain members of Parliament who opposed the trial of Charles I. Col. Pride, at the head of two parliamentary regiments, on 6 Dec. 1648, effected the 'purge'.

Prime Minister. This office existed in England, *de facto*, from 1710, but its existence was first officially recognized and its holder given a definite precedence,

1905. A deputy P.M. was officially named for the first time, 13 June 1962.

Prime Ministers (British), (since the beginning of the modern cabinet system).

George I:
Sir Robert Walpole, 1721.
George II:
Sir Robert Walpole, 1727.
John Carteret, Lord Carteret, Feb. 1742.
Hon. Henry Pelham, Nov. 1743.
William Pulteney, Earl of Bath, 10–12 Feb. 1746.
Hon. Henry Pelham, Feb. 1746.
Thomas Pelham Holles, Duke of Newcastle, Apr. 1754.
William Pitt, Nov. 1756.
Thomas Pelham Holles, Duke of Newcastle and William Pitt as Secretary of State, known as the Coalition Ministry, 19 June 1757.
George III:
Thomas Pelham Holles, Duke of Newcastle, 1760.
Earl of Bute, May 1762.
George Grenville, Apr. 1763.
Marquess of Rockingham, July 1765.
William Pitt, Earl of Chatham, Aug. 1766.
Duke of Grafton, Dec. 1767.
Frederick, Lord North, Jan. 1770.
Marquess of Rockingham, Mar. 1782.
Earl of Shelburne, July 1782.
Duke of Portland, Lord North, and Charles James Fox, known as Coalition Ministry, Apr. 1783.
William Pitt, the Younger, Dec. 1783.
Henry Addington, Mar. 1801.
William Pitt, May 1804.
Lord Grenville ('All the Talents' Ministry), Feb. 1806.
Duke of Portland, Mar. 1807.
Spencer Perceval, Oct. 1809.
Earl of Liverpool, June, 1812.
George IV:
Earl of Liverpool, Jan. 1820.
George Canning, Apr. 1827.
Visc. Goderich, Sept. 1827.
Duke of Wellington, Jan. 1828.
William IV:
Earl Grey, Nov. 1830.

Visc. Melbourne, July 1834.
Provisional government during absence of Sir Robert Peel, Nov. 1834.
Sir Robert Peel, Dec. 1834.
Visc. Melbourne, Apr. 1835.
Victoria:
Visc. Melbourne, June 1837.
Sir Robert Peel, Sept. 1841.
Lord John Russell, July 1846.
Earl of Derby, Feb. 1852.
Earl of Aberdeen, Dec. 1852.
Visc. Palmerston, Feb. 1855.
Earl of Derby, Feb. 1858.
Visc. Palmerston, June 1859.
Lord John Russell, Oct. 1865.
Earl of Derby, June 1866.
Benjamin Disraeli, Feb. 1868.
William Ewart Gladstone, Dec. 1868.
Benjamin Disraeli, Earl of Beaconsfield, Feb. 1874.
William Ewart Gladstone, Apr. 1880.
Marquess of Salisbury, June 1885.
William Ewart Gladstone, Feb. 1886.
Marquess of Salisbury, July 1886.
William Ewart Gladstone, Aug. 1892. (Gladstone resigned Mar. 1894), succeeded by Earl of Rosebery.
Marquess of Salisbury, June 1895.
Edward VII:
Arthur James Balfour, 12 July 1902.
Sir Henry Campbell-Bannerman, 5 Dec. 1905.
Herbert Henry Asquith, 16 Apr. 1908.
George V:
Herbert Henry Asquith, Dec. 1910.
David Lloyd George, 7 Dec. 1916.
Andrew Bonar Law, 23 Oct. 1922.
Stanley Baldwin, 22 May 1923.
James Ramsay MacDonald, 22 Jan. 1924.
Stanley Baldwin, 4 Nov. 1924.
James Ramsay MacDonald, 8 June 1929.
James Ramsay MacDonald, 24 Aug. 1931.
Stanley Baldwin, 6 June 1935.
Edward VIII:
Stanley Baldwin, 22 Jan. 1936.
George VI:
Stanley Baldwin, 4 Dec. 1936.
Arthur Neville Chamberlain, 28 May 1937.
Winston Spencer Churchill (Coalition), 10 May 1940.
Winston Spencer Churchill (without Labour Party), 26 May 1945.

Clement Richard Attlee, 27 July 1945.
Clement Richard Attlee, 23 Feb. 1950.
Winston Spencer Churchill, 25 Oct. 1951.
Elizabeth II:
Winston Spencer Churchill, 8 Feb. 1952.
Anthony Eden, 7 Apr. 1955.
Harold Macmillan, 13 Jan. 1957.
Sir Alec Douglas-Home (formerly 14th Earl of Home), 19 Oct. 1963.
Harold Wilson, 16 Oct. 1964.
Harold Wilson, 31 March 1966.
Edward Heath, 19 June 1970.
Harold Wilson, 12 Mar. 1974.
James Callaghan, 5 Apr. 1976.
Margaret Thatcher, 4 May 1979.
Margaret Thatcher, 9 June 1983.
Margaret Thatcher, 11 June 1987.
John Major, 28 Nov. 1990.
John Major, 9 Apr. 1992.

Prime Ministers' Meetings, 1937, superseded the *Imperial Conference. Since 1944 these took place at increasingly irregular intervals and were later replaced by the bi-annual *Commonwealth Conferences.

Primitive Methodism. See METHODISTS.

Primrose League. Conservative association founded, 1883, in memory of Disraeli.

Prince Edward Island, Canada. Discovered by Cabot, 1497; possessed by French, 1603; captured by Great Britain from French, 1758; admitted to Dominion of Canada, 1873.

Prince William Sound, Alaska, USA, where the oil tanker *Exxon Valdez* ran aground, March 1989, causing extensive oil pollution and consequent environmental damage. See OIL POLLUTION.

Princess Royal, courtesy title awarded by the British sovereign to his or her eldest daughter. It was first held by a daughter of Charles I, 1640. Princess Anne, daughter of Elizabeth II, created P.R. in June 1987, she being the seventh to hold the title. The title was also used by the Prussian royal family up to 1918.

Princeton, New Jersey, USA. University founded, 1746. Moved from Elizabethtown to P., 1756. Women admitted, 1969.

printing, origins of. Practised by the Chinese in very early times (*see* ENGRAVING); the origin of the European system seems to be very doubtful, though recent evidence points not to Gutenberg (1397–1468), once accepted as the first printer from movable type, but to Laurens Coster of Haarlem, who printed from wood blocks in 1440. Gutenberg, however, appears to have been the first European to make a practical business of P. from movable types.

privateering. See LETTERS OF MARQUE.

privatization, practice of selling state undertakings into private hands. Followed extensively in UK since 1979; in Europe since 1990s, notably in the former Communist bloc. See NATIONALIZATION.

Privy Council (England). By an Act passed, May 1612, P. Councillors took precedence after Knights of the Garter; dissolved on the demise of the crown; in 1679 the council was remodelled and the P. Councillors by this Act held office for six months after the sovereign's death. (*See* COUNCIL.) The whole P.C. has not met except at an accession since 1839, when Queen Victoria's impending marriage was declared in Council.

prize money originated in England before 1243. Paid for the last time in the Royal Navy, 1945.

probate court established under the Court of Probate Act, 1857, and merged with the Supreme Court, 1875.

probation for first offenders first introduced in Massachusetts, 1878. Became legally recognized in Britain under the Probation of Offenders Act, 1907; many modifications since. 1991 Criminal Justice Act established P. as a sentence in its own right.

Production, Ministry of, set up, 1942. Merged with *Board of Trade, 1945.

profiteering. Act to check excessive

profits passed, Aug. 1919. Attempts to stop P. during World War II by Prices of Goods Act, 1939, and the Goods and Services (Price Control) Act, 1941.

Profits Tax. First introduced as a temporary tax, and called the National Defence Contribution, by Neville Chamberlain, 1937. Named P.T., 1946. Repealed, 1958.

Prohibition. Scottish Temperance Act, 1920, resulted in some local P. P. introduced in Sweden, 1922, and in modified form in Norway, 1922. Abolished in Finland, 1932; in Norway, 1946; in Sweden, 1955. P. in America lasted from 1919 until 1933; some states retained local P. until 1966. P. in theory virtually total in India from 1950 onwards but not in practice: but in force in such Muslim countries as Saudi Arabia, Libya, Pakistan and Iran. *See* USA, CONSTITUTION OF.

Promenade concerts, first given in Queen's Hall, 10 Aug. 1895, and continued there until the hall's destruction by bombing, 1941. Since then held in the Albert Hall.

Propaganda or *De Propaganda Fide.* An institution of the Roman Catholic Church at Rome, founded for the propagation of the Roman Catholic faith originally by Pope Gregory XIII (1572–84), but more fully developed by Gregory XV, 1622.

Propaganda, Ministry of. Established in Germany under Goebbels, 1936–45.

Propagation of the Gospel, Society for, founded by royal charter, 1701.

proportional representation. Principle set out by C. C. G. Andrae of Denmark, and Thomas Hare and John Stuart Mill of Britain in the mid-19thC. After World War I, it was adopted in several European states. In Britain, principle advocated by Liberals (later Liberal Democrats) from 1950s and by some Labour politicians from 1990s. Italian P.R. system increasingly discredited by political scandals from 1980s and in 1993 after April referendum electoral reforms proposed that would abolish most of the P.R. element. However, in New Zealand a referendum, Nov. 1993, voted in favour of change to P.R. system of elections in future.

protectorates, British (many of which have since had a change of name and all of status). Basutoland,* 1868; Bechuanaland,* 1895; Brunei, 1888; Johore, 1914; Malay States, Federated (Perak, Selangor, Pahang, Negri Sembilan), 1874; Malay States, Unfederated (Kedan, Perlis, Kelantan, Trengganu), 1909; N Borneo, 1881; Nyasaland, 1891 (called British Central Africa until 1907); Solomon Islands, 1893; Somaliland, 1884; Swaziland, 1890; Tonga Island, 1899; Uganda, 1894; Zanzibar, 1890.
*[Nominally not P., but High Commission Territories.]

Protestant Episcopal Church, now (1995) more commonly known as the **Episcopal Church of the USA. (ECUSA).** American form of Anglicanism, introduced into Virginia, 1607. Movement for union of all its American branches began *c.* 1784. Its first bishop (of New York) consecrated in London, 1786.

Protestantism. *See* REFORMATION.

Provençal and Catalan Literature. Prominent writers include

Aldobrandini of Florence, Provençal (Italian), 13thC.
Anellier, Guillaume, Provençal, *fl. c.* 1280.
Aribau, Carlos, Catalan, 1798–1862.
Bernard of Ventadour, Provençal, mid-12thC.
Bertan de Born, Provençal, *c.* 1170–1200.
Brueys, Claude, Provençal, 1570–1650.
Brunetto Latini, Provençal (Italian), 13thC.
Carner, José, Catalan, *b.* 1554.
Cortete, Fançois de, Provençal, 1571–1655.
Costa y Llebera, Miguel, Catalan, 1854–1922.
Daniel, Arnaut, Provençal, late 12thC.
Favre, Abbé, Provençal, 1729–83.
Folquet of Marseilles, Provençal, *c.* 1150–1231.
Gaillard, Augor, Provençal, 1530–95.
Ganas, Gaston Pey de, Provençal, *fl.* 1565.

Ganulin, Faidit, Provençal, late 12thC.
Girant of Borneil, Provençal, 12thC.
Goudelin, Pierre, Provençal, 1579–1649.
Guimerá, Angel, Catalan, 1849–1924.
Iglesias, Ignacio, Catalan, 1871–1928.
Lull, Ramon, Catalan, c. 1235–1315.
Maragall, Juan, Catalan, 1860–1911.
Marcubru, Provençal, fl. 1140.
March, Ausias, Catalan, 1379–1459.
Metge, Bernat, Catalan, ? 1350–after 1410.
Mila y Fontanals, Manuel, Catalan, 1818–84.
Mistral, Frédéric, Provençal, 1830–1914.
Mutaner, Ramon, Catalan, 1265–1336.
Peter of Auvergne, Provençal, 12thC.
Rigaud, Auguste, Provençal, 1760–1835.
San Jordi, Jordi de, Catalan, end 14thC–before 1430.
Satoly, Nicholas, Provençal, 1614–75.
Verdagner, Mosén Jacinto, Catalan, 1845–1902.
Vidal de Besalù, Raimon, Provençal, mid-early 12th–13thC.
Vidal of Toulouse, Peire, late 12thC.
William IX, Count of Poitiers, Provençal, 11thC.

Provisors, Statue of, passed 1350, to prevent papal pretensions to the disposition of ecclesiastical benefices in England.

Prussia. See BRANDENBURG. Albert of Hohenzollern, Grand Master of the Teutonic Knights, converts P. into a secular duchy, 1525. Treaties of mutual succession with Silesia, 1537. Pomerania, 1571. Arrangement of Gera, 1599. P. comes under Brandenburg as a Polish fief, 1618. Poland renounces suzerainty at Treaty of Wehlau, 1657. Defeat of Swedes at Fehrbellin, 1675. Frederick of Brandenburg crowned king of P., 18 Jan. 1701. By Treaty of Stockholm with Sweden acquires W Pomerania, 1720. P. guarantees *Pragmatic Sanction, 1728. Frederick the Great invades Silesia, 1740. Obtains Silesia by Treaty of Berlin, 1742. Second Silesian War, 1744–6. Treaty of Aix-la-Chapelle, 1748. Frederick invades Saxony and starts the Seven Years War, 1756–63. Austria finally recognizes Prussian acquisition of Silesia at Treaty of Hubertusburg, 1763. First Partition of Poland, 1772. Second Partition of Poland, 1793. Third Partition of Poland, 1795. Joins Northern Confederacy against Britain, 1800. Occupies Hanover, 1801. Defeated by Napoleon at Jena and Auerstädt, 1806. Congress of Vienna gave P. large additions in Rhineland and Saxony, 1815. Organizes the *Zollverein 1818 onwards.
War with Denmark, 1848. Convention of Olmütz, 1850. Austro-Prussian attack on Denmark, 1864. Austro-Prussian War, 16 June–26 July 1866. Franco-Prussian War, 19 July 1870. King William I proclaimed German Emperor at Versailles, 18 Jan. 1871. (See GERMANY.) Proclaimed a republic, 9 Nov. 1918. Nazis take over by force, 20 July 1932. P. liquidated by Allied Control Council, Feb. 1946. Of the territory called P. at its greatest extent, E P. was joined to Russia in 1945, W P. (Pomerelia) to Poland at the same date.

Kings of Prussia:
Frederick I 1701–13
Frederick William I 1713–40
Frederick II 1740–86
Frederick William II 1786–97
Frederick William III 1797–1840
Frederick William IV 1840–61
William I (became German Emperor, 1871) 1861–88

Public Debt. See NATIONAL DEBT.

Public Health Acts in England and Wales passed 1848, 1875, 1936, 1961 and 1984.

Public Lending Right Act, giving authors revenue from the borrowing of their books in libraries, in operation from Sept. 1982.

Public Order Act, banning political uniforms, etc., passed, 1936. Fell into desuetude but subsequently revived and scope widened by a section of the Race Relations Act, 1976, and by the P.O.A. of 1986.

Public Prosecutor. Office separated from that of Solicitor to the Treasury, 1908, and known as the **Director of Public Prosecutions.**

Public Record Office. *See* RECORD OFFICE, PUBLIC.

public schools (British). First P.S. said to have been St Peter's, York, founded by Alcuin in 627. Several subsequently wealthy foundations, e.g. *Eton and *Harrow began as charitable schools for poor scholars.

Public Trustee office opened, 1908, under Official Trustee Act, 1906.

Puerto Rico, formerly **Porto Rico,** discovered by Columbus, 1493; explored by Ponce de León, 1508. Ceded to USA by Spain, 1898. Constitution established by 'Jones Act', 1917; amended, 1947. Governor elected quadrennially, from 1948. Considerable emigration to US mainland since 1930. 'Commonwealth status' since 1952.

Pulitzer Prizes. US series of annual awards for outstanding journalism and literature, established under the will of Joseph Pulitzer (1847–1911), newspaper proprietor, and administered by the trustees of Columbia University. Eight prizes for journalism and five for literature are awarded each year; a music prize was added from 1943. The 1993 P.P. for fiction was awarded to Robert Olen Butler for *A Good Scent from a Strange Mountain* (short stories) and in 1994 to Edward Albee (his third P.P. award).

Pullman coaches. Invented by G. M. P. of New York (1831–97). First car built, 1849.

Punch. See NEWSPAPERS.

Punic Wars: between Carthage and Rome. First: 264–41 BC. Second: 218–01 BC. Third: 149–46 BC. All resulted ultimately in the defeat of Carthage: after the third, Carthage was utterly destroyed. *See* CARTHAGE.

Punjab. Invaded by Alexander the Great, 326 BC. Devastated by Genghiz Khan, AD 1221. Ruled by Mogul emperors, 1556–1707. Sikh kingdom under Ranjit Singh, 1799–1820. *See* SIKHS. War against the British, 1845 and 1848–9, who annexed P., 1849. Severe plagues between 1896 and 1910. Partitioned between India, and Pakistan, 14 Aug. 1947, into E and W P. Serious unrest among Sikh separatists in 1980s led to Indian government sending the army into the Golden Temple at Amritsar, 1984, and subsequent assassination of Mrs Gandhi by Sikhs. Further unrest in 1990s.

Purchase Tax imposed first by the Finance Act, 1940. Came into effect, 21 Oct. 1940. Replaced by *Value Added Tax, 1973.

Puritans. Name first derisively given to Anglicans who, between 1564 and 1569, wished to purge the established ecclesiastical system from so-called popish abuses. Earliest P. thus a party within the established Church. In the later 17thC the term came to be applied to Dissenters outside the Church of England, e.g. Congregationalists, Baptists, Quakers, etc.

Purple Heart, initiated by George Washington in 1782, and the USA's oldest military decoration. It appears to have been awarded only three times during the US War of Independence, and then virtually lapsed. Revived, 22 Feb. 1932, on 150th anniversary of its inception: awarded many times since, for valour in World War II, Korea, Vietnam, the Gulf War, etc.

Pythian Games, originally held every nine, later every four, years. Regulated by Amphictyonic Council after 586 BC. Coincided with the third year of each Olympiad (*see under* OLYMPIA). Laurel wreath first awarded to victor, 582.

Pyx, Trial of. *See* TRIAL OF THE PYX.

Qatar, state in the Persian Gulf, its relations with Britain governed by the treaty of 3 Nov. 1916, until it achieved full independence on 3 Sept. 1971. Emir of Q. deposed in bloodless coup by his son, June 1995.

Quadi, a tribe living to the E of the Marcomanni, and classified by Latin writers as 'Suevi', i.e. nomadic Germans. They rebelled against Rome, AD 167, and again, 171, but were finally crushed, 173.

quadrille.
1. Country dance of French origin, introduced into England, 1818.
2. Card game, became fashionable in England *c.* 1726, and remained so until superseded by *whist.

Quadruple Alliance.
1. Britain, France, Austria, Holland, 1718.
2. Britain, Austria, France and Russia, 1813.
3. Britain, France, Portugal, and Spain, 1834.

Quakers or **Society of Friends.** Founded by George Fox between 1647 and 1666; the name 'Quaker' was given to the sect by Mr Justice Bennet, 1650, who was admonished by Fox to tremble at the word of the Lord; first meeting-house was opened in London, 1650. Q. in America, 1656. Their 'affirmation of the truth' was declared by Act of Parliament to be sufficient in place of the usual oaths in courts of justice, 1696; and for municipal offices, 1828 and 1837. Nobel Peace Prize awarded jointly to the American Friends' Service Committee and the Friends' Service Council, in recognition of Quaker work for international reconciliation, 1947. In 1990s, estimated over 200,000 Q. world-wide, over 18,000 in UK.

quango. Acronym for quasi-non-governmental organization. Word first used in USA, 1967; in Britain, 1973. Qs. multiplied in Britain from 1970s onwards and government promised to review, 1994. There were over 3,000 Qs. in Britain in 1979; but number only down to 2,018 by 1993, despite public concern.

quantum theory. First expounded by Max Planck, 1900. Applied by Niels Bohr, 1913, to gases and the frequency of light emitted. New Q.T. evolved by de Broglie, 1924.

Quarter Sessions. Established, 1363. Regulated, 1831. Abolished, 1972.

Quarterly Review. First published by John Murray to counteract the Whig *Edinburgh Review*, Feb. 1809. Ceased publication, 1967.

Quebec, Canada. Town and province. Town founded by Champlain, 1608; captured by Britain, 1629; restored to France, 1632; finally captured by British under Gen. Wolfe, 13 Sept. 1759; formally ceded to Britain by Treaty of Paris, 1763; the 'Quebec Act' of 1774 gave the French-Canadians the right to exercise their customs, laws and religion. Province united with Ontario, 1841. Separated and made a province of the new dominion, 1867. Boundary extended, 1912. Separatism became a political force in the province after 1945: foundation of '*parti québécois*', 1968. In power in Q., 1985–9 but continued to influence separatist legislation in Q. after that. From 1993, separatist '*bloc québécois*' party longest opposition party in Canada, and announced it hoped Q. would secede from Canada by 1995. Boosted by successes in 1994 elections, but narrowly failed to win referendum in Q. on separatist issue, Oct. 1995.

Queen Anne's Bounty. Instituted in 1703 for the relief of the poor clergy. Queen

Anne devoted the funds arising from first-fruits and tithes which were at her disposal to this object. United with the Ecclesiastical Commissioners, 1947, since when functions of both bodies have been exercised by the Church Commissioners.

Queen Charlotte Island. *See* BRITISH COLUMBIA.

Queen Elizabeth 2 (QE2). British passenger liner launched, 1967; maiden voyage, 1969. Threatened by terrorists, 1972; 1977–8, troubles following German refit. Struck rock off Massachusetts, Aug. 1992. Further troubles following German and British refit, Dec. 1994. QE2 was intended as successor in transatlantic crossing traffic to the *Queen Elizabeth*, which when launched in 1938 was the biggest passenger liner ever built. This ship was a war transport during World War II, but a transatlantic liner, 1946–68. Sold for conversion into a floating university in 1969, it sank in Hong Kong harbour, Jan. 1972, during refitting.

Queen Mary Land, in Antarctica, was discovered by the Australasian Antarctic Expedition of 1911–14. The Shackleton expedition took possession of Q.M.L. for the British crown, 1912.

Queen Mary's Army Auxiliary Corps. Formed, 1917. Disbanded, 1920.

Queen Maud Land, in Antarctica, is Norwegian territory, with effect from 14 Jan. 1939. The Anglo-Scandinavian Antarctic expedition was based there, 1949–51.

Queen Victoria Memorial (outside Buckingham Palace). Unveiled, 16 May 1911.

Queen's Award (for Export and Industry), originally called the Queen's Award for Industry when established in 1966. Name changed, 1972. Awards announced annually on Queen's (official) birthday.

Queensberry rules of boxing drawn up by 8th Marquess of Q., 1867.

Queensferry was the site of the earliest bishopric in Scotland from 681 to 685.

Queensland, Australia. Visited by Capt. Cook, 1770. Explored, 1823. Divided from New S Wales, 1859 and made a separate state. National party in power there for record 32 years (1957–89).

Queens of England. *See* ENGLISH SOVEREIGNS AND CONSORTS.

Queen's University, Belfast, established 1908; chartered, 1909.

Quetta, Pakistan. British Residency established at, 1876. Earthquake at, 31 May 1935.

***Quia Emptores*,** a statute passed in 1290 to stop the practice of subinfeudation.

Quintuple Treaty, guaranteeing Belgian integrity, signed by Austria, France, Britain, Russia and Prussia, 1839.

quisling, term synonymous with traitor, derived from the Norwegian Nazi Vidkun Quisling, *b.* 1887; puppet-ruler 1940–5; executed, 1945.

Quito, capital of Ecuador. Inca settlement *c.* 1470; Spanish captured it, 1534.

quoits originated in the 15thC. Still occasionally played in Scotland and N England.

R101. *See* AIRSHIPS.

rabies. Vaccine discovered, 1885. Anti-R. Serum being developed from 1954. Suggestions that UK might end anti-R. quarantine rules, 1994.

Race Relations Acts. The Acts of 1965 and 1968 have been repealed and replaced by the Act of 1976.

racial discrimination, existed in limited form in *S Africa from 1912, but from 1948 extended and codified, being based on successive Nationalist governments' policy of *'apartheid', which Nationalists translated as 'separate development'. Began to break down in 1980s, partly due to pressure of international economic sanctions against S Africa. Basic elements of R.D. repealed by de Klerk, 1991 and equal voting rights for all races from 1994, resulting in election of a government led by Nelson Mandela. R.D. in the USA had no legislative basis and from the 1950s declined rapidly, largely due to the 'desegregationist' rulings of the Supreme Court under the Eisenhower administration (1952–60) and to the Civil Rights legislation under Johnson (1963–8). In Britain R.D. is outlawed by the Race Relations Acts of 1965, 1968 and 1976. S African and US R.D. was primarily based on colour, (hence historic phase 'colour bar') but in Nazi Germany, 1933–45, R.D. operated against Jews, gypsies, etc. and resulted in the barbaric extermination of millions (see HOLOCAUST, etc.) In 1990s R.D. has surfaced in conflicts in the Balkans in Serb/Croat/Muslim conflicts, resulting in *'ethnic cleansing' policies. It has also surfaced in civil conflicts in Africa (e.g. Rwanda, 1994). Historically R.D. has been the result of anti-Semitism, tribal conflicts, assertion of supremacy by a conquering race over another, and, notably in the 20thC, fear of pressure of foreign immigration.

Racial Equality, Commission for, established 1977, under the Race Relations Act of 1976. It replaced the *Community Relations Commission.

rack. This instrument of torture is thought to have been introduced into England by John Holland, Duke of Exeter (1352–1400). Its use declared illegal in 1628.

radar (for **Radio Detection and Ranging**). The principle – that of reflected short-range wireless waves – was first proved by the German Heinrich Hertz *c.* 1899, but early attempts to apply it, 1904, not successful. It became more widely known in the 1920s. The Appleton Layer from which waves are reflected was discovered in 1928. Sir Robert Watson-Watt projected aircraft detection apparatus, 1935, and first R. station in world set up in Britain. Belt of coastal systems almost complete in 1939. A German radar system (Freya) was established later that year. Germans captured intact Coastal Command anti-submarine R. set, 1942, enabling U-Boats to carry counter-device which was defeated, 1943, by new shorter-wave detection beam carried in aircraft. After 1945, R. was developed for civilian navigation, astronomy and meteorology. A US-Canadian R. network (SPADATS) developed during the 1980s for identifying and monitoring man-made *satellites.

Radcliffe College (Cambridge, Massachusetts, USA). Originally a college for women only, founded 1878, and part of Harvard University; named after Annie R., the first woman who left money to Harvard University.

Radiation. Theory first developed by Max Planck (1858–1947), 1900.

Radical. The word applied to a political party probably originated in a speech by Charles J. Fox in 1797, when he referred to the necessity for 'R. reform'.

radio, formerly known as **wireless**. Broadcasting boom began in USA, 1921 (opening of KDKA broadcasting station at Pittsburgh). In Apr. 1922 British Postmaster-General announced a scheme for providing licences and for broadcasting from seven stations. Long-distance R. tested, Aug. 1922. Music from America heard in England, 28–9 Dec. 1923. Anglo-S African beam system opened, 3 July 1927; first broadcast from Australia to England, 4 Sept. 1927; beam service to India opened, 5 Sept. 1927. Regular foreign broadcasts begun, 1937 (now the World Service). Frequency modulation (FM) discovered by Edwin Armstrong, 1933 but not generally applied in R. until after World War II. First transistor R. produced in Japan, 1952. Commercial R. stations established in UK from 1970s, many with local connections. Classic FM station, 1992 (commercial). There were over 140 local R. stations in 1993, and more were planned; additionally there were 40 BBC local R. stations. *See also* BRITISH BROADCASTING CORPORATION.

radioactivity discovered, 1896, by Henri Becquerel (1852–1908).

Radio Authority, established Jan. 1991, one of two bodies which succeeded the Independent Broadcasting Authority. Duties include granting of licences for independent radio services, monitoring radio output, planning radio frequencies, etc.

radio-carbon dating, or **carbon-14 dating,** a method of detecting the age of buildings, artifacts, fossils, etc., devised by the US physicist Willard Libby in 1946. Can approximately date objects from 500 to 50,000 years old.

Radio Luxemburg, was for many years the UK's only commercial radio channel. It started broadcasting, 3 Dec. 1933. Ceased, 30 Dec. 1992.

radiometer invented, 1873–6, by Sir W. Crookes.

radium. Marie Curie's investigations, on her taking the principle of radioactivity as subject for her doctorate degree, led her and her husband Pierre (1859–1906) to the discovery, in 1898, of R. Its burning effect on human tissue accidentally discovered by Becquerel, 1901; and a 'Laboratoire biologique du R.' was established in Paris in 1906; similar laboratory in London in 1909. Mme Curie (1867–1934) and André Debirne isolated metallic R. from its chloride in 1910. *See also* CANCER.

radon, colourless and odourless chemical element produced by the radioactive decay of radium. Seepage of R. can occur from certain rocks and by the 1980s the seepage of R. into houses built over such rocks was recognized as a potential health hazard (cancer-inducing). Radon 220 discovered by Owens and Rutherford, 1899; Radon 222 by Dorn, 1900; Radon 219 by Giesel and Debirne, 1904. Compound radon difluoride identified, 1962.

ragged schools, first opened in Portsmouth, 1820. R.S. Union founded, 1844, by Earl of Shaftesbury (then Lord Ashley). Discontinued after the *Education Act, 1870. *And see* SUNDAY SCHOOLS.

ragtime, syncopated music, developed in the USA in the late 19thC, a forerunner of *jazz.

railways (Britain). First line opened for passenger and general traffic was Stockton-Darlington, 1825. Except for metropolitan R., grouped in four main systems: London, Midland, and Scottish; London and N Eastern Railway; Great Western Railway, and the Southern Railway by Act of 1921 as from 1 Jan. 1923. Metropolitan systems were united under the London Passenger Transport Board as from 1 July 1933 (replaced by London Transport Executive, 1948, now (1995) London Regional Transport. All R. were nationalized by Act of 1947 as from 1 Jan. 1948, as British R. Beeching Reports, 1963 and 1965. Many allegedly unprofitable branch lines closed,

1963–70. Docklands Light Railway opened, 1987. R. Privatization Act, 1993, provided for selling of franchises for rail lines and operations and British Rail break-up began, 1 April 1994. Extension of Jubilee line to Docklands approved 1993. Proposals to privatize Railtrack, Nov. 1994; first franchises offered for sale, 1995. *See also* ELECTRIC RAILWAY.

Rajasthan, union of Indian states initially approximately the same as the former Rajputana. First nine states united, Apr. 1948. Jaipur, Jodhpur, Bikaner and Jaisalmer then joined union, and formal inauguration celebrated, 30 Mar. 1949. Extension of state boundaries, 1956.

Ramblers' Association, established 1935, challenged some landowners' closures of public rights-of-way. Its headquarters are at 1–5 Wandsworth Rd. London SW8 2XX.

Rand. *See* TRANSVAAL, SOUTH AFRICA.

Ranelagh pleasure garden at Chelsea laid out, and wooden rotunda built, 1742. Decline set in *c.* 1788. Closed down, 1804.

Rangoon, or (since 1989) **Yangou,** made Burmese capital, 1752, on site first inhabited, AD 746, near Shwe Dagon Pagoda; this building last modified in 16thC AD. Known as R. from 1755. E India Co. factory established, 1790. Town rebuilt, 1841. Captured by British, 1852. Captured by Japanese, 8 Mar. 1942. Reoccupied by British and Indian troops, 3 May 1945. Instrument of surrender for all imperial Japanese forces in Burma signed here, 13 Sept. 1945.

Rapallo, Treaty of.
1. Between Italy and Yugoslavia. Settled Italo-Yugoslav frontiers, Nov. 1920.
2. Between Germany and the Soviet Union, for the mutual renunciation of reparations and the re-establishment of diplomatic and economic relations, 18 Apr. 1922.

rape (within marriage), became a criminal offence in England and Wales, 1991.

Rastafarianism, religious movement (with political overtones) of W Indian origin, deriving from ideas of Marcus Garvey (1887–1940), in the 1950s. It has a number of adherents in Britain.

rationing. *See* FOOD CONTROL.

Ravenna. Became seat of Western Roman Empire, AD 404; mausoleum built, 446; conquered by Belisarius, 540, and seat of the exarchs of the Eastern Roman Empire from 553 until 752, when it was sacked by the Lombards. Pepin forced the Lombard king to bestow the exarchate on the Pope, 756. Subject to Venice, 1441; again part of the papal states, 1509.

Reading, England. Danish Army under Ivar and Ubbe quartered here, 871. Abbey founded, 1121; consecrated, 1164. University College became University of R., 1926.

Receiver in Bankruptcy. The Official R.'s department was established in 1914, and its administration regulated by Acts of that year, of 1926, and of 1929. Supreme Court Act, 1981, repealed and replaced previous legislation. Effect unchanged.

Recife, or **Pernambuco,** Brazil. Founded, 1504. Occupied by Dutch, 1624–54, when it was recaptured by the Portuguese.

Reconstruction, in the USA, term applied to the years 1865–77, following the Civil War.

Record Office, Public. Established in London as result of the P.R.O. Act of 1838 when it was put under the Master of the Rolls; the publication of the Calendars of State papers was commenced in 1856. 1958, Public Record Acts transferred control to the Lord Chancellor. 1967, Public Record Act established that government records should normally be open to public inspection after 30 years had passed. Parallel offices opened at Kew in 1970s. The P.R.O. became an executive agency, 1 Apr. 1992. The Scottish R.O., in Edinburgh, dates from 1774.

Record Offices (other), include the House of Lords R.O., established 1946, with records going back to 1497; and the City of

London R.O., at the Guildhall, holding records going back to the reign of William the Conqueror. ·

record player, superseded the *gramophone in the 1950s, and by the 1980s, with introduction of music centers, *compact discs, etc., itself obsolete.

Red Army, name given to the USSR's military force, 1917, officially abandoned, 1946, but in popular usage until dissolution of Soviet system, 1991.

Red Army Faction. *See* BAADER-MEINHOF GANG.

Red Army, Japanese, terrorist group active in Japan and elsewhere in first half of 1970s. Caused bombing and shooting outrage at Lod Airport, Israel, 30 May 1972, when 27 killed and 76 wounded (mostly Filipino Christian pilgrims), in show of solidarity with Arab Palestinian cause.

Red Brigade, Italian left-wing urban terrorist group, allegedly founded by Renato Curcio (*b.* 1945). It was active from 1970, beginning a campaign of bombing, followed by kidnappings. In 1978 it kidnapped and murdered former Italian premier Aldo Moro. In 1981 it captured a US NATO officer and held him prisoner for 42 days. Curcio was captured in 1974, escaped, and was recaptured 1976. The R.B. ceased to be a major force from the early 1980s.

Red Cross. As a result of the efforts of the Swiss Henri Dunant (1829–1910), the Geneva Conference, 1863–4, by the Convention of 1864, set up the International Committee of the R.C. with its headquarters at Geneva. The British R.C. Society was founded, 1870, and incorporated, 1908. The American National R.C. was founded, 1881, and reincorporated, 1893. In Muslim countries, the R.C. adopted the name Red Crescent, 1906. The International Federation of R.C. and Red Crescent Societies founded 1919, and in 1994 had societies in over 150 countries. The International Conference of R.C. and Red Crescent Societies meets every four

years. Awarded Nobel Peace Prize, 1963.

Red River Settlement in the present Manitoba province, Canada, was made on land sold to Thomas Douglas, the 5th Earl of Selkirk (1771–1820) by the Hudson's Bay Co., 1811. Intermittent fighting between Indians and local inhabitants, continued up to its amalgamation with the Hudson's Bay Co., 1821.

Red Sea Expedition, sent by Wellesley from India to expel the French from Egypt, 1800.

Redundancy Payments Act, 1965, was replaced, 1978, by the Employment Protection (Consolidation) Act, without significant change.

Reform Acts.
1. The 'Great' R. Act introduced by Lord J. Russell, 1 Mar. 1831, but defeated on amendment. Reintroduced, June 1831, but rejected by the Lords. Introduced a third time, Dec. 1831, but amended out of recognition by the Lords. Government persuaded William IV to threaten wholesale creations of peers, 15 May 1832. Passed by Lords, 4 June, and received royal assent, 7 June 1832.
2. The Second R. Act passed by Disraeli's government, 1867, conferred household and lodger franchise in boroughs.
3. The Third R. Act by Gladstone, 1884, made household and lodger franchise uniform in UK. It was followed by a drastic Redistribution of Seats Act, 1885. *See also* REPRESENTATION OF THE PEOPLE ACTS.

Reformation. Martin Luther (1483–1546) issues the 95 Theses at Wittenberg in protest against the sale of indulgences, 31 Oct. 1517. He refuses to recant before Cardinal Cajetan at Augsburg, 12 Oct. 1518. He disputes with Eck at Leipzig, 27 June–16 July 1519. He burns papal bull of excommunication, 10 Dec. 1520. Lutherans outlawed by Edict of Worms and Luther retires to the Wartburg, May 1521. Zwingli carries out a R. in Zürich, 1519–25; killed in battle, 1531. Luther's translation of the New Testament appears, Sept. 1522. Philip of Hesse joins the R., 1523. R. in Sweden, Denmark and Lüneburg, 1527. Henry VIII of England proclaimed Supreme Head of the Church in England, Feb. 1531. Act of Supremacy in England, 1534. Dissolution of English monasteries, 1536–9. Calvin goes to Geneva, 1536, and his movement supersedes Zwinglianism as the main Protestant force in Switzerland. Cardinal Contarini's attempt at reconciliation, 1540. Calvin organizes the Geneva Church and Knox begins R. in Scotland, 1541. Cardinal Beaton murdered in Scotland, 1546. The *Interim* of Augsburg, 15 May 1548. First English Act of Uniformity and Prayer Book, 9 June 1549. Second English Act of Uniformity and Prayer Book, Jan. 1552. Treaty of Passau annuls *Interim*, 2 Aug. 1552. Queen Mary I's counter-R. in England, 1553–8. Religious peace of Augsburg, 25 Sept. 1555. First Covenant signed in Scotland, Dec. 1557. Elizabethan Act of Supremacy, 8 May 1559. Issue of the Gallican Confession by the French Calvinists, May 1559. Scots Parliament abolishes papal jurisdiction, Aug. 1560. Knox establishes Scottish Church, 1561. Netherlands Confession of Faith, 1562. Queen Elizabeth I excommunicated, 25 Feb. 1570. Thirty-nine Articles sanctioned, 1571. Massacre of French Protestants (St Bartholomew), 23–4 Aug. 1572. Presbyterian system established in Scotland, 1592. Edict of Nantes grants toleration to the Huguenots, 13 Apr. 1598. Authorized Version of the Bible appears, 1611. Calvinist Synod of Dort, 1618–19.

Regency, in Great Britain, denotes period between 1810 and 1820, when George IV was regent during incapacity of George III.

Regency Acts (Great Britain).
1. 1751, on death of Frederick, Prince of Wales, appointing Princess of Wales regent in the event of George II's death before the Prince of Wales (i.e. George III – to be) was 18.
2. 1765, on the recovery of George III from his first attack of mental disease.
3. 1788, during the second mental attack of George III.
4. 1810, when the mind of George III finally gave way.
5. 1830, Duchess of Kent appointed regent during minority of Victoria should the latter succeed to the throne before the age of 18.
6. 1837, provided for the carrying-on of the Government by lords justices in the event of the Duke of Cumberland, the heir-presumptive, being abroad.
7. 1840, on the marriage of Queen Victoria with Prince Albert; it enacted that in the event of Victoria's demise, and any child of hers succeeding to the throne under the age of 18, Prince Albert should act as regent.
8. 1910, appointed Queen Mary regent in the event of a child of George V's succeeding to the throne before the age of 18.
9. Acts providing for a regency in the event of the Sovereign dying and leaving an heir who is a minor have subsequently been passed at the beginning of the reigns of George VI and Elizabeth II, the most recent being the Act of 1953, designating the Duke of Edinburgh as regent, should a regency have arisen during the minority of Queen Elizabeth II's children.

Regent's Park, London. Laid out by John Nash for the Prince Regent, 1812. Park opened to the public, 1838.

reggae, type of W Indian music, in vogue since 1970s. Has connections with the religious movement known as *Rastafarianism.

Regicides, The. Those who tried and condemned Charles I in 1649; the Bill of Indemnity in 1660 ordered severe penalties against the R.

regiments of the British Army (UK Establishments). The following is a historic list of British Cavalry and Infantry R. of the line and of the Household, with the dates when they were first raised, and the numbers they bore up to 1881.

Horse		Dragoon Guards		Dragoons	
1	1661 Tangier			1	1693 Royals
2	1678	1	1746 King's	2	1691 Scots Greys
3	1685	2	1746 Queen's Bays	3	1685 King's Own
4	1685	3	1746 Prince of Wales's	4	1685 Queen's Own
			(3/6)*		
5	1685	4	1788 (4/7)	5	1685 Disbanded, 1799
6	1685	5	1788 Inniskilling (5/6	6	1689 Inniskilling (5/6
			Dragoon Guards)		Dragoon Guards)
7	1685	6	1691 Carabiniers (3/6)	7	1690 Queen's Own
8	1688	7	1788 (4/7)	8	1693
				12	1715

Light Dragoons		Hussars		Lancers	
3	1715	3	1859		
4	1715	4	1859		
				5	1859 Re-raised (16/5)
7	1715	7	1805		
8	1715	8	1822		
9	1715			9	1806
10	1715	10	1806		
11	1715	11	1840		
12	1768 (Prince of Wales's)			12	1806
13	1715	13	1861		
14	1715	14	1861		
15	1759	15	1806		
16	1759			16	1806 (16/5)
17	1759			17	1806 (17/21)
18	1763	18	1807		
19	1759	19	1861 } Ex-E India		
			Co's 1st, 2nd,		
20	1759	20	1861 } and 3rd European		
			Cavalry		
21	1760	21	1861 }	21	1896 (17/21)
22	1760 Disbanded 1799				
23	1781			23	1816 Disbanded
				27	Raised 1941

*3rd Carabiniers from 1929.

Household Cavalry:
First Life Guards, 1660, and Second Life Guards, 1661: Amalgamated, 1922. Each became a *regiment* (not troop as before), 1788.
Horse Guards, 1661 (Ex-Cromwellian Crook's Regiment).
Foot Guards:
Scots Guards (Third Foot Guards), 1641. Totally destroyed at Worcester, 1651.

Re-raised, 1661, in Scotland. On British Establishment, 1707.
Grenadiers (First Foot Guards). *Émigré* regiment raised, 1656, re-formed, 1660.
Coldstream (Second Foot Guards). Monk's Regiment (1650) entered Charles II's service, 1660.
Irish Guards, 1902.
Welsh Guards, 1915.

No.	Date Raised	Title in 1881
Infantry:		
1	1633	Royal Scots.
2	1661	Queen's Royal West Surrey.
3	1665	Buffs (East Kent).
4	1680	Lancaster
5	1685	Northumberland Fusiliers.
6	1673	Warwickshire (now Royal Warwickshire Fusiliers).
7	1685	Royal (English) Fusiliers.
8	1685	King's Liverpool.
9	1685	Norfolk.
10	1685	Lincolnshire.
11	1685	Devon.
12	1685	Suffolk.
13	1685	Somerset Light Infantry.
14	1685	West Yorkshire.
15	1685	East Yorkshire.
16	1688	Bedfordshire and Hertfordshire.
17	1688	Leicestershire.
18	1684	Royal Irish.
19	1688	The Green Howards.
20	1688	Lancashire Fusiliers.
21	1678	Royal Scots Fusiliers.
22	1689	Cheshire.
23	1689	Royal Welch Fusiliers.
24	1689	South Wales Borderers.
25	1689	King's Own Scottish Borderers.
26	1689	1st Cameronians (Scottish Rifles) (*see* 90).
27	1690	1st Inniskilling Fusiliers (*see* 108).
28	1694	1st Gloucestershire (*see* 61).
29	1694	1st Worcestershire (*see* 36).
30	1702	1st East Lancashire (*see* 59).
31	1702	1st East Surrey (*see* 70).
32	1702	1st Duke of Cornwall's Light Infantry (*see* 46).
33	1702	1st West Riding (*see* 76).
34	1702	1st Border (*see* 55).
35	1701	1st Royal Sussex (*see* 107).
36	1701	2nd Worcestershire (*see* 29).
37	1702	1st Hampshire (*see* 67).
38	1702	1st South Staffordshire (*see* 80).
39	1702	1st Dorset (*see* 54).
40	1712	1st South Lancashire (Prince of Wales's Volunteers) (*see* 82).
41	1719	1st Welch (*see* 69).
42	1743	1st Black Watch (*see* 73).
43	1741	1st Oxford and Buckinghamshire Light Infantry (*see* 52).
44	1741	1st Essex (*see* 56).
45	1740	1st Sherwood Foresters (*see* 95).
46	1741	2nd Duke of Cornwall's Light Infantry (*see* 32).
47	1741	1st North Lancashire (*see* 81).
48	1741	1st Northamptonshire (*see* 58).
49	1741	1st Royal Berkshire (*see* 66).
50	1755	1st Queen's Own Royal West Kent (*see* 97).
51	1755	1st King's Own Yorkshire Light Infantry (*see* 105).
52	1741	2nd Oxford and Buckinghamshire Light Infantry (*see* 43).
53	1755	1st Shropshire Light Infantry (King's) (*see* 85).
54	1755	2nd Dorset (*see* 39).
55	1755	2nd Border (*see* 34).
56	1755	2nd Essex (*see* 44).
57	1755	1st Middlesex (*see* 77).
58	1750	2nd Northamptonshire (*see* 48).
59	1755	2nd East Lancashire (*see* 30).
60	1755	King's Royal Rifle Corps (formerly Royal Americans).
61	1756	2nd Gloucestershire (*see* 28).
62	1757	1st Wiltshire (*see* 99).
63	1756	1st Manchester (*see* 96).
64	1756	1st North Staffordshire (was 2nd/11th till 1758) (*see* 98).
65	1756	1st York and Lancaster (*see* 84).
66	1756	2nd Royal Berkshire (*see* 49).
67	1756	2nd Hampshire (*see* 37).
68	1756	1st Durham Light Infantry (*see* 106).
69	1756	2nd Welch (*see* 41).
70	1758	2nd East Surrey (*see* 31).
71	1766	1st Highland Light Infantry (*see* 74).
72	1778	1st Seaforth Highlanders (*see* 78).
73	1786	2nd Black Watch (*see* 42).
74	1787	2nd Highland Light Infantry (*see* 71).
75	1787	1st Gordon Highlanders (*see* 92).
76	1787	2nd West Riding (*see* 33).
77	1787	2nd Middlesex (*see* 57).

No.	Date Raised	Title in 1881
78	1793	2nd Seaforth Highlanders (*see* 72).
79	1793	Cameron Highlanders.
80	1793	2nd South Staffordshire (*see* 38).
81	1793	2nd North Lancashire (*see* 47).
82	1793	2nd South Lancashire (*see* 40).
83	1793	1st Royal Irish Rifles (*see* 86).
84	1793	2nd York and Lancaster (*see* 65).
85	1794	2nd Shropshire Light Infantry (King's) (*see* 53).
86	1799	2nd Royal Irish Rifles (*see* 83).
87	1793	1st Royal Irish Fusiliers (*see* 89).
88	1793	1st Connaught Rangers (*see* 94).
89	1794	2nd Royal Irish Fusiliers (*see* 87).
90	1794	2nd Cameronians (Scottish Rifles) (*see* 26).
91	1794	1st Argyll and Sutherland Highlanders (*see* 93).
92	1794	2nd Gordon Highlanders (*see* 75).
93	1800	2nd Argyll and Sutherland Highlanders (*see* 91).
94	1800	2nd Connaught Rangers (*see* 88).
95	1816	2nd Sherwood Foresters (*see* 45).
96	1800	2nd Manchester (*see* 63).
97	1798	2nd Queen's Own Royal West Kent (*see* 50).
98	1824	2nd North Staffordshire (*see* 64).
99	1824	2nd Wiltshire (*see* 62).
100	1858	1st Leinster (*see* 109).
101	1861	1st Munster Fusiliers (*see* 104).
102	1861	1st Dublin Fusiliers (*see* 103).
103	1861	2nd Dublin Fusiliers (*see* 102).
104	1861	2nd Munster Fusiliers (*see* 101).
105	1861	2nd King's Own Yorkshire Light Infantry (*see* 51).
106	1861	2nd Durham Light Infantry (*see* 68).
107	1861	2nd Royal Sussex (*see* 35).
108	1861	2nd Inniskilling Fusiliers (*see* 27).
109	1861	2nd Leinster (*see* 100).

No.	Date Raised	Title in 1881
	1800	1st Rifle Brigade; 1805, 2nd Rifle Brigade, up to 1816 known as 1st and 2nd Battalions, 95th R; 1855, 3rd Rifle Brigade; 1857, 4th Rifle Brigade.

Nos. 101–109 were formerly the European element of the E India Co.'s Army. Between 1958 and 1994 considerable amalgamations of R. took place, and the total number is now much reduced.

registers, parish, were regularly kept in France from about 1308, but in England only from 1538, and then, erratically. From 1837 they record only baptisms, marriages and deaths.

Registrar-General first appointed, 1836, to conduct census (carried out every 10 years from 1841, excluding 1941) and carry on **Registration of Births, Marriages, and Deaths**, which was first generally enforced in England by the Registration Act, 1837, and extended to Scotland, 1855, and Ireland, 1864. Consolidating Act, 1874, gave rise to the General Registry at Somerset House. Optional shortened form of birth certificate issued, from 1947, which omitted details of parentage. In 1970 the Office of Population, Censuses and Surveys was established by merging the General Register Office and the Government Social Survey Department and offices transferred to St Catherine's House, Kingsway.

regium donum (royal gift). Originally an annual grant to Nonconformist bodies in Britain and Ireland by the king. In 1690 William III first made a grant of £1,200 a year to the Presbyterian ministers in Ireland; which continued, and increased till it ceased on passing of Irish Church Act, 1869. This grant was also paid to English Nonconformist clergy from 1721, but withdrawn by mutual consent in 1857.

Regius Professor. All these chairs endowed by Henry VIII, 1546, except that of Modern History at Oxford which George I founded, 1724.

Regulating Act. Introduced by Lord North in 1773 to cause the British Government to interfere in the administration of India.

Regulating Act. Passed by Parliament, 1774, for the subversion of the charter of Massachusetts. It was one of the causes of the subsequent War of Independence.

Reichsrat, or Imperial Council, second chamber of several European legislatures, but especially the Upper House of the German legislature, set up under the Weimar Constitution, 1919, as a council of Federal republics; it survived, in theory, until 1945.

Reichstag, a modern form of the *Imperial Diet, revived under the regime of Bismarck as the legislature of the N German Confederation (1867) and then of the German Empire (Reich: 1871). The name and the institution continued little altered under the Weimar Constitution of 1919; though the power of the Upper House (*Reichsrat) was curtailed, the R. never had the initiative that the English Commons in Parliament have had, and in 1933 it yielded to Hitler practically without a struggle. Following the R. elections of 5 Mar. 1933, alleged agents of the Comintern were tried on charges of causing the fire whereby the R. building was largely burnt out, 27 Feb. 1933. The R., originally built 1884–94, was extensively damaged during World War II. Following German reunification, 1991, plans to reconstruct R. building as eventual new parliamentary assembly.

relativity, theory of. Einstein's paper on the Special Theory of R. published, 1905. On the General Theory, 1915.

Remonstrance, The Grand. A petition drawn up by Parliament against the cruelty and injustice of Charles I; presented, 1 Dec. 1641.

Remonstrants. The Dutch Protestants who, in 1610, after the death of Arminius, presented to the states of Holland and Friesland a remonstrance in which the doctrines of Calvinism were repudiated; their confession of faith was drawn up in 1621; they were persecuted, 1625–52, and officially recognized, 1795.

Renaissance. The great cultural movement in Europe after the Middle Ages, generally seen as representing the emergence of the modern age. It was much more than a revival of old forms, as its name might imply, and its span is such that it is difficult to fix it with dates. The following, however, are relevant: Cimabue's *Madonna della Trinità* completed, 1260. Roger Bacon's *Opus Majus* completed, 1266. Dante completed *La Vita Nuova*, 1292, and *De Monarchia*, 1313, and *Divina Commedia*, 1321. Boccaccio finished the *Decameron*, 1353. Manuel Chrysoloras lectured on Greek at Florence, 1396. Lorenzo Valla, humanist, 1405–57. Printing reached Italy, 1456. St Mark's, Venice, completed, 1484. St Peter's, Rome, commenced, 1513.

Rennes, capital of Brittany from the 9thC, became an episcopal see in the 5thC. Burnt down and radically replanned, 1720. Second trial of *Dreyfus took place here, 1899.

Rent Restriction Acts. Had their origins in the Act of Dec. 1915. Rent tribunals established under the Furnished Houses (Rent Control) Act, 1946. Rent Act of 1957 drastically cut the number of houses protected by R.R. The Rent Acts, 1965 and 1968 reintroduced R.R. in many cases; the Rent Act and the Protection from Eviction Act of 1977 repealed these. Further modifications under Housing Act, 1988.

reparations. Germany's reparation debt put at £6,600 million, 1920. Allied ultimatum, 1921. Germany applied for reductions, Dec. 1921. Moratorium granted, Jan. 1922. London Conference, Aug. 1922. Abortive negotiations among Allies, 1922. French and Belgian forces advanced into the Ruhr, Jan.–Feb. 1923. German passive resistance in Ruhr, Feb.–Sept. 1923. (Lord Curzon's speech, Imperial Conference, 5 Oct. 1923). *Dawes Plan, 1924. *Young Plan, 20 Jan. 1930. Obligations cancelled, 1932.

Representation of the People Acts. Women over 30 enfranchised, 1918. Extended to all women over 21, 1928. Extension of local franchise, 1945. Act of 1948 abolished plural voting. Act of 1969 gave votes to all those over 18, from 1970.

Republican Party (USA) was formed in 1828 when a faction seceded from the Democratic Party. Modern R.P. dates from 1854, beginning as a union of elements opposed to slavery. First National Convention held, 1856. First R. president – Abraham Lincoln – elected, 1860. Dwight D. Eisenhower, R. candidate, elected president, 1952; held office until 1960 after which the Democrats filled the presidency until 1969, when the R. Richard Nixon was elected. He resigned, 1974. R.P. defeated, 1977, but regained presidency under Reagan, 1981, losing it again, 1992. Made sweeping gains in 1994 mid-term elections, winning both houses of Congress.

resale price maintenance. The Restrictive Trades Practices Act, 1956, outlawed collective price maintenance in Britain. Resale Prices Act, 1964, was intended to abolish R.P.M. except in specified cases.

Rescissory Act. Passed by Scottish Parliament, 1661; it was proposed by Sir Thomas Primrose with the object of annulling the Acts establishing Presbyterianism in Scotland.

Restoration, in English context, means the return of Charles II, his family and court to England in 1660, and his coronation. In French history, means the R. of the Bourbons, and the reigns of Louis XVIII and Charles X (1814–30).

Resurrectionists, c. 1826–30, provided anatomical specimens for surgeons, especially in Scotland, by robbing graves; after Burke and Hare were hanged, 1829, for murdering people as an easier alternative to digging, public attention was directed to the R., and an Act of 1832 required licences to be procured for the dissection of human bodies.

retirement pensions. *See* OLD AGE PENSIONS.

Réunion or **Bourbon.** Indian Ocean. Discovered, 1513, by Portuguese navigator, Pedro Mascarenhas; formally possessed by French, 1643; attacked and captured by British, 1810; restored to France, Apr. 1815. Overseas *département* of France, 1946; overseas region, 1972.

Reuters News (originally **Telegraph Agency**), founded by Baron Julius Reuter (1816–99), who in 1849 at Aachen began to transmit commercial intelligence by pigeon post, and transferred his agency, now working by electric telegraph, to London, 1851. Became a limited liability company, 1865, and a private trusteeship, 1918. In 1947 the company became the joint property, together with the Press Association, of British, Australian and New Zealand newspaper concerns, joined in 1949 by the Press Trust of India. Stock Exchange flotation, 1984.

Reval. *See* Tallin.

Revolutionary Tribunal, The. Established in Paris, Oct. 1793, for the trial of criminal cases; suppressed, 31 May 1795.

Reykjavik, capital of Iceland since 1918. The first settler on the site of the town was Ingolf, who landed in 874. *See* ICELAND.

Rhaetia, Central Alpine region conquered by the Romans, 15 BC, and organized, as a province. Enlarged by addition of Vindelicia, late 1stC AD. Divided into R. Prima and R. Secunda in the reign of Diocletian, AD 284–305. R. Prima corresponded to the present Swiss cantons of Grisons, St Gall, Appenzell, Thurgau, Glarus, parts of Zürich and Schwyz, the Austrian provinces of Vorarlberg and Tirol and the Italian province of Bolzano. R. Secunda, or Vindelicia, consisted of Swabia and Bavaria N to the Danube and E to the Inn. *See* articles on all of the above provinces.

Rheims or **Reims,** France. *Durocortorum* mentioned by Julius Caesar as the capital of the Remi; Clovis baptized at, 496; from

1179 to 1825 the sovereigns of France were crowned here. Cathedral built between 1211 and 1430; restored, 1877 *et seq.*; damaged by German bombardment, Sept. 1914; restored and consecrated, 1937; reopened, July 1938. Eisenhower received formal surrender of German High Command at, 7 May, 1945. Ceremony of Franco-German 'reconciliation' held at Rheims, in presence of Adenauer and de Gaulle, July 1962.

Rhine, Confederation of the. *See* CONFEDERATION OF THE RHINE.

Rhineland-Palatinate, a German region corresponding to Rhenish Prussia (*see* PRUSSIA). Demilitarized under terms of Versailles Treaty; French efforts to form a separatist R. state finally failed in 1924. The demilitarized zone was reoccupied by the Wehrmacht, 7 Mar. 1936. Heavily bombed by the Allies, 1942–5.

Rhode Island, USA. Explored by the Dutch, 1614; commonwealth of R.I. founded, 1636, by Roger Williams; patent for the government of the settlement granted, 1644; first General Assembly met, 1647; patent confirmed by Cromwell, 1655; charter granted by Charles II, 1663; ratified National Constitution of USA, 29 May 1790.

Rhodes, Dodecanese Islands. Early settlement by Dorians. Enrolled in Delian League, 5thC BC. Revolted from Athens, 412. City of R. built, 408. Great prosperity from 330 onwards. Successful resistance to Demetrius Poliorcetes, 304. Colossus completed, 280; destroyed, 224. In alliance with Rome, 180–160. Sacked by C. Cassius, 43. Ruined by earthquakes, AD 155. Occupied by Saracens, 653–8 and 717–18. Conquered by Knights of St John, 1309. Turkish siege, 1480. Turkish conquest, 1522. Occupied by Italians, 1912 (*see* DODECANESE ISLANDS). Ceded to Greece, 1947.

Rhodes scholarships, places at Oxford University instituted under the will of Cecil Rhodes (1853–1902) and originally for 20 male scholars annually from the then British Empire (now Common-

wealth). R.S. later extended to students from the USA and Germany. In 1976 terms of the original settlement varied to include women. Past R.S. of distinction, their year of entry to Oxford and later professions include:

J. H. Hofmeyr, 1910 (Deputy Prime Minister of S Africa)
Edwin Hubble, 1910 (US astronomer)
Norman Manley, 1914 (Prime Minister of Jamaica)
Lord Florey, 1921 (Australian-born scientist and Nobel Prize winner)
E. F. Schumacher, 1930 (German economist)
Dean Rusk, 1931 (US Secretary of State)
Dom Mintoff, 1939 (Maltese Prime Minister)
Bob Hawke, 1953 (Australian Prime Minister)
Kris Kristofferson, 1958 (US film-maker and song-writer)
William (Bill) Jefferson Clinton, 1968 (US President)

Rhodesia, Southern, name, until 1980, of * **Zimbabwe.**

Rhodesia and Nyasaland, Federation of, existed 1953–63, when, after concentrated African opposition, it was dissolved.

Rhodesia, Northern. *See* ZAMBIA.

Rhodesia, earlier, **Southern Rhodesia.** *See* ZIMBABWE.

Richborough, England, the Roman *Rutupiae*, was the beachhead of Claudius's invasion, AD 43. A monumental building in honour of the Emperor Domitian, final conqueror of Britain, was erected, 85. The port was heavily fortified *c.* 287–93 against Saxon pirates. In 1943–4 units of the Mulberry harbour and the cross-channel petrol supply pipe, 'PLUTO', were made at R.

Richter scale, named after Charles Richter (1900–85), US seismologist, used to measure earthquakes since 1935.

Ridings, historical division (into three) of the county of Yorkshire, deriving from the Danish conquest in the 8–9thC. The R. abolished under local government reorganization, 1974: plans to restore partially, 1993.

Ridolfi Conspiracy. A Roman Catholic plot instigated by Roberto R., in which the Duke of Norfolk was involved, against Queen Elizabeth, 1571. It arose out of the papal bull *Regnans in Excelsis* against Queen Elizabeth, 25 Feb. 1570. Norfolk was executed with others, June 1572.

Rievaulx Abbey (England). Founded by Cistercians, 1131.

rifle. Invention of spiral groove attributed among others to J. Koller of Vienna, 15thC. Such a rifled weapon is recorded at Guastalla (Italy), 1476. Occasionally found, especially among French troops, in 17thC. Introduced by Swiss colonists into America, 1721. A. R. factory existed in Pennsylvania, 1754. The British 95th Regiment armed with the Baker R., 1800. General introduction of breechloading Rs. into Prussian Army, 1841–8. Smooth bores abolished in British Army *c.* 1852. Magazine Rs. used in American Civil War, 1861. Lee-Enfield R. introduced to Britain, 1895; some semi-automatic Rs. (the Garand) used in World War II. British Army changed to Belgian FN.30 Rs., 1954. By 1960s, assault Rs. fully automatic. Most famous of these the Soviet Kalashnikov or AK47 (= Russian for *automatic Kalashnikov*). This was invented in 1947 by Mikhail Kalashnikov (*b.* 1919). In 1980 Warsaw Pact countries replaced the AK47 with the AKM which had better sights than the original. By the 1990s these made in many countries, notably eastern Europe, and in use world-wide.

Riga, founded, 1201, by Bishop Albert of Livonia, seat of an archbishopric from 1225. Joined Hanseatic League, 1282. Came into possession of the Teutonic Knights, 1330, adopted Protestant faith (Lutheran), 1522. Free City of the Empire from the decay of the Teutonic Knights' dominions (1561) until 1582, when it became Polish. Passed to Sweden, 1621; to Russia, 1710; to Latvia, 1919 when it became capital. *See* Treaties. Leased to USSR as military base, 3 Oct. 1939; taken by Germans, 1 July 1941; by Russians, 13 Oct. 1944. Capital of independent Latvia since 1991.

Rights, Bill of (Britain), Oct. 1689, confirmed the Declaration of R. made to William and Mary, Feb. 1689. It affirmed the liberties of the subject and settled the succession.

Rights, Bill of (USA). The collective name given to the first 10 amendments to the US Constitution passed together, 15 Dec. 1791.

Rights of Man, Declaration of. Proclaimed by the French National Assembly, 4 Aug. 1789.

Rijeka (Italian **Fiume**). Part of the Holy Roman Empire, 1471. Joined to Hungary, 1870. Granted to Italy by secret Pact of London, 1915. Seized by d'Annunziano, who proclaimed provisional government, Sept. 1919. Recognized as a free city by treaty of Rapallo, 1920. Italy annexed R., 9 March 1924. Ceded to Yugoslavia, 1947: since Croatian independence, 1991–2, in Croatia.

Rio de Janeiro, Brazil. Discovered, 1502, by Coelho. City founded, 1566. Capital of Brazil, 1763–1960. Venue of 'Earth Summit', June 1992.

Rio de Janeiro, Treaty of, 2 Sept. 1947, for the mutual defence of the Americas.

Riot Act (Britain), **1714.**

Ripon, Treaty of, 1640; ended the war between England and Scotland; peace was finally concluded in London, Aug., 1641.

Road Safety Act, 1967, provided for breath-tests for drivers involved in traffic offences.

Robert Gordon University, The, Aberdeen. Was until 1992 the Robert Gordon Institute of Technology.

robot (from Czech *robotnik*, worker), a term invented by Karel Čapek in his play *R.U.R.*, 1923. *See* Czech Literature.

Rochelle, La, France. Became part of English possessions by marriage of Henry II to Eleanor of Aquitaine; taken by Louis VIII of France, 1224; ceded to England, 1360; retaken by France, 1372; resisted siege as Huguenot stronghold, 1573; besieged (1627) and taken by Richelieu, 1628.

Rochester, England. Bishopric founded, 604, by St Augustine; present cathedral founded, 1077–1107; earliest city charter, 1189; castle of very early construction, captured by King John, 1215; besieged in vain by Simon de Montfort, 1264; captured by Wat Tyler, 1381.

rock and roll, type of popular music which reached its peak in the 1950s–60s, pioneered by Bill Haley (1927–81). Its most famous exponent was Elvis Presley (1935–77); others of note include 'Jimi' Hendrix (1942–70) and 'Buddy' Holly (1936–59).

Rockefeller Foundation, endowed by John Davison R. (1839–1937). Chartered, 1913.

Rocket, The. Steam locomotive built by Stephenson, which in Oct. 1829 won the Rainhill competition, and so inaugurated the use of locomotives on the Liverpool and Manchester Railway.

rockets. As a firework and missile, invented by the Chinese, 12th–13thC AD. A small rocket missile used by the British in India at the end of the 18thC. Modern interest in Rs. dates from *c.* 1920. First flight of a liquid-propelled R. made at Massachusetts, 1926. Germany did much work on Rs. after 1933 and Rs. were used against Britain in Second World War (*see* PEENEMUNDE). Subsequent research carried out on space Rs. and military Rs. by USA and Russia, and by an unknown number of other countries. First man in space in a R. was a Russian, Yuri Gagarin (1934–68), 12 Apr. 1961; he orbited the earth. *See also* SPACE FLIGHTS.

Roman Catholics in England. Absolved from allegiance to Henry VIII by Pius III, 1535; to Queen Elizabeth I by Pius V, 1570. Excluded from the throne, 1689. Laws against repealed, 1780, 1791. Catholic Emancipation Act, 13 Apr. 1829. Episcopate re-established 1850.

Roman emperors before the division of the Empire. Dates of accession only:

Augustus 27 BC
Tiberius AD 14
Caligula 37
Claudius 41
Nero 54
Galba ⎫
Otho ⎬ 68
Vitellius ⎭
Vespasian 68
Titus 79
Domitian 81
Nerva 96
Trajan 98
Hadrian 117
Antoninus Pius 138
Marcus Aurelius 161
Commodus 180
Pertinax ⎫
Didus Julianus ⎬ 193
Niger ⎭
Septimus Severus 193
Caracalla ⎫ 211
Geta ⎭
Macrinus 217
Elagabalus 218
Alexander Severus 222
Maximin I 235
Gordian I and II ⎫
Balbinus ⎬ 238
Pupienus ⎭
Gordian III 238
Philip 244
Decius 249
Gallus 251
Aemilian ⎫
Valerian ⎬ 253
Gallienus ⎭
Gallienus alone 260
Claudius II 268
Aurelian 270
Tacitus 275
Florian 276
Probus 276
Carus 282

Carinus ⎫
Numerian ⎬ 284
Diocletian 284
  (abdicated 305)
Maximian associated with Diocletian 286
Constantius ⎫
Galerius ⎬ 305
Severus 306
Constantine the Great ⎫
Licinius │
Maximin │
Galerius ⎬ Jointly 309
Maxentius │
Maximian ⎭
Constantine alone 323
Constantine II ⎫
Constantius II ⎬ 337
Constans
Constantius II (alone) 353
Julian 361
Jovian 363
Valens ⎫
Valentinian I ⎬ 364
Valentinian I ⎫
Gratian ⎬ 367
Gratian ⎫
Valentinian II ⎬ 375
Theodosius the Great 379–95

See also ROMAN EMPERORS (LATER WESTERN)
and ROMAN EMPIRE, EASTERN.

Roman emperors (Later Western).
(Usurpers in italics.) (See also ROMAN
EMPERORS.)

Honorius 393–423
Constantine III 407–11
Constantius III 421
John 423–25
Valentinian III 425–55
Maximus 455
Avitus 455–56
Majorian 457–61
Severus 461–65
Anthemius 467–72
Olybrius 472
Glycerius 473
Julius Nepos 473–80
Romulus 475–76

NOTE: Romulus surnamed Augustulus is
wrongly known as the last R. emperor in
the W; he was never recognized in the E,
and Julius Nepos survived him.

Roman Empire. Organization of by Augustus, 30 BC–AD 14. Defeat of Romans by
Germans under Arminius, AD 9. Annexation of Mauritania, 41–2. Of Britain, 43–5.
Boudicca's rebellion in Britain, 61. Batavian rising, 69–71. Fortification of the German frontier, 96. Empire reaches its widest
extent under Trajan, 98–117. The *Perpetual
Edict* of Julius Salvianus drawn up c. 130.
Germanic invasion of Italy, 161. Beginning
of serious praetorian interference in central government, 193. *Constitutio Antonini-
ana* extends Roman citizenship to all
freeborn subjects, 212. Defeat of Emperor
Valerian by Sapor I of Persia, 260. Defeat
of the Goths at Nish, 269. Diocletian organizes the R.E. into two great circum-
scriptions (E and W), 285. Britain
independent under Carausius, 286–93,
and under Allectus, 293–6. Constantine
legalizes Christianity by the *Edict of Milan*,
313. Defeat of Emperor Valens by
Visigoths at Adrianople, 378. Definite partition of the Empire at death of Theodosius
the Great, 395.

Roman Empire, Eastern, or **Byzantine
Empire**. The name given to that part of the
R.E. whose capital was at Constantinople
and which continued after the end of the
Western Imperial line in AD 476. For previous history see ROME, ROMAN EMPIRE, etc.
First schism between Eastern and Western
Churches begins, 484. Justinian closes Athens University, 529. Belisarius reconquers
N Africa, 533–4. Invades Italy, 535–40.
Narses makes Italy a Byzantine province,
552–5. Hagia Sophia Cathedral consecrated, 563. War with Persia, 572–91. Persians conquer Syria and Palestine, 614;
Egypt, 618–19. Heraclius recovers Jerusalem, 629. Arabs under the Caliph Omar
defeat Byzantines at battle of the Yarmuk,
634; take Damascus, 635; Jerusalem, 638;
Egypt, 639–40; Tripoli, 647; Cyprus, 649.
They begin conquest of N Africa, 670. Arab
siege of and defeat at Constantinople,

673–7. Arab raids on Constantinople, 717–19. Lombards take Ravenna from Byzantines, 751. The Iconoclastic controversy, 726–842. Arabs take Crete, 826; and invade Sicily, 827; and S Italy, 838. Cyril and Methodius convert the Bulgars, 864, Basil I recovers S Italy, 867–80. Arabs expel Byzantines from Sicily, 902. Saracens attack Salonika, 904. Romanus I (Lecapenus) extends Byzantine Empire to the Euphrates, 920–44. Crete reconquered, 961; and Cyprus, 964–6. Victorious wars under John Zimisces and Basil II (Bulgaroktonos – 'Kill-Bulgars') against Bulgars, 971–1025. Conquest of Armenia, 1045. Disastrous defeat of Romanus IV (Diogenes) by Seljuk Turks at Manzikert and loss of central Anatolia, 1071. Norman invasion of the Balkans, 1081–5. Alexius Comnenus defeats Petchenegs at Leburnium, 1091; and the Cumans at Adrianople, 1095. (*See* CRUSADE (FIRST), 1096–9). Commercial agreements with Venice, 1126. Venetian merchants excluded, 1171. Seljuks defeat Manuel I at Myriokephalon. 1176. Cyprus becomes independent, 1184. (*See* CRUSADE (THIRD), 1189–93, and CRUSADE (FOURTH) which, led by Venice, captures Constantinople and establishes a Latin Empire, 1204.) (*See* TREBIZOND.) Theodore Lascaris established at Nicaea, 1208. Vatatzes expels Latins from Anatolia, 1224; and captures Salonika, 1246. Michael VIII Palaeologus retakes Constantinople and overthrows Latin Empire, 1261. Osman I (Ottoman) defeats Byzantines at battle of Baphaion, 1301. He takes Brusa, 1326. John VI Cantacuzene, Turkish-supported candidate for imperial throne, 1347–54. First Turkish settlement in Europe, 1353. Turks take Adrianople, 1357. John V visits the W to get aid against the Turks, 1366. Final loss of Anatolia, 1390. Defeat by Turks at battle of Nicopolis, 1396. First Turkish siege of Constantinople, 1422. Turks storm Constantinople and bring the Eeastern R.E. to an end, 29 May 1453. *See* OTTOMAN EMPIRE.

Eastern Roman Emperors from the Foundation of Constantinople, AD 330.
(Usurpers in italics. Constantine II and Constans I are not included, as they never exercised effective power in the E.)

Constantinian Dynasty:
Constantine I, the Great *d.* 337
Constantius 337–61
Julian, the Apostate 361–63
Jovian 363–64
Valens 364–78
Theodosian Dynasty:
Theodosius I, the Great 379–95
Arcadius 395–408
Theodosius II 408–50
Marcian 450–57
Leonine Dynasty:
Leo I 457–74
Leo II 474
Zeno 474–91
Basilicus 475–76
Anastasius I 491–518
Justinian Dynasty:
Justin I 518–27
Justinian I 527–65
Justin II 565–78
Tiberius II 578–82
Maurice 582–602
Theodosius, co-Emperor 590–602
Phocas 602–10
Heraclian Dynasty:
Heraclius I 610–41
Constantine III 613–41
Heracleonas 638–41
Constantine III 641
Heracleonas 641
Constans II 641–68
Constantine IV 659–68
Heraclius 659–81
Tiberius 659–81
Constantine IV, Pogonatus 668–85
Justinian II, Rhinotmetus 685–95
Leontius 695–98
Tiberius III, Apsimar 698–705
Justinian II, Rhinotmetus 705–11
Tiberius 706–11
Philippicus, Bardanes 711–13
Anastasius II, Artemius 713–16
Theodosius III 716–17
Isaurian Dynasty:
Leo III, the Isaurian 717–40
Constantine V, 720–40
Constantine V, Copronymus 740–75
Leo IV 750–75

Leo IV, the Chazar 775–80
Constantine VI 776–80
Constantine VI 780–97
Irene 797–802
Nicephorus I 802–11
Stauracius 811
Michael I, Rhangabe 811–13
Leo V, the Armenian 813–20
Amorian Dynasty:
Michael II, the Amorian 820–29
Theophilus 821–29
Theophilus 829–42
Michael III, the Drunkard 842–67
Basil I 866–67
Macedonian Dynasty:
Basil I the Macedonian 867–86
Constantine 869–80
Leo VI 870–86
Alexander 871–912
Leo VI, the Wise 886–912
Constantine VII 911–13
Alexander 912–13
Constantine VII, Porphyrogenetus 913–19
Romanus I, Lecapenus 919–44
Constantine VII 919–44
Christopher Lecapenus 921–31
Stephen Lecapenus 924–45
Constantine Lecapenus 924–45
Constantine VII, Porphyrogenetus 944–59
Romanus II *c.* 950–59
Romanus II 959–63
Basil II 960–63
Constantine VIII 961–1025
Basil II, Bulgaroctonus 963
Nicephorus II, Phocas 963–69
Basil II 963–76
John I, Tzimisces 969–76
Basil II, Bulgaroctonus 976–1025
Constantine VIII 1025–28
Romanus III, Argyrus 1028–34
Michael IV, the Paphlagonian 1034–41
Michael V, the Caulker 1041–42
Zoe and Theodora, Porphyrogenetae 1042
Constantine IX, Monomachus 1042–55
Theodora, Porphyrogeneta 1055–56
Michael VI, Stratioticus 1056–57
Isaac I, Comnenus 1057–59
Ducas Dynasty:
Constantine X, Ducas 1059–67
Michael VII *c.* 1060–67
Michael VII, Parapinaces 1067–68

Romanus IV, Diogenes 1068–71
Michael VII 1068–71
Michael VII, Parapinaces 1071–78
Nicephorus III, Botaniates 1078–81
Comnenian Dynasty:
Alexius I, Comnenus 1081–1118
Constantine, Ducas 1081–90
John II 1092–1118
John II, Calojohannes 1118–43
Alexius 1119–42
Manuel I 1143–80
Alexius II 1172–80
Alexius II 1180–83
Andronicus I 1182–83
Andronicus I 1183–85
Angelus Dynasty:
Isaac II, Angelus 1185–95
Alexius III 1195–1203
Alexius IV 1203–04
Isaac II 1203–04
Alexius V, Murtuphlus 1204
Latin Emperors:
Baldwin I 1204–05
Henry 1206–16
Peter of Courtenay 1216–17
Robert 1221–28
Baldwin II 1228–37
John of Brienne 1228–37
Baldwin II (alone) 1237–61
Lascarid Dynasty (Nicaean Empire, 1204–61)
Theodore I, Lascaris 1204–22
John III, Ducas Vatatzes 1222–54
Theodore II, Lascaris Vatatzes 1254–58
John IV, Ducas Vatatzes 1258
Palaeologan Dynasty:
Michael VIII, Palaeologus 1258–82
Andronicus II 1272–82
Andronicus II 1282–1328
Michael 1295–1320
Andronicus III 1325–28
Andronicus III 1328–41
John V 1341–47
John VI, Cantacuzene 1347–55
John V 1347–55
Matthew Cantacuzene 1348–55
Andronicus IV 1376–79
John VII 1376–90
John V 1379–90
Andronicus IV 1379–85
Manuel II 1386–91
John VII 1390

John V 1390–91
Manuel II 1391–1425
John VII 1399–1412
John VIII 1423–25
John VIII 1425–48
Constantine XI, Palaeologus 1448–53

Roman Empire (Later Western). The Vandal mercenary Stilicho seizes power, AD 395. Alaric's first invasion of Italy, 401–3. Capital moved to Ravenna, 401–3. Assassination of Stilicho, 408. Rome three times besieged by Alaric, 408–10. *Visigoths settle in Gaul, the Vandals and Suevi in Spain, 415–23. *Vandals invade and settle N Africa, 429–42. Aetius defeats Huns at battle of 'Châlons' or the Catalaunian Fields (probably near Troyes), 451. Odoacer rules Italy, 473–89; Italy conquered by Theodoric the Ostrogoth, 489–93. Belisarius reconquers Italy, 536–49. Byzantine rule established, 552–5.

Romania. Came into existence by the union of Moldavia and Wallachia under Alexander Cuza, 23 Dec. 1861. Cuza succeeded by Charles of Hohenzollern, 22 Feb. 1866. Independent of Turkey, 13 July 1878. Proclaimed a kingdom, 26 Mar. 1881. Alliance with Austria, 30 Oct. 1883. Balkan Wars, 1912–13. Crushed by German-Austrian offensive, 1–9 Dec. 1916. Bessarabia proclaims union with R., 9 Apr. 1918. Treaty of Bucharest with Germany, 9 May 1918. Transylvania proclaims union with R., 30 Nov. 1918. Treaty of Bucharest annulled by treaties of St Germain, 10 Sept. 1919 and Trianon, 4 June 1920. R. acquires N Bukovina, 1920. Joins Little Entente, 17 Aug. 1920. First accession of King Michael, 20 July 1927. Ex-Crown-Prince Carol ordered to leave England, 1928. He is elected king instead of Michael (his son), 8 June 1930. Joins Balkan Pact, 9 Feb. 1934. Bessarabia and N Bukovina ceded to USSR, 28 June 1940. S Dobrudja to Bulgaria, 21 Aug. 1940. Vienna Award cedes half of Transylvania to Hungary, 30 Aug. 1940. Gen. Antonescu appointed leader (*Conductor*), 5 Sept. 1940. Second accession of King Michael, 6 Sept. German

military occupation, Oct. 1940. Axis pact signed, 23 Nov. R. attacks USSR, 22 June 1941. Britain declares war on R., 7 Dec. 1941. Russians invade R., 2 Apr. 1944. King Michael overthrows Antonescu dictatorship, 23 Aug. 1944. Declares war on Germany, 25 Aug. 1944. Russians capture Bucharest, 31 Aug. 1944. King Michael abdicates and R. proclaimed a People's Republic, 30 Dec. 1947. Ex-King Carol *d.* Apr. 1953. From 1947–89 R. dominated by Communist party under a number of ruthless leaders and economy ruined. Ceaucescu, president of R. from 1967, overthrown by popular revolution, Dec. 1989 and he and his wife executed. Free elections, May 1990 brought Iliescu to power but resulting National Salvation Government (mostly ex-Communists) brought down, Oct. 1991. In 1992 elections former Communist Iliescu re-elected president of R. and ruled with combination of ex-Communists and nationalists. Regime remained relatively authoritarian.

Kings of Romania, 1881–1947:
Carol I 1881–1914
Ferdinand 1914–27
Michael 1927–30
Carol II 1930–40
Michael (again) 1940–47

Roman Republic. Foundation of Rome, 753 BC. Expulsion of the Tarquin dynasty, 510. First dictatorship, 501. Enactment of the XII Tables, 451–450. Rome sacked by the Gauls, 390. Final subjection of the Latin League, 338. Publication of the *Jus Flavianum*, 304. *Lex Hortensia* gives the plebs concurrent power of legislation by plebiscite, 267. First Punic War with Carthage is indecisive, 264–41. Conquest of Sardinia, Corcyra, and Lombardy, 241–18. Second Punic War, 218; ends with defeat of Hannibal at Zama, 202. Conquest of Syria, 190; Macedon, 168. In Third Punic War Carthage is destroyed, 149–6. Greece conquered, 146. Rise and fall of the Gracchi, 135–23. Marius defeats the Cimbri and Teutones, 106–01. The Social War, 91.

Sulla crushes the Marians, 88. Defeats Mithradates of Pontus, 84. Institutes the proscriptions, 82. Resigns dictatorship, 79. *Lex Cornelia*, 67. First Triumvirate (Caesar, Pompey, Crassus), 63. Caesar conquers Gaul, 58–51. He crosses the Rubicon, Jan. 49. He defeats Pompey at Pharsalus, 48. Is murdered, 15 Mar. 44. Second Triumvirate (Octavius, Antony, Lepidus), 43. Defeat of Antony at Actium, 2 Sept. 31. Octavius changes his name to Augustus, 16 Jan. 27.

Romantic movement, as a conscious literary school, had its first English manifesto in the preface to the *Lyrical Ballads* (the second edition, of 1800) by Wordsworth. The word *romantic* when given a literary connotation is of English origin, but was first introduced into the German language by Novalis *c*. 1795, and as used by him and Wieland and reintroduced into English by Coleridge, Southey, etc., came to have the anti-classical and medievalizing association of the R.M. which is largely the result of interaction between English, French and German literature and philosophy; its influence on and derivation from the literature of the Mediterranean countries is negligible. France was drawn into the R. orbit last of the three, and Mme de Staël's *De l'Allemagne*, 1813, shows the origin of French R. ideas. R. traditions lasted longer in France than elsewhere, at least until the 1850s, perhaps because of the longevity and continued vigour of the chief French R. poet, novelist, and playwright, V. Hugo, who did not die until 1885. The R. heyday in Germany and England may be said to have come to an end *c*. 1832 with the deaths of Scott and Goethe.

Rome, City of. (*See also* ROMAN REPUBLIC; ROMAN EMPIRE, etc.; also PAPACY and ITALY.) Traditionally founded, 753 BC. Capitol founded *c*. 614. Sacked by Gauls, 390. Aqua Appia built, 312. Aqua Julia, 33. Pantheon, 27. Colosseum begun, AD 72. Trajan's column, 114. Charlemagne crowned at, 25 Dec. 800. Sacked by Saracens, 846. By the Emperor Arnulf, 896. By the Normans under Guiscard, 1084.

Taken by Barbarossa, 1167. University founded, 1245. Rienzi's republic at R., 1347. St Peter's new cathedral begun, 1513. Sacked by the Spaniards, 1527. Consecration of St Peter's, 1626. Walls restored, 1749. Proclaimed a republic by the French, 1798. Restored to Pope, retaken, and restored, 1799–1801. Annexed to Napoleon's kingdom of Italy, 1808. Restored to Pope, 1814. Garibaldi's Roman republic suppressed by French, 1848–9. Became capital of Italy, 1870. Papal temporal authority restored in Vatican City, 1929, modified, 1984. Mafia bomb outrages in, 1993.

Rome, Treaty of, signed, 25 Mar. 1957, between Belgium, France, Federal Germany, Italy, Luxemburg and the Netherlands, which instituted the *European Economic Community.

Roses, Wars of the. Collective name for the English Civil Wars which broke out in 1455 and ended at battle of Bosworth, 1485. Red Rose = Lancaster; White Rose = York.

Rosetta Stone, inscribed *c*. 200 BC; dug up, 1799. True contents recognized, and demotic text partially translated, 1816, by Dr Thomas Young (1773–1829). The whole deciphered, 1822, by Jean François Champollion (1790–1832). Ceded to Britain, 1801.

Rosicrucians. Rosicrucian tracts published soon after 1600 claim the existence of Rosicrucian societies in the 14thC. They first became widely publicized by Johann Valentin Andreae (1586–1654).

Roskilde, Roeskilde, was capital of Denmark until 1443. Most of the Danish kings from Harald Gormsson (*d*. 986) onwards are buried here in the cathedral which was consecrated, 1084, but the present building was erected, 1191–1200.

Rostock, founded, 1160, by the Polish Prince Pribislav, across the river from a Wendish castle, joined the Hanseatic League, 1218. Became part of Duchy of Schwerin, 1695.

Rostov-on-Don. Founded by Slavs in 862, R. is first mentioned in a document of 988;

was an independent principality from the 10th to the 14thC; assimilated by the Grand Duchy of Moscow, 1389. Fortified, 1761. Changed hands four times in World War II, the last time in Feb. 1943, when the retreating Germans destroyed most of the older buildings; since restored.

Rosyth, Scotland, was the residence of Margaret, sister of Edgar Atheling, wife of King Malcolm Canmore; she *d.* 1093. The naval base here was first laid down, 1903.

Rotary International, founded, 1905, in Chicago by P. P. Harris (*d.* 1947). New York R. Club founded, 1909. First non-American R. Club in Dublin, 1911. British Association of R. Clubs formed, 1914; known as the R.I. in Britain and Ireland since 1938.

Rotterdam, Holland. John I in 1299 granted various privileges to burghers of, and this date marks the origin of the present town; Erasmus *b.* at, 1467; plundered by Spaniards, 1572. Linked by canal to N Sea, 1866–90. Building of Waal harbour, 1906–30, made R. world's largest dredged harbour. Heavily bombed by the Germans, May 1940, and town centre destroyed; rebuilt after 1945.

Rouen, France. Originally *Ratuma*, latinized as *Rotomagus*. An archbishop's see in AD 260; became capital of Normandy, 912; death of William the Conqueror at, 1087; Joan of Arc burned at, 1431; sacked by Huguenots, 1562; occupied by Germans, Dec. 1870–July 1871 and June 1940–Aug. 1944.

Round Table Conferences (in London). Three were concerning government of India: first, Nov. 1930–Jan. 1931; second, Oct.–Dec. 1931; third, Nov.–Dec. 1932. Besides these, a Burma R.T. Conference was held, Nov. 1931–Jan. 1932, and there was a Malta R.T. Conference, 1955.

Royal Academy of Arts (London). Originally the Society of Incorporated Artists, founded by Hogarth *c.* 1739; first exhibition held, 21 Apr. 1760; the present institution founded, Dec. 1768, with Sir Joshua

Reynolds as president; first exhibition held at Burlington House, 3 May 1869. The following are the presidents, with their dates of inauguration:

Sir Joshua Reynolds, 1768.
Benjamin West, 1792.
James Wyatt, 1805.
Benjamin West, 1806.
Sir Thomas Lawrence, 1820.
Sir Martin A. Shee, 1830.
Sir Charles Eastlake, 1850.
Sir Edwin Landseer, 1866.
Sir Francis Grant, 1866.
Sir Frederick Leighton, 1878.
Sir John Everett Millais, ⎫
Sir Edward John Poynter, ⎬ 1896.
Sir Aston Webb, 1919. ⎭
Sir Frank Dicksee, 1924.
Sir William Llewellyn, 1928.
Sir Edwin Lutyens, 1938.
Sir Alfred Munnings, 1944.
Sir Gerald Kelly, 1949.
Sir Albert Richardson, 1954.
Sir Charles Wheeler, 1956.
Sir Thomas Monnington, 1966.
Sir Hugh Casson, 1976.
Sir Roger de Grey, 1984.
Sir Philip Dowson, 1993.

Royal Air Force. Formed by Act of Parliament, 1 Apr. 1918, by amalgamation of the R. Naval Air Service and R. Flying Corps. *Women's Royal Air Force merged with R.A.F., 1 Apr. 1994.

Royal Assent, last refused by Queen Anne in 1702, when she declined to sign the Scottish Militia Bill.

Royal Automobile Club (RAC), founded 8 Dec. 1897, as the Automobile Club of Great Britain and Ireland. Became RAC, 1907. Moved to Pall Mall premises, 1911.

Royal Bounty, part of the Civil List, was fixed at £13,200 in 1837. Payment from R.B. to subjects whose wives are delivered of three or more children at one birth discontinued, 1957.

Royal Commissions. The first R.C. was

established to enquire into Civil establishments and offices of State and reported in 1887.

Royal Exchange (London). *See* EXCHANGE, ROYAL.

Royal Flying Corps. *See* ROYAL AIR FORCE.

Royal George, flagship of Admiral Kempenfelt, sank suddenly in Portsmouth harbour, 29 Aug. 1782.

Royal Greenwich Observatory. *See* GREENWICH OBSERVATORY.

Royal Hospital (Chelsea). *See* CHELSEA HOSPITAL.

Royal Institution of Great Britain. Founded, 1799. R. charter, 1800. Act of Parliament, 1810.

Royal Marriage Act arose out of the marriages of the Duke of Cumberland (1745–90) and the Duke of Gloucester (1743–1805) to Mrs. Horton and Lady Waldegrave respectively. By this Act, passed in 1772, all descendants of George II, other than the issue of princesses married into foreign R. families, must obtain the sovereign's consent before marriage, which is otherwise void.

Royal Military Academy, founded at Woolwich, 1741. In 1946 it amalgamated with the R.M. College, which was established at Sandhurst in 1813; the R.M. College buildings date mostly from 1911.

Royal Naval Air Service. *See* FLEET AIR ARM; ROYAL AIR FORCE.

Royal Naval College. Opened at Osborne, 1903; closed, 1921. Another, at Greenwich, 1873. Another, at Dartmouth, 1905.

Royal Regiment of Artillery formed, 24 May 1716.

Royal Society. Originated 1660. Incorporated, 22 Apr. 1662.

Royal Society for the Prevention of Cruelty to Animals (RSPCA), established 1824.

Ruanda Urundi, annexed by Germany as part of German E Africa, 1884, was awarded to Belgium, as mandatory of the League of Nations, 1919. United administratively to the then Belgian Congo, 1925. Trusteeship territory from 1946. Became independent on 1 July 1962 as the two states of *Rwanda and *Burundi.

Rugby League. Seceded 1895 from *Rugby Union. First known as Northern Union, and took its present name in 1922. First rule changes, 1895. Manningham club first champion, 1896. First Test Match (1908) against New Zealand. International R.L. Board founded at Bordeaux, 1948. R.L. Challenge Cup inaugurated, 1897. First won by Batley. Wigan has won it annually, 1987–95. Yorkshire Challenge Cup, 1905–06; Regal Trophy, 1971–2; R.L. Charity Shield, 1985–6.

World Cup R.L. first staged, 1954. Winners since then: Great Britain, 1954, 1960 and 1972; Australia, 1957, 1968, 1970, 1975, 1977, 1985–8, 1989–92, 1995. In the Great Britain–Australia Tests, A. has won every series since 1970, including 1994 (2–1). New superleague formed, comprising 12 British and two French clubs, to play during summer, starting in Mar. 1996. Amalgamation of several other clubs to form a new first division.

Rugby School (England). Founded by Laurence Sheriff, 1567. Rebuilt, 1809. Thomas Arnold, headmaster, 1828–42. Rugby football originated here in 1823.

Rugby Union, founded, 1871, by adherents of a game played according to rules similar to those codified at R. School (*see* above) in 1846. The characteristic R.U. tactic of *carrying* the ball was first adopted by W. W. Ellis, in 1823. Rules amended several times, including 1875, 1877, 1886, 1893 and 1953. Scottish R.U., 1873; Irish R.U., 1879; Welsh R.U., 1881. Australian R.U., 1874; S Africa, 1889. First New Zealand club formed, 1871. French introduced to R.U. by British in Le Havre, 1872 and since World War II have won several rugby internationals. Calcutta Cup played between England and Scotland since 1878.

Internationals played since 1871. First Oxford *v.* Cambridge University match, 1872. R.U. World Cup won by New Zealand, 1987; by Australia, 1991. Women's R.U. from 1990s. England won Grand Slam for record 11th time, 1995. World Cup played in S Africa following ending of *apartheid, 1995 and won by S Africa. Next World Cup to be played in Wales, 1998. International Rugby Football Board decided, Aug. 1995, that professional players could now play R.U.

Rumania. *See* ROMANIA.

Rump. MPs remaining after *Pride's Purge, 1648.

runes. The earliest decipherable runic inscriptions to which a date can be assigned are at Vimose, Fynen, Denmark, and date from *c.* AD 250. R. spread to Norway before 300, and thence to Sweden; they spread to the W Germanic area (Germany, eastern France and England) during the 5thC. Early R. found in the Rhineland all date from 450 to 550. The Franks casket (Anglian, probably Northumbrian work) was inscribed with R. before 650, and R. were extensively used in England until *c.* 860. The Old English *Rune Song*, a versified ABC of R., must have been composed before 900, though the only MS known, burnt in 1731, was of the 11thC. The runic alphabet achieved its final form in Scandinavia *c.* 1100, and was in use in the N generally for certain purposes, until the Reformation. As to the origin of R., according to Marstrander they were first adapted by Gothic traders or mercenaries on the Black Sea from the Greek alphabet: this would imply AD 150 at earliest. The theory of von Freisen derives them from a N Etruscan alphabet current in Noricum, and adapted by the Marcomanni of Bohemia: this could have happened *c.* AD 1.

Russia. 1) *Up to the Revolution of 1917.* Rurik comes from Sweden, and his successors found the principality of Kiev, 864. Vladimir of Kiev marries Anna, a Byzantine princess, 988. Is baptized, and sets about conversion of R., 990–1015. Conversion continued by Jaroslav, 1015–54. Sack of Kiev and foundation of Vladimir by Andrew Bogolinski of Suzdal, 1169. R. overwhelmed by Mongols at the battle of the Kalka, 1224, and of the Oka and the Sit, 1238. Batu established Empire of the Golden Horde, 1242. The reign of Alexander Nevski, 1252–63. Moscow becomes the leading feudatory under Ivan Kalita, 1328–41. Rise of Lithuania, 1315–77. Dimitri Donskoi defeats the Golden Horde of Kulikovo, 1380. The Horde is attacked by Tamerlane, 1390–4. Ivan the Great (1462–1505) proclaims himself tsar and overthrows the Golden Horde, 1480. He conquers Kazan, 1487. Russo-Polish War, 1512–22. Ivan the Terrible conquers Astrakhan, 1554. Boris Godunov regent, 1588. End of the dynasty of Rurik, 1598. The 'False Dimitriy', 1605–6. The Time of Troubles, 1606–13. Michael Romanov elected tsar, 1613. Serfdom of the peasantry legally established, 1649. Alexis takes Smolensk, 1654. Treaty of Vilna with Poland, 3 Nov. 1656. Truce of Andrussov with Poland secures Smolensk and Kiev, 1667. Peter the Great, founder of the pre-revolutionary Russian state and empire captures Azov from Turks, 1696. He destroys the Streltzi (Musketeers), 1698. Is defeated by Swedes at battle of Narva, 1700. He founds St Petersburg, 1703. He decisively defeats Charles XII of Sweden at Poltava, 8 July 1709. He obtains Baltic provinces from Sweden by the Peace of Nystad, 10 Sept. 1721. R. obtains S Finland from Sweden by Treaty of Aabo, 1743. R. enters *Seven Years War against Prussia, 1757. Peace with Prussia, 1762. First Partition of Poland, 1772. Treaty of Kuchuk Kainardji with Turkey, 1774. R. obtains N Black Sea coast by Treaty of Jassy, 1792. Second Partition of Poland, 1793. R. suppresses Kosciuszko's rising in Warsaw, Mar. 1794. Third Partition of Poland, 1795. R. defeated at Zürich, 1799. Defeat at Austerlitz, 1805; at Eylau, 1807. Treaty of Tilsit, 9 July 1807. Napoleon's invasion of R., May–Dec. 1812. Congress of Troppau, 1820. Frontier treaty with USA, 1824. Treaty of Adrianople with Turkey, 1829. Straits Convention, 1841. Poland made a Russian province, 1847. Assists Austrians to crush Hungarian nationalists at Vilagos, 13 Aug. 1849. Crimean War, 1853–6. Serfs emancipated, 3 Mar. 1861. Hereditary priesthood abolished, 1869. Russo-Turkish War, 1877–8. Murders of prominent ministers: Bogolepoff, 1901; Sipyagin, 1902; Plehve, 1904. Russo-Japanese War, 1904–5. Revolt in St Petersburg, Jan. 1905. In Sebastopol, Oct. 1905. First Duma meets, 10 May 1906. Slow progress of reform halted by outbreak of World War I, Aug. 1914. Riots in Petrograd, abdication of tsar, Nicholas II, 1917. R. becomes the Russian Socialist Federal Republic, 1918, and under the Soviet constitution of 1923, one of the republics of the USSR. See also WORLD WARS I and II; and USSR for history up to 1991.

2) *Since 25 Dec. 1991.*

Sovereign republic, based on the territory of the former Russian Federal Republic. R. inherited the USSR's seat at the UN, 13 Mar. 1992, treaty signed between R. central government and its autonomous republics, but Tatarstan and Chechenya refused to sign and declared independence (not recognized by R.) and Sverdlovsk and Maritime Territory regions declared republic status, July 1993. Yeltsin, president of R. had powers limited by 1988 constitution and a hostile parliament. Policy of economic reform hindered by hard-line opposition from 1992 and popular discontent at hardships: in April 1993, Yeltsin won a referendum, safeguarding his position, but not giving him authority to call new elections. Policy of disarmament since 1991: founder member of the *CIS. Attempted 'hard-line' rebellion against Yeltsin, Sept/Oct. 1993 by Parliament members based in *White House crushed, 4 Oct., when Russian troops stormed White House and opposition surrendered. Subsequent crackdown on provincial resistance centres. R. ends pledge not to use nuclear arms first, Nov.; presses *Ukraine to hand over nuclear warheads for dismantling by 1 Jan 1994. Yeltsin announces he will serve out presidential term (till 1996), Nov. 1993; new constitution draft allows stronger presidential government. Elections, Dec. for approval of new constitution and election of new lower house of Parliament (Duma) result in approval for constitution but parliamentary victory for ultra-right-wing 'Liberal Democrats' under Zhirinovsky on relatively low poll. President Clinton holds summit with Yeltsin in Moscow, Jan. 1994: USA and Russia agree to cease targeting nuclear missiles at each other's countries, and agreement with *Ukraine for dismantling of latter's nuclear arsenal. Russian parliament grants amnesty to 1991 and 1993 plotters, Feb. 1994 Agreement with Ukraine to split Black Sea fleet, Apr.: Solzhenitsyn returns to R., May; R. signs 'Partnership for Peace' with NATO, June: Elizabeth II pays state visit to R., Oct. Economic difficulties persist: rouble drastically weaker, summer 1994. Launches military attack against breakaway Chechen republic, Dec. (*see* CHECHENYA). After capture of Chechen capital *Grozny in Feb. 1995, Chechen resistance confined to guerilla activity. But R. criticized nationally and internationally for its military action. Yeltsin loses confidence vote in Russian parliament over handling of Chechen war, June 1995. July: Russia signs trade agreement with European Union. Parliamentary elections announced for Dec. Burial of remains of last Tsar and his family planned to take place in St Petersburg in 1996. Yeltsin in hospital, Aug. and Oct./Nov.: Bosnian 'Summit' cancelled.

Russian Federal Security Agency, replaced the *KGB in parts of former USSR controlled by Russia in 1991.

Russian literature. The following is a list of prominent Russian authors:

Akhmatova, Anna, 1889–1966, poet.
Aksakov, Ivan, 1823–86, poet and miscellaneous writer.
Aksakov, Serge Timofieievich, 1791–1859, novelist.
Andreiev, Leonid Nicolaievich, 1871–1919, novelist.
Artsibashev, Mikhail Petrovich, 1878–1927, novelist.
Babel, Isaak, 1894–1941, short-story writer.

Bakunin, Mikhail, 1814–76, anarchist writer.

Baratinksy, Evgen Abramovich, 1800–44, poet.

Bashkirtsev, Marie, 1860–84, diarist.

Batiushknov, Constantine, 1787–1855, poet and translator.

Bely, Andrey, 1880–1934, novelist and poet.

Belinsky, Vissarion, 1811–48, critic and philosopher.

Blok, Alexander Alexandrovich, 1880–1921, poet.

Bunin, Ivan Alexeyevich, 1870–1953, poet and novelist.

Chekhov. *See* TCHEKHOV.

Derzhavin, Gabriel Romanovich, 1743–1816, poet.

Dmitriev, Ivan Ivanovich, 1760–1837, poet.

Dolgorukaia, Princess Natalia, 1713–70, memoir writer.

Dostoevsky, Fedor Mikhailovich, 1822–81, novelist.

Ehrenburg, Ilya, 1891–1967, poet, novelist and journalist.

Fadeyev, Alexander Alexandrovich, 1901–56, novelist.

Gogol, Nikolai Vasilievich, 1809–52, novelist.

Gontcharov, Ivan Alexandrovich, 1812–91, novelist.

Gorky, Maxim (the pen name of Alexei Maximovich Pyeshkov), 1868–1936, novelist.

Herzen (or Gertsen), Alexander Ivanovich, 1812–70, novelist, etc.

Kantemir, Antiochus Dmitrievich, 1708–44, poet and satirist.

Karamzin, Nikolai Mikhailovich, 1766–1826, historian.

Kheraskov, Mikhail Matvieievich, 1733–1807, epic poet.

Khomiakov, Alexis, 1804–60, poet and theologian.

Kirieievsky, Ivan Vasilievich, 1806–56, critic.

Koltzov, Alexis Vasilievich, 1808–42, poet.

Korolenko, Vladimir Galaktionovich, 1853–1921, novelist.

Kostomarov, Nikolai Ivanovich, 1817–85, historian.

Kovalevsky, Sonya, 1850–1901, novelist.

Krylov, Ivan Andreievich, 1768–1844, fabulist.

Kuprin, Alexander Ivanovich, 1870–1938, novelist.

Lermontov, Mikhail Yurevich, 1814–41, poet.

Leskov, Nikolai Semenovich, 1831–95, novelist.

Lomonosov, Mikhail, 1711–65, poet and prose writer.

Lukin, Vladimir Ignatievich, 1757–1824, dramatist.

Maïkov, Apollonius Nicolaievich, 1821–98, poet.

Mandelstam, Osip, 1892–1941, poet.

Merezhkovsky, Dmitri Sergeievich, 1866–1941, poet.

Nékrasov, Nikolai Alexeievich, 1821–77, poet.

Nestor, *c.* 1050–*c.* 1100, historian.

Nikitin, Ivan Savich, 1826–61, poet.

Novikov, Nikolai, 1744–1818, prose writer and social reformer.

Ostrovsky, Alexander Nicolaievich, 1823–86, dramatist.

Pasternak, Boris, 1890–1960, poet and novelist.

Polotsky, Simeon, *fl.* 17thC, poet and dramatist.

Pososhkov, Ivan, *c.* 1673–1726, reformer and miscellaneous writer.

Prokopovich, Feofan, 1681–1736, ecclesiastic reformer, controversialist, author of prose works and poems.

Pushkin, Alexander Sergeievich, 1799–1837, poet.

Pyeshkov, Alexei Maximovich *See* GORKY.

Romanovna, Princess Dashkov, 1743–1810, prose writer and editor, for some years president of the Academy of Science.

Ratushinskaya, Irina Borisovna, 1954–, poet.

Saltykov, Shtchedrin Mikhail Evgrafovich, 1826–89, novelist.

Sholokhov, Mikhail, 1905–84, novelist.

Sologub, Fedor (pseudonym of Fedor Kuzmich Tchernikov), 1863–1927, novelist and poet.

Soloviev, Sergei Mikhailovich, 1820–79, historian.

Soloviev, Vladimir Sergeievich, 1853–1900, philosopher.

Solzhenitsyn, Alexander, 1918–, novelist.

Sumarokov, Alexis Petrovich, 1718–77, dramatist.

Tchadaev, Peter Yakovlevich, 1793–1855, writer and critic.

Tchekhov, Anton, 1860–1904, dramatist and novelist.

Tchernishevsky, Nikolai, 1828–89, critic, philosopher, and novelist.

Tiutchev, Fedor Ivanovich, 1803–76, poet.

Tolstoy, Alexei Nikolaievich, 1883–1945, novelist.

Tolstoy, Alexis Constantinovich, 1817–1875, novelist, etc.

Tolstoy, Leo Nikolaievich, 1828–1910, novelist, etc.

Trediakovsky, Vasili, 1703–69, poet and prose writer.

Turgenev, Ivan Sergeievich, 1818–83, novelist.

Yesenin, Sergei, 1895–1925, poet.

Yevtushenko, Yevgeniy Alexandrovich, 1933–, poet.

Zhukovsky, Vassili Andreievich, 1783–1852, poet.

Russian secret police. Tsarist designation, Okhrana; under the Soviet regime, 1917–91, *see* CHEKA, MVD, NKGB, NKVD, etc.

Russian tsars. The R. rulers from 864 till 1169 were Grand Princes of Kiev. From 1169 to 1328 they were Great Dukes of Vladimir, and from 1328 till 1480 Grand Dukes of Muscovy. Ivan the Great proclaimed himself tsar, 1480. This list therefore begins with him.

House of Rurik:
Ivan III (the Great) 1462–1505
Vassili III 1505–33
Ivan IV (the Terrible) 1533–84
Theodore I 1584–98
House of Godunov:
Boris 1598–1605
Theodore II 1605
Interregnum 1605–13
House of Romanov:

Michael 1613–45
Alexis 1645–76
Theodore III 1676–82
Ivan V 1682–89
Sophia (regent) 1682–89
Peter I (the Great) 1682–1725
Catherine I 1725–27
Peter II 1727–30
Anne 1730–40
Ivan VI 1740–41
Elizabeth 1741–62
Peter III 1762
Catherine II (the Great) 1762–96
Paul 1796–1801
Alexander I 1801–25
Nicholas I 1825–55
Alexander II 1855–81
Alexander III 1881–94
Nicholas II (abdicated) 1894–1917

Ruthenia. Ruthenians, or Little Russians, or Ukrainians, are a linguistic division of the Slavs, the most south-westerly of the E Slav group, whose language was identical with that of the other E Slavs (Great Russians, White Russians) until *c.* 1240. All alike spoke Old Russian. From 1321 to 1772 the greater part of R. was under Lithuanian, then under Polish, dominion, while from 1772 to 1917 it was divided under Russian, Austrian, Hungarian and occasionally Turkish suzerainty. In 1918 the easternmost province of the newly set-up Czechoslovak Republic was named R., or Sub-Carpathian Russia. In 1938 it was isolated by the defection of the Slovaks from the republic, and was occupied by the Hungarian Army and annexed to Hungary. In 1945 the Ukrainian SSR, which had already acquired the territories of Galicia from Poland and N Bukovina and Bessarabia from Romania, obtained the cession of the province from Czechoslovakia. *see* UKRAINE.

Ruthenian Church is a name for the Uniate Catholic Church (Catholics of Slavonic rite but Roman allegiance), whose followers are spread over Polish, Russian (especially in Galicia), Slovak and Romanian territory. The Little Russians, for the most part, became Christian during the reign of Vladimir the Great of Kiev (980–1015), and at the time of the schism, 1054, sided with the Greek faction. But after numerous overtures they became attached to the Roman allegiance by the union of Brest-Litovsk, 1594. In 1946 about 3½ million members of the R.C. in Soviet territory withdrew their allegiance to Rome, under duress, and submitted to the Orthodox Patriarchate in Moscow. Some attempts to return to Roman allegiance since 1989.

Rutland. English county, dating from the 13thC, whose absorption into Leicester was recommended, 1961; proposal abandoned, 1963, but adopted under the Local Government Act of 1972. Announced, 1995, R. to be revived under recommendations of Local Government Commission.

Ruthven, Raid of. A *coup d'état* which involved kidnapping the boy James VI of Scotland from his guardians, the Duke of Lennox and the Earl of Arran; this was done by the Earls of Gowrie and Mar, Lord Lyndsay of the Byres, and the Master of Glamis, in 1582.

Rwanda, Africa. Independent republic created by the granting of independence to *Ruanda-Urundi on 1 July 1962. Military government, 1973–80. Intertribal fighting from 1989 despite frequent official ceasefires and adoption of multiparty constitution 1991. Famine already apparent when president and premier of R. killed in air crash, 6 April 1994, regarded as assassination. Civil war followed between Tutsi and Hutu tribes with atrocities on both sides and hundreds of thousands of refugees fleeing to Zaire. UN approved a two-month French intervention and 'safe zone', June. By end of July Tutsis controlled most of R. and announced a new government. International aid provided food and medicine for R. and those in refugee camps, and UN urged refugees to return home. But majority still refusing to do this in 1995 and signs that some camps increasingly dominated by militants. Many executions, violation of human rights occurring, 1995, and refugee problem remained acute.

Ryder Cup, golfing trophy presented by Samuel Ryder and first competed for officially by British and US teams, 1927. British team expanded to Britain and Ireland, 1973; became a European team from 1979. To date (1995) scores are: USA 23, Great Britain/Europe 6, Halved, 2.

Rye House Plot. A conspiracy formed in 1683 to assassinate Charles II and the Duke of York; the plot was frustrated soon after its origin.

Ryswick, Treaty of, 1697. Ended the war between France and the coalition composed of England, Spain, Brandenburg, Holland and the Empire.

Ryuku Islands (which include *Okinawa) S of Japan, which seized them from the Chinese, 1609. China gave up claim to 1895. Taken by the USA, 1945. Part of group returned to Japan, 1953; the remainder in 1972.

SA (Sturmabteilungen). *National, Socialist 'assault detachment' formed in Germany about 1922 for the purpose of breaking up meetings by rival parties, etc. Its chief of staff, Roehm, shot, 30 June 1934, when its influence largely ceased.

Saarland (for earlier history *see* PALATINATE) was placed under control of League of Nations from 10 Jan. 1920 by Treaty of Versailles (*see end* of WORLD WAR I) for 15 years, viz. until 1935, when plebiscite decided for return to Germany. From May 1945 occupied by French troops. New Landtag, elected Oct. 1947, passed constitution making S. an autonomous state, economically united to France, Nov. 1947; ratified by French National Assembly, Feb. 1948. Agreement on future status of S. signed by France and Federal Germany, 23 Oct. 1954; this rejected by the Saarlanders in a referendum, Oct. 1955. Widespread agitation for unification with Federal Germany resulted in France and Federal Germany signing an agreement in Oct. 1956, whereby S. returned to Germany on 1 Jan. 1957.

Sabah, formerly known as North Borneo (*see* BORNEO), ceded to a British syndicate by local ruler, 1877–8, which transferred to the British N Borneo Co., chartered 1881. Joined Malaysian Federation, 16 Sept. 1963, when name was changed to S.

Sacco and Vanzetti were accused of a double murder committed, 15 Apr. 1920, in USA. Trial began, 31 May 1921, verdict of guilty given, 14 July. Celestino Madeiros confessed to the murder, 18 Nov. 1925. Judge Thayer refused re-trial and sentenced S. and V. to death, 9 Apr. 1927. Sentence executed, 23 Aug. 1927.

Sa-Ch'e. *See* YARKAND.

SADC (South African Development Community). Emerged from original meeting of 10 African countries in Tanzania, July 1979, which wished to reduce their economic dependence on S Africa. Formally established, Aug. 1992. In Aug. 1994, following establishment of multiracial democratic rule in S Africa, S Africa itself became a member and SADC's aims expanded to include future establishment of a common market area and a common defence policy.

Sadler's Wells Opera Company. *See* ENGLISH NATIONAL OPERA COMPANY

Sadler's Wells Royal Ballet Company. *See* BIRMINGHAM ROYAL BALLET COMPANY.

Safad, Safed, N Galilee, Israel. After 1492 became centre of Jewish learning and the residence of Isaac Luria ben Salomon (Ashkenazi) (1534–72) and other Cabbalistic scholars. First Palestinian printing-press installed, 1563. Severe earthquake, 1837.

Safety of Sports Grounds Act, 1975. Extended after Bradford football club disaster, May 1985 and Hillsborough disaster, 1989.

Sahara, first crossed by Europeans: Hornemann, 1798–1800; Oudney, Denham, and Clapperton, 1822–4; Laing, 1826; Caille, 1828; Davidson, 1836; Richardson, 1845; Barth, 1850–5; Rohlfs, 1865–7; Nachtigal, 1869–70; Lenz, 1880; Flatters (perished), 1881; Buchanan, 1922, all with animal transport. Laperrine lost his life attempting to fly across the desert, 1919. First motor-car crossing by de Prohuk, 1920. Up to 10,000 years ago much of the present S. was part grassland. Estimated that desert area extended by over 250,000 square miles, 1940–90 and famine caused by drought now endemic to the S. *See* SAHEL.

Sahara, Western. *See* WESTERN SAHARA.

Sahel, area to S of the Sahara, has suffered severe drought, resulting in famines since 1968. There was virtually no rain at all in 1972, 1983–85. *See also* FAMINES.

Saigon. *See* HO CHI MINH CITY.

Salford, University of, established 1967.

St Albans, England. Present town, containing many ancient buildings, and near site of Roman *Verulamium*, is called after St Alban, a Roman soldier martyred there, AD 303. Monastery erected *c.* 793; dissolved, 1539. Abbey (cathedral since 1877) consecrated, 1115. Battles at during Wars of the Roses: 1. 22 May 1455; 2. 17 Feb. 1461.

St Andrews, Scotland. Royal burgh after 1140. Cathedral commenced in 1162; consecrated, 1318; desecrated by Protestant mob, 1559. University founded, 1411. Robert Bruce held his first Parliament at, 1309. Royal and Ancient Golf Club instituted, 1754.

St Bartholomew, St Barthélemy Island, was first settled by Frenchmen from St Kitts in 1648. Taken by English, 1689; restored to France, 1697. Retaken, 1746, restored, 1748. Ceded to Sweden, 1785, but bought back, 1878.

St Bartholomew's Hospital. *See* BARTHOLOMEW, ST.

St Bartholomew's Massacre. *See* BARTHOLOMEW, MASSACRE OF SAINT.

St Bernard Pass, runs between Switzerland and Italy. Great S.B.P. contained the hospice of St Bernard of Mentone (923–1108), built 962, and served by Augustinian canons since 13thC. Hospice handed over to French, 1947; now a retreat centre. Crossed by Napoleon's army, 1800. Carriage road opened, 1895. Tunnel opened, 19 Mar. 1964. Little S.B.P. used by Hannibal's army, 218 BC.

St David's, Wales. St David founded monastery at and *d.* at, 6thC. Present cathedral dates back to 12thC and additions from then to 19thC. 14thC bishop's palace ruins. S.D. made a city, July 1994.

St Gothard Pass, runs between Switzerland and Italy. First opened to wheeled traffic, 1820–4. Railway (and tunnel) constructed, 1872–82. Road tunnel (10 miles long) opened, 1980.

St Helena, Island of, S Atlantic. Discovered by the Portuguese on St Helena's Day, 21 May 1502; possessed by E India Co., 1659; Napoleon *d.* at, 1821; became a British colony, 1834. Island of Ascension annexed to, 1922; Tristan da Cunha, 1938.

St Helens, Mount, Washington state, USA. Volcano dormant from 1857 till major eruption, 1980, caused widespread devastation, climatic interferences, and top of mountain blown away, reducing total height by over 1200 ft/390 m.

St James's Palace, London. Built by Henry VIII, 1530–6. Extended by Charles II, 1668; by George IV, 1827. Official residence of the sovereign from 1698 until 1837.

St John, Knights of. *See* MALTA, KNIGHTS OF.

St Kilda. Sold by The Macleod, 1779; bought back, 1871; evacuated by remnant of population, 1930. First wedding for 70 years at, June 1993.

St Kitts, W Indies. Discovered by Columbus, 1493. Ceded to Britain, 1713; independent (with *Nevis) 19 Sept. 1983.

St Lawrence Seaway. Complex of dredged channels, locks and Great Lakes, linking centre of the American mainland to the Atlantic Ocean for sea-going vessels, started 1954, opened officially by Queen Elizabeth II, 26 June 1959.

St Louis, Missouri, USA. Named after Louis IX of France, and founded in 1764 by Laclède. Possessed by Spain, 1768; by USA, 1803.

St Lucia. Discovered by Columbus, 1502. French, 1635. English settlement established, 1639; captured by English, 1664; English evacuated, 1667. Finally ceded to Britain, 1814. Independent, 22 Feb. 1979.

St Paul's Cathedral (London). A church built in the early 7thC, traditionally on the site of a demolished Roman basilica, was burnt down in 1087. New cathedral completed about 1287; in 1561 the spire was struck by lightning. About 60 years later Inigo Jones was entrusted with restoration, but in 1666, after its destruction by the Great Fire, Christopher Wren was commissioned to re-build the cathedral; in 1675 the foundation-stone of the new building was laid, and the whole was completed, 1710. A 'dangerous structure' notice, in regard to the dome, served by the City of London, 6 Jan. 1925. Eastern part of cathedral cleared for five years while the building was made safe. Damaged by bombing, 1940–1; restored and renovated after 1945.

St Paul's School (London). Founded by Dean Colet in 1509, the school-house was destroyed by fire, 1666, and rebuilt by Wren; removed to Hammersmith, Apr. 1884: to Barnes, Sept. 1968.

St Peter's (Rome). Church originally erected by the Emperor Constantine AD 324 on the site of a chapel built over the tomb of St Peter by Pope Anacletus at the beginning of the 2ndC; the present church (the largest Catholic church in the world) was designed by Bramante, Michelangelo, Maderno and others, and in 1506 the first stone was laid by Pope Julius II; building began in earnest, 1513; the church was consecrated, 18 Nov. 1626.

St Petersburg, Russia. Founded by Peter the Great, 27 May 1703; became seat of government, 1712–1918. Peace of, between Russian and Prussia, signed 5 May 1762; treaty of alliance signed at, between Bernadotte and the Emperor of Russia, Alexander, 24 Mar. 1812. Name changed to **Petrograd**, 1914–24; to **Leningrad**, 1924–91, since when it has reverted to S.P. Kirov assassinated at, 1934. Withstood German siege, 21 Aug. 1941–18 Jan. 1944, during which approximately one million civilians died. Academy of Fine Arts, 1757. Winter Palace (fifth on site) built, 1754–62 by Rasbelli, destroyed by fire, 1837 and rebuilt in same style, 1839. Only the *Hermitage survived the fire, now an art museum. Summer Palace, 1710–14. Cathedral of SS Peter and Paul, built 1712–33 by Trezzini, contains tombs of all Tsars from Peter the Great (except Peter II and Nicholas II; plans to bury remains of Nicholas II there, 1996). Neva Gate, 1787. Statue of Peter the Great by Falconet, 1782. *Aurora* cruiser, moored in Neva, now a museum and training ship. Blank shot from it, 1917, signalled storming of Winter Palace.

St Pierre and Miquelon Islands. First occupied by French, 1635; fortified, 1700. In British hands for the following periods: 1702–63; 1778–83; 1793–1802; 1803–14. Overseas *département* of France 1976; made a *collectivité territoriale*, June 1985.

St Sophia, Constantinople. Founded in the 4thC by Constantine; rebuilt by Theodosius (415) and Justinian (538–68); Muslim mosque, 1453–1927; museum since 1927.

St Thomas, Virgin Islands. *See* CHARLOTTE AMALIE.

St Thomas's Hospital. *See* THOMAS'S, ST, HOSPITAL

St Vincent and the Grenadines. Became independent of Britain, 27 Oct. 1979.

Sakhalin, island off the SE coast of Russia. First settled by Russians, 1855, and Russian sovereignty extended over whole island, 1875; partitioned with Japan, 1905; penal settlement abolished, 1907; northern half occupied by Japanese, 1917–25; whole ceded to Russia, 1945. Severe earthquake, May 1995, over 2000 killed.

Salamanca, Spain. Captured by Hannibal, 222 BC; Moors expelled from, 1055; university founded, 1243; library of the university founded, 1254; cathedral begun, 1513; defeat of French by Wellington, 1812.

Sale of Goods Act, 1893, repealed and replaced by **Sale of Goods Act**, 1979.

Salem, Massachusetts, USA. Founded, 1626; settlement under Endicott, who gave the place its present name, 1628; famous witchcraft trials, 1692.

Salerno, Italy. University, traditionally founded in the 9thC, and said to be the oldest in Europe; closed by order of Napoleon, 1811. S. beach was the scene of bitter fighting in Sept. 1943, when British and American forces fought to establish a beachhead there.

Salette-Fallavaux, La, France. Miracle at, 19 Sept. 1846. Missionaries of Our Lady of La Salette founded, 1852.

Salisbury, England. Founded, 1219, when the clergy were removed by Bishop Poore from Old *Sarum. Present cathedral built, 1220–58, except the spire. Spire built *c.* 1330–60. Walls of Old Sarum demolished, 1608. Cathedral destructively restored, 1782–1791. Spire repaired and summit rebuilt, 1950–1; spire again in danger and new appeal launched, 1990.

Salisbury, Zimbabwe. *See* HARARE.

Salisbury (England). **Councils held at.**
1. Summoned by William the Conqueror to take the oath of allegiance to himself, 1086.
2. Summoned by Henry I to swear to the succession of Prince William (1103–20), 1116.
3. National councils, 1296, 1328, 1384.

Salk vaccine, against *poliomyelitis, was developed by the American scientist Jonas Salk (1914–95) in 1954.

Salonika, Greece. Rebuilt by Cassander on the site of Therme and named Thessalonika, 315 BC; surrendered to the Romans, 168 BC; made a free city, 42 BC; St Paul preached there, AD 52; taken by the Saracens, 904; by the Normans of Sicily, 1185; by the Turks, 1430; Young Turk revolution broke out here, 1908; captured by the Greeks, 8 Nov. 1912, during the First Balkan War. Assigned to Greece by Treaty of London, 30 May 1913. Venizelist revolutionaries here declared war on Germany and Turkey, 23 Nov. 1916. French and British forces used S. as base for their operations against Bulgaria until end of World War I. Extensively damaged by fire in 1890, 1898, 1910 and 1917; by earth-quake in 1978. 60,000 Jewish community deported by Germans, 1941: few survived.

Salt Lake City, Utah, USA. Founded by the *Mormons, 1847. Became a city, 1851.

SALT Treaties. First strategic arms limitation treaty (SALT I) signed between USA and USSR, May 1972. Second (SALT II) was signed in June 1979 but never ratified by the US Senate.

Salvador, Brazil, founded 1510, was capital of Brazil, 1549–1763.

Salvador, El. Conquered, 1526, by Spaniards under Pedro de Alvarado, who built capital San Salvador, 1528; formed part of Guatemala until 1821, of Mexico until 1823, and of Central American Federation, 1823–39; became independent, 1841. Dispute with Honduras erupted into the 'Football War', July 1969, followed by border-skirmishes. Left-wing coup, 1979, followed by right-wing military ascendancy. Archbishop Romero murdered by right-wing extremists, 1980, and civil war began. Civilian rule from 1984, but constitution not accepted by the FMLN guerillas. Cease-fire signed with FMLN in Mexico City, 16 Jan. 1992, allowing FMLN to become legal political movement. Monitoring by UN. 15 military leaders dismissed for human rights abuses, July 1993. Elections, 1994.

Salvation Army, The. Founded by William Booth, 1865. First known as the Christian Mission; adopted name S.A. in 1878. In 1995 has about 1½ million members world-wide, about 55,000 in the UK.

Salzburg, Austria. Bishopric founded *c.* 700 by St Boniface. Mozart *b.* here, 1756. The S. music festival was founded in 1870; it became an annual event from 1920 onwards.

Samara, Russia, founded as fortress, 1586. Town, 1688; provincial capital, 1851. Industrialized from 19thC. During World War II many government departments and foreign embassies evacuated to S. Known as **Kuibishev,** 1935–91.

Samaria. City (modern, **Sebastiyeh**) founded by King Omri (*c.* 887–76 BC), and extended by Ahab (*c.* 876–53 BC), kings of Israel. Destroyed by Assyrians, 721. Colonized by Alexander, 331. Burnt down, AD 66; but rebuilt, mostly by Herod the Great (39–4 BC), who renamed it Sebaste. 20thC excavations have revealed the remains of Ahab's palace.

Samarkand, Uzbekhistan, dates from *c.* 4thC BC. Known to the Greeks as Macaranda. Seat of Muslim learning by 10thC AD. Tamerlane made it his capital. Noted for its Muslim architecture (10th–16thC).

Sam Browne belt. Named after its inventor Sir Samuel Browne (1824–1901). The British Army discarded it for field service after 1939.

Samoan Islands, Pacific. Visited by the Dutch, 1721–2; by Bougainville, 1768; Christianity introduced, 1830; independence recognized by European powers, 1889. Treaty of 1899 divided Pacific Islands between England, Germany and the USA; W Samoa ceded to Germany and Tutuila to USA. W Samoa was mandated to New Zealand, 1920 and became independent 1 Jan. 1962. Swain's Island ceded to the USA, 1925, and considered an integral part of American Samoa. American Samoa an unincorporated territory of the USA; constitution, 1960; revised, 1967. Universal suffrage following referendum of 1990; elections, 1991.

Samos, Aegean island, colonized by Ionian Greeks, 11thC BC. Oligarchy overthrown, 535; tyranny of Polycrates, 535–522; then subject to Persia until 479, when it regained independence and joined the Delian League. Seceded in 440, but reduced by Athens and became tributary to her. Under Spartan domination, 404–394; again subject to Persia from 387 until its recovery by Athens, 366. Subsequent history uncertain until given by Rome to Eumenes II of *Pergamum in 189 BC. Genoese colony, AD 1346–1560; then Turkish until 1834, when it became a virtually in-

dependent principality. Annexed to Greece, 1912.

San Antonio, Texas, founded, 1718. Modern city built around Alamo fort site.

sanctions. Use of term became current in present sense, 1919. S. were first applied, 1921: at Düsseldorf by the French, and later, in 1935, against Italy. Used against Rhodesia, 1966–80; other countries where S. applied against include Libya, Iraq, S Africa and Serbia, 1992–5.

sanctuary, right of. Abolished by law in 1624, so far as felons were concerned, although debtors were able to take refuge in London and elsewhere until the end of the 17thC.

Sandhurst. *See* ROYAL MILITARY ACADEMY.

San Diego, California, first sighted by Europeans, 1542, and named San Miguel. Renamed S.D., 1602. Presidio and first of Californian missions (restored 1931) founded there, 1769. Mexican till 1846. Modern S.D. sprang from site S of presidio, 1867. Santa Fe rail link brought growth, 1884. Naval base established at, 1917.

Sandwich Islands. *See* HAWAIIAN ISLANDS.

Sandringham, England. Estate purchased by the Prince of Wales, 1862. House rebuilt, 1871. King George VI *d.* here, 6 Feb. 1952.

San Francisco, California, USA. Formerly **Yerba Buena**. Spanish mission arrived at, 27 June 1776; American settlement, 1836; name changed to present one, 1847; discovery of gold, 1849; subject to USA, 1850; disorder in and vigilance committee appointed, 1851; single-span bridge across S.F. Bay completed, 1937; earthquakes at, 1868, 1872, 1906 and 1989.

San Francisco Conference opened, 25 Apr. 1945. Broke up, July 1945.

San Marino City founded, AD 885. Republic reputedly dates from second half of 4thC AD. Treaty relations with Italy established, 1862. Left-wing coalitions ruled,

1947–86; 'grand' coalition of all parties since 1986. UN member, 1992.

Sans Souci (Potsdam), built and laid out by G. W. von Knabelsdorff for Frederick the Great, 1745–7.

Santa Cruz de Teneriffe. Spanish fleet destroyed by Blake, 1657; attacked by Nelson, who here lost his arm, 1797.

Santiago, capital of Chile, founded 1541.

Santiago (de Compostella), Spain. Sacked by Moors, AD 995, who held it till taken by Ferdinand III, 1235; university founded at, 1532; captured by French, 1809; restored, 1814. S. has been the shrine of St James and a place of pilgrimage since the 9thC. Cathedral (housing shrine) begun in 11thC.

Santo Domingo.

1. *See* DOMINICAN REPUBLIC.
2. The oldest European town in the Americas, founded, 1496, by Bartholomew Columbus. From 1936 until 1961 it was known as **Ciudad Trujillo**. It is the capital of the *Dominican Republic.

São Paulo, Brazil, founded by Jesuit missionaries, 1554; in 1995 said to be second largest metropolis in the world.

São Tomé and Principe, is in the gulf of Guinea. Former Portuguese colony which became an independent republic, 12 July 1975.

Sarajevo, capital of *Bosnia-Herzegovina. Town existed here in Roman times, but developed rapidly under Turkish rule from 16thC. Under Austrian rule, 1878–1918. Archduke Franz Ferdinand, heir of Emperor Franz Josef and his wife Sophie assassinated in S., 28 June 1914, the event which led to the outbreak of World War I. After 1918, in Yugoslavia; following declaration of Bosnian independence, 1991, S. became focal point of fighting between Muslims and Serbs from early in 1992. From March, under siege by Serbs. Heavy damage and casualties; UN aid airlifted in. Proposal to put S. under UN administration in event of peace settlement, 1993.

Siege declared officially over in Aug. 1993 but S. remained largely isolated by surrounding Serb forces and dependent on UN airlifts and UN land corridors which were regularly threatened. Fresh shelling by Serbs, Feb. 1994 caused threat of NATO air reprisals; situation subsequently relatively stable throughout rest of year. Fighting around S. resumed, Apr. 1995. NATO airstrikes, May, results in Bosnian Serbs taking UN soldiers hostage (all released by June). UN aid flights suspended, later resumed. Serb bombardment of S., 22 Aug. 1995, resulted in prolonged NATO action against Serbs, and siege of S. effectively over by early Oct., 1995. To be united city under peace agreement of Nov. 1995

Sarawak. By cession from the sultanate of Brunei (see BORNEO). James Brooke became Rajah of S., 24 Sept. 1841. Independence recognized by Britain, 1863. British protectorate, 1888. Japanese occupation, 1941–45. Ceded by Rajah Sir Charles Brooke to Britain, Feb. 1946. Part of *Malaysia since 1963.

Sardinia, Island of. Conquered by *Vandals, 435. Conquered by the Byzantines *c.* 540. Conquered by Saracens, 10thC. Successful revolt against Saracens, 1052, and acquired by Norman kingdom of Naples *c.* 1060. Came under Hohenstaufen rule, 1189. To Aragon, 1323. Placed under Spanish viceroys, 1478–1713. To Austria, 1713. To Duke of Savoy, 1720, who then took the title of King of S. *See* SARDINIA, KINGDOM OF and SAVOY.

Sardinia, Kingdom of. At the acquisition of S. by the dukes of *Savoy, the latter proclaimed themselves kings of S., 1720. Deprived of their mainland territories by Napoleon, 1796, but reinstated with Genoa added by Congress of Vienna, 1814. Merged in Italy when the kings of S. became kings of Italy, 1861.

Sardinian Convention, 1855, between Britain, France and Sardinia, by which the King of Sardinia agreed to furnish troops for the Crimea.

Sargasso Sea. First observed by Columbus, 1492.

Sark (Sercq), Island of, became fief of English crown, 1066. Seigneurie of S. established under Elizabeth I. Demilitarized and occupied by Germans, 1 July 1940. Raided by British Commandos, night 3–4 Oct. 1942. German garrison capitulated, 9 May 1945. New harbour opened, 23 June 1949.

Sarum, Old, became seat of bishopric formerly at Sherborne, in 1078. A cathedral, begun 1067, was burned down, 1092. See removed to New Sarum (i.e. Salisbury), 1219. Parliamentary 'rotten' borough abolished, 1832.

SAS. *See* SPECIAL AIR SERVICES.

Saskatchewan, province of *Canada. Name means 'Rapid River' in the language of the Crees, who before 1869 were almost the sole inhabitants. In the 1870s a settlement began, partly by people of mixed race who took part in Riel's second rebellion, 1885. Constituted a province, 1905. University of S., at Saskatoon, incorporated, 1907.

satellites. First four man-made earth S. put into orbit were *Sputnik I,* 4 Oct. 1957; *Sputnik II,* 3 Nov. 1957 (both Russian); *Explorer I,* 31 Jan. 1958, and *Vanguard I,* 17 Mar. 1958 (both from the USA). Since then many S. launched by Britain, USA, Russia, France, etc., *see* ROCKETS and SPACE FLIGHTS.

satellite television, available in Britain from 1989.

satellite towns, since World War II known as *New Towns. See GARDEN CITY.

Saudi Arabia. Nominally a dependency of Turkish Empire from 1871. As Nejd, consisted of two emirates, Eastern and Western Nejd, until 1892, when Eastern defeated and absorbed Western. Ibn Saud, who seized the emirate in 1905, annexed province of Hasa, on the Persian Gulf, 1914. Inactive during World War I, by 1920 he had annexed parts of Asir; in 1921 Hail and other places. He subdued the new

kingdom of Hejaz, 1925; proclaimed King of Hejaz, 1926, and Sultan of Nejd, 1927. The enlarged realm, in 1932, was named S.A. First oil concession agreement, 1933. Ibn Saud *d.* Nov. 1953; succeeded by his son, Saud ibn Abdul-Aziz. Treaty with Jordan, 1962. Prince Feisal, the new Prime Minister, announced the end of slavery in S.A., 6 Nov. 1962. King Saud deposed, 2 Nov. 1964, and his brother Prince Feisal became king. S.A. became leader of moderate Arab opinion from 1960s: and dominated *OPEC. By 1970s controlled virtually all own oil supplies and country extremely wealthy. Feisal assassinated, 1975; Khalid (ruled 1975–82) succeeded by Fahd, May 1982. Joined allied coalition in *Gulf War, 1991. King announced new Basic Law, 1992; some modifications, 1993. Border tensions with Yemen, Jan. 1995. Terrorist outrage in Riyadh kills Americans, Nov.

Saurashtra, India. Confederation of former princely states of W India set up, Mar. 1948. Part of Maharashtra since 1960.

Savannah, Georgia, USA. Taken by British, 1778. Americans and French repulsed, 1779. British evacuation, 1782. First steamship (the *Savannah*) to cross the Atlantic sailed from S. to Liverpool, 1819.

Save the Children, British charity, founded 1919, with worldwide as well as UK aims.

savings banks. First suggested by Defoe, 1697, but first practical scheme started by Rev. J. Smith, who instituted a S.B. for his parish, 1799. Post Office S.B. established, 1861 (*see* NATIONAL SAVINGS BANK.) In USA first S.B. at Boston and Philadelphia, 1816. New York, 1819.

Savoy. Duchy founded by Umberto Biancamano, 1034. Piedmont acquired by marriage, 1056. Dukes of S. became kings of *Sardinia, 1720. District of S. annexed by France, 1792, but returned to Sardinia, 1814. In 1860 it was finally ceded to France.

Savoy Conference. For the purpose of discussing changes in the liturgy of the

*Church of England; it was attended by Church and Puritan parties, and sat, 15 Apr.–24 July 1661.

Savoy Palace (London). Built by Peter of Savoy, 1245; burnt by Wat Tyler, 1381; restored by Henry VII; used as a hospital till 18thC; finally taken down, 1817. The chapel survives, having twice been considerably restored.

Saxony. Ancient tribal duchy in NW Germany broken up, 1180. The name survived in districts of Lauenburg (annexed to Hanover, 1680) and Wittenberg, which with Thuringia and Meissen became under Frederick of Meissen the nucleus of the modern S. in E Central Germany, 1423. Ravaged by Hussites, 1429–1430. S. divided between Ernestine and Albertine families at Partition of Leipzig, 1485. John Frederick (Ernestine) forced to transfer the electoral title to the Albertine branch (capitulation of Wittenberg), 1547. Treaty of Naumburg results in foundation of the five Thuringian duchies, 1554. Devastated in Thirty Years War, 1618–48. Augustus the Strong, Elector of S., elected King of Poland, 1697. Polish connection continues till 1762. S. joins the *Fürstenbund*, 1785; Frederick Augustus I assumes title of king, 1806, and becomes Duke of Warsaw, 1807. Half S. annexed by Prussia, 1815. Revolutions, 1848–9. In alliance with Austria against Prussia, 1866. Last king abdicates, 9 Nov. 1918. Since 1945 'S'. has appeared in the name of three German *Länder*, two of which were in E Germany until reunification in 1990.

saxophone, patented, 1846, by Adolphe Sax (1814–94), popularized in the 20thC in jazz.

Scala, La (Opera House, Milan), completed 1778; restored, 1878, 1922; severely damaged, 1943; reopened, 1947.

Scapa Flow. Adm. Reuter scuttled interned German fleet, 21 June 1919. German submarine penetrated the basin, 14 Oct. 1939, and sank the battleship *Royal Oak* with the loss of 810 lives.

Scarborough, England. Site of Roman signal station *c.* 370. Viking settlement in 10thC. S. castle begun 12thC: besieged five times, including (1644–5) during Civil War. Quaker founder George Fox imprisoned here, 1665–6. 12thC parish church damaged in Civil War and rebuilt, 1669. Anne Brontë buried here, 1849. Museum of Regional Archaeology, 1829. Grew from fishing village following spa development, 1626 and sea-bathing fashion in 18thC. 1845: rail links with industrial centres led to rapid expansion. Shelled by German warships, 16 Dec. 1916. Its theatre made famous by Alan Ayckbourn from 1970. Land slippage causes hotel at S. to collapse into sea, June 1993.

Schism Act, 1714. Replaced by Occasional Conformity Act, 1719.

schizophrenia, term first used in a medical journal, 1912, to describe this form of mental disorder.

Schleswig-Holstein. Convention of Gastein, 1865, provided that H. should be under Austrian occupation and S. under Prussian; by the Treaty of Prague, 1866, Austria resigned her rights; it was stipulated that N S. should be reunited to Denmark if the people wished it; but the two countries were organized as a single Prussian province, 1867. After plebiscites of the inhabitants of N and S S., N S. was assigned to Denmark, and renamed S Jutland, 1919. S S., with Holstein, remained German and is now an administrative *Land*.

Schmalkalden, League of. Formed by the Protestants of Germany, who met at the town of S. on 22 Dec. 1530. It was finally organized in Dec. 1531.

Schneider Trophy. First race, 1913. Annual till 1927, when it became biennial; the trophy was won outright by Britain in 1931, and there have therefore been no contests since.

Schools, Brothers of the Christian. A Roman Catholic congregation for the education of the poor, founded, 1679, and organized by the Abbé de la Salle in France, 1683; papal acknowledgement; 1725.

Scientists, Among the most prominent are:

Abbe, Enst, 1840–1905
Abel, Sir Frederick Augustus, 1827–1902
Adrian, Baron, 1889–1977
Agassiz, Alexander, 1835–1910
Ampère, André Marie, 1775–1836
Aquinas, St Thomas, 1225–74
Archimedes, 287–12 BC
Aristotle, 384–222 BC
Arrhenius, Straute Augustus, 1859–1927
Avogadro, Amedeo, 1776–1856
Bacon, Roger, c. 1214–94
Baird, John L., 1889–1946
Banting, Frederick Grant, 1891–1941
Berthelot, Marcelin, 1827–1907
Black, Joseph, 1728–99
Bohr, Niels, 1885–1962
Boyle, Hon. Robert, 1627–91
Bragg, Sir William, 1862–1942
Braun, Wernher von, 1912–77
Broglie, Louis de, 1892–1987
Bunsen, Robert, 1811–99
Calne, Sir Roy, 1930–
Cavendish, Henry, 1731–1810
Celsius, Anders, 1701–44
Clausius, Rudolf, 1822–88
Cockcroft, Sir John Douglas, 1897–1967
Copernicus, Nicolaus, 1473–1543
Crick, Francis, 1916–
Crookes, William, 1832–1919
Curie, Marie, 1867–1934
Curie, Pierre, 1859–1906
Dalton, John, 1766–1844
Darwin, Erasmus, 1731–1802
Darwin, Charles, 1809–82
Davy, Sir Humphry, 1778–1829
Descartes, René, 1596–1650
Dewar, Sir James, 1842–1923
Doppler, Christian, 1803–53
Dyson, Sir Frank, 1868–1939
Eddington, Sir Arthur, 1882–1944
Edison, Thomas, 1847–1931
Ehrlich, Paul, 1854–1915
Einstein, Albert, 1879–1955

Euclid, c. 330–283 BC
Fabre, Jean Henri, 1823–1915
Faraday, Michael, 1791–1867
Fermi, Enrico, 1901–54
Fleming, Sir Alexander, 1881–1955
Florey, Lord, 1898–1968
Galileo, Galilei, 1564–1642
Gauss, Karl Friedrich, 1777–1855
Gell-Mann, Murray, 1929–
Green, Michael, 1946–
Haeckel, Ernst, 1834–1919
Hahn, Otto, 1879–1968
Haldane, John B. S., 1892–1964
Haldane, John Scott, 1860–1936
Hawking, Stephen, 1942–
Herschel, Sir William, 1738–1822
Hewish, Anthony, 1918–
Hipparchus of Nicaea, 16–125 BC
Hodgkin, Dorothy, 1910–94
Hounsfield, Sir Godfrey, 1919–
Humboldt, Alexander von, 1769–1859
Huxley, Thomas Henry, 1825–95
Huxley, Sir Julian, 1887–1975
Jeans, Sir James, 1877–1946
Jeffreys, Sir Alec, 1950–
Joliot-Curie, Pierre, 1900–58
Josephson, Brian, 1940–
Kepler, Johannes, 1571–1630
Landsteiner, Karl, 1868–1943
Lavoisier, Antoine, 1743–94
Leibnitz, Gottfried Wilhelm, 1646–1716
Lemaitre, Georges Edouard, 1894–1966
Linnaeus, Carolus, 1707–78
Lodge, Sir Oliver, 1851–1941
Low, Archibald Montgomery, 1888–1956
Marconi, Marchese Guglielmo, 1874–1937
Mayer, Julius Robert, 1814–78
Mendel, Gregor, 1822–84
Newton, Sir Isaac, 1643–1727
Nobel, Alfred Bernhard, 1833–96
Ohm, Georg Simon, 1789–1854
Oppenheimer, John Robert, 1904–67
Paracelsus, Theophrastus, 1493–1541
Pascal, Blaise, 1623–62
Pasteur, Louis, 1822–95
Pauli, Wolfgang, 1905–58
Pauling, Linus, 1901–94
Penney, Lord, 1909–1991
Piccard, Auguste, 1884–1962
Poincaré, Jules Henri, 1854–1912
Priestley, Joseph, 1733–1804

Robinson, Sir Robert, 1886–1973
Röntgen, Wilhelm Konrad, 1845–1923
Ross, Sir Ronald, 1857–1932
Rutherford, Lord, 1871–1937
Ryle, Sir Martin, 1918–1984
Sabin, Albert, 1906–93
Sakharov, Andrei, 1921–89
Salk, Jonas Edward, 1914–95
Sanger, Frederick, 1918–
Saussure, Horace Bénédicte de, 1740–99
Schrödinger, Erwin, 1887–1961
Siemens, Werner S., 1816–92
Steptoe, Patrick Christopher, 1913–1988
Taube, Henry, 1915–
Thomson, Sir Joseph John, 1856–1940
Vinci, Leonard da, 1452–1519
Volta, Count Alessandro, 1745–1827
Wallace, Alfred Russell, 1823–1913
Wallis, Sir Barnes, 1887–1979
Walton, Ernest, 1903–95
Watson, James, 1928–
Watson-Watt, Sir Robert, 1892–1973
Watt, James, 1736–1819
Whittle, Sir Frank, 1907–
Wilkins, Maurice, 1916–
Wilson, Charles Thomson Rees, 1869–1959
Zeeman, Pieter, 1865–1943
Zuckerman, Lord, 1904–93

Scientology (Church of), religio-scientific movement, originating in the USA and formally instituted there, 1954. It derived from the ideas of L. Ron Hubbard (1911–86). Spread to Europe, where its recruitment methods questioned, and UK arm based in Sussex. Less influential after founder's death in 1986.

Scilly Islands (Sillinae). Conquered by Athelstan, 938. Given to the abbey of Tavistock by Henry I. Became crown property on dissolution of monasteries, 1539; leased to Francis Godolphin, 1571; civil power granted him, 1593; Godolphin leases ended, 1830; leases granted by Duchy of Cornwall to Augustus John Smith, 1834; his successors, the Dorrien-Smiths, in 1920 surrendered all except Tresco, Samson and Tean. Exemption from income tax ended by Finance Act, 1953.

Scone, Stone of, taken to Westminster by Edward I, 1296. Taken away by Scottish Nationalists on Christmas Eve, 1950. Handed to the curator of Arbroath Abbey, Apr. 1951. Returned to Westminster Abbey, Feb. 1952.

Scotland. St Columba founds Iona and begins the conversion of the Picts, 563. Rise of the Scots under Constantine I, 789–820. Kenneth McAlpine unifies S S. and founds kingdom of S. proper, 832–60. Malcolm I conquers *Strathclyde, 946. Malcolm II conquers Lothian, 1018. Duncan killed by Macbeth, 1040. Macbeth defeated by Siward and Malcolm Canmore at Dunsinane, 1054, and killed, 1057. Malcolm Canmore becomes king, 1058. He does homage to William I of England, 1070. David defeated by English at battle of the Standard, 1138. Malcolm IV subdues Galloway, 1160. Defeat of Haakon of Norway at battle of Largs, 1263. Acquisition from Norway of Hebrides and Isle of Man at Treaty of Perth, 1266. Margaret, the 'Maid of Norway', dies, 1290. Edward I awards throne of S. to John Baliol, 1292. Franco-Scots alliance, 1295. Wallace defeats English at Stirling Bridge, 1297. Wallace defeated at battle of Falkirk, 1298. Wallace captured, 1304. Robert Bruce crowned king, 25 Mar. 1306. Accepted by clergy, 1310. Defeats Edward II at Bannockburn, 1314. Edward Bruce invades Ireland, 1315–18. Anglo-Scots truce, 1323. Battle of Halidon Hill, 1333. David II captured at Neville's Cross, 1346. David released by Treaty of Berwick, 1357. Robert II, first of the Stuarts, succeeds to the throne, 1371. Battle of Chevy Chase (Otterburn), 1388. James I murdered at Perth, 1437. James II killed at Roxburgh, 1460. James III annexes Orkneys and Shetlands, 1471. James III murdered, 1488. James IV killed at battle of Flodden, 1513. Knox begins Reformation, 1541. Defeat at battle of Solway Moss, 1542. English sack Edinburgh, 1544. Henry VIII of England instigates the murder of Cardinal Beaton, 1546. Knox flees to France, 1547. The Covenant signed, 1557. Treaty of Berwick, 1560. Papal jurisdiction abolished, 1560. Mary Queen of Scots marries Darnley, 1565. Rizzio murdered,

1566. Darnley murdered, 1567. Mary flees to England, and is imprisoned by Elizabeth, 1568. James VI takes over government, 1578. He signs the second Confession of Faith, 1581. Mary beheaded at Fotheringhay, 1587. Presbyterianism established, 1592, but king reintroduces episcopacy, 1597. James VI becomes King of England as James I, 1603. Charles I authorizes new book of canons, 1635. First Bishops' War, 1637. National Covenant, 1638. Second Bishops' War, 1639–40. The Solemn League and Covenant, 1643. Covenanters' rebellion defeated by Monmouth at Bothwell Brig, 1679. Jacobites defeated at Killiecrankie, 1689. Massacre of Glencoe, 1692. Legislative Union with England, 1707. *See* ENGLISH HISTORY and GREAT BRITAIN, JACOBITES, etc. English rule consolidated after failed Jacobite uprisings of 1715 and 1745. Highland Clearances, 18th and 19thC; industrialization of several urban areas from late 18thC. Widespread emigration, 19thC. Growth of nationalist home rule movement from 20thC. Scottish National Party founded, 1934: wins first parliamentary seat, 1945. Directly-elected Scottish assembly rejected in 1979 referendum but nationalist movement gathered impetus in 1990s, with Liberal Democrats and Labour parties supporting its aims in varying degrees by 1993. Labour announces renewed support for an independent Scottish parliament, 1995. Conservatives routed in local elections, 1995, having control of none of the 32 new unitary authorities which would take over power, 1996.

Scotland, Sovereigns of:
Constantine I 789–820
Kenneth I (McAlpine) 832–60
Donald 860–63
Constantine II 863–77
Eocha 881–89
Donald I 889–900
Constantine III 900–42
Malcolm I 942–54
Indulf 954–62
Dubh 962–67
Cullean 967–71

Kenneth II 971–95
Cuilean 967–71
Kenneth II 971–95
Constantine IV 995–97
Kenneth III 997–1005
Malcolm II 1005–34
Duncan 1034–40
Macbeth 1040–57
Lulach 1057–58
Malcolm III (Canmore) 1058–93
Donald Bane 1093
Duncan II 1094
Donald Bane (again) 1094–97
Edmund 1094–97
Edgar 1097–1107
Alexander I 1107–24
David I 1124–53
Malcolm IV 1153–65
William the Lion 1165–1214
Alexander II 1214–49
Alexander III 1249–86
Margaret ('the Maid of Norway') 1286–90
Interregnum 1290–92
John Baliol 1292–96
Interregnum 1296–1306
Robert I (Bruce) 1306–29
David II (Bruce) 1329–72
Robert II (Stuart) 1372–90
Robert III 1390–1406
James I 1406–37
James II 1437–60
James III 1460–88
James IV 1488–1513
James V 1513–42
Mary (abdicated) 1542–67
James VI 1567–1603
James VI became James I of England, 1603.
See ENGLISH SOVEREIGNS AND THEIR CONSORTS.

Scotland, Church of. Founded by John Knox (1505–72) and Andrew Melville (1545–1622). First Assembly ratified Confession of Faith, 20 Dec. 1560. Act of Scottish Parliament establishing the C. of S. passed, 1592. Episcopacy finally abandoned, 1690. Union with United Free Church of Scotland, 3 Oct. 1929.

Scotland Yard, the London palace of the Scottish kings, was demolished soon after

1603. Last Scottish sovereign to use it had been Queen Margaret (née Tudor) (*d.* 1541). Police office set up, 1829, which moved to New S.Y. and became HQ of the Metropolitan Police, 1891. Move to new building at Broadway, off Victoria St., SW1, 1967

Scott Enquiry. *See* MATRIX CHURCHILL AFFAIR

Scottish National Heritage, established 1 Apr. 1992 under the National Heritage (Scotland) Act, 1991, and formed from the merger of the Countryside Commission for Scotland and the Nature Conservancy Council for Scotland.

Scottish National Party (SNP), resulted from merger of two existing nationalist groups, 1934. First parliamentary success, Apr. 1945 (Motherwell). Impact then declined until 1960s. Reached parliamentary high point in 1974 (11 MPs). Returned 3 MPs in 1992 general election and another in a by-election in 1995. Has local government representation and campaigns for Scottish Home Rule.

Scrabble, word-game invented, 1931, by Alfred M. Butts (1900–93) of Rhinebeck, New York. First called Criss-Cross; renamed S., 1948 and became a national, then international best seller from 1952.

SDLP. *See* SOCIAL AND DEMOCRATIC LABOUR PARTY

Sea Fish Conservation Act, 1992, limited the hours fishermen could remain at sea, in conformity with EC law, and caused widespread opposition in Britain, provision suspended, 1994, pending appeal hearing in European Court.

Seal of England, Keeper of the Great. First keeper, Richard, a chaplain, 1116; joined to Lord Chancellorship, 1563.

Seal of the United States, Great. Design adopted by Congress, 20 June, 1782.

Sears Center, Chicago. *See* CHICAGO.

seatbelts, in cars (Britain). Compulsory to wear front seatbelts from 31 Jan. 1983.

Wearing of back seatbelts (where fitted) made compulsory for children under 14 in 1989, and for adults from July, 1991.

Seattle, Washington, USA, named after the American Indian chief S. *c.* 1790–1866 who befriended first European settlers. First European settlement at, 1851; town laid out, 1853. Serious fire, 1889. Rapid growth after arrival of railway, 1893. By mid-20thC a major Pacific port. World Fair, 1962. Present prosperity based on the aircraft industry. Boeing Company founded at S., 1916.

SEATO. *See* SOUTH-EAST ASIA TREATY ORGANIZATION.

Sebastopol. A town in the Crimea, built in 1784; famous for the 11 months' siege by the English and French in 1854–1855, after which it was largely rebuilt, and the siege by the Germans, 1941–2, which also resulted in widespread destruction of the town.

Second Empire. Dec. 1852–4 Sept. 1871. *See* FRANCE.

Second Republic. 24 Feb. 1848–Dec. 1852. *See* FRANCE.

Secretary of State (USA). First appointment (that of Thomas Jefferson) made, 1789.

Secretary of State for Scotland appointed under terms of the Act of Union, 1707, but office abolished in 1746, when its duties devolved on the Home Secretary. In 1827 these were delegated to the Lord Advocate; Secretaryship created, 1885, and offices of S. of S. re-established, 1926.

secret service. *See* CENTRAL INTELLIGENCE AGENCY: MI5, MI6, etc.

sedan chairs. First used in England, 1581; in general use, 1649.

Sederunt, Act of, 1532. James V of Scotland conferred on the Scottish Court of Session the power to regulate Courts of Law by means of A. of S. Power confirmed, 1540.

Seditious Meetings Act. Introduced by William Pitt in 1795. It prohibited the meeting of more than 50 persons (except county and borough meetings duly called) for the consideration of petitions or addresses for reform in Church or State. S.M. and Assemblies Bill, 1817.

Selangor, state of the Malaysian Federation, since 1963. Commercial treaty with E India Co., 1818; accepted British resident and protection, 1874.

selective employment tax (SET) type of 'pay-roll tax' instituted by the Labour Government, 1966. Abolished, 1972.

Self-Denying Ordinance. A measure introduced into the Long Parliament on 9 Dec. 1644. It was to enact 'that no member of either House of Parliament should during the war enjoy or execute any office or command, military or civil'. It was passed 3 Apr. 1645. Essex and other Presbyterians were removed and replaced by Cromwell's nominees, and since, under the Ordinance as finally passed, reappointment was allowed, Cromwell became cavalry commander.

Seljuk, Turkish dynasty, was descended from eponymous chieftain who *fl.* 950 as first Muslim Emir of Bokhara. His grandson, Toghrul Beg, became Shah of Persia, and established new capital at Merv, 1040; he captured Baghdad, 1055. Toghrul Beg's successor, Alp Arslan, defeated and captured the Emperor Romanus at Manzikert, 1071. On death of Malik Shah (1092) the S. domains were split among four branches of the dynasty, the last of which was supplanted by the Ottomans *c.* 1300.

Sellafield, nuclear power station in Cumbria, known as Windscale until 1971. Fire in a plutonium producing reactor resulted in radioactive release, 1957. A large quantity of plutonium was discharged into the Irish Sea from S., 1969–79, but in 1980s substantial investment made in new plant to prevent this recurring. *Calder Hall is located here. Plan to reprocess spent nuclear fuel from Thorp plant at S. given approval by government, Dec. 1993, after

years of controversy; start-up allowed by High Court, Mar. 1994.

Selsey, original seat of the S Saxon bishopric, founded by Wilfrid of Ripon *c.* 683, removed to Chichester, 1079.

semaphore invented by Edgeworth, 1767; adapted by Chappe, 1794; by Sir G. Murray, 1795; Sir H. Popham's system adopted by Royal Navy for sea service, 1816, but replaced by Pasley's system, 1827. Present system not fully evolved until 1890.

Semtex, plastic explosive, manufactured in the former Czechoslovakia. Used by IRA and Arab terrorists from 1970s. Believed to have been used in the *Lockerbie air disaster, 21 Dec. 1988. In 1991 Czechoslovakia announced S. no longer being made: it was estimated that stocks held throughout the world could last for several decades.

Senate, Roman, first mentioned, 509 BC, as having 300 members, all patricians; plebeians admitted shortly before 401 BC. It existed, though largely deprived of effective power, as long as the Western *Roman Empire.

Senegal. First European explorer in modern times was Jean de Béthencourt (1406). French factories established, 1626, but displaced by English; returned, 1677; again displaced by British, 1720–63: this settlement confirmed, 1783; abandoned between 1789 and 1815, the colony was re-established and re-explored, 1824. *Dakar founded by Gen. Faidherbe, who landed, 1852, and became governor, 1854. S. became an independent republic on 20 Aug. 1960, after having been a partner (with the Sudan) in the Federation of Mali from Jan. 1959 until Aug. 1960. On 1 Feb. 1982 joined with *Gambia to form Confederation of Senegambia; this dissolved, 1989.

Seoul made capital of *Korea by King Ni Taijo (*fl.* AD 1392). Scene of heavy fighting during the Korean War, 1950–1. Rapid growth since 1960s.

Sepoy Rebellion, alternative name for the *Indian Mutiny, 1857–8.

Septennial Act, passed, 1716, in force until 1911.

Sepulchre, Church of the Holy, Jerusalem. The first building, commissioned by Constantine, 326, was combined with other small early churches in one building at the time of the *Crusades. Largely rebuilt, 1799 and 1810. E dome damaged in earthquake, 1927. Rockefeller Founda- tion undertook repairs as result of Harvey Report (1932). Damage caused in battle between Arab Legion (Jordan Army) and Israeli forces, 1947–8, and in the fire of 1949.

Sepulchre, Knights of the, received papal sanction, 1113.

Serbia. Serbs settled in present S. *c.* 610–40. Zhuponiya period, 6th–9thC. Visheslav dynasty, early 9thC to 890. Bulgarian supremacy, 890–924. Yovan Vladimir captured by Bulgars, 989. Michael Voislavich king, 1077. S. united and independent under Nemanyich dynasty, 1159–1331. Zenith under Tsar Stephen Dushan, 1331–55. After great Turkish victory at Kossovo Polje (The Field of Blackbirds), S. becomes tributary to Turks, 15 June 1389. Despotate of S., 1389–1459, suppressed by Sultan Mohammed II, 1459. S. a Turkish Pashalik, 1459–1805. Karageorge storms Belgrade, 1805. Limited international recognition of Treaty of Bucharest, 1812. Turkish reconquest, 1813–15. Miloš Obrenović frees S., 1815–17. Becomes hereditary prince, 1830. Milos abdicates, 1839. Alexander Karageorgević elected prince, 1842. International guarantee by Treaty of Paris, 1856. Miloš Obrenović returns, 1858. Succeeded by Michael, 1860. Michael murdered, 1868. Milan elected prince, 1868. Regency till 1872. War with Turkey, 1876–8. Full independence recognized by Treaty of Berlin, 1878. Proclaimed a kingdom, 1882. War with Bulgaria, 1885–6. Milan abdicates, 1889. Alexander Obrenović deposes the regents, 1893. Assassination of Alexander and Queen Draga, 1903. Peter Karageorgević elected king, 15 June 1903. Austria annexes Bosnia, 1908. For history up to 1990, *see* BALKAN WARS; WORLD WARS I and II; YUGOSLAVIA. A constituent republic of Yugoslavia from 1945 until break-up of Yugoslav federation, 1989/90. *Serbia since 1990*: Central authority in Yugoslavia began to collapse from 1989, resulting in aggressive reassertion of Serb nationalism in S. proper and elsewhere. In July 1990 S. reduced the autonomy of the Kosovo and Vojudina regions (with non-Serb majorities). Elections, 1990, won by nationalist hardliner Milosevic's Socialists (former Communists). Sept. 1990: S. adopted a new constitution declaring S. 'united and sovereign on all its territories' (which were unspecified). Following declarations of independence from *Croatia and *Slovenia, Serb forces (allegedly acting as Yugoslav forces) attempted to reverse both, 1991–2. Cease-fire, 1992, left Slovene boundaries intact but after fierce fighting, Croatia lost considerable territory to S. In Apr. 1992 S. and Montenegro announced a federation which they invited Serbs in Bosnia and Croatia to join, giving rise to fear that S. was planning a 'Greater S.'. From 1992 civil war in *Bosnia-Herzegovina between Bosnian Serbs and predominantly Muslim Bosnian government with S. supporting Serbs. International sanctions against S. followed but in Dec. 1993 Serb leader Milosevic won elections. Subsequently S. followed a more conciliatory policy, establishing relations with *Croatia and when Bosnians Serbs rejected international peace plan, Aug. 1994, officially withdrawing support from them. Supports Carter-brokered cease-fire, Dec. During 1995 adopted ambivalent attitude towards Bosnian question, but criticized NATO airstrikes. Played important part in achieving Bosnian cease-fire, Oct.; Milosevic attended peace-talks in USA, Nov. S. initialled agreement to end Bosnian war 21 Nov. Subsequently UN lifts sanctions against S.

Serbo-Croatian language, spoken in the western half of the Balkan peninsula since its penetration by the Slavs in the 7thC AD.

Seringapatam. British defeated Tipu Sahib of Mysore, 15 May 1791. In a later war S. was stormed by Madras Army and Tipu killed, 4 May 1799. *See* MYSORE.

Serious Fraud Office (SFO), established 1988 on recommendation of the Roskill Commission.

Serjeant at Law. This rank became obsolete in 1873.

Settlement, Act of, 1662. Relating to the forfeiture of estates by Irish rebels. Repealed, 1689. Restored, 1690.

Settlement, Act of, 1701. Secured the succession to the throne to the house of Hanover in default of Protestant heirs to the house of Stuart.

Seven Bishops. *See* BISHOPS, SEVEN.

Seventh Day Adventists, Christian church founded in the USA in 1863. It has (1995) about 6 million members world-wide, with about 18,000 in Britain.

Seven Years War, 1756–63.
1756: Anglo-Prussian alliance, 16 Jan. Franco-Austrian alliance, 1 May. Britain declares war on France, 15 May. Black Hole of Calcutta, 19 June. French take Minorca, 28 June. French take Oswego (Canada), 14 Aug. Prussia invades Saxony, 29 Aug. Saxon Army capitulates, 15 Oct.
1757: Clive takes Calcutta, 2 Jan. Russia, Poland, Sweden, and the Empire declare war on Prussia, 10 Jan. Austrians defeat Prussians at Kolin, 18 June. Clive wins victory at Plassey, 23 June. French defeat British at Hastenbeck, 26 July. Russians and Swedes invade Prussia, Aug.–Sept. British capitulate at Kloster Zeven, 8 Sept. Great Prussian victories at Rossbach over French and Imperialists, 5 Nov.; at Leuthen over Austrians, 5 Dec.
1758: British agree to finance Prussia, 13 Apr. French defeated at Krefeld, 23 June. British take Louisburg, 24 July. Prussians defeat Russians at Zorndorf, 25 Aug. Austrians defeat Prussians at Hochkirch, 14 Oct. British conquer Pittsburgh and French Senegal and Clive forces Dutch in India to surrender at Chinsura, Nov.
1759 (*Annus Mirabilis*): British take Masulipatam, 7 Apr. British defeat French at Minden, 1 Aug. Austro-Russians defeat Prussians at Künersdorf, 12 Aug. British

capture Quebec, 18 Sept. British destroy French fleet at Quiberon, 20 Nov. Prussians defeated at Maxen, 21 Nov.
1760: Decisive French defeat in India at Wandewash, 22 Jan. Prussians defeated at Landshut, 23 June. Prussian victory at Liegnitz, 15 Aug. British capture Montreal, 8 Sept. Prussian victory at Torgau, 3 Nov.
1761: British victory at Patna, 15 Jan. British take Pondicherry, 16 Jan. Franco-Spanish alliance (Third Family Compact), 15 Aug. Austro-Russian invasion of Prussia, Oct.–Dec.
1762: Britain declares war on Spain, 4 Jan. British clear the W Indies, Jan.–Apr. British cease to subsidize Prussia, Apr. Sweden and Russia make peace with Prussia, May. Prussia defeats Austrians at Bürkersdorf, 21 July. French capitulation at Kassel, 1 Nov. Truce between Prussia, Austria, and Saxony, 24 Nov.
1763: Peace of Paris between Britain, France, Spain, and Portugal, 10 Feb. Peace of Hubertusburg between Prussia and Austria, 15 Feb.

Severn Road Bridge, opened by Queen Elizabeth II, Sept. 1966. A second S.R.B. due to be completed in 1996.

Seville (ancient *Hispalis*; Latin *Julia Romula*), taken by Julius Caesar, 45 BC. Became Roman colony. Taken AD 411, by Vandals, 441 by Visigoths, 712 by Moors. Reconquered 1248 by Castilians. Building of cathedral lasted 1402–1519, though some parts like the Sacristy (1532) were added later, and parts of the older Moorish mosque were incorporated, such as the Orangery and the quadrangular Giralda tower (1184). Other buildings include Alba Palace, 1483; University, 1502; Town Hall, 1527–64; and Exchange, 1583. Site of Expo 92, 1992.

Sèvres porcelain first manufactured, 1756. Treaty of S. signed, 10 Aug. 1920.

sewing-machine first built by Thomas Saint, 1790 (for shoemakers); for tailoring by Madersperger, 1814; B. Thimonier, 1830; Walter Hunt, 1834; Elias Howe, 1845; I. M. Singer, 1851; A. B. Wilson, 1852.

Mechanical models gradually superseded by electric ones from 1920s.

Sex Discrimination Act, 1974. *See further under* EQUAL OPPORTUNITIES COMMISSION.

Sexual Offences (Amendment Act), 1992, extended law which gave statutory anonymity to victims of rape to victims of other sexual offences.

Sexual Offences Acts. 1) of 1956 made it an offence to live off a prostitute's earnings: 2) 1985 made kerb-crawling an offence.

Seychelles, discovered by Portuguese, 1505. Explored by French, 1742 and 1744, and captured by the British, 1794. Ceded to Britain, 1814. Politically separated from *Mauritius, 1897. Leaders of Arab revolt in Palestine exiled here, 1937. Archbishop Makarios of Cyprus banished to S., 1956–7. Independent republic, 29 June 1976; left-wing coup, 5 June 1977 and one-party state till Dec. 1991, when multiparty system reintroduced. New constitution, 1993, followed by elections.

SFO. *See* SERIOUS FRAUD OFFICE.

Shaba. *See* KATANGA.

Shakers (United Society of Believers in Christ's Second Appearing) founded *c.* 1747 in England. Moved to America, 1774. Community of Mt Lebanon, New York State, founded 787.

Shakespeare's works. Shakespeare was *b.* in 1564 and *d.* in 1616. First collected edition of his works, 1623, in folio. The first plays produced about 1590, in which Shakespeare himself took part; the Globe Theatre, Southwark, was the scene of most of the early productions. Shakespeare's plays with conjectural dates of composition are: *Titus Andronicus* and *Love's Labour's Lost,* 1590; *The Two Gentlemen of Verona,* 1591; *Henry VI, The Comedy of Errors, Romeo and Juliet,* and *A Midsummer Night's Dream,* 1592; *Richard II* and *Richard III,* 1593; *King John,* 1594; *The Merchant of Venice* and *The Taming of the Shrew,* 1596; *Henry IV, Henry V,* and *The Merry Wives of Windsor,* 1598; *Julius Caesar,* 1598–9; *Much Ado about Nothing* and *As You Like It,* 1598–1600; *Twelfth Night,* 1600; *All's Well that Ends Well,* 1601; *Hamlet,* 1602; *Troilus and Cressida,* 1603; *Othello* and *Measure for Measure,* 1604; *Macbeth* and *King Lear,* 1606; *Timon of Athens,* 1607; *Pericles* and *Antony and Cleopatra,* 1608; *Coriolanus,* 1609; *Cymbeline,* 1610; *The Winter's Tale* and *The Tempest,* 1611; *Henry VIII,* 1612. Poems, with dates of publication:
Venus and Adonis, 1593; *The Rape of Lucrece,* 1594; *The Passionate Pilgrim* (partly Shakespeare's), 1599; *The Phoenix and the Turtle,* 1601, Sonnets, and *A Lover's Complaint,* 1609.

Shanghai first settled by Europeans under terms of Treaty of Nanking, 1842. Central Bank of China opened, 1928. Battles between Nationalists and Japanese, 1932 and 1937. Occupied by Japanese, 1938, and International Settlement taken over by them, 1941. Treaty rights of European powers abandoned, 1947. S. captured by Communist Chinese, 1949. By 1990s again prominent commercial and banking centre, handling half China's international trade. Expansion of port and harbour facilities, 1950–82; considerable state housing programme, 1950–90. Heavy industry of 1950s largely replaced by lit industry and service industries by 1970s. Stock Exchange reopened, 1990.

Shan States, annexed to Burma, 1885. Council of Chiefs instituted, 1922; combined with Wa States into single S. State, 1947.

Sharpeville, S Africa. On 21 Mar. 1960, 67 Africans here were killed when police opened fire on a crowd agitating against the Pass Laws.

Sheerness (England). A royal dockyard in Kent, made by Charles II in 1663; taken by the Dutch under De Ruyter in 1667; Nore mutiny here, 1798; new dockyard, 1814: closed 20thC and S. now seaside resort.

Sheffield, England. First charter, 1297. Famous for iron-smelting from 12thC and for knife-making in 14thC. Steelworks began, 19thC. Borough, 1843; city, 1882. S.

University founded, 1905. S. Hallam University, 1992, was formerly S. polytechnic.

sheriffs became important in English provincial administration after 1066. Yearly tenure of office introduced, 1100; confirmed, 1258. Ceased to command county militia, 1557. Modern practice regulated by Sheriffs' Act, 1887.

Sherman Act (USA), against trusts, passed 1890 at instance of John S. (1823–1900).

Shetland Islands. Written sources state Scandinavian settlement began c. AD 800, but contact with Scandinavia probably much earlier than this. Early Norse form of S. place-names indicates occupation before 700. Annexed to Norway, AD 875. Came under Scottish rule, 1466. Economy transformed by oil industry from 1960s, with Sullom Voe built in 1970s, Europe's largest oil terminal, 1993. Wreck of oil tanker *Braer* off S. I., Jan. 1993 caused ecological damage and call for restrictions on tanker coastal routes.

ship. Roman *corvus* in use, 260 BC. Light galleys became standard Mediterranean warships after battle of Actium, 31 BC. Large warships built in England, 1413. Success of galleasses at battle of Lepanto, 1571. *Royal George* launched, 1756; *Victory*, 1765. Earliest iron ship built at Foss (Yorkshire), 1777. Transatlantic packets began, 1816. First genuine clipper, 1832. First power boat, 1786. First paddle steamer, *Charlotte Dundas*, 1801. First screw steamer, *Archimedes*, 1839. Twin-screw ship, *Flora*, 1862. Steam turbine, *Turbinia*, 1894. First diesel and electric ship, *Wandal*, 1903. First gas-turbine driven ship, 1948. First nuclear-powered vessel, the US submarine *Nautilus*, 1955.

ship-money was first levied by Ethelred, 1007. Specifically forbidden by Petition of Right, 1628, but declared legal by a majority of judges of the Court of Exchequer, 1637. Abolished by statute, 1641.

Shipping, Ministry of, formed, 1916, wound up, 1919.

shoguns of Japan. Originally a military Commander in Chief, the first shogun was Otomo Otomaro, 794. When Yoritomo became shogun in 1192 the shogun was the political ruler of Japan. The shogunate was itself under a regency, 1205–1333. The office was held by the Ashillaga family, 1338–1500. Oda Nobunaga seizes shogunate, 1568. Succeeded by Hideyoshi, 1582. With the appointment of Iyeyasu in 1603 the office became hereditary in the Tokugawa family until its abolition, 1867. The following are the Tokugawa S.:

Iyeyasu	1603
Hidetada	1616
Iyemitsu	1622
Iyetsuna	1651
Tsunayoshi	1680
Iyenobu	1709
Iyetsugo	1713
Yoshimune	1716
Iyeshige	1745
Iyeharu	1760
Iyenari	1786
Iyeyoshi	1838
Iyesada	1853
Iyemochi	1858
Yoshinobu (Kei-Ki)	1866–67.

Shop Hours Acts (Britain), first passed, 1886, frequently amended thereafter. Variations in Scotland. Move to liberalize grew from 1990s when unions abandoned opposition to Sunday trading, and Sunday Trading Act, July 1994, radically altered law in England and Wales. From 1 Dec. 1994, most legal restrictions on S.H. in England and Wales (previously based on legislation of 1950) abolished.

Shops and Offices Act, 1963, legislated to improve working conditions of white-collar workers. Much amending legislation since.

Shoreditch (London). First public theatre in England built here, 1576.

shorthand, first known form invented by ancient Greeks (Xenophon), 4–5thC BC. The Roman Marcus Tullius Tiro invented a S. system, 63 BC and there were other systems in England and elsewhere in 16th and 17thC, including one invented and used by Samuel Pepys. First commercial S. set out by Isaac Pitman in *Stenographic Shorthand*, 1837: subsequently used worldwide. Gregg S. system, 1888.

Siam. *See* THAILAND.

Siberia. Explored by Russians in 1483. Tatar khanate, whose capital was Sibir on the Irtish, formed in 16thC. Russian conquest begun by Yermak, 1579. Tobolsk built on site of Sibir, 1587. Traders reached Sea of Okhotsk, 1639. Russians reached the Amur, 1651. Treaty of Nertchinsk established boundary between Russia and China, 1689. S. First used as place of banishment, 1710. *Sakhalin occupied, 1853. Petropavlovsk abandoned, 1855. Convention of Aigun, making the Amur boundary between Russia and China, 1857. Country between Ussuri and the sea secured by Treaty of Pekin, and Vladivostok founded, 1860. Construction of Trans-Siberian Railway begun, 1891. Russia occupied Liaotung peninsula and established Port Arthur and Dalny, 1895. Trans-Siberian Railway was completed, partly through Chinese territory, in 1896. The Russo-Japanese War, 1904–5; Port Arthur fell, Jan. 1905, and Japan gained footing on mainland. Exile system abolished, 1914 (but after 1917 revolution S. housed Soviet camps for political prisoners until final dissolution of Soviet system in 1991). A new line made the Trans-Siberian Railway complete on Russian territory, 1916. In the struggles that began in Nov. 1917, the Bolsheviks of S. were driven out by Czechs. Britain and France landed contingents at Vladivostok, Aug. 1918, and followed by Japanese, 12 Aug.; on the fall of Chita, 6 Sept., Bolshevik government disappeared from S. The leader of the reaction, Adm. Koltchak, became dictator after a *coup d'état* at Omsk, 18 Nov. On the resurgence of Bolshevism, Koltchak lost Omsk in Nov. 1919; he was caught and shot, 7 Feb. 1920, following which S. was absorbed into the Soviet system. Industrial development

since 1950s, based on natural gas and oil resources: also nuclear plant, where deficiencies revealed since 1990s (including serious nuclear accident at Tomsk, in S., April 1993). Now part of Russia.

Sicilian Vespers. Massacre of the French began, 30 Mar. 1282.

Sicily. The Phoenicians founded colonies here in 735 BC, and the Greeks 200 years later; made a Roman province, 241 BC; taken by Belisarius, AD 535; by Saracens, 832; in Norman possessions, 1072–1194; made one kingdom with Naples, 1130; Charles of Anjou King of the Two Sicilies, 1266; 'Sicilian Vespers', massacre of French at Palermo, 1282; became a Spanish dependency, 1501; revolution in, 1848; Garibaldi landed at Marsala, 1860; defeated Neapolitans at Milazzo, 1860; annexation with Sardinia and arrival of King Victor Emmanuel, 1860; annexation to kingdom of Italy, 1860; earthquake at Messina, 1908. In World War II Germans driven out by British, American and Canadians, 10 July–17 Aug. 1943. Mafia extortion in S. since 1945: increased from 1980s, with several murders of policemen, judges, etc. Government attempts to suppress, from 1990s. *See also* NAPLES.

sieges:

Acre, 1189–12 July 1191; 16 Mar.–20 May 1799; April–24 June 1832; 3–4 Nov. 1840.
Adrianople, Oct. 1912–26 Mar. 1913.
Alesia, 52 BC.
Algeciras, 1324–24.
Algiers, 1682–83; 26–27 Aug. 1816; 14 June–5 July 1830.
Almeida, 17 Aug. 1810.
Amiens, 1597.
Ancona, Oct.–13 Nov. 1799.
Antwerp, 1584–5, Dec. 1832; 1914.
Arras, 1640.
Avignon, 10 June–13 Sept. 1226.
Badajoz, 1385; 1396; 1542; 1705; Mar. 1811; Apr. 1812.
Baghdad, 1258.
Barcelona, 1471; 1697; 1705; 1706; Sept. 1714.

Bataan, Jan.–Apr. 1942.
Belgrade, 1456; Aug. 1521; Aug. 1717; Oct. 1789.
Belle Isle, June 1761.
Bergen-op-Zoom, 1588; 1622; Sept. 1747, Mar. 1814.
Berlin (blockade), June 1948–May 1949.
Berwick, 1296; 1333; 1481.
Besançon, 1668; 1674.
Bethune, 1710.
Bilbao, 1835; 1874; 1937.
Bois-le-Duc, 1601, 1603, 1794.
Bologna, 1506; 1796; 1799.
Bomarsund, 1854.
Bonn, 1689; 1703.
Bordeaux, 1451; 1453.
Bouchain, Aug.–Sept. 1711.
Boulogne, Sept. 1544.
Breda, 1625; Feb. 1793.
Brescia, 1512; 1849.
Breslau, 1807.
Brisach, 1638.
Brussels, 1695; 1746.
Budapest, July 1541; Sept. 1686; Dec. 1944– 13 Feb. 1945.
Burgos, Sept.–Oct. 1812; June 1813.
Cadiz, 1812.
Calais, Sept. 1346–Oct. 1347; 1558; 1596; 22–7 May 1940.
Calvi, 1794.
Candia, 1667–9.
Capua, 211 BC; 1501; 1799.
Cartagena, 1706; Nov. 1873–Jan. 1874.
Chalus, 1199.
Charleroi, 1672; 1690.
Charleston, USA, 1780; Aug. 1863–Feb. 1865.
Chartres, 1568.
Cherbourg, 1418, 1758.
Chester, 1643–46.
Chillon, 1536.
Chitral, Mar.–Apr. 1895.
Ciudad Rodrigo, June–July 1810; 1812.
Colchester, June–Aug. 1648.
Como, 1127.
Compiègne, 1430.
Condé, 1676; 1793; 1794.
Coni, 1691; 1744.
Constantinople, 1453.
Copenhagen, 1658; 1801; 1807.
Cordova, 1012.

Corfu, 1536; 1716–18.
Corinth, 1205; 1209.
Cracow, 1702, 1794.
Cremona, 1702.
Cumae, 553.
Danzig, 1734; 1793; 1807; 1813–14.
Delhi, 1857.
Dien Bien Phu, Apr.–May 1954.
Douay, 1710.
Dresden, 1756; 1760; 1813.
Drogheda, 1649.
Dublin, 1170; 1500; 1649.
Dunkirk, 1646; 1793.
Edinburgh, 1093; 1296.
Edinburgh Castle, 1571.
Exeter, 1136.
Famagusta, 1571.
Flushing, Aug. 1809.
Fredrikshald, 1718.
Gaeta, 1707; 1734; Nov. 1860–Feb. 1861.
Genoa, 1684; 1747; 1800.
Gerona, 1808–9.
Ghent, 1706.
Gibraltar, 1704; 1779; 1782–3.
Glatz, 1622; 1742; 1807.
Gloucester, Aug.–Sept. 1643.
Göttingen, 1760.
Granada, 1491–2.
Groningen, 1594; 1678.
Haarlem, Dec. 1572–July 1573.
Harfleur, 1415.
Heidelberg, 1688.
Herat, 1837–8; 1856.
Humaitá (Paraguay), 1868.
Ismail, 1770; 1790.
Janina, 1913.
Jerusalem c. 1400 BC; 588 BC, AD 70; 637; 1099.
Kandahar, 1521, 1839–42.
Kars, 1855.
Kehl, 1796–7.
Khartoum, 1884–5.
Kimberley, Oct. 1899–Feb. 1900.
Komárom or Komorn, 1849.
Ladysmith, Nov. 1899–Feb. 1900.
La Motte, 1634.
Landau, 1702; 1703; 1793.
Landrecies, 1712; 1794.
Leipzig, 1547; 1642.
Leith, 1560.
Leningrad, 21 Aug. 1941–18 Jan. 1943.

Lerida, 1647; 1707; 1810.
Leyden, 1574.
Liège, 1468; 1702; 1914.
Lille, 1708; 1792.
Limerick, 1651; 1690–91.
Londonderry, 1689.
Lucknow, 1857.
Luxemburg, 1795.
Lyons, 1793.
Madrid, 1936–39.
Maastricht, 1579; 1673; 1703; 1748; 1793–94.
Mafeking, Oct. 1899–May 1900.
Magdeburg, 1631; 1806.
Mainz, 1689; 1793.
Malaga, 1487.
Malta, 1565; 1798; 1800; June 1940–Nov. 1942.
Mannheim, 1793.
Mantua, 1796–97.
Messina, 1282; 1719; 1848.
Metz, 1552–53; 1870.
Missolonghi, 1822; 1823; 1825–26.
Mons, 1691; 1709; 1746; 1792.
Montargis, 1427.
Montauban, 1621.
Montevideo, 1807; 1814.
Mostar, Bosnia, May–Aug. 1993.
Namur, 1692; 1695.
Naples, 1495; 1799; 1806.
Nice, 1705.
Numantia, 134–133 BC.
Olivenza, 1811.
Olmütz, 1741; 1758.
Orleans, 1428–29; 1563.
Ostend, July 1601–Sept. 1604; 1706; 1745; 1798.
Oudenarde, 1708.
Padua, 1509.
Pampeluna or Pamplona, 1813.
Paris, 885–86; 1594; Sept. 1870–Jan. 1871.
Pavia, 1525; 1655.
Pekin legations, 1900.
Perpignan, 1542; 1642.
Phalsbourg, 1814; 1815; 1870.
Phillipsburg, 1644; 1676; 1688; 1734; 1799–1800.
Plevna, 1877.
Pondicherry, 1748.
Port Arthur, 1904.
Prague, 1741–44.
Quebec, 1759.

Quesnay, 1793–94.
Rheims, 1359.
Rhodes, 1306–09; 1480; 1522.
Richmond (Virginia), 1864–65.
Riga, 1700; 1710.
Rochelle, 1573; 1628.
Rome, 1527; 1849.
Romorantin, 1356.
Rouen, 1419; 1449; 1591.
Roxburgh, 1460.
Saguntum, 219 BC.
Saint-Quentin, 1557.
*Sarajevo, 1992–93.
San Sebastian, 1813.
Saragossa, 1710; 1808; 1809.
Schweidnitz, 1762; 1807.
Scio, 1822.
Srebenica, Bosnia, 1992–93.
Scutari, 1913.
Sebastopol, Oct. 1854–Sept. 1855; 1941–42.
Seringapatam, 1792; 1799.
Seville, 1248.
Silistria, 1854.
Smolensk, 1611; 1812.
Stalingrad, Aug.–Nov. 1942.
Stralsund, 1715.
Strasbourg, 1870.
Tarragona, 1813.
Temesvar, 1716.
Thérouanne, 1303; 1479; 1513.
Thionville, 1792.
Thorn, 1703.
Tobruk, Apr.–10 Dec. 1941; 18–20 June 1942.
Toledo, 1936.
Tortosa, 1810–11.
Toulon, 1707; 1793.
Toulouse, 844; c. 848; 1229.
Tournai, 1340; 1513; 1581; 1667; 1709; 1792.
Tunis, 1270, 1535.
Turin, 1640; 1706.
Valencia, 1812.
Valenciennes, 1677; 1793; 1794.
Vannes, 1342.
Venice, 1849.
Verdun, 1792; 1916.
Vicksburg, 1863.
Vienna, 1529; 1683; 1848.
Vukovar, 1991.
Warsaw, 1831; 1939; 1944.

Westerplatte, 1939.
Xativa, 1246; 1707.
Xeres, 1262.
York, 1644.
Ypres, 1648; 1794.
Zürich, 1544.
Zutphen, 1586.
*Though limited international relief admitted, S. effectively cut off from rest of Bosnia from March 1992; siege declared 'officially' over, Aug. 1993. Blockade by Bosnian Serbs effectively ended, Oct. 1995.

Siegfried Line.
1. (Or **Hindenburg Line**.) German line of defence in France in Sept. 1918.
2. German fortifications, properly called the W Wall, stretching from the Dutch to the Swiss frontiers, partly on the E bank of the Rhine, completed, 1939.

Sierra Leone, W Africa. Discovered, 1462, by the Portuguese navigator, Pedro de Sintra. Became a settlement for freed slaves, 1786. British colony of S.L. originated in sale of land by native chiefs to some English settlers, 1788. Crown colony, 1808; protectorate, forming the hinterland of the colony, 1896. New constitution, 1958. Became an independent member of the Commonwealth, 27 Apr. 1961; republic, 19 Apr. 1971. One-party state from 1978; in Apr. 1992, an army coup brought down the regime and promised return to multiparty system by 1995. Civil unrest led to kidnapping of foreigners, 1994–5. British and other foreign hostages freed, Apr. 1995. Elections promised for Feb. 1996.

Sikhs, religious order founded by Nanak (1469–1539). Became politically independent of the Moguls, 1764. Ranjit Singh became overlord of the confederation of Sikh states, 1805; in 1849 the Punjab, home of all S., came under British rule. Patalia and E Punjab Union, a Sikh state forming part of the republic of India, was set up, 5 May 1948, but reorganized as the Punjab, 1956. Sikh agitation against alleged Indian discrimination, 1961–2, and again from 1980s. After Indian army attacked S. Golden Temple at Amritsar in attempt to quell unrest, militant Sikhs assassinated Mrs Gandhi, Indian Premier, 1984.

Sikkim or **Denjong** suffered in 18thC from aggression by *Nepal, which was ended by alliance with Britain against Nepal (1814). Site of Darjeeling sold to British for 180,000 Rs., 1835. Protected state of India from 1947; monarchy abolished, and S. made Indian state, 1975.

Silchester, England, formerly *Calleva Atrebatum*, was laid out as a Roman town in the 1stC AD. Excavated 1890–1909, 1938–9, and from 1954. Results of excavation set out at Calleva Museum, S., established 1957.

Silicon Valley, name popularly given, since 1960s, to the area of W central *California which occupies the San Jose and Santa Clara valleys, and where electronic and computer business multiplied in a previously agricultural area. District transformed in 1970s and 1980s. By 1990s emphasis changing from manufacturing to research and suffering some recession.

Silesia. Mutual succession pact between Hohenzollems (of Prussia) and the Piasts (Rulers) of S., 1537. Last Piast dies and S. seized by the emperor as a Bohemian fief, 1675. Hohenzollern claims renounced in return for Schwiebus, 1686. Schwiebus returned to Austria, 1694. Seized by Frederick the Great of Prussia, 1740. Cession to Prussia finally recognized by Austria, 1763. After plebiscites Teschen ceded to Czechoslovakia and Upper S. partitioned between Germany and Poland, 1920. Teschen taken by Poland, 1938. S. E of the Neisse taken by Poland, 1945, and most of the German population expelled.

silk. Silkworms introduced into Europe from China in 552 by two Persian monks; manufactured in Italy, Spain, and S France, 1510; first S. mills in England, 1604; formerly all S. was brought from abroad.

silver coinage. Until Dec. 1920 contained 92.5 per cent silver. Coinage Act, 1920, authorized 50 per cent only. New Coinage

Act of 1946 did not legally abolish S. as coinage, but for all practical purposes meant that S. coins were to be replaced by cupro-nickel.

Simplon Pass, Switzerland. Road built by Napoleon, 1800–7. Tunnel built, 1898–1906, at which time it was longest rail tunnel in the world (12½ miles).

Sinai Peninsula, occupied by Israel after war of 1967. Returned to Egypt, 1982, under terms of 1979 treaty. Sinaitic Inscriptions discovered there by Flinders Petrie, 1904–5.

Sinaiticus, Codex, incomplete Greek MS of Old and New Testaments and some other writings, on vellum. Probably copied in Egypt or Palestine c. 350. Tischendorf (1815–74) found the MS in the monastery of St Catherine, Mt Sinai, 1844 and 1859; he published it in facsimile type, 1862. Photographic reproductions appeared, 1911 and 1922; about 340 leaves of MS were bought for the British Museum from the Soviet Government, 1933.

Sind, Scinde, annexed to British India, 1843. Autonomous province of Pakistan, 1947–55, when it was integrated into Pakistan.

Singapore, the old Malay city, fl. in the 14thC AD, but had been destroyed by 1391. Settlement founded by Sir Stamford Raffles, 1819; placed under Bengal Government, 1823; part of Straits Settlements, 1836–1946. British land forces in Malaya retired into S., 30 Jan. 1942. Japanese landed on S. Island, 8 Feb. 1942; garrison surrendered, 15 Feb. Reoccupied by British forces, 5 Sept. 1945. An agreement reached in London in Apr. 1957 provided for an internationally self-governing S. and the creation of a S. citizenship. A referendum on 1 Sept. 1962 produced a majority in favour of an autonomous S. within the projected *Malaysia, but the arrangement led to stresses and on 9 Aug. 1965 S. seceded from Malaysia by mutual agreement. S. became a republic within the Commonwealth, 16 Oct. 1965 and has since enjoyed increased growth and prestige as an international commercial and financial centre.

Single European Act, signed by all EC members, Feb. 1986, in force from 1 July 1987. It confirmed and in practice extended the objectives first set out in the Treaty of Rome, 1957, including increased use of majority voting in decision-making, and lessening of power of an individual state to use veto.

Single Market, officially existed in the *EC from 1 Jan. 1993.

Sinkiang (Uighur, or **Xinjiang Uygur)** formerly Chinese Turkestan, became a separate province at the territorial reorganization of the Manchu Empire, 1882. Russian influence increased steadily from 1911 until 1941, but officially Chinese since 1942.

Sinking Fund first adopted, 1716, increased, 1727, exhausted, 1786, and new fund started. S.F. on new principle started, 1792; modified by Vansittart, 1813. Legislation on S.F.s repealed, 1866; another new fund started, 1875; modified by Lloyd George, 1910. Other S.F.s started by Baldwin, 1923, and Churchill, 1928.

Sinn Fein, Irish nationalist movement, formed about 1905, which, in the period before 1922, aimed at economic and political separation from England. Since 1960s regarded as the political wing of the *Irish Republican Army (IRA). It won one seat at Westminster in the general elections of 1983 and 1987, but failed to win any in 1992. It has some local government representation in N Ireland itself (1993). Talks between SF and SDLP, 1993. Revealed that secret communication between British government and S.F. representatives had been taking place during 1993, Nov. and Anglo-Irish Declaration, 15 Dec. 1993, envisaged S.F. taking part in talks in future if IRA renounced violence permanently; following IRA ceasefire announcement, Aug. 1994. Irish government met S.F. leaders and Britain lifted broadcasting ban and exclusion orders. British government representatives met S.F. leaders at Stormont,

Dec. and subsequently, but in 1995 British/S.F. talks stalling on question of 'decommissioning' of terrorist weapons.

SIS (Secret Intelligence Service). *See* MI6.

Sino-Japanese Agreement. Signed, 16 May 1918, to counteract common danger of German penetration towards E Russia.

Sistine Chapel, built for Pope Sixtus IV, 1473–81; Michelangelo painted the ceiling, 1508–12, and the E wall, 1534–41. Controversially restored, 1990.

Sizewell, England, site of two British nuclear power stations. 1) S. A was one of Britain's first Magnox power stations, being commissioned in 1966. It first supplied power to the National Grid, 21 Jan. 1966, and has two reactors. 2) S. B is Britain's first pressurized water reactor (PWR). Work started on building in June 1987: completion, mid-1994. (the first prototype PWR power station in the world was brought into operation in the USA at Shippingport in 1957). Plans for a technical replica of S. B in twin-form, to be known as S. C, were being developed in the 1990s, and application made to build, 1993. S. B started up, 31 Jan. 1995, after the longest public inquiry in British history.

Skopje, capital of Illyria in pre-Roman times and of an independent kingdom of Macedonia, 10th and 11thC. Seriously damaged by earthquake, 1963. Capital of independent Macedonia since 1993.

Skye, Inner Hebrides. 'Bonnie Prince Charlie' escaped to, 1746. Bridge linking S. to mainland begun, 1993. Party of schoolchildren allowed to cross, 9 June 1995. Bridge officially opened, 16 Oct. 1995.

slavery. In England S. began, 1562; abolished, 25 Mar. 1807. Abolition of, in British colonies in 1833, and owners compensated; S. in British possessions terminated following year; the abolition in USA announced, 1863; effective from 1865.

Slovakia. Under Hungarian domination until 1918, when the Slovaks united with the Czechs of Bohemia, Moravia and Silesia to form *Czechoslovakia. A German puppet-state, 1938–45. Became an independent republic, 1 Jan. 1993.

Slovene literature. Following are some Slovene authors of the modern period:

Jurij Dalmatin, *fl.* 1584, translator (Old Testament).
Tomaz Hren, 1560–1630, theologian.
Matthias Kastelic, 1620–88, theologian.
Marko Pohlin, 1735–1801, grammarian.
Leopold Wolkmer, 1741–1815, fabulist.
Anton Linhart, 1757–95, dramatist.
Valentin Vodnik, 1758–1819, poet.
Jernej Kopitar, 1780–1844, philologist.
Matthias Čop, 1797–1835, critic.
France Preseren, 1800–49, poet.
Janez Blajvajs, 1808–81, essayist.
F. Levstik, 1851–87, popular lyricist.
S. Jenko, 1835–69, lyricist.
J. Stritar, 1836–1923, poet and critic.
J. Jurjic, 1844–81, novelist.
S. Gregorcic, 1844–1906, lyricist.
Stanislas Skrabec, 1844–1918, critic.
I. Tivcar, 1851–1923, novelist.
J. Kersnik, 1852–97, short story writer.
A. Askerc, 1856–1912, novelist.
I. Cankar, 1856–1918, short story writer.
Zofka Kveder, 1878–1926, novelist.
Prezhikov Voranc, 1893–1950, poet.

Slovenes migrated from the W Carpathians to the valley of the Drava (Drau) about AD 600. Threatened by the Avars they appealed for protection to the Franks, to whom they became subject about 790, first under the counts of Friuli and dukes of Carinthia, then, from 1056 onwards, under the counts, later dukes, of Styria. From 1260 to 1282 they formed part of the kingdom of Bohemia (Ottakar II); then passed under Hapsburg dominion, which was finally consolidated in 1335. No major political change took place until 1918 (*see* YUGOSLAVIA). Their language became separated from Croatian between AD 600 and 900, and its earliest written monument, the Freising Leaves, dates from the 11thC. New Testament rendered into Slovene by

Primoz Trubar (1508–86), 1582. First grammar, 1584, by Adam Bohoric, and quadrilingual dictionary, 1592, printed at Wittenberg.

Slovenia. In 1918 S. was formed out of Lower Styria, Carniola, and a small part of Carinthia. The term went out of official use in the internal reorganization of Yugoslavia, 1922, the nearest geographical equivalent being the Banat of the Drava. In 1945 the Federal Republic of S. was constituted, including the same area as in 1918, but including parts of Istria and Venezia Giulia. Constitutional changes, 1989, allowed a referendum calling for secession from Yugoslavia, and S. declared its independence, June 1991. A brief struggle with Yugoslav (Serb) forces ended in cease-fire and UN recognition of Slovene independence, 1992, since when S. has remained free from the fighting in other areas of the Balkans.

smallpox. *See* Vaccination.

Smith Act (USA), formerly the Alien Registration Act, 1940. This made it a criminal offence to advocate the overthrow of the government by violence, or to be a member of any organisation advocating thus. After World War II the S.A. formed basis of a series of prosecutions against Communists and others in the USA.

Smithfield. A cattle market in 1150 till 11 June 1855; a meat market, 1 Dec. 1868. Famous as a place of Protestant martyrdom, notably during the reign of Mary Tudor, 1553–8.

Smithsonian Institute (USA), endowed by bequest of James Smithson (1765–1829) dated 1826. Formally organized, 1846, first buildings completed, 1854.

Smyrna (Turkish **Izmir**), founded by Greeks *c.* 1000 BC; passed into possession of Colophon and thence into the Ionian confederation, *c.* 690 BC; captured by Lydians, 630 BC; besieged by Timur-i-leng (Tamerlane), AD 1402; taken by Turks, 1424; occupied by Greek army, 1919; awarded to Greece (for a trial period of five years) by Treaty of Sèvres, 1920; Greeks expelled, 1922; awarded to Turkey by Treaty of Lausanne, 1923.

Snettisham, England. A hoard of Roman gold and silver coins discovered here declared treasure trove and acquired by the British Museum, 1991, when it was the largest hoard yet found in Britain.

snooker, game derived from *billiards, said to have been invented by British soldiers in India, *c.* 1870. First world professional championships, 1927. Popular 'TV sport' since 1970s.

Soane Museum (13 Lincoln's Inn Fields, London). Formed by Sir John Soane; opened, 1833.

soccer. *See* Football; Football Association, English etc.,

social credit, the economic theory of C. H. Douglas, enunciated in his books *Credit Power and Democracy* and *Economic Democracy*, 1920, and *Social Credit*, 1933. S.C. parties in Canada have held power in Alberta and British Columbia and held balance in national parliament, 1962–3 (and seats there, 1935–80) but after elections in 1991 held only seven seats in British Columbia.

Social Chapter, section of the *Treaty of Maastricht, 1992, from which Britain had gained exemption, Dec. 1991.

Social Democratic Party, (Britain), formed 26 Mar. 1981 initially mainly by disenchanted members of the Labour Party (Commons representation of SDP initially 13 ex-Labour MPs and 1 ex-Conservative MP). Roy Jenkins first leader: succeeded 1983 by David Owen. Electoral Alliance with Liberals, 1981. In 1988 the majority of SDP agreed to merge with the Liberals. A few (including David Owen) continued as a separate party. Party organization wound up, June 1990, after which three remaining SDP MPs sat as independent SD members. All three lost seats at 1992 general election.

Social Democratic and Labour Party (SDLP), N Irish political party, founded 1970, and is main party representing moderate republican and nationalist aspirations of the Roman Catholic minority in N Ireland. It returned four MPs to Westminster in the 1992 general election. They vote with the Labour Party on most issues, and are widely represented in local government in N Ireland. Leader John Hume had talks with *Sinn Fein, Sept. 1993, and is considered to have been pivotal in securing end to violence in N Ireland, 1994.

Social Security, Ministry of, name given to the former **Ministry of Pensions and National Insurance,** 1966–8 when it was merged in the Department of *Health and Social Security and again from 1988 when it reverted to being a separate department.

Society Islands, so named in honour of the Royal Society, his patrons, by James Cook, 1769. Consists of the Leeward and Windward Islands.

Sofia, anciently *Serdica,* occupied by the Romans, AD 29; sacked by the Huns, 447; taken by Bulgars, 808; conquered by Turks, 1382; liberated, 1877; became Bulgarian capital, 1878.

Sokol movement (Panslav athletic youth clubs) founded, 1861, by Miroslav Tyrs (1832–84) and subsequently spread to the USA.

solar power, generation of electricity or heat from sun, used increasingly commercially and domestically since the 1960s. Plane *Solar Challenger* flew English Channel using only S.P., 1989.

soldiers and sailors. The following is a selective list of outstanding military and naval commanders prior to 1900. Where not otherwise specified, their distinction is specifically military.

Alexander the Great, 356–323 BC, Greek.
Attila the Hun, *c.* 400–53.
Belisarius, *c.* 505–65, served Byzantium, probably *b.* in Illyria.
Berwick, James Fitzjames, Duke of, 1670–1730. English-born marshal of France.
Blake, Robert, 1598–1657, English soldier and sailor.
Blücher, Gebhard, Leberecht von, 1742–1819, Prussian.
Caesar, Gaius Julius, 102–44 BC, Roman.
Charles XII of Sweden, 1682–1718.
Clive, Robert, 1725–74, English.
Condé, Louis II de Bourbon, 1621–86, French.
Cromwell, Oliver, 1599–1658, English.
Drake, Sir Francis, *c.* 1545–96, English sailor.
Prince Eugene of Savoy, 1663–1736, French-born but served the Empire.
Frederick II the Great of Prussia, 1712–1786.
Garibaldi, Guiseppe, 1807–82, Italian.
Genghiz Khan, 1162–1227, Mongol emperor.
Gordon, Charles George, 1833–85, British.
Grant, Ulysses Simpson, 1822–85, American.
Grenville, Sir Richard, *c.* 1541–91, English sailor.
Gustavus VI Adolphus of Sweden, 1594–1632.
Hannibal, 247–*c.* 183 BC, Carthaginian.
Henry V of England, 1387–1422.
Howard of Effingham, Baron Charles, 1536–1624, English sailor.
Howe, Earl Richard, 1726–99, English sailor.
Hunyadi, John Corvinus, *c.* 1387–1456, Hungarian.
Jackson, Thomas Jonathan 'Stonewall', 1824–63, American.
Jones, John Paul, 1747–92, Scots-born American sailor.
Marlborough, John Churchill, Duke of, 1650–1722, English.
Napoleon I Bonaparte, 1769–1821, French.
Nelson, Horatio, Viscount, 1758–1805, English sailor.
Ney, Michel, 1769–1815, French.
Peter I the Great of Russia, 1672–1725.
Roberts, Frederick Sleigh, 1st Earl, 1832–1914, British.
Rupert of Bavaria, Prince, 1619–82 (served England).

Ruyter, Michael Adriaanszoon, 1607–1676, Dutch sailor.

Tamerlane (Timur-i-leng), 1335–1405, Mongolian.

Tilly, Johann, Count von, 1559–1632, Flemish-born, served the Empire.

Tromp, Martin Harpertszoon, 1597–1653, Dutch sailor.

Turenne, Henri de la Tour d'Auvergne, Vicomte de, 1611–75, French.

Wallace, Sir William, c. 1272–1305, Scots.

Wallenstein, Albrecht von, 1583–1634, Bohemian-born, served the Empire.

Washington, George, 1732–99. American.

Wellington, Arthur Wellesley, Duke of, 1769–1852, British.

Wolfe, James, 1727–59, English.

Wolseley, Garnet, Viscount, 1833–1913, British.

Xerxes, c. 519–465 BC, Persian.

---

soldiers, sailors and airmen of this century. The following is a list of military, naval and air commanders noted for their service since 1900.

American:

Clark, Mark, W., 1896–1984, general.

Doolittle, James 1896–1993, general (air force).

Eisenhower, Dwight David, 1890–1969, general.

Marshall, George, 1880–1959, general.

MacArthur, Douglas, 1880–1964, general.

Nimitz, Adam Chester, 1885–1966, admiral.

Patton, George Smith, 1885–1945, general.

Pershing, John Joseph, 1860–1948, general.

Powell, Colin Luther, general, 1937–

Ridgway, Matthew, general, 1895–1993.

Schwartzkopf, H. Norman, general, 1934–

Stillwell, Joseph W., 1883–1946, general.

Australian:

Blamey, Sir Thomas, 1884–1951, field marshal.

Hobbs, Sir Talbot, 1864–1938, general.

Monash, Sir John, 1865–1931, general.

British:

Alanbrooke, Alan Francis Brooke, 1st Viscount, 1883–1963, field marshal.

Alexander, Rupert Leofric George, 1st Earl, 1891–1969, field marshal.

Allenby, Edmund Henry Hynman, Viscount, 1861–1936, field marshal.

Beatty, David, 1st Earl, 1871–1936, admiral.

de la Billière, Sir Peter, 1934–, general.

Birdwood, William Riddell, 1st Baron, 1865–1951, field marshal.

Carton de Wiart, Sir Adrian, lieutenant-general, 1880–1963.

Cunningham, Sir Andrew, 1st Viscount, 1883–1963, admiral.

Cunningham, Sir John, 1885–1962, admiral.

Dempsey, Sir Miles Christopher, 1896–1969, general.

Dowding, Hugh, 1st Baron, 1882–1970, air chief marshal.

Freyberg, Sir Bernard Cyril, 1st Viscount, 1890–1963, general.

Gough, Sir Hubert de la Poer, 1870–1963, general.

Haig, Douglas, 1st Earl, 1861–1928, field marshal.

Hamilton, Sir Ian, 1853–1947, general.

Harris, Sir Arthur, 1892–1984, air marshal.

Ironside, Sir William Edmund, 1st Baron, 1880–1959, field marshal.

Ismay, Lord, 1887–1964, general.

Jellicoe, John Rushworth, 1st Earl, 1859–1935, admiral.

Keyes, Roger John Brownlow, 1st Baron, 1872–1945, admiral.

Kitchener, Horatio Herbert, Earl, 1850–1916, field marshal.

Lawrence, Thomas Edward, 1888–1935, lieutenant-colonel.

Methuen, Paul, 3rd Baron, 1845–1932, field marshal.

Milne, G. F., 1st Baron, 1866–1948, field marshal.

Montgomery, Viscount, 1887–1976, field marshal.

Mountbatten, Earl Louis, 1900–79, admiral.

Mountevans, Sir Edward, 1st Baron, 1881–1957, admiral.

Plumer, Herbert, Viscount, 1857–1932, field marshal.

Tedder, Arthur William, 1st Baron, 1890–1967, marshal of the RAF.

Trenchard, Hugh Montague, first Viscount, 1873–1956, Marshal of the RAF.

Wavell, Archibald, 1st Baron, 1883–1950, field marshal.

Wingate, Francis Reginald, 1861–1953, general.

Wingate, Orde Charles, 1903–44, major-general.

Ypres, John French, 1st Earl of, 1852–1925, field marshal.

Cuban:

Castro, Fidel, 1927–, general.

Finnish:

Mannerheim, Baron, Carl Gustaf Emil von, 1867–1948, marshal.

French:

Darlan, Jean, L. X. F., 1881–1942, admiral.

Foch, Ferdinand, 1851–1929, marshal of France.

Gallieni, Joseph, 1849–1916, general.

Gamelin, Maurice Gustave, 1872–1958, general.

Gaulle, Charles de, 1890–1970, general.

Giraud, Henri, 1879–1949, general.

Joffre, Joseph C., 1852–1931, marshal of France.

Juin, Alphonse Pierre, 1888–1967, marshal of France.

Lattre de Tassigny, Jean-Joseph Marie de, 1889–1952, marshal of France.

Leclerc de Hautecloque, Philippe, 1902–47, marshal of France.

Lyautey, Louis H. G., 1854–1934, marshal of France.

Marchand, J. B., 1863–1934, general.

Nivelle, Robert G., 1856–1924, general.

Pétain, Philippe, 1856–1951, marshal of France.

Sarrail, Maurice P. E., 1856–1929, general.

Weygand, Maurice, 1867–1965, general.

German:

Bock, Fedor von, 1880–1945, colonel-general.

Bülow, Karl von, 1846–1921, general.

Doenitz, Karl, 1891–1981, admiral.

Falkenhayn, Erich von, 1861–1922, general.

Fritsch, Werner von, 1880–1939, colonel-general.

Goering, Hermann, 1893–1946, field marshal.

Guderian, Heinz, 1889–1954, colonel-general.

Hindenburg und Beneckendorf, Paul von, 1847–1934, field marshal.

Hipper, Franz von, 1863–1932, admiral.

Kesselring, Albert, 1885–1960, field marshal.

Kluck, Alexander von, 1846–1934, general.

Kluge, Günther von, 1882–1944, field marshal.

P. von Lettow-Vorbeck, 1870–1964, general.

Liman von Sanders, Otto, 1855–1929, general.

Ludendorff, Erich, 1865–1937, general.

Mackensen, August von, 1849–1945, field marshal.

Paulus, F., *d.* 1957, field marshal.

Rommel, Erwin, 1891–1944, field marshal.

Raeder, Erich, 1876–1960, admiral.

Rundstedt, Gerd von, 1875–1953, field marshal.

Seeckt, Hans von, 1866–1936.

Tirpitz, Alfred von, 1849–1930, grand admiral.

Greek:

Metaxas, John, 1871–1941, general.

Papagos, Alexander, 1883–1955, marshal.

Italian:

Aosta, Amadeo Umberto Duca d', 1898–1942, general.

Badoglio, Pietro, 1871–1956, marshal.

Balbo, Italo, 1896–1940, marshal.

Cadorna, Luigi, Count, 1850–1928, general.

Diaz, Armando, marshal, 1861–1928.

Graziani, Rodolpho, Marchese de, 1882–1955, marshal.

Japanese:

Togo, Heihachiro, Count, 1847–1934, admiral.

Tojo, Hideki, 1884–1948, general.

Polish:

Anders, Wladyslaw, 1892–1970, general.

Bor-Komorowsky, *d.* 1966, general.

Pilsudski, Josef, 1867–1935, marshal.

Sikorski, Wladyslaw, 1881–1943, general.

Russian:

Alexeiev, Mikhail, 1857–1918, general.

Brussilov, Alexei, 1853–1926, general.

Budenny, Semyon Mikhailovitch, 1883–1919, marshal.

Krylenko, Nikolai Vasilievitch, 1885–1938, general.

Malinovski, Rodion Yakovlevich, 1898–1967, marshal.

Nikolai Nikolaievich, Grand Duke, 1856–1929, general.

Rennenkampf, Paul, 1854–1918, general.

Sokolovski, Vasilij Danilovich, 1897–1968, marshal.

Timoshenko, Semyon Konstantinovich, 1895–1970, marshal.

Tolbukhin, Fyodor, 1894–1949, marshal.

Tukhachevski, Mikhail Nikolaievitch, 1893–1937.

Voroshilov, Kliment E., 1881–1969, marshal.

Zhukov, Georgi Konstantinovich, 1896–1978, marshal.

South African:

Cronje, Piet, 1835–1911, general.

Botha, Louis, 1862–1919, general.

Smuts, Jan, 1870–1950, field marshal.

De la Rey, Jacobus, 1847–1914, commandant-general.

De Wet, Christian, 1854–1922, general.

Spanish:

Francisco Franco, 1892–1975, general.

Turkish:

Fevzi Chakmak, 1876–1950, marshal.

Mustapha Kemal Pasha (Kemal Atatürk), 1880–1938, marshal.

Yugoslav:

Mihailovich, Draza, 1893–1946, general.

Tito, Josip Broz, 1892–1980, marshal.

Solemn League and Covenant. Drawn up by Scots against Charles I's religious interferences, 1638. Agreed by English parliament, 1643. Declared illegal, 1661.

Solidarity, free Polish trade union movement established 1980, as a result of industrial and political unrest based on the Gdansk shipyards. Banned, 1982–9, it was important in helping to remove Communist government from Poland. Leader, Lech Walesa (b. 1943) awarded the Nobel Peace Prize, 1983 and became president of Poland, 1990.

Solomon Islands, first visited by Alvaro de Mendaña c. 1568, then by Carteret, 1767, and sighted by Bougainville, 1768. British protectorate recognized by treaties with Germany, 1886 and 1893, extended to more northerly islands, 1898–9: further islands transferred from German protectorate, 1900. Japanese invaded, Jan. 1942. American counter-attack began, Aug. 1942. Operations taken over by Australian forces, Dec. 1944; reconquest of islands completed, 1945. Independent, 7 July 1978.

Somalia (formerly British and Italian Somaliland). Conquered by Portuguese in the 16thC, and by the Sultan of Zanzibar, 1866, became an Italian protectorate by treaty, 1889. The former Italian colony was incorporated in the government of Italian E Africa, 1936; conquered by British, 1941 (Feb.–May); territory occupied by British troops from 1941 to 1 Apr. 1950 was handed over to Italians, UN trusteeship to expire in 1960. On 1 July 1960 S. became an independent republic, formed by the merger of S. with British Somaliland (*see* next article). One-party state from 1970. War with Ethiopia, 1978–8 led to civil war in S. and disintegration of the country, with the NE announcing secession, 1991. Country run by 'warlords' and famine followed. UN intervention to relieve famine spearheaded by US troops, Dec. 1992. Over 20 Pakistani UN peacekeepers, killed in S., June 1993; consequent UN air and military reprisals, and US contingent increased, Aug. Attempts to capture warlord Aidid failed, but caused heavy civilian casualties in *Mogadishu. Following further heavy fighting US announced change of policy in S., Oct. with less emphasis on capturing Aidid, who then released captured UN personnel. Virtual cease-fire in Mogadishu followed, and UN Secretary-General visited S. Hunt for Aidid officially over, Nov. and US troops began leaving S. All UN troops being withdrawn, Mar. 1995 and signs that civil war in S. might restart.

Somaliland, British. Made a British protectorate, 1884. Conquered by Italians, Aug. 1940. Regained, Mar. 1941. Merged with *Somalia, 1 July 1960, to form an independent Somali republic.

Somaliland, French. *See* DJIBOUTI.

Somerset House (London). Founded, 1549, on the site of some old churches. Its founder, the Protector Somerset, was executed and his house fell to the crown; demolished in 1775 and a new building erected. The E wing forms King's College, and was built, 1833. Formerly housed the General Registry, transferred 1970 to St Catherine's House, Kingsway; now holds Registers of Divorce, Wills and Probate, and the Inland Revenue. Courtauld Art Collection based at, since 1990.

South Africa, Republic of, formerly the **Union of**. Union formed, 31 May 1910, with Botha as premier. Rebellion began Sept., ended Dec. 1914. S. African Military Command terminated, 1 Dec. 1921, when responsibility for defence devolved on the Union. Anti-Asiatic measure in Parliament; Colour Bar Bill passed, May 1926. Status of the Union Act, 1934. 1939: Hertzog moved declaration of neutrality, but Smuts's amendment declaring war on Germany carried, so the Hertzog ministry resigned, 4 Sept.; Smuts formed ministry, 5 Sept. 1948: Malan became prime minister as leader of the Nationalist Party. *Apartheid* the basis of government domestic policy from 1948. 1949: Merger of Afrikaner Party and Nationalists. Natives Representative Council abolished. Separate Representation of Voters Act passed. Nationalist majority now deemed permanent. Virtual incorporation of SW (former German) territory, July. *Sharpeville incident, Mar. 1960. 1961: S.A. announced her intention of leaving the Commonwealth, 16 Mar.; then became an independent republic. Gave independent white Rhodesia economic support, 1966–80. Verwoerd assassinated, 1966. S.A. increasingly barred from international sport because of her apartheid policies from 1970 onwards. Soweto riots, 1976. Muldergate scandal, 1978–9. First 'black homeland' (Transkei) established, 1976. Limited liberalization of *apartheid* under Botha, premier from 1978 and executive president from 1984; Fifth Amendment of 1981 provided for limited non-white participation in government.

Growing international condemnation and increased black agitation led to state of emergency, 1986–90. International sanctions against S.A. applied in varying degrees from 1987. In Sept 1989 Premier Botha replaced by F. W. de Klerk and from then on a reform programme rapidly accelerated. Ban on *African National Congress lifted, Feb. 1990 and its leader Nelson Mandela freed from gaol. By end 1991 many aspects of apartheid had been abolished and in Mar. 1992 a referendum among white voters approved political reform by 69% to 31%. By end 1993 most sanctions against S.A. lifted and international sporting links restored. Talks between government and ANC on a future multiracial, one person, one vote, regime continued, 1993, despite being broken off several times due to violence (e.g. assassination of black leader Chris Hani by white extremists, April 1993). Plan for elections based on universal suffrage, 27 Apr. 1994, with powersharing between black majority and whites for five years after that. This approved by S. African parliament, 23 Sept. 1993. Mandela addressed UN assembly in New York, 25 Sept. and called for removal of remaining sanctions and for IMF loans to revive S. African economy. In Oct. killers of Hani sentenced to death. But continuing divisions between ANC and *Inkatha, caused sporadic but serious outrages and white 'separatists' threatened secession after Apr. 1994. President de Klerk and Nelson Mandela signed new constitution officially ending three centuries of white minority rule in S.A., 17 Nov. 1993. Constitution ratified by S. African parliament, 22 Dec. Following the elections of Apr. 1994, which were won by the ANC, Mandela became president of S.A., 10 May. S.A. rejoined the Commonwealth, and joined the OAU. In Feb. 1995 Mandela announced he would step down in 1999. Winnie Mandela dismissed from government posts, Mar. 1995: also in Mar., Queen Elizabeth visits S.A. for first time since 1947. Rugby World Cup played in S.A., June and won by S.A. Local elections, Nov.; Nationalist ex-defence minister accused of murder.

Governor-Generals of Union of South Africa, 1910–61:
Viscount Gladstone 1910–14
Earl Buxton 1914–20
HRH Prince Arthur of Connaught 1920–24
Earl of Athlone 1924–31
Earl of Clarendon 1931–37
Sir Patrick Duncan 1937–43
N. J. de Wet (acting) 1943–45
G. B. van Zyl 1946–50
Dr E. G. Jansen 1951–59
C. R. Swart 1960–61
State Presidents of the Republic of South Africa since 1961:
C. R. Swart 1961–67
T. E. Donges 1967
J. F. T. Naudé (acting) 1967–68
J. J. Fouché 1968–75
B. J. Vorster, 1978–79
M. Viljoen, 1979–84
P. J. Botha, 1984–89
F. W. De Klerk 1989–94
Nelson Mandela 1994–

See also CAPE PROVINCE; ORANGE FREE STATE; TRANSVAAL.

South African Development Community. *See* SADC.

South African War. 1899: Ultimatum sent by Boers, 9 Oct. Lord Roberts appointed C.-in-C. after British reverses, 23 Dec. 1900: Relief of Kimberley, 15 Feb.; Cronje's surrender at Paardeberg, 27 Feb.; relief of Ladysmith, 28 Feb.; relief of Mafeking, 17–18 May; Transvaal Republic annexed to Great Britain, 1 Sept.; formally annexed, 25 Oct. 1902: Peace of Vereeniging, 31 May.

Southampton, England. A Roman town (*Clausentium*) and a Jutish port (*Hamwih*) existed in the suburbs of modern S., but the first town on the present centre was built shortly before 1066. Present system of wharves, begun 1927; oil tanker terminal, 1951. The University College became S. University in 1952.

South Australia was surveyed by Tasman, 1644, and Flinders, 1802. Murray River explored, 1828. First settlement made, 1834. Province proclaimed, 28 Dec. 1836. Copper discovered, 1842 and 1845. Constitution adopted, 1856. Became a state of the Australian Commonwealth, 1901. Controversial nuclear testing took place at, 1963.

South Bank University, London. Name and status of former South Bank Polytechnic from 1992.

South Carolina, USA, first permanently settled as proprietary government, 1670. Charleston founded, 1680. One of 'founder' states of USA. Seceded from Union, 1861; readmitted, 1868.

South Dakota, USA, first explored by brothers Verendrye, 1743. First permanent building by white men, 1794. Sold to U.S.A. by France, 1803, as part of Louisiana Purchase. Dakota Territory created, 1861. Gold struck in the Black Hills, 1874. Separated from N. Dakota and admitted to Union, 1889.

South-East Asia Treaty Organization (SEATO). Arose from the South-East Asia Collective Defence Treaty, SE Asian counterpart to the *N Atlantic Treaty, signed in Manila, 8 Sept. 1954, between Britain, the USA, Australia, New Zealand, Pakistan, France, Thailand and the Philippines. France took little part after 1964; S.E.A.T.O. gradually phased out after 1975, and non-military functions taken over by *Association of South East Asian Nations.

Southern Yemen. *See* YEMEN.

South Georgia, S Atlantic island, dependency of the *Falkland Islands till 1985. Argentine force landed on S.G., 19 Mar. 1982; British recaptured island, 25 Apr. 1982. Since 1985 a crown colony administered with the S Sandwich Islands.

South Korea. *See* KOREA.

South Ossetia, formerly part of USSR, whose autonomy was abolished by Georgia, 1989, conducting campaign since 1990 to become independent; cease-fire, June 1992 but intermittent fighting since.

South Pacific Forum, first met 5 Aug.

1971, at Wellington, New Zealand. Conference of heads of government of S Pacific states. Since then has held regular meetings: that in 1985 declared the S Pacific a 'nuclear-free zone'; 'green-house effect' a major topic at 1992 meeting. The **South Pacific Forum Secretariat** was established in 1973 as the South Pacific Bureau for Economic Co-operation, changing its name in 1988. It promotes economic co-operation between the participating states. Trade liberalization measures, 1981, 1985, 1987, etc.

South Pole. First reached, 16 Dec. 1911, by the Norwegian, Roald Amundsen. Scott reached it 17 Jan. 1912. *See* ARCTIC AND ANTARCTIC REGIONS.

South Sea Bubble. The financial scheme under which the S.S. Co. (incorporated 1710) offered in 1720 to pay off the national debt and to buy up the irredeemable annuities granted in the two previous reigns. Parliament accepted the offer, and a number of other bubble companies competed. Shares rose to fantastic prices and then slumped, the stock of the S.S. Co. which had risen to 1,000 falling to 135. Sir Robert Walpole tried to restore credit by arranging to assign £9,000,000 of S.S. stock to the Bank of England, a like amount to the E India Co., and to repay the bonus of £7,500,000 which the Government had received.

Southwark, though retaining its identity as a borough, was annexed to the city of London, 1327. Diocese of S. created, 1905.

South-West Africa. *See* NAMIBIA.

sovereigns when first minted (1503) were worth 22*s*. 6*d*., later 10*s*. and 11*s*. In 1817 the value was fixed at £1, which remained constant until 1917, when they were re-called by the bank. In 1949 some 100,000 S. were minted in order to preserve the art and craft of gold coining. Small numbers now increasingly made for commemorative occasions e.g. coronation of Queen Elizabeth, 1953; 1975 (last coin struck at London Mint); 1992 etc.

Sovetsk. *See* TILSIT.

Soviet. *See* USSR.

Soweto, was a racially segregated black urban settlement (South West Township) near Johannesburg, S Africa which grew rapidly after 1948 and became a centre of black nationalism prior to 1994. Soweto Riots, 1976, resulted in many deaths.

Spa, in Belgium, where mineral springs were discovered in 1326, gave its name to an establishment for curative waters. Was seat of the Armistice Commission, 1918–19, and venue of a conference, 1920, on German reparations.

space flights (manned). Yuri Gagarin (USSR) was the first man to orbit the earth (once: in 1 hr. 48 min.) on 12 Apr. 1961. Alan Sheppard made the first US space flight (sub-orbital) on 5 May 1961; John Glenn was the first American to orbit the earth (three times) on 20 Feb. 1962. Valentina Tereshkova (USSR) was the first woman to orbit the earth, 16 June 1963. On 12 Oct. 1964 Russia put the first 3-man spaceship into orbit. On 18 Mar. 1965 Leonov (USSR) left a 2-man space craft and became the first man to 'walk' in space. On 23 Mar. a spaceship was pilot-manoeuvred for the first time by the Americans, Grissom and Young. In 1968 US Apollo 8 made 10 orbits of the moon, transmitting the first live television pictures of the lunar orbit; in 1969 the Russian Soyuz 4 (one man) and Soyuz 5 (three men) linked up in space. The US Apollo 11 (Armstrong, Collins, Aldrin) was launched, 16 July, and on 21 July Armstrong became first man to walk on the moon. Soyuz-Apollo link-up, 17 July 1975, was a joint US-Soviet project. In 1978 (11 Jan.) two Soviet space craft docked with an orbiting laboratory constituting the first triple space docking. In 1984 the American Bruce McCandless (from *Challenger*) became the first man to walk in space without being attached to his space craft (7 Feb.). US space-shuttle *Challenger* exploded on take-off, Jan. 1986: crew killed and US space programme put back several years. Unmanned S.F. by the

USA and USSR first concentrated on moon-probes (1960–70) and subsequently on probes to Mars and Venus. Defence and communications played major part in un-manned S.F. from 1970s. *European Space Agency established 1975. Since 1984 the European Communication and Satellite Programme (ECS), funded by 26 countries, has launched satellites to establish tele-communication networks and collect as-tronomical data. US launched the *Hubble space telescope, 1990. In May 1993 space agencies from the USA, Russia, France, Britain, etc., agreed to pool resources for the exploration of Mars. US Mars space-probe lost contact, Aug. 1993. US space shuttle *Endeavour* sent to repair Hubble telescope, Dec. 1993, and returned after 11-day journey and five space walks last-ing 35 hrs., 28 min., a world record. 67th space shuttle launch (*Discovery*), 3 Feb. 1995. This was first piloted by a woman (Eileen Collins, USA) and first where a British-*b.* astronaut space-walked (Michael Foale: first Briton in space had been Helen Sharman on Anglo-Russian space mission lasting eight days, 1991). *Discovery* made rendezvous with Russian space station *Mir*, 2 Feb. 1995. Space shuttle *Atlantis* docked with Russian *Mir*, 29 June 1995.

Spain (*Hispania*). Occupied (S of the Ebro) by Carthaginians, 238–10 BC; after which the country was slowly subjugated by Rome. S. was divided into two provinces after the second Punic War, and into three by Augustus. Overrun by the Vandals, Alans and Suevi, AD 409. Visigoths over-run S. and establish kingdom, 416–18. Vandals migrate to Africa, 429. Visigothic state overthrown and S. conquered by Arabs, 711–18. Abdurrahman (I) founds the Ommayad caliphate of Cordoba, 755, which reaches its zenith in the reign of Abdurrahman III (912–61). Christian reconquest begins in earnest under Sancho I of Leon, 962. Civil war destroys caliphate, 1031. Alfonso VI of Castile takes Toledo, 1085. Muslim revival under *Almoravides, 1086. Aragonese defeat at Fraga, 1134. Muslim revival under Almohades at battle of Alarcos, 1185. Great Christian victory at

Navas de Tolosa, 1212. Cordoba captured, 1236. Moors confined to Granada by 1257. Permanent union of Aragon and Valencia, 1309. Muslim defeat at battle of the Salado, 1340. French expel Pedro the Cruel from Castile and substitute Henry of Trastamara, 1366. English expel Henry and restore Pedro, 1367. Henry defeats Pedro at Montiel, 1369. John I of Portugal defeats Castilians at Aljubarotta, 1385. Union of Aragon and Castile under Ferdi-nand and Isabella, 1479. Granada con-quered, 2 Jan. 1492. Treaty of Tordesillas, 1494. Cortez conquers Mexico, 1519–21. Victory over French at Pavia, 1525. Treaty of Câteau Cambrésis, 1559. Spanish sack of Antwerp, 1576. Annexation of Portugal, 1580. English defeat of the Armada, 1588. Portugal again independent, 1640 (*see* PARTITION TREATIES). War of Spanish Succession, 1701–13. Treaty with France against Britain ('First Family Compact'), 1733. Second Family Compact, 1743. Third Family Compact, 1761 (*see* SEVEN YEARS WAR). S. at war with Britain, 1779–83. Al-liance with France and war with Britain, 1796. Destruction of Franco-Spanish fleet at battle of Trafalgar, 21 Oct. 1805. French driven out by Wellington, 1812. Revolu-tion, 1820, suppressed by French, 1823. First Carlist War, 1830–40. Second Carlist War, 1872–6. War with USA, 1898. Primo de Rivera military dictator, 1923–30. Riff War in Morocco, 1924–5 (*see* MOROCCO). Revolution and flight of King Alfonso, Mar. 1931; republic declared. *Spanish Civil War 1936–39*: Popular front won elections, 16 Feb. 1936 and civil war, led by Army began in Morocco, 18 July; Gen. Mola set up Falangist government at Burgos, 24 July; seaplanes brought Falangist rein-forcements from Morocco, 26 July; Falan-gist captured Badajos, 14 Aug.: Republicans evacuated San Sebastian, 13 Sept.; the Alcazar of Toledo blown up by Republican forces, but Falangist defenders continued to resist, 18 Sept.; Republicans withdrew from Alcazar after two months' siege, 28 Sept.; Gen. Franco, head of Falangist government, 30 Sept.; Republi-can government granted autonomy to Basque provinces, 1 Oct.; Republican government moved to Valencia, 7 Nov.; Franco recognized by Germany and Italy, 18 Nov. In 1937 the Falangists captured Malaga, 8 Feb.; Guernica, ancient Basque capital, destroyed by Falangists, who captured Durango, 27 Apr.; Bilbao captured by Falangists, 19 June, and all Asturias surrendered by Nov. By April 1938 Catalonia was cut off from France; struggle for Ebro ceased, 18 Nov. Barcelona fell to Franco, 26 Jan. 1939, and there was a mass exodus of refugees into France. President Azana resigned in Feb. and Madrid and Valencia fell to Franco in March: civil war ended in Franco's victory, 2 Apr.

Spain since the Civil War: S. neutral in World War II: ex-King Alfonso XIII *d.*, 1941. Cortes re-established on corporate lines, 1942. After referendum in 1947 in favour of a future monarchy, Franco told the Cortes, 1957 that the monarchy would be restored on his death or withdrawal from power. Concordat with Papacy, 1953; US bases in S., 1953. From 1960 government liberalized; phenomenal growth in tourist trade. Franco *d.* 1975 and S. reverted, to constitutional monarchy under King Juan Carlos I. Unsuccessful military coup, 1981: Socialist government under Felipe Gonzalez elected, 1982. Church in Spain disestablished, 1978 and 17 autonomous regions established under new constitution. S. settled *Gibraltar dispute with Britain, 1985; but some difficulties still remained, 1995; joined EEC, 1 Jan 1986. Severe recession in early 1990s followed expansion in 1980s. Three devaluations within eight months, 1992–3. General election, June 1993; Socialists lost absolute majority but remained largest party. Corruption scandals, 1993–5 threatened to bring down government. Wedding in Seville of King's daughter, Mar. 1995. *ETA attempt on life of opposition leader, Madrid, April. In May Socialists lost heavily in local and municipal elections. Catalan party announced withdrawal of support from government, July. Unsuccessful *ETA plot to assassinate King Juan Carlos, Aug.

Spain, sovereigns of, from the Union of Castile and Aragon, 1479, under Ferdinand of Aragon and Isabella of Castile.

Isabella *d.* 1504
Ferdinand *d.* 1516
House of Hapsburg:
Charles V (Emperor) I 1516–56 (abdicated)
Philip II 1556–98
Philip III 1598–1621
Philip IV 1621–65
Charles II 1665–1700
House of Bourbon:
Philip V 1700–1724 (abdicated)
Luis Jan.–Aug. 1724
Philip V (again) 1724–46
Ferdinand VI 1746–59
Charles III 1759–88
Charles IV 17–1808 (abdicated)
Ferdinand VII 1808
Joseph Bonaparte 1808–12 (abdicated)
Ferdinand VII (again) 1813–33
Isabella II 1833–68 (flees)
Interregnum 1868–74
Alfonso XII 1874–85
Alfonso XIII 1886–1931 (abdicated)
Juan Carlos I* 1975–
*General Franco was Head of State 1936–75.

Spanish literature. The following is a list of Spanish (and of Spanish-speaking S American) authors:

Aguilera, Ventura Ruiz, 1820–81, poet.
Alarcón, Juan Ruiz de, *c.* 1581–1639, dramatist.
Alarcón, Pedro Antonio de, 1833–91, prose writer of tales, etc.
Alemán, Mateo, 1547–*c.* 1613, prose writer, author of the popular *Guzman de Alfarache*.
Alfonso X, the Learned, of Castile and Leon, 1226–84, poet and patron of letters.
Álvarez Quintero, Joaquin, 1873–1944, dramatist.
Álvarez Quintero, Serafin, 1871–1938, dramatist.
Argensola, Bartolomé Leonardo de, 1562–1631, historian and poet.
Argensola, Lupercio Leonardo de, 1559–1613, poet and dramatist.

Avilia, Juan de, 1500–69, mystic and prose writer.

Ayala, Adelardo López de, 1828–79, poet, and dramatist.

Ayala, Pero López de, 1332–1407, poet and prose writer.

Ayala, Ramón Pérez de, 1880–1962, poet, critic and novelist.

Balmes y Uspia, Jaime, 1810–48, controversial writer.

Bazan, Emilia Pardo de, 1851–1921, novelist.

Becquer, Gustavo Adolfo, 1836–70, poet and tale writer.

Benavente y Martinez, Jacinto, 1866–1954, dramatist.

Berceo, Gonzalo de, 1198?–1264?, poet

Boscan Almogavér, Juan, c. 1490–1542, poet and prose writer.

Bretón de los Herreros, Manuel, 1796–1873, dramatist.

Caballera, Fernán (pseudonym of Cecilia Böhl von Faber), 1797–1877, novelist.

Cadalso y Vázquez, José de, 1741–82, poet and dramatist.

Calderón de la Barca Henao de la Barreda y Riaño, Pedro, 1600–81, poet, dramatist, and prose writer.

Carrasquilla, Tomás, 1851–1941, Colombian novelist.

Castillejo, Cristobal de, d. 1556, poet.

Castro y Bellvis, Guillén de, 1569–1631, dramatist.

Celaya, Gabriel (Rafael Múgica), poet, 1911–

Cervantes Saavedra, Miguel de, 1547–1616, author of *Don Quixote*, poet, dramatist and prose writer.

Cota de Maguaque, Rodrigo, *fl.* late 15thC poet.

Cruz y Cano, Ramón de la, 1731–95, dramatist.

Darío, Rubén, 1867–1916, Hispano-American poet.

Diaz de Castillo, Bernal, *fl.* second half 16thC, historian of the conquest of Mexico.

Echegaray y Elizaguirre, José, 1832–1916, dramatist.

Espinel, Vicente Martinez, 1551–1624, poet and novelist.

Feijoo y Montenegro, Benito Jerónimo, 1677–1764, prose writer and critic.

Figueroa, Francisco de, *d.* 1620, poet.

Fuentes, Carlos, 1928–, Mexican novelist.

Galdos, Pérez, 1842–1920, novelist.

Gallego, Juan Nicasio, 1777–1853, poet.

Gana, Alberto Blest, 1830–1920, Chilean novelist.

García Gutiérrez, Antonio, 1812–84, dramatist.

Garcia Marquez, Gabriel, 1928–, Colombian novelist.

Garcilaso de la Vega. *See* VEGA, GARCILASO DE LA.

Garcilaso the Inca, 1539–1616, Inca *b.*, historian.

Gómez de Avellaneda, Gertrudis, 1816–73, poet, dramatist and novelist.

Góngora y Argote, Luis de, 1561–1627, poet.

Gracián, Baltasar, 1601–58, prose writer, Jesuit epigrammatic moralist.

Granada, Luis de, 1505–88, mystic and religious writer.

Guevara, Antonio de, c. 1480–1545, chronicler and moralist.

Guevara, Luis Velez, 1570–1644, dramatist.

Herrera, Fernando de, 1534–97, poet and critic.

Ibañez, Vicente Blasco, 1867–1928, novelist.

Iriarte y Oropesa, Tomás de, 1750–91, fabulist.

Isidore of Seville, St c. 560–636, encyclopaedist and Doctor of the Church.

Isla y Roja, José Francisco de, 1703–81, humorous prose writer.

Jáuregui y Aguilar, Juan Martínez de, c. 1570–c. 1641, poet and translator.

Jimenez, Juan Ramón, 1881–1958, poet.

Jove-Llanos, Gaspar Melchior de, 1744–1811, poet, dramatist and prose writer.

Juan de la Cruz, 1542–91, mystic, poet and prose writer (St John of the Cross).

Juan Manuel, Infante, 1282–1349, poet and miscellaneous writer; his chief prose work was *El Conde Lucanor*, a collection of tales.

Llosa, Mario Vargas, 1936–, Peruvian writer.

López de Gómara, Francisco, 1519–60, historian of the conquest of Mexico.

Lorca, Federico García, 1899–1936, poet.

Loyola, St Ignatius, 1491–1556, author of the *Exercitia Spiritualia* and the *Constitutiones. See also* JESUITS.

Lucena, Juan de, *fl.* 15thC prose writer.

Lully, Raymond ('Ramon Lull'), 1235–1315.

Luzán Claramunt de Suelves y Gurrea, Ignacio, 1702–54, critic and poet.

Machado y Ruiz, Antonio, 1875–1939, poet and dramatist.

Machado y Ruiz, Manuel, 1874–1947, poet and dramatist.

Manrique, Gómez, 1412–91, poet.

Manrique, Jorge, 1440–79, poet.

Mariana, Juan de, *c.* 1535–1623, historian.

Martínez de la Rosa, Francisco, 1789–1862, poet, dramatist and novelist.

Martínez de la Toledo, Alfonso, 1398–1466?, prose writer and moralist.

Martínez Ruiz, José (Azorín), 1874–1967, novelist and critic.

Meléndez Valdés, Juan, 1754–1817, poet and dramatist.

Mendoza, Diego Hurtado de, 1503–75, poet and scholar.

Mistral, Gabriela (Lucila Godoy y Alcayaga), 1889–1957, Chilean poet and prose writer.

Molinos, Miguel de, *c.* 1640–96, author of the *Spiritual Guide*.

Montemayor, Jorge de, *c.* 1520–61, author of the prose pastoral, *Diana Enamorada*.

Morales, Ambrosio de, 1513–91, historian.

Moratin, Leandro Fernández, 1760–1828.

Moreto y Cabaña, Agustin, 1618–69, dramatist.

Naharro, Bartolomé Torres. *fl.* early 16thC, dramatist.

Nebrija, Elio Antonio de, 1444–1522, humanist.

Neruda, Pablo, 1904–73, Chilean poet.

Nuñez de Arce, Gaspar, 1833–1903, poet and dramatist.

Otero, Blas de, 1916–, poet.

Padilla, Juan de, 1468–1522?, poet.

Palacio Valdés, Armando, *c.* 1854–1938, novelist.

Paravicino y Arteaga, Hortensio Félix, 1580–1633, poet.

Pereda, José Maria de, 1833–1906, novelist.

Pérez Andrés ('Francisco Lopez de Ubeda'), *fl.* early 17thC, picaresque novel writer.

Pérez, Antonio, 1540–1611, miscellaneous writer.

Pérez de Guzmán, Fernán, 1378–1460, poet and historian.

Pérez de Montalban, Juan, 1602–38, dramatist.

Pérez Galdós, Benito, 1843–1920, novelist and dramatist.

Ponce de León, Luis, 1529–91, poet.

Pulgar, Hernando de, 1436–92?, historian.

Quevedo y Villegas, Francisco Gómez de, 1580–1645, poet and prose writer.

Quintana, Manuel José, 1772–1857, poet, dramatist, and prose writer.

Rivas, Duque de. *See* SAAVEDRA.

Rodo, José Enrique, 1872–1917, Uruguayan essayist.

Rojas, Fernando de, *fl.* late 15thC.

Rojas Zorrilla, Francisco de, 1607–48, poet and dramatist.

Rueda, Lope de, *c.* 1510–65, dramatist.

Ruiz de Alarcón, Juan. *See* ALARCON, JUAN RUIZ DE.

Ruiz, Juan *fl.* 14thC, poet.

Saavedra, Angel de (Duque de Rivas), 1791–1865, poet and dramatist.

Samaniego, Félix Maria de, 1745–1801, fabulist.

San Martin, Juan Zorrilla, 1855–1931, Uruguayan poet.

Sancho IV, *d.* 1295, author of *Castigos y Documentos*, and patron of letters.

Santillana, Iñigo Lopez de Mendoza, Marqués de, 1398–1458, poet and prose writer.

Sem Tob, *fl.* 14thC, author of a collection of proverbs and maxims in verse.

Silvestre, Gregorio, 1520–70, poet.

Solis y Rivadeneira, Antonio de, 1610–86, dramatist and historian.

Teresa d'Avila, St, 1515–82, poet and prose writer.

Tirso de Molina, *c.* 1584–1648, poet, dramatist and prose writer.

Torre, Alfonso de la, *fl.* 15thC, didactic prose writer.

Torre, Francisco de la, 1534?–94, poet.

Unamuno, Miguel de, 1864–1936, novelist.

Urrea, Pedro Manuel de, 1486–1530?, poet.

Valdés, Armando P. *See* PALACIO VALDÉS.

Valdés, Juan de, *c.* 1500–44, mystic, scholar and prose writer.

Valera, Juan de, 1824–1905, novelist and critic.

Vega Carpio, Lope Félix de, 1562–1635, poet, novelist, dramatist and miscellaneous writer.

Vega, Garcilaso de la, 1503–36, poet.

Velez Guevara, Luis, *See* GUEVARA, LUIS VELEZ.

Villamediana, Conde de, 1582–1622, poet.

Villegas, Esteban Manuel de, 1596–1669, poet.

Villena, Enrique de, 1384–1434, poet, prose writer and translator.

Yañez, Rodrigo, *fl.*, 14thC, author of an epic work known as the 'Rhymed Chronicle', *Poema de Alfonso Onceno.*

Zorilla, José 1817–93, poet and dramatist.

Zurita, Jeronimo de, 1512–80, historian.

For certain other writers of Spanish nationality who did not write in Spanish, *see* PROVENCAL AND CATALAN LITERATURE.

Spanish Succession, War of, 1701–13. Alliance of Britain, Holland, Austria, Prussia and the Empire against Louis XIV, 1701.

Sparta or **Lacedaemon,** between 750 and 650 BC conquered the whole of Laconia, and by 550 the greater part of the Peloponnese. Defeated Athens in Peloponnesian War, 431–404, but after being beaten by the Thebans at Leuctra (371) the military decline of S. began, and became more rapid after about 335. It nominally retained its sovereignty after conquest by the Romans in 146. A village still exists on the site, which was the seat of a Frankish Count from AD 1212–62.

Spartacists. Organized a revolutionary movement in Germany, 1918–19. Leaders, Karl Liebknecht and Rosa Luxemburg, killed, Jan. 1919. Movement crushed, Apr. 1919, by Ebert's provisional Government, but from it modern German Communism began.

Speaker of the House of Commons existed as an office, though perhaps not a title from about 1326. The first member known to have performed the functions of a S. was William Trussell, who *d.* 1346, though he is not yet referred to as *Parlour* or S., a title first definitely ascribed to Sir Thomas Hungerford in 1377. Sir Thomas More the last S. to die by violence (1535). First woman S., 1992. The names of all Ss. since 1600 are known; since World War II Ss. have been:

D. Clifton-Brown 1943–51
W. S. Morrison 1951–59
Sir Harry Hylton-Foster 1959–65
Dr Horace King 1965–70
Selwyn Lloyd 1971–76
George Thomas 1976–83
Bernard Wetherill 1983–92
Betty Boothroyd 1992–

Speaker's Corner. *See* HYDE PARK.

Special Air Services (SAS) crack military group with origins in World War II élite UK Special Forces. Much operational secrecy: but has taken part in Malaysia in 1950s; N Ireland since 1970s; Falkland War, 1982; Gulf War, 1991. Also in separate incidents, e.g. Iranian embassy siege, London, 1980, and 'Death on the Rock' shooting of IRA members, March 1988, in Gibraltar.

Special Branch, British police section established 1883, originally to deal with Fenian terrorists; some duties taken over by intelligence services, 1992.

spectrum (solar). Treated of by Newton in his *Optics*, 1704; chemical analysis by means of a S. invented by Bunsen and Kirchhoff, 1860

Spiritualism, has its modern origins in a sect which developed in New York, USA, 1848.

Spitalfields (London), named after the hospital of St Mary Spital (corruption of 'hospital'), founded 1197. Many silk-weaving Huguenots settled there after the revocation of the Edict of Nantes, 1685. Market received its original charter from Charles II in 1682. Moved to new site at Hackney Marshes, 1991.

Spitsbergen (Svalbard), so called by Dutch explorers, 1596. Placed under Norwegian sovereignty by Treaty of Sèvres, 9 Feb. 1920, to which Russia adhered, 1925. Canadian raid, Sept. 1941, destroyed mining installations and evacuated population. German naval landing, 1943. Russian mining camps reoccupied, 1947.

Split (Italian **Spalato**; Serbo-Croatian **Spljet**), Byzantine port opened *c*. AD 639 by refugees from *Salona. Municipal rights granted, 1239. Venetian territory from 1420 to 1797 Occupied by Italians, 1918. Yugoslav since 1920, now (1995) part of Croatia.

Spode chinaware, first manufactured, 1770.

squash, or **squash rackets,** was invented at the end of the 19thC at Harrow School and derives from rackets. The S.R. Association was formed, 1929; the International S.R., 1967. Women's S.R. Association, 1934. The S.R. Open Championship established 1930; became a knock-out competition from 1946. British domination of S. broken in 1950s. S. an increasingly popular game from 1970s. A US alternative to S.R. called **squash tennis** evolved at the same time as S.R. in Britain, invented at a boys' school in New England. There have been squash tennis contests since 1911.

Sri Lanka, formerly **Ceylon**. Portuguese landed, 1505: first Portuguese settlement, 1517. Taken by Dutch, 1656–8: by English, 1795–6. Ceded to Britain by Treaty of Amiens, 1802. HQ of Supreme Commander, Far E, in World War II. Became a Dominion, 4 Feb. 1948. British naval and air bases phased out, 1954–7. Bandaranaike, prime minister, assassinated by Buddhist extremists, 1957. New constitution, making S.L. a republic, 1972, amended to allow for presidential system, 1978. Tamil separatist agitation from 1981 erupted into civil war, 1983. Indian troops sent to try to enforce peace; pact between S.L. and India, 1988. Indian troops withdrew, 1990. President Premadasa assassinated by Tamils, 1 May 1993. Elections won by Mrs Kumaratunga, 1994, after increased tension and assassination of opposition leader by Tamil extremists: she subsequently became president of S.L. Moves to end civil war, 1995 but Tamil attacks ended 14-week cease-fire, Apr. and more fighting followed, June onwards, with assault on Jaffna, Tamil stronghold, Nov.

SS (Schutzstaffel = 'Protection Squads'), militant branch of German *National Socialist Party, formed by separation from *SA, 1928. Heinrich Himmler (1900–45) became commander, 1929. One branch of SS responsible for state security and played major role in persecution of Jews, etc.

Staffordshire University, name and status, since 1992, of the former Staffordshire polytechnic.

Stage Carriage Act, 1832 required number of passengers carried to be painted on the vehicle. Revenue Act, 1869, defined S.C. as any public vehicle other than a railway carriage (*see also* HACKNEY COACHES). Under Road Traffic Act, 1960 a stage carriage is defined as a public service vehicle carrying passengers at separate fares, not being an express carriage.

Stalingrad, known until 1925 as **Tsaritsin** and since 1961 as *Volgograd. The siege of S. by the Russians began in Aug. and ended Nov. 1942, with the capitulation of the German commander von Paulus and his army and was a turning-point in the Russo-German campaign of World War II. *See* SIEGES: VOLGOGRAD: WORLD WAR II.

Stamp Acts. That of 1765, which was a contributory cause of the American Revolution, was repealed in 1766. Present law relating to stamp duties is founded in the Stamp Act, 1891, and in various subsequent Finance and Revenue Acts.

Standard, Royal, bore only three leopards passant in 1200, which were quartered with the arms of France in 1340. The latter were removed and replaced by the arms of Ireland, then of Scotland, 1603. From 1714 to 1837 the R.S. also bore the arms of

Hanover until the accession of Victoria (1837), when it assumed its present form.

Standards Institution, British. *See* BRITISH STANDARDS INSTITUTION.

standard time. Different countries began to adopt S.T., based on a variation of a number of hours from Greenwich mean time, in 1883. EC suggestion, 1993, that Britain should adopt Central European Time, based on the principle of S.T.

Stansted, London's third airport. First constructed as a US airbase, July 1942 and by end of World War II was largest 9th USAAF base in East Anglia. Runway extended by USAF 1953–6 to present length (3048 m.). Civilian airport from 1957. First terminal built, 1969; extended, 1972 and 1979. S. confirmed as London's future third airport, 1979; development approval, 1985. New airport and terminal opened by Queen Elizabeth II, 15 March 1991. Capacity of eight million passengers per year; outline approval (1993) for 15 million passengers per year. During 1985–91 construction, 10 new archaeological sites found including an Iron Age village and two Roman burial sites excavated. Seven listed buildings moved to make way for new terminal.

Star Chamber. Prerogative court going back at least to the reign of Edward III (1327–77) and abolished by Parliament, 1641.

Star-spangled Banner, national anthem of the USA. Words written, 1814, by Francis Scott Key, during the war with Britain. Tune is by J. Stafford Smith. It was officially adopted as the US national anthem in 1831, replacing the earlier *Hail Columbia* (*c.* 1800).

START (Strategic Arms Reduction Talks) began in Geneva, 1982, between USA and USSR with aim of agreeing to reciprocal reduction of their nuclear capabilities. Signing of Intermediate Nuclear Forces Treaty (INF), 1987. Talks continued after Soviet disintegration. START I signed in Moscow, 1991. In Dec. 1992, in Geneva, US-Russian agreement for draft treaty on START II: this signed, Jan. 1993, in Moscow. In Nov. 1993 the Ukraine, heavily involved in nuclear matters since breakup of USSR, finally signed START I.

Star Wars (Strategic Strategic Defense Initiative, SDI), sophisticated US defence system against a theoretical Soviet nuclear assault, with extra-terrestrial dimensions. First proposed by President Reagan in a television address, 23 Mar. 1983. Its practicability appeared increasingly limited from 1988 and by 1990 it had cost nearly 17 billion dollars, whilst collapse of Soviet system meant Russia no longer perceived as a threat. In May 1993 Clinton government announced S.W. programme to be scaled down, implying its virtual abandonment, though there were Republican suggestions that it might be revived, 1995. Scaled-down spin-off, THAAD (Theatre High-Altitude Area Defense) still being developed, 1995. Yeltsin accepted US development of THAAD as within the limits of 1972 ABM (Antiballistic Missile) treaty, May 1995.

State Department. *See* SECRETARY OF STATE (USA).

States-General (France). Last meeting before *French Revolution was in 1614. It met at Versailles on 5 May 1789. The *Tiers État* declared itself the National Assembly, 17 June 1789.

States-General (Holland). Began *c.* mid-15thC, established permanently at The Hague, 1593. Abolished with convocation of the National Assembly, 1 Mar. 1796. Name used since 1814 as the title of the Dutch Parliament.

statesmen and -women and politicians of the 20th century. The following list of political personalities, not now living, were all prominent in the present century, though not necessarily heads of state or of administrations:

Albanian:
Hoxha, Enver 1908–85

Argentine:
Peron, Juan 1895–1974
Australian:
Curtin, John 1885–1945
Chifley, Joseph 1885–1951
Evatt, Herbert 1894–1965
Hughes, William Morris, 1864–1952
Lyons, Joseph Aloysius 1879–1939
Menzies, Sir Robert Gordon 1894–1978
Austrian:
Bauer, Otto 1881–1938
Dollfuss, Engelbert 1892–1934
Renner, Karl 1870–1951
Brazilian:
Vargas, Getulio 1882–1954
British:
Asquith, Violet Bonham-Carter, Baroness 1887–1969
Astor, Nancy, Viscountess 1879–1964
Attlee, Clement Richard, 1st Earl 1883–1967
Baldwin, Stanley, Earl of Bewdley 1867–1947
Beaverbrook, Lord 1879–1964
Bevan, Aneurin 1897–1960
Beveridge, William, 1st Baron 1879–1963
Bevin, Ernest 1881–1951
Birkenhead, Earl of 1872–1930
Bondfield, Margaret 1873–1953
Brown, George, Lord George-Brown 1914–85
Burns, John 1858–1943
Butler, Lord 1902–82
Carson, Edward, Lord 1854–1935
Chamberlain, Sir Austen 1863–1937
Chamberlain, Joseph 1836–1914
Chamberlain, Neville 1869–1940
Churchill, Sir Winston 1874–1965
Cripps, Sir Stafford 1889–1952
Curzon of Kedleston, Marquess 1859–1925
Eden, Anthony, Earl of Avon 1897–1977
Gaitskell, Hugh 1906–63
Grey of Fallodon, Edward, Viscount 1862–1933
Grimond, Jo, Lord 1913–93.
Haldane, Visc. 1856–1928
Halifax, Earl of 1881–1959
Henderson, Arthur 1863–1935
Home, Lord (Sir Alec Douglas-Home) 1893–1995
Joseph, Lord (Sir Keith Joseph) 1918–94

Law, Andrew Bonar 1858–1923
Lloyd George, David 1863–1945
MacLeod, Iain 1913–1970
MacDonald, James Ramsay 1866–1937
Morrison of Lambeth, Herbert, Lord 1888–1965
Mosley, Sir Oswald 1896–1980
Oxford and Asquith, Earl of 1852–1928
Pankhurst, Dame Christabel 1880–1958
Pankhurst, Emmeline 1858–1928
Reading, Rufus, Marquess of 1860–1935
Salisbury, 5th Marquess of 1893–1972
Samuel, Herbert Louis, 1st Viscount 1870–1963
Smith, John 1938–94
Snowden, Philip, Visc. 1864–1937
Stockton, Harold Macmillan, Earl of 1894–1986
Wilkinson, Ellen 1891–1947
Wilson of Rievaulx, Harold, Lord 1916–95
Woolton, 1st Earl 1883–1964
Bulgarian:
Dimitrov, Georgi 1882–1949
Liaptcheff, Andrea 1866–1933
Malinoff, Alexander 1867–1938
Stambolisky 1879–1923
Canadian:
Borden, Sir Robert L. 1854–1937
King, William Lyon Mackenzie 1878–1950
Laurier, Sir Wilfrid 1841–1919
Pearson, Lester Bowles 1897–1972
Strathcona, Donald Alexander Smith, Baron 1820–1914
Chilean:
Allende, Salvador 1908–73
Chinese:
Chiang Kai-Shek 1887–1975
Mao Tse-Tung 1893–1976
Sun Yat-Sen 1866–1925
Cypriot:
Archbishop Makarios 1913–77
Czech:
Benes, Edward 1884–1948
Dubček, Alexander 1921–92
Gottwald, Klement 1896–1953
Masaryk, Jan 1886–1948
Masaryk, Tomáš Garrigue 1850–1937
Egyptian:
Nasser, Gamal Abdel 1918–70
Sadat, Anwar 1918–81

Filipino:
Aquino, Benigno d. 1983
Marcos, Ferdinand, 1917–89
Finnish:
Mannerheim, Carl 1867–1951
French:
Auriol, Vincent d. 1966
Barthou, Jean Louis 1862–1934
Blum, Léon 1872–1950
Briand, Aristide 1862–1932
Clemenceau, George Benjamin 1841–1929
Darlan, J.L.X.F. 1881–1942
de Gaulle, Charles 1890–1970
Delcasse, Théophile 1852–1923
Doumer, Paul 1857–1932
Doumergue, Gaston 1863–1937
Herriot, Édouard 1872–1957
Laval, Pierre 1883–1945
Maginot, André 1877–1932
Monnet, Jean 1888–1979
Painlevé, Paul 1863–1933
Pétain, Philippe 1856–1951
Poincaré, Raymond 1860–1934
Pompidou, Georges 1911–74
Reynaud, Paul 1878–1966
Schumann, Robert 1886–1963
Thomas, Albert 1878–1932
Thorez, Maurice 1900–64
German:
Adenauer, Konrad 1876–1967
Bernstorff, Count Johann Heinrich 1852–1939
Brandt, Willy 1913–92
Ebert, Friedrich 1871–1925
Erhard, Ludwig 1897–1977
Goebbels, Joseph 1897–1945
Goering, Hermann 1893–1946
Heuss, Professor Theodor 1884–1963
Hitler, Adolf 1889–1945
Honecker, Erich 1912–94
Pieck, Wilhelm 1876–1960
Rathenau, Walther 1967–22
Schumacher, Kurt 1895–1952
Strauss, Franz-Josef 1915–88
Strésemann, Gustav 1878–1929
Ulbricht, Walther 1893–1973
Wörner, Manfred 1934–94
Ghana:
Nkrumah, Kwame 1909–72
Greek:

Konduriotis, Adam Paul 1855–1935
Metaxas, John 1871–1941
Papandreou, George 1888–1968
Papagos, Alexander 1883–1955
Venizelos, Eleutherios 1864–1936
Hungarian:
Apponyi, Count Albert 1846–1933
Horthy, Nicholas 1868–1957
Karolyi, Count Michael 1875–1955
Nagy, Imre 1896–1958
Tisza, Count Istvan 1861–1918
Indian:
Gandhi, Indira, Mrs 1917–84
Gandhi, Mahatma 1869–1948
Gandhi, Rajiv, 1944–91
Morarji, Desai, 1896–1995
Nehru, Jawaharial 1889–1964
Indonesian:
Sukarno, Achmed 1901–70
Iraqi:
Nuri es-Said 1888–1958
Kassem, Abdul Karim 1914–63
Irish:
Collins, Michael 1890–1922
de Valera, Eamon 1882–1975
Hyde, Douglas 1860–1949
McBride, Maude (Gonne) 1866–1953
McNeill, James 1869–1938
Israeli:
Begin, Menachem 1913–92
Ben-Gurion, David 1886–1973
Meir, Golda 1898–1978
Rabin, Yitzhak 1922–95
Weizmann, Chaim 1874–1952
Italian:
Badoglio, Pietro 1871–1956
Balbo, Italo 1896–1940
Ciano, Caleazzo 1903–44
Gasperi, Alcide de 1881–1954
Giolitti, Giovanni 1842–1928
Mussolini, Benito 1883–1945
Orlando, Vittorio Emanuele 1860–1952
Sforza, Carlo 1873–1952
Togliatti, Palmiro 1893–1964
Kenyan:
Kenyatta, Jomo c. 1889–1978
Korean:
Rhee, Syngman 1875–1965
Kim Il-Sung, 1912–94
Japanese:
Tojo, Hideki 1884–1948

Yamamoto, Count 1852–1933
New Zealand:
Fraser, Peter 1884–1950
Holland, Sir Sidney 1893–1957
Holyoake, Sir Keith 1904–83
Nash, Walter 1882–1968
Savage, Michael 1872–1940
Pakistani:
Jinnah, Mohammed Ali 1876–1948
Liaquat Ali Khan 1896–1951
Bhutto, Zulfilkar Ali 1928–79
Zia-ul-Haq, Mohammed, 1924–88
Polish:
Beck, Josef 1894–1944
Sikorski, Wladislaw 1881–1943
Portuguese:
Salazar, Antonio de Oliveira 1889–1970
Romanian:
Antonescu, Ion 1882–1946
Averescu, Alexander 1859–1938
Bukharin, N.I. 1880–1938
Ceausescu, Nicolai 1918–89
Duca, Ion 1879–1933
Gheorgiu-Dej, Georgei 1901–1965
Russian:
Andropov, Yuri, 1914–1984
Beria, Lavrenti 1899–1953
Brezhnev, Leonid 1906–82
Chernenko, Konstantin 1911–85
Gamsakhurdia, Zviad (Georgian), 1939–94
Kamenev, Lev B. 1883–1936
Kerensky, Alexander 1881–1970
Khruschev, Nikita 1894–1971
Lenin, Vladimir Ilyitch Ulyanov 1870–1924
Litvinov, Maxim Maximovitch 1876–1951
Molotov, V.H., 1890–1986
Stalin, Josef V.D. 1880–1953
Trotsky, Lev 1879–1940
Zinoviev, Grigori 1883–1936
S African:
Botha, Louis 1862–1919
Hertzog, J. B. M. 1866–1942
Malan, Daniel 1874–1959
Smuts, Jan Christiaan 1870–1950
Strijdom, Johannes 1893–1958
Verwoerd, Hendrik 1901–66
Spanish:
Franco, Francisco 1892–1975
La Pasionara (Dolores Ibarruri Gomez), 1895–1989
Primo de Rivera, Miguel 1870–1930

Swedish:
Hammarskjöld, Dag 1905–61
Turkish:
Atatürk, Mustafa Kemal 1881–1938
Gursel, Cemal 1896–1966
Menderes, Adnan 1899–1961
Ozal, Turgot 1927–93
USA:
Bingham, Robert Worth 1871–1937
Bryan, William Jennings 1860–1925
Coolidge, Calvin 1872–1933
Dulles, John Foster 1888–1959
Eisenhower, Dwight David 1890–1969
Hoover, Herbert 1874–1964
House, Edward Mandell 1858–1938
Kellogg, Frank Billings 1856–1937
Kennedy, John Fitzgerald 1917–63
Kennedy, Robert Francis 1925–68
King, Martin Luther 1929–68
La Follette, Robert M. 1855–1925
Long, Huey Pierce 1893–1935
MacCarthy, Joseph 1909–57
Marshall, George 1880–1959
Morrow, Dwight Whitney 1873–1931
Nixon, Richard 1913–94
Roosevelt, Eleanor 1884–1962
Roosevelt, Franklin Delano 1882–1945
Roosevelt, Theodore 1858–1919
Root, Elihu 1845–1937
Rusk, Dean 1909–94
Stevenson, Adlai 1900–65
Taft, Robert 1890–1953
Taft, William Howard 1857–1930
Truman, Harry S. 1884–1972
Vandenberg, Arthur 1884–1972
Welles, Sumner 1892–1961
Wilson, Thomas Woodrow 1856–1924
Vietnamese:
Ngo Dinh Diem *d.* 1964
Ho Chi-Minh 1892–1969
Yugoslav:
Kidrić, Boris 1912–53
Mihailovich, Draza 1893–1946
Tito, Josip Broz 1892–1980

Stationers' Hall. Incorporated, 1556.

Stationery Office, Her Majesty's, established, 1786.

steam navigation. *See* SHIP.

Stellaland, short-lived Boer republic set up in N Cape Province, 1882. Declared British protectorate, 1884.

Stettin. *See* Szczecin.

Stirling, University of, established 1967.

Stock Exchange (London), 1773. Constitution regulated by Deed of Settlement, 27 Mar. 1802, modified by Deed of 31 Dec. 1875. Complete restructuring with 'Big Bang', 1986. Rules further altered to comply with EEC requirements, 1990. Originally at Throgmorton St. new building there, 1854. Moved to new building in Old Broad St. opened by Queen Elizabeth II, 1972. Slight damage by IRA attack, 20 July 1990. 'Taurus' (paperless transfer system) scheme abandoned, 1993. Oldest existing S.E. in the world claimed to be Antwerp (1460), but this is now less important in Belgium than the Brussels S.E. (1801).

Other S.E.s include:

Argentina: 1854
Australia: Melbourne, 1865
             Sydney, 1871
Austria: Vienna, 1771 (suspended during World War II)
Canada: Montreal, 1874
             Toronto, 1852 (incorporated 1878)
Chile: Santiago, 1893
France: Paris, modern origins, 18thC: modernized during 1980s.
Germany: Frankfurt, regular trading started 18thC, but an exchange office there, 1402. Closed early 1945: reopened Sept. 1945.
Berlin: 1685. Closed 18 April 1945 (building destroyed): reopened 11 Mar. 1952. New building in progress, 1995.
Hong Kong: first S.E., 1866, formalized, 1891. Subsequently three S.E.s formed, but by 2 Apr. 1886 all merged into the S.E. of Hong Kong Ltd.
India: Bombay, began informally, 1830s; formalized during 1880s.
Italy: Milan, 1808
Japan: Tokyo, 1878 (suspended, 1945: restarted 1947)
Korea: 1956 (but some share activity 1911–40)
Malaysia: Kuala Lumpur, wholly independent from 1973.
Mexico: 1895
Netherlands: Amsterdam, 1611
New Zealand: Auckland, 1870s; formalized 1902, 1908.
Nigeria: 1960
Pakistan: 1947
Singapore: 1930; joined to Kuala Lumpur S.E., 1964: two S.E.s separated and Singapore wholly independent from 1973
South Africa: Johannesburg, 1886
Spain: Madrid, 1831
Switzerland: Basle, 1876
                     Geneva, 1850
                     Zurich, 1877
Thailand: 1960, reorganized, 1975
Turkey: Istanbul, 1986
USA: New York, 1792 (constitution, 1817)
          Mid-West (as Chicago S.E., 1882, merged with other minor S.E.s to form Mid-West, 1949, now (1995) fastest growing S.E. in USA)
Venezuela: Caracas, 1947 (some informal trading since 1905)

European S.E.s in Communist countries were closed while the system lasted: they have been reopening since the late 1980s, e.g. in Hungary, Budapest S.E. began operating again, 1989, officially reopened, 21 July 1990.

There were three S.E.s in Moscow in 1993, all founded 1991. They were the Moscow Central S.E.; the Moscow International S.E.; and the Moscow Financial S.E. There were *c.* 160 S.E.s in the whole of Russia but most trade still carried on outside the S.E.s. In China, S.E. activity also revived from late 1980s. The Shanghai Securities Exchange (the S.E.) opened Dec. 1990: the Forex Forward Market, June 1992.

Stockholm, capital of Sweden, grew up around a fortress in the 13thC. Cathedral dates from 13thC. Royal palace, 18thC. S. has grown extensively since beginning of 20thC. City Hall, 1923. Underground system started, 1950. S. the venue of many international conferences including the S. Conference of European Social Democrats held at, Aug. 1917. Arms limitation talks at, 1984.

Stoics. The disciples of Zeno (335–263 BC), whose school was held in a portico (Greek *stoa*).

Stonehenge, Wiltshire. Excavation since 1950 suggest three Ss.:
1. S. 1., *c.* 3,100 BC which was used for about 500 years and then reverted to scrubland.
2. S. 2. *c.* 2,100 BC.
3. S. 3. *c.* 2,000 BC.

The 'Avenue' was extended *c.* 1100 BC. Function of S. remains unknown, but generally thought to be religious. Though incomplete now it ranks as one of Europe's finest ancient monuments.

Stormont, E Belfast, which is the site of the N Ireland Parliament buildings and S. House. Official residence of the N Ireland prime minister until introduction of direct rule from Westminster in 1972. The parliament buildings date from 1928–32. Debating chamber destroyed by fire, Jan. 1995.

Strand (London), first mentioned in Anglo-Saxon Chronicle, *sub anno* 1052. Business area from 19thC.

Strasbourg or **Strassburg.** Capital of Alsace. Taken by France, 1681; captured by Germany, 1870; returned to France, 1918; Germany, 1940; France again, 1944. Contains a celebrated university, founded in 1538. HQ Council of Europe, 1949: subsequently periodical meeting place of European Parliament.

Strategic Arms Limitation Treaties. *See* SALT.

Strategic Arms Reduction Talks. *See* START.

Strategic Defense Initiative (SDI). *See* STAR WARS.

Stratford-on-Avon, England. Shakespeare born at 1564. Shakespeare Memorial Theatre built, 1877–9; burnt down, 1926; rebuilt, 1932.

Strathclyde, Scottish administrative region since 1972, with HQ at Glasgow. Government proposals to abolish, 1993, to be enacted 1996.

Strathclyde, Celtic kingdom of the Clyde Valley and parts of Galloway, at times linked to that of Cumbria, founded *c.* AD 560. Became subject to Northumbria about 650, but regained independence after the defeat of King Ecgfrith, by the Picts at Nectansmere, 685. Alcluith (Dumbarton), the capital, stormed by Picts, 736. King Eadberht of Northumbria conquered and annexed SW S., 750, and temporarily subdued the whole kingdom, 756. Dumbarton sacked by the Danish king, Ivarr Ragnarsson, 870, and again invaded by him, 875 (*see* VIKING AGE). Thereafter more frequently invaded, and partly settled, by Norwegian Vikings. Submitted to Edward the Elder, King of England, about 921. Ceded by Edmund, King of England, to Malcolm I of Scotland, 946, but again became independent before 971. Last mention of a king of S. (Owen), as ally of Malcolm Canmore, 1018. Independence finally lost before 1100.

Strathclyde University, Glasgow. Established 1864.

Statue of Liberty, gift of the French people to the USA. Sculpted by Bartholdi from 1875. In 1885 shipped to USA and erected in New York Harbor. Officially dedicated by President Cleveland, 28 Oct 1886. National Monument since 1924, Museum of Immigration (1972) in its base. Repaired in 1980s for 1986 centenary.

Street Offences Act. Came into force, 16 Aug. 1959. Made soliciting in streets or public places illegal.

streptomycin. Isolated, 1943, by Waksman, a Russian-born scientist, who was awarded the Nobel Prize, 1952.

Stresa Conference, 11–14 Apr. 1935. Britain, France and Italy agreed to maintain independence of Austria.

Strike, the General. *See* GENERAL STRIKE.

strong nuclear force, discovered, 1935, by Hideki Yukawa, a Japanese physicist.

Stuttgart. Originated around a stud farm (hence name), *c.* 950. Chartered in 1250. Became capital of the dukes of Württemberg in the 15thC. Declined after 1648 until industrial expansion began, 19thC. Major centre of German car industry since early 20thC. Heavily damaged during World War II: rebuilding includes some notable 20thC architecture. Town hall, 1954–6; TV Tower (633 ft/201 m), 1955; Liederhall, 1954–6. Port opened, 1958.

Styria (Steiermark). Came under Frankish domination about 780, but only as part of Duchy of *Carinthia. Made a separate mark in 1056, and bestowed on Count Ottokar of Steyr, whence its name. Became a duchy in 1180, and was attached to the Duchy of Austria, 1192; belonged to Bohemia from 1260 to 1282, thereafter to the Hapsburg empire. Formed one province (*Land*) of the Austrian Federal Republics of 1918 and 1945.

Submarines. First practicable submarine was demonstrated by the American Bushnell in 1775, the next by Robert Fulton in 1800; both capable of placing limpet charges. S. were first used in action in the American Civil War, 1863. First British submarine launched, 1901. First nuclear-powered submarine was the USS *Nautilus*, 1955. First nuclear-powered British submarine, the *Dreadnought*, commissioned 1963. *See also* TRIDENT.

Sudan, N Africa, sovereign independent republic since 1 Jan. 1956, formerly Anglo-Egyptian territory. The area corresponds more or less to the territory anciently called Nubia (i.e. the Nile valley S of the First Cataract – Aswan), which was penetrated by Egyptian influence as early as the Old Empire, almost 4000 BC. Colonies and military posts were established regularly in the 12th dynastic period (2700–2500 BC), and the conquest S to the Fourth Cataract consolidated under the 18th dynasty. (*c.* 1350 BC). About 200 years later fugitive priests of Amen from Thebes founded a new state, with sub-Egyptian culture, with its capital at Napata in S. An independent Nubian civilization arose *c.* 800 BC, and for a time its kings dominated Egypt (from 749 to 667). The borrowed Egyptian culture declined after the withdrawal of Nubian rulers from Egypt, and the capital Napata was supplanted by Meroë *c.* 300. For three centuries thereafter Nubia was virtually independent of the Ptolemaic rulers of Egypt, but the Romans who succeeded them also conquered the S., and established their southern frontier to the S of Wadi Halfa. Only at the end of the Romano-Nubian period (*c.* 550) was Christianity introduced. Moslem invasions began, 652, but strong Christian kingdoms persisted until *c.* 1350, and many Nubians professed Christianity until the 16thC. The triumph of Islam was due to direct migration from Arabia, led by the Beni Omayya tribe from the 8thC onwards. S. was conquered by Mehemet Ali, 1821. Gen. Gordon was appointed (Egyptian) governor-general, 1873–80; revolt of Sudanese under the Mahdi, 1882; annihilation of Hicks Pasha's forces, 1883; Gordon killed at Khartoum, 1885; battle of Omdurman, 1898. Anglo-Egyptian agreement on condominium, 19 Jan. 1899, determined the manner of S. administration for the first half of the 20thC. Anglo-Egyptian agreement, Feb. 1953, acknowledged the right of S. to self-determination, the population to choose, in 1955, between independence and union with Egypt. The Sudanese Parliament voted for independence immediately, 19 Dec. 1955, and a republic was proclaimed, 1 Jan. 1956. Increasing Islamicization from 1960s led to civil war in S. between Christians and central government in which whole communities have been exterminated. General discontent resulted in military coup, 7 Apr. 1985, when Numeiri, S.'s dictator, ousted. The civilian government of 1986 overthrown by military coup, 1989. Civil war continued and famine in S. since *c.* 1980 estimated to have caused over one million deaths up to 1995 (*see* FAMINES). Islamicization and anti-Christian policies increased from 1989; archbishop of

Canterbury's decision to visit only S S., Dec. 1993, caused friction between Britain and S. and British ambassador in Khartoum asked to leave.

French S.: the designation from 1920 until 1960 of Upper Senegal-Niger, a French colony formed in 1904. A partner (with Senegal) in the Federation of Mali, Jan. 1959–Sept. 1960. On 22 Sept. 1960 the territory became the independent republic of *Mali.

Sudetenland, district taking its name from the Sudetic Mountains in Bohemia and Moravia, and before 1945 largely inhabited by Germans from Saxony, Bavaria and Franconia, whose immigration began shortly after AD 1100. Sudeten German *Heimatfront* (local Nazi and other Pan-German parties amalgamated) formed by Konrad Henlein (1898–1945), 1933. S. incorporated in German Reich, Oct. 1938. Some 3,700,000 S. Germans, out of an estimated 4,000,000, were expelled from Czechoslovakia, 1945, after the Allied victory.

Suevi. *See* SWABIA.

Suez Canal. Permission for its construction under de Lesseps, 1854; company formed, 1856; work begun, 1859; opened to traffic, 1869. Britain buys shares in, 1875. Under Article 8 of the Anglo-Egyptian Defence Treaty, 1938, Britain was responsible for defending the S.C. zone; but in Nov. 1955 Egypt took over. The last British troops left the zone, 31 Mar. 1956. Nasser nationalized the S.C., 26 July 1956. Anglo-French planes began bombing canal installations, Oct. 1956, and (Nov.) invaded the zone (*see* EGYPT). Egypt blocked the S.C. and it was not opened to traffic again until 30 Apr. 1957. Shareholders of the S.C. Company accepted compensation terms offered by Egypt, July 1958. S.C. was blocked by Egypt during the 'June War', 1967, and remained so till 1975. Two-stage development begun, 1976. Israeli ships again allowed to use S.C., 1979.

suicide, ceased to be defined as a crime in Britain, under S. Act of 1961.

Sullom Voe, *see* SHETLAND ISLANDS.

Sumatra was a Hindu kingdom from *c.* AD 600–1300. First European (Portuguese) settlement, 1509, was replaced by Dutch settlement *c.* 1600. Occupied by Japanese 1941–45, part of Indonesia since then.

Sumer, early civilization based in area between rivers Tigris and Euphrates, in S Mesopotamia. Probably first settled *c.* 4500 BC but Semitic 'Sumerians' arrived *c.* 3300 BC and civilization lasted till *c.* 1850 BC. See UR.

Summer Time, formerly known as **Daylight Saving**. Summer Time Act, 1916, partly due to example of Germany, which had adopted system earlier in the year, but principally to efforts of W. Willert (1856–1915) who first proposed it, 1907. British S.T. lasted continuously from 25 Feb. 1940 to 31 Dec. 1944 and for all but three months of 1945. During these years, and again in 1947, double S.T. in force from Apr. to Oct. With the British Standard Time Act, 1968, S.T. extended throughout the whole year for a trial period but met much opposition. Summer Time Act, 1972, reinstated S.T. to run from March to Oct. Efforts from 1990s by EU to persuade UK and Ireland to synchronize S.T. dates with those in other member countries; for 1996 and 1997. S.T. in whole EU will end at same date, but no decision reached for after that.

Sunday Observance Acts, 1625–1780, modified by the S. Entertainment Act, 1932, S. Trading Act, 1870 and Shops Act, 1950 and after. Efforts to reform in England and Wales from 1980s. 8 Dec. 1993, Commons voted on liberalizing Sunday shop opening hours. Legislation passed, 1994. Moves to reform S.O.A. in respect of public houses and licensing laws, 1994: alcohol laws relaxation on Sundays, in Scotland, from Dec. 1994 and in England from 1995; on-course Sunday betting allowed in England from 1995; bookmakers open on Sundays, 1995.

Sunday schools. Originally in Milan under St Charles Borromeo, 1580, and in England under Robert Raikes and Rev. Stocks, 1780.

Sunderland, developed from Monkwearmouth (monastery there, 674). Chartered from 12thC: a borough from 1634. Development of coal trade from 17thC and from mid-18thC to mid-20thC a major ship-building centre, but this subsequently replaced by other industries (e.g. car building) in 1980s onwards. Sunderland polytechnic became Sunderland University 1992. S. made a city, 1993.

sunspots were discovered by Galileo, 1610. Periodicity of 11 years deduced by Schwabe, 1843.

supersonic speed, first attained by John Derry of de Havillands, 6 Sept. 1948.

supertax first imposed by Lloyd George in Finance Act, 1909, and levied until 1929. *See* SURTAX.

Supply, Ministry of, 1939–59.

Supremacy, Act of, 1534, declared Henry VIII head of the English Church. Denial of this doctrine declared treasonable under Edward VI, 1457. Repealed by Philip and Mary, 1554. Restored in slightly modified form by Elizabeth I, 1559.

Supreme Council. British, French and Italian Governments set up a S. War C. at Versailles, Nov. 1917. In 1919–20 it acted as the Executive Committee of the *Peace Conference.

Supreme Court (USA), is the final court of appeal in the USA and expositor of the constitution. Established in 1787, size set by Congress, which must approve its composition and has rejected some presidential nominees. Since its inception, one justice has been impeached (1805, but acquitted) and one resigned (1969, for financial reasons).

Supreme Court of Judicature. The Judicature Act of 1873 formed one supreme court for England and Wales. The S.C. consists of the High Court and the Court of Appeal, and, since 1971, the Crown Court.

Surinam, formerly **Dutch Guiana**. First European settlement attempted by the English, 1630. Sugar planters (Dutch and Portuguese) entered the country, 1644. English settlement, 1650; capitulated to the Dutch, and exchanged for New Amsterdam (now New York) the following year. Again in English hands, 1799–1802 and 1804–16. Independent, 1975. Marxist coup, 1982. New constitution, 1987; military coup, 1990. New Front leader Venetiaan elected president, Sept. 1991, and less authoritarian rule envisaged. Peace agreement between government and main guerrilla groups, Aug. 1992.

Surrey, University of. Established at Guildford, 1966.

surtax replaced *supertax in 1929. Ceased to be a separate tax, 1971.

Sussex, Kingdom of. 477, Aelle and his sons Cymen, Wlencing, and Cissa landed at place chronicled as *Cymenes ora*, 485. Battle between Aelle and the Britons, 491. Aelle and Cissa besieged Andredesceaster (i.e., Anderida, now Pevensey), and killed the garrison, 514. Aelle died, 661–c. 685. Aethelwalh, King of Sussex, killed by Caedwalla of Wessex, c. 685. References to two kings of Sussex, Berthun and Andhun, who resisted Caedwalla. About 687 Caedwalla seems to have become effective rule of S. *See* SELSEY. Later history suggests that S. was ruled by a number of sub-kings, probably subject to Wessex and then to Mercia.

Sussex University, established at Brighton, 1961.

suttee. Suicide of an Indian widow on the husband's funeral pile. Forbidden by the British administration, 1829.

Sutton Hoo, England. Site where a 7thC ship-burial discovered, Aug. 1939. The landowner presented the entire treasure found there to the British Museum. In the 1980s further excavations carried out on the site: six further burial mounds excavated by 1992.

Sverdlovsk, 1) region of Russia, in the Urals, which declared itself a republic, 1993.
2) *see* EKATERINBURG.

Swabia (Schwaben), originally an ethnic rather than geographical term denoting the land of the Suevi or Swabians. It is not clear that the term Suevi when used by Tacitus (AD 55–120) is anything more than a vague term for nomadic tribes at a rather lower cultural level than other Germans to the S and W; but by about AD 600, Swabians had come to mean tribes speaking the W or Alemmanic variant of the High German language, and their country the rough rectangle between the Main, the Rhine, Lake Constance and the Lech. It was a 'tribal' duchy under the Carolingian Empire (751–987) and came into possession of the Stauffen dynasty, 1079, who retained it until 1268, when it was partitioned among the local nobility. The 'Swabian League', a confederation of Swabian cities formed in 1488, disintegrated, 1534. *See also* BADEN and WÜRTTEMBERG.

Swaziland. Independence recognized by Boer republics in Conventions of 1881 and 1884. Dual control by British and Boers set up, 1890; administration taken over by Transvaal, 1894; British protectorate declared, 1906. Independent dominion, 1968. New constitution, 1978. King *d.*, 1982; crown prince confirmed as successor, 1986. Constitution amended, 1992–3.

'sweating'. A term first applied in 19thC to underpaid and overworked labour. Cradley Heath chainmakers' sufferings disclosed, 1889; Anti-Sweating League formed, 1889; Blue Book published, 1890.

Sweden. S. originated in the Sver Kingdom N of Lake Mälar and the Gothic Kingdom in south S. which coalesced after the battle of Bråvalla (? *c.* 650) under the Uppsala Yngling dynasty. Swedes under Rurik found Novgorod *c.* 862. Ynglings die out and are succeeded by the Gothic Stenkil's dynasty, 1060. The Christian Sverker's dynasty follows, 1130–55, when civil war between Sverker's and Eric's dynasties follows till 1250. Folkung dynasty established by the jarl, Birger Magnusson, 1250 till 1387. By the Union of *Kalmar S. comes under Danish rule, 1397.

Engelbrekt Engelbrektsen raises revolt in Dalecarlia, 1434. He calls the first Riksdag (Parliament) at Arbog, 1435, and is murdered, 1436. Sten Sture the Elder defeats Danes at Brunkeberg, 1471. Papal charter granted to Uppsala University, 1477. Christian II of Denmark carries out massacre at Stockholm, 1520. Gustavus Vasa raises national revolt in Dalecarlia, Jan. 1521. Elected king by Riksdag at Stränghäs, 6 June 1523. *Reces* and *Ordinantia* of Västerås establish power of the Vasa monarchy and regulate church affairs, 24 June 1527. Pact of Succession, 1544. Eric XIV deposed, 1568. S. seize Novgorod, 1611. Peace of Stolbova, 1617. Gustavus Adolfus conquers Baltic provinces, 1621–2; Pomerania, 1630. Defeats Tilly at battle of Breitenfeld, 1631. Is killed at battle of Lützen, 6 Nov. 1632. New constitution, 1634. Abdication of Queen Christina, 1654. Defeat by Russians at Poltava, 1709, and collapse of Swedish Baltic Empire, 1709–18. Peace of Nystad with Russia, 1721. By *Riksdags ordningen* ('Parliamentary constituent'), Riksdag organized into Four Estates, 1723. Marshal Bernadotte elected Crown Prince, 1810. Norway transferred to Swedish crown, 1814. Bernadotte succeeded to throne as Charles XIV, 1818. Union with Norway dissolved, 1905. Prohibition introduced, 1922; abolished, 1955. Changed to driving on the right, Sept. 1967. S. neutral in both world wars. Under constitution of 1975 sovereign merely Head of State and inheritance passes to eldest child. Premier Palme assassinated, 1986. Recession in 1990s; first applied to join EC, 1991; referendum voted in favour, Nov. 1994; became member of EU, 1 Jan. 1995.

Sweden, Kings of, from c. 850–1951:
Olaf and Emund *c.* 850–*c.* 882
Eric Emundsson *c.* 882–*c.* 905
Bjorn Ericsson and Ring *c.* 905–*c.* 950
Eric the Victorious *c.* 950–*c.* 993
Period of confusion c. 993–999
Olaf Scatt-King 999–1022
Anund Jacob 1022–50
Edmund the Old 1050–60

Stenkil 1060–66
Period of confusion 1066–80
Halstan *c*. 1080–*c*. 1093
Inge the Good *c*. 1090–*c*. 1118
Inge II Halstansson *c*. 1118–1130
Sverker *c*. 1132–55
Eric IX (St) 1150–60
Charles VII 1160–67
Knut Ericsson 1167–96
Sverker Carlsson 1196–1205 (?)
Period of confusion: rival kings 1205–50
Valdemar 1250–75
Magnus I Ladulas 1275–90
Birger 1290–1318
Magnus II 1319–65
Albert of Mecklenburg 1365–88
Margaret (as 'Lady of Sweden') 1389–97
Eric of Pomerania (XIII) 1397–1439
Christopher of Bavaria 1440–48
Charles VIII Knutsson Bonde 1448–57
Christian I 1457–64
Charles VIII (again) 1464–65 and 1467–70
Regency under Sten Sture the Elder 1470–97
John II 1497–1501
Regency under Sten Sture the Elder 1501–03
Regency under Svante Sture 1504–12
Regency under Sten Sture the Younger 1512–20
Christian II 1520–23
Gustavus I (Vasa) (of Sweden only) 1523–60
Eric XIV 1560–68
John III 1568–92
Sigismund 1592–99
Charles IX 1600–11
Gustavus II, Adolphus 1611–32
Christina 1632–54
Charles X 1654–60
Charles XI 1660–97
Charles XII 1697–1718
Ulrica Eleonora 1718–20
Frederick I 1720–51
Adolphus, Frederick 1751–71
Gustavus III 1771–92
Gustavus IV, Adolphus 1792–1809
Charles XIII 1809–18 and of Norway 1814–18
Charles XIV, John (Bernadotte) 1818–44
Oscar I 1844–59
Charles XV 1859–72
Oscar II (renounced throne of Norway, 1905) 1872–1907
Gustavus V 1907–50
Gustavus VI, Adolphus 1950–73
Charles XVI, Gustavus 1973–

Swedenborgians, followers of Emanuel Swedenborg (1688–1772), more properly called the New (Jerusalem) Church, founded in England, 1788; their propaganda organ, the Swedenborg Society, instituted, 1810.

Swedish literature. The following is a list of prominent Swedish authors:

Almqvist, Carl Jonas Ludvig, 1793–1866, novelist.
Atterbom, Per Daniel Amadeus, 1790–1855, poet.
Bellman, Carl Mikael, 1740–95, poet.
Benedictsson, Victoria ('Ernst Ahlgren'), 1850–99, novelist.
Bengtsson, Frans, 1894–1956, novelist and biographer.
Bergman, Hjalmar, 1883–1931, novelist.
Dahlgren, Karl Fredrik, 1791–1844, humorist and poet.
Dahlsjerna, Gunno (Eurelius), 1661–1709, poet.
Dalin, Olaf von, 1708–63, poet and historian.
Franzén, Frans Mikael, 1772–1847, poet.
Geijer, Erik Gustaf, 1783–1847, historian and poet.
Geijerstam, Gustaf af, 1858–1909, novelist and dramatist.
Gyalenborg, Gustaf Fredrik, 1731–1808, poet and dramatist.
Hansson, Ola, 1860–1925, poet.
Heidenstam, Verner von, 1859–1940, poet, novelist and critic.
Kellgren, Johan Henrik, 1751–95, poet.
Konsenstjerna, Agnes von, 1894–1940, novelist.
Lagerlöf, Selma, 1858–1940, novelist.
Lundegård, Axel, 1861–1930, novelist.
Messenius, Johannes, 1579–1636, poet and dramatist.
Molander, Harald Johan, 1858–1900, dramatist.

Munthe, Axel Marten Fredrik, 1857–1949, miscellaneous writer.

Nordenflycht, Hedvig Charlotte, 1718–63, poetess.

Petri, Olaus, 1493–1552, historian.

Rosenhane, Gustaf, 1619–84, poet.

Runeberg, Johan Ludvig, 1804–77, poet.

Sjöberg, Erik ('Vitalis'), 1794–1828, poet.

Snoilsky, Count Carl Johan Gustaff, 1841–1903, poet.

Stagnelius, Erik Johan, 1793–1823, poet.

Stjernhjelm, Georg (Göran Lilja), 1598–1672, poet.

Strindberg, Johan August, 1849–1912, novelist and dramatist.

Swedenborg, Emanuel, 1688–1772, philosopher and scientist.

Tegner, Esaias, 1782–1846, poet.

Wägner, Elin, 1882–1949, novelist.

The following though writing in Swedish were born and lived in Finland, and regarded themselves as of Finnish nationality:

Hemmer, J., 1893–1944, poet.

Lybeck, M., 1864–1925, poet.

Numers, G. von, 1848–1913, playwright (also in Finnish).

Procope, H., 1868–1927, poet.

Runeberg, J. L., 1804–77, poet.

Schildt, R., 1888–1925, novelist and playwright.

Södergran, Edith, 1892–1923, poet.

Stenbäck, J., 1811–70, poet.

Tavastjerna, K. A. 1860–98, poet and novelist.

Topelius, Z., 1818–98, poet.

Wecksell, J. J., 1838–1907, playwright.

Swiss Guard (French). Raised, 1616; ceased to exist after 1792, when they suffered heavy losses in the defence of the Tuileries.

Swiss Guard (papal). Raised by Julius II, 1506. Had heavy casualties (two-thirds of total strength) at the sack of Rome, 1527. New establishment ordered by Paul III, 1548. Disbanded in 1794, reformed, 1825, by Leo XII. Now form part of Vatican security forces.

Switzerland. Struggle for independence against the *13th–14thC Hapsburgs; victories at Morgarten, Sempach, and Näfels, 1315, 1386, and 1388; overthrow of Burgundians at Granson and Morat, 1476; defeated by French at Melegnano, 1515; religious wars during 16thC; Calvin at Geneva, 1536, till his death; declared independent at Peace of *Westphalia, 1648; Peasants' Revolt, 1653; first Villemergen War, 1656; second Villemergen War, 1712; Helvetic Society founded, 1762; alliance with France, 1777; Helvetic Republic proclaimed, 29 Mar. 1798; independence secured by Treaty of Vienna, 1815; the Sonderbund Civil War, Oct.–Nov. 1847; Romansch declared an official language, 1937. Women's suffrage, 1971. New canton (Jura) established, 1979. Referendum voted against S. joining UN, 1986. Economic and financial changes since 1990. 'Money-laundering' an offence, 1990; complete banking anonymity abolished, and foreigners able to buy shares in Swiss companies, 1991. In May 1992, Swiss narrowly voted to apply for EC membership, but referendum, Dec. 1992, rejected S. joining European Economic Area. Cult mass suicides in S., Oct. 1994, with over 40 deaths. For early history, *see* articles on separate cantons and WALDSTÄTTE.

Sydney, capital of New S Wales, was founded by Capt. Arthur Philip, 1788 named after the then British Home Secretary and was originally a penal colony. Developed into a town under Governor Macquarie, 1810–21. Enormous growth 1850–90 and biggest city in Australia by 1911. First railway at, 1855; underground begun, 1926. Stock exchange, 1871. S. Harbour Bridge officially opened, 1932. Capt. Cook Dock completed, 1945. Opera House, 1961; opened officially, 1973. Wool Centre, 1975. Olympics to be held at, 2000. Threatened by bushfires, Jan. 1994.

Synod, General. *See* GENERAL SYNOD.

synods. Convened formerly by the emperors, and afterwards by the Pope; rendered illegal in England except by royal permission, 1533. The Synod of Dort was held from Nov. 1618 to May 1619.

Syracuse, founded *c*. 734 BC as Corinthian colony. Beat off Carthaginians at Himera, 480 BC; defeated Athenian expedition, 414–413; allied to Carthage in second Punic War and taken by Romans, 212, despite brilliant defence by Archimedes (*b*. 287 BC), the chief engineer. Taken by Arabs, AD 878, and Normans, 1085.

Syria. Mandated to France in 1920. French commander in S., loyal to Vichy Government, announced cessation of hostilities with Germany, 28 June 1940. British and Free French forces carried through occupation of S. against Vichy opposition, 8 June–21 July 1941, and declared the independence of S., but in 1945 disagreements arose with the French which led to fighting. Independent republic, 12 Apr. 1946. With Egypt, formed the *United Arab Republic, 1958–61. S. joined in the 'June War', 1967, on the side of Egypt but lost important strategic territory to Israel thereby. Invaded Jordan, Sept. 1970, but troops repulsed and withdrew. Coup in 1970 brought Assad to power. Fought against Israel, 1973, but heavily defeated: in 1980s intervened decisively in *Lebanon on side of the anti-government forces. Originally considered linked with Arab terrorism, S. exerted increasingly benign influence from late 1980s, and instrumental in securing release of Western hostages in Lebanon. On allied side in *Gulf War, 1991. Had assisted establishment of relatively stable government in Lebanon, 1990 and in May 1991, Treaty of Brotherhood, Co-operation and Co-ordination with Lebanon codified Syrian influence there. *See* LEBANON. Remained in dispute (1994) with Israel over territories lost in 1967. Talks between Presidents Clinton and Assad in Geneva, Jan. 1994, and in Damascus in Oct. to attempt to settle Syrian–Israeli problem inconclusive, as S. insistent on return by Israel of Golan Heights. EU lifted 8-year trade embargo with S., Nov. 1994. Talks to secure formal Syrian–Israeli peace treaty so far unsuccessful, 1995.

Szezecin (German **Stettin**) grew up round a Wendish stronghold *c*. AD 1200; received municipal charter, 1243, ceded to Sweden, 1648; to Prussia, 1720. In 1945 it was ceded to Poland.

table tennis, game said to have been derived from tennis, and invented in 1890s by British officers serving in India. Popularly first known as 'ping-pong'. It became very popular from 1920s and spread world-wide. World T.T. championships first held, 1926, and bi-annually since 1957.

Tabuearan. *See* FANNING ISLAND.

Tahiti, Pacific, discovered by Spaniard, de Quiros, 1607; French protectorate formally accepted by native ruler, 1847; French colony, 1880. Since 1970s economy boosted by French nuclear development; but resumption of French underground nuclear testing at *Mururoa, July 1995, caused rioting in T. and boosted support for Tahitian independence movement.

Tai-Pings. Followers of the Christian Hung Hsinchwan in the Chinese rebellion of 1851. Captured Nanking, Mar. 1853; Nanking retaken by the Imperialists under direction of Charles Gordon (later killed at Khartoum), 19 July 1864; and rebellion suppressed, 1865.

Taiwan, formerly **Formosa**. Colonized by Dutch, 1624. Spanish landed, 1626, and called the island Formosa, but expelled by Dutch. Dutch expelled by Chinese, 1662. Invaded by Japanese 1874: ceded to Japan 1895. Returned to Nationalist China, 1945. Since 1949 seat of a Chinese Nationalist government under Chiang Kai-Shek, initially, and the only territory controlled by it. USA and others ceased diplomatic relations with T. on recognition of China in

1970s, though close commercial links continued. Chiang Kai-Shek *d.*, 1975. Martial law lifted in T., 1987. Chiang Kai-Shek's son, Chiang Ching-Kuo, who had succeeded his father, *d.* 1988; succeeded by Lee Teng-hui and T. democratization began. First free elections, 1989. *De facto* recognition of Communist China, Apr. 1991 when 'civil war officially ended', and constitutional reforms. Kuomintang won elections, Dec. 1992, but opposition got 30% of vote. T. and China held high-level talks in Singapore, Apr. 1993, paving way for eventual Chinese reunification. T. one of the most economically prosperous territories in SE Asia from 1950s. France recognized T. as part of integral China, Jan. 1994.

Taizé, France. Religious community founded at, 1944, by Roger Schutz. Originally wholly Protestant, it subsequently attracted members of other Christian denominations and non-Christians for long or short stays: internationally known.

Tajikistan, republic of, originally part of Soviet Turkmenistan. Autonomous republic, 1924 and constituent republic of the USSR, 1929. Declared independence, 6 Sept. 1991 and subsequently joined CIS. From inception clashes between (former Communist) rulers and fundamentalist Muslim opposition. Civil war from end 1991; many refugees fled to Afghanistan, where a 'resistance government in exile' formed. Russia sent troops to help government, and by 1994 civil war largely over, with former Communists in control and seeking closer ties with Russia. Position confirmed in elections, Nov. 1995.

Taj Mahal (India), built by Shah Jehan, 1630–52, as a mausoleum for his favourite wife, Mumtaz, who *d.* 1629. In danger of ultimate destruction by industrial pollution, 1995.

Tallage, a Norman tax, was placed under the control of the Commons, 1297, which abolished it, 1340.

Tallies were used by the exchequer for accounting purposes until 1826, though an

Act for their abolition was passed, 1782. An unsupervised bonfire of old T. was the cause of the greater part of the Palace of Westminster being burnt down, 1834.

Tallin (German **Reval),** fortress founded by Danes in 1219, joined the Hanseatic League, 1248. Ceded to Sweden, 1561, by the Teutonic Knights, who had obtained possession in 1346. Ceded, 1710, to Russians, who made it capital of the government of *Estonia, 1783. Capital of the independent republic of Estonia, 1919–40. Ceded to Russia as a naval base, 28 Sept. 1939. Taken by Germans, Aug. 1941, and retained until the spring of 1945 when, with the rest of Estonia, it became part of the USSR; capital of independent Estonia since 1991.

Talmud. The civil and religious code of the Jews. The T. dating from the 5thC is the one in use, an earlier one having become unintelligible. It is divided into the Mishna and the Gemara. The first complete copy was published at Venice, 1520.

Tamil Nadu, state of S India, formed, 1956, from former Madras province. *See* MADRAS.

Tammany Society. A powerful Democratic association of New York, founded in 1789; chartered, 1805. Named after Tammany, a 17thC Delaware Indian chief. Composition of T.S. radically altered from 1817 by Irish immigrant membership: influence declined after it withheld support from Roosevelt, 1932, and thereafter.

Tanganyika. Formerly German E Africa; mandated to Britain under the peace treaty, 1919. Became an independent dominion, 9 Dec. 1961. On 9 Dec. 1962 became a republic, within the Commonwealth, with Nyerere as President. British troops called in to put down an army mutiny, Jan. 1964; in Apr. 1964 T. united with Zanzibar to form the republic of *Tanzania.

Tangier or **Tangiers,** *Morocco. The Roman *Tingis.* Captured by Portuguese, 1471; given to Charles II on his marriage to Catherine of Braganza, 1662; evacuated by English, 1684; bombarded by French, 1844; terrorized by Raisuli in early years of 20thC; policed in 1906 as a result of Algeciras Convention. By treaty of Fez (Nov. 1912) T. to become centre of an international zone. Finally formed into an internationally governed neutral port, 18 Dec. 1923, by France and Britain (Spain acceded to the agreement, 1924). Spanish troops occupied T., 14 June 1940, and in Sept. T. was incorporated into Spanish Morocco. Spanish troops withdrew and former status restored, 1945. France agreed to terminate treaty of Fez, 1956. Spanish protectorate abolished, and T.'s international status was terminated 1 Jan. 1957, when it became an integral part of Morocco. Free port, 1962.

tanks. British War Office began experiments, 1915. First went into action on the Somme, 15 Sept. 1916.

Tanzania, formed by the union of *Tanganyika and *Zanzibar, 27 Apr. 1964, though the name T. was not officially adopted until 29 Oct. 1964. Nyerere became president of the new state, which became a one-party one in 1977. Constitution revised, 1984 and Nyerere retired, 1985. In June 1992 President Mwinyi endorsed bill legalizing multiparty politics in T. First multiparty elections for 32 years held, Oct. 1995.

tape recorders. Principle of magnetic recording first demonstrated by Poulsen (Denmark), 1900. Much developed by Germany, USA and Britain for military use during World War II. High-quality reproduction by late 1940s. Used for data storage from 1950. Videotape recorder developed, USA, 1956.

Taoism. One of the three religions of China. The system was founded by Lao-tsze in the 6thC BC.

tapestry. Introduced into Flanders during 10thC; Arras chief centre during 14th and 15thC; *Gobelin factory founded in Paris, 16thC; famous T. factory founded at Mortlake by Sir Francis Crane, 1619;

existed till 1703; another factory existed at Windsor, 1872–88. Revival of tapestry in 20thC exemplified by one behind the high altar of the rebuilt Coventry Cathedral. It depicts 'Christ in Glory' and was designed by Graham Sutherland and woven, 1958–61, at the Aubusson factory in France. *See* also BAYEUX TAPESTRY.

Tara, Hill of, was the residence of the High Kings of Ireland until AD 560. The Danes were defeated there (*see* VIKING AGE), 980.

Taranto (Latin *Tarentum*; Greek *Taras*), Italy, founded 708 BC by Spartans. Assisted by Pyrrhus in war against Romans, 281 BC; captured by Romans, 272 BC; became ally of Rome, but went over to Hannibal, 213 BC, and on being recaptured by Fabius, 209 BC, was severely punished. Roman colony, 123 BC. Taken by the Saracens, AD 830; by the Normans, 1083. British air raid on Italian fleet, 11 Nov. 1940.

Tariff Reform League. Inaugurated, July 1903.

tariffs (Britain). Bill to promote Imperial Preference, passed first reading, Nov. 1919, and was then dropped. Government proposals for Imperial Preference introduced at Imperial Conference, Oct. 1923. First protective measures passed by National Government, Nov. 1931. Import Duties Act, 1932. Reprisal Quotas (for imports) were instituted, 1934. Drastic tariff modifications since World War II through GATT, the *European Economic Community (Single European Market within EC existed from 1 Jan 1993 and European Economic Area, comprising EU and EFTA states except Switzerland, in being, 1 Jan. 1994) and the *European Free Trade Association and trading areas established in the Americas, SE Asia, etc.

Tarsus, Asia Minor. Founded by Ionian Greeks, *c.* 900 BC. Occupied by Assyrians, 850. Birthplace of Saul (Paul the Apostle). Capital of the Roman province of Cilicia, AD 72. Captured by Arabs *c.* 660; taken by Tancred in First Crusade, 1099; under Turks since *c.* 1500.

tartan. The word, which is not Gaelic and first appears in English usage in 1500, may be of French origin. The characteristic setts denoting clans and septs evolved probably during the 17thC. The wearing of T. was prohibited by law from 1746 to 1782, under the Highland Garb Act.

Tashkent, capital of Uzbekhistan. Important trading centre since 11thC. Taken by Tamerlane, 1361. Khanate of Kokand, 1809. Taken by Russia, 1865. Serious earthquake, 1966 and major rebuilding since.

Tasmania. Discovered in 1642 by Abel J. Tasman. Penal settlement till 1853. Granted local government, 1856. Name then changed from Van Diemen's Land to T. United with the mainland states to form the Commonwealth of Australia, 1901.

Tatar or **Tartar Republic,** former autonomous republic of the USSR, formed in 1920 on the territory of the 15thC T. kingdom of Kazan. Declared its independence in Aug. 1991, since when it has refused to recognize the authority of the Russian republic.

Tate Gallery (London). Opened, 1897. Turner Wing (Duveen Gallery) opened, 1920. Sculpture hall opened, 1927. Damaged during World War II, but re-opened, 1946, and repairs completed, 1949. Further extension, 1979. Clore Gallery (to house Turner collection) opened by Queen Elizabeth II, 1 April 1987. Tate Gallery, (Liverpool), May 1988. Tate Gallery (St Ives), 1993. Announced, 1994, that former Bankside Power Station to be converted to a T. museum of modern art; awarded National Lottery money for this, 1995.

Taunton, England. Castle first built by King Ine *c.* 710; rebuilt *c.* 1100; defended by Blake, 1644–5; 'Bloody Assize' opened by Judge Jeffreys, 1685.

taxation (Britain). Income and property tax first levied by Parliament during the civil war, 1642. William Pitt the Younger introduced an income tax, 1798, which was repealed, 1815, and revived by Peel, 1842. Supertax introduced, 1914–18. Surtax

replaced supertax, 1929; ceased to be separate tax, 1971.
Land tax first levied, 1690. Made perpetual but redeemable, 1798. Land Value Tax, 1909. Abolished, 1920. Purchase tax introduced, 1940. A 'once-and-for-all' Special Contribution, similar to a capital levy, imposed, 1948. Capital Gains Tax, 1965. Selective Employment Tax, 1966–72. Value Added Tax, 1973.

Tay Bridge (Scotland). Rail bridge first opened, 1877. Famous disaster, 28 Dec. 1879. New bridge opened, 1887. Road bridge opened, Aug. 1966.

Tbilisi, formerly **Tiflis.** Capital of Georgia, founded 5thC AD, conquered by Arabs, 645. Residence of Armenian Kings, 1121–6. Disputed between Turkey and Persia until seized by Russia in 1801. Capital of Georgia since 1922. Scene of violent anti-Russian demonstrations in 1989. Railway links to Black Sea, 1872; to Caspian, 1883. Underground system, 1966.

tea. Used in China in 3rd millenium BC. Introduced in Europe, 16thC, but not into England until 1657. Indian T. plantations date from 1830s.

Teeside, University of, name and status, since 1992, of the former Teeside Polytechnic.

Tehri-Garhwal, small tributary kingdom which in Mar. 1949 the Indian Government combined with *Garhwal as part of the United Provinces (known as Uttar Pradesh since 1950).

Tehran, or **Teheran,** capital of Iran. The ancient capital of *Rayv* has been discovered S. of modern T. (destroyed by Mongols, 1220). T. developed from 14thC AD, and capital of Persia under the Qajars (1779–1925). Subsequently expanded and modernized by the Pahlevis (1925–79). The T. Conference of Allied leaders held at T., (28 Nov.–1 Dec. 1943). US Embassy at T. stormed by revolutionaries, and hostages held, 1979–80.

Tel-Aviv, founded in 1909, originally as a garden city by Jewish residents of Jaffa, received its present name in 1910. T.-A. became the principal economic centre of *Palestine in 1930, and the largest town in the country in 1936. It was the provisional capital of *Israel, 1948–50. Jaffa was absorbed into T.-A., 1950.

telecommunications. *See* TELEGRAPHY; TELEPHONE etc.

telegraphy. Proposal to use electricity as means of communication made as early as 1753. First serviceable telegraphic device invented by Chappe (France), 1792. Ronald (England) produced his pith-ball telegraph, 1816. Morse constructed an instrument in 1835, and Steinheil in 1837. Cooke and Wheatstone's, 1837. Earliest trial, 1837, on LNW Railway. First public line from Paddington to Slough, 1843; London and Paris connected, 1851. Radiotelegraphy invented by Marconi, 1895. Post Office took over telegraph systems on 5 Feb. 1870; acquired by British Telecom, 1981. First transatlantic stations, Poldhu, Cornwall and St John's, Newfoundland, Dec. 1901; first installed in ships, Feb. 1902. Internal telegrams in Britain abolished, 1 Oct. 1982; replaced by telemessages. *See* RADIO.

telepathy. So named by F. W. H. Myers (1843–1901), 1882.

telephone. Wheatstone's 'Magic Lyre' (for reproducing sounds by means of sound-boards connected by a rod), 1831. Philipp Reis's experiments to reproduce human speech, 1861. Alexander Graham Bell (1847–1922) invented electric T., 1876; patented, 1876. Edison patented an invention of his, July 1877. The T. Co. formed, 1878; Edison T. Co. formed, 1879. Action by British postmaster-general against Edison for infringement of monopoly, 1879. National T. Co. (amalgamation of various separate concerns) formed, 1889; trunk wires transferred to Post Office, 1896; Government, by agreement of 2 Feb. 1905, obtained the whole undertaking of the National T. Co., 31 Dec. 1912. Automatic system developed in USA from 1889 (Strowger's invention). Communication between London and Paris established, 1 Apr. 1891. First automatic exchange in UK, Newport, 14 Aug. 1915. Service between New York and London opened, 7 Jan. 1927. Switch to subscriber trunk dialling in Britain, 1959 onwards. First public telephone call by *Telstar London–New York, 19 July 1962. Telephone service transferred to British Telecom, 1981; telemessage service started, 1982. T. system electronic from 1980s. Telecommunications Act, 1984 removed British Telecom's T. monopoly: establishment of Mercury. Cellular T. systems from 1985; over one million mobile Ts. in UK by Jan. 1994.

telescope. Traditionally, invented by Roger Bacon, in the 13thC. Giambattista della Porta probably first to construct some form of instrument, 1558; Leonard Digges is also said, in a book published in 1571, to have arranged glasses so as to obtain 'miraculous effects'. First practical instruments constructed by Lippershey and Jansen in Middelburg, 1608; Galileo constructed his first T., 1609, and began astronomical observations at the beginning of 1610. Lord Rosse's at Birr, 1844; Greenwich T. erected, 1860; Lick Observatory, California, 1880; Pulkowa, Russia, 1885; Yorkes Observatory, Chicago, 1897; Mount Palomar, California, 1949; Jodrell Bank, Cheshire, 1958. Mount Semirodriki, Caucasus, 1976; Los Muchachos, Canaries (William Herschel T.), 1987; Keek T., Mauna Rea, Hawaii, 1992; Hubble Space T., 1992. Largest T. so far, planned for Paranal, N. Chile, to start working *c.* 1995.

teletext, system started in Britain, 1974.

television (TV) was first practically demonstrated by J. L. Baird (1888–1946) in 1926, though means of transmitting images electronically had been suggested by Boris Rosing (1905) and Campbell-Swinton (1911). Still pictures were experimentally diffused by the *British Broadcasting Corporation in 1928. In Nov. 1936 a high-definition transmission station opened at Alexandra Palace. Baird system discontinued, 1937. T. ceased, Sept. 1939; transmissions resumed, 7 June 1946.

Baird's contemporary in the USA was C. F. Jenkins. There were five stations transmitting in the USA in 1939, where T. was not forced to close down during hostilities. In 1946 stations in New York State and Pennsylvania were linked by cable. Columbia Broadcasting System demonstrated colour T., 1940, and colour T. began to be used in the USA from 1949. Eurovision started, 1953. T. Act of 1954 established commercial T. in Britain, under the *Independent T. Authority. T. first shown 'live' between Europe and the USA via *Telstar, July 1962. Britain began changing her line definitions from 405 to 625 lines from 1964. First British colour T. on BBC 2, 1 July 1967: first live T. pictures from the lunar orbit transmitted by *Apollo* 8, Dec. 1968. Cable T. started in USA in 1950s; proliferated in W Europe during 1970s: In Britain Cable and Broadcasting Act established cable T., 1984. Teletext in Britain from 1974. BBC World T. service established, 1991. Videos became established in 1980s. Satellite T. in Britain from 1989. Shake-up in independent T. franchises, 1 Jan. 1993. Debate as to whether Britain would adopt high-definition T. system favoured by Europe or USA settled, June 1993, when EC agreed to fund European wide-screen HDTV. Many restrictions on ITV franchise ownership removed, Nov. 1993. Multi-channel digital TV in Britain envisaged within two years, 1995. Channel 5 Broadcasting awarded fifth TV channel, Oct. 1995; award subsequently challenged.

telex, national and international system of transferring messages by teleprinter, first applied in Germany in 1930s. Teleprinter invented in 1890s by Frederick Creed (British) but first commercial one by Krumm in the USA, 1907. USA established national T. network, 1962, and rest of developed world rapidly followed.

Telstar. US satellite launched from Cape Canaveral, Florida, 10 June 1962. A television picture from Andover, Maine, 'bounced off' T. and was picked up at Goonhilly, Cornwall, at 1 a.m. on 11 July 1962, and at Brittany (even more clearly) on 12 July. Pictures from France and England transmitted to the United States via T. First live television show from United States seen in Europe via T., 23 July 1962. Goonhilly visitors' centre opened, 1987. Now (1995) handles over 50,000 simultaneous telephone messages a day, operating to 110 countries and brings over 4000 TV news items to Britain annually.

Templars, Knights. Order of knighthood founded under Baldwin II of Jerusalem in AD 1118 by Hugues de Payen and Geoffroi de Saint-Adhémar for the protection of pilgrims to the Holy Land. Statutes drawn up at the Council of Troyes, 1128. Rendered independent of any bishop's authority by a bull dated 1172. Reached England *c*. 1185. By order of Philip the Fair, Oct. 1307, the Order was persecuted in France with great cruelties, and was abolished in 1312 by the Council of Vienne. *See also* TEMPLE CHURCH (London).

Temple Bar (London). Wren's gate built, 1670–2. Removed, 1878–9. Erected at Theobalds Park, Cheshunt, 1888. In 1985 suggestion that T.B. be re-sited in St Paul's Churchyard – nothing done by 1995.

Temple Church (London). Built *c*. 1250.

Tennessee, originally a part of N Carolina, was first explored by Spaniards in 1540. Though forming part of the grant made to Sir Walter Raleigh in 1584, it was next explored by the French *c*. 1670–80. Settlement by British colonists began about 1750, and in 1776 the territory was annexed to N Carolina under the name of Washington District, later Washington County. Admitted to the Union as the 16th state, 1 June 1796. Seceded from the Union, June 1861; readmitted, 24 July 1866.

Tennessee Valley Authority (TVA), created by an Act of Congress, May 1933.

tennis. Played in France from the 12thC onwards; popular in court circles in England from 15thC. Lawn T. evolved from real T., *c*. 1870. First Wimbledon 'All-England' men's championships, 1877; first women's, 1893. Lawn Tennis Association founded 1886. New premises, 1922. Lawn T. Association tournaments open from 1968. T. museum at Wimbledon, 1977.

Among leading male personalities in T. are the following:

Ashe, Arthur (USA), 1943–93
Becker, Boris (Germany), 1967–
Borg, Björn (Sweden), 1956–
Borotra, Jean (France), 1898–
Connors, Jimmy (USA), 1952–
Courier, Jim (USA), 1970–95
Edberg, Stefan (Sweden), 1966–
Gonzalez, Pancho (USA), 1928–95
Laver, Rod (Australia), 1938–
Lendl, Ivan (Czech), 1960–
McEnroe, John (USA), 1959–
Patty, Budge (USA), 1924–
Perry, Fred (UK), 1909–95
Sampras, Pete (USA), 1971–
Stich, Michael (Germany), 1968–
Tilden, Bill (USA), 1893–1953

Notable women T.-players include:
Bueno, Maria (Brazil), 1939–
Connolly, Maureen (USA), 1934–69
Godfree, Kitty (UK), 1896–1992
Graf, Steffi (Germany), 1969–
Jacobs, Helen (USA), 1908–
King, Billie Jean (USA), 1943–
Lenglen, Suzanne (France), 1899–1938
Lloyd-Evert, Christine (USA), 1954–
Marble, Alice (USA), 1913–90
Moody, Helen Wills (USA), 1905–
Navratilova, Martina (Czech, then USA), 1956–
Round, Dorothy (UK), 1909–82
Seles, Monica (Serb. *b*.), 1973–
Wade, Virginia (UK), 1945–

The holders of the Wimbledon singles' championships since 1980:
1. Men.
1980 Borg, Björn (Sweden)
1981 McEnroe, John (USA)
1982 Connors, Jimmy (USA)
1983 McEnroe, John (USA)
1984 McEnroe, John (USA)
1985 Becker, Boris (Germany)
1986 Becker, Boris (Germany)

1987 Cash, Pat (Australia)
1988 Edberg, Stefan (Sweden)
1989 Becker, Boris (Germany)
1990 Edberg, Stefan (Sweden)
1991 Stich, Michael (Germany)
1992 Agassi, André (USA)
1993 Sampras, Pete (USA)
1994 Sampras, Pete (USA)
1995 Sampras, Pete (USA)
2. *Women.*
1980 Goolagong-Crawley, Evonne (Australia)
1981 Evert-Lloyd, Christine (USA)
1982 Navratilova, Martina (USA)
1983 Navratilova, Martina (USA)
1984 Navratilova, Martina (USA)
1985 Navratilova, Martina (USA)
1986 Navratilova, Martina (USA)
1987 Navratilova, Martina (USA)
1988 Graf, Steffi (Germany)
1989 Graf, Steffi (Germany)
1990 Navratilova, Martina (USA)
1991 Graf, Steffi (Germany)
1992 Graf, Steffi (Germany)
1993 Graf, Steffi (Germany)
1994 Martinez, Conchita (Spain)
1995 Graf, Steffi (Germany)

An outstanding T. commentator was Dan Maskell (UK), 1908–92

ten-pin bowling. World championships held since 1923. Held every four years since 1963 (when women first competed).

Ten Thousand, Expedition of the. Evacuation of Iraq by Greek mercenaries, formerly in the pay of the Persian King Cyrus, 401 BC. The leader of the operation, Xenophon (427–355 BC), wrote an account of it (*Anabasis*).

Territorial. T. Force formed 1908 from *Volunteers and Yeomanry. Became T. Army, 1920. Re-formed, Jan. 1947, to include conscripts. Further reorganizations, 1956, 1958, 1966, 1984, and 1992. Aim to reduce T. force to 65,000 by 1995.

territorial waters. An act of 1878 gives British courts jurisdiction over offenders arrested in British T.W., viz. within three sea-miles of the coastline of the UK. T.W.

for fishery purposes extended to 12 miles by Acts of 1964 and 1968 but drastically modified as result of British entry into EEC, after 1973.

Temperance League of America. *See* ANTI-SALOON LEAGUE.

Terrorism, Prevention of. *See* PREVENTION OF TERRORISM.

terrorism. For modern T., *see* BAADER-MEINHOF GANG; IRISH REPUBLICAN ARMY; RED ARMY, JAPANESE; RED BRIGADE etc.

Tesina (German **Teschen**; Polish **Cieszyn**), town and environs in Silesia, was a principality of the Empire, since 1290 under Bohemian suzerainty. Became part of Bohemia, 1625. Passed to Austria, 1723. Divided, 1920, between Poland and Czechoslovakia, the whole territory was seized by Poland in 1938, but recovered by Czechoslovakia, 1945. Now Czech.

TESSA. (Tax-Exempt Special Savings Account), introduced by John Major when Chancellor of the Exchequer, 1991.

'test-tube babies'. *See* ARTIFICIAL INSEMINATION.

Teutonic Knights. Order of Military Knights, established 1189–91, for succouring the sick and wounded in the Holy Land; later they fought in parts of NE Germany and the Baltic lands for the Christianizing of the country; headquarters at Acre, 1191–1291, but transferred to Marienburg (now Malbork, Poland), 1308. Prestige hit by defeat at Tannenberg by Poles and Lithuanians, 1410. Grand Master of the Order, Albert of Brandenberg, became a Protestant, 1525, and the order was secularized; its last remaining possessions were taken by Napoleon in 1809.

Texas, USA, first permanently settled by the French, 1685, was surrendered to Spain, 1713, and became part of Mexico when the latter declared its independence, 1821. Heavily settled by English-speaking cattle-ranchers, T. broke away from Mexican rule and declared itself an independent republic in 1836. It joined the USA at the request of the Texans, Dec. 1845. The resultant war with Mexico over the Texan boundary lasted until 1848. T. seceded from the Union in 1861. The last battle of the civil war was fought at Palmito, T., 13 May 1865. Readmitted to the Union, Feb. 1870.

Thailand (Siam). Present kingdom founded when Ayuthia became capital, 1350. Burmese storm Ayuthia and conquer T. *c.* 1555. Independence re-established by Phra Naret, 1560–80. Siege and destruction of Ayuthia by Burmese, 1765–7. Phaya Tak Sin establishes new government at Bangkok, 1767–8. Succeeded by Phaya Chakri, 1782. Establishment of British interests in T. by John Burney, 1822–4. E territories ceded to France, 1893. Anglo-French convention *re* T., 1895. Further cessions to France, 1902. Middle-class revolution establishes constitution, 1932. Name changed to T. from Siam, 1939. Japanese occupation, 8 Dec. 1941–45. King Ananda Mahidol murdered, 9 July 1946; succeeded by Bhumibol Adulyadej. Military coup, 1947; civilian government, 1973–6 then further military coup. Restricted civilian government, 1983, overthrown by army, Feb. 1991. Elections, March 1992, disputed, as result maintained military rule: there was rioting, May, and government fell. Elections, Sept. 1992, won by pro-democracy movement and return to civilian rule. Much economic expansion since mid-1980s.

thaler. *See* DOLLAR. The official unit of currency of the German Monetary Union from 1857–1873.

thalidomide. Proprietary name of tranquillizing drug developed in Germany and introduced into Britain, 1958. Withdrawn by the makers as the result of evidence that when taken in early pregnancy it was liable to cause deformities in babies, Nov. 1961. Feb. 1968: in a High Court settlement, the British manufacturers of T. agreed to settle 'very substantial damages' on the British T. children affected. Used to treat leprosy in 38 countries since 1970s, and children born to sufferers adversely affected. Use in some treatment of *Aids suggested, 1993.

Thames. Conservation of the 'stream' given to the mayors of the city of London, 1489; conservators fixed by Act of Parliament, 1857; abolished, 1973. T. Tunnel, 1843, now part of the modern Underground system. First T. Conservancy Act, 1894. Steamboat service opened, 1905; discontinued, 1909. Port of London Authority instituted, 31 Mar. 1909. River bus service started, 1948. Thames Water Authority established, 1973. Thames Barrier opened, 8 May 1984.

Thames Embankment. N side (Victoria) constructed, 1862–70; S (Albert), 1866–70; Chelsea, 1871–4.

Thames Polytechnic. *See* GREENWICH, UNIVERSITY, of.

Thames Valley University, name and status since 1992 of the former Polytechnic of West London.

Thanksgiving Day, USA, originated Nov. 1621 when the Pilgrim Fathers gave thanks for their first harvest. Gradually adopted by whole country and proclaimed public holiday, 1863. Celebrated since 1941 on fourth Thursday of each November; in Canada, T. D. made a public holiday in 1879, now celebrated on the second Monday in October.

theatres (London). Licence granted to Burbage, 1576: the 'Theatre' and the 'Curtain', 'Blackfriars', and 'Globe' were among the T. extant in the time of Elizabeth I, and were all used by Shakespeare. Some prominent theatres still existing, with dates of opening include:

Her Majesty's (as Queen's) 1705
Haymarket 1720
Covent Garden 1732
Sadler's Wells 1764–65; rebuilt 1931
Old Vic (as Coburg) 1818
Coliseum 1904
Royal Court 1871
Savoy 1881; rebuilt after fire 1993
Garrick 1889
Aldwych 1905
Globe 1906 (*renamed Gielgud 1994)

Piccadilly 1928
Phoenix 1930
Whitehall 1930
Mermaid 1959
National Theatre 1976
Barbican 1982
*This change of name left the S bank theatre begun by Sam Wanamaker on the Shakespearean site, 1989, and planned to open, 1996, as the only theatre named *'Globe'.

Some notable British provincial theatres include:
Birmingham Repertory Theatre 1913
Bristol Old Vic 1943
Cambridge Arts Theatre 1936
Chichester Festival Theatre 1962
Coventry, Belgrade Theatre 1958
Yvonne Arnaud Theatre, Guildford 1965
Liverpool Playhouse 1911
Theatre Royal, Norwich 1768 – new premises 1826, 1934; local authority owned since 1967
Nottingham Playhouse 1948
Oxford Playhouse 1938
Stephen Joseph Theatre in the Round, Scarborough 1955; new premises 1970
Theatre Royal, York 1734; present building c. 1900

A notable Irish theatre is the Abbey, Dublin 1904.

The following actors and actresses are among famous theatre performers. From the 1920s, actors and actresses have increasingly made their reputation in films and, subsequently, in television as well as on the stage, so see also list of performers under CINEMATOGRAPHY.

Ashcroft, Dame Peggy, 1907–91
Attenborough, Richard (Lord), 1923–
Jean Louis, Barrault, 1910–94
Bernhardt, Sarah, 1845–1923
Bracegirdle, Anne, 1673–1748
Branagh, Kenneth, 1960–
Burton, Richard, 1925–84
Campbell, Patrick Mrs, 1865–1940
Cibber, Colley, 1671–1757

Cusack, Cyril James, 1910–93
Dench, Dame Judi, 1934–
Du Maurier, Sir Gerald, 1873–1934
Evans, Dame Edith, 1888–1976
Ffrangcon-Davies, Dame Gwen, 1891–1992
Garrick, David, 1717–79
Gielgud, Sir John, 1904–
Guinness, Sir Alec, 1914–
Hicks, Sir Seymour, 1871–1949
Hiller, Dame Wendy, 1912–
Hordern, Sir Michael, 1911–95
Irving, Sir Henry, 1838–1905
Jacobi, Sir Derek, 1938–
Kean, Edmund, 1787–33
Kemble, Charles, 1773–1854
Kemble, John, 1757–1823
Kemble (Mrs Siddons), Sarah, 1755–1831
Laughton, Charles, 1899–1962
Leigh, Vivien, 1913–67
McKellen, Sir Ian, 1939–
Marceau, Marcel, 1923–93
Miles, Sir Bernard, 1907–91
Mills, Sir John, 1908–
Olivier, Lord (Laurence), 1907–89
Nazimova, Alla, 1879–1945
Redgrave, Sir Michael, 1908–85
Richardson, Sir Ralph, 1902–83
Robson, Dame Flora, 1902–84
Rutherford, Dame Margaret, 1892–72
Scofield, Paul, 1922–
Smith, Dame Maggie, 1934–
Stephens, Sir Robert, 1931–95
Terry, Dame Ellen, 1847–1928
Thompson, Emma, 1959–
Thorndike, Dame Sybil, 1882–1976
Vestris, Lucy Eliza, 1797–1856
Wanamaker, Sam, 1919–93
Welles, Orson, 1915–85
Woffington, Peg, 1714–60
Wolfit, Sir Donald, 1902–68

Thebes, Egypt, *fl.* 1600–1100 BC as capital of Upper Egypt. Partly burnt by Persians, 525 BC, captured and sacked by Greeks, 85 BC.

Thebes, Greece, capital of Boeotia, founded about 1100 BC. For a short time after 371 BC T. became the strongest city in Greece, but lost her supremacy after 362. Razed to the ground by Macedonians under Alexander, 335, restored 316. Captured by Demetrius Poliorcetes, 290 BC. Repatriated Greeks from Asia settled in T., 1922.

Theosophists, a sect founded by Helena Petrovna Blavatsky (1831–91), whose principal disciple was Mrs. Annie Besant (1847–1933). The Theosophical Society was founded in America, 1875.

thermometer. Invention of attributed to Galileo (1564–1642). General change from Fahrenheit to Centigrade in Britain during 1960s, to Celsius in 1980s.

***Thetis* disaster.** British submarine *Thetis* failed to resurface, 1 June 1939. Ninety-nine men died, and there were four survivors. Submarine was eventually beached, 3 Oct. 1939, recommissioned, and renamed the *Thunderbolt*; lost during World War II off Sicily, 13 Mar. 1943, with all hands.

Third Reich, descriptive term applied to Nazi Germany, 1933–45 and coined by Hitler.

Third World, term invented by the French demographer Alfred Sauvy, 1952 ('tiers monde'), when he compared the undeveloped world with the pre-Revolutionary Third Estate in France. It subsequently passed into general use. Sauvy's thesis was: 'the third world is nothing, but wants to be something.'

Thirty-nine Articles of Religion. (*see* ARTICLES OF RELIGION (ANGLICAN)). Were agreed by the Convocation held in London, 1562, and subsequently reduced to 39 and confirmed, 1571 and 1604.

Thirty Years War, 1618–48. Waged between the Protestants and Catholic Imperialists of Germany; Frederick, Elector Palatine, the prince to whom the Bohemian Estates had offered the imperial succession which was the immediate *casus belli*, defeated at the White Mountain (*Bela Hora*), 8 Nov. 1620. English intervention against Spanish Netherlands, 1625. Protestant effort mainly directed by Denmark, 1625–30, thereafter by Gustavus Adolphus of Sweden, until his death in action at Lützen, 16 Nov. 1632. Wallenstein, recalled to command imperialist forces, 1632, murdered, 1634. From 1632 French intervention became the dominant factor, and the native Protestant leadership, such as it was, devolved on Bernard of Saxe-Weimar (*d.* 18 July 1639). *See* WESTPHALIA, PEACE OF.

Thomas's, St, Hospital. Founded in 1213 as an alms-house; enlarged by the Mayor of London in 1551; rebuilt, 1693; and 1868; extended after World War II.

Thorp. *See* SELLAFIELD.

Three Choirs Festival held annually at cathedrals of Gloucester, Worcester and Hereford in rotation since 1724.

Three Mile Island, Pennsylvania, USA, where a major accident at a nuclear power station, 1979, resulted in reassessment of official US policy on peaceful use of nuclear energy.

Thugs. Indian fanatics, a caste of professional thieves who strangled victims in honour of the goddess Bhowani (Mother Kali). Suppressed by British, 1830.

Thule. *See* FAIR ISLE.

Tiananmen Square, Peking, China, where in June 1989 pro-democracy demonstrators massed and were dispersed by the army, 3–4 June, resulting in over 1,000 deaths. The suppression marked end of pro-democracy movement, and victory of government hard-liners, and drew international condemnation.

Tianjin. *See* TIENTSIN.

Tibet. First king Lhato Nyan-tsen. Fourth Nam-ri Song-tsen, *d.* AD 630, and was succeeded by Song-tsen Gampo, who founded the secular monarchy of T. Nepalese rebellion, 703. Zenith of Tibetan power under Tisong Detsen, 743–89. War with China, 810–21. End of the dynasty of religious kings at assassination of Ral-pa-Chen, 838. Kingdom divided, 841 onwards. Dharmapala arrives from India, 1013. Atisha also, 1026. Rule of the abbots of Sakya under Mongol protection, 1270–

1340. Pakmodu founds dynasty *c.* 1350. Tsong Ka-pa founds Yellow Hat Order *c.*. 1370–1380. System of priestly incarnation established, 1474. End of Pakmodu's dynasty, 1635. Fifth Dalai Lama established as ruler of T., 1641. Chinese resident established at Lhasa *c.* 1710. War with Gurkhas, 1788–92. Chinese resident insists on closure of T. to foreigners, 1792. Dogra invasion repelled, 1841. Gurkha invasion and treaty of friendship, 1855. Younghusband mission, after fighting, reaches Lhasa, 1906. Chinese occupation, 1910. Chinese expelled, 1911. New Dalai Lama enthroned, 1940; assumed full powers, 1950. Treaty of Peking, 23 May 1951, gave the Tibetans theoretical national regional autonomy within China, but increasing Chinese repression resulted in Tibetan revolt against China, Mar. 1959; T. declared herself independent. Chinese troops crushed the revolt and on 31 Mar. the Dalai Lama was granted political asylum in India. In T. monasteries closed, religion suppressed. Communist regime established, 1965: T. made autonomous region of China. Opposition continued in T. and there was bloodshed in 1989 and from 1993. Nobel Peace Prize awarded to Dalai Lama, 1990.

Tichborne Case. Sir J. F. Doughty T., *d.,* 1862. In 1872 a claimant to the estate, representing himself to be Sir Roger T., son of Sir Doughty, involved the T. family in litigation which cost them £70,000. In 1874 he was exposed as a butcher named Thomas Castro, and sentenced to 14 years' penal servitude for perjury.

Ticino (German **Tessin**). After the break-up of the Roman Empire the canton was part of the temporal domains of the Bishop of Como and the Chapter of Milan, taken over between 1100 and 1400 piecemeal by the secular communes of Milan and Como. The conquest of T. by the 12 'old' cantons of Switzerland was gradual, and complete by 1512. In 1798 the Helvetic Confederation set up cantons of Lugano and Bellinzona, which fused, 1803 to form the canton of T.

tides. Theory of T. first made clear by Kepler, 1598, but had been studied by Posidonius of Apamea, 79 BC; completely explained by Sir Isaac Newton, 1683.

Tientsin, or **Tianjin**, China, port opened to foreign trade, 1860. Occupied by Japanese, 1937–45. Industrial and oil centre since 1950s.

Tierra del Fuego, S America, discovered by Magellan, 1520.

Tiflis. *See* TBILISI.

Tigré, or **Tigray**, Ethiopian province, where rebellion against Ethiopian government (for more autonomy locally) started, 1978. Serious famine there from 1985. Falashas (who practised Judaism), airlifted to Israel, 1984–5 and 1989. Virtual autonomy since 1989.

Tilbury Docks (England) were opened, 1886.

Tilsit (Lithuania) noted for the peace treaty between the emperors, Alexander of Russia and Napoleon, 1807. It was founded by the Teutonic Knights in 1288 and was named **Sovetsk** from 1946 during period when it was part of USSR, and when most of its German population was expelled. Reverted to Lithuania, 1991.

***Times, The,* newspaper.** First issued as *The Times*, 1788, but had been published as the *Daily Universal Register* since 1785. Founded by John Walter (1739–1812). Controlling interest bought by Lord Northcliffe, July 1907. On the death of Northcliffe, 1922, the paper was bought by John Walter the fourth and Maj. J. J. Astor. Acquired by Lord Thomson, 1966: by Rupert Murdoch, 1982.

Timor was divided between the Dutch and Portuguese colonial empires, 1859, by a boundary rearranged by arbitration, 1914. Both parts of the island were occupied and used by the Japanese as an air base, 1942–5. Dutch T. became part of *Indonesia, 1950; Portuguese (E) T. declared its independence, 1975, but was absorbed by Indonesia, 1976 and renamed **Loro Sae**.

Persecution of Christians there since 1976, and acquisition not recognized by UN. Estimated at least half-million killed since 1976 by Indonesian troops. R.C. bishop of T. condemned Indonesian policy, July 1994; agitation during visit of President Clinton, Nov. UN condemnation, Dec.

tin. One of the earliest known metals, having been imported from England by the Phoenicians more than 1,000 years BC.

Tirol (also **Tyrol**, but not locally). Trent becomes fief of Bishops of Trent, 1004. Bolzano (Bozen) and Vintschgau (Val Venosta) added, the rest of the area being given to the Bishops of Brixen, 1027. Bishops delegate authority to the Lords of T. Castle (near Merano) from which T. takes its name, *c.* 1100. They become counts in Trent, 1150. Acquire lands in Brixen, 1248. Finally displace the episcopal authorities, 1271. Family became extinct and T. passed to Austria, 1363. Held as an apanage of a junior line of the Hapsburgs till 1665. Ceded to Bavaria by Peace of Pressburg, 1805. Andreas Hofer's rising against French and Bavarians, 1809–10. Restored to Austria by Treaty of Paris, 1814. S T. annexed to Italy, 1919. Agreement between Italy and Austria on local autonomy of S T., 6 Sept. 1946, and this incorporated into the Italian Peace Treaty of 1957.

Titanic. White Star ocean liner lost after striking iceberg near Cape Race, near Newfoundland, 14 Apr. 1912, with over 1,500 casualties. Wreck located and televised, 1986. Salvage teams at work from 1987.

tithes were commonly paid to monasteries up to 1215, but thereafter only to parish priests. The T. Act of 1936 (amended by the T. Act of 1951) was designed to replace T. by the payment of T. Redemption annuities which will cease to be payable, 1996.

Tlatelolco, Treaty of, 1967, aimed to ensure prohibition of nuclear weapons in Latin America.

TNT *See* TRINITROTOLUENE.

tobacco. First observed in Cuba, 1492; brought to England in 1565 or 1586 by Sir John Hawkins or Sir Walter Raleigh; cultivation in England was prohibited, 1684, and allowed in Ireland, 1779; Pure Tobacco Act, 1842; permission to cultivate T. in England under certain conditions was granted, 1886. Royal College of Physicians' Report, 'Smoking and Health', suggested a causal relationship between cigarette-smoking and lung cancer, Mar. 1962. Cigarette advertising banned on British television, Aug. 1965; further media restrictions since. US Environmental Protection Agency said 'passive smoking' from T. killing 3000 Americans a year, Jan 1993; and out-of-court settlement in UK to woman who claimed health damaged by this, Jan 1993. Larger health warnings on cigarette packets in UK, June 1993. Commons committee recommended ban on tobacco sponsoring of broadcast or televised sports events, 1994.

Tobruk, Libya, occupied by Italy, 1911. Captured by British forces, 1941; besieged 1941 and 1942, finally recaptured by British, Nov. 1942. *See* SIEGES.

Toc H (for **Talbot House**) took its name from a military chapel and soldiers' club opened at Poperinghe, Flanders, Dec. 1915.

Togo. W African republic since 1960, before which it was French *Togoland. Its first president was assassinated, 1963, since when there have been a number of coups and failed coups. Struggle since 1991 between army-backed President and pro-democratic premier. Eyadema (president since 1967) again returned, 1993, but elections alleged to be flawed.

Togoland became a German protectorate, 1884. Became a League of Nations mandated territory, under British and French administration, 1920. British T. united with *Ghana when the latter achieved independence in 1957. French T. became the independent republic of *Togo on 27 Apr. 1960.

Tokyo. Capital of *Japan since 1868. Formerly called Yedo; castle, built 15thC.

Practically destroyed by earthquake in Sept. 1923 (over 50,000 deaths), when *Yokohama was completely demolished. Heavily bombed by the Americans, 1945, and since reconstructed on American 'skyscraper' lines. *See also* EARTHQUAKES.

Toledo, Spain, was small fortified town when captured by Rome, 193 BC. Became important Roman colony, later Visigothic capital (534–712). Moorish, 712–1085 (Tulaytulah) and home to many Mozarabics and Jews. Taken by Alfonso VI, 1085. Declined after 1560, when *Madrid made Spanish capital. 18 Church Councils held at T. between 400 and 702. Cathedral begun, 1226. Alcazar begun *c.* 1531, was famous for its defence by Falangists in Civil War, 1936.

Toleration, Act of, 24 May 1689, for the relief of Dissenters. Roman Catholics included, 13 Apr. 1829. *See* NONCONFORMISTS.

tolls. The first T. in England were collected in London, 1267; toll gates were instituted, 1663; from 1827 to 1893 toll gates were gradually abolished, and now (1995) very few remain in England. T. have, however, been applied to help finance certain new roadworks (e.g. the Severn, Humber and Dartford bridges) since 1955 but up to 1995 suggestions for British motorway tolls not taken up. In the USA T. are levied to pay for several of the 20thC motorways, as is the case in France, etc.

Tolpuddle Martyrs. Six labourers living at the village of T., Dorset, convicted at Dorchester of 'administering unlawful oaths' (i.e. trade union activity), 19 Mar. 1834, and sentenced to seven years' transportation. Following nation-wide agitation, they were pardoned two years later. Later all except one emigrated to Canada.

tomatoes were introduced into England, 1596, though not extensively consumed in Britain before 1900.

Tomsk, Siberia, with a pop. of *c.* 500,000, possesses one of several nuclear centres kept secret under former Soviet regime,

until 1991. Serious explosion at T. plant reported, April 1993.

Tonga or **Friendly Islands** were first explored by the Dutch under Cornelius Schouten and Jacob le Maire, 1616, then by Tasman, 1643. The first Englishman to land was Wallis (1767). Cook landed several times, 1773–7. In 1831 Tupou, the King of T., was baptized and took the name of George, his consort that of Salote (i.e. Charlotte). By 1845 he had extended his rule over the whole group; he *d.* 1893, aged 96. His successor, George Tupou II, signed a treaty of friendship and protection with Britain 1900. Salote, daughter of George Tupou II, came to the throne on his death, 1918; she *d.* 1965, and was succeeded by her son, Taufa'ahau Tupou IV, who was crowned 4 July 1967. Independent within Commonwealth, 1970. In 1993 elections, the party wishing to reduce royal powers gained ground.

tonnage and poundage first levied, 1371, and abolished, 1787.

tontines. Instituted by Tonti, a Neapolitan; first used in Paris, 1653. A tontine was a fund to which a group subscribed and out of which each member received an annuity, increasing as the group diminished through deaths, until the last survivor was left with the whole fund. The last English public tontine was in 1789.

Tonton Macoutes, secretive execution squads controlled by the Haitian president, F. Duvalier 1957–71 and his son, J.C. Duvalier, 1971–86, responsible for a reign of terror and hundreds of deaths in Haiti.

Torgau, League of. Between the Elector of Saxony and the Landgrave of Hesse to uphold the opinions of Martin Luther, concluded at Gotha, Feb. 1526.

Toronto, site chosen as seat of government for Upper Canada, 1793. Occupied by US forces, 1813, and legislative buildings burned. The mace carried away on that occasion was returned by Franklin D. Roosevelt, 1934. The city, first named York, adopted the present name, 1834. T.

Univ. originated, 1827. New city hall (1958) among extensive new building and expansion, 1950 onwards. Influx of European immigrants, 1950s and 1960s: from 1970s many from SE Asia and the W Indies. C.N. tower in T. built, 1973–5.

torpedoes. The word originally signified *mines*, and was so used till *c*. 1868. First T. devised by Whitehead, 1866. Modern Ts., basically homing missiles, were developed first by the Germans, 1941–5.

Torres Vedras, Portugal, was captured by the Portuguese from the Moors, 1149, and was the seat of the Cortes in 1441. Wellington built a strong defensive position here, covering Lisbon, into which he retired at the end of 1810. The French under Masséna closed up on the lines of T.V., but were unable to storm them, and compelled to retreat in Mar. 1811.

Tory (Irish for a persecutor, robber, or outlaw). Nickname for any supporter of the Duke of York, 1679. From 1689 any opponent of the Whigs or Hanoverian party. Since about 1833, colloquially, a Conservative.

totalisator. First T. machine was set up at Christchurch, New Zealand, 1880, based on the *pari mutuel* system which was invented in France, 1872. The first machine in Europe operated at Longchamps, 1929, in Britain in the same year following establishment of Race Course Betting Control Board, 1928. This reconstituted as Horserace Totalisator Board, 1961. Constituted as a body corporate, 1963. Further amended under the Horserace Totalisator and Betting Levy Boards Act, 1972. In Maryland, USA, T. machines were first used, 1930.

Toulon (ancient *Telo Martius*), France, docks and arsenal were begun by Vauban (1633–1707). The town was taken by the British, Aug. 1793, who destroyed the military and naval installations before the Republicans (under the young Napoleon) retook them in Dec. Fire and explosion of battleship *Liberté* destroyed 200 ships in T. harbour, 1911. French fleet scuttled in the harbour, 27 Nov. 1942, before German occupation of the port.

Toulouse, in Roman times *Tolosa*, chief city of Gallia Narbonnensis, was colonized by the Romans in 106 BC, became capital of a Visigothic kingdom, AD 419, and was captured by the Franks, 506. Became capital of Aquitaine, 630, then of a virtually independent county, one of whose rulers, Raymond IV (count from 1088 to 1105), was a principal commander in the First *Crusade, and refused the crown of Jerusalem. In 1271 the royal house of France inherited the county and its independence ceased. In 20thC, centre of French aircraft industry, and supersonic commercial plane *Concorde* built here in 1960s.

Tour de France, first and most famous national stage-cycling race, established 1903 by Henri Desgranges as a six-stage 2410 km race. Later extended, the longest T. de F. was in 1919. At same date, yellow jersey awarded to stage leaders. From 1971 T. de F. restricted to 20 shorter stages. Idea copied by other countries e.g. Britain where Milk Race (covering approx 1300 m in 13/15 days over England and Scotland) begun, 1951. Part of 1994 T. de F. took place in England, to mark opening of *Channel Tunnel. See also CYCLING.

Touraine, ancient province of France, roughly approximating to the *département* of Indre-et-Loire; became an independent county, 941, subject, 1040, to the counts of Anjou, and hence, 1154, to the English crown. From 1205 did homage to the French crown; won back by Joan of Arc; finally incorporated in France as a *gouvernement*, 1541.

Tours, ancient capital of *Touraine, was an episcopal see in the 4thC. It was captured by the Visigoths, 473, by the Franks in 507. Charles Martel defeated the Saracens near T., 732. Destroyed by Vikings, 853 and 903. From *c*. 1400 to 1685 centre of the silk industry in France. Seat of French Government, 13 Sept.–10 Dec. 1870, and June 1940.

Tower Bridge (London), built 1886–94. Proposal to demolish it in improvement scheme caused protests, 1961 and plan abandoned. Extensive repair caused several months' closure, 1993.

Tower of London. *See* LONDON, TOWER OF.

town and country planning. An Act of 1943 provided for the appointment of a minister to perform plannings, functions formerly devolving on the Minister of *Health and the Minister of *Works. Since 1970, these duties have devolved upon the Deptartment of the *Environment.

Toynbee Hall (England), opened, 1885. Named after Arnold T., 1852–93.

Tractarianism. Arose from *Tracts for the Times*, dealing with Church matters; published, 1833–41.

Trade, Board of. *See* BOARD OF TRADE.

trade boards for settlement of wage disputes were authorized by the T.B. Acts of 1909 and 1918. Abolished, 1945.

trade marks in the UK were formerly regulated principally by the T.M. Acts of 1905–1950 (notably that of 1938) and by the Trades Descriptions Act, 1968, which replaced the Merchandise Marks Acts, 1887–1953. A new T.M. Bill, which replaced existing T.M. legislation, introduced, 1993. Became law, 1994.

trade unions. Instituted, 1825, to withstand the influence of capital and competition. A commission of inquiry into the working of T.U. was held, 1867; an Act to protect the funds of T.U. was passed, 1869. To counteract T.U. a Federation of Employers was founded, 1873. First agricultural T.U. founded by Joseph Arch (1826–1919), 1874. T.U. instituted in France, 1834, and USA, before 1833. In the USA the American Federation of Labour and the Congress of Industrial Organizations merged, 1955. Polish T.U. *Solidarity established, 1980. British T.U. allowed to spend funds on parliamentary representation by T.U. Act, 1913. Act passed making illegal non-industrial strikes and lock-outs, and the demanding of political contributions from the members that had not volunteered to make

such, 29 July 1927. This Act was repealed, 1945. Trade Union and Labour Relations Act, 1974. Secondary picketing made illegal by Employment Act of 1980; further legislation in 1980s further restricted T.U. powers. T.U. voting influence on Labour party decreased by resolution of 1993.

Trade Unions, International Conference of Free. *See* INTERNATIONAL CONFERENCE OF FREE TRADE UNIONS.

Trades Union Congress (TUC) originated, 1868. A conference organized by the TUC, 1900, gave rise to the formation of the Parliamentary *Labour Party. The General Council of the TUC formed, 1920. Withdrew from World Federation of Trade Unions, 1949 and joined International Confederation of Free Trade Unions. Had c. 7¾ million members, 1992. The **Scottish TUC**, founded 1897, functions similarly to the TUC. The TUC's general secretary from 1926–46, Walter (Lord) Citrine, greatly increased its standing and influence. TUC General Secretaries since 1960:

George Woodcock, 1960–69
Victor (Lord) Feather, 1969–73
Len (Lord) Murray, 1973–84
Norman Willis, 1984–93
John Monks, 1993–

Radical restructuring of TUC, Mar. 1994: its numbers approximately halved, 1995 from 1979 peak.

Trafalgar Square (London), laid out by Sir Charles Barry, 1840–3, to commemorate the naval victory. Statue of Nelson placed on column, 1843. Bronze lions by Landseer, placed on the N side, 1876. Torsos of Admirals Jellicoe and Beatty erected, and N side replanned, 1950. Norwegian Christmas Tree in T.S. each year since 1947. T.S. refurbished, 1987–9. Move to control pigeons in T.S., 1993.

Training Corps, Officers'. Founded, 1908. Merged in Army Cadet Force, 1940.

trams. First street T. operated in New York, 1832; in Paris, 1853; in London, 1861.

Electric T. inaugurated in Leeds, 1891. Last T. in London ran on 6 July 1952. Continued to run in Blackpool: and revived in Manchester in 1992 and in Sheffield in 1994. Planned to have a T. service in Croydon by 1997.

Transdniestr, on E bank of Dniestr river, proclaimed itself autonomous republic, and independent of *Moldova in 1991. Fighting ended in cease-fire, June 1992, but political solution not yet found (1995).

Transjordan. *See* JORDAN.

Transkei, S Africa, 'black homeland' established 1963; 'independent', 1976. Ruler integrated T. with S Africa, 1994.

transplant surgery, became well-known after first heart transplant operation (in S Africa), 1967. By 1995 these were relatively routine. World's longest surviving heart transplant patient (20 years 4 months after operation) *d.* in USA (from cancer), June 1993. Kidney, liver transplants, etc. increasingly successful from 1970s (though first kidney T. dates back to 1957). First liver/bowel transplant in UK, Apr. 1993. Gene transplant therapy being experimented on in USA, 1993. Claim that pig hearts could be transplanted into humans by 1996 made, 1993. Human ear grown on mouse (for subsequent transplant) in US laboratory, Oct. 1995.

Transport, Ministry of. Established, Sept. 1919 to exercise the powers and duties of various existing government departments relating to public aspects of transport.

transportation was first used as a punitive measure in England at time of Charles II (1600–85). It was legalized under an Act of 1719. The first shipment of convicts to Botany Bay, Australia, was in 1783, the last in 1840. Convicts continued to arrive in Tasmania until 1853. The practice finally ceased in 1864. The French government sent no new shipments of convicts to Guiana after 1938. T. to Siberia existed in Tsarist Russia and was continued up to the dissolution of the Soviet system, 1991, though much reduced from 1985.

tranquillizers, popular name for a range of drugs, developed since 1950s for treating anxiety, depression and tension. Term first used in this sense by Aldous Huxley (1956) and taken up by *The Times*, 1958.

Trans-Siberian Railway. Single track begun, 1891; completed, 1905. New line built, 1974–84.

Transvaal. Founded by Boers, 1836–48; Britain recognized the independence of the territory, 1852; Volksraad elected M. W. Pretorius first president of the territory named the S African Republic, 1857; under British protection, 1877; declared crown colony, 1879; Boers revolt and established republic, 1880; battle of Majuba Hill, 27 Feb. 1881; Orange Free State proclaimed neutrality, Feb. 1881; peace, 24 Mar. 1881; Paul Kruger president, 1883; Jameson Raid, 1 Jan. 1896; ultimatum from Boers, 9 Oct. 1899; war declared, 11 Oct. 1899; annexation of T., 25 Oct. 1900; Milner appointed High Commissioner, 4 Mar. 1901; new constitution on representative lines, Dec. 1906; Botha Premier, 1907; became province of Union of S Africa, 31 May 1910. *See* SOUTH AFRICAN WAR and SOUTH AFRICA, REPUBLIC OF.

Transylvania. Ceded to Romania by Hungary, Dec. 1918. Returned to Hungary by Hitler's 'Vienna Award', 30 Aug. 1940. Occupied by Russians, Aug. 1944. Returned to Romania, 10 Mar. 1945, and this decision confirmed in the peace treaties between the Allies and Hungary and Romania, 1947.

Trappists, a branch of the Cistercian order; founded, 1664, by Armand Bouthillier de Rancé (1626–1700), at the abbey of La Trappe in Normandy.

treadmill. First used as an instrument for irrigation by the Chinese. Introduction into English prisons by Sir William Cubitt, and first used in Buxton prison, 1818; in disuse by 1910.

treason. Defined by Statute of Treasons, 1351. Other important definitions: 1800 and 1945.

Treasury. A Board of Commissioners, appointed for the first time in 1612, instead of a Lord High Treasurer as hitherto. Lords Commissioners of the T. have functioned continuously since 1714. The practice of combining the office of Prime Minister and First Lord of the T. arose, 1721. Reorganization of T., 1962; further modifications in 1990s.

Treasury Bills first introduced, 1877.

Treaties. The following is a list of major historical treaties:

Abo, 1743. Aberdaron, 1406. Aix-la-Chapelle, 1668–1748. Algeciras, 1906. Altmark, 1629. Alton, 1101. Altranstädt, 1706. Amiens, 1527, 1802. Amsterdam, 1717. Anagri, 1176. Antananarivo, 1895. Aquisgran, 1749. Aranjuez, 1752. Ardes, 1546. Arras, 1482. Athis, 1305. Augsburg, 1686.

Badajoz, 1801. Baden, 1714. Baghdad, 1955. Bagnolo, 1484. Barcelona, 1493, 1529. Bärwalde, 1631. Basel, 1499. Belgrade, 1739. Berlin, 1728, 1850, 1878. Berwick, 1560. Björkö, 1905. Blois, 1504, 1505. Bologna, 1515. Boulogne, 1550. Breda, 1667. Brest, 1435. Bretigny, 1360. Bretton Woods, 1944. Brigham, 1290. Brömsebro, 1645. Bruges, 1521. Brussels, 1516, 1522, 1948. Bucharest, 1886. Beczacz, 1672.

Caen, 1091. Calais, 1416, 1520. Cambrai, 1529. Campo Formio, 1797. Câteau Cambrésis, 1559. Charlottenburg, 1723. Cherasco, 1631. Clayton-Bulwer, 1850. Cognac, 1526. Compiègne, 1624. Constantinople, 1479, 1573, 1724, 1889, 1897. Corbeil, 1258.

Delft, 1428. Dordrecht, 1489. Dunkirk, 1947. Durham, 1136. Düsseldorf, 1624.

Edinburgh, 1560. Eisenburg, 1664. Escorial, 1733.

Ferrara, 1428. Fontainebleau, 1785. Fredericksborg, 1720. Frederickshamn, 1809. Fürstenberg, 1373.

Gandamak, 1879. Gastein, 1865. Gerstungen, 1074. Gisors, 1180. Grosswardein, 1538. Guérande, 1365. Guillon, 1360.

Hagenau, 1330. Hague, 1625, 1716, 1790. Hampton Court, 1562. Herrenhausen, 1725. Hubertusburg, 1763.

Jassy, 1792.

Kalisz, 1343. Kardis, 1661. Kaschau, 1374. Khaeroed, 1613. Kuchuk Kainardji, 1774.

Labian, 1656. Lambeth, 1217. Lateran, 1929. Lauf, 1453. Lodi, 1454. London, 1518, 1839, 1954. Lorris, 1243. Lübeck, 1629. Lunéville, 1801. Lyons, 1504, 1601.

Maastricht, 1992. Madrid, 1618, 1630, 1715. Manila, 1954 (South-East Asia Collective Defence Treaty). Meaux, 1229. Mechlin, 1513. Melfi, 1059. Mersen, 870. Montebello, 1175. Moscow (Nuclear Test Ban Treaty), 1963 (START I), 1991; (START II), 1993, 1994. Mürzsteg, 1903.

Nanking, 1842. Nettuno, 1925. Newcastle, 1334. Nicolsburg, 1886. Nijmegen, 1678–9. Northampton, 1328. Noyon, 1516. Nystad, 1721.

Oléron, 1287. Oliva, 1660. Olmütz, 1850. Ouchy, 1912.

Panama, 1977. Paris, 1259, 1303, 1320, 1657, 1763, 1898, 1947, 1954, 1963 ('Franco-German reconciliation'). Passarowitz, 1718. Passau, 1552. Peking, 1860, 1901. Perth, 1266. Picquigny, 1475. Prague, 1635. Pressburg, 1490, 1626, 1805. Pretoria, 1881. Pyrenees, 1659.

Rastatt, 1714. Redon, 1489. Reichenbach, 1790. Reval, 1488. Riga, 1920, 1921. Rome, 1957. Roskilde, 1658. Roxburgh, 1332. Ryswick, 1697.

St Claire, 911. St Germain, 1331, 1570, 1679. St Omer, 1782. St Petersburg, 1805. Salbai, 1782. Salisbury, 1289. San Germano, 1230. San Ildefonso, 1796. San Stefano, 1878. Saragossa, 1529. Schönbrunn, 1805. Senlis, 1493. Seville, 1729. Shimonoseki, 1895. Shrewsbury, 1267. Sistova, 1791. Stettin, 1570. Stockholm, 1720, 1724, 1959 (European Free Trade Association Convention). Stolbova, 1617. Sutri, 1111.

Tangier, 1844. Tarascon, 1291. Teschen, 1779. Thorn, 1466. Tientsin, 1858. Tilsit, 1807. Toledo, 1480, 1539. Tordesilhas, 1494. Trent, 1501. Troyes, 1420, 1562. Tyrnau, 1615.

Uccialli, 1889. Utrecht, 1474, 1712–13.

Valençay, 1813. Vancelles, 1556. Venice, 1177. Verdun, 843. Vereeniging, 1902. Versailles, 1756, 1783, 1919–20. Vervins, 1598. Vienna, 1731, 1738, 1814–15, 1864, 1955.

Villafranca, 1859. Vincennes, 1330. Vossem, 1673.

Waitangi, 1840. Wallingford, 1153. Warsaw, 1955 (Eastern Security Treaty). Washington, 1846, 1949 (North Atlantic Treaty). Wedmore, 878. Westminster, 1654, 1716, 1756. Westphalia (2), 1648. Windsor, 1899. Worms, 1743. Wusterhausen, 1726.

Xanten, 1614.

Zsitva-Torok, 1606. Zurawna, 1676. Zürich, 1859.

Trebizond, or **Trabzon**, the Greek city of *Trapezos*, originated, 600 BC, in a colony from Sinope. Mentioned in connection with the retreat of the *Ten Thousand. At the time of the Fifth Crusade, when Constantinople was stormed by the Latins, the Byzantine refugee, Alexius Comnenus, founded an empire at T., which endured until the capture of the city by the Turks, 1462. Scene of the Armenian massacres, 1895.

Trelleborg, archaeological site of the *Viking Age in W Zealand, Denmark. A large barracks or permanent camp occupied between 950 and 1050, presumably by the followers of Kings Svein Forkbeard and Knut (*see under* DENMARK), was excavated, 1932–42.

Trengganu, state of Malaysia since 1963, was a Muslim kingdom *c.* 1300. Did homage to the kingdom of Siam from 1776 to 1909. Entered into treaty relations with Britain, 1910.

Trent (Italy). The first Council of T., sat from 1545 to 1563; its decisions laid down the main lines of Roman Catholic development in post-Reformation times up to the changes of the 1960s and were confirmed by Pope Pius IV in 1564.

Trial of the Pyx, testing of coinage. Regular testing began in reign of Henry I (1154–89). By 13thC T. of P. had begun to take modern form. Early T. of P. held at Westminster Hall, then in Star Chamber and later in the Exchequer and Goldsmith's. By Coinage Act, 1870, Goldsmith's Hall became established place for T. of P., to be presided over by Queen's Rembrancer.

trials and *causes célèbres*. Among the most notable are:

Sir Thomas More, 1 July 1535; beheaded 6 July.

Mary Queen of Scots: 14 Oct. 1586; executed, 8 Feb. 1587.

Sir Walter Raleigh: treason, 17 Nov. 1603; executed, 29 Oct. 1618.

Guy Fawkes and others: 27 Jan. 1606; Guy Fawkes executed, 31 Jan. 1606.

Charles I: 20–25 Jan.; executed, 30 Jan. 1649.

Dame Alice Lisle: treason, before Jeffreys; beheaded, 2 Sept. 1685.

Lord Lovat: treason; executed, 9 Mar. 1747.

Mary Blandy: murdered father by arsenic, 3 Mar. 1752.

Eugene Aram: murder, 3 Aug.; hanged, 6 Aug. 1759.

Earl Ferrers: murder of his steward; executed, 16 Apr. 1760.

John Wilkes MP: for obscene poem *Essay on Woman*, 21 Feb. 1764 and 18 June 1768; expelled from House of Commons.

Elizabeth Brownrigg: murder of her apprentice; hanged, 12 Sept. 1767.

Duchess of Kingston: for bigamy, 15 Apr. 1776 and left the country.

Lord George Gordon: treason; acquitted, 5 Feb. 1781.

Warren Hastings: high crimes and misdemeanours, 13 Feb. 1788; acquitted, 23 Apr. 1795.

Thomas Paine: libel in *The Rights of Man*; guilty, 18 Dec. 1792.

Louis XVI of France, in French Convention: 19 Jan.; beheaded, 21 Jan. 1793.

Marie Antoinette, Queen of France: 14 Oct.; executed, 16 Oct. 1793.

Wolfe Tone: for treason, 10 Nov.; condemned to death but committed suicide, 19 Nov. 1798.

Queen Caroline, wife of George IV: for adultery, 16 Aug.–10 Nov. 1820, but case abandoned in face of popular protest.

Burke and Hare: body-snatchers, 24 Dec. 1828; Burke executed, 28 Jan. 1829.

Dr Pritchard: murder of wife and mother by poison; guilty, 2–7 July 1865.

Tichborne Case: plaintiff claimed to be Sir

Roger Tichborne, lost at sea, entitled to estates worth £24,000 a year. Trial began 11 May 1871, claimant nonsuited, 6 Mar. 1872. Trial of claimant for perjury began, 23 Apr. 1872; claimant sentenced, 28 Feb. 1874 on two counts to two cumulative terms of seven years penal servitude each.

Penge Case: Louis Staunton, his brother Patrick, Elizabeth Ann, his wife, and her sister, Alice Rhodes, mistress of Louis, for murder by starvation of Louis's wife; 19–26 Sept, all convicted; respited, 13 Oct.; Alice Rhodes pardoned; others, penal servitude for life, 30 Oct. 1877.

Whistler *v.* Ruskin: for libellous criticism in *Fors Clavigera*; one farthing damages, 25–26 Nov. 1878.

City of Glasgow Bank Directors: for fraud; all convicted, 20 Jan.–1 Feb. 1879.

Charles Peace: murder; guilty, 4 Feb. 1879 and hanged.

Florence Maybrick: murder of husband by arsenic; convicted, 21 July–7 Aug.; commuted to life imprisonment, 22 Aug. 1889.

Tranby Croft Case: Sir W. Gordon-Cumming *v.* Mr. and Mrs. Lycett Green and others. Gordon-Cumming charged them with cheating at baccarat at Tranby Croft, near Hull. Prince of Wales (Edward VII) gave evidence; verdict for defendants, 1–9 June 1891.

Dreyfus Case: Alfred Dreyfus, French soldier, for treason. Convicted, degraded and sent to Devil's Island, 1894. Case reopened, 1898; again convicted, but sentence reduced and free pardon given almost at once. Proceedings against D. quashed, 1906.

Wilde Case: Oscar Wilde (1854–1900) *v.* Marquess of Queensbury, for libel, 1895; following the failure of this, he was convicted of immoral behaviour and sentenced to two years' imprisonment.

Oscar Slater: for murder of Miss Gilchrist, 3–6 May; found guilty, commuted to life sentence, 25 May 1909. Released 14 Nov. 1927; given government grant of £6,000. Conviction quashed, 20 July 1928.

H.H. Crippen: murder of wife; convicted, 18–22 Oct. 1910 and hanged.

Brides in the Bath Case: George Joseph Smith, for murder of Misses Mundy,

Burnham and Lofty; guilty, 22–30 June 1915 and hanged.

Sir Roger Casement: treason; convicted, 17 May; executed, 3 Aug. 1916.

Désiré Landru: in France, for murder of ten women; convicted, 7–28 Nov. 1921; guillotined, 23 Feb. 1922.

Ronald True: murder; convicted 1–5 May. Sent to Broadmoor, 8 June 1922.

Edith Thompson and Frederick Bywaters: murder of Percy Thompson; guilty, 6 Dec. 1922; both hanged, 9 Jan. 1923.

Nicolo Sacco and Bartolomeo Vanzetti (USA): murder; first trial, 31 May–14 July 1921. Conviction affirmed, 12 May 1926. Sentence imposed, 9 Apr. 1927. Both executed, 23 Aug. 1927.

Teapot Dome Scandal (Oil Reserves or Elk Hill Scandal): rocked USA from early 1920s. Concerned secret leasing of federal oil reserves by Albert B. Fall, Interior Secretary of State, in return for gifts. Senate investigations, 1923–4. In 1929 Fall found guilty of accepting a bribe, sentenced to one year's imprisonment and fine of $100,000. Of accomplices, Doheny acquitted and Sinclair spent just over six months in gaol for contempt of court and contempt of US Senate.

Clarence Hatry: fraud; 20–24 Jan. 1930; 14 years' penal servitude.

Blazing Car Murder: Arthur Alfred Rouse, murder of unknown man, 26–31 Jan. 1931. Guilty and hanged.

Metropolitan-Vickers Trial in Moscow: Thornton, Cushny, Gregory, Monkhouse and Macdonald; for espionage and sabotage in USSR. Thornton three years, Gregory acquitted, Macdonald two years. Monkhouse and Cushny expelled from Russia, Apr. 1933.

Lindbergh Baby Case: Bruno Hauptmann, for kidnapping and murder of child of Charles Lindbergh; guilty, 14 Feb. 1935 and executed by electrocution. Hauptmann's guilt subsequently questioned by many.

Alma Victoria Rattenbury and George Percy Stoner: murder of Mr Rattenbury, 27–31 May; Mrs Rattenbury discharged; Stoner convicted. Mrs Rattenbury committed suicide, 3 June. Stoner reprieved, 25 June 1935.

Dr Buck Ruxton: murder of wife and maid; guilty, 2–13 Mar. 1936. Hanged.

Ex-Marshal Pétain of France: for treason; found guilty, 1945, and sentenced to death, subsequently commuted to life imprisonment.

'Lord Haw-Haw' (William Joyce): for treason by broadcasting, 17–19 Sept. 1945. Hanged, 3 Jan. 1946.

Nürnberg Trials: Nov. 1945–Oct. 1946; of German war criminals: several including Ribbentrop hanged. Goering committed suicide before execution, Hess sentenced to life imprisonment, *d.* in gaol, 1987.

Japanese War Criminals' Trials: 1946–8. The seven Japanese war-leaders condemned to death were hanged, 23 Dec. 1948.

Timothy John Evans: tried for the murder of his baby daughter: guilty and hanged, 1950. Given a posthumous free pardon, 1966. *See* EVANS CASE.

Derek Bentley and Christopher Craig: tried for murder of a policeman in 1952 in Croydon. Found guilty. Craig, who fired shot, was 16 and too young to be hanged. He was released, 1963. Bentley was hanged, 28 Jan. 1953. In July 1993 Bentley posthumously granted 'a conditional pardon'.

Rosenberg Trial: Julius Rosenberg (1918–53) and his wife Ethel (1915–53) were arrested in New York, May 1950, accused of spying for the Soviet Union since the 1940s. Found guilty, 6 March 1951, under the Espionage Act of 1917 and sentenced to death. Both executed at Sing Sing Prison, New York, 19 June 1953 after several failed appeals: they were the first US civilians to be put to death for espionage.

John Reginald Halliday Christie: for murder of his wife, but also for murders of several other women on the file; guilty and hanged, 1953. *See* EVANS CASE.

Adolf Eichmann: in Israel, for crimes against the Jewish people; 11 Apr.–15 Dec. 1961; found guilty and hanged.

George Blake, former British vice-consul in Seoul, found guilty of espionage, 1961, and sentenced to 42 years' imprisonment, the longest sentence ever imposed in Britain. Escaped from Wormwood Scrubs Prison, Oct. 1966, and went to live in Russia.

Gordon Lonsdale, a Soviet citizen: tried in London for espionage; found guilty and sentenced to 25 years' imprisonment, 1961; subsequently exchanged for Greville Wynne. (*See* below.)

Greville Wynne, a British business man, and Oleg Penkovsky, a Russian scientist and civil servant, in Moscow for espionage, 7 May 1963; Wynne found guilty and sentenced to eight years' imprisonment; Penkovsky found guilty and executed. Wynne subsequently exchanged for Lonsdale. (*See* above).

Stephen Ward, a London osteopath, on charges of procuring and of living on immoral earnings, in London, July 1963; Ward found guilty on two charges of living on immoral earnings. Verdict reached in his absence, as he was in hospital after taking an overdose of drugs. He died on 3 Aug., and was never sentenced.

Great train robbery trial: 12 men tried and found guilty of being involved in the £2½ million mail train robbery of 8 Aug. 1963. Apr. 1964: sentences totalling 307 years were imposed. Two of the convicted men subsequently escaped from prison.

Moors Murder Case: Ian Brady and Myra Hindley tried for murders of Edward Evans, John Kilbride, etc., 1966; found guilty and sentenced to life imprisonment.

Guildford Four: On 5 Oct. 1974, two IRA bombs killed five people in two Guildford public houses. 7 Nov. 1974, two killed in IRA bomb attack on a Woolwich public house. Subsequent arrests of three men and one woman, all charged with murder. All four convicted of Guildford and Woolwich murders and sentenced to life imprisonment, 22 Oct. 1975. Appeal rejected, Oct. 1977. Review of case begun, 1987; case referred back to Court of Appeal, Jan. 1989. On 19 Oct. 1989 all four released because of irregularities in police evidence. Three detectives involved charged with conspiracy to pervert the course of justice, but cleared, 20 May 1993.

Birmingham Six: Six Irishmen arrested after IRA bombing of two Birmingham public houses on 21 Nov. 1974, in which 21 people died. Tried, June–Aug. 1975 and all six convicted on 21 murder counts and sentenced to life imprisonment. Subsequent appeals dismissed, 1976 and 1987–8. New enquiry and appeal, 1990–1, when all six said to have been wrongly convicted and freed, March 1991. Three police officers in case accused of perjury, 1993, but case abandoned.

Bridgewater Murder: Four men tried, 1978, for murder of Carl Bridgewater, a 13-year-old newspaper boy, at a Staffordshire farm. Three convicted of murder, one of manslaughter and aggravated burglary (he died in gaol). Subsequent campaign for convictions to be declared unsafe: Home Secretary re-examining dossier, 1993.

Peter Sutcliffe, 'The Yorkshire Ripper': convicted of the murder of 13 women, 1981. Sentenced to life imprisonment (to Broadmoor, 1984).

Geoffrey Prime, former officer at the Government Communications Headquarters in Cheltenham: convicted of spying for the Soviet Union, Nov. 1982 and sentenced to 35 years imprisonment.

Dennis Nilsen, found guilty of the murder of six young men and two attempted murders at Highgate: sentenced to life imprisonment, Nov. 1983.

Demjanjuk Case: In 1986 John Demjanjuk, a Ukrainian-*b*. US citizen and retired car-worker, was extradited to Israel after being accused of being 'Ivan the Terrible', a Nazi guard at the Treblinka concentration camp during World War II who had been responsible for the deaths of thousands of Jews. He was stripped of his US citizenship and was condemned to death by the Jerusalem District Court, April 1988, and sentenced to death. Demjanjuk appealed and in 1991 new evidence presented to the Israeli Supreme Court claimed case rested on mistaken identity. Demjanjuk was cleared, July 1993, and allowed to return to the USA, Sept.

Saunders Case: Ernest Saunders, chief executive and chairman of Guiness plc 1986–7, was charged, 1987 and found guilty, Aug. 1990, on 12 charges of conspiracy, theft and false accounting. Five-year prison sentence halved by Appeal Court, May 1991; released on health grounds, June 1991. Guinness case sent back to Court of Appeal, Dec. 1994.

Barbie Case: Klaus Barbie, former German Gestapo officer, the 'Butcher of Lyons', extradited from S America and tried in France, 1987, for 'crimes against humanity', which included sending thousands of French Jews to their deaths during World War II. Found guilty and sentenced to life imprisonment. Died in prison, 1991.

Noriega Trial: Antonio Noriega (*b*. 1910), effective dictator of Panama from 1983, accused of drug smuggling by the USA, 1988. Deposed after US invasion, 1989 and extradited to Miami to face drugs charges, Jan. 1990. In April 1992, a US court found him guilty on eight out of 10 drugs charges (money laundering, cocaine manufacture and racketeering and building a drug laboratory in Panama); he was sentenced to 40 years' imprisonment.

Allitt Case: Beverley Allitt, 24, a nurse in a children's ward at Grantham, Lincs., was found guilty, 17 May 1993, of being responsible over a two-month period in 1991 of the murder of four children, attempted murder of three children and of grievous bodily harm to six children in her care. Received 13 life-sentences, 28 May 1993.

Bulger Case: James Bulger, aged 2, abducted from a Bootle, Liverpool shopping centre, 12 Feb. 1993 and found murdered two days later on a railway line 2½ miles away. Two 10-year-old boys, Robert Thompson and John Venables, charged with abduction and murder. Trial (defendants then aged 11), Nov. 1993. Found guilty, Nov 24; sentenced to be detained during Her Majesty's Pleasure. Youngest convicted murderers in modern British criminal history.

O. J. Simpson Case: Former wife of American football celebrity O. J. Simpson and her lover murdered in California, USA, 12 June 1994. O. J. Simpson arrested after chase in Los Angeles, 17 June. Ordered to stand trial for the murders, 8 July. Opening statements in trial, 23 Jan. 1995, in Los Angeles followed by televised proceedings. Simpson acquitted, 3 Oct. 1995, after prosecution evidence raised doubts.

Rosemary West: tried at Winchester, Oct./Nov. 1995 and convicted for the murder of 10 women and young girls in Gloucester over period of years up to 1987 (her co-defendant and husband, Frederick West, charged with 11 murders, committed suicide in prison, Jan. 1995). Britain's record female serial killer to date.

Trident, US ballistic missile, launched from submarines, developed in 1970s. Trident I, 1979. Trident IIs carried by British submarines since 1994 (with British-made nuclear warheads). Devonport to refit British Trident submarines from 1993; their firepower to be cut, Nov. First British test of T. off USA, May 1994.

Triennial Parliaments were established by Act, 1641. The Long Parliament of 1640–63 broke this Act, and it was repealed, 1664. A similar Act of 1694 was repealed, 1716, when the limit was increased to seven years (which in turn was reduced to five by the Parliament Act, 1911).

Trieste, the Roman colony of *Tergeste*, was settled by the Romans in 178 BC and was an established port some time between AD 69 and 79. Submitted to the Hapsburg Duke Leopold III, 1382. Free port, founded 1719. Held by French, 1797–1805, and by the puppet kingdom of Illyria, 1809–13. Returned to Austria, and became an imperial city, 1849. Ceded to Italy, 1918 (*see* VENETIA GIULIA). In Apr. 1945 the German forces retreating from the Balkans passed through T.; their rearguard was driven out by two independent local guerrilla forces, Slovene and Italian, 30 Apr. Anglo-US occupation followed. In Sept. 1947 a Free State consisting of T. and its environs was set up. On 25 Oct. 1954 T. city was handed over to Italy, less one small strip, which then passed under Yugoslav (now Slovene) civil administration.

Trinidad and Tobago, republic of. Trinidad was discovered and annexed to Spain by Columbus, 1498, but no settlement was made until the 1530s. Retained by the Spaniards, who by a new colonial policy, implemented in 1783, attracted large numbers of able foreigners to the cocoa industry, especially Frenchmen. The colony capitulated to Britain, 1797, and was formally ceded 1802. T. and T. joined, 1889. US leased defence bases there for 99 years, 1941 (but given up except for one tracking station, 1960). After the dissolution of the *Caribbean Federation T. and T. became an independent dominion of the Commonwealth on 31 Aug. 1962. Republic, 1976. 1980: Tobago granted increased self-administration from Trinidad. Failed anti-government coup, 1990.

trinitrotoluene (TNT), chemical explosive, solid organic nitrogen and very stable. Invented, Europe, *c.* 1906.

Trinity House, London, UK. An institution for regulating pilots; founded in its present form by Sir Thomas Spert, who was the first master, 1512, and given its first charter, 1514. The maintenance of lighthouses and buoys is also one of the duties of the brethren of T.H.

Tripartite Pact. Extension of German-Italian Axis Pact to include Japan signed in Berlin, 27 Sept. 1940; mutual cooperation in 'New World Order'. Hungary signed, 20 Nov. 1940; Romania and Slovakia signed, 23 Nov. 1940; Bulgaria signed, 1 Mar. 1941; Yugoslavia signed, 25 Mar. 1941.

Triple Alliance, 1668. Was ratified for the protection of the Spanish Netherlands, the contracting parties being the States-General and England (Sweden joined later) against France. Other T. As. have been: 1717, England, France, and Holland against Spain; 1795, England, Russia, and Austria; 1882, Germany, Austria, and Italy. The last came to an end, as regards Italy, in May 1915. The Germano-Austro-Hungarian Alliance was dissolved in 1918 at the end of World War I.

Tripoli, Libya, founded by Phoenicians 7thC BC, and important under Rome. Bombed during World War II, 1941–2; and in 1986 by US, as reprisal for Libya's alleged terrorist involvement.

Tristan da Cunha, S Atlantic. Discovered by Portuguese, 1506. Taken over by a British garrison, 1816, during Napoleon's residence at St Helena. When the garrison was withdrawn, 1817, Corporal William Glass and his wife elected to remain; they were joined by two ex-naval men and some shipwrecked sailors, and formed the nucleus of the T. colony. Attached, 1938, to St Helena Dependencies. An administrator appointed, 1948. Crawfishing company began operations there, 1949. In Oct. 1961 the volcano on the island erupted, destroying most of the settlement. All the inhabitants were evacuated and attempts made to settle them in Britain. Most had returned to T. by 1963, to live at the settlement of Edinburgh. New constitution with increased self-government, 1969.

Trondhjem or **Trondheim.** The town of *Nidaros* (then sometimes called *Kaupangen*) was founded, 996, on an existing market site by Olaf Tryggvason, who was elected king here. Kings of Norway began to be crowned here again from 1814. Name T. adopted during the Middle Ages. Seat of archbishopric of Norway from 1152, but importance waned after the Reformation. German U-boat base, 1940–4.

troubadours. Poets of Provence and Catalonia in 11th to 14thC. *See* PROVENÇAL AND CATALAN LITERATURE.

Troy. The five earliest of the cities which *fl.* on the site at Hissarlik in Asia Minor have been dated about 3000–1900 BC. The Homeric siege appears to have ended *c.* 1300 BC (Troy VIIa). The site was abandoned *c.* 1100–750 BC, and then occupied by settlers from mainland Greece. It survived until about 350 AD. 'Priam's Treasure', found at T. by Schliemann, 1873, and subsequently displayed in a Berlin museum, removed to Russia after World War II and held in Moscow. Negotiations to return it to Berlin begun, 1993 but so far inconclusive (1995). McLaren identified the site, 1822. Excavations by Schliemann began, 1870, and lasted until 1890; Dörpfeld's from 1893 to 1894; Cincinnati University, 1932–8.

Truce of God (*Treuga Dei*). A device of the Church in the Middle Ages to check private warfare, by limiting the periods within which fighting would not be sacrilegious. Inaugurated at Tuluges in Roussillon by a synod, 1027. By 1041 the movement had spread all over France; soon afterwards it reached England, and, by the end of the 11thC, only about 80 days in the year remained unaffected. Confirmed by Urban II in 1095 at the Council of Clermont. Extended to the whole Church by ecumenical council of 1179. Fell into disuse during the 13thC.

Truck Acts, requiring payments of wages to be made in current coin of the realm only, and not in goods, were passed in 1831, 1887 and 1896; they also forbid fines, except under special conditions. The Truck Act, 1940, forbids the provision of canteen meals in lieu of wages. One effect of the T.A. in modern society was to prevent manual workers being paid by cheque; after 31 Mar. 1963 payment by cheque in such cases was permitted, subject to the recipient's specific agreement.

trusts (USA), commercial, first established by John D. Rockefeller (Standard Oil T.), 1882. Congress passed Sherman Anti-T. Act, 1890, and Supreme Court ordered dissolution of Standard Oil T., 1911. Clayton Anti-Trust Act, 1914, amended by the Robinson-Patman Act, 1936, basis of present US anti-trust law.

Tsaritsin. *See* VOLGOGRAD.

tuberculosis. The organism causing this disease isolated by Koch, 1882. Vaccine developed *c.* 1920. First anti-T. drug, 1944. In developed world T. declined in first half of 20thC. Upsurge in 1990s has been partially linked to *AIDS and in the West, to increase in homelessness. World Health Organisation called T. a 'global emergency', Apr. 1993.

tubular bridge. The first T. bridge was built over the Menai Strait, 1846–60.

Tuileries Palace (Paris). Begun, 1564. Built by Catherine de' Medici, Henry IV and Louis XIV. Stormed, 1792; and ransacked, 1830 and 1848. Destroyed by the Communards, 25 May 1871.

Tunis, N Africa. Probably older than Carthage, and in 800–909 was a residence of the Agylabite dynasty. Repeatedly pillaged during 10thC. Turks captured it, 1533. French occupation, 1881. Deep-water channel to harbour opened, 1893. Captured by Allies from Germans, 7 May 1943. Capital of independent *Tunisia since 1956.

Tunisia corresponds in area with the Roman province of Africa, conquered by the Moslems in 698, and called by them Ifrikiya. Hussein ben Ali became Bey in 1705, acknowledging Turkish suzerainty, which was terminated by the Treaty of Bardo, 12 May 1881, and the Convention of La Marsa, 8 June 1883, which established the French protectorate. Important theatre of operations in *World War II. Nationalist agitation after the war resulted in France giving T. full independence, 20 Mar. 1956. The monarchy was abolished, 1957, and Bourguiba became T.'s first president; made president for life, 1975. Bourguiba deposed, 1987; succeeded by Ben Ali, who was re-elected, 1989. 1994 elections confirmed existing regime.

tunnels. *See* CHANNEL TUNNEL; also separate entries under BLACKWALL TUNNEL; DARTFORD etc.

turbines. *See* SHIPS and AVIATION.

Turin. Capital of Italy, 1861–5. Besieged by the French, 1706; taken by French, 1798, but they were expelled by the Russians and Austrians in the following year; again surrendered to the French, 1800; restored to Sardinia, 1814.

Turkestan, Chinese. *See* SINKIANG.

Turkestan, Russian. *See* TURKMENISTAN.

Turkish Republic. (For previous history of the Turks *see* OTTOMAN EMPIRE.) National-ist government set up under Mustafa Kemal Atatürk at Ankara, Oct, 1920. He refuses to accept the Treaty of Sèvres, Nov. 1920. Declares sovereign power to reside in National Assembly of the T. nation (*Kamutay*), Jan. 1921. Greek attempt to take over E Anatolia resisted, June 1921. Greeks driven out, Sept. 1922. Mudania armistice, Oct. 1922. Sultanate abolished and Turkey becomes a republic, Oct. 1923. Muslim religion disestablished and *caliphate abolished, 3 Mar. 1924. Treaty of Lausanne ratified with Allies, 1 Apr. 1924. Constitution passed, 21 Apr. 1924. Wearing of fez prohibited, 1925. Monogamy and civil marriage instituted, 1926. Latin alphabet supersedes Arabic, 1929–30. Refortifies Dardanelles, under League authority obtained; 20 July 1936. Atatürk *d.*, 10 Nov. 1938. Declares war on Germany and Japan, 23 Feb. 1945. Genuine opposition parties allowed, 1945 onwards; growth of Democratic party under Menderes. T. joined NATO, 1952. Menderes became premier, 1950. In May 1960 the Menderes regime was overthrown by an army revolt. Menderes was executed, 1961. Parliamentary government re-established during 1961; T. invaded *Cyprus, 1974 and has subsequently maintained troops in Turkish part of island; army took over power, 1980–82. In elections, Nov. 1983, Ozal, leader of Motherland party, elected. T. supported Turkish Cypriots' declaration of independence, Nov. 1983. Ozal won elections again, 1987; became president, 1989, but *d.* 1993. Succeeded by Demirel. T. supported Allies in Gulf War, 1991. Kurdish unrest in SE T. during 1990s rigorously suppressed. Tansu Ciller became T.'s first woman premier, June 1993 but resigned, Sept. 1995; elections, Dec.

Turkmenistan, republic of. This area of N Asia was conquered by the Russians, 1866–73. Part of Turkestan Soviet Socialist autonomous republic, 1921; constituent republic, 1924. Proclaimed its independence, 1991. Joined UN, 1992. Increased inter-ethnic tension, as Russian abolished as official language, May 1992. In 1995 the president's powers were extended to 2002.

Turksib (i.e. Turkestan-Siberian) **Railway**, from Novosibirsk to Tashkent, begun 1927, was connected to the Transib, 1929, and opened to traffic, 1930.

Turner's Legacies. Pictures which J. M. W. Turner, the landscape painter, bequeathed to the nation, 1851. Since the opening of the Clore wing in the *Tate Gallery, 1987, these have been more fully displayed.

Turner Prize was established in 1984 by the Tate Gallery's Patrons of New Art. Its intention was 'to promote public discussion of new developments in contemporary British art'. Awarded annually; value £20,000; winner must be under 50 years old. In 1993 controversially awarded to Rachel Whiteread for her sculpture 'Untitled (Room)', a development of 'Ghost', 1990; in 1994 to Antony Gormley, a figurative sculptor, for 'Testing a World View'. First winner, 1984, was Malcolm Morley.

Tuscany, in area corresponding roughly to the ancient *Etruria, was in the Middle Ages a margravate of the Frankish Empire established about 800, but dissolving into a loose league of city republics of which by the 13thC Florence was the leader. The family of Medici, who usurped power in the Florentine republic, became dukes of T., 1532, and grand dukes, 1557. On the death of the last Medici, 1737, T. fell to the Duke of Lorraine who, as consort of the Empress Maria Theresa, bequeathed it to the Austrian crown, which retained it until 1800, when Napoleon set up the puppet kingdom of Etruria. From 1808 to 1814 T. formed part of the French Empire. The Hapsburg-Lorraine restoration lasted peaceably until 1848, after which date it was only maintained by Austrian troops, who were driven out, 1859. T. was incorporated in the kingdom of Italy, 1861.

Turin Shroud, or **Holy Shroud of Turin,** first heard of in France, 1354, when in possession of Geoffroi de Charnay. His descendant gave it to House of Savoy, 1453, at Chambéry: moved to Turin, 1578 and after that exhibited on special occasions (e.g. 400th anniversary of arrival in Turin, 1978). Traditionally said to be the winding sheet in which Christ's body was wrapped following the Crucifixion, carbon-dating and other tests made by three different universities implied, 1988, that T.S. made sometime between 1260 and 1390. Examination of pollen found on it suggested as showing T.S. had come from Middle East; 1993. T.S. continues to be venerated as showing an inspiring pictorial representation of Christ.

Tussaud's, Madame. Marie Tussaud (1761–1850) brought her collection of French Revolution death-masks to UK, 1802. Exhibition toured country until established in Baker St, London, 1833. 'Chamber of Horrors' coined by '*Punch*', 1845. Moved to Marylebone Road, 1884. Destroyed by fire, 18 Mar. 1925. Reopened, 1928. Damaged by bombing, 1940, but subsequently restored.

Tutankhamen's tomb. Located near Luxor by Lord Carnarvon and Howard Carter, 1922, and opened Feb. 1923. Contents now in a Cairo museum.

Tuvalu, formerly the **Ellice Islands**, became independent under name of T., 1 Oct. 1978.

TV. *See* TELEVISION.

Twelve Tables, The, a code of laws collected and formulated by a decemvirate of the Roman Republic, 451–449 BC.

Tyburn (London). Here criminals were executed *c.* 1388–1783. Many Catholics died here for their faith during the 16th and 17thC. The gallows were near the present Marble Arch.

Tyler's Insurrection, 1381. *See* PEASANTS' REVOLT.

Tynwald, parliament and supreme court of Isle of Man, meets on T. Hill, consisting originally of three estates, now effectively only of the House of Keys. A characteristically Scandinavian legislative body dating from Norse occupation (800–1266). *See* MAN, ISLE OF and VIKING AGE.

typewriters invented in the USA by Scholes, Glidden and Soulé, 1868 (although an embryonic T. design had been patented by the Englishman, Henry Mills, 1714). First manufactured in commercial quantities, 1873. First lower- and upper-case model, 1878. Portables were available from 1909, but not popular until 1940s. First electric T. invented by Edison, 1872; commercially produced, 1920, but not in general use until 1950s. Electronic Ts. from 1980s.

tyres, pneumatic, were first fitted to horse-drawn vehicles by R.W. Thompson, 1845. Reinvented by J.B. Dunlop for bicycles, 1888. Pneumatic tyres for cars first made by Michelin, 1895, and for aeroplane undercarriages by Dunlop, 1910. Pneumatic tyres were first fitted to lorries, 1917, and to tractors, 1930.

'U-2' incident. On 5 May 1960 Khruschev told the Supreme Soviet that an American Lockheed U-2 aeroplane had been shot down over Soviet territory on 1 May and its pilot captured; on 7 May the US government admitted that the plane had been carrying out an intelligence mission. The incident was used by Khruschev to humiliate the US president and break up the Summit Conference in Paris on 17 May. Subsequently the pilot, Gary Powers, was convicted of espionage at a 'show' trial in Moscow; in 1962 he was released in exchange for a Russian spy held by the USA.

U-boats (German *Unter-seebooten*), *see* SUB-MARINES, which were so called when used by the German navy from 1914.

UEFA (Union of European Football Associations), established 1954. It is responsible for numerous inter-European football competitions, of which the best known is the European Football Championship, which was established in 1958, and the first final held in 1960. Winners of the European Football Championship:

1960: Soviet Union
1964: Spain
1968: Italy
1972: West Germany
1976: Czechoslovakia (on penalties)
1980: West Germany
1984: France
1988: Holland
1992: Denmark

Uffizi Gallery (Florence), contains one of the world's leading art collections. Cosimo Medici I commissioned Vasari, 1560, to design present structure on site of 15thC building, as administrative centre for Grand Duchy of Tuscany. Completed, 1560. Reached present size, 1658. Since 1852 has held the Tuscan state archives. Damaged by terrorist bombing, May 1993.

Uganda, E Africa, assigned to Britain by Anglo-German Treaty, 1890. Civil war, 1891. Protectorate declared, 1894. Rebellion, 1897. Treaty with dominant Buganda tribe, 1900. On 10 Oct. 1962 U. became a self-governing dominion within the Commonwealth. In 1966 the premier of U. Obote, deposed the president, Mutesa II of Buganda, and took over his functions (monarchy restored. July 1993: *see* BU-GANDA). Republic, 1971 and Obote deposed by Idi Amin, 1971, and reign of terror followed. Amin deposed, 1979: in Dec. 1980 the Uganda People's Congress under Obote gained power in elections. Unrest from 1980: Obote overthrown in military coup, 1985; subsequent power-sharing between military and civilian interests ended, 1986, when civilian Museveni became president. U. has been heavily affected by the *AIDS epidemic since the 1980s. Ban on political parties set to remain until 2000.

Ukraine, republic of. As the principality of Galicia-Volhynia, was independent *c.* 1300–20; part of Lithuania, 1321–1569; then Polish until 1772 (pro-Russian revolt under Hetman Khmielnitzky, 1648); until World War I U. was divided between Russia and Austria-Hungary. Encouraged by Germany U. declared itself independent, 20 Nov. 1917. Union of E and W U., Jan. 1919. Invasion by Bolsheviks, Feb. 1918. Fall of Kiev, Feb. 1918. Spoliation by German forces, 1917–18. Generals Petliura and Vinnichenko drove out the government established by Germany and set up dictatorship at Kiev, Nov.–Dec. 1918. Second Soviet government set up, Mar. 1919; Denikin's troops overthrew Soviet government June; Soviet forces recaptured Kharkov and Kiev, Dec 1920; Odessa taken by Soviet troops, and third Soviet government set up, Feb. 1920; by Treaty of Riga, Poland and Russia recognized independence of U., 12 Oct. 1923: U. joins USSR., 6 July: collectivization leads to mass starvation 1932–4. In 1938 on being granted self-government, the Ruthenian province of Czechoslovakia called itself 'Carpatho-U.', Oct. In 1939, Carpatho-U. annexed by Hungary, 14 Mar. The German-Soviet partition of Poland gave Polish (W) U. to Russia, 28 Sept. Bessarabia ceded by Romania, 1940, united to Soviet U. Heavy Ukrainian casualties 1941–5: estimated 5 million *d*. Carpatho-U. joined Soviet U., 1945. World's worst nuclear accident occurred at *Chernobyl in the U., 1986. Nationalism, suppressed under Soviet regime, revived in 1980s. U. elected Kravchuk president and declared its independence, Dec. 1991. Founder member of *CIS.

Ukraine since 1991: Friction between U. and Russia regarding allocation of defence forces and resources, previously centrally controlled from Moscow, notably U.'s nuclear warheads. U. finally ratified *START I, Nov. 1993. Agreement to split Black Sea fleet with Russia, 1994 quickly disintegrated. Running dispute with Russia over status of *Crimea since 1991. Economic difficulties caused serious strikes, 1993, and falling popularity of nationalist government. In Jan. 1994, US agreed to help pay for dismantling of U's nuclear arsenal. Success of former Communists and pro-Russians in 1994 elections and in July in presidential run-off Kravchuk defeated by Kuchma, favouring closer cooperation with Russia. In Nov. U. acceded to the *Nuclear Non-Proliferation Treaty. New agreement, June 1995, over Black Sea fleet signalled strengthening of 'strategic partnership' between Russia and U.

Ukrainian or **Little Russian Language** became finally differentiated from Great Russian about the middle of the 13thC. The use of U. as a vehicle of instruction in Russian schools was forbidden by an imperial edict in 1863, and in 1876 it became a criminal offence to print or publish U. material in the tsar's dominions. The use of the written language again became legal in 1905. An official orthography was published by the U. Academy of Sciences, 1946.

Following are some better-known U. authors:

Ivan Kotlyarevsky, 1769–1838, satirist.
Pantaleimon Kulish, 1819–97, novelist, poet and translator.
Taras Shevchenko, 1814–69, poet.
Marko Vovchok, 1834–1907, novelist.
Leonid Hlibov, 1827–93, lyrical fabulist.
Oleksander Konysky, 1836–1900.
Mihailo Drahomaniv, 1841–95, philologist.
Ivan Franko, 1856–1916, poet.

Ulm, Germany. Peace signed, 1620. Cathedral built, 1377–1494. 550-ft. spire completed, 1894.

Ulster. Colonization of forfeited land, 1611. Rebellion, 1641. U. Convention against Home Rule, 17 June 1892. U. Convention League formed, Aug. 1892. Accepted under protest Government of Ireland Act, 1920, which set up two legislatures in Ireland. For later events *see* IRELAND, NORTHERN.

Ulster Democratic Unionists, political party formed, 1972. Its leader since 1974 has been the Rev. Ian Paisley. In 1994 the U.D.U. had three MPs at Westminster and was widely represented in local government in N Ireland. The U.D.U. tends to be more hardline than the *Ulster Unionists but both wish to preserve the Union.

Ulster Freedom Fighters and **Ulster Volunteer Force (UVF),** two of a number of illegal and paramilitary Protestant organizations which sprang up in N Ireland from the early 1970s. Their methods of violence and intimidation were similar to those of the IRA and INLA, but applied against Catholics, and confined to the Irish mainland. Their power increased from the late 1980s. U.F.F. banned 1973; UVF, 1975. Following IRA cease-fire, Aug. 1994 the U.F.F. and UVF followed suit.

Ulster King of Arms. This office joined to that of Norroy King of Arms in 1943.

Ulster Unionists, political party which controlled the N Irish Parliament in *Stormont from 1920 until the imposition of direct rule from London in 1972. Originally linked to the Conservative Party (from 1886) and representing the Protestant majority in Ulster, the U.U.'s links with the Conservative party have been abandoned in practice following the events of 1972, and its monopoly of Protestant votes in Ulster challenged by the emergence of the *Ulster Democratic Unionists. However it retains wide support in Ulster and had nine MPs at Westminster in 1995 when its leader since 1974, James Molyneaux, stood down and was replaced by David Trimble.

umbrella. Appears on Assyrian bas-reliefs, 8thC BC. First habitual user in London was Jonas Hanway (*d.* 1786).

Uncle Sam, nickname for the US government, first used in the *Troy Post* for 7 Sept. 1813.

underground railway. First in the world was that opened in London in 1863. New York, 1868; Paris, 1900; Berlin, 1902; Madrid, 1919; Moscow, 1935; Stockholm, 1950; Peking, 1972. Worst U.R. accident *Baku, 1995 (over 300 dead).

UNESCO (United Nations Educational, Scientific and Cultural Organization) set up, 16 Nov. 1945. Became operative, Nov. 1946. USA withdrew membership, 1984; Britain and Singapore in 1985.

Ungava, interior territory of Labrador, round U. Bay, joined to province of Quebec, 1912.

UNICEF (United Nations Childrens' Fund) set up as United Nations International Childrens' Emergency Fund, 1946.

Uniformity, Act of, 15 Jan. 1549, ordered use of the Common Prayer Book. Confirmed, 1552. Repealed by Queen Mary, 1553. Restored by Queen Elizabeth, 1559. Formed basis of the stringent Act of Charles II, which came into force, 24 Aug. 1662.

UDI (Unilateral Declaration of Independence), made by Rhodesia (now Zimbabwe) on 11 Nov. 1965. Ian Smith, Rhodesian premier, declared Rhodesia an independent dominion, but Britain refused to recognize this. Ended, Dec. 1979. *See* GREAT BRITAIN; ZIMBABWE.

Union, Act of, with Scotland, 1707.

Union, Act of, with Ireland, 1801.

Union Jack. British flag, made up of: English flag, red cross on white ground (St George); Scottish flag, diagonal white cross on blue (St Andrew), incorporated, Apr. 1606; Irish flag, diagonal red cross on white (St Patrick), incorporated, Jan. 1801.

Union Jack club. Opened by King Edward VII, 1907, for British soldiers and sailors, as memorial to men killed in China and S Africa.

Union of European Football Associations. *See* UEFA.

Union of Soviet Socialist Republics. *See* USSR

unit trusts. First in Britain formed, 1931. Became widely used from 1950s.

Unitarians. Sect founded by Socinus in Italy, 1546. English U. trace their descent from those mainly Presbyterian congregations whose ministers were ejected in 1662, many of whose chapels are now in Unitarian hands. The specifically Unitarian doctrines of these congregations became current *c.* 1700. International Unitarian Council, Geneva, 1905. General Assembly of Unitarian and Free Christian Churches formed, 1928. US U. merged with the national organization of Universalist churches, 1961.

United Arab Emirates, formed 2 Dec. 1971 from the Trucial States of Abu Dhabi, Dubai, Sharjah, Ajmaw, Umm al Qawain, Fujairah and Ras al Khaimah. Joined UN coalition against Iraq in *Gulf War, 1991.

United Arab Republic. State formed on 1

Feb. 1958 by the union of *Egypt and *Syria. The *Yemen federated temporarily with the U.A.R. on 8 Mar. 1958. Syria seceded from U.A.R. after anti-Egyptian revolt, 28 Sept. 1961. Yemen subsequently broke connection with U.A.R., but Egypt continued to be known as the U.A.R., finally reverting to name 'Egypt' on 2 Sept. 1971.

United Free Church of Scotland, formed by union of the United Presbyterian Church and the Free Church of Scotland, 1900. Further united with the *Church of Scotland, 1929.

United Irishmen, formed, 1791, by Wolfe Tone (1763–98), organized risings in Northern Ireland, 1797 and 1798. Tone committed suicide when the latter rising failed.

United Kingdom, from 1801 to 1921, was styled 'United Kingdom of Great Britain and Ireland', since then, 'United Kingdom of Great Britain and Northern Ireland.' *See* GREAT BRITAIN, HISTORY OF etc.,

United Kingdom Atomic Energy Authority. *See* ATOMIC ENERGY AUTHORITY, UNITED KINGDOM.

United Nations Organization (UN). Charter signed at San Francisco, 26 June 1945. Sufficiently ratified to begin existence, 24 Oct. 1945. First meeting of General Assembly: London, 10 Jan. 1946; New York, 23 Oct. 1946. Among UN's major international involvements have been the Korean War, 1950; the Gulf War, 1991; the Balkans' conflict since 1992; Somalia, from 1992–4; and Rwanda, 1994.

Secretaries-General of the UN:
Trygve Lie (Norway) 1946–1952
Dag Hammarskjöld (Sweden) 1953–1961
U Thant (Burma) 1962–1972
Kurt Waldheim (Austria) 1972–1982
Javier Perez de Cuellar (Peru) 1982–92
Boutros Boutros Ghali (Egypt) 1992–

United Presbyterian Church. Restoration, in 1712, of patronage in the Church of Scotland, led, in 1733, to formation of a Secession Church, which, in 1747, split over the scripturality of the burgess oath. The Burgher Auld Lichts were organized, 1799; the Anti-Burgher Auld Lichts, 1806. The two New Licht churches were united, 1820; the two Auld Lichts in 1842 as the Original Seceders. Meanwhile, in 1761, the Establishment had lost, by another anti-patronage secession, a group called the Relief Church. Secession Church and Relief Church amalgamated as U.P.C., 1847. This, in 1900, was amalgamated with the Free Church, the result being the *United Free Church.

United Provinces (of Agra and Oudh). Designation adopted, 1902. Now *Uttar Pradesh (since 1950).

United Reformed Church, formed 1972, from a union of the Congregational Church in England and Wales and the Presbyterian Church in England and Wales.

United States of America. First American combined opposition to Stamp Act, Oct. 1765. Chests of tea destroyed at Boston and New York, 16 Dec. 1773. Declaration of Rights, Oct. 1774. First battle between British and Americans (Lexington), 19 Apr. 1775. Battle of Bunker Hill, 17 June 1775. Act of Perpetual Union of States, 20 May 1775. Declaration of Independence, 4 July 1776. Articles of Confederation proposed by John Dickinson, 1776. Submitted to States, Nov. 1777. Battle of Saratoga, 17 Oct. 1777. Alliance with France, 6 Feb. 1778; ratified, Mar. 1781. Lord Cornwallis surrendered at Yorktown, 19 Oct. 1781. Peace signed at Paris, 3 Sept. 1783. Constitution proposed by Convention of Philadelphia, Sept. 1787; ratified, 21 June 1788. Death of Washington, 14 Dec. 1799. Louisiana Purchase, 30 Apr. 1803. Importation of slaves prohibited, 1 Jan. 1808. War with Britain, 18 June, 1812–24 Dec. 1814. Missouri Compromise, defining boundaries of slave area, 1820. Monroe Doctrine proclaimed, 1823. Texas annexed, 1845. Mexican War over the annexation of Texas, 1845–8. Mormons settled in Utah, 1847.

Fugitive Slave Bill, 1850. Commercial treaty with Japan, 1854. Civil war in Kansas, 1856–7. Attack on Harper's Ferry by John Brown, 16 Oct. 1859. Execution of John Brown, 2 Dec. 1859. Republican convention at Chicago, 1860. S Carolina, State Convention passed ordinance of secession, 20 Dec. 1860. Secession of Mississippi (9 Jan.), Florida (10 Jan.), Alabama (11 Jan.), Georgia (19 Jan.), Louisiana (26 Jan.), and Texas (1 Feb.), Jan.–Feb. 1861. 'Confederate' States' delegates met at Montgomery, Alabama; elected Jefferson Davis President, 9 Feb. 1861, and formed constitution, 11 Mar. 1861. Civil war began by an attack on Fort Sumter by the Confederates (S), 12 Apr. 1861. Lincoln issued proclamation of blockade of southern ports, 19 Apr. 1861. N Carolina and Arkansas seceded, May 1861. Battle of Bull Run, 21 July 1861. Battle of Ball's Bluff, 21 Oct. 1861. Jefferson Davis elected President of Southern Confederacy, Nov. 1861. Paper currency ('green-backs') adopted, 25 Feb. 1862. Battle of Pea Ridge, 6–8 Mar. 1862. Battle of Winchester, 23 Mar. 1862. Battle of Pittsburg, 6–7 Apr. 1862. Battle of Fredericksburg, 10 Dec. 1862. Homestead Act passed, Dec. 1862. Abolition of slavery proclaimed, Jan. 1863. Battle of Chancellorsville, 2 May 1863. 'Stonewall' Jackson mortally wounded by his own troops in mistake at the battle of Chancellorsville; *d.* 10 May 1863. Fugitive Slave Act repealed, 13 June 1864. Gen. Lee surrendered to Gen. Grant at Appomattox, 9 Apr. 1865. President Lincoln assassinated, 15 Apr. 1865. Proclamation of amnesty, 29 May 1865. End of rebellion proclaimed by President Johnson, 3 Apr. 1866. Civil Rights Bill passed, 9 Apr. 1866. Impeachment of President Johnson carried in House of Representatives, 25 Feb.; acquitted by Senate, 26 May 1868. Engagement with Indians at Little Big Horn River, 25 June 1876. Edmunds's Anti-Polygamy Act, Mar. 1882. Chinese Exclusion Act passed, Apr. 1882. Nicaragua Canal Bill passed, Feb. 1889. McKinley Tariff Bill (protectionist) passed, Oct. 1890. Railway strikes at Chicago, much rioting, June–July 1894. Dingley Tariff Bill (highly protectionist) passed, July 1897. Hawaii annexed, 7 July 1898. *Maine* explosion, 15 Feb. 1898. Ultimatum sent to Spain, 19 Apr. 1898. War began, 21 Apr. 1898. Treaty of Paris between Spain and America, 10 Dec. 1898. McKinley assassinated, 1901. Panama Canal Bill passed, 26 June 1902. Alaska Boundary Treaty, 11 Feb. 1903. Riots in Chicago, May 1905. Acts for reform of tariffs and for creating federal reserve of currency passed, 1913. War declared on Germany, 6 Apr. 1917. Wilson enunciated his '14 points', Jan. 1918. Wilson announced League constitution, Feb. 1919. Wilson presented peace treaty in Congress, July 1919; eventually rejected by the Senate, which meant that the USA did not join the League of Nations. Women's suffrage, 1920. Prohibition came into effect, 1920; repealed, 1933. Immigration quota system started, 1921. 1927: Sacco and Vanzetti (Communists) convicted, on doubtful evidence, of a murder committed Apr. 1920; executed 23 Aug. at Charlestown, near Boston. 1929: New York Stock Exchange slump. 1930: London Naval Treaty signed by President Hoover, 22 July. 1932: Olympic Games (10th), Los Angeles, Aug. Franklin D. Roosevelt, Democrat, elected President, on the promise of a 'New Deal'. 1933: Gold standard suspended, 5 June; USSR recognized, 17 Nov. Acts passed included the Economy Act; the National Industrial Recovery Act; the Agricultural Adjustment Act. 1935: Federal judge decided National Recovery Act invalid (confirmed by Supreme Court, 1936); dust bowl over Kansas, Mar–Apr.; Huey Long of Louisiana shot 8 Sept. at Baton Rouge, *d.* 10 Sept; Roosevelt re-elected, 1936. USA refused to recognize German annexation of Czechoslovakia, 21 Mar 1939; George VI and Elizabeth of England visit the USA, 8 June; President appealed for peace to Italy, Germany and Poland, Aug.; signed three proclamations relating to US neutrality, 5 Sept.; Neutrality Revision Bill law, 4 Nov. Arms production for Britain increased, 1940; Conscription Bill enacted, 16 Sept.; Roosevelt elected for a third term. Lease-Lend Act passed, 11 Mar. 1941; Atlantic Charter issued by Churchill and Roosevelt, 11 Aug; Japanese attacked Pearl Harbor, 7 Dec.; Germany and Italy declared war on USA, 11 Dec. (*see further under* WORLD WAR II). 1942: Washington Pact, 1 Jan; Anglo-American Combined Chiefs of Staff appointed, Feb. 1943; Cairo meeting, 22–26 Nov., Teheran meeting, 26 Nov.–2 Dec. 1944: Roosevelt elected for fourth term. 1945: Yalta Conference, Feb.; death of Roosevelt, 25 Apr. succeeded by Vice-President Harry S. Truman; San Francisco Conference, May–June; Potsdam Conference July–Aug.; Congress ratified UN Charter, 28 July, marking end of isolationism as a political force in the USA for next 30 years. Truman re-elected, 1948. North Atlantic Treaty signed in Washington, 4 Apr. 1949. Korean War (*see* KOREA) began 25 June 1950. Constitutional amendment limiting president's tenure of office to two terms passed, Feb. 1951; Eisenhower elected Republican President, 1952; Korean cease-fire, 1953. Supreme Court ruled racial segregation in schools unconstitutional, 1954, and McCarthy's influence faded. Suez crisis of 1956 caused temporary rift in Anglo-US relations. US troops intervened temporarily in Lebanon, 1958. 1960: Summit Conference in Paris attended by Eisenhower broke up over *U-2 Incident; Kennedy elected Democratic President, 9 Nov. 1961: Bay of Pigs' fiasco, Apr.; disarmament talks with Russia. Settlement of Cuban missile crisis (*see* CUBA), Oct. 1962 and in Feb. 1962 first American (Glenn) orbited the earth in space. Kennedy assassinated, Dallas, 22 Nov. 1963 and Vice-President Lyndon Johnson succeeds. Civil Rights Act becomes law, 2 July 1964. US intervention in Vietnam escalates; bombing of N Vietnam by US planes, Feb. 1965 and anti-war student riots in USA. Martin Luther King assassinated, Apr. 1968 and Robert Kennedy in June. Johnson orders halt to US Vietnam bombing, 1 Nov. 1968; Nixon elected Republican president, 6 Nov. Decade 1970–80 great period of space progress in USA; consoli-

dation of civil rights. But Vietnam dominated US politics until 1974–5, when the war officially ended. Nixon forced to resign over *Watergate scandal, 1974; succeeded by Vice-President Ford. Jimmy Carter became Democratic President in 1976. Diplomatic relations established between Communist China and USA. But Carter's term plagued by domestic problems of inflation and unemployment and hostage crisis in Iran, 1979–80. His major success the Camp David agreement of 1979 between Israel and Egypt. Carter defeated by right-wing Republican Reagan, 1979. Reagan re-elected 1984, 'Irangate' scandal broke, 1986 and Reagan image tarnished thereafter. Stock market crash, 1988 and following economic recession. Invasion of Panama, 1988. Vice-President Bush elected President, Nov. 1988; US troops sent to Gulf, 1990 and won *Gulf War, 1991. Democratic landslide, 1992 and Bill Clinton president with a radical domestic programme. Recession ending, 1993 and US announced ending of *Star Wars programme. Clinton first pursued aggressive policy in Somalia (following involvement there by Bush, 1992) but later relaxed this and US personnel all withdrawn by 1994. Health Care proposals revealed, 1993. Clinton meets Chinese leader in Seattle, Nov.; *NAFTA approved by Congress, 17 Nov.; Brady (Gun Control Bill) passed, 24 Nov. GATT Uruguay Round (*see* GATT) concluded, Dec. Jan. 1994: Clinton visits Europe but popularity in USA increasingly threatened by domestic scandals, notably the 'Whitewater Affair' (into which enquiry begun, July); foreign policy successes regarding Cuba, Korea, Haiti, Middle East and Eastern bloc during 1994 failed to halt slide in presidential unpopularity. In Sept. Health Care Bill abandoned for present session. In Nov. mid-term elections Republicans gained control of both houses of Congress for first time since 1950 and also won several state governorships. Republican gains increased US hawkish attitude to Bosnian crisis: USA announced it would not continue to enforce arms embargo there, Nov.

Former president Carter negotiated Bosnian cease-fire, Dec. but this did not last. 1995: Bombing in Oklahoma City, Apr.; Congress refuses to endorse President's nominee as Surgeon-General. Senate votes to lift arms embargo on Bosnia, 26 July. US reopens Vietnam embassy, Aug.; announces it will end nuclear tests. Congress hearings leave 'Whitewater' Affair unresolved. Efforts of US negotiator instrumental in producing further Bosnian cease-fire, Oct., and Clinton offers US troops to enforce a future peace settlement. USA brings about initialling of peace agreement between Bosnia, Croatia and Serbia to end Bosnian civil war, Dayton, Ohio, Nov. 1995.

United States of America, Constitution of, passed, 17 Sept. 1787. Came into force, 21 June 1788. The following amendments have been made: (1) Freedom of religion, expression and assembly. (2) Freedom to keep arms. (3) Quartering of troops illegal. (4) General warrants illegal. (5) No deprivations or punishments without trial. (6) Trial by jury secured in criminal offences. (7) Trial by jury secured in most civil cases. (8) Fines and bail not to be excessive; punishments not to be cruel or unusual. (9) Rights enumerated in the Constitution not to deny other rights retained by the people. (10) Rights not specifically given to the Union to be retained by states or people. The above, collectively known as the Bill of Rights, were passed, 15 Dec. 1791. (11) Alteration of powers of the Supreme Court, 1798. (12) Alteration of method of election of President and Vice-President, 1804. (13) Slavery abolished, 1865. (14) Definition of citizenship. Apportionment of representation in House of Representatives. Former rebels excluded from office. Confederate debt repudiated, 1868. (15) Voting rights not to be denied on account of colour, 1870. (16) Income tax legalized, 1913. (17) Senators to be directly elected, 1913. (18) Prohibition instituted, 1918. (19) Female suffrage, 1920. (20) Alteration in election and terms of office of President, Vice-president, etc., 1933. (21) Prohibition to be left to state legislation, 1933; in effect, the repeal of the Eighteenth Amendment.

(22) Limiting the President's tenure of office to two terms, or to two terms plus two years in respect of a Vice-President who has succeeded to presidential office, 26 Feb. 1951. (23) Giving citizens of the District of Columbia the right to vote in national elections, 30 Mar. 1961. (24) Banning the use of a poll-tax in federal elections, 4 Feb. 1964. (25) Dealing with Presidential disability and succession, 10 Feb. 1967. (26) giving citizens over the age of 18 the right to vote, 22 June 1970.

United States of America, Presidents of. Those marked V.-P. were Vice-Presidents and took office in the first instance by succession and not by election.

George Washington 1789–97
John Adams 1797–1801
Thomas Jefferson 1801–09
James Madison 1809–17
James Monroe 1817–25
John Quincy Adams 1825–29
Andrew Jackson 1829–37
Martin Van Buren 1837–41
W.H. Harrison Mar.–Apr. 41
John Tyler (V.-P.) 1841–45
J. Knox Polk 1845–49
Zachary Taylor 1849–50
Millard Fillmore (V.-P.) 1850–53
Franklin Pierce 1853–57
James Buchanan 1857–61
Abraham Lincoln 1861–65
Andrew Johnson (V.-P.) 1865–69
Ulysses S. Grant 1869–77
Rutherford Hayes 1877–81
James Garfield 1881
Chester Arthur (V.-P.) 1881–85
Grover Cleveland 1885–89
Benjamin Harrison 1889–93
Grover Cleveland (again) 1893–97
William McKinley 1897–1901
Theodore Roosevelt (V.-P.) 1901–09
William Howard Taft 1909–13
Woodrow Wilson 1913–21
Warren Harding 1921–23
Calvin Coolidge (V.-P.) 1923–29
Herbert Hoover 1929–33
Franklin Delano Roosevelt 1933–45
Harry S. Truman (V.-P.) 1945–53

Dwight David Eisenhower 1953–61
John Fitzgerald Kennedy 1961–63
Lyndon Baines Johnson (V.-P.) 1963–69
Richard Milhous Nixon 1969–74
Gerald Ford (V.-P.) 1974–77
James Earle Carter 1977–81
Ronald (Wilson) Reagan 1981–89
George Herbert Walker Bush, 1989–93
William (Bill) Jefferson Clinton, 1993–

United States Marine Corps. *See* MARINE CORPS USA

Universities. Salerno, reputed to have been founded in 9thC, is the earliest of which there is record; Cordoba, 968; Bologna, 1116; Paris, 1200; Padua, 1222; Salamanca, 1243; Rome, 1245; Sorbonne, Paris, 1253; Cracow, 1364; Vienna, 1365; Prague, 1384; Heidelberg, 1386; Leipzig, 1409; Ingolstadt, 1472 (transferred to Landshut, 1800, to Munich, 1826); Uppsala, 1477; Wittenberg, 1502 (absorbed, 1694, by Halle); Strasbourg, 1538; Jena, 1558; Douai, 1563; Leyden, 1575; Utrecht, 1636; Harvard, 1638; Innsbruck, 1669; Besançon 1676; Göttingen, 1734; Bonn, 1786 (*See* CAMBRIDGE UNIVERSITY and OXFORD UNIVERSITY.) The other historic U. of Great Britain and Ireland, with dates of foundation, are:

St Andrews 1411
Glasgow 1450
Aberdeen 1495
Edinburgh 1583
Dublin (Trinity College) 1591
Durham 1832
London 1836
Manchester 1880
Wales 1893
Birmingham 1900
Liverpool 1903
Leeds 1904
Sheffield 1905
Ireland, National University of 1908
Queen's, Belfast 1908
Bristol 1909
Reading 1926
Nottingham 1948
Southampton 1952

Hull 1954
Exeter 1955
Leicester 1957
Sussex (at Brighton) 1961
Keele 1962
East Anglia (at Norwich) 1963
Newcastle upon Tyne 1963
York 1963
Essex (at Colchester) 1964
Lancaster 1964
Strathclyde (at Glasgow) 1964
Kent (at Canterbury) 1965
New University of Ulster (at Coleraine) 1965
Warwick 1965
Aston (at Birmingham) 1966
Bath 1966
Bradford 1966
Brunel (at Uxbridge) 1966
City (London E.C.2), 1966.
Heriot-Watt (at Edinburgh) 1966
Loughborough University of Technology 1966
Surrey (at Guildford) 1966
Dundee 1967
Salford 1967
Stirling 1967
Open University 1969
Buckingham 1976

Under a royal charter, 1967, the Royal College of Art, London SW7, also ranks as a U., able to confer its own degrees: the Cranfield Institute of Technology obtained similar status in 1969. Luton College of Higher Education was granted U. status, 1993. It was expected that other colleges of higher education would follow, and also apply for U. status.

In 1992 polytechnics were granted university status, enabling them to award their own degrees. They are now known as follows:

Anglia Polytechnic University (at Chelmsford)
University of Central England at Birmingham
Bournemouth University
Brighton University

University of the West of England at Bristol
University of Westminster
City of London University
Coventry University
University of East London
Hertfordshire University
University of Huddersfield
University of Humberside
Kingston University
De Montfort University (at Leicester)
Leeds Metropolitan University
Liverpool John Moores University
Manchester Metropolitan University
Middlesex University
University of Northumbria (at Newcastle)
Nottingham Trent University
University of North London
Oxford Brookes University
University of Plymouth
University of Portsmouth
Sheffield Hallam University
South Bank University
University of Sunderland
University of Teeside
University of Greenwich
University of Glamorgan
University of Wolverhampton
Thames Valley University
Glasgow Caledonian University
Napier University (at Edinburgh)
University of Paisley
Robert Gordon University (Aberdeen)

Universities, American. Privately endowed U. include: Harvard, 1633; William and Mary, 1693; Yale, 1701; Princeton, 1746; Washington and Lee, 1749; Columbia, 1754; Brown, 1764; Rutgers, 1766; Dartmouth, 1770; Miami and Ohio, 1809; Emory, 1837; Ohio Wesleyan, 1841; Notre Dame, 1842; Wilberforce, 1856; Atlanta, 1865; Cornell, 1865; Des Moines, 1865; Johns Hopkins, 1876; Drake, 1881; Stanford, 1885; Chicago, 1890; Duke, 1924.
The characteristic American U. originally founded for women are privately endowed; some of the better known are: Mount Holyoke, 1837; Elmira, 1853; Vassar, 1865; Wells, 1868; Humber, 1871; Smith, 1871; Wellesley, 1871; Radcliffe,

1879; Bryn Mawr, 1881; Barnard, 1889. Most of these are now (1995) co-educational.
State U. are mostly of 19thC foundation, but a few date back to colonial times. In 1862 the federal government passed an Act setting aside public lands for the endowment of U. The following are some of the better-known state U.: Pennsylvania, 1751; Georgia, 1785–1801; North Carolina, 1789; Virginia, 1819; Alabama, 1820; Indiana, 1838; Michigan, 1841; Missouri, 1841; Iowa, 1847; Mississippi, 1848; Wisconsin, 1848; Utah, 1850; Minnesota, 1851; Louisiana, 1860; Kansas, 1866; Illinois, 1867; West Virginia, 1867; California, 1869; Nebraska, 1871; Arkansas, 1872; Oregon, 1872; Nevada, 1873; Ohio, 1873; Colorado, 1877; South Dakota, 1882; Wyoming, 1886; Arizona, 1891; New Hampshire, 1891; New Mexico, 1892; Oklahoma, 1892; Montana, 1895; Florida, 1903; Kentucky, 1908; North Dakota, 1918; Maryland, 1920; Delaware, 1921.

University of Central England at Birmingham. *See under* BIRMINGHAM.

University of the West of England at Bristol, *see under* BRISTOL.

UNRRA (United Nations Relief and Rehabilitation Administration). Formed, 1943. Its major tasks were virtually complete early in 1947, the first shipload of its supplies having been dispatched, Mar. 1945.

UNSCOB, a special and temporary committee, established 21 Oct. 1947, by the General Assembly of the UN, charged with solving the problems then involving Greece and neighbouring states.

Upper Volta. *See* BURKINA FASO.

Uppsala, or **Upsala,** Sweden. University founded, 1477. New buildings, 1879–86. The cathedral was built, 1230–1435.

Ur of the Chaldees was founded shortly before 4000 BC. Its recorded history begins not later than 2500 BC. Its resplendent Third Dynasty came to an end, *c.* 2000 BC. Houses *c.* 1800 BC discovered (period of

Abraham). Revival of U. under Nebuchadnezzar II, 605–562 BC and much rebuilding, but city declined and then disappeared c. 300 BC. Excavated by Taylor, 1854; Campbell Thompson and Hall, 1918–19; and Sir Leonard Woolley, 1922–1934.

Uranus, planet discovered by Sir William Herschel, 13 Mar. 1781.

Uriconium Viroconium, near the site of the present village of **Wroxeter,** Shropshire at the crossing of Watling Street over the Severn. A Roman camp here appears to have been laid out c. AD 48 as the quarters of the XIV Legion. When the Legion was transferred to Chester in AD 70 the site continued in civil occupation and expanded to become the tribal capital of the Cornovii. A forum was completed by 130. Extensive damage caused by fire c. 300, but town continued in occupation until c. 350. Further important discoveries announced, July 1995.

Ursuline Nuns. Founded by St Angela Merici, 1535; approved as a religious order by Pope Paul V, 1612.

Uruguay. In 1603 Hernando Arias, the first American-born Spanish governor of La Plata, explored the eastern bank of the Plate River. Portuguese expedition, 1680. The Spaniards in 1726 erected a fort on the site of Montevideo. In 1810 the Creoles of Montevideo joined in the general rising against the Spanish royal garrisons, and besieged Montevideo with the help of republicans from the Argentine. It fell in 1814 to the Argentine General Alvear. The Portuguese invaded the territory from the N in 1816, and from 1820 to 1825 U. was under Brazilian occupation. The war between Brazil and the Argentine republic was terminated at the instance of Britain and France by a treaty of 1828, making U. independent of either. Series of constitutional innovations since 1900, aimed at preventing dictatorship and resulting in periods of collegiate government, e.g. 1917–33, and 1951–66. Army in control, 1978–84, when presidential government re-established.

Sanguinetti (Colorado party) elected president, Nov. 1994.

USSR (Union of Soviet Socialist Republics; Soviet Union), officially existed from the adoption of the constitution, July 1923, to the proclamation of the C.I.S. in Dec. 1991. It originated in the revolution of 1917.

1917: Riots at Petrograd, tsar abdicated, provisional government formed under Prince Lvov, Mar.; Council of Workers and Soldiers formed at Petrograd, Baltic and Black Sea fleets mutinied, Apr.; autonomy granted to Finland and Ukraine, June; National ministry under Kerensky, 6 Aug.; a republic proclaimed, 15 Sept.; 'the *October Revolution', 7 Nov; Kerensky overthrown by Lenin and Trotsky, rise of the Russian Socialist Federal Soviet Republic, Nov.–Dec. Treaty of Brest-Litovsk ends war with Germany, 3 Mar. 1918; tsar and family murdered at Ekaterinburg, 16 July. Civil war, 1919–22 ends in Bolshevik victory; constitution of USSR adopted, 6 July 1923, Lenin d., 1924. Struggle for power followed: Trotsky expelled from Communist party, 1927 and exiled, 1929 (murdered on Soviet orders in Mexico, Aug. 1940) and Stalin in control. Enforced collectivization of land, 1932–4 leads to famine and mass starvation, especially in the Ukraine; programme of industrialization undertaken. Trials of foreign nationals, 1933, and purge of Communist officials and army officers, 1934–8. USSR aids government forces in *Spain 1936–9.

Clashes with Japan in Far E settled, 1939; Russo-German pact signed, 23 Aug. and USSR invades Poland, 17 Sept. and occupies E half of it, forces Baltic States to grant concessions. Invades Finland, 30 Nov. War with Finland ended, 13 Mar. 1940; USSR. occupies Romanian provinces of Bessarabia and N Bukovina, June and Baltic States annexed, Aug.

1941: Germany attacks USSR, 22 June (*see under* WORLD WAR II).

1942: Anglo-Russian 20 Year Treaty;

1943: Teheran meeting of Stalin, Roosevelt and Churchill, Yalta. 1945: World War II ends with USSR in control of E Europe including E Germany.

1948: Berlin blockade; quarrel begins with Tito's *Yugoslavia. Increasingly repressive régime ended with Stalin's death, 5 Mar. 1953; Beria, Minister of the Interior, executed in July. Rise to power of Khruschev from 1955: German prisoners in Russia released and diplomatic relations established between USSR and FGR. Khruschev denounced Stalin in speech to congress of Communist party, 25 Feb. 1956 and dissolution of Cominform announced, 17 Apr. Some liberalization at home, but Russian troops savagely crushed Hungarian revolt (*see* HUNGARY), Nov. USSR making great progress in nuclear development and in space technology. Khruschev addressed UN, 18 Sept. 1959 but Paris Summit of 1960 broke up over *U-2 incident. Berlin Wall built, 1961. Worsening in Soviet-Chinese relations. Cuban crisis settled by Khruschev and Kennedy, Oct. 1962. Nuclear Test Ban Treaty signed by USSR, 1963. Khruschev fell from power, 1964: rise of Brezhnev. In 1968–9 Soviet troops crushed liberal movement in Czechoslovakia. Campaign against dissidents continued but some allowed to settle in W. Relations with USA worsened after Russia invaded Afghanistan, 1979. From 1980 USSR exerted pressure on *Poland to prevent liberalization. Brezhnev *d.*, 1982, and power passed to Andropov. Increased propaganda campaign against NATO; breakdown of arms limitation talks in Geneva, 1983. Andropov *d.*, 1984: succeeded by Chernenko who was succeeded by Gorbachev, 1985. Talks between Gorbachev and US President Reagan in Geneva, 1985; further meeting in Iceland, 1986, ends in failure. Apr. 1986: serious accident at nuclear power station at *Chernobyl. Gorbachev (who was president of the Supreme Soviet, 1988–91 and head of state, 1989–91) introduced many liberal reforms within the USSR including steps towards free market economy. Release of many political prisoners. Arms limitation policy followed abroad; lessening of grip on other Communist states. Economic problems from 1989 and collapse of Soviet system outside the USSR. In Russia itself, rise of Yeltsin from 1991. Attempted coup to oust Gorbachev failed, Aug. 1991, but Gorbachev's hold on power broken thereafter, and Yeltsin the dominant figure. Break-up of the USSR formalized, 21 Dec. 1991, by the formation of the *Commonwealth of Independent States, and resignation of Gorbachev four days later. Russia then assumed USSR's former place at UN. *See further* under RUSSIA.

Effective Soviet leaders 1917–91
Vladimir Ilyich Lenin 1917–24
Joseph Stalin 1924–53
Nikita Khruschev 1953–64
Leonid Brezhnev 1964–82
Yuri Andropov 1982–84
Konstantin Chernenko 1984–85
Mikhail Gorbachev 1985–91

Uttar Pradesh, Indian state, the name, since 1950, of the former *United Provinces.

usury laws. In England, legal maximum interest first fixed, 1545. Interest on loans limited to 8 per cent, 1623; 6 per cent, 1651; 5 per cent, 1713. Restraint removed, 1854.

Utah, USA. Mormons under Brigham Young entered the Salt Lake Valley, 1847. Mexico ceded the territory to the USA, 1848, and territorial government was organized in 1850. State admitted to Union, 4 Jan. 1896. *See* MORMONS.

Utopia, by Sir Thomas More, published in Latin, 1516. In English, 1551.

Utrecht, in the Netherlands, was a bishopric, 696; chartered, 1122. From 1527–77 controlled by the Hapsburgs; subsequently Protestant stronghold. Cathedral built, 1254–1517. The *Paushouse* was completed, 1523 for Adrian VI, the only Dutch b. (in U.) pope. University, 1636. Archbishopric, 1559; suppressed, 1580; revived, 1851.

Utrecht, Treaty of. Between Britain, the United Provinces, and France to end the War of the Spanish Succession, 11 Apr. 1713.

Uzbekistan, republic of, became constituent republic of USSR, 1925. Declared independence, 1991, and joined C.I.S. The area comprising modern U. was overrun by Mongols in 13thC and in 14thC was centre of Timurid empire. Kingdom of *Bokhara from 16thC; absorbed by Russia in 19thC. U. assisted *Tajikistan in war against Muslim fundamentalists, 1993. Indecisive election results, with regional party gains, Dec. 1994. President succeeds in getting vote to postpone next presidential election from 1997 to 2000, Mar. 1995.

vaccination (against smallpox). Conceived and developed by Sir E. Jenner, 1796. Made compulsory in UK, 1853, but no longer so after 1948. Discontinued altogether after *World Health Organization pronounced official global eradication of smallpox, 1980. Proposals to destroy remaining laboratory specimens, 1993. V. developed since 1930s against diphtheria, tetanus, whooping cough, measles, tuberculosis, etc. In the UK V. regulated by the National Health Service Act, 1977. Use of genetically engineered Vs. increasing in 1990s.

Vaccine Damage Payments Act, 1979, gives persons severely disabled as result of vaccination for diseases as prescribed under the Act (e.g. diphtheria, tetanus, rubella, etc.) the right to compensation.

Vagrancy Acts, constituted, with the *Poor Laws, the greater part of English social legislation down to the end of the 18thC, especially under the Tudors. The Act of 1459 authorized the imprisonment of vagrants, that of 1530 whipping, that of 1535 mutilation, to which by the Act of 1597 all entertainers unless employed by some nobleman were also subject. Transportation was authorized by Orders in Council, 1603 and 1662. In 1713 previous Acts were consolidated and rationalized, and branding ceased to be legal. Previous legislation repealed by Consolidation Act, 1740, amended by Vagrancy Acts, 1822, 1824, 1838, etc. Amendments under Sexual Offences Act, 1956, deal with males living on prostitutes' earnings; and Fraudulent Mediums Act, 1951, with persons claiming

to foretell the future. There were further modifications in 1981 and 1982.

Valencia, Spain, mentioned by Livy as existing, 132 BC. Visigothic capital, 413. Captured by Moors, 714 and in 1021 capital of Moorish independent kingdom of V. Taken by El Cid, 1092; retaken by Moors, 1102. In 1238 captured by James I of Aragon; united with Castile, 1479. Government capital during Spanish civil war 1936–9. Cathedral built, 1262–1482. University founded. 1501.

Valencia, Venezuela, was founded, 1555 and was capital of Venezuela in 1812, 1830 and 1858.

Valenciennes, France. Philippa of Hainault married Edward III of England at, 1328. French from 1678. Heavily damaged in both World Wars. V. lace flourished c. 1700–80. There were machine versions from 1850s, and attempts to revive hand-made V. lace in 20thC.

Valetta or **Valletta,** capital of Malta since 1570, constructed 1565, named after Jean de la Valette, Grand Master of the Knights of Malta. Knights expelled. 1798. British took V., 1800 and it was a naval base, 1800–1979; since then converted to commercial use. Italian fleet surrendered at V., 1943. University, 1592. Palace of Grand Masters (1574), now residence of Maltese president.

Valladolid, first mentioned, 1072, as having been recovered from the Moors a hundred years earlier. Residence of Castilian kings from c. 1400. Cathedral begun, 1585.

Valparaiso, Chile. Founded 1536 by Juan de Saavedra; captured by Sir Francis Drake, 1578; sacked by the Dutch, 1600; severe earthquakes, 1730, 1822, 1839, 1873 and 1906.

value added tax (VAT) in Britain, replaced *Purchase Tax, 1973. It is administered by Customs and Excise, not the Inland Revenue. First extended to cover domestic fuel from Apr. 1994; but proposed further extension abandoned after government defeat, Dec.

Van Allen radiation belts, discovered by US physicist James A. Van Allen, 1958.

Vancouver, British Columbia, Canada, originated as a saw-milling centre called Granville in the 1870s; began to be an important commercial city about 1885 on becoming terminus of Canadian Pacific Railway. Incorporated, 1886, and, re-named V. Largely rebuilt after fire, 1886. Third largest city in Canada by 1939. University of British Columbia. 1968; Art Gallery, 1931; Stadium, 1983. Expo, 1986. Much development since 1980 and influx of settlers from Hong Kong.

Vancouver, oldest city in Washington, USA, was founded 1825 as Hudson's Bay Co. trading post; taken over by USA, 1846. City, 1857.

Vancouver Island, British Columbia, discovered and circumnavigated, 1792, by Cap. George Vancouver. (1757–98)

Vandals. Earliest references to V. in Roman authors do not denote any particular people but generally all E Germanic tribes, such as Burgundians and Goths. About AD 330 they were defeated by the Goths, and moved into Pannonia (now Hungary), whence in 406 they migrated via Mainz across Gaul to Spain, where they gave their name to Andalusia ('Vandalitia'), 409. Another detachment settled in Galicia. In May 429 the V. under King Gaiseric, about 160,000 strong, crossed to Africa (Tunisia). They had captured nearly all the principal cities of Africa by 433. By treaty of 30 Jan. 435 the Emperor Valentinian ceded to Gaiseric the whole Roman territory of Africa except Carthage and its province. Gaiseric seized Carthage, 19 Oct. 439, and took and sacked Rome in 455. He built a large navy and conquered the Balearics. Carthage retaken by Count Belisarius, 533, to whom the last known Vandal king, Gelimer, surrendered, 534. No mention of V. made by historians after 536.

Vanuatu, formerly **New Hebrides,** visited by Spaniard de Quiros, 1606; by Bougainville, 1768; and Cook, 1774. Franco-British condominium, 1906; independent, 30 July 1980, as Republic of V. Joined Spearhead Group, 1988.

Vanzetti. *See* SACCO.

Varangian Guard, marine infantry corps of the Byzantine Army performing the same functions as the praetorian cohorts of the old Roman Army. Originally recruited in Sweden by Vladimir the Great, Grand Duke of Kiev, about 977–84, they were transferred by him to the service of Byzantium under Constantine VIII, 999. From then till 1066 the preponderance of recruits from Sweden and the Baltic diminished in favour of Norwegians, Icelanders and other W Scandinavians: after Oct. 1066 Englishmen in increasing numbers joined the V.G., and eventually they and other westerners completely displaced the Swedish and Russian element; they had heavy losses against the Normans at Durazzo, 1082; Edgar Ætheling, who renounced the throne of England, joined the V.G. in 1097. Up to 1453 the regiment still existed, but was exclusively English.

VAT. See VALUE ADDED TAX.

Vatican. A Roman hill, on which a palace, commenced in 1146, became the residence of the Pope in 1377; it is said to contain 7,000 rooms. The popes made the V. their voluntary prison, 1870–1929. Established as a sovereign state, 7 June 1929, as consequence of Mussolini's concordat with the papacy. This treaty was embodied in the constitution of the Italian Republic, 1947, amended Feb. 1984, whereby V. City lost its territorial rights and the Catholic Church in Italy many of its privileges. Diplomatic accord with Israel, 1993.

Vatican Councils. *See* COUNCILS OF THE CHURCH.

Vaud (German **Waadt**), canton of Switzerland. Burgundians settled there, AD 443. Acquired by Counts of Savoy about 1268. Alternated between Savoyard and Bernese rule, 1536–1617, then finally ceded to Berne. Republic of Leman declared, 1798. Entered the Confederation, 1803. Canton

V. replaced designation Canton Leman, 1803.

Vauxhall Gardens (London). Laid out on the S bank of the Thames, 1661. With George IV's permission called Royal, 1822. Closed, 1859.

V-E Day, 8 May 1945, marked end of Second World War in Europe. The anniversary is marked each year in France by a public holiday.

Venetia, originally the land of the Veneti, an Illyrian tribe, who entered the area between 200 and 100 BC; then name applied to same area, as being the metropolitan territory of the republic of *Venice. It consists of three regions of Italy.
Venezia Tridentina (Trentino Alto Adige), ceded by Austria (provinces of Trento and Bolzano, formerly part of Tirol), 1918.
Venezia proper, or *Veneto,* Austrian only from 1815 to 1866, Italian since then.
Venezia Giulia, now known as *Friuli-Venezia Giulia,* acquired in 1918, then comprised the provinces of Fiume, Gorizia, Pola, Trieste and Zara. It was partly occupied by Yugoslav troops in 1945, and by the settlement of 1947 Istria, the Forest of Ternova, and the upper Isonzo valley passed to Yugoslavia (*see* SLOVENIA), reducing the region more or less to the boundaries of medieval Friuli (provinces of Udine and Gorizia), while *Trieste and its surroundings remain under neutral occupation. The agreement of 5 Oct. 1954, however, restored Trieste to Italy, while its surroundings were assigned to the then Yugoslavia.

Venezuela. Became independent of Spain as part of the Federal Republic of Gran Colombia, 1811. Separated from Colombia and set up a separate constitution, 1830. Petroleum production began, 1917. Exports of iron ore (by Bethlehem Steel Corporation) began, Mar. 1951. Venezuelan capital began to enter the country's oil industry, 1956. New constitution 1961. Unrest due to economic problems sporadic since 1988. President Perez changed with corruption, 1993; Velasquez appointed acting president for remainder of term, with special powers from Aug. 1993. Populist Caldera elected, Dec.
Following is a list of heads of the Venezuelan State since 1945:

Betancourt 1945–48
Gallegos (deposed) 1948
Delgado (assassinated) 1948–50
Suarez 1950–52
Perez 1952–58
Larrazabal 1958
Sanabira 1958–59
Betancourt (again) 1959–63
Leoni 1963–69
Caldera 1969–74
Pérez 1974–79
Herrera 1979–84
Lusinchi 1984–89
Perez 1989–93
Velasquez 1993
Caldera 1994–

Venice, Italy. Founded *c.* AD 452. First Doge, Paolo Zucio Anafesto, 697. Beginning naval power under D. Orso Ipato, 726. Venetian navy assists in overthrow of the Lombards, 787. At peace of Aix-le-Chapelle Charlemagne cedes suzerainty of V. to the Byzantines, 810. Seat of government moved from Malamocco to Rialto, 811. St Mark's bones brought to V., 828; present structure of St Mark's church dates from 10th cent, with additions, 13th–17thC cents. Defeat by Muslims in naval battle of Taranto, 839. Death of D. Pietro Candiano I at battle of Zara, 888. Venetian protectorate of Istria established under D. Pietro Candiano II, 932–9. D. Pietro Orseolo II conquers Dalmatia, 999–1000. 'Blessing of the Sea' first instituted, 1001. Commercial and political treaty with Byzantium concedes practical independence, 1081. Defeat of the Normans at Butrinto, 1085. Venetian fleet under D. Vitale Michiel I deserts the First Crusade, 1100. Capture and settlement of Tyre, 1124. Fourth Crusade diverted by D. Enrico Dandolo against Byzantium, 1204. Genoese defeated at Trapani, 1264. Sequins first coined, 1284.

Defeat by Genoese at Curzola, 1297. The Great Council established, 1297. Council of Ten established, 1310. Doges' palace built, 1309–1447. The 'Closure' (*Serrata*) of the Great Council, 1315. Complete defeat of Genoa in the War of Chioggia under D. Andrea Contarini, 1378–81. Acquisition of Padua, 1406; Ravenna, 1441. Commercial treaty with Turks, 1453. Loss of Negropont to the Turks, 1470. Turkish victory at Prevésa, 1530 Loss of Cyprus, 1570. Victory over Turks at Lepanto, 1571. Present Rialto bridge built, 1588–91. Siege and loss of Candia (Crete), 1648–69. Decline of the republic after death of D. Francesco Morosini, 1694. Republic extinguished by Napoleon and ceded to Austria, 1797. Annexed to Italy, 1805. To Austria, 1814. Finally to Italy, 1866. Environmental deterioration of V. evident from 1950s and campaigns for its preservation from 1960s. Solutions to problems included tests on a prototype for a flood barrier in 1988. St Mark's crypt (built *c.* 925) and walled up since 1580, restored and reopened, Dec. 1993. *See also* VENETIA.

The following is a list of doges:

Paolo Zucio Anafesto 697–717
Marcello Tegaliano 717–26
Orso Ipato 726–37
Six masters of soldiers 737–42
Orso Diodato 742–55
Galla Gaulo 755–56
Domenico Monegario 756–65
Maurizio Galbaio 765–87
Giovanni Galbaio 787–804
Obelerio de'Antenori 804–09
Angello Participazio 809–27
Giustiniano Participazio 827–29
Giovanni Participazio I 829–36
Pietro Tradonico 836–64
Orso Participazio I 864–81
Giovanni Participazio II 881–87
Pietro Candiano I 887–88
Pietro Tribuno 888–912
Orso Participazio II 912–32
Pietro Candiano II 932–39
Pietro Participazio 939–42
Pietro Candiano III 942–59
Pietro Candiano IV 959–76

Pietro Orseolo I 976–77
Vitale Candiano 977–78
Pietro Memmo 978–91
Pietro Orseolo II 991–1008
Otho Orseolo 1008–25
Domenico Centranico 1026–32
Domenico Flabianico 1032–43
Domenico Contarini I 1043–71
Domenico Selvo 1071–84
Vitale Falier 1085–96
Vitale Michiel I 1096–1102
Ordelafo Falier 1102–17
Domenico Michiel 1117–30
Pietro Polani 1130–48
Domenico Morosini 1148–56
Vitale Michiel II 1156–72
Sebastiano Ziani 1173–78
Orio Malipiero 1178–92
Enrico Dandolo 1193–1205
Pietro Ziani 1205–29
Giacomo Tiepolo 1229–49
Marin Morosini 1249–52
Renier Zeno 1253–68
Lorenzo Tiepolo 1268–75
Jacopo Contarini 1275–80
Giovanni Dandolo 1280–89
Pietro Gradenigo 1289–1311
Giorgio Marin 1311–12
Giovanni Soranzo 1312–28
Francesco Dandolo 1329–39
Bartolomeo Gradenigo 1339–42
Andrea Dandolo 1343–54
Marino Falier 1354–55
Giovanni Gradenigo 1355–56
Giovanni Dolfin 1356–61
Lorenzo Celsi 1361–65
Marco Cornaro (Corner) 1365–68
Andrea Contarini 1368–82
Michele Morosini 82
Antonio Venier 1382–1400
Michele Steno 1400–13
Tomaso Mocenigo 1414–23
Francesco Foscari 1423–57
Pasquale Malipiero 1457–62
Cristoforo Moro 1462–71
Nicolo Tron 1471–73
Nicolo Marcello 1473–74
Pietro Mocenigo 1474–76
Andrea Vendramin 1476–78
Giovanni Mocenigo 1478–85
Marco Barbarigo 1485–86
Agostino Barbarigo 1486–1501

Leonardo Loredano 1501–21
Antonio Grimani 1521–23
Andrea Gritti 1523–39
Pietro Lando 1539–45
Francesco Donato 1545–53
Marc'antonio Trevisano 1553–54
Francesco Venier 1554–56
Lorenzo Priuli 1556–59
Girolamo Priuli 1559–67
Pietro Loredano 1567–70
Alvise Mocenigo I 1570–77
Sebastiano Venier 1577–78
Nicolo da Ponte 1578–85
Pasquale Cicogna 1585–95
Marin Grimani 1595–1606
Leonardo Donato 1606–12
Marc'antonio Memmo 1612–15
Giovanni Bembo 1615–18
Nicolo Donato 1618
Antonio Priuli 1618–23
Francesco Contarini 1623–24
Giovanni Cornaro (Corner) I 1624–30
Nicolo Contarini 1630–31
Francesco Erizzo 1631–46
Francesco Molin 1646–55
Carlo Contarini 1655–56
Francesco Cornaro 1656
Bertuccio Valier 1656–58
Giovanni Pesaro 1658–59
Domenico Contarini II 1659–74
Nicolo Sagredo 1674–76
Luigi Contarini 1676–83
Marc'antonio Giustinian 1683–88
Francesco Morosini 1688–94
Silvestro Valier 1694–1700
Alvise Mocenigo II 1700–09
Giovanni Cornaro II 1709–22
Alvise (Sebastiano) Mocenigo III 1722–32
Carlo Ruzzini 1732–35
Luigi Pisani 1735–41
Pietro Grimani 1741–52
Francesco Loredano 1752–62
Marco Foscarini 1762–63
Alvise Mocenigo IV 1763–79
Paolo Renier 1779–89
Ludovico Manin 1789–97

Verden. *See* BREMEN (3).

Vermont, USA, first settled by French under Samuel Champlain, 1609. English and Dutch infiltration began with the 18thC and a British fort was built at Battleboro in 1724. Intensive settlement began after the cession of Canada, 1760. Between then and the revolution the territory was disputed between the states of New York and New Hampshire. Independence declared, 1777; but state not admitted to Union (14th) until 1791.

Verner's Law. Phonetic law propounded, 1875, by the Danish philologist, Karl Adolf Verner (1846–96).

Verona, Italy, was a Roman colony in 89 BC. Captured by Charlemagne, 774; became an independent republic, 1107. Mastino and Cangrande Scaliger, Lords of V., entertained the exiled Dante, 1291–1329. Added to Milanese territory under Galleazzo Visconti, 1387; but passed to Venice, 1405. Ceded to Austria, 1797; part of Italy since 1866. The last of the Scaligers, Brunoro della Scala, *d.* at Vienna, 1434. Heavily damaged in World War II. Congress of V. at, 1822. *See also* VENICE.

Versailles. A town in NW France near Paris; here Louis XIII built a hunting-box on the site of which Louis XIV erected a palace, 1661–87; First Treaty of V., 1783; surrendered to Germans, 1870 and German Kaiser crowned there, 1871. Seat of French government, 1871–9 and constitution of Third Republic proclaimed at, 1875. *See end of* WORLD WAR I for Second Treaty. Church of Notre Dame began, 1684; church of St Louis, 1743–54 is now the cathedral of V.

Verulamium, near St Albans, England was the tribal capital of the Catuvellauni, established about AD 1. Roman *municipium c.* AD 45. Boudicca (Boadicea) sacked V. in the Icenian rising, 61, but it continued to develop until about 200. St Alban martyred near, 303. St Germanus found it still inhabited in 429. The theatre was excavated in 1847; parts of the forum in 1898. In 1930 a comprehensive excavation scheme was begun, which has made it possible to trace the complete plan of the Roman town; and excavations continue, 1995.

Vesuvius (Italy). Volcano on the Bay of Naples. An eruption in AD 79 totally destroyed Pompeii and *Herculaneum. Last considerable eruption, 1944.

Vice-Chancellor. The first judicial V.-C., Sir Thomas Plumer (1753–1824), appointed, 1813; two additional V.-Cs. appointed, 1841; they became judges of the High Court of Justice, 1873. The last V.-C. was Sir James Bacon (1798–1895), appointed, 1870; retired, 1886.

Vichy, France, celebrated for its mineral waters. Known to the Romans, but did not become famous till the 17thC. French puppet government established here after capitulation of France, 1 July 1940, and the word V. became synonymous with 'collaborator'.

Victoria, state of Australia, became a colony separate from New S Wales, 1851. Following on the reports of Capt. Cook, who did not, however, land there, a party of convicts was sent out in 1785, to the site of Port Jackson. First permanent settlement by Edward Henty at Portland Bay, 19 Nov. 1834. Melbourne founded, 1835. Civil Government established, 1839. Responsible government conferred, 23 Nov. 1855. State, 1901.

Victoria, British Columbia, Canada, founded, 1843, by Hudson's Bay Co., and called Fort Camosun. Named Victoria, and made capital of Vancouver Island colony, 1849. Ceased to be capital when Vancouver Island was united with British Columbia, 1866; but capital status restored, 1868.

Victoria and Albert Museum (London). Originated as the Museum of Ornamental Art, 1852; merged in the S Kensington Museum, 1857. Foundation stone of present building laid in 1899 by Queen Victoria; opened in 1909 by King Edward VII and Queen Alexandra. Indian gallery, 1990; Chinese gallery, 1991.

Victoria Cross. For bravery in the forces, instituted 1856. The cross was manufactured out of the cannon taken from the Russians at Sevastopol, until the supply

ran out in 1942. The colour of the ribbons, originally blue for the Navy and red for the Army, was changed to crimson for all services in 1918.

Victoria Falls or **Mosi-oa-Tunya Falls** (on the Zambesi, Africa). Discovered by Livingstone in 1855; spanned by a bridge of the Cape to Cairo railway, 1905. Hydroelectric station 1938.

Victoria Falls Conference. 28 June-4 July 1963, held to wind up the Federation of *Rhodesia and Nyasaland.

Victoria, (now **Victoria-Nyanza) Lake**, Africa. Discovered by Speke, 1858; Wilson and Smith first voyaged across the lake, 1877; divided between England and Germany, 1890. Germans driven out, 1916.

Victory, HMS, was launched at Chatham, 7 May 1765; commissioned, 1778. Flagship of Howe, 1782; Hood, 1793; and Nelson, 1797–1805. Paid off from active service, 1812. Became flagship of C.-in-C., Portsmouth. 1825; permanently placed in dry dock, 1922, and restored throughout and re-rigged.

video-cameras, use in criminal cases confirmed, 1993, when arrests were made as the result of evidence on Vs. in a child murder case in Merseyside, and relating to a terrorist bombing outside Harrods in London (in 1992).

Vienna (Wien) capital of the Austrian republic, was an inhabited site when the Romans laid out the camp of Vindobona, AD 180. Name appears in something like its modern form in documents of 881. The Babenberg margraves of Austria chose V. for their seat, 1142, and granted charters, 1221. Became an imperial free city, 1237. Capital of Hapsburgs, 1278. University founded, 1365. After Austrian empire fell, V. counted as a province equal to the other Austrian provinces. 12thC cathedral destroyed by fire and rebuilt, 14th–16thC; damaged during World War II. Its 20-ton bell cast from captured Turkish cannons, 1711. Vienna State Opera House, 1865, destroyed, 1945; rebuilding finished, 1955. V.

was occupied by Russian forces, April 1945 and from then till 1955 divided into four zones. Austrian State Treaty, signed in V., May 1955, led to Austrian independence and withdrawal of foreign troops.

Vienna, Congress of. Opened, 1 Nov. 1814. Closed, 8 June 1815. Representatives of all the powers of Europe, led by Britain, Austria, Prussia, Russia and France, met to settle the internal frontiers, etc., of Europe after the Napoleonic Wars. By it Poland was placed under Russian suzerainty. N Italy was largely restored to Austria, Prussia received the Rhineland and part of Saxony, and Hanover, E Frisia and Hildesheim. The German confederacy was organized under Austrian presidency, and Cracow made an independent republic.

Vienne, Council of, 1311–12. Decided the abolition of the *Templars.

Viet Cong, a guerrilla force opposed to the official government of S Vietnam from the 1950s, and subsequently to the USA (till 1973). In 1960 the V.C. became the military arm of the National Liberation Front. It was supplied from N Vietnam, though the bulk of its members came from the S.

Viet Minh, established in China by Ho Chi Minh, May 1941, and fought the Japanese in Vietnam from 1943. After France refused to recognize the Democratic Republic of Vietnam, 1946, V.M. directed campaign against France. Absorbed into other organizations from 1950, some elements joining the *Viet Cong.

Vietnam, at first under Japanese protection, intermittently at war with France (1945–9) when by unification of the provinces of Tongking, Annam and Cochin China, V. became an integral part of the French Union. Convention signed between France and the Emperor Bao Dai, Dec. 1949. France transferred all sovereign rights to V., Dec. 1954, but retained military authority there until 1956. The civil war between Communists and anti-Communists split V. into N and S zones from 1946, the French influence extending

only over the S zone. During 1951–3 the Communists in the N made gains at the expense of the S. The Geneva Agreement of 20 July 1954 brought about a cessation of official hostilities between N and S. South V. became a republic in Oct. 1955, with Ngo Dinh Diem as president. He was assassinated, 1963, and a series of unstable régimes, with partial US backing, followed. From 1959 a state of civil war existed between N V., led by the veteran Communist Ho Chi Minh until his death in 1969, and S V. American 'advisers' sent to help the S, 1960. In 1965 American troops committed to fighting in V.: by the end of the year there were nearly ¼ million US troops there. American planes bombed N V. War had debilitating effect on US morale at home; agreement signed in Paris, 27 Jan. 1973, ending the war and US troops withdrawn. But fighting between N and S continued until final defeat of the S in 1975. President Thieu resigned 21 Apr. and S V. Army surrendered to the N, 30 Apr. Marxist régime for whole country adopted; new constitution, Dec. 1980. Poor relations with China from 1979 and open hostilities, 1979–80. Expulsion of 'boat-people', during 1980s: some returned from Hong Kong in 1990s. New constitution, 1992, remained Marxist but allowed for free market economics, which applied increasingly from 1989. Increased liberalization from 1990 onwards with an elected National Assembly meeting, 1992; but effective power remaining in hands of Communist party. USA lifted trade embargo on V., Feb. 1994 and reopened embassy in V., Aug. 1995. V. joined *Association of South East Asian Nations in July 1995.

Viking Age proper extended from the 8th to the 11thC. But excursions of Scandinavian pirates, though less frequent, did occur earlier. Thus a seaborne raid of the Gautar (Geatas) under their King Hugleikr (Chocilaicus or Hygelac) was made on Frisia about AD 530. Irish sources describe Scandinavian raids on the Hebrides and coast of Donegal in the 7thC. Danes began intermittent land warfare with the Franks after giving asylum to Wittekind of

Saxony, 777. Three ships from Hordaland in Norway raided Dorset about 790; Lindisfarne sacked, 793; Jarrow sacked, 794; Norwegians in Skye, 795; Man, 798; Iona, 802; and Sligo, 807; Armagh sacked, 832. Turgeis (Thorgest) made himself King of Ulster, 841; but drowned by Irish, 844.

Danish attacks on England began, 833; on Ireland, 849; on Holland, 833; on Seine valley, 841; on Spain, Portugal, Morocco, 844; Paris besieged, and Hamburg sacked, 845. Danes under Björn and Hasteinn first entered Mediterranean from the W, 860, and ravaged Provence, the Balearics, Liguria, parts of Tuscany and Morocco until 862. Danish penetration of Frisia and Rhineland stopped by King Lothair II (855–69). Raids in Flanders, 882–5. Paris besieged again, 885–6, but Danes defeated at Verdun in June, and by Duke Alan in Brittany, 888. Evacuated to Kent, 892. Returned, 902, reinforced by Norwegians under Rollo (Hrolfr), who did homage for the fief of Normandy at Clair Sur-Epte, 911. Cork settled (by Danes) about 900.

Campaigns in England by the sons of Ragnar, 855–6 (mainly in Kent), by Guthrum (Guttorm), 866–78. King Edmund martyred, 870; truce in 876. Treaty of Wedmore, 878, gave most of Northumbria and Mercia to Danes. English recover London and W Essex, 886. Campaign by Hasteinn's army (*see* above), 892–7; the army beaten by Alfred and disbanded. The Danelaw reconquered, 914–20. Svein Forkbeard, allied to Olaf Tryggvason (*see* NORWAY), attacks Ethelred, 994–1014; Svein's son Knut succeeds to English crown, 1016. *See* DANEGELD and SHIP-MONEY.

Norwegian: the court of the Norse king of Dublin described by an embassy sent to Abd-er-Rahman II, Emir of Cordoba (*d.* 852). Norse settlements in Ireland plundered by Danes, 851. Olaf the White arrived in Ireland, 853; became joint King of Dublin; went back to Norway, 873. Dublin captured by the Irish, 902, and Vs. expelled, but returned, 914, to capture Waterford and (916) Dublin. Norwegians kill the High King Niall Glundubh at Kilmashogue, 919. Norse-Welsh-Scottish confederacy beaten at Brunanburh (in Galloway?), 938. Irish resistance stiffens about 940 under King Muirchertach of Ailech, and in 980 the High King Maelsechlainn II defeated the Dublin and Hebridean Norsemen at Tara. Brian Boru beats Ivar of Limerick at Sulcoit (968) and becomes King of Munster, 976, and High King, 1002. He captured Dublin, 1000, but returned it to his son-in-law, Sigtrygg Silkbeard, whom he defeated again, together with a Norse coalition, including Earl Sigurd of Orkney, at Clontarf on Good Friday, 1014.

Punitive expedition by King Harald Fairhair of Norway, following on his victory at Stiklestad (872), established his suzerainty over the W coast of Scotland, Man, the Hebrides and all N Atlantic islands except Iceland, 873. Earl Sigurd of Orkney and Thorsteinn the Red conquer Scotland as far S as Strath Oykel, 874. Sigurd the Thick (*d.* 1014) conquered Scotland as far S as Strath Spey – Moor of Rannoch – Strath Fillan – Loch Long. The last Norse earl of Orkney *d.* 1231, but Scottish earls continued to do homage to the King of Norway (*see* LORD OF THE ISLES). Hebridean sovereignty renounced by King Magnus Hakonarson of Norway, 1266, as result of battle of Largs, 1263, which date is usually taken as end of V.A.

Swedish expansion, exclusively E across the Baltic, is first recorded in 853 (attempt to reconquer Kurland from Danes, whose king, Gorm the Old, 900–40, made wide conquests in Pomerania). Danish base at Jomsborg set up by Harald Bluetooth (936–86) was destroyed, 1043, by the Norse King Magnus the Good. Russian chronicles first mention Swedish raiders in 859. Expelled in 862, they returned to Russia (to which they gave their name) at the invitation of certain Slav clans in the same year, when Rurik became prince of Novgorod. In 865 Rurik absorbed two other principalities, and Hoskuld and Dir founded Kiev, which was conquered by Oleg (Helgi) of Novgorod, 882. Commercial treaties with Byzantium, 911 and 944. Swedish-Russian habits described in detail by the Arab diplomat Ibn Fadhlan, 921. 'Varangians' mentioned for the last time in Russian chronicles, 1043, by which time (reign of Yaroslav of Kiev, 1036–54) the Scandinavian ruling class had become Slavonic in language and Greek Orthodox in religion. *See also* Man, Isle of; Hebrides; Orkney Islands; Norway; Denmark; Sweden; Ireland; Normandy; East Anglia; Mercia; Northumbria, Kingdom of; Varangian Guard.

Vilnius (Russian **Vilnyus**, formerly **Vilna**: Polish, **Wilno**) was founded *c.* 1100, became capital of the Grand Duchy of Lithuania *c.* 1323. Partially destroyed by the Teutonic Knights, 1377. Became an episcopal see, 1387 (when the Catholic cathedral of St Stanislaus was begun); after Lithuanian union with Poland, under Casimir IV, 1427–92, V. became a centre of Polish culture. In the Third Partition of Poland (1795) V. and its province fell to the Russian share. Occupied by German troops, 1915-Dec. 1918, during which time (Feb. 1918) the independence of Lithuania was proclaimed, with V. as capital. V. assigned to Poland by Entente council of ambassadors, 15 Mar. 1923. On collapse of Poland in 1939, the USSR handed over V. to the republic of Lithuania. Russian 1940–91 except for German occupation, 1941–5. V. scene of Russian-Lithuanian conflict, 1991 prior to recognition of Lithuanian independence, since when it has again been made capital.

Vimy Ridge Memorial to Canadian soldiers killed storming the ridge, 9–10 Apr. 1917; unveiled by Edward VIII, 1936.

Vindictive. British cruiser which figured in Sir Roger Keyes's attack on Zeebrugge mole, 23 Apr., and was sunk in the blocking attack on Ostend, 9–10 May 1918.

Virginia, USA. The first permanent English settlement in N America, 1607, by members of the London Co., led by John Smith. African slaves first imported, 1619. Indian raids, 1622, 1644, 1676. Became a crown colony, 1624. Williamsburg became the state capital, 1699. Founder member of the Union. Seceded from the Union, 1861, (Richmond becoming the Confederate capital), whereupon Federal sympathisers set up the separate state of W V. From 1867 until its readmission to the Union in 1870, V., as 'military district No. 1', was governed by a Federal general.

Virgin Islands, W Indies. Discovered by Columbus, 1493. Some probably included in Charles I's grant of the Caribbean Islands to Earl of Carlisle, 2 July 1627. First settlement by Dutch buccaneers, in Tortola, 1648; ousted by British, 1672 and British V. I. retain colonial status (1995). Denmark made first permanent settlement (in St Croix, St Thomas and St John), 1672. Spain had Culebra, Culebrita and Vieques. The Spanish islands passed to USA, 1898. Danish islands bought by USA, 1917. The United States' V.I. are governed under rules passed by the US Congress, 1954. Since 1970 there have been popular elections for government. Plans for a referendum at some future date to determine V.I. future status not yet finalized, 1995.

Visigoths, the western group of the tribes collectively known as *Goths separated from the eastern or Ostrogothic branch *c.* AD 376, when most of the V. followed their king Frithigern across the Danube into Moesia. By a treaty of 381 the V. entered the Roman service as *foederati*, and their king Athanaric was received with honour at Constantinople in that year. On the death of the Emperor Theodosius, 395, the V. elected Alaric (*d.* 410) king, and turned against the Empire: they besieged Rome itself in 408, 409 and 410, the last time they sacked the city. Alaric was succeeded by Ataulfus, who married the Emperor Honorius's sister, Placidia, and led the V. into SW Gaul and to Spain, where he was murdered in 415. His successor, Wallia, set up a Visigoth kingdom, centring upon Toulouse. At the battle of Chalons, 451 (*see* Ostrogoths), Theodoric I, king of the V., was killed leading them against the Huns and their Germanic vassal tribes. Under Euric (466–85) the centre of gravity of the Visigoth state shifted to Spain. Though now much romanized the V. adhered to the Arian heresy (*see* Arianism), and in 507, under Alaric II, were defeated by the more barbarous but Catholic Franks, but protected by the Ostrogothic King Theodoric; they did not become a separate kingdom again until he *d*. in 526. The most successful Visigoth kings in Spain were Leovogild (568–86) and his son Recared (586–601), the latter of whom by becoming Catholic reconciled the Roman interests with his own, though at the cost of abandoning the *Gothic language. A code of Visigoth laws, issued *c*. 654 under Recceswinth, survives. The Visigoth kingdom finally perished at the hands of the Muslim emirs, 711.

Vitoria. Capital of Alava, Spain. Founded, 581, by Leovogild, King of the Visigoths. A decisive victory, which freed Spain from France, was fought here during the Peninsular War, 1813.

V-J Day, 15 Aug. 1945, marked formal conclusion of Second World War conflict with Japan.

Vlachs, name applied to the Latin-speaking Provincials of *Dacia; the bulk of them withdrew southwards over the Danube, AD 270, and in the 6th and 7thC inhabited Macedonia, Thrace and parts of Epirus. Continually displaced by Avars, Magyars and Slavs they became pastoral nomads, and are mentioned as such by Byzantine sources in 976. They set up an independent empire which reoccupied part of Dacia, and came to an end, 1257. Another branch inhabited Thessaly about 1050, and were conquered by the Turks, 1393. About 1150 there was a Vlach colony in Dalmatia, and another in Montenegro. *See* ROMANIA and BESSARABIA.

Vladivostok. Founded as a Russian military port, 1860 and in 1872 became Russia's principal Pacific naval base. Town since 1875. Grew rapidly after railway developments, end of 19thC; E terminus of Trans-Siberian Railway. Occupied by foreign troops, 1918. When these finally left, 1922, Soviet government established in V. In Sept. 1993, the parliament of the Maritime Territory, meeting in V., voted to declare itself a republic.

Vlöne, Albania (Italian **Valona**: Greek **Avlona**; anciently *Aulon*). Occupied by Robert Guiscard the Norman, AD 1080. Retaken by Byzantines, 1085. Passed by marriage to kingdom of Sicily, 1295; thereafter alternately under Serbian rule or that of local despots, subject to Venice. Turkish, 1691–1912. Temporary capital of Albania, 1913. Occupied by Italians, 28 Dec. 1915 and 7 Apr. 1939. Reverted to Albania, 1945.

Vojvodina, nominally autonomous region of Serbia with only half its population ethnic Serbs. Serbia abolished V.'s autonomy in practice in Sept 1990. Rioting followed in 1991 and 1992 but was suppressed.

volcanoes. Major historic volcanic eruptions include:

Mt Mazama, Oregon, USA, *c*. 5000 BC
Island of Thera, Greece, *c*. 1450 BC
Mt Vesuvius, Italy, 79
Mt Etna, Sicily, 1169
Mt Vesuvius, Italy, 1631
Mt Etna, Sicily, 1669
Mt Unzen-Dake, Japan, 1792
Mt Tamboro, Indonesia, 1815
Mt Krakatoa, Indonesia, 1883
Mt Pelée, Martinique, 1902
Mt St Helens, Washington, USA, 1980
Mt Etna, Sicily, 1983
Mt Nevado el Ruiz, Colombia, 1985
Mt Hudson, Chile, 1991
Mt Pinatubo, Philippines, 1992
Mt Mayon, Philippines, 1993

Effects of Vs. on global weather conditions and ozone layer have been increasingly monitored and understood since 1970s. Estimated that 1980 Mt St Helens eruption affected climate globally; that 1991 Mt Hudson eruption wiped out 15% of Antarctic ozone layer; and that 1992 Mt Pinatubo eruption also caused global climatic reactions into 1994.

Volga German Republic. *See* GERMAN VOLGA REPUBLIC.

Volkssturm, German home defence force raised at the instance of Heinrich Himmler

(1900–45) in his capacity as C.-in-C. Home Forces and Reinforcements, 18 Oct. 1944.

Volgograd name, since 1961 of *Stalingrad which in turn called **Tsaritsin** until 1925. Originally a military outpost, built 1589 to protect farmers from predatory nomads, it was captured by the Cossack mutineer, Stenka Razin. 1670. In 1918 defended by Stalin and Voroshilov against anti-Bolsheviks. Industrialized 1923–39, and population grew 20-fold. Devastated during World War II: rebuilt and population approaching 1 million, 1995.

Volsci. The greatest enemies of Rome during the first century of the Roman Republic; they lived in S Latium. They were subdued by Rome, 338 BC, and enjoyed Roman citizenship by 304.

Volturno, Italy. The colony of Volturnum was founded here, 194 BC, by the Romans. In 1860 the Neapolitans were defeated at the V. River by Garibaldi's army. German defensive position on V. forced by Anglo-American Fifth Army, Oct. 1943.

Voluntary Service Overseas (VSO). Started by Alec Dickson, 1958, with idea of young Britons devoting a year between school and university to work overseas helping local projects including building, teaching, etc. Initially no government funding. 14 volunteers to three countries in first year. 1959, first government aid and 61 volunteers to 18 countries. In 1962 Community Service Volunteers (CSV) established to organize similar voluntary service in UK. British Council became overseer for overseas projects. By 1971 1500 volunteers working overseas. In 1982 privately raised funds first topped £1 million. In 1995 VSO had volunteers extending into three-year programmes, with average age 30, but increased appeal to those over 50. Active all over Third World. VSO probable inspiration for US *Peace Corps.

Volunteers (English). Honourable Artillery Co. granted charter by Henry VIII in 1537; V. organized on a larger scale, 1757; English and Scottish V. were disbanded,

1783, but raised again, 1794; National Volunteer force established, 1860; in 1900 V. supplied many service companies for the S African War; converted into the Territorial force, 1908. For Local Defence V. *see* HOME GUARD.

Voodoo, Haitian cult, dates from French colonization of Haiti and importation of African slaves in 17thC. Combination of Catholic and pagan beliefs deriving from W Africa. Prominent during rule of the Duvaliers, 1957–86, but influence continues after.

Voortrekkers. The Great Trek of Afrikaners out of Cape Colony began in 1836. Columns under Pieter Uys and Hendrik Potgieter defeated the Matabele king, Moselekatze, 1837. Zulus decisively defeated by Andries Pretorius at Blood River, 16 Dec. 1838. Republic of Natal proclaimed, 1840; the whole country N to the Limpopo open to European settlement by *c.* 1848. Monument to the V. at Voortrekkerhoogte, near Pretoria, dedicated, 1949.

Vorarlberg, province of Austria, acquired piecemeal by Hapsburgs, 1375–1765, consolidated by Maria Theresa. Josef II amalgamated it with *Tirol, 1782. Ceded to Bavaria, 1805, but retroceded, 1814.

Voronezh, Russia. Founded in 1586 to rebuff Tatars, but burned by them, 1590; here Peter the Great built boats for conquest of Azov; three times almost destroyed by fire: 1703, 1748, 1773. Heavy fighting in 1919, and 1942–3.

Votes. *See* FRANCHISE.

Vryheid, town and county in Natal, were ceded to a group of Boers (Lukas Beyer and others) by the Zulus, 1884. Independent republic until 1888.

VSO. *See* VOLUNTARY SERVICE OVERSEAS.

Vukovar, Croatian port, surrendered to Serb forces after three-month siege in 1991, during which it was virtually destroyed.

Vulgate. Latin version of the Bible prepared by St Jerome during the last quarter of the 4thC. First printed *c.* 1455; first dated edition, 1462; critical edition issued by order of Sixtus V, 1590; superseded by that of Clement VIII, 1592; translated by Wycliffe and his followers, 1356–84. Authorized Catholic translations into English: New Testament, Rheims, 1582; Old Testament, Douai, 1609–10; by R. A. Knox, New Testament, 1943; Old Testament, 1948–9. 'Jerusalem Bible', 1966.

Vyborg (Russian), **Viborg** (Swedish), **Vipuri** (Finish), grew up round a Swedish castle built by Torgils Knutsson, 1293. Became Russian, 1710, and Finnish, 1917. Ceded to Russia, 31 Mar. 1940; recaptured by Finns in the autumn of 1941; retaken by Russians, 21 June 1944.

Waco, Texas, USA, scene of an FBI siege of a compound containing armed and unarmed members of an extreme religious sect, which lasted 51 days. It began 18 Feb. 1993 and ended 19 April in the mass suicide of the 80 cult members still in the compound, several of whom were British. Some of the survivors prosecuted for alleged murder, 1994, and two Britons jailed for 40 years, June.

Wadai. Once a powerful native state in the Sudan. Kingdom founded, 1635. Notorious as a slave-raiding state; came under French influence, 1899; annexed by France, 1909. Part of Chad Republic since 1960.

Wadi Halfa, Sudan. The British base in 1884 in the operations for the unsuccessful relief of General Gordon.

wages. First fixed by Act of Parliament, 1350. Act prohibiting payment of miners' wages in public houses, 1872; extended to wages generally, 1883. Wages payable by cheque from 31 Mar. 1963. Present W. legislation in Britain includes Equal Pay Act, 1970; Sex Discrimination Act, 1975; Race Relations Act, 1976; Employment Protection (Consolidation) Act, 1978; Wages Act, 1986. *See also* next article. *See* TRUCK ACTS.

Wages Councils, established 1909 in the UK; fixed statutory minimum wages for the lowest paid. W.C. for 16–21 year olds abolished, 1986; remaining W.C. abolished, 1993 (with exception of Agricultural Wages Board: this reprieved, 1994). Labour party proposed reinstatement of W.C., 1994.

Wahabis. Muslim Puritan sect founded by Mohammed ibn Abd al Wahhab (1703–87), son of a shepherd in Central Arabia. He converted Mohammed ibn Sa'ud, ruler of Derayeh, who married his daughter, and *d.* 1765: the Wahabi dynasty began with that daughter's son, Abd al Aziz, who spread Wahabi doctrines throughout Arabia. Wahabi rule established in E Arabia, by Faizul, 1830. Wahabi Army in India crushed at Balakot, 1831. The remnants retired to Mahában on NW Frontier, whither punitive expeditions were sent against them in 1853 and 1858; Indian W. finally defeated at Ambéla Pass, 15 Dec. 1863.

Wailing Wall, Jerusalem. Fighting between Jews and Muslims, Aug. 1929. In Old City, occupied by Jordan during and after Israelite-Arab War, 1948–9; after 'June War' of 1967 Israel recovered access to W.W.

waits. A wait was a city watchman, who sounded his pipe or trumpet during the night. As early as 13thC a small band of wind-musicians maintained by a city was called W. By 18thC the name was applied to those who went round at Christmas time playing and singing carols.

Walcheren Island, Holland. British expedition under the second Earl of Chatham and Sir R. Strachan after capturing Flushing, 1809, came to a disastrous end and was withdrawn. Flooded and severely damaged in the course of allied reconquest, Nov. 1944. Monument to British Commandos unveiled, June 1952. Dykes burst again, Jan.–Feb. 1953.

Waldeck, a German county of the 12thC, was united with Pyrmont, 1621, and became a principality, 1712; joined the Germanic League, 1815. From 1919 to 1928 W. was a separate province of the Weimar republic, but was absorbed by Prussia, 1929.

Waldenses or **Vaudois.** A sect founded, 1176, at Lyons by Peter Waldo. Their doctrine prohibited by the Lateran Council, 1179; and W. included in an excommunicating Bull by Lucius III, 1184. Majority driven from France at time of the persecution of the *Albigenses, 1209, they took refuge in Piedmont, where their persecution began, 1220. Again ex-communicated, 1231. Many went to Calabria in 14thC and 15thC. About 1532 they joined the Reformation. Those left in France again persecuted, 1545–55. Those in Piedmont attacked, 1655, when Cromwell obtained some respite for them. Persecutions recommenced, 1685, on revocation of Edict of Nantes. Many went to Switzerland from Piedmont. In 1689 they tried to recover their Piedmont valleys. Received permission to return, 1694; again exiled, 1698–?1740. They had liberty of conscience, 1799–1814. Civil and religious liberty accorded, 1848, in kingdom of Sardinia.

Waldstätte. 'Forest Cantons' Uri, Schwyz and Unterwalden united in Perpetual League, 1291, to form the nucleus of Switzerland.

Wales. Occupied at the time of the Roman invasion, 55 BC, by five tribes, the Gangani and Decangi, the Ordovices, the Demetae and the Silures; Caractacus defeated by the Romans, AD 43, taken prisoner to Rome, 50; conquest of Silures and Ordovices by Julius Frontinus and Agricola, 78; Welsh became Christian c. 300, and maintained this faith when the rest of the island was repaganized; withdrawal of Romans, early 5thC; warfare with the Saxons: St David preaching in, c. 550; battle of Deorham, 577; with the Angles: battle of Chester c. 613; battle of Hatfield and death of Edwin, King of the Angles, 633; Cadwallon slain soon after in battle; continued dissension among the Welsh princes; the N Welsh king Rhodri the Great (844–78) defeated the Danes; peaceful reign of Hywel the Good, who drew up a code of laws, 10thC; Gruffydd ap Llewelyn became king of Gwynedd, 1039, and killed (1044) Howel ap Edwin; defeated Gruffydd ap Rhydderch and became king of all W., 1055, and was finally crushed and slain by Harold and Tostig, 1063; gradual conquest of country by William the Conqueror and his sons; expedition into, under Henry I,

1121; general uprising under Ap Rhys, 1135, and victory over English at Cardigan, 1136; N and S divided between his sons and those of Ap Cynan; expedition into of Henry II, 1157, and peace concluded with princes of the N and S; later unsuccessful raid, 1169; peace made with Rhys ap Gruffydd, the ruling lord of S W.; Llewelyn ap Iorwerth became powerful in the N and married King John's bastard daughter Joan, 1206; joined the rebelling barons, became Prince of All W., d. 1240; disputes between various claimants to the kingship, among them Prince Edward, Henry III's son; victory of Llewelyn ap Gruffydd over English at Dynevor, 1255; peace concluded with Henry, 1267, and Llewelyn declared Prince of W.; Llewelyn refused homage to Edward I; invasion by the English king, and Llewelyn starved into submission, 1277; oppression of natives by English officers, and fresh rising under Llewelyn and Dafydd; English put to flight at the Menai Straits, and Llewelyn finally slain near Builth, 1282; completion of conquest by Edward I, 1283; Statute of Rhuddlan enacted, 1284; Owain Glyndwr's rebellion, 1400–15; Richmond (Henry VII) landed in Pembroke, 1485; Council of W. under Bishop Rowland Lee, 1534; W. incorporated into England, Act of 1535; Monmouthshire detached, 1536; great sessions established, 1542: Welsh Bible translated, 1567–88; Council abolished, 1689; circulating schools, 1730; Growth of Methodism in W., 18thC; industrialization in S Wales, 19thC, and Welsh language increasingly threatened; but moves to preserve and revive it from second half of 19thC, strengthened in 20thC. Intermediate Education Act, 1889; Welsh Land Commission, 1893–4; investiture of Prince of W. at Caernarvon Castle, 1911; Welsh National Library begun, 1911; Welsh nationalism took political form with foundation of *Plaid Cymru, 1925. Cardiff made capital of W., Dec. 1955. Prince Charles invested as Prince of W. at Caernarvon, 1 July 1969. Office of Secretary of State for Wales created, 1964. Local government reorganization in 1972 returned some border territories to W.

Rundown of coal and heavy industries in W. from 1970s: growth of light industry in S. Referendum in W. 1979, rejected Home Rule. Welsh language given equal standing with English in W., 1992. Local government reform to divide W. into 22 unitary authorities, 1996. *See also* WELSH LITERATURE.

Wales, Calvinistic Methodist Church of, arose *c.* 1735. Its connection with English Methodism ceased before 1750.

Wales, Church in. There being no separate Welsh administration, either religious or secular, under the Tudors, its origin has the same date as the *Church of England. Bills for the Disestablishment of the (Anglican) Church in Wales were introduced in 1895 and 1909; a third Act, passed in 1914, did not become operative until 31 Mar. 1920. As a result of this the Welsh dioceses were increased to six by the creation of the sees of Monmouth and Swansea and Brecon in 1921 and 1923. In 1993 the church's Governing Body passed second reading of Bill for *ordination of women, but rejected the measure at third reading in April 1994. 120,000 members and over 1,700 parishes in 1994. Question of women's ordination again being voted on, 1995. *See also* CATHEDRALS, CHURCH IN WALES.

Wales, Princes of: *Welsh Princes only:*

Maelgwn Gwynedd ?–550
Rhun ap Maelgwn 547–84
Cadvan 584–617
Cadwaladr ap Cadwallon 617–34
Idwal ap Cadwaladr 634–61
Rhodri Molwynog 661–728
Cynan and Hywel 728–55
Mervyn Frych 825–44
Rhodri the Great 844–77
Anarawd, Cadell, and Mervyn 877–943
Idwal Foel 915–43
Hywel Dda, the Good 909–50
Ieuan and Iago 948–79
Hywel ap Ieuaf 979–84
Cadwallon II 984–86
Meredith ap Owen 986–99

Idwal (II) ap Meyric ap Idwal Foel 992–97
Aedan (usurper) 998
Llewelyn ap Seisyll 1018–23
Gruffydd ap Llewelyn ap Seisull 1039–63
Bleddyn, Rhiwallon, Meredith ap Owain 1067–73
Trahaiarn ap Caradoc 1073–79
Meilir 1073–79
Caradoc 1073–79
Gruffydd ap Cynan 1079–1137
Rhys ap Tewdwr 1079–1137
Cadwgan ap Bleddyn 1079–1137
Iorwerth ab Bleddyn 1079–1137
Owain Gwynedd 1137–69
Howel ab Owain Gwynedd 1169–94
Daffydd ap Owain Gwynedd 1169–94
Llewelyn (II) ap Iorwerth, the Great 1194–1240
Dafydd ap Llewelyn 1240–46
Llewelyn (III) ap Gruffydd ('Llewelyn y Llyw Olaf') 1246–82

From 1301 the Prince of Wales has always been the eldest son of the English sovereign.

Wales, University of. Received full charter, 1893; the university then consisted of three colleges: Aberystwyth, 1872; Cardiff, 1883; and Bangor, 1884. To these have been added: University College of Swansea, 1920; University College of Medicine (Cardiff), 1931; St David's University College, Lampeter, 1971.

Wallace Collection (London). Opened, 1900; consists of art treasures collected by the 3rd and 4th Marquesses of Hertford.

Wallachia. *See* ROMANIA and VLACHS.

Wall Street, Manhattan, New York, USA, named after an earth wall built by the Dutch against the English, 1653. It was a financial centre from the beginning of the 19thC, and the New York stock exchange is there.

Wall Street Crash, occurred between 24 Oct and 29 Oct. 1929, when millions of shares on Wall Street changed hands in panic selling. It marked the start of the 'Great Depression' of the 1930s.

Walsingham. The shrine of Our Lady of W., Norfolk, much resorted to by pilgrims in the Middle Ages, was built in 1061. Destroyed during 16thC. Reformation; Catholic shrine (Slipper Chapel) officially reopened, 1934; Anglican shrine, 1934. Catholic Chapel of Reconciliation, 1981.

Waltham Abbey, Waltham Cross. The Church of the Holy Cross, founded 1061 by Harold Godwinsson; an abbey in 1184; dissolved at Reformation; reputed burial place of Harold (killed at Hastings, 1066).

wampum. Shell money of N American Indians, its value depending on colour; used by whites as well as Indians, and current in Connecticut in 1704.

War Crimes Act, 1991. First person charged in Britain under the Act, July 1995 (for alleged war crimes in World War II).

War Crimes Commission, United Nations, established, Oct. 1943. International Military Tribunal established, Aug. 1945. Suggestion that a new kind of W.C.C. should be convened to try alleged Balkan war-crimes, 1991 onwards, and first prosecutions, 1994, by a Danish court. International Court at the Hague indicts Bosnian Serb leaders Mladic and Karadzic for alleged war crimes, July 1995.

Warsaw (Polish **Warszawa**). The date of its foundation is unknown, but a castle was erected there as early as the 9thC; not mentioned in writings before 1224. Compact of W., 1573, guaranteed religious freedom for Polish Protestants. Capital of Poland, 1595; being taken by Sweden, 1655; retaken by Poles, 1656; taken again by Sweden, 1702; by Russians, 1764; and in 1806 was occupied by Napoleon's troops; taken finally by Russia, 1813; an insurrection in favour of independence took place, 1863; further insurrection, 1905–6. Surrendered, after siege, to Germany, 27 Sept. 1939. Ghetto uprising in W., 19 Apr.–16 May 1943 ended with destruction of the Great Synagogue and deportation of W.'s Jewish community (most subsequently perished in concentration camps). Polish rising against Germans, 1

Aug. 1944. Crushed after the Russians had refused assistance, 2 Oct. 1944. Russians entered Warsaw, 11 Jan. 1945. Old city largely destroyed during World War II, but rebuilt to replicate its original form after 1945.

Warsaw, Duchy of, independent state created by Napoleon, 1806–15. *See under* POLAND.

Warsaw Pact. Signed between USSR and the eastern bloc countries, as a 20-year-treaty of friendship and collaboration, on 14 May 1955. It represented the Soviet answer to the *North Atlantic Treaty Organization. Following the dissolution of eastern bloc Communism, the unified command of this Soviet-dominated organization was dissolved, March 1991. The remaining political remnants of the W.P. abolished, July 1991.

Wartburg. A castle in Thuringia, built by Landgrave Louis *c.* 1070. A poem written about 1280 describes the 'Tourney of Grief' which, however, did not really take place. W. was seat of landgraves until 1460. Luther was brought here for safety in 1521, and here he completed his translation of the New Testament.

Warwick, University of. Established at Coventry, 1965.

Washington, originally part of the Oregon territory (*q.v.* for earlier history), was ceded to the USA by Great Britain, 1846. Made a territory, 1853, and admitted to the Union, 1889. Eruption of Mt St Helen, 1980.

Washington, DC, USA. Made capital of the USA by an Act of Congress, 1790; the American government removed here in 1880. In 1814 the town was taken by the British, and the Capitol and President's house burned. A centre of operations during the civil war. Coextensive with the *District of Columbia, 1895. Local residents got right to vote in national elections, 1961.

Washington Conference, the, on naval armaments, opened Nov. 1921; on 1 Feb.

1922, treaties for limitation of naval armaments and for prohibiting submarine attacks on merchant vessels received the assent of USA, Britain, France, Italy and Japan.

Washington, Treaties of, 1846, settled the boundary question between USA and British America; 1854, a trade and fishery treaty with Canada; 1871, with Britain for the settlement of all causes of difference; 1922, *see* preceding article.

watches. Invented in Germany *c.* 15thC, when they were known as 'Nürnberg Eggs'. The greatest advance was the invention of the deadbeat escapement by T. Tompion (1639–1713), an Englishman.

Waterford, Ireland, founded by Danes or 'Ostmen' (*see* VIKING AGE), was taken from them by the Norman, Strongbow, 1170. King John gave it a charter, 1205.

Watergate Affair, name given to incident in June 1972 when Democratic Party Offices in the Watergate Building, Washington, were burgled. Several of President Nixon's staff subsequently implicated and convicted: W.A. eventually led to resignation of Nixon in Aug. 1974.

Waterloo Bridge (London). Originally built by Rennie, 1811–17. London County Council rebuilding scheme rejected by Parliament, 1932. L.C.C. persist, begin demolition, 1934. Construction begun, 1937; half-width opened to traffic, 1942. Bridge formally opened for full use, 1945.

Wazzan, N Morocco. Celebrated for manufacture of coarse woollen cloth and as burial-place of the Moorish saint, Idrisi Sharif, who lived there, 1727.

weather forecasts, first regularly issued by the Admiralty, 1860. First radio W.F.s in Britain, 1923; first television W.F.s, 1953. *See also* METEOROLOGICAL OFFICE.

weaving. First practised in China; during the 10thC the Flemings were important wool weavers, and during the 14thC England supplied them with most of the raw material; the first mention of W. in England is at York, 1331; early English centres of the industry were Canterbury, Colchester and Norwich. Power-looms, 1786, transformed W. industry.

Wedgwood china. Josiah W. (1730–1795) first established own pottery, 1759. Brought out patent for porcelain, 1763. Factory moved to Barlaston, Staffs., 1940.

Wedmore, Treaty of, between Alfred the Great of England and the Danes, by which England was divided between the English to the S and the Danes to the N of Watling Street, 878.

weights and measures. The shekel of Babylonia and Israel is traceable back to the 11thC BC; it was about one-sixtieth of a pound avoirdupois. The cubit, or length of forearm, was a favourite measure in Egypt, Phoenicia and Greece. A king of Argos, Pheidon, was renowned as having introduced a new system, the Aeginetan, into the Peloponnesus; but even his century is uncertain, probably 8thC BC. A standard of English measure was made in 972, and kept at Winchester; the first official examination of W. and M., 1795; an Act to enforce uniformity over the UK was passed, 1878, and is the basis of all subsequent amending legislation; a metric system Act was passed, 1897, but was not applied. Britain transferred to metric system, 1965 onwards and in response to EU directive metric system compulsory in Britain for all packaged goods from 1 Oct. 1995. Pint and mile exempt from metrication in Britain.

Wei-hai-wei. Held by Japan pending payment of war indemnity by China, Jan. 1895, till leased to Britain, 1 July 1898, for so long as Port Arthur remained in occupation of Russia. Restored to China, 1 Oct. 1930.

Weimar, Germany. As capital of Saxe-W.-Eisenach from 1547 it *fl.* as a centre of German classical culture *c.* 1775–1828. The constitution of the German republic was drawn up here in 1919. Hence the name W. Republic which existed 1919–33.

Welfare State. Term said to have been used by Sir Alfred Zimman in the 1930s. First written reference, in William Temple's *Citizen and Churchman* of 1941, and adopted to describe the British state as it evolved following the social reforms of the Labour governments, 1945–51. Many features dismantled from 1979 onwards under successive Conservative governments.

Welland Ship Canal, between Lakes Ontario and Erie, Canada, the first built, 1824–9; the second completed, 1932. Further improvements finished, 1972.

Wellington, capital of New Zealand, founded, 1840 after first Britons had explored the site for timber, 1826. Borough, 1842; municipality, 1853. Seat of government transferred to W. from Auckland, 1865.

Wells, England. King Ine of Wessex is said to have founded first church here, 704. Work on the cathedral began before 1200, and the greater part was finished, 1242.

Welsh language, declined in use from the 17thC and more particularly the 19thC, especially in the S of Wales and the towns. Bible translated into Welsh, 1567–88. Revival began in mid-19thC and accelerated in 20thC, assisted by sympathetic legislation. W.L. given equal status with English, 1992, when estimated nearly 20% of Welsh population spoke it.

Welsh laws. Code drawn up by Hywel Dda *c.* 943. For Statute of Rhuddlan, and later English statutes, *see* WALES.

Welsh literature. The following is a list of Welsh authors, in chronological order, not now living:

Aneurin, *c.* 560, poet.
Taliesin, *c.* 570 (*d.* 601), poet.
Myrddin, *c.* 570, poet.
Llywarch Hen, *c.* 580, poet.
Meilyr, *c.* 1137, poet.
Caradoc of Llancarvan, *c.* 1150, historian.
Gwalchmai, *c.* 1157, poet.
Owain Cyveiliog, *c.* 1165, poet.

Hywel ab Owain Gwynedd, *c.* 1169, poet.
Einion, *c.* 1175, poet.
Dafydd Benvras, *c.* 1230, poet.
Elidir Sais, *c.* 1230, poet.
Cynddelw, 1250, poet.
Llywarch ap Llewelyn, *c.* 1250, poet.
Einion Wann, *c.* 1200–50, poet.
Phylip Brydydd, 1250, poet.
Einion ap Gwgan, 1260, poet.
Edeyrn Dafod Aur, *c.* 1270, grammarian.
Llygad Gwr, *c.* 1270, poet.
Einion ap Madoc, *c.* 1270, poet.
Y Prydydd Bychan, *c.* 1275, poet.
Howel Voel, *c.* 1280, poet.
Bleddyn Fardd, *c.* 1284, poet.
Gruffydd ab yr Ynad Coch, *c.* 1284, poet.
Gwilym Ddu o Arfon, *c.* 1300, poet.
Dafydd ap Gwilym, *c.* 1340–1400, poet.
Gruffudd ab Meredydd, *c.* 1380, poet.
Hywel ap Einion Llygliw, *c.* 1390, poet.
Iolo Goch, *c.* 1400, poet.
Llywelyn Goch ab Meurig Hen, *c.* 1400, poet.
Gruffudd Llwyd ab Dafydd ab Enion Llygliw, *c.* 1400, poet.
Rhys Goch Eryri, *c.* 1410, poet.
Sion Cent, *c.* 1410, poet.
Rhys Goch ap Rhiccert, *c.* 1420, poet.
Gutto'r Glyn, wrote 1430–60, poet.
Lewis Glyn Cothi, 1440–90, poet.
Meredydd ap Rhys, *c.* 1450, poet.
Dafydd Nanmor, *c.* 1460, poet.
Howel Swrdwal, *c.* 1460, poet.
Ieuan Brydydd Hir Hynaf, *c.* 1460, poet.
Ieuan ap Howel Swrdwal, *c.* 1460, poet.
Llawdden, *c.* 1460, poet and prosodist.
Ieuan Deulwyn, 1460–90, poet.
Dr Morris Clynnog, *d.* 1580–1, catechist.
Dr Richard Davies, 1501–81, translator.
Sir John Prys, 1502–54, historian and miscellaneous writer.
Humphrey Llwyd, 1527–68, historian, etc.
Gruffud Hiraethog, 1530–66, poet.
Owain Gwynedd (or Owain Ifan), *d.* 1590, poet.
Dr Thomas Huet, ?–*d.* 1591, translator.
Maurice Kyffin, *d.* 1598, translator.
Dr David Powel, *d.* 1598, historian, etc.
William Cynwal, 1530–1600, poet.
Dr Sion Dafydd Rhys, 1534–*c.* 1600, poet, grammarian, etc.
William Llyn, 1535–80, poet.

Sion Tudur, 1535–1602, poet.
Edward Kyffin, *d.* 1603, translator.
Edmund Prys, 1541–1623, poet and translator.
Sion Phylip, 1543–1620, poet.
Rhys Cain, 1545–1614, poet and painter.
Simwnt Fychan, 1546–1606, poet and grammarian.
Dr Roger Smyth, 1546–1625, translator.
Dr William Morgan, 1547–1604, translator.
Sion Brwynog, 1550–67, poet.
Dr Gruffydd Roberts, *fl.* 1555–95?, grammarian and philosopher.
Dr Richard Parry, 1560–1623, translator.
Henry Parry, 1561–1617, grammarian.
Henry Salesbury, *b.* 1561, grammarian.
Huw Lewys, 1562–1634, translator.
Edward James, 1570–1610, translator.
Dr John Davies, *c.* 1570–1644, grammarian.
John Salisbury, 1575–1625, translator.
Thomas Prys, *d.* 1634, poet.
William Salesbury, *c.* 1575, translator and lexicographer.
William Phylip, 1577–1669, poet.
Vicar Prichard, or Rhys Prichard, 1579–1644, religious poet.
William Myddelton, or Gwilyn Canoldref, *c.* 1590, poet, translator, etc.
Rowland Vaughan, *d.* 1667, miscellaneous writer.
Richard Jones, 1604–73, translator.
Thomas Gouge, 1605–81, educationist.
Morgan Llwyd o Wynedd, 1619–59, miscellaneous writer.
Stephen Hughes, 1622–88, translator, etc.
Edward Morus, *d.* 1689, poet.
Huw Morus, 1622–1709, poet.
Charles Edwards, *c.* 1628, religious writer.
Robert Llwyd, *c.* 1640, translator.
James Davies (Iago ab Dewi), 1648–1722, poet and translator.
Edward Lhuyd, 1660–1709, philologist.
Elis Wyn o Lasynys, 1671–1734, author of the *Barrd Cwsg.*
Edward Samuel, 1674–1748, miscellaneous writer.
Griffith Jones, Llanddowror, 1684–1761, educationist, etc.
Moses Williams, 1686–1742, translator.
Theophilus Evans, 1693–1767, historian.
Lewis Morris, 1700–79, poet and miscellaneous writer.

Daniel Rowland, 1713–90, religious writer and translator (?).
William Williams of Pantycelyn, 1717–91, hymn writer.
Joshua Thomas, 1719–97, historian.
David Lewis, *c.* 1720, philosopher.
Gcronwy Owen, 1722–69, poet.
Simon Thomas, *c.* 1730, historian.
Evan Evans (Ieuan Brydydd Hir), 1731–1788, poet, etc.
Thomas Edwards (Twm o'r Nant), 1739–1810, interlude writer.
Owen Jones (Owain Myfyr), 1741–1814, poet.
Edward Williams (Iolo Morganwg), 1746–1826, poet.
Dr Owen Pughe, 1759–1835, lexicographer.
David Thomas (Dafydd Ddu Eryri), 1760–1822, poet.
Edward Jones, Maesyplwm, 1761–1836, religious poet.
John Jones (Sion Glanygors), 1767–1821, poet.
Robert Davies (Bardd Nantglyn), 1769–1835, poet.
David Saunders, Merthyr, 1769–1840, translator.
John Jones, LL.D., 1772–1837, historian, etc.
Evan Evans (Ieuan Glan Geirionydd), 1795–1855, poet.
William Williams (Caledfryn), 1801–69, poet.
Jane Williams (Ysgafell), 1806–85, poet.
Robert Ellis (Cynddelw), 1810–75, poet.
John Jones (Talhaiarn), 1810–69, poet.
Rosser Beynon (Asaph Glan Taf), 1811–1876, poet.
Roger Edwards, 1811–86, poet and miscellaneous writer.
Thomas Jones (Glan Alun), 1811–66, poet.
Edward Davies (Iolo Trefaldwyn), 1819–87, poet.
Edward Roberts (Iorwerth Glan Aled), 1819–67, poet.
Thomas E. Davies (Dewi Wyn o Essyllt), 1820–91, poet.
Evan Jones (Ieuan Gwynedd), 1820–52, poet.
Ellin Evans (Elen Egryn), *fl.* 1850, poet.
Thomas Rowlands, 1824–84, grammarian.

John C. Hughes (Ceiriog), 1832–87, poet.
W. Thomas (Islwyn), 1832–78, poet.
Richard Davies (Mynyddog), 1833–77, poet.
John Davies (Ossian Gwent), 1834–92, poet.
Richard Foulkes Edwards (Rhisiart Ddu o Wynedd), 1836–70, poet.
Daniel Owen, 1836–95, novelist.
John Robert Pryse (Golyddan), 1841–63, poet.
David Griffiths (Dewi Eifion), d. 1871, poet.
Emrys ap Iwan, 1851–96, critic.
Mary Olwen Jones, 1858–93, novelist.
Sir Owen Morgan Edwards, 1858–1920, critic.
Eivion Wyn, d. 1926, poet.
Sir John Morris-Jones, 1864–1929, poet.
Thomas Gwynn Jones, 1872–1949, poet.
H. Elvet Lewis (Elfed), 1860–1953, poet.
W.J. Gruffydd, 1881–1954, poet.
Alun Lewis, 1915–44, poet.
Dylan M. Thomas, 1914–53, poet.

Welwyn. *See* GARDEN CITY.

Wembley, British Empire Exhibitions at, 1924, 1925. Many events of 1948 Olympic Games held at W. stadium; used for Cup Finals and other major events, including 'pop concerts' and religious meetings.

Wends or **Sorbs,** Slavonic tribes who are mentioned by the English missionary Winfrith (*alias* Boniface), who d. 754. Under German rule from about AD 900, they formed part of the Polish kingdom, 1002–32, and were united under the Bohemian crown from the 15thC until 1621 when the region was partitioned between Saxony and Brandenburg.

Wesleyans. *See* METHODISTS.

Wessex, kingdom of the W Saxons, the political nucleus of which arose out of the Gewissae (i.e. Confederates); this confederacy, military and perhaps also religious, was led into Britain, 495, by Cerdic, and his son Cynric. In 519 Cerdic and Cynric 'undertook the government of the W Saxons ... from that day have reigned the

children of the W Saxon kings.' Bede, mentioning the W Saxons for the first time, a century later, says they were 'formerly called Gewissae,' and were converted to Christianity in 635 by the Italian bishop Birinus (d. 690). Cerdic's grandson Ceawlin obtained possession of the country between the upper Thames and lower Severn, 571–578. The territory of the Hwicce (Worcestershire, Gloucestershire, SW Warwickshire) was lost to the militant pagan Penda, king of Mercia, 630. Somerset was conquered from the Britons of Cornwall about 660, and the Isle of Wight, 686. Ine, whose code of laws still survives, extended the W. dominions W to include most of Devonshire. During the 8thC the kingdoms of Sussex and Kent were eliminated and annexed piecemeal by W., which then subdued its final internal enemy, Mercia, 825–9. Thereafter *see* ENGLAND.

Wessex, Kings of, c. 552–839:
Cynric *fl.* 552–*d.* 560
Ceawlin 560–92
Ceol 591–97
Coelwulf 597–611
Cyneglis 611–43
Cenwalh 643–45
Penda (of Mercia) 645–48
Cenwalh (restored) 648–72
(Queen) Seaxburg 672–74
Escwine 674–76
Centwine 676–85
Caedwalla 685–88
Ine 688–726
Ethelheard 726–40
Cuthred 740–56
Sigeberht 756–57
Cynewulf 757–86
Beorhtric 786–802
Egbert, KING OF ENGLAND 802–39
See further under ENGLISH SOVEREIGNS AND THEIR CONSORTS.

West Bank, area on W bank of river Jordan, taken by Jordan, 1948; captured by Israelis, 1967. Populated by Arabs, it became a base of Palestinian resistance thereafter. Israeli settlements on W.B. since

1980s. Negotiations for Israeli troop withdrawals from Arab areas of W.B. settled by PLO–Israeli agreement, 1995.

West Bengal, state of NE India since 1947. Cooch Behar joined to, 1950; Chandernapore, 1954. Further accretions following reorganization of 1956.

Western Australia was first explored by the Dutch under Dirk Hartog, 1616. The first Englishman to land was William Dampier, 1688. Formal possession taken on behalf of the English crown by Vancouver, 1791. A settlement of convicts was sent from New S Wales, 1826. Swan River Settlement founded, 1829. Responsible government granted, 1890; state, 1901.

Western Sahara, former Spanish Sahara, which was divided between Mauritania and Morocco, 1976, after Spanish withdrawal, 1975. In 1979 Mauritania gave up claim to W.S., and Morocco took over but opposed by Polisario guerrillas. Morocco and the Polisarios accepted UN peaceplan, 1988, proposing a referendum on future of W.S.

Western Samoa. *See* SAMOAN ISLANDS.

Western Union had its beginnings in a 50-year treaty signed in Brussels on 17 Mar. 1948 by Britain, France, the Netherlands, Belgium and Luxemburg. European Council established, May, 1949. In Dec. 1949 the W.U. defence organization was incorporated with the N Atlantic Treaty command. Enhanced status of W.U. envisaged as EU countries' defence policies increasingly cohered while not always in line with those of the USA, from 1993. In 1995 John Major supported revival of W.U. mechanism as a way of enhancing EU defence cooperation.

West Indies, Federation of. *See* CARIBBEAN FEDERATION.

Westminster. The abbey was founded *c.* 7thC, and refounded by Edward the Confessor *c.* 1050–65. The 'city' was governed by the abbots till 1547. St Margaret's was founded *c.* 1100. The W. Hall was built, 1097–1100. Law Courts established in W.

Hall *c.* 1200. Abbey rebuilt, 1245–69. Further additions *c.* 1350–1528, and *c.* 1722–40. The school attached to the abbey from early times was chartered by Henry VIII, but only properly endowed by Queen Elizabeth I. The abbey was converted into barracks for a time, 1643. First W. Bridge opened, 1750. W. Palace (Houses of Parliament) burned down, 1834. New palace completed, 1867. New bridge built, 1862. Law Courts removed from, 1883. Created a city and a metropolitan borough, 1899. Roman Catholic cathedral opened, 1903; consecrated, 1910. University of W., 1992.

Westminster Assembly. The Long Parliament, having in 1641 expelled the bishops, summoned an assembly of 121 divines, who, with 30 laymen from Parliament, formed the body that was to inaugurate a Presbyterian establishment for England and Wales. Meetings held in W. Abbey: the first, 1 July 1643; the last, 22 Feb. 1648; in all, 1,163 meetings. The assembly adopted the *Solemn League and Covenant, 25 Sept. 1643. It submitted to Parliament: a 'Directory of Public Worship' to supersede the Book of Common Prayer, 20 Apr. 1644; a 'Confession of Faith' and two Catechisms, both approved by Parliament, 15 Sept. 1648. The Commons ordered, 13 Oct. 1647, that Presbyterianism be tried for a year, bishops having been abolished, 9 Oct. 1643. Presbyterianism soon gave place to Independency in England. All the Assembly's work in England and Wales was swept away at the Restoration, but the Confession and the Shorter Catechism remained binding in the Church of Scotland.

Westminster, Provisions of, drawn up, 1259. Re-enacted as the Statute of Marlborough, 1267.

Westminster, Roman Catholic Archdiocese of. Prior to 1850, Westminster had been briefly an Anglican bishopric, created by Henry VIII, 1540, and absorbed into the see of London in 1550. In 1850, Pope Pius IX revived the Catholic hierarchy in England, despite protests from Protestant bodies. Its centre was established at Westminster, which was made an archdiocese. Westminster Cathedral built, 1895–1903. Archbishops of Westminster since 1850:

Nicholas Wiseman, 1850–65
Henry Edward Manning, 1865–92
Herbert Vaughan, 1892–1903
Francis Bourne, 1903–35
Arthur Hinsley, 1935–43
Bernard Griffin, 1943–56
William Godfrey, 1956–63
John Heenan, 1963–75
Basil Hume, 1976–

It is customary for the archbishop of W. to receive a cardinal's hat soon after his elevation.

Westminster, University of, name and status since 1992 of the former polytechnic of central London. It is in Regent St, London W1.

Westminster, Statutes of.
I. 1275. A miscellaneous code on revenue, etc., matters.
II. 1285. Part of this is called *De Donis Conditionalibus*, and legalized the creation of entailed interests.
III. 1290. Part of this is called *Quia Emptores*, and abolished further subinfeudation.
IV. 1931. This Act created the legally independent sovereign status under the crown of the British Dominions.

Westphalia, Kingdom of, created by Napoleon, 1807. Dissolved, 1814. *See* BONAPARTE.

Westphalia, Peace of, 1648. This consisted of two treaties, which ended the Thirty Years War, negotiated at Münster and Osnabrück, and signed at Münster, 21 Oct. 1648.
1. A treaty of alliance between France, the Empire and Sweden against Spain.
2. A treaty of peace by which Sweden received W Pomerania, Bremen and Verden; France received Metz, Toul, Verdun, and Alsace; and the independence of Switzerland and the United

Provinces of the Netherlands was guaranteed. Religious toleration was granted to Calvinists as well as Lutherans in Germany, but the principle was not extended to the Hapsburg territories. The peace marks the failure of the Austro-Spanish effort to restore Roman Catholicism in Central Europe, and the beginning of a period of French hegemony in Europe.

West Point Military Academy, USA. A resolution of Congress, Oct. 1776, proposed the establishment of a military academy, but no bill was passed until 1802. A further Act of 29 Apr. 1812 increased the establishment, and in 1817 a system of admitting a fixed proportion of cadets from each state was adopted. Women admitted, 1976.

West Virginia was admitted to the Union in 1863 by fissure from *Virginia.

West Wall. Between 1936 and 1940 the Germans constructed a continuous fortified belt from Lörrach in the S to a point opposite the junction of their frontier with those of Belgium and Luxemburg. From 1939 to 1945 it was extended to protect the S flank from Lörrach to Lake Constance.

Wexford, Ireland. Founded by Vikings in the 9thC, was taken from their descendants by the Normans, 1169; received a charter, 1318; besieged by Cromwell, 1649; held by Williamites, 1690. During the second rising of the *United Irishmen, 1798, W. was the headquarters of the civil administration.

whaling. English and Dutch commercial W. fleets important from 17thC. Forced further afield from 18thC. US W. in Pacific from 19thC. In 20thC Japan became major W. nation. Modern W. started with invention of harpoon containing an explosive charge by Svend Foyn (Norway) in mid-19thC. Conservationists and others increasingly opposed to W. In 1985 the International W. Commission secured international agreement to a moratorium on commercial W; in 1993 Norway and Japan announced they would abandon this, and some W. recommended by them subsequently. Antarctica a W. sanctuary from end of 1994.

wheel, breaking on the. Continental form of torture first used in Germany, 1535, then abolished, 1827; used in Edinburgh, 1604. In France in use still in 18thC: abolished at Revolution.

Whig. A term of contempt under Charles II, probably of Scottish origin. It eventually became the honoured party name of those who took the lead in establishing William III and George I on the throne. *See* LIBERALS.

Whipsnade Park. *See* ZOOLOGICAL SOCIETY OF LONDON.

Whisky Insurrection, 1794, in western Pennsylvania against the enforcing of the excise law by the Federal Government.

whist is first mentioned about 1621, but only became fashionable in the latter part of the 18thC, being displaced towards 1900 by *bridge which evolved from it though it retains some popular appeal still (1995).

Whitbread Prize. British literary award, founded 1971, with a value of £21,000. Won for third time in 1995 by the novelist William Trevor.

Whitby, England, so called in the 9thC by Scandinavians, who used the harbour called by the English Streoneshalh, where a monastery, built by St Hilda in 656, was the scene of a council, since called the Synod of W., in 664, attended by St Wilfrid (634–709) and St Colman (*d.* 676) in the Roman and Celtic interests respectively. The extant ruins of the abbey on the E cliff date from 1220 and were further damaged when the Germans shelled W., 16 Dec. 1914. James Cook, the navigator, sailed in a W. brig about 1745, and the *Endeavour*, in which he set out to New Zealand in 1768, was a collier of local pattern built in a W. shipyard.

Whiteboys. Irish secret organization, founded *c.* 1860. It was of the type known as Ribbonism. The Westmeath Act (1871)

declared Ribbonism illegal. The movement died out about 1885.

Whitehall (London). York House, the residence of the Archbishop of York, stood on this site, *c.* 1250. It was later acquired by Henry VIII, who made it a royal residence. A new hall was designed for James I, but only partially completed, 1622; through this hall Charles I passed to execution, 1649; and when the old palace was burned down in 1698 the hall was the only part to survive. The street now called W. was called King Street until the destruction of the palace.

White House (Moscow, Russia). Built 1981, to house the (then) Soviet parliament. So called from its white exterior: 19 storeys high. In 1991 scene of resistance to coup against Gorbachev: but in Sept./Oct 1993 centre of a rebellion by hard-line deputies against Yeltsin, who had dissolved it. Resistance crushed by the Russian army, 4 Oct. 1993, when the building was largely gutted.

White House (Washington, DC). Built between 1792 and 1799. Partly burnt out by British troops, 1814. Condemned as unsafe, 1949; repairs were completed in 1952 and much internal renovation was later done under the supervision of the wives of Presidents Eisenhower and Kennedy.

White Russia. *See* BELARUS.

Whitewater Affair, US government scandal based on alleged dealings of President Clinton and his wife prior to Clinton's presidency, surfaced 1993; and resignation of Clinton aides resulted 1993/4. Official enquiry into W.A. begun July 1994, but had reached no conclusion, 1995.

White Wednesday. *See* BLACK WEDNESDAY.

'Who's Who', biographical reference work first published, 1848, by Alfred Baily. Acquired, 1896, by Adam and Charles Black.

Wildlife and Countryside Act, 1981, marked important step in government recognition of importance of conservation.

Wilhelmshaven, the chief naval station of Germany on the N Sea, was founded in 1853, at the time of the origin of the Prussian Navy; the harbour was opened in 1869; many important additions made to the naval station from 1900 onwards; the dry dock was destroyed by the RN in 1948; the naval installations having been heavily damaged by RAF bombing between 1942 and 1945. Since 1950s an oil harbour (pipeline link with Cologne) and industrial centre.

Wilkes's case. Trials of John Wilkes, alderman of London, for printing obscene poem, *Essay on Woman*, and publication of *North Briton*, 21 Feb. 1764 and 18 June 1768.

Williamsburg, Virginia, USA, settled 1633 (as Middle Plantation). College of William and Mary, 1693. Capital of Virginia, 1699, and renamed after William III. Declined after state government moved to Richmond, 1780. Battle of W., 1862. Restoration of colonial W. begun, 1926, with grant from Rockefeller family: restored town now covers over 3,000 acres. Patrick Henry's historic speech against the Stamp Act at W., 1765.

Wilton House (Wiltshire), built by 1st Earl of Pembroke (1506–70) on site of abbey founded in 9thC by King Alfred. Largely destroyed by fire, 1647; subsequently rebuilt from designs by Inigo Jones and Philip Webb. Philip Sidney wrote *Arcadia* at W.H., 1590. Houses UK's largest private collection of Van Dyk paintings.

Wimbledon, England, where 'All-England' Tennis Championships held since 1877. *See* TENNIS.

Winchester (Roman *Venta Belgarum*). A city in Hampshire. The first bishop was Hedda (d. 705), but no traces of the Saxon cathedral remain. Present cathedral begun in 1079; nave reconstructed, 1380–1400; major restoration, 1905. Public school at W. founded by William of Wykeham 1382, opened 1394.

Window Tax, 1697. Brought in by William III to atone for the deficiency on damaged coin; repealed, 24 July 1851.

Windsor. Family name of the British royal house, adopted 1917, when George V renounced all German titles for himself and his family, together with the dynastic name of Saxe-Coburg-Gotha, acquired through Queen Victoria's marriage with Prince Albert. Retained by Elizabeth II and her descendants, despite her marriage to Lieutenant Philip Mountbatten (now Prince Philip, Duke of Edinburgh) in 1947.

Windsor Castle. The building was begun in wood by William I; stonework begun by Henry I *c.* 1110; in 1344 the Round Tower was built, and in 1356 practically the whole castle was rebuilt by Edward III, who was *b.* there, 1312; additions were made by (*inter alia*) Henry VIII, Elizabeth I and Charles II. St George's Chapel was built, 1473–1519 (begun by Edward IV); it was carefully restored by George III, 1787. Extensive alterations, 1824–30 and in the present century; serious fire caused extensive damage, 20 Nov. 1992. Permission given for exploratory oil drilling in grounds of, Jan. 1995.

Winnipeg, Manitoba, first reached by white travellers, 1738. NW Co.'s trading post, founded 1810, was replaced by a Hudson's Bay Co. post, named Fort Garry, 1822. On the creation of the province of Manitoba in 1870 its capital was sited at W., which was chartered as a city in 1873. University of Manitoba at, 1877. Canadian Pacific Railway reached W., 1881. Serious flooding, 1950, resulted in construction of Red River Floodway, 1967. Boundaries extended, 1972.

Wireless. *See* RADIO.

Wisconsin, USA, was first entered by a European, Jean Nicolet, 1634. First permanent settlement, 1701. It was admitted to the Union, 1848.

witchcraft. A Bull against W. was issued by Pope Innocent VIII in 1484, whilst in England Acts against it were passed in 1542, 1562 and 1601. Last person to be tried under these Acts was Jane Wenham of Walkern, Hertfordshire, 1712, but a woman was actually burned alive in

Sunderland as late as 1722. An Act of 1736 penalizes *'pretending* to use W., etc.' The Vagrancy Act of 1824 was amended in 1950 to cover cases of reputed W. As late as 1895 (15 Mar.) a woman was burned as a witch in Ireland, at Cloneen, County Tipperary and a case of (illegal) witch burning was reported in Mexico, June 1963 and in S Africa, 1983. Charities in S Africa set up 'safe houses' for women accused of being witches, 1990s.

Witenagemot or **Witan.** The Anglo-Saxon royal council; in 7th and 8thC separate Ws. were possessed by Wessex, Kent, Mercia and Northumbria; there was no fixed meeting-place, but the king was always present; meetings were held three times a year: at Easter, Whitsun and Christmas. The most celebrated meetings were at Luton, 931, and Winchester, 934.

Wittenberg, Saxony. Mentioned, 1180; here, in the Augustinian monastery, Luther dwelt; in 1508 he was appointed professor of philosophy, and in 1517 he affixed his celebrated 95 Theses to the church door; bombarded by Austrians, 1760; taken by France, 1806; taken by Prussians, 1814.

Witwatersrand. S Africa. Gold discovered there, 1854.

Wolverhampton, University of, name and status since 1992 of the former Wolverhampton polytechnic.

Women's Auxiliary Air Force. *See* WOMEN'S ROYAL AIR FORCE.

women's colleges, English. Tennyson's *Princess,* written against women's higher education, 1847. Earliest W.C. were at London University (Queen's and Bedford), 1848 and 1849. Most higher education establishments originally founded for women co-educational from 1990s.

women's franchise. *See* FRANCHISE, ELECTIVE and USA, CONSTITUTION OF.

Women's Institutes originated in Canada in 1897, and were introduced to the UK in 1915 by a Canadian, Mrs Alfred Watt (1868–1948), who founded a branch at Llanfairpwllgwyngyll, Anglesey. The National Federation of W.I. was founded, 1917.

Women's Land Army raised, 1917. The W.L.A. came into being again in Sept. 1939, organized by committees set up in May of that year. Disbanded, 1950.

women's ordination. *See* ORDINATION OF WOMEN.

Women's Royal Air Force.
1. An ancillary service of the RAF formed 1 April 1918 and disbanded in 1920.
2. A force formed round the nucleus of certain ATS (*see* WOMEN'S ROYAL ARMY CORPS) companies which had been attached to the RAF since 1938, and in June 1939 were permanently transferred. It was known as the Women's Auxiliary Air Force until Feb. 1949, when the designation W.R.A.F. was adopted, merged with RAF, 1 Apr. 1994.

Women's Royal Army Corps, designation adopted from 1 Feb. 1949, by the former Auxiliary Territorial Service, the formation of which was proclaimed by royal warrant, 9 Sept. 1938. Disbanded, Apr. 1992, and merged with the Army.

Women's Royal Naval Service.
1. Raised, 1917; disbanded, Oct. 1919.
2. Re-formed, 1939; placed on permanent basis, Jan. 1949. Using weapons, from 1989. From Feb. 1990 role expanded to include service at sea. Adopted naval rank titles, Dec. 1990. Disbanded, 1993, and members integrated into the Royal Navy.

Women's Royal Voluntary Services, an association formed, 16 May 1938, by the Marchioness of Reading, and established on a permanent basis by the Home Office in May 1947. Originally the W.V.S., received addition of 'Royal' after World War II.

wonders of the world. The seven W. of the W. were
1. the Egyptian pyramids, *c.* 4700 BC;
2. the tomb of Mausolus, 353 BC;

3. the Ephesian temple of Diana, *c.* 550 BC;
4. the walls and hanging gardens of Babylon, work of Nebuchadnezzar, *c.* 604–562 BC;
5. the Colossus of Rhodes, 280 BC;
6. the statue of Zeus at Olympia, *c.* 450 BC;
7. the pharos of Ptolemy Philadelphus, *c.* 282 BC.

Woolsack. The seat of the Lord Chancellor in the House of Lords; placed there in the reign of Edward III as a reminder of the importance of the wool industry; the earliest authentic mention of the W., however, is in the reign of Henry VIII.

Woolwich, England, mentioned, 1064. Already an important royal dockyard in 15thC. The *Great Harry* launched at, 1515. Batteries erected against the Dutch, 1667. Royal Arsenal, 1805. Royal dockyard closed, 1869. Royal Military Academy, which was established 1741, was amalgamated with the Royal Military College at Sandhurst, 1946.

Woomera rocket range, Australia. Developed since 1946. In early 1960s ELDO (European Space Vehicles Launcher Organization) established at W.; first successful launch from there, 1964.

Worcester, England, became an episcopal see, 680. Benedictine church built by St Oswald (*d.* 992), 964, extensively rebuilt by Wulfstan the bishop (1012?–95), 1084, as his cathedral church. He also founded the Hospital of St Wulfstan, still standing now, but converted from its original purpose, 1541. Grammar School, 1541, chartered 1561. Battle of W., 1651. King John is buried in the cathedral. Last material addition to cathedral was Prince Arthur's Chantry, built by Henry VII. First bridge across Severn at W., 1313. Porcelain works (founded by John Wall) were opened, 1751; W. Royal Porcelain from 1864.

word processor. Prototypes in existence in 1930s, but breakthrough was development in USA in 1946 of a high-speed, automatic typewriter with a magnetic tape data storage unit, etc. However W.P.s not

in general commercial use until 1970s, and refinements continue.

Workmen's Compensation. W.C. Act, 1897, introduced principle of compulsory insurance by employers in a limited number of trades. All W.C. Acts were superseded by the National Insurance (Industrial Injuries) Act, 1946 etc.

Works, Ministry of, H.M. Office of W. first so called, 1852. Ministry status, 1940; part of the Department of the *Environment since 1970.

World Bank. *See* INTERNATIONAL BANK FOR RECONSTRUCTION AND DEVELOPMENT.

World Trade Center, Manhattan, New York, USA. This twin-towered building of 110 floors completed, 1972. Damaged by a bomb, 27 Feb. 1993, in which several people killed. Islamic extremists blamed and subsequently charged and four convicted, Mar. 1994.

World Council of Churches, other than Roman Catholic, held its first assembly at Amsterdam, Aug. 1948. Most recent assembly (7th) at Canberra in 1991.

World Cup (Football). *See under* FIFA.

World Health Organization. Constitution drawn up, 22 July 1946; came into effect, 1948. The W.H.O.'s status as a specialized agency of the United Nations Organization was recognized, 1950.

World Trade Organization, superseded the *SATT, 1 Jan. 1995. HQ, as with SATT at Geneva.

World War I. *Declaration of War*
1914: Austria-Hungary on Serbia, 28 July; Germany on Russia, 1 Aug.; Germany on France, 3 Aug.; Britain on Germany, 4 Aug.; Germany on Belgium, 4 Aug.; Montenegro on Austria-Hungary, 7 Aug.; France on Austria-Hungary, 10 Aug.; Britain on Austria-Hungary, 12 Aug.; Japan on Germany, 23 Aug.; Britain on Turkey, 6 Nov.
1915: Italy on Austria, 23 May; Italy on Turkey, 20 Aug.; Britain on Bulgaria, 15 Oct.; France on Bulgaria, 16 Oct.; Italy on Bulgaria, 19 Oct.

1916: Albania on Austria, 11 Jan.; Germany on Portugal, 9 Mar.; Romania on Austria, 27 Aug.; Italy on Germany, 28 Aug.; Germany on Romania, 28 Aug.; Turkey on Romania, 30 Aug.; Bulgaria on Romania, 1 Sept.

1917: USA on Germany, 6 Apr.; Cuba on Germany, 7 Apr.; Austria on USA, 8 Apr.; Bulgaria on USA, 9 Apr.; Panama on Germany, 10 Apr.; Siam on Central Empires, 22 July; China on Germany, 14 Aug.; China on Austria, 11 Sept.; Brazil on Germany, 26 Oct.

Military Events

France and Flanders:

1914: German invasion of Belgium begun, 4 Aug.; Brussels entered, 20 Aug.; Namur captured, 23 Aug.; Antwerp taken, 9 Oct. Battles: Mons, 23–24 Aug.; Le Cateau, 26 Aug.; Marne, 6–12 Sept.; Aisne, 12–15 Sept.; Ypres, 19 Oct.–22 Nov.

1915: Battles: Neuve-Chapelle, 10–13 Mar.; Ypres, 22 Apr.–25 May (first German attack with gas, 22 Apr.); Festubert, 15–25 May; Loos, 25 Sept.–8 Oct.

1916: Battles: Verdun, begun 21 Feb. (Douaumont, 25 Feb. and 24 Oct.); Somme, 1 July–18 Nov. (Beaumont-Hamel, 13 Nov.); Verdun, 15 Dec.; Ancre, 13–18 Nov.

1917: German retreat to Hindenburg Line, 14 Mar.–5 Apr. Battles: Arras, 9 Apr.–4 May (Vimy Ridge, 9–14 Apr.; Scarpe, 9–14, 23–24 Apr., 3–4 May); Chemin des Dames, 5 May; Bulle-court, 3–17 May; Messines, 7–14 June; Ypres, 31 July–10 Nov. (Passchendaele, 12 Oct., 26 Oct.–10 Nov.); Verdun, 20 Aug.; Cambrai, 20 Nov.–3 Dec.

1918: Battles: Somme, 21 Mar.–5 Apr.; Lys, 9–29 Apr. (Kemmel Ridge, 17–19 Apr.); Aisne, 27 May–6 June; Marne, 18 July; Ourcq, 23 July–2 Aug.; Amiens, 8–11 Aug.; Bapaume, 21–31 Aug.; Somme, 21 Aug.–3 Sept.; Arras, 26 Aug.–3 Sept. (Drocourt-Quéant, 2–3 Sept.); Saint-Mihiel, 12 Sept.; Hindenburg Line, 12 Sept.–9 Oct. (Épéhy, 18 Sept.; Cambrai, 8–9 Oct.); Argonne, 26 Sept.–2 Nov.; Ypres, 28 Sept.–2 Oct.; Selle River, 17–25 Oct.; Valenciennes, 1 Nov.; Sambre, 4 Nov.

Prussia – Poland – Russia – Austria-Hungary:

1914: Battles: Tannenberg, 26–30 Aug.; Lemberg, 1–3 Sept.; Augustovo, 1–4 Oct.; for Warsaw, 15–20 Oct.; 18 Nov.–28 Dec.; Lodz, 1–5 Dec.

1915: Przemysl surrendered to Russians, 22 Mar.; recaptured, 3 June; Lemberg retaken, 22 June; third battle for Warsaw, 19 July; Warsaw evacuated by Russians, 5 Aug.; Kovno stormed, 7 Aug.; battle of Brest–Litovsk, 26 Aug.; battle of Tarnopol, 7–8 Sept.; Vilna taken by Germans, 17 Sept.

1916: Battle of Lake Narotch, Mar.–Apr.; Russian offensive in Ukraine, 4 June; in E Galicia, 8 June; near Baronovitchi, 13 June; near Brody, 15 July.

1917: Russian offensive at Brzezany, 1 July; battle of Halicz, 10 July, 23 July; fall of Riga, 3 Sept.

1918: Odessa occupied by Germans, 13 Mar.

Romania:

1916: Invasion of Transylvania, 28 Aug.; Silistria taken by Bulgarians, 12 Sept.; Constanza taken by Bulgarians, 22 Oct.; Bucharest occupied by Germans, 7 Dec.

1917: Evacuation of the Dobrudja, 8 Jan.; Galatz evacuated, 11 Jan.

Dardanelles:

1915: Landing at Cape Helles, 25–26 Apr.; battles for Krithia, 28 Apr., 6–8 May, 4 June; Anzac battles, 25 Apr.–30 June; landing at Suvla, 6–15 Aug.; Suvla battles, 6–21 Aug. (Sari-Bair, 6–10 Aug.). Evacuation of Dardanelles declared, 8 Dec.

1916: Evacuation completed, 8 Jan.

Italy:

1915: First battle of the Isonzo, 2–29 July.

1916: Battle of Trentino, 14 May–16 June; battle of Gorizia, 6–14 Aug.

1917: Italian offensive on Isonzo, 14 May–10 June; Italian attack between Tolmino and sea, 19 Aug.; battle of Caporetto, 24 Oct.–18 Nov.

1918: Battle of Piave, 15–23 June, 26 Oct.; battle of Vittoria Veneto, 24 Oct.–4 Nov.

Balkans:

1915: Allied landing at Salonika, 5 Oct.; fall of Üsküb, 22 Oct.; battle of Kachanik, 4 Nov.; fall of Monastir, 2 Dec.

1916: Cettinje taken, 1–3 Jan.; Durazzo taken, 24 Feb.; Monastir retaken, 23 Nov.

1917: Battle of Doiran, 24–25 Apr., 8–9 May.

1918: Battle of the Vardar, 15–25 Sept.; battle of Doiran, 18–19 Sept.; Üsküb retaken, 30 Sept.

Egypt, Palestine, and Arabia:
Operations against the Senussi, Nov. 1915–Feb. 1917; battle of Romani, 3–4 Aug. 1916; battles of Gaza, 26 Mar.–7 Nov. 1917; capture of Jerusalem, 7–9 Dec. 1917; of Jericho, 19–21 Feb. 1918; Arab rising against Turks began, 7 June 1918; Mecca taken, 10 June 1918; battle of Megiddo, 19–25 Sept. 1918.

Mesopotamia – Persia:
1915: Battle of Kut, 28 Sept.; battle of Ctesiphon, 22–24 Nov.
1916: Kermanchah taken by Russians, 26 Feb.; Battle of Sanna-i-Yat, 6–22 Apr.
1917: British occupied Baghdad, 11 Mar.; Samaria, 19 Sept.; Ramadi taken, 28 Sept.; battle of Sherghat, 30 Oct.

Africa:
E Africa: Tanga operations, Nov. 1914; surrender of Mafia Island, 12 Jan. 1915; Tanga occupied, 7 July 1916; Dar-es-Salaam surrendered, 4 Sept. 1916; final surrender, 25 Nov. 1918.
SW Africa: Luderitzbucht occupied, 18 Sept. 1914; occupation of Windhoek, 12 May 1915; German capitulation, 9 July 1915.
Cameroons: Capture of Duala, 24 Sept. 1914; of Mora, 8 Sept. 1916.
Togoland: Lome captured, 8 Aug. 1914.
S Africa: Rebellion began, 15 Sept. 1914; surrender at Reitz, 4 Dec. 1914.

Caucasus:
Erzerum taken, 12 Feb. 1916, retaken, Mar. 1918; Trebizond taken, 18 Mar. 1916, retaken, Mar. 1918; Erzingan taken, July 1916, retaken, Mar. 1918; Batum occupied, Apr. 1918; Baku evacuated by British, 14 Sept. 1918.

N Russia – Siberia:
Kem occupied, 7 June 1918; Irkutsk occupied by Czechslovaks, July 1918; Dukhovskaya, 23 Aug. 1918; Archangel occupied, 1 Aug. 1918; Troitsa, 10 Aug. 1919; British evacuation, 27 Sept. 1919.

Naval Events
1914: *Goeben* and *Breslau* reach Turkey, 11 Aug.; blockade of Kiaochow, 27 Aug.; battle of Heligoland Bight, 28 Aug.; siege of Tsingtao, 23 Sept.–5 Nov.; HMS *Aboukir, Hogue* and *Cressy* torpedoed, 22 Sept.; battle of Coronel (Admiral Cradock's squadron lost), 1 Nov.; Kiaochow surrendered, 7 Nov.; German cruiser *Emden* destroyed, 9 Nov.; battle of Falkland islands (Spee's squadron sunk), 8 Dec.; Germans bombard Yorkshire coastal towns, 16 Dec.; seaplane raid on Cuxhaven, 25 Dec.
1915: Battle of Dogger Bank, 24 Jan.; German submarine blockade of Britain opened, 18 Feb.; British attack on Dardanelles forts, 19 Feb.; again, 4–7 Mar.; German cruiser *Dresden* sunk, 14 Mar.; *Lusitania* torpedoed, 7 May; *Königsberg* destroyed in Rufiji River, 11 July.
1916: Germans bombard Lowestoft, 25 Apr.; battle of Jutland, 31 May; HMS *Hampshire* with Kitchener aboard mined off Orkneys, 5 June; Allies bombard Athens, 1 Sept.; blockade of Greece, 19 Sept.
1917: Suffolk coast bombarded, 26 Jan.; Germans begin unrestricted submarine warfare, 1 Feb.; HMS *Swift* and *Broke* figure in a destroyer action in the Channel, 23 Apr.; Ramsgate shelled, 27 Apr.; first US destroyers arrive, 3 May; British naval success in Kattegat, 2 Nov.
1918: Germans bombard Yarmouth, 14 Jan.; British blocking attack on Zeebrugge and Ostend, 22–23 Apr.; another on Ostend, 9–10 May; German naval meeting at Kiel, 10 Nov.; Allied fleet passed through Dardanelles, 12 Nov.; German fleet surrenders, 21 Nov.

Armistices and Treaties
Armistices: Central Powers – Russia, 29 Nov. 1917; Romania – Central Powers, 7 Dec. 1917; Central Powers – Ukraine, 9 Feb. 1918; Allies – Bulgaria, 29 Sept. 1918; Allies – Turkey, 30 Oct. 1918; Allies – Austria-Hungary, 3 Nov. 1918; Allies – Germany, 11 Nov. 1918.
Peace Treaties: Brest-Litovsk, between Russia and Germany, 2 Mar. 1918; preliminary peace between Romania and Central Powers, Buftea, 5 Mar. 1918; ratified, 7 May 1918; annulled at Versailles, 1919. Versailles, signed by the Allies and Germany, 29 June 1919; ratified in Paris,

10 Jan. 1920. Saint-Germain, between Allies and Austria, signed, 10 Sept. 1919; ratified in Paris, 16 July 1920. Trianon, between Allies and Hungary, signed, 4 June 1920. Neuilly, between Allies and Bulgaria, signed, 27 Nov. 1919; ratified in Paris, 9 Aug. 1920. Sèvres, between Allies and Turkey, signed, 10 Aug. 1920 (never ratified). Lausanne, between Allies and Turkey, signed, 24 July 1923; ratified, autumn 1923.

World War II 1939: Germany invades Poland, 1 Sept.; Britain, New Zealand, Australia, and France declare war on Germany, 3 Sept.; Canada and S Africa declare war: Russia invades Poland, 17 Sept.; Poland partitioned between Germany and Russia, 28 Sept.; *Royal Oak* sunk in Scapa Flow, 14 Oct.; Anglo-Turkish pact, 19 Oct.; US 'Cash and Carry Act' repeals the arms embargo, 4 Nov.; Russia invades Finland, 30 Nov.; battle of the River Plate, 13 Dec.; *Admiral Graf Spee* scuttled, 17 Dec.

1940: *Altmark* incident, 17 Feb.; Russo-Finnish Peace, 13 Mar.; Reynaud French Premier, 20 Mar.; Germans attack Denmark and Norway, 9 Apr.; Germans invade the Low Countries, 10 May: Churchill forms coalition government, 10 May; Dutch Army surrenders and German victory at Sedan, 15 May; Belgian Army surrenders, 28 May; Dunkirk evacuation, 26 May–3 June; British evacuate Norway and Italy declares war on Allies, 10 June; Spain seizes Tangier and Germans enter Paris, 14 June; French reject British offer of union and Pétain becomes Premier, 16 June; French surrender, 22 June; Russians seize Bessarabia from Romania, 28 June; Romania denounces Anglo-French guarantee, 1 July; British disable the French fleet in N Africa at Oran, 3 July; Italians invade the Sudan, 4 July; Vichy breaks off relations with Britain, 5 July; British closes Burma road, 18 July; Lithuania annexed by USSR, 3 Aug.; Italians invade British Somaliland, 4 Aug.; USSR, annexes Estonia and Latvia, 5 Aug.; battle of Britain, 8 Aug.–6 Sept.; Vienna award dismembers Romania, 30 Aug.; British obtain 50 destroyers from USA in return for bases in W Indies, 2 Sept.; beginning of the London blitz, 7–8 Sept.; Italians invade Egypt, 13 Sept.; British attack on Dakar fails, 25 Sept.; the 'New Order' Pact (Germany, Italy, Japan), 27 Sept.; Germans occupy Romania, 7 Oct.; Italy attacks Greece, 28 Oct.; Italian fleet severely damaged by British air attack at Taranto, 11 Nov.; blitz on Coventry, 14 Nov.; Wavell opens victorious offensive against Italians in N Africa, 8 Dec. (till 8 Feb. 1941).

1941: Italian forces placed under German control, 20 Jan.; Germans occupy Bulgaria, 9 Feb.; Britain breaks off relations with Romania, 10 Feb.; British capture Mogadishu, 26 Feb.; Bulgaria joins Axis, 1 Mar.; US Lease-Lend Act becomes law, 11 Mar.; Rommel's counter-attack in Libya begins, 24 Mar.; General Simovic overthrows pro-Axis government in Yugoslavia, 27 Mar.; British naval victory over Italians at Cape Matapan, 28 Mar.; Rashid Ali's pro-Axis revolt in Iraq, 3 Apr.; British capture Addis Ababa, 5 Apr.; Germans invade Yugoslavia and Greece, 6 Apr.; Germans capture Sollum, 26 Apr.; Athens, 27 Apr.; Hess flies to Scotland, 10 May; Italians surrender at Amba Alagi, 19 May; German conquest of Crete, 19 May–1 June; HMS *Hood* sunk, 24 May; *Bismarck* sunk, 27 May; British and French occupy Syria, 8 June–14 July; Germany invades USSR, 22 June; USA occupies Iceland, 7 July; British and Russians occupy Iran, Aug.–1 Sept.; Reza, Shah of Iran, forced to abdicate, 16 Sept.; Germans reach Leningrad, 4 Sept.; capture Kiev, 19 Sept.; second British offensive in Libya, 18 Nov.; final Italian surrender in Ethiopia at Gondar, 27 Nov.; Three-Power Conference at Moscow, 29 Nov.; Japanese attack Pearl Harbor, 7 Dec.; Japanese occupy Thailand and invade Malaya, 8 Dec.; HMS *Prince of Wales* and *Repulse* sunk, 10 Dec.; Japanese take Guam and Axis declare war on USA, 11 Dec.; Hitler takes immediate command of German Army, 19 Dec.; Japanese take Wake Island, 23 Dec.; Hong Kong, 25 Dec.

1942: United Nations Pact at Washington, 1 Jan.; Japanese take Manila, 2 Jan.;

Japanese naval victory in Macassar Straits, 23–25 Jan.; Japanese invade Burma, 8 Feb.; capture Singapore, 15 Feb.; Rangoon, 8 Mar.; Java, 10 Mar.; American raid on Tokyo, 18 Apr.; fall of Corregidor, 6 May; Japanese naval victory in the Coral Sea, 7–11 May; second German offensive in Libya opens, 12 May; first 1,000-bomber raid (on Cologne), 30 May; battle of Midway, 3–6 June; Japanese attack Aleutians, 3 June; Gen. Eisenhower C.-in-C. US forces European theatre, 25 May; Germans reach El Alamein, 1 July; Germans take Sevastopol, 2 July; Americans attack Guadalcanal, 7 Aug.; British raid on Dieppe, 18–19 Aug.; first all-American air raid on Europe, 17 Aug.; Germans enter Stalingrad, 5 Sept.; British victory at Alamein, 23 Oct.–3 Nov.; allied landing in N Africa, 8 Nov.; Germans occupy Vichy France, 11–12 Nov.; Russian counter-offensive at Stalingrad begins, 19 Nov.; French fleet scuttled at Toulon, 27 Nov.; Germans driven from Agheila, 13 Dec.; Russian victory at Kotelnikovo, 29 Dec.

1943: Casablanca Conference, 14–26 Jan.; British take Tripoli, 23 Jan.; Russians take Voronezh, 25 Jan.; final German surrender in Stalingrad, 2 Feb.; Gen. Eisenhower allied C.-in-C. N Africa, 6 Feb; Russians take Kursk, 8 Feb.; Americans finally clear Guadalcanal, 9 Feb.; battle of the Bismarck Sea, 1–3 Mar.; battle of the Mareth, 21–29 Mar.; Allies take Tunis, 7 May; Axis surrender in N Africa, 13 May; breaching of Möhne and Eder dams by RAF, 18 May; Allies take Pantelleria, 11 June; Battle of Kursk begins, 5 July; Allies conquer Sicily, 9 July–7 Aug.; Mussolini resigns, 25 July; Russians take Orel, 4 Aug.; Kharkov, 23 Aug. signalling defeat of German Kursk offensive; Mountbatten becomes allied C.-in-C. SE Asia, 25 Aug.; Allies land in Italy and Italy surrenders, 9 Sept.; allied landing at Salerno, 9 Sept.; Russians take Bryansk, 17 Sept.; Smolensk, 25 Sept.; Kiev, 6 Nov.; Allies allowed to use Portuguese Azores bases, Oct.; Americans capture Tarawa, 21–25 Nov.; Cairo Conference, 22–26 Nov.; Teheran Conference, 26 Nov.–2 Dec.; USA and Britain give aid to Tito, 20 Dec.

1944: Ciano executed, 11 Jan.; Russian offensive in Leningrad area begins, 15 Jan.; allied landings at Nettuno and Anzio, 22 Jan.; Americans capture Kwajalein, 1–6 Feb.; battle of Cassino, 1 Feb.–18 May; Japanese defeat in Manipur, 13 Mar.–30 June; Russians reach Polish and Romanian frontiers, 2 Apr.; capture Sebastopol, 9 May; Allies enter Rome, 4 June; allied landings in Normandy, 6 June; flying bomb attacks on London begin, 15 June; break-through at St Lô, 27 July; Polish rising in Warsaw begins, 1 Aug.; battle of the Falaise gap, 7–23 Aug.; allied landings in S of France, 15 Aug.; Allies capture Paris, 24–25 Aug.; Brussels, 3 Sept.; Americans take Palau Island, 15 Sept.–13 Oct.; battle of Arnhem, 17–26 Sept.; Russians invade Hungary, 6 Oct.; Americans invade Philippines, 20 Oct.; decisive Japanese naval defeat in Philippine Sea, 23–25 Oct.; armistice with Bulgaria, 28 Oct.; British land on Walcheren, 1 Nov.; last German offensive in the Ardennes, 16–22 Dec.; Hungary changes sides, 30 Dec.

1945: Russians take Warsaw, 11 Jan.; Yalta Conference, 4–11 Feb.; Russians take Budapest, 13 Feb.; Turkey declares war on Germany and Japan, 23 Feb.; Americans cross the Rhine at Remagen, 7 Mar.; Russians denounce the neutrality pact with Japan, 5 Apr.; President Roosevelt dies, 12 Apr.; Russians occupy Vienna, 13 Apr., and reach Berlin, 21 Apr.; Russians and Americans meet near Torgau, 26 Apr.; Mussolini shot, and German plenipotentiaries in Italy sign terms of surrender, 29 Apr.; Hitler's death announced, 1 May; Berlin surrenders and armistice in Italy effective, 2 May; German forces in NW Europe surrender, 5 May; all German forces surrender, 7 May; Americans capture Okinawa, 21 June; atomic bomb on Hiroshima, 6 Aug.; Russia attacks Japan, 8 Aug.; atomic bomb on Nagasaki, 9 Aug.; Japan surrenders, 14 Aug.; Japanese forces in China surrender, 9 Sept.; in SE Asia, 12 Sept.

Peace Treaties

1946: Between Britain and India on the one hand, and Thailand on the other. Between

Australia and Thailand. Between France and Thailand.

1947: Between the Allies and the German satellites, signed and ratified, namely with Italy, Hungary, Romania, Bulgaria and Finland (the USA had not been at war with the last of these).

1951: Between Japan and 48 allied countries.

1955: Between Austria and the Allies. The Western powers terminated the state of war with Federal Germany in 1951; the USSR did the same in 1955. This considered to apply to the whole of reunited Germany from 1990, though no formal peace treaty signed.

Worms, on the site of a Roman town *Borbetomagus*, was the capital of the Burgundian kingdom from AD 416 to 444. More than 100 Imperial Diets met in W., including those of 1122 and 1521 (*see* next two articles). Except for one cathedral (the oldest external parts of the present structure date from 1110, some internal parts of the structure built 1000–25), the whole town was destroyed by the French, 1689. Ceased to be an Imperial Free City, 1801, and became part of Hesse, 1815. An episcopal see, 614–1801.

Worms, Concordat of, 1122, abolished lay investiture of bishops and abbots in favour of election by cathedral chapter.

Worms, Edict of. Luther was summoned before the Imperial Diet and was warned by Spalatin against entering W. His writings were recognized, but he had to remain in hiding. He was put under an imperial ban, 26 May 1521.

Writers to the Signet. Scottish law agents corresponding to English solicitors; by an Act of 1868 they prepare all crown writs.

Wroclaw, Poland, formerly **Breslau**. Bishopric, 10thC and from 1163 capital of a duchy of Silesia. Destroyed by Mongols in the 13thC, but rebuilt by German settlers, and joined Hanseatic League. Acquired by the Hapsburgs, 1526. Jesuit College founded 1702. Captured by Frederick the Great, Jan. 1741, and became part of Prussian territory. University established, 1861. Extensively bombed in World War II and besieged by Russians for nine weeks in 1945. Conceded to Poland for occupation by *Yalta Conference. Most German inhabitants driven out, 1945–6, and name changed to Wroclaw.

Wroxeter. *See* URICONIUM.

Württemberg, Germany. War between W. and the Swabian cities, 1377–88. Formation of Swabian League, 1488. W. raised to a dukedom, 1495. Ulrich Duke of W. expelled from W. by Swabian League, 1519. W. sold to the Emperor Charles V by Swabian League, 1520. Ulrich restored, with French support, 1534. Napoleon made W. into kingdom, 1806, which endured until 1918. Joined the S German Zollverein, 1828–31. Joined the Prussian Zollverein, 1833. Fought Prussia in alliance with Austria, 1866. Fought against France, 1870. Joined German Empire, 1871. Combined with Baden in a SW province of the German Federal Republic, 1950.

Wyatt's Insurrection, 1554. A futile revolt led by Sir Thomas W. the Younger (1521?–54), in opposition to the marriage of Queen Mary with Philip of Spain. He collected forces in Kent, marched to Blackheath, 29 Jan.; entered Southwark, 3 Feb.; then marched to Kingston, 6 Feb.; through Kensington to Hyde Park, 7 Feb.; by Charing Cross to Ludgate, turned back, and was arrested at Temple Bar, 8 Feb.; beheaded on Tower Hill, 11 Apr.

Wyoming, USA, explored by Spaniards in the 17th, and French in the 18thC, was first entered by an American, John Colter, 1807. Part of it was acquired by the USA in the Louisiana Purchase, 1803, part from the British Oregon territory, 1846, part ceded by Mexico, 1848, and part annexed (with Texas), 1854. The first woman state governor in the USA took office in W., 1925. Admitted to the Union, 1890.

Xanthica. Named after Xanthicus, a month in Macedonian calendar, corresponding to Apr.; it was a military festival instituted 392 BC.

Xanthus, Asia Minor. Twice sustained sieges which ended with the self-destruction of the inhabitants; first by the Persians under Harpagus (*c.* 546 BC), and secondly by the Romans under Brutus (43 BC).

xenon. Discovered by Sir William Ramsay (1852–1916), 1898.

Xeres or **Jerez**, SW Spain. The word sherry is the English corruption of X. Roderic, the last Visigothic king of Spain, was killed here by the Saracens in 711.

Xinjiang Uygur. *See* SINKIANG UIGHUR.

X-rays. Discovered by Wilhelm Konrad von Röntgen (1845–1923) in 1895.

Y

yacht. The word was used in England in the forms yeaghe, yoathe, etc., from 1557. Charles II had a Y. named *Mary*. The first Y. club was the Cork Harbour Water Club, 1720. First English Y. club, Cowes, 1815. Royal Thames Y. club, 1830. Became popular in USA, Canada, Australia, etc. from 19thC. Ocean Y.-racing began, 1866, from Connecticut, USA to Isle of Wight. Y.-Racing Association, 1874 (Royal from 1952). International Y. Racing Union, 1907. Y.-racing in Olympics from 1900 (1904 excepted). Single-handed transatlantic Y. races since 1960; first yachtsman to circumnavigate globe alone, Sir Francis Chichester, 1966–7.

Yakutsk, Siberia. Celebrated for its great trade in furs; founded in 1632; capital of the autonomous republic of Yakut in USSR, 1922–91, since then in Russia.

Yale University (Connecticut, USA). The third oldest university in the USA; founded in 1701 by ministers selected by the churches of New Haven county. Took the name of Yale College, 1718, after Elihu Yale (1648–1721), its great benefactor, Charter, 1745. Known as Y.U. since 1887.

Yalta Agreement concluded allied conference, 4–11 Feb. 1945.

Yanaon. A former French settlement in India, founded, 1750. Administration transferred to India, 1954; treaty of cession, May 1956.

Yangon. *See* RANGOON.

Yangstekiang or **Chang Jiang,** longest river in China. The 'Y. Incident' occurred 20 April 1949 when British frigate *Amethyst* detained on the Y. while on a mercy mission. In July the *Amethyst* slipped moorings and escaped to the open sea.

'Yankee'. Used in Cambridge, Massachusetts, *c.* 1713, as a term of excellence. Derived by Thomas Anburey, 1789, from *eankee*, Cherokee for slave or coward; by J. G. E. Heckewelder, 1818, from American Indian pronunciation of the word *English*. But possibly a Dutch diminutive of *Jan*: the personal name *Janke* is found in the Calender of State Papers, Colonial Series (1898), under date 1683. Derisively applied to the New Englander by British troops during the War of Independence; by the Confederates to the Union troops during the Civil War.

Yarkand, historic name of **Sa-ch'e**, or **Sache**, walled town in Sinkiang, China; visited by Marco Polo, 1271, and by the Portuguese Goes, 1603; Chinese from 18thC, little known to the outside world till Adolf Schlagintweit visited it in 1857.

yellow fever. First authentic account from Barbados, 1647. Cause discovered by Walter Reed, 1901. Preventive serum first used, 1919. World Health Organization confirmed its existence in Kenya, Feb. 1993 (first time in *c.* 50 years).

Yellowknife, capital of NW Territories, Canada, since 1967. Gold discovered there in 1930s.

Yellowstone National Park, Wyoming, USA. Covers 3,469 sq. miles. Occupied by Sheepeater Indians when area was first visited by John Colter, 1807. First received publicity through account of Henry D. Washburn, surveyor-general of Montana, 1870. Made a public park and nature reserve 1872. Serious fires damaged it, 1988.

Yemen (*Arabia Felix*) settled before 1000 BC. Conquered by Muslim tribes, AD 631; by Turks, 1517. Imam Yahya became independent of Turkish rule, 1918. Imam Yahya and the two emirs, his sons, murdered, Feb. 1948. Republican revolt, Sept.

1962; civil war ended with republican victory, 1968. Renamed People's Republic of Y., 1970. Fighting between Y. and the Yemen People's Democratic Republic took place sporadically from 1971–2 and from 1978–9. Unification agreement between Y. and the Yemen People's Democratic Republic signed, 1979; co-operation agreement, 1988; unification finally achieved, 22 May 1990, when the two Ys. became known as Republic of Y. Elections, April 1993. Civil war erupted between N and S Y., May 1994. S Y. declaring its independence, but the war ended with the N Y. forces capturing Aden, 6 July and thereby reasserting control over all Y.

Yemen People's Democratic Republic, established 30 Nov. 1967 and comprised the former federation of S Arabia and *Aden. United with the People's Republic of Y. (*see* preceding article), 22 May 1990.

Yeomanry (British). Mounted volunteers. First units organized under Volunteer Act of 1794; served in the S African War in Imperial Y. battalion, 1899–1901; merged in Territorial Force, 1980.

Yeoman of the Guard. A king's bodyguard instituted, 1485; the oldest professional military body in England; properly called Y. Warders of the Tower, they were nicknamed 'Beef-eaters' *c.* 1669; their services, originally most comprehensive, are now largely ceremonial.

Yerevan, capital of Armenia, founded in the 7thC. From 1440, variously Turkish or Persian; Russian 1827–1991. Scene of violent anti-Russian and anti-Azeri demonstrations, 1988.

Yeti. *See* ABOMINABLE SNOWMAN.

Yezidis. Kurdish sect, found in Armenia, N Iraq and the Caucasus; their sacred book is Al-Yalvah, interpreted by Sheikh Adi *c.* 1200.

Yokohama. Japanese seaport on W of Tokyo Bay. Opened to foreigners, 1859; it was then little more than a village. Three-quarters of the town destroyed by the earthquake of 1 Sept. 1923. Severely damaged by bombing, 1945; rebuilt, and population 1995 over three million.

Yom Kippur War, name of war between Israel and Egypt (aided by Syria), Oct. 1973. Won by Israel, and named after the Jewish holy day on which the Egyptian attack began.

York, Archbishopric of. Date of foundation of the see uncertain: probably *c.* 625. Independent till subordinated to Canterbury by papal decree, 1073. Scottish bishops asserted independence from 1176. Following are the dates of investiture of the Archbishops of York:

Paulinus 625
Wilfrid I 664
Cead 664
Bosa 678
John of Beverley 705
Wilfrid II 718
Egbert 732
Ethelbert 766
Eanbald I 780
Eanbald II 796
Wulfsige ? 812
Wigmund 837
Wulfhere 854
Ethelbald 900
Redewald *c.* 928
Wulfstan *c.* 931
Osketyl 958
Oswald 972
Ealdulf 992
Wulfstan II 1003
Aelfric 1023
Kinesige 1051
Ealdred 1060
Thomas I 1070
Gerard 1101
Thomas II 1109
Thurstan 1119
William 1143
Henry Murdac 1147
Roger 1154
Geoffrey 1191
Walter Gray 1215
Sewal de Bovil 1256
Godfrey 1258
Walter Giffard 1266

Wm. Wickwain 1279
John le Roman 1286
Henry Newark 1298
Thos. Corbridge 1300
Wm. Greenfield 1306
Wm. Melton 1317
Wm. Zouche 1342
John Thoresby 1352
Alex. Neville 1374
Thos. Arundel 1388
Robt. Waldby 1397
Richd. Scrope 1398
Henry Bowett 1407
John Kemp 1426
Wm. Booth 1452
Lawrence Booth 1476
Thos. Rotherham 1480
Thos. Savage 1501
Christopher Bainbridge 1508
Thos. Wolsey 1514
Edward Lee 1531
Robt. Holgate 1545
Nicholas Heath 1555
Thos. Young 1561
Edmund Grindal 1570
Edwin Sandys 1576
John Piers 1589
Matt. Hutton 1595
Tobias Mathew 1606
George Monteigne 1628
Samuel Harsnett 1628
Richd. Neile 1632
John Williams 1641
Vacant 1650–60
Accepted Frewen 1660
Richd. Sterne 1664
John Dolben 1683
Thos. Lamplugh 1688
John Sharp 1691
George Neville 1464
Sir Wm. Dawes Bart. 1714
Lancelot Blackburne 1724
Thos. Herring 1743
Matt. Hutton 1747
John Gilbert 1757
Robt. Hay Drummond 1761
Wm. Markham 1777
Edward Harcourt 1807
Thos. Musgrave 1847
Chas. Thos. Longley 1860
Wm. Thomson 1862
Wm. Connor Magee 1891

Wm. Dalrymple Maclagan 1891
Cosmo Gordon Lang 1908
Wm. Temple 1929
Cyril Forster Garbett 1942
Arthur Michael Ramsey 1956
Fredk. Donald Coggan 1961
Stuart Blanche 1974
John Stapylton Habgood 1983
David Hope 1995

York, City of, England (Latin *Eboracum*;
Danish **Jorvik**). In Roman times the headquarters of the IXth Legion till AD 120;
thereafter of the VIth. Hadrian visited Y.,
120. Severus *d.* at, 211. Constantine the
Great proclaimed Emperor at, 306. Captured by the Deiran Angles, *c.* 520. Edwin
of Northumbria baptized by St Paulinus
at, 627. First cathedral *c.* 625. Present structure built between 1070 and 1472; seriously
damaged by fire, 1984. Stormed by Penda
of Mercia and Cadwallon the Welshman,
653. Renowned as a seat of learning in the
8thC. Conquered by Danes, 867. Sigtrygg
Ivarsson (*d.* 927), Danish King of Y., 921.
Y. burnt by William I, 1068. Incorporated,
12thC. Many medieval buildings include
Merchant Adventurer's Hall, 1357; Guildhall, 1446–8 (rebuilt after bombing in
World War II;) St William's College, 1453.
Council of the North established at, 1537.
Besieged by Parliamentarians, 1644. Mansion House, 1726; Assembly Rooms, 1735;
Bar Convent, 1784. Present Castle Museum built as a women's prison, 1780. Re-
newed prosperity due to growth of
railways after 1850. Industries in 19thC
included railway workshops and confec-
tionery. University of Y. opened, 1963.
Yorkshire Museum, 1830; City Art Gallery,
1879 (rebuilt after bombing, 1948); Railway
Museum, 1975. Major excavation of Viking
Y., 1978–83 led to establishment of a Jorvik
Centre in the 1980s.

Yosemite Valley, California, USA. Discovered, 1851. Made a state park, 1864;
national park, 1890.

Young Men's Christian Association,
founded 1844 by Sir George Williams

(1821–1905). World Alliance of Y.M.C.A.s established, 1855.

Young Offenders' Institutions, replaced *Borstal, 1988.

Young Plan. Despite the *Dawes Plan, Germany stopped paying reparations, etc. 1929. A committee of experts sat in Paris, 11 Feb. 1929, and one of them, Owen D. Y. (*d.* 1962), of USA, propounded a plan that they accepted, 7 June. This, with modifications, signed at The Hague by 15 nations, 20 Jan. 1930. In fact, Germany stopped paying reparations, June 1931, and whole idea abandoned, 1932.

Young Women's Christian Association, founded, 1855. Independent English branches amalgamated, 1887. World Y.W.C.A. established, 1894.

Youth Hostels Association of England and Wales formed, 1930. Scottish and N Ireland Y.H.A. formed, 1931.

Ypres, medieval capital of W Flanders. Cloth Hall built, 1201–1342. Belgian since 1830. Belonged to France between 1678 and 1715 and between 1794 and 1814; to Holland, 1814–30. Devastated by three battles in First World War. Menin Gate memorial built, 1927. *See* BATTLES.

Yucatan, Mexico. Discovered, 1517; became a state (boundaries later reduced), 1824.

Yugoslavia. (For history before 1918 *see* SERBIA, MONTENEGRO, BOSNIA, CROATIA, SLOVENIA, MACEDONIA, etc.) King Nicholas of Montenegro deposed and Montenegro united with Serbia, 29 Nov. 1918. Yugoslav kingdom under the Serbian monarchy proclaimed, 1 Dec. 1918. D'Annunzio seizes Fiume for Italy, 12 Sept. 1919. Treaty of Rapallo with Italy gives Zara to Italy and makes Fiume independent, 12 Nov. 1920. Italy annexes Fiume, 9 Mar. 1924. King Alexander murdered at Marseilles, Oct. 1943; succeeded by Peter II and Regent Paul. Y. joins Axis, 25 Mar. 1941; Simovic coup, 26–27 Mar.; Paul flees and Peter assumes full powers; German invasion, 6 Apr. and official Yugoslav resistance ends, 17 Apr.

'Independent' Croatia formed and house of Savoy offered crown, 18 May; Dalmatia annexed to Italy, 21 May. *See* WORLD WAR II for events 1941–45. Underground resistance effective by end of 1941 but hampered by existence of two rival groups, under Mihailovic and Tito respectively. After 1944 the West gave support exclusively to Communist Tito and country effectively under his control when war ended. Federal Republic proclaimed, 29 Nov. 1945; trial and execution of Mihailovic, June–July 1946; internationalization of *Trieste accepted, 3 Sept., ex-king and family deprived of nationality and property, Mar. 1947; peace treaty with Italy. Bitter conflict begun between Y. and Soviet Russia, 1948; US supplied credit as Y. isolated by E bloc; harshness of régime relaxed. New constitution, 1950; Tito elected president and visits England; in 1954 Y. a party to the Trieste Agreement. Y. retained independent position after relations with Russia resumed, 1962. From 1960s considerable liberalization of régime and a tourist boom from western Europe. Tito *d.* 1980; and collective leadership followed. Economic difficulties and break-up of Communist system in other parts of Europe fuelled nationalist agitation in Y.'s different republics from 1988 onwards. In 1991* Slovenia and *Croatia declared their independence. This signalled break-up of Y. and although it continued to exist in theory, its power in effect passed to Serbia which by 1992 controlled the rump Yugoslav presidency and selected its president. In April 1992 Serbia and Montenegro announced a new Yugoslav federation and invited other Serbs to join. This had no international recognition and lost any meaning after Serbia disowned action of Bosnian Serbs in 1994. *See further under* SERBIA etc.

Yukon, Canada. Organized as a separate territory, 1898. Klondike gold rush, 1896–8: over by 1900, when Y.'s prosperity declined. Klondike Highway completed, 1979; railway closed, 1982. Administrative reorganization, 1966. Tourism growing industry since 1960s.

Zadar (Serbo-Croatian) (Italian **Zara**, Latin *Jadera*), former capital of Dalmatia, taken from Byzantine Empire by Venetians *c.* 990, from which time till 1409 Z. alternated between Venetian and Hungarian sovereignty; captured and then bought by Venetians, 1409. Became Austrian, 1797, then part of Illyrian kingdom (*see* ILLYRIA), 1809–13, then again Austrian. Ceded to Italy, 1918, and to Yugoslavia, June 1947. Heavily bombed in World War II.

Zagreb (Serbo-Croatian) or (German **Agram**). Centre of Slav nationalism in 19C. Capital of Croatia from 1867, ceded to Yugoslavia by Hungary, 1918. Seat of Catholic diocese, 1093, from which period the still-extant Kaptol (fortified Old Town) dates. Capital of puppet state of Croatia, 1941–3; and of independent Croatia since 1991.

Zaire, African republic, formerly known as the **Congo**, or **Belgian Congo,** became independent of Belgium, 30 June 1960. The colony originated with annexation of *Congo Free State, 1908. *Katanga province declared itself independent of the government in Leopoldville (Kinshasa) and the central government appealed for UN help, 11 July 1960. UN troops arrived in Z., 15 July. Army coup, 15 Sept. Premier Lumumba kidnapped by Katanga tribesmen and murdered, Feb. 1961. In Jan. 1963 President Tshombe of Katanga formally agreed to Katanga's reintegration into Z. From 1964–5 Tshombe was premier of Z. Dismissed by Kasavubu, Oct. 1965: in Nov. 1965 Kasavubu deported by Mobutu, who

took over the government as president, with far-ranging powers. Name changed to Z., 1971. Uprisings crushed in Shaba, 1977–8. Economic and political chaos increased from late 1980s; end to one-party government announced, 1990, but Mobutu held on to power. Serious rioting, with many dead, 1991 and 1993, as president and premier disputed power. International negotiation withheld from premier appointed by president, April 1993. Z. economy further affected by enormous influx of refugees into Z. during Rwandan civil war, 1994. UN attempts to settle political crises, 1994–5. Ebola virus kills estimated 200, May 1995.

Zambesi. The first European to explore the Z. river was Livingstone in 1851–3.

Zambia, formerly **Northern Rhodesia**. Capital moved from Livingstone to Lusaka, 28 May 1935. Part of Federation of *Rhodesia and Nyasaland, 1953–63. Federation dissolved, Dec. 1963. Became republic within the Commonwealth under the name of Zambia, 24 Oct. 1964, with Kaunda as president. Trouble with the Lumpa Church, 1965. One-party rule established, 1972; ended after widespread discontent, primarily economically based, 1991, when Chiluba became president after multiparty elections.

Zante Island, Greece (ancient *Zacynthos*), traditionally belonged to Ulysses. Peopled by Achaeans *c.* 1390 BC. Naval base for Athenians in Peloponnesian War. Attacked by Lacedaemonians, 430 BC. Headquarters of Dion's Syracusan expedition, 357 BC. Seized by Philip V of Macedon, 217 BC. Taken by Romans, 211 BC, but restored; annexed by Rome, 191 BC. In AD 11thC it passed to the Norman kings of Sicily. After the 12thC it belonged at different times to despots of Epirus, emperors of Constantinople, and counts of Cephalonia. In hands of Tocco family, 1357–1482; then Venetian possession ceded to France, 1797. Briefly occupied by a Russo-Turkish fleet, 1799; then British ceded to Greece, 1820.

Zanzibar, E Africa. Mentioned by Arab

writers, 1328; fell into hands of the Portuguese in 15thC, and taken by Turks in 17thC; proclaimed a British protectorate, 1890. Slavery abolished, 1897. On 10 Dec. 1963 Z. became an independent state within the Commonwealth. A left-wing revolt in Jan. 1964 deposed the Sultan, and a republic was declared. In April 1964 Z. united with *Tanganyika in a single state, subsequently named *Tanzania.

Zaragoza, Spain, former capital of Aragon. Captured by Moors, *c.* 714. Taken by Alfonso I of Aragon, 1118, who made it his capital. Two cathedrals; one built *c.* 1120–1520; the other, Nuestra Senora del Pilac, begun 1681, to commemorate traditional appearance of the Virgin Mary on a pillar in Z. University, 1474.

Zeebrugge, Belgium. Canal linking Z. to Bruges completed, 1907. British naval raid on Z., 23 April, 1918. On 6 March 1987 188 of those on the British cross-channel car ferry *Herald of Free Enterprise* died when it sank after sailing from Z. with its bow doors open.

Zend-Avesta. The book of the religion of Zoroaster; mentioned by Hermippus in the 3rdC BC.

zeppelin. *See* AIRSHIPS.

Zimbabwe, formerly **Rhodesia**, earlier **Southern Rhodesia**. Named after Cecil Rhodes (1853–1902), who founded the British S Africa Co.; chartered 1889. The company administered both N and S Rhodesia until 1923 when S Rhodesia received responsible (white) self-government. After dissolution of Federation of *Rhodesia and Nyasaland, Rhodesian whites' demand for independence increased. Talks with Britain broke down and on 11 Nov. 1965 the Rhodesian premier, Smith, made a unilateral declaration (*UDI), of Rhodesia's independence. Britain did not recognize this and unsuccessfully imposed exchange and trade sanctions. A republic was declared in 1970. Economic difficulties, plus increasing black resistance to white rule, led by Nkomo and Mugabe, 1970–80, amounting to virtual

civil war, led to the Lancaster House talks in London, 1979. UDI was ended and Rhodesia became the Republic of Zimbabwe, under Mugabe, with black majority rule, on 18 Apr. 1980. Bills of 1987 amended the constitution, abolishing the 20 parliamentary seats reserved for whites and establishing an executive presidency, Dec. 1987. Mugabe made president, and merger of ZANU and ZAPU parties created a one-party state in effect. Mar. 1990: government won 117 of 120 seats in elections and one-chamber legislature created. State of emergency, existing from 1965, lifted 1990. Economic problems and droughts caused discontent: in June 1991 government renounced Marxism and liberalization of economy began. Elections, 1995; Mugabe won but elections were boycotted by main opposition parties.

zinc. Used in early times as a component of brass (referred to by Pliny); known to the ancients only in the carbonates and silicates called calamine. The word Z. first used by Paracelsus; and described by Libavius in, 1597.

Zinoviev Letter, the. Allegedly sent by Zinoviev, head of the *Comintern on 15 Sept. 1924, to Russian *chargé d'affaires* in London, advising agitation for a violent revolution in Britain. Published in London press, 25 Oct. 1924, just before General Election; possibly helped cause a Labour defeat.

Zionism. Congress of Basel, 1897, convened by Theodor Herzl (1860–1904), author of *The Jewish State*, 1896, who founded organization with headquarters first in Vienna, but from 1904 to 1911 in Cologne under David Wolfssohn (*d.* 1914). Practical work begun by actual purchase of land in Palestine, 1908, financed by Jewish National Fund, which was founded, 1901. Organization moved to Berlin for period, 1911–14. Balfour Declaration, 2 Nov. 1917, prompted by Chaim Weizmann (1874–1952) and Nahum Sokolow (1861–1936). The organization from 1917 to 1929 was identical with the Jewish Agency for Palestine, but thereafter other bodies participated in the agency. *See* Israel and Palestine, Modern.

Znaim, or **Znojmo**, Moravia. Founded, 1226, by Ottakar I of Bohemia. The armistice between Napoleon I and the Archduke Charles was concluded here after the battle of Wagram, 1809.

zodiac, signs of the. Names assigned by Anaximander *c.* 560 BC.

Zollverein (*Customs Union*), term used especially of those economic alliances binding various German states between 1818 and 1871.

zoological nomenclature. First applied with any accuracy by Linnaeus in his *Systema Naturae*, the first sketch of which appeared in 1735.

Zoological Society of London. Founded, 1826. Gardens opened at Regent's Park, 1828. Royal charter, 1829. Threatened with closure in 1990s; in 1993 reform plans included reduction in number of animals held and increased emphasis on conservation. Whipsnade Park opened, 1931.

Zoroastrianism. Founder Zoroaster lived *c.* 800 BC. Z. became national religion of Persia *c.* 550 BC to *c.* AD 650.

Zouaves. Former French African infantry. First corps raised in Algeria, 1831; saw service outside Africa for first time in Crimean War (1855).

Zuider Zee, Holland. Formed by series of storms in the 13thC and 14thC. Bill to reclaim passed, 1918. Work on dam begun, 1924. Completed and name of Z. Z. changed to *Ijssel Meer, 1932. Partly reflooded by Germans, 1944–5, but largely reclaimed by the end of 1945. Flooding caused by high tides and storms, 1953. Reclamation complete in 1980's.

Zululand. Annexed by Britain, 1887; annexed to Natal, 1897. Since the 1970s most of the former Z. known as **Kwa Zulu**. Planned merger with Natal in new constitution, Nov. 1993, but this opposed by *Inkatha, and Kwa Zulu eventually given special status. *See next article.*

Zulus migrated southwards to the hinterland of Delagoa Bay during 17thC, and overran Natal, 1823, under King Chaka (*b.* 1783), who was murdered by his brother, Dingaan, who succeeded him, 1829. After Dingaan's defeat at Blood River (1838) by the *Voortrekkers he was deposed by his brother Umhanda (Jan. 1840), and fled to Swaziland, where he was murdered. Civil war, 1856, won by Cetewayo, who succeeded his father Umhanda, 1873. Boundary dispute between Cetewayo and the Transvaal Republic (later Colony) led to Zulu War of 1879. Cetewayo captured and deposed, 27 Aug. 1879. Restored by British, 1882; *d.* of wounds, 1884. His son Dinizulu led a rebellion, June–Aug. 1888, and was exiled, but allowed to return by the Natal Government, 1898. In 1975 Z. formed the *Inkatha movement led by Chief Buthulezi (*b.* 1928), who has been chief minister of Kwa Zulu since 1976. Increasing stresses between Buthulezi and Zulu monarch from 1993. Z. particular status reorganized in new S African constitution, 1993, but underlying unrest since national ANC election victory of 1994, despite Buthulezi being allotted a position in the central government.

Zürich, Switzerland. Celtic Helvetii settlement; conquered by Rome *c.* 58 BC. Imperial free city, 1218. Canton revised its constitution, 1336, and joined Swiss Confederation, 1351. Its subjects made free citizens of the Empire in 1262, granted complete autonomy within the Empire, 1400. Centre of *Zwinglianism in early 16thC. Grossmunster started by Charlemagne, 8thC. University of Z, 1833; Swiss National Museum, 1898. Internationally important financial centre in 20thC. Joined Helvetic Republic, 1798.

Zutphen, Holland. Sir Philip Sidney killed at battle of, 1586. Taken by Spaniards, 1587. Recovered by Dutch, 1591.

Zwinglianism. Followers of Swiss reformer Ulrich Zwingli (1484–1531). Now known as Swiss Evangelical Church. Since their defeat at the battle of Kappel, 1531, Zwinglian influence has been confined to Zürich and neighbouring cantons.

CHRONOLOGY OF EVENTS
30,000 BC to the present day

c. 30,000–3500 BC

Date	History, Politics and People	Economics and Sociology
c. 30000 BC	Last Ice Age: Old Stone Age Culture. First men reach N America by land bridge then existing across Bering Sea.	
c. 15000 BC	Men reach S America.	
c. 10000 BC	Middle Stone Age – nomadic societies.	Bows and arrows in SW Asia.
c. 9000 BC	Beginning of New Stone Age (Neolithic) in SW Asia – start of more fixed agricultural society. Evidence of first occupation of Jericho site.	
c. 8000 BC		
c. 7000 BC		Mud-brick building in Mesopotamia and grain being grown there.
c. 4999–4500 BC	Sumerians in Lower Mesopotamia (cf. carbon-dating of settlement remains).	Boomerang in Australia. Grain being grown in Mexico.
c. 4449–4000 BC	New Stone Age culture reaches Mediterranean. Foundation of Ur as permanent settlement.	
c. 3999–3500 BC	Sumerians settle on historic site of Babylon.	

Religion, Education and Philosophy	Science, Exploration and Technology	*c.* 30,000–3500 BC Music and the Arts
		Earliest known surviving paintings, France/Spain. (e.g. Lascaux and Grotte Chauvet, France 25,000–20,000 BC.)
	Copper being used.	
		Pottery in Japan.
	Boats with sails in Egypt.	Saharan rock paintings. Flutes & lyres in Egypt. Painted pottery in Mesopotamia.
	Start of Julian Calendar (4241 BC).	
	First map, on clay, showing R. Euphrates. Copper alloys used by Egyptians & Sumerians. Gold & silver smelted. Beginning of Jewish calendar (3760 BC). By 3500 BC, bronze alloys in Egypt & Sumeria.	

c. **3499–1000** BC

Date	History, Politics and People	Economics and Sociology
c. 3499–3000 BC	Sumerian civilization at peak. 1st and 2nd Dynasties in Egypt (till 2780 BC). Stonehenge I. *c.* 3100 BC. Historic Jericho being settled by 3000 BC.	Sumerian urban society, using the wheel, with a fixed agricultural base.
c. 2999–2500 BC	First settlement at Troy. Phoenicians settle on Syrian coast. Semitic tribes in N Assyria. Old Egyptian Kingdom, 3rd–6th Dynasties (2780–2270 BC). China: 'Sage King' period begins.	Lake dwellings in central Europe. Sumerians using coins, instead of grain, for trading.
2499–2000 BC	Maya civilization in Mexico begins. Semitic tribes settle in Palestine: Abraham leaves Ur about 2000 BC. Sargon establishes empire in Mesopotamia 2350–2100 BC. Yao and Shun Dynasties in China (till 2205 BC). Hsia Dynasty (2205 till 1766 BC). Early Minoan civilization in Crete. Indus civilization in India. End of Old and beginning of Middle Kingdom in Egypt, 11th and 12th Dynasties (2100–1788 BC). Dynasty of Pharaohs, 2200–525 BC. Stonehenge II and III 2100–2000 BC.	
1999–1500 BC	Hittites unite in one kingdom. Rise of Persian Empire. Rise of Babylonian Empire. End of Egyptian Middle Kingdom. Shang Dynasty in China (1766–1122 BC). Bronze Age in Western Europe.	Legal Code in Babylon (under Hammurapi).
1499–1000 BC	Mycenaean culture in Crete. Bronze Age in Scandinavia. Ganges culture in India. Building of Chiapa de Carzo, earliest known settlement in Mexico Trojan War: destruction of Troy (*c.* 1300 BC). Israelites leave Egypt for Canaan: Saul first king (1002–1000 BC). Demise of Babylonian Empire: foundation of Assyrian Empire under Tiglath-Pileser 1 (*c.* 1120 BC).	Phoenicians principal trading power in Mediterranean: establishing chain of trading ports.

Religion, Education and Philosophy	Science, Exploration and Technology	*c. 3499–1000* BC Music and the Arts
	Potter's wheel in Sumeria. Mayan chronology: first date 3372 BC.	Cuneiform in Sumeria.
Fertility religions (based on mother-goddess dominate): in Egypt, Pharaoh regarded as a god-king.	Foundations of astronomy in Egypt, Assyria and China. Iron first manufactured.	Evidence of Sumerian poetry. In Egypt, building of the Great Sphynx of Gizeh and the Cheops Pyramid. In England, Avebury built.
Resurrection doctrine propounded in Egypt (cult of Isis and Osiris). Beginnings of Judaism.	Papyrus used in Egypt. Cotton being grown in Peru.	Libraries in Egypt. Script changes from Sumerian to Semitic style.
	Mercury used in Egypt. Irrigation to harness Nile floods. Geometry highly developed in Babylon.	Dancing used in Cretan religious ceremonies. Trumpets in Denmark. First palace at Mycenae: first at Knossos.
In Egypt Akhnaton establishes Monotheism, 1385: old gods re-established by successor, Tutankhamen. Ten Commandments brought down from Sinai by Moses: reassertion of Jewish Monotheism.		Harp developed in Egypt. Sculpting of head of Nefertiti: building of Abu-Simbel Temple. Erection of Cleopatra's Needle. Early Greek alphabet at Knossos. First Chinese dictionary has 40,000 characters. Avenue at Stonehenge

999–500 BC

Date	History, Politics and People	Economics and Sociology
	19th Dynasty in Egypt (1350–1200 BC): Memphis made capital. 20th Dynasty in Egypt (1200–1090 BC): decline begins. 21st Dynasty: 1090–945 BC. Ethiopia independent of Egypt.	
999– 900 BC	Under kings David and Solomon (1000–925 BC). Israel at height of power: Jerusalem capital. Decline follows.	Hut-culture in S California.
899– 800 BC	Teutonic tribes begin moving W across Europe.	
799– 700 BC	Estruscans enter Italy. Rome founded (traditionally, 753 BC). Greek settlements in S Italy. Tiglath-Pileser III (745–727 BC) founds Nineveh: Assyria conquers Hittites, Israelites, Egypt and Judah. Celtic migration to Britain.	Olympic Games first dated at 776 BC: may have existed earlier. In Israel, prophets attack social and moral abuses.
699– 600 BC	Assyrian tyranny: Babylon, Thebes and Memphis destroyed. Medes, Babylonians and Scythians destroy Nineveh: Assyrian Empire ends, 612 BC. Judah made tributary by Nebuchadnezzar II: 'The Babylonian Captivity'. Rise of Greek city-states. Traditional date of foundation of Japanese Empire, 660 BC.	
599– 500 BC	Rise of Persian Empire under Cyrus II 553–529 BC: conquest of Lydia, Medea, Babylonia (Israelites freed and repatriated) and Egypt. Rome a republic, 510 BC.	Sophisticated banking system in Babylon.

Religion, Education and Philosophy	Science, Exploration and Technology	999–500 BC Music and the Arts
		extended *c.* 1100 BC. Temple of the Sun, Teotihuacan, Mexico. 'Gilgamesh Epic' written down (*c.* 1200 BC).
Pantheism in India. Classical paganism fully developed in Greece.	Sophisticated mathematics in China.	Temple of Hera, Olympia. Solomon builds Temple at Jerusalem: origins of Hebrew literature and religious music in present forms.
Early Jewish prophets: temporary reversion to paganism suppressed by Elijah.		*Iliad* and *Odyssey* written (Homer).
Jewish Messianic prophecies.	10 month calendar established in Rome. Hallstatt culture in Europe using horses and wheel.	'Book of Songs' contains earliest known Chinese poetry. Sumerian hymn found on cuneiform tablet. Greek music permeating general as well as religious life.
Dracon's Code in Athens, 621 BC. Zoroastrianism in Persia. Brahminism in India.	Sophisticated irrigation schemes in Nineveh. Kaleus sails through Straits of Gibraltar.	Famous library at Nineveh. End of Indian Vedas. Age of Greek classical literature begins: Sappho, Alcaeus, etc. Building of Acropolis begun at Athens.
Confucianism in China. Buddhism in India. Peak of Delphic influence in Greek religion. Solon's Laws promulgated in Athens, 594 BC.	Phoenicians, patronized by Egyptian Pharaoh, circumnavigate Africa. Babylonian astronomy starts applying modern calculation methods. Greek mathematical progress – Pythagoras.	At Jerusalem, Temple rebuilt. Greek art and literature flourish: Aesop, Aeschylus, etc. Theatre built at Delphi: and at Ephesus. Greek music influenced by Pythagoras and Pindar.

499–250 BC

Date	History, Politics and People	Economics and Sociology
499–450 BC	Etruscans reach height of power in Italy: formation of Latin League, led by Rome, starts Etruscan decline. Ionian War, 499–494 BC. Persian Wars with Greek states, 490–449 BC: Thermopylae, 480: Persian fleet destroyed at Salamis, 480: start of Persian decline. Athens becomes ascendant state. Rise of Pericles, 462.	Paid civil service in Athens c. 460 BC.
449–400 BC	Continued Roman expansion in Italy. except where Greek colonies exist (in S). Spartan challenge to Athens leads to Peloponnesian War (431–404) leading to Athenian defeat and Spartan supremacy.	
399–350 BC	Retreat of Ten Thousand under Xenophon, 400 BC. Coalition of cities against Sparta leads to Spartan overthrow, 371. Rise of Macedon under Philip (352–336). Rome sacked by Gauls, 390 BC. 30th (last native) Dynasty in Egypt, 380–341 BC. In Mexico, Indian dominance ends.	
349–300 BC	Philip of Macedon dominates Greece after Chaeronea, 338: his son Alexander crushes Persia, occupies Jerusalem, Babylon, etc., invades India, 327, dies, 323 when his Empire divided among his officers. In Italy, Samnite Wars, 343–341 and 327–304, increase Rome's power. Egyptian dynasty founded by one of Alexander's generals, Ptolemy Soter, will last till Cleopatra.	
299–250 BC	Third Samnite War, 298–290: Etruscans submit to Rome. Most of S Italy subject to Rome by c. 260. First Punic War, 264–241, ends in stalemate between Rome and Carthage.	First public gladiatorial fights in Rome (264 BC).

Religion, Education and Philosophy	Science, Exploration and Technology	Music and the Arts
Continuing flowering of Greek philosophy and learning under Sophocles, Pythagoras, Socrates. Twelve Tables of Roman Law, 451–449 BC	Carthaginian exploration of W African coast.	Temple of Castor and Pollux, Rome, 484 BC. Greek literature flourishes: Aeschylus, Pindar, Herodotus, Euripides. Further musical development under Pindar. Greek theatre flourishes.
The Torah, basis of Jewish morality, written.		Rebuilding of Acropolis in Athens, with sculptures, including 'Elgin Marbles' by Phidias.
Age of Plato and Aristotle in Greece.	Hippocrates revolutionizes Greek medicine.	Beginning of theatre in Rome.
Alexandria now a centre of Greek learning.	Pytheas reaches Britain, c. 325. First Roman coins, c. 340. Appian Way started, 312. Euclid's treatise on geometry, c. 300.	'Hellenic' period in art and letters. Aristotle defines musical theory.
Septuagint (Old Testament in Greek) written.	Greek medical theory and practice spreads to Rome.	Colossus at Rhodes completed, 280. 'New Comedy' literature in Greece. Sun Temple in Mexico (Teotihuacan) built.

Date	History, Politics and People	Economics and Sociology
249– 200 BC	2nd Punic War, 218 ends in defeat of Hannibal at Zama, 202. Greeks ally with Carthage.	Chinese rationalize weights and measures: build Great Wall of China, *c.* 220–210. Romans build first prison, *c.* 245.
199– 150 BC	Rome conquers N Italy: in wars against Greece, conquest of Macedon at Pydna, 168, marks start of Roman Empire. Revolt of the Maccabees, 167.	Foreign slaves become basic part of Roman economy after Greek subjugation.
149– 100 BC	Third Punic War, 149–146, ends in total destruction of Carthage and Greece subjugated. By 133 BC, Roman Empire has eight Provinces, including two Spains, Africa and Asia Minor. Decline of democracy in Rome.	Social and moral decadence in Rome exemplified in writings of Sallus, etc.
99–50 BC	Civil war in Roman Republic from 90: culminates in First Triumvirate under Caesar, Pompey and Crassus, 63. Wars in Spain and Gaul. Caesar invades Britain, 55 and 54. All Gaul subjugated by 50. Pompey conquers remainder of Syria and Palestine by 60.	Foreign and native slaves now a cornerstone of Roman economy, in Italy and elsewhere.
49 BC–0	Civil war in Rome: Caesar crosses Rubicon, 49: *de facto* dictator, 45: murdered, 44. 2nd Triumvirate, 43 ended by Octavian's Egyptian victories and suicide of Mark Anthony and Cleopatra, 31: Egypt absorbed in Empire and Octavian (Augustus) becomes Emperor (Caesar), 30. Herod king of Judaea, 40: Judaea annexed by Rome, 6.	Foreign troops used in increasing numbers in Roman armies.

Religion, Education and Philosophy	Science, Exploration and Technology	249 BC–0 Music and the Arts
Chinese classical philosophy ends with death of Sun Tsi (233). Asoka's Laws in India.		Beginnings of classic Roman literature with Plautus and Ennius.
Jews persecuted by Antiochus IV: this leads to Revolt of Maccabees, 167.	Water wheel used in irrigation.	Roman theatre flourishes under Plautus and Terence.
		Venus de Milo dates from this period.
Caesar writing his Histories.		Great age of Roman oratory – Cicero.
Jesus born in Bethlehem, c. 4 BC.	Julian Calendar adopted.	Age of Virgil, Horace and Ovid. Roman Pantheon begun, 27.

1–300

Date	History, Politics and People	Economics and Sociology
1–50	Roman Army destroyed in Teutoburg Forest, German, by Arminius, 9. Roman annexation of Mauretania, 41–2: of Britain, 43–5: capture of Caractacus. Goths advance W across Vistula.	
51–100	Emperor Claudius (poisoned, 54) succeeded by Nero (suicide, 68). Boudicca's rebellion in Britain, 61. Under Trajan (98–117) Empire reaches greatest limits: German frontier fortified, 96, in attempt to stem Teutonic advance. Jewish revolt: Jerusalem destroyed, 70.	
101–50	Emperor Hadrian (117–38) visits Britain: Hadrian's Wall built, 122–6.	
151–200	German invasion of Italy, 161: beginning of serious praetorian involvement in imperial choice, 193. Romans attempt subjugation of Scotland, but forced to retreat behind Hadrian's Wall, 180.	Plague sweeps Roman Empire 160–80
201–50	Goths invade Asia Minor and Balkans, 220. Roman citizenship extended to all freeborn subjects, 212. End of Han Dynasty in China, 220: start of Epoch of Three Kingdoms.	
251–300	Defeat of Valerian by Persia, 260. Goths reach Black Sea, 255, but defeated by Romans at Nish, 269. First partition of Empire into E and W by Diocletian, 285.	

Religion, Education and Philosophy	Science, Exploration and Technology	Music and the Arts
Jesus baptized by John the Baptist, probably 27: crucified outside Jerusalem, probably 30. St. Paul starts his mission, about 45, and Christianity begins to organize into a church.		
First Roman persecution of Christians starts, 64; executions in Rome of St Peter (first Pope) and St Paul. Four Gospels probably written down in this period. Ming Ti, Chinese Emperor, introduces Buddhism to China.		
Christianity, as an underground religion, spreads throughout Roman Empire.		Tacitus writes his *History*. Earliest known Sanskrit inscriptions in India.
Neo-Platonist philosophy dominates schools of learning. Pope (bishop of Rome) achieves predominant position in Christian church.	Ptolemy draws his maps of known world.	Cultural revival in Rome under Emperor Marcus Aurelius, 161–80. Oldest Mayan monuments.
Increased persecution of Christians: martyrs now being named as saints: catacomb burials.	Diophantus of Alexandria writes algebra textbook.	
Mani, founder of Manichaenism, crucified, 277.		Diocletian's palace at Ragusa (modern Dubrovnik) built.

301–500

Date	History, Politics and People	Economics and Sociology
301–350	Constantine the Great becomes Emperor, 309: reunites Empire. Makes Constantinople capital, 330. Is baptized on deathbed, 337, having tolerated Christians from 313. Empire again split, 340. First Gupta Emperor of N India, 340.	Constantine forbids public gladiatorial combat.
351–400	Scottish invasion of Britain, 360, defeated by Romans, 368. Theodosius the Great reunites Roman Empire, 392: permanently divided into E and W, 395. Visigoths under Alaric ravage Greece, 396: pressure growing on W Empire from all sides and first evacuations from Britain, c. 390. Defence of W Empire in hands of Germanic generals. Japanese historical records begin, 400.	Theodosius bans Olympic Games. Non-Romans control civil service and military commands.
401–50	Visigoths invade Italy, 401: Alaric sacks Rome, 410. Visigoths settle in Gaul, Vandals and Suevi in Spain, 415–23. Vandals in N Africa, 429–42, establish a kingdom there. Romans abandon Britain, c. 429: renounce all responsibility for defence, 446. Raids by Germanic tribes: Romano-British withdrawal westwards, decay of Roman urban civilization and temporary abandonment of Christianity in NW Europe except in extreme W.	
451–500	End of Roman Empire in West, 476: Odoacer king of Italy till 489, then country ruled by Theodoric the Ostrogoth. Permanent Anglo-Saxon settlements in Britain: but advance westward temporarily halted by Romano-British victory at Mount Badon, c. 500. Clovis founds Frankish Merovingian dynasty, 481, becomes Christian, 496.	

Religion, Education and Philosophy	Science, Exploration and Technology	Music and the Arts
Edict of Milan: Christianity tolerated in Roman Empire, 313. Council of Nicaea, 325, condemns Arianism. First St Peter's, Rome, built.		
Attempt by Julian the Apostate to revive paganism in Empire fails, 361–3. Caves of Thousand Buddhas founded in Kansu, 360. Books replacing scrolls.		Hymns introduced into Christian worship by St Ambrose, 386.
St. Augustine writes *City of God*, 411. St Patrick's mission to Ireland, *c.* 432. Goths and Vandals adopt Arian Christianity.	Alchemy begins: search for 'Philosopher's Stone'.	Mausoleum at Ravenna, 446.
First schism between E and W Christians begins, 484 (till 519). Armenian Church secedes, 491. First Shinto shrines in Japan, 478.		

501–600

Date	History, Politics and People	Economics and Sociology
501–20	Death of Clovis the Great, 511: Frankish kingdom divided between his four sons. Wu Ti Emperor of China, 517.	
521–40	Death of Theodoric, Ostrogoth king of Italy, 526. Accession of Justinian I as Byzantine Emperor, 527: his general Belisarius quells internal revolts, conquers Vandals in N Africa and Ostrogoths in Italy, 533–40 Totila the Ostrogoth regains Italy, 540. Persia enjoys renaissance under Chosroes I (531–79). Arthur of Britain said to have been killed, c. 538.	
541–60	Byzantines under Narses regain Italy, 552–5. Frankish kingdom reunited under Clothair I, 558. Ethelbert becomes king of Kent, c. 560. Beginning of Turkish and Slav migration westwards.	Plague from Middle E reaches Constantinople and spreads W, 542. Silk made a state monopoly in Byzantium 553.
561–80	Byzantines driven from N Italy by Lombards, 565–8. Frankish kingdom partitioned into three, 567. War with Persia, 572 (till 591).	
581–600	Whole of Spain a Visigothic kingdom by 585. Ethelbert of Kent baptized by St Augustine, 597: Kent becomes Christian. Tibet emerges as a single state. End of century marks end of Teutonic invasions in W.	Plague in Europe dying out (estimated to have cut population by one-third or over).

Religion, Education and Philosophy	Science, Exploration and Technology	Music and the Arts
End of First Schism between E and W churches. Buddhism reaches central China.		Century of Celtic literary and artistic achievement.
Justinian closes Athens University, 529: his first Law Code promulgated. Boethius executed for treason, Rome, 524. Benedictine Order founded by St Benedict at Monte Cassino, 529.		St Sophia's, Constantinople, built. Tombs of Theodoric and Gallia Placida at Ravenna. Poetry flourishing in Wales. Earliest pagoda at Honan, China.
St David preaching in Wales, c. 550.		Zenith of Byzantine art and literature.
Buddhism introduced to Japan. Birth of Mohammed, 571. St Sophia consecrated, 563. St Columba establishes monastery at Iona, 563, begins converting Picts.		
First Buddhist monastery in Japan, 587. Visigoths and Lombards became Catholic. Pope Gregory sends Augustine to England, 596: he baptizes Ethelbert of Kent, 597. Irish missionaries in France.		

600–99

Date	History, Politics and People	Economics and Sociology
600–19	Revived Persian Empire spreads: overruns Palestine, Syria and Egypt, 614–19.	
620–39	First Norse raids on Irish coast. Byzantine defeat Persians at Nineveh, 627: Persia in decline. Advance of Arabs, bringing with them Islam, from 632: they conquer Persia, Syria, Egypt and Armenia, and capture Jerusalem, 637.	
640–59	End of Persian Empire, 641: Arabs impose Islam which replaces Zoroastrianism as Persian religion. Arabs spread to Mediterranean: capture Cyprus, 649. In England, heathen Penda of Mercia killed by Oswiu, 655.	
660–79	Ommayads become caliphs, 660: Arabs begin conquest of N Africa, 670. Bulgarian Empire on Danube, c. 668 recognised by Byzantium, now threatened from W and E.	
680–99	Franks united again under Pepin, 687: Clovis III king of Franks, 691. Growing power of Wessex in S England. N Africa conquered by Arabs, 697.	First Arab coinage, 695.

Religion, Education and Philosophy	Science, Exploration and Technology	Music and the Arts
Irish missions in N England, Switzerland, Italy. Mohammed's vision on Mount Hira, 610.		Isidore of Seville compiling Roman and Greek classics. Height of Egyptian Coptic Art. Chinese artists settle in Japan.
The Hegira, 622: Mohammed's flight from Mecca to Medina. Start of spread of Islam over Asia Minor. In Byzantium, start of Monothelite controversy, 622. Spread of Christianity in Northumbria, E Anglia and Wessex.	622 is Year 1 in Muslim calendar.	Sutton Hoo ship burial, England, shows high quality of Anglo-Saxon art.
Arabs destroy School at Alexandria: library dispersed. Whitby Abbey founded, 656.		Dome of Rock in Jerusalem begun, 643.
Synod of Whitby, 664: Christian Britain adopts Roman, not Celtic, Christianity.	'Greek fire' first used against Arabs at siege of Constantinople, 673–7: first weapon of modern warfare.	
Anglo-Saxon missionaries travel to Europe.		Great period of Anglo-Saxon Christian art and literature begins: poet Caedmon and historian Bede flourished.

700–99

Date	History, Politics and People	Economics and Sociology
700–19	Caliphate of Walid I: Arabs invade Spain across Straits of Gibraltar and kill last Visigothic king, 711, and by 718 control of all Spain except NW corner. Leo III of Byzantium withstands Arab siege and defeats their fleet, 718. A Muslim state established in India (Sind).	Jews in Spain, previously persecuted, enjoy toleration and cultural revival under Islamic rule.
720–39	Arabs cross Pyrenees and capture Narbonne, 719; sweep north till blocked by defeat by Charles Martel at Tours, 732.	
740–59	Byzantium defeats Arabs, 745: Lombards take Ravenna from Byzantium, 751. Caliphate of Cordoba founded, 756. End of Merovingians in France: Franks recover Narbonne, 759. Abbasids overthrow Ommayads, 750. Arabs intervene in Chinese affairs, 751.	
760–79	Increased power of Tibet a threat to China. Charlemagne unites Franks, 771, subdues Saxony, conquers Lombardy, but defeated by Basques at Roncevalles, 778. Offa of Mercia leading English king, 780.	
780–99	Empress Irene defeat Iconclasts, 780: takes sole power, 797. Charlemagne extends power in Germany and Italy. Slav tribes cross Oder. First Viking raids on Britain about 790: Lindisfarne sacked, 793, Jarrow 794.	

Religion, Education and Philosophy	Science, Exploration and Technology	Music and the Arts
Christianity virtually eradicated in N Africa (except Egypt).		Earliest Islamic art. Cultural revival in China: first Japanese history written.
Iconoclast controversy in Byzantium, 726–842, leads to excommunication of emperor, 730. Germany converted to Christianity by St Boniface (from England).		Chinese music develops 5-note scale.
Islam divides into four sects, 751.	Science and medicine flourish in Muslim Spain.	Gregorian Church Music in W Europe: music school at Fulda, 746.
York the major seat of European learning under Alcuin. Islamic purge begins, 775. Christian Nestorian missions in China.		Books of Kells in Ireland: Chinese poetry flourishes. Arabs begin translation of Greek classics.
Empress Irene defeats Iconoclasts, 780.	Arabs develop chemistry as distinct from alchemy.	Golden period of Arab culture under Haroun al Rashid: Building of the Great Mosque at Cordoba begins, 785. Charlemagne patronizes arts: builds chapel at Aix-la-Chapelle.

800–919

Date	History, Politics and People	Economics and Sociology
800–19	Charlemagne crowned first Holy Roman Emperor by Pope Leo III at Rome, 25 Dec. 800. Dies, 814. Emperor Nicephorus killed by Bulgars, 811. Iona sacked by Vikings, 802.	Growth of feudalism in W Europe. W European unity does not survive death of Charlemagne.
820–39	End of Mercian supremacy in England: king of Wessex 'overlord of the Heptarchy' 829. Danish raids on England increase. Arabs take Sicily, Sardinia, Crete and invade S Italy.	
840–59	Slav confederation in central Europe, c. 840. Treaty of Verdun, 843, divides Frankish Empire. Arabs sack Rome, 846. Vikings found Dublin, c. 840: plunder Rouen and reach Paris, 841. Rurik, a Viking, from Sweden, invades Russia: his descendants found Kiev, 864. Other Vikings raid Mediterranean.	
860–79	Viking power extends: they sack Paris, Cologne and Aix: start settling permanently in England and found Viking kingdom at York 867; Alfred of Wessex defeats them at Edington, 878 and Vikings accept Christianity in return for control of E England, 'the Danelaw'. Vikings found Novgorod, 862. Decline of Tibetan power.	
880–99	Permanent separation of France and Germany, 887. Magyars settle in Hungary, c. 889. Under Alfred, united England becomes major power in Europe.	Alfred establishes a navy and a militia.
900–19	In England, Danelaw largely reconquered, 900–25. In Spain, beginning of Christian Reconquest under Alfonso III of Castile. Rise of Fatimids in Egypt.	Growth of castles in W mainland Europe as power bases of kings and nobles.

Religion, Education and Philosophy	Science, Exploration and Technology	Music and the Arts
	School of Astronomy at Baghdad.	Doge's Palace in Venice started.
Harold of Denmark, baptized at Mainz, returns to propagate Christianity in Scandinavia.	Ptolemy's System translated into Arabic.	Founding of St Mark's, Venice, c. 828.
	Arabs perfect astrolabe.	First attempts at polyphonic music. *Edda* poem cycle written down c. 855.
SS Cyril and Methodius start conversion of Slavs, 864 and invent Cyrillic alphabet. Vikings in England accept Christianity, 878. Much original Arabic philosophy.	Iceland discovered c. 870. High period of Arabic medicine.	Angkor Thom, Cambodia, started c. 865.
		Anglo-Saxon Chronicle traditionally started by Alfred the Great. Chinese and Japanese cultures separate about this time.
10th century a low-point in papal authority: many scandals, 904–74. Abbey of Cluny founded, 910.		*Thousand and One Nights* – Arabian stories – begin to appear.

920–1039

Date	History, Politics and People	Economics and Sociology
	Rome in almost permanent state of civil unrest during this century. Vikings settle in N France: Rollo 1st duke of Normandy, 912.	
920–39	Holy Roman Emperor Henry I makes gains in E and N Germany: subdues Bohemia. English defeat Danes and Scots at Brunanburh c. 937. Civil war period starts in Japan, 937. Byzantine revival: Romanus I extends Empire to Euphrates, 920–44.	
940–59	Otto I quells Bohemia and acquires Lombardy. Renewed Danish attacks on England.	
960–79	Byzantines recapture Crete and Cyprus from Arabs: victories against Bulgars from 971. Cordoba Caliphate at zenith: Sancho I of Leon pursues Christian Reconquest from 962. Renewed Viking attacks on Ireland.	
980–99	England under weak Ethelred tries to buy Danish peace by levying Danegeld (from 991). St Vladimir Prince of Kiev, 980: baptized, 988. First Viking colony in Greenland under Erik the Red, c. 982.	Italy (i.e. cities of Venice and Genoa) doing extensive trade with Arabs.
1000–19	English massacre Danes, 1002: England overrun by Danes by 1013 and Canute King of England, 1016. At Clontarf, 1014, Norse rule in Ireland ended. Henry II (Holy Roman Emperor) campaigns in Italy, crowned in Rome, 1014. Cordoba Caliphate in decline.	Danegeld tax in England marks embryonic general taxation system.
1020–39	Henry II defeats Byzantium in Italy: Byzantine decline. Canute conquers Scotland and Norway and dominates N Europe till death in 1035, when possessions	

Religion, Education and Philosophy	Science, Exploration and Technology	Music and the Arts
Cluniac discipline, 927.	Cordoba becoming principal centre of Arab science and medicine.	
St. Dunstan carries through monastic revival and church reform in England. Cordoba University, 968.		Great period of Icelandic literature. Cluniac movement affects European architecture and art.
E Christianity introduced to Kiev area by St Vladimir, 988. Norway and Sweden become Christian. Canonizations become official.		Beginning of main building at Cluny. Famous 400-pipe organ at Winchester.
Christianity spreads to Iceland and Greenland. Avicenna, Arabic philosopher, flourishes.	Leif Ericson said to have discovered N America, 'Vinland' c. 1000.	English heroic poem *Beowulf* written. Art reviving in Italy but much influenced by Byzantine conventions. Music of Berno of Reichenau.

1040–1139

Date	History, Politics and People	Economics and Sociology
	divided between three sons. Poland becomes an imperial fief.	
1040–59	Rise of Seljuk Turks: Togrul Beg Shah of Persia, 1040, captures Baghdad, 1055. Edward the Confessor King of England, 1042: power fluctuates between pro-Saxon and pro-Normans. Increasing power of Norman duchy vis-à-vis England and France: Normans under Guiscard found Norman kingdom, 1053, in S Italy. Holy Roman Emperor no longer to choose Pope, 1059.	
1060–79	Seljuks conquer Armenia, Syria, Palestine and capture Emperor Romanus IV at Manzikert, 1071. Edward the Confessor dies, 1066: Harold Godwinson succeeds but William of Normandy invades and kills Harold at Hastings, 14 Oct. 1066: crowned king of England 25 Dec. at Westminster Abbey. In Italy, struggle between Guelphs and Ghibellines begins, 1073. Emperor Henry IV does penance before Pope Gregory VII at Canossa, 1077.	Gradual imposition of Norman feudalism in England. After 1080 few great native English nobles remain.
1080–99	Christians capture Toledo from Moors' 1085, but Almoravids revive Arab kingdom in S Spain, 1086. Henry IV renews quarrel with Pope: War of Investiture, 1077 (till 1122) and storms Rome.	Normans build castles in England. *Domesday Book*, 1086 (compiled for fiscal and administrative purposes).
1100–19	Baldwin I, Latin King of Jerusalem, 1100–18: Crusaders capture Acre, 1104. Beginning of colonization and forcible Christianization of E Germany. Constant wars between England and France. Decline of Seljuk power.	
1120–39	Civil war in England from 1139, result of succession dispute of Matilda and Stephen.	Anarchy in England, 1135–54: baronial excesses and

Religion, Education and Philosophy	Science, Exploration and Technology	1040–1139 Music and the Arts
Schism between E and W Churches permanent, 1054. Monasteries built around Kiev. From 1059, cardinals only to elect Popes.	Astrolabes reach Europe from E.	Building of Westminster Abbey begun. Writing of the *Mabinogion*—Welsh folk tales. Polyphonic singing replaces Gregorian chant.
Gregory VII (Hildebrand) Pope, 1073: reforms Papacy. Excommunication of married priests, 1074. Denounces Lay Investiture, 1075. Humiliates Emperor, 1077. Lanfranc and Anselm reform English Church. School of Moorish philosophy in S Spain.	Halley's Comet seen.	Omar Khayyam, Persian poet, flourished. Distinctive Romanesque architecture in England ('Norman'). Making of Bayeux Tapestry.
Paris a centre of learning under Peter Abelard. First Cistercian monastery at Cîteaux, 1098.		
Era of Scholasticism in W Europe begins.	Arabic science in decline	*Chanson de Roland*, heroic French poem. First mystery plays performed in England. French and English languages start to emerge in their modern forms. Start of French Gothic architecture.
First Lateran Council, 1123, condemns simony.		Troubadours in France. Great period of English monastic chroniclers (till *c.* 1400).

1140–1219

Date	History, Politics and People	Economics and Sociology
	Byzantines defeat Serbs and Hungarians: sign trade treaties with Venice. Attempts to solve differences between Emperor and Papacy inconclusive.	considerable social hardship.
1140–59	Second Crusade begins, 1146: fails, 1147. Henry II, son of Matilda, king of England 1154: by marriage to Eleanor of Acquitaine, England controls more of France than the French king. Henry imposes strong rule, leading to clashes with Church under Becket, Archbishop of Canterbury. End of Toltec Empire, Mexico, *c*. 1150.	
1160–79	Quarrel between Henry II of England and Becket begins, 1163, ends with Becket's murder, 1170: Henry does penance, 1174. Wars with Queen Eleanor and with France. Byzantium defeats Seljuks, 1176: Barbarossa allies with Venice against Byzantium. Saladin conquers Egypt and Syria.	Sophisticated exchequer system organised by Normans in England.
1180–99	Quarrel between Emperor and Papacy recommences. Florence an independent republic, 1198. Third Crusade, 1189–93: joined by Richard I of England who is imprisoned by the Emperor, 1192–4. Saladin *d*. 1193 at height of power. Second Mayan culture in S America.	
1200–19	Rise of Genghiz Khan: he seizes Peking, 1214 and conquers Persia, 1218. Pope places England under Interdict, 1208, and excommunicates King John, 1209; baronial revolt leads to him signing Magna Carta at Runnymede, 1215. John *d*. and France invades England, 1216–7. France defeats England and Empire at Bouvines, 1214: English territory in France diminished. Fourth Crusade, 1202–4: Constantinople sacked by Crusaders at Venetian instigation and Latin Empire established. Fifth Crusade, 1217–28. Delhi Sultanate, 1206.	'Children's Crusade' phenomenon, 1212.

Religion, Education and Philosophy	Science, Exploration and Technology	1140–1219 Music and the Arts
Carmelites founded, 1155. Nicholas IV, only English Pope, 1154–9. Oxford University traditionally founded *c.* 1149.		Courtly poetry in France and Germany.
Thomas Becket murdered at Canterbury, 1170: canonized, 1173. St Francis of Assisi born, 1182. Anti-Semitism in England and France. Beginning of Waldensian movement in S France.		First *eisteddfod* in Wales, 1176. Walter Map systemizes Arthurian legends.
Pope Innocent III, 1198–1216: a reformer, anxious to reassert papal authority.		Early English architectural style. Scandinavian *Edda*: German *Nibelungenlied*: French *fabliaux*.
Franciscan order of friars founded, 1209; Poor Clares, 1212. Albigensian heresy growth leads to Albigensian 'Crusade' in S France and foundation of Dominician Order to combat heresy, 1216.		Golden age of German epic poetry: von Eschenbach's *Parsifal* and von Strassburg's *Isolde*. Century of finely illuminated books in W Europe: *Books of Hours*, etc.

1220–99

Date	History, Politics and People	Economics and Sociology
1220–39	Mongols under Genghiz Khan invade Russia, 1223: overrun it, seizing Moscow, 1237. Cordoba falls to the Castilians, 1236. 1238: Sixth Crusade. Moorish kingdom of Granada founded, 1238.	Leprosy arrives in Europe (from Middle E).
1240–59	At Liegnitz, 1241, Mongols defeat Germans, invade Poland and Hungary. Then abandon Europe and 'Golden Horde' settles on Lower Volga, 1242. Kublai Khan governor of China, 1251, and Mongol ruler, 1259. Yuan dynasty established. War starts between Venice and Genoa, 1256, resulting in eventual decline of Genoese power. Seventh Crusade, 1245: Louis IX of France captured by Saracens, 1250.	
1260–79	Eighth Crusade on which Louis IX *d.*, 1270. Misgovernment in England leads to Barons War, 1262: leader, Simon de Montfort, killed at Evesham, 1265. English possessions in France further depleted. Michael VIII Palaelogus regains Byzantium from Latins, 1261. Death of Kublai Khan, 1294.	Florence becomes world banking centre.
1280–99	Edward I of England seizes Scottish throne, 1296; moves Stone of Scone to London. Attempts to conquer Wales and Scotland. 'Model Parliament', 1295. Sicilian Vespers: French massacre in Sicily, 1282. End of Crusading era: Mamelukes take Acre, 1291. Teutonic Knights subdue Prussia. Osman I, founded of Ottoman Empire, succeeds, 1288.	

Religion, Education and Philosophy	Science, Exploration and Technology	Music and the Arts
Cambridge University founded (first charter, 1231). Franciscans reach England, 1224. Inquisition against Albigensians in Toulouse, 1229; Dominicians control Inquisition from 1233.	Porcelain manufacture begins in Japan. Arab geographic. encyclopaedia compiled.	
Collegiate system taking shape at Oxford, Cambridge and Paris (there by nationality). Period of English mystical writing (till c. 1400). Albigensians defeated and liquidated, 1245: Inquisition officially sanctions torture.	Roger Bacon, most notable scientist of his century flourished. Recorded existence of gunpowder substance.	Start of Alhambra, Granada, and modern Cologne Cathedral. Church of St Francis at Assisi finished.
Thomas Aquinas flourished. Scholasticism at height. Flagellant movement begins in Germany, spreads to France. Roger Bacon imprisoned for heresy (1277).	Marco Polo travels to China, 1271; enters service of Kublai Khan, 1275–92.	Italian art flourishes with Cimabue and Giotto. First school of mastersingers (Mainz). Motet form evolves. Dante flourished. Lohengrin written.
	Marco Polo returns to Italy, 1292, starts writing account of travels from prison.	Much building and art activity in Florence, financed by banking wealth.

1300–99

Date	History, Politics and People	Economics and Sociology
1300–19	Edward names his son Prince of Wales, 1301: Scots defeat Edward II at Bannockburn, 1314, and regain independence. Council of Ten established in Venice, 1310. Start of Swiss struggle for independence from the Empire, 1307. Osman I defeats Byzantines, 1301.	Salic Law adopted in France, 1317, excluding women from succession to crown.
1320–39	Edward II deposed and murdered, 1327: his son Edward III claims French crown and Hundred Years War starts, 1338. First Valois king succeeds in France, 1328 (Philip VI). Height of Arabic civilization in Granada kingdom. Greater Serbia founded by Stephen Dushan, 1331. Aztecs build Mexico City.	First descriptions of bubonic plague (India).
1340–59	English win battles of Crecy, 1346 and Poitiers, 1356, when French king taken prisoner. Treaty of London, 1359. Hapsburgs sign Treaty with Swiss League, 1358. Ottoman Turks advance into Europe, 1353. Revolution in Rome under Rienzi, 1347: Rienzi murdered, 1354. Golden Bull, 1356, establishes electoral constitution of Holy Roman Empire.	Black Death reaches Europe, decimates England, 1349–51, then reappears sporadically. Exacerbates feudal decline and social changes. Edward III founds Order of Garter, *c.* 1346–8.
1360–79	England allies with Burgundy, 1360 against France: truce between England and France 1375–8. Stewarts accede to Scottish throne, 1371. Ming Dynasty replaces Yuan in China, 1368. Tamberlaine ascends throne of Samarkand, 1368.	Prolonged war with France leads to unrest and breakdown of social order in England.
1380–99	In England, Peasants' Revolt, 1381, suppressed: England losing war in France. Richard II deposed and murdered, 1399: accession of Henry IV, son of John of Gaunt. Norway, Denmark and Sweden unite in Union of Kalmar, 1397.	Poll taxes levied in England – early attempt at centralized personal taxation.

Religion, Education and Philosophy	Science, Exploration and Technology	1300–99 Music and the Arts
Christianity tolerated in China. Clement V establishes Papacy at Avignon, 1309, beginning of the 'Babylonian Captivity'. Templars' Grand Master burnt for heresy in Paris, 1314.	Growth of medical studies in Germany.	Building of modern Doge's Palace in Venice.
Universities being founded all over Europe during next century. John Wyclif born, 1328.		Boccaccio and Petrarch flourished. Alhambra, Granada, extended. Counterpoint music developed.
	Hundred Years War leads to development of archery, resulting in crossbow: and development of heavy cannon.	Papal Palace at Avignon built.
Scholastic debates at Oxford alarm Church. Pope Gregory XI returns to Rome: beginning of Great Schism in Church, 1378. John Hus b.c. 1370.	Crossbow first used in warfare.	Growth of vernacular literature. Chaucer, Langland in England, Froissart in France. Age of great Flemish Primitive painting.
Wyclif expelled from Oxford, 1382 and doctrines condemned. Hus lectures in Prague.	Gutenberg, traditional inventor of European printing, b. 1397	Wyclif's Bible in English written.

1400–59

Date	History, Politics and People	Economics and Sociology
	Turkish advance continues: capture Sofia, 1382. Byzantium loses last possessions in Asia Minor, 1390. Defeated at Nicopolis, 1396.	
1400–19	Growing power of Florence and Venice. Tamerlane's conquests in Middle East, 1405 temporarily halt Ottoman threat to Byzantium. Sigismund becomes Emperor 1410: war between Empire and Hussites starts, 1419 (–36): Sigismund gains Bohemia. In France, civil war between Crown and Burgundy, 1406: Joan of Arc *b.*, 1412. Henry V of England reasserts claim to French throne, invades and defeats French at Agincourt, 1415. Collapse of French forces – country devastated.	Rise of Medici in Florence: they dominate European finance: Papal bankers from 1414.
1420–39	Henry V recognized as heir to French throne by Treaty of Troyes, 1420, but *d.* and succeeded by infant Henry VI and Regency: French rally under Joan of Arc, 1427, but she is captured by Burgundians (English allies) and burned at Rouen, 1431. French-Burgundian peace at Arras, 1435 and henceforth English steadily driven back. Hussites defeated by Emperor: Compact of Iglau, 1436: Bohemia subjugated. First Turkish siege of Constantinople, 1422. Growth of Aztec Empire in Mexico. Inca Empire founded *c.* 1435.	Exotic Burgundian court influences courtly life all over Europe: Order of the Golden Fleece founded, 1429.
1440–59	Turks advance into Europe: rise of the Hunyadis in Hungary, who defeat them at Varna, 1444; Belgrade, 1456. Byzantium falls to Turks, 1453 and last E Emperor, Constantine XI, killed: end of Eastern Empire. Athens captured and Acropolis sacked, 1458. English lose all French possessions except Calais and Hundred Years War ends, 1453: Wars of Roses start, 1455. Sforzas become dukes of Milan, 1450. In Empire, Turkish raids start after Kossovo, 1448. In Bohemia, temporary Hussite revival under Podebrad (1456–71).	African slave trade to Europe begun by Portuguese. Breakdown of law and order due to civil wars and aftermath all over W Europe.

Religion, Education and Philosophy	Science, Exploration and Technology	1400–59 Music and the Arts
Height of Lollard heresy in England: burnings, 1401–19. Hus burned for heresy at Constance, 1415. Council of Constance: Martin V elected Pope in Rome, 1417: end of Great Schism. Age of Flemish mysticism: Thomas à Kempis flourished.		'Early Renaissance' period. Golden Age of Burgundian court music and arts. Froissart flourished.
Empire persecutes Hussites in Bohemia and Germany.	Beginning of era of Portuguese exploration: Cabral discovers Azores, 1431–2. Heavy guns increasingly used in warfare by Byzantines.	French poet François Villon flourished.
Virtual elimination of Christianity in Asian Byzantium after 1453: Islam spreads to Turkish-occupied E Europe. St Sophia's becomes a mosque. Pope Pius II, 1458–64: 'humanist' Pope. General decline of religious orders in West.	Tristao discovers Cape Verde, 1443. Coster printing from wooden blocks, Haarlem, 1440: Constance Mass Book printed by Gutenberg (movable type), 1450.	Eton and King's College Cambridge founded by Henry VI: King's College Chapel begun, 1446. Vatican Library begun, 1450.

1460–1519

Date	History, Politics and People	Economics and Sociology
1460–79	In England, Edward of York crowned Edward IV, 1461: defeats Lancastrians and has Henry VI murdered, 1471. Turks spread to Balkans: take Bosnia and Herzegovina. 1477: marriage contract ensures future union of Burgundy and Empire. 1479: union of Castile and Leon under Ferdinand and Isabella (married 1469). Age of *condottieri* in Italy.	Growth of German banking: Fuggers become Hapsburg bankers.
1480–99	In England, Tudors under Henry VII replace Plantagenets after defeat and death of Richard III at Bosworth, 1485: government centralized. Charles VIII of France invades Italy, 1494–5 and Italy becomes battlefield between France and Empire for next 50 years: Brittany joined to France, 1499. Spain conquers Granada, 1492: end of Moorish rule in Spain. Marriage between Joanna of Castile and Philip of Burgundy, 1496, foreshadows union of Spain and Empire. Swiss independence ensured by Treaty of Basel, 1499. Venice seizes Cyprus, 1489: but fleet defeated by Turks, 1499 and Venice in decline.	Syphilis ravages W. Europe: brought from Naples by invading French army, 1494.
1500–19	In England, Henry VIII succeeds, 1509, and marries Catherine of Aragon: with Wolsey, tries to make England a major world power: defeats Scots at 1513. Pope confirms that German king henceforth automatically Holy Roman Emperor, 1508: attempts to reform Imperial government founder. Pope Julius II tries to drive French from Italy but Francis I conquers Milan, 1515. Archduke Charles becomes King of Spain, 1516, and Emperor (as Charles V), 1519. Empire at height of territorial power. Turkish expansion continues in E, with conquest of Egypt and Arabia. Spanish Empire in S America founded: Cortes received by Montezuma in Mexico, 1519.	African slaves introduced to S America by Portuguese *c.* 1510.

Religion, Education and Philosophy	Science, Exploration and Technology	1460–1519 Music and the Arts
Beginning of Humanism in W Europe. Erasmus born, 1465; Thomas More, 1478; Machiavelli, 1469. Inquisition moves against Jews in Spain.	Gold Coast (Ghana) discovered by Portuguese. Caxton prints first book in English, Bruges, 1474: in England, 1477. Age of invention: Leonardo da Vinci, etc. Oxford University Press founded.	Papacy becomes major art patron.
Italian campaigns, and papal involvement in them, detract from papal spirituality. Spanish Inquisition under joint control of Crown and Church from 1481: Jews expelled from Spain, 1492, from Portugal, 1496. Puritanical rule of Savonarola in Florence. Humanism begins to verge on religious dissent.	1492, Columbus, under Spanish patronage, discovers N American continent. 1493: Pope Alexander III divides New World between Spain and Portugal. Cabots commissioned by Henry VII to find new trade route to Asia. Revised study of algebra astronomy etc.	Explosion of artistic activity in Italy and the Empire: Leonardo, Michaelangelo, Holbein, Dürer, etc.
Luther nails theses on door of Wittenberg church, 1517, marking start of Reformation – touched off by Indulgence sales. Zwingli attacking papal doctrines in Zurich, 1519. 'New Learning' flourishes in England, especially at Cambridge: More, Colet and Fisher advocate reform within the Catholic Church. Erasmus publishes New Testament with Greek and Latin text, 1516, More writes *Utopia*.	Portuguese explore Africa and Brazil: reach China, India and E Indies. Magellan begins voyage to circumnavigate globe, 1519. Spanish explore W Indies, S and central America. Copernicus states earth revolves round sun, 1512. Printing flourishing in W Europe.	Beginning of rebuilding of St Peter's Rome, 1513 (leads to Indulgences sales to finance it – one factor resulting in the Reformation). 'High Renaissance' in Italy.

1520–59

Date	History, Politics and People	Economics and Sociology
	Fluctuating international treaties mark emergence of modern doctrine of 'balance of power'.	
1520–39	Henry VIII's failure to obtain papal consent to divorce from Catherine of Aragon results in Henry declaring himself Supreme Head of the Church in England, 1531; Cranmer archbishop of Canterbury, and Henry marries Anne Boleyn, 1533. English Reformation effective from 1536: monasteries dissolved, 1536–40. Luther excommunicated, 1520, but sheltered by German princes dissatisfied with Imperial rule: Protestant Union against Charles V, 1524; Prussia secularized, 1525; German Peasants' Revolt savagely put down, 1524–5; Anabaptists in Munster, 1534; suppressed, 1535. Swiss Protestant and Catholic cantons at war, 1531; Zwingli killed. Calvin in Geneva, 1536; expelled, 1538. Protestantism spreads to France, Flanders and Scandinavia. Suleiman the Magnificent succeeds, 1520: defeats Hungarians at Mohacs, 1526; besieges Vienna, 1529. Imperialists sack Rome, 1527; imperial control of papacy results in denial of Henry VIII's divorce (from Emperor's aunt), hence English Reformation. 1533, Ivan IV, the Terrible, Tsar of Russia (aged 3). End of Aztec Empire in Mexico after Cortes's victory, 1521; in Peru, Pizarro crushes Incas, 1533.	Dissolution of monasteries in Protestant countries leads to deprivation and revolts (e.g. England and Germany). Severe inflation in W Europe. Increased fluidity of social structures, especially in England and Low Countries. Beginnings of modern nationalism and capitalism.
1540–59	War in Germany between Protestant princes and Emperor ended by Peace of Augsburg, 1555; Lutheran states to have same rights as Catholic. Charles V abdicates, 1556; Empire goes to brother Ferdinand I and Spain to son Philip II. Henry VIII *d.*, 1547. Succeeded by Edward VI, till 1553, and extreme Protestant regime. Catholic reaction under Mary Tudor, 1553–8, with many Protestants burned. Elizabeth succeeds, 1558 and Act of Settlement establishes Church of	

Religion, Education and Philosophy	Science, Exploration and Technology	1520–59 Music and the Arts
Reformation in England, Scandinavia, parts of France, Germany and Scandinavia: ideas spread to Italy and Poland. Luther translates Bible into German: Tyndale's translation of New Testament printed abroad, 1525. Growth of Anabaptism in German. Universities in Protestant countries secularized. Beginnings of Counter-Reformation: Jesuit Order founded by Ignatius Loyola, 1534.	Cartier discovers St. Lawrence River, 1534. Name 'America' first used by Mercator, 1538.	In Protestant countries, destruction of monastic buildings, shrines, etc. but expansion of church music among Catholics and Protestants. Luther a leading hymn-writer. Use of vernacular in Scriptures encourages learning down social scale in Protestant countries.
Calvin institutes Protestant theocracy in Geneva, 1541: John Knox leads Scottish Reformation. Spanish Inquisition burns Protestants, 1543. Council of Trent, 1545–63, establishes principles of Counter Reformation.	Chancellor visits Russia via Archangel, 1553. Spaniards penetrate SE of N America. Servetus discovers pulmonary circulation of the blood, 1540.	Literary and musical renaissance in France and England: Ronsard, du Bellay in France: Wyatt, Howard, in England.

1560–99

Date	History, Politics and People	Economics and Sociology
	England in modern form, 1559, the 'Via Media'. England loses Calais, 1558. Reformation in Scotland from 1541; Catholic Mary Stuart becomes Queen of Scotland, 1542. In France, Protestants (Huguenots) increasingly powerful among nobility. Peace between Venice and Turkey, 1540; between Turkey and Empire, 1545. Calvin returns to Geneva, 1541, which becomes a Calvinist theocracy till his death (1564).	
1560–79	Civil wars of religion in France: Henry of Navarre leader of Huguenots from . 1577 Massacre of St Bartholomew, 1572. Mary Stuart returns to Scotland, 1562; civil war there results in her fleeing to England, where she is imprisoned, 1567, and becomes focus for Catholic unrest. Irish rebellions against English rule; Reformation resisted in Ireland after early compliance. Duke of Alba governor of the Spanish Netherlands, 1567, and active revolt against Spain follows: Spanish sack Antwerp, 1576; England supports rebels against Spain and Drake attacks Spanish ships and W Indies' possessions. In Russia, Ivan IV attacks power of boyars. Turkey makes gains in Mediterranean; but fleet defeated by John of Austria at Lepanto, 1571 and forced to lift siege of Malta, 1565.	Slave trade introduced to W Indies from W Africa by English.
1580–99	Spain absorbs Portugal: is defeated in Netherlands where William of Orange (*d.* 1584) becomes effective ruler of N Netherlands (Holland), 1583. Spain intervenes in French civil wars but at Peace of Vervins, 1598 renounces claims to French throne: suffers increasing English harassment in Netherlands, Americas and Mediterranean (e.g. Drake attacks Vigo, 1585) and Armada, sent to invade England, destroyed, 1588. Philip II *d.* 1598 and Spain now in decline. End of Valois dynasty in France, 1589	In Spain, economy falls into imbalance due to bullion imports from New World: outflow of younger sons to New World to colonize S and Central America. Inquisition in Spain stifles enterprise in all fields. Colonial acquisitions make transportation a European punishment:

Religion, Education and Philosophy	Science, Exploration and Technology	Music and the Arts
Jesuit missions in Japan and S America. Grammar Schools founded and refounded in England under Edward VI: secular colleges at Oxford and Cambridge.		
Influx of Protestant refugees to England from Low Countries: growth of Puritanism within English Church. Counter-Reformation in Poland. Congregation of the Oratory founded by Philip Neri in Rome, 1564. Index published, 1564. Pope excommunicates Elizabeth I, 1570: first Jesuits reach England and are executed. Jesuits make many converts in Japan. Period of Spanish mysticism: St John of the Cross, St Teresa of Avila.	Francis Drake starts on voyage round world, 1577. Medical advances by Paré in France. Map-making science improves as discoveries enhance knowledge: Mercator flourished.	Shakespeare *b*. 1564: growth of London theatre. Evolution of distinctive Elizabethan domestic architecture and gardens.
Execution of Jesuits in England, including Edmund Campion (1581). Growth of secularist-based philosophy in Europe. Elizabeth I founds Trinity College, Dublin, 1591. Catholic revival in Ireland, linked with nationalism.	England founds Newfoundland colony, 1583; Raleigh discovers Virginia, 1584. Dutch active in E Indies. Exploration boom leads to revolution in navigational theory and instruments. Hakluyt writes his navigational works. Galileo professor of	Shakespeare's plays being performed: Marlowe, Sidney, etc. flourished. In Spain, devotional art of El Greco. Byrd (England) and Palestrina (Italy) notable for church music.

1600–39

Date	History, Politics and People	Economics and Sociology
	Protestant Henry of Navarre succeeds: war continues but in 1593 Henry becomes Catholic, crowned 1594. Huguenots tolerated and peace established. Empire fights off Turkish threats, but Turks reach Hungary. Empire resists claims of a revived Poland and Protestant threats in S Germany. England gains international status by defeat of Armada: extends influence in New World. Executes Mary Stuart, 1587 and many Catholics over period. In Japan, dictatorship of Hideyoshi 1585–98: shogunate then revived (till 1867).	in England from 1597.
1600–19	Elizabeth I *d.* 1603, succeeded by James of Scotland: England and Scotland united. Spanish army helping Irish rebels surrenders, 1602: rebellion collapses and N Ireland resettled by Protestants from Scotland and England. Gunpowder Plot, 1605. Michael, first of Romanov Tsars, accedes, 1613. Growth of Sweden as military power: becomes Protestant champion in Continental Europe. Empire attempts to assert authority and maintain Catholic dominance, especially in Hungary and Bohemia: 'Defenestration of Prague', 1618 leads to outbreak of Thirty Years War (till 1648) which devastates large parts of Germany. War between Turkey and Persia, 1602 (till 1627). Jesuit state in Paraguay, 1608–11.	England and Netherlands become dominant trading nations. First African slaves arrive on N American mainland (Virginia, 1619). Tobacco and potatoes reach Europe. Native societies of S and Central America being destroyed by Spanish and Portuguese English Poor Law System founded, 1601.
1620–39	Empire defeats Bohemia at White Mountain, 1620: Thirty Years War then moves to Germany proper. Gustavus Adolphus of Sweden, Protestant champion, defeats Empire at Lutzen, 1632, but is killed. After Peace of Prague, 1635, France intervenes on Protestant side against Hapsburgs: start of 150 years' conflict between France and Austria.	Period marks consolidation of power of landed gentry and successful London tradesmen in England (as opposed to Crown and large landowners the established hereditary nobility).

Religion, Education and Philosophy	Science, Exploration and Technology	1600–39 Music and the Arts
Bodley starts restoring and extending 15thC library at Oxford. First Christian persecutions in Japan.	mathematics at Pisa, 1589. Italian interest in antiquities: catacombs (part) and Pompeii rediscovered. Archery in warfare obsolete in Europe.	
Attempts at Counter-Reformation in Scandinavia (unsuccessful) and Poland (ultimately successful). Persecution of Bohemian Protestants by Empire. Growth of Protestant dissent in England. Authorized Version of the Bible, 'King James', published London 1611. In Spain, expulsion of Moriscos, 1609–14.	Astronomic cooperation of Brahe and Kepler at Prague, 1600 onwards. Galileo's telescope, 1608, but G. prohibited from working by the Church after 1616. John Speed's maps, 1610. Hudson Bay explored, 1610. Harvey's discovery of blood circulation, 1619.	In Spain, more secular art: Velasquez. In Netherlands, emergence of Protestant trading houses brings a new type of art patron.
Disputes in England between High and Low Church parties. Persecution of Dissenters, leading to emigration to New England. Religious intolerance in several Puritan New England colonies. Harvard founded, 1638.	Dutch colonies in America: French colonial growth. Kepler's teachings censured by Catholic Church. Thirty Years' War produces advances in armaments.	Building of Taj Mahal by Shah Jehan c. 1630–52. Century of literary brilliance in England and France: Charles I patron of art and invites Van Dyck to England. Golden age of painting in Italy, Netherlands and Spain.

1640–79

Date	History, Politics and People	Economics and Sociology
	In France, Richelieu crushes Protestant revolt at La Rochelle: centralizes government. James I of England *d.* 1625, and Charles I attempts to govern without Parliament but unrest grows on fiscal, constitutional and religious issues. First Bishops' War (against Scots), 1639. Several crown colonies founded in America, e.g. Virginia and Maryland in reply to Puritan foundations, e.g. Pilgrim Fathers leave Plymouth in Mayflower, 1620, to found Plymouth Colony, New England. Shah Jehan becomes Great Mogul of India, 1627.	
1640–59	Outbreak of English Civil War, 1642: initial Royalist victories but eventual defeat by Parliament and Charles I executed, 1649. England proclaimed a Commonwealth, Cromwell Lord Protector, 1653; *d.* 1658. Trade wars with Dutch. Cromwell defeats Royalists in Ireland; savage repression there, 1649–50. Peace of Westphalia, 1648 ends Thirty Years War: religious toleration in Germany excluding Hapsburg territories. Independence of Netherlands and Switzerland guaranteed. French gains mark beginning of French hegemony in Europe. In France, Mazarin crushes power of nobility in wars with Fronde, 1648–53: Louis XIV accedes, 1643. Beginning of rise of Brandenburg in N Germany. End of Ming dynasty in China: Manchus come to power, 1644 (till 1912). Japan closed to foreigners (except limited access to Dutch) from *c.* 1640.	Under Bourbons, state monopolies feature of French economy. Tea appears in Europe Colonization of N America marks start of displacement of N American Indians. Puritan laws on Sunday observance in England.
1660–79	Restoration of Charles II in England, 1660: he attempts tolerant rule but many Catholics die in Popish Plot, 1678; he obtains French money secretly after Treaty of Dover, 1670, which gives him some independence of Parliament. Peace of Oliva, 1660, recognizes	Great Plague in England especially London, 1665 Great Fire of London, 1666.

Religion, Education and Philosophy	Science, Exploration and Technology	Music and the Arts
Age of Donne, Bacon, in England: Descartes in France. Christianity virtually obliterated from Japan, 1637–40: but missionaries welcomed in China.		
Limited religious toleration in non-Hapsburg Germany after 1648. Episcopacy in England abolished under Commonwealth but Dissent tolerated and Jews tolerated by Cromwell. Rise of Jansenism in France. Quakers founded by George Fox c. 1647. Descartes, Pascal, Hobbes flourished. English replaces Latin in all legal documents, 1649. Civil war controversies encourage political writing at all levels: embryonic socialism of Levellers and Diggers.	Tasman discovers Tasmania and New Zealand, 1642: parts of Australia chartered, 1644. Aggressive colonizing brings conflicts between England and Holland, England and France: Dutch settle in S Africa, English in S India, 1639.	Milton flourished in England. Bernini working in Rome. Charles I's art collection sold by the Commonwealth and dispersed. Destruction of English stained glass and statuary in churches and cathedrals by Puritan extremists.
Restoration of episcopacy in England. Much religious writing: Bunyan, Watts, Burnet. 1662 Prayerbook issued. Charles II fails to get official toleration for	French explore Mississippi valley. Isaac Newton flourished: Greenwich Observatory built, by Wren, 1675.	Great period of English Restoration theatre: actresses play female parts for first time. Rebuilding of St Paul's (designed by Wren) and many City

1680–1719

Date	History, Politics and People	Economics and Sociology
	Brandenburg sovereignty over E Prussia. Rise of Sweden as major power. Louis XIV attempts to crush Dutch from 1667; Peace of Nijmegen, 1678. Turks invade Slovakia, 1663; truce with Empire, 1664. Capture Crete from Venice, 1669. Defeated by Poles 1673. French build up colonial Empire in N America.	
1680–99	Catholic James II succeeds Charles II, 1685: defeats Monmouth but deposed in 'Glorious Revolution', 1688 which establishes William III of Orange on English throne. Beginning of 'Whig Supremacy'. England becomes involved in Dutch struggle against France. William III Irish crushes Jacobite rebellion at Battle of Boyne, 1691. Turks besiege Vienna unsuccessfully, 1683; Turkish decline begins. Emperor occupies Belgrade, 1688–90. Russia under Peter the Great attacks Turkey; captures Azov, 1696. Russia becomes champion of Balkan Christians occupied by Turkey. Louis XIV revokes Edict of Nantes, 1685 and Huguenots leave France: settle especially in Prussia and England. Peace of Ryswick, 1697, concludes wars with Holland.	Bank of England founded, 1691. National Debt in England begins, 1692. 'Modernization' of Russian society forcibly carried out by Peter the Great.
1700–19	Great Northern War starts, 1700; Charles XII of Sweden builds an Empire extending into Poland and Russia but defeated by Peter the Great at Poltava, 1709, captured by Turks, 1713–14, killed, 1718. Thereafter Sweden declines. Elector Frederick III of Brandenburg crowns himself King of Prussia, 1703. In England Act of Settlement, 1701 provides for Protestant Succession: Anne rules, 1702–14. Union with Scotland, 1707. George I of Hanover succeeds, 1714: unsuccessful Jacobite Rising, 1715. Charles II of Spain *d.* 1700: Philip V,	Last witchcraft execution in England, 1712. Centring of court life on Versailles by Louis XIV and XV finally destroys French nobility's links with peasantry and Crown's links with Paris and intelligentsia. In England coffee houses play important part in political and business life.

Religion, Education and Philosophy	Science, Exploration and Technology	1680–1719 Music and the Arts
Catholics. French send missions to N American Indians. Trappist Order founded, 1664. Spinoza flourished. Royal Society founded, 1660.		churches after Great Fire. Diarists Pepys and Marvell in England. Purcell dominated English music. Louis XIV great art patron: age of Molière and Corneille. Building of Versailles, 1661–87.
Edict of Nantes revoked by Louis XIV: Huguenots leave France, 1685. Pennsylvania founded as Quaker colony, 1682. New England Salem witch-trials, 1692. SPCK founded, 1698.	Newton's theory of gravity, 1683. Calcutta founded by British, 1687. Dampier explores NW Australia, 1698.	
Century of 'Rationalism' and 'Reason'. Russia expels Jesuits, 1719. Age of Locke, Leibnitz, etc. Growth of news-sheets.	Newton president of Royal Society, 1703. Fahrenheit's temperature scale, c. 1712 Edmund Halley flourished.	Bach, Handel flourished: modern opera and oratorio evolve. In France court and country life typified by Watteau and Chardin. In England, Clarendon's *History* published (1702): Professorship of Poetry, Oxford, founded 1708. Distinct Georgian church and country house architecture evolves.

1720–59

Date	History, Politics and People	Economics and Sociology
	grandson of Louis XIV, heir to Spanish throne. War of Spanish Succession, 1702–13 – France against England, Empire, Prussia, Holland. Military successes by Marlborough and Prince Eugène. English take Gibraltar, 1704. Peace of Utrecht, 1713, ends war: France and Spanish Bourbons separate: French military power in Europe shattered. France bankrupted by wars and court extravagance: Camisard revolt, 1702–6. Louis XIV *d.* 1715. 1713: Pragmatic Sanction, an attempt to ensure Maria Thérèsa's succession to Empire. Empire and Russia make progress against Turkey: Turks leave Hungary, 1716; Eugène defeats Turks at Belgrade, 1716. Russia acquires Finland, 1710–11.	
1720–39	Pragmatic Sanction receives assent of major powers. Maria Thérèsa marries Francis of Lorraine, 1736, and Empire gets Tuscany, 1737. Poland increasingly unstable and intrigued against. Frederick William I of Prussia builds up army. France and England quarrel increasingly over American and Indian possessions. Russian expansion halted temporarily after Peter I's death, 1725; Turkish decline also halted, they drive Imperial army back to Belgrade, 1738. Persians sack Delhi, 1739. Tibet absorbed by China, 1720.	England establishes trade links with Russia. England becomes major financial centre: South Sea Bubble crisis, 1720–1. Lloyd's list issued, from 1726. Gin drinking in England a major social evil, especially in London. Evolution of a 'prime minister' in English government (from Sir Robert Walpole, 1721 ff).
1740–59	1740: death of Charles VI and accession of Maria Thérèsa leads to War of Austrian Succession 1741–8. Francis of Lorraine elected titular emperor, 1745 and Treaty of Aix recognizes Pragmatic Sanction but Prussia keeps Silesia, captured, 1741. Frederick II succeeds in Prussia, 1740: attacks Austria and gains Silesia, 1741. England allies with Austria against France and Prussia. 1756: outbreak of Seven Years War:	Wearing of Scottish tartans prohibited in Britain, 1746–82. Anti-semitic pogroms in Russia. Cotton being imported to Britain from E. Smuggling a major 'black' industry in Britain for next 50 years. Hambledon cricket club, 1750.

Religion, Education and Philosophy	Science, Exploration and Technology	1720–59 Music and the Arts
John and Charles Wesley found Methodist group at Oxford, 1730. Papal Bull against Freemasonry, 1738. Rationalism expounded by Hume, Butler, Pope, Voltaire. 'Exclusion' policy in China from 1722: Christian teaching prohibited.	Kay patents flying shuttle loom, 1733. Glassmaking starts at Murano, 1736. Linnaeus flourished. Revolutionary husbandry system begun in Norfolk by Townshend c. 1730– beginning of the Agricultural Revolution.	10 Downing St. London, becomes official residence of British prime minister. Covent Garden opened (as theatre), 1732. In Italy, Vivaldi flourished.
Encyclopaedists in France: Diderot, Rousseau flourished. Frederick the Great encourages French philosophers to his court: Kant writing. In England, Burke putting forward progressive views; in America, Franklin.	1752: Britain adopts Gregorian calendar. Centigrade thermometer, 1742. French explorers reach Rockies. Dutch explore S Africa beyond Orange River. Halley's comet, 1758.	Sans Souci, Berlin, begun, 1745. In England, school of portrait and landscape painting: Reynolds, Gainsborough, etc. Johnson leading London literary figure. Emergence of the novel in England: Fielding, Richardson, etc.

1760–99

Date	History, Politics and People	Economics and Sociology
	England allies with Prussia against France and Austria. England makes gains against France in New World and India. Clive arrives in India. 1744, Black Hole of Calcutta, 1756. 1759: British take Montreal and gain Quebec from France. In England, 2nd Jacobite Rising, 1745 under Charles Stuart ends in Jacobite defeat at Culloden, 1746. Catherine (Sophia of Anhalt) marries Peter II of Russia, 1744: Russia allies ineffectually with Austria against Prussia, 1757.	
1760–79	1762 Catherine II becomes Empress of Russia: 1st Polish Partition, 1772, between Russia and Prussia, marks start of Poland's disappearance as an independent state. Russia conquers Crimea, 1771. Peace of Paris, 1763, confirms Britain's acquisitions in America, W Indies and India. France militarily and economically weakened. George III succeeds, 1760: Britain now has vast overseas Empire. 1765: Stamp Act for taxing American colonies passed: opposed in Britain and America ('no taxation without representation') and repealed, 1766, but friction persists and American War of Independence breaks out, 1775, in New England. England uses German troops to fight colonists: France (under Lafayette) and Holland intervene on American side. In S America, Portuguese colonies organized in one unit, with Rio de Janeiro as capital, 1763.	Canal boom begins in England. Agricultural changes multiply – drift to towns and beginning of Industrial Revolution. (Similar processes start rather later in Europe.) American Congress stops importing of slaves, 1778. Papacy starts draining Rome marshes, 1779. Some social awakening in England: John Howard writes on prison reform.
1780–99	Britain defeated in N America: 1783, war over with Peace of Versailles: Britain recognizes independence of USA. Loyalists emigrate to Canada (Ontario). First US Congress meets, 1789 and Washington first President. In Britain, Grattan demands Home Rule for Ireland, 1780; Pitt forms ministry, 1783, but progressive policy halted by	First building society in Birmingham c. 1780. French Revolution overturns society: estates broken up, church property seized. Metric system introduced, 1795. Income tax introduced

Religion, Education and Philosophy	Science, Exploration and Technology	1760–99 Music and the Arts
Jesuits expelled from several countries and Order dissolved by Clement XIV, 1773. Spread of Methodism (not yet defined as such) in England and Wales. Rousseau's *Social Contract*, 1762: Smith's *Wealth of Nations*, 1776. American problems encourage liberal political thought in England: Burke, Fox, Priestley, etc. General spiritual decline in Europe.	New period of discovery in Pacific: Cook discovers Botany Bay, 1770, Hawaii, 1778. De Bougainville discovers Tahiti, Solomons and New Guinea. Age of scientific enquiry in Britain: Priestley, Watts. Watts perfects steam engine, 1776.	Revival of historical interest in Britain with Hume, Gibbon, etc. Royal Academy, London, founded, 1768. Hogarth painting commentaries on English social scene. Vienna becomes world musical centre with Haydn and Mozart.
Religious freedom in Empire declared by Joseph II, 1781: Christian religion banned in France, 1793 but toleration from 1795. Revolutionary philosophies of Thomas Paine, William Godwin.	In Britain, inventions aid Industrial Revolution: Watt's engine in Nottingham cotton mill, 1785; iron being exported from 1790s. Threshing machine, 1784. First steam-driven mill,	Growth of romanticism in music and arts: in Germany, Goethe and Schiller, in Britain, Blake and Burns. Louvre becomes French national art gallery: David paints the French Revolution.

1800–19

Date	History, Politics and People	Economics and Sociology
	threat from French Revolution after 1789. at war with France, 1793–1802. Nelson destroys French fleet, 1798 at Aboukir Bay. In France, economic and political unrest forces Louis XVI to recall States General, 1789: outbreak of French Revolution and storming of Bastille. Feudalism abolished, Republic proclaimed, 1792. Jacobins seize power, Louis tried and executed. French revolutionary army declares war on Austria, Prussia and Sardinia, 1792: first Coalition against France, 1793. Reign of Terror ends with Robespierre's execution, 1794, and establishment of Directory, with Napoleon as C-in-C, 1795. Napoleon's Italian victories, 1796–8: in Middle East, 1799. Directory overthrown, 1799: Napoleon Consul. In Russia, Catherine the Great conquers the Crimea, 1783. 2nd Partition of Poland, 1793; 3rd, 1795: Poland absorbed by Russia, Austria and Prussia.	in Britain (as temporary measure), 1799. Serfdom abolished in Austria, 1781: slavery abolished in French colonies, 1794. Malthus' treatise on population growth, 1798. Transportation to Australia from 1783.
1800–19	Holy Roman Empire officially ended, 1806. French wars halt with Peace of Amiens, 1802, but war with Britain renewed, 1803. Battle of Trafalgar, 1805. France defeats Prussia, 1806. Napoleon Emperor, 1804: crowned in Paris in Pope's presence. By 1810 Napoleon controls most of continental Europe but Russian campaign fails 1812–13 and Prussian victories 1813–14 lead to Napoleon's abdication and banishment to Elba, 1814. Congress of Vienna starts, 1814. 'Hundred Days': Napoleon escapes from Elba but defeated by Allies at Waterloo, 1815 and exiled to St Helena. Congress of Vienna settles Europe along conservative lines: Swedish throne to Bernadotte. French Revolution leads to independence movements in S and Central America. Britain acquires some French colonies and India almost totally British. Anglo-US war, 1812–14: White House burned by British.	In Britain, Wilberforce's Act abolishing slavery passed, 1801. Rapid growth of industry in Britain: slowly spreads to France, Germany, etc. Growth of modern union concept: held down initially by establishment fears of Jacobin revolution. Large-scale European emigration to N America begins. Potato now staple Irish diet.

Religion, Education and Philosophy	Science, Exploration and Technology	Music and the Arts
German philosophic school led by Kant and Fichte. Gordon Riots (anti-Catholic) in England, 1780: Catholic Relief Act, 1781. Compulsory education from age of 6 in France, 1793. Finding of Rosetta Stone in Egypt makes possible deciphering of hieroglyphics, 1799.	Manchester, 1789. Cotton gin, 1793. Montgolfiers build air balloon, 1782: Channel crossed by balloon, 1785. Steamboat on Delaware, 1787. Mont Blanc climbed, 1786. Jenner introduces smallpox vaccination, 1796.	Beethoven's first works published: modern piano and orchestra evolves. *Times* first published under this name, 1788. M.C.C. founded 1787.
Irish Union of 1801 does not lead to promised Catholic Emancipation. Methodism spreads in Britain, and Evangelical revival in Church of England, with social implications. Baptist Union, 1812. Evangelical Union in Prussia, 1817. Code Napoleon, 1804. Philosophy tends to discount religion. Karl Marx *b.* 1818.	First practical submarine built by Fulton, 1800. Stephenson builds first practical steam engine at Killingworth Colliery, 1814. Davy's safety lamp, 1816. Much research into electricity. Source of Ganges discovered, 1808.	Elgin Marbles bought for the British Museum, 1816. In English literature, period of Romantic poets: Byron, Shelley, Keats, Wordsworth; novels of Scott and Jane Austen. Realist paintings of Goya contrast with general romantic trend (Ingres, Turner, etc.)

1820–59

Date	History, Politics and People	Economics and Sociology
	In England, fears of Jacobinism lead to first anti-union laws: Luddites attempt to wreck new machines, 1811–15. Corn Laws instituted, 1815: depression follows end of war. Union of Ireland with England, 1801: rebellion, 1803, fails. Modern Egypt established when Mehemet Ali proclaimed Pasha, 1806, marking decline of Turkey's Middle East empire.	
1820–39	Period dominated by conservative reaction in Continental Europe (Metternich), but revolts against despotism in France, Spain, Portugal and Italian states, 1830. In France Charles X abdicates 1830 and more liberal rule of Louis Philippe follows: Belgian independence and neutrality guaranteed, 1830. In England, Great Reform Act of 1832 reforms electoral system. Burning of Houses of Parliament, 1834. Accession of Victoria, 1837. Canning becomes champion of Greek independence: Greek independence assured, 1827: Serbia autonomous state by 1830. In Middle East Turks lose territory to Egypt. S American states successfully gain independence. Britain first occupies Falkland Islands, 1822. In USA, push W and S continues. Texas independent of Spain, 1836: battle of Alamo, 1836. Dutch advance N from Cape in S Africa: 'The Great Trek', 1836. German unity being advanced *de facto* by the Zollverein from 1830 onwards. Colony established, S Australia, 1834: colonization of Australia and New Zealand begins in earnest.	Chartists flourish in England: word 'socialism' current in Europe by 1830s. Population explosion in W Europe: cholera scourge of many industrial cities from 1830s (arriving from Asia). Suttee abolished in British India, 1829. Poor Law in Britain amended, drastically, 1834. Registration of births, deaths and marriages in England and Wales from 1837 (Scotland 1855, Ireland 1864). 'Penny post' in England, 1839. Anti-slavery agitation growing in USA.
1840–59	In England, Victoria marries Albert, 1840: 'Victorian Age' proper begins. Britain acquires Hong Kong after Opium	In England Whigs and Tories now generally known as Liberals and

Religion, Education and Philosophy	Science, Exploration and Technology	1820–59 Music and the Arts
In England, Repeal of Test Acts, 1828: Catholic Emancipation Act, 1829. Growth of Oxford Movement in Church of England. Plymouth Brethren, 1827: Mormons, 1830. Philosophic dominance of Germany and Britain: Carlyle, Hegel, Ranke, Bentham. Emerson in USA.	Advances in all fields of science and invention: great strides in mechanical engineering, electricity, photography. Stockton-Darlington railway carries first passengers, 1825. British industrial products widely exported: industrial revolution taking place in Germany and France and USA. Darwin's survey and expedition in S America and Australasia, 1831–6.	Period of Beethoven's greatest work. Building of West End of London (Nash).
Growth of modern British 'public school' (many based on old	Much medical advance: Lister, Pasteur flourished. Chloroform	Great age of the English novel begins: Dickens, Brontes, Eliot, Trollope,

1860–79

Date	History, Politics and People	Economics and Sociology
	War with China, 1840–2. Indian Mutiny, 1857. Aim of Britain to protect Turkey from Russian expansion – 'the Eastern Question', so sides with Turkey in Crimean War, 1854–6. In Europe, 1848 year of revolution: Louis Napoleon comes to power in France (emperor from 1852). Hungary fails to win independence. Nationalist movements growing all over Austrian Empire. In Germany, Prussian influence growing: German National Association formed, 1859. US-Canadian boundaries – 49th Parallel – defined, 1842: USA acquires Texas, New Mexico Slavery question dominates north-south state relations: 'Battle of Harper's Ferry' (John Brown), 1859. Opening of Japan started by Perry, 1854: leads to rapid superficial westernization of Japan. China weakened by internal decay and further conflict with Britain. Africa being carved up between major European powers, especially Britain and France. Austria declining: defeated by France (champion of Italian independence) at Magenta and Solferino, 1859.	Conservatives. Repeal of Corn Laws, 1846. In Ireland, disastrous potato famines from 1846 exacerbate nationalism: population declines through starvation and emigration (to Britain and USA). End of transportation to New South Wales, 1840. Era of industrialisation in cities of US north. First popular newspaper, *Daily News* (Dickens the editor) started, 1846, in London. Great Exhibition, London, 1851. Hospital reforms as result of Crimean experiences of Florence Nightingale.
1860–79	Progress towards Italian unity under Piedmont and Sardinia. Garibaldi takes Palermo and Naples, 1860 and proclaims Victor Emmanuel II King of Italy. Papal troops defeated: King of Naples surrenders to Garibaldi, 1861: Italy an independent kingdom, gains Venice from Austria after 1866 war, Rome capital from 1870. Lincoln elected US president, 1860: southern states secede, 1861, and Civil War begins: Emancipation Proclamation, 1863: Lincoln assassinated, 1865, war ends in Union victory and 13th Amendment abolishes slavery. Decline of Austria: after defeat of 1866 loses territory to Prussia and Italy. Rise of	Russian serfs freed, 1861: American slaves, 1865. US industrial expansion in N: S declines. Industrial growth in Europe leads to modern unionism: first TUC Congress at Manchester, 1868. Red Cross founded, 1864: Krupp starts arms production, Essen, 1861. In sport, baseball popular in USA from *c.* 1860: All-England Lawn Tennis

Religion, Education and Philosophy	Science, Exploration and Technology	Music and the Arts
foundations). Newman becomes a Catholic, 1845: Bernadette's vision at Lourdes, 1858. Doctrine of the Immaculate Conception promulgated, 1854. Socialist writings of Marx, Engels and Lasalle. Anticlericalism in Europe: agnostic writings of Renan, etc.	used, 1847. Darwin's *Origin of the Species*, published 1859, revolutionized views on natural science. Railways being constructed world-wide: steam taking over from sail in ships. Growth of the electric telegraph. Celluloid patented, 1855.	Thackeray, etc. In France, Napoleon III patron of arts, starts reconstruction of Paris. Pre-Raphaelite school of painting in Britain. Rebuilding of Houses of Parliament in present style. Romanticism in music: Chopin, Mendelssohn, Schubert, Schumann, etc. Great period of Italian opera: Verdi
Revival of Catholicism in Britain. Doctrine of Papal Infallability, 1871. Kulturkampf in Prussia, 1871. Seventh Day Adventists, 1863; Salvation Army, 1865: Christian Science, 1866. In philosophy, Mill, Spencer, Marx: Newman a major Catholic apologist. Historians Bagehot, Lecky, Gardiner, etc. Educational progress throughout western world: first women's colleges at Oxford and Cambridge.	Exploration continuing in Africa, Arctic and Antarctica. Pasteurization, 1864: antiseptics (Lister), 1865. Mendel's Law on heredity, 1865. Bell invents telephone, 1876; Nobel invents dynamite, 1866. Start of London Underground, 1863. Bicycles popular from 1860s. Whymper climbs Matterhorn, 1865.	Russian ballet now world-famous. Opera flourishing in France, Italy, Germany, (Wagner) and Britain (Gilbert and Sullivan). First Impressionist Exhibition, Paris, 1874. Russian novel flourishes with Tolstoy, Turgenev, Dostoievsky: Strindberg and Ibsen make Scandinavian theatre world-famous. Folklore expands with Grimms and Hans Andersen.

1880–99

Date	History, Politics and People	Economics and Sociology
	Prussia under direction of Bismarck: gets Schleswig-Holstein, 1864, further German territory, 1866. Franco-Prussian War, 1870 ends in Prussian victory, annexation of Alsace-Lorraine and proclamation of German Reich. France's Mexican policy 1863–7 ends in French humiliation and execution of Emperor Maximilian, France's nominee, Mexico again a republic. French defeat in Franco-Prussian War, 1870, leads to abdication of Napoleon III and establishment of Third Republic. Paris Commune, 1871. Treaty of Berlin, 1878, intended to halt Russian expansion at Turkish expense: Turkish massacre of Bulgarians, 1876. In S Africa, friction between British and Boers: Zulu wars, 1879. Prince Albert *d*. 1861: parliamentary reform, 1867: Dominion of Canada established, 1867: Victoria Empress of India, 1877.	Championship starts at Wimbledon, 1877. Football Association, 1863. First cricket Test Match between Australia and Britain, 1877. Elementary education in Britain compulsory from 1876: moves to ameliorate working-class poverty: Salvation Army founded, 1865, Barnardo's first home in Stepney, 1866. Bank Holidays established in England and Wales, 1871.
1880–99	In Britain, further parliamentary reforms: Dock Strike, 1889, first Labour MP, 1892. Increased Irish agitation for Home Rule. In S Africa, outbreak of Boer War, 1899. In Sudan, Mahdi takes Khartoum and kills Gordon, 1885: Kitchener reconquers Sudan, 1898. Corruption in French government: Dreyfus Case begins, 1894 Spain in decline: Cuba rebels 1895 and USA supports her, defeats Spain and acquires Cuba, Puerto Rico, Guam and Philippines, 1898. Brazil a republic, 1889. First Indian National Congress, 1886. start of modern Indian nationalism. Young Turk movement formed in Geneva, 1891: Crete proclaims union with Greece, 1897 and Greece defeats Turkey. Fall of Bismarck in Germany but German arms build-up continues: attempts at late colonial expansion. Korea and Japan attack China and defeat her, 1894.	Growth of left-wing and anarchist parties in Europe. Germany pioneers social insurance for workers, 1883. Discovery of gold leads to rise of Johannesburg, 1886. Klondike Gold Rush, 1896. Local government reform in Britain: London County Council established, 1889. Death duties introduced in Britain, 1894. First modern Olympic Games in Athens, 1896. Growth of women's suffrage movement especially in Britain.

Religion, Education and Philosophy	Science, Exploration and Technology	1880–99 Music and the Arts
Church of Ireland disestablished, 1869.	Horsedrawn trams in London from 1861.	US literature and art with James, Longfellow, Whistler, etc., has world acclaim. Albert Hall and Memorial built in Britain. Japanese art introduced to Europe at Paris World Fair, 1867.
Persecution of Russian Jews leads to emigration to Britain and USA and growth of Zionism, 1897. Fabian Society, 1883: London School of Economics, 1895. Nobel Prizes founded, 1896. Secularist philosophy dominates, interest in anthropology and sexual behaviour – Havelock Ellis, Frazer, etc. Christian missions in Africa, India and Asia at height of influence.	Medical advances include rabies vaccine, 1885; phenacetin, 1887; X-Rays, 1895; radium 1898. Electric lighting from 1880s. Start of modern motorcar: Diesel internal combustion engine, 1892; Henry Ford makes first car, 1893. Marconi invents radio-telegraphy, 1895; magnetic sound recording, 1899. First airship built, 1898. World communication much improved, journey-times shortened. Mass-travel possible. Paris Metro opens, 1898.	Realist school of literature (Hardy, Wells, Zola, etc.) exists alongside Romantics (Tennyson, Kipling, Maeterlinck). English theatre flourishes with Wilde, Pinero, Shaw. Zenith of English music hall and French cabaret. Romanticism dominates music: Richard Strauss, Dvorak, Smetana, Sibelius, Elgar, etc. Art nouveau influential from 1890.

1900–19

Date	History, Politics and People	Economics and Sociology
1900–09	Queen Victoria *d.* 1901. British military successes in S Africa, 1900–01: Boer War ends with British victory, 1902: Union of S Africa, 1908. Australia a Commonwealth Dominion, 1900: New Zealand, 1907. Boxer Rising against Europeans in China, 1900; Sun Yat-Sen begins campaign against Manchus, 1905. In France, Dreyfus rehabilitated, 1906; Entente Cordiale between Britain and France, 1904. Lords reject Lloyd George's Finance Bill, 1909. Japan defeats Russia in war, 1904; allies with Britain, 1905. Korea a Japanese protectorate, 1907. Norway separates from Sweden, 1905. Turkey surrenders Sinai to Egypt, 1906; Turkey and Serbia recognise Austrian annexation of Bosnia and Herzegovina, 1909. Treaty on US rights over Panama Canal, 1903; US occupies Cuba, 1906–8. Russian Socialists split into Mensheviks and Bolsheviks, 1903; *Potemkin* mutiny and localized revolts, 1905, followed by some reforms.	Rapid growth in popularity of motorcar: first British traffic laws, 1903; first Ford T-model, 1908. Oil drilling starts in Iran, 1909. Synthetics and mass production lead to cheaper clothing, furniture etc., in W world. Arms race between Britain and Germany accelerates. San Francisco earthquake, 1906. Boy Scout Movement founded by Baden Powell, 1908.
1910–19	In Britain, Parliament Act, 1911; suffragette violence, 1913. After World War I, women get limited vote and Lady Astor first woman MP to take seat, 1919. Home Rule for Ireland, 1914, suspended for duration of war. Rebellion in Dublin, 1916; Home rule bill abandoned, 1918. Italy defeats Turkey and annexes Tripoli and Cyrenaica, 1911: Balkan Wars 1912–13 further weakens Turkey. Revolution in China, 1911, overthrows Empire. Sun Yat-Sen president: rapid modernization and industrialization in major cities. June 1914: assassination of Franz Ferdinand at Sarajevo causes start of	Sinking of *Titanic*, 1912, on maiden voyage. Woolworths founded, 1912. Socio-economic upheaval in W Europe and USA as a result of World War I: diminution of class distinctions in varying degrees everywhere, and enhancement of women's position. Population imbalances as result of heavy war casualties.

Religion, Education and Philosophy	Science, Exploration and Technology	Music and the Arts
	First moving pictures, New York, 1890.	
Modernism in Catholic Church condemned by Pope, 1907: Jesuit reforms, 1906. Church and State in France separated, 1906. Reunion of British Methodists, 1907. Anthroposophy founded by Steiner, 1901. In Japan, Shintoism reinstated, 1900. Cult of violence in philosophy: Liebknecht, Lenin, Wallas. Psychoanalysis developed by Freud and Jung.	Quantum theory, 1900; Special Theory of Relativity, 1905. First motorcycles, 1901; Rolls Royce Company founded, 1904. Typewriters in common office use: women office workers become general. Wright brothers in USA fly powered aeroplane, 1903; Bleriot flies the English Channel 1909. Invention of bakelite (1908: USA) heralds age of plastics. Decade of the silent film: development of cinemas – 'picture-palaces'.	Picasso's 'Blue Period': sculptors Rodin and Epstein flourished. Steel increasingly used in industrial and commercial building. Light opera flourished especially in Vienna: ragtime develops into jazz, originating in the southern USA (from New Orleans.)
Rapid spread of Marxism after Russian revolution of 1917: attempt to suppress religion in USSR. In Germany, separation of Church and State, 1919. In Britain, Church of Wales disestablished, 1920. Philosophic advocacy of sexual freedom in Europe and USA. World War sees growth of pacifism in all	Amundsen reaches S Pole, 1911; Scott, 1912. World War I results in advances in production of arms, motor-vehicles, ships and aeroplanes: and communications' systems. First helicopter flown, 1918. Poison gas first used, 1915; tanks first used (by British, on the Somme), 1916. Medical advances in treatment of serious physical injuries and	Modernism in art and music: Picasso, Modigliani, Matisse, Spencer: Bartok, Prokoviev. Popular spread of jazz: major composers include Kern and Berlin. War causes reaction against literary romanticism: Owen, D. H. Lawrence, Sassoon, Remarque, Sinclair Lewis, Barbusse. Irish nationalism encourages literary

1920–29

Date	History, Politics and People	Economics and Sociology
	World War I in Aug. major participants, France, Britain, Russia and Japan (later Italy and USA) against Germany, Austria and Turkey. (*See Dictionary article*: World War I). 1914: Germans occupy much of Belgium, invade France: first battle of Ypres. Russians defeat at Tannenberg, 1915: war further destabilizes Russia. *Lusitania* sunk by U-boat, 1915. U-boat warfare a major factor in war: first air attacks on Britain. Gallipoli, 1915–16. 1916: battle of Somme. 1917: Bolshevik revolution leads to Russo-German armistice. USA enters war on Allied side. Middle East campaigns ending in Allied victories against Turks, aided by dissident Arabs. 1918: Allied victory, armistice November 11. Collapse and disintegration of German, Austrian and Turkish empires: emergence of such states as Czechoslovakia, Jugoslavia, Poland and Finland. Versailles Peace Treaty, 1918. Bolshevik regime in Russia has Russian royal family murdered, 1918.	Keynesian economics in embryo: Keynes's *Economic Consequences of the Peace*, 1919.
1920–29	League of Nations founded, 1920: confirmed, with HQ at Geneva, 1921, but USA did not join. Hague seat of International Court of Justice, 1921. In Britain, Zinoviev Letter influenced election results, 1924: first Labour government, 1929. Government of Ireland Act established two Irelands, 1920, but war existed between Britain and S Ireland till 1922 when Irish Free State proclaimed. In Germany, reparations burden helped cause galloping inflation, 1921: political instability led to sporadic Communist uprisings and eventually to (at first insignificant) rise of Nazism. Hindenburg president, 1925. Mussolini marched on Rome, 1922 and	Post-war inflationary boom period in W followed by financial collapse, 1929, leading to world depression, deflation and mass unemployment. Tariffs again being applied. Further growth in women's rights in W: women gained vote in USA, 1920: forcibly emancipated in Turkey, 1926. USA adopted prohibition, 1920 (till 1933): organised crime

Religion, Education and Philosophy	Science, Exploration and Technology	Music and the Arts
participating countries, given philosophic basis by such scholars as Bertrand Russell. Non-violence adopted as a political weapon by Gandhi in India.	mental illness: shell-shock, neuroses, etc. Alcock and Brown make first flight across the Atlantic, 1919. Atom first split by Rutherford, 1919.	revival: Yeats, Joyce. Abbey Theatre, Dublin becomes world famous.
Joan of Arc canonized, 1920. Presbyterian churches in Scotland reunited, 1929. Anti-Semitism in Germany, Poland, Austria: adds impetus to Zionist growth. In Mexico, systematic campaign to eradicate Catholicism eventually abandoned. In W aftermath of war sees acceleration in decline of religious observance, especially in Protestant countries. New exposition of	Medical advances swift, notably in neurosurgery tuberculosis, diabetes, tropical diseases, anaemia. Fleming discovers penicillin, 1928. Basic principle of autogyro developed, 1923: Lindbergh flies monoplane solo nonstop from New York to Paris, 1927. De Forest produces process for moving pictures with sound tracks, 1923: first colour movies, 1928.	Golden period of the 'Jazz Age'. Modernism dominates music and the arts: era of the skyscraper New York Empire State Building started, 1929. In Europe, Bauhaus concept influenced public building. Restless but productive literary period: Shaw, Galsworthy, Virginia Woolf, O'Neill, Maugham, Eliot, Pound. European ballet revival greatly influenced by influx of dancers leaving

1930–39

Date	History, Politics and People	Economics and Sociology
	formed Fascist government. Economic and political difficulties and fear of Bolshevism led to right-wing regimes in several European countries e.g. Poland, Greece, Rumania, Austria. In USA political corruption rife: era of isolationism began. Financial boom, followed by collapse of stock market. 28 Oct. 1929, resulting in world depression. Kemal Ataturk made Turkey a republic, 1922: modernization from 1926. In Middle East, stability of Arab emergent states affected by increased vociferousness of Zionism: and by impact of oil-based economy on those possessing vast oil-reserves. Civil war in USSR ended 1920 with Bolshevik victory: Lenin *d.* 1924, and Stalin subsequently rose to power. Gandhi became leader of Indian nationalism: Round Table Conference on possible Dominion status for India convened, 1929. Beginnings of nationalism in several African and Asian colonies belonging to European powers, notably in Dutch E Indies and French Indo-China.	flourished. Hoover made head of FBI, 1924. Great Exhibition, Wembley, 1923. Football increasingly popular. Motorcar availability widens: rail importance begins to decline. Expansion of air travel. BBC formed, 1922: radio soon generally available in average homes in W. 'Apartheid' term first used in S Africa during this decade.
1930–39	Period of high unemployment in W world. Britain abandons gold standard, 1931; Edward VIII abdicates, 1936. Chamberlain flies to Munich–'peace in our time', 1938. Britain declares war on Germany, 3 September, 1939. Nazis gain most seats in German elections, 1932; Hitler Chancellor, 1933, assumes dictatorial powers. Concentration camps established. Germany rearms, begins building Siegfried Line, 1936. Occupies Austria, Sudetenland, 1938; rest of Czechoslovakia, 1939 and invades and occupies Poland, 1939. Alliance with USSR to partition Poland, 1939. Spanish Civil War 1936–9 ends with Franco's victory and formation of Fascist corporate state.	Spread of radio and cinema leads to growing public awareness of international issues. Development of propaganda techniques in Germany. Mass advertising in USA and Europe changes selling techniques. In W, revised divorce laws affect family structures. From mid-1930s rearmament leads to steady decline in unemployment in Britain: despite

Religion, Education and Philosophy	Science, Exploration and Technology	Music and the Arts
Protestantism by Barth. Logical positivism propounded, 1922. Socialist historical writing, begun by Wells, developed further by Tawney, Russell. Literacy continues to grow: colonial powers encourage foundation of higher education institutions in their overseas territories.	Baird transmits television pictures, 1926. Much astronomic research: embryonic work on space rockets. Further exploration in Tibet and at Poles. Gregorian Calendar established in USSR, 1923. Geneva Convention, 1925, banned poison gas in warfare.	Bolshevik Russia.
Anti-semitism in Germany; Protestant, Catholics and Socialists also imprisoned from 1933. Growth of Existentialism. Neo-Thomist school of Catholic philosophy founded by Gerson, Maritain, etc.	Radar detection set up in Britain, 1935; aircraft development, especially in Germany. First jet engine built by Whittle, 1937. Much progress in fields of anaemia, kidney and liver therapy. Insulin used to control diabetes from 1937. RH factor in blood discovered, 1939. Boulder Dam, USA, completed, 1936, creating the then largest reservoir in world. Public television service in Britain, 1936.	Talking pictures superseded silent films; colour used increasingly. Cinema reaches standards of best theatre: Greta Garbo, Charlie Chaplin, Marlene Dietrich, Ingrid Bergman, etc. 'Swing' music becomes popular. Novel continues to dominate literature: German art and literature decline under Nazi censorship and many artists emigrate. British music flourishes:

Date	History, Politics and People	Economics and Sociology
	Japan attacks China, 1937; rapid advances and Chungking becomes nationalist capital. Round Table Conference fails to solve Indian question: Gandhi's passive resistance campaign continues. Italy invades and conquers Ethiopia, 1936–36; international failure to act marks effective collapse of League of Nations. Italy occupies Albania, 1939. Roosevelt elected Democratic president in USA, 1933, 'New Deal' policy, with attempts at widespread social and economic reform. Prohibition abolished, 1933. Stalin purges his opponents, 1934 onwards; alliance with Hitler, 1939; invades Finland: forcible collectivization1932–4 leads to mass-starvation, notably in Ukraine.	recession, improved mass-production processes lead to higher living standards for many. From 1934 German persecution of Jews results in mass-exodus to Britain and USA.
1940–49	World War II (*see Dictionary section article*: World War II). 1940: Finland signs armistice with USSR; Germany occupies Norway and Denmark; Churchill becomes premier of National Government in Britain. Germany invades and conquers Belgium, Holland and France and British army evacuated from Dunkirk. Battle of Britain in air, Aug.–Sept. Italy joins war on German side. 1941: Yugoslavia, Greece and Crete invaded by Germans: they occupy rest of Balkans. June: Germans invade Russia; Japanese attack Pearl Harbor 7 Dec. and USA and Britain declare war on Japan who sweeps through Asia up to Indian frontier. 1942: Tide turns for Allies with battle of El Alamein, Oct.–Nov. 1943: Allies reconquer N Africa and invade Sicily and Italy, which surrenders. Heavy day and night bombing of Germany by Allies. Germans in retreat in Russia: surrender at Stalingrad. USA begins offensive against Japan in Pacific.	At end of World War II most countries institute some form of women's suffrage. Great diminution of class distinctions in W countries: increased power of State almost everywhere. Emergence of the 'Welfare State' in Britain and elsewhere in W Europe. Decade of full employment. Vast increase in availability of higher education. Marshall Plan, 1947, aids recovery of W Europe. By end of decade Germany and Japan becoming very prosperous. Keynesian economic theory dominates European economic strategies.

Religion, Education and Philosophy	Science, Exploration and Technology	Music and the Arts
		Bax, Beecham, Henry Wood, Britten, etc. Royal Academy holds major international exhibitions in London.
Shintoism reformed in Japan, 1945. Persecution of Catholic Church by Communists after 1945; Hungarian primate imprisoned for treason, 1949. Protestant theologians e.g. Niebuhr, Bonhoeffer, influential. Mass-extermination of Jews by Nazis, 1940–45. In former colonial territories, reaction against Christianity; Buddhist and Muslim revivals. Church of S India formed from union of major Protestant churches after Indian independence. First Dead Sea scrolls discovered Existentialism popularized by Sartre.	War causes inventive and technological surge: aircraft vastly improved. Atomic bombs on Japan, Aug. 1945, followed by nuclear advances in military and civil fields. VI and VII German weapons forerunner of future space programmes. First complete electronic computer built in America, 1939–44; transistor first developed, 1947. Major advances in antibiotics and plastic surgery. Aerial and underwater photography greatly developed.	Existentialist literature of Camus, Sartre, etc. World War II sees popularity of radio and cinema at height. In Britain, vogue for 'social history': G.M. Trevelyan, Realist school of literature: Priestley, Steinbeck, Graham Greene: satirists like Waugh and Wodehouse. Mass-rebuilding after war gives impetus to new forms: 'pre-fabs' and the 'tower block'. Much art religiously inspired: Spencer, Sutherland, Epstein. In contrast, mature work of Picasso. Age of mass-market publishing arrives.

1950–59

Date	History, Politics and People	Economics and Sociology
	1944: Allied invasion of Europe, D-Day June 6; offensives on of all fronts. Unsuccessful attempt to assassinate Hitler. 1945: British, Chinese and US offensives in Asia gather strength, Russians and Allies sweep forward in Europe. Germany surrenders May; atom bombs dropped on Japan 6 and 9 August; Japan surrenders. War ends with Russia in control of E Europe and China with civil war between Nationalists and Communists. Roosevelt *d.* After war, dismantlement of colonial empires. India independent, 1947, and partitioned between India and Pakistan. Dutch E Indies independent. French Empire breaks up. Communists take control in China, 1949; Nationalists withdraw to Taiwan. Communist rebellion, Malaya, 1946. United Nations created, 1945. Civil rights movement, USA. Yugoslavia independent of USSR after 1949; Germany divided into E and W Berlin airlift, 1948–9. Israel created, 1948. In Britain, Labour gain sweeping victory, 1945, and radical programme of nationalization and social reform instituted. In Europe, war leads to growth of left-wing nfluences in most countries: but civil war in Greece, 1946, ends in Communist defeat. Italy a republic. NATO formed, 1949, to counter Russian threat. Apartheid dominates S Africa after 1948.	
1950–59	Decade dominated by Communist threat: June, 1950 N Korean forces invade S. Korea; UN force (mainly US) opposes them; China intervenes; armistice, July 1953, restores status quo. Communist uprising in Malaya crushed by 1955. Communist nationalists defeat French at	Period of rapid economic growth in West. In USA Civil Rights movement gains widespread white liberal support: in S Africa, machinery of apartheid

Religion, Education and Philosophy	Science, Exploration and Technology	Music and the Arts
Doctrine of the Assumption proclaimed, 1950. Pope John XXIII elected, 1959; convenes first Vatican Council since 1870.	Medical advances include antihistamines, tranquillizers and contraceptive pill. First suggestions of connection between smoking and lung cancer, 1953.	Cheaper mass-produced records begin a western world boom in 'pop music'. Theatre, films and literature become more sexually explicit.

1960–69

Date	History, Politics and People	Economics and Sociology
	Dien Bien Phu, 1954; N Vietnam then Communist. Anti-Communist uprising, Hungary, 1957, crushed by Soviet intervention. In 1959 leftist revolutionary movement led by Fidel Castro gains power in Cuba. Fear of Communism leads to McCarthyism in USA, 1953–4. Further growth of civil rights movement in USA, racial segregation in schools ruled unconstitutional, 1954. Britain reelects Conservatives, 1951; George VI *d.* 1951, Elizabeth II succeeds. With France, intervenes in Egypt, 1956 and humiliated. Nationalist unrest in many British colonies. Cyprus a republic, 1959. In France, nationalist war in Algeria leads to overthrow of republic and return to power of de Gaulle. Fifth Republic inaugurated. In USSR, *d.* of Stalin, 1953 and rise of Khruschev. Warsaw Pact, counter to NATO, 1955. Egypt becomes a republic and nationalizes Suez Canal, 1956: war with Israel. Israel-Arab conflict increasingly dominates Middle East politics. Under Nehru, India leads 'uncommitted nations'. In Europe, Treaty of Rome, 1958, establishes the European Economic Community: non-EEC countries, led by Britain, form EFTA, 1959.	tightened. Rapid growth of mass international air travel, leading to increases in tourism (new tourist areas, e.g. Spain) and start of considerable 'New Commonwealth' immigration to Britain. World population explosion, with serious food and health problems in 'Third World'. Full employment in the West, but rapid inflation.
1960– 69	Kennedy President of USA, 1960; Bay of Pigs fiasco in Cuba, 1962 and Cuban missile crisis settled by Kennedy and Khruschev, 1963. Kennedy assassinated, Dallas, 22 Nov. 1963; Johnson president and carries on Kennedy's civil rights' programme but increasingly involved in Vietnam, where US advisers now replaced by US troops. Liberal and student opposition to US involvement there becomes important; marches on the White House. In 1968 Nixon (Republican) elected president,	American involvement in Vietnam leads to moral crisis at home; youth reaction involves overthrow of traditional values, rapid spread of drug abuse, which then spreads to Europe. Age of 'hippies' and 'flower-power'. 'Women's Liberation Movement', aggressively feminist,

Religion, Education and Philosophy	Science, Exploration and Technology	Music and the Arts
Protestant churches attempting closer ties. Christians playing increasing part in political issues, e.g. controversy over nuclear weapons and racial issues in USA and S Africa. Evangelist movement in USA started by Billy Graham, 1954, spreads to Europe. Several modern Biblical translations.	Nuclear advances: electric power first produced from atomic energy, 1951; first hydrogen bomb exploded by USA, 1953; USA launch first nuclear-powered submarine, 1955. Space programmes: USA and USSR establish space agencies: Van Allen discovers radiation belts round earth. US launches rocket to moon, 1959, which travels 79,000 miles/ 126,400 km up; Russians launch rocket with two monkeys aboard, 1959. Russian rocket reaches moon, 1959. Vertical take-off invented: British 'flying bedstead', 1954. International Geophysical Year, 1957. Hillary and Tensing climb Everest, 1953. Pollution begins to be a recognised threat: Carson's *The Sea Around Us*, 1959.	US literature influential with Bellow, Vidal, Hersey, Wouk, Tennessee Williams. 'New' Coventry Cathedral begun, 1956. Painting and sculpture dominated by innovators like Hepworth, Moore, Chagall, Picasso. Television growth exerts increasing influence on all arts; cinema begins popular decline in west.
Vatican Council 1962–3 results in radical changes in Catholic structure and practices. Vernacular replaces Latin in liturgy and theology more liberal, but Pope reaffirms Church opposition to artificial contraception, 1968. Frequent Papal visits overseas. Growing cooperation	Space physics makes great advances: Gagarin (USSR) orbits the earth, 1961. Subsequently USA and USSR successfully launched many manned flights. In 1969, US, astronauts land and walk on the moon. Progress also in fields of communication, meteorology and	'The Swinging Sixties': growth of a 'pop culture' typified by the Beatles in Britain (1962 onwards) and Dylan and Baez in the USA. Abolition of theatre censorship in Britain, 1968. Cult of protest literature in literature and theatre in W. In USSR, growth of

1970–79

Date	History, Politics and People	Economics and Sociology
	promising end of Vietnam war and rapprochement with China. In S Vietnam, government overthrown, 1963, and situation from then on increasingly unstable. Britain fails to join EEC: 'Profumo affair', 1963, and Labour under Wilson in power from 1964. Several former colonies gain independence but S Rhodesia declares UDI, 1965. S Africa leaves Commonwealth, 1961. Republican agitation in N Ireland from mid-1960s and British troops sent to keep peace, 1969. Emigration from E Germany through Berlin stopped by Berlin Wall, 1961; Czech revolt against hard-line Communism, 1968, ended by Russian intervention, 1969. Khruschev falls from power, 1964, rise of Brezhnev. In France student riots, 1968, lead ultimately to resignation of de Gaulle, 1969. In China, 'Cultural Revolution' begins, 1966. War between Israel and major Arab states, 1967, ends in Israeli victory and occupation by Israel of W bank of Jordan including all Jerusalem. Arab campaign against Israeli subsequently more violent, Jordan main Palestinian base. Nazi criminal Eichmann hanged in Israel, 1962. Some progress in quest for world peace: Nuclear Test Ban treaty signed by Britain, USA and USSR, 1963.	spreads from USA to Europe. Terrorism adopted by Irish and Arab extremists. Death penalty abolished in Britain, 1965. Oil boom brings rapid prosperity to several states in Middle East and Africa (Libya; Nigeria).
1970–79	Nixon, US president, withdraws US forces from Vietnam and effects rapprochement with China but forced to resign over Watergate Scandal, 1974. All Vietnam effectively Communist from 1975. Carter, US president from 1976, effects Camp David Agreement between Israel and Egypt, 1979 (after further war, 1973). Overthrow of Shah of Iran by militant Muslims, 1979, and failure of USA to get release of US hostages in Iran helps	Steep rise in oil prices, 1973 helped to produce recession in W Europe and USA. This had global effects, with severe inflation in several countries (e.g. 25% in Britain in 1975) and hyperinflation in less developed ones. Famines in Africa. Growing power of feminism in USA and W Europe. In Britain

Religion, Education and Philosophy	Science, Exploration and Technology	1970–79 Music and the Arts
between Catholics and Protestants but sectarian violence in Ulster; rising influence of the IRA. Women's rights movement affects all churches: first woman priest ordained in Sweden, 1960. Pope Paul VI formally exonerates Jews from blame for death of Jesus, 1965. Growth of a 'philosophy of violence' propagated by Marcuse, etc. Urban guerrilla movements in W Europe often led by university graduates.	military surveillance. Development of supersonic aircraft: Concorde makes flight, 1969. Britain starts gas and oil exploration in N Sea, 1964. In medicine, thalidomide causes malformation of babies, from 1962; in 1962 Royal College of Surgeons report links cigarette smoking lung cancer. In S Africa, Barnard performs first heart transplant, 1967, and transplant surgery subsequently becomes routine in USA, Britain and France. 'CS' gas used in riot control.	literary protest against regime as typified by Pasternak and first Solzenitzhin. Thriller achieves classic status with Greene, Le Carré, Fleming. Aldeburgh becomes a leading musical centre. British opera revived by Britten, and British ballet leads internationally with Fonteyn, Markova and with Helpmann.
Closer relations between Catholic and Protestant churches; but signs of religious decline in many W. countries. Revival of militant Islam in Libya, Iran, Egypt, etc., Student unrest in W much diminished after end of Vietnam War. Christians divided on question of	Further advances in space science: USA and USSR continue massive space spending programmes. In medicine, heart transplants now have high success rates; kidney and liver transplants routine in developed countries.	Revival of 'entertainment' school in literature and the theatre. Cinema in the West in popular decline due to television and video competition. 'Pop' music a worldwide culture, with its leading performers and composers becoming

1970–79

Date	History, Politics and People	Economics and Sociology
	succession of Republican Reagan as president, 1979. In China, Cultural Revolution ends, 1972. Mao Tse Tung dies, 1976. Power struggle follows. Limited liberalization. Reign of terror in Cambodia, 1975–9, causes a possible million deaths and mass exodus of refugees. Hardline Communism in Soviet Union and Eastern bloc continues. Some dissidents (e.g. Solzenitzhin) allowed to leave. Expansionist Soviet Union intervenes directly or indirectly in Angola, Ethiopia, and notably and directly in Afghanistan. Britain joins EEC, 1973 (also Denmark and the Irish Republic). Margaret Thatcher first British woman prime minister (Conservative), 1979, when Conservatives defeat Labour after period of economic and social difficulties and increasing disillusionment with trade union powers. In N Ireland, numerous deaths from IRA campaign of violence: bomb outrages there and in mainland Britain from 1971. Indira Gandhi dominates Indian politics. Bangladesh independent, 1971. In Pakistan, Bhutto overthrown and executed, 1979. Last remaining European colonies in Africa independent. Rhodesian settlement, 1979, paves way for independent Zimbabwe. But white minority rule continues in S Africa. Left-wing coup in Portugal (later modified) leads to Angola and Mozambique becoming independent (with subsequent civil wars). Franco *d.* 1975 and Spain moves peacefully to constitutional monarchy. Jordan expels Palestinians, 1970, who then make Lebanon (in state of civil war) their main base for attacks on Israel. In S America, conservative regimes generally prevail. Leftist Allende government overthrown in coup, 1973; military regime in Argentina, 1976. But in Central America Somoza dictatorship	increased disillusionment with post 1945 style of interventionist government, notably in second half of decade, (resulting in Conservative victory, 1979): but 'permissive society' increasingly accepted. Left-wing guerrilla movements in Germany and Italy. Kidnapping becomes a relatively common crime in Italy where Mafia influence also growing. Growth in drug trafficking and addiction most notably in USA and W Europe: rise of the Colombian 'drug barons'. Rise in crime, much drug-related, in W world, and, after 1989, in former Soviet-dominated territories.

Religion, Education and Philosophy	Science, Exploration and Technology	1970–79 Music and the Arts
permissibility of nuclear warfare. Right-wing philosophers prominent in much W thinking and growing influence of monetarism: but religious philosophy more radical, with Kung challenging traditional Catholicism, and 'liberation theology' gaining ground, notably in Central America.	Fertility drugs and 'test-tube baby' techniques developed. But in Third World infant mortality high, life expectancy low in many countries and African famines prime cause of premature deaths. Video growth affects cinema, television and recording industries. Era of the 'silicon chip': increasing use of computers in offices and factories. Japan pioneers large-scale use of robots in industry and challenges the W's superiority in electronics, the motor industry, etc. In countries such as Britain and Mexico, new oil discoveries boost the economies, but following the oil-price rises of 1973 and growth of the 'Green' movement in the W, energy conservation becomes of increasing concern in Europe and the USA and the use of nuclear power for industry starts to be questioned.	'cult figures' and amassing fortunes.

1980–95

Date	History, Politics and People	Economics and Sociology
	overthrown by left-wing forces, 1979. Japan's economic growth and prosperity makes her increasingly important throughout the decade.	
1980–95	In Britain, Thatcher government organizes successful military and naval campaign to expel Argentine forces from Falkland Islands, 1982; defeats miners' strike, 1984–5 and curbs trade-union powers. Free-market philosophy encouraged, but divide between rich and poor increased after start of recession, 1989, while increased social welfare spending led to questioning of original welfare state concept from 1990s by all major political parties. Margaret Thatcher fell from power after 11 years premiership, Dec. 1990. John Major succeeded her and won Conservatives a fourth consecutive term in power against predictions in general election, Apr. 1992. British part of UN force in Gulf War, 1991. Britain signed Maastricht Treaty, 9 Feb. 1992; sterling crisis and Britain left E.R.M., Sept. 1992. Sent peacekeeping force to Bosnia, 1992 and took part in NATO bombing of Bosnian Serbs, 1994 and 1995. Continuing violence in N Ireland and bomb outrages on British mainland, but in Dec. 1993 agreement between British and Irish government held out peace hopes in N and in Aug. 1994 the IRA announced a cease-fire, followed soon after, by similar declaration by Loyalist paramilitaries. 'Peace process' continuing at end of 1995. By end of 1994 Britain slowly emerging from recession but government deeply unpopular. Prince and Princess of Wales (married 1981) announced separation, 1992. Queen pays tax on personal income from 1993. Federalism dominated EC (known from 1991 increasingly as the EU and joined by Greece, Spain and Portugal during 1980s	In Britain, inner-city riots in early 1980s: later in the decade, riots in London and elsewhere against the Community Charge which was subsequently dropped. Miners' failed strike, 1984–5, marked declining power of British trade unions, further curbed by fresh legislation. Privatization of many nationalized industries led to wider share-ownership. Extended Sunday trading legalized, 1994. Period of boom ended 1989 by onset of worst economic recession since 1930s, with unemployment reaching three million, but falling, and economy improving, by end of 1994. Further decline in family life. Campaign for Nuclear Disarmament in Britain lost impetus after break-up of Soviet Union, 1989 onwards, and end of 'cold war'. Economic depression also affected USA and W Europe. In 1993, GATT agreement ended Uruguay Round and gave hope of future world economic growth. During 1980s urban guerrilla movements in Europe, notably in W Germany and Italy, committed kidnappings and murders, while at same time Arab extremists in Lebanon

Religion, Education and Philosophy	Science, Exploration and Technology	1980–95 Music and the Arts
Pope John Paul II makes several visits abroad, e.g. Britain, Ireland, US. Unsuccessful attempt on his life, Rome, 13 May 1981. Encyclical *Veritatis Splendor*, 1993. Continuing decline in influence of 'mainstream' Christianity in many W countries, matched by continuing increase in power of Islamic fundamentalists (e.g., assassination of President Sadat of Egypt, 1981; and President Boudiaf of Algeria, 1992). Persecution of Christians in Sudan and Timor. Move to ordain women threatened split in Church of England; General Synod voted in favour, Nov. 1992; first women priests ordained, 1994. English continued to increase dominance as world's international language. Large increase in number of universities worldwide. Rebirth of nationalism in Europe and beyond (e.g. break-up of Soviet Union from 1989 and of Yugoslavia from 1991. Tribalism caused continuing bloodshed in Africa, e.g. Somalia; Rwanda. Final extinction of	Following US space disaster, Jan. 1986, when *Challenger* exploded on take-off, killing entire crew, US manned programme curtailed. In Soviet Union economic pressures also led to space scale-down. Unmanned probes continued. In Apr. 1990 Hubble space telescope placed in orbit round earth. Mars probe failed, Mar. 1993, but in Dec., US manned mission repaired faults in Hubble and created space-walk record. Poison and nerve gas used by Iraq against Kurds in 1980s and 'marsh Arabs' in 1990s. Chernobyl nuclear disaster in Ukraine, 1986, affected global thinking on nuclear power. Collapse of USSR revealed long-standing instability in nuclear installations and considerable areas of contamination. In Britain Sizewell B power station completed, 1993, and Thorp nuclear reprocessing plant at Sellafield given government go-ahead, 1994. AIDS infection a major	British dominance of light music shows continued, e.g. *Les Miserables, Amadeus, Phantom of the Opera, Miss Saigon*. 'Pop' music a multi-billion dollar world industry. During 1980s increasingly large prices paid at auction for art works, notably Impressionists, e.g. Van Gogh's *Sunflowers* fetched £24 million in Mar. 1987. In W 'high-rise' architecture retained favour in such developments as London Docklands, but reaction and return to neo-Classicism in such buildings as Sainsbury National Gallery extension, opened 1991. States, major companies and charitable foundations increasingly replacing private individuals as principal patrons of the arts.

1980–95

Date	History, Politics and People	Economics and Sociology

and by Austria, Finland, Sweden (but not Norway) on 1 Jan. 1995 but held back temporarily by onset of recession in Europe, 1989 and problems caused by German reunification and Soviet collapse in 1990s. Formal reunification of Germany, 3 Oct. 1990.

Relations between E and W Europe improved after rise to power in Soviet Union of Gorbachev from 1984. He ended Soviet expansionism in Afghanistan, Africa, etc., and tried to liberalize Soviet economy and government. Collapse of Communism in Soviet Union led to Gorbachev's resignation, Dec. 1991 (after failed coup against reform in Aug.) and emergence of Commonwealth of Independent States, with Yeltsin dominant in Russia (he survived attempt by hardline parliamentarians to overthrow him, 1993). More liberal regimes throughout former Communist bloc and former Baltic states again independent, but there were subsequently serious conflicts in parts of the former Soviet Union from 1991 onwards (e.g. Georgia, Azerbaijan, Armenia, Tajikistan) as nationalism and religious fundamentalism revived. Yugoslavia fell apart and there was heavy fighting there, notably in Bosnia: international peacekeeping force there from 1992, and NATO bombing of recalcitrant Serbs from 1994; cease-fire Oct. 1995; peace-talks in USA, Nov.

Economic hardship following attempts to promote free-market economy caused political reactions in several E European countries (e.g. Poland, Lithuania, Hungary and in Russia itself, 1993–4).

In USA Republican presidential power, 1980–92, ended with election of Democrat Bill Clinton, Dec. 1992. Republicans had promoted interventionist foreign policy and better understanding with Communist countries; this continued by Democrats. But Clinton's radical domestic programme caused Republican landslide

carried out kidnappings of Westerners, this ending in 1992.

While economic prosperity eluded most of S America and Africa, Far E countries such as Japan, Singapore, Taiwan and S Korea increased their economic and financial muscle, though Japan itself experiencing economic problems by early 1990s.

The recession led to growing questioning of the long-term viability of the free-market theory. At the same time, economic and demographic pressures in several W countries threatening survival of the 'Welfare State'. European Economic Area (comprising countries of the EU and EFTA excepting Switzerland) came into being, 1 Jan. 1994. Question of European Monetary Union again being pressed by end of 1994: opposed by many in Britain and, increasingly, in other parts of the EU.

Religion, Education and Philosophy	Science, Exploration and Technology	Music and the Arts
apartheid with election of a multiracial government in S Africa, April, 1994, with Nelson Mandela as president. Growth of 'political correctness', notably in the USA from 1980s onwards.	concern first in USA and W Europe from early 1980s: AIDS virus discovered, April 1984. Reached epidemic proportions in parts of Africa. No cure or vaccine found by 1995. Further developments in genetic engineering offered future hopes of eradication of some major diseases, e.g. cancer: but also raised moral problems. DNA 'finger-printing' invented by Jeffreys, 1985, first used in murder trial, 1987. Transplant surgery became more common; first liver and bowel transplant in Britain, 1993. Channel Tunnel between Britain and France begun, 1986; official opening, May 1994. Destruction of ozone layer causing concern throughout this period: attempts to address problem at international 'Earth Summit' in Rio de Janeiro, 1992 but depletion continued. Massive oil resources in seas of S Antarctic (off Falkland Islands) found, 1993; Argentina and Britain agree on joint oil exploration, 1995.	

in midterm elections, Nov. 1994, with Republicans controlling both houses of Congress for first time for 50 years. USA led UN forces in Gulf War, 1991. Work towards Middle East peace settlement led to freeing of last European hostages in Lebanon by 1992 and in 1994 Israel signed peace agreements with both the Palestine Liberation Organization and Jordan. Arab self-government in the Gaza Strip, Jericho and W Bank, 1994–5. Israeli premier Rabin assassinated by Jewish extremist, Nov. 1995. US intervention led to restoration of elected president and downfall of military regime in Haiti, 1994. Islamic fundamentalism increased in several areas. Fundamentalists gained control in Sudan during 1980s and threatening governments in Egypt and Algeria in 1990s. Iran remained fundamentalist stronghold despite increased commercial links with W. Several African states attempted return to multiparty rule in late 1980s and 1990s and Marxism declined. But there was civil war in several countries (e.g. Angola, Liberia, Somalia, Rwanda). Estimates that several millions died from effects of war and/or famine between 1980 and 1995. In S Africa apartheid system still dominant at start of 1980s and country isolated internationally. Apartheid relaxations followed rise to power of de Klerk from 1989. Release of ANC leader, Mandela, Feb. 1990. Remnants of apartheid abolished, 1993; elections held, Apr. 1994, on basis of universal suffrage led to a multi racial government led by Mandela and S Africa's isolation ended.

In Asia, economic dominance of Japan in 1980s being challenged in 1990s by emergence of S Korea, Taiwan, Thailand, Singapore, etc., as major industrial powers. Tokyo, Hong Kong and Singapore important world financial centres. Indian subcontinent relatively peaceful despite assassination of Indira Gandhi, 1984 and continuing conflict with

Religion, Education and Philosophy	Science, Exploration and Technology	1980–95 Music and the Arts

Date	History, Politics and People	Economics and Sociology
	separatist Sikhs and Kashmiris. In China, popular moves towards political liberalization ended in government crackdown, 1989, and student massacre in Peking's Tianenmen Square. But economic liberalization continued, with massive industrial growth and reopening of stock exchanges (e.g. Shanghai, 1990). China continued ruthless repression in Tibet. British agreement, 1984, to hand back Hong Kong to China in 1997, but subsequently there were differences regarding future Hong Kong democratic 'safeguards' and these unresolved at end of 1995. Instability in parts of the Far East; notably in Cambodia, despite official ending of civil war there; and in Burma, where military dictatorship continued. N Korea attempted to defy international community on nuclear issues, 1994, but a settlement brokered by USA, 1995.	

Religion, Education and Philosophy	Science, Exploration and Technology	1980–95 Music and the Arts